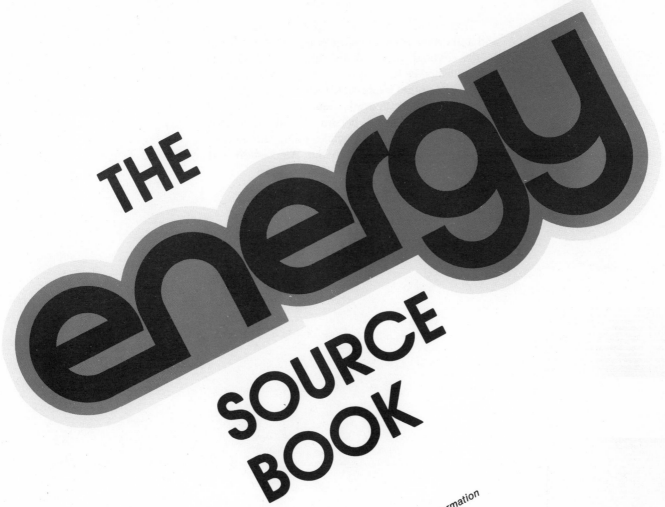

THE energy SOURCE BOOK

EDITORS
Alexander McRae
The Center for Compliance Information
Janice L. Dudas
The Center for Compliance Information

CONSULTING EDITOR
Howard Rowland
The Rowland Company

A publication of
THE CENTER FOR
COMPLIANCE INFORMATION

AN ASPEN PUBLICATION

Copyright © 1977 by Aspen Systems Corporation

Library of Congress Catalog Card Number: 77-99086
ISBN: 0-89443-030-0

Printed in the United States of America.

1 2 3 4 5

CONTENTS

CHAPTER FIVE—GUIDELINES FOR INDUSTRY 487

PREFACE

The adequacy of America's energy supply has become one of the most frequently discussed subjects in the business and professional communities. Though most of us may not be involved in global decisions that will affect our nation's future use of the various available energy sources, many of us are involved in important energy decisions affecting individual businesses and industries. Energy use decisions made this year may well determine the survival or failure of a company and the employment status of hundreds or thousands of people next year and beyond. Decisions this important require the fullest possible availability of readily usable information from both public and private sources. But—this kind of information is not always easy to obtain.

The vast body of energy-related material produced by government and private agencies contains enormous amounts of raw, unorganized information which is not readily available to or easily assimilated by industrial users. The Center for Compliance Information was formed to serve the growing need of industry for easily-accessible information on vital issues. In this volume, the Center has compiled background information and guidelines from those current documents and reports most likely to facilitate sound energy management and prudent corporate decisions. The Energy Sourcebook is a direct result of the Center's extensive research in the areas of energy supply availability and regulation.

The government and non-government source material featured here has been selected for its potential contribution to supply evaluations, conservation and the decision-making process involving all areas of energy regulation. In scope and sequence the material is designed to provide a detailed review of the energy problems facing industry and a prospectus of the available energy source options through 1990 and beyond. It presents and analyzes President Carter's proposed methods for dealing with the country's energy problems. And—it provides data on the guidelines for commercial and industrial energy conservation efforts.

The volume's appendixes contain the text of the law, signed by President Carter on August 4, 1977, establishing the Department of Energy. They also include information on state energy policy considerations and a General Accounting Office review of energy issues facing the 95th Congress.

The energy crisis gives no indication of going away or even of diminishing. Instead, it shows every sign of increasing in severity and complexity in the months and years to come. We believe the information and guidelines presented in this book will help today's energy decision-maker to meet the critical challenge of current and long-term energy management.

Alexander McRae   Janice L. Dudas

December 1977

CHAPTER ONE

CARTER'S ENERGY PROPOSALS
AND
CONGRESSIONAL ACTIONS

THE NATIONAL ENERGY PLAN *

Overview

The diagnosis of the U.S. energy crisis is quite simple: demand for energy is increasing, while supplies of oil and natural gas are diminishing. Unless the U.S. makes a timely adjustment before world oil becomes very scarce and very expensive in the 1980's, the nation's economic security and the American way of life will be gravely endangered. The steps the U.S. must take now are small compared to the drastic measures that will be needed if the U.S. does nothing until it is too late.

How did this crisis come about?

Partly it came about through lack of foresight. Americans have become accustomed to abundant, cheap energy. During the decades of the 1950's and 1960's, the real price of energy in the U.S. fell 28 percent. And from 1950 until the quadrupling of world oil prices in 1973-1974, U.S. consumption of energy increased at an average annual rate of 3.5 percent. As a result of the availability of cheap energy, the U.S. developed a stock of capital goods—such as homes, cars, and factory equipment—that uses energy inefficiently.

The Nature of the Problem

The most critical increase in demand has been for oil, the most versatile and widely used energy resource. To meet that growing demand, the U.S. has turned increasingly to imports. In January and February of 1977, the U.S. imported about 9 million barrels of oil per day, half of total domestic oil consumption. By 1985, U.S. oil consumption could equal 12 to 16 barrels per day.

U.S. domestic oil production has been declining since 1970. New production from Alaska, the deep Outer Continental Shelf, and new recovery methods should reverse the decline, but will be unable to satisfy the projected growth in U.S. demand. Other major additions to domestic oil supply are unlikely.

The principal oil-exporting countries will not be able to satisfy all the increases in demand expected to occur in the U.S. and other countries throughout the 1980's. In 1976, the 13 OPEC countries exported 29 million barrels of oil per day. If world demand continues to grow at the rates of recent years, by 1985 it could reach or exceed 50 million

barrels per day. However, many OPEC countries cannot significantly expand production; and, in some, production will actually decline. Thus, as a practical matter, overall OPEC production could approach the expected level of world demand only if Saudi Arabia greatly increased its oil production. Even if Saudi Arabia did so, the highest levels of OPEC production probably would be inadequate to meet increasing world demand beyond the late 1980's or early 1990's.

There are physical and economic limits on the world's supply of oil. A widely used geological estimate of total recoverable world oil resources, past and present, is about 2 trillion barrels. More than 360 billion barrels have already been consumed. Current proved crude reserves are 600 billion barrels. World consumption of oil has grown at an average annual rate of 6.6 percent since 1940, and it grew by as much as 8 percent annually during the 1960's.

If it could be assumed that world demand for oil would grow at an annual rate of only 3 percent, and if it were possible (which it is not) that production would keep pace with that rate of growth, the world's presently estimated recoverable oil resources would be exhausted before 2020. At a conjectural growth rate of 5 percent, those resources would be exhausted by 2010. Despite some uncertainty about the exact size of recoverable world oil resources, and about the rate of increase of productive capacity, this fundamental fact is clear: *within about four generations, the bulk of the world's supply of oil, created over hundreds of millions of years, will have been substantially consumed.*

Of course, actual physical exhaustion of oil resources will not occur. Even today, well over half the oil in existing fields is being left in the ground because additional recovery would be too expensive. As production by conventional methods declines and oil becomes more scarce, its price will rise and more expensive recovery methods and novel technologies will be used to produce additional oil. As this process continues, the price of oil will become prohibitive for most energy uses. Eventually the nations of the world will have to seek substitutes for oil as an energy source, and oil will have to be reserved for petrochemical and other uses in which it has maximum value.

The world now consumes about 20 billion barrels of oil per year. To maintain even that rate of consumption and keep reserves intact, *the world would have to discover another Kuwait or Iran roughly every three years, or*

* Executive Office of the President, Energy Policy and Planning, April 1977

another Texas or Alaska roughly every six months. Although some large discoveries will be made, a continuous series of such finds is unlikely. Indeed, recent experience suggests that, compared to world oil consumption, future discoveries will be small or moderate in size, will occur in frontier areas, and will yield oil only at very high cost. Obviously, continued *high rates of growth* of oil consumption simply cannot be sustained.

Natural gas supplies are also limited. In the U.S., natural gas constitutes only 4 percent of conventional energy reserves, but supplies 27 percent of energy consumption. Gas consumption grew about 5.7 percent per year between 1960 and 1970. From 1970 to 1974, however, consumption dropped 1.3 percent. The demand for gas is considerably higher than the amount that can be supplied. Hence, gas is rationed by prohibitions on hook-ups for new homes in many areas.

Gas is not only in short supply, but its allocation across the country is distorted, and its distribution among end-uses is unsatisfactory. Federal regulation of the wellhead price of natural gas in interstate commerce has discouraged its distribution from gas producing States to other States, and has encouraged consumption of this premium fuel for less essential uses. Industry and utilities currently consume almost 60 percent of U.S. natural gas, despite the fact that other fuels could be used in a majority of cases.

During the 1973-75 period, only 19 percent of new gas reserve additions were made available to the interstate market, and much of that gas was from the Federal domain. Since the price of intrastate gas is not regulated, there are strong economic incentives to sell gas within the producing States. *The existing distinction between intrastate and interstate sales has given intrastate users first claim to natural gas.*

Strategies and Objectives

The U.S. has three overriding energy objectives:

- as an immediate objective that will become even more important in the future, to reduce dependence on foreign oil and vulnerability to supply interruptions;
- in the medium term, to keep U.S. imports sufficiently low to weather the period when world oil production approaches its capacity limitation; and
- in the long term, to have renewable and essentially inexhaustible sources of energy for sustained economic growth.

The U.S. and the world are at the early stage of an energy transition. Previous energy transitions in the U.S. were stimulated by new technologies, such as the development of the railroad and the mass production of automobiles, which fostered the use of coal and oil, respectively. The latest transition springs from the need to adjust to scarcity and higher prices.

To make the new transition, the U.S. should adhere to basic principles that establish a sound context for energy policy and provide its main guidelines. The energy crisis must be addressed comprehensively by the Government and by a public that understands its seriousness and is willing to make necessary sacrifices. Economic growth with high levels of employment and production must be maintained. National policies for the protection of the environment must be continued. Above all, the U.S. must solve its energy problems in a manner that is fair to all regions, sectors and income groups.

The salient features of the National Energy Plan are:

- conservation and fuel efficiency;
- rational pricing and production policies;
- reasonable certainty and stability in Government policies;
- substitution of abundant energy resources for those in short supply; and
- development of nonconventional technologies for the future.

Conservation and fuel efficiency are the cornerstone of the proposed National Energy Plan. Conservation is cheaper than production of new supplies, and is the most effective means for protection of the environment. It can contribute to international stability by moderating the growing pressure on world oil resources. Conservation and improved efficiency can lead to quick results. For example, a significant percentage of poorly insulated homes in the United States could be brought up to strict fuel-efficiency standards in less time than it now takes to design, build, and license one nuclear powerplant.

Although conservation measures are inexpensive and clean compared with energy production and use, they do sometimes involve sacrifice and are not always easy to implement. If automobiles are to be made lighter and less powerful, the American people must accept sacrifices in comfort and horsepower. If industry is required to make energy-saving investments and to pay taxes for the use of scarce resources, there will be some increases in the cost of consumer products. These sacrifices, however, need not result in major changes in the American way of life or in reduced standards of living. Automobile fuel efficiency can be greatly improved through better design and use of materials, as well as by producing lighter and less powerful cars, without inhibiting Americans' ability to travel. With improved energy efficiency, the impact of rising energy prices can be significantly moderated.

Energy conservation, properly implemented, is fully compatible with economic growth, the development of new industries, and the creation of new jobs for American workers. Energy consumption need not be reduced in absolute terms; what is necessary is a slowing down in its rate of growth. By making adjustments in energy consumption now, the U.S. can avoid a possibly severe economic recession in the mid 1980's.

The U.S. has a clear choice. If a conservation program begins now, it can be carried out in a rational and orderly manner over a period of years. It can be moderate in scope, and can apply primarily to capital goods, such as homes and automobiles. If, however, conservation is delayed until world oil production approaches its capacity limitation, it will have to be carried out hastily under emergency conditions.

It will be sudden, and drastic in scope; and because there will not be time to wait for incremental changes in capital stock, conservation measures will have to cut much more deeply into patterns of behavior, disrupt the flow of goods and services, and reduce standards of living.

Pricing policies should encourage proper responses in both the consumption and the production of energy, without creating any windfall profits. *If users pay yesterday's prices for tomorrow's energy, U.S. resources will be rapidly exhausted. If producers were to receive tomorrow's prices for yesterday's discoveries, there would be an inequitable transfer of income from the American people to the producers, whose profits would be excessive and would bear little relation to actual economic contribution.*

Currently, Federal pricing policy encourages overconsumption of the scarcest fuels by artificially holding down prices. If, for example, the cost of expensive foreign oil is averaged with cheaper domestic oil, consumers overuse oil, and oil imports are subsidized and encouraged. Consumers are thus misled into believing that they can continue to obtain additional quantities of oil at less than its replacement cost.

Artificially low prices for some energy sources also distort interfuel competition. The artificially low price of natural gas, for example, has encouraged its use by industry and electric utilities, which could use coal, and in many areas has made gas unavailable for new households, which could make better use of its premium qualities.

These misguided Government policies must be changed. But neither Government policy nor market incentives can improve on nature and create additional oil or gas in the ground. From a long-term perspective, prices are an important influence on production and use. As long as energy consumers are misled into believing they can obtain energy cheaply, they will consume energy at a rate the U.S. cannot afford to sustain. Their continued overuse will make the nation's inevitable transition more drastic and difficult.

A national energy policy should encourage production. The energy industries need adequate incentives to develop *new* resources and are entitled to sufficient profits for exploration for *new* discoveries. But they should not be allowed to reap large windfall profits as a result of circumstances unrelated to the marketplace or their risk-taking.

The fourfold increase in world oil prices in 1973-74 and the policies of the oil-exporting countries should not be permitted to create unjustified profits for domestic producers at consumers' expense. By raising the world price of oil, the oil-exporting countries have increased the value of American oil in existing wells. That increase in value has not resulted from free market forces or from any risk-taking by U.S. producers. *National energy policy should capture the increase in oil value for the American people.* The distribution of the proceeds of higher prices among domestic producers and consumers must be equitable and economically efficient if the United States is to spread the cost fairly across the population and achieve its energy goals.

The pricing of oil and natural gas should reflect the economic fact that the true value of a depleting resource is the cost of replacing it. An effective pricing system would provide the price incentives that producers of oil and natural gas need by focusing on harder to find new supplies. The system should also moderate the adjustment that households will have to make to rising fuel costs. It should end the distortions of the intrastate-interstate distinction for new natural gas, which is a national resource. It should also promote conservation by raising the ultimate price of products made by energy-intensive processes.

Reasonable certainty and stability in Government policies are needed to enable consumers and producers of energy to make investment decisions. A comprehensive national energy plan should resolve a wide range of uncertainties that have impeded the orderly development of energy policy and projects. Some uncertainties are inherent in a market economy, and Government should not shelter industry from the normal risks of doing business. But Government should provide business and the public with a clear and consistent statement of its own policies, rules, and intentions so that intelligent private investment decisions can be made.

Resources in plentiful supply should be used more widely as part of a process of moderating use of those in short supply. Although coal comprises 90 percent of United States total fossil fuel reserves, the United States meets only 18 percent of its energy needs from coal. Seventy-five percent of energy needs are met by oil and natural gas although they account for less than 8 percent of U.S. reserves. This imbalance between reserves and consumption should be corrected by shifting industrial and utility consumption from oil and gas to coal and other abundant energy sources.

As industrial firms and utilities reduce their use of oil and gas, they will have to turn to coal and other fuels. The choices now for electric utilities are basically coal and nuclear power. Expanding future use of coal will depend in large part on the introduction of new technologies that permit it to be burned in an environmentally acceptable manner, in both power plants and factories. Efforts should also be made to develop and perfect processes for making gas from coal.

Light-water nuclear reactors, subject to strict regulation, can assist in meeting the United States energy deficit. The 63 nuclear plants operating today provide approximately 10 percent of U.S. electricity, about 3 percent of total energy output. That contribution could be significantly increased. The currently projected growth rate of nuclear energy is substantially below prior expectations due mainly to the recent drop in demand for electricity, labor problems, equipment delays, health and safety problems, lack of a publicly accepted waste disposal program, and concern over nuclear proliferation. The Government should ensure that risks from nuclear power are kept as low as humanly possible, and should also establish the framework for resolving problems and removing unnecessary delays in the nuclear licensing process.

To the extent that electricity is substituted for oil and gas, the total amounts of energy used in the country will be somewhat larger due to the inherent inefficiency of electricity generation and distribution. But conserving scarce oil and natural gas is far more important than saving coal.

Finally, *the use of nonconventional sources of energy must be vigorously expanded.* Relatively clean and inexhaustible sources of energy offer a hopeful prospect of supplementing conventional energy sources in this century and becoming major sources of energy in the next. Some of these nonconventional technologies permit decentralized production, and thus provide alternatives to large, central systems. Traditional forecasts of energy use assume that nonconventional resources, such as solar and geothermal energy, will play only a minor role in the United States energy future. Unless positive and creative actions are taken by Government and the private sector, these forecasts will become self-fulfilling prophecies. Other technologies that increase the efficiency of energy use should also be encouraged, such as cogeneration, the simultaneous production of industrial process steam and electricity.

A national energy plan cannot anticipate technological miracles. Even so, nonconventional technologies are not mere curiosities. Steady technological progress is likely, breakthroughs are possible, and the estimated potential of nonconventional energy sources can be expected to improve. Some nonconventional technologies are already being used, and with encouragement their use will grow.

Because nonconventional energy sources have great promise, the Government should take all reasonable steps to foster and develop them.

The National Energy Plan is based on this conceptual approach. It contains a practical blend of economic incentives and disincentives as well as some regulatory measures. It strives to keep Government intrusion into the lives of American citizens to a minimum. It would return the fiscal surpluses of higher energy taxes to the American people.

Finally, the Plan sets forth goals for 1985 which, although ambitious, can be achieved with the willing cooperation of the American people. These goals are:

- reduce the annual growth of total energy demand to below 2 percent;

- reduce gasoline consumption 10 percent below its current level;

- reduce oil imports from a potential level of 16 million barrels per day to 6 million, roughly one-eighth of total energy consumption;

- establish a Strategic Petroleum Reserve of 1 billion barrels;

- increase coal production by two-thirds, to more than 1 billion tons per year;

- bring 90 percent of existing American homes and all new buildings up to minimum energy efficiency standards; and

- use solar energy in more than 2 1/2 million homes.

The Plan would reverse the recent trend of ever-rising oil imports and ever-increasing American dependence on uncertain foreign sources of supply. It would prepare the United States for the time when the world faces a limitation on oil production capacity and consequent skyrocketing oil prices. It would achieve substantial energy savings through conservation and increased fuel efficiency, with minimal disruption to the economy, and would stimulate the use of coal in a manner consistent with environmental protection.

The United States is at a turning point. It can choose, through piecemeal programs and policies, to continue the current state of drift. That course would require no hard decisions, no immediate sacrifices, and no adjustment to the new energy realities. That course may, for the moment, seem attractive. But, with each passing day, the United States falls farther behind in solving its energy problems. Consequently, its economic and foreign policy position weakens, its options dwindle, and the ultimate transition to scarce oil supplies and much higher oil prices becomes more difficult. If the United States faces up to the energy problem now and adopts the National Energy Plan, it will have the precious opportunity to make effective use of time and resources before world oil production reaches its capacity limitation.

The energy crisis presents a challenge to the American people. If they respond with understanding, maturity, imagination, and their traditional ingenuity, the challenge will be met. Even the "sacrifices" involved in conservation will have their immediate rewards in lower fuel bills and the sense of accomplishment that comes with achieving higher efficiency. By preparing now for the energy situation of the 1980's, the U.S. will not merely avoid a future time of adversity. It will ensure that the coming years will be among the most creative and constructive in American history.

Summary of the National Energy Plan

Conservation

In the transportation sector, the Plan proposes the following major initiatives to reduce demand:

- a graduated excise tax on new automobiles with fuel efficiency below the fleet average levels required under current legislation; the taxes would be returned through rebates on automobiles that meet or do better than the required fleet averages and through rebates on all electric automobiles;

- a standby gasoline tax, to take effect if total national gasoline consumption exceeds stated annual targets; the tax would begin at 5 cents per gallon, and could rise to 50 cents per gallon in 10 years if targets were repeatedly exceeded by large or increasing amounts; the tax would decrease if a target were met; taxes collected would be returned to the public through the income tax system and transfer payment programs; States would be compensated for lost gasoline tax revenues through sources such as the Highway Trust Fund;

- fuel efficiency standards and a graduated excise tax and rebate system for light-duty trucks;

- removal of the Federal excise tax on intercity buses;

- increase in excise tax for general aviation fuel, and elimination of the existing Federal excise tax preference for motorboat fuel;

- improvement in the fuel efficiency of the Federal automobile fleet, and initiation of a vanpooling program for Federal employees.

To reduce waste of energy in existing buildings, the Plan proposes a major program containing the following elements:

- a tax credit of 25 percent of the first $800 and 15 percent of the next $1,400 spent on approved residential conservation measures;

- a requirement that regulated utilities offer their residential customers a "turnkey" insulation service, with payment to be made through monthly bills; other fuel suppliers would be encouraged to offer a similar service;

- facilitating residential conservation loans through opening of a secondary market for such loans;

- increased funding for the current weatherization program for low-income households;

- a rural home conservation loan program;

- a 10 percent tax credit (in addition to the existing investment tax credit) for business investments in approved conservation measures;

- a Federal grant program to assist public and non-profit schools and hospitals to insulate their buildings;

- inclusion of conservation measures for State and local government buildings in the Local Public Works Program.

The development of mandatory energy efficiency standards for new buildings will be accelerated. In addition, the Federal Government will undertake a major program to increase the efficiency of its own buildings.

The Plan proposes the establishment of mandatory minimum energy efficiency standards for major appliances, such as furnaces, air conditioners, water heaters, and refrigerators.

The Plan proposes to remove major institutional barriers to cogeneration, the simultaneous production of process steam and electricity by industrial firms or utilities, and to provide an additional 10 percent tax credit for investment in cogeneration equipment. Encouragement will also be given to district heating, and the Energy Research and Development Administration (ERDA) will undertake a study to determine the feasibility of a district heating demonstration program at its own facilities.

To promote further industrial conservation and improvements in industrial fuel efficiency, an additional 10 percent tax credit for energy-saving investments would be available for certain types of equipment (including equipment for use of solar energy) as well as conservation retrofits of buildings.

The Plan also contains a program for utility reform, with the following elements:

- a phasing out of promotional, declining block, and other electric utility rates that do not reflect cost incidence; declining block rates for natural gas would also be phased out;

- a requirement that electric utilities either offer daily off-peak rates to customers willing to pay metering costs or provide a direct load management system;

- a requirement that electric utilities offer customers interruptible service at reduced rates;

- a prohibition of master metering in most new structures;

- a prohibition of discrimination by electric utilities against solar and other renewable energy sources;

- Federal authority to require additional reforms of gas utility rates;

- Federal Power Commission (FPC) authority to require interconnections and power pooling between utilities even if they are not now subject to FPC jurisdiction, and to require wheeling.

Oil and Natural Gas

Government policy should provide for prices that encourage development of new fields and a more rational pattern of distribution; but it should also prevent windfall profits. It should promote conservation by confronting oil and gas users with more realistic prices, particularly for those sectors of the economy where changes can be made without hardship. To promote these ends, the Plan proposes a new system for pricing oil and natural gas.

The proposal for oil pricing contains the following major elements:

- price controls would be extended;

- newly discovered oil would be allowed to rise over a 3 year period to the 1977 world price, adjusted to keep pace with the domestic price level; thereafter, the price of newly discovered oil would be adjusted for domestic price increases;

- the incentive price for "new oil" would be applicable to oil produced from an onshore well more than $2^1/2$ miles from an existing well, or from a well more than 1,000 feet deeper than any existing well within a $2^1/2$ mile radius; the incentive price would be applicable to oil from Federal offshore leases issued after April 20, 1977;

- the current $5.25 and $11.28 price ceilings for previously discovered oil would be allowed to rise at the rate of domestic price increases;

- stripper wells and incremental tertiary recovery from old fields would receive the world price;

- all domestic oil would become subject in three stages to a crude oil equalization tax equal to the difference between its controlled domestic price and the world oil price; the tax would increase with the world price,

except that authority would exist to discontinue an increase if the world price rose significantly faster than the general level of domestic prices;

- net revenues from the tax would be entirely returned to the economy: residential consumers of fuel oil would receive a dollar-for-dollar rebate, and the remaining funds would be returned to individuals through the income tax system and transfer payment programs;

- once the wellhead tax is fully in effect, the entitlements program would be terminated, along with certain related activities, but would be retained on a standby basis.

The proposal for natural gas pricing contains the following major provisions:

- all new gas sold anywhere in the country from new reservoirs would be subject to a price limitation at the Btu équivalent of the average refiner acquisition cost (before tax) of all domestic crude oil;

- that price limitation would be approximately $1.75 per thousand cubic feet (Mcf) at the beginning of 1978; the interstate-intrastate distinction would disappear for new gas;

- new gas would be defined by the same standards used to define new oil;

- currently flowing natural gas would be guaranteed price certainty at current levels, with adjustments to reflect domestic price increases;

- authority would exist to establish higher incentive pricing levels for specific categories of high-cost gas, for example, from deep drilling, geopressurized zones and tight formations;

- gas made available at the expiration of existing interstate contracts or by production from existing reservoirs in excess of contracted volumes would qualify for a price no higher than the current $1.42 per Mcf ceiling; gas made available under the same circumstances from existing intrastate production would qualify for the same price as new gas;

- the cost of the more expensive new gas would be allocated initially to industrial rather than residential or commercial users;

- Federal jurisdiction would be extended to certain synthetic natural gas facilities;

- taxes would be levied on industrial and utility users of oil and natural gas to encourage conservation and conversion to coal or other energy sources.

The Plan contains the following additional proposals for oil and natural gas:

- to encourage full development of the oil resources of Alaska. Alaskan oil from existing wells would be subject to the $11.28 upper tier wellhead price and would be treated as uncontrolled oil for purposes of the entitlements program; new Alaskan oil finds would be subject to the new oil wellhead price;

- production from Elk Hills Naval Petroleum Reserve would be limited to a ready reserve level at least until the west-to-east transportation systems for moving the surplus Alaskan oil are in place or until California refineries have completed a major retrofit program to enable more Alaskan oil to be used in California;

- the Outer Continental Shelf Lands Act would be amended to require a more flexible leasing program using bidding systems that enhance competition, to assure a fair return to the public, and to assure full development of the OCS resources;

- shale oil will be entitled to the world oil price;

- the guidelines established by the Energy Resources Council in the previous administration would be replaced by a more flexible policy: projects for importation of liquified natural gas (LNG) should be analyzed on a case-by-case basis with respect to the reliability of the selling country, the degree of American dependence the project would create, the safety conditions associated with any specific installation and all costs involved; imported LNG would not be concentrated in any one region; new LNG tanker docks would be prohibited in densely populated areas;

- Federal programs for development of gas from geopressurized zones and Devonian shale would be expanded;

- the Administration hopes to eliminate gasoline price controls and allocation regulations next fall; to maintain competition among marketers, it supports legislation similar to the pending "dealer day in court" bill;

- as part of the extension of oil and natural gas price controls, the Administration would urge that independent producers receive the same tax treatment of intangible drilling costs as their corporate competitors;

- a Presidential Commission will study and make recommendations concerning the national energy transportation system.

To provide relative invulnerability from another interruption of foreign oil supply, the Strategic Petroleum Reserve will be expanded to 1 billion barrels; efforts will be made to diversify sources of oil imports; contingency plans will be transmitted to the Congress; and development of additional contingency plans will be accelerated.

Coal

Conversion by industry and utilities to coal and other fuels would be encouraged by taxes on the use of oil and natural gas.

The Plan also contains a strong regulatory program that would prohibit all new utility and industrial boilers from burning oil or natural gas, except under extraordinary conditions. Authority would also exist to prohibit the burning of oil or gas in new facilities other than boilers. Existing facilities with coal-burning capability would generally be prohibited from burning oil and gas. Permits would be required for any conversion to oil or gas rather than to coal. By 1990, virtually no utilities would be permitted to burn natural gas.

While promoting greater use of coal, the Administration will seek to achieve continued improvement in environmental quality. A strong but consistent and certain, environmental policy can provide the confidence industry needs to make investments in energy facilities. The Administration's policy would:

- require installation of the best available control technology in all new coal-fired plants, including those that burn low sulfur coal;

- protect areas where the air is still clean from significant deterioration:

- encourage States to classify lands to protect against significant deterioration within 3 years after enactment of Clean Air Act amendments;

- require Governors to announce intent to change the classification of allowable air quality for a given area within 120 days after an application is made to construct a new source in that area;

- require States to approve or disapprove the application within 1 year thereafter.

Further study is needed of the Environmental Protection Agency's policies allowing offsetting pollution trade-offs for new installations. A committee will study the health effects of increased coal production and use, and the environmental constraints on coal mining and on the construction of new coal-burning facilities. A study will also be made of the long-term effects of carbon dioxide from coal and other hydrocarbons on the atmosphere.

The Administration supports uniform national strip mining legislation.

An expansion is proposed for the Government's coal research and development program. The highest immediate priority is development of more effective and economic methods to meet air pollution control standards. The program will include research on;

- air pollution control systems;

- fluidized bed combustion systems;
- coal cleaning systems;
- solvent refined coal processes;
- low BTU gasification processes:
- advanced high Btu gasification processes;
- synthetic liquids technology;
- coal mining technology.

Nuclear Power

It is the President's policy to defer any U.S. commitment to advanced nuclear technologies that are based on the use of plutonium while the United States seeks a better approach to the next generation of nuclear power than is provided by plutonium recycle and the plutonium breeder. The U.S. will defer indefinitely commercial reprocessing and recycling of plutonium. The President has proposed to reduce the funding for the existing breeder program, and to redirect it toward evaluation of alternative breeders, advanced converter reactors, and other fuel cycles, with emphasis on nonproliferation and safety concerns. He has also called for cancellation of construction of the Clinch River Breeder Reactor Demonstration Project and all component construction, licensing, and commercialization efforts.

To encourage other nations to pause in their development of plutonium-based technology, the United States should seek to restore confidence in its willingness and ability to supply enrichment services. The United States will reopen the order books for U.S. uranium enrichment services, and will expand its enrichment capacity by building an energy-efficient centrifuge plant. The President is also proposing legislation to guarantee the delivery of enrichment services to any country that shares U.S. nonproliferation objectives and accepts conditions consistent with those objectives.

To resolve uncertainties about the extent of domestic uranium resources, ERDA will reorient its National Uranium Resources Evaluation Program to improve uranium resource assessment. The program will also include an assessment of thorium resources.

The United States has the option of relying on light-water reactors to provide nuclear power to meet a share of its energy deficit. To enhance the safe use of light-water reactors:

- the Nuclear Regulatory Commission (NRC) has already increased the required number of guards at nuclear plants and the requirements for the training that guards receive;
- the President is requesting that the NRC expand its audit and inspection staff to increase the number of unannounced inspections and to assign one permanent Federal inspector to each nuclear power plant;
- the President is requesting that the Commission make mandatory the current voluntary reporting of minor mishaps and component failures at operating reactors;
- the President is requesting that the NRC develop firm siting criteria with clear guidelines to prevent siting of nuclear plants in densely populated locations, in valuable natural areas, or in potentially hazardous regions.

The President has directed that a study be made of the entire nuclear licensing process. He has proposed that reasonable and objective criteria be established for licensing and that plants which are based on a standard design not require extensive individual licensing.

To ensure that adequate waste storage facilities are available by 1985, ERDA's waste management program has been expanded to include development of techniques for long-term storage of spent fuel. Also, a task force will review ERDA's waste management program. Moreover, improved methods of storing spent fuel will enable most utilities at least to double their current storage capacity without constructing new facilities.

Hydroelectric Power

The Department of Defense (Corps of Engineers), together with other responsible agencies, will report on the potential for installation of additional hydroelectric generating capacity at existing dams throughout the country.

Nonconventional Resources

America's hope for long-term economic growth beyond the year 2000 rests in large measure on renewable and essentially inexhaustible sources of energy. The Federal Government should aggressively promote the development of technologies to use these resources.

Solar Energy

Solar hot water and space heating technology is now being used and is ready for widespread commercialization. To stimulate the development of a large solar market, a tax credit is proposed. The credit would start at 40 percent of the first $1,000 and 25 percent of the next $6,400 paid for qualifying solar equipment. The credit would decline in stages to 25 percent of the first $1,000 and 15 percent of the next $6,400. The credit would be supported by a joint

Federal-State program of standards development, certification, training, information gathering, and public education. Solar equipment used by business and industry would be eligible for an additional 10 percent investment tax credit for energy conservation measures.

Geothermal Energy

Geothermal energy is a significant potential energy source. The tax deductions for tangible drilling costs now available for oil and gas drilling would be extended to geothermal drilling.

Research, Development and Demonstration

An effective Federal research, development and demonstration program is indispensable for the production of new energy sources. The Federal Government should support any research options in their early stages, but continue support into the later stages only for those that meet technical, economic, national security, health, safety, and environmental criteria. Research and development should be accompanied by preparation for commercialization so that successful projects can rapidly be put to practical use.

Additional research, development and demonstration initiatives are proposed, with emphasis on small, dispersed and environmentally sound energy systems.

An Office of Small-Scale Technologies would be established to fund small, innovative energy research and development projects. The office would enable individual inventors and small businesses to contribute to the national energy research and development effort.

Information

A three-part energy information program is proposed. A Petroleum Production and Reserve Information System would provide the Federal Government with detailed, audited data on petroleum reserve estimates and production levels. A Petroleum Company Financial Data System would require all large companies and a sample of small firms engaged in crude oil or natural gas production to submit detailed financial information to the Federal Government. Data required from integrated companies would permit evaluation of the performance of their various segments by providing vertical accountability. An Emergency Management Information System would provide the Federal and State governments with information needed to respond to energy emergencies.

Competition

Effective competition in the energy industries is a matter of vital concern. The Under Secretary for policy and evaluation in the proposed Department of Energy would be responsible for making certain that policies and programs of the Department promote competition. Although at this time it does not appear necessary to proceed with new legislation for either horizontal or vertical divestiture of the major oil companies, their performance will be monitored. The proposed information program would greatly assist that effort.

A present anomaly in the availability of the tax deduction for intangible drilling costs within the oil industry would be removed as part of the program for extending oil and natural gas price controls.

Emergency Assistance for Low-Income Persons

Existing emergency assistance programs are deficient in assisting low-income persons to meet sharp, temporary increases in energy costs due to shortages or severe winters. A redesigned program will be completed promptly and submitted to the Congress.

Chapter I.—The Origins of the U.S. Energy Problem

Abundant, cheap energy has been a decisive element in the creation of modern America. Since the industrial revolution, fossil energy has increasingly replaced human labor in the workplace, supported a growing population, and led to a spectacular growth in productivity and higher standards of living for Americans. Today, the entire stock of capital goods—from poorly insulated buildings to heavy and powerful automobiles—is tailored to plentiful and cheap energy.

But the days of abundance are now drawing to a close, and American society faces sobering new energy realities. Domestic reserves of oil and natural gas, the nation's predominant energy sources since World War II, have been declining since 1970. Imported oil and other possible substitutes for oil and gas are now expensive. As a result, the available supply of cheap oil and gas is being rapidly exhausted, and consumption of them cannot continue to grow at the pace to which Americans have become accustomed. Fundamental changes in the supply and cost of oil and gas will reshape the United States during the remainder of this century.

Today, America's primary source of energy is oil, which provides nearly half the energy consumed and is used in all sectors of the economy. Oil was developed originally as a source of artificial light and as a lubricant. In the 1870's and 1880's, illumination from new forms of gas manufactured from coal began to appear, and Edison invented the incandescent light. By the outbreak of World War I, industrial and residential heating had become the principal use of oil.

In the early years of this century, the age of the mass-produced automobile—and the age of oil—really began. The number of registered automobiles increased from 8,000 in 1900 to over 1 million in 1913, 10 million in 1922, and 27.5 million in 1940. American oil production rose from 64 million barrels in 1900 to 1.4 billion barrels in 1940. By 1950, oil had replaced coal as the predominant energy source in the United States.

Demand for natural gas followed a similar course. Gas was originally a discarded by-product of oil extraction, but its consumption grew with the development of pipeline systems that could deliver it cheaply to nationwide markets.

Between 1945 and 1960, gas became the predominant fuel for residential heating, and began to replace oil and coal as a boiler fuel for industry and electric utilities. Its cleanness and extremely low price induced both industrial and residential users to switch from coal and become heavily dependent on natural gas. Today, natural gas meets about one-fourth of U.S. energy needs.

During the period from 1950 to 1970, the real cost of energy in the United States decreased 28 percent. Much of the decrease resulted from declining real prices for oil imports, which grew from 900,000 barrels per day in 1950 to 3.4 million barrels per day in 1970. The expansion of imports was made possible by new production from large reservoirs of oil overseas, and by the development of an efficient, economic international oil transportation system.

During the two decades of falling real energy prices, America's gross national product rose an unprecedented 102 percent or 3.6 percent per year, and domestic energy consumption grew at an average annual rate of 3.5 percent, for a total increase of 98 percent. The effects of increased affluence and energy demand were felt throughout society, as Americans in homes, farms, factories, and offices turned to energy-consuming machines and appliances for liberation from daily drudgery.

Buildings generally were constructed with little or no insulation or regard for energy-saving design. Air-conditioners became commonplace. Automobile weight and horsepower increased. Cheap automobile transportation helped to shape major metropolitan areas with widely distributed suburban development and inadequate mass transportation. Petroleum-based plastics and textiles replaced many natural fibers, wood, and other materials.

Energy Consumption Per Unit of GNP

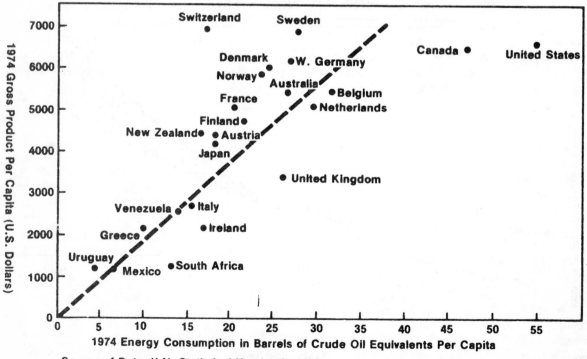

Source of Data: U.N. Statistical Yearbook, 1975

Figure I–1

Wider use of electricity resulted in generally less efficient use of oil, gas, and coal because three units of primary energy are consumed in the generation and transmission of every unit of electricity energy. During the entire post-war period—until the quadrupling of world oil prices in 1973-74—almost all economic and technological developments were premised on cheap energy, while the costs of other factors of production increased.

Today, America consumes far more energy than any other nation. With less than 6 percent of the world's population, the United States consumes more than 30 percent of the world's energy. As Figure I-1 shows, the United States uses more energy per dollar of gross national product than any other industrialized nation. America consumes twice as much energy per capita as West Germany, which has a similar standard of living.

America's rapidly growing demand for energy has not resulted entirely from broad economic and social developments. With some exceptions, such as the restrictions on oil imports during the period when foreign oil was cheap, Government policies have generally stimulated energy demand. Tax benefits to producers and regulation of prices to consumers have kept the price of energy below its true replacement cost, and thereby promoted consumption and waste. Large-volume consumers of electricity and natural gas have been given discounts. Government policy has subsidized and protected energy-inefficient truck and air transportation. The interstate highway system has encouraged automobile use. Local highways have drawn people, businesses, and industry out of central cities into suburbia. Thus, the American people have been led to believe that the oil and gas they consume will remain cheap, when in fact new additions to oil and gas supply already are expensive and inevitably will become more so.

Compound growth of demand for energy can produce striking results within a surprisingly short time. If demand for energy increases at the long-term annual average of 3 percent, it doubles in 24 years. Compound growth at an annual average of 4.3 percent, the rate prevailing from 1963 to 1973, would double energy consumption in 16 years. At 7 percent, the rate at which electricity consumption grew during the 1960's, energy consumption would double in 10 years. The difference between a U.S. growth rate of 3.5 percent (the 1950-73 average) and a growth rate of 2.3 percent (the 1968-76 average) would result in the consumption of 20 million additional barrels of oil equivalent per day in the year 2000.[1] (See Figure I-2.) That would be an increment of more than one-half of total 1976 daily energy consumption.

The domestic sources of energy which have largely satisfied growing U.S. demand since World War II are declining. U.S. oil production has been falling since 1970. Alaskan oil will boost U.S. production for a few years; but

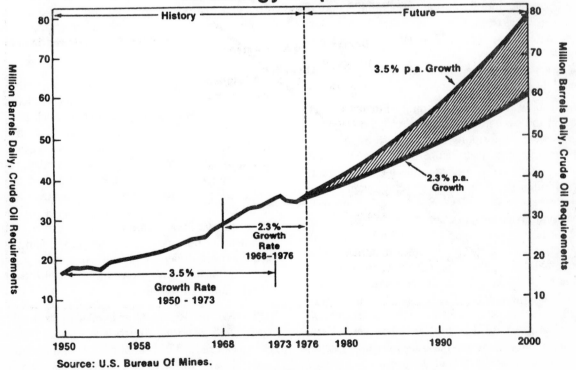

A Lower Growth Rate Can Make A Large Difference In Energy Requirements

Source: U.S. Bureau Of Mines.

Figure I-2

The United States Has Shifted to Different Fuel Use Patterns

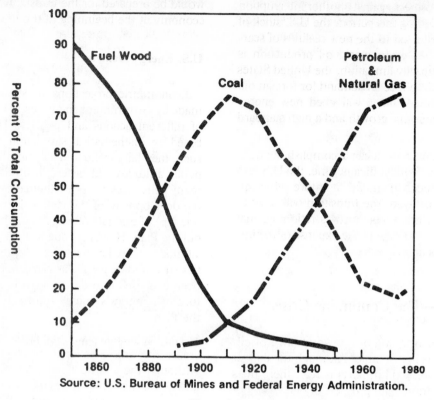

Source: U.S. Bureau of Mines and Federal Energy Administration.

Figure I-3

then, without significant new discoveries, production will decline or remain static. World production of oil is likely to approach its capacity limitation by the mid-1980's, so the United States cannot look to an expanding supply of imported oil as it has in the past. U.S. natural gas production has been declining since 1973. In sum, the supplies of oil and natural gas now available to the United States cannot possibly serve to sustain continued growth of demand at rates like those of recent years.

America is now at an historic turning point as the post-war era of oil and gas comes to a close. America has made two major energy transitions in the past, but in very different circumstances (see Figure I-3). After the Civil War, wood, waterwheels, and windmills largely gave way to coal. Although these resources were abundant, technological progress made it feasible and more economical to use coal in railroad transportation, for industrial process heat, and for home heating. Coal supplied more than half of U.S. energy needs from about 1885 to about 1940. During the 1950's, the transition from coal to oil and natural gas was completed, and they became America's predominant energy sources. This second transition, from one abundant fuel to two others, also resulted from technological progress, as well as the lower cost, cleanness, and ease of handling of oil and natural gas. The transition did not result from any shortage of coal, which even today is a vast resource.

The energy crisis that now faces America results from the divergence between its historically increasing energy demand and its decreasing supplies of oil and natural gas. To meet this crisis, America must make a new kind of energy transition—from a period of abundant, cheap oil and gas to a period when these resources will be in short supply.

Historically, the United States has depended on technological progress to solve many of its problems. There is hope that technological developments will provide long-term solutions to the energy problem. But, in the energy field, technologies develop slowly. Someday, the U.S. probably will be able to rely on such abundant resources as solar energy, geothermal energy, and, and perhaps, fusion; but, even under the most optimistic estimates, those resources will not become major suppliers of energy until after the year 2000. America landed a man on the moon in a decade, but finding substitutes for oil and natural gas is a far more difficult and time-consuming job that must be accomplished within economic, social, health and environmental constraints.

The coming energy transition can be made in three stages. In the short term, from now until 1985, the United States can reduce its rate of growth of demand for energy generally and for oil in particular, reallocate natural gas to high priority uses, increase the use of abundant conventional energy sources, and build up the Strategic Petroleum Reserve to protect against another interruption of foreign oil supply. During this period, the U.S. stock of capital goods can be adjusted to the new realities of scarcity. By the mid-1980's, when world oil production is likely to approach its capacity limitation, the United States could be in a position to reduce its demand for foreign oil. Beyond 2000, the United States will need new energy sources to maintain economic growth and a high standard of living.

If America takes action now, it can accomplish the transition in an orderly way. With sufficient time, the U.S. can modify its capital stock to make it more efficient. However, if action is delayed, the transition will have to be made abruptly with measures, such as rationing, that operate directly on behavior and at the expense of the immediate flow of goods and services.

Chapter II.—The Continuing Crisis

Another sudden quadrupling of the world price of oil, like that in 1973-74, is improbable. Although the danger of another interruption of oil imports is real, there does not appear to be any immediate prospect of one. Another winter as cold as 1976-77 does not seem likely.

In the absence of energy traumas, it is easy to forget. But the real energy crisis does not lie in intermittent supply interruptions or shortages during abnormally cold winters. These are simply dramatic symptoms of the underlying conditions of energy demand and supply that are worsening slowly, but inexorably, day by day.

This invisible crisis arises from the pressure of growing demand on finite resources of oil and natural gas. Over time, economic growth and increases in population add large increments to an already large base of consumption. However, the resources from which the demand must be satisfied are limited.

In the short run, the growing gap between consumption and domestic supply will have to be filled by increasing oil imports unless effective actions are taken to reduce demand and increase domestic supply. Import dependence produces economic and political vulnerability. The energy demand of other nations is also growing, and world oil production is likely to approach its capacity limitation in the near future. Thus, even if the United States were willing to accept the consequences of increasing dependence on imports, in the future the world's oil supply will no longer be able to satisfy growing American demand.

In the long term, research and development will provide supply options not available now. Until then, the basic task for the American people is to adjust energy consumption patterns to reduce pressure on domestic oil and

gas resources and reduce oil imports. Thereby, the U.S. would be prepared for the transition to a different energy economy at the beginning of the next century.

U.S. Energy Demand

Econometric projections of supply and demand are made by Government and industry to analyze the impacts of different actions and policies. These projections are based on mathematical simulation of past behavior. As such, they fail to take into account the changing nature of public attitudes and tastes, institutional constraints, and many other factors. A mathematical model was used in the development of the National Energy Plan to provide one type of estimate of what would happen with and without the Plan. However, due to the inherent limitations of all models, care has been taken to set forth the uncertainties surrounding particular projections, and judgment has been exercised in order to provide the most reliable picture of America's energy future, both with and without the Plan.

The President's economic goals imply a 46 percent increase in gross national product (GNP) by 1985. Although there is no fixed relationship between energy and GNP, this growth does imply a substantial increase in energy consumption unless effective conservation measures are taken.

The model projects that, with a high rate of economic growth and no new conservation initiatives, total U.S. energy demand would grow between 1976 and 1985 at an average annual rate of 3 percent. Consumption would rise from the equivalent of 37 million barrels of oil per day in 1976 to more than 48 million by 1985, a 31 percent increase. Under favorable assumptions and with no new initiatives, domestic energy supply is projected to increase from the equivalent of 30 million barrels of oil per day in 1976 to 37 million in 1985. Thus, the overall gap between demand and domestic production would grow from 7 million barrels of oil equivalent per day to about 12 million.[2]

These projections could be unduly optimistic: they could understate demand and overstate domestic supply. If Americans disregard the energy crisis, demand could easily increase at a rate higher than projected; and experience suggests that domestic supply could easily be below the projected level.

Energy consumption is projected to grow at different rates in the three sectors of the economy from 1976 to 1985. The industrial sector's consumption of energy, 37 percent of the total in 1976, is projected to increase the most by more than 5 percent per year. Residential and commercial demand, also 37 percent in 1976, is projected to increase at an average annual rate of about 2 percent.

Transportation demand, 26 percent in 1976, is projected to increase at an average annual rate of 1 percent, assuming successful implementation of the present fuel efficiency standards and driver response to higher gasoline prices.

These projected growth rates are substantially different from those of the recent past. From 1950 to 1973, when energy consumption increased at an average annual rate of 3.5 percent, industrial use rose at a rate of only 3.0 percent; residential and commercial use grew at a rate of 4.3 percent; and use in the transportation sector grew at a rate of 3.4 percent. Since the 1973-74 embargo, energy use by industry has actually decreased, and energy use in the residential and commercial sector and the transportation sector has increased only slightly.

In addition to considering total demand and the demand of individual sectors, it is important to recognize that the various energy sources have different qualities and ranges of use and are more valuable in some uses than in others. Oil is heavily used by all three sectors, but is needed most for the transportation sector, where no substitute is currently available. Although natural gas is heavily used in industry, it is the premium fuel for residential and commercial use because it is an efficient, clean, and convenient source of heat. Coal is used principally by electric utilities and industry, and nuclear energy is suitable only for electricity generation. (Figure II-1 shows the fuels used by each sector.)

Substantial opportunities exist for reducing demand in all sectors. In the transportation sector, large savings can be achieved by improving the efficiency of automobiles and trucks. Sizable savings are also attainable in the industrial sector through more efficient processes and other energy-saving measures. With better insulation of homes and more efficient appliances, significant savings can be made in the residential sector.

Oil

Oil is the nation's major energy source, but neither domestic supplies nor imports from the rest of the world will be able to satisfy indefinitely continued high rates of growth.

Since World War II, U.S. oil consumption grew at an average annual rate of 4.4 percent until 1973. From 1969 to 1973, utilities and industrial users of coal responded to increased environmental concerns by converting to oil and natural gas. OPEC's fourfold increase in oil prices in 1973-74 created an immediate incentive for conservation. Consumption fell during the 1973-75 recession, but has

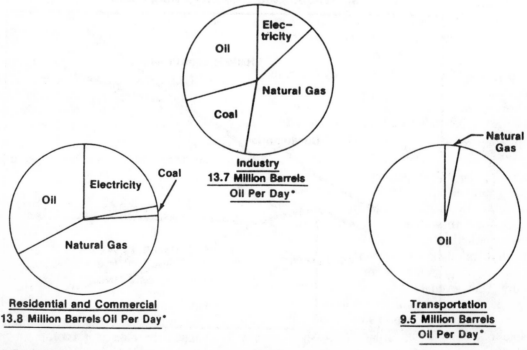

U.S. Energy Consumption By Sector, 1976

Industry
13.7 Million Barrels
Oil Per Day*

Residential and Commercial
13.8 Million Barrels Oil Per Day*

Transportation
9.5 Million Barrels
Oil Per Day*

*Oil Equivalent
(Electricity Losses Allocated)

Source: Federal Energy Administration.

Figure II-1

now resumed its upward trend, and grew 6.7 percent in 1976.

Without further action, U.S. demand for oil will continue to increase in the future (see Figure II-2). Even taking into account various constraints, the mathematical model projects that demand will rise from 17.4 million barrels per day in 1976 to 22.8 million in 1985, a 3 percent annual increase. Without constraints, U.S. oil demand probably would grow at the postwar rate of 4 percent per year, and reach 25 million barrels per day by 1985.

Domestic oil supply cannot possibly meet that growing demand. Domestic oil reserves constitute only 3.7 percent of U.S. conventional energy reserves, but provided 27 percent of U.S. energy consumption in 1976. Current domestic production is 10 million barrels per day.[3] With rising prices, the model projects total U.S. production of around 11 million barrels per day in 1985,[4] assuming a new contribution of about 3 million barrels per day from Alaskan oil, Outer Continental Shelf development, and tertiary recovery. Nevertheless, these new sources will be far from sufficient to satisfy the projected growth in U.S. demand.

Other major additions to domestic oil supply are unlikely. For more than 17 years, domestic oil discoveries have been outpaced by domestic consumption, except for the discovery of oil on the North Slope of Alaska. In 1940, U.S. proved reserves were sufficient for 14 years of consumption. Today, U.S. proved reserves amount to less than 10 years of production at the current level, which is only 5 years of current total domestic oil consumption. In the face of falling domestic oil reserves and production, oil companies increasingly engage in high-risk, high-cost development in such frontier areas as Alaska and the deep Outer Continental Shelf.

As a result of these postwar trends in demand and domestic supply, the United States has increasingly turned to imported oil. In 1947, the United States became a net importer of oil, but domestic excess production capacity exceeded the level of imports. By the mid-1960's, the United States had become dependent on imports: domestic excess capacity could no longer match the level of imports. Imports rose from 21 percent of U.S. oil consumption in 1965 to 37 percent in 1974. In 1976, imports averaged 7.3 million barrels per day, or 42 percent of U.S. oil consumption. In February of 1977, oil imports jumped to 9.6 million barrels per day. Increasing consumption of imported oil has led to deepening dependence on the world oil market and growing vulnerability to a supply interruption.

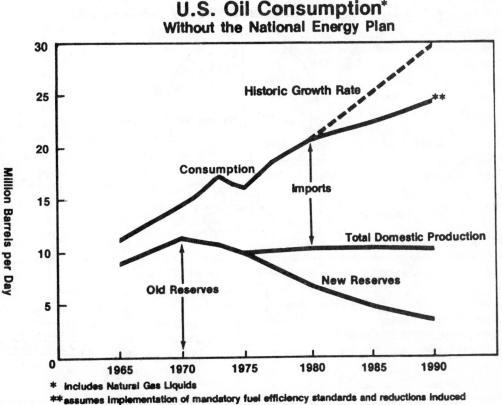

U.S. Oil Consumption*
Without the National Energy Plan

* Includes Natural Gas Liquids
** assumes implementation of mandatory fuel efficiency standards and reductions induced by higher gasoline prices
Source: U.S. Bureau of Mines and Federal Energy Administration.
Figure II-2

A major increase in imports will occur by 1985 unless demand is curbed. If demand for oil were to grow freely, it could reach 25 million barrels per day in 1985. Domestic oil production could well be only about 9 million barrels per day, 2 million below the model's projection. Oil imports would then be 16 million barrels per day. If current measures to increase fuel efficiency in automobiles are successful and if higher gasoline prices reduce driving, it is likely that demand for oil would be closer to 23 million barrels per day and imports closer to 14 million. If, by 1985, demand were in fact 23 million barrels per day and domestic oil production were to increase by 1 million barrels per day, to 11 million, oil imports would then be 12 million barrels per day. Although estimates vary widely, the most reasonable range of estimates of 1985 oil imports is 12 to 16 million barrels per day.

Even apart from considerations of vulnerability, the United States cannot rely indefinitely on growing oil imports to meet its domestic deficit. In coming years, several factors will limit the availability of world oil for U.S. consumption. Ultimately, there are physical and economic limits on world oil resources. The approach to these limits will be hastened by increasing demand in other countries. During the 1980's, the oil-exporting countries will approach their capacity limitation.

The availability and cost of oil imports to the United States will be influenced by the rate of growth in demand for oil throughout the world. As the economies of other industrialized countries grow, their demand for world oil will increase. It is probable that, during the 1980's, demand for oil will outpace production in the Soviet Union and Eastern Europe, and their excess demand will aggravate the growing pressure on world oil supply. As developing countries make economic progress, they, too, will need additional oil. Iran, Venezuela, Nigeria, and other oil-exporting countries may well experience economic growth that will create substantial domestic demand for oil and cause them to limit exports, even if they maintain or increase production.

The oil-exporting countries probably will not be able to satisfy the increases in demand now projected to occur in the 1980's. In 1976, the 13 OPEC countries exported 29 million barrels of oil per day. If world demand continues to grow at the rates of recent years, by 1985 it could reach or exceed 50 million barrels per day. The United States alone the most profligate of the world's energy users, would require a substantial part of that total. However, many OPEC countries cannot significantly increase production. In some, production will actually decline. Thus, as a practical matter, overall OPEC production could approach the expected level of world demand only if Saudi Arabia greatly increased its production. Even if Saudi Arabia did so, the highest levels of OPEC production probably would be inadequate to meet increasing world demand beyond the late 1980's or early 1990's.

Finally, there are physical and economic limits on the world's supply of oil. There is considerable uncertainty and debate about the size of the world's oil resources. A widely used geological estimate of total recoverable world oil resources, past and present, is about 2 trillion barrels. More than 360 billion barrels have already been consumed. Current proved crude reserves are 600 billion barrels. World demand for oil has grown at an average annual rate of 6.6 percent since 1940. It grew by as much as 8 percent annually during the 1960's. If it could be assumed that world demand for oil would grow at an annual rate of only 3 percent, and if it were possible (which it is not) that production would keep pace with that rate of growth, the world's estimated recoverable oil resources would be exhausted by 2020. At a conjectural growth rate of 5 percent, those resources would be exhausted by 2010.

In reality, world production would not continue to grow until the last drop was recovered. Rather, the growth of world consumption would be stopped by limitations on productive capacity. Despite the uncertainty about the exact size of recoverable world oil resources and about the rate of increase in productive capacity, this fundamental fact is clear: within about four generations, the bulk of the world's supply of oil, created over hundreds of millions of years, will have been substantially consumed.

Of course, actual physical exhaustion of oil resources will not occur. Even today, well over half the oil in existing wells is left in the ground because additional recovery would be too expensive. As production by conventional methods declines and oil becomes more scarce, its price will rise and more expensive recovery methods and novel technologies will be used to produce additional oil. As this process continues, the price of oil will become prohibitive for most energy uses. Eventually, the nations of the world will have to seek substitutes for oil for most energy uses, and oil will have to be reserved for petro-chemical and other uses in which it has maximum value.

The world now consumes over 20 billion barrels of oil per year. To maintain *even that rate of consumption* and keep reserves intact, the world would have to discover another Kuwait or Iran roughly every 3 years, or another Texas or Alaska roughly every 6 months. Although some large discoveries will be made, the likelihood of a continuous flow of large discoveries is small. Indeed, recent experience suggests that, from the perspective of world oil consumption, future discoveries will be small or moderate in size, will occur in frontier areas, and will yield oil only at very high cost. Obviously, continued high rates of *growth* of oil consumption simply cannot be sustained.

Natural Gas

The opportunities for supplementing domestic production of natural gas with imports are small. It is far more expensive to transport gas overseas than oil. The presently available supplements to domestic natural gas are limited amounts of Canadian gas, imported liquefied natural gas (LNG), and synthetic natural gas (SNG). The availability of Canadian gas is becoming increasingly uncertain, and LNG and SNG are very expensive. Therefore, the growing imbalance between America's domestic natural gas resources and its annual consumption is of particular concern. (See Figure II-3.)

Natural gas constitutes only 4 percent of domestic conventional energy reserves. In 1973 it furnished 30 percent of U.S. energy consumption, the equivalent of about 11.2 million barrels of oil per day.[5] By 1976, its share had dropped to 27 percent, equivalent to 10 million barrels per day.

Gas consumption grew by about 5.7 percent per year between 1960 and 1970. From 1970 to 1974, however, consumption declined by 1.3 percent, mainly because declining production caused prohibitions against the use of gas in new homes and buildings, and because industrial and electric utility users of interstate natural gas could not obtain adequate long-term commitments for new supplies.

Domestic production of gas, having peaked at 22.2 trillion cubic feet in 1973, has been declining. Last year, only 19.0 trillion cubic feet were produced.

Between 1976 and 1985, total U.S. production of natural gas is projected by the model to decrease from the equivalent of 9.5 million barrels of oil per day to 8.2 million barrels. Consumption, however, is projected to be equivalent to 9.4 million barrels of oil per day. Consumption would increase to a much greater extent if supply were not limited. The difference between the estimated consumption and the estimated domestic production would be made up by imports, amounting to the equivalent of 1.2 million barrels of oil per day.

Federal regulation of the wellhead price of natural gas in interstate commerce has encouraged consumption of this premium fuel for nonessential uses and has discouraged its distribution from gas producing States to other States. Recent contract prices for new gas in the intrastate market range from $1.60 per Mcf to $2.25, while the highest price ever allowed for long-term interstate gas purchases is $1.45.

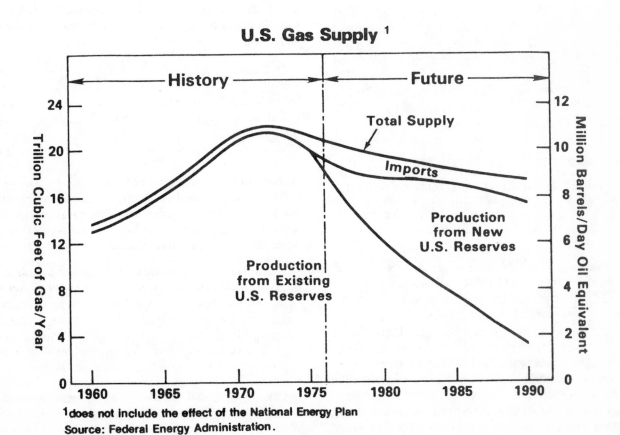

U.S. Gas Supply [1]

[1] does not include the effect of the National Energy Plan
Source: Federal Energy Administration.

Figure II-3

Last year, natural gas in the interstate market sold at wellhead rates that were 25 percent of the Btu equivalent price[6] of imported crude oil. At that price, natural gas was highly attractive to industry and utilities, and they used the equivalent of about 6 million barrels of oil per day, while new households had to turn to electricity.

Since Federal regulation covers only the interstate market, new onshore gas production has gone primarily to the unregulated intrastate market, where it has received higher prices. From 1973 to 1975, only 19 percent of new reserve additions were committed to the interstate market, and much of that gas was from the Federal domain. The existing distinction between intrastate and interstate sales has given intrastate users first claim on new natural gas.

By 1985, gas from existing reservoirs will be able to satisfy only 55 percent of natural gas demand. It is doubtful that even substantial price increases could do much more than arrest the decline in gas production.

The gap between demand and production in the lower 48 States will have to be filled from new sources, such as Alaskan gas; the Outer Continental Shelf; deeper, tighter onshore formations; the geopressurized zones along the Gulf Coast; synthetic natural gas; and imported liquefied natural gas. In the short term, the new sources of natural gas will not be able to reverse the downward trend in total U.S. production. Supplies for the residential and commercial sector will have to be obtained by diverting gas from electric utilities. However, from the mid-1980's onward, the prospects for gas supply could improve if significant discoveries are made on the Outer Continental Shelf, and if technological advances make possible the exploitation of the deeper, tighter onshore formations, Devonian shale, and geopressurized zones.

Implications For The United States

The United States would be profoundly affected by a continuation of current trends of oil and gas demand and supply. To sustain continuation of the rate of growth of demand, the U.S. would be forced to expand domestic production greatly or to increase its already high level of imports, or pursue a combination of both. These courses of action would present serious problems in the short run. But short-term impacts would be eclipsed by even greater problems if U.S. petroleum demand is still growing at the time OPEC production levels off.

Supply disruptions in the 1976-77 winter caused short-term unemployment for more than 1 million workers nationally. They have also encouraged firms to consider moving plants, and jobs, to the Sun Belt to assure stable supplies of energy. But these near-term effects are minor compared to the loss of millions of jobs should future energy prices increase dramatically as a result of a continuing upward trend of demand combined with static or declining production.

The United States could face repeated jolts as energy supplies become increasingly unreliable and actual shortages occur more frequently. Regional disruptions could result from unusual weather, failure to bring electricity generating capacity on line, and many other factors. In some cases, the American people could experience mere inconvenience; in others, real suffering, as economic activity ground to a halt. It is difficult to predict which region would encounter problems and when, but future supply disruptions would be very likely.

Some industries, such as the recreation industry, are particularly dependent on a continuing supply of energy. Short-term limitations on energy use are disruptive to these industries. If action is taken now to curb demand, they will continue to flourish. If action is not taken, their very survival may come into question in the future.

A crash program to meet growing demand through increased domestic production would have very serious adverse consequences. Oil, the most critical energy resource, would be drained rapidly, and therefore the nation would not have adequate protection against future shortfalls in energy supply. It would be unwise to solve a problem of short-term vulnerability arising from dependence on oil imports by creating a problem of long-term vulnerability arising from depletion of America's resources.

A production effort intended to eliminate oil and gas imports would also harm the environment. The Outer Continental Shelf, Alaska, oil shale, and synthetic fuels would have to be developed as rapidly as possible. Even more coal-fired and nuclear plants would be needed. Major energy production facilities would have to be developed without adequate attention to adverse impacts on public health, society and the environment.

The capital investment required to meet a domestic production level of 48 million barrels of oil equivalent per day by 1985 would exceed $550 billion, about 37 percent of total U.S. expenditures for all plant and equipment throughout the economy. In recent years, energy production has already been drawing a disproportionate share of capital. From 1973 through 1975, the United States invested $112 billion in plant and equipment to produce energy, about 35 percent of all such expenditures throughout the economy. Previously, the share of investment going to energy production had ranged between 25 and 30 percent.

Finally, an all-out production effort would raise questions of regional equity and balance. Actual and potential producing States would be pressed to deliver increasing quantities of energy at the expense of their environment and, in some areas, a distinctive way of life. Nonproducing States would be pressed to carry out increasingly drastic conservation programs.

If the United States pursued the course of accepting ever increasing imports, it would face a set of difficult problems. In the past, the United States has enjoyed flexibility in formulating and executing its foreign policy. If, however, the United States continues to increase its dependence on oil imports, its position as a world leader will be weakened. The current vulnerability to supply interruptions affects the whole structure of international relations. Although greater cooperation among the industrialized nations is needed to deal with the energy crisis, the crisis itself raises the specter of future competition among political allies for diminishing oil supplies. Because the United States is the country most wasteful of energy, and because it has been increasing its demand for world oil, the United States has not been able to provide leadership to restrain the growth of world demand.

Reliance on oil imports beyond the short term would also make the U.S. economy even more vulnerable to sudden large oil price increases. Price vulnerability is as harmful to long-term economic and political interests as supply vulnerability. A precipitous increase in energy prices would place significant inflationary pressures on the economy.

The high level of oil imports has already increased the U.S. merchandise trade deficit from $2.0 billion in 1971 to $14.8 billion in 1976. In 1971, oil imports cost $3.7 billion; in 1976, they cost $36.4 billion.

The foregoing discussion addressed the most likely developments in U.S. energy demand and supply. The actual situation could be either better or worse. If growth in demand is reduced and significant new discoveries of oil are made, the leveling off and decline of world production would be deferred for a time.

However, one need not engage in fantasy to contemplate a far worse case. Under a set of unfavorable circumstances, U.S. payments for imported oil theoretically could run as high as $175 billion in 1985. Foreign oil producers might reduce exports to the United States or the world generally for their own economic or political reasons. Some producer nations might choose to conserve their remaining reserves rather than supply world demand. Moreover, a disruption of oil exports from the Persian Gulf would be a disaster for all oil-importing countries, including the United States.

The consequences would be grave if the United States were unable to purchase all the oil it needs. The United States would most likely experience a dramatic interruption of economic activity akin to a depression, and real income would plummet. Rationing and other Government controls would be necessary, leading to an unprecedented Government intrusion into the lives of American citizens.

In developing public policy toward the energy crisis, all three possibilities—the most likely case, the optimistic case, and the pessimistic case—should be considered. It would be foolhardy to base public policy on the most optimistic possibility. Even if the future should prove to be brighter than now appears likely, steps taken to curb demand and increase use of abundant resources would still have been justified to meet the immediate need to reduce vulnerability. In formulating public policy toward energy, the prudent course is to act on the basis of the most likely assumptions about the future, and to bear in mind that the pessimistic set of assumptions is a real possibility.

Implications For The International Community

Although the United States faces very serious problems, they are far less severe than those faced by most other nations. The 1973-74 embargo and fourfold increase in oil prices have already demonstrated the industrialized countries' vulnerability to arbitrary supply and price manipulation. The industrialized nations continue to suffer from supply and price vulnerability, large and increasing balance of payment deficits, and resulting constraints on economic growth.

The dramatic 1973-74 OPEC price increases contributed significantly to the worst global recession since the Great Depression. Unemployment, for example, increased 4 percentage points in the U.S. In 1973, the OECD countries and the OPEC countries each had a small surplus in current account balances with the rest of the world, but in 1974 that situation was radically altered. The OECD countries experienced a $33 billion deficit on current account, while the OPEC surpluses increased to $70 billion. Since 1973, the oil-importing countries have paid over $300 billion in oil imports bills to the 13 OPEC countries. Today, each 10 percent price increase adds an additional $14 billion to the growing OPEC balances.

The massive oil price increases since 1973 have most adversely affected those developing countries that lack domestic oil supplies. Their expenditures for oil rose from about $4 billion in 1973 to $12 billion last year. The indirect cost to their economies was even more pronounced. The recession and inflation in the industrialized countries slackened their demand for the developing countries' exports, and raised the prices of the developing countries' imports. From 1973 to 1975 the foreign debt of these developing countries rose from $67 to $117 billion.

The developing nations cannot significantly reduce their energy consumption since they are not large energy users. As increasing amounts of scarce foreign exchange are expended for energy imports, other development needs suffer. Many developing countries have reached or even surpassed the limits of their creditworthiness.

The quadrupling of oil prices introduced a massive structural distortion into the international payments mechanism. That distortion has not abated. Debt service amounts to 15 percent of the world's export receipts in 1976. As a result, many countries are finding it more difficult to obtain additional loans from the commercial capital markets. The balances held by OPEC countries have been invested in the industrialized countries, largely in short-term securities, although a shift to longer-term investments is occurring. Most of these funds are invested in the United States and Europe, with only limited amounts flowing to the weaker developed and developing countries. Ironically, it is these very countries that suffer most from the energy crisis and have the greatest need for a compensating flow of capital.

The oil-exporting countries and the oil-importing countries share a number of long-term interests. Both need a growing global economy and a liberal trading system to ensure the availability of future markets for their products. All nations, including the oil exporters, will someday have to meet their energy needs from resources other than oil and gas. Hence, all nations are part of the coming energy transition, even though they will be affected very differently.

The prognosis for the United States and the world is serious if current growth in demand for oil continues. In the short term, American vulnerability to a supply interruption would increase. By the mid-1980's, the United States could be vying for scarce oil against its allies and other consuming nations, including the Soviet Union. Then, prices could increase dramatically as a result of tremendous pressure on world oil supply.

During the last years of the 20th century, the United States will have to reduce significantly its reliance on oil, and make greater use of abundant energy sources. For the long term, the United States and other nations will need to develop renewable and essentially inexhaustible sources of energy. If steps are not taken now to prepare for this transition, the United States and the world will face serious economic and political problems.

Chapter III.—Principles and Strategy of the National Energy Plan

Broad public understanding of the gravity of the energy problem, a commitment to action, and a willingness to endure some sacrifice are all indispensable to the success of a national energy plan. In the present circumstances, an energy plan that demanded nothing from the American people would be no energy plan at all, but merely a prescription for chaos at a later date.

Changes in energy demand and supply have long lead-times, and, therefore, the coming energy transition cannot be made overnight. For the transition to be made without serious economic and social disruptions, it will have to take place over a period of years. If the United States is to be prepared for the time when world oil production approaches its capacity limitation and then begins to level off, it must take action now.

The ultimate question is whether this society is willing to exercise the internal discipline to select and pursue a coherent set of policies well in advance of a threatened disaster. Western democracies have demonstrated such discipline in the past in reacting to immediate, palpable threats to survival, as in time of war. But they have had less success in harnessing their human and material resources to deal with less visible and immediate threats to their political and economic systems. When dangers appear incrementally and the day of reckoning seems far in the future, democratic political leaders have been reluctant to take decisive and perhaps unpopular action. But such action will be required to meet the energy crisis. If the nation continues to drift, it will do so in an increasingly perilous sea.

Principles

The principles set forth in this chapter provide a framework not only for present policies, but also for development of future policies. Planning is necessarily an ongoing process. The National Energy Plan will have to be adjusted continually as new experience and knowledge are gained, as government programs take effect, as new technologies develop, and as the world's political and economic circumstances change.

The following 10 principles divide into two groups. The first five establish the context in which energy policy must be formulated. The remaining five are fundamental to the proposed comprehensive National Energy Plan.

The first principle is that the energy problem can be effectively addressed only by a Government that accepts responsibility for dealing with it comprehensively, and by a public that understands its seriousness and is ready to make necessary sacrifices. The declining availability of oil and natural gas will affect virtually all energy prices and consumption patterns in the United States, for the various energy supplies are all part of an integrated energy market. Therefore, in this democratic society, a solution can be found only in comprehensive Government policy-making informed by public comment and supported by public understanding and action.

The Federal Government can pass laws and encourage action. State and local governments can play active roles. But this society can function at its best only when citizens voluntarily work together toward a commonly accepted goal. Washington can and must lead, but the nation's real energy policy will be made in every city, town and village in the country.

The second principle is that healthy economic growth must continue. It is an axiom of public policy that full employment be promoted. The energy problem can be solved without turning off or slowing down America's economic progress. In developing energy policy, measures should be designed to minimize adverse economic and fiscal consequences by returning to the economy funds collected to carry out energy policy. National energy policy can move toward economic rationality while protecting jobs, avoiding rampant inflation, and maintaining economic growth. Conservation initiatives, for example, not only contribute to productivity, but also create a large number of new jobs. Indeed, in the long run, the nation can continue to enjoy economic health only if it solves its energy problems.

The third principle is that national policies for the protection of the environment must be maintained. Energy policy should sustain and improve the quality of life of the American people. It would be ironic if, in moving toward that objective, the nation unnecessarily degraded the quality of the environment and made this country and the planet a less healthful place in which to live.

Virtually every available source of energy has its disadvantages. Storage and combustion of hydrocarbons can pollute the air. Oil imports and drilling on the Outer Continental Shelf present a risk of spills. Strip mining of coal scars the landscape, and deep mining causes deaths through accidents and black lung disease; coal combustion also presents risks to health; liquefied natural gas poses safety problems, as do light-water nuclear reactors. In energy planning, it is necessary to recognize hazards and risks and to reduce them to relatively low levels.

In the long run, there is no insurmountable conflict between the twin objectives of meeting energy needs and protecting the quality of the environment. The energy crisis and environmental pollution both arose from wasteful use of resources and economic and social policies based on the assumption of unlimited and cheap resources. The solutions to many energy and environmental problems follow a parallel course of improving efficiency and harnessing waste for productive purposes.

The fourth principle is that the United States must reduce its vulnerability to potentially devastating supply interruptions. Although conserving energy in general is an important goal, conserving oil has an even higher priority. Continued high vulnerability to interruptions of foreign oil supply is unacceptable.

Considerations of national security, as well as the problem of funding ever-increasing balance of payments deficits, suggest rejection of any "solution" to the energy problem through unrestrained growth of oil imports. Continued growth of imports would erode the nation's economic security, promote dissension with allies, and jeopardize America's world leadership. Moreover, the time is approaching when world oil production will no longer be able to supply the United States with increasing levels of imports.

The solution to the problem of vulnerability does not lie in a crash program of production to achieve energy independence. There is no justification for massive, reckless development of all U.S. energy resources, depletion of critical domestic oil and gas reserves, pollution of the environment, draconian conservation measures, and rejection of the substantial economic benefits of oil imports, all in the name of energy independence.

An appropriate and far more sensible goal is relative invulnerability. The United States should be prepared to import foreign oil for a number of years because it is an available source of supply that does not deplete domestic resources. Through effective conservation and increased use of abundant domestic resources such as coal, oil imports can be reduced to a manageable level. A large Strategic Petroleum Reserve, diversification of foreign sources of oil, and contingency plans should help to deter interruptions of foreign oil supply and protect the economy should an interruption occur.

The fifth principle is that the United States must solve its energy problems in a manner that is equitable to all regions, sectors, and income groups. No segment of the population should bear an unfair share of the total burden, and none should reap undue benefits from the nation's energy problems. In particular, the elderly, the poor, and those on fixed incomes should be protected from disproportionately adverse effects on their income. Energy is as necessary to life as food and shelter.

The energy industries need adequate incentives to develop new resources and are entitled to sufficient profits to encourage exploration and development of new finds. But they should not be allowed to reap large windfall profits as a result of circumstances not associated with either the marketplace or their risk-taking. The fourfold increase in world oil prices in 1973-74 and the policies of the oil-exporting countries should not be permitted to create unjustified profits for domestic producers at consumers' expense. By raising the world price of oil, the oil-exporting countries have increased the value of American oil in existing wells. National energy policy should capture that increase in value for the American people. However, where incentives are legitimately needed to stimulate new production, energy policy should allow adequate returns to producers. The distribution of the proceeds of higher prices among domestic producers and consumers must be equitable and economically efficient if the nation is to spread the costs fairly across the population and meet its energy goals.

Some regions of the country, particularly the Gulf Coast States and Appalachia, are large energy producers. Other regions, such as the Rocky Mountain and Great Plains States, have large energy resources which have not yet been extensively developed. And still other regions, such as New England and California, import most of their energy from other regions and other nations. The Plan must assure that policies are equitable across the country, and that the special needs of each region are met. Prices for energy should be reasonably uniform to prevent economic dislocations and unjustified variations in consumer costs.

The environmental quality of producing States and States with untapped resources should be protected by strict standards effectively enforced. Producing States should be fairly compensated, and consuming States should be assured a fair share of energy supplies at reasonable prices.

The Federal Government can enact national policies to further these goals, and can recognize that the States also have important responsibilities for the formulation and execution of energy policy. But States within the various regions must also accept their share of the responsibility for national equity if the U.S. is to avoid ''energy Balkanization.'' It would be desirable for States to develop energy policies that complement the Plan while meeting local and regional needs.

The sixth principle, and the cornerstone of National Energy Policy, is that the growth of energy demand must be restrained through conservation and improved energy efficiency. Conservation and improvement in energy efficiency is the most practical course of action for the United States and for the nations of the world. Conservation is cheaper than production of new energy supplies, and is the most effective means for protection of the environment.

Conservation and improved efficiency can lead to quick results. A significant percentage of poorly insulated homes in the United States could be brought up to strict fuel efficiency standards in less time than it now takes to design, license, and build one nuclear powerplant.

Although conservation measures are inexpensive and clean compared with energy production, they do involve sacrifice and are sometimes difficult to implement. If automobiles are to be made lighter and less powerful, the American people must accept some sacrifice in comfort and horsepower. If industry is required to make energy-saving investments and to pay taxes on the use of scarce fuels, there will be some increases in the cost of consumer products. These sacrifices, however, need not result in major changes in the American way of life or in a reduced standard of living. Automobile fuel efficiency can be

greatly improved through better design of cars, and thus gasoline consumption could be significantly reduced without inhibiting Americans' ability to travel. With improved energy efficiency, the impact of rising energy prices can be significantly moderated. Energy conservation, properly implemented, is fully compatible with economic growth, the development of new industries, and the creation of new jobs for American workers. Energy consumption need not be reduced in absolute terms; what is necessary is a slowing down in its rate of growth.

If a conservation program is instituted now, it can be carried out in a rational and orderly manner over a period of several years. It can be moderate in scope, and can apply primarily to capital goods, such as homes, automobiles, factories, equipment, and appliances. If, however, conservation is delayed until world oil production approaches its capacity limitation, it will have to be carried out hastily under emergency conditions. It will then be drastic; and, because there will not be time to wait for incremental changes in capital stock, conservation measures will have to cut much more deeply into patterns of behavior, disrupt the flow of goods and services, and reduce standards of living.

Finally, conservation in America can contribute to international stability by moderating the growing pressure on world oil resources. Indeed, reduction of America's demand for world oil would be a form of assistance to the developing countries.

The seventh principle underlying the National Energy Plan is that energy prices should generally reflect the true replacement cost of energy. Energy prices should move toward a level that reflects the true value of energy in order for market signals to work in harmony with conservation policy. When the cost of expensive foreign oil is averaged with cheaper domestic oil, consumers overuse oil. Government policy that promotes overuse by artificially holding down prices misleads consumers into believing that they can continue to obtain additional quantities of oil at less than its replacement cost.

Artificially low prices for particular energy sources also distort interfuel competition. The artificially low price of natural gas, for example, has encouraged its use by industry and electric utilities, which could use coal, and has made gas unavailable for new households, which could make better use of its premium qualities.

Neither Government policy nor market incentives can create additional oil or gas in the ground. But from a long-term perspective, prices are an important influence on production and use. As long as energy consumers are enticed into believing that they can continue to pay yesterday's prices for tomorrow's energy, they will continue to use more energy than the nation can really afford, U.S. resources will be rapidly exhausted, and continued overuse will make the inevitable transition more sudden and difficult.

Although producers need incentives for exploration and new development, pricing policies should not give them windfall profits unrelated to their economic contribution. If producers were to receive tomorrow's prices for yesterday's discoveries, there would be an inequitable transfer of income from the American people to the oil and gas producers, and producers' profits would be excessive.

The eighth principle is that both energy producers and consumers are entitled to reasonable certainty as to Government policy. An inadequately organized Federal Government, conflicting signals from different Federal agencies, and unwieldy and confusing regulatory procedures have resulted in major bottlenecks in the development of energy resources. The Plan should resolve a wide range of uncertainties that have impeded the orderly development of energy policy and projects. Some uncertainties are inherent in a market economy, and Government cannot and should not shelter industry from the normal risks of doing business. But government can and should provide business and the public with a clear and consistent statement of its own policies, rules, and intentions, so that intelligent private investment decisions can be made. In order to be able to provide certainty and consistency in energy policy-making, the Federal energy agencies should be organized into a Department of Energy.

The ninth principle is that resources in plentiful supply must be used more widely, and the nation must begin the process of moderating its use of those in short supply. Although coal comprises 90 percent of domestic fossil fuel reserves, the United States meets only 18 percent of its energy needs from coal. Seventy-five percent of energy needs are met by oil and natural gas although they account for less than 8 percent of U.S. reserves. This imbalance between reserves and consumption should be corrected by shifting from oil and gas to coal and other domestic energy sources.

If the United States is to preserve its scarce reserves of oil and gas and still reduce the growth of imports, policies must be forged to reduce consumption of oil and gas, particularly by automobiles, industry, and electric utilities. As industry reduces its use of oil and gas, it will have to turn to coal and other fuels. The choices for electric utilities for the foreseeable future will be coal and nuclear power.

Expanding future use of coal will depend in large part on the introduction of new technologies that permit it to be burned in an environmentally acceptable manner, in both power plants and factories, for electricity, for process steam, and for heat. Efforts must also be made to perfect processes for low Btu gasification of coal and to develop new technologies for advanced high Btu gasification.

Light-water nuclear reactors, subject to strict regulation, can assist in meeting the nation's total net energy deficit. The 63 nuclear plants operating today provide approximately 10 percent of U.S. electricity, about 3 percent of total energy consumed. That contribution could be significantly increased. The currently projected growth rate of nuclear energy is substantially below prior expectations due mainly to the recent drop in demand for electricity, labor problems, equipment delays, health and safety problems, lack of a publicly accepted waste disposal program, and concern over nuclear proliferation. The Government should ensure that risks from nuclear power are kept as low as possible, and should also resolve problems and unnecessary delays in the nuclear licensing process.

To the extent that electricity from coal is substituted for oil and gas, the total amounts of energy used in the country will be somewhat larger due to the inherent inefficiency of electricity generation and distribution. But conserving scarce oil and natural gas is more important than saving coal.

The tenth principle is that the use of nonconventional sources of energy must be vigorously expanded. Relatively clean and inexhaustible sources of energy are a hopeful prospect, as supplements to conventional energy resources in this century, and as major sources of energy in the next. Many of these sources permit decentralized production, and thus provide alternatives to large, central systems. Traditional forecasts of energy use assume that nonconventional resources, such as solar and geothermal energy, will play only a minor role in the energy future. Unless positive and creative actions are taken by Government and the private sector, these forecasts will become self-fulfilling prophecies. Other technologies that increase efficiency of energy use, such as cogeneration of industrial process steam and electricity, should also be encouraged.

The Plan should not be premised on technological miracles. But nonconventional technologies are not mere curiosities. Steady technological progress is likely, breakthroughs are possible, and the estimated potential of nonconventional energy sources can be expected to improve. Many nonconventional technologies are already being used, and with encouragement their use will grow. Because nonconventional energy sources have great promise, the Government should take all reasonable steps to foster and develop them.

The Broad Perspective

The U.S. has three overriding energy objectives. As an immediate objective, which will become even more important in the future, the U.S. must reduce its dependence on foreign oil to limit its vulnerability to supply interruptions. In the medium term, the U.S. must weather the stringency in world oil supply that will be caused by limitations on productive capacities. In the long term, the U.S. must have renewable and essentially inexhaustible sources of energy for sustained economic growth. The strategy of the Plan contains three major components to achieve these objectives.

First, by carrying out an effective conservation program in all sectors of energy use, through reform of utility rate structures, and by making energy prices reflect true replacement costs, the nation should reduce the annual rate of growth of demand to less than 2 percent. That reduction would help achieve both the immediate and the medium-term goals. It would reduce vulnerability and prepare the nation's stock of capital goods for the time when world oil production will approach capacity limitations.

Second, industries and utilities using oil and natural gas should convert to coal and other abundant fuels. Substitution of other fuels for oil and gas would reduce imports and make gas more widely available for household use. An effective conversion program would thus contribute to meeting both the immediate and the medium-term goals.

Third, the nation should pursue a vigorous research and development program to provide renewable and other resources to meet U.S. energy needs in the next century. The Federal Government should support a variety of energy alternatives in their early stages, and continue support through the development and demonstration stage for technologies that are technically, economically, and environmentally most promising.

The Plan seeks to achieve the overriding objectives by other means as well. To reduce vulnerability, the Strategic Petroleum Reserve should be expanded, foreign sources of oil should be diversified, and contingency plans should be put in place. To help weather the approaching capacity limitations on world oil production, incentives should be provided to encourage new production in Alaska, on the Outer Continental Shelf, and from advanced recovery techniques. Potential new sources of gas hold great promise and should be developed. Conversion from oil and gas to coal should be facilitated by development of more environmentally acceptable methods for using coal.

The 10 principles of the National Energy Plan provide a realistic framework for these actions. By pursuing conservation, bringing energy prices into line with replacement costs, and expanding the use of coal, the U.S. can reduce oil imports to an acceptable level and prepare for the coming stringency in oil supplies. Backed by a large Strategic Petroleum Reserve, a more diversified set of foreign oil suppliers, and contingency plans, the United States can reduce its vulnerability to supply interruptions to an acceptable level. Measures can be designed to assure that American workers, the poor, and the elderly do not suffer

as a result of rising prices. Economic growth can be promoted and inflationary pressures kept within bounds. Regional and environmental imbalances can be recognized and corrected with maximum equity. And nonconventional sources of energy can be promoted to meet long-term needs.

The United States is at a turning point. It can choose, through piecemeal programs and policies, to continue the current state of drift. That course would require no hard decisions, no immediate sacrifices, and no adjustment to the new energy realities. That course may, for the moment, seem attractive. But, with each passing day, the nation falls farther behind in solving its energy problems. Consequently, its economic and foreign policy position weakens, its options dwindle, and the ultimate transition to stringency in oil supplies and higher oil prices becomes more difficult.

An alternative to continued drift is the comprehensive National Energy Plan, set forth in the next five chapters. Chapter IV describes the Plan's conservation and fuel efficiency program. Chapter V contains proposals for the pricing of oil and natural gas and for resolving other issues affecting those resources. Chapter VI presents the Plan's program for conversion to coal and other fuels, and its programs for nuclear and hydroelectric power. Chapter VII presents initiatives for the development of nonconventional resources and sets forth the Administration's policy toward energy research and development. Chapter VIII addresses the role of government and the public in formulating and carrying out energy policy. It discusses, in particular, the establishment of national energy goals, the creation of the Department of Energy, the development of a national energy information system, competition within the energy industries, the role of the States, assistance to people with low incomes, and public participation. Finally, Chapter IX discusses the impacts of the Plan.

Chapter IV—The National Energy Plan: Conservation And Energy Efficiency

The cornerstone of the National Energy Plan is conservation, the cleanest and cheapest source of new energy supply. Wasted energy—in cars, homes, commercial buildings and factories—is greater than the total amount of oil imports. By reducing the need for additional oil imports, conservation and improved efficiency in the use of energy can contribute to national security and international stability. By reducing the need for additional domestic energy production, conservation can contribute to environmental protection and to an adequate supply of capital for balanced economic growth.

America needs to embrace the conservation ethic. The attitudes and habits developed during the era of abundant, cheap energy are no longer appropriate in an era of declining supplies of America's predominant energy sources. Conservation offers vast opportunities for American creativity and know-how. The challenge of saving energy should galvanize the ingenuity and talents of the American people. As individual Americans find new ways to save energy in their daily lives, they will reduce their own energy bills and contribute to the future well-being of the country.

In buying durable goods, in deciding how to travel to work or how to spend leisure time, and in making countless other decisions, Americans will have to be conscious of the rising price of energy, and will have to emulate the shrewdness and practicality of earlier generations. For example, when buying a home, a car, or an appliance, consumers ought to consider not only an item's initial cost, but also its annual operating cost—including its energy consumption. In many cases, an item that is initially more expensive will actually prove to be cheaper over a period of years.

If vigorous conservation measures are not undertaken and present trends continue, energy demand is projected to increase by more than 30 percent between now and 1985. Americans can eliminate energy waste through effective conservation and improved energy efficiency in transportation, buildings, and industry.

Transportation

Transportation consumes 26 percent of U.S. energy, and about half of that is used by automobiles. About 5 million barrels of oil per day are consumed by automobiles. Domestically manufactured automobiles use considerably more gasoline than imported cars. (See Figure IV-1.) More efficient, lighter, and less powerful cars would save a substantial amount of gasoline. Carpooling could also save significant quantities of gasoline. If 4 commuting cars out of 10 carried 1 additional passenger, 2.5 percent of total oil consumption, about 400,000 barrels per day, could be saved. No serious energy policy can ignore these opportunities for large savings.

Overseas, there is no greater symbol of American energy waste than the heavy, powerful, accessory-laden American automobile. An average new car in Europe weighs about 1,900 pounds; in the United States, about 3,300. From the perspective of energy efficiency, a major problem with American cars is their weight and power, not necessarily their interior size. With better design and other improvements, family size cars could be considerably more fuel efficient.

In late 1975, the Congress enacted legislation requiring that the average mileage of new cars be 20 miles per gallon

Fuel Economy For New Automobiles

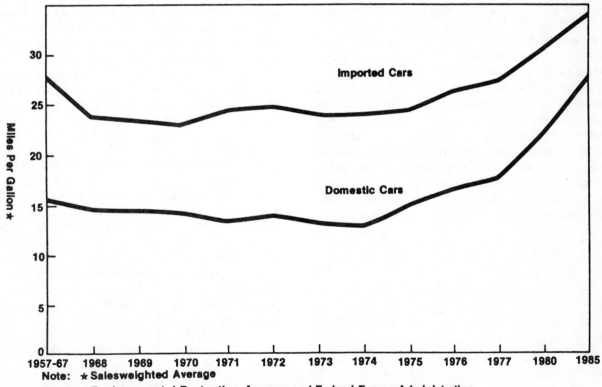

Note: ★ Salesweighted Average

Source: Environmental Protection Agency and Federal Energy Administration.

Figure IV-1

by 1980, and 27.5 miles per gallon by 1985, compared to 14 miles per gallon actually achieved in 1974. However, many consumers still appear to prefer heavier cars with high acceleration and low fuel efficiency. It is questionable whether the penalties for noncompliance by manufacturers are strong enough to assure that the current statutory standards will be met. The present legislation, is, therefore, insufficient to ensure the kind of reductions that are needed in the transportation sector. Reduction in gasoline consumption is necessary. Accordingly, the Plan proposes a national goal to reduce gasoline consumption 10 percent by 1985.

To help achieve that goal, a graduated excise tax would be imposed on new automobiles with fuel efficiency below the fleet average levels required under current legislation. Graduated rebates would be given for new cars with mileage better than the standard. The tax schedule would be fixed by statute, and taxes would rise from 1978 to 1985 and remain constant thereafter. The rebate schedule would be set by the Internal Revenue Service so that total estimated rebate payments would be equal to estimated tax receipts, with no gain or loss to the Treasury. The rebate schedule would be fixed in advance so that manufacturers and consumers would know the exact amount of tax or rebate for every car. Rebates would be available for cars purchased after May 1, 1977. These rebates would be paid from taxes collected on 1978 fuel inefficient vehicles.

Examples for the model year 1985 illustrate the operation of the tax-rebate system. In that year the statutory standard will be 27.5 miles per gallon. A car with at least 20.5 miles per gallon but less than 21.5 would bear a tax of $610; and a car with less than 12.5 miles per gallon would bear a tax of $2,488, the maximum under the proposed system. In the same year, a car with 30.5 miles per gallon would earn a rebate of $176; a car with 34.5 miles per gallon would earn a rebate of $362; and a car with 38.5 miles per gallon or above would earn a rebate of $493. The statutory maximum would be $500. Actual rebates might differ from these estimates, depending on the estimate that will be made in 1984 of the composition of new car sales during the 1985 model year, and the tax receipts that would result from that composition.

Cars manufactured in the United States or Canada would be eligible for rebates; for cars manufactured in other countries, rebates would be provided only after agreements were reached with individual countries. The President's Special Representative for Trade Negotiations will work with other nations to develop equitable rebate agreements.

Electric vehicles would be eligible for the maximum rebate. These vehicles consume no gasoline and are a clean method of transportation for intra-urban use. Electric delivery trucks have long been used in Europe.

The Administration intends to continue the progress that has been made to date on automobile fuel efficiency. The Secretary of Transportation will begin the analytic work necessary to examine how his authority should be used to raise mileage standards above 27.5 miles per gallon beyond 1985.

The tax on fuel inefficient new cars will not reach old cars, and it will not directly influence the number of miles driven. A further measure is necessary to help meet the goal of a 10 percent reduction in gasoline consumption by 1985. Accordingly, a program is proposed to establish annual targets for gasoline consumption, backed by a standby tax on gasoline.

A gasoline tax is a highly effective measure for conservation because it affects all cars and all drivers. However, in order to provide maximum scope for citizen action, the tax would not be imposed as long as Americans achieved specified annual gasoline consumption targets. The proposal would challenge the American people to reduce gasoline consumption through use of more efficient cars, increased use of car pools and van pools, compliance with the 55-miles-per-hour speed limit, more efficient driving, regular maintenance, and reduced use of cars. If the American people join together to meet this challenge, the standby tax will never take effect.

The targets established in the standby tax program would permit limited annual increases in gasoline consumption from 7.35 million barrels per day in 1978 to 7.45 million in 1980. From 1980 to 1987, when fuel-efficient cars will become a sizable share of the total automobile fleet, the program would require annual reductions in gasoline consumption. The target in 1985 would be 6.60 million barrels per day.

Under the program, no tax could go into effect until 1979. In 1979 or any subsequent year, the tax would go into effect if gasoline consumption in the preceding year exceeded the target by at least 1 percent. The amount of the tax would equal 5 cents for each percent that gasoline consumption exceeded the target in the preceding year. The tax could be reduced by 5 cents a year based on the formula in the legislation. The tax could not increase or decrease more than 5 cents per year and it could never exceed 50 cents.[7]

Funds collected from the standby gasoline tax would be rebated progressively to the public. For each five cents of tax imposed, nearly $6 billion in revenue would be generated. These revenues would be rebated on a per capita basis in the amount of $25 to each person per year on a payment of $100 for a family of four. If a tax of twenty-five cents were to be imposed, each citizen would be eligible for a payment of $125, or $500 for a family of four.

Passenger automobiles are not the only wasteful vehicles. Under the Energy Policy and Conservation Act, the

Secretary of Transportation plans to promulgate by next July efficiency standards for light-duty trucks weighing 6,000 pounds or less. Once those standards are in effect, these vehicles will become subject to a tax-rebate system similar to that for automobiles. The President has directed the Secretary to commence a proceeding to cover trucks weighing over 6,000 pounds.

Legislation is requested to remove the 10 percent excise tax on intercity buses. Buses, like railroads, are fuel-efficient forms of transportation that deserve encouragement.

The existing Federal gasoline tax on aviation fuel would be raised to 11 cents per gallon except for use by commercial airlines and in farming. The current rebate of half of the Federal excise tax on fuel used by motorboats would be eliminated. Revenues from the elimination of that rebate would go to the Land and Water Conservation Fund.

The Federal Government itself must set an example in reducing gasoline consumption. The President is issuing an Executive Order requiring that the Federal fleet of new cars meet an average mileage standard that will rise from 2 miles per gallon above the average fuel economy standard applicable in 1978 to 4 miles per gallon above in 1980 and thereafter. This initiative not only will save gasoline, but also will provide incentives for the development of more fuel-efficient vehicles.

The Federal Government will also initiate a major van pooling demonstration program in areas not served by mass transit. About 6,000 vans will be purchased by the Federal Government and made available to Federal employees. All costs of the program will be repaid to the Federal Government by the riders.

If it should appear that the goal of a 10 percent reduction in gasoline consumption by 1985 is not being achieved, additional measures, including a tax on commuter parking and minimum automobile mileage standards, would have to be considered.

Beyond this Federal program, States and localities can promote gasoline conservation through local initiatives. Observance of the national 55-miles-per-hour speed limit should be vigorously enforced by States and municipalities. The Secretary of Transportation has authority to withhold Highway Trust Fund revenues from States not enforcing the 55-miles-per-hour speed limit. If the widespread noncompliance and lack of enforcement continue, the Secretary may find it necessary to exercise that authority.

Inspection and maintenance programs to determine compliance with the Clean Air Act can also provide gasoline savings. In areas where air quality indicates a need for inspection and maintenance, gasoline savings of 2 percent can be achieved.

Reduction in gasoline consumption will entail a loss of revenues to the States from their taxes on gasoline, which are used to operate and maintain highways. A way needs to be found to ease this additional burden on State treasuries. The Administration will develop a program to compensate them for this loss through sources such as the Highway Trust Fund.

In the long run, mass transit by bus and rail must play a significant role in reducing energy consumption in the transportation sector. Reliable, inexpensive mass transit is needed to serve existing, spread out metropolitan areas. New development patterns based on public transportation can bring homes and offices, churches and schools, shops and other community buildings together, and at the same time conserve energy. The nation must begin to explore a system of incentives for more efficient transportation just as it is creating disincentives for inefficient transportation.

Buildings

Currently, there are approximately 74 million residential units in the United States, and 1.5 million nonresidential buildings with some 29 billion square feet of floor space. Almost 20 percent of U.S. energy is used to heat and cool buildings. Some of these buildings needlessly waste as much as half of that energy. The hermetically-sealed glass and steel skyscraper is the analogue of the gas-guzzling automobile. The energy inefficiency of American buildings is a direct result of the cheap energy era in which most of these structures were built.

The potential savings from improving the energy efficiency of the nation's stock of buildings are enormous. Installation of ceiling and roof insulation, weatherstripping of doors and windows, caulking of cracks, installation of clock thermostats, and simple furnace modifications could result in substantial energy savings.

The Plan includes a national program designed to bring 90 percent of all residences and many public and other buildings up to minimum Federal standards by 1985. The program contains the following elements:

First, homeowners would be entitled to a tax credit of 25 percent of the first $800 and 15 percent of the next $1,400 spent on approved conservation measures. The credits would be available for measures undertaken between April 20, 1977, and December 31, 1984. A list of eligible measures will be included in proposed legislation.

Second, State public utility commissions would be required to direct their regulated utilities to offer their residential customers a "turnkey" conservation service, financed by loans repaid through monthly bills. Utilities would also inform customers of other available conservation programs, and advise them how to obtain financing, materials, and labor to carry out conservation measures themselves. Other fuel suppliers will be encouraged to offer similar programs, with the help of State energy offices.

Third, the Federal Government will remove the barriers to opening a secondary market for residential energy conservation loans through the Federal Home Loan Mortgage Corporation and the Federal National Mortgage Association. This action should help to ensure that capital is available to homeowners at reasonable interest rates for residential energy conservation through private lending institutions.

Fourth, increased funds would be available to aid people with low incomes to weatherize their homes. Under this proposal, $130 million would be provided in fiscal 1978, $200 million in 1979, and $200 million in fiscal year 1980. The Secretary of Labor has been directed to take all appropriate steps to ensure that recipients of funds under the Comprehensive Employment Training Act (CETA) will supply labor for the weatherization effort. The CETA program's employment levels, as proposed by the Administration, would meet the labor requirements of the low-income weatherization program.

Fifth, the Department of Agriculture has begun a rural home conservation program in cooperation with rural electric cooperatives with loans provided through the Farmers Home Administration.

Sixth, businesses would be entitled to a 10 percent tax credit for investments in approved conservation measures, in addition to the existing investment tax credits. A list of approved measures would be included in the legislation. The credit would be available to owners of apartment buildings, and tenants should benefit from the impact of reduced energy costs on rents.

Seventh, a Federal grant program would assist public and nonprofit institutions such as schools and hospitals in conservation. The program would be funded at the rate of $300 million per year for 3 years.

Eighth, the Local Public Works Program, under which the Federal Government provides funds for public works projects for State and local government units, will include repair of State and local government buildings. The Department of Commerce, which administers the program, will strongly encourage State and local governments to include in their proposals actions that will contribute to energy conservation.

Except for participation by electric and gas utilities, the proposed national program is a voluntary one. It does not initially include any intervention by the Federal Government into the homes of individual Americans. The American people already have ample incentives for improving the energy efficiency of their homes. Home heating and cooling bills have risen dramatically in recent years, and the prices for all fuels used in home heating and cooling

will rise even more in the future. The program provides the means for carrying out conservation measures: tax credits, federally encouraged loans, and the assistance of utilities. If, however, the present reliance on voluntary measures is insufficient to achieve widespread residential energy conservation, then mandatory measures will be considered, such as a requirement that homes be insulated before they are sold.

New buildings should also be energy efficient. The President is directing the Department of Housing and Urban Development to advance by 1 year, from 1981 to 1980, the effective date of the mandatory standards required by the Energy Policy and Conservation Act. Funds will be made available to States to help them in this effort.

The President is issuing an Executive Order to upgrade the efficiency of Federal buildings. He is directing all Federal agencies to adopt procedures which aim at reducing energy use per square foot by 1985 by 20 percent from 1975 energy consumption levels for existing Federal buildings and by 45 percent for new Federal buildings. Investments which are not cost-effective would not be funded under the program. The Director of the Office of Management and Budget and the Administrator of the Federal Energy Administration will implement this program.

Finally, the Administration will request appropriations of up to $100 million over the next 3 years to add solar hot water and space heating to suitable Federal buildings to reduce consumption of conventional fuels and demonstrate the feasibility of widespread solar energy use.

Appliances

Major home appliances such as furnaces, air-conditioners, water heaters, and refrigerators account for 20 percent of the nation's energy consumption.[8] Most of these appliances could achieve significant reductions in energy use with relatively small increases in cost. Current legislation relies mainly on voluntary efforts to meet industry-wide average targets, and permits the establishment of mandatory standards only after long delays. New legislation is proposed to streamline the regulatory process. The present voluntary program will be replaced by mandatory minimum standards on certain major home appliances as soon as possible. The National Bureau of Standards will continue to develop procedures to test the energy efficiency of appliances. The Federal Energy Administration will continue to promulgate test procedures. The Federal Trade Commission will establish labeling requirements.

U.S. Industry Energy Efficiency Compared to West Germany, for Major Energy-Intensive Industries

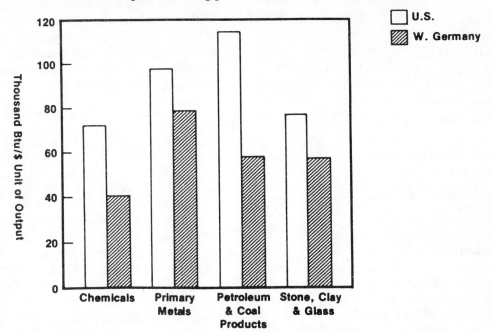

Source: Comparison of Energy Consumption Between W. Germany & the U.S., Stanford Research Inst., June 1975.

Figure IV-2

Fuel Efficiency in Industry

Industry accounts for 37 percent of the nation's energy consumption. Since the 1973-74 oil supply interruption, industry has done better than other sectors in conserving energy, but still has a large potential for further savings. For example, various U.S. industries are substantially less fuel efficient than their West German counterparts. (See Figure IV-2.) Industrial firms have an incentive to make energy-saving investments that are cost-effective from their own perspective. The price industry pays for much of the energy it consumes is not the marginal cost of energy, but rather a "rolled in" average cost, and often industrial firms receive volume discounts. In many cases, energy costs are small relative to the first costs of energy-saving investments. Therefore, energy-saving investments frequently have a lower value to industry than to society.

The oil and gas pricing program, described in Chapter V, and the taxes on industrial and utility use of oil and gas, described in Chapter VI, would provide substantial improvement in overall industrial energy efficiency.

To achieve greater savings within the industrial sector, an additional 10 percent investment tax credit would generally be available for investments in energy-saving equipment, including solar energy systems. A list of types of eligible investments would be included in the legislation. The Secretary of the Treasury would have authority to add items to the list and to delete items that do not effectively conserve energy after consultation with the Administrator of the Federal Energy Administration.

Cogeneration And District Heating

About three-quarters of the energy used by industry actually performs useful work; the rest is waste heat. In addition, two-thirds of the energy used in electricity generation and distribution is wasted. In 1975, waste heat from these sources was equivalent to over 7 million barrels of oil per day.

One way to use this waste heat is through cogeneration, the simultaneous production of process steam and electricity. Cogeneration provided 15 percent of U.S. energy as recently as 1950, but now contributes only 4 percent.

Although cogeneration is economical today and will become increasingly attractive as energy prices rise, a variety of institutional barriers impede its development. A program is proposed to remove these barriers by assuring that industrial firms generating electricity receive fair rates from utilities for both the surplus power they would sell and for the backup power they would buy. Industries using cogeneration to produce electricity could be exempted from State and Federal public utility regulation, and would be entitled to use public utility transmission facilities to sell surplus power and buy backup power. An additional tax credit of 10 percent above the existing investment tax credit would be provided for industrial and utility cogeneration equipment. Finally, industrial firms and utilities which invest in cogeneration equipment could be exempted from the requirement to convert from oil and gas in cases where an exemption is necessary for cogeneration. Cogeneration would reduce the capital requirements of electric utilities.

Another productive use of waste heat which should be fully explored is district heating. State public utility commissions should give close attention to this option in their processing of applications for new utility generating capacity.

The Government proposes to demonstrate a commitment to district heating by funding in fiscal 1978 a program to make use of the large quantities of waste heat generated by facilities of the Energy Research and Development Administration. ERDA would recover the waste heat for use on site and would also pipe steam and hot water to nearby households, industry, and agriculture. After a study of the feasibility of this concept, actual implementation of the program could occur at ERDA's facilities at Oak Ridge, Tennessee; Paducah, Kentucky; Portsmouth, Ohio; and Savannah River, South Carolina.

The Plan seeks to achieve the large savings available from productive use of waste heat through positive incentives. Careful review will be made of progress in the use of waste heat. If industry and utilities do not respond adequately, consideration will be given to a tax on waste heat or other direct measures to reduce this loss of energy.

Utility Reform

Conventional utility pricing policies discourage conservation. The smallest users commonly pay the highest unit price due to practices such as declining block rates. Rates often do not reflect the costs imposed on society by the actions of utility consumers. The result is waste and inequity.

Electrical energy is difficult and expensive to store, so a utility's need for plant and equipment is determined by its peak demand. If electricity consumption during peak periods were reduced, fewer costly new additions to utility capacity would be needed. Equally important, since peaking units commonly burn oil and gas, a reduction in peak demand would save these scarce fuels.

Accordingly, comprehensive utility reform legislation is proposed. State public utility commissions would require their regulated utilities to reform rate structures in the interest of conservation and equity. Such reform would be a prerequisite to future rate increases. The program includes the following elements:

- Electric utilities would be required to phase out promotional, declining block, and other rates that do not reflect costs; gas utilities would also be required to phase out declining block rates.

- Electric utilities would be required to offer either daily off-peak rates to each customer who is willing to pay metering costs, or provide a direct load management system. Off-peak rates would provide a strong incentive for customers, particularly industrial customers, to shift energy use from peak to off-peak periods. Similarly, homeowners would have an incentive to wash dishes and clothes at night when rates were lower, or to install equipment that stores energy during off-peak hours for use during peak hours.

- Electric utilities would be required to offer lower rates to customers who are willing to have their power interrupted at times of highest peak demand.

- Master metering—the use of a single meter for multi-unit buildings or complexes—would generally be prohibited in new structures. Individual metering induces energy conservation, in some cases as much as 30 percent.

- Electric utilities would be prohibited from discriminating against solar and other renewable energy sources.

- The Federal Government would be authorized to adopt, and require implementation of, similar policies applicable to gas utilities.

Utility interconnections and power pools make possible economies of scale, reduction of aggregate capacity requirements, and sharing of power during emergencies. Expansion of interconnections and achievement of maximum efficiency from pools are primarily the responsibility of the utility sector, which has been active in this area.

The Federal Government will follow closely the further progress of the utility sector. A proposed amendment to the Federal Power Act would remove a major gap in the authority of the Federal Power Commission by authorizing it to require interconnections between utilities even if they are not presently under FPC jurisdiction. The FPC would also be authorized to require wheeling the transmission of power between two noncontiguous utilities across another utility's system.

Savings From Conservation

Many conservation measures can be implemented with relatively little cost. Conservation involves sacrifice mainly where a cherished prerogative is given up. Many American drivers have come to enjoy instant acceleration, but as oil becomes increasingly scarce, the highly powered automobile will become increasingly anachronistic. Some moderate sacrifice today will help avoid major jolts and far more painful sacrifices in the future.

There are many ways that individual Americans can save energy beyond those specific measures included in the National Energy Plan. Individuals can keep their homes at 78°F. during the summer and at 65°F. during the winter. They can walk or ride bicycles or join carpools, instead of driving alone. They can combine several shopping trips into one. And, they can maintain their energy-using equipment—furnace, car, appliances—in good operating condition, so as to reduce energy waste.

The value of the proposed conservation program can be illustrated by comparing the cost of savings from conservation with the cost of oil imports. Conservation reduces the need for imported oil costing about $13.50 per barrel through investment in insulation, lighter automobiles, clock thermostats, and other capital equipment. The costs of the capital equipment can be expressed in terms of the cost of each barrel of oil equivalent which the equipment saves. The resulting costs vary. For example, the effective cost of a barrel of oil equivalent saved under some of the Plan's proposed conservation measures are: less than $2 for cogeneration; $3.50 for mandatory standards for new commercial construction; and about $7.50 for tax credits for commercial and industrial investments in energy-saving retrofits or mandatory standards for new residential construction. In short, conservation pays.

Chapter V — The National Energy Plan: Oil and Natural Gas

Oil and natural gas are currently the nation's primary energy sources. They provide three-quarters of U.S. energy consumption, but constitute less than 8 percent of domestic reserves. National policy toward oil and gas has been erratic, complex, and ineffective. Continuing uncertainties, particularly as to price, have retarded both production and conservation investment. The United States needs a clearly defined oil and gas policy that provides both producer incentives and consumer protection.

The Context Of Oil And Natural Gas Pricing

Both oil and natural gas are now priced domestically below their marginal replacement costs, and as a result they are overused. By holding down the price of domestic oil and "rolling in" the higher price of foreign oil, the United States has actually subsidized oil imports. The entitlements program, designed to equalize the cost of foreign and domestic oil to U.S. refiners, has become an administrative nightmare. Current mandatory oil price controls are scheduled to expire in 1979: and there is great uncertainty as to what system of controls, if any, will exist in the future.

As a result of present price controls on natural gas, discount rates offered by gas utilities, and environmental concerns, large quantities of natural gas are burned by industry and utilities. Consequently, it has become unavailable for use in new homes in many areas of the country. The movement of natural gas from producing to nonproducing States has been discouraged; and serious regional shortages, like the one in the 1976-77 winter, could occur in the future.

The time has come to recognize that, regardless of Government policy, the production of oil and natural gas will cost more in the future than it has in the past. Newly discovered fields are more expensive to develop than existing fields, and additional recovery from existing fields by nonconventional means is more expensive than recovery by conventional means.

It is also time to face up to the realities of the price of foreign oil. It has sometimes been argued that the oil-producing countries should not determine the price of oil in the United States. But, despite all the rhetoric and protestations to the contrary, the fact is that as long as a large percentage of U.S. oil consumption is imported, the world price of oil will continue to be the real cost to the U.S. economy of every extra barrel consumed.

In 1973-74, the oil-producing countries raised the world oil price fourfold. Deregulation of oil and gas prices would make U.S. producers the beneficiaries of those arbitrary price rises, and yield windfall profits from the increased value of oil and gas in existing fields. The producers have no equitable claim to that enhanced value because it is unrelated to their activities or economic contributions.

Government policy must now address the fundamental economic facts of oil and natural gas supply, and the deficiencies and uncertainties of the current system of price controls. It should provide for prices that encourage development of new wells through a more effective distribution of production incentives, but should also prevent windfall profits. It should protect consumers from profiteering, but should also promote conservation by confronting them with the real cost of oil and gas in the energy marketplace.

To achieve these purposes, a new system for pricing oil and natural gas is required. The Administration is proposing a system under which price controls would be made more consistent with national energy policies. Producers would be given adequate price incentives for development of new fields. A crude oil equalization tax would bring the cost of domestic oil up to the world price. It would raise the price of oil to its true replacement cost, and thereby encourage conservation. The proceeds of the tax, which represent the enhancement of value of domestic oil caused by OPEC price increases, would be distributed to the American people on an equitable basis.

Price controls on natural gas would be reformed as a first step toward market pricing through a formula that relates the price of gas to the price of oil.

Oil Pricing

Under the Energy Policy and Conservation Act (EPCA) passed in December of 1975, producers generally are subject to a price ceiling of either $11.28 per barrel for new oil, or $5.25 per barrel for old oil. These pricing regulations encourage additional production from existing fields. However, oil from higher cost new field development is denied the full incentive of the $13.50 world price.

The President's position has been that price controls on oil should be retained as long as world oil prices remain subject to arbitrary control, and domestic supplies are insufficient to meet domestic needs. Therefore, the Plan calls for creation of a new long-range pricing system.

The price of newly discovered oil would be allowed to rise over a 3 year period to the current 1977 world oil price, adjusted to keep pace with the domestic price level. Thereafter, the price of newly discovered oil would be adjusted for subsequent inflation. This measure would establish a domestic incentive price for frontier oil, separate from post-1977 OPEC world prices.

The incentive price would be limited to new discoveries by a definition of "new oil" applicable to oil produced from any well more than 2½ miles from a currently existing onshore well. A well more than 1,000 feet deeper than any existing well within a 2½-mile radius would also qualify for the new oil price. Offshore, only oil discovered on new Federal leases granted on or after April 20, 1977, or old leases which had been abandoned and are subjected to re-leasing by the Government would qualify for this new price.

This price should provide all the incentives needed for the development of new oil production in the United States. It would yield one of the highest production incentives available to producers anywhere in the world. It is more, for example, than the level of producer revenues in the North Sea, where exploration takes place in extremely deep water and thirty-foot waves are commonplace.

There is little or no basis for the assertion that the only reasonable price for all domestic production is the world oil price. In addition to enjoying under this program one of the highest incentives for new oil production available to any producers in the world, the domestic oil industry would find it difficult in the short-run to utilize additional incentives due to physical limitations on the availability of drilling rigs and related equipment. It would make little sense to provide incentives that could not be fully used. This pricing approach would provide the incentives in the future that would produce more energy, rather than increasingly expensive energy.

The increase in producer revenues from new discoveries of oil would provide an incentive for new production, while ensuring that there would be no windfall profits on conventional production from existing wells. Total deregulation would result in a massive transfer of income from the American public to the oil and gas producers, amounting to $14 or $15 billion, nearly 1 percent of the U.S. gross national product.

The $5.25 and $11.28 price ceilings for previously discovered oil would be allowed to rise at the rate of inflation. Where it could be shown on a case-by-case cost basis that the $5.25 ceiling makes production from a marginal well uneconomic, that well would be eligible for the $11.28 price ceiling.

Stripper wells and new tertiary recovery from old fields would receive the world oil price.

In order to ensure that market decisions by consumers are based on the real value of oil, all domestic oil would become subject at the wellhead in three stages over a 3 year period to a crude oil equalization tax equal to the difference between its controlled price and the world price. The first increment of the tax would be applied on January 1, 1978, with two subsequent increments on January 1, 1979 and January 1, 1980. Once the full tax was in place, it would increase in accordance with the world price of oil. However, authority would exist to prevent increases in the tax if the world price increased significantly faster than the level of domestic prices.

To protect consumers, net revenues from the equalization tax would be returned to them in the form of a per capita energy credit against other taxes or in the longer run as part of general tax reform. These "energy payments" would result in lower withholding from weekly paychecks to make it unnecessary to wait a full year for the benefit of the energy credit. The poor who do not pay taxes would also be entitled to their per capita share of these tax revenues. Most would receive their payment through existing income maintenance programs. The remainder would collect their energy payment by applying to one of the existing State agencies through which Federal funds are now distributed. It would be up to each State to designate which agency, or group of agencies, would have the responsibility for distributing energy payments. If the funds from the equalization tax were distributed on this basis in 1980, when the tax is fully in effect, a family of four would receive $188 in energy payments. Home heating oil users would receive an additional share of the equalization tax as a dollar-for-dollar reduction in price when they buy fuel oil.

The oil tax would establish a more realistic energy pricing system, with no net gain to the Treasury, and no net loss to consumers as a group. Once the tax is fully in effect, all domestic oil would have the same price (after tax), the entitlements program would be terminated, and certain related regulatory activities could be phased out. The entitlements program would be retained in a standby status.

Natural Gas Pricing

The Natural Gas Act never contemplated the dramatic increase in demand for natural gas which has resulted from the sudden quadrupling of the world price of oil in 1973-74 and from growing environmental concern in recent years. As a result of regulation under that Act, natural gas is now substantially underpriced, and there is excess demand. Existing supplies are being wasted on nonessential industrial and utility uses. A pricing policy which evolved at a time when gas was a surplus by-product of oil production is no longer sensible in a world where gas is a premium fuel in short supply.

Natural gas price regulation based on historic costs was workable when there were abundant supplies of natural gas. Similarly, the distinction between the unregulated intrastate and regulated interstate markets made little practical difference as long as gas was a cheap, surplus fuel. Producer claims that historic cost-based regulation is no longer appropriate for a premium fuel in short supply are fundamentally correct. But for precisely the same reason, the intrastate-interstate distinction has also become unworkable, indeed intolerable, as the limited amount of new gas increasingly flows to the unregulated intrastate market at the expense of interstate consumers. The shift in the natural gas market from surpluses to shortages requires the abandonment of historic cost-based regulation and of the artificial distinction between interstate and intrastate markets.

Therefore, a new commodity value pricing approach is proposed that applies to all new gas wherever it is used. It recognizes that prices should reflect the costs and the degree of risk associated with finding replacement supplies. This approach also recognizes the need to provide a sufficient incentive for the development of future supplies with substantially higher long-range development costs. By helping bring natural gas supply and demand back into balance, this pricing proposal would be a first step toward deregulation. If the natural gas market could be brought into better balance by the mid-1980's, it might be possible

and desirable to move further toward establishing full market pricing.

Under this proposal, all new gas sold anywhere in the country from new reservoirs would be subject to a price limitation at the Btu equivalent of the average refiner acquisition price (without tax) of all domestic crude oil. That price would be approximately $1.75 per thousand cubic feet (Mcf) at the beginning of 1978. New gas entitled to this incentive price would be limited to truly new discoveries. Gas from onshore wells more than 2$1/2$ miles from an existing well, or 1,000 feet deeper than any existing well within 2$1/2$-mile radius, would qualify for the new gas price. Offshore, only gas produced from wells on new Federal leases granted on or after April 20, 1977, or old leases which had been abandoned and are subject to releasing by the Government would qualify for this new price.

The country would also move toward a single national market for gas, like that now existing for oil. For new production the interstate-intrastate distinction would be eliminated, together with the resulting distorting effect on both production and distribution. Currently flowing natural gas would be guaranteed price certainty at levels currently set by the Federal Power Commission, with adjustments in accordance with changes in the GNP deflator. The Government would have authority to establish higher incentive pricing levels for specific categories of high-cost gas, such as gas from deep drilling, geopressurized zones, and tight formations.

The Federal Power Commission would be given new, more flexible standards for determining the price of natural gas made available at the expiration of existing interstate contracts or by production from existing reservoirs in excess of contracted volumes, but in no case would such gas qualify for a price in excess of the $1.42 per Mcf ceiling (plus inflation). Gas made available under the same circumstances from existing intrastate production would qualify for the same price as new supplies of gas, that is, a price no greater than the domestic oil Btu equivalent. Existing intrastate contracts would not be affected. Because States already regulate intrastate pipelines, Federal jurisdiction would not be extended to them except for purposes of allocation during national supply emergencies. This new gas pricing system would increase the supply of gas in the interstate market without precipitously drawing gas away from the intrastate market.

Federal pricing policy would also discourage use of gas by industry and utilities. The wellhead cost of the more expensive new supplies would all be allocated initially to industrial users, not to residential and commercial users, because the latter have far less capacity than industrial consumers to convert to other fuels.

In addition to these wellhead pricing changes, taxes would be levied on the use of oil and gas by industry and utilities, in order to encourage conservation and conversion to coal and other fuels. High volume industrial and utility users of natural gas, except for fertilizer manufacturers and certain agricultural users, would be subject to a use tax. The tax would increase the price of gas to industrial and utility users by about one-third above the Btu equivalent price of world oil over the next 5 years. Utility and industrial users of oil would also be subject to a phased-in conservation and conversion tax ranging from 90 cents to $3.00 per barrel. These measures are discussed in more detail in Chapter VI.

Federal Power Commission jurisdiction would be extended to certain synthetic natural gas facilities. However, the higher price of synthetic natural gas would not be rolled in with the price of natural gas, but rather would be allocated to industrial customers.

It will be at least 3 years before these proposals can significantly improve the natural gas supply situation. Until then, the U.S. will remain vulnerable to natural gas supply emergencies during the coldest months of the year. Because it was needed to keep American homes warm in the 1976-77 winter, the current emergency gas allocation authority would be extended for another 3 years. The need for that authority will be reviewed as the natural gas market comes into better balance.

This pricing approach acknowledges that the true economic value of a depleting resource is its replacement cost. The proposed pricing system would provide the price incentives natural gas producers need and protect homeowners from natural gas prices in excess of levels needed to maintain production.

For both oil and gas, this approach establishes an integrated pricing system that places the incentives on harder to find, new supplies, while ending the distortions of the interstate-intrastate distinction for new natural gas. It provides no reward to any firms that may have withheld natural gas last winter. Under the Plan, there would be about as much gas, oil, and conservation as would result under total deregulation. But, in addition, windfall profits would be prevented, realistic market prices for energy would be established, and part of the higher retail price of oil would be distributed to the American people.

Alaskan Oil

By the end of 1977, the Alaska pipeline terminal in Valdez, Alaska, should be receiving approximately 1.2 million barrels of oil per day. The current capacity for absorbing additional crude oil on the West Coast is no more than 600,000 to 800,000 barrels per day, leaving another 400,000 to 600,000 barrels of Alaskan oil as surplus.

Active Federal and State involvement will be necessary to assure expedited construction of the best project or combination of projects for receiving Alaskan oil on the the West Coast and moving it in an environmentally sound way to inland markets where it is needed. A Federal project coordinator has been designated to coordinate Federal involvement and to work with States in ensuring timely and thorough review of all proposals in order to expedite projects. The Administration will consult with the Canadian Government to encourage timely Canadian consideration of projects that could be constructed in that country.

As the United States reviews its options for transporting Alaskan oil, it is important that the needs of midcontinent and northern tier refiners be taken into account along with those of refiners on the West Coast. The establishment of a long-term transportation system for supplementing supplies in these regions is a matter of high priority. An assessment will also be made of all options that would enable the U.S. to benefit from Alaskan oil in the short term until permanent transportation systems are in place. The options include transshipment of surplus crude to Gulf Coast markets as well as exchanges with other nations.

The 500,000 barrels per day of imports now expected to arrive on the West Coast could also be phased out by a refinery retrofit program that, over the course of the next several years, would enable more high-sulfur Alaskan oil to be refined in California.

In order to reduce the West Coast oil surplus, legislation will also be sought to provide authority to limit production from the Elk Hills Naval Petroleum Reserve to a ready reserve level. This action could reduce the West Coast surplus until the west-to-east transportation systems for moving the West Coast crude surplus are in place or California refiners have completed a major retrofit program. In the meantime, studies will be undertaken to determine the feasibility of producing and selling natural gas from Elk Hills to supply California markets.

Without a comprehensive oil pricing approach, inclusion of Alaskan North Slope oil production in the domestic composite price would introduce a degree of unnecessary uncertainty into domestic crude oil pricing. Because the large volume of new Alaskan oil would initially be moving into the composite average at a wellhead price considerably below the current average, its inclusion could allow price increases in other tiers in the short term. Under the Plan's proposed regulations, this problem would be eliminated. The $5.25, $11.28, and new oil pricing tiers would be guaranteed increases consistent with inflation. Alaskan oil from already developed fields would be subject to an $11.28 wellhead ceiling price, would be exempt from the equalization tax, and would be treated like uncontrolled oil for purposes of the entitlements program until that program is terminated. New Alaskan discoveries would be subject to the new oil wellhead price.

This program grants maximum and certain wellhead price incentives for Alaskan oil production.

Outer Continental Shelf

Oil and gas under Federal ownership on the Outer Continental Shelf (OCS) are important national assets. It is essential that they be developed in an orderly manner, consistent with national energy and environmental policies. The Congress is now considering amendments to the OCS Lands Act, which would provide additional authorities to ensure that OCS development proceeds with full consideration of environmental effects and in consultation with States and communities. These amendments would require a flexible leasing program, using bidding systems that will enhance competition, ensure a fair return to the public, and promote full resource recovery. The Administration strongly supports passage of this legislation.

The President has also directed the Secretary of the Interior to undertake a review of OCS leasing procedures. This review will establish a sound basis for the leasing program and assure adequate production from the OCS, consistent with sound environmental safeguards.

Shale Oil

Billions of barrels of oil may some day be recovered from shale deposits in Western States if environmental and economic problems can be overcome. Several private firms have announced that they believe they can solve these problems, and that they are prepared to proceed with shale oil development. These commercial ventures should provide valuable information about the viability of a shale oil industry.

Due to the high risks and costs involved in shale oil development, the Government should establish a pricing policy that provides adequate incentives to producers. Accordingly, shale oil will be entitled to the world price of oil.

Liquefied Natural Gas

The Energy Resources Council in the previous administration proposed guidelines to limit imports of liquefied natural gas to 2 trillion cubic feet per year. Of that, no more than 1 trillion cubic feet could be imported from any one country. Applications for LNG contracts now pending before the Federal Power Commission already approach the 2-trillion-cubic-feet limitation, with over 1.2 trillion cubic feet proposed to come from Algeria.

Due to its extremely high costs and safety problems, LNG is not a long-term secure substitute for domestic natural gas. It can, however, be an important supply option through the mid-1980's and beyond, until additional gas supplies may become available.

The previous Energy Resources Council guidelines are being replaced with a more flexible policy that sets no upper limit on LNG imports. Under the new policy, the Federal Government would review each application to import LNG so as to provide for its availability at a reasonable price without undue risks of dependence on foreign supplies. This assessment would take into account the reliability of the selling country, the degree of American dependence such sales would create, the safety conditions associated with any specific installation, and all costs involved. This action could add as much as 500 billion to 1 trillion cubic feet annually to U.S. gas supply through the 1980's, without making an open-ended commitment for large volumes of this expensive resource.

The new policy further provides for distribution of imports throughout the nation, so that no region would be seriously affected by a supply interruption. It also provides for the development of contingency plans for use in the event of a supply interruption. In cases where the proposed supplier retains a unilateral right to cut off supply, consideration should be given to conditioning FPC certification on recognition of a reciprocal right to cancel on the part of the U.S. purchaser.

Finally, strict siting criteria would foreclose the construction of other LNG docks in densely populated areas.

Synthetic Natural Gas

The nation's current policy toward synthetic natural gas (SNG) made from petroleum feedstocks is not satisfactory. Existing regulations favor the allocation of naphtha and other potential SNG feedstocks to the petrochemical industry, and effectively preclude their use by gas utilities. This policy has discouraged the construction of new SNG plants. Yet, the 13 SNG plants that were operating in 1976-77 provided the additional margin of natural gas supply that kept several areas of the country from shutting off residential users during the coldest months.

Therefore, a Federal task force will be created to work with the gas utilities to identify those areas of the country where a limited number of additional SNG plants should be built to help meet the critical peakload needs for gas over the next 5 to 7 years. Federal Energy Administration regulations will be revised to provide a priority for SNG feedstocks to those plants approved by the task force. This regulatory change will give pipeline companies and utilities the reasonable certainty they need to make investments for this short-term source of gas supply.

SNG plants could contribute almost 1 trillion cubic feet of gas annually in the 1980's.

New Sources of Natural Gas

Additional funding in fiscal year 1978 is proposed to encourage private efforts to tap the potential of two resources that may produce considerable quantities of natural gas in the near and mid-term.

To evaluate the technology and economic viability of Eastern Devonian shale deposits, a number of wells will be drilled and advanced recovery will be tested. In addition, the institutional and regulatory arrangements needed to assure effective use of this resource will be studied.

ERDA will assess the dissolved gas potential in the geopressurized zones along the coast of the Gulf of Mexico. The proposed research program is designed to provide a reliable assessment of this resource and to help resolve corrosion and other problems associated with it. The significant environmental and institutional barriers to extensive development of the geopressurized resource will also be examined.

New gas from these sources could materially alter the outlook for U.S. gas supply. Successful development of these resources could provide enough additional gas to assure supplies for residential and commercial use for years to come.

Study Of The National Energy Transportation System

During the era of cheap energy, the United States developed a national energy transportation system principally for moving oil and natural gas from the South and the Texas Panhandle to the North and Northeast. With growing prospects for increased supplies of oil and gas from the Outer Continental Shelf, as well as the anticipated increases in coal production, the nation urgently needs to reassess its energy transportation system. It is clear that the energy transportation routes built in the first half of this century will have to be supplemented by new routes capable of moving the projected mix of energy supplies in 1985 to market. Therefore, the President will create a commission to study the nation's energy transportation needs and to make recommendations to him by the end of this year. One purpose of the study will be to develop means to encourage use of energy supplies nearest to consuming markets, such as eastern coal, in order to reduce the need for long-distance transport.

Gasoline Decontrol

Gasoline allocation and price controls are another major area of unsettled oil policy. Gasoline prices have never reached their allowable controlled ceilings, and marketers have contended for some time that deregulation of

gasoline would increase competition by allowing them to shop among suppliers. There is little question that gasoline allocation and price controls have distorted what at times has been a competitive market.

In order to assure the maintenance of such competition in the gasoline marketplace, the Administration will support legislation similar in concept to the pending "dealer day in court" bill that would protect service station dealers from arbitrary cancellation of their leases by major oil suppliers. In addition, the Administration currently hopes to eliminate gasoline price controls and allocation regulations at the end of the peak driving season this coming fall. Gasoline prices and market competition will be closely monitored between now and then to assure this policy is appropriate. If gasoline were to be decontrolled, controls could be reimposed if prices rose above a predetermined level. This standby authority would permit the elimination of controls while protecting consumers.

Oil Imports

In February and March of this year, United States imports reached a level of about 9 million barrels of oil per day. The measures proposed in the Plan would reduce total oil demand by 4.5 million barrels per day, resulting in oil imports in 1985 averaging about 7 million barrels per day, 2 million below the levels of February and March of 1977. Even with a reduction of oil imports to under 6 million barrels per day, the United States would have to take additional steps to reduce its vulnerability to supply interruptions.

As explained in Chapter III, the sensible policy goal for oil imports is relative invulnerability, not independence. The United States continues to import foreign oil because, even at the high prices set by the oil-exporting countries, it is cheaper than domestic sources of synthetic oil. To eliminate imports would be to sacrifice an economic benefit of major proportions. Imports also reduce the depletion of America's own critical oil reserves. Moreover, by substituting for domestic production, and by obviating the need for immediate massive development of all energy sources simultaneously, imports help maintain the quality of the environment. The United States has no reason to pay the very high cost of trying to achieve energy independence. Even if the U.S. itself were independent, its allies could not be, and the U.S. would have to assist them in the event of an international oil shortage.

The key to a tolerable level of oil imports lies in reducing vulnerability by means of an adequate strategic oil reserve, diversification of foreign sources of supply, and contingency plans. The reserve must be large enough to impose substantial revenue losses on countries imposing an embargo, and to enable the United States to deal with the consequences of any supply interruption. The ability to ride out a supply interruption may reduce the likelihood that any nation or combination of nations would impose one. The availability of the Strategic Petroleum Reserve would help offset the adverse economic effects of a supply interruption.

Accordingly, the U.S. plans to expand the Strategic Petroleum Reserve from the currently projected 500 million barrels to the 1 billion barrel level. Assuming that vigorous conservation measures, including rationing, would be undertaken during a supply interruption, and assuming further that a number of OPEC and non-OPEC nations would not participate in the supply interruption, the reserve is designed to supply somewhat more than 3 million barrels per day. Under these assumptions, a 1 billion barrel reserve would last at least 10 months. This reserve is the best kind of insurance the United States could buy, since it is unlikely that the price of oil will fall in the foreseeable future.

An effective policy to reduce vulnerability to supply interruptions also requires diversification of the sources of oil imports. Some developing countries with major petroleum reserves find it difficult to deal directly with multinational oil companies. Yet such countries need capital and sophisticated technology of the kind U.S. firms could supply, as well as the revenues that resource development would bring. The United States recognizes that government-to-government negotiations may be helpful in dealing with the wide variety of potential obstacles that currently prevent these nations from making a significant contribution to world oil supplies.

Finally, the United States must put in place effective contingency plans. The Administration is transmitting to the Congress a standby rationing plan and demand restraint plans to be available in the event of a national emergency resulting from a supply interruption. The impacts on particular industries and sectors of society would be substantial. But the contingency plans would be implemented only under conditions of extreme national emergency, when substantial sacrifices in the national interest would be justified. In addition, the Administration is accelerating the preparation of additional contingency plans. These plans would reach all sectors of American life: industry, commerce, transportation, residences, and the public sector. Should a national energy emergency occur and the plans have to be invoked, the burdens would be shared widely and fairly among all Americans.

Chapter VI. — The National Energy Plan: Coal, Nuclear, and Hydroelectric Power

Even with vigorous conservation, America's demand for energy will continue to grow. The United States will need increased domestic energy production if it is to avoid shortages and unacceptable levels of imports. The U.S. eventually will make extensive use of solar and other non-conventional energy sources. During the remainder of this century, however, it will have to rely for the bulk of its energy supply on the conventional sources now at hand: oil, natural gas, coal, nuclear, and hydroelectric power. Federal policy should stimulate the expanded use of coal, supplemented by nuclear power and renewable resources, to fill the growing gap created by rising energy demand and relatively stable production of oil and gas.

Coal: Conversion to Coal and Alternative Fuels

Industry and utilities consumed 4.8 million barrels of oil per day and 5.9 million barrels of oil equivalent per day in the form of natural gas in 1976. Oil and natural gas are scarce, and generally they are needed more by other sectors of the economy. Industry and electric utilities can convert to other energy sources more readily than can other users; therefore, a large-scale conversion by industry and utilities from oil and gas to more abundant resources is needed.

Coal constitutes 90 percent of U.S. conventional energy reserves, but currently supplies only 18 percent of energy consumption. It is generally acknowledged that the coal industry can expand production significantly, and currently has a small amount of excess capacity. (See Figure VI-1.) Full utilization of America's coal resources has been hindered principally by constraints on demand, rather than by lack of supply.

Questions have been raised about the adequacy of the nation's transportation system to deliver increased quantities of coal. With the exception of a few areas, it appears that railroads could transport the additional coal. The coal transportation situation will be considered as part of the study of the national energy transportation system. In addition, the Federal Government will monitor coal transportation carefully; and if problems should appear, it will take appropriate action.

Coal development and production is most economical when it is near major markets. Although coal production will expand in many areas, there should be large production increases in the highly populated Eastern and Mid-West regions, where coal use in industry and utilities could grow considerably in the future. The required use of best available control technology for new powerplants should stimulate even greater use of high sulfur Mid-Western and Eastern coals.

Expansion of U.S. coal production and use is essential if the nation is to maintain economic growth, reduce oil imports, and have adequate supplies of natural gas for residential use. Accordingly, to stimulate an increase in demand for coal and other alternatives to gas and oil, the

U.S. Coal Supply

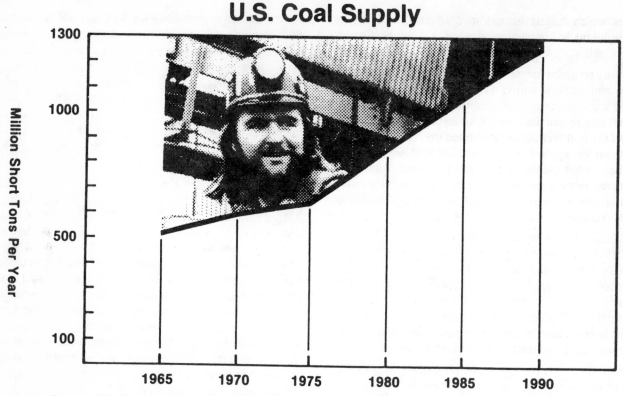

Source: U.S. Bureau of Mines and Federal Energy Administration.

Figure VI-1

Plan proposes a coal conversion program consisting of tax and regulatory measures.

The tax measures are designed to raise the cost of gas and oil to industrial and utility users, and to provide positive incentives for conversion to other sources of energy. A tax would be levied on industrial and utility use of natural gas and petroleum products. Beginning in 1979, high volume industrial users of natural gas (except fertilizer manufacturers and certain agricultural users) would be affected. They would be taxed an amount equal to the difference between their average cost of natural gas and a price target keyed to distillate oil (without the proposed tax on utility and industrial use of petroleum products). The price of distillate is one third higher than the world price of crude oil. The target level for the first year's tax in 1979 in constant dollars would be $1.05 below the Btu equivalent price of distillate. The target price would rise to the distillate prices in 1985 and beyond.

Thus, in 1979, an industrial user who paid $1.65 per Mcf for gas would pay a tax of $0.30 per Mcf to bring the total cost of gas up to the target level of $1.95 per Mcf, assuming the Btu equivalent price of distillate would be $3.00. By 1985, the target level would rise to approximately $3.30 per Mcf, the projected Btu equivalent price for distillate, resulting in an average tax of $1.10 per Mcf based on a projected actual gas cost of $2.20 per Mcf.

Utility users of natural gas would be similarly taxed starting in 1983, at an amount that would bring their cost of gas to a level of $0.50 per Mcf below the Btu equivalent price of distillate. The tax would rise so that by 1988 their cost of gas would equal the cost of the Btu equivalent amount of distillate. The later starting date for the tax on utility use of natural gas reflects the longer lead time required by utilities to convert to coal.

Industrial and utility users of petroleum products would be taxed at a flat rate since, unlike natural gas prices, petroleum prices are relatively uniform nationwide. Beginning in 1979, industrial use would be taxed $0.90 per barrel; the tax would rise to $3.00 per barrel by 1985. A tax on utility use of petroleum products would begin in 1983 at $1.50 per barrel and remain at that level thereafter.

Industry would generally be eligible, at its election, for either an additional 10 percent investment tax credit for conversion expenditures or a rebate of any natural gas or petroleum taxes paid, up to the amount of any expenditures incurred for conversion to coal or other fuels. With tax liability delayed until 1979 for industry and 1983 for utilities, prudent investors undertaking an aggressive conversion program should be able to accumulate enough conversion credits to eliminate, or minimize, the actual amounts of tax paid. Only those industrial firms and utilities which lagged behind in conversion would pay substantial taxes.

The Plan also proposes a revised and simplified regulatory program for oil and natural gas conversions. Industry and utilities would be prohibited from burning natural gas and petroleum products in new boilers, with limited environmental and economic exceptions. Industrial firms also could be prohibited from burning gas or petroleum in new major fuel-burning installations other than boilers, by regulations applicable to categories of installations, or on a case-by-case basis. Such orders would be subject to the same limited environmental and economic exceptions.

Existing facilities with coal-burning capability could be prohibited from burning gas or oil, where the burning of substitue fuels would be economically feasible and environmentally acceptable. Facilities burning coal would be required to obtain a permit in order to shift to petroleum or natural gas. Utilities burning gas would require a permit to shift to petroleum instead of coal. By 1990, virtually no utility would be permitted to burn natural gas.

Any industrial firm or utility prohibited from using natural gas would be allowed to sell its contract to purchase gas at a price that would compensate it fully for shifting to petroleum on an interim basis or to coal on a longer term basis.

These regulatory proposals closely resemble a bill sponsored by Senators Jackson, Humphrey, and Randolph. The Administration looks forward to working closely with the Congress to develop an effective fuel conversion program.

Environmental Policy

Attainment and maintenance of the environmental goals set out in the Clean Air Act, the Federal Water Pollution Control Act, and the National Environmental Policy Act are high national priorities. The Administration intends to achieve its energy goals without endangering the public health or degrading the environment.

The Administration has indicated its position regarding a series of amendments to the Clean Air Act. Utilities and industrial facilities will be asked to convert to coal without sacrifice of air quality standards. It is recognized that, in areas with serious air pollution problems, it may be necessary to continue burning oil in order to protect public health. The Administration is conducting a research and development program that will produce new technologies that allow the clean burning of coal more efficiently.

A strong but consistent and certain environmental policy can provide the stability needed to encourage investment in new energy facilities. The Administration has taken a position that all new facilities, including those that burn low sulfur coal, should be required to use the best available control technology.

The Administration has also supported an amendment to the Clean Air Act which would prevent significant deterioration of air quality in areas where air is now cleaner than required by air quality standards. It is committed to protecting national parks and other pristine Federal lands. In order to provide a necessary measure of certainty for the development of new energy facilities, the Administration has recommended adoption of a provision which would encourage States to classify their lands into the various categories within 3 years for protection against significant deterioration. After these initial designations are made, a new energy facility would be subject to those classifications and requirements in effect at the time of application, unless the Governor of the State served notice of an intent to change the classification within 120 days. If a classification is to be changed, the State would be required to complete the redesignation within 1 year. By reducing the amount of time during which the ground rules for locating energy facilities can change, Government would enable energy planning to proceed in a more orderly and expeditious way.

The Environmental Protection Agency will review its current policies allowing offsetting pollution tradeoffs for new installations locating in areas which violate the primary ambient air quality standards. Although the current policy may prove to be the most reasonable strategy for permitting new growth while maintaining progress toward attainment of air quality goals, alternatives should also be explored. The Administration has recommended that no new legislative requirements be adopted in this area until the review is completed. In the interim, the existing EPA policy will be retained.

Some uncertainty will continue over the environmental impacts of an increasing number of coal-burning plants, even those equipped with the best available control technology. Accordingly, the President will appoint a special committee to study the health effects of increased coal production and use, and the environmental constraints on coal mining and on the construction of new coal-burning facilities. The committee will report to the President by next October. In addition, nearly $3 million is being requested to study the long-term effects on the atmosphere of carbon dioxide from coal and other hydrocarbons.

The Administration has recognized the need to protect land and water quality against unwarranted damage resulting from inadequate reclamation of strip mined areas. It continues to support uniform national strip mine legislation that would fully protect the nation's land while permitting the production of coal that is needed to meet national energy objectives.

Coal Research

Coal will meet the greatest portion of increased U.S. energy needs. A comprehensive coal research and development program is a high priority. The program should focus on meeting environmental requirements more effectively and economically, and should seek to expand the substitution of coal for natural gas and petroleum products.

In the short term, most coal will continue to be burned directly. Hence, the highest immediate priority is the development of more effective, economical methods to meet air pollution control standards. Some flue-gas desulfurization (FGD) systems, or "scrubbers", are already in commercial use. Work will continue on overcoming generic operating problems encountered by these systems. A number of new systems are under development, and the Government will undertake a 6 month review to determine whether the new technologies offer sufficient environmental, cost and reliability advantages to justify accelerating the RD&D program. Research into fluidized-bed combustion systems for the direct burning of coal in an environmentally superior manner is being expanded.

In addition, increased research will be devoted to developing means to control the fine particulate and sulfur oxide emissions associated with coal burning. In many situations, front-end coal cleaning by grinding and washing can reduce the free sulfur and ash content and thereby reduce the cost of meeting environmental standards. Accordingly, the Government will expand its current research and demonstration program for coal cleaning to determine what additional efforts are needed to meet sulfur oxide and particulate standards more economically.

Solvent refined coal processes use chemical means to remove even more of the sulfur content. The Government will initiate the design of a commercial-size demonstration solvent refined coal plant in fiscal 1978. If, as expected, pilot plant technical and economic feasibility is demonstrated, construction of a commercial-size plant will proceed.

Pursuant to the Administration's February budget revisions, the Government is proceeding with demonstration projects to develop on a commercial scale techniques for deriving low Btu gas from coal. For example, a large gasification project at a Minnesota ore plant and another at a Pennsylvania zinc smelter have been selected for government and industry cost-sharing demonstrations. Low Btu gasification processes produce a coal-derived industrial quality fuel that avoids the need for back-end sulfur oxide and particulate control. That fuel could be a major aid in meeting coal conversion objectives.

In the long run, high Btu synthetic gas produced from coal may provide a substitute for declining natural gas supplies. The Administration will pursue an active RD&D program for high Btu coal gasification using advanced technologies. The program will be conducted with the urgency required to ensure that the new technology will be ready when needed.

The basic Federal role in this process is research, development and demonstration of new technologies. In general, the Government seeks to avoid subsidization of existing technologies, although circumstances may sometimes merit an exception to that policy.

The technology for producing synthetic crude oil is not as well developed as synthetic gas technologies. An active RD&D program, including pilot plant demonstrations, will be pursued. The Federal Government currently is providing some of the funding for a 600-ton per day, coal-to-oil pilot facility in Kentucky.

Funding authority for the overall coal program would amount to $527 million in fiscal 1978, and would continue at substantial levels. The success of this program in developing and commercializing new coal technologies will reduce the pressure on dwindling oil and gas supplies. The new coal technologies are critical to the National Energy Plan, both as an immediate aid in converting from scarce to abundant resources and as a future source of synthetic oil and gas.

Nuclear Power

Many countries view nuclear power as their only real alternative to dependence on costly and uncertain oil and gas imports. The United States is in a better position, primarily because of its vast coal resources. Coal does, however, have economic, environmental, and health and safety limitations; and, therefore, the United States also must continue to count on nuclear power to meet a share of its energy deficit.

Light-water reactors provide a proven technology to produce needed electrical power. However, more advanced forms of nuclear power may entail significant risk, and must therefore be developed cautiously. The United States has been concentrating on the development of a breeder reactor that uses plutonium, a by-product of uranium in nuclear reactors. In addition, the United States has been developing reprocessing technology to recover the uranium and plutonium in the spent fuel from light-water reactors. Access to plutonium, or even the capacity to recover or isolate it, can lead to the risk of diversion of material that could be used for nuclear explosive devices. The United States should develop advanced nuclear technologies that minimize the risk of nuclear proliferation, but with the knowledge that no advanced nuclear technology is entirely free from proliferation risks.

It is the President's policy to defer any U.S. commitment to advanced nuclear technologies that are based on the use of plutonium, while the United States seeks a better approach to the next generation of nuclear power than is provided by plutonium recycle and the plutonium breeder. At the same time, because there is no practicable alternative, the United States will need to use more light-water reactors to help meet its energy needs. The Government will give increased attention to light-water reactor safety, licensing, and waste management so that nuclear power can be used to help meet the U.S. energy deficit with increased safety.

Proliferation is a world-wide problem. The President announced on April 7, 1977 that the United States will make a concerted effort in association with other countries to find better solutions to this problem. For its part, the United States has adopted two policies. First, it will refrain from proceeding with nuclear technologies that present a high risk of proliferation. To this end, the United States will defer indefinitely commercial reprocessing and recycling of plutonium, as well as the commercial introduction of the plutonium breeder. Second, the President is proposing to reduce the funding for the existing breeder program and to redirect it toward evaluation of alternative breeders, advanced converter reactors, and other fuel cycles, with emphasis on nonproliferation and safety concerns. He also is proposing to cancel construction of the Clinch River Breeder Reactor Demonstration Project and all component construction, licensing, and commercialization efforts. The design work would be completed, and a base level program would be maintained, including the Fast Flux Test Facility. These actions would not seriously affect long-term energy supplies in the United States. There is, of course, some price to be paid in redirecting this program but that price is clearly outweighed by the dangers of proceeding.

The United States hopes that these actions will encourage other nations to pause in their development of plutonium-based technology and to examine alternative methods of meeting their future energy needs.

The United States recognizes that for this pause to be feasible, other nations must have assured supplies of slightly enriched uranium required for light-water reactors. The United States must restore confidence in its willingness and ability to supply enrichment services. The Administration, therefore, is prepared, in cooperation with the Congress, to take three steps that will substantially improve confidence in the U.S. position:

- reopen the order books for U.S. uranium enrichment services;
- adopt legislation to guarantee the delivery of enrichment services to any country that shares U.S. nonproliferation objectives and accepts conditions consistent with those objectives;

- expand U.S. enrichment capacity.

Current U.S. enrichment capacity consists of three gaseous diffusion plants which use a technology first developed more than 30 years ago. The time has come to move to the new gaseous centrifuge technology, which consumes less than 10 percent as much electrical power as a diffusion plant of equivalent capacity. In addition, a centrifuge plant has the potential for producing enriched uranium at lower cost. Therefore, the next U.S. enrichment plant, for which funds are already in the proposed fiscal 1978 budget, will be a centrifuge plant.

Light-water reactors require a supply of natural uranium. Current estimates of U.S. uranium resources range between 1.8 and 3.7 million tons. The uncertainties about the extent of domestic uranium resources should be resolved. The Energy Research and Development Administration will reorient its National Uranium Resources Evaluation Program to improve uranium resources assessment. The program will also include thorium, which may be used to breed fuel in some of the advanced nuclear technologies. This program will be a cooperative effort with industry, the States and the U.S. Geological Survey.

Today, 63 nuclear power plants provide about 10 percent of the U.S. supply of electricity. By 1985, an additional 75 nuclear plants already planned or in construction could be in operation, and nuclear power could provide as much as 20 percent of electricity supply.

Thus, the United States has the option of relying on light-water reactors to provide nuclear power to offset a share of the nation's energy deficit without undue risk of proliferation. However, as with any energy technology, there are risks in the operation of light-water reactors. Although the safety record of light-water reactors has been good, several additional actions can be taken to improve safety.

To protect against possible diversion of nuclear material and against sabotage, the Nuclear Regulatory Commission has already increased the required number of guards at plants and the requirements for the training that guards receive. To improve the overall safety of light-water reactors, the President is requesting that the Commission expand its audit and inspection staff to increase the number of unannounced inspections and to assign one permanent Federal inspector to each nuclear power plant. The President is also requesting that the Commission make mandatory the current voluntary reporting of minor mishaps and component failures at operating reactors, in order to develop the reliable data base needed to improve reactor design and operating practice.

In addition, the President is requesting that the Commission develop firm siting criteria with clear guidelines to prevent siting of future nuclear plants in densely populated locations, in valuable natural areas, or in potentially hazardous locations. Proper siting will substantially reduce the risks of a nuclear accident and the consequences should one occur.

Reform of the nuclear licensing process is clearly needed. The present process is unsatisfactory to all participants: industry, intervenors, and the Federal Government. The President has directed that a study be made of the entire nuclear licensing process. He has proposed that reasonable and objective criteria be established for licensing and that plants that are based on a standard design not require extensive individual licensing.

In addition to licensing problems, construction delays have also contributed to the long lead-times needed to build U.S. nuclear plants. A national industry-labor agreement could lead to a substantial reduction in construction time and increase the willingness of utilies to invest in nuclear power plants.

Finally, the waste generated by nuclear power must be managed so as to protect current and future generations. Improved methods of storing spent fuel will enable most utilities at least to double their current storage capacity without constructing new facilities. Two actions have been taken to ensure that long-term waste storage facilities are available by 1985. The Energy Research and Development Administration's waste management program has been expanded to include development of techniques for long-term storage of spent fuel. Prototype technologies, complete designs, and initial environmental criteria for waste repositories will be developed by 1978. Licensing of the first repository should be completed by 1981. There will be an opportunity for thorough public review at each of these stages. A task force under the direction of the Assistant to the President for energy will review the entire ERDA waste management program.

Hydroelectric Power

New or additional hydroelectric generating capacity at existing dams could be installed at less than the cost of equivalent new coal or nuclear capacity. Many of these sites are small, but could generate 3 to 5 megawatts, and are located near major demand centers currently dependent on imported fuel oil. Installation of additional generating capacity at existing sites could conceivably add as much as 14,000 megawatts to the nation's generating potential.

The Department of Defense (Corps of Engineers) and other responsible agencies, have, therefore, been directed to report to the Assistant to the President for energy on the potential for additional hydropower installations at existing dam sites throughout the country.

Chapter VII. — The National Energy Plan: Non-conventional Sources and Energy Research

America's hope for energy to sustain economic growth beyond the year 2000 rests in large measure on the development of renewable and essentially inexhaustible sources of energy. Many diverse solar, geothermal, biomass and other technologies are in various stages of development. Some technologies, such as solar hot water and space heating, can make contributions now. Others, such as the solar electric technologies and some forms of geothermal energy, have great promise for the future. Fusion still requires significant scientific progress before its feasibility can be demonstrated. The Government should aggressively promote the development of nonconventional resources despite the fact that they face many uncertainties. The danger of too much initial skepticism is that it may become a self-fulfilling prophecy.

Solar Energy

Solar hot water and space heating technology is now being used, and is ready for more widespread commercialization. A temporary Federal program of financial incentives and public education is needed to stimulate the development of a larger solar market. As manufacturers, installers, and consumers become more familiar with solar energy equipment, and as economies of scale are achieved, prices should be reduced. Therefore, a tax credit supported by a Federally funded public education program is proposed. The credit would start at 40 percent of the first $1,000 and 25 percent of the next $6,400 (for a maximum of $2,000) paid for installation of qualifying solar equipment. The credit would decline in stages to 25 percent of the first $1,000 and 15 percent of the next $6,400. The credit would be available for expenditures between April 20, 1977, and December 31, 1984. The public education initiative would consist of a joint Federal-State program of standards development, certification, training, and information gathering and dissemination.

This initiative should help launch the solar heating industry. The industry would be further aided by the inclusion of investments in solar equipment among the approved conservation measures eligible for the proposed 10 percent tax credit for energy-saving investments by business. This investment tax credit should encourage the use of solar energy for industrial and agricultural process heat and for commercial operations. Solar energy is likely to be particularly attractive for use in crop drying and other agricultural applications.

The results of the solar demonstration programs being carried out by the Energy Research and Development Administration and the Department of Housing and Urban

Development and the equipment performance standards being developed by HUD should help provide a basis for warranties, insurance, and mortgage valuations. Moreover, the Federal Government will demonstrate its confidence in solar technology by undertaking a 3 year program of up to $100 million for installation of solar equipment in Federal buildings.

The States should also support widespread use of solar energy. A number of them have already amended their property tax laws to exempt solar installations from assessments. It is desirable that the other States do so as well. The States are also encouraged to enact legislation to protect access to the sun and to promote consumer education in the solar field. Under the proposed utility reform program, State public utility commissions would develop guidelines to prevent utilities from discriminating against users of solar energy.

Energy from the sun can also be used without any equipment at all. Through building orientation and design, choice of materials, location of trees and hedges, and other means, "passive" solar systems can be used to obtain heat from the sun when it is needed and to reject it when it is not. More widespread use of passive solar systems would help to reduce fuel bills and conserve conventional fuels.

Solar energy can also be used to generate electricity. The solar electric technologies are in varying stages of development. Photovoltaic systems, using cells developed in the space program, are economic today for certain small, decentralized applications. These systems have a potential for dramatic price reductions that would make them economical for a broader range of applications. Increased funding is proposed to accelerate the development of economic photovoltaic systems. Longer term development is proceeding on central station solar electric power systems. Collection of solar energy by space satellites has been proposed, and the concept deserves further study.

Various technologies make indirect use of solar energy, in the form of wind, agricultural and forestry residues ("biomass"), and ocean thermal energy (the heat captured by the ocean surface). Wind and biomass can make significant regional contributions in the medium term. Wind systems can supply energy to small utilities, hydroelectric systems, and dispersed users of power. Agricultural and forestry residues already are used as fuel, and that use can be increased by improved collection methods and by energy farms, in which crops are grown specifically for use as energy. In addition, biomass can be used to produce liquid and gaseous fuels for a variety of uses.

The Plan's fuel conversion program would be an incentive for use of biomass, as well as coal. Industry and utilities would have strong reasons to shift away from oil and gas to other energy sources. Tax credits would be pro-

vided for investments in facilities to use nonconventional energy sources, as well as to use coal. The environmental problems associated with coal combustion should lead businessmen to take a close look at the advantages of using nonconventional energy sources.

Finally, the Plan's research and development program includes increased funding for biomass, small wind systems, solar cooling, and other solar technologies.

Municipal Solid Waste

Municipal solid waste is a valuable energy resource. Its use for energy production also helps to solve environmental problems and reduce municipal disposal costs. Energy can be obtained from municipal solid waste both through direct combustion and through systems for converting wastes into liquid, gaseous, and solid fuels ("refuse-derived fuels").

Greater use of energy recovery systems has been hindered by the availability of cheap, open dumps and by technological and institutional difficulties. However, some plants burning solid waste or producing fuel from it already operate successfully, and present barriers to more widespread use should be overcome with coordinated action by Federal, State and local governments and private firms.

The Plan's fuel conversion program would provide incentives for use of municipal solid waste and refuse-derived fuel as energy sources. Through implementation of the Resource Conservation and Recovery Act of 1976, the Federal Government will continue to help States and local governments to overcome the present barriers to more widespread use of municipal solid waste.

Geothermal Energy

Geothermal energy, the natural heat in the Earth's crust, has a large potential for direct thermal use and for electricity generation, particularly in the Western States. It occurs in many forms, only one of which is currently used to a significant extent. Dry geothermal steam from The Geysers in California provides more than 500 MWe for northern California.

Hydrothermal (liquid-dominated) sites are found throughout the West, some at high temperatures adequate for electricity generation, and others at lower temperatures suitable for heating of buildings. At present, several hundred buildings use geothermal heat. With expected technological progress, hydrothermal sources should begin to make a significant contribution in the 1980's.

Geopressurized resources, located along the Gulf Coast, contain potentially significant amounts of hot water and dissolved methane, which may become accessible in the 1980's. Hot dry rock may become a significant source of energy in the 1990's.

To stimulate the development of geothermal resources, legislation is proposed to extend to geothermal drilling the tax deduction for intangible drilling costs that is now available for oil and gas drilling. The purpose of this proposal is to bring about equality of treatment among activities which compete for capital. The issues concerning the overall allowance of deductions for intangible drilling costs will be reviewed as part of the President's tax reform program.

The Plan's research and development program provides additional funding to evaluate the geopressurized and liquid-dominated hydrothermal resources and to promote the use of geothermal energy in nonelectric applications.

Finally, the Department of the Interior, the Department of Agriculture, and the States will be encouraged to streamline their leasing and environmental review procedures to remove unnecessary barriers to development of geothermal resources.

Fusion

Research in controlled thermonuclear reactions ("fusion") has been a major element in energy research and development programs. However, despite many years of active research, scientific feasibility has yet to be demonstrated, though steady progress has been made in satisfying each of the individual criteria for achievement of breakeven power (the production of more power than is consumed).

Current research on magnetic confinement systems seeks to demonstrate the simultaneous attainment of temperature, density, and confinement time necessary for breakeven. Inertial confinement (laser or beam) systems, a newer technology, may lag behind magnetic systems in achieving breakeven power. Once a demonstration of breakeven is made, extensive engineering efforts would be required to design a commercial system.

However, even without achievement of breakeven power, either fusion system may be able to produce usable energy as part of a hybrid fusion-fission cycle. The fusion process produces neutrons which might breed fuel for light-water nuclear reactors more easily than it produces electricity.

The revised budget submitted by the Administration last February provides for continued work on fusion on an orderly basis.

Research, Development, and Demonstration

An effective Federal research, development and demonstration (RD&D) program is indispensable for the production of new energy sources. Research is not an end in itself. The purpose of RD&D is to produce technologies for practical use. The final stage of a successful RD&D program is commercialization, the movement of a functioning technology into the marketplace.

The groundwork for eventual commercialization should generally be laid during the RD&D stage. Before embarking on costly research projects, the Government should have the best possible information on prospects for economic success and institutional acceptance. As scientific and technical advances are made, economic and institutional barriers to commercialization should also be addressed, so that if technical success is achieved in the RD&D program, commercialization can take place rapidly.

However, Government support of scientific research and engineering development does not constitute a commitment to subsequent demonstrations of technologies that do not meet technical, economic, national security, health, safety, and environmental criteria. The Government should support multiple parallel technological options in their early stages, but it should not drift unwittingly into a long-term guarantee of support for all options initially pursued. Only those technologies that satisfy criteria for practical success should be supported into the demonstration stage. Recognition that early Government support should not be regarded as a blank check for the future should benefit the entire RD&D program.

Commercialization activities, and in particular commercial demonstration projects, also must not become a hidden subsidy of technically feasible but economically uncompetitive technologies. Where subsidies are justified, they should be awarded in an open process that is responsive to national priorities.

A balanced RD&D program should have near-term as well as long-term benefits, should promote conservation and nonconventional resources as well as conventional resources, should support small-scale as well as large-scale projects, and should enlist the talents of individual inventors and small business as well as major corporations. In its revisions of the fiscal year 1978 budget, the Administration began the process of reorienting RD&D priorities to meet the country's real needs. The Administration proposed additional funding for the following items:

- programs to develop improved methods of energy conservation;

- solar heating and cooling demonstrations, mainly in residential buildings;

- application of solar energy in agricultural and industrial processes, including more than 60 agricultural projects in more than 30 States;

- development of improved ways to use agricultural and forestry residues, water-based energy crops, and animal wastes; and

- development and demonstration of the use of solar and wind energy to operate irrigation pumps and for other rural applications.

In accordance with the priorities set forth in the National Energy Plan, additional funds will be provided for research and development projects for conservation and small-scale energy systems. A new Office of Small-Scale Technologies is also proposed, in order to tap more fully the potential of individual inventors and small business firms.

Additional conservation projects are proposed. The Energy Research and Development Administration will conduct a feasibility study of waste heat recovery and district heating at several of its own facilities. To conserve natural gas, the Government will also fund programs for additional work on gas-fired heat pumps and small fuel cells for residential and commercial heating and cooling.

Other programs may add significantly to the nation's near-term natural gas supply. The Government will provide additional funding to accelerate the investigation of methane recovery from the geopressurized zones along the Gulf Coast and gas from Eastern Devonian shale.

The Government will add several initiatives to its research program to support the Plan's emphasis on increased use of coal, as described in Chapter VI.

The Government will provide increased funding for solar cooling and allied technology and for small wind energy conversion systems. It will also support a project to demonstrate the use of wood-derived biomass as a substitute for fuel oil. These projects could yield significant regional benefits.

New initiatives are proposed for geothermal energy. Additional funding will be provided to identify new liquid-dominated hydrothermal fields which could be tapped for direct thermal use. The Government will also support field experiments of direct, nonelectric uses of geothermal energy for residential space conditioning and industrial and agricultural process heat in areas where this resource has not previously been exploited.

The Plan's additional research and development program focuses on projects with near-term and mid-term potential. It emphasizes small, dispersed, and environmentally sound production and use of energy, particularly renewable energy. It also seeks to redress the advantage enjoyed by big business in the Government's current research and development program.

Chapter VIII.—The National Energy Plan: The Role of Government and the American Public

Government at all levels has a critical role to play in guiding the course of energy production and use. In addition to proposing specific initiatives, the Federal Government should:

- establish clear national energy goals;

- organize itself to administer national energy policy effectively;

- create a comprehensive, reliable repository of energy information;

- ensure competition in the energy industries generally and among the major oil and natural gas companies in particular; and

- provide assistance to low-income people during energy emergencies.

State and local governments will be asked to assume major responsibilities in cooperation with the Federal Government. Nongovernmental organizations and individuals can also make significant contributions to the success of energy policies. The private sector will continue its primary role as the major producer and consumer of energy resources.

National Energy Goals

There is no quick or easy solution to the energy problem. The reorientation of American society to the newly recognized energy realities will occur only as a result of a multitude of measures over many years. An important part of the Plan is Congressional adoption of specific national energy goals, so that progress can be monitored and assessed. The proposed goals, to be achieved between now and 1985, are:

- reduce the rate of growth of energy consumption to below 2 percent per year;

- reduce gasoline consumption by 10 percent below the 1976 level;

- reduce oil imports to less than 6 million barrels per day, about one-eighth of total energy consumption;

- establish a Strategic Petroleum Reserve of 1 billion barrels;

- increase coal production by about two-thirds, to more than 1 billion tons annually;

- insulate 90 percent of American homes and all new buildings; and

- use solar energy in more than 2-1/2 million homes.

The Plan does not seek illusory goals, such as energy independence. Rather, it seeks goals that are ambitious, but that are achievable in light of the present widespread waste of energy, and the large potential for conversion from oil and natural gas to coal. However, the proposed conservation goals do not reflect merely what can be achieved by the measures formally proposed in the Plan. These goals are set at more demanding levels in order to take account of voluntary actions outside the scope of the specific measures in the Plan, such as keeping buildings at 78° in the summer and 65° in the winter, carpooling instead of driving alone, and spending leisure time in ways that consume less energy. The goals challenge the American people to go beyond the Plan through voluntary actions.

If the proposed goals are adopted, then, beginning 2 years after enactment of the National Energy Plan, the President will submit to the Congress biannually a report on the nation's progress in moving toward the 1985 goals. The report will recommend any changes in the existing Plan, or any additional measures needed to meet the 1985 goals.

The Department Of Energy

The initiatives presented in the National Energy Plan underscore the importance of creating at the earliest possible date a Department of Energy. Legislation to create this Department has been sent to the Congress by the Administration, and hearings have been held in both the House and Senate.

Although organizational changes alone will not solve any energy problem, creation of the Department of Energy is a necessity if the elements of the Plan are to be carried out in a coherent and effective manner. The Plan proposes a unified policy. The Department would carry out this policy through a unified organization that would coordinate and manage energy conservation, supply development, information collection and analysis, energy regulation, and research, development, and demonstration. Only through creation of a Department that combines the skills and expertise now dispersed through numerous Federal agencies will the Government obtain the comprehensive overview of interrelated energy problems and the organizational coherence needed to implement the National Energy Plan.

By consolidating more than 100 important energy data collection programs in the Federal Government, the Department of Energy would provide comprehensive and reliable energy information. An Energy Information Administration within the Department would organize and analyze information so that it could be used by governments, industry, and the public.

In addition, the ability of the Federal Government to administer the regulatory process when market forces do not suffice would be significantly enhanced by unification of most of the responsibilities for economic regulation of energy. The Department of Energy, operating within congressional mandates, would be able to avoid the inconsistencies and uncertainties inherent in a situation where agencies operate in isolation and sometimes at cross-purposes.

The Department of Energy would enable the Federal Government to coordinate its research, development, and commercialization activities within a policy-planning process that takes full account of the importance of conservation and near-term resource development. The Department would be the most effective means for ensuring that the priorities established in the National Energy Plan are translated into the Government's ongoing research, development, and commercialization efforts.

Finally, by combining the conservation programs of various agencies, the Department would be in a position to ensure that the strong emphasis of the Plan on fostering genuine conservation and improved energy efficiency will not be frustrated by a mass of competing, conflicting, and overlapping jurisdictions in the Executive Branch.

Information

The Federal Government needs more detailed and reliable information on energy matters than is now available. Much of the nation's remaining reserves of oil and natural gas are located on Federal lands and belong to the American people. More information is needed on the size of particular reserves and the rates at which they are being depleted. To identify and assess possible anticompetitive behavior on the part of major oil companies, the Government needs detailed data on their operations. To deal swiftly and effectively with energy emergencies, such as an interruption of foreign oil supply or a natural gas shortage, governments need information on local energy supplies and consumption patterns.

Accordingly, a three-part energy information program is proposed. It would include a Petroleum Production and Reserve Information System, a Petroleum Company Financial Data System, and an Emergency Management Information System.

For the Petroleum Production and Reserve Information System, the Federal Government would assume the data collection responsibilities now performed by the American Gas Association and the American Petroleum Institute. The oil and gas industries would be required to open their reserve estimation processes to Federal officials, who would supervise the collection and preparation of reserve data. Information collected and submitted to the Federal Government through these processes would be verified and randomly audited at the company level. Existing law regarding the protection of confidential proprietary information would not be changed.

The Petroleum Company Financial Data System would require all large companies, and a sample of small firms, engaged in the oil or gas business to submit detailed financial information to the Federal Government. Companies would have to conform to specified accounting principles and to report capital expenditures and operating results by geographical region and type of fuel. They would be required to submit information relating to functional areas, including refining, production, marketing and distribution, and information relating to foreign as well as domestic operations.

This comprehensive reporting program would enable the Government to assess the performance of the industry and individual firms, by providing a system of vertical accountability of the operations of integrated oil companies. The reporting program would restore confidence within the Congress and among the American people that the Government, not the oil industry, is in charge of national energy policy.

The Emergency Management Information System would provide governments with up-to-date information on local energy supplies and consumption. Such information is needed to respond if there should be an interruption of foreign oil supply, a natural gas shortage, or other energy emergencies. State energy offices, assisted by the Federal Government, would collect and maintain the data. As further preparation for possible electrical power shortages in the West this coming summer and natural gas shortages in future winters, the Administration is formulating contingency plans for submission to the Congress under the Energy Policy and Conservation Act.

Competition

Promotion of competition is a critical component of public policy. Since energy is an essential commodity for all Americans, effective competition within the energy industries is a matter of vital concern. Continuous vigilance is needed to ensure that the structure, behavior, and performance of the energy industries are vigorously competitive.

The Federal Trade Commission and the Antitrust Division of the Department of Justice will continue active programs of enforcement of the antitrust laws in the energy industries. Moreover, the promotion and maintenance of competition would be a major objective of the proposed Department of Energy, and would be the responsibility of a high-ranking official with appropriate staff support.

A prime responsibility of the Under Secretary for policy and evaluation would be to make certain that policies and programs of the Department promote competition. In particular, the Under Secretary would monitor resource leasing policies and rules, and research, development, demonstration, and commercialization programs to ensure that they are carried out in accordance with the purposes of the antitrust laws.

The Under Secretary would also direct an active program to monitor the structure, behavior, and performance of the energy industries. The conduct of individual firms, prices, profits, concentration ratios, and similar matters would be closely reviewed; and any indication of a lessening of competition would elicit a prompt response.

In recent years, trends and practices in the energy industries have created substantial public concern. Attention has focused particularly on the oil and natural gas industries, with special reference to vertical and horizontal integration, as well as joint ventures and the international activities of the major multinational firms.

Public policy toward vertically integrated firms, those that span exploration, production, refining, and marketing of petroleum products, has long been a matter of dispute. The Federal Trade Commission is currently litigating a vertical integration case that addresses some of the relevant legal issues. In recent years, concern about vertical integration has increased due to the possibility that Federal oil price regulations have not held down ultimate prices to consumers, but instead have led to abnormally high profits for refiners. Further investigation is needed to determine whether in fact vertically integrated firms have manipulated profit margins of their various operations in order to circumvent regulations or to exercise market power for anticompetitive purposes.

Horizontal diversification by oil and gas producers, particularly into the coal and uranium industries, has led to concern that the major firms will be able to restrict the development of alternative energy sources. The potential exercise of such power could be detrimental as the nation increases its reliance on coal, uranium, and renewable energy sources.

Traditionally, the structure of the coal industry has been extremely competitive. It is still relatively unconcentrated compared to industries such as steel and automobiles. Nevertheless, recent trends have caused legitimate concern. A total of 32 oil and gas companies accounted for 16 percent of total U.S. coal production in 1974, a 48 percent increase over their share in 1967. These companies accounted for more than 18 percent of coal shipped to electric utilities in 1974, a 27 percent increase over their share in 1967. In 1974, they held 5 percent of total U.S. coal resources, compared to 1 percent in 1967. These figures do not indicate that the oil and gas companies have a dominant position or even significant market power in the coal industry. But the trend of oil and gas company entry into coal mining and the companies' activities and performance merit continuous attention to make sure that a competitive industry does not become noncompetitive.

At this time it does not appear necessary to proceed with new legislation mandating either vertical or horizontal divestiture in order to promote or maintain competition in the energy industries. However, the performance of the energy industries will be closely monitored to make sure that prices are in line with costs and that costs are reasonable. Armed with an efficient organizational structure and new information-gathering programs, the Department of Energy would have an active analysis and evaluation program to study these matters in depth. The proposed Petroleum Company Financial Data System would provide needed vertical accountability for major energy companies. In particular, as the oil and gas companies receive additional incentives, this system would show whether the benefits are being passed through to the public or are being captured as excessive profits by firms with undue market power. If it should appear that there are anticompetitive problems in the energy industries that cannot be reached under current laws, new legislation would be proposed.

The uranium industry is another area of concern that will merit continued attention. Recent rapid increases in uranium prices have raised questions about competition in that industry. In addition, private litigation has produced information that suggests possible anticompetitive actions. Effective competition in the uranium industry must be a matter of high national priority.

The competitive structure of the energy industries depends significantly on the independent producers of oil, natural gas, coal, and solar energy equipment and on the independent refiners and marketers of petroleum products. The Administration supports legislation similar to the pending "dealer day in court" bill. The Department of Energy would seek to preserve the competitive viability of independents in all segments of the energy industries.

Finally, a problem has resulted from the Tax Reform Act of 1976, which changed the tax treatment of intangible drilling costs. Some independent oil and gas producers have lost a tax deduction for such expenses, while corporate producers continue to enjoy the deduction. The law has thus put those independent producers at a competitive disadvantage and has adversely affected their exploratory drilling. This anomaly should be removed as part of the President's program for extending oil and gas price controls. As part of that program, the Administration would urge that independent oil and gas producers receive the same tax treatment for intangible drilling costs that their corporate competitors receive. However, investors who finance oil and gas exploration in order to obtain a tax shelter for income earned in other occupations should not receive such a benefit.

State And Local Government Participation

A National Energy Plan can be built only on a foundation of partnership and understanding among the Federal Government, the States, local governments, and the nation's Indian tribes, which regulate or own a substantial part of U.S. energy resources.

Many of the programs proposed in the Plan cannot succeed without the active cooperation of State and local governments. The assistance of State and local governments will also be needed to harmonize the varying interests of the different regions of the country, all of which are affected by national energy policy. State and local governments performed admirably during the recent natural gas shortage, and their role in energy matters should increase in the future.

The States will play a critical role in developing an adequate repository of information for energy decision-making. The States' role in the proposed Emergency Management Information System is particularly important. That system should be of great value to both the Federal Government and the States in dealing with energy shortages. The utility reform program is another instance where the State role is crucial.

The Federal Government is willing to do its part to assist States, localities, and Indian tribes in coping with new energy developments, principally from coal utilization, that will occur under the Plan. Large-scale development places heavy demands on local communities for schools, roads, sewage treatment facilities, and other municipal improvements. Without proper planning for such developments, small communities may be overwhelmed and may be unable to prevent serious social and environmental problems.

A variety of existing Federal programs can assist States, communities, and Indian tribes in coping with development of major energy producing installations. A review will be conducted of these programs, and the views of States, local governments, and Indian tribes will be sought. If it should appear that there are gaps in coverage, additional legislation will be proposed.

Emergency Assistance For Low-Income Persons

Government at all levels has the responsibility for protecting low-income citizens from the most severe effects of the energy crisis. The Plan contains several programs to carry out that responsibility.

The weatherization program, by insulating large numbers of low-income homes, would moderate the effect of rising fuel costs on low-income families. Proceeds from the crude oil equalization tax and the standby gasoline tax would be distributed in a progressive manner that benefits low-income people. Protection for low-income people from the long-term increase in energy prices lies in a reformed welfare system, on which the Administration is hard at work.

The remaining major problem is the possibility of future supply disruptions, such as the natural gas shortage last winter or another oil supply interruption. Such events could cause temporary, but sharp increases in basic energy costs in some regions, or to users of particular fuels. Such increases are particularly harmful to low-income people, who have little or no discretionary income with which to meet energy price rises. Present programs are deficient in meeting this need. Therefore, the Department of Health, Education, and Welfare will promptly complete a redesigned emergency assistance program for submission to the Congress.

Public Participation

The general strategy of the National Energy Plan reflects the tenor of comments received from the public during the preparation of the Plan. As a general matter, members of the public who expressed views preferred voluntary to regulatory measures, though not uniformly so. The public placed strong emphasis on conservation, stockpiling of oil to reduce vulnerability, and development of solar energy and other renewable or essentially inexhaustible resources. A summary of the public participation in the development of the Plan appears in a separate report.

The announcement of the National Energy Plan marks only the beginning of the effort to deal with the energy problem comprehensively. As the Plan's legislative proposals are considered by the Congress and as its administrative proposals are implemented, they will be the subject of extensive public comment. The Administration encourages broad national discussion of the Plan and its specific elements.

The President will meet periodically with the Governors to discuss actions that the States can take to deal with the energy problem. The Federal Government will also sponsor additional town meetings and other public events to encourage citizen comment on national energy policy. Private organizations are also encouraged to sponsor seminars and meetings to consider the energy problem and how to deal with it.

But public participation can go far beyond discussion. There is much that individual Americans can do to help the country solve the energy problem. American families can reduce energy waste and their own fuel bills by investing in insulation and other energy-saving home improvements, and by reducing their use of air-conditioners during the summer. Individuals can use public transportation where it is available instead of automobiles, or, if they must drive, go in car pools or van pools and observe the 55-miles-per-hour speed limit. Schools can help young people understand the energy problem and develop the conservation ethic. Employers can make conservation a high priority in incentive awards and suggestion programs. Business can develop better processes and practices to use energy more efficiently.

In sum, meeting the nation's energy goals should be a great national cooperative effort that enlists the imagination and talents of all Americans. At home, on the road, at work, and elsewhere, all Americans can do their part to help solve the energy problem.

Chapter IX—The National Energy Plan and the Future

To be successful, the National Energy Plan must squarely address the energy crisis and propose actions consistent with the President's principles. The Plan seeks to:

- reduce U.S. dependence on oil imports and vulnerability to interruptions of foreign oil supply;
- lower the rate of growth of total U.S. energy demand and make the U.S. stock of capital goods more energy efficient;
- shift industrial and utility consumption of oil and natural gas to coal and other abundant resources;
- provide incentives for new oil and natural gas discoveries;
- advance the development of new energy sources for the long-term future.

The Plan should be assessed by comparing its results with the likely situation without it. The year 1985 has been selected for the purpose of comparison. The middle of the next decade now appears likely to be the critical time when world oil production will approach the limit of readily expandable capacity. At that time the United States should be prepared for the subsequent period of growing oil stringency.

In some instances, the results of the measures proposed in the Plan may not be sufficent to achieve the goals proposed in Chapter VIII. These goals are ambitious. Their achievement will require voluntary action in addition to the Plan's specific legislative and administrative measures. In some instances, mandatory measures would be considered if voluntary actions are insufficient. The energy savings projected to be achieved by specific proposals in the Plan should be regarded as a basic minimum. Achievement of the Plan's more ambitious goals could be materially aided by the accomplishments of a purposeful citizenry or, perhaps, by unforeseen developments, such as technological improvements in transportation or exploitation of new gas supplies.

Achievement of the goals and strategy of the National Energy Plan could demonstrate the benefits of indicative planning. If private decision-makers voluntarily act within the framework proposed in the Plan, the United States could achieve its energy and economic goals with relatively little direct Government regulation of economic activity.

The Impact Of The Plan On The Energy Crisis

The first test of the Plan is whether it would make a significant improvement in the trends in energy usage that have produced the energy crisis.

The projections of future impacts are based on certain assumptions about population and economic growth. The U.S. population is projected to increase from 216 million people today to 235 million by 1985. The projections are also based on the assumption that the President's economic goals will be achieved, and that, accordingly, the gross national product (GNP) will increase about 46 percent by 1985.

Without the Plan and without any other Government restraints, U.S. demand for oil could be as much as 25 million barrels per day in 1985. The model projects oil demand in 1985 to be 22.8 million barrels per day, if the automobile efficiency standards under present law are met and if higher gasoline prices since 1973-74 reduce driving. The Plan would reduce oil demand by 4.5 million barrels a day, 20 percent below the projected level of demand without the Plan. Industrial consumption of oil would be reduced from 7 million barrels per day to 4 million.

If U.S. demand for oil were 25 million barrels per day in 1985, oil imports could be as much as 16 million barrels per day. At the level of 22.8 million barrels per day of oil demand, oil imports would be about 12 million barrels per day. The Plan would reduce imports to 7 million barrels per day. Voluntary conservation could achieve a further reduction to the national goal of below 6 million barrels per day.

The Plan is projected to reallocate natural gas to high-priority uses and to stimulate additional domestic production, as shown in Figure IX-1. Total natural gas consumption in 1985 would be the equivalent of 9.4 million barrels of oil per day, with or without the Plan, but the distribution of gas among energy consumers would be altered. Under the Plan, the residential and commercial sector would consume the equivalent of 4.1 million barrels of oil per day instead of 3.8 million, and electric utilities would consume 0.5 million instead of 0.9 million. Total industrial consumption would stay the same, with some industrial shifts of gas use to coal, and some shifts from oil to gas within the total. The Plan would also stimulate additional domestic gas production equivalent to 600,000 barrels of oil per day.

As a result of the conservation initiatives, the United States would achieve an annual rate of growth of energy demand of less than 2 percent by 1985. With additional voluntary conservation efforts, energy demand could be reduced even further.

The Plan would increase the use of coal in 1985 by the equivalent of 2.4 million barrels of oil per day (200

Figure IX-1

Fuel Balances by Sector

[Millions of barrels of oil equivalent per day]

	1976	1985 without Plan	1985 with Plan	1985 Plan plus additional conservation
Demand	37.0	48.3	46.4	45.2
Residential and commercial:				
Oil	3.5	3.2	2.7	
Natural gas	3.9	3.8	4.1	
Electricity	6.3	9.1	8.4	
Coal	.1	(1)	(1)	
Total [2]	13.8	16.1	15.2	
Industry:				
Oil	3.2	7.0	4.0	
Natural gas	4.4	4.5	4.5	
Electricity	4.2	7.2	7.1	
Coal	1.9	2.7	5.0	
Total [2]	13.7	21.4	20.6	
Transportation:				
Oil	9.2	10.6	10.2	
Natural gas	.3	.2	.3	
Total [2]	9.5	10.8	10.5	
Electricity: [3]				
Oil	1.6	2.0	1.3	
Natural gas	1.5	.9	.5	
Coal	4.9	8.2	8.3	
Nuclear	1.0	3.6	3.8	
Other	1.5	1.6	1.6	
Total [2]	10.5	16.3	15.5	
Supply	37.0	48.5	46.4	45.2
Domestic:				
Crude oil [4]	9.7	10.4	10.6	
Natural gas	9.5	8.2	8.8	
Coal	7.9	12.2	14.5	
Nuclear	1.0	3.7	3.8	
Other	1.5	1.7	1.7	
Refinery gain	.4	.9	.6	
Total [2]	30.0	37.1	40.0	
Imports/exports (−):				
Oil	7.3	11.5	7.0	5.8
Natural gas	.5	.5	.6	
Coal	−.8	−1.2	−1.2	
Total [2]	7.0	11.5	6.4	5.2

[1] Less than 0.05 million barrels of oil equivalent per day.
[2] Detail may not add due to rounding.
[3] Included in previous sectoral totals.
[4] Includes natural gas liquids.

Figure IX-2
Balances by Fuel [1]
[Millions of barrels of oil equivalent per day]

	1976	1985 without Plan	1985 with Plan	1985 Plan plus additional conservation
Oil:				
Consumption	17. 4	22. 8 [2]	18. 2	17. 0
Domestic supply [3]	9. 7	10. 4	10. 6	10. 6
Refinery gain	. 4	. 9	. 6	. 6
Imports	7. 3	11. 5	7. 0	5. 8
Natural gas:				
Consumption	10. 0	9. 4	9. 4	
Domestic supply	9. 5	8. 2	8. 8	
Imports	. 5	1. 2	. 6	
Coal:				
Consumption	6. 8	10. 9	13. 3	
Domestic supply	7. 9	12. 2	14. 5	
Exports	. 8	1. 2	1. 2	

[1] Detail may not add up to total due to rounding.
[2] Assuming compliance with automobile efficiency standards under current law, and reduced driving as a result of higher gasoline prices. Without these assumptions, consumption would be 25 million barrels per day.
[3] Includes natural gas liquids.

million tons) above the level without the Plan, and 6.5 million barrels per day (565 million tons) above the 1976 level. The effects of the Plan on consumption and supply are shown in Figures IX-1 and IX-2.

Significant progress would be made to prepare the country for the period of oil stringency beyond the mid-1980's. The rate of growth of total energy demand and oil imports would both be brought down to manageable levels. The projections of the effects of the conservation program imply that the U.S. capital stock would have become more energy efficient. The reductions in industrial and utility use of oil and natural gas, and the increase in the use of coal together would represent a very important shift from scarce to abundant resources.

The reduction of oil imports, together with the expansion of the Strategic Petroleum Reserve, the diversification of U.S. sources of foreign oil supply, and the development of contingency plans would significantly reduce U.S. vulnerability to a supply interruption.

Finally, implementation of the Plan would enable the United States to make a contribution to the maintenance of economic progress and political stability throughout the world. By reducing its own demand for world oil, the United States would help reduce the economic dislocations and political tensions that would result from an intense scramble for diminishing world supplies of oil.

The Economic Consequences Of The Plan

The macroeconomic impacts of the Plan would be quite small in a $2 trillion economy. In view of the range of un-

certainty surrounding any econometric projection across a period of 8 years, the following projections should be regarded as merely indicative of the direction of the consequences of the Plan, rather than as precise forecasts.

Various macroeconomic analyses have been examined. From these analyses it appears that the program would not have a negative economic impact. Some analyses indicate the Plan could be slightly stimulative. The effects on employment are consistent with the impact on GNP. The standby gasoline tax, if triggered, would have a slightly dampening effect compared to base conditions.

Inflation would increase on the order of one-quarter to one-half a percent per year over the next 4 years. The smaller number would occur if the standby gasoline tax were not triggered, and the larger number would be more likely if the gasoline tax were in effect.

It is important to emphasize that with or without the Plan, the price of fuels will rise. The Plan would increase the price of fuels somewhat. However, the conservation program would moderate the impact on energy bills and might even offset the increases.

The program is designed to stimulate capital investment in conservation and coal conversion. Between now and 1985, coal conversion would require an additional capital investment of more than $45 billion beyond what would otherwise be required. Four billion dollars of additional capital investment would be required for coal mining. The Plan could reduce new capacity requirements for electric utilities by as much as $40 billion. Thus, the net additional investment required for coal conversion and for new electrical generation capacity could be reduced.

A substantial part of the investment generated by the Plan would go to make homes energy efficient. Estimating the capital cost of that effort is exceedingly difficult. However, the total additional investment probably would be around $20 billion.

The effect of the Plan on domestic automobile sales would be small, but probably positive. However, due to the large uncertainties involved, it is extremely difficult to predict the exact level of new car sales. If the standby gasoline tax were triggered, sales would be slightly lower compared to base conditions.

It should be emphasized once again that all of these projections are subject to a substantial range of uncertainty. They suggest that the National Energy Plan would not adversely affect economic growth. There would be a moderate increase in the rate of inflation. But this disadvantage is outweighed by the impacts on energy use. The future availability of energy has significant economic implications that are not captured by current projections of the GNP or other economic indicators. Standard projections implicitly assume energy will continue to be available at reasonable prices. If it were not available at reasonable prices, all economic activity would be severely affected. An assessment of the economic consequences of the National Energy Plan cannot be made without taking into account the benefit of adequate supplies of energy to maintain the very health of the economy. The economic and social advantages of solving the energy problem are obvious.

The Impact Of The Plan On Citizens And The Environment

The Plan is based on the principle of equity. Revenues from the crude oil equalization tax would be returned to the economy progressively, as would any revenues from the standby gasoline tax. Although the major price, tax, and regulatory burdens would fall on industry rather than on individuals, those economic burdens would be reflected in higher priced goods and services.

Although energy costs would be generally higher, consumers would receive specific benefits from the Plan. The residential energy conservation program would be available for all households to help reduce energy waste and moderate high energy costs. Residential consumers of natural gas would have more assured supplies, would be protected from the cost of higher priced new gas, and would benefit from the gas utility reform program. Residential consumers of fuel oil would receive an additional share of the equalization tax proceeds as a reduction in price when they buy fuel oil. All users of electricity would benefit from reductions in new capacity construction brought about by conservation, and residential users would also benefit from the electric utility reform program, which would result in improved utility load curves and, therefore, lower costs. All consumers would also receive, through energy payments from the equalization tax revenues, the bulk of the surpluses generated in bringing oil prices up to the true replacement cost.

American workers would benefit from more assured supplies of energy and a reduced risk of factories shutting down for lack of fuel. There would also be less incentive for industrial firms to move from one part of the country to another in search of reliable fuel supplies. The Plan would also create jobs directly through specific programs such as residential energy conservation, and might have positive indirect effects, as well.

The special needs of the poor and the elderly are addressed. Expansion of the existing Federal weatherization program would particularly benefit the poor and the elderly. The existing HEW Federal-State emergency assistance program would be revised to meet energy emergencies. The progressive nature of the energy payment system is also a benefit. The long-term needs of the poor and the elderly for protection from rising energy prices will be met through a reformed welfare system.

Small firms in the energy industries would benefit from the Plan's emphasis on competition and from the reorientation of the Federal Government's research, development and demonstration programs. Commercial establishments that consume natural gas would benefit from the Plan's pricing proposals.

Businesses would benefit from creation of a single market for natural gas instead of the segmented market that has resulted in the anomaly of plentiful but high priced gas in the intrastate market and cheap but scarce gas in the interstate market. Energy prices would be sufficient to elicit a flow of capital for investment in the energy industries. Investment decisions throughout the business sector would be facilitated by stability and predictability in pricing, environmental and other policies. A healthy business climate for the long run can be preserved only through an effective response to the energy crisis.

Many of the proposed measures would help preserve the quality of the environment. The conservation measures, the support for stringent environmental standards, the emphasis on solar energy and improved technologies for the use of coal, and the measures to increase the safety of light-water reactors are all positive steps.

Implementation of the conservation program clearly is the most important action that could be taken to protect environmental quality while allowing for continued economic growth. The quality of the nation's air would be preserved despite increasing use of coal. The development of solar energy systems would have a modest short-term impact, but over the long run should make a valuable contribution. The proposed steps for siting criteria for nuclear plants, plant inspectors, and waste management, would make important contributions to nuclear safety and safeguards.

Despite the strong environmental measures discussed in the Plan, some uncertainty will continue over the impacts of increasing coal utilization. The President will appoint a special committee to study the health effects of increased coal production and use. In addition, the Government's coal research and development program will be expanded. The program will focus on meeting environmental requirements more effectively and economically.

The Future Beyond 1985

The period from 1985 to the end of the century will test the success of the National Energy Plan. If oil importing countries have failed to restrain their demand by the time world oil production levels off, prices are likely to skyrocket and critical shortages are likely to develop. Reduction in the rate of growth of energy demand, combined with additional domestic energy production, should enable the United States to make the energy transition successfully without major dislocations.

More than two-thirds of the additional private investment required to carry out the Plan is projected to be made before 1985, but many of the benefits, particularly of the conservation programs, are much larger after 1985.

Steps taken during the next few years should produce much greater efficiency in vehicles, buildings, and factories. It is realistic to envision a period of growth for the U.S. economy for the remainder of this century, together with a steady reduction in the amount of energy required to drive a car, heat a home, or run a factory. The lower birth rate of recent decades will also reduce energy requirements after 1985. Fewer Americans will be entering the family-forming age group, which creates the largest demand for housing, automobiles, and energy intensive appliances.

If the National Energy Plan is adopted promptly, the nation's energy requirements per dollar of GNP will steadily decline. The United States will have the time it needs to develop sources of supply to build a more reliable energy base for continued economic growth in the 21st century. Growth rates in energy consumption during the 1985 to 2000 period will be significantly below those projected up to 1985.

The present and future markets for energy can be divided roughly into three categories. The first is transportation, which now is wholly dependent on petroleum. The second is high quality, high temperature energy such as electricity or high temperature steam, which is used for most industrial processes and such household needs as lighting and appliances. The sources of high quality energy currently are fossil fuels and nuclear power. Solar electric technologies and certain geothermal resources can also produce high quality energy. The third category is low-grade heat—temperatures below the boiling point of water—which can be used to heat and cool buildings and provide about one-third of the process heat for industry.

Roughly two-thirds of energy consumption requires petroleum or other high-quality energy in the form of fossil fuels or electricity. It is the low-quality energy requirements that could substantially be met by decentralized solar heating and cooling systems, waste heat from power plants, direct use of geothermal energy, or other diffused and less concentrated energy sources. Over the long run, it is wasteful to use high-grade energy sources, such as fossil fuels and electricity, for end-uses that can be satisfied by low-grade heat.

The strategy of the Plan beyond 1985 is twofold. First, it seeks to encourage dispersed solar energy systems, waste heat, and, within geographical limits, direct use of geothermal energy for those uses for which such low temperature energy is adequate. These uses constitute roughly one-third of the total energy market. Second, the Plan seeks to promote the economical, environmentally sound

use of various forms of coal, supplemented by nuclear power, for the high temperature needs of powerplants and industry. A variety of other energy sources—solar electric, biomass, municipal solid waste, high temperature geothermal resources and others—would be developed to supplement coal and nuclear power as sources of high grade industrial heat and electricity.

It is possible that by 1985 a significant share of new buildings in the United States will be incorporating solar technology as the primary source of energy for water and space heating and perhaps cooling. Solar energy can also supply some of the low grade process heat needed by industry and agriculture. Geothermal energy, a virtually untapped but potentially large resource, could meet many direct thermal needs in areas near geothermal resources. Both resources could also, during the 1990's, supplement the light-water reactor and coal for generating electricity.

Some very important questions currently remain unanswered. It is not yet clear what energy source will replace petroleum in transportation. Coal can be converted to petroleum products, as Germany demonstrated during World War II, but current synthetics are extraordinarily expensive, more than double the world price of oil. Perhaps electric cars, buses, and trains will be part of a long-term solution for reducing oil consumption. Methanol, an alcohol even now sometimes used for fuel, could also make a major contribution as a substitute or additive to gasoline. New opportunities no one can foresee may appear during the next two decades. The United States will need to pursue research and development on all promising options to determine whether any of them can fill the petroleum gap.

Another major question for the future is the long-term source of electric power. The year 2000 is a short period away in terms of the time required to develop new sources of energy. Nuclear energy was discovered 38 years ago, but today provides only about 3 percent of total U.S. energy. Experience with nuclear energy teaches that the development of a new energy source is not simply a matter of solving technical problems. Assessment of an energy system from the perspectives of health and safety, economics and environmental quality must also be an integral part of any research and development program.

Under the Plan, the Federal Government will pursue a diversified effort to develop new sources that can meet electricity generating needs beyond the turn of the century. The major options include the nuclear breeder technologies, nuclear fusion, centralized solar energy and hot dry rock geothermal resources.

Many countries are developing breeder technologies. These technologies could be made commercial by the end of the century. However, the proliferation risk from a plutonium economy and the availability of energy alternatives make it advisable to defer further development of the plutonium breeder technology. Alternative breeder technologies that do not raise the same proliferation concerns are in the very early stages of development. A diversified breeder research effort should be continued as an option for future energy supply, providing insurance if other alternatives fail.

Fusion power remains an enigma. If proven feasible, it could provide a virtually limitless source of energy. Its scientific feasibility, however, has yet to be established despite years of intensive research, and it may bring environmental problems of its own, which have yet to be evaluated. Fusion research should be pursued in a deliberate and careful manner. The United States cannot now count on fusion power to meet energy needs.

Solar energy is also a possible source of electrical energy for the future. The options available are to generate electricity through photovoltaic systems, power plants in the desert, ocean thermal gradients, biomass or perhaps even space satellites. The economics of all these options are poor at this early stage of development. Solar electric technologies also present various environmental problems that require evaluation.

The current economics of solar electric systems do not doom them for the future. The research and development effort has hardly begun, and the costs of alternative sources of electrical power are rising. Moreover, conventional economics do not reflect solar's major advantages—the absence of the problems of proliferation and safety inherent in most of the nuclear technologies. Even so, it must be recognized that solar electric—as distinguished from decentralized solar—is still an unproved technology. It, too, is not yet an option on which society can rely.

Finally, hot dry rock geothermal resources may provide substantial quantities of high grade energy during the next century. Hot dry rocks deep in the earth contain vast quantities of heat, but no fluid with which to bring the heat to the surface. Before this resource can be tapped, difficult engineering problems will have to be solved.

In sum, the long-term future of electrical energy in America is still open. It is critical that the United States develop a broad range of nonconventional technologies to assure that in the future it will have energy options that are reasonably priced and environmentally acceptable.

Conclusion

Implementation of the National Energy Plan would enable the United States to achieve the President's goals in a manner consistent with his 10 principles. The United States would reduce its short-term vulnerability to a supply interruption by reducing oil consumption and imports, by expanding the Strategic Petroleum Reserve, and by proceeding with diversification of foreign oil supplies and the development of contingency plans. Through effective conservation programs, the United States would upgrade the efficiency of its stock of capital goods so that it could weather the period when world oil production approaches its capacity limitation. Thereby, the United States would avoid sudden and possibly severe interruptions in the flow of goods and services resulting from shortages of energy. By proceeding with research, development and, when appropriate, early commercialization of renewable energy sources, the Plan would do much to prepare for the time when oil and gas will be virtually unavailable for energy use and alternative energy sources will be needed.

The effort to achieve the major objectives of the Plan would provide a sense of mission to the American people. Previous generations of Americans have faced major challenges—settling the frontier, industrialization, war, depression. This generation is discovering that it faces a challenge that is equally great—the energy crisis. Meeting this challenge will require sacrifice, hard work, skill and imagination on the part of the American people. It will require a new national ethic that values energy efficiency and condemns energy waste. And it will require a degree of cooperation that the United States has attained only in meeting the great challenges of the past. As the President stressed in his address on April 18, 1977, "This difficult effort will be 'the moral equivalent of war'— except that we will be uniting our efforts to build and not to destroy." The prospect of America organizing to meet the energy crisis is not grim. It is exciting.

ENDNOTES

[1] Throughout this report, quantities of energy are expressed in terms of barrels of oil (petroleum product) per day. One million barrels of oil per day equals 1.96 trillion cubic feet of natural gas per year, or 88 million tons of coal per year.

[2] The numbers do not add up due to rounding.

[3] Including natural gas liquids (NGL's) and refinery gains.

[4] Including refinery gains.

[5] Excluding natural gas liquids.

6 The Btu equivalent is the price paid for quantities of various energy sources that have the same heat value.

7 The tax would increase if an annual target is exceeded and would decrease if an annual target is met. For example, if standby tax legislation is enacted in 1977, the first target would be for 1978. If the target is exceeded by 0.5 percent in 1978, no tax would go into effect for 1979, because the tax is triggered only by an excess of at least 1 percent. If the 1979 target is exceeded by 10 percent, a 5-cents-per-gallon tax would go into effect for 1980; regardless of the amount of excess, no increase in the tax can be more than 5 cents for any year. If the 1980 target is exceeded by 1 per-cent, the 5-cents-per-gallon tax would remain in effect without any increase because the tax can reach 10 cents per gallon only if the excess in the previous year was at least 2 percent. If the 1981 target is exceeded by 2 percent, the tax would increase to 10 cents per gallon for 1982. If in 1982 consumption is 25 percent below the target, the tax for 1983 would decrease from 10 cents per gallon to 5 cents per gallon. No decrease in the tax can be more than 5 cents per gallon for any year.

8 This figure includes the heating and cooling of buildings.

PRESIDENT CARTER'S ENERGY PROPOSALS: A PERSPECTIVE*

Summary of Report on Carter's Proposals

The energy plan submitted by President Carter to the Congress contains more than 100 interdependent proposals aimed at reducing consumption of petroleum, converting from oil and natural gas to coal as an energy source, and increasing domestic supplies of energy. These proposals are designed to reduce imports of crude oil from a potential 11.5 million barrels a day to 7.0 million barrels by 1985. Of these projected 4.5 million barrels a day saved, the Administration estimates that approximately 2.1 million would be attributable to conservation and 2.4 to the substitution of coal for oil and gas.

This report analyzes five major sets of proposals in the Administration's plan:

- Pricing of crude oil,
- Pricing of natural gas,
- Conversion to coal,
- Automobile-related proposals, and
- Tax credits for home insulation and solar heating equipment.

The Administration estimates that altogether, these sets of proposals would achieve a reduction in oil imports of 3.2 million barrels a day by 1985. The analysis conducted by the Congressional Budget Office and presented in this report, however, indicates that this saving is overly optimistic; CBO estimates that the proposals would be likely to save closer to 2.3 million barrels a day. About 0.6 of the 0.9-million-barrel difference results from lower estimates of coal conversion potential; the remaining 0.3-million-barrel discrepancy is due to differing estimates of the results from the home insulation and solar equipment tax credits. The Administration asserts that an additional savings of 1.3 million barrels a day (over and above the savings from the five main proposals) can be expected to result from various proposals such as new building standards; these have not been analyzed by CBO. On the assumption that these unanalyzed savings will be realized, however, the total oil import savings achieved by the Administration's plan are estimated by CBO to be about 3.6 million barrels a day, rather than the Administration's

* Congressional Budget Office, U.S. Congress, June 1977

estimated 4.5 million barrels. The Administration's plan leaves open the possibility of future measures not included in the present proposed legislation that could help close this gap.

The Need For An Energy Plan

The need for a national energy plan arises from both immediate and long-run problems. The long-run problem is simply that the growth in oil and gas consumption exceeds the growth in proven reserves—both domestic and foreign. Before long, we will have to shift to new energy sources or face drastic reductions in our standard of living. The more immediate problem is that U.S. imports of oil have increased substantially—from 3.5 to 7.3 million barrels per day between 1970 and 1977. The fact that almost half of the oil consumed in the United States is now imported creates national security risks and makes our economy highly vulnerable to shocks from outside, especially because the supply and price of oil are to a great extent dictated by an international cartel.

The major reason for the substantial increase in our dependence on imports is the current system of price controls on oil and gas, which have kept the domestic price of these fuels artificially below world levels. Over the past four years, this regulatory system has served to cushion Americans from the dramatic shifts in consumption, and in turn in lifestyles, that might otherwise have been caused by the abrupt quadrupling of world oil prices by the OPEC cartel in 1973-1974. Artificially low prices have also tended to encourage energy consumption and discourage the search for and production of new domestic resources—thereby further increasing our dependence on potentially unreliable foreign suppliers.

The Administration's Strategies

To reduce our dependence on imports, the President has proposed three major strategies:

- Reduce the long-term growth in energy demand by imposing various excise taxes that would serve to raise the price of petroleum and related products to world levels or near world levels. New regulatory standards are also proposed, and special efforts are made to reduce the growth in demand for gasoline.

- Increase large industries' and utilities' use of coal instead of oil or natural gas by taxing their use of the latter two fuels. Regulations are designed to prohibit most new industrial and utility use of oil and natural gas.

- Increase domestic supplies by reintroducing market pricing, or near market pricing, for truly new energy supplies. Accelerated development of new energy sources, however, is not stressed.

A critical element in the President's proposal is the effort to raise the price of petroleum and natural gas by predictable increments so that consumers and businesses can begin to make decisions on the basis of higher future energy prices. The theme of the plan is that the transition to a less energy-intensive economy is a long and complex process. Incentives established now to alter consumption and investment decisions regarding energy will only begin to yield significant savings within the next few years. Truly large-scale energy savings will not show up until the middle of the next decade or later.

Energy price increases under the plan would be achieved mainly by a system of taxes to be rebated to consumers. Such taxes are preferred to simple increases in private-sector prices because the taxes capture windfall profits for the public rather than for industry. These tax revenues would then be rebated in order to maintain the real purchasing power of consumers. Since the taxes would have raised energy prices relative to others, however, it is expected that most of the rebates would be spent on other goods; energy would thus be saved.

Conclusions Of The Study

The general conclusion of the CBO analysis is that the strategies proposed by the Administration would be effective in reducing energy use and dependence on oil imports, but that the Administration's estimates of the magnitudes of import savings are overoptimistic.

One of the costs of the plan would be a rise in the general price level, but the inflationary effect would be small and gradual compared to that of the OPEC price increases of 1973-1974. The plan would redistribute real income from some groups to others, but on the average, lower-income people would be protected. The shift to a more energy-efficient economy envisioned by the plan would not involve dramatic adjustments in American lifestyles; for example, the increase in miles driven per household would be slowed but not reversed.

Crude Oil Pricing

The Administration's plan would retain controls on prices received by domestic oil producers, but it would allow the controlled price of newly discovered oil to rise over three years to the 1977 world price with subsequent adjustments for domestic inflation. This price would offer substantial incentives to increase production of domestic oil, but actual increases in production are likely to be relatively small. CBO estimates that the rise in price for newly discovered oil would increase production by about 100,000 barrels a day by 1985; the Administration's estimate of increased production is slightly higher.

To discourage consumption of oil, the plan would raise prices paid by domestic consumers to world levels by imposing a "crude oil equalization tax" equal to the difference between world and domestic prices. This tax would capture for the public the windfall profits associated with higher prices on already discovered oil and would return those profits to consumers in the form of rebates.

The equalization tax on crude oil will increase the price of petroleum products by an estimated 4 to 5 cents per gallon (in current dollars) by 1980; this amount is in addition to the increase of 4 to 5 cents per gallon projected under existing legislation. The tax would also lead to the elimination of the so-called "entitlements program," and would thereby reduce some of the regulatory burden on the industry. The equalization tax appears to be an effective mechanism for equalizing foreign and domestic oil prices and capturing windfall profits. It would provide a light incentive for consumers to reduce consumption or convert to alternative sources. Proposed user taxes on oil provide additional incentives for industry and utilities to convert to coal.

Natural Gas Pricing

The pricing proposal for natural gas eliminates the current distinction between interstate and intrastate markets by placing all gas under federal jurisdiction; it places a cap on the price of new gas at $1.75 per thousand cubic feet. In addition, a special excise tax is placed on use of natural gas by industries and public utilities. The purpose of these proposals is three-fold:

- To protect residential consumers against high prices and shortages,

- To make gas expensive for industries that can convert to coal, and

- To increase new supplies but reduce the possibilities of producers' gaining excessive profits on previously discovered gas.

With the exception of the degree of coal conversion, CBO finds that the natural gas proposals will attain the stated objectives. The proposals would generally reallocate the existing supplies of natural gas; no energy savings would therefore be attributable to this proposal according to either the Administration or CBO.

Coal Conversion

Since the goal for conversion of utilities from oil and gas to coal is generally consistent with current trends, CBO concurs wth the Administration's conversion estimates in this area. A major discrepancy exists, however, in estimates of the likelihood of attaining the goal for industrial conversion. If present policy were continued to 1985, only 12 percent of new industrial demand would burn coal. The President's plan envisions that industrial consumption of coal would more than double by 1985. Accomplishing the Administration's goal would require that 10 percent of all existing oil and gas used for industry be converted to coal and that 44 percent of all new potential users would convert to coal. This report agrees with the President's 10 percent conversion of existing industrial use but projects only 33 percent of new uses to be converted to coal. (The reasons for this lower estimate include the logistics of transporting coal, concerns about protecting the environment, and problems of scheduling new coal facilities to maximize the benefits of rebates, all of which will impede new conversion.) This would result in total coal consumption by industry of 360 million tons by 1985—50 million tons below the Administration's estimate.

In terms of equivalents in barrels of crude oil, CBO's estimate translates into a savings in imported oil of 1.8 million barrels a day, which is 0.6 million below the Administration's figure. To some extent, however, the attainment of the goal would depend upon the future actions of the Administration since it could control both the specification of coal regulations and their subsequent enforcement.

Auto-Related Proposals

The automobile-related provisions of the President's energy package are aimed at reducing gasoline consumption through production and sales of vehicles with greater fuel efficiencies, and through price-induced reductions in the number of miles driven. The goal of the plan is to reduce total gasoline consumption by 10 percent from current levels by 1985. This is an ambitious goal, considering that motor gasoline consumption has increased at 4.5 percent per year between 1965 and 1975, but its attainment would be aided substantially by existing legislation. In particular, the Energy Policy and Conservation Act of 1975 set fuel economy standards for new cars under the threat of civil penalities. While CBO does not expect these standards to be met in every year, it does anticipate that they would have significant effects on automobile gasoline use—in 1985, holding it within one percent of the present level. CBO estimates that adoption of the President's plan would reduce automotive gasoline consumption further, but to 5 percent beneath its present level, not 10 percent below as projected by the Administration.

Three programs in the President's plan contribute to gasoline savings. More than half of the savings come from the President's proposed "gas-guzzler" taxes and rebates based upon a new car fuel economy. This program is estimated to yield fuel savings of 215,000 barrels a day in 1985. Second, standby gasoline tax could be triggered as early as 1982 according to CBO projections, and assuming that it is triggered then, it would produce gasoline savings of 65,000 barrels per day in 1985. Finally, the crude oil equalization tax is expected to contribute an additional 25,000 barrels a day of gasoline savings in 1985. Taken together, these three programs would yield total gasoline savings of 305,000 barrels a day in 1985, less than a tenth of the energy savings produced by the President's plan as a whole.

CBO's estimate of the fuel savings for the gas-guzzler excise tax and rebate program is slightly higher than the Administration's, and the Administration has not yet computed comparable estimates for the standby gasoline tax and crude oil equalization tax. The Administration has indicated, however, that without the standby gasoline tax, 1985 gasoline consumption would be 350,000 barrels per day above target. While CBO expects that 1985 gas consumption would most likely exceed the target by more than this, the excess above target in both sets of projects is greater than the estimated 65,000-barrel savings of the standby gasoline tax, implying that the President's goal of a 10 percent gasoline reduction by 1985 appears unlikely.

Future gasoline consumption by trucks introduces considerable uncertainty as to whether or when the President's goal would be met. At present, trucks account for more than 20 percent of the nation's gasoline consumption, and their future share of gasoline use could rise if their fuel economy improvement does not keep pace with that of autos. The fuel economy of light trucks is expected to improve as a result of existing legislation as well as through the President's gas-guzzler proposal as it would apply to light trucks. But both existing and proposed legislation in this area are keyed to a set of standards that have not yet been specified, so that assessment of their conservation impact is impossible at this stage. CBO analysis indicates that these future developments in the fuel economy of trucks would have a major effect on the triggering of the standby gasoline tax, and could delay it from 1982, as projected above, to 1983 or 1984. Policies related to trucks play a key role in shaping an effective and evenhanded policy for transportation fuel conservation.

Insulation Tax Credit

The proposed insulation tax credit is likely to encourage some additional homeowners to upgrade the insulation in their homes. With sharp rises in fuel prices since 1973, however, many homeowners have already reinsulated or have decided to do so in the future. For example, about 3 million homeowners chose to upgrade their insulation in 1976. With current energy prices, insulation is already a good investment since the savings in fuel bills are about three times the cost of the insulation. The proposed credit would increase this ratio of savings to cost to 4 to 1.

Between now and 1985, an estimated 24 million home-owners and renters are likely to reinsulate their dwellings. CBO estimates that nearly 8 million of the 24 million would be an increase attributable to the tax credit. The 24 million translates into a total of 70 percent of all residential homeowners as opposed to the 90 percent projected by the President. CBO estimates the energy savings attributable to these nearly 8 million households would be approximately 120,000 barrels of oil a day.

The Administration, on the other hand, estimates that a savings of 480,000 barrels would be due to the credit and related programs. The major difference is that CBO estimates that an additional 280,000 barrels a day will be saved by reinsulation that people would do anyway without the Carter plan, adding up to total of 400,000 barrels per day from all insulation. The Administration assumes that a total of 480,000 barrels a day savings would be induced by the plan.

Short-Run Impacts on the Economy

President Carter's package would have a major impact on energy markets, a noticeable but small impact on the overall rate of inflation, and only a minor impact on total output and employment. CBO estimates that the President's plan would add about 1.6 percent of the level of consumer prices by 1980 or about half a percentage point a year to the rate of inflation from 1978 through 1980. The output effect is estimated to reduce constant-dollar gross national product by no more than 0.7 percent by the end of 1980, thus adding 0.2 percent to the unemployment rate. These estimates do, however, assume that there will be no new investment for conversion during the next two years. The total impacts on unemployment and real growth could therefore be partially offset if additional investment is forthcoming.

Distribution Effects

A final issue addressed in this study is the combined impact that the energy proposals and tax rebates would have on various groups of Americans. Assuming that the various taxes would be passed on to consumers almost entirely, close to $12 billion would be paid by 1980 (in 1977 price levels) in higher energy prices. Primarily

because the natural gas and oil excise taxes are not rebated to consumers, the total rebate is estimated to be about $9 billion, leaving a net reduction in real puchasing power of approximately $3 billion.

In addition to this total effect, the energy proposals would redistribute purchasing power from persons in the upper four income quintiles to the lowest quintile in 1980 and from the upper two quintiles to the lowest three in 1985.

Other shifts are likely to take place as well. For example, people who do not own automobiles would gain at the expense of automobile owners. Homeowners would gain at the expense of renters, and city dwellers with access to public transportation would gain at the expense of persons in suburbs and rural areas.

Petroleum and Its Effects on Industry

In Table 1 the effects of the President's proposals on consumption of refined products are displayed. As a result of the crude oil equalization tax, the automobile related proposals, the insulation tax credit and the coal conversion program, consumption in 1980 would be 4 percent lower in the President's plan than under present policy. By 1985 the difference is estimated to be 17 percent. Because the crude oil equalization tax would operate in tandem with many of the other proposals within the plan, however, no independent estimates are made of this particular proposal.

Generally, the impact of all the proposals by 1980 is uniform among the sectors—the Carter plan decreased consumption in each sector in comparison with a continuation of present policy. The plan would decrease consumption in the residential and commercial sector in absolute terms. After 1980, the plan would also lead to the reduction of the amount of oil used by electrical utilities.

An important point in this regard is that the industrial consumption of oil continues to grow from present levels in both cases. Under the President's plan, industrial consumption in 1985 is 44 percent above consumption for 1977. This implies an average annual growth rate in the industrial sector of 4.6 percent per year. By 1985, however, the number of industrial boilers burning oil would decline, whereas consumption of petroleum as feedstocks would continue to expand.

Since most of the oil price increases in the residential sector will be rebated, the President's plan will not substantially affect residential consumption of oil. However, implementation of the home insulation tax credits would reduce consumption in this sector. But because increased use of insulation is cost-effective, with or without the proposed tax credit, demand for residential fuel would decline after 1980 in both cases.

TABLE 1.   PROJECTED CONSUMPTION OF REFINED OIL PRODUCTS:
IN MILLIONS OF BARRELS PER DAY

		1980		1985	
	1977	Present Policy	Carter Plan	Present Policy	Carter Plan
Residential/Commercial (90 percent distillate)	3.4	3.4	3.3	3.2	2.8
Industrial (70 percent residual)	3.2	4.2	3.8	7.0	4.6
Transportation (70 percent gasoline)	9.7	10.3	10.2	10.6	10.2
Utilities (90 percent residual)	1.6	1.8	1.6	2.0	1.3
Total Refined Products	17.9	19.7	18.9	22.8	18.9
Equivalent Amount of Crude Oil	17.5	19.2	18.4	22.3	18.4

SOURCE: Congressional Budget Office.

The largest use of petroleum is for transportation. Demand for all fuels for transportation expands slowly in both cases, but reaches a plateau in the early-1980's under the President's proposals. Demand for gasoline for automobiles may then start declining between 1982 and 1984.

The Petroleum User Tax

The Tax On Industry.   The President's plan proposes a tax on industrial consumers of petroleum products that would go into effect in 1979. A similar tax on utilities would be implemented in 1983. The user tax is graduated according to consumption, so that consumers of less than 500 billion BTU of oil per year pay no tax and consumers of more than 1,500 billion BTU pay tax on their entire consumption.

The tax is planned to start at 95 cents per barrel of residual fuel oil and 87 cents per barrel of distillate. The

tax doubles in 1980 and then rises each year to $3.15 and $2.90 for residual and distillate respectively by 1985. In terms of real change, the tax increases fuel prices to industry by 12.9 percent in 1980 and 21.5 percent in 1985 relative to a price without the tax. The price and revenue impacts of the user tax on industry are displayed in Table 2.

The costs of using petroleum in new plants are already higher on a BTU basis than competing coal prices. Thus it is doubtful whether the user tax provision taken alone would influence many consumers to convert to coal. Perhaps more important than the negative incentive of the user tax is the positive incentive of the proposed rebate provision for new industrial investment for conversion to coal.

Industry is eligible under the President's plan for either an additional 10 percent investment tax credit for expenditures to convert to coal or a rebate of user taxes (on either natural gas or petroleum) for the amount of expen-

TABLE 2.   THE INDUSTRIAL USER TAX: IN 1977 DOLLARS

	Quantity Consumed a/	Approximate Taxable Use a/	Average Price Before Tax b/	Price After Tax b/	Revenue c/
Revenue in 1980					
Residual Fuel	2.66	2.39	12.15	14.05	1.7
Distillates	1.14	0.68	22.26	24.00	0.4
Total	3.80	3.07	14.40	16.26	2.1
Revenue in 1985					
Residual Fuel	3.22	2.90	12.15	15.30	3.3
Distillates	1.38	0.83	22.26	25.16	0.9
Total	4.60	3.73	14.40	17.50	4.2

SOURCE: Congressional Budget Office.

a/   Millions of barrels per day.

b/   Dollars per barrel.

c/   In billions of dollars.

ditures incurred during conversion. In order to encourage accelerated investment in conversion, there is a carry-forward provision in the proposed tax amendment which would enable industry (and in later years, utilities) to accumulate credits in advance which could be used later to reduce the tax.

The Tax On Utilities. The corresponding user tax for utilities would go into effect in 1983 at a flat rate of 25 cents per million BTUs. Based on the assumption that 90 percent of utility oil consumption would be residual fuel and that 1.4 million barrels per day in 1985 would be consumed, the tax revenues are estimated to be approximately $470 million in that year.

Increases in Production of Oil

The President's proposals attempt to provide incentives to seek new oil production by allowing the price of newly discovered oil to escalate within three years to 1977 world prices, adjusted for domestic inflation. The plan correctly states that the revenues per barrel collected by the oil industry would be higher than in any other oil producing countries due primarily to the low production taxes or royalties permitted United States producers. Because domestic costs of production are also high relative to other countries, however, producers still argue that additional incentives are necessary.

CBO believes that the amount of oil produced in response to small price increases seems very limited. The increase in oil and gas prices since 1973 has been several times larger than the increase proposed by the plan, yet increases in production have been modest. It is questionable whether price increases above those proposed in the President's plan would stimulate substantial additional investment in exploration and development. Second, incentives such as decontrol of old oil would not necessarily be an efficient means of stimulating new production as this decontrol would not represent a rate of return on the new exploration and development, but mainly a windfall profit. It could, however, be argued that decontrol would improve the cash flow position of the industry. Most economists agree, however, that investment is influenced most heavily by the price of new oil (discovered after April 20, 1977) rather than by the average prices. Unless an industry cannot attract credit, and the oil industry has few such problems, the price of newly discovered oil would generally be the most important determinant of new investment. The National Energy Plan correctly states that the marginal prices proposed in the plan ($14.69 per barrel) would yield among the highest revenues per barrel available to the industry anywhere in the world.

In conclusion, it is possible that some huge new discoveries in virgin areas (the Atlantic, the Gulf of Alaska) could change the entire outlook. However, without those discoveries, the increase in production of oil will come from increased development of known but costly fields and advanced recovery from older fields.

This report projects that 200,000 barrels per day additional oil would be produced in 1980 as a result of the President's energy plan. About half of the increase is from advanced recovery, and half is from increased drilling of known but subcommercial pools or extensions. New discoveries as a result of enactment of the President's proposals could not be developed by 1980.

By 1985, production could be increased substantially but it is virtually impossible to make a prediction of how much at this time. There are few additional incentives that are efficient which can be created by using market mechanisms without explicit subsidies. Although the President's proposals have been criticized because they allegedly provide a few incentives for increased production, in fact, the plan does virtually decontrol prices of new oil and thereby rewards exploration and new production. The effects of the incentives will probably be modest but may be the best that can be expected. No amount of additional incentive is likely to substantially change the situation.

Natural Gas and Its Effects on Industry

With or without implementation of the National Energy Plan, natural gas prices will be higher in the future and slightly less gas might be available. If enacted, however, the plan would make a difference in how high prices would be, what regions would bear the burden of the price increases, and what regions would receive the limited supplies.

Enactment of the Administration's proposal would mean that customers served with interstate gas would find more gas available, but at somewhat higher prices. However, the gas that intrastate consumers received would be less expensive under the plan.[1] For the nation as a whole, natural gas prices will be slightly lower with enactment of the plan.

Effects of the Proposals on Consumers

As shown in Tables 3 and 4, the President's natural gas proposals will affect various groups of consumers in different ways. This section will discuss the effects of these proposals on the availability of gas and the prices that would be paid by various groups of consumers. The subsequent section will discuss the effect of the proposed user tax on prices for industries and utilities.

Residential and Commercial. Residential and commercial users of natural gas would have slightly more gas available with enactment of the proposals. Furthermore, in both 1980 and 1985 implementation of the President's proposals would significantly reduce average fuel bills paid by residential and commercial customers compared to what they would pay under continuation of present policy, particularly those served by intrastate sources. The gas prices paid by these groups would, on average, be 22 percent lower. Furthermore, both residential and commercial groups would be protected against curtailment of supply.

It should not be expected, however, that the availability of natural gas will permit many new homes to be serviced by gas.

Industry. In recent years, because of federal and state gas emergency allocation priorities, interstate industrial customers have borne the brunt of gas service curtailments. Because more gas would be available to consumers now served by the interstate systems than would be available under present policy, interstate industrial customers would have more gas available to them with the President's proposals. The additional supplies, however, will be at much higher prices than at present.

If the incremental pricing proposal were enacted, industries using gas would pay significantly higher prices than they would under present policy because the new higher prices would be passed on to them and to utilities and not to residential and commercial customers. The proposed user tax would further increase the price of gas for industry and utilities.

Industries served by interstate pipelines would receive less gas in 1980 under the Carter proposals than they do now, but as a result of general conservation measures in other sectors, gas supplies to industrial customers could increase after 1980. In the long run, the supply position of industries using interstate gas would be much better with implementation of the plan. Intrastate industry would have more gas available in 1980 and 1985 than it has in 1977, but less in 1980 and 1985 than it would have under present policy.

Electric Utilities. The proposed user tax on utilities burning gas is intended to encourage a significant number

TABLE 3.   PROJECTED CONSUMPTION OF NATURAL GAS IN TRILLIONS OF CUBIC FEET

	1977	1980 Present Policy	1980 Carter Proposal	1985 Present Policy	1985 Carter Proposal
Residential and Commercial					
Intrastate	2.0	2.1	2.2	2.1	2.3
Interstate	5.5	5.7	5.7	5.5	5.9
Total	7.5	7.8	7.9	7.6	8.2
Industrial					
Intrastate	3.6	4.2	4.2	6.0	4.8
Lease and Plant	1.6	1.1	1.1	0.9	0.9
Interstate	3.3	2.4	2.7	2.1	3.3
Total	8.5	7.7	8.0	9.0	9.0
Transportation					
Total	0.6	0.5	0.5	0.4	0.5
Utilities					
Intrastate	2.0	2.3	1.9	1.8	1.1
Interstate	0.8	0.4	0.4	0.1	0.1
Total	2.8	2.7	2.3	1.9	1.2
Grand Total	19.4	18.7	18.7	18.9	18.9

SOURCE: Congressional Budget Office.

TABLE 4.   PROJECTED CONSUMER PRICES OF NATURAL GAS BEFORE USER TAXES: IN CENTS PER THOUSAND CUBIC FEET

	1977	1980 Present Policy	1980 Carter Proposal	1985 Present Policy	1985 Carter Proposal
Residential Commercial					
Intrastate	192	249	202	305	222
Interstate	223	242	221	286	242
Industrial					
Intrastate	112	169	161	225	196
Lease and Plant	97	154	146	210	181
Interstate	118	137	170	180	237
Transportation					
Total	105	130	123	165	220
Utility					
Intrastate	112	169	141	225	196
Interstate	123	142	130	185	242

SOURCE: Congressional Budget Office.

of utilities to convert from gas (and oil) to coal. However, if this user tax were implemented, it would not go into effect until 1983. Thus any significant conversions by utilities would not take place until after 1983. At present the prices paid by utilities using intrastate gas are actually substantially lower than the prices they would have to pay for alternative fuels. By 1985, however, electric utilities would be using about 37 percent less gas with the plan.

The Effect of the User Tax on Natural Gas Prices

If the President's plan were enacted, a user tax for industrial consumers of natural gas would go into effect in 1979. In 1979, the tax would be the difference between the specific price charged the industrial consumer, and a target level which would be set at about $1.05 per thousand cubic feet below that of competing liquid fuels (distillate fuel oil would sell for the equivalent of about $3.05 per thousand cubic feet). The target level would escalate each year until 1985 when it would equal the price of distillate. The expected prices and tax revenues for industrial users (gas use in transportation is not included) are summarized in Table 5.

By 1980, the price of distillates is expected to be equivalent to about $3.09 per thousand cubic feet, and the target price would be $2.69 per thousand cubic feet. Industrial prices should range from a low of about $1.46 per thousand cubic feet for field use of intrastate gas to about $1.70 per thousand cubic feet for average interstate gas. The tax (the difference between the specific price and $2.69 per thousand cubic feet) would therefore apply to virtually all marketed gas in 1980 except for that proportion exempted for small consumers. Total revenue to the treasury is expected to be about $6.1 billion in 1980 (in 1977 dollars).

In 1985, the price of distillates is expected to be about $3.32 per million BTU, and the target price in that year equals the distillate price. Virtually all industrial gas would be sold at delivered prices below the target and would therefore be subject to the user taxes. Revenue in 1985 would be approximately $8.0 billion.

In summary, natural gas prices paid by industrial users would more than double from 1977 to 1980. Of the increase in prices, about one third would be due to increased prices in the field—much of which would occur even without implementation of the President's plan. The remainder of the increase is due to the user tax. Prices would increase another 23 percent in real terms by 1985. Furthermore, despite differences in wellhead prices for intra and interstate gas, all classes of industrial users would be paying identical gas prices under the President's plan.

As stated earlier a similar user tax is proposed for electrical utilities, beginning in the year 1983. By the year 1985, utilities would pay a tax based on the difference between the price of distillates, less $.50 per thousand cubic feet, and the specific price of gas paid by the utility. On average, interstate utilities should expect prices averaging about $2.42 per thousand cubic feet in 1985, and intrastate utilities should expect prices of about $1.96 per thousand cubic feet. As a result, interstate utilities will be taxed about $.40 per thousand cubic feet on the average. The tax for intrastate utilities would be about $.86 per thousand cubic feet. Because some specific interstate utilities might have contracts in excess of the target, only 90 percent are estimated to pay taxes. Virtually all intrastate utilities would pay taxes. Total tax revenues are estimated to be about $1.0 billion in 1985.

Coal and Its Effects on Industry

Several of the proposals in the National Energy Plan involve encouraging or requiring the substitution of coal for oil and natural gas in industrial and public utility use. In fact, more than half of the anticipated savings in imported oil by 1985, projected in the President's plan, would be the result of coal conversion.

Although, CBO is in general agreement with the President's estimates of public utility uses, it is skeptical that the amount of industrial conversion envisioned by the Administration will be forthcoming by 1985. The President's plan anticipates an increase in the industrial consumption of coal from 156 million tons in 1977 to 410 million tons in 1985. Most of the increase would take place in non-metallurgical coal which would have to increase from 70 million tons in 1977 to 305 million tons in 1985. The Administration estimates that the attainment of this goal would require that 10 percent of all existing industrial facilities burning oil or gas and 44 percent of newly constructed industrial facilities would have to convert to coal. This contrasts with the continuation of current policy where only 12 percent of new industrial facilities would burn coal in 1985.

CBO agrees with the Administration's estimate of a 10 percent conversion of existing industrial facilities, but projects only a 33 percent increase in new industrial uses with implementation of the President's proposals. A 33 percent increase would result in total coal consumption by industry of 360 million tons by 1985—50 million tons short of the Administration's projections. In terms of barrels of crude oil equivalents, CBO conversion estimates translate into oil import savings of 1.8 million barrels per day which is 0.6 million barrels below the President's estimate.

The lower estimate of industrial coal conversion provided by CBO is based on the difficulties of altering existing planned construction, the problems that may arise with transporting coal to the factory, environmental

TABLE 5.   PROJECTED INDUSTRIAL PRICES AND TAX REVENUES

	Quantity Subject to Tax a/	Average Price Before Tax b/	Average Price After Tax b/	Average Tax b/	Revenue (In billions of dollars)
For 1980					
Intrastate	2.8 c/	161	269	108	3.0
Lease & Plant	0.6 c/	146	269	123	0.7
Interstate	2.4 c/	170	269	99	2.4
				Total Revenue	$6.1
For 1985					
Intrastate	3.2 c/	196	332	136	4.4
Lease & Plant	.5 c/	181	332	151	0.8
Interstate	3.0 c/	237	332	95	2.8
				Total Revenue	$8.0

a/ In trillion cubic feet.

b/ In cents per thousand cubic feet.

c/ An estimated 25 percent of intrastate gas would be exempt from user taxes (petrochemical and fertilizer feedstocks, agriculture uses, or field use) and about 50 percent of lease and plant uses would be exempt. Furthermore, about 10 percent of intrastate and interstate consumption would not be "taxable use" as defined in Sec. 4992 of the proposed National Energy Act.

restrictions and the desire of industry to take full advantage of the rebate system by stretching out new construction.

It is possible, however, that the additional 50 million tons of coal production estimated by the Administration could be achieved if more stringent regulations regarding future burning of oil and gas were imposed by the Administration, or if the above problems prove easier to solve.

Proposed Policies

The immediate goal of the President's proposed coal program is to increase the production of coal, presently at about 680 million tons per year, by 400 million tons per year by 1985. This increase is to be encouraged primarily through the use of price incentives and regulation, implemented without adverse effects in the environment.

A second goal is to provide efficient, economically feasible technologies for the longer term that will support the substitution of coal for oil and gas.

Two types of taxes have been proposed to further the incentive to conversion to coal. The first is designed to increase the price of domestic oil. The second, a users tax plus rebates is designed specifically to encourage the use of coal in new and existing facilities.

If this users tax is implemented, industrial users of oil would be taxed beginning in 1979 at about $.90 per barrel. This tax would increase to about $3.00 per barrel by 1985. Industrial users of natural gas would also be taxed. This tax would be imposed in 1979 and would be the difference between the average price of natural gas and a target price that would be set in 1979 at about $1.05 per thousand cubic feet below the price of other liquid fuels—such as distillate oil. The target price would increase incrementally each year until 1985. At that time, the price of natural gas would equal that of distillate.

Public utilities would also be taxed under the President's plan but the tax on utilities would not be implemented until 1983. At that time, an additional tax of about $1.50 per barrel would be applied to all oil burned by utilities.

Utilities burning natural gas would pay a tax based on the difference between their cost of gas and the equivalent BTU price of distillate. This tax would also begin in 1983 and would be imposed in the same fashion as the tax on industrial users of gas except that the target price would be set at about $0.50 per thousand cubic feet below the price of distillate oil.

Since it is less feasible for economic reasons for small industrial users to convert to coal, users consuming less than 500 billion BTUs per year—about 90,000 barrels of oil per year—would not be required to pay tax.

A major component of the proposed user tax is the existence of tax rebates to industries that convert to coal. An industrial user would have the option of either using an additional 10 percent investment tax credit or taking a rebate of up to that year's oil or gas tax and investing the rebate in coal conversion. Utilities would have the option of receiving a rebate on the user tax paid to be used for new construction which would help accelerate the retirement of facilities burning gas or oil.

President Carter's coal conversion program also includes restrictions on the burning of natural gas:

- With only limited exception, no new boilers would be constructed that burned either oil or natural gas.

- Other industrial facilities could be prohibited from burning natural gas.

- Existing boilers capable of burning coal could be prohibited from burning oil or natural gas.

- Utility boilers would be prohibited from burning gas after 1990, with certain limited exceptions.

- Any industrial facilities burning coal would need permits to shift to oil or gas, and utilities would need permits to shift from gas to oil.

An integral part of any coal conversion program is a policy regarding the effects of conversion on the environment. The President's plan would require that the best available technology be applied to clean up all coal burning plants. At present, this requirement would make scrubbers (flue gas disulfurization) mandatory in all large coal-fired facilities whether or not low sulfur coal is used, thus reducing the pressure to use low sulfur western coal.

Although not a part of the present energy plan before the Congress, proposals to fund expanded research and development (R and D) in the area of coal technology will eventually become part of an overall energy policy. New R and D initiatives would probably include accelerated research on ways to clean coal before it is burned and to clean the smoke from coal burning; plus demonstrations of new ways to process and burn coal (e.g., fluidized bed combustion and low BTU coal gasification). These efforts would not include subsidies for existing BTU gasification technologies.

Energy Impacts

Unless converted to liquid or gaseous form, coal is inconvenient to use except as fuel for relatively large, stationary boilers. Consequently, the market for coal is likely to be greatest for the electric utilities and large industrial consumers that have such boilers. Demand for coal is sensitive to its price and availability and to that of alternative fuels. Air pollution regulations, and the cost of coal-fired facilities and related coal handling equipment also affect its use.

In 1976, U.S. coal production was 681 million tons, which included 459 million tons for electric utilities, 6 million tons for household and commercial consumers, 156 million tons for industrial users, and 60 million tons for export. Total domestic coal consumption was 621 million tons.

Different assumptions about factors affecting coal demand can give rise to very different projections of coal consumption in 1985. Various estimates project that under present policy, domestic coal consumption in 1985 could be as low as 730 million tons, or as high as 1,305 million tons.

The projections of present policy assume that oil price controls will be continued, interstate natural gas will be regulated at $1.42 per thousand cubic feet by the Federal Power Commission, air pollution standards will require either scrubbers or low sulphur coal, coal conversions required under present law are carried out, world oil prices are constant in real dollars, and real coal prices rise at about 2 percent per year.

The projections for the President's coal conversion proposals assume that the wellhead taxes on crude oil and industrial and utility user taxes will be implemented, the rebates will be available, and regulatory restrictions on burning oil and gas will be implemented. The major variables affecting coal demand that are not components of any of the above assumptions are: the relative capital cost of coal and the use of nuclear power by utilities. Consequently, considerable uncertainty about coal demand remains.

Utility Coal Consumption

For the present policy projections, coal demand by electric utilities has been estimated to increase to about 768 million tons by 1985, resulting in an annual rate of increase of 5.9 percent.

Under the President's proposals utility demand for coal has been estimated to increase to about 777 million tons by 1985 which is in general agreement with present policy projections.

Electric utilities will find coal superior to oil and gas as fuel for new base-load facilities given almost any set of energy prices.[2] The level of coal demand for new baseload facilities will depend on total electricity demand and on the coal-nuclear mix. Under present policy, construction of new coal-fired power plants to substitute for existing oil-fueled base-load facilities will probably also be economically attractive to utilities.

However, substitution of coal for oil in intermediate-load facilities is less likely to be attractive until oil price controls are removed and domestic oil prices rise. The price of utility fuel would have to go substantially above current world coal prices before it would become attractive to construct new coal-fired facilities to substitute for existing oil-fired plants in intermediate load service.[3]

There are various reasons why implementation of the President's coal conversion program would result in only a small increase in the use of coal in utilities by 1985. In brief, these reasons relate to proposed requirements for protecting the environment, and long lead times associated with building new facilities.

Environmental Restrictions. The proposed environmental standards for coal use would require the best available pollution control technology for all new facilities (including those burning low sulfur coal), thus increasing the capital cost of coal-fired plants. Consequently, because of these restrictions, a slightly larger number of utilities would turn to nuclear power than is anticipated under present policy. However, this factor will not be of any great significance until after 1985.

Long Lead Times. Over the past few years, construction of a significant number of coal-fired power plants has already begun, many of which are scheduled to begin operation in 1978-1981.[4] However, it is not likely that these plants will be affected by the President's proposals. Any concentrated effort to construct new coal-fired plants, resulting from the coal conversion program, will mean that these plants will not become operational until well after 1985, because of the long lead time needed to construct the facilities. However, conversion of existing facilities, when technically feasible, may occur more quickly.

Industrial Coal Consumption

The key to the President's coal conversion program is the conversion of industrial facilities from oil and gas to coal. The success of industrial conversion will account for nearly all of the difference between present policy projections of coal consumption and projections of the President's proposals. Industrial consumption of metallurgical coal will increase somewhat, but will be the same in 1985 whether the coal conversion program is enacted or not.

Fossil fuels are presently used in industrial settings in four ways:

- to generate steam
- to generate electric power
- as a source of direct heat
- as feedstocks

The major growth in demand for coal will be for those uses, exclusive of feedstocks, which in 1968 resulted in 89 percent of all industrial fossil fuel consumption.[5]

The economics of coal transportation and combustion technology make the costs of burning coal much higher for smaller installations than for larger ones. Therefore, it is not feasible to anticipate that all industrial facilities could convert to coal to generate steam and electric power in the foreseeable future. Furthermore, small installations may find meeting air quality standards more difficult if they convert to coal.[6] There will be further difficulties in converting to coal as a source of direct heat because of elements in the coal—such as sulfur—that may contaminate the product being heated.

Projections of present policy indicate that industrial demand for non-metallurgical coal will increase by 4 percent a year reaching about 100 million tons by 1985. Combining all industrial uses for coal will create a demand for about 206 million tons in 1985, under present policy.

President Carter's energy proposals for coal conversion combine economic incentives with user taxes and regulatory restrictions to convince various energy sectors to convert both new and existing facilities to the use of coal. However, projections of energy use in industry indicate that even if gas were taxed at a rate higher than that proposed by the President, most industrial facilities would still substitute gas for coal if the gas were available. Consequently, oil and gas taxes and conversion incentives by themselves may be ineffective in discouraging the use of gas as a primary energy source in industry.

On the other hand, direct regulatory restrictions on gas use, also proposed by the President, would transfer the demand for gas to oil or coal.

The Administration estimates that the President's proposals would result in the conversion of about 10 percent of existing industrial facilities from oil and gas to coal plus the substitution of coal for oil and gas in about 44 percent of new facilities by 1985.

This conversion and substitution is estimated by the Administration to result in industrial non-metallurgical coal consumption of nearly 305 million tons by 1985, a growth rate of 16 percent per year. This is an increase of 200 million tons over estimated demand under present policy. About 50 million tons of the increase is due to conversion of existing facilities and about 150 million tons would result from the substitution of coal for oil and gas in new facilities.

CBO analysis concurs with Administration estimates of a conversion to coal by 10 percent of existing facilities by 1985. However, CBO estimates conclude that 33 percent of new facilities would substitute coal for oil and gas by 1985 instead of the 44 percent estimated by the Administration, if the President's proposals were implemented. Various problems exist which CBO believes may affect the Administration estimates. These include the exemption of user taxes on small facilities, facilities already planned or under construction which may not be able to convert to coal, difficulty in meeting environmental standards, difficulties in transporting coal to newly constructed facilities, and the stretching out of construction of new facilities beyond 1985 to gain optimal benefits from tax incentives. However, it is possible that a strong regulatory program which simply prohibited most non-coal facilities and strong government efforts to solve the aforementioned problems could increase coal production closer to the Administration estimates.

CBO estimates that if the President's coal conversion proposals were implemented, non-metallurgical industrial coal consumption in 1985 would be about 150 million tons more than consumption estimated under present policy, resulting in a growth rate of about 14 percent. Although CBO estimates indicate 50 million tons less in industrial coal consumption by 1985 than the Administration estimates, it is likely that if these estimates were projected to 1990, CBO and the Administration estimates would differ only slightly.

The export of coal would, on the whole, not be affected by the President's proposals. Thus, estimates of exports under present policy and with implementation of the President's proposals do not differ. The projections suggest an increase in the amount of coal exported from about 60 million tons in 1976 to 90 million tons by 1985. Estimated coal consumption for various sectors, both under present policy and under CBO estimates of the President's proposal, is shown in Table 6.

Supply of Coal

The success of conversion from gas and oil to coal is more likely to be constrained by inadequate demand than by inadequate supply.

U.S. coal reserves are concentrated in the Ap-

TABLE 6. COAL CONSUMPTION (MILLIONS OF TONS)

Coal Consumers	Current Policy 1976	1985	Carter Policy 1985
1) Electric Utilities	459	768	777
2) Household/Commercial	6	2	2
3) Industrial	156	206	360
4) Exports	60	90	90
Total	681	1,066	1,229

SOURCE: National Energy Plan and Congressional Budget Office.

palachians, the Midwest, and the Northern Great Plains. Most Appalachian and midwestern coal has higher heating value and higher sulfur content than does Great Plains coal. Appalachian and midwestern coal is also more expensive to mine, because it is found in thinner, deeper seams than the Great Plains coal which can be easily strip-mined. However, Great Plains coal is located farther from major electricity markets, and thus, carries higher transportation charges. Great Plains coal reserves are also sufficiently large and of such even quality that production can be expanded without increasing unit costs. Costs of producing coal in other regions are likely to rise as it becomes necessary to utilize less accessible and lower-quality reserves. The amount of western coal that finds its way to eastern markets will depend on relative production costs in the different regions, transportation costs, and on the premium users are willing to pay for low-sulfur coal.

Financing for coal mine expansion has been cited by some authorities as a potential constraint to increasing coal production. However, financing is readily available to any mining concern with long-standing contracts with its customers. These contracts can be used as collateral to provide financing for new operations. If the demand for coal continues to increase, the desire for contracts by coal users will also increase,[7] as will the collateral.

If conversion to the use of coal is undertaken to the extent estimated in the President's proposals, coal production could fall short in the short term. And the mismatch of short-term demand and supply could cause sharp coal price increases which could, in turn, create decreases in future coal demand. The phasing in of user taxes as proposed may greatly mitigate such effects.

In all of these projections of the increase in coal supply one very large uncertainty remains. The effect of an increase in coal production in the West from about 100 million tons now to near 400 million tons in 1985 will require a great effort to mitigate adverse effects on the environment, transportation systems, and the life of western communities. To the extent that these issues cannot be easily solved, coal prices may rise and production may be reduced. Since utility consumption has to be contracted in advance, it is likely that any net reduction of western pro-

duction that may occur will reduce the conversion of industries which are more dependent on shorter-term commitments. Of course if this results in simply a shift to eastern coal, industry may still have adequate coal, at somewhat higher prices.

Consequence of Environmental Restrictions

The most significant problems associated with future coal use relate to the adverse effects on the environment of coal production and use.

Strip-mining of coal is a very visible example of the deleterious effects to the environment of coal production. Strip-mining necessitates excavating very large land areas. This land must be completely restored and revegetated in order to be used for other purposes. There is some question about the feasibility of restoring strip-mined land in the Great Plains coal fields; eastern strip mines can be restored, but at a cost that could be as high as $4.85 per ton of coal mined.[8] Mining can also adversely affect water supply and quality. More sulfur oxides and particulates are emitted into the atmosphere by typical coal-burning installations than would be emitted by similar facilities burning oil or gas. Measures that would mitigate these effects are available, at a cost.

The stringent application of environmental regulations, coupled with the desire to increase dramatically the use of coal in all energy sectors, creates a paradox. Furthermore, should environmental goals become even more ambitious, it is possible that expanded use of coal will become relatively less desirable.

This could be true particularly for use of coal by small industrial facilities, or in facilities that do not have a long history of pollution control.

However, for the time being it is likely that coal use and production will respond to government incentives whether stringent or lenient environmental regulations are chosen. But stringent standards and rapid development may be consistent only if substantial expenditures to compensate for higher coal costs or penalties on the use of other fuels are imposed.

ENDNOTES

[1] It is often misleading to use average prices for the intrastate market. Many industrial customers are served directly by producers so that their rates will increase abruptly as new contracts are negotiated. In the interstate market, customers are usually served by distributors who co-mingle cheap and expensive gas so that prices charged to consumers often reflect average gas prices.

[2] Council on Wage and Price Stability Staff Report, *A Study of Coal Prices,* March 1976, pp. 52-53.

[3] Federal Energy Administration, *1976 National Energy Outlook,* p. 182.

[4] R. L. Gordon, *The Future of Western Coal,* Chapter 5; and *Marketing Prospects for Western Coal,* a report to the National Science Foundation, Grant Number

OEP-75-20827, December 1976, Chapter 5, pp. 31-34.

[5] R. L. Gordon, *Historical Trends in Coal Utilization and Supply,* August 1976, prepared for U.S. Bureau of Mines, Chapter 7, pp. 3-5.

[6] If new technology, such as the fluidized bed combustion passes the demonstration stage soon, industry may be able to use more coal in small installations.

[7] Mitre Corporation, *Report on Potential Constraints to Coal Supply,* January 1975.

[8] Council on Environmental Quality estimates cited in Council on Wage and Price Stability, *Study of Coal Prices,* p. 79.

AN ANALYSIS OF THE DEPARTMENT OF ENERGY ORGANIZATION ACT*

Introduction

This memorandum analyzes the recently enacted Department of Energy Organization Act, Public Law No. 95-91, (the Act) and the accompanying Conference Report. The memorandum describes the structure and jurisdiction of the new Department of Energy (DOE) and, where appropriate, notes any significant clarifying or explanatory language contained in the Report. The length of the memorandum is occasioned by the importance of the new Department to the energy regulatory scene. Furthermore, because it is anticipated that there will be tremendous confusion during the first months of the DOE's existence, it is vital to have a clear understanding of the legislative history of the Act. For the full text of the Act, see *Appendix B* page 629.

Section 1. The Act is to be cited as the "Department of Energy Organization Act."

Section 2. Defines the terms "department," "function," "perform," and "Federal lease" used throughout the Act.

Title I
Declaration Of Findings And Purposes

Section 101. Statement of findings on why the Act is necessary, including increasing energy shortages, increasing dependence on foreign energy supplies, need for a strong national energy program to meet the present and future energy needs of the nation, need to centralize responsibility for energy policy, regulations and research in one agency, and need to integrate major Federal energy functions into a single department in the Executive Branch.

Section 102. Sets out purposes of the Act and includes almost every conceivable goal. Some of the more important purposes of the Act are:

1. Creation of a "comprehensive energy conservation strategy that will receive the highest priority,"

2. Continuation and improvement of the effective-

ness and objectivity of "central energy data collection and analysis,"

3. Establishment of an effective strategy for distributing and allocating fuels in times of short supply,

4. Implementation of policies regarding "international energy issues,"

5. Fostering competition in the supply of energy and fuels,

6. Incorporation of "national environmental protection goals" in energy programs, and

7. Fostering the continued good health of small business firms, public utility districts, municipal utilities, and private cooperatives.

Significantly, the Report states that the language emphasizing that a purpose of the Act is to foster and insure competition in the energy area is "declarative of present law which requires agencies to give attention to antitrust principles in formulating regulatory policies and decisions."

Another important and potentially troublesome purpose of the Act is to "promote the interests of consumers through the provision of an adequate and reliable supply of energy at the lowest reasonable cost," which, according to the Report, confirms the purposes of the Natural Gas Act and the Federal Power Act, as they have long been defined for "meaningful consumer protection."

Section 103. Requires the DOE to give, anytime a proposed action conflicts with a State's energy plan, due consideration to the needs of the State and, if practicable, to resolve conflicts through consultations with appropriate State officials. This section also provides that nothing in the Act shall affect the authority of any State over matters exclusively within its jurisdiction.

Title II
Establishment Of The Department

Section 201. Establishes the DOE in the Executive Department with a Secretary of Energy appointed by the President and with the advice and consent of the Senate.

Section 202. Establishes principal officers of the DOE, a Deputy Secretary, who shall act for and exercise

* Linda Elizabeth Buck, Attorney, Patton, Boggs & Blow, Washington, D.C., August 1977

the functions of the Secretary during his absence or disability, an Under Secretary, and a General Counsel, who shall perform the functions and duties prescribed by the Secretary. The Under Secretary will bear primary responsibility for energy conservation.

Section 203.   Provides for eight Assistant Secretaries. Their functions are specified but are not assigned to specific Assistant Secretaries. At the time the President nominates an Assistant Secretary, he must specify his functions. The functions which will be assigned to the Assistant Secretaries include, but are not limited to, the following:

1. Energy resource applications, including functions dealing with management of all forms of energy, production, and utilization (includes leasing);

2. Energy research and development;

3. Environmental responsibilities;

4. International programs and international policy;

5. National security;

6. Intergovernmental policies and relations;

7. Competition and consumer affairs;

8. Nuclear waste management responsibilities;

9. Energy conservation;

10. Power marketing; and

11. Public and congressional relations.

Section 204.   Establishes the Federal Energy Regulatory Commission (FERC). The Chairman and members must be specially qualified to assess fairly the needs of all interests affected by Federal energy policy.

Section 205.   Establishes an Energy Information Administration (EIA) headed by an Administrator who is specially qualified to manage an energy information system. He is responsible for carrying out an energy data and information program to collect, evaluate, assemble, analyze, and disseminate relevant energy information. The purpose of the EIA is to eliminate existing duplication and overlap in energy information programs.

The Secretary must delegate to the Administrator, on a non-exclusive basis if so desired, his authority under section 11 of the Energy Supply and Environmental Coordination Act of 1974. Further, the Administrator may act in the name of the Secretary for the purpose of obtaining enforcement of any delegated functions. The Administrator must also perform the functions assigned to the Director of the Office of Energy Information and Analysis under Part B of the Federal Energy Administration Act of 1974. The provisions of sections 53(d) and 59 of that Act are applicable to the Administrator. These provisions relate to making information available to Congress.

The Administrator will act independently and does not have to obtain any DOE official's approval in his collection and analysis of information or publication of reports.

The EIA will be subject to an annual professional audit review of performance as described in section 55 of Part B of the Federal Energy Administration Act of 1974 and must provide necessary information to other parts of the DOE. Any information gathered by the EIA must be made available to the public in a form and manner adaptable for public use, except that information which is exempt from disclosure under 5 U.S.C. §552(b) is not required to be disclosed—Freedom of Information Act (FOIA) exemptions. Other statutory restrictions on the disclosure of trade secrets or other proprietary information will apply, such as section 1(d) of the Energy Supply and Environmental Coordination Act and section 17 of the Federal Non-Nuclear Energy Research and Development Act of 1974. Any other applicable law relevant to the confidentiality of information will also continue to apply in the same manner as before transfer to the DOE of the authority to collect the information.

This may well prove to be one of the most important departments within the DOE because of the Administrator's extensive authority to collect many different kinds of information. The following statement from the Report is relevant to how he may exercise that authority:

> This provision makes it clear that the Administrator is to exercise his independent professional judgment with respect to the methodology he uses in the collection or analysis of energy information. The Secretary and other officers of the Department may require services of the Administrator or require the Administrator to collect certain data. Further, it is not intended to exempt the Energy Information Administration from the provisions of the Federal Reports Act or the discipline of the budgetary and appropriations process. . . . It is also the conferees' intent to assure and maximize the independence of the data collection and analysis functions within the Department.

It should be noted that the Act contains no definition of "energy information".

Section 205(h).   Charges the Administrator with developing and implementing a system of mandatory reporting by "major energy-producing companies" of information relating to the economics of the energy industry. While this provision does not expand or limit the basic authority of the Federal government to gather energy information, it requires that certain information be collected on a systematic basis from major energy-producing companies. Previous discretionary authority to collect this type of information has not been used by the Federal Energy Administration (FEA).

The Report suggests that, in fulfilling this responsibility, reporting should not be census-type reporting but statistically reliable data series describing the economics of the energy industry, accomplished by gathering information from the largest companies and sampling the smaller ones. The Administrator must first identify and designate "major energy-producing companies" (companies which alone or with their affiliates are involved in "one or more lines of commerce in the energy industry"). The aim is to provide a "statistically accurate profile of each line of commerce in the energy industry in the United States." The Administrator is directed to use reliable statistical sampling techniques and to minimize the reporting of energy information by small businesses.

The Act contemplates that the information will be gathered on the basis of the energy resource being produced by each line of commerce, such as the oil or coal industry. The Report suggests that the Administrator make a determination in his designation of major energy-producing companies, selecting those companies which are the largest engaged in a given line of commerce and working toward smaller companies.

The Administrator might, for example, distribute the new questionnaire to the largest producer of a given resource, and collect data from that and other companies in descending order of their production until 3/4 of the total production is covered, provided he determines the reporting from this 75 percent of the universe of producers will provide a valid profile of production economics.

A reporting form must be developed for use during the second full calendar year after the enactment of the Act. The reporting form must show, for the energy-related activities of major energy-producing companies, the following:

1. Evaluation of company revenues, profits, cash flow and investments in total, for the pertinent energy-related lines of commerce and for all significant energy-related functions;

2. Analysis of the competitive structure of sectors and functional groupings within the energy industry;

3. Segregation of energy information, including financial information, describing company operations by energy source and geographic area;

4. Determination of costs associated with exploration, development, production, processing, transportation, and marketing and other significant energy-related functions within such company, and

5. Any other necessary analyses or evaluations.

For integrated companies, it is not intended that these efforts be expanded beyond their energy-related activities.

The Administrator is required to consult with the Chairman of the Securities and Exchange Commission with respect to the development of accounting practices

for crude oil and natural gas producers as required by the Energy Policy and Conservation Act of 1975 (EPCA). He also is directed to require the designated major energy-producing companies to file these reports annually and to include a summary of the information gathered under his authority in the DOE annual report.

Section 205(h)(6). Defines "energy-producing company," as "any person engaged in ownership or control of energy resources: extraction, refining or otherwise processing energy resources; storage of fuel; generation, transmission or storage of electricity: transportation of fuels; wholesale or retail distribution of fuels or electricity."

Section 205(h)(7). Applies the criminal penalties in 18 U.S.C. §1905 to disclosure of any information obtained by the Energy Information Administration.

Section 206. Establishes an Economic Regulatory Administration (ERA) headed by an Administrator with the necessary qualifications.

The Secretary must by rule provide for a "separation of regulatory and enforcement functions" within the ERA. The purpose of this language is to require that separate offices within the ERA be responsible for the preparation of regulations and for the bringing of individual enforcement actions. The Secretary may use the ERA to administer any function which he deems appropriate, except for functions falling exclusively within the jurisdiction of the FERC.

Section 207. Provides that the General Accounting Office (GAO) shall perform for the entire DOE the functions it now performs under section 12 of the Federal Energy Administration Act of 1974, including studies of existing statutes and regulations governing DOE programs, review of policies and practices of DOE, and reviews and evaluations of particular projects and programs.

Section 208. Establishes an Office of Inspector General headed by an Inspector General (IG) and a Deputy IG. While under the general supervision of the Secretary, the IG shall be indpendent in carrying out his functions and responsibilities, which include auditing and investigating the activities of the DOE in order to "promote efficiency and prevent fraud and abuse."

The IG must appoint an Assistant IG for audits and an Assistant IG for investigations and must submit an annual report to the Secretary, to the FERC, and to the Congress summarizing his office's activities. The report must include an identification and description of significant problems, a description of recommendations for corrective actions, an evaluation of progress made in implementing recommendations, and a summary of matters referred to prosecuting authorities.

The IG must report immediately to the Secretary and to the FERC, and within 30 days thereafter to the appropriate committees and subcommittees of the Congress, any particularly serious or flagrant problems, abuses or deficiencies relating to the administration of programs and operations of the DOE. The IG is only responsible for investigative activities relating to the promotion of economy and efficiency in the administration of or the prevention or detection of fraud or abuse in the programs and operations of the DOE and not in the enforcement of the programs of the DOE. The IG must coordinate his activities with those of the GAO to the extent possible.

The IG does not have to get clearance of any reports, information, or documents required to be transmitted to the Secretary, the FERC or to Congress. Also, the IG has direct and prompt access to the Secretary and to all materials within the DOE which relate to his responsibilities. He can require by subpoena the production of any necessary information and can seek enforcement of a subpoena in a United States District Court.

Section 209. Establishes an Office of Energy Research (OER), headed by a Director whose duties include administration of the Energy Research and Development Administration's (ERDA) physical research program, advising the Secretary regarding undesirable gaps or duplication in energy, research and development, management of the multipurpose laboratories, education and training related to research, financial assistance for research, and carrying out additional assigned duties supportive of research.

Section 210. Establishes a Leasing Liaison Committee composed of an equal number of members appointed by the Secretary of DOE and the Secretary of the Interior. Although the Act does not spell out the responsibilities or the purpose of the Committee, so as not to limit the avenues of cooperation, Congress recognized that the separation of mineral leasing responsibilities is somewhat unique and thus determined that it would be helpful to provide the DOE with an institutional coordinating mechanism. Among the activities which may take place are consultations on leasing matters, establishment of long-term energy leasing goals, energy resources on the public lands, and other information relevant to leasing decisions and procedures.

Title III
Transfers Of Functions

Section 301. Transfers to the Secretary all of the functions vested in the Administrator of the FEA, the FEA, the Administrator of ERDA, ERDA, and any offices and components of either Administration. Except as provided in Title IV, the functions of the Federal Power Commission (FPC) are transferred to the Secretary.

Section 302. Transfers certain functions of the Secretary of the Interior under section 5 of the Flood Control Act of 1944, the Southeastern Power Administration, the Southwestern Power Administration, the Bonneville Power Administration, and the Alaska Power Administration. Establishes a new Administrator to administer functions transferred from the Bureau of Reclamation and the Falcon and Amistad Dams.

Section 302(b). Transfers to the DOE from the Secretary of the Interior authority under the Outer Continental Shelf Lands Act, the Mineral Lands Leasing Act, the Mineral Leasing Act for Acquired Lands, the Geothermal Steam Act of 1970, and the Energy Policy and Conservation Act which relate to:

1. Fostering competition for Federal leases;
2. Implementation of alternative bidding systems for the award of Federal leases;
3. Establishment of diligence requirements for operations of Federal leases;
4. Setting rates for production for Federal leases; and
5. Specifying procedures, terms and conditions for obtaining and disposing of Federal royalty interests taken in kind.

Section 302(c). Transfers to the DOE the authority of the Secretary of the Interior to establish production rates for all Federal leases.

Section 302(d). Transfers to the DOE the functions of the Secretary of the Interior exercised by the Bureau of Mines which are limited to fuel supply and demand analysis and data gathering, research and development related to increased efficiency of production technology of solid fuel mining, and coal preparation analysis. Mine health and safety matters stay with the Department of the Interior (DOI).

Section 303(a). Provides that no transfers from the DOI shall affect Indian lands and resources or any responsibilities for those lands and resources.

Section 303(b). Directs the Secretary of the DOE to consult with the Secretary of the Interior during preparation of regulations relating to administering Federal leases and affords the Secretary of the Interior 30 days prior to publication an opportunity to comment on proposed regulations.

Section 303(c). Directs the Secretary of the Interior to afford the Secretary of Energy 30 days prior to granting a Federal lease an opportunity to disapprove any term or condition of the lease. No such term or condition shall be included if disapproved by the Secretary. If the Secretary disapproves, he must provide a detailed, written statement of his reasons and of acceptable alternatives.

Section 303(d). Provides that the DOI shall be the lead agency for preparation of an environmental impact statement required by section 102(c) of the National Environmental Policy Act for any action with respect to Federal energy mineral leases, unless the action involves matters within the exclusive authority of the DOE.

Section 304. Provides for the transfer from the Secretary of Housing and Urban Development (HUD) to the Secretary of Energy the authority to develop and promulgate energy conservation standards for new buildings pursuant to section 304 of the Energy Conservation Standards for New Buildings Act of 1976 (42 U.S.C. §§6833 *et seq*). All other responsibilties under that Act relating to the implementation of the standards remain with the Secretary of HUD, who must provide the Secretary of Energy with the necessary technical assistance and keep him informed about implementation of the standards. This section also provides for the transfer to the Secretary of Energy from the Department of Housing and Urban Development the $200 million national energy conservation demonstration program designed to test various forms of financial assistance to encourage energy conservation in existing residences.

Section 305. Amends section 502 of the Motor Vehicle and Cost Savings Act to provide that the Department of Transportation (DOT) shall consult with the DOE with regard to DOT's development of average fuel economy standards. Before issuing a notice proposing to establish or change a standard, the DOE shall have not less than 10 days to provide written comments to DOT concerning the impacts the proposed standards may have upon conservation goals. If DOT does not take such comments into account, then DOT must include the unaccommodated comments in the notice. Before taking action on any final standards, DOT must provide the DOE with a reasonable period of time to comment. The details of the consultation process will be left to the two Secretaries to develop and adapt as the need arises. The provision is not intended to add bureaucratic delay to fuel economy rulemakings.

Section 306. Provides that, except as provided in Title IV, the functions set forth in the Interstate Commerce Act as they relate to transportation of oil by pipeline are transferred to the Secretary of Energy. The term "transportation of oil by pipeline" includes pipeline transportation of crude and refined petroleum and petroleum by-products, derivatives and petrochemicals. The authority transferred includes that under the Interstate Commerce Act as well as under other statutes vesting authority in the Interstate Commerce Commission (ICC), such as the Trans-Alaska Pipeline Authorization Act of 1973, the Elkins Act, and the Clayton Act, as those statutes relate to the transferred functions.

The current ICC oil pipeline functions which are transferred to DOE are in Chapter 1 of Title 49: Sections 1(4), (5), and (6), Section 2, Section 3, Section 4, Section 5(1), Section 6(7), Sections 15(1), (3) and (7), Section 19a, Sections 20(1), (3), (4) and (5).

Section 307. Transfers to the DOE jurisdiction vested in the Secretary of the Navy under 10 U.S.C. Chapter 641 for three naval petroleum reserves and three oil shale reserves. In administering these functions, the Secretary must consider national security factors. The DOE may enter into interagency agreements with the DOI concerning the surface management of these reserves.

Section 308. Transfers to the DOE the industrial energy conservation programs administered by the Office of Energy Programs of the Department of Commerce.

Section 309. Assigns the Division of Naval Reactors from ERDA to the Assistant Secretary of DOE who will handle energy research and development. The division will be an organizational unit of the DOE. The Division of Military Applications and the Military Liaison Committee are transferred to the DOE and assigned to the Assistant Secretary responsible for national security functions. They also will be DOE organizational units.

Section 310. Transfers to the DOE the responsibility of the FEA to promote van-pooling and car-pooling arrangements under section 381 (b) (1) (B) of the Energy Policy and Conservation Act.

Title IV
Federal Energy Regulatory Commission

Sections 401 (a) and (b). The FERC is composed of five members appointed by the President, one of whom shall be designated as Chairman. The members shall hold office for a term of four years and may be removed by the President only for inefficiency, neglect of duty or malfeasance. The Act provides for staggered times of expiration of the members first taking office. No more than three members of the Commission may be members of the same political party. Any commissioner appointed to fill a vacancy may only serve out the term of his predecessor, but he may continue to serve after the expiration of his term until a successor has taken office but not for more than one year. Members of the FERC cannot engage in any other business, vocation or employment while serving on the FERC.

Section 401(c). Sets out the responsibilities of the Chairman, which include appointment of hearing examiners, administration of personnel, distribution of business, and procurement of services of experts and consultants.

Section 401(d). Provides that members, employees or other personnel of the FERC shall not be responsible to any other person or office of DOE.

Section 401 also establishes other administrative details of the FERC. Importantly, the FERC is authorized to establish procedural and administrative regulations. Until changed by the FERC, any procedural and administrative rules applicable to particular functions over which the FERC now has jurisdiction will continue in effect.

The FERC is authorized to hold hearings, sign and issue subpoenas, administer oaths, examine witnesses, and receive evidence at any place in the United States which it designates, and may conduct any of these proceedings through agents. For the purposes of 5 U.S.C. § 552(b), the FERC will be deemed to be an agency. The FERC may appoint its own attorneys to represent it in any civil action, except in the case of litigation before the Supreme Court. It is not contemplated that this authority will be employed to litigate independently of the Department of Justice cases arising under administrative statutes which apply government-wide, such as the Freedom of Information Act (FOIA) or the Privacy Act of 1974.

Section 401(j). The FERC is intended to have an independent existence from the DOE. Thus, this section provides that the DOE must indicate any difference between the amount requested by the FERC and the amount intended by the DOE for the support of the FERC when it submits its budget estimates to Congress. For the FERC to play the effective role intended for it, it must receive all the budgetary resources it needs to carry out its responsibilities. Congress must therefore have an opportunity to obtain the FERC's own assessment of its budgetary needs. The procedure established will also assure the Secretary and the President an adequate time to evaluate the FERC request and to place it in the context of the DOE's overall budgetary needs.

Whenever the FERC submits to the Secretary, the President or the Office of Management and Budget (OMB), any legislative recommendation or testimony of comments on legislation, which are prepared for submission to Congress, the FERC shall concurrently transmit a copy to the appropriate committee of Congress. Any advice requested by the Secretary from the FERC on legislative questions would not be subject to the provisions of this section. However, if Congress asks the FERC directly for such legislative recommendations, comments, or testimony, or if the FERC prepares such material on its initiative, this provision applies. This provision also applies when a document is submitted to the Secretary, the President, or the OMB, even if it is not the final document which the FERC intends to submit to Congress.

Section 402. Establishes the jurisdiction of the FERC. The underlying principle of the FERC is that major pricing and licensing matters should be made by an independent collegial body appointed for a fixed term, rather than by a single, political entity, while at the same time preserving for the Secretary the opportunity to initiate and, where appropriate, to participate in the FERC's decision-making process.

Section 402(a). Describes the exclusive jurisdiction of the FERC over certain functions transferred from the FPC. These functions are the sole responsibility of the FERC to consider and to take final agency action on without further review by the Secretary or any other executive branch official. These functions include:

1. The issuance and renewal of hyroelectric licenses under part I of the Federal Power Act,

2. The establishment, review, and enforcement of rates and charges for the transmission or sale of electric energy, including determinations on construction work in progress, under part II of the Federal Power Act, and the interconnection, under section 202(b) of the Act, of facilities for the generation, transmission, and sale of electric energy (other than emergency interconnection),

3. Establishment and enforcement of rates and charges for the transportation or sale of natural gas by a producer or gatherer or by a natural gas pipeline or other natural gas company under sections 1, 4, 5 and 6 of the Natural Gas Act,

4. Issuance of certificates of public convenience and necessity, including abandonment of facilities or services and the establishment of physical connections under section 7 of the Natural Gas Act,

5. Establishment, review and enforcement of curtailments, other than the establishment and review of priorities of such curtailments, under the Natural Gas Act, and

6. The regulation of mergers and securities acquisitions under the Federal Power Act and the Natural Gas Act.

In addition to these functions, section 402(a) is worded to make it clear that the FERC will have exclusive jurisdiction over related matters necessary to carry out its responsibilities, even where they are not referred to specifically in the Act. For example, sections 402(a)(1)(B) and (C) give the FERC jurisdiction over the establishment of rates and charges for wholesale sales of natural gas and electricity. The conferees purposely deleted the Senate language which would have given the FERC jurisdiction only where the FERC action *directly* established the rates or charges. At the same time the Act specifies that the FERC should have jurisdiction over rules governing construction work in progress, as well as the power to enforce and review rates and charges established by it. Thus, the proposed action need not directly establish rates or charges or directly issue permits or licenses to be within the exclusive jurisdiction of the FERC.

Similarly, section 402(a)(2) provides a broad list of authorities contained in the Natural Gas Act and the Federal Power Act which the FERC may rely upon in carrying out the functions within its exclusive jurisdiction. The Report states:

It is the intent of the Conference that this provision confer upon the Commission the right to take on its own, without review by the Secretary, rulemaking or other actions under these authorities, even though not specifically referred to in Section 402(a)(1), where the Commission determines such action should be taken in order to carry out the Commission's responsibility over the licensing and pricing and other regulatory matters described in Section 402(a)(1).

Those provisions of the Natural Gas Act which are referred to in section 402(a)(2) include, among other things, authority to prescribe a system of accounts for natural gas companies, to require that depreciation and amortization accounts be kept in accordance with regulations, to allow States, municipalities or state commissions to file complaints against natural gas companies, and to provide for judicial review and penalties.

According to the Report, the Secretary's own direct jurisdiction over the functions transferred from the FPC is derived from two sources. Section 301(b) of this Act provides generally that any functions not placed in the FERC by Title IV shall be within the authority of the Secretary. This includes, but is not limited to, the collection and analysis of energy information under sections 304 and 311 of the Federal Power Act and sections 10 and 110 of the Natural Gas Act, the regulation of interlocking directorates, and the establishment of regional districts or other coordination and interconnection of facilities under section 202(a) of the Federal Power Act. Additionally, sections 402(a) and (f) of this Act explicitly exempt certain matters from the FERC's jurisdiction, thereby placing responsibility for these matters with the Secretary. These matters include exports and imports of natural gas, exports and imports of electricity, emergency interconnections under part II of the Federal Power Act, and establishment of curtailment priorities.

Significantly, both the Secretary and the FERC may use the "incidental" powers contained in the Federal Power Act and the Natural Gas Act. For example, the Secretary may invoke the enforcement provisions or adopt accounting rules so long as they are limited to what is necessary to carry out the functions vested exclusively in him.

Section 402(b). Establishes that all of the functions and authority of the ICC are transferred to the FERC where those regulatory functions establish rates and charges for the transportation of oil by pipeline or establish the valuation of any such pipeline.

Section 402(c)(1). Provides that the FERC has jurisdiction to consider any proposal by the Secretary to amend any regulations required to be issued under section 4(a) of the Emergency Petroleum Allocation Act of 1973 (EPAA) which is required by section 8 or 12 of the EPAA to be transmitted by the President and reviewed by the Congress under section 551 of the Energy Policy and Conservation Act (EPCA) — an "energy action". However, in the event the President determines that there is an emergency situation, the President may direct the Secretary to assume sole jurisdiction over the promulgation of such rule. The authority granted in this provision includes amendments to provide for adjustment to the composite price for domestic crude oil at a rate in excess of 10 percent per year, amendments to remove up to 2 million barrels a day of crude oil transported through the trans-Alaska pipeline from the composite price limitation and to specify the price for such crude oil, and amendments to exempt crude oil, residual fuel oil, or any refined petroleum product from the allocation or price regulations.

The Report makes it plain that Congress intends that the Secretary shall be the only one who proposes to take an "energy action." Once he decides to do so, however, the matter must be immediately referred to the FERC, which will be responsible for considering the proposal and holding hearings. After studying the proposal, the FERC may (1) concur in the proposed energy action, (2) concur in adoption of the proposed rule if certain amendments are made, or (3) recommend that the rule not be adopted. The Secretary may take any one of these actions, each of which would constitute final agency action. If the FERC proposed changes, the Secretary may issue the rule only if it conforms to the FERC's amendments. If the FERC has disapproved the rule, the Secretary may not issue the rule in any form. The Secretary may decide not to issue the rule regardless of the FERC's conclusion. The current procedure for submission to Congress of any "energy actions" as defined in section 551 of EPCA is retained.

Importantly, the Secretary or his delegate, not the FERC, will continue to carry out the administration and enforcement of the oil pricing and allocation programs.

Section 402(d). Establishes that the FERC has jurisdiction over any matters arising under any function of the Secretary which involve an agency determination which is required by law to be made on the record or any other agency determination which the Secretary determines shall be made on the record. Specifically exempted, however, are certain formal hearings related to the Secretary's leasing functions, especially the setting of lease production rates pursuant to sections 105 and 106 of the Energy Policy and Conservation Act.

Section 402(e). Grants jurisdiction to the FERC over any other matter assigned to it by the Secretary after public notice or referred to the FERC pursuant to section 404 of the Act.

Section 402(f). Exempts from the FERC's jursidiction authority over exports and imports of natural gas and electricity unless the Secretary assigns those functions to the FERC.

Section 402(g). Establishes that any decision of the FERC involving any function within its jurisdiction, other than actions referred to it pursuant to section 404, is final agency action for purposes of judicial review.

Section 402(h). Grants the FERC authority to prescribe rules, regulations, and statements of general applicability in performance of its functions.

Section 403. Provides the Secretary an opportunity to participate actively in the FERC's decision-making process and assures expeditious FERC consideration of important regulatory matters.

Section 403(a). Specifies that either the Secretary or the FERC may propose a rule to carry out functions within the Board's exclusive jurisdiction.

Section 403(b). Authorizes the Secretary to set reasonable time limits for the completion by the FERC of any rulemaking proceeding.

Section 403(c). Specifies that the FERC may use informal rulemaking procedures, rather than formal, on-the-record proceedings, to establish rates and charges under the Federal Power Act and the Natural Gas Act. Individual enforcement actions, however, will continue to be decided under more formal procedures. This section also provides that such rulemaking procedures must ensure full consideration of the issues and opportunity for interested persons to present their views and explore the issues. The Report suggests that this include, at a minimum, a legislative-type hearing where there is no formal presentation of evidence or cross-examination of witnesses and that the FERC should have the discretion to limit the length of oral and written presentations.

In some proceedings cross-examination would be appropriate. This would be the case if it has been demonstrated by a party that a particular factual question is essential to the Commission's decision in the rulemaking and that the question can only be resolved through cross-examination.

Section 403(d). Encourages but does not mandate the FERC's use of additional procedures to provide interested persons a reasonable opportunity to submit written questions to other persons in rulemakings to establish the wellhead price of gas. Such procedures will help ensure all parties an opportunity to obtain the facts they need to comment effectively on the proposed rule but will avoid the delay resulting from a full, on-the-record proceeding.

Section 404. Recognizes that there may be actions proposed by the Secretary to carry out the functions vested in him which may "significantly affect" the FERC's exercise of its authority. In the case of overlap,

the Act assures the FERC an opportunity to consider the Secretary's proposals. Whenever the Secretary is contemplating publishing notice of a proposed rule, he must notify the FERC and give it a reasonable length of time to conclude whether the rule is one which will significantly affect any of its functions. If it so finds, the Secretary must immediately refer the matter to the FERC, which must provide an opportunity for public comment. Following the comment period, the FERC may, as in the case of "energy actions," concur in the proposal, concur with amendments, or recommend against adopting the rule. The Secretary, if the FERC has recommended concurrence, may promulgate the rule in the form recommended by the FERC. The rule may not be promulgated by the Secretary either where the FERC's conclusion is that no such rule be issued or where the Secretary in his discretion declines to do so. Any decisions taken by the Secretary will constitute final agency action.

Section 405. Authorizes the Secretary to intervene in any proceeding before the FERC whether adjudicatory or rule-making in nature. The Secretary must comply with all procedural rules applying to intervention, and his intervention or participation does not affect the obligation of the FERC to assure procedural fairness for all participants.

Section 406. The FERC is to be deemed an independent regulatory agency for purposes of 5 U.S.C. Chapter 9, which prohibits the President from using the reorganization plan procedures to abolish independent regulatory agencies.

Section 407. The Secretary, each officer of the DOE, and all Federal agencies must provide the FERC upon request any existing information it may require. The FERC must demonstrate that it needs the information to carry out its responsibilities under the Act. Moreover, the Secretary in administering the information gathering authority under the Federal Power Act (sections 304 and 311) and the Natural Gas Act (sections 10 and 11), must include matters requested by the FERC and provide the FERC with the results of his investigations.

Title V
Administrative Procedures And Judicial Review

Includes administrative and procedural provisions governing rulemaking and other proceedings by the DOE. The present law governing judicial review of actions taken under functions transferred to the DOE is preserved.

Section 501. States that the requirements of the Administrative Procedure Act will apply to proceedings conducted by the Secretary and the FERC, unless the FERC is exempted by other law. Because the well-established administrative rules and procedures already in use in connection with the regulatory functions transferred to the

FERC will continue to apply, the additional rulemaking procedures contained in this Act shall apply to functions carried out by the DOE but not by the FERC. Where the rulemaking procedures tranferred to the FERC do not provide for as great an opportunity for notice and public comment as do the new rules established by this Act, the FERC may decide in its discretion to adopt the new rules.

Section 501(a) (1). Provides that where other applicable law establishes administrative procedural requirements in addition to those specified in section 501 of this Act, those rules will continue to apply to the exercise of the functions to which they relate. Thus, section 501 provides only a minimum set of procedures. For example, the longer period for public comment and other additional procedural requirements established by sections 325 and 326 of the EPCA would continue to apply.

Section 501 (a)(2). Provides that the new rulemaking procedures apply to the FERC in any actions under section 402(c)(1) of this Act considering any proposal by the Secretary to amend regulations under the EPAA or which the Secretary has assigned to it under section 402(e).

Section 501 (b)(1). Establishes that notice must be given of any proposed rule, regulation or order in the *Federal Register*, accompanied by a statement of available information in support of the proposed rule. Directs the Secretary to use other effective means to notify concerned or affected persons. In any case, a minimum 30-day notice period must be provided.

Section 501 (b)(2). Any rule, regulation or order which is promulgated by officers of a State or local government agency pursuant to a delegation by the Secretary must be given public notice by publication of the proposed rule in at least two newspapers of state-wide circulation or, if not practicable, in some other manner to assure wide public notice.

Section 501 (b)(3). Provides that DOE regulations relating to public property, loans, grants or contracts will be subject to the Administrative Procedure Act. Regulations pertaining to agency management or personnel are exempt.

Section 501 (c)(1). Provides that an opportunity for oral presentation of views need not be provided if the Secretary determines that no "substantial issue of fact or law" exists and that the proposal is unlikely to have a substantial impact on the nation's economy or on large numbers of individuals or businesses. However, it is anticipated that the broad test established by this provision will require the Secretary in most instances to provide the public with an opportunity for oral presentation of views.

Section 501 (c)(2). Provides that any person who would be adversely affected by the implementation of a proposed rule who wishes an opportunity for oral presen-

tation of views and argument may submit material supporting the existence of substantial issues or impact.

Section 501 (c)(3). Requires that a transcript be made of all oral presentations.

Section 501 (d). Provides that the Secretary may promulgate a rule after notice and comment if the rule is accompanied by an explanation responding to the major comments, criticisms, and alternatives offered during the comment period.

Section 501 (e). Authorizes the Secretary to waive the rulemaking procedures where he finds that it would be likely to cause serious harm or injury to the public health, safety or welfare. His findings must be set out in detail in such a rule, regulation, or order. Where the period for notice and comment is waived because of an emergency, the requirements must be satisfied within a reasonable period of time following the promulgation of the rule.

Section 501(f). Requires local public hearings if any rulemakings are confined primarily to a single unit of local government or its residents, a single geographic area within a State or its residents, or a single State or its residents.

Section 501 (g). Prescribes notice and comment procedures where the Secretary lawfully delegates authority to a State or local government agency to carry out certain functions.

Section 502. Provides for judicial review of DOE action. Review of any action taken under transferred jurisdiction shall be made in the manner specified by such law. The District Courts of the United States shall have exclusive original jurisdiction of all other cases or controversies arising under this Act, except regarding any actions taken to implement or enforce rules issued by a State or local government agency. If, in a proceeding in a State court, an issue is raised of the unconstitutionality of this Act or the validity of agency action under this Act, the case is subject to removal by either party to a District Court of the United States. Cases or controversies arising under any rule of a State or local government agency may be heard in either an appropriate State court or a District Court of the United States. The DOE's litigation is subject to the supervision of the Attorney General, who may authorize any DOE attorney to conduct any civil litigation except in the Supreme Court.

Section 503. Concerns remedial orders, a highly controversial subject under the FEA's regulations.

Section 503(a). Provides that a remedial order may be issued to any individual, association, company, corporation, partnership or other entity who the Secretary believes has violated any regulations promulgated pursuant to the EPAA of 1973—price and allocation regulations. The remedial order must be in writing and describe with particularity the nature of the violation, including a reference to the regulations alleged to have been violated.

Section 503(b). Provides that the remedial order becomes effective if within 30 days after the receipt of the order the person fails to notify the Secretary that he will contest it. The order will then be a final order not subject to judicial review.

Section 503(c). Provides that if a person does notify the Secretary within 30 days that he intends to contest a remedial order, the Secretary must immediately advise the FERC. The FERC shall then stay the effect of the order, unless it finds the public interest requires immediate compliance. Upon request, the FERC shall afford opportunity for hearing, including, at a minimum, the submission of briefs, oral or documentary evidence, and oral argument. If, in its discretion, the FERC determines that cross-examination is required, it may afford that right. The FERC shall then issue an order, based on findings of fact, affirming, modifying or vacating the Secretary's order, or directing other appropriate relief. This order will constitute final agency action for purposes of judicial review. Enforcement and judicial review of such action will be the responsibility of the Secretary.

Section 503(d). Provides that the Secretary may set reasonable time limits for the FERC to complete its actions.

Section 503(e). Provides that these procedures do not affect any procedural action taken by the Secretary prior to or incident to initial issuance of a remedial order, although such procedures are reviewable in a hearing.

Section 503(f). Provides that these procedures are applicable only with respect to proceedings which are initiated by a "notice of probable violation" issued after the effective date of this Act. Thus, section 503 applies only prospectively.

The Report contains some interesting language regarding the deletion of a provision in the Senate bill which would have delayed the effect of a remedial order for 30 days before a decision on the appeal of an order became final. In deleting the provision, the conferees intended that whatever preexisting law on the matter provided should continue to apply.

Section 504. Requires the Secretary to provide for the making of adjustments to any rules or regulations issued under the Federal Energy Administration Act, the Emergency Petroleum Allocation Act of 1973, the Energy Supply and Environmental Coordination Act of 1974, or the Energy Policy and Conservation Act which are necessary to prevent "special hardship, inequity, or unfair distribution of burdens." The Secretary must also establish procedures available to persons who wish to seek interpretations, modifications, recissions, exceptions or exemptions from the regulations.

The decision on any application or petition requesting an adjustment must specify the standards upon which any disposition was made and must demonstrate a specific application of the standards to the facts contained in the application or petition. Any person aggrieved or adversely affected by denial of a request for adjustment can appeal to the FERC. The FERC must establish appropriate administrative procedures, including the granting of a hearing, to provide for such review. Action by the FERC is final agency action. Any litigation involving judicial review of the action is the responsibility of the Secretary.

The Report discussed the criteria for adjustments, which are identical to those included in the FEA Act of 1974. However, the reenactment of those standards is not to be taken as a validation of the FEA's narrow application of them.

> The FEA has been applying criteria carried forward from the Cost of Living Council despite different language in the FEA Act and ECPA of 1976. While these more restrictive standards may have been appropriate for an emergency price control program, the establishment of the Department of Energy and the recognition of a more permanent energy regulatory program requires that the standards specified by Congress be fully and accurately applied, with each criterion given its separate and intended meaning. The Managers want to emphasize that adjustments should be granted, consistent with the other purposes of the relevant Acts, whenver an applicant meets any one of the three grounds for relief, and that relief, including *retroactive relief* where fairness and the public interest requires, should be of the degree and duration necessary to alleviate the special hardship, inequity, or unfair distribution of burdens. (emphasis added)

The office administering the adjustments program should communicate to the Economic Regulatory Administration suggested rule changes when it appears that a rule is impacting large numbers of persons inequitably or unfairly.

Sections 503 and 504 place responsibility for appeals from remedial orders or denials of requests for adjustments in the FERC. The purpose of this is to guarantee "a separation of the prosecutorial and judicial functions relating to enforcement."

All notices of probable violation issued and outstanding on the effective date of the Act will be completed without regard to the new statutory requirements, unless the Secretary chooses to apply them to preexisting proceedings. While this could result in inconsistent rulings by the FERC until action is completed on all pending proceedings, the Secretary is expected to conform his rulings to precedents enunciated by the FERC.

Also important is language from the Report concerning the due process rights of those persons involved in enforcement actions or proceedings which will not get the benefit of the new rules.

Congress always intended that the notions of fair play and due process be followed in the administrative process. Although the effect of the provisions in this Act on remedial orders and adjustments is prospective only, the Department should adhere to the principles of due process while completing action on pending proceedings not subject to these provisions.

Section 505. Requires the Secretary within 1 year to submit to Congress a report reviewing the implementation and effectiveness of the new administrative procedures.

Title VI
Administrative Provisions

Part A. Conflict of Interest Provision

The Act is designed to eliminate or minimize conflicts of interest by employees of the DOE. Thus, top DOE employees cannot hold any assets of an energy concern, must make public disclosure of their financial interest in an energy concern, must disclose certain previous or future employment with an energy concern, and cannot have any post-employment contact with the DOE for a period of time after leaving the DOE.

Section 601(a). Defines a supervisory employee as an individual who holds a position at or above GS-16 or the equivalent, an expert or consultant who works for 90 days or more, the top two officers of any State or regional office, and any employee who has primary responsibility for grants or awards. Requires the Secretary to include in the definition any employee or officer who exercises sufficient decision-making or regulatory authority.

Section 601(b). Defines an "energy concern" as a profit-making entity which devotes a significant proportion of its operations to energy-related activities. If only an insignificant proportion of an entity's activities are energy-related, it would not be included. Additionally, the definition includes any non-profit-making entity if the entity receives any financial assistance from the DOE. The definition also includes any person holding an interest in property from which an energy product is obtained or purchased (royalty owners.)

Section 601(c). Requires the Secretary to publish a current list of energy concerns and provides that an employee may request a determination whether a particular entity is an energy concern and should be on the list. If an entity is not on the list, an employee will not be excused from the disclosure and divestiture requirements if he knows or should know that the entity engages in energy-related activity.

Section 601(d). Provides that if an employee "should have known" of a particular interest or activity, he will be presumed to have known of it. An employee may not evade the requirements of this Title by transferring a financial interest in an energy concern to a spouse or dependent during the six months prior to the time he comes to work for the DOE or during the time he is employed by the DOE. An employee will be presumed to have knowledge of any financial interest in an energy concern which is in a trust of which he is a beneficiary.

Section 602. Prohibits a supervisory employee from having a known financial relationship with an energy concern. Personnel transferring to the DOE have 6 months to comply with the Act's divestiture requirements and 30 days after the date of transfer to notify the Secretary of the relationship.

Section 602(c). Allows the Secretary to waive the divestiture requirements if already totally vested or where exceptional hardship would result. Exceptional hardship applies to unusual circumstances where the financial injury to the person far out-weighs the potential harm that could be caused by any possibility of a conflict of interest or an appearance of a conflict. A waiver may only be for a certain specified period and when a waiver does occur, the grounds for the waiver must be published in the *Federal Register.*

Section 602(d). Provides that supervisory employees who receive income from an energy concern or own property directly or indirectly in an energy concern must comply with the disclosure requirements of section 603.

Section 603. Provides disclosure requirements which apply to all DOE employees except those that are below the level of GS-13 and which are employed in positions or classes of positions which are specifically designated by the Secretary as of a non-regulatory or non-policymaking nature. DOE employees must file 30 days after beginning service and by May 15 of each of the following calendar years a report with the Secretary regarding direct or indirect sources of income from energy concerns. Employees who leave the DOE are required to file a financial disclosure report within 30 days after termination of employment.

Section 604. Requires a separate report on prior employment with an energy concern which must be filed within 60 days after an individual becomes an employee of the DOE identifying the name and address of any energy concern that paid the supervisory employee more than $2,500 in any of the preceding five calendar years, the period during which such income received, the title or position held, and a brief description of duties performed. No confidential information from a legally privileged relationship need be disclosed. If the employee was a member of a firm or association, no information with respect to any clients must be filed unless the employee was directly involved in the work for the clients.

Section 605. Prohibits a former supervisory employee from having contact on any DOE matter for one year after termination of DOE service. The prohibition extends to both oral and written communications and to new matters that arise after the employee leaves service, as well as to matters which were before the DOE while the individual was employed. There is no requirement that there be a formal proceeding in the DOE before the prohibition applies. However, before the prohibition applies, there must be an intention by the former employee to influence the action of the DOE in some way. It does not apply where the former employee appears in response to a subpoena nor when the sole subject matter of the communication is personal and individual and of a non-business nature. Furthermore, a former employee with outstanding scientific or technological qualifications is not prohibited from making a formal appearance or written communication on a particular matter in that field if there is a certification that the appearance is in the national interest published in the *Federal Register.*

Each former supervisory employee must file a report on May 15 for two years after leaving the DOE, describing any employment with an energy concern during the two-year period. If an employee specifies at the time he leaves the DOE any contract of agreement for future employment with an energy concern and files a report within 30 days after leaving the DOE, the requirement is satisfied. The report must be amended if there is a change of employment within the two year period.

Section 606. Provides that for a period of 1 year after leaving an energy concern, a supervisory employee shall not knowingly participate in a DOE proceeding in which his former employer is substantially, directly, or materially involved (other than a general rulemaking proceeding). Furthermore, a supervisory employee, for a period of 1 year after commencing service with the DOE, may not knowingly participate in any DOE proceeding for which within the previous 5 years he had direct responsibility or in which he participated substantially or personally while working for an energy concern. The Secretary may waive these provisions, if, in a particular circumstance, there would be an exceptional hardship upon the supervisory employee or if imposing the restriction would be contrary to the national interest. Any waiver must be filed with the record of the DOE proceeding for which the waiver is granted.

Section 607. Requires the DOE to make these reports and any waivers available to the public and to retain them for 6 years. Requires the Civil Service Commission to perform random audits to monitor the reporting procedures.

Section 608. Provides criminal penalties for any individual who knowingly violates the disclosure provisions of not more than $2,500 or imprisonment of not more than 1 year or both. Any individual who violates any of the other conflict of interest provisions will be subject to a civil penalty not to exceed $10,000 for each violation.

In the event of any violation of the prohibition against post-employment contacts, the violation must be considered in deciding the outcome of any related proceeding. None of the provisions of this Title limit in any way the operation of the general, government-wide conflict of interest prohibitions contained in 18 U.S.C. §§207-208.

Part B. Personnel Provisions

These provisions will be dealt with briefly because they will not have the impact which the substantive provisions of the Act will have on a firm's energy operations.

Section 621. Allocates to the DOE a certain number of supergrade positions, of which a number may be hired outside the Civil Service, and establishes the percentages which may be placed at each grade level.

Section 622. Provides for the appointment of 14 additional executive level personnel.

Section 623. Authorizes the Secretary to obtain the services of experts and consultants.

Section 624. Permits the Secretary to establish necessary advisory committees, subject to the provisions of the Federal Advisory Committee Act, and provides for travel expenses and *per diem* allowances for the members.

Specifies that section 17 of the FEA Act of 1974 shall be applicable to all advisory committees chartered by the Secretary or transferred under the Act. Section 17 concerns balanced representation of members, requirements for open meetings and other procedural requirements, and provides that a meeting may be closed in the interests of national security. Section 624 furnishes an additional basis for closing certain kinds of advisory committee meetings, by providing that where an advisory committee advises the Secretary on matters pertaining to research and development, the Secretary may determine that the meeting be closed because it comes within the scope of exemption 4 of the Government in the Sunshine Act "is likely to disclose trade secrets and commercial or financial information obtained from a person and is privileged or confidential."

If the Secretary chooses to close all or part of a meeting, he must demonstrate a maximum effort to close no more of the meeting than may properly be closed and to open the remainder to the public and must distinguish in a written statement the national security and trade secrets reasons for justifying closure.

Section 625. Permits the Secretary limited use of the services of military personnel.

Part C. General Administrative Provisions

Section 641. Authorizes the Secretary to perform any functions transferred by the Act and to exercise any authority available by law to the official or agency from which such function was transferred.

Section 642. Provides that the Secretary, unless otherwise prohibited, may delegate his functions.

Section 643. Allows the Secretary authority to reorganize the DOE unless the organzational units are established by this Act.

Section 644. Authorizes the Secretary to prescribe necessary procedural and administrative rules and regulations.

Section 645. Confers upon the Secretary the same powers and authorities as the FTC has to issue subpoenas under section 9 of the Federal Trade Commission Act.

Section 646. Authorizes the Secretary to enter into and perform contracts, leases, cooperative agreements, or other similar transactions with public agencies, private organizations and persons.

Sections 647 and 648. Authorize the Secretary to construct and improve necessary facilities for employees and dependents of DOE.

Section 649. Pertains to the DOE's use of government facilities.

Section 650. Allows the Secretary to establish and change State, regional, local or field offices.

Section 651. Authorizes the Secretary to acquire copyrights and patents.

Section 652. Authorizes the Secretary to accept and use gifts and bequests for DOE.

Section 653. Authorizes a working capital fund.

Section 654. Directs the Secretary to cause a seal of office to be made.

Section 655. Provides that the Governors may establish Regional Energy Advisory Boards for their regions with such memberships as they may determine. Representatives of the Secretaries of Energy, of Commerce, of the Interior, the Chairman of the Council on Environmental Quality, the Commandant of the Coast Guard, and the Administrator of the EPA shall be entitled to participate as observers in the deliberations of the Boards. If a Board makes specific recommendations, the Secretary is required to publish his reasons for not adopting such recommendations.

Section 656. Provides that the Secretaries of Defense, Commerce, Housing and Urban Development, Transportation, Interior, Agriculture, as well as the Administrator of General Services and the U.S. Postal Service, must designate an Assistant Secretary or Assistant Administrator as the principal energy conservation officer responsible for coordinating with the DOE on energy matters.

Section 657. Directs the Secretary to make an annual report to Congress on the activities of the DOE. The report must include a statement of the Secretary's goals, priorities and plans for the DOE, together with an assessment of the progress made toward the attainment of the goals, the management of the DOE, and progress made in coordination of its functions with other departments and agencies. The report must also include:

1. The projected U.S. energy needs,

2. Estimate of domestic and foreign energy supply,

3. Current and foreseeable trends in various aspects of energy resources,

4. Summary of research and development efforts,

5. Review and appraisal of the adequacy and appropriateness of technology,

6. Summary of cooperative and voluntary efforts mobilized to promote conservation and recycling.

7. Summary of substantive measures taken by the DOE to stimulate and encourage the development of new manpower resources,

8. Summary of activities by companies or persons which are foreign owned or controlled and which own or control U.S. energy sources and supplies.

Section 658. Requires the Secretary of the Interior to submit a report on the organization of the leasing functions as well as any recommendations for reorganizing such functions within 1 year after the date of enactment of this Act.

Section 659. Authorizes the Secretary to transfer funds from one appropriation to another within the DOE, but no appropriation may be either increased or decreased more than 5 percent.

Section 660. Requires annual authorization for all DOE appropriations.

Title VII
Transitional, Savings, And Conforming Provisions

Section 701. Provides for the transfer and allocation of appropriations and personnel to the DOE.

Section 702. Provides protection for transferred personnel.

Section 703. Provides for the termination of any agency whenever all the functions vested in it by law are terminated or transferred by this Act.

Section 704. Requires the Office of Management and Budget to make necessary determinations regarding the transfer of functions and to make such incidental disposition of funds as necessary.

Section 705. (Savings provision). Continues the effect of agency actions and applies to any action taken pursuant to functions transferred by this Act. Such actions shall continue in effect until changed in accordance with law and include rulemakings in progress as well as all other types of proceedings. Authorizes the Secretary and the FERC to issue regulations for the transfer of proceedings to the DOE.

This provision continues all proceedings or applications for any license, permit, certificate or financial assistance which are pending at the time this Act becomes effective. Orders issued in such proceedings and appeals will continue until modified, superseded, or revoked by a duly authorized official, a court of competent jurisdiction, or by operation of law.

Section 706. The standard separability provision.

Section 707. Provides that references in other laws to other agencies shall be deemed changed to reflect the transfer of functions to the DOE.

Section 708. Provides that nothing in the Act except as provided in Title IV shall in any way limit the authority of the President.

Section 709. Details the laws which are amended by this Act.

Section 710. Provides for certain administrative amendments in other laws, such as placing the Secretary in the line of succession to the President.

Section 711. Provides that, with the consent of the appropriate department or agency head concerned, the Secretary may use for a reasonable period of time the services of those agencies from which functions have been transferred.

Section 712. Directs the Civil Service Commission to prepare a report to Congress on the effect on employees of the reorganization under this Act.

Section 713. Provides that the transfer of functions under Titles III and IV shall not affect the validity of any draft environmental impact statement published before the effective date of this Act.

Title VIII
Energy Planning

Section 801. Requires the Secretary to prepare and submit a proposed National Energy Policy Plan which establishes energy production, utilization and conservation objectives and identifies strategies and recommendations for action in accordance with the energy needs of the United States for 5 and 10 year periods. The Plan must also recommend legislative and administrative actions necessary to achieve the objectives of the proposed Plan. Accompanying the Plan must be a report with data and analysis to support the Plan's conclusions and recommendations. The first proposed Plan must be submitted by April 1, 1979, and updated Plans must be submitted biennially thereafter. This section sets forth explicit requirements for the proposed Plans.

Section 802. Requires that the proposed Plan be referred to the appropriate committees of Congress and that the committees review the proposed Plan and fully consider the need for action on the proposal. Their action could be in the form of a Joint Resolution or otherwise enacting the National Energy Policy Plan into law. Any legislation reported could contain alternatives to, modifications of, or additions to the proposed Plan.

Title IX
Effective Date And Interim Appointments

This Title provides that the Act shall take effect 120 days after the Secretary first takes office or earlier, as the President may prescribe. It also provides for interim appointments and other related matters.

Title X
Sunset Provisions

This Title requires the President to submit to the Congress a comprehensive review of each program in the DOE by January 15, 1982, which shall be made available to the committee or committees of the Senate and the House of Representatives having jurisdiction with respect to the annual authorization of funds for such programs for the fiscal year beginning October 1, 1981.

Section 1001. Prescribes the necessary contents for each comprehensive review prepared for submission by the President.

CHAPTER TWO

THE NATIONAL ENERGY SCENE

THE ENERGY OUTLOOK *

Introduction

Considerable time has passed since publication of the first *Project Independence Report*. It has been a dynamic, controversial, and important period with respect to energy. Several events have occurred that will shape our future energy situation. This report is another look at America's ability to achieve energy independence, and the problems we face in attaining that goal.

A number of trends have become clearer that help us to forecast future energy demand and supply. Some of these make the situation appear worse, such as downward revisions in oil reserves; and some make it appear better, including upward revisions in Northern Alaskan rate of development.

In this reassessment of America's energy future, the implications of these trends have been taken into account in a set of revised forecasts. Major improvements in FEA's forecasting techniques have also been incorporated. Further, in order to sharpen the discussion of policy alternatives, the effects of alternative price regulation policies, environmental controls, and shifts in energy resource mix have been explicitly evaluated.

This chapter reviews the historical context of our present energy situation, evaluates the implications of the past year's events and then summarizes the major findings of this year's forecasts.

Recent Energy Trends

Oil   Until the 1960's, the United States was essentially independent of foreign oil supplies. This nation produced and consumed more oil than any other country; its domestic supply was plentiful and proven reserves were growing. However, as production from older fields peaked and new exploration and development diminished because of the availability of less expensive imported oil, domestic petroleum production began to decline after 1970.

Declining supply, combined with a continued 4 percent annual growth rate in consumption, resulted in a dramatic rise in our reliance on imported oil. Import dependency has grown from 18 percent in 1960 to about 37 percent in

* The National Energy Outlook, Federal Energy Administration, February 1976

1975. Direct imports from OPEC now constitute about two-thirds of all imports, with Nigeria, Canada, Venezuela, Saudi Arabia, and Indonesia supplying most of our imported oil.

The rise in imports and the increase in the price of oil have placed severe burdens upon America's balance of payments for energy. In 1970, the United States paid about $3 billion for foreign oil; in 1975, our import bill was about $27 billion. Further, our vulnerability to an embargo continues to rise. Another supply cut-off could result in a large reduction in GNP and considerably greater unemployment.

As a consequence of the Arab oil embargo and OPEC price increases, both domestic crude oil and imported crude oil prices rose dramatically during the latter part of 1973 and the first quarter of 1974. Although price changes have been more gradual since then, they continued to increase. The higher prices affected all petroleum products, including motor gasoline, home heating oil, and residual fuel oil. The average retail price of gasoline has increased by about 50 percent since the onset of the embargo.

Higher crude oil prices have stimulated greater exploration activities. For the second successive year, oil wells drilled and drilling rigs in use increased; wells drilled have risen from 26,600 in 1973 to about 37,000 in 1975. The number of rotary rigs in operation in the United States increased from about 1200 in 1973 to over 1600 in 1975. However, despite the increased drilling activity, the lead-time from exploration to production is often several years; hence, the Nation's oil production continues to decline. In the two years since the Arab oil embargo, domestic production has dropped by nearly one million barrels per day (MMB/D) to a low of 8.2 MMB/D in December 1975 (See Figure I-1). In 1974, for the first time, the United States was surpassed as the world's largest oil producer— by the Soviet Union. The completion of the Trans-Alaskan Pipeline in 1977, which will bring about two million barrels per day of North Slope oil to the "Lower 48" States, will only lift domestic production to levels reached in the early 1970's.

The higher oil prices experienced since the 1973 embargo have also had an important effect on petroleum consumption. Domestic oil demand fell by 4 percent in 1974 and an additional 2.5 percent in 1975—a startling reversal from the trend in recent years. Had pre-embargo

Figure I-1

Domestic Production Of Crude Oil

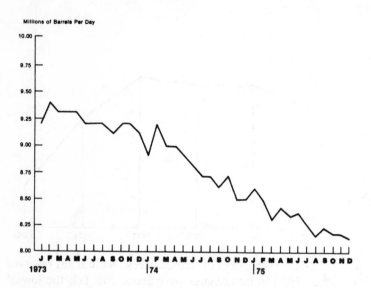

Millions of Barrels Per Day

trends continued, demand would have been about three million barrels per day higher than it was in 1975 (see Figure I-2). Although much of the decrease in demand is due to lower economic activity, significant reductions are a result of consumer response to higher prices. As evidence of the consumer reaction to higher prices, sales of

Figure I-2

Petroleum Demand Forecast vs. Actual Demand

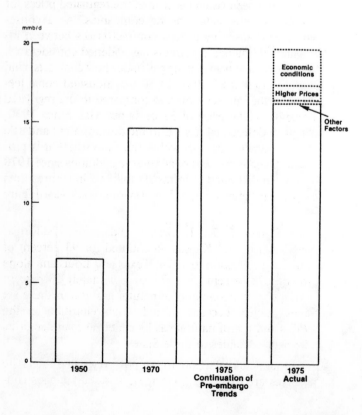

sub-compact cars have increased considerably and the average fuel efficiency of new cars has increased from 15.6 miles per gallon (mpg.) in the 1975 model year to an estimated 17.6 mpg. in 1976.

The major legislative events affecting oil supply and demand were passage of the Energy Policy and Conservation Act (EPCA) and partial removal of the oil depletion allowance. The effects of these measures, as well as the impacts of the lower estimates of reserves published by the United States Geological Survey, are discussed later in this report.

Coal   Coal production has remained essentially level during the past five years (see Figure I-3). Production in 1970 was 603 million tons; in 1974, it was still 603 million tons and rose to about 640 million tons in 1975. Coal production could have been higher in 1974, but about 40 million tons of production were lost due to work stoppages in that year.

Over the past 20 years coal consumption has declined in the industrial and residential sectors, while the use of coal as a boiler fuel by utilities has increased. The regulated price for interstate natural gas, the removal of import controls on residual fuel oil and its cheap imported price until the embargo, and the continued development of nuclear power have limited the growth of coal use. In the late 1960's and early 1970's, State and local air pollution regulations discouraged the burning of coal in many situations. The uncertainty about environmental issues such as interim use of intermittent control systems, reliability and cost of stack gas scrubbers, litigation over significant deterioration regulations, compliance deadline exten-

Figure I-3

Annual U.S. Coal Production and Consumption

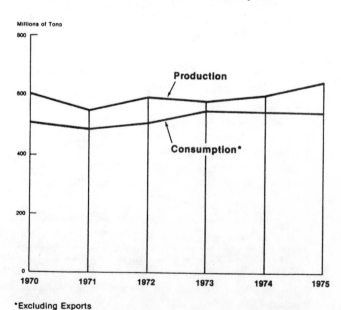

Millions of Tons

*Excluding Exports

sions, legislative changes to the Clean Air Act and surface mining reclamation laws is still affecting the growth in coal use.

While oil prices rose dramatically, coal prices for long-term contracts have been relatively stable. Spot coal prices rose rapidly to about $32 per ton in the latter part of 1974 in anticipation of a coal strike, but then declined markedly in 1975 (see Figure I-4). Contract coal prices have increased steadily in the last two years.

Natural Gas   Natural gas supplied about 30 percent of the Nation's energy last year and about 40 percent of our non-transportation uses. Approximately 21 trillion cubic feet (Tcf) were consumed in 1974. Although pipeline imports from Canada are an important source of natural gas in some regions, e.g., the Pacific Northwest, they account for less than 5 percent of annual consumption.

Because of the clean burning properties of natural gas, its low regulated price compared to alternate fuels and, until the late Sixties, abundant supply, demand has been increasing. Marketed natural gas production, however, peaked in 1973 at 22.6 Tcf, and dropped significantly for the first time in 1974. This pattern continued in 1975 with production down another 7 percent, to 20.1 Tcf (see Figure I-5).

Since 1968, the "Lower 48" States have been consuming more natural gas each year than producers have been

Figure I-5

U.S. Natural Gas Annual Marketed Production

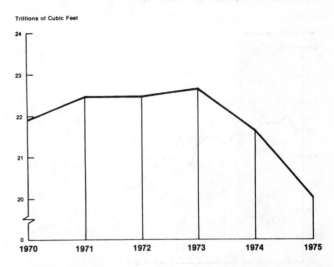

finding in the form of new reserves. Natural gas reserves for 1974 in these States were about 208 Tcf, the lowest level since 1952. Except for 26 Tcf discovered in Alaska in 1970, annual additions to reserves have failed to equal marketed production for the past seven years. Moreover, the Alaskan reserves will not provide significant amounts of gas until the 1980's due to the absence of necessary transportation facilities.

Low regulated prices have encouraged consumption and discouraged the search for new gas to supply the interstate market. Within the past five years, intrastate prices have been rising faster than the regulated prices for gas sold to interstate pipeline companies. As a consequence, the disparity in new contract prices between intrastate and interstate markets has widened considerably. Producers have been selling gas under new contracts at an average price of $1.00 to $1.50 per thousand cubic feet (Mcf) in the intrastate market compared to the regulated interstate ceiling price of 52 cents per Mcf. Since 1970, this price differential has led to the development and sale of most new natural gas within the state where it is produced. Over 90 percent of all reserve additions since 1970 have been dedicated to intrastate markets in contrast to a 60 percent figure for the five previous years (see Figure I-6).

Six States—Texas, Louisiana, Oklahoma, California, New Mexico, and Kansas—accounted for 93 percent of domestic production in 1974; Texas and Louisiana alone provided 73 percent. In 1974, approximately 50 percent of domestic consumption of natural gas was in these six States, largely because of industrial relocation in the 1960's and use of natural gas by chemical manufacturers and electric utilities in these States.

Curtailments of supply to the price regulated interstate pipelines are expected to increase as total supplies con-

Figure I-4

Average Coal Prices
(F.O.B. Plant)

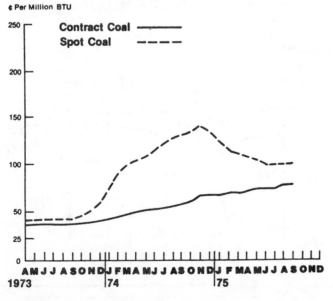

Source: FPC

Figure I-6

Average Annual Reserve Additions of Natural Gas

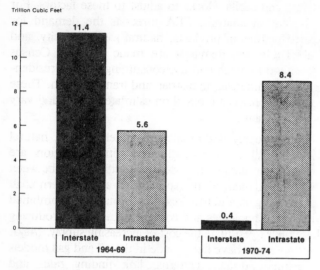

Trillion Cubic Feet

Source: American Gas Association, Federal Power Commission.

tinue to decline and available gas is dedicated to the unregulated intrastate market. In 1970, curtailments reported by interstate pipelines were less than 1 percent of requirements. By 1974, curtailments increased to 10 percent of total requirements, and were forecast to rise to as much as 15 percent in 1975. The economic impacts of this shortage, however, were greatly mitigated by the switching of industrial users from natural gas to higher priced alternative fuels (propane, residual or distillate oil); mild weather conditions; conservation; limited emergency gas deliveries; and a Federal Power Commission ruling that enabled high priority, curtailed industrial users of natural gas to purchase uncommitted gas directly from producing States at unregulated prices.

The major economic effects of the curtailments in the East and Midwest resulted from the higher costs of alternative fuels. These costs reduced the ability of industrial firms to compete with similar firms in other areas that did not have to utilize high-priced alternate fuels. In addition, curtailments have led to widespread adoption of restrictions on new natural gas connections of residential and commercial space heating.

Electric Power   The increased fuel prices of the past two years have had a significant impact on the electric utility industry. The higher fuel costs, combined with already escalating plant construction and operating costs, have forced higher rates for electricity causing consumer unrest and demands for changes in rate structures. With today's oil prices and the natural gas shortages, the economics of new plants has shifted to coal and nuclear power. Higher prices have also reduced demand and this, in turn, is likely to reduce future capacity needs. These

effects, coupled with continuing debate over environmental, siting and safety issues, and financial problems in the utility industry, have introduced significant uncertainties into the outlook for electricity growth.

For many years, electric power demand grew at an annual rate of about 7 percent. Additions to generating capacity planned for the years through the early 1980's were based on this pre-embargo rate of demand growth. In 1974, however, the growth rate for electricity fell to zero and only increased by about 2 percent in 1975. This phenomenon is largely attributable to reduced consumption in response to higher prices and the economic slowdown.

Prices have risen most significantly in regions which rely heavily on residual oil for electric power. New England and the Mid-Atlantic, for instance, recorded price increases averaging more than 35 percent in 1974 and consumption declined significantly.

The financial situation of electric utilities has been dramatically affected by higher fuel costs, which necessitated large rate increases and hardened resistance to further rate adjustments. At the same time, lower capacity utilization, lengthening times of licensing and construction, and high inflation associated with new plant construction required even greater rate increases if utilities were to finance new plants. When these were not forthcoming, their ability to raise new debt or equity was impaired, and the cash shortage caused cancellation or deferral of many new plants. While the situation has improved somewhat in the past year, financial problems are still evident.

The fuels used to generate electricity have shifted in recent years, with the nuclear share of electricity production growing sharply from 4.5 percent in 1973 to about 8.6 percent estimated for 1975 (see Figure I-7). Although nuclear power has the lowest variable operating costs and

Figure I-7

Nuclear Power Generation by Year
(Percentage of Total Electric Power Generation)

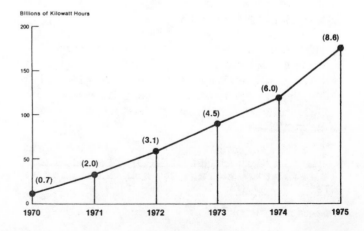

Billions of Kilowatt Hours

is insensitive to oil price fluctuations, nuclear plants require the largest capital investment and the longest construction leadtime of any type of electric generating plant. Consequently, they have been the most heavily affected by recent plant deferrals and cancellations. Since June 1974, orders for over 100,000 megawatts of planned nuclear capacity have been cancelled or postponed. These cancellations and deferrals amount to almost 70 percent of planned additions. Nevertheless, with the drop in electricity growth and the additions of new plants, reserve capacity is now 34 percent, compared with a traditional level of 20 percent.

International Energy Perspective   The shock wave felt throughout America and the rest of the oil importing countries at the onset of the Arab embargo has subsided. Consumer nations have reacted sharply to the higher world oil prices. The International Energy Agency (IEA) was established under the aegis of the Organization for Economic Cooperation and Development. Supply security has been a primary concern, but considerable attention has also been given to the issue of higher oil prices and longer-term energy matters. The IEA has developed an emergency program which calls for a coordinated response in the event of a future oil embargo. IEA members have also developed plans for long-term cooperation on conservation, research, resource development, and access to supply.

As higher prices and conservation reduced world oil demand, OPEC has been forced to reduce production to prevent prices from falling. Excess OPEC productive capacity has increased greatly since the embargo and now amounts to an estimated 10-12 million barrels per day, or one-third of total OPEC capacity. OPEC production, which had increased steadily for nine years, declined from 31.2 million barrels per day in 1973, to about 27 million barrels per day in 1975. The major cutbacks were absorbed by Saudi Arabia, Libya and Kuwait. Nevertheless in 1975, OPEC's members approved a 10 percent increase in the price of Saudi Arabian marker crude oil, from $10.51 per barrel to $11.56.

Forecasting Our Energy Future

The Analytical Base   Against this background of energy developments, a number of changes were made in this year's analysis. The FEA forecasting model—the Project Independence Evaluation System (PIES)—was improved to reflect current energy data and new strategies were evaluated.

The PIES system is a model of the technologies, lead-times, costs and geographical locations which affect energy commodities from the point of discovery, through production, transportation, conversion to more useful forms, and ultimately consumption by all sectors of the economy.

Consumption (final demand) for a particular fuel depends on prices for that fuel, the prices of substitute fuels, the general level of economic activity, and the ability of consumers and capital stocks to adjust to these factors. For each year of analysis, FEA forecasts the demand for refined petroleum products, natural gas, electricity, and coal. These fuel demands are made for each Census region and for each end-use consuming sector—residential and commercial, industrial, and transportation. These demand forecasts are based on estimated prices and vary as prices change.

Energy supply is estimated separately for oil, natural gas, and coal. For each fuel, many different regions are separately evaluated to assess the differences between OCS and Alaskan oil or Appalachian and Western coal. For each region and fuel, reserve estimates are combined with the technologies and costs of finding and producing these fuels to estimate the cost of increasing supply. Major improvements have been made in the oil and gas models to estimate drilling patterns, link finding rates and enhanced recovery directly to revised research estimates, and account for changes in the depletion allowance. The coal supply estimates distinguish between various sulfur and Btu contents.

The PIES then attempts to match these energy demands as a function of fuel, sector, and price with the available supply in the regions which can supply these needs at the lowest price to find a balance or equilibrium. If supply is not available to satisfy the specific demands in an area, the prices are allowed to vary until supply and demand are brought into balance.

Alternative Scenarios   While there are an infinite number of possible energy policy strategies for the United States, last year's report examined four alternatives—business as usual, accelerated supply, accelerated conservation, and a combination of accelerated supply and conservation. These four broad scenarios were chosen because they depicted a range of feasible actions that could be expected to lead to very different energy outcomes by 1985.

The scenarios discussed in this report still evaluate the impacts of accelerated development and conservation, but the scope has been expanded to include different government price controls and regional growth restrictions, expectations about geologic and resource potential, and the effects of a greater use of electricity. These energy scenarios do not represent FEA or Administration policy recommendations. They are neither comprehensive, nor mutually exclusive. Each is intended to illustrate a major trend or impact of a possible policy direction and to show the implications of some of the more extreme energy policies being considered. The intent is to provide a spectrum of alternatives that can be used to evaluate specific proposals.

Energy Through 1985: The FEA Forecast

International Oil Price   Any analysis of the domestic energy outlook must begin with a perspective on future world oil prices. The world oil price will greatly influence domestic energy demand and the economic feasibility of producing various high cost sources of domestic supply. The events of the past two years have indicated an ability by the oil producing cartel to maintain the high prices of oil established during the embargo, even in the face of substantial declines in world oil demand due to the high prices and reduced rates of world economic growth. It seems clear that little can be done between now and 1980 to alter the supply and demand relationships between OPEC and consuming nations enough to weaken the cartel's exclusive control over prices. Thus, there is no significant likelihood of a considerably lower price for OPEC oil in this period.

Nevertheless, there are political factors which are likely to be as important in determining the viability of the cartel as economics. The dynamic relationships among producers and consumers will be crucial during this period. Further, the major consumer nations have each initiated programs to cope with higher energy prices and excessive dependence on foreign oil. Although consumer nations have not yet implemented all these programs to apply downward pressure on cartel prices, pressure can be brought by aggressive resource development and conservation actions to stabilize prices.

Recognizing the uncertain nature of world oil price dynamics, FEA continues to forecast at various world oil prices. It is almost certain that the era of $3-4 per barrel oil is over, and thus our analysis considers a range which brackets current prices ($8-16). Most of the analytical emphasis, however, is placed on a continuation of current prices (about $13 per barrel c.i.f. United States, in 1975 dollars). The $8 and $13 prices are almost equivalent to the $7 and $11 prices (in 1973 dollars) used in last year's report, accounting for inflation.

Energy Consumption   The analysis of our energy future begins with a discussion of one set of forecasts of what can reasonably be expected to happen if present government policies and market forces are allowed to operate. In most respects, the Reference Scenario in this analysis is similar to last year's Base Case and is designed to illustrate the major technical and data changes between 1974 and the present. Numerous assumptions are needed to make this forecast; the impacts of changing these assumptions are described later in the chapter.

If current prices continue, energy demand should increase from 72.9 quadrillion Btu (quads) in 1974 to 98.9 quads in 1985 (see Table I-1). This is a growth rate of 2.8

Table I-1

ENERGY DEMAND BY SECTOR, 1985
(Reference Scenario at $13 Imported Oil)
(Quadrillion Btu)

	Coal	Petro-leum	Nat-ural Gas	Nu-clear	Other	Total Gross Inputs	Utility Elec-tric Distri-buted
Household/ Commercial	0.1	8.2	6.4	--	--	14.8	6.4
Industrial	4.8	8.2	14.0	--	--	27.1	3.9
Transportation	--	22.4	0.8	--	--	23.2	--
Electrical Generation	15.4	2.7	3.1	8.7	3.9	33.7	(10.3)
Other	0.3	--	(0.2)	--	--	0.1	--
Total	20.6	41.5	24.1	8.7	3.9	98.9.	--

percent, compared with the recent historical rate of 3.6 percent.

The greatest growth will occur in electric generation, which will continue to grow at about twice the rate of total energy consumption (or about 5.4 percent annually), although more slowly than in the past. In the Electric Sector, however, the forecast of additions to nuclear capacity has been reduced considerably from last year's levels, as will be discussed later in this chapter.

The rate at which energy demand will grow and distribution of demand by end-use sector is highly sensitive to the price of imported oil. For example, in the Reference Scenario, at $13 prices, demand grows at 2.8 percent annually; if world prices drop to $8 per barrel, the growth rate would be increased to 3.2 percent.

There are major changes in the growth rate to be experienced in each end-use sector. The most pronounced change is in the Household/Commercial Sector which is expected to experience a considerable reduction in growth (1.7 percent at $13 oil prices, as compared to 3.8 percent in recent history). This lower growth rate is in response to higher prices and slower projected population growth in the coming decade. Since about 30 percent of industrial use of oil is insensitive to price (feedstock), industrial energy use will grow at about the historic rate in spite of higher prices. Whereas total energy use for transportation grew historically at 3.1 percent, it is expected to grow at about only 2.1 percent through 1985 if today's high oil prices continue (see Table I-2). The figures in Table I-2 assume net electricity distributed among sectors, but not inputs of electricity. Since about two-thirds of the energy used to generate electricity is lost before end-use, the growth rate would be higher in some sectors (particularly

Household) if gross electricity inputs were accounted for in the Table.

Petroleum Consumption Petroleum demand is naturally most sensitive to oil prices. This is particularly evident in the Electric Sector, where petroleum and coal are readily substitutable in new facilities based on their relative economics. For example, at $8 oil prices, in 1985, 8.3 quads (about 3.8 MMB/D) of petroleum are used to generate electricity whereas only 2.7 quads of petroleum are forecast for this sector at $13 prices. As a result, coal replaces oil in electric generation at higher import prices, and coal use in utilities increases by over 137 million tons if oil prices shift from 8 to 13 dollars per barrel. This shift occurs because electricity from a new baseload coal plant is cheaper than from an oil-fired plant if oil is above $9 per barrel. Further, when oil is above $10.50 per barrel, it is economic to build a new coal plant for baseload and to shift an existing oil-fired plant to intermediate load.

Overall, the 1985 forecast use of petroleum is 20.7 MMB/D at $13 prices, but would be 4.9 MMB/D higher at $8 prices (see Table I-3).

Even at $13 per barrel import prices in 1985, there is still a considerable amount of petroleum being utilized in the Industrial and Electric Generation Sectors. The electric use is mainly in currently existing powerplants used solely for intermediate or peak loads. These facilities are still attractive, despite the higher operating costs, because they are run relatively infrequently, and because the cost of construction has already been incurred.

The industrial demand for petroleum tends to be relatively insensitive to price since about 30 percent of the use is as a raw material, where alternative fuels cannot be physically substituted. The Transportation Sector accounts

Table I-2

ENERGY GROWTH RATES BY SECTOR, REFERENCE SCENARIO
(Percent/Year)

	1952-1972	1974-1985 at $8/bbl.	1974-1985 at $13/bbl.
Household/Commercial	3.8	2.4	1.7
Industrial	2.6	2.9	2.6
Transportation	3.4	2.9	2.1
Electrical Generation	7.3	5.2	5.4
Total	3.6	3.2	2.8

Table I-3

PETROLEUM CONSUMPTION ACROSS PRICES
REFERENCE SCENARIO
(MMB/D)

	1974 Usage	1985 Demand at $8/bbl. (growth rate)	1985 Demand at $13/bbl. (growth rate)
Household/Commercial	3.4	4.8 (4.6)	4.0 (2.8)
Industrial	3.1	4.6 (3.8)	4.2 (3.1)
Transportation	8.7	12.4 (3.3)	11.5 (2.1)
Electrical Generation	1.5	3.8 (8.3)	1.2 (-2.3)
Total	16.6	25.6 (4.0)	20.7 (2.0)

for more than half of petroleum demand. Higher gasoline prices, along with recent enactment of mandatory auto fuel efficiency legislation, should bring about the purchase of more efficient automobiles.

Petroleum demand is also greatly affected by the policy scenario chosen. Demand could range from about 18.7 MMB/D in 1985 if stringent conservation measures are taken (thermal efficiency standards, expanded industrial program and other actions in the Conservation Scenario) to 23.2 MMB/D in the $13 Supply Pessimism Scenario in which oil prices are regulated below import prices, thereby encouraging greater use. The increased demand in the regulation case occurs in the Electric Generation Sector, where demand for oil rises from about 750,000 barrels per day to over 3.1 million barrels per day by 1985.

The recent enactment of the Energy Policy and Conservation Act in December, 1975, is expected to reduce petroleum demand by about 2.5 MMB/D. This reduction is due primarily to automobile fuel efficiency standards, appliance labeling, and state conservation programs contained in the Act.

Electricity Consumption Electricity has been growing about twice as fast as the total of all energy sources in the last twenty years and will continue to do so, although at a slower overall rate. In the Reference Scenario, FEA estimates that electricity will grow at a rate of 5.4 percent from 1974-1985, if present world oil prices continue.

The demand for electricity is one of the large uncertainties in our energy future and affects coal, nuclear, oil, and gas consumption. If electricity grows more slowly or quickly than expected, coal demand could be affected dra-

matically. Electricity tends to displace direct use of oil and natural gas in households and industry, and since nuclear growth through 1985 is constrained by long leadtimes for new plants, the next cheapest source of electric power—coal—becomes the economic fuel for swing capacity. For each 1 percent change in the electricity growth rate from 1974-1985, coal consumption changes by 150 million tons in 1985, provided that coal plants can be completed in time.

An area of key concern with electricity forecasts is the impact of forecasting errors. The capital intensity of electric power generation and the leadtimes for new construction can make errors in this sector particularly expensive, both in financial terms and in the effects on import dependence. If actual consumption grows more slowly than forecast, utilities may have overbuilt and find themselves with idle capacity. This idle capacity is expensive for consumers, since the carrying and overhead costs must be paid whether or not the equipment is used. For example, if demand growth is actually 1 percent below forecast, utilities could have almost $50 billion of excess capacity in 1985, and the added cost of carrying extra capacity could be $7.2 billion annually, requiring an 8 percent increase in electric utility revenues.

Equally important, if not more critical, are the costs if consumption will be higher than forecast. In such a situation there are two possibilities. First, utilities recognizing possible shortages may build oil or gas fired plants to meet the demand. These plants can be built relatively quickly (3-5 years), are less capital intensive than coal or nuclear plants, but involve higher fuel costs, will raise consumer bills, and utilize fuels that will have to be imported, contrary to a goal of reduced vulnerability. For example, if demand growth is 1 percent faster than expected and oil and gas plants must be used to meet the extra needs, imports could rise by over one million barrels per day in 1985. Moreover, it is possible that gas turbine manufacturing capacity could be limited as manufacturers close existing facilities because of poor initial market conditions.

A second possibility, which may occur if demand surges in a 2-3 year period, is low reserve margins that could imperil supply reliability. Reserve margins should remain adequate in most areas through the 1970's, since many additions to capacity have continued despite low demand growth. However, adequacy is less certain for the 1980's.

In any event, there is a wide range of policy actions that can be taken to change the course of electricity growth. A strong conservation program could reduce electricity growth to less than 5 percent annually. Alternatively, if a strong shift toward greater use of electricity occurs (Electrification Scenario), demand could grow at almost 6.5 percent per year. Under this scenario, coal production would increase by about 220 million tons over the Reference Scenario, energy demand would be 101.5 quads, but imports would be reduced by only about 1 MMB/D.

Electricity provides major advantages in deliverability and in utilization of domestic rather than foreign fuel sources, but in many cases it represents a less efficient use of coal, oil, or natural gas than direct use and is more expensive as a source of heat unless used with a heat pump or similar device.

The mix of utility fuels will vary with the different scenarios and at different world oil prices. The role of oil could range from 4.5 percent in the Electrification Scenario to 16 percent in the Regional Limitation Scenario (see Figure I-8). As the price of oil is regulated or in cases where coal use is restricted or made more expensive, such as in the Regional Limitation Scenario, oil becomes relatively more attractive for powerplant use. The Regional Limitation Scenario reduces coal and nuclear power's share of electric generation from 71.3 percent to 59.6 percent largely due to an assumed partial nuclear moratorium, with concomitant increases in the shares of oil and gas (increases from 17 percent to 28.1 percent).

Coal Consumption The bulk of the 72 percent increase forecast for coal consumption in the 1974-1985 period will occur in the Electric Utility Sector (see Table I-4).

The greatest increases in electric generation from coal are expected to be in the East, Midwest, and Southwest. This indicates that the trend towards oil burning plants in the East will be reversed and that natural gas baseload plants in the Southwest will be phased out. The actual coal

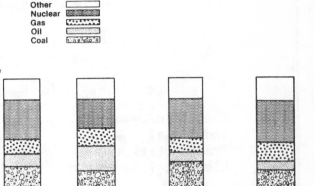

Figure I-8

1985 Utility Fuel Mix
($13 Imported Oil)

consumption in the Electric Sector will depend upon environmental standards, availability of coal transportation, surface mining regulations, and other factors discussed later in this chapter.

Other sectors are anticipated to have little growth potential for coal. Opportunities for coal consumption by the Industrial Sector are limited by the cost of complying with air pollution control requirements and the diseconomies of scale for handling coal in small quantities. In addition, synthetic fuels from coal are not yet competitive at $13 per barrel prices and are not expected to develop substantially until the late 1980's.

Natural Gas Consumption Natural gas usage is projected to increase slightly through the next ten years, assuming deregulation of new natural gas prices. Natural gas usage under the Reference Scenario would be 23.4 Tcf in 1985 (this assumes marketed domestic production of 22.3 Tcf in 1985, with the balance being met by LNG imports and Canadian pipeline imports), as compared to about 21 Tcf in 1974. If present regulations continue and the maximum feasible level of gas imports is allowed, consumption would be about 20.9 Tcf in 1985, and could be even lower if LNG is not available. Natural gas use is constrained by the limited availability of inexpensive supply. Much of the more readily accessible domestic source is already dwindling before liquefied natural gas (LNG) imports, synthetic fuels, and Alaskan gas can have much impact.

Table I-4

1985 COAL CONSUMPTION AT $13 OIL PRICES, REFERENCE SCENARIO
(Million Tons)

	1974*	1985	Growth Rate (Percent/Year)
Electric Utilities	390	715	5.7
Household/Commercial	11	5	-6.9
Industrial	94	151	4.4
Metallurgical	63	73	1.3
Synthetics	0	16	--
Exports	60	80	2.4
Total	618	1040	4.8

* Coal consumption in 1974 was greater than production due to changes in inventory.

There is also considerable uncertainty with respect to the distribution of natural gas among consuming sectors. FEA forecasts that gas consumption in industry will grow and that residential use will be reduced. This has been the national trend in the past few years, but in some regions the pattern of growth has been different. The sectoral distribution of gas use is an area of major uncertainty requiring further analysis.

Residential consumption declined in 1972-1975 mainly because gas deliveries to the interstate market, particularly in the Mid-Atlantic and Midwest, have been declining; weather was considerably warmer than usual in 1974 and 1975; and new residential natural gas connections have been restricted in many areas. On the other hand, the intrastate market, where most of the industrial demand is located, continues to be strong. With industrial users of natural gas in the interstate market generally having the lowest priority during curtailments, many industries are voluntarily switching from natural gas to electricity, coal, or in some cases, oil to assure supply reliability.

The FEA Reference Scenario forecast of natural gas use is made under the assumption of deregulation and market clearing prices. The higher natural gas prices would reduce demand, as natural gas prices increase more than those of other fuels. There is a large uncertainty concerning the relative proportion of natural gas, heating oil, and electricity use in the Household/Commercial Sector. Distribution costs for gas to this sector are higher than for oil, and could make gas more expensive to consumers. Electricity prices are expected to remain relatively constant (in real terms) in the Household/Commercial Sector, whereas natural gas prices under deregulation would increase significantly, and thus electricity could penetrate further in this sector. Industrial users, however, may retain the flexibility to use gas if its relative price is lower than other fuels.

The ultimate choices made by consumers depend greatly on their perception as to gas availability in the future. The distribution of a commodity such as natural gas is a major policy question. If natural gas prices continue to be regulated, curtailments of service will persist and most industrial use may have to be severely limited. The FEA analysis, with its uncertainty in this sector, indicates that in a higher price environment, the Household/Commercial Sector may move away from natural gas more than the Industrial Sector.

Effects of Conservation It is clear that energy demand can vary substantially depending upon policy actions taken to change consumption patterns. In particular, the actions assumed in the Conservation Scenario can reduce demand by the equivalent of about 2.9 million barrels per day (6 quads) and imports by about 2 million barrels per day. (See Table I-5 on next page.)

Table I-5

IMPACT OF ENERGY CONSERVATION ACTIONS

	1985 Energy Savings (MMB/D)	1985 Oil Import Reductions (MMB/D)
Transportation Sector:		
Auto Efficiency Standards	1.0	1.0
National Van Pool Program	0.1	0.1
Improved Airline Load Factors	0.1	0.1
Household/Commercial Sector:		
Thermal Efficiency Standards for New Buildings	0.3	0.3
Appliance Standards for Labeling	0.2	0.1
Insulation Tax Credit	0.1	0.1
Elimination of Gas Pilot Lights	0.2	0.2
Industrial Sector and Others:		
Industrial Energy Conservation Program	0.6	0.3
Increased Dispersed Solar Equipment	0.1	--
Solid Waste Energy Combustion	0.2	--
Total	2.9	2.2

The measures in this Scenario are not all proposed by the President or intended to represent the only possible conservation program. They are, however, an indicator of the level of energy savings which an aggressive program can achieve. The conservation measures described in Table I-5 include several measures which have already been enacted in the EPCA. The EPCA includes the automobile fuel efficiency standard of 20 miles per gallon (mpg.) in the 1980 model year and 27.5 mpg. in 1985 (with possible changes if auto emission standards place too heavy a burden on fuel efficiency), which is the single most significant conservation measure. It can save about one million barrels per day by 1985. The Act also includes appliance labeling and efficiency improvement goals, voluntary industrial conservation, and a Federal/State conservation program. The EPCA could reduce 1985 demand by the equivalent of about 2.5 MMB/D.

The national thermal efficiency standards for all new residential and commercial buildings and insulation tax credit have been proposed by the President and have passed the House of Representatives. The van pool program involves encouragement of an increasingly attractive commuting concept in which vans are purchased either by a firm or by a group of commuters; a monthly fee is paid by the riders to cover operating costs and the depreciation of the vans. Experience to date has shown that transportation costs to and from work are reduced, and in addition, some individuals no longer require second cars.

The industrial conservation program delineated in Table I-5 involves an expanded system of energy accounting and technical assistance whose scope and coverage of firms goes well beyond the program for industry established by the EPCA, establishing extensive reporting requirements. Similarly, the elimination of gas pilot lights in new appliances and equipment, mandatory retrofit of existing residential pilot light systems by 1980, and changes in airline load factors do not represent policy recommendations, but are only included for analytical purposes.

Table I-6

**EFFECTS OF CONSERVATION ACTIONS
AT $13 IMPORTED OIL PRICES
(Quadrillion Btu)**

	Reference Scenario Growth Rate 1974-1985 (percent/year)	Conservation Scenario Growth Rate 1974-1985 (percent/year)
Household/Commericial	1.7	0.8
Industrial	2.6	2.2
Transportation	2.1	1.1
Electrical Generation	5.4	4.3
Total	2.8	2.2

Although the conservation actions described above would reduce demand by about 3 MMB//D, adoption of load management practices in the Electric Utility Sector could tend to increase demand. Load management techniques are actions which lead to shifts in electricity demand from peak hours of use to times when existing capacity is not fully utilized. The use of time-of-day meters (i.e. peak load pricing), ripple control systems, storage devices, and other innovations will shift the utilization and efficiency of the total capacity. Since a utility must have sufficient reserve capacity to meet expected peak demand, significant reductions in maximum demand through deferral or increased efficiency of on-peak loads can lessen requirements for expensive new capacity, improve generation efficiency and fuel mix, and eventually lower electricity costs. However, lower electricity costs not only benefit customers, but result in a small increase in the demand for electricity.

The Conservation Scenario reduces overall consumption by over 6 quads, with the greatest growth rate reductions in the Transportation Sector, as a result of the automobile fuel efficiency standards (see Table I-6). While these actions cut the growth in all Sectors, in no case is the growth rate zero. In the non-industrial sectors, however, the growth rates are already substantially below their historic rates. The Industrial Sector, although sensitive to higher prices, cannot reduce consumption much further without curbing economic activity.

Oil Supply Domestic oil production, which has been declining since 1970, will stabilize and then increase in the next few years as approximately 2 MMB/D of Alaskan production can be transported to the Lower-48 States. Production will further increase as enhanced recovery projects and OCS leasing of the last few years begin to yield tangible results. By 1980, production could reach 12.8 MMB/D (at $13 prices) providing that investments are made now assuming at least $11 per barrel (in real prices) for new oil through early 1979, and no price controls thereafter (as provided for in the EPCA). Production is expected to be 13.9 MMB/D in the Reference Scenario in 1985, if prices stay at $13, but will start to decline by 1990.

The reserves from which most of today's oil is being produced—mainly onshore in the Lower-48 States—will decline by almost two-thirds by 1985 and about 80 percent by 1990 (see Figure I-9). New crude production onshore at today's prices will largely result from more intensive use of secondary and tertiary recovery in existing fields and the exploration and development of many new, relatively small fields. By 1985, the diminished supply from existing fields can just about be replaced by oil production from these other sources. Increases above historical levels will largely come from Alaska (onshore and offshore) and greater OCS development. Crude production in Northern Alaska will be limited primarily by available transportation infrastructure (pipeline capacity) and high costs. Although at least 1.6 MMB/D can be produced from proved reserves at Prudhoe Bay, and about 1.5 MMB/D could be produced from the Beaufort Sea and other areas on the Alaskan OCS and North Slope by

Figure 1-9
1985 Oil Production (Reference Scenario)

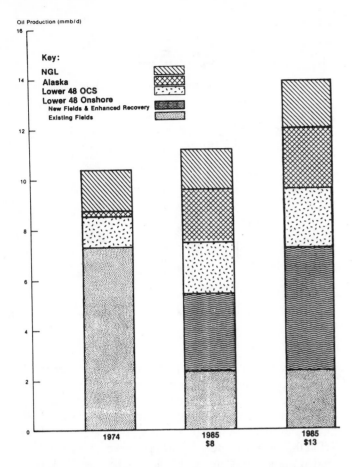

Oil Production (mmb/d)

Key:
NGL
Alaska
Lower 48 OCS
Lower 48 Onshore
New Fields & Enhanced Recovery
Existing Fields

1974   1985 $8   1985 $13

Most of the actual decrease occurs onshore in the Lower-48 States, where many new fields and more sophisticated tertiary recovery techniques are not economic at $8 per barrel. The effects of higher or lower prices tend to magnify over time and by 1990, the difference in potential production could be as much as 4 MMB/D between $8 and $13 prices. This widening difference occurs because although higher prices bring forth new and more expensive production, it normally takes many years to move from planning to production.

It is likely that physical and institutional bottlenecks may constrain production as well as prices. The increases in oil production at $13 per barrel are based upon levels of domestic drilling activity that approach the peaks reached in the mid-1950's. Drilling activities are estimated at about 120 million feet per year from 1975-1990 at $13 oil prices, as compared to an annual average of almost 110 million feet in the last fifteen years. However, drilling has declined from a peak of 137 to 75 million feet per year in this period, and a compound growth rate of almost 7 percent will be needed to achieve Reference Scenario levels. The projected drilling profile reverses the declining trend and peaks at about 160 million feet in 1984. While these levels of drilling are economically attractive at today's world oil prices, they will only occur under a favorable regulatory and legislative climate.

Expanded drilling, although less productive than historical drilling, must result in large additions to reserves to achieve the projected production. The Nation will have to prove 41 billion barrels of reserves out of an estimated 89 billion barrels that are economic to produce, and an additonal 9 billion barrels from sub-economic reserves. Since about 50 billion barrels would be consumed during this period, it is possible that total proved reserves in 1985 could approximate current levels. However, uncertainty is increased because much of these reserves are in areas that have not been drilled previously and many require new technology to meet environmental protection standards.

While significant increases in oil production are forecast, the outcome would be appreciably different depending upon assumptions about the ultimate level of recoverable reserves; delays in OCS leasing schedule; extent of investment tax credit allowed; new Alaskan development; and extent of price controls.

The 1985 domestic oil production forecast ranges from a low of 9.6 MMB/D under a scenario of price regulation at $9 per barrel in 1975 dollars and a pessimistic assessment of resource availability to a high of 17.6 MMB/D in the Accelerated Supply Scenario (see Figure I-10). The latter scenario assumes a more aggressive OCS lease schedule, an optimistic assessment of resource potential, development of NPR-4, greater Alaskan pipeline capacity, and a more optimistic assessment of the potential

1985, production could probably not be sustained long enough to make further pipeline investment economic. While further Alaskan production from Naval Petroleum Reserve No. 4 would change this evaluation, it is not considered in the Reference Scenario. Hence, Northern Alaskan production is estimated to be about 2.0 MMB/D by 1985.

Production from the Lower-48 Outer Continental Shelf may double by 1985 if the current leasing schedule is met and the United States Geological Survey's expectations about OCS resources prove correct. If this occurs, this area could account for about 15 percent of crude production in 1985 (over 2 MMB/D). Gulf of Mexico production will require substantial additions to reserves to compensate for expected declines from today's reserves. While Pacific OCS production could increase substantially, Atlantic OCS production is expected to proceed slowly given the long leadtimes from leasing to production of expected reserve additions. Lower-48 OCS production is constrained more by leasing and leadtimes than price levels.

The expected decrease in oil supply in 1985, if prices drop from $13 to $8 per barrel, is about 2.5 MMB/D.

Figure I-10

Domestic Oil Production Under Different Scenarios
($13 Imported Oil)

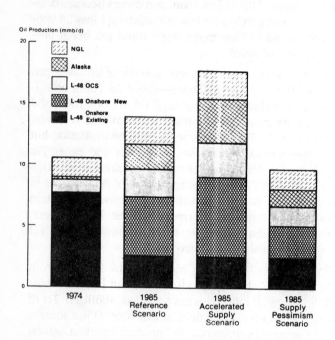

Figure I-11

Natural Gas Production Under Different Scenarios ($13 Oil)

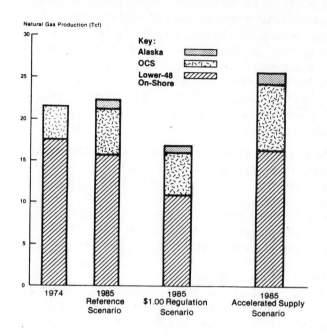

for tertiary recovery. Alaska accounts for about half of the difference in production possibilities (see Table I-7).

Natural Gas Supply Although natural gas production will continue to decline in the next few years, 1985 marketed production will be 22.3 Tcf (slightly above current levels) if new gas prices are deregulated. If completion of an Alaskan gas transportation system is accelerated and more favorable reserves are assumed, production

could only rise to 25.3 Tcf (Accelerated Supply Scenario). However, without a significant increase in the price of natural gas, production is expected to fall dramatically by 1985. If present regulation of the interstate market continues through 1985, production would decline to 17.9 Tcf in that year. Further, if natural gas regulation were extended to the intrastate market at about $1 per Mcf, production in 1985 would decline to 17.0 Tcf (see Figure I-11 for consumption of the production under different scenarios).

Table I-7

FACTORS AFFECTING OIL PRODUCTION ESTIMATES
(MMB/D)

	1985 Potential Crude Oil Production	
	Optimistic Cast	Pessimistic Case
Geological	+ 1.1	- 0.7
Drilling	+ 0.3	- 0.1
Leasing	+ 0.9	- 0.4
Alaska and Other	+ 1.8	- 1.6
Total Impact of Factors	+ 4.1	- 2.8

Most of the increase in natural gas production at higher prices comes from more intensive production of onshore fields in the West Texas and Western Gulf regions. However, despite deeper drilling and other efforts in these regions, onshore production will decline from current levels by 1985. In fact, if United States gas production were to continue only from existing fields, production would decline by about 60 percent by 1985. Natural gas supply is further limited by the inability to extract much more gas through advanced recovery techniques, such as tertiary recovery in the cost of oil.

The greatest increase in production under deregulation (as compared to today's levels) will be in the Gulf of Mexico as a result of recent and expected OCS leasing activities, increasing from about 4 Tcf now to about 5.3 Tcf in 1985. The OCS leasing schedule is the prime determinant of offshore gas production at higher prices; that is, if leasing could be accelerated, more gas could be produced.

Natural gas supply is affected most significantly by the extent and level of gas price regulation. As indicated above, continuation of present regulations would reduce production to 17.9 Tcf by 1985. Of even greater importance than the absolute decline in production is the fact that continued price regulation would drastically reduce the interstate share of the market (from about 62 percent currently to about 42 percent in 1985). Such a reduction would hasten the migration of industry to the producing areas and would ultimately lead to much higher residential fuel bills in the East and Midwest as residential users are forced to turn to electricity and oil as a replacement.

Future natural gas supply also depends greatly on the policies adopted with respect to oil pricing, Alaskan development, and synthetic fuels. If world oil prices decline or domestic oil prices are regulated, gas production associated with the recovery of crude oil will decline. For example, if imported oil prices drop from $13 to $8 per barrel, gas production would be lowered by almost 10 percent (about 2 Tcf). This reduction occurs because drilling for oil wells would be less attractive and less oil production would in turn mean less natural gas being produced from oil wells.

Alaska has the largest known reserves of undeveloped natural gas in the United States—about 26 Tcf of associated gas in the Prudhoe Bay area, 2 Tcf in Cook Inlet, and 2 Tcf in other areas. Substantial undiscovered reserves, estimated at 76 Tcf are also believed to be in Alaska, but all of the reserves will require a complex and expensive transportation system to deliver the resulting production to the Lower-48 States. Transportation of Alaskan gas to the Lower-48 States is the subject of intense competition between two proposed alternative routes. Nevertheless, with either transportation approach, as much as 1.2 Tcf could be available by the early 1980's.

Synthetic fuels including high and low Btu gas from coal, are not likely to be produced without Federal financial incentives. If incentives are provided, about 1.1 Tcf of supplemental gas supply could be available. Other sources of supplemental supply include imported liquefied natural gas (LNG), which could supply 0.4 Tcf from currently approved projects, and up to a maximum of about 2 Tcf by 1985. The availability of substitute gas from petroleum products (SNG) will depend greatly on the price of oil, availability of feedstocks, and methods of pricing, but could supply 1.0 Tcf by 1985. These and other supply sources are delineated in Table I-8.

Coal Supply Coal production in the long run is largely contingent on the growth in electricity, as well as

---

Table I-8

POTENTIAL NATURAL GAS SUPPLY SOURCES

Source	1985 Supply (Tcf)
Lower-48 and Alaska	22.3
Accelerated OCS Leasing	0.5
Synthetic Gas from Coal	1.1
SNG from Petroleum Products	1.0
Imported LNG	0.4-2.1
Gas from Tight Formations and Devonian Shale	0.1-0.8
Total	25.4-28.3

the price of oil. If imported oil prices drop to $8 per barrel, coal production in the Reference Scenario (including coal for exports) would be 894 million tons in 1985; whereas at today's oil prices, coal production could reach 1040 million tons. The 1985 coal production level at $13 per barrel represents a 5.1 percent compound annual growth rate over 1974 levels. This compares to the relatively constant coal production in the last five years.

The growth in coal is faster in the 1980-1985 period (5.4 percent) than in the period from 1974-1980 (4.8 percent), as a result of relatively few new coal powerplants now scheduled for completion prior to 1980 (coal plants have a 5-8 year leadtime and many utilites in the early 1970's decided that in view of the low price of imported oil and in view of Clean Air Act restrictions it was better to burn other fuels). The analysis assumes that plants ordered for completion after 1980 can be accelerated to meet projected electricity demand.

Most of the growth in coal production will be in low-sulfur coal as industry strives to meet sulfur emission limitations (see Table I-9). While air quality standards permit the use of high sulfur coal accompanied by flue gas desulfurization equipment (scrubbers), it is likely that existing coal users will choose to use low-sulfur coal as much as possible.

A large part of the increased production will come from the Northern Great Plains and Central Appalachia, the two major areas with low-sulfur coal reserves (see Figure I-12). The Northern Great Plains has large low-sulfur, relatively inexpensive coal reserves. Large-scale development in this area, as is implied by about a 600 percent increase in production (about 260 million tons more than at present) could have significant social and environmental

Figure I-12

Regional Growth In Coal Production

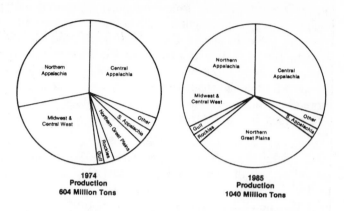

1974
Production
604 Million Tons

1985
Production
1040 Million Tons

effects, or may be inhibited by state or regional restrictions. Central Appalachia is the only producing area in the East, near to many newly planned coal-fired powerplants, with substantial low-sulfur coal.

In addition to the large increase in coal production in the Western part of the country, there will be a significant increase in surface mine production. The proportion of coal produced from surface mines will increase from 54 percent in 1974 to 63 percent in 1985 at $13 oil prices (in the Reference Scenario). While surface mining will about double in the next 10 years, underground production will also increase by 39 percent, primarily in the East (see Table I-10). This is a reversal of recent trends, but is expected because inexpensive eastern strippable reserves are being depleted and the demand for eastern coal will still grow. The increase in surface mining is largely a function

Table I-9

SULFUR DISTRIBUTION OF PRODUCTION
(Millions of Tons Per Year)

	1974	1985	Increase
Metallurgical Coal	114	138	24
Low-sulfur Steam Coal	90	477	387
High-sulfur Steam Coal*	400	425	25

* Defined as any coal that does not meet new source performance standards (0.6 lbs. or sulfur per million Btu)

Table I-10

SURFACE/UNDERGROUND MINING FORECAST
AT $13 OIL, RERERENCE SCENARIO*
(Million of Tons)

Area	1974 Surface	1974 Underground	1974 Total	1985 Surface	1985 Underground	1985 Total
East	245	267	512	292	368	661
West	81	11	92	362	17	379
Total	326	277	603*	655	385	1040

* Totals do not add due to rounding

of the substantially increased western coal production from reserves which can be mined relatively cheaply, but only with surface mining techniques.

Since coal production is largely a function of electricity demand, which is stable among many scenarios, the alternatives examined have little effect on the levels of expected production. With the exception of the Electrification Scenario, in which the electricity growth rate rises from 5.4 to about 6.5 percent and coal requirements rise from 1040 to 1263 million tons in 1985, all strategies forecast coal demand within a range of about 100 million tons (at current oil prices). The Electrification Scenario includes efforts to switch large boiler use to coal in both utilities and industries (industrial coal consumption increases by about 75 million tons).

The major variation in regional coal production among different scenarios occurs in the Northern Great Plains,

where production drops from 305 to 221 million tons in 1985 under the Regional Limitation Scenario (still a large increase from current levels), and increases from 305 to 438 million tons under the Electrification Scenario. The increase in this region under Electrification occurs since this is the only region that has relatively inexpensive additional reserves to meet the greater demand for low-sulfur coal. The increase implies growth from 43 million tons in 1974 to 438 million tons in 1985, a growth rate of 23.5 percent per year. Such growth would be unprecedented and could potentially cause significant socioeconomic and environmental problems.

The reduction in Northern Great Plains production under the Regional Limitation Scenario occurs despite the fact that eastern coal production is kept relatively constant (see Table I-11). The shift of emphasis from West to East is mainly caused by the assumed 30 percent severance tax

Table I-11

REGIONAL COAL PRODUCTION, 1985

	Reference Scenario Million Tons	(Percent)	Regional Limitation Scenario Million Tons	(Percent)
East	661	(64)	662	(69)
West	379	(36)	296	(31)
Total	1040	(100)	958	(100)

applied to all western production in this scenario. This assumption makes western coal less competitive with midwestern coals in the midwestern electric power markets.

The shift from West to East caused by a severance tax would have been even greater if reclamation costs under this strategy were not much higher in the East. Actual coal development in the West will be largely dependent on transportation rates, severance taxes, reclamation requirements, and air pollution control requirements. Either the severance tax or higher reclamation costs alone would have a more pronounced regional shift. As a result of the West to East movement, the Regional Limitation Scenario also decreases the percentage of coal that is surfaced mined.

Despite requiring all new coal-fired powerplants to burn low-sulfur coal and install scrubbers, the Regional Limitation Scenario reduces low-sulfur coal production more than high-sulfur production. This occurs because the cost of building a new plant with low-sulfur coal and scrubbers renders new plant generation costs so high that utilities in some areas would prefer to maximize the use of less expensive existing plants burning high-sulfur coal.

Nuclear Power   Despite considerably lower forecasts this year than last, the growth in nuclear power in the next ten years is expected to be substantial. Additions to nuclear capacity by 1985 are limited by the long construction and licensing period (about ten years), and thus projections of maximum capacity for 1985 are well determined already.

The 1975 *Project Independence Report* projected that nuclear capacity could increase from about 36,000 megawatts (MWe) currently, to about 204,000 megawatts by the end of 1984; whereas FEA's current forecast is that the maximum total capacity if current licensing conditions remain the same is about 152,000 megawatts (new capacity of about 116,000 megawatts).[1]

About 105,000 megawatts of new nuclear capacity were deferred or cancelled in the last 18 months. This cutback affected almost 70 percent of planned additions and has occurred because of lower projections of electricity demand, financial problems experienced by utilities, uncertainty about government policy, and continued siting and licensing problems. Nuclear power, even at these reduced levels, will still grow to almost 26 percent of electric power generation in 1985 (see Figure I-13). This compares with 8.6 percent in 1975.

The reduced forecast of nuclear power reflects constraints rather than economic desirability or technical potential. Nuclear energy is the cheapest source of baseload electric power, although not much cheaper than coal. If its growth were not constrained, there would be much more nuclear power projected and American consumers would

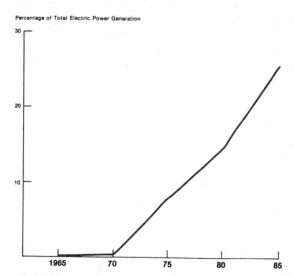

Figure I-13

Nuclear Power's Role in Generating Electricity

Percentage of Total Electric Power Generation

experience lower electricity prices. FEA estimates that the cost of using baseload nuclear power is about 18 mills/kWh., as compared to coal which is almost 22 mills/kWh., at 70 percent capacity factors. The projected differential in prices is lower this year than last because the cost of capital has remained high, penalizing the more capital intensive nuclear plants.

Although nuclear power estimates in the Reference Scenario are considerably lower than last year's forecast, policy and regulatory decisions could dramatically change these estimates. For example, if the leadtime from inception to operation of a nuclear plant could be reduced from 10-12 years to 5-7 years, the effects of inflation would be reduced, capital costs would decline, and more nuclear plants would be built. FEA estimates that under such an accelerated nuclear strategy, about 142,000 MWe. of new nuclear capacity could be added by the end of 1984, rather than 116,000 MWe. in the Reference Scenario. The additional nuclear capacity would reduce electricity costs by about 3 percent.

On the other hand, if nuclear capacity expansions are limited by moratoria on new growth or by continued financial problems in the electric utility industry, the economic costs to the nation will be considerable. In the Regional Limitation Scenario, FEA assumed that capacity was limited to plants already granted construction permits, resulting in an upper limit of 61,000 megawatts of new capacity by the end of 1984. Under this case, electricity costs would be higher than under the Reference Scenario.

A nationwide moratorium on new nuclear power could increase coal requirements by more than 200 million tons, in addition to the 400 million ton increase already projected for 1985. Such an increase would place further environmental and socioeconomic pressures on parts of the

West and worsen air quality in many areas. It could also strain the coal delivery system. If coal capacity could not make up the difference needed because of the moratorium, oil imports would have to increase by about 2 MMB/D. The economic and environmental costs of this strategy are significant by 1985, and the 1990 implications are even more severe. For example, 1990 coal production might have to increase to more than three times today's levels, if nuclear power were restricted.

Emerging Technologies Production from emerging technologies, such as solar, geothermal, and synthetic fuels, under business as usual conditions, is not expected to be significant by 1985. Solar electricity capacity is expected to amount to about 500 megawatts; geothermal power to about 1650 megawatts. In addition, solar heating and cooling could represent the equivalent of 60,000 barrels per day by 1985. Synthetic fuels production could reach the equivalent of 280,000 barrels per day excluding urban waste; less than one percent of oil and gas demand. The latest analysis of the economics of synthetic fuels indicates that little if any production can be expected in the next 10 years unless financial incentives are provided. The FEA forecast assumes that environmental problems associated with synthetic fuels can be overcome.

Each of these sources becomes more important in 1990 and the years beyond, and a strategy which accelerates development of solar, geothermal, and synthetic energy sources can substantially increase their contribution by 1985. FEA estimates that 6100 megawatts of geothermal capacity and 2550 megawatts of solar electric capacity could be available in 1985 under an accelerated development program (about 1 percent of total electric power generation). The solar projections do not include solar heating and cooling, which are accounted for directly in the Residential and Commercial sector. Both geothermal and solar power have technological, environmental, and economic questions to resolve to meet these 1985 targets.

Synthetic fuels, excluding urban waste, could supply as much as 880,000 barrels per day by 1985 (about 3 percent of total oil and gas consumption), if additional Federal financial assistance is provided. Since the major synthetic processes are not economic at $13 per barrel (with the possible exception of shale oil which is marginally economic at this price, but still risky given the uncertainty with respect to world prices), additional production is not likely to occur without loan guarantees, price supports, or other Federal financial support. Even with financial assistance, there are environmental and socioeconomic problems to be overcome before this potential could be reached.

The Projected Import Situation The FEA forecast indicates that higher world oil prices and phasing out of oil price controls should lead to significant increases in domestic oil production and lower than historical demand. Nevertheless, if current import prices continue, 5.9 MMB/D of imports would be needed in 1985 (about the same as 1975 levels). This level is about 2.6 MMB/D higher than under a comparable case in the 1975 *Project Independence Report*, with the difference being caused mainly by an increase in expected demand of about 1.6 MMB/D and about a 1.0 MMB/D lower supply estimate.

These import levels are very dependent on world oil prices, reaching 13.5 MMB/D if oil prices drop to $8, or declining to 3.3 MMB/D if oil prices rise to $16 per barrel during the next ten years (see Table I-12). The rise in oil consumption at lower prices will result in lower coal consumption. Figure I-14 describes overall domestic supply and import trends at different world oil prices.

Table I-12

1985 EXPECTED OIL IMPORTS
REFERENCE SCENARIO
(MMB/D)

Import	Oil Consumption	Domestic Crude Oil Production*	Oil Imports
$8/bbl.	25.5	11.4	13.5
$13/bbl.	20.7	13.9	5.9
$16/bbl.	19.4	15.0	3.3

* Excludes refinery gain and shale oil

Figure I-14

Energy Outlook Under Different Oil Prices

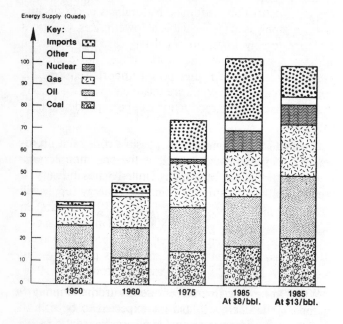

Oil import projections are as much a function of government policy actions as price (see Table I-13). For example, an accelerated OCS leasing program, greater production from shale oil and tertiary recovery tech- niques, and more optimistic resource estimates, could reduce imports to essentially zero by 1985 (1.7 MMB/D of imports, mainly from the Caribbean, are still used because of proximity and relative security of supply). An aggressive conservation program alone would reduce demand by about 2 MMB/D and thus cut imports to 3.8 MMB/D. Alternatively, if all oil prices are regulated at a maximum of $7.50 per barrel, imports could be 11.3 MMB/D (even at $13 import prices) due to the reduced domestic production and greater petroleum use encouraged by lower prices (would be as high as 13.5 MMB/D to satisfy unfeasible gas import levels).

The Energy Policy and Conservation Act will also affect our import situation. Its impact depends upon the period oil price controls are in effect. The law provides for a statutory domestic composite crude oil price of $7.66 per barrel that may be escalated by an adjusted GNP deflator and other incentives to increase production. The price control authorities convert from mandatory to standby after 40 months (the Reference Scenario is designed with a similar phase-out of controls). If price controls expire in 40 months and world oil is at $13 per barrel, the conservation measures in the EPCA would reduce import needs to 3.4 MMB/D by 1985. If price controls remain in effect through 1985, imports would be 6.5 MMB/D. However, if present natural gas price regulations are also continued, imports under these alternative oil price control cases would be 6.2 and 8.3 MMB/D, respectively.

Table I-13

1985 OIL IMPORTS UNDER DIFFERENT SCENARIOS
$13 IMPORTED OIL
(MMB/D)

Scenario	Consumption	Domestic* Oil Production	Imports
Reference	20.7	13.9	5.9
Accelerated Supply	20.3	17.6	1.7
Conservation	18.7	14.0	3.8
Accelerated Supply/ Conservation	18.3	15.6	1.7
$7.50/bbl. Oil Regulation	22.1	9.9	11.3
Supply Pessimism	23.2	9.6	12.6

* Oil production figures exclude shale oil and refinery gain

Energy Prices Coal and electricity prices are expected to remain relatively stable in real terms, even if import prices change (see Table I-14). Coal prices are stable because in the long-term, coal production can be substantially increased at little or no increase in costs. It should be noted that these conclusions might not hold if large production increases were needed in the next few years. Spot coal prices would then increase until new mines were opened. Long-run electricity prices remain stable because about half of the cost is fixed investment, and as oil prices increase, utilities can switch to nuclear power or coal, which are priced lower than oil. These conclusions, of course, are highly dependent upon national, State and local energy actions. It should also be noted that constant real prices would imply $21 per barrel oil in nominal dollars in 1985 and similar changes for other fuels.

Oil prices would vary directly with import prices if domestic price controls are removed. Thus, distillate oil would be $9.84 per barrel at $8 prices and $14.16 per barrel at $13 prices. As long as world oil prices increase no faster than the rate of inflation and decontrol is gradual, large increases in domestic product prices should not occur.

Natural gas prices are expected to increase significantly if prices are deregulated and to track oil prices in the long run. However, residential fuel bills are expected to rise regardless of whether natural gas prices are deregulated, since if gas is unavailable to some consumers in the interstate market, they will have to use expensive oil or electricity. Energy prices vary significantly in the alternative scenarios. The Accelerated Supply/Conservation Scenario actually lowers natural gas and electricity prices dramatically (gas lowered from $2.03/mcf to $1.35/mcf;

electricity from 29.73 mills/kWh to about 26 mills/kWh). Electricity prices decline due to the more efficient use of equipment and resulting lower capital costs (load management), and to lower costs on new plants because of shorter construction leadtimes. Natural gas prices decline as more supply is made available at lower prices. Oil prices are considerably lower in regulated cases as domestic prices are held below the world price; however, the greater percentage of higher priced imports reduces this price advantage. Coal prices are relatively invariant among strategies because the production can be expanded at little extra cost.

Capital Requirements A possible constraint on increasing domestic energy supply is the enormous capital requirement that will be faced by United States industry. It is expected that investments to increase energy supply will amount to about 580 billion dollars (in 1975 dollars) in the next ten years (or almost $800 billion in nominal dollars). These investments will represent about 30 percent of total business fixed investment in this period—about equal to the almost 29 percent average from 1947-1974.

While these investments represent a tremendous flow of capital, the energy industry is expected to be able to raise the funds for investments in all areas except possibly the electric utility and synthetic fuels sectors. The electric utility industry, which requires the most capital intensive plants, will need to invest between 215 and 323 billion dollars depending upon the policy strategies. Also, because utilities are not expected to generate much of these funds from profits, they will continue to be the most intensive users of capital markets to finance expenditures. In recent years, about 70-75 percent of the utility capital expenditures are financed externally. Investments of this

Table I-14

ENERGY PRICE FORECAST, REFERENCE SCENARIO
(1975 Dollars)

	1985 at $8/bbl.	1985 at $13/bbl.	1985 at $16/bbl.
Distillate oil ($/bbl.)	9.84	14.16	16.95
Coal* ($/ton)	26.47	27.82	28.11
Natural Gas ($/Mcf)	1.79	2.03	2.07
Electricity (mils/kWh)	28.17	29.73	30.15

* Includes $12/ton surcharge to represent scrubbing costs.

Figure I-15

Cost of Energy Supply Investments

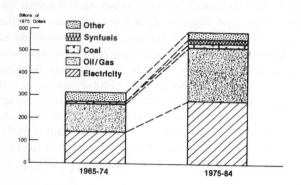

magnitude could be difficult to accomplish since in many cases the utility industry has reached its maximum debt carrying capacity given the revenues currently allowed by regulatory commissions, and in many cases their stocks are at depressed levels, making new equity issues unattractive.

Synthetic fuel investments may not be forthcoming due to the economic and technological risks of the processes and institutional uncertainties (see Figure I-15 for sectoral distribution of all energy investment needs).

A further area of investment not previously considered is the investment that could be required over the next 10 years to utilize higher priced energy more efficiently, i.e., the investment to conserve energy. Using a return on investment consistent with that used to judge the viability of investments in energy supply, a midrange investment estimate of 250 billion dollars is consistent with the savings anticipated both from higher prices and governmental actions. To illustrate, investments will be made: by industry to purchase more efficient process equipment, by homeowners and building managers to add insulation and improve heating and lighting, and by auto manufacturers to produce more efficient cars. Thus, increased initial outlays will be required to reduce expected fuel costs, but if conservation investments proceed they must make economic sense. Financing these conservation investments will not be difficult since they are spread throughout the economy and are often an integral part of investments made for other purposes.

Environmental Impacts The environmental impacts of a specific energy scenario are hard to measure without performing an analysis of existing environmental quality and potential changes at individual energy producing or consuming locations. However, general trends can be depicted. At higher oil prices, less oil and more coal are consumed. Thus, despite the reduced levels of demand at $13 oil prices, air emissions of nitrogen oxides, for example, are likely to be significantly higher in some regions.

Reduced forecasts for nuclear power growth will tend to increase coal use and could adversely affect air quality near powerplants, and create greater land and water quality problems in the Western States.

The Conservation Scenario exhibits the lowest levels of air pollution, whereas the Electrification Scenario has the highest air emissions (as measured by an FEA model of environmental discharges). The Regional Limitation Scenario results in the lowest levels of sulfur oxides from coal-fired powerplants, but these levels are offset by increased emissions from oil- and gas-fired powerplants and greater use of existing coal-fired plants in baseload. Since powerplant emission requirements are less stringent for existing plants, their use is expanded.

The major environmental issues associated with energy will focus on regional development questions. These include OCS development, oil and gas production from Alaska, western coal development, commercialization of synthetic fuels, and nuclear power growth. The resolution of these issues will largely determine the future of energy production.

Post-1985 Trends and Issues In the 1975 *Project Independence Report*, FEA did not assess the post-1985 period. Although a 1990 forecast was included in 1976, the forecast should be considered as indicative of trends, rather than precise. The forecast was designed to capture the most important trends in oil and gas production, coal consumption, and major demand uncertainties. It forecasts that energy consumption would grow at about a 2.8 percent rate from 1975 through 1985, if oil prices are about $13 per barrel. This compares to the 1952-1972 rate of 3.6 percent. However, as consumers adjust to higher energy prices, the growth rate should increase to about 3.3 percent in the 1985-1990 period.

Electricity is expected to continue to increase its penetration. It could represent about 37 percent of energy use in 1990, as compared to 27 percent in 1974. The major economic choice in electricity generation by 1990 will still be between nuclear power and coal. However, actual capacity additions will be determined by other factors as well, such as environmental standards, financial health of utilities, and infrastructure to transport coal. Coal and nuclear power could amount to 77 percent of electric generation in 1990, as compared to 71 percent in 1985 and 50 percent in 1974 (see Figure I-16 on next page).

If electrical energy grows at the anticipated rate, there will be a strong need to increase coal production and to resolve the nuclear fuel cycle problems. Coal production in the $13 Reference Scenario will have to increase to about 1.6 billion tons in 1990, with most of the additional increase in the Northern Great Plains, and Northern and Central Appalachia. These areas will supply 80 percent of the coal, with the Northern Great Plains alone supplying about 40 percent. Nuclear capacity additions will have to

Figure I-16

Electricity Generation By Energy Source
(Reference Scenario, $13 Oil)

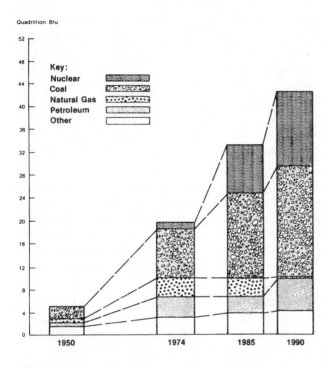

Quadrillion Btu

Key:
Nuclear
Coal
Natural Gas
Petroleum
Other

1950   1974   1985   1990

occur at greatly accelerated rates in the 1985-1990 period to meet electrical generation needs. Installed nuclear capacity in 1990 could be as high as 227,000 megawatts in the Reference Scenario.

The oil and gas supply projections for 1990 depend greatly on geology and institutional constraints. If the price of domestic oil is below $10 per barrel, oil production by 1990 will be below 1985 levels. Even if higher prices are maintained, however, production would begin to decline around 1990; Alaskan production would also decline in this period, unless significant NPR-4 reserves are proved and produced. Natural gas production declines even sooner—in the 1980's—at all prices reviewed by FEA.

With demand increasing and supply of oil and gas either stable or declining, oil imports in 1990 could be 9.7 MMB/D at $13 import prices, unless synthetic fuels or other new technologies expand more rapidly than anticipated.

This scenario indicates a rapidly increasing requirement for imported oil if the projected demand pattern is to be satisfied. However, by 1990, a number of existing OPEC countries can be expected to have dropped out as exporters of large quantities of oil. Many of the countries will have passed their peak of production and/or will have developed domestic markets of such size that they will not have substantial production available for export. The reduced number of major exporters could present a physical difficulty in meeting U.S. import requirements by 1990, unless major new sources of oil are found in countries that are not currently active as exporters.

The 1990 Reference Scenario raises several major national issues, and suggests three basic directions for the future domestic energy economy. The first would be to develop an aggressive program to provide more liquid and gaseous hydrocarbon sources to feed existing demand patterns as they expand. The second would be to substitute ever increasing amounts of electricity where possible for some of the expected hydrocarbon fuel demand and thereby substitute coal and uranium. Finally, there is the option to reduce the rate of growth of total demand. These options are not necessarily mutually exclusive.

The first approach would be that of finding means for providing artificial sources of liquid or gaseous hydrocarbons. While synthetic fuels hold promise for the long term, there are technical, economic, and environmental problems to be overcome before it can be a major source of energy, even by 1990.

The second option is greater use of electricity. The success of this approach depends on overcoming several problems. First, there are a limited number of possibilities for substituting electricity for substantial amounts of oil or natural gas unless a major breakthrough is made in electrifying transportation and in storage technology for electricity. Also, this approach is the most capital intensive of the available alternatives, which might place additional burdens on the Nation's capital markets. The expected energy investments as a percentage of total investments are near the high end of historical levels. In addition to the investment required for the generation of electric power, there will also be significant new investment to convert users of other fuels to electric power. Finally, electrification would prove expensive to consumers. The major areas of potential substitution would be in residential, commercial, and industrial heating. While widespread use of heat pumps would reduce the cost differential by making electricity use more efficient, the cost of the capital needed to generate and transfer the electricity would still have to be paid, raising prices at the consumer levels. However, many of the technological developments that could improve efficiency and make such options more attractive are still in early stages of development.

The third option open to the Nation is the option of reducing demand through an aggressive conservation program in order to use the remaining supplies of the available fuels as judiciously as possible. The existing and proposed conservation program can reduce growth significantly. However, these conservation programs involve extensive regulation and are largely designed to reduce aggregate energy usage, but not necessarily directed to conserving the specific fuels that will be in short supply.

Natural gas appears to be the fuel most likely to be in short supply in the 1975-1990 period. Unless an economically feasible approach can be found for producing synthetic gas from coal in large quantities, either growing quantities of imported liquid natural gas may have to be used or conservation will have to be pursued intensively for this fuel.

In order to conserve petroleum, it is clear that the major attention must be paid to the Transportation Sector. Almost half of total petroleum usage in 1974 was for transportation and this percentage is expected to remain unchanged through 1990, unless major modifications are made in the transportation system. While automobiles are likely to be made much more efficient over the next decade, gasoline demand will ultimately increase again as the number of autos increase, unless a basic change in the pattern of usage is made or transportation fuel use is shifted, probably to electricity. Both alternatives involve large capital investment, technological uncertainties, and difficult social and environmental decisions.

In summary, the Nation faces difficult decisions relating to the post-1985 period. The choice is among a continuation of existing energy demand patterns, while substituting synthetic fuels for declining natural sources; attempting to shift end-use patterns to electricity generated from coal, nuclear, solar, and geothermal sources; or greater efforts to conserve energy. Each of these alternatives involves difficult technical, economic, environmental, and social choices; but the longer we delay, the more difficult and expensive the transition. If these policies are not successful the result will be greater reliance on foreign energy imports. The choice is difficult; none of the alternatives are easy. But the course that is set will determine the well-being of future generations.

ENDNOTE

[1] Actual capacity expected in 1985 (all capacity figures are as of December 31, 1984) under current conditions is about 142,000 megawatts, as about 10,000 megawatts of possible additions are not utilized due to reduced demand. The lower demand estimates are centered in the Western part of the country and could be a result of estimating errors caused by power curtailments experienced in the Northwest and California in 1973 and 1974 (these are the starting point years from which the forecast is based).

U.S. AND WORLD ENERGY FORECAST THROUGH 1990*

Major Findings

Demand

1. Assuming long-term real GNP growth in the United States of 3.5 percent per year for the period 1976-90, CRS base case projects 2.9 percent average annual energy growth rates. The energy demand forecast assumes no supply constraints but higher prices for oil and gas compared with the present.

2. Imposition of a gradually escalating Btu tax could result in bringing average annual energy growth rates down considerably, but the price to be paid for lower energy growth will be dependent on the ability of the economy to substitute labor, capital and other materials for energy. If there is enough flexibility in the economy, GNP growth rates and employment will only be marginally affected; if, on the other hand, there is little flexibility in the economy, the Btu tax could result in substantially lower GNP growth rates and higher unemployment. This is currently a matter of some controversy.

Domestic Supply

3. Under optimistic political and economic assumptions, domestic oil production could rise from 10.0 million barrels per day (b/d) in 1976 to 10.4 million b/d in 1980, 10.9 million b/d in 1985, and 11.4 million b/d by 1990. These supply figures assume—among other things—decontrol of oil and an aggressive OCS development plan. It seems more probable that the political and economic climate will be less favorable and finding rates lower than projected in the base case. This could result in production of 9.5 million b/d in 1980 and 1985 and 10.1 million b/d in 1990.

4. Under similar optimistic political and economic assumptions, natural gas production is projected to decline only gradually from 19.7 trillion cubic feet (TCF) in 1976 to 17.4 TCF in 1980, and 16.9 TCF each in 1985 and 1990. These supply figures assume early decontrol of new natural gas; an aggressive OCS development plan; a com-

* Project Interdependence, Congressional Research Service, Library of Congress, June 1977

pleted natural gas pipeline for Alaskan gas by 1985; very high-finding rates in frontier areas between 1976 and 1990. Under less optimistic, but currently more probable political and economic assumptions and continuing decline in gas findings in the lower 48 States, production is likely to decline faster to 16.3 TCF in 1980, 15.7 TCF in 1985, and 15.5 TCF in 1990.

5. Of all potential sources of synthetic fuels, only synthetic gas from coal is projected to make a substantial contribution to supply in 1985 (0.5 TCF) and 1990 (1.5 TCF). Potentially promising nonconventional sources of methane—such as methane occluded in coal, geopressure zones, natural gas from Devonian shale and tight formation—are not expected to make a substantial contribution to U.S. energy supply between 1976 and 1990. Shale oil is projected to supply 75,000 b/d in 1985 and 200,000 b/d by 1990.

6. While coal reserves are huge, production is likely to be limited to 775 million tons in 1980, 940 million tons in 1985, and 1,225 million tons by 1990. Of these figures, about 80 million tons are projected for exports in 1980, and 90 million tons may be exported by 1985 and 1990. In terms of Btu's, production increases are lower due to the higher proportion of low-Btu western coal, as compared with current production from primarily higher Btu eastern coal. Coal production and utilization is subject to numerous constraints, and the domestic production and utilization figures used in the base case of this study assume that some impediments to higher coal use will be removed soon.

7. During the period of our forecast, the main constraint to expansion of nuclear power capacity is the rate of licensing new nuclear powerplants. The base case assumes that licensing will be speeded up from a recent low of about one plant every 8 weeks to about one plant every 5 weeks.

8. All other domestic energy sources: hydropower has been projected to increase slowly; geothermal is not likely to gain a role of significance during the next 15 years; and, solar energy is projected to supply about 1 percent of total U.S. energy demand in 1985 and 2 percent by 1990. The projected solar energy contribution assumes substantial government support for solar energy in the form of tax incentives.

Capital

9. Uncertainties about energy policy have delayed investment decisions in many sectors of the energy industry. Capital requirements to meet projected energy supply are substantial, but can be met assuming prices will not be regulated to the extent of preventing a fair return on investment. Some form of government support in the form of price floors or loan guarantees might be needed to encourage development of high-risk energy sources such as shale oil, tar sands, synthetic gas, and other alternative energy resources.

Oil and Natural Gas Imports

10. Under base case demand and supply conditions laid down in this report, natural gas imports are expected to grow from 0.9 TCF in 1976 to 1.5 TCF in 1980, 2.1 TCF in 1985, and 2.4 TCF by 1990. Oil imports—crude oil and oil products—are projected to increase from 7.2 million b/d in 1976 to 10 million b/d in 1980, 11.8 million b/d in 1985, and 12.9 million b/d by 1990. The strategic oil storage program is projected to add another 0.4 million b/d in 1980 and 0.3 million b/d in 1985.

11. Additional oil imports will come primarily from Arab countries in the Middle East and North Africa. Total U.S. imports from the Middle East and North Africa are projected to grow from about 2.5 million b/d in 1976 to 6.6 million b/d in 1980, 7.4 million b/d in 1985, and 7.9 million b/d by 1990. The adverse effects of another oil embargo on the economy at current and projected Arab oil import levels could be anywhere between very substantial and disastrous.

12. The implications of a dependence on the Middle East and North Africa in 1985 equal to total oil imports in 1976 are manifold and include: (*a*) potential oil supply interruptions as a result of war in the Middle East, or confrontation with the Soviet Union or, acts of sabotage by terrorist groups; (b) unknown effects of the accumulation of vast monetary reserves in Saudi Arabia and a few other Arab Gulf countries on the world economy; (c) potential conservation policies of Saudi Arabia or other Arab Gulf countries with limited capital absorptive capacity, resulting in escalating oil prices; (d) reduced leverage in the exercise of U.S. foreign policy in the region; (e) possible friction within the western alliance systems related to potential competition for available Middle East oil supplies.

13. World oil productive capacity can meet total world demand for oil throughout most of the decade of the 1980's, if the Soviet bloc does not become a major importer of oil. Sometime between the late 1980's and middle 1990's productive capacity of world oil is likely to peak, followed by declining world oil production (conventional oil sources only).

14. In spite of the production capacity there is no guarantee that producer states—in particular Saudi Arabia and a few smaller producers in the Arab Gulf region with low capital absorptive capacity—will continue to increase oil production. For political and economic reasons world oil demand could outpace supply as early as the early 1980's or as late as the early or middle 1990's. A few producer states—in particular Saudi Arabia—are likely to be in a position to determine when world oil production levels will peak. This action will be followed by subsequent world oil price increases.

15. Economic incentives by themselves are not likely to encourage the Saudis and other Arab Gulf producers with limited capital absorptive capacity to continue to increase oil production. A key incentive to a general atmosphere of cooperation between the industrial world and OAPEC is early progress toward a comprehensive peace settlement in the Arab-Israeli dispute. Other incentives to encourage

U.S. Energy Demand and Supply Projections 1970 - 1990 - Base Case (In Quads)

QUADRILLION BTU

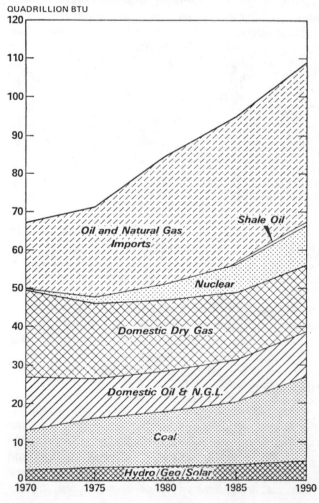

FIGURE 1

TABLE 1.—U.S. ENERGY DEMAND AND SUPPLY: 1977-90, PROJECTIONS [In million barrels per day oil equivalent]	1977	1980	1985	1990
Supply:				
Oil and NGL	9.6	10.4	10.9	11.4
Natural gas	9.2	8.5	8.3	8.3
Shale oil			.08	.2
Nuclear power	1.5	2.3	3.4	5.0
Coal (supply for domestic)	6.7	6.8	7.7	10.5
Hydro/solar/geo	1.3	1.7	1.9	2.4
Total U.S. supply	28.3	29.7	32.3	37.8
Demand:	36.9	40.4	45.1	51.9
Imports:				
Natural gas	.5	.7	1.0	1.2
Crude oil and products	8.1	10.0	11.8	12.9
Oil for oil storage program	.1	.4	.3	
[In conventional units]				
Supply:				
Oil and NGL (million b/d)	9.6	10.4	10.9	11.4
Natural gas (TCF/yr)	18.6	17.4	16.9	16.9
Shale oil (million b/d)			.08	.2
Nuclear power (gigawatts)	54	81	131	175
Coal (million short tons/yr utilization)	630	695	850	1.135
Hydro/solar/geo (gigawatts)	2.8	3.5	4.0	5.0
Imports:				
Natural Gas (TCF/yr)	.99	1.5	2.1	2.4
Crude oil and products (million b/d)	8.1	10.0	11.8	12.9
Oil storage (million b/d)	.1	.4	.3	

further growth in OAPEC oil exports include: (a) progress in the ''North-South'' dialogs; (b) favorable foreign investment policy in the industrial world, encouraging surplus nations to produce more oil and invest their surpluses in the rest of the world; (c) assistance in modernization of developing oil-producing states, leading toward further interdependence between consumer and producer states.

16. There seems no practical way to avoid development and implementation of energy policies in the industrial world—spearheaded by the United States—leading to an aggressive conservation ethic and a major program of energy resource development. If the industrial nations can show that they are willing to make adequate sacrifices at home, leading to reduced long-term reliance on imported oil, the Gulf States may be convinced to fill the energy gap in the transition period. A considerable degree of cooperation and understanding of interdependence can only be avoided at great cost.

17. The Soviet bloc is not expected to become a major net exporter or importer of energy throughout the 1980's. The Peoples Republic of China is projected to export 0.5 million b/d in 1980 and 1 million b/d by 1985.

Oil Reserves, Resources, And Production

Oil and natural gas have been the dominant sources of energy since the 1940's, when coal was replaced by oil and gas as the most important sources of energy in the United States. Today, oil and natural gas comprise 75 percent of U.S. energy consumption, a figure which is likely to decline to between 65 and 70 percent by 1990. In view of serious constraints on the liquid fossil fuel resource base, the share of coal and nuclear power—as a percentage of total energy consumption—is likely to rise during the next 15 years, from about 20 percent in 1976 to more than 30 percent in 1990.

There continues to be a great deal of uncertainty about the size of the oil and natural gas resource base, and the approximate location of undiscovered recoverable resources. This is particularly true for the frontier areas in the Outer Continental Shelf and in Alaska. Moreover, one cannot determine when and where new fields will be found, and what the size of those fields will be. All of these uncertainties can be factored into the actual future oil and natural gas production projections to the early 1980's with some confidence, but the accuracy of production projections tends to diminish the further one projects into the future.

Our projections of oil and natural gas production for the next 15 years are based on the best available geological information, actual data on reserves, historical trends, current and projected technological progress, price expectations, and the general political environment affecting oil and natural gas exploration and development.

Oil Reserves

Petroleum reserves are those quantities of oil-in-place that have been identified and are considered, on the basis of engineering and geological knowledge, to be recoverable or producible under current economic conditions.[1] Thus, price increases and improved technology will increase petroleum reserves, even without exploratory action on the part of the oil operators. The reason for this is that a higher percentage of the oil-in-place can be produced with advanced technology when prices rise. At present, the average percentage of the oil-in-place that can be recovered from reservoirs in the United States is 32 percent—in some fields much more, in others significantly less. Of the 32 percent, about 20 percent is produced from primary recovery—oil that will flow unaided from oil reservoir rock into an oil well—and the remaining 12 percent must be produced with the assistance of secondary and tertiary recovery techniques. These techniques require that water, steam, or chemicals be pumped back into the reservoir to enable oil to flow toward the existing well. Estimates of the ultimate potentially recoverable oil-in-place range from a nationwide average of 40 to 50 percent, but most engineers believe that the lower figure is more likely to be the accurate one.

Between 1973 and 1975, the average wellhead price of domestic oil rose from $3.39 to $6.85. Drilling activity showed a sharp increase, but contrary to expectations total proved reserves continued the decline which began in 1971. It may, however, take several years before the effects of high oil prices on reserve additions will be known.

The reserve figures per December 31, 1976, as released by the American Petroleum Institute, indicate a domestic crude oil reserve of 30.9 billion barrels, down

TABLE 2.—ANNUAL ESTIMATES OF PROVED CRUDE OIL AND NATURAL GAS LIQUIDS RESERVES IN THE UNITED STATES
(In thousand barrels per day)

Year	Proved reserves at end of the year (crude oil)	Production crude oil	Proved NGL reserves end of the year	Production of NGL	Proved natural gas reserves	Production of natural gas
1946	20,873,560	1,726,348	3,163,219	129,262	159.7	4.0
1950	25,268,398	1,943,776	4,267,663	227,411	184.6	6.3
1955	30,012,170	2,419,300	5,438,565	320,400	222.5	9.4
1960	31,613,211	2,471,464	5,816,059	431,379	262.3	12.8
1965	31,352,391	2,686,198	8,023,534	555,410	286.5	16.0
1970	39,001,335	3,319,445	7,702,941	747,812	290.4	21.9
1971	38,062,957	3,256,110	7,304,227	746,434	278.8	22.5
1972	36,339,408	3,281,397	6,786,559	755,941	266.1	22.5
1973	35,299,839	3,185,400	6,454,707	740,831	250.0	22.5
1974	34,249,956	3,043,456	6,350,449	724,099	237.1	21.4
1975	32,682,127	2,886,292	6,267,830	701,123	228.2	19.7
1976	30,942,166	2,825,252	6,401,967	700,629	216.0	19.5

Source: American Gas Association, American Petroleum Association, Canadian Petroleum Institute, Reserves of Crude Oil, Natural Gas Liquids, and Natural Gas in the United States and Canada as of Dec. 31, 1975, Washington, D.C., 1976, pp. 23 and 122.

almost 1.7 billion barrels from the previous year. The American Petroleum Institute estimates that an additional 5 billion barrels might be added to these reserves when and if enhanced recovery techniques are successfully applied to known reserves.

Since the discovery of the vast Prudhoe Bay field in 1970, oil reserves have continued to decline, and it is even more disturbing that with the exception of the North Slope find, new field discoveries have been rather small since the late 1960's. Most reserve additions came from extensions and revisions of reserves in oil fields.

Natural gas liquids were estimated by the American Gas Association at 6,401 million barrels as of December 31, 1976.[2] This was up slightly from the 6,267 million barrels estimate of a year earlier.

The drop in proved reserves of crude oil continued a steady decline which has been evident over the past several years, and which has been broken only by the Alaskan North Slope discoveries. The 1975 decline was registered in spite of a 17.5 percent increase in the number of wells drilled. Proved reserves of crude oil have declined by about 9 billion barrels, almost 25 percent since the end of 1970, because new discoveries have not been able to offset depletion of oil fields.

Natural gas reserves were estimated by the A.G.A. at 216 trillion cubic feet as of December 31, 1976. This represents a decline of 12 trillion cubic feet as compared with December 1975 natural gas reserves. The year 1976 represents the 6th year of decline in the Nation's total natural gas reserves and the 10th year of decline in reserves in the lower 48 States.

Reliability of Reserve Estimates

The reserve estimates are prepared annually by one or more subcommittees of the American Petroleum Institute Committee on Reserves. The subcommittees, which are responsible for determining annual reserve estimates, are composed of geologists and engineers who represent various segments of the producing industry, with broad experience in the estimation of reserves and an intimate knowledge of the areas and the more significant sized fields assigned to them. The subcommittees are expected to make multiple assignments of selected fields to their members in cases where it will contribute to the quality of reserve estimates and promote the exchange of expert views. The subcommittee reports are reviewed by the Committee on Reserves, which is composed of at least 15 professionally competent individuals selected from the management of the petroleum industry, industry-associated companies, or State Agencies, with a balance attempted between industry function, company representation, and geographic location. The Committee on Reserves of API works closely with the Committee on Natural Gas Reserves of the American Gas Association to report total liquid hydrocarbon reserves. Representatives of the Federal Government are also included in the Committee on Natural Gas Reserves of the AGA.

The reliability of estimates of the proved productive area of new discoveries or partially developed reservoirs varies according to the amount of geological information that is available at the time the estimate is being prepared. Such important factors as the areal extent of the geological structures, the average thickness of the producing reservoirs, the oil column within the reservoir, and the continuity of the reservoir characteristics cannot be determined accurately without sufficient subsurface information. The ultimate size of newly discovered reservoirs—in new or old fields—is seldom determined in the year of discovery.

Thus, first year estimates of proved reserves in new reservoirs are often much smaller than the total that will eventually be assigned to the new reservoirs. It follows that reserves credited to discoveries in any given year are usually less than the total extensions and revisions for the same year, since the extensions and revisions represent adjustments of reserves as additional drilling is done. Estimates of ultimate recovery and original oil-in-place for recently discovered fields are often subject to substantial upward revisions in subsequent years based on information provided by additional drilling, production performance, and the use of improved recovery techniques. For this reason it is necessary to exercise caution in interpreting the most recent data of this kind.

The reserve figures compiled by the American Petroleum Institute and the American Gas Association are generally accepted throughout industry and government as being reliable estimates of domestic oil and gas reserves. These figures are used by the U.S. Geological Survey to derive their statistics for measured and indicated hydrocarbon reserves.

The Federal Energy Administration estimated U.S.-proved reserves in a report to the President issued on October 31, 1975. Based on a survey of all oil and gas field operators in the United States, the FEA estimated domestic proved crude oil reserves to be 38 billion barrels as of December 31, 1974. The American Petroleum Institute listed comparable crude oil reserves at 34.2 billion barrels, or 10 percent less than the FEA survey. The two estimates are considered by FEA to vary no more than that which may be expected when comparing estimates from different sources.

The FEA estimate of indicated crude oil reserves, quantities of oil believed to be economically producible from known reservoirs by use of proven but not as yet installed recovery technology, was 4.1 billion barrels as of December 31, 1974.

The API estimated comparable indicated reserves at 4.6 billion barrels, a 12 percent higher figure than the FEA survey. About half of the difference between the crude oil reserve figures of the FEA and those of the API can be attributed to FEA's inclusion of 2 billion barrels of heavy crude oil which the API does not count because it is not considered economically and technically recoverable by them at this time. As a part of FEA's effort to prepare reserve and productive capacity estimates of oil and natural gas, the Administration contracted for and performed geological engineering analyses of 59 major oil and gas fields in the United States. These fields were studied to serve as an audit of the operators survey; as a test of the feasibility of expanding estimates from the major fields in conjunction with estimates from other sources to arrive at national reserve and productive capacity estimates; as a means of increasing the understanding of reserve and productive capacity estimates of our domestic major oil and gas fields; and as a test of the capabilities of Federal Government agencies and private contractors in developing independent field estimates. The reserve estimates from the major field studies when compared with those from the operators survey varied significantly, but neither tended to be consistently higher. The overall difference for crude oil was less than 2.5 percent, and therefore the operator's survey tended to be verified as an acceptable technique of reserve estimation.

The FEA survey has not yet satisfied all congressional critics. A recent study by the Subcommittee on Oversight and Investigations of the House Committee on Interstate and Foreign Commerce suggests that the FEA failed to include several new natural gas fields representing reserves of several trillion cubic feet. The subcommittee study stated that the FEA study had left out at least 3.4 trillion cubic feet in natural gas reserves, which could have produced some 500 billion cubic feet. In view of total natural gas reserves and production in the United States—respectively 228 and 21 TCF in 1975—the difference be-

tween AGA, FEA, FPC, and other estimates is not very large.

Undiscovered Recoverable Oil And Natural Gas Resources

Half of all the oil that has ever been produced has been taken from the earth in the last 10 years. This gives a perspective on the escalating growth in world energy demand. Even in the OPEC countries, as in most producing basins of the world, most of the oil has already been found. So great is the accelerating demand for energy that the years of abundant supply of conventional liquid hydrocarbons will be relatively few, and this has caused, among other things, an increased urgency in estimating the amount of remaining undiscovered recoverable hydrocarbon resources in order to better formulate future energy policy.

Estimates of undiscovered recoverable oil and natural gas resources in the United States have undergone significant changes in recent years,[3] ranging from a high of 590 billion barrels of oil (USGS-Zapp, 1962) to a low of 72 billion barrels (Hubbert, 1974), and a high of 990 to 2,000 TCF (USGS, 1974) to a low of 443 TCF (Mobil, 1974).

The difference in the estimates of oil and natural gas resources is due to different techniques used in analyzing remaining undiscovered resources. The 1962 and 1974 USGS estimates are based on volumetric and geological province analysis studies which assumed that an equal volume of oil would be found in equal volumes of drilled and undrilled sediments. Even if this assumption is cut in half—one-half as much oil as assumed to be found in a given volume of undrilled sediments as was found in the same volume of drilled sediments—the result in terms of undiscovered resources would still be relatively high because the most promising areas are drilled first and the sediments in the United States (onshore) which remain undrilled after 100 years and 2½ million wells, are those which, for a number of geological and economic reasons, are not very promising.

The Mobil and Exxon figures were derived by more sophisticated combined geological and statistical model

TABLE 3.—UNDISCOVERED DOMESTIC OIL AND NATURAL GAS RESOURCES

	Liquid petroleum (billion barrels)	Natural gas (trillion cubic feet)
U.S. Geological Survey:		
Zapp (1962)	590	
McKelvey (1974)	200–400	990–2000
Miller et al. (1975)	50–127	322–655
M. King Hubbert (1974)	72	540
National Academy of Sciences (1975)	113	530
Mobil Oil (1974)	88	443
Exxon (1976)	118	582

methods. These, and the figures of M. King Hubbert, which result from extrapolation of past production performance, are more conservative and appear to be safer projections on which to base public policy. The recent studies by Mobil, Exxon, and Hubbert are in agreement with the latest USGS oil and natural gas resources estimates, published in 1975. The 1975 USGS study combines geological and statistical model methods, such as the extrapolation of known producibility into untested sediments of similar geology; volumetric techniques using geologic analogs and setting of upper and lower yield limits through comparisons with a number of known areas; volumetric estimates with an arbitrary general yield factor, used when direct analogs are not known; graded series of potential-area categories; and comprehensive comparisons of all published estimates for each area to all estimates generated by the above method.

The 1975 USGS oil and natural gas resources survey is the most comprehensive and sophisticated ever undertaken by the Survey. The need for resources studies with a high degree of accuracy arose in the early 1970's when policymakers became aware that with limits to the resource base and high exponential growth rates of oil and natural gas production of the post World War II era, available resources will result in oil and gas production peaking out before the end of this century. Studies by the USGS prior to 1975 suggested that oil and gas production in the United States could be expanded and would not peak out until well into the 21st century.

Oil Production Estimates: 1975-90

Production of petroleum liquids in the United States steadily increased until it peaked at 11,297,000 b/d—of which 9.180 million b/d are crude oil and the remainder natural gas liquids—in 1970. From 1970 onward, production has gradually declined to 9.6 million b/d in 1976. Production of oil and natural gas liquids in traditional areas in the lower 48 States is expected to continue to decline, but Alaskan production and production from new onshore and offshore fields in the lower 48 States are expected to gradually increase total production to about 1 million b/d above current production by 1985. It will require major efforts from the side of the oil industry, and a favorable economic and political climate to increase domestic oil production to the levels projected in this study. Without a combination of favorable economic and political stimuli, oil and natural gas liquids production may actually be slightly below current levels of production 10 years from now. On the other hand, a very favorable political and economic climate, coupled with very high finding rates in frontier areas and more successful application of tertiary recovery techniques in old fields, could increase production of petroleum liquids possibly as much as 2

million b/d over and above current production by the middle or late 1980's.

In the base case projections of domestic petroleum liquids production for the period 1975-90 the following methodology was used: (*a*) elaborate questionnaires were sent to the 15 largest integrated oil companies in the United States—taken from Fortune's largest 500 companies; (*b*) data supplied by 12 companies responding to the questionnaire were compared, and analyzed; (*c*) the mean figure of total production of petroleum liquids as projected by the companies was then compared with U.S. oil and natural gas liquids reserves and resources to see if the mean production figure was reasonable in view of required additions to reserves of petroleum liquids for the next 15 years. The result, explained in more detail below, suggests that the oil and natural gas liquids production projected in this study for the period 1975-90 is within the realm of the attainable, but possibly a little on the high side.

Major oil company projections.—The CRS questionnaire asked the major oil companies to project the domestic production levels of oil and natural gas liquids for 1977, 1980, 1985, and 1990. Companies were asked to use their own data on reserves and resources expectations, drilling and finding rates, and projected leadtimes between leasing and production. The CRS questionnaire asked the companies to include the following political assumptions in their base case analysis: (1) decontrol of the price of all domestic oil after May 1979—assumes current EPCA controls terminated after May 1979—and no new windfall profit taxes added; (2) decontrol of new natural gas; (3) current OCS leasing system; (4) annual

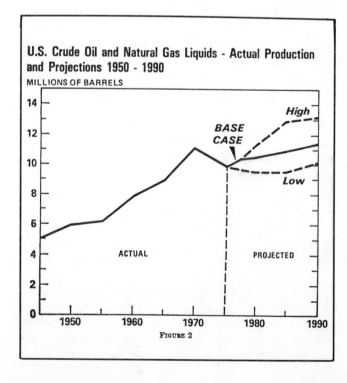

U.S. Crude Oil and Natural Gas Liquids - Actual Production and Projections 1950 - 1990

MILLIONS OF BARRELS

FIGURE 2

TABLE 4.—U.S. PRODUCTION PROJECTIONS FOR CRUDE OIL AND NATURAL GAS LIQUIDS: 1980, 1985, 1990 (In million barrels per day)				
	1975	1980	1985	1990
Lower 48 onshore	8.4	7.4	6.5	5.7
Lower 48 offshore	1.4	1.2	1.6	2.1
Alaska onshore		1.7	2.0	2.0
Alaska offshore	.2	.1	.8	1.6

average of 1.5 to 2 million acres of Outer Continental Shelf leased by the Government; (5) no vertical divesture; (6) Naval Petroleum Reserve No. 4 to be leased by the Department of the Interior on terms similar to OCS leasing.

On the basis of these assumptions, the average U.S. domestic production level of petroleum liquids—crude oil and natural gas liquids—as forecast by 12 leading international and national oil companies was as follows: 9.6 million b/d in 1977, and 10.4 million b/d in 1980, 10.9 million b/d in 1985, and 11.4 million b/d by 1990. Production estimates varied considerably among the 12 companies for 1985 and 1990. The difference between the high and low production estimates for 1985 was about 3 million b/d. This was mainly due to one particularly high and one very low estimate. Most companies' production projections were no more than 500,000 b/d higher or lower than the mean. The difference between the high and low estimates for 1990 was also about 3 million b/d, but most company production projections were between 10.5 and 11.5 million b/d.

Required reserve additions.—Production of 10.9 million b/d in 1985 and 11.4 million b/d by 1990 would mean a total cumulative oil production of about 62 billion barrels between 1975 and 1990. Moreover, in order to keep the reserve production ratio at about 10 years—slightly below the current ratio—reserves must total about 40 billion barrels by 1990.

The total resource base is estimated at 160.7 billion barrels.[4] The total cumulative production to arrive at 11.4 million b/d of oil production in 1990, is about 62 billion barrels. This, plus 40 billion barrels of proved reserves in 1990 in order to keep an R/P ratio of 10, adds up to a requirement of 102 billion barrels. Thus, 102 billion barrels out of a total recoverable resources of 160.7 billion barrels will have to be found, and 62 billion barrels produced between 1975 and 1990, in order to achieve a production level of 11.4 million b/d by 1990. This requires a major drilling effort and a great deal of success in locating new fields in the frontier areas of the lower 48 States and Alaska.

To get to the most optimistic and highly unlikely output of 13.1 million b/d by 1990, an additional 930 million barrels would have to be added to reserves annually between 1975 and 1990, a truly gigantic task in view of past experiences. The lower production levels, resulting in pro-

duction of 10.1 million b/d by 1990 would require that 90.7 billion barrels out of total recoverable resources would be found between 1975 and 1990.

The base case, projecting oil production to rise to 10.9 million b/d in 1985 and 11.4 million b/d in 1990 can be called a cautiously optimistic forecast. Major changes in the key political assumptions and/or disappointing finding rates could very well lead to production levels of 9.5 and 10.1 million b/d respectively by 1985 and 1990. The maximum supply case appears highly unlikely at this point.

Synthetic Oil

Oil from shale and coal will not become commercially available until the middle 1980's. Some Government intervention may even be necessary to achieve an oil production of only 150,000 b/d respectively by 1985 and 1990. Speeding up shale oil production by 100,000 barrels or more by 1985 would probably require additional Government incentives in the form of direct support or tax incentives, and a compromise on offsite plant location and spent shale disposal. A high production target of about 500,000 b/d would probably require legislation to: (*a*) permit near-term development of supplemental water impoundment capacity, (*b*) modify existing air and water quality standards or other environmental regulations, and (*c*) provide priorities to energy producing industries in procurement of necessary construction or machinery.

With currently available mining technology and aboveground processing, some 80 billion barrels of oil may be extracted from shale under favorable economic conditions. However, numerous economic, environmental and institutional constraints are likely to keep shale oil production in the United States down to less than 500,000 b/d by 1990.

Natural Gas Production

Proved natural gas reserves in the United States peaked in 1967, the year prior to the discovery of the Prudhoe Bay oil and gas field.[5] While reserve additions in the lower 48 States had peaked in 1956, substantial additions of North Slope reserves in AGA/API statistics—and total reserves were still high enough to increase production of natural gas through 1973. In that year natural gas production peaked at 22.6 trillion cubic feet.

The Nation was warned of the pending production declines as early as 1948 when reserves were at 173 TCF, and production at only 6 TCF (1976 yearend reserves were at 216 TCF, production 19.5 TCF). These warnings of future exhaustion of natural gas were repeated by the President's Material Policy Commission in 1952, and by the National Academy of Sciences in 1962. In a followup report released in February 1972, the FPC's Bureau of Natural Gas predicted that gas production would peak in the middle 1970's—it did peak in 1973-74—and that shortages would be of long duration leading to supply deficiencies of 9 TCF in 1980 and 17 TCF in 1990, even after optimistic allowance for new supply from supplemental sources such as coal gasification and gas imports.

In retrospect FPC forecasts have proved to be somewhat optimistic, but they have also been basically indicative of our national supply posture. The CRS natural gas production projection for the period 1975-90 further largely supports the earlier warnings by the Bureau of Natural Gas. Until very recently the Nation did not accept the imminent prospect of supply constraints. It was felt that ultimate recoverable resources of natural gas as estimated prior to 1975 were high enough to warrant continued production expansion. The price elasticity of supply was assumed to be very high in most studies published prior to 1975. After the most comprehensive oil and natural gas resource survey ever published by the USGS was circulated in 1975 natural gas production forecasts were scaled down considerably in most post-1975 studies.

Natural gas production data in the 1977 CRS study are based on the same methodology employed to project oil production levels for the period 1975-90.

Companies were asked to provide production projections for "domestic dry gas to domestic use," a term used by the Bureau of Mines in its annual natural gas production statistics. It represents the dry natural gas after all the liquids have been taken out of the produced wet gas, and transmission losses, storage, and exports are accounted for. Natural gas liquids were discussed in the previous section on petroleum liquids—crude oil and natural gas liquids. In order to calculate the volume of domestic natural gas which will be available to end users in the major sectors of the economy, one has to deduct from the domestic dry gas to domestic use figure used here, the volume used for pipeline fuel and lease and plant fuel. In 1974, this was about 2 trillion cubic feet.

On the basis of the same basic assumptions listed in the previous section, the average projections derived from the responses of 12 leading oil and natural gas producing companies for the volume of dry natural gas production is as follows: 18.6 TCF in 1977; 17.4 TCF in 1980; 17.1 TCF in 1985; and, 17.1 TCF by 1990.

Production estimates varied among the 12 companies. The difference between the highest and the lowest estimate for 1985 was 8 trillion cubic feet, enough to meet 1976 demand for natural gas by the industrial sector. However, two-thirds of the companies estimated natural gas production by 1985 at between 15 and 18 TCF. The difference between the highest and lowest estimate for 1990 was 11.3 TCF, or equal to the 1976 demand for natural gas by the industrial sector and the electric utilities

combined. It is difficult to explain such differences other than to argue that there are major differences in view—even among the oil and gas producers—about the effects of higher prices on finding rates. Of the 12 companies projecting 1990 natural gas production, 8 estimate natural gas production by 1990 at between 15 and 18 TCF. Hence, most of the companies project natural gas production to continue its current decline until the middle 1980's, followed by a period of stabilization or slow increase of production until 1990, the final year of our forecast.

Reserve additions required.—Production of domestic dry gas to domestic end use of respectively 16.9 TCF in 1985 and 16.9 TCF in 1990, would mean gross withdrawals from oil and gas wells of approximately 19.1 TCF in 1985 and 1990—compared with 22.850 in 1974. To arrive at gross withdrawals of natural gas production of 19.1 TCF in 1985 and 1990, about 243 TCF will have to be added to reserves during the 1977-90 period. On the basis of the estimated resource base alone these reserve addition figures are not unreasonable. The USGS estimated in 1976 that natural gas reserves were 216 TCF, and inferred reserves stood at 201 TCF. Adding to this the weighted mean of undiscovered recoverable resources of natural gas of 484 TCF, the total remaining resource base is 901 TCF. Hence about 40 percent of the not yet discovered recoverable resources would have to be found during the next 15 years. Assuming that inferred reserves of 201 TCF as quoted in USGS circular 725 are too high as many geologists now maintain, a total of between 45 and 50 percent of the remaining resources would have to be discovered between 1975 and 1990. In view of our recent experience onshore and offshore, this would require major drilling efforts in frontier areas and a great deal of success in the early stages of drilling.

In the 30 years from 1946-75, some 290,000 wells were drilled and a total of about 470 TCF were added to reserves. During the early part of the 30-year period finding rates were high, but in the latter part finding rates were very low. Also, about 50 percent of current gas reserves are located in about 100 large fields, which is less than 2 percent of the total. With the exception of the Prudhoe Bay find in 1968, very few large fields have been found in the United States after 1967.[7] In the traditional areas new reserves are likely to be added from small fields. It will take an ever-growing drilling effort to add a little more to reserves in those areas. It is feasible that major new gas fields will be found in due time in the frontier areas.

On the basis of the experience in natural gas drilling of the past 30 years, it would take about 150,000 wells to find the 243 TCF of gas needed to achieve the average dry natural gas production of 16.9 TCF in 1985 and in 1990 as projected by the 12 companies. On an annual basis, about 10,000 exploratory and development wells would have to be drilled between 1976 and 1990. This is well

TABLE 5.—U.S. NATURAL GAS PRODUCTION PROJECTION, 1980,1985,1990 (DOMESTIC DRY GAS PRODUCTION USE) (In trillion cubic feet per year)	1980	1985	1990
Lower 48 States onshore	13.1	11.0	8.8
Lower 48 States offshore	3.9	4.5	5.6
Alaska onshore		1.1	1.5
Alaska offshore	.4	.3	1.0
Total	17.4	16.9	16.9

within the average of the past few years. The major immediate problem to increase production over the next 15 years is not so much related to the total estimated resource base or the total projected drilling rate. The projected failure to increase natural gas production during the next decade is primarily related to the exhaustion of old provinces onshore in the lower 48 States, and the leadtimes required to find additional reserves in the frontier areas offshore and in Alaska. No Alaskan natural gas is likely to be available in the lower 48 States prior to 1985 (pipeline), and leadtimes between leasing and development of discovered resources in the offshore Atlantic and Pacific are such that early discoveries of large reserves are needed to expect major production from those areas by 1985.

In spite of the substantial increases in drilling rates in recent years—in response to higher interstate prices—finding rates in the lower 48 States traditional areas continued their general downward trend. Drilling productivity has continued to decline from 536,000 cubic feet of gas per foot drilled in 1966 to 220,000 cubic feet per foot drilled in 1975. In 1976, reserve additions were again substantially below 1975 reserve additions, in spite of the higher price allowed for interstate gas.

Natural gas production is almost certain to decline in the lower 48 States onshore and even assuming successful exploration and development of the frontier areas offshore Atlantic, Pacific, and Alaska, the trend in the direction of lower production is not likely to be reversed. Successful exploration and development in the frontier areas could at best stabilize production, probably during the period from the middle 1980's to the early 1990's.

This forecast may be considered optimistic for the following reasons: it assumes that additions to reserves in the traditional gas producing areas in the lower 48 States will increase substantially above the 1968-76 annual average of 8.6 trillion cubic feet; and, that between now and 1990 about 90 percent of the maximum undiscovered recoverable natural gas resources in the Atlantic and Pacific OCS as quoted in the USGS circular 725, will in fact be found. Moreover, these projections assume a most favorable political and economic climate.

If additions to natural gas reserves in traditional areas onshore and offshore in the lower 48 States are not going

to respond significantly to higher prices and subsequent higher drilling rates, in the years to come production would decline more rapidly in our projections to 16.3 trillion cubic feet in 1980, 15.7 trillion cubic feet in 1985, and 15.5 trillion cubic feet by 1990.

In the event that finding rates respond very favorably to higher prices in the traditional natural gas-producing areas, maximum production could possibly rise to 17.8 trillion cubic feet in 1980, and thereafter slowly decline to 17.6 trillion cubic feet in 1985 and 17.4 trillion cubic feet in 1990. At this point the high production scenario seems highly unlikely.

In view of the constraints on the resource base in the traditional gas-producing areas, where a great deal of gas remains to be found in smaller fields, it seems unlikely that the traditional areas will contribute much more than our already optimistic base case scenario indicates. The Atlantic and Pacific Outer Continental Shelf are projected to produce 0.1, 1.7, and 3.2 trillion cubic feet, respectively, in 1980, 1985, and 1990. Such production figures would already exhaust most of the natural gas resources said to be located in that area under favorable conditions—see USGS Circular 725. Very little additional drilling for natural gas will take place in Alaska until more is known about the route of the proposed gas pipeline and when it is expected to be completed. It is unlikely that more natural gas will be produced and transported to the market than projected in the base case.

There is always an element of surprise in any efforts to project future oil and gas production on the basis of resources other than proved reserves. It for that reason that a more pessimistic and a more optimistic scenario have been developed.

U.S. Dry Natural Gas Production: Actual and Projected, 1950 - 1990

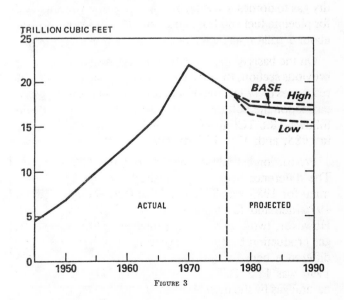

FIGURE 3

Nonconventional Sources of Gas

The only source of methane gas other than natural gas produced today, is produced from oil. Its future is not entirely clear, but in view of declining oil resources in the country, this form of methane is projected to decline during the 1980's and early 1990's. Current production is 0.4 trillion cubic feet per year.

Methane gas occluded in coal, gas from stimulation of tight formation, methane from bioconversion and gas dissolved in formation water—though promising potential resources—are not likely to make a significant contribution to the Nation's gas production during the next 15 years.

Of all nonconventional sources of gas, synthetic gas from coal has the best prospects during the 1975-90 period. Production projections of synthetic gas from coal in this study assume that political, environmental, and above all economic constraints to development will be overcome soon.

The Future Of Natural Gas

Total gas supply from domestic and foreign conventional and nonconventional sources in the United States may be stabilized at current levels at least until the middle 1980's, and possibly well into the 1990's. During the next 15 years it does not seem likely that total supply of gas from conventional and nonconventional sources will increase much, and it is possible that total gas supply may decline substantially in the period from 1977-90.

Stabilization of total gas supply—natural gas and nonconventional sources of gas—would be possible under the following assumptions:

No further decline in natural gas discoveries in traditional areas in the lower 48 States onshore and offshore. In fact, reserve additions would have to increase beyond the annual average of the past decade.

Early successful exploratory and development drilling for natural gas in the frontier areas of the Pacific (southern California) and the Atlantic (in particular the mid-Atlantic).

TABLE 6.—U.S. NONCONVENTIONAL SOURCES OF METHANE
(In trillion cubic feet)

	1976	1980	1985	1990
Methane from oil	0.4	0.4	0.3	[1] 0.2
Syngas from Coal		(²)	.5	1.5
Total		.4	.4	.8	1.7

[1] Syngas from oil not separately listed in tables of total energy supply. In total energy supply tables syngas from oil is included in oil figures.
² Negligible.

TABLE 7.—TOTAL GAS SUPPLY PROJECTIONS FOR THE UNITED STATES: CONVENTIONAL AND NONCONVENTIONAL SOURCES OF GAS
(In trillion cubic feet)

	1976	1977	1980	1985	1990
Domestic natural gas	19.0	18.6	17.4	16.9	16.9
Syngas from oil	.4	.4	.4	.3	.2
Syngas from coal				.5	1.5
Canadian dry gas imports	1.0	1.0	1.0	.9	.7
Liquid natural gas		(¹)	.5	1.2	1.7
Total gas supply	20.4	20.0	19.3	19.8	21.0

¹ Negligible.

Completion of a natural gas pipeline to transport Alaskan gas to the markets in the lower 48 States.

Natural gas pricing policy must reflect higher costs of exploration and development, in particular in the frontier areas and for deep drilling in traditional areas.

A favorable economic and political climate to expect capital investments to be available to achieve a production of 0.5 TCF of syngas from coal in 1985, and 1.5 TCF by 1990.

No significant decline in Canadian dry natural gas exports to the United States until 1985. After 1985, Canadian exports are expected to decline gradually from 0.9 TCF to 0.7 TCF by 1990. After 1990, Canadian exports are expected to decline rapidly unless large new discoveries are made in Canada..

No major institutional barriers raised to the development of syngas from coal, and to facility siting in the coastal zone to allow liquid natural gas imports to rise to about 0.5 TCF in 1980, 1.2 TCF in 1985, and 1.7 TCF by 1990.

Coal Utilization And Production

Resources and reserves.—Domestic coal[8] resources—all coal known or expected to be in the Earth's crust—and reserves—that small part of the total resources which is mineable with today's technology and economic situation—although huge and adequate for the near- and mid-term, are not nearly so large when considered from a long-range standpoint.

Tons of coal in the ground must be discounted on the basis of (l) recoverability during mining and (2) Btu (heat) content. Thus, the commonly cited numbers for the U.S. coal reserve base—434 billion tons total or 427 billion without anthracite—become only 266 billion tons of recoverable coal. Or, if the commonly applied recoverability factors— 50 percent for underground mining and 85 percent for surface mining—are reduced to more reasonable percentages (perhaps as low as 30 and 45 percent, respectively, according to Schmidt, 1976) then the total recoverable U.S. coal reserve can become as low as 150 billion tons.

A large amount of U.S. coal reserves, and an increasing amount of domestic coal production, are in the Western States where the Btu content is substantially lower—sub-bituminous coal and lignite, instead of bituminous—these tonnage numbers could be reduced on an equivalent-Btu basis to 140 billion. Thus the commonly projected life of U.S. coal reserves, based on the 1974 production of 600 million tons would be reduced from the very large number of 711 years for the total reserve base, to 443 years recoverable—or only 250 years at Schmidt's recoverability factors—and to 410 years on an equivalent-Btu basis—or 230 years if Schmidt is correct.

Our complacency for the long-term future is thus stirred as we contemplate the possibility of exhaustion of our available coal reserves at an earlier date than projected in previous studies. Increases in annual demand—which are projected to occur—above the 600 million tons used in the foregoing calculations shorten the time period substantially, although compensating increases in the coal reserve base will take place as exploration for new coal deposits and as new technology meets with success.

In addition, the regional distribution of usable coal reserves in the ground is reversed from the tonnage-basis numbers of 47 percent East of the Mississippi River and 53 percent West, to 52 percent in the East and only 48 percent in the West, because of (1) Btu content and (2) sulfur content. Those percentages are likewise subject to further modification if the recoverability is closer to Schmidt's numbers of only 45 percent for surface mining and 30 percent for underground mining—on the basis of how much surface mining and what degree of sulfur content society will permit.

Production.—Production of bituminous coal and lignite, which had risen from 603 million tons in 1970 to 648 million in 1975—and an estimated 665 million in 1976—is expected to increase as the demand increases. The demand is predicated on an increase in coal usage by the electric utility consuming sector, which in 1975 used about three-quarters of the domestic bituminous coal and lignite produced.

Constraints.—As with all forecasts, projections of coal production are based on a number of assumptions—and, most importantly, must be considered in the light of several constraints.

Serious deterrents to the capability of the U.S. coal industry to meet our production forecasts include:

1. Lack of availability of capital because of numerous uncertainties;

2. Lack of availability of trained manpower and the diminishing productivity of coal miners;

3. Inadequacy of the transportation network, and capital requirements to rectify the situation;

4. Environmental enhancement measures—their kinds, severity and rigor, timing and capital requirements;

5. Delays in gaining access to the massive coal resources and reserves on Federal lands; and

6. Uncertainty of the market because of environmental regulations that regulate coal out and thus create uncertainties on the supply side and a reluctance to invest.

The foregoing constraints apply generally throughout most—or all—of the United States— except for No. 5, which will affect coal mainly in the Western States and Alaska. Others will likewise have more serious effects in certain areas or regions of the country than in others. In addition, events that will likely hinder the production timetable of the coal industry are:

7. Shortages of certain kinds of equipment, both for surface and underground mining;

8. Labor problems—particularly wildcat strikes, such as during the summer of 1976;

9. Inclement weather, such as during the period, January-February, 1977.

The severity of the aforementioned constraints—and possibly others—can be lessened if the United States were to have an accommodating energy policy and programs, which are mutually agreed to by both the Congress and the executive branch. Governmental incentives can help alleviate the effects of many of the disincentives resulting from the constraints mentioned above.

In the absence of a comprehensive energy policy and programs, together with incentives, it is highly unlikely that the coal utilization goals of the administration will be reached. In fact, a more likely set of numbers for coal production is seen to be considerably lower than the sights which had been set in 1974 and are still being repeated by most seers today.

Our estimates are that U.S. coal production given moderately favorable conditions will rise to 775 million

TABLE 8.—U.S. PRODUCTION AND UTILIZATION OF BITUMINOUS COAL AND LIGNITE
(Million tons and quadrillion Btu)

	Million tons		Quadrillion Btu	
	Domestic utilization	Exports	Domestic utilization	Exports
Low:				
1977	610	65	13.2	1.7
1980	640	80	13.2	2.1
1985	760	90	14.9	2.4
1990	1,020	90	19.9	2.4
Median:				
1977	630	65	14.0	1.7
1980	695	80	14.3	2.1
1985	850	90	16.3	2.4
1990	1,135	90	22.2	2.4
High:				
1977	660	65	14.4	1.7
1980	730	80	15.1	2.1
1985	940	90	18.5	2.4
1990	1,250	90	24.5	2.4

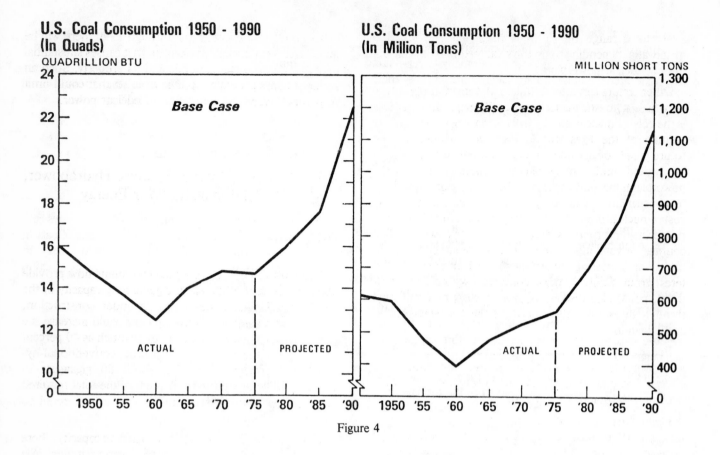

U.S. Coal Consumption 1950 - 1990 (In Quads)

QUADRILLION BTU

Base Case

ACTUAL   PROJECTED

U.S. Coal Consumption 1950 - 1990 (In Million Tons)

MILLION SHORT TONS

Base Case

ACTUAL   PROJECTED

Figure 4

tons in 1980, 940 million tons in 1985, and 1,225 million tons in 1990. Coal exports are expected to be: 80 million tons in 1980, and 90 million tons in 1985 and 1990. In order to achieve these coal utilization figures, many of the aforementioned constraints will have to be eased or removed, otherwise the low projections below will have greater validity.

Coal output measured in short tons/year increases more rapidly than output measured in Btu's. This is due to the fact that the average Btu per ton of coal is projected to continue to decrease when we move from high Btu Eastern to low Btu Western coal. Estimated Btu's per ton: 11,100 in 1977; 10,600 in 1980; 10,100 in 1985; and 10,000 in 1990.

Nuclear Power

Through 1990 the expansion of nuclear power in the United States probably will be less than forecasted by ERDA and the nuclear industry and will be limited primarily by the rate at which the Federal Government can license construction and operation of additional nuclear powerplants because this constraint is the one least controllable by the nuclear and electrical industries. This factor will probably limit nuclear generating capacities by

TABLE 9.—NUCLEAR POWER CAPACITY: 1977-90

	1977		1980		1985		1990	
	GWe	Btu	GWe	Btu	GWe	Btu	GWe	Btu
Base case	54	3,240	81	4,860	131	7,560	175	10,560
Low supply	52	3,120	70	4,200	100	6,000	130	7,800
High supply	56	3,360	92	5,520	162	9,120	222	13,320
Maximum	56	3,360	92	5,520	212	12,720	332	19,950

U.S. Nuclear Power Capacity - Actual and Projected 1957 - 1990 (In GWe)

CAPACITY — GIGAWATTS ELECTRICAL

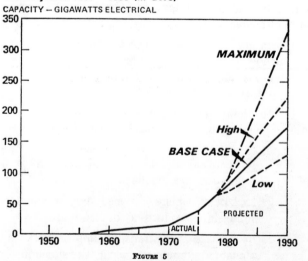

MAXIMUM

High

BASE CASE

Low

ACTUAL   PROJECTED

FIGURE 5

1990 to a range of 130,000 megawatts to 332,000 megawatts, depending upon the sustained rate of licensing of new nuclear powerplants.

Other factors can also stimulate or constrain the future growth of domestic nuclear energy. Principal among these is the role of nuclear energy in U.S. energy policy and the attitude of the President and his administration. The future supply of uranium and enrichment services probably would limit any substantial increase in nuclear powerplants beyond those now being built or committed to construction. The comparative capital and operating cost of nuclear power too can become a limiting factor and numerous uncertainties in costs of nuclear power can discourage private investment in new construction. Continued or increased opposition to nuclear power by interest groups, notably those concerned with the environment, could also discourage new nuclear commitments through threats of intervention in the licensing process and litigation.

Federal and State legislation to expand the role of State governments in decisions on siting, environmental effects, and operation of nuclear powerplants also could become a substantial new constraint.

Factors that seem unlikely to limit use of nuclear energy through 1990 include reprocessing and recycling of nuclear fuels, demonstration of the plutonium breeder, storage of spent fuel, terminal storage of high-level radioactive wastes, and the capacity of the nuclear industry to build nuclear powerplants. Table 10 summarizes the likely effects of several factors on prospective nuclear energy.

Factors which could accelerate the growth of nuclear power include further increases in the price of imported oil, increased prices for coal, technical and regulatory problems in generating electricity from coal, and national policy to limit or reduce imports of oil and natural gas. In particular, widespread public opposition to deep and strip mining of coal can be expected to make nuclear power more attractive to the electricity industry.

This overview assumes that through 1990 there will be no accident in a nuclear powerplant that causes substantial injury or damage to the public and its property. Such an accident could generate a public reaction that could limit or perhaps even stop generation of nuclear power.

Other Domestic Energy Sources: Hydropower, Geothermal and Solar Energy

Hydropower

Conventional hydroelectric developments now provide about 15 percent of the electric generating capacity in the contiguous United States. Projects under construction, planned, and possible of development could increase the developed hydroelectric capacity by as much as 40 percent by the end of the century. At that time, conventional hydroelectric projects, providing about 80 gigawatts of capacity, could account for 5 percent of the total required capacity and about 4 percent of the annual required electricity generation.

In addition to the projected hydroelectric capacity, there is significant underdeveloped hydroelectric potential in a large number of projects for which investigations of various levels have been made. Development of some of these projects may be precluded by wild and scenic rivers or similar legislation. Excluding such projects, and selecting those appearing to be most favorable of development during the next quarter of a century, as much as 36 gigawatts of capacity with an annual generation of 100 billion kilowatt-hours could be provided by potential developments of 25 megawatts or greater. The FPC estimates that such generation would represent an annual saving of 160 million barrels of oil over equivalent production by thermal plants. If existing facilities are extensively modified by increasing dam heights or reservoir storages, current estimates of feasible potential could be increased.

Conventional hydroelectric projects are attractive since they utilize a renewable resource and produce electric power over long service lives without consuming fuel resources or creating air and water pollution. They are especially suited to provide peakload and reserve capacity.

Geothermal Energy

The geothermal resource base is huge. Cost and technological considerations will restrict its near-term utilization to the Western part of the country and perhaps the

Factor	1990	2000
Industrial capacities:		
Uranium production	No	Maybe.
Uranium enrichment	No	Do.
Fuel reprocessing	No	Do.
Fuel recycle, LWR	No	Do.
Spent fuel storage	No	No.
Terminal waste storage	No	No.
Use of the breeder	No	Yes.
Reactor production	No	No.
Social:		
Public reaction to nuclear power	Yes	Yes.
Public interest group action on nuclear power	Yes	Yes.
Governmental actions:		
Administration's policy for nuclear power	Yes	Yes.
Licensing and regulation; Federal	Yes	Yes.
Licensing and regulation; State	Maybe	Maybe.
Nonproliferation regulation	No	Do.
Further technological development	No	Yes.
Federal legislation	Maybe	Maybe.
Economic:		
Comparative cost of nuclear powerplants	do	Yes.
Comparative cost of nuclear fuel cycle	do	Yes.

TABLE 10.—FACTORS AFFECTING FUTURE OF NUCLEAR POWER IN THE UNITED STATES

gulf coast, but if cost is disregarded and major technological advance is assumed, the geothermal resource which underlies the entire country would have immense potential. However, the exact size of the geothermal resource base is not now as important as the current and near-term use of the most accessible of geothermal deposits for electrical power and heating and industrial purposes. The geothermal resources clearly merit judicious development.

There are a number of projections of future geothermal energy utilization. The more recent of these are less optimistic concerning future geothermal energy utilization and tend to converge on a few thousand megawatts of geothermal production for 1985, and a few tens of thousands megawatts of geothermal electrical production for the year 2000. These modest estimates may even tend to be too optimistic as the development of geothermal resources has been slowing down. Progress appears to be impeded for the most part by uncertainty of profitability and institutional barriers such as leasing arrangements which seem counterproductive, and long delays in obtaining governmental permits at all levels. It is possible that Federal incentives such as loan guarantees, depletion allowances, intangible drilling expense writeoffs, geothermal reservoir investment indemnities, and perhaps even direct subsidies may be needed if even the more recent utilization estimates are to be realized.

Solar Energy

It is widely recognized that solar energy is received on the Earth in sufficient quantities to make a major contribution to the future energy needs of the United States and the world. However, solar technologies are in such limited use today that it is yet uncertain when the means will be available for making practical use of solar energy on a large scale.

A number of factors over which there is little direct control affect the extent to which solar energy will be used over the next several years. Possibly the most important and yet the one which we seem to have the least control over is the cost and availability of established energy sources. It is said that the energy shortages caused by the severe winter of 1976-77 did more for the solar market than anything else the industry could have hoped for.

Another important factor which is controllable to some extent is the Federal Government's role in the development and commercialization of solar technologies. This factor is considered by many to be the key to the future use of solar energy. With a continued strong Federal commitment to the development of solar technology and with the introduction of moderate economic incentives at the Federal level, it is estimated that the combined contribution of all solar technologies could reach about 1 percent of the national energy demand by 1985 (0.9 quad). Assuming that cost competitive hardware is available by the early to mid-1980's, the combined contribution might reasonably be expected to grow to 2 to 3 percent (2 quads) of the national demand by 1990.

Without an active Federal role in commercialization, however, solar technologies will probably contribute substantially less to the national energy supply by 1985 or 1990 than indicated. If solar energy is indeed a desirable alternative to established energy sources and worth pursuing at this time, then a moderate Federal incentive does seem necessary to improve the economic position of marginally competive hardware and spur the growth of the industry. Without a Federal incentive, the ability of solar technologies to compete on the open market with established energy sources in a significant way is in doubt because of their relatively high initial cost.

The solar industry is not sufficiently advanced at this time to allow a simple extrapolation to future use based on the growth rate of the present market.

Therefore, any projection of future use must be based on assumptions which in time may prove to be incorrect. The major assumptions used to arrive at the projections stated above are: (1) The price of established energy sources will rise at a moderate rate, and (2) the Federal Government will institute moderate financial incentives to accelerate the widespread commercial use of solar hardware as it becomes technically and economically competitive with established energy sources. No attempt is made to consider possible scenarios whereby the Federal Government, in a more aggressive role, would either institute disincentives for the continued use of established sources or make the use of solar hardware so economically attractive that these systems would be put into use in greater numbers and at a faster rate than is presently envisioned. If the Government chooses to substantially subsidize solar hardware, or if the cost of conventional energy sources rises precipitously, then any projections based on moderate assumptions, such as those made here, should be adjusted upward.

The Present Status and Near-Term Outlook

The present use of solar energy is negligibly small, but the prospects for expanded use of certain technologies in the next few years appear good, particularly if combined with conservation measures and Federal economic incentives.

Recent studies indicate that solar space and water heating are now competitive with electric space and water heating in some regions over the lifetime operation of the system. Space cooling by solar thermal means is not as advanced and will require further development. The applications of similar technology for industrial and agricultural applications also show promise for expanded near-term use.

In certain situations the conversion of organic materials (bioconversion) into useful energy forms, or the direct combustion of such materials for their energy content, is economically more attractive than ordinary waste disposal.

Small wind energy machines are being installed in increasing numbers in situation where line power is not practical. Large machines for use by utilities are under development but not expected to be available for commercial use before the early 1980's.

Photovoltaic systems, which convert sunlight directly into electricity, are expensive now but can be cost effective in remote areas where a low-level power source is needed.

Two other solar technologies are systems which convert solar thermal energy into electricity and systems which operate power generators on the temperature difference between the surface and deep waters of the oceans—ocean thermal energy conversion. These are still in the research and development stage and are not expected to be available for commercial application for several years.

Thus, the solar hardware now on the market is either low-temperature equipment or special purpose equipment which fills a limited need: it generally is not well suited for widespread implementation at this time. Its use is restricted because of relative high cost and by its dependence on such factors as local climatic conditions, the existence of a solar market infrastructure—supply, finance, service, et cetera—and the availability of alternate energy supplies. Even with moderate Federal incentives to reduce first cost, the aggregate contribution of all solar technologies will probably not exceed the 1 percent goal set for 1985. The market infrastructure for solar products is almost nonexistent at this time. Over the next few years, possibly into the 1980's, the market for such solar products as space and water heating for residential and commercial buildings and for agricultural and industrial applications is expected to develop slowly on a regional basis as one element of the market infrastructure catches up to the next.

ENDNOTES

1 Oil-in-place is oil deposits whose existence has been discovered through exploration.

2 Natural gas liquids are hydrocarbons present in gaseous form or in solution with reservoir oil that are recoverable as liquids by condensation or absorption processes.

3 Undiscovered recoverable resources are resources estimated to be economically recoverable yet undiscovered, in favorable geological setting.

4 Proved reserves at the end of December 1975 were 38.9 billion barrels; the A.P.I. estimate of potential recoverable oil from old fields with enhanced recovery techniques is 24 billion barrels (mean); undiscovered recoverable resources of petroleum liquids are estimated by the USGS at 97.8 billion barrels—50 percent chance of discovery. Hence, total recoverable resource base is 160.7 billion barrels.

5 Prudhoe Bay field was discovered in 1968, but oil and gas reserves were first entered in AGA/API statistics in 1970 report year.

6 Cumulative production of approximately 272 TCF for 1975-90 needed to achieve gross withdrawal rates of 19.1 TCF in 1985 and 1990. Assuming a reserve/production ratio of 10:1 (current) by 1990, 463 TCF of natural gas would be required to meet projected production and maintain an R/P ratio not lower than today's. In December 1976 reserves were 216 TCF. Hence, 463−216=247 TCF would have to be found between 1977 and 1990.

7 A large or class A-type field contains more than 300 billion cubic feet of gas.

8 Coal is used in this larger sense to include anthracite, bituminous coal, subbituminous coal, and lignite. Anthracite, whose U.S. reserves constitute only 1.6 percent of the total domestic coal reserves, is often excluded from consideration in general discussions of U.S. coal. Coal is found in bedded deposits, which are much easier to measure than fluids like oil. Hence, our estimates of coal resources tend to be more accurate than those of oil and gas resources.

CHAPTER THREE

THE SOURCES OF ENERGY

ESTIMATES OF FUTURE PRODUCTION*

Oil

Introduction

The forecasts of future oil supply contained in the *Project Independence Report* were conditioned upon numerous policy assumptions and a forecasting technique with many inherent uncertainties. In the ensuing year, several events occurred in rapid succession that affected the basic assumptions and methodology and changed this year's analysis:

- The Tax Reduction Act of 1975 modified the tax and depletion situation.

- Resource estimates were revised downward substantially by the Federal Energy Administration (FEA) and the U. S. Geological Survey (USGS).

- The schedule changed for Federal leasing of Outer Continental Shelf (OCS) lands.

- The rate of development envisioned for Northern Alaska was revised upward.

- The oil and gas price controls debate led to more intensive evaluation of their effects.

The purpose of this chapter is to estimate future oil production possibilities over a range of geological assessments and under different policy assumptions. To do this, an historical perspective is established; the analytical techniques used to forecast oil supply possibilities are explained and areas of uncertainty are identified; and the implications of this analysis for future policy are discussed.

Perspective

The outlook for domestic oil supply is clouded with uncertainty. The extent and availability of domestic resources, Federal OCS leasing policy, form and duration of oil price controls, success of tertiary recovery techniques, and participation of State and local governments will determine our future production possibilities.

In recent years, significant changes have occurred in domestic crude oil production, reserves, imports, prices, and consumption. This section discusses the present oil supply situation, the events leading up to it, and the short-term supply and demand outlook.

* The National Energy Outlook, Federal Energy Administration, February 1976

The Present Situation The present oil supply situation is best characterized by the following:

- The United States now imports almost 40 percent of the oil it consumes.

- Price controls on domestic production have been in effect since 1973.

- Proved reserves have been steadily declining since 1970 (when nearly 10 billion barrels were added in North Alaska, but no oil has yet been produced).

- Domestic production levels have been decreasing since 1970, but may be beginning to fall more slowly.

- Federal leasing of OCS lands has been stepped up.

- Drilling effort for oil has been increasing since 1972, after declining for 15 years.

- Domestic oil consumption has declined from 1973 levels.

The relevant historical perspective behind these observations can be divided into two parts; the dividing point is the Arab oil embargo of 1973.

Pre-Embargo Period Three major factors shaped domestic oil supply from the Fifties to the early Seventies:

- Crude oil prices remained relatively flat (actually declining when adjusted for inflation; see Figure II-1).

- Conservation practices in major producing states held crude oil production well below full capacity until about 1970.

- A large amount of cheap foreign crude oil overshadowed the world petroleum market; its import into the United States, however, was limited severely by mandatory oil quotas.

These factors created a pre-embargo domestic oil supply situation with a number of important features:

- Oil drilling declined steadily after 1959 for two major reasons (see Figure II-2): decreased profitability of domestic production in mature producing areas (because of rising costs and flat oil prices in the face of cheap foreign oil); and the lack of access to Federal lands in frontier areas (OCS and Alaska).

- In response to decreased drilling, domestic oil reserves declined steadily after 1966 (except for North Alaskan reserves added in 1970; see Figure II-3).

Figure II-1

Average Wellhead Price of U.S. Crude

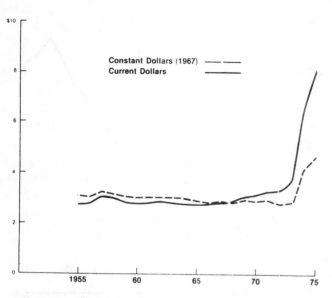

Constant Dollars (1967) ———
Current Dollars ———

Source U.S. Bureau of Mines, U.S. Bureau of Labor Statistics, American Petroleum Institute and Federal Energy Administration

Figure 11-2

Oil Drilling Trends

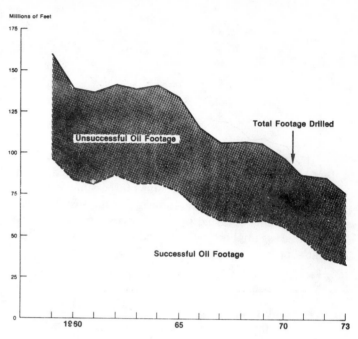

Millions of Feet

Unsuccessful Oil Footage

Total Footage Drilled

Successful Oil Footage

Source : American Petroleum Institute.

Figure II-3

U.S. Proved Reserves of Crude Oil

(Billions of Barrels)

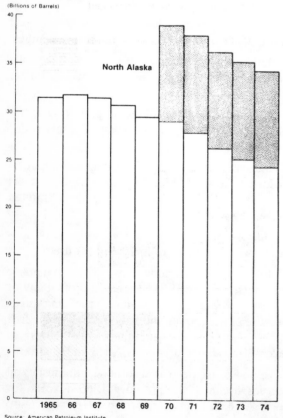

North Alaska

Source American Petroleum Institute.

- Until 1970, production increased, at which point full capacity was reached. After the 1970 peak, domestic production began to follow reserves downward (see Figure II-4).

- Meanwhile, domestic oil consumption increased steadily in the face of this production trend, reaching a pre-embargo peak in 1973 of over 17 million barrels per day (MMB/D) (see Figure II-5).

- In turn, the widening gap between domestic oil consumption and domestic production was filled with increasing quantities of cheap oil imports (see Figure II-6).

- These growing U. S. imports soon caused Western Hemisphere sources to reach their production capacities. Afterwards, the importance of the Western Hemisphere began to decline as an increasing percentage of imports came from the Eastern Hemisphere (see Figure II-7).

- Finally, the makeup of the imports shifted from crude to products, as a by-product of import quota exemptions, environmental requirements for low sulfur fuel oil, and various incentives imbedded in price controls (see Figure II-8).

Post-Embargo Period   The changes in the oil supply situation caused by the 1973 Arab oil embargo cannot be overemphasized. They have caused a rethinking, at a high national priority, of the entire domestic energy situation.

Figure III-4

U.S. Crude Oil Production

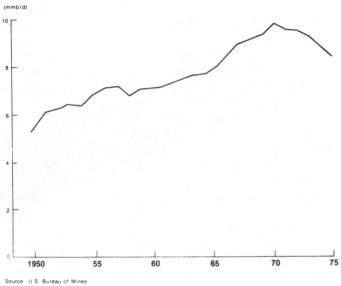

Source: U S Bureau of Mines.

Figure II-5

U.S. Petroleum Products Consumption

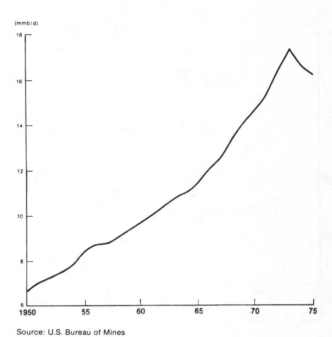

Source: U.S. Bureau of Mines

Figure II-6

U.S. Oil Consumption By Source

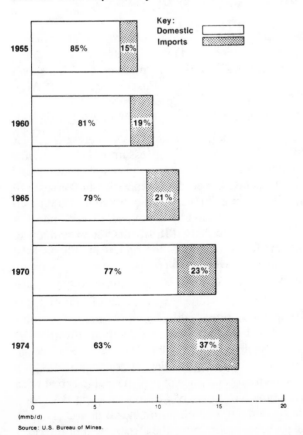

Source: U.S. Bureau of Mines.

Figure II-7

Total U.S. Petroleum Imports by Regional and Organizational Sources

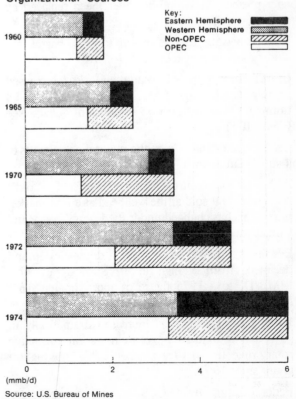

Source: U.S. Bureau of Mines

Figure II-8

Petroleum Imports

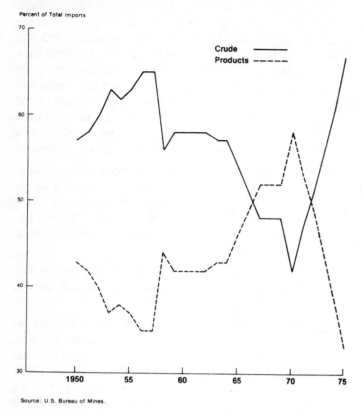

Source: U.S. Bureau of Mines.

After 1973, the three major pre-embargo factors were no longer present; they had, however, been replaced by others:

- Imports became expensive—up to $12 a barrel, excluding any import fees.

- In response, domestic crude oil prices increased sharply, on average from around $3 to over $8 nominally and to nearly $5 in constant dollars (see Figure II-1).

These two factors have been the major determinants of the oil supply situation in 1974 and 1975:

- Although price controls remained in effect for "old" oil, "new" oil sold at the wellhead at a free market price. This has changed under the Energy Policy and Conservation Act (EPCA).

- For the first time in recent history, domestic demand declined, from a high in 1973 of about 17.3 MMB/D, to a 1975 figure of approximately 16.2 MMB/D (see Figure II-5).

- Drilling activities for oil increased dramatically in 1974 and again in 1975. As an indication, the active rotary rig count in 1975 reached 1,877, the highest count since 1962.

- Federal leasing on the OCS stepped up markedly.

- Higher prices stimulated consideration of tertiary processes to increase crude oil recovery.

- Domestic crude oil production began to slow its decline in 1975.

Effects of the Energy Policy and Conservation Act of 1975   The short-term outlook for supply and demand for crude oil in the United States is in transition, due to changes of oil price controls required by the EPCA. The precise course of near-term consumption and production is uncertain, because the effects will be closely related to final implementation of the legislation. EPCA's possible effects, however, cannot be ignored. Domestic consumption will increase in the short term regardless of the EPCA as the economy recovers. However, the lowering of crude oil prices under EPCA will increase demand even further. Because production will remain relatively level in the next two years, imports would have reached 8.0 MMB/D in this period had several conservation measures not been in effect. The impact of these measures will be to reduce expected imports to between 6.0 and 7.0 MMB/D in 1977-1978. Uncertainties remain with respect to inclusion of Alaskan production in the calculation of the average price, the future levels of the production incentive factor, and the final effect of the program on petroleum industry decision-making.

Business-As-Usual Supply Outlook

The future oil supply outlook is estimated for a range of geological assessments and under different policy assumptions. This range of outlooks is indicated by three supply forecasts, entitled: *Pessimistic, Business-as-Usual* (BAU), and *Optimistic*. These represent three points on a spectrum of potential future oil supply levels.

Equally important, these forecasts represent supply "possibilities," in light of the assumptions underlying each outlook and different import prices of crude oil and its coproducts (associated-dissolved gas and natural gas liquids). These "possibilities" are converted into an estimate of actual production by the overall Project Independence Evaluation System (PIES), after consideration of the demand for crude and its coproducts as well as of the major costs incurred to convert crude to products useful to energy consumers (e.g., transportation, refining, distribution, etc.).

Among these three outlooks, the forecast resulting from the BAU Outlook is the central one. From an oil supply perspective, this outlook reflects the U. S. Geological Survey (USGS) geological assessment which it believes has a 50-50 chance of proving-out in actual practice over time.[1] In terms of assumptions, the BAU outlook is moderately optimistic in several areas: (1) OCS leasing proceeds according to the Department of Interior's announced leasing schedule; (2) tertiary oil recovery methods prove successful technically and economically and are applied at a moderately optimistic pace; (3) oil and gas deregulation occurs over the next few years; and (4) the present provisions of the Federal tax code which affect crude oil economics remain unchanged.

Oil supply estimates are made primarily on the basis of a set of assumptions which are considered most likely. The assumptions that make up the BAU supply possibility outlook are summarized in Table II-1. These assumptions and the uncertainty surrounding them are discussed in subsequent sections of this chapter.

The Optimistic and Pessimistic outlooks differ from BAU with respect to level of geological success, the rate of leasing offshore, the degree of success and pace of application of tertiary oil recovery, and the fate of the investment tax credit. The specific assumptions underlying each supply outlook are detailed in a later section.

Within the overall PIES, these oil supply outlooks become building blocks of a variety of comprehensive energy scenarios. The connections between PIES *scenarios* and BAU oil *supply possibilities* are shown in Table II-2 (the other two oil supply outlooks are also reconciled with PIES scenarios).

Two of these energy scenarios (Regulatory and Supply Pessimism) reflect price regulation. These price regulation scenarios illustrate the way PIES converts supply possibilities into an estimate of actual future oil production. For scenarios which envision price regulation, PIES excludes from the production estimate the supply possibilities which are not economically viable at the regulated oil price.

Business-as-Usual Supply Possibilities[2] Under any one oil supply outlook—for example, BAU—future oil supply possibilities vary over time between geographical areas, between the portion of the overall resource base from which they may be withdrawn (e.g., newly dis-

covered fields versus known fields), and between the mix of recovery technology employed (e.g., primary, secondary and tertiary methods). Along each of these dimensions the quantities in any future year also vary with the prices of crude and coproducts that the producing industry expects will prevail. At $13 and under BAU conditions, a number of important observations emerge concerning the make-up of future oil supply possibilities (see Table II-3 which shows the BAU supply possibilities estimated to be available if the industry expects $13 per barrel import prices [in constant 1975 dollars] and identical prices, on a BTU-equivalent basis, for the crude and its coproducts):

- The main source of today's domestic crude production—lower-48 onshore initial reserves—will shrink by two-thirds by 1985 and by 80 percent by 1989. Before crude production on the lower-48 can expand, the withdrawals which account for this decline must be replaced.

- Sufficient new lower-48 onshore production can become available to approximately sustain today's production rate through 1985.

Through 1980, withdrawals from today's proved reserves will be replaced mainly by fluid injection projects, extensions, and revisions applicable to known fields (labeled Old Field Secondary in Table II-3). By 1985, however, new fields, and more elaborate tertiary recovery technology must replace the further decline in production from existing onshore reserves. This replacement is estimated to occur as follows: 40 percent from new fields, 40 percent from technically straightforward expansion of the production capacity of known fields and 20 percent from tertiary recovery. After 1985, production from new fields and tertiary recovery must accelerate in order to counter the dwindling potential of primary recovery methods in old fields.

Since the lower-48 onshore can just offset further decline at $13 and under BAU conditions, growth in total

---

Table II-1

BUSINESS-AS-USUAL SUPPLY OUTLOOK ASSUMPTIONS

Resource Estimates	USGS Statistical Mean.
OCS Leasing (1975-1984)	26.8 million acres.
Investment Tax Credit	10% through 1977; 7% thereafter.
Alaskan pipeline capacity	2.0 MMB/D in 1980; 2.5 MMB/D in 1985.
Price Controls	Removed within a few years.
Tertiary Recovery	Tertiary methods prove out, but are applied at a moderate pace.

Table II-2

OIL SUPPLY OUTLOOKS AND PIES ENERGY SCENARIOS

Energy Scenario	Pessimistic	BAU	Optimistic
Accelerated			X
Reference		X	
Conservation		X	
Regional Limitation		X	
Regulatory		X	
Electrification		X	
Supply Pessimism	X		

domestic oil supply at $13 must come from less mature provinces. Two areas, the lower-48 OCS and Alaska (onshore and offshore), are expected to provide growth. Of the two, Alaska has the greater potential.

- In 1985 under BAU assumptions, potential Alaskan crude production is estimated to equal 3.1 MMB/D, or about one-fourth of total domestic production (see Table II-3).

- Of this, at least 1.6 MMB/D—from reserves already proven at Prudhoe Bay—is reasonably well assured. The balance—0.8 MMB/D from the Beaufort Sea and other areas on the Alaskan OCS plus 0.7 MMB/D from other North Slope regions—depends upon reasonable geological fortune, new technology, and substantial institutional effort.

Without more accelerated effort in Alaska and successful results from additional oil search, continued withdrawal of today's proved reserves on the North Slope will cause Alaskan production to decline slightly between 1985 and 1989. One Alaskan area likely to provide growth in response to accelerated effort is NPR-4, whose development is excluded from the BAU Outlook (but is included in the Optimistic Outlook). In Alaska, the areas next in importance are on the Alaskan OCS, especially the Gulf of Alaska and the Beaufort Sea.

The lower-48 OCS is the second most important area for expanding domestic production.

- Assuming that the BAU leasing schedule is achieved and the geological potential of the OCS has been assessed correctly, lower-48 OCS production can almost double by 1985. If so, this area will account for 16 percent of total crude production that year (see Table II-3).

- Similar to onshore, OCS production growth must follow after replacement of withdrawals from today's OCS reserves—principally in the Gulf of Mexico. For example, the net increase of 0.4 MMB/D in the Gulf of Mexico by 1985 requires gross additions of productive capacity of 1.1 MMB/D.

- By 1985 the balance of the lower-48 OCS increase— 0.5MMB/D— should come from the Atlantic and Pacific.

As will be emphasized later, the assumed rate of leasing limits the lower 48 OCS production estimate over the period of the BAU Outlook. Consequently, an inadequate leasing rate can cause a decline in lower-48 OCS production after 1985.

The balance of any increase in crude production is envisioned to stem from NPR-1 and heavy hydrocarbons. Both make an important contribution to future supply, but certainly one that should be dwarfed by Alaska, the lower-48 OCS and even by replacement of today's productive capacity on the lower-48 onshore.

Finally, the balance of total conventional petroleum liquids available domestically is expected to consist of coproducts of crude production (liquid derivatives of associated-dissolved gas) and of non-associated gas. These additional liquids—NGL's—are expected to account for about 12 percent of total production (see Table II-3).

Effects of Price on BAU Supply   The overall level of BAU oil supply possibilities changes substantially if price expectations are higher or lower than $13 (see Table II-4). This change is the result of different price effects in various geographical areas, different components of the resource base, the rate of drilling and changes between alternative oil recovery methods.

Table II-3

BAU OIL PRODUCTION POSSIBILITIES AT $13*
(MMB/D)

	1975	1980	1985	1989
Lower-48 Onshore				
New Field Primary/Secondary	--	0.8	1.9	2.2
Old Field Secondary	--	2.0	2.0	1.8
Tertiary	--	0.5	1.0	1.3
Initial Reserves	7.0	4.2	2.4	1.5
Subtotal	7.0	7.5	7.3	6.8
Lower-48 OCS				
Pacific	0.2	0.6	0.6	0.5
Gulf of Mexico	1.0	1.4	1.4	1.1
Atlantic	--	0.1	0.1	0.1
Subtotal	1.2	2.1	2.1	1.7
Alaska				
Beaufort Sea	--	--	0.4	0.8
Other OCS	0.2	0.3	0.4	0.4
North Slope	--	1.7	2.3	1.7
NPR-4	--	--	--	--
Subtotal	0.2	2.0	3.1	2.9
Other				
NPR-1	--	0.2	0.2	0.2
Tar Sands	--	--	--	--
Heavy Hydrocarbons	--	0.1	0.2	0.3
Subtotal	--	0.3	0.4	0.5
Total Crude	8.4	11.9	12.9	11.9
Natural Gas Liquids (NGL)**	1.6	1.9	1.8	1.8
Total Liquids	10.0	13.8	14.7	13.7

---

* Throughout this chapter, domestic production is presented as a supply possibility at a given equivalent imported oil price. For the actual solutions from the main PIES supply and demand model, which may be different from the supply possibilities at that price, see Chapter I.

** Excludes NGL's produced at refineries.

Table II-4

1985 BAU OIL PRODUCTION AT ALTERNATIVE IMPORT PRICES (MMB/D)

Source	Expected Oil Price		
	$8	$13	$16
Lower-48, Onshore	4.4	7.3	7.7
Lower-48, OCS	1.9	2.1	2.3
Subtotal	6.3	9.4	10.0
Alaska	2.3	3.1	3.1
Other	0.4	0.4	0.6
Total Crude	9.0	12.9	13.7
NGL's	1.1	1.8	2.4
Total Liquids	10.1	14.7	16.1

In 1985, several things concerning the potential response of oil supply to price are important to note (see Figure II-9):

- Between $8 and $13, the estimated crude supply response is large—4.0 MMB/D by 1985.

- Through 1980, however, time lags are estimated to make the response smaller (1.6 MMB/D). By 1985 major time delays should be resolved; thereafter continuing decline in the quality of resources found causes the difference between $8 and $13 to grow further (to 5.3 MMB/D in 1989).

The largest share (75 percent) of the 4.0 MMB/D growth in response to price by 1985 occurs onshore in the lower-48. In these onshore areas, the supply response from $8 to $13 stems from new fields and from more sophisticated tertiary recovery methods.

- The 2.9 MMB/D price response onshore in the lower-48 is made up of 2.0 MMB/D from new fields, primary and secondary, and 1.0 MMB/D from tertiary recovery.

- This indicates that replacing today's productive capacity in the lower-48 states—by 1985 and to an even greater extent beyond 1985—depends on the more expensive components of potential future supply.

The next most important contributions to the supply response between $8 and $13 are Alaska (20 percent) and the lower-48 OCS (5 percent).

The components of future supply which are price insensitive by 1985 need careful interpretation.

- The assumed rate of leasing constrains the estimate from the lower 48 OCS through 1985 (and, generally, through 1989 also).

- This suggests that the result of less leasing is a greater reliance on higher-priced foreign supply sources in lieu of lower cost domestic resources offshore.

- In the case of tertiary recovery, price insensitivity above $12 is a function of the pace of technical development as well as the rate of application of new technology in the field. This conservation represents a judgment in response to the speculative nature of tertiary recovery technology.

- In the case of Alaska, the mild price response reflects the joint effects of leasing rates and pipeline capacity constraints. The supply response in later years, however, could be greater.

There are also two other implications of constraints other than price. First, careful scrutiny is needed to insure that an unrealistically conservative estimating bias does not exist. The other is that relieving supply bottlenecks—of both a physical and institutional nature—may become a

Figure II-9

Crude Oil Production at Three Prices (BAU)

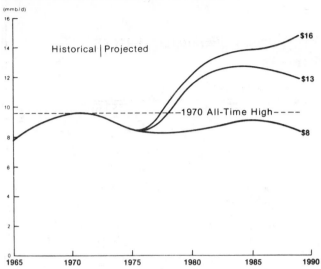

These proved reserves of crude oil represent the most definitive source for future production, but as they are drawn down by production, the reserve pool must be supplemented by other categories of resources in order for production not to continually decline. It is proving these other resource categories that will supply future production.

Indicated reserves are those reserves as yet unproven but believed recoverable from known fields using known fluid injection techniques. According to the USGS Circular 725, they amount to 4.7 billion barrels. Inferred reserves are those inferred from demonstrated reserves (measured plus indicated) and are, therefore, more speculative. Circular 725 has inferred reserves amounting to 23 billion barrels. These additions are due to extensions, revisions, and new horizons within the defined limit of an oil field.

The USGS also reports assessments of undiscovered recoverable resources based on historical and geological data. To emphasize the uncertainty involved with these assessments, they are reported not as point estimates, but rather as a range of quantitites and probabilities. The statistical mean of the range of quantities is USGS's estimated point where there is a 50-50 chance of the actual amount being above or below that quantity. The 95 percent point is the USGS estimate that there is a 95 percent chance that there is *at least* this amount, and the 5 percent point is where there is only a 5 percent change that there is *at least* this amount. As an example of this technique, the USGS estimate for economically recoverable oil resources in the United States has a statistical mean of 89 billion barrels, a 95 percent point of 50 billion barrels, and a 5 percent point of 127 billion barrels (see Table II-5).

Crucial to the modeling effort for projecting future oil production is the capability of the model to 'capture' this entire range of the resource base. The USGS, in Circular 725, delineates the resource base into the various categories (see Figure II-10).

The FEA oil supply model performs six production calculations for each expected price in each region during each year. These six 'types' of production correspond to these resource categories into which the domestic resource base is divided by the USGS. The labels the model uses to designate production from each of these categories is also shown in Figure II-10.

Several observations emerge regarding reserve and resource assessments (see Table II-5):

• Using the USGS 'statistical mean' for undiscovered resources, 151 billion barrels of 'undiscovered' and 'identified' (demonstrated plus inferred) resources remain economically recoverable. Another 197 billion barrels potential (classified as sub-economic) might ultimately become recoverable at prices

more important and cost-effective policy as prices rise to very high levels.

Reserves and Resources   A crucial assumption underlying the analysis of oil production estimates is the assessment of the resources, both discovered and undiscovered, from which production must ultimately come. The resources assessments fall into three categories: proved reserves, indicated and inferred reserves, and undiscovered recoverable resources. Each of these categories will be discussed, followed by a description of their use in the FEA oil supply model.

Past estimates of U.S. petroleum reserves have been characterized by a high degree of uncertainty resulting in a broad range of estimates, none of which could be considered definitive. Recognizing that a key element in formulating a national energy policy is the development of a reliable estimate of remaining domestic crude oil and natural gas reserves, the Federal Energy Administration Act of 1974 required FEA to prepare a "...complete and independent analysis of actual oil and gas reserves and resources in the United States and its Outer Continental Shelf..." The FEA report on reserves was submitted to the Congress in October, 1975. The FEA survey of reserves estimated that proved oil reserves were 38 billion barrels, with most of the potential contained in Texas, Alaska, California, and Louisiana.

This contrasts with an assessment by the USGS which, using data supplied by the American Petroleum Institute (API), estimated United States crude oil reserves at 34 billion barrels. Even though proved reserves is the category of resources about which the most is known, some differences still exist between the two estimates, which is even further magnified in trying to assess correctly the entire resource base.

Table II-5

USGS-725: RESERVES AND UNDISCOVERED RESOURCES
(Billions of Barrels)

Region	Reserves Demonstrated Measured	Reserves Demonstrated Indicated	Inferred	Resources Undiscovered Recoverable Statistical Mean	Resources Undiscovered Recoverable 95%-5% Range
Economic Resources*					
Lower-48 onshore	21.1	4.3	14.2	44	29-64
Lower-48 offshore	3.1	0.4	2.6	18**	11-28
Alaska offshore	0.2	0	0.1	15	3-31
Alaska onshore	9.9	negligible	6.1	12	6-19
Subtotal-Economic	34.3	4.7	23.0	89	50-127
Sub-Economic	120	negligible	20	57	44-111

* Economic at pre-embargo prices.
** Adjusted for resources at water depths greater than 200 meters.

above pre-embargo levels with new technology and time. Both amounts compare to cumulative domestic oil production to date of about 105 billion barrels.

- Of these potential resources, the indicated and inferred portion (which are considered to be more nearly assured) are large. Ultimately, 80 percent of the withdrawals from today's proved or 'measured' reserves might be replaced from these two categories.

- The uncertainty associated with undiscovered recoverable resources is large (indicated by the wide spread of the 95 to 5 percent range). The quantity represented by this range amounts to plus or minus more than 40 percent of the 89 billion barrels which have a 50-50 chance of being discovered and recovered. As will be shown later, this resource uncertainty causes future production estimates to be equally uncertain.

- Over half of the 89 billion barrels of the statistical mean of undiscovered recoverable resources reside in immature regions with little or no production or

cost history (Alaska and offshore). This fact further increases the uncertainty of oil supply projections.

- Finally, the quantity of resources which the USGS considers 'sub-economic' at pre-embargo prices is very large—197 billion barrels. Higher prices, new technology and time may make a substantial portion of this resource attractive for production. This fact, too, significantly complicates the problem of estimating future oil supplies, especially at prices substantially above pre-embargo levels.

The adequacy of the resource base to provide projected reserve levels is illustrated by the quantities of resources that must be proved as reserves to achieve the BAU forecasts at different prices during the 15-year time span of the projections (see Table II-6). The quantities are derived from results of the oil supply model. Several points concerning the adequacy of the resource base to provide projected reserve levels are important:

- In order to capture the production from inferred reserves, the 'secondary recovery from old fields' production category has been expanded to include all production from the economic portions of both indi-

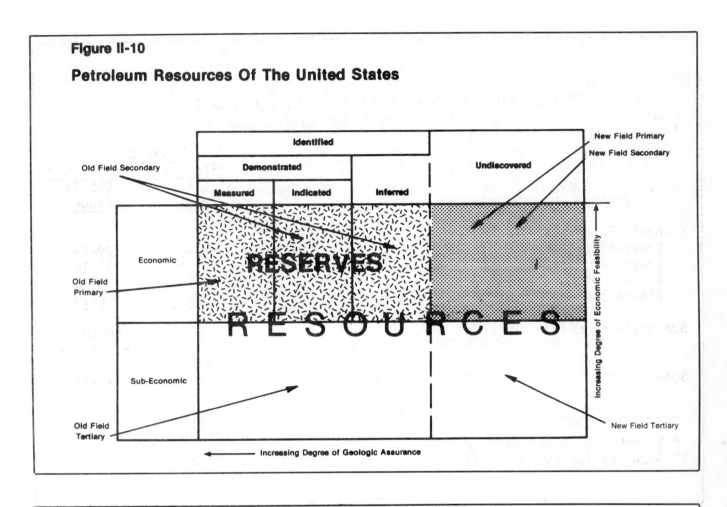

Figure II-10

Petroleum Resources Of The United States

Table II-6

BAU PROVED RESERVES ADDED, 1975-1989
(Billions of Barrels)

	USGS-725 Mean	Expected Oil Price					
		$8		$13		$16	
		Bbl.	%	Bbl.	%	Bbl.	%
USGS "Economic"							
New Field Primary and Secondary	73.6*	10.8	14	26.7	35	32.0	43
Old Field Secondary	21.5	14.4	67	14.4	67	14.4	67
Sub-total	98.1	27.2	28%	41.1	42%	46.4	47%
USGS "sub-economic"							
New Field Tertiary	57.0	0.0		0.3		0.7	
Old Field Tertiary	120.0	0.6		7.5		10.2	
Sub-total	177.0	0.6		7.8		10.9	
Total	275.1	27.8		48.9		57.3	

---

* Alaska onshore and Beaufort Sea excluded. Lower-48 OCS adjusted for resources at water depths greater than 200 meters.

cated and inferred reserves. This includes primary production from inferred reserves. Tertiary production from old fields is considered sub-economic at pre-embargo prices, and stems from the sub-economic reserve category.

- At $13, about 55 percent of the total of 48.9 billion barrels of reserves added is through primary and secondary development of new fields (discovered subsequent to 1/1/75).

- A little less than a third more comes from secondary development of old fields (the definition of which has been enlarged to include inferred reserves).

- The final sixth of the reserves added is due to development of tertiary recovery processes, which were sub-economic at pre-embargo prices.

- Even at $16, less than half of the economically recoverable resources available are proved as reserves, which is only about 21 percent of the total resources available (both economic and sub-economic).

- Tertiary reserves, which are derived from a resource category of potentially enormous size (177 billion barrels), has reached only a very low level by 1989 (10.9 billion barrels).

The results of the fifteen year projections depend upon the resource base assumptions and also on the effort required to convert resources into reserves and subsequently to produce them.

OCS Leasing   During 1974, 1.8 million acres of OCS lands were leased, or about 26 percent of the total of 6.8 million acres leased between 1964 and 1974. The assumed Business-as-Usual OCS leasing will amount to 34.4 million acres between 1975 and 1989 (see Table II-7).

The schedules were based on assumptions concerning lease sales and the attractiveness of the areas offered to the industry. These assumptions include:

- There will be six sales per year through 1990.

- 800,000 acres will be offered in each sale.

- The percentage of acres leased of those offered in each sale will be:

  - 1976 and 1977   75%
  - 1978 through 1982   55%
  - 1982 through 1989   35%

The rationale for the higher percentage leased figure in the early years is based on the fact that the early nominations of acreage will be those with the most attractive structures.

Table II-7

BUSINESS-AS-USUAL LEASING
(Millions of Acres)

Period	Total MM Acres	% of Total	Alaska* MM Acres	California MM Acres	Gulf of Mexico MM Acres	Atlantic MM Acres
1975-79	15.8	46	4.5	3.1	4.1	4.2
1980-84	11.0	32	2.6	0.9	4.6	2.9
1985-89	7.6	22	2.0	0.6	2.8	2.2
Total	34.4	100	9.1	4.6	11.5	9.3
Percent of total			26%	13%	33%	27%

* Excludes Beaufort Sea

Several points are important:

- The percentage of acreage leased assumption leads to nearly half of the acreage to be leased in the first five years.

- The acreage leased in the 15-year period is divided almost equally between mature and frontier areas, i.e., 46 percent in California and the Gulf of Mexico, and 54 percent in Alaska and Atlantic areas.

- The lead time between acres leased and production is long; consequently the effects of the increased leasing in the early years is not felt until much later.

- The number of sales per year and percentage of acres leased may be optimistic in light of recent experience.

Drilling Capacity   Annual drilling rates respond to many factors, including:

- Industry expectations of oil price and its translation into demand for drilling equipment.

- Present supply of drilling rigs and their expected usage over time.

- Current rig manufacturing capability.

- Capability of the rig-producing industry to expand capacity over time.

Several points concerning the BAU drilling profiles, are important.

- Drilling at $8 oil prices will be much lower than at higher prices since little onshore oil from new fields is economic at $8 (see Figure II-11). The bulk of the drilling in the first 5-year period (1975-1979) is utilization of existing rigs, and in the latter years, drilling is exclusively off-shore.

- The large jump in drilling between $8 and $13 reflects the fact that the lower-48 onshore regions have a large amount of undiscovered oil that is economic only at prices above $8.

- In the preceding 15-year period (1959-1973), drilling activities for oil declined steadily from over 150 million feet to a low of 75 million feet per year. The $13 drilling trajectory reverses that decline and peaks in 1985 at nearly 160 million feet. Drilling activities for oil at $13 in the period 1975 to 1989 are expected to average about 120 million feet per year, compared to a yearly average in the preceding 15 years of about 108 million feet.

Figure II-11

Drilling Activities for Oil (BAU)

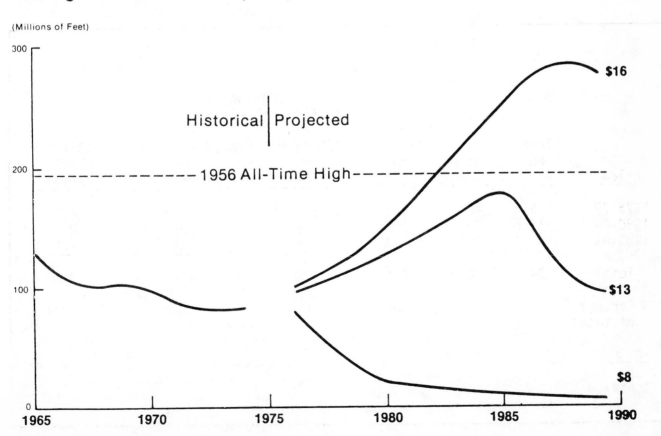

(Millions of Feet)

- At an expected oil price of $16, drilling is constrained early by rig availability. The greatest production response at $16 occurs later in the forecast as $13 opportunities decline.

Enhanced Recovery   Any discussion of enhanced oil recovery first requires a clarification of the terms involved, due to the current differences regarding definitions. For the purpose of this report the following apply:

Secondary Recovery:	Waterflooding and non-miscible gas injection, including pressure maintenance
Tertiary Recovery:	All thermal techniques, including:

- Cyclic steam injection (steam soak, huff & puff)
- In Situ combustion
- Steam drives

Improved water or gas drives

- Surfactant (miceller slug, caustic, etc.)
- Miscible (carbon dioxide, high pressure gas, etc.)
- Polymer

Enhanced recovery projects generally are initiated while the field is still producing under primary drive. Thus, while approximately 50 percent of U.S. production, or 4.25 MMB/D, is currently being produced from fields under enhanced recovery, only about 25 percent (slightly over 2 MMB/D) is attributable incrementally to the enhanced recovery projects. In the FEA forecasts, only the incremental amount of oil produced from a field under enhanced recovery is that directly attributable to the technique.

Several observations emerge:

- Enhanced recovery production rises to approximately 26 to 30 percent of total crude production—a slight increase over the present 25 percent (see Table II-8).

- The bulk of enhanced recovery production remains secondary methods; these are generally feasible in old fields at prices below the $8 level.

- Tertiary methods show a large price response between $8 and $13. Above $13, tertiary production in 1985 is constrained by lags in research, planning and commercialization, not prices.

Increased tertiary production is expected to be largely the result of steam or CO_2 injection which, of all the tertiary techniques, are best understood and provide the fastest response. This outlook, however, remains specula-

tive due to the dearth of data and the range of theories concerning tertiary recovery potential.

Available data suggest that near-term production rates (1980) from tertiary recovery cannot be increased by increasing the expected oil price (see Table II-9). The reason for short-term production constraints is that tertiary recovery is essentially in the research and planning stage as a commercial recovery technique.

Several years must be spent in screening prospective fields, designing displacement mechanisms, customizing chemicals, conducting pilot projects, lining up equipment, materials, and trained manpower. Thereafter, a delay of one to four years will occur while the recovery agent works its way through the reservoir, displacing the oil toward the producing wells. This short term delay, however, does not mean that higher prices are unproductive with regard to tertiary technology. A higher price immediately will accelerate the overall rate of tertiary recovery applications so that more sophisticated tertiary projects will yield production by 1985, rather than in some later period.

North Alaskan Development   In mid-1975, Alaskan crude production averaged 190 thousand barrels per day. This production occurred almost entirely within state waters offshore in South Alaska.

Under the BAU Outlook and with $13 import prices,[3] Alaskan crude production possibilities reach 3.1 MMB/D by 1985—a sixteen-fold increase in ten years (see Table II-3). Of these, 2.7 MMB/D depend upon North Alaskan development, principally in and around the Prudhoe Bay area of the North Slope. Major producing areas expected in North Alaska and the route of the Trans Alaska Pipeline System (TAPS) are shown in Figure II-12.

These North Alaskan supply possibilities account for about 21 percent of total potential domestic BAU crude production in 1985. Without further effort, however, fully exploiting these possibilities by 1985 would lead by 1989 to a production decline of 0.6 MMB/D in North Alaska. This factor—coupled with the economics of North Alaskan oil and gas logistics—complicate the Alaskan outlook, and require the careful evaluation of the reserve development potential and the difficult transportation problems.

Onshore Alaska oil production possibilities—as well as those from the Beaufort Sea—are estimated outside of the FEA model through field-by-field engineering assessments. (This methodology, however, produces economically comparable results plus more geographical detail.)

Of the 27 billion barrels of undiscovered, recoverable resources estimated by the USGS to exist onshore and offshore in Alaska, the overwhelming share of the potential stems from northern Alaska (see Table II-5). At $13, the BAU outlook envisions that North Alaskan develop-

Table II-8

1985 BAU PRODUCTION FROM ENHANCED RECOVERY AT ALTERNATIVE OIL PRICES
(MMB/D)

Type Recovery	Crude Oil Price		
	$8	$13	$16
Secondary			
Old fields*	2.2	2.2	2.2
New fields	0.4	0.4	0.4
Subtotal	2.6	2.6	2.6
Tertiary			
Old fields	0.1	0.9	0.9
New fields	negligible	negligible	negligible
Subtotal	0.1	1.0	1.0
Total Enhanced	2.7	3.6	3.6
Total Crude Production	9.0	12.9	13.7
% Enhanced of Total	30%	28%	26%

———————————

* Also contains production from inferred reserves.

Table II-9

POTENTIAL TERTIARY RESERVE ADDITIONS AND PRODUCTION

Marginal Oil Price	Incremental Reserves Added (Billions of Barrels)	Total Tertiary Production (MMB/D)		
		1980	1985	1989
$ 8	0.6	0.1	0.1	0.1
10	3.4	0.4	0.6	0.5
12	3.9	0.4	0.9	1.3
14	3.1	0.4	0.9	1.9

Figure 11-12
North Alaska Production Areas

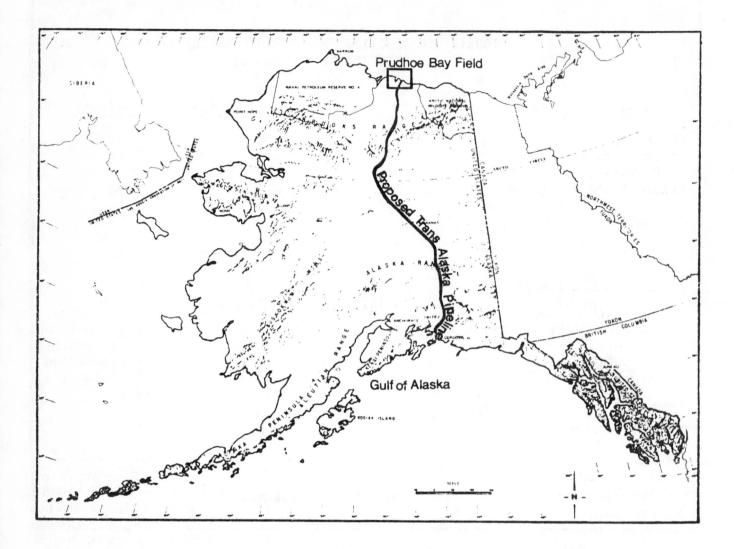

ment will convert approximately 50 percent of this resource potential into proved reserves by 1989.

In turn, about 9.6 billion barrels in the Prudhoe Bay field is well-assured with respect to its actual existence and to its economic viability. The confidence associated with the balance of the reserves envisioned under BAU contrasts sharply with the Prudhoe Bay Field (see Table II-10). The majority of the remainder (Other North Slope Private) is discovered, but its extent—and, consequently, the ultimate volume of reserves forthcoming—is only partially delineated. In turn, its performance under production (especially the producing rate of each well, to which economics in north Alaska are critically sensitive) mainly is assumed by analogy with Prudhoe Bay. Consequently, its economics tend to be speculative.

The final portion (the Beaufort Sea) underlies waters not yet leased. Accordingly, not only is its existence

geologically uncertain and its economic performance in question, but its accessibility is speculative.

Production possibilities in North Alaska depend upon the amount of reserves available at various minimum acceptable import prices for crude and its coproducts. The economics of north Alaska logistics, however, generally will control the rate at which production *possibilities* are translated over time into *actual* production.

Pipeline capacity to serve North Alaska oil fields must be bought in large increments, each of which represents a large capital expenditure. For example, TAPS (2.0 MMB/D of pipeline capacity) is expected to cost about $6 billion in 1975 dollars. A two-step looping program—that is, adding loops to increase the flow in uphill segments to expand TAPS to 3.0 MMB/D —would require an additional $3 billion. Additional capacity would necessitate a

Table II-10

POSSIBLE NORTH ALASKA RESERVES AT $13
(Billions of Barrels)

Area	Reserves** Expected	Status Discovered	Delineated	Developed
Prudhoe Bay	9.6	Yes	Yes	10%
Other North Slope	3.2	Yes	Partially	No
Private*				
Beaufort Sea	2.3	Not Leased	No	No
Subtotal: BAU	15.1			
NPR-4***	4.0	No	No	No

  * Consists of four fields: Gwndyr Bay, North Prudhoe, Kuparuk, and Lisburne.
 ** Higher prices and technology could increase this amount by about 2.4 billion
    barrels. Of this, half is estimated to be too expensive at $13; it consists
    of undiscovered oil around Kavik and a heavy hydrocarbon deposit overlaying
    the Prudhoe Bay Field. The balance is technically infeasible, awaiting the
    capacity to drill in waters deeper than 20 feet in the Beaufort Sea.
*** NPR-4 which is included only under the Optimistic Outlook, is also
    illustrated here.

second pipeline, perhaps, at an additional $6 billion, or more, depending on its route.

Normally, outlays for pipeline capacity are planned to be recovered over an operating life of no less than 10 years; a 15-year life, however, is more typical. Consequently, the reserves to keep full existing planned capacity (2.0 MMB/D) as well as to sustain the incremental capacity (0.5 MMB/D) for a minimum of 10 years must be reasonably well in hand in order to promote consideration of looping TAPS.

The key features for North Alaskan development and likely evolution of TAPS' capacity under the BAU Outlook are as follows:

- Expansion of TAPS under the BAU Outlook (and in turn, the actual crude production to be expected from Alaska in the 1980's) depends on the Beaufort Sea (see Figure II-13).

- Even if the Beaufort Sea proves prolific, and is exploited according to the moderately optimistic schedule envisioned under BAU, north Alaska production barely can fill a 2.5 MMB/D TAPS for the minimum 10-year economic life of the first loop.

- Any looping of TAPS above 2.5 MMB/D (and, perhaps even occupying fully its 2.5 or 2.0 MMB/D capacity) depends on greater geological fortune from the already discovered fields as well as on substantial new findings to add production during the post-1985 period. Potential sources of additional north Alaska production possibilities, such as NPR-4, are discussed further under the Optimistic Outlook.

- Maintaining the flow through a looped TAPS after 1985 is particularly dependent upon production from new findings. New findings must occur soon, because construction lead times generally require that the looping decision be made within the next three to four years.

Since construction of TAPS was initiated in 1973, the pace of development at the Prudoe Bay field in North Alaska has accelerated dramatically. To complete the development of Prudhoe and to further attain the BAU outlook, the current pace must quicken substantially.

Several things concerning the BAU development effort in North Alaska are important to note:

Figure II-13

North Alaska Crude Production (BAU)

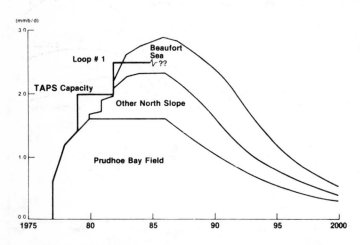

- First, the effort requires substantially faster drilling than experienced through 1975. Developmental drilling from 1975 through 1989 (about 1,765 wells) must be more than 20 times larger than has been accomplished to date (75 wells).

- Three sizeable pipeline projects must be substantially completed by 1982 (a Beaufort Sea link to TAPS, a gas pipeline, and the first TAPS loop; see Figure II-14).

- The development capacity—ignoring the effects of new discoveries—is both front-end loaded and highly peaked. That is, development drilling will increase rapidly until 1983 and will quickly decline thereafter (see Figure II-14).

The major observation with respect to North Alaskan development is that the BAU oil supply outlook is far from the status quo. The results expected from the outlook require an expeditious mobilization of effort, encompassing institutional steps such as leasing and substantial money and 'bricks and mortar.'

Development of Alaska beyond the BAU outlook will require more than large capital investments, geological success, and extensive drilling and logistics; it could also involve large-scale construction and influx of population in many sensitive areas. Any Alaskan development will need careful consideration of attendant environmental and socioeconomic impacts. Such consideration implies a high degree of cooperative effort among Federal, State and local officials, and private parties.

Supply Uncertainties: The Optimistic and Pessimistic Supply Outlooks The description of the BAU supply outlook discussed the influence of geology on the price response of lower-48 onshore supply. It also

noted the non-price constraints which bind tertiary recovery supply possibilities (e.g., speculative technology) as well as the lower-48 OCS (e.g., leasing rate) and Alaska (e.g., logistics). The combined effect of these major estimating assumptions is large.

Consequently, a large degree of uncertainty surrounds the central, BAU supply possibilities forecast. This uncertainty consists of three elements: geological potential, technology (in the case of tertiary recovery), and the policy environment (evidenced in the leasing rate and achievable rates of development in Alaska). Of the many questions which pervade any attempt to estimate future oil supply, these are three of the most important and fundamental ones.

To delineate the uncertainty about the future oil supply, the BAU Outlook is bracketed by two others. One, Pessimistic, reflects a geological outlook which has approximately four chances out of five of actually being at least this amount. The Pessimistic Outlook couples this more certain (but lower) resource potential with less successful and less aggressively applied tertiary recovery technology. Finally, this outlook envisions a lower rate of leasing and a slower buildup of Alaskan facilities.

The other outlook, Optimistic, reflects lower geological confidence, one which has about one chance in five of actually containing this amount of resources. Geological optimism is coupled with comparable optimism regarding tertiary recovery, the leasing rate, and the attainable pace of Alaskan development. The estimating assumptions un-

Figure II-14

North Alaska Drilling and Logistical Effort (BAU)

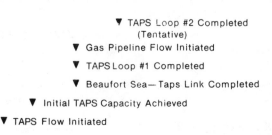

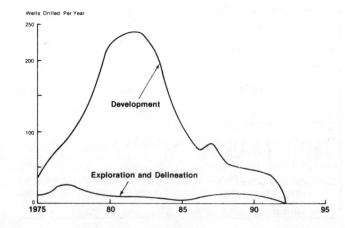

derlying both of these additional outlooks are summarized in Table II-11.

Uncertainty Effects on Total Crude Production

There is considerable variation in crude production possibilities as assumptions are modified:

- In 1980 and at $13 the Optimistic Outlook is 3.9 MMB/D higher than the Pessimistic Outlook (see Figure II-15).

- This difference of 3.9 MMB/D represents almost twice the production expected from the Alaskan North Slope in 1980.

The implications of uncertainty are large by 1980, and continue to increase over time. By 1985 at $13, the Optimistic forecast is almost 70 percent higher than the Pessimistic, and the difference continues to increase.

These two factors—uncertainty and its increasing influence as estimates reach farther and farther into the future—produce widely varying outlooks for the direction of domestic oil supply and prices in the longer term. Specifically:

- At $8, all but the Optimistic Outlook show a steady decline from today's production levels throughout the forecast period.

- At $13, all outlooks evidence some potential supply increase through 1980. After 1980, however,

Figure II-15

Crude Oil Production Under Alternative Outlooks

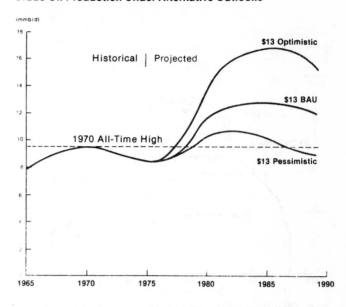

Pessimistic declines rapidly and BAU remains steady. The Optimistic Outlook increases until 1985, then a slow decline commences (see Figure II-15).

- At $16, the Pessimistic Outlook still reflects a supply potential somewhat akin to today's levels through

Table II-11

OPTIMISTIC AND PESSIMISTIC OUTLOOK ASSUMPTIONS

	Pessimistic	BAU	Optimistic
Resource Assessment*	USGS "Mean" minus one standard deviation	USGS "Mean"	USGS "Mean" plus one standard deviation
OCS Leasing (1975-1984)	18.2 million acres	26.8 million acres	38.2 million acres
Investment Tax Credit	10% through 1977; 7% thereafter	10% through 1977; 7% thereafter	10% throughout
Alaskan Pipeline Capacity	2.0 MMB/D in 1980 2.0 MMB/D in 1985	2.0 MMB/D in 1980; 2.5 MMB/D in 1985	2.0 MMB/D in 1980 4.5 MMB/D in 1985
Prince Controls	Removed within a few years	Removed within a few years	Removed within a few years

*
The USGS mean value for undiscovered, recoverable resources was shown in Table II-5 with a 95-5% confidence level. To reflect pessimism, the mean value minus one standard deviation was utilized, and to reflect optimism the mean plus one standard deviation was used. This amounts to generally an 80-85% confidence level for the Pessimistic Outlook, and a 15-20% confidence level for the Optimistic Outlook.

1989. The other two outlooks increase over the entire forecast period.

Components of Oil Supply Uncertainty The changes in the oil supply possibilities across the three supply outlooks have geographical, resource base, and recovery method implications (see Table II-12). The following observations are important:

- Most importantly, uncertainty occurs evenly across all of the major components of potential supply, on both the Pessimistic side and the Optimistic side of BAU.

- On the Pessimistic side, however, less fortunate geological experience on the lower-48 onshore (0.8 MMB/D), the rate of OCS leasing (0.4 MMB/D),

Table II-12
ALTERNATIVE 1985 PRODUCTION AT $13 PRICE
(MMB/D)

	Supply Outlook		
	Pessimistic	BAU	Optimistic
Lower-48 Onshore			
New Field Primary/Secondary	1.3	1.9	2.1
Old Field Secondary	2.0	2.0	2.7
Tertiary	0.8	1.0	1.5
Initial Reserves	2.4	2.4	2.4
Subtotal	6.5	7.3	8.7
Lower-48 OCS			
Pacific	0.5	0.6	0.9
Gulf of Mexico	1.1	1.4	1.9
Atlantic	0.1	0.1	0.2
Subtotal	1.7	2.1	3.0
Alaska			
Beaufort Sea	--	0.4	0.7
Other OCS	0.3	0.4	0.5
North Slope	1.4	2.3	2.7
NPR-4	--	--	0.9
Subtotal	1.7	3.1	4.8
Other			
NPR-1	--	0.2	0.2
Tar Sands	--	--	--
Heavy Hydrocarbons	0.2	0.2	0.3
Subtotal	0.2	0.4	0.5
Total Crude	10.1	12.9	17.0
Natural Gas Liquids	1.7	1.8	2.1
Total Liquids	11.8	14.7	19.1

and the production rate which can be sustained on the North Slope (0.9 MMB/D) stand out as the major uncertainties. These three elements account for 75 percent of the lower supply possibilities represented in the Pessimistic Outlook.

● Alternatively, on the Optimistic side, better tertiary recovery results combine with more fortunate geological experience to cause a 1.4 MMB/D higher estimated supply potential. Offshore leasing (0.9 MMB/D) and the combination of access to and successful results in NPR-4 (0.9 MMB/D) add another 3.2 MMB/D to the Optimistic Outlook compared to BAU. These three elements again account for about 75 percent of the elevated potential estimated under the Optimistic Outlook.

An important twofold message lies behind these widely varying production outlooks. First, geological uncertainty of the magnitude reflected in USGS Circular 725, coupled with the economic unknowns in untried frontier areas, produce major uncertainty in future production estimates. It may be that even very large sums expended in refining geological assessments and hypothetical petroleum engineering estimates could not reduce substantially the intrinsic uncertainty underlying domestic oil resource potentials.

Second, a large degree of this uncertainty is not intrinsic to nature but rather is policy-determined. Geological uncertainty may not respond dramatically to a much larger effort; the reliability of tertiary technology and the availability of supply from the OCS and Alaska—through

leasing and more intensive development—probably will. Thus the importance of resolving outstanding policy questions on these subjects is very clear.

Major Areas of Uncertainty in the Oil Supply Outlook The four major areas of uncertainty in the oil supply outlook are the resource base, drilling effort, OCS leasing schedules, and enhanced recovery. The Optimistic and Pessimistic supply possibilities incorporate different assumptions concerning these factors. The incremental impact on 1985 crude oil production at $13 varies with these assumptions (see Table II-13).

Several points to be noted concerning resource levels chosen for each scenario are (see Table II-14):

● The Optimistic resource levels are determined statistically and correspond to about a one in five chance that they are this high.

● The Pessimistic resource levels have approximately a four in five chance to be at least this much.

● The higher inferred reserve level in the Optimistic supply outlook is a result of subjective judgment by the USGS concerning inferred reserves in East Texas, which departed from its normal statistical procedure to report a more optimistic quantity. The more conservative statistical estimate was used for the BAU and Pessimistic outlooks.

There are several important points with respect to drilling levels:

Table II-13

CONTRIBUTION TO ESTIMATING UNCERTAINTY FROM GEOLOGIC, DRILLING, LEASING AND ALASKA SCENARIOS
(1985 Crude Oil Production (MMB/D)

	Scenario	
	Optimistic	Pessimistic
BAU Base Production	12.9	12.9
Geological*	+1.1	-0.7
Drilling	+0.3	-0.1
Leasing	+0.9	-0.4
Alaska and other	+1.8	-1.6
Scenario production	17.0	10.1

* Enhanced recovery is implicit in these figures.

Table II-14

USGS-725:   ALTERNATIVE GEOLOGICAL OUTLOOKS
(Billions of Barrels)

	Pessimistic	BAU	Optimistic
Measured Reserves	34.3	34.3	34.3
Inferred Reserves	18.5*	18.5*	23.1
Subtotal: Reserves	52.8	52.8	57.4
Undiscovered Recoverable			
Lower-48 Onshore	28.0	44.0	60.0
OCS**	15.6	33.0	49.6
Alaska - Onshore	7.7	12.0	16.3
Subtotal	51.3	89.0	125.9
Total	104.1	141.8	183.3

 * Adjusted to reflect lower East Texas inferred.
** Adjusted to include water depths greater than 200 meters.

Table II-15

IMPACT OF ALTERNATIVE SUPPLY OUTLOOKS ON DRILLING ACTIVITY AT $13
(Millions of Feet Drilled: 1975-1985)

	Pessimistic	BAU	Optimistic
Lower-48 Onshore	833.4	1,144.3	1,405.8
OCS	151.8	212.1	297.0
Total	985.2	1,356.4	1,702.8

- Increased drilling is largely the result of the higher resource base, but also the result of other factors which are varied for each outlook (see Table II-15).

- OCS drilling increases because of increased leasing which will be discussed as the next area of uncertainty.

- The largest part of the drilling difference onshore occurs late in the forecast as drilling 'builds up' or 'runs down,' which consequently lessens the impact on 1985 production (see Figure II-16).

The difference in OCS leasing schedules occurs solely because of a variance in the assumed acreage per lease

Figure II-16

Drilling Activities for Oil Under Alternative Outlooks

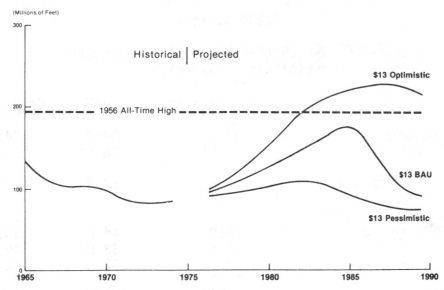

sale. The BAU Outlook assumed 800,000 acres per sale would be offered; whereas the Optimistic assumed 1,200,000 acres and the Pessimistic 500,000 acres (see Table II-16).

There are considerable differences of opinion among experts as to which enhanced recovery techniques are applicable to which reservoirs, or whether they are applicable at all. These differences account for the variations in projected reserves and production rates for specific times in the future.

To reflect this uncertainty, the Pessimistic and Optimistic supply outlooks have different levels of enhanced recovery (see Table II-17).

Several points concerning enhanced recovery are worth noting:

- Secondary recovery from old fields remains at the same level for both Pessimistic and BAU outlooks, as it is targeted to USGS indicated and inferred reserves.

- Tertiary recovery shows a large range of possibilities—from 0.6 MMB/D to 1.3 MMB/D in 1985 at an expected import price of $13 per barrel. These production quantities were based on high and low estimates, given that tertiary recovery processes prove out in practice.

- Enhanced recovery in the Optimistic outlook increases from a 1975 high of around 2.0 MMB/D to 5.0 MMB/D. However, enhanced production still accounts for only 30 percent of total production, a figure only slightly up from the present 25 percent.

Table II-16

OCS LEASING SCHEDULES UNDER ALTERNATIVE SCENARIOS
(Millions of Acres Leased)

Period	Pessimistic	BAU	Optimistic
1975-79	11.3	15.8	21.7
1980-84	6.9	11.0	16.5
1985-89	4.7	7.6	11.8
Total	22.9	34.4	50.0

Table II-17

1985 PRODUCTION FROM ENHANCED RECOVERY UNDER
ALTERNATIVE OUTLOOKS AT $13
(MMB/D)

Type Recovery	Outlook		
	Pessimistic	BAU	Optimistic
Secondary			
Old Fields	2.2	2.2	3.3
New Fields	0.3	0.4	0.4
Subtotal	2.5	2.6	3.7
Tertiary			
Old Fields	0.6	0.9	1.2
New Fields	negligible	negligible	0.1
Subtotal	0.6	1.0	1.3
Total Enhanced Production	3.1	3.6	5.0

- The timing of production from enhanced recovery technology is affected by many variables which are not yet fully understood. One of these key variables is economics, which is an especially important consideration since there is a 3-5 year time lag between investment and oil recovery. Economic factors, however, still remain speculative since so few field-wide commercial applications have been undertaken that there is an insufficient data base for generalization. Also, some techniques require chemicals or compounds which are not currently available on a large scale.

Alaskan crude production in 1985 at $13 was shown to vary from 1.7 MMB/D (Pessimistic) to 4.8 MMB/D (Optimistic), as indicated in Table II-12. This difference represents 45 percent of the total swing between outlooks in potential domestic crude supply in 1985. North Alaska makes up 2.9 MMB/D of this difference. Three things account for the large uncertainty there: geological fortune, rate of development, and accessibility to NPR-4 (itself additionally contingent upon geological success and rate of development).

Each of the alternative outlooks varies from BAU to a large extent due to the rate of development. Both, however, do represent varying degrees of geological fortune. In the Pessimistic case, worse geological experience occurs in the fields envisioned to prove productive and economically viable under BAU (see Table II-18).

For the Optimistic case, the BAU fields are worked more quickly; no greater amounts of reserves are expected. In contrast, NPR-4 reflects the joint effects of geological fortune and an expeditious development program. It can be argued that the fate of NPR-4 hinges on future geological fortune, because 30 years of geological work in NPR-4 has yet to establish a single 'reserve' in the sense applied anywhere else across the domestic petroleum resource picture.

Under BAU conditions, the coordination required between production capacity and logistical capacity was described. The coordination problem, of course, becomes even more delicate in the face of widely varying uncertainty about the magnitude of resources available in North Alaska, the timing of accessibility to them, and rates of productive capacity build-up that might be achieved (see Figure II-17 which portrays trajectories of the three alternative production possibilities for North Alaska as well as the implications of the Optimistic Outlook for TAPS capacity requirements).

Table II-18

1985 COMPONENTS OF NORTH ALASKA UNCERTAINTY
(MMB/D)

	Alternative Outlook	
	Pessimistic	Optimistic
Business-as-Usual	2.7	2.7
Geological Fortune	-0.5	--
Rate of Development	-0.8	+0.7
NPR-4	--	+0.9
Alternative Outlook	1.4	4.3

The most important points which emerge from the figure concern the maximum production likely to be realized under the Optimistic Outlook. Although peak production *possibilities* of about 4.5 MMB/D are estimated, expansion of TAPS beyond loop No. 2 (3.0 MMB/D) looks doubtful for two major reasons:

- Coincident production peaks, caused by rapid buildup of North Alaskan production from all likely fields through 1985, lead to an equally sharp decline thereafter.

- Since achieving the 4.5 MMB/D peak requires bringing 60 percent of the USGS-estimated resource base into play, finding reserves to fill another pipeline more than temporarily, while maintaining 3.0 MMB/D throughput for a doubly-looped TAPS, will be difficult.[4]

From this perspective, the likelihood of loop No. 2 appears to depend heavily on either NPR-4 or the portion of the resource base not covered in this outlook. The same point made earlier under BAU concerning TAPS loop No. 1 pertains equally here: The expansion of TAPS' capacity to 3.0 MMB/D by 1985 requires that the reserves to support it be identified soon.

Toward the Pessimistic end of the spectrum of North Alaskan production possibilities, incremental TAPS capacity is a lesser issue. There, it appears that the disposition of NPR-4—with institutional difficulty due partly to the requirement for a major, 400-mile pipeline required to link up with TAPS—may control the future of loop No. 1.

The major point here, however, concerns the uncertainty, not the wisdom of any one specific TAPS capacity.

At this juncture, the question of appropriate TAPS capacity for 1985 is impossible to calculate. The key to the solution is more tangible knowledge about the resource base, both how much is there, and at what price it becomes economically viable. In turn, obtaining tangible knowledge requires geological/geophysical work and exploratory drilling.

Figure II-17

Outlooks for North Alaska Crude Production

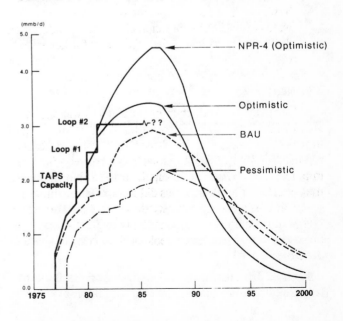

The Estimating Approach And The FEA Model

The BAU estimating assumptions are converted to oil supply estimates through two separate estimating tools. Oil supply estimates for the lower-48 states and most of the Alaskan OCS are derived using an FEA model, which deals in aggregate fashion with twelve large geographical areas.

The most speculative, immature areas (the Alaskan North Slope, Beaufort Sea, and the Naval Petroleum Reserves) are estimated through individual engineering-oriented assessments. These engineering-oriented assessments provide geographical detail, but otherwise calculate supply possibilities consistent with the FEA model.

The original FEA oil supply model, utilized in the 1974 *Project Independence Report,* used subjective judgments about resources, drilling levels, recovery rates, decline rates, costs, and other factors to produce annual production quantities for each of twelve petroleum regions. Since these estimates, the model has been improved in four major ways:

- Total oil drilling is estimated within the model, and its allocation among regions is derived rather than judged subjectively.

- Finding rates and enhanced recovery rates are linked formally to USGS estimates of the domestic resource base.

- OCS leasing schedules are translated into drilling schedules and production levels using regional parameters which better represent the unique geological characteristics of each OCS area.

- All other estimating factors have been reviewed and substantially revised, based on an additional year of actual supply experience.

The major inputs to the model are:

- *Resource assessments.* These data consist of existing oil in place, reserve levels, and estimates of future reserves potentially available from both known fields and newly discovered fields.

- *Recovery factors.* These regional factors are based on historical analysis, and estimate the percentage of oil in place found which will consequently be produced. There are, in fact, six recovery factors for each region, one for each 'type' of production.

- *Depletion fractions.* These regional factors are based on 1974 production history, and pertain to the rate that crude oil is produced from reserves. These factors provide for a systematic dwindling of existing reserves which have to be replaced by new discoveries in order to maintain production levels.

- *Costs.* Costs are of two types: drilling costs and other investments necessary to find oil and convert it to proved reserves, and operating costs necessary to produce the oil from reserves, once proved. These cost factors have been estimated from historical analyses and from judgmental decisions concerning cost escalation due to, say, deep wells.

These four major inputs (and many other less critical factors) permit the model to derive annual regional production figures at different price levels. Briefly, the calculation procedure consists of six broad steps:

- The expected oil price and drilling rig supply parameters combine to determine the total domestic oil drilling over time and its allocation among twelve oil regions.

- Finding rates, derived from USGS resource assessments, then combine with drilling to determine the amount of oil-in-place found by the drilling process.

- Regional recovery rates—one for each of three recovery methods in old and in new fields—combine with various lead time factors to allocate successive portions of this oil-in-place into proved reserves.

- As each portion of the oil-in-place is proved, the minimum-acceptable price at which it becomes economically attractive is calculated. The calculation consists of a discounted cash flow analysis of each reserve addition. This calculation considers the investment required to prove it, the operating costs subsequently required to produce and sell it (e.g., royalties), and the time profile over which it will be produced and sold.

- Depletion fractions—or decline rates— are used to calculate future annual production resulting from proved reserves added each year at each minimum-acceptable price.

- Finally, in each year the production which is available at successively higher prices is cumulated to produce a curve of production versus price (or a supply curve).

Long Term Demand Forecast

The Project Independence Evaluation System (PIES) links the supply projections delineated in this chapter with demand scenarios for each sector of the economy. The linkage is accomplished in the main PIES linear programming model which finds an equilibrium solution for domestic consumption and total supply of all energy resources. It determines this equilibrium solution by considering the flow of energy resources from areas of supply to areas of consumption, and supplements any shortfall in domestic production with imports. The PIES model does this for a range of energy scenarios and for several prices.

Under the PIES Reference Scenario, there is a wide variation between demand growth rates at three imported oil prices: $8, $13, and $16 (see Figure II-18). This growth is based on BAU supply possibilities at these same prices. Several points are important:

- At $8 world oil prices, domestic consumption rises at a compounded growth rate of 3.9 percent between 1974 and 1985. Imports of nearly 14.0 MMB/D must be brought in to fill the gap between consumption and domestic production.

- At $13 domestic consumption increases at about half the historical pace, or about 2.0 percent compounded annually. Domestic production fills 70 percent of this demand in 1985, and imports of only about 6.0 MMB/D are necessary to fill the gap.

- At $16 world oil prices, consumption grows at a slower rate of only 1.4 percent per year, and domestic production supplies all but about 3.0 MMB/D of that amount by 1985.

These same consumption solutions can also be broken down by consuming sector (see Figure II-19).

Several observations regarding sector demand at $13 world oil prices are important (see Table II-19):

Figure II-19

Outlook for Petroleum Consumption by Sector (Reference Scenario)

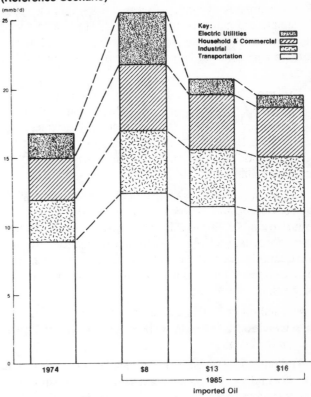

Figure II-18

Projected Petroleum Consumption (Reference Scenario)

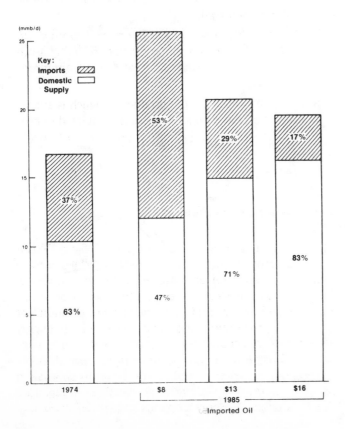

- The transportation sector is quantitatively the largest of the final consuming sectors, accounting for about half of total oil demand. The trend towards smaller, more fuel-efficient automobiles is expected to continue and to have a major impact in reducing demand growth between now and 1985.

- At $13 world oil prices, consumption of oil by electric utilities is expected to decline substantially as coal and nuclear plants replace oil in base-loaded generation. At higher or lower prices, electric utilities show the greatest level of demand elasticity of all the sectors, and at $8, consumption by this sector rises from 6.5 to 16.0 percent of total consumption.

- In the household/commercial sector, the effect of a substantial rise in delivered oil prices is partially offset by an equivalent rise in decontrolled natural gas prices, thus maintaining oil's share for heating in the 1974-85 period.

- About 30 percent of petroleum consumption in the industrial sector is for raw materials and coking, and is not very sensitive to price. This reduces the impact of rising prices on consumption.

Table II-19

HISTORICAL AND FORECASTED ANNUAL OIL DEMAND GROWTH RATES, BY ECONOMIC SECTOR

	1960-72	1972-74	Reference Scenario 1974-85*
Transportation	4.3%	1.3%	2.1%
Electric Utilities	15.4	5.4	-2.3
Household/Commercial	2.6	-4.7	2.8
Industrial	3.7	2.1	3.1
Total	4.2%	0.7%	2.0%

* At $13 per barrel imported oil.

Summary and Implications Of Alternative Outlooks

The preceding sections of this chapter put domestic oil supply in perspective, and presented three alternative outlooks for how our domestic oil supply possibilities may evolve over the next 15 years.

Several things are important to note concerning BAU oil supply possibilities (see Figure II-20):

- The effects of price are large and cumulative; today's price expectations set a course of activity whose results are not felt immediately, but, once felt, continue indefinitely.

- Under $13 expectations domestic oil supply can regain its pre-1970 upward trend.

- Under the assumed BAU conditions (leasing constraints, moderate tertiary technology success, and a large, but not crash, Alaskan development effort), supply possibilities at $13 will have peaked in 1985 and will trend downward once again.

- At a low price of $8, BAU crude oil production maintains current levels.

- At a higher price of $16, crude oil production until 1985 proceeds on a slightly higher trajectory than at $13, averaging about 0.5 MMB/D higher. By 1985, however, when the $13 supply trajectory peaks and begins to decline, supply possibilities at $16 continue to trend upward to peak at a point beyond 1990.

The effort necessary to produce these BAU oil supply possibilities is large by historical standards (see Figures II-21 through II-23):

- A massive exploratory and developmental drilling effort is required. Annual oil drilling must more than double by 1985, to approach its all-time high reached in 1956.

- In addition to drilling, accomplishment of these supply possibilities requires a high level of Federal OCS leasing.

- The most comprehensive measure of the total effort is the capital required to fuel it. Capital expenditures for oil must more than double (in constant 1975 dollars) by 1985.

Figure II-20

Crude Oil Production at Three Prices (BAU)

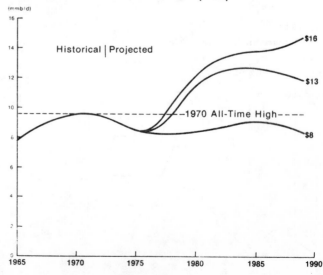

Figure II-21

Drilling Activities for Oil (BAU)

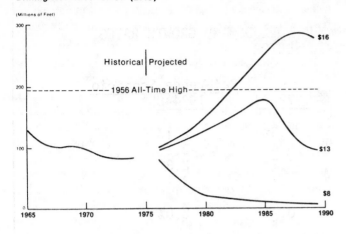

Figure II-23

Capital Expenditures by the Petroleum Industry

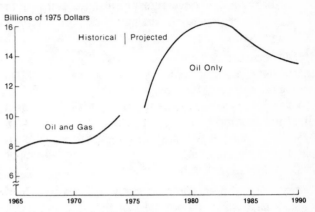

Source: Annual Financial Analysis of a Group of Petroleum Companies. 1974 Energy Economics Division. Chase Manhattan Bank, September 1975. Projections from PIES Oil Supply Model

Figure II-22

Outer Continental Shelf Leasing Schedules

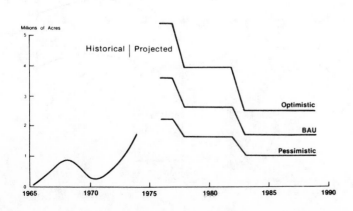

Figure II-24

Crude Oil Production Under Alternative Outlooks

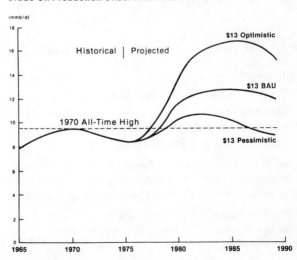

- Tertiary recovery must succeed technically and economically, and must be applied at a moderately brisk pace.

- North Alaskan development must proceed at a rate capable of expanding Alaskan crude production sixteen-fold over ten years.

With respect to the oil supply possibility outlooks estimated here, the final results will depend on three things: geological fortune, technology (in the case of tertiary recovery) and the policy environment. It is in these areas that the large uncertainty in future potentials appears impossible to resolve at this point. Unfortunately, the implications of this range of outcomes for oil supply possibilities is very large (see Figure II-24).

Previous comments on uncertainty bear repeating here. First, a large share (about half) of this variation across outlooks accurately portrays the fundamental geological unknowns inherent in the oil business. These are revealed directly in USGS Circular 725. These geological unknowns—and the economic uncertainty they create in a forecast dominated as is this one by frontier areas—can only be expected to produce an uncertain forecast of oil production possibilities 15 years forward in time. Large geological/geophysical expenditures and hypothetical petroleum engineering estimates of economic potential may not substantially reduce the uncertainty intrinsic to domestic oil resources.

A large degree of uncertainty, however, is not natural, but rather, is policy-determined. Geological uncertainty may not respond dramatically to our will. In contrast, policy-determined uncertainty should respond to effort.

Natural Gas

Introduction

Natural gas is a vital source of energy for the United States, supplying about 30 percent of our total energy needs and 44 percent of non-transportation, direct uses. Concern regarding its continued role as a major U.S. energy supply source has risen because consumption has exceeded additions to proven reserves from the lower continental 48 States since 1968, and because interstate natural gas pipeline companies have been increasingly unable to meet their contracted delivery requirements to customers in many regions of the country.

Based on declining proven reserves of oil and natural gas, it is evident that a transition will take place over the next few decades from these less abundant domestic sources, to more abundant sources, such as coal, solar, and nuclear energy. However, the prospect of increased supplies of natural gas supplements, including synthetic

gas from coal and pipeline-quality substitute gas from petroleum products, brightens the outlook for the natural gas industry. Also prospects for improving the natural gas reserves base through development of advanced recovery techniques or new exploration could be significant.

In response to the recent natural gas shortages, the FEA, in cooperation with other Federal agencies, has performed intensive analyses into the short-term, mid-term, and long-term projected supply and demand for natural gas, including supplemental sources such as imported liquefied natural gas (LNG) and synthetic natural gas produced from coal and petroleum products. The major conclusion derived from these studies is that some fundamental decisions must be made now that will affect the contribution of natural gas and its pipeline supplements during the remainder of this century. The results of these studies and FEA's revised long-term forecasts are the basis for this Chapter.

Natural Gas—Background And Current Situation

Consumption Demand for natural gas has steadily increased during the last half century because of its clean-burning properties, low cost, and until recently, availability. After World War II, the availability of abundant supplies of natural gas—most of it found in the search for oil—and improved quality of pipe for high-pressure, long-distance delivery enabled the gas utility industry to expand rapidly and widely. Total U.S. energy consumption of natural gas increased from 4 percent in 1920, to 18 percent in 1950, and exceeded 30 percent in 1974 (see Figure III-1), growing at an average of 6.5 percent

Figure III-1

Growth in U.S. Natural Gas Consumption 1920—1974

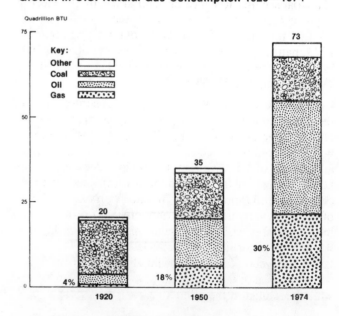

Table III-1

SECTORAL GROWTH IN NATURAL GAS CONSUMPTION
(Tcf)

	1960	1970	1974	Annual Growth Rate 1960-1970	Annual Growth Rate 1970-1974
Residential	3.10	4.83	4.78	4.5	-0.3
Commercial	1.02	2.05	2.26	7.2	2.4
Industrial	4.34	7.87	8.29	6.2	1.3
Utility	1.73	3.89	3.41	8.5	-3.2
Total*	10.19	19.02	19.08	6.4	0.1

* Totals slightly exceed sum of four sectors due to inclusion of "Other Consumers" in BOM data and rounding.

Source: Bureau of Mines Mineral Industry Surveys--Delivered gas consumption

annually in the 1950's and 1960's. In 1974, it was consumed in over 40 million residences, in almost 3.4 million commercial establishments, and by over 193,000 industrial users.

Natural gas now accounts for over 50 percent of direct fossil fuel inputs to both the household/commercial and industrial sectors. Reliance on natural gas by the electric utility industry peaked in 1970, when natural gas accounted for almost 25 percent of total energy input. By 1974, natural gas generated only 17 percent of electricity, as curtailments and an inability to obtain long-term supply commitments affected its use.

The growth rate of natural gas consumption was reduced dramatically in the 1970's as compared to the previous decade. In particular, residential gas consumption declined in the early 1970's, following an annual growth rate of 4.5 percent in the previous decade (see Table III-1). Several factors accounting for this reduction include: the imposition of local moratoria on new additions of buildings to natural gas distribution lines for space heating, to offset rising interstate pipeline curtailments; warmer than normal weather in 1973 and 1974; voluntary conservation effects following the 1973 oil embargo; and a reversal in the decline in real prices for natural gas which prevailed in the 1960's.

Government moratoria restricting new additions of residential consumers during 1974 were extensive (see Table III-2). There were only 17 States without restrictions; these were predominantly in areas where population is relatively sparse (Mountain States) or where gas is being produced and sold at unregulated prices (the West South Central region). However, 20 other States, principally those in areas served by interstate pipelines undergoing severe curtailments (Middle Atlantic, South Atlantic, and East North Central), had restrictions covering more than 50 percent of their residential gas utility customers.

The effect of warmer weather cannot be measured precisely. Although the weather in 1974 was colder than in 1973, natural gas consumption declined, primarily due to a reaction to the embargo, higher prices, and the recession. Further, real prices for natural gas in the residential sector declined by 1.5 percent annually between 1968 and 1972; but in 1973 and 1974 real prices increased by 0.7 percent annually.

Natural gas consumption within the commercial sector also grew at a much less rapid rate in the early 1970's, as compared to the preceding decade. Nevertheless, the commercial sector maintained positive growth in natural gas consumption from 1970-1974, growing by 2.4 percent annually.

Table III-2

EXTENT OF HOUSING CUSTOMER RESTRICTIONS, 1974*

Region	% of Utility Customers Covered By Restrictions	% of Utility Customers Not Covered By Restrictions	% of Utility Customers Not Covered By Survey	Number of States With Over 50% of Utility Customers With Restrictions	Number of States With 0% of Surveyed Utility Customers With Restrictions	Number of States in Region
New England	43	14	43	1	1	6
Middle Atlantic	97	0	3	3	0	3
East North Central	43	53	4	3	0	5
West North Central	22	66	12	1	1	7
South Atlantic	62	23	15	7	0	9**
East South Central	39	37	24	2	1	4
West South Central	0	79	21	0	4	4
Mountain	44	25	31	2	6	8
Pacific	3	96	1	1	3	5

* Customer restrictions refer to either restrictions imposed voluntarily by utilities in anticipation of supply shortages or those imposed upon the utility by state or municipal public utility commissions. The percentages cited above refer to the percentage of the total customers of a state that are served by utilities which restrict new customers for either reason and in any fashion.
** Includes District of Columbia.

Source: American Gas Association, Gas Heating Survey, 1975.

The growth rate of natural gas consumption in the industrial sector declined in the 1970's principally due to the recession and to curtailments imposed by interstate pipelines and related gas utilities. The Middle Atlantic States experienced the largest decline in industrial natural gas consumption, dropping from a growth of 5.6 percent annually in the 1960's to a decline of 2.3 percent annually in the 1970's, principally due to the effects of pipeline curtailments.

However, the most dramatic change in growth of natural gas consumption occurred in the utility sector. Electric utilities in the Middle Atlantic and South Atlantic states in the 1970's shifted away from natural gas mainly because of pipeline curtailments (see Table III-3). In the same period, gas consumption in utilities located in the gas producing states in the West South Central region continued to grow at 3.8 percent annually. However, even in these producing states, utility consumption growth rates were lower than the 10 percent annual rates experienced in the previous decade in response to higher prices, the slower economy, and an inability to obtain long-term commitments for supplies.

Most of the residential use of natural gas is for space heating (over 70 percent) and water heating (about 20 percent). The largest industrial gas users are chemical and allied products (about 24 percent), petroleum and coal products (16 percent), and primary metal industries (about 13 percent). Almost 40 percent, about 3.5 trillion cubic feet (Tcf), of the industrial gas use is for fueling boilers in the chemical, petroleum, food, and paper industries, mostly in the South. Gas also plays an important role as a feedstock and process fuel in the manufacture of ammonia, fertilizer, and methanol.

The greatest natural gas use occurs in the West South Central census region (Texas, Louisiana, Oklahoma, and Arkansas). This area accounts for over 30 percent of the country's natural gas use and more than half of the gas used by electric utilities. Alternatively, New England consumes less than two percent of the natural gas (see Figure III-2 for the distribution of delivered natural gas consumption by region in 1974).

Natural Gas Production and Distribution Industry The U.S. natural gas industry is composed of producers, interstate and intrastate pipelines, distributors, and end-users. Currently there are about 12,000 oil and gas producers in the United States. In 1974, however, 34 companies accounted for 96 percent of the interstate volume, and the 25 largest interstate pipelines carried over 95 percent of the interstate gas (see Figure III-3).

Domestic production is derived from six major producing states (accounting for 93 percent of production):

Figure III-2

Regional Distribution of Natural Gas Consumption, 1974

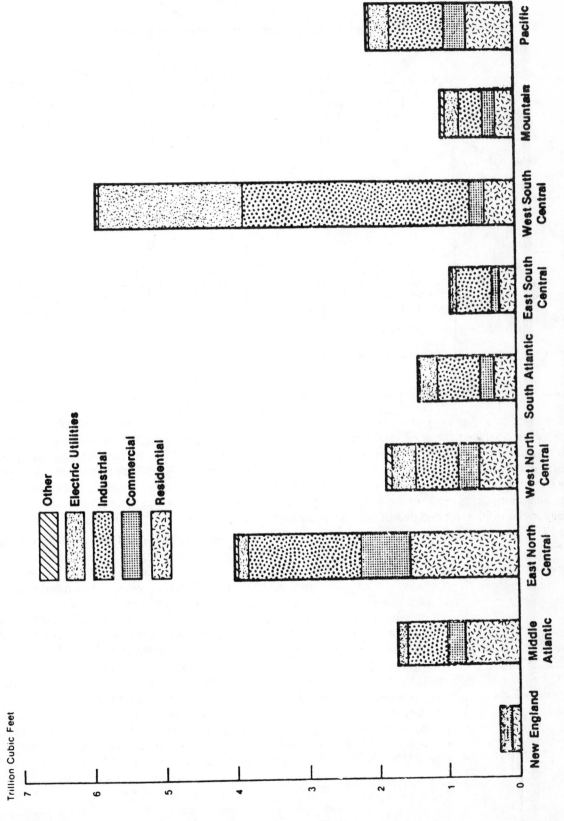

Trillion Cubic Feet

Note: Consumption Excludes Extraction Losses, Lease and Plant Fuel, Pipeline Fuel, and Transmission Losses.
Source: Mineral Industry Surveys, Bureau of Mines, Delivered Gas Consumption.

Figure III-3

Overview—U.S. Natural Gas System 1974
(Bcf)

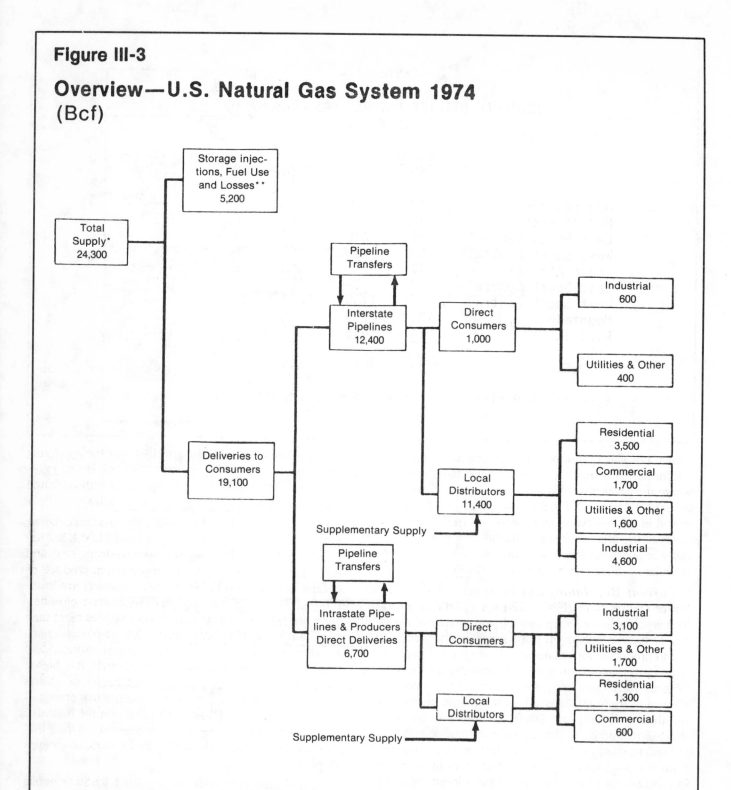

*Supply includes U.S. marketed production, withdrawals from storage, and imports.

**Gas for such purposes as lease and plant fuel, pipeline compressor fuel, extraction loss, and transmission losses.

Note Divisions between interstate and intrastate volumes are estimated.

Source: Based primarily on data from "Natural Gas Production and Consumption 1974" (Washington, DC: Bureau of Mines, Mineral Industry Surveys, 1975).

Table III-3

REGIONAL UTILITY NATURAL GAS CONSUMPTION
(Bcf/yr)

	Consumption			Growth Rate	
	1960	1970	1974	60-70	70-74
New England	13	8	11	(-4.7)	8.3
Mid Atlantic	89	161	61	6.1	(-21.5)
East North Central	61	245	167	14.9	(-9.1)
West North Central	245	420	365	5.5	(-3.4)
South Atlantic	147	343	240	8.8	(-8.5)
East South Central	53	139	53	10.1	(-21.4)
West South Central	657	1733	2012	10.2	3.8
Mountain	135	199	210	4.0	1.3
Pacific	324	645	310	7.1	(-18.0)
U.S.	1725	3894	3429	8.5	(-3.2)

Source: BOM Mineral Industry Surveys - Delivered Gas Consumption

Texas, Louisiana, New Mexico, Oklahoma, Kansas, and California. Some natural gas is produced from reservoirs where the gas is dissolved in or associated with crude oil. In 1974, 82 percent of the gas was withdrawn from wells drilled in gas reservoirs (gas wells) and the rest from oil wells; of the total wellhead production, 19 percent of the gas was produced from wells on Federal lands, the remainder on State and privately owned lands.

Current Regulatory Environment   The Federal Power Commission (FPC) exercises Federal regulatory jurisdiction over interstate transmission and sale of natural gas. It sets the maximum price a pipeline company may pay to producers for gas dedicated for resale to the interstate market, and controls the resale price of gas delivered to local distributing companies. Currently, a pipeline is allowed to pay a producer a maximum base price of 52¢ per thousand cubic feet (Mcf) for new gas, except on short-term emergency purchases by pipelines or purchases of uncommitted gas by curtailed, high priority customers from intrastate sources, when higher prices may be paid. In contrast, unregulated prices for gas sold on the intrastate market usually range between $1.00 and $1.50 per Mcf.

Aside from controlling prices, the FPC regulates various other aspects of the interstate natural gas market, including the rates charged for the transportation of gas delivered into interstate commerce. Since 1970, when shortages first developed, the FPC has been responsible for establishing curtailment priorities and for approving curtailment plans filed by affected pipelines. It also regulates, through a certification process, the construction and abandonment of pipeline and storage facilities.

Because of its authority to control imports and exports, the FPC also has jurisdiction over imported LNG, but has jurisdiction over synthetic gas (syngas) from coal and substitute natural gas (SNG) from petroleum products or natural gas liquids only when these products are commingled with regular natural gas in interstate pipelines. Since each of these supplements costs pipelines more than natural gas, the FPC decides on a case-by-case basis whether they can be incrementally priced to individual purchasers of the supplement, or whether the higher prices will be averaged among all purchasers of natural gas. The FPC has ruled in favor of incremental pricing in projects reviewed to date, thereby lowering the incentive to obtain more gas from these sources, but assuring that new users pay the real marginal price for these costly supplements.

Natural gas distributors are regulated by State public utility commissions or municipal governments. This regulation covers the utility's service territory, the rates charged its customers, the construction of new facilities, and local curtailment priorities.

Natural Gas Production and Reserve Additions: The Basis for the Shortages   Natural gas marketed production peaked at 22.6 Tcf in 1973 and declined significantly for the first time to 21.6 Tcf in 1974, a decline of nearly 5 percent. This decline in 1974 production was equivalent to about 170 million barrels of crude oil. Preliminary data from the Bureau of Mines indicates that the natural gas production decline was accelerated in 1975, dropping 7 percent to about 20.1 Tcf. Additions to the inventory of natural gas reserves in the lower 48 States failed to equal or exceed production for the seventh consecutive year in 1974, leaving these reserves at their lowest level since 1952 (see Figure III-4). The only major reserve additions in recent years have been the Alaskan reserves of 26 Tcf, added in 1970. Both regulation over wellhead prices and a depletion of natural gas drilling prospects onshore, within the lower 48 States, contributed to the peaking of natural gas reserves in 1967.

Price regulation of producers at low price levels for wellhead production has affected both demand and supply of natural gas. Regulated natural gas prices are lower than oil, coal, or electricity on a Btu basis, and demand has been stimulated. Environmental regulations also have made "clean" natural gas desirable. Exploratory gas well completions peaked in 1959 and began a decline which continued until the early 1970's. However, in the early 1970's, increases in the unregulated prices for natural gas in the intrastate market stimulated a sharp increase in exploratory activity.

Figure III-4

U.S. Natural Gas Reserves
(Excluding Alaska)

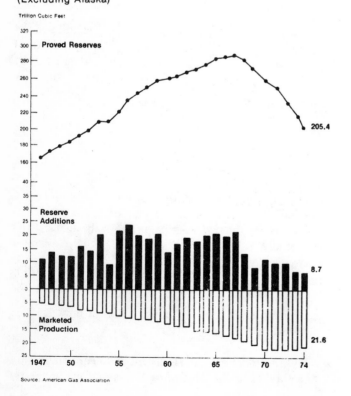

Source: American Gas Association

Figure III-5

Average Annual Reserve Additions of Natural Gas

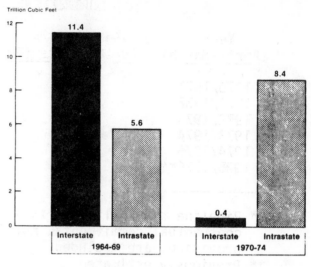

Source: American Gas Association, Federal Power Commission.

The depletion of prime natural gas drilling prospects also hastened the onset of natural gas shortages. The first natural gas areas explored are those least costly to drill and with the greatest likelihood of discovery of large fields. By 1974, the average reserve additions per foot drilled for exploratory and developmental wells was 170 Mcf per foot, compared to 485 Mcf per foot in 1970.

The interstate natural gas pipelines have suffered both from a decline in the total amount of reserves added to the inventory and from a decline in the share of reserves acquired by these systems. Since natural gas produced and sold within the same State is not regulated by the Federal Power Commission, the share of new reserve dedications to pipelines crossing State boundaries has fallen, while the intrastate market share has risen (see Figure III-5).

Curtailments to Date   Due to a continually increasing demand and a relatively stable rate of production, the demand for gas exceeded its supply in the 1970's. Many gas distribution companies have found it necessary to deny gas service to new customers and to curtail some existing customers. Firm curtailments (generally defined as contractual requirements less deliveries) as reported by the interstate pipelines grew from 0.1 Tcf in the 1970-71 delivery year (April-March) to 2.0 Tcf in 1974-75 (see Table III-4). For the delivery year 1975-76, firm curtailments were projected by the FPC at 2.9 Tcf, or 19 percent of requirements.

In 1970-71, when the Federal Power Commission began compiling data on curtailments, 12 of the 48 major interstate pipelines experienced curtailments. More

Table III-4

CURTAILMENT TRENDS*

Year (April-March)	Annual Firm Curtailments (Tcf)	Heating Season (Nov.-Mar.) Firm Curtailments (Tcf)
1970/1971	0.1	0.1
1971/1972	0.5	0.2
1972/1973	1.1	0.5
1973/1974	1.6	0.6
1974/1975	2.0	1.0
1975/1976**	2.9	1.3

* Pipeline to pipeline curtailments not included in 1974/1975 data; contractual commitments, not incorporating an interruptible supply provision, are included.

** Previously estimated

pipelines with curtailments have been added to the list in each subsequent year. By the 1975-76 heating season, 31 of the 48 pipelines were projecting curtailments. However, six of these accounted for about 65 percent of projected firm curtailments and about 40 percent of the total firm requirements.

A few key pipelines experiencing substantial curtailments serve the States most affected (see Figure III-6). These States are the Atlantic States stretching south from New York; several Mid-Western States, such as Ohio and Kentucky; and California. Estimates of the natural gas shortages in the 21 States most affected are shown in Table III-5.

Due to increasing curtailments, the FPC in March 1973, promulgated a uniform, nine-tier curtailment priority schedule based on the end use of the gas and size of the customer. Under this schedule, residential and small commercial users are afforded the highest priority during service curtailments, followed by large commercial users and industrial users who cannot switch to alternate fuels.

The priority of distribution in the final market usually depends on policies established by the State regulatory agencies, which vary substantially among States. A recent survey of 21 States[5] indicated that only six had statewide uniform curtailment policies. Seventeen of the States imposed curtailments on an end-use basis, curtailing industrial, commercial, and residential customers in that order. The others approved pro rata curtailment plans, usually curtailing the larger volume users on an equal share basis, and not distinguishing between industrial and commercial usage. Nineteen out of 21 States also distinguished between firm and interruptible contracts in assigning curtailment priorities. However, all States provided residential users the highest priority for continuous gas service.

Curtailments on the interstate pipeline system have not caused large adverse economic impacts to date. Most of the curtailments have been absorbed by industrial users on firm contracts, but having alternate fuel use capabilities. Customers on interruptible contracts frequently absorbed curtailments through shifts in production schedules and through use of alternate fuels. However, curtailments beginning in the winter of 1974-75 reached into levels of the industrial market sector which either could not use alternate fuels by nature of their processes, or which have not yet installed alternate fuel use capability.

There is, of course, an economic impact involved in the shift to alternate fuels. Industrial plants must eventually recoup the cost of higher-priced alternate fuels, as well as the capital costs of installing alternate fuel burning facilities, through higher product prices. In addition, the increased demands for alternate fuels by natural gas curtailees have intensified supply problems in other sectors of the energy industry, especially in the propane market.

In the winter of 1974-75, very little unemployment and few plant shutdowns occurred directly as a result of natural

Table III-5

PROJECTIONS OF NATURAL GAS SHORTAGE DURING WINTER OF 1975-1976 IN MOST-AFFECTED STATES

| | Total Curtailments | | Increase Over Last Winter |
	Bcf	Percent of Requirements	Bcf
Arizona	22	24	2
California	370	34	46
Delaware	1	12	0
Florida	50	49	10
Georgia	63	29	11
Indiana	17	6	5
Iowa	36	18	4
Kansas	60	23	5
Kentucky	13	10	6
Maryland/D.C.	14	12	1
Missouri	35	15	5
Nevada	24	51	6
New Jersey	21	11	(-10)
New York	41	10	6
North Carolina	41	46	6
Ohio	78	12	11
Pennsylvania	37	9	10
South Carolina	59	55	4
Tennessee	31	22	9
Virginia	12	14	(-1)
West Virginia	12	13	3

Source: FEA/FPC Distributor Survey, updated December 1975

gas unavailability. Most plant closings occurred primarily because of the recession and many shutdowns were avoided by the use of alternate fuels (propane, butane, distillate, or residual oil), emergency diversion of natural gas, mild weather, or conservation. There were reports of scattered plant closings for brief periods during the heating season in Virginia, North Carolina, New Jersey and other States.

Near-Term Outlook

The natural gas supply available to the interstate pipelines will continue to decline throughout the next several years in the absence of a major shift in supplies from the intrastate market. The FPC has predicted that, based on the total gas reserves committed to the interstate pipelines at the end of 1974 under all contracts and commitments, the annual decline in deliveries would be about 1 Tcf through 1979 if these supplies were not augmented (see Table III-6), or a doubling of current curtailments within three years. Potential supply additions include increased production from newly dedicated reserves to the interstate market, increased supplies from the intrastate market through emergency and short-term contracts, and increased imports.

Table III-6

GAS SUPPLY AND DELIVERABILITY
DEDICATED TO INTERSTATE PIPELINE COMPANIES THROUGH 1974
(Bcf/yr)

	Produced and/or Purchased 1974	Projected Deliveries				
		1975	1976	1977	1978	1979
A. Domestic Gas Supply						
Company Owned and Long Term Producer Contracts	12,513	11,606	10,595	9,557	8,517	7,579
Warranty Contracts	226	218	248	250	235	224
Emergency/Limited Term Contracts	226	0	1	0	0	0
Total Domestic	12,965	11,824	10,844	9,807	8,753	7,803
Domestic % of Total	93.5	92.8	92.1	90.1	87.4	85.8
B. Pipeline Imports						
Canada	900	922	927	930	932	933
Mexico	0	0	0	0	0	0
Total Pipeline Imports	900	922	927	930	932	933
Pipeline Imports % of Total	6.5	7.2	7.9	8.5	9.3	10.3
C. LNG Imports						
Algeria	-0-	-0-	-0-	146	332	360
LNG Imports % of Total				1.4	3.3	3.9
D. Total All Sources, All Contracts and commitments	13,866	12,746	11,772	10,883	10,016	9,097

Source: Federal Power Commission-Preliminary Data

The volume of new reserve additions is likely to be insufficient to replace the 1 Tcf/year expected decline, even if all production from new reserves was dedicated to the interstate market, an unlikely event. The outlook for increased imports through 1979, either by pipeline from Canada or in the form of LNG, is exceedingly unlikely because of recent declarations of energy resource conservation from Canada and the long lead times needed to obtain project approval and to construct LNG gasification terminals. Also, even if prices increase under deregulation, production levels will not increase for at least the next few years, although more gas would be available in the interstate market.

FEA estimates a substantial increase in the natural gas shortage in 1976-77 as the economy reaches normal levels of activity. Forecast is an increase of about 1.3 Tcf for the delivery year and 0.8 Tcf for the winter heating season as compared to the corresponding period in 1975-76. In addition, severe weather conditions (equivalent to the coldest winter in the last 10 years) could increase the natural gas shortage by about 200 Bcf in any winter.

The states most affected by shortages this year will experience greater impacts in the winter of 1976-77 as the supply situation of the interstate pipelines serving them continues to deteriorate. Although the shortage is not projected to reach the residential sector, the industrial and electric utility sectors will experience even greater shortfalls as the economy recovers.

Several factors can substantially reduce the effects of natural gas curtailments. The most important factor will be the availability and cost of alternate fuels. Others include the heating demand by residential and commercial customers which is a function of the temperature; the extent to which industrial activity dependent on natural gas has recovered from the economic downturn, the actual supply deficits, emergency purchases of uncommitted gas, and fuel savings by conservation efforts. As an example, the warm weather in the early part of the 1975-76 heating season relieved the pressure in some areas, reducing by December 1975 the forecast of curtailments by about 160 Bcf in the most seriously impacted States.

Long-Term Outlook For Natural Gas

The interstate pipeline curtailment problem facing the country in the near term is but a symptom of a fundamental long-term inability of domestic natural gas supplies to meet demand at the presently regulated price levels. The resulting shortage is thus focused and amplified in several States due to the structure of the current pricing regulations. The long-term outlook for natural gas supply and demand is uncertain and dependent on several factors.

Long-Term Outlook for Natural Gas Demand

The potential demand for natural gas in the long term is influenced by the following:

- The world pricing strategy for oil, since natural gas and oil are close substitutes in both the utility and industrial sectors;

- The degree and structure of price regulations over domestic oil;

- Government conservation initiatives, particularly those directed to buildings and industry, and the degree of commercialization of existing energy-saving technologies in these sectors;

- Government policy regarding the availability of natural gas for use in utility and industrial boilers;

- The status of local government moratoria.

The long-term forecasts for natural gas demand are highly uncertain since natural gas average prices have never been in the high ranges estimated for the 1985 strategies, and the effects of both government-induced and voluntary conservation cannot be established with precision. In addition, the response to higher prices in each consuming sector is uncertain since projections are based on current consumption patterns which are a derivative of over 20 years of price regulations, and the establishment of two distinct markets for gas—the controlled interstate and unregulated intrastate markets.

Natural gas demand in the Reference Scenario is expected to increase from the actual consumption of 21.2 Tcf measured in 1974 to 23.4 Tcf by 1985 (see Table III-7). However, combining reported interstate curtailments of 1.9 Tcf with actual consumption provides an indication of the "unconstrained" demand for natural gas of about 23.1 Tcf for 1974. Thus, aggregate demand for natural gas in 1985 will remain about the same as the unconstrained demand observed in 1974, if world oil prices remain at current levels and both new natural gas and oil prices are deregulated.

Aggregate demand for natural gas in 1985 is not heavily influenced by the world price of oil, decreasing by only 8 percent (to 21.5 Tcf) if world oil prices drop to $8 a barrel, and increasing by only 1 percent (to 23.7 Tcf) if world oil prices increase to $16 per barrel.

Although there will be little change in aggregate demand for natural gas from the unconstrained demand level observed in 1974, large changes can occur in individual sectors. The industrial sector is shown in the $13 Reference Scenario to increase consumption by 3.7 Tcf

Table III-7

1985 NATURAL GAS DEMAND BY SECTOR AND WORLD OIL PRICE
(Tcf/yr)

Reference Scenario	1974	Oil Import Price ($/bbl)		
		$8	$13	$16
Residential & Commercial	7.3	6.4	6.2	6.3
Industrial	9.9	13.9	13.6	13.6
Transportation	0.6	0.8	0.8	0.8
Utility	3.4	0.5	3.0	3.2
Total Demand	21.2	21.5	23.4	23.7

Note: Totals exclude about 0.2 Tcf of synthetic gas consumed by the sectors.

(or 37 percent) over 1974 levels, while usage in the residential/commercial sector decreases by 1.1 Tcf (15 percent).

Although these sectoral forecasts are consistent with trends of recent years, the forecast for natural gas consumption in the residential/commercial sector may be understated since the economic forecasting techniques employed are projecting from a baseline—the first half of the 1970's—that has been affected by local government moratoria on connections of gas lines to new buildings, interstate pipeline curtailments, and warm weather. Thus, the baseline does not represent a true unconstrained demand condition, from which the unconstrained demand under unregulated conditions is being forecast.

The Reference Scenario sectoral forecast should instead be viewed in terms of the combined potential growth in natural gas consumption in the residential and industrial sectors. The actual distribution of the gas consumption in these sectors will depend on several factors, particularly the rate in which the local government restrictions on space-heating additions are removed. The forecast indicates that about 2.6 Tcf of growth will be distributed in these sectors.

At current world oil prices, natural gas usage in the Utility Sector declines by 13 percent to 3.0 Tcf. This means that with new natural gas and oil prices decontrolled, virtually no new gas driven turbines will be used to generate electricity. Available gas will instead be used by industry and in buildings.

An increase in the world price of crude oil from $13 to $16 per barrel will not have much effect on sectoral natural gas consumption. However, with new natural gas prices deregulated, a decrease in world oil prices to $8 per barrel will drive most natural gas out of utilities. Utility gas consumption would decline to 0.5 Tcf as the lower oil price causes extensive switching from natural gas to oil in power plants.

Unconstrained natural gas demand does not vary significantly as different government actions are implemented due to the compensating movement of natural gas prices (see Table III-8). However, natural gas domestic production declines significantly if natural gas price controls remain, leaving large shortfalls which must be satisfied by oil or gas imports.

The projected aggregate demand for natural gas cannot be met in all scenarios combining projected domestic pro-

Table III-8

1985 NATURAL GAS DEMAND AT $13/BBL OIL IMPORTS
(Tcf/yr)

PIES Scenario	U.S. Demand	Production	Imports	Average Price***
Reference	23.4	22.1	1.3	$2.03
BAU Supply with/ Conservation	23.1	21.8	1.3	$1.87
Accelerated Supply Without Conservation	26.6	25.3	1.3	$1.48
Supply Pessimism	24.7	17.2	7.5*	$1.84
Continued Current Regulation	23.4**	17.9	5.5*	$1.88
Gas Price Ceiling of $1/Mcf ($7.50 Regulatory)	24.2	17.0	7.3*	$1.83

  * Exceeds maximum available natural gas imports and would have to be replaced by oil imports or electricity.
 ** Estimated.
*** Average prices shown consist of a weighted average of domestic natural gas wellhead prices from all producing regions and imports, including transportation costs to the city gates, to satisfy all demand regions.

duction with a realistic estimate of natural gas imports. Natural gas imports in 1985 will be composed principally of imported LNG and Canadian pipeline gas. Canada is expected to provide about 0.87 Tcf/year based on the Canadian Natural Energy Board's current schedule of deliveries. Imported LNG is expected to vary between 0.4 Tcf and 2.1 Tcf annually, depending on the level of government encouragement as demonstrated through subsequent policy statements and further project approvals. Thus, realistic estimates of natural gas imports available by 1985 lie within the range of 1.0 to 3.0 Tcf per year.

As shown in Table III-8, in the Regulatory and Supply Pessimism Scenarios, the projected natural gas import requirements far exceed those which can realistically be considered attainable. Import requirements above 3.0 Tcf will be manifested as pipeline curtailments, and this unsatisfied natural gas demand will have to be satisfied through the use of alternate fuels, predominantly natural gas liquids, petroleum products, and perhaps electricity.

Long-Term Outlook for Supplies of Natural Gas and Pipeline Supplements The long-term supplies available through natural gas pipelines include domestic natural gas production (including Alaskan gas and supplies obtainable from tight gas formations, Devonian shale, and offshore areas), pipeline imports from Canada, liquefied natural gas imports and natural gas manufactured from petroleum products (SNG) or coal (syngas).

In viewing the total potential for natural gas supplies and its pipeline supplements in the long term, price, and therefore the degree of price regulation, is a critical factor. However, there are other factors that could greatly affect domestic exploration and production, including government policy concerning:

- Leasing of Outer Continental Shelf areas;

- Timing and ultimate construction of an Alaskan transportation system to transport production from the vast gas reserves at Prudhoe Bay;

- Acceptable LNG import levels and price;

- Pricing of SNG and construction of SNG plants;

- Research and Development to extend the natural gas resource base, including recovery from tight formations and Devonian shale;

- Possible financial support and regulatory control over the commercialization of synthetic gas from coal.

The Nation's total gas production is derived from gas wells which produce no oil (nonassociated gas), and from oil wells which produce both gaseous and liquid hydrocarbons (associated-dissolved gas). The supply of nonassociated gas is most sensitive to wellhead prices, while the supply of associated gas is primarily dependent upon the price of crude oil. Therefore, two separate models are used to estimate supply from these two sources to obtain FEA projections for production from the lower 48 States and the Outer Continental Shelf.

The FEA model for nonassociated gas supply activities has been designed to independently treat production rates, reserves depletion, exploration, drilling rates, and investment costing on a regional basis, given estimates of the undiscovered natural gas resource base. Provision has also been made to account for additional complexities inherent with exploration behavior under the influence of changing prices, and to capture distortions in drilling patterns that occur when very large gas fields are discovered in newly developed areas. Independent engineering estimates for a few special geographic gas regions and geologic formations are included to complete the regional supply curves for nonassociated gas production over the next 15 years.

A second model is utilized to estimate associated gas supply. Essentially, historical data from each region are utilized to derive a ratio of associated gas production to oil production, and the resulting supply curve for associated gas is a derivative of the oil model's supply curve for oil.

In comparison to the 1975 *Project Independence Report*, the price levels required to retain present production rates of nonassociated gas will be substantially higher. This is chiefly because the USGS reduced estimates of the resource base, smaller gas finding rates per unit of drilling were assumed, and the model was adjusted to account for the recent alterations in the depletion allowance. Further, new procedures were incorporated into the model which both related and extended estimates of the drilling and gas production responses to higher prices, removing simplifications in the original methodology.

Previously, the level of drilling was determined using one drilling curve available for all prices. This curve was selected to approximate the drilling that would be forthcoming at wellhead prices of $.80/Mcf in 1973 dollars. This simplification was used in the original study because the judgments at that time were that these prices and quantities would be sufficient to achieve equilibrium, and the focus was on evaluating fuel substitution—not the evaluation of supply increments at higher prices. Other improvements in FEA demand estimates have altered the equilibrium price calculations and motivated the more extensive treatment summarized here.

The revised supply model produces estimates of natural gas production which recognize the difference in costs and, therefore, prices of producing from reserves of different size and quality. This price sensitivity is essential in evaluating the impacts of fuel competition or in assessing the potential supply results from gas price deregulation.

This section describes the impact of prices on natural gas supply, including gas produced from domestic sources but excluding liquefied natural gas, synthetic gas from petroleum or coal and imported natural gas.

If new natural gas prices are deregulated and real uncontrolled oil prices remain at their current level, FEA estimates that total domestic production will be 22.3 Tcf in 1985 at an average price of $2.03/Mcf. If current natural gas regulation persists, production would decline to 17.9 Tcf and the interstate share of this production would be reduced drastically. Alternatively, if natural gas prices are set at $1.00/Mcf at the wellhead in both the interstate and intrastate markets, this supply estimate could drop to 17.0 Tcf. The sensitivity of these aggregate estimates can be displayed by separating the discussion into the contribution of total supply that comes from nonassociated gas and that which comes from associated gas.

Nonassociated supplies are very price sensitive, and could reach 1974 levels of 17 Tcf by 1985 under Business-as-Usual (BAU) assumptions if prices are permitted to rise above $2.00 per Mcf (see Table III-9). However, if price controls were extended to the intrastate market and maintained at the $.52/Mcf level (which amounts to a significant rollback of current intrastate prices), nonassociated natural gas production would fall to 5.8 Tcf by 1985, or 66 percent below 1974 levels.

The nonassociated gas component is forecast to decline to about 13.5 Tcf in 1985 from 17 Tcf in 1974 if prices are

Figure III-7

Non-Associated Natural Gas Production from the Lower-48 States and the O.C.S. at Three Wellhead Price Levels

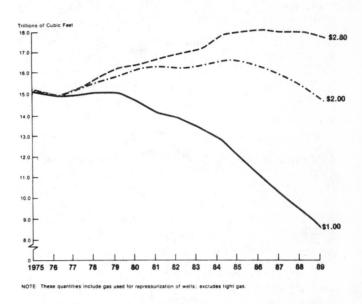

NOTE: These quantities include gas used for repressurization of wells; excludes tight gas.

restrained at the $1/Mcf level, averaged over all marketed production.

Natural gas production would begin to decline in the mid-1980's under BAU assumptions, even at $2 per Mcf, as remaining reserves in onshore areas are depleted. For

Table III-9

1985 NONASSOCIATED NATURAL GAS SUPPLY RESPONSE--BUSINESS-AS-USUAL
(Tcf)

Price $/Mcf	Nonassociated Gas*	Nonassociated Gas in Special Regions**	Total Nonassociated Natural Gas
$0.52	5.86	.00	5.86
1.00	13.31	.17	13.48
1.70	16.12	.46	16.58
2.00	16.64	.46	17.10
2.80	18.20	.46	18.66

* Excludes special regions. Quantities of nonassociated natural gas are presented for a Btu-equivalent petroleum price.
** Southern Alaska and tight gas. The non-responsiveness of supply at higher prices is due to logistic and institutional constraints.

this same reason, production at prices as high as $2.80 per Mcf under BAU assumptions peaks in 1986 and declines thereafter (see Figure III-7).

Most of the production response to price increases above $1 per Mcf comes from more intensive production on onshore fields. As natural gas prices vary from $1/Mcf to $2/Mcf, production would increase by 25 percent in the Western Gulf Basin and Mid-Continental regions and about 100 percent in the West Texas area (see Table III-10).

However, Gulf of Mexico offshore yields are constrained by the acreage leased by the government for exploration and drilling, which is assumed independent of price. The OCS leasing schedule is the prime determinant of frontier OCS gas production (given fixed geological expectations) at prices above about $.80 per Mcf. In addition, the long lead times required for production in some frontier areas constrain the supply response to price seen through 1985, and thus a greater elasticity of supply may actually be shown in the post-1985 period.

At $2 per Mcf, production from Louisiana and Texas would decline from 1974 levels by about 1 Tcf, but this loss is projected to be offset by increased production from the Gulf of Mexico, bringing total nonassociated gas production to near-1974 levels.

The sensitivity of these production estimates to factors other than price has been examined under two separate sets of assumptions other than BAU. The important pessimistic or optimistic assumptions are summarized in Table III-11.

The Optimistic and Pessimistic cases reflect the considerable uncertainty as to the size of the natural gas resource base of the United States. In recent years, the USGS has substantially reduced its estimates of our total undiscovered gas (including Alaska), from 2100 Tcf in 1972 to a 1000 to 2000 Tcf range in 1974, and then to its most recent estimate of 322 to 655 Tcf, made in 1975. The mean estimate, adjusted for water depths greater than 200 meters, is the primary natural gas data source utilized in the BAU cases. The major source of reserves is still located onshore in the lower 48 States (see Table III-12). Optimistic and Pessimistic geological outlooks vary considerably in offshore areas which are largely unexplored (see Table III-13). Historically most of the search for new reserves has focused on oil rather than natural gas, and thus the uncertainty surrounding the gas reserve estimates far exceeds that for oil reserves.

Although estimates of undiscovered resources are unimportant for short-term (1- to 5-year) production projections, they become increasingly important for longer-term analysis. If the U.S. production were to continue only from existing reserves through 1985, nonassociated production would drop to 5.6 Tcf in 1985 and to 3.4 Tcf in 1989 (see Table III-14). Thus, the currently unknown amount of gas that actually exists will begin to bear heavily upon discovery and production rates in the mid-1980's and beyond, and becomes the driving factor in long-range supply projections.

The Optimistic and Pessimistic cases also reflect the influence that changes in the rate of leasing of the offshore

Table III-10

NON ASSOCIATED GAS PRODUCTION ESTIMATES--BUSINESS-AS-USUAL
(Bcf/yr)

Code	Region	Actual 1974 Production	1985 Production Price ($/Mcf) 1.00	1985 Production Price ($/Mcf) 2.00	Difference in Production Estimates $2 From $1 Price	Difference in Production Estimates $2 price from 74 Actual
2	Pacific Coast States	156	53	62	9	(-94)
2a	Pacific Ocean (OCS)	20	0	48	48	28
3	Western Rocky Mountains	626	318	465	147	(-161)
4	Eastern Rocky Mountains	311	462	662	200	351
5	West Texas-E. New Mexico	2201	887	1839	952	(-362)
6	Western Gulf Basin	6422	4368	5545	1177	(-877)
6a	Gulf of Mexico (OCS)	3528	4493	4493	0	965
7	Mid Continent	3269	2569	3221	652	(-48)
8&9	Mich Basin, E. Interior	103	33	46	13	(-57)
10	Appalachians	331	129	255	126	(-76)
11	Atlantic Coast	0	0	0	0	0
11a	Atlantic Ocean (OCS)	0	0	0	0	0
	Total	16967	13312	16636	3324	(-331)

Table III-11

OPTIMISTIC AND PESSIMISTIC OUTLOOK ASSUMPTIONS

	Pessimistic	BAU	Optimistic
Resource Assessment	USGS "Mean" Minus 36%*	USGS "Mean"	USGS "Mean" Plus 36%*
OCS Leasing**	18.7 Million Acres	27.7 Million Acres	39.7 Million Acres
Investment Tax Credit	10% through 1977; 7% thereafter	10% through 1977; 7% thereafter	10% throughout

* These represent ± 1 standard deviation around the USGS "statistical" mean.
** Oil leasing not separated from gas leasing here.

Table III-12

RESERVES AND UNDISCOVERED RESOURCES OF NATURAL GAS
FOR THE UNITED STATES*
(Tcf)

	Reserves		Undiscovered Recoverable Resources	
	Measured	Inferred	Statistical Mean	95%-5% Range
Lower 48 Onshore	169	119	345	246-453
Alaska Onshore	32	15	32	16-57
Total Onshore	201	134	377	264-506
Lower 48 Offshore	36	67	101	42-178
Alaska Offshore	0	0	44	8-80
Total Offshore	36	67	145	50-248
Total U.S.	237	202	522	338-722

* Lower 48 States offshore estimates have been adjusted for OCS resources at greater than 200 meters, increasing mean estimate by 38 Tcf; includes associated-dissolved and nonassociated gas.

Table III-13

ALTERNATIVE GEOLOGICAL OUTLOOKS*
(Tcf)

Category	Pessimistic	Business-as-Usual	Optimistic
Measured Reserves	237.1	237.1	237.1
Inferred Reserves	201.6	201.6	201.6
Subtotal: Reserves	438.7	438.7	438.7
Undiscovered Recoverable			
Lower-48 Onshore	247	345	443
Lower-48 Offshore	52	101	150
Alaska Onshore	19	32	45
Alaska Offshore	9	44	79
Subtotal	327	·522	717
Total	766	961	1156

* Includes associated-dissolved and nonassociated natural gas; adjusted for water depths greater than 200 meters.

Table III-14

NONASSOCIATED GAS PRODUCTION FROM RESERVES EXISTING IN 1974

Year	Production
1975	15.1
1977	12.9
1980	9.6
1985	5.6
1989	3.4

areas can have on nonassociated production. However, changes in geological expectations are the dominant factor driving differences in the production response in both the Pessimistic and Optimistic cases as compared to the BAU case.

Under Optimistic conditions, total gas production in 1985 is estimated to increase above the BAU case by 2.5 Tcf (15 percent) at $2 per Mcf prices, and 2.3 Tcf (17 percent) at the $1 per Mcf price (see Table III-15). The Gulf of Mexico offshore region, most sensitive to these altered assumptions, increased 43 percent at the $2/Mcf price and

36 percent at the $1/Mcf price level (see Table III-16). Almost three-fourths of the increased production from the Gulf of Mexico at either price level is attributable to Optimistic resource estimates, virtually all of the remainder due to accelerated leasing.

Optimistic conditions delay the decline in nonassociated natural gas production (see Figure III-8 for production estimates for all three cases through 1989 at $2/Mcf). Under Optimistic conditions production reaches over 19 Tcf in 1986, while under BAU production declines after reaching 16.7 Tcf in 1984. By 1989, production only

Table III-15

NONASSOCIATED GAS PRODUCTION--1985
(Tcf)

Wellhead Price (1975 $)	Pessimistic	BAU	Optimistic
$1.00	12.0	13.3	15.6
$2.00	15.2	16.6	19.1
$2.80	16.2	18.1	20.9

drops 0.6 Tcf from 1985 levels under Optimistic resource assessments, while under BAU, production drops over 1.8 Tcf from 1985 levels. Under Pessimistic conditions, production rises slightly after 1976 to about 15.7 Tcf in 1980, and then drops to about 14.0 Tcf by 1989.

Drilling is expected to be extremely sensitive to price changes under all three outlooks. In 1974, the footage

drilled for gas wells (with dry holes allocated) totaled about 63 million feet. However, in the BAU case at $2 per Mcf, the average annual footage drilled is projected at 87 million feet from 1975 through 1980, and 92 million feet from 1981 through 1985.

The cumulative drilled footage doubles from 1975 through 1985 in the BAU case as the price is increased

Table III-16

NONASSOCIATED GAS PRODUCTION ESTIMATES--1985
(Bcf/yr)

Code	Region	$1/Mcf BAU	$1/Mcf Optimistic	$2/Mcf BAU	$2/Mcf Optimistic
2	Pacific Coast States	53	53	62	62
2a	Pacific Ocean (OCS)	0	35	48	53
3	Western Rocky Mountains	318	361	465	504
4	Eastern Rocky Mountains	462	546	662	732
5	West Texas-E. New Mexico	887	1193	1839	2059
6	Western Gulf Basin	4368	4391	5545	5688
6a	Gulf of Mexico (OCS)	4493	6103	4493	6413
7	Mid Continent	2569	2773	3221	3343
8&9	Mich. Basin, E. Interior	33	33	46	46
10	Appalachians	129	129	255	269
11	Atlantic Coast	0	0	0	0
11a	Atlantic Ocean (OCS)	0	0	0	0
	Total	13312	15617	16636	19169

Figure III-8

Non-Associated Natural Gas Production from the Lower-48 States and the O.C.S. Under Three Sets of Assumptions

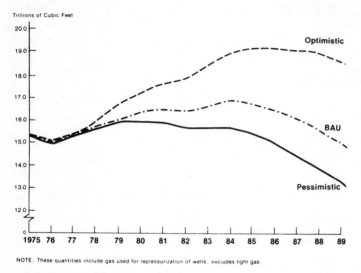

NOTE: These quantities include gas used for repressurization of wells, excludes tight gas.

from $1 to $2 per Mcf (see Table III-17). Drilling increases by 136 million feet (14 percent) in 1985 at the $2 price level under the Optimistic case, as compared to BAU conditions. In the Pessimistic case drilling drops 57 million feet as compared to BAU at $2/Mcf.

The drilling response to increased prices results in larger additions to proved reserves. Most added reserves will occur in the onshore and offshore Gulf Coast area (see Table III-18). Additions in the Gulf of Mexico, for example, could almost double current reserves, while reserve additions in the Western Gulf Basin will not exceed proved reserves in 1974. The annual average additions to reserves computed over 11 years from 1975 through 1985 at $2 per Mcf are comparable to the reserve additions that occurred prior to 1970, about 15 Tcf annually.

While most natural gas is supplied from wells devoted solely to producing gas, large amounts of production are possible from oil wells. In 1974, this associated gas production amounted to 4.2 Tcf. At current world oil prices and with domestic oil prices deregulated, associated gas production is forecast at 4.9 Tcf in 1985. However, both the degree of control over domestic oil prices and the world price of oil will affect associated gas production. For

Table III-17

PROJECTED FOOTAGE DRILLED FOR GAS WELLS, CUMULATIVE FROM 1975*
(Millions of Feet)

	Wellhead Price	1980	1985	1989
Business-As Usual	$1.00	308	404	419
	$2.00	521	982	1381
	$2.80	586	1275	1970
Optimistic	$1.00	446	618	618
	$2.00	551	1118	1632
	$2.80	623	1443	2301
Pessimistic	$1.00	285	333	335
	$2.00	509	925	1210
	$2.80	561	1105	1606

* Includes dry holes allocated to gas wells.

Note: In 1974, a total of 63.5 million feet were drilled for gas wells, including dry holes allocated.

Table III-18

NONASSOCIATED REGIONAL GAS RESERVE ADDITIONS (Tcf)
(BAU)

Region	1974 Proved Reserves	Reserves Added 1975-1985 Wellhead Prices ($/Mcf)		
		0.60	1.00	2.00
Eastern Rocky Mountain (4)	4.6	0.0	4.4	11.3
W. Texas - E. New Mexico (5)	14.4	0.0	8.9	26.2
W. Gulf Basin (6)	59.8	0.0	17.3	38.1
Gulf of Mexico OCS (6a)	30.9	11.6*	51.1	51.1
Mid Continent (7)	30.8	0.0	22.6	31.5
Other	21.7	0.0	1.0	9.8
Totals	162.2	11.6	105.3	168.0

* Drilling in region 6a commences for four years and then ceases.

instance, if world oil prices drop from about $13/bbl currently to $8/bbl, and domestic oil is decontrolled, associated gas production in 1985 could decrease 0.8 Tcf to 4.1 Tcf, because drilling for exploratory oil wells would decline from projected levels. In addition, if world oil prices remain at $13/bbl, but domestic oil is controlled at $7.50/bbl through 1985, then associated gas production will be only 3.5 Tcf in 1985, again due to the induced reduction in domestic drilling for new oil wells.

A reduction of natural gas prices at constant oil prices through establishment of a ceiling would affect oil production in addition to both associated and nonassociated gas production. For instance, if world oil prices were maintained at $13 per barrel, domestic oil prices were uncontrolled, and a natural gas price ceiling was established at $1 per Mcf, combined associated gas and oil production would be reduced by 2.8 Tcf, with about 65 percent of this loss being reduced oil production. This occurs because of the reduced exploration activity in geological areas which produce both gas and oil due to reduced expected revenues by oil and gas companies.

The BAU supply curve is input into the PIES model to determine the Reference Scenario—that is, the market clearing price at which supply and demand are at

Table III-19

REFERENCE SCENARIO PRODUCTION

World Oil Price $/bbl	1985 Domestic Production (Tcf)			Price $/Mcf*		
	Nonassoc.	Assoc.	Total	Nonassoc.	Assoc.	Avg.
$8	16.3	4.1	20.4	$1.90	$1.67	$1.79
$13	17.4	4.9	22.3	$2.13	$1.93	$2.03
$16	17.4	5.1	22.5	$2.16	$1.97	$2.07

* The average price is the city gate price for domestic gas and imports; prices for nonassociated and associated gas reflect marginal wellhead prices for new gas.

equilibrium in an uncontrolled market or deregulated condition. At current world oil prices, about 22.3 Tcf of natural gas would be produced domestically in 1985 at an average price of $2.03 per Mcf (see Table III-19). Of this production, 78 percent would be nonassociated gas including 165 Bcf from tight formations. Of the remaining 4.9 Tcf of associated gas, 835 Bcf would be transported from Northern Alaska by a pipeline expected to be operational in the early 1980's (see later discussion in this Chapter).

In addition to this domestic production, 1.27 Tcf of natural gas imports are purchased at the import price of $2.14 per Mcf. This represents 0.4 Tcf of liquefied natural gas already contracted for and approved by the FPC, and 0.87 Tcf of pipeline imports from Canada pursuant to the Canadian National Energy Board's current schedule of deliveries.

If oil prices drop from $13 per barrel to $8 per barrel, natural gas prices are pulled down to approximate a Btu-equilibrium with lower priced oil in the utility sector, and the total production of natural gas declines. However, as world oil prices increase to $16 per barrel, little effect is noted on natural gas production and prices as compared to the $13/bbl case, since no significant fuel switching response in the utility sector is stimulated.

To project prices and production levels in 1985 if current regulations over natural gas were maintained, a special methodology had to be constructed to model the effects of maintaining two distinct markets—the unregulated intrastate market and the regulated interstate market. A regulated supply curve was constructed and allowed to equilibrate with a regulated demand curve to produce a new production and price level. The following assumptions were made:

- All West South Central gas consumption was considered intrastate gas.
- The 1974 ratio of OCS to non-OCS contracts will be maintained under continued regulation.
- The West South Central intrastate market can be assumed representative of all domestic intrastate markets.
- Quantities under existing interstate contracts will continue to decline at a rate of 7 to 8 percent per year.
- The ratio of non-West South Central, non-Alaskan production to West South Central production will continue at its 1974 level.
- The intrastate demand curve for West South Central will be stable under deregulation, i.e., the regulated and deregulated intrastate equilibria are on the same demand curve.

In the Continued Regulations Scenario only the intrastate market will be in equilibrium. Gas from the onshore areas would be produced until demand in this market is satisfied at a new contract price of about $1.80/Mcf. Offshore and Alaskan gas production, on the other hand, would be restricted by an assumed FPC field price ceiling

Table III-20

PROJECTED INTERSTATE/INTRASTATE SALES UNDER DIFFERENT POLICIES--1985

| | Marketed Production | | Sales | |
	Gross	Net*	Interstate*	Intrastate*
Actual 1974	21.6	18.8	11.6	7.2
Present Regulation - 1985	17.9	15.9	6.6	9.3
Deregulation - 1985 (Reference Scenario)	22.3	20.0	12.1	7.9

* Gas consumed by end-users from domestic sources, excluding liquefied natural gas, synthetic fuels, and imported natural gas. Total gas consumption (including these other sources) would be greater.

Table III-21

NATURAL GAS PRODUCTION AND PRICES FOR ALTERNATIVE SCENARIOS
($13 Oil Imported)

| Scenario | 1985 Production Tcf | | | Price $/Mcf | |
	Nonassoc.	Assoc.	Total	Nonassoc.*	Avg**
Reference	17.4	4.9	22.3	$2.13	$2.03
BAU Supply With/ Conservation	16.9	4.9	21.8	$1.98	$1.87
Accelerated Supply Without Conservation	19.0	6.3	25.3	$1.59	$1.48
Supply Pessimism	14.2	3.0	17.2	$1.12	$1.84
Continued Current Regulation	13.9	4.0	17.9	$1.81	$1.88
Gas Price Ceiling of $1/Mcf	13.5	3.5	17.0	$1.04	$1.83

* Marginal price across all gas production regions of new nonassociated gas only.
** Average is weighted average of domestic natural gas and imported gas, transported to city gate for all demand regions.

of about $.60/Mcf plus any cost-of-living adjustments. Total marketed production is forecast at 17.9 Tcf for the Nation, although only 6.6 Tcf of this would be allocated to the interstate market (see Table III-20). Curtailed industrial users would be forced to purchase imported oil.

The differences between deregulation and regulation are substantially more pronounced for interstate supply than for total national production. With the continuation of the present regulations at today's prices (in constant dollars), interstate supply would decline about 5.0 Tcf below its 1974 level of 11.6 Tcf—a reduction of 43 percent. If new gas is deregulated, the higher gas prices would allow large volumes of gas to enter the interstate market, because not only will more offshore and Alaskan gas be produced but also some onshore gas will be bid away from the intrastate market. Under these conditions, the decline in interstate sales would be halted, resulting in slightly more sales than its present level by 1985.

FEA analyzed the effects of a number of possible policy variations on natural gas production, consumption, and price. If development of resources is accelerated by increasing leasing and if geology is favorable, production possibilities could increase to more than 25 Tcf and price would decline (see Accelerated Supply Scenario on Table III-21). The lower prices result because lower cost production is made available to meet demand. In economic terms, the supply curve is shifted to the right on a

relatively elastic demand curve, yielding increased supplies at lower prices.

Government conservation measures tend to reduce demand, thereby reducing production requirements to meet demand and lowering prices. For instance, conservation measures added to the Reference Scenario result in the lower average natural gas prices observed in the BAU Supply with Conservation Scenario $1.87/Mcf as compared to $2.03/Mcf in the Reference Scenario.

Although price regulations shown in the $1.00 Regulation Scenario and the Supply Pessimism Scenario succeed in holding down domestic wellhead prices, average natural gas (or equivalent fuel) prices will not be reduced significantly below those of the Reference Scenario, due to large quantities of imports needed to meet demand.

Delivering Alaskan Natural Gas Although estimates for associated gas from the North Slope of Alaska were included in the Reference Scenario projections already discussed, a separate section is devoted here to the special problems involved in accessing this gas.

Alaska has the largest known U.S. reserves of undeveloped natural gas potential: 26 Tcf of associated gas in the Prudhoe Bay area, 1 Tcf in the Cook Inlet area, and 2 Tcf in other areas. The National Petroleum Council and the U.S. Geological Survey estimate undiscovered resources ranging between 16 and 57 Tcf onshore, and between 8 and 80 Tcf offshore (95 percent probability of at least the first; 5 percent probability of as much as the second number in each range).

In addition to the North Slope gas, there are some 3.6 Tcf of proved nonassociated gas reserves in Canada's Mackenzie Delta area; another 2.8 Tcf are expected to be added to the proven reserves for this area in the near term. Estimated future potential of Canada's Mackenzie Delta is an additional 49 Tcf.

Transportation in the Arctic presents unusual challenges because of the cold climate, remoteness, long distances, and the permafrost. The land is permanently frozen in the Arctic (in some places to a depth of 2,000 feet) except for an active surface layer of a foot or two which thaws in summer. Permafrost problems are most severe near rivers and deltas. When the moisture-laden surface layer thaws during the summer, these areas become spongy swamps over which ground transport is often impossible.

If the surface layer of moss lichen and other small plants is disturbed for any reason, the summer heat penetrates to the permanently frozen ground underneath and the ground melts. Water runoff erodes the area and disturbs more of the surface layer. A small wash can quickly become a 20-foot-deep mud slough, which will continue to spread each summer. Off northern Alaska, ice conditions become so severe that in some places the sea is open for navigation only one or two weeks a year.

Figure III-9

Proposed Arctic Gas System

— ARCTIC GAS SYSTEM
--- proposed companion systems
..... existing systems owned or
served by participating firms

Figure III-10

Proposed El Paso System

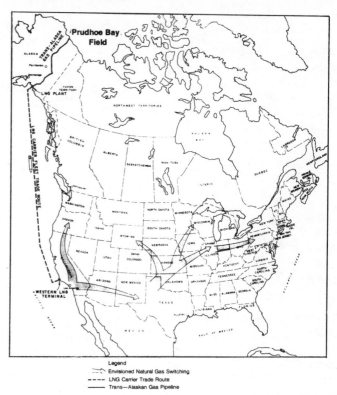

Legend
⌐⌐⌐ Envisioned Natural Gas Switching
--- LNG Carrier Trade Route
— Trans—Alaskan Gas Pipeline

Transportation of Alaskan gas to the lower 48 States is the subject of intense competition between two proposed alternative routes. Issues include the relative economics of the systems, Alaskan/Canadian environmental concerns, Alaskan economic development policy, U.S.-Canada relations, Canadian domestic policies, financing, possibility of delay, location of natural gas delivery, and lower 48 safety concerns.

The *Arctic Gas* consortium proposes about 200 miles of line eastward from Prudhoe to the Canadian border, 2,400 miles of Canadian line from the Yukon-Alaska border to South Alberta and two branches of line in the United States: 1,600 miles in Montana, North and South Dakota, Minnesota, Iowa, Illinois, Indiana, Ohio, West Virginia to Delmont, Pennsylvania; and about 280 miles through Idaho and Washington to Stanfield, Oregon (see Figure III-9).

The *El Paso* group proposes 809 miles of pipeline from Prudhoe along the Alyeska corridor to a gas liquefaction plant and terminal in Southern Alaska. From there, the LNG would be shipped by cryogenic tanker to a receiving terminal and regasification plant in Southern California (see Figure III-10). Although the Alaskan gas would be introduced at the West Coast, El Paso expects to make increasing supplies of natural gas available to the Mid-West and East Coast by switching present East-to-West supplies of Gulf Coast natural gas from West Coast markets to the East (this concept is known as displacement). This would require construction of an additional 540 miles of pipeline in the lower 48 States.

Further, an all-Canadian proposal by (Maple Leaf) *Foothills Pipeline*, Ltd., from the Mackenzie Delta south to Alberta, is being considered by the Canadian government.

Recently Arctic Gas has estimated its pipeline capacity in Alaska at 0.8 Tcf/yr; El Paso designed its proposed system to fit a projected Prudhoe supply of 1.2 Tcf/yr. If one system is expedited and encounters no serious delays, the lower 48 could be receiving 0.8 to 1.2 Tcf/yr (2.1 to 3.2 Bcf/day) of Prudhoe gas by 1985—at an estimated cost of $2.50 to $3 per Mcf including transportation to U.S. borders.

Final details of the two routes to the lower 48 States have not yet been settled. Accurate cost comparisons are not possible because each of the two groups used not only a different assumed gas supply from Prudhoe, but also differing base year dollar values. However, extrapolation from information available last fall indicated that the Arctic Gas proposal could cost between $8.5 and $9.7 billion (in 1975 dollars) and the El Paso proposal between $7.5 and $9 billion. Canada's cost share of the Arctic Gas proposal could be $1.3 to $1.7 billion.

The two proposals differ fundamentally, and each offers its own set of benefits. El Paso maintains that its proposed system bypasses any possible complications arising from routing the Arctic Gas line through Canada. El Paso points out the advantage to the U.S. economy and the Treasury of having all the payments for construction and operation of its system accrue solely to the United States. El Paso also says its system will give a bigger economic boost to Alaska. Arctic maintains that the Canadian route for Alaskan gas that also accesses Canada's Mackenzie reserves offers better economies of scale and cheaper ultimate costs to U.S. consumers.

Each system has its own set of potential environmental difficulties and possible sources of delays. The Arctic proposal could threaten disruption of the Arctic National Wildlife Range in Northeast Alaska, while the El Paso plan may increase maritime traffic in the Gulf of Alaska and Prince William Sound. Delays in project completion under the Arctic plan could be caused by difficulties in resolving Canadian taxing issues and Northwest Territories native claims, and by the larger requirement for construction activities to be undertaken north of the Arctic Circle. El Paso faces possible engineering delays because it would utilize larger liquefaction facilities and LNG tankers than have been previously built.

Among the most important unresolved issues is the regional impact of each competing system. Alaska,

California, Midwestern, and North Central States all have a direct interest in the decision, as do the shipbuilding states where El Paso's LNG tankers would be built.

Whereas the Arctic Gas line would run only 195 miles through uninhabited Alaskan terrain, the El Paso line would lay four times as much pipe and build an expensive liquefaction plant in Alaska—thus, continuing the Alyeska oil line boom in southern Alaska.

The El Paso system would require a terminal, regasification plant, and pipeline in California to link up with existing lines. The Arctic Gas line would include pipeline construction in Montana, North Dakota, South Dakota, Minnesota, Iowa, Illinois, Indiana, Ohio, and Pennsylvania. In Montana and western North Dakota, pipeline construction would draw out-of-state construction workers and shift workers into construction from other occupations.

In summary, although the choice between competing pipeline proposals cannot be made until the relative costs and benefits of the systems are more clearly defined, the construction of a natural gas pipeline from Prudhoe Bay is critical to the U.S. economic and energy interests. The 0.8 to 1.2 Tcf that could be available in 1982 could reduce oil import requirements by about 500,000 barrels a day.

The Role of Imported Liquefied Natural Gas (LNG) LNG is natural gas of pipeline quality (1000 Btu/cf or higher) which is converted to liquid form by reducing the gas temperature to -259 degrees F. The liquefaction process reduces volume by a factor of 623:1, and consumes approximately 15 percent of the gas energy supplied at the liquefaction plant. Additional energy losses are incurred through production, gathering, and transmission from the wellhead to the liquefaction plant.

Large scale liquefaction and ocean shipment of gas as LNG are relatively recent developments, resulting from the fact that countries such as Abu Dhabi, Algeria, Indonesia, Iran, Libya, and Nigeria have developed sizable proved reserves of natural gas, but have no means at present to deliver this gas by pipeline to potentially large consuming markets.

An average sized LNG project in international trade would deliver approximately 1 Bcf/day or over 0.3 Tcf per year. For a U.S.-Algeria trade project delivering 1 Bcf/day and using current design technology, one liquefaction facility, eight 125,000-cubic meter tankers (8,000-mile round trip trade) and a terminal facility capable of handling one ship every 2½ days would be needed. The following is an estimate of the investment cost for such a system delivering gas in 1980 from Algeria to an East Coast port:

Table III-22

OIL AND GAS DATA FOR POTENTIAL LNG SUPPLY SOURCES

Country	Oil Reserves (Billion Barrels)	Gas Reserves (Tcf)	Gas: Oil Reserve Ratio	Oil Production (1975 MB/D)
Algeria	7.4	126.0	17.0	935
Indonesia	14.0	15.0	1.1	1,300
Iran	64.5	329.5	5.1	5,600
Libya	26.1	26.3	1.0	1,400
Nigeria	20.2	44.3	2.2	1,850
Abu Dhabi	29.5	20.0	0.7	1,500

Source: Oil and Gas Journal, December 29, 1975

Investment Items	Cost—$Million, 1975 Rate
Liquefaction Facility	1,000
8 Tankers (8,000 mile round trip, Algeria U.S.)	1,300
Receiving Terminal and Regasification Facility	300
Total	2,600

This investment cost of about $2.6 billion results in considerable additions to the wellhead price of the exported natural gas for liquefaction, transportation, and regasification. Consequently, at current world prices the producer country's 'take' (profit) from LNG exports is considerably less than the equivalent 'take' from the export of crude oil. Based on F.O.B. prices of $1.30/Mcf for LNG, North Africa, and $11.51/barrel for marker crude, Persian Gulf, producer country 'takes' are $.30/Mcf and $11.00/barrel respectively, or 23 percent vs. 96 percent of F.O.B. price.

The pricing strategy of some LNG exporters has been to seek an oil Btu equivalent price for LNG at the port of embarcation. This has been the Libyan strategy to date, although it has encountered severe resistance in buying markets. A strategy currently being followed by the Algerians in negotiations with U.S. companies is to price against a competing fuel in the consuming country.

A major factor in determining the demand for imported LNG will be the manner in which the FPC allows LNG to be priced domestically. In the only two cases previously approved by the FPC, imported LNG was to be priced on an incremental basis, thereby disallowing averaging in the higher costs of LNG with cheaper domestically produced natural gas.

Although Iran and Algeria have large gas reserves, Algeria is the only one of these nations actively seeking a large LNG export market because of its substantially higher gas/oil reserve ratio and low oil export revenues (see Table III-22). One country with large reserves not listed on Table III-19 is the U.S.S.R. (estimated reserves in excess of 800 Tcf).

It is unlikely that new LNG projects will be able to come on stream until after 1985 unless they are in the initial planning stages at this time, due to the long lead times for the regulatory process and for construction of tankers and facilities. Thus, maximum LNG import quantities in 1985 are now defined, and several alternative levels can be assumed.

- Most conservatively, it could be assumed that only the projects already unconditionally-approved by the FPC will materialize, i.e., the Distrigas I and El Paso I ventures; this would result in annual LNG imports of 0.4 Tcf in 1985 (LNG Supply Case I).

- Alternatively, it could be assumed that in addition to the above ventures, projects which have been submitted to the FPC for approval would also materialize; annual supply by 1985 would total 1.5 Tcf (LNG Supply Case II).

- Finally, projects announced in Iran and Nigeria but not yet submitted to FPC for their review could be developed, resulting in a 1985 supply level of 2.1 Tcf (LNG Supply Case III).

In all three cases, Algeria emerges as the major source of LNG imports for the United States, ranging in 1985 from 100 percent of supply in Case I to about 70 percent in Case III. This results not only from Algeria's advantageous location with respect to consuming markets, but also from its determination to market its vast gas reserves, since its oil reserves are relatively limited.

The possible levels of U.S. LNG imports in 1980 and 1985 are shown below:

```
         Table III-23

ALTERNATIVE LNG SUPPLY CASES
          (Tcf/yr)

                 1980    1985

   Case I         .4      .4
   Case II       0.9     1.5
   Case III      1.3     2.1
```

Determining regional dependence on LNG imports is difficult because most of the companies that import gas serve more than one region and also sell to transmission companies serving other regions.

Although regional dependence could go as high as 10 percent, the dependence of customers served by the importing pipeline companies will be much greater. Of the seven projects filed with the FPC, individual pipeline company import dependence could range between 9 and 29 percent of current annual sales. Regional and company dependence are important because of the potential for sudden interruption or abrupt increase in price.

Although dependence, vulnerability, and pricing are the significant major issues associated with LNG, there are several other potential problems. While exporting countries have traditionally constructed and owned the liquefaction facilities, the financing of such facilities has originated within the importing country through government agencies such as the Export-Import Bank of the United States. These Export-Import Bank loans for liquefaction facilities, along with Maritime Administration loan guarantees and subsidies for LNG tankers, must be reviewed and coordinated with national policy towards LNG. Safety and environmental concerns have delayed the use of some terminals, particularly in densely populated harbor areas such as the New York Harbor.

In summary, it is clear that some supplemental LNG imports will probably be required in the next decade or two to assist the United States in meeting energy demands placed on the natural gas pipeline and distribution system. However, excessive dependence on the supplies must be avoided due to the consequent vulnerability to arbitrary price increases and sudden interruptions in supplies, as in the case of oil imports.

Synthetic Gas From Coal The extraction of methane from coal has been demonstrated in several pilot plants, both in the United States and abroad. This process offers the U.S. a mid-term capability to make greater use of coal reserves to supplement domestic natural gas supplies.

However, the commercial viability of a high Btu synthetic gas venture has not yet been demonstrated in the United States. Present estimates indicate that an investment of about $1 billion will be required to construct a high Btu gas plant capable of producing 0.08 Tcf/yr (assuming a debt/equity ratio of 75:25). About $525 million would be required to finance construction of a low Btu gas plant producing the equivalent of 0.05 Tcf/yr (assuming a debt/equity ratio of 50:50). The full costs (i.e., without incentives of both high and low Btu synthetic gas processes, expressed in 1975 dollars on an F.O.B. gasification plant basis) are expected to range as shown in Table III-24.

Additional costs will be incurred in transmitting the high Btu gas output to consuming areas; these costs will vary depending on the proximity of the synthetic plants to natural gas transmission networks and consuming markets. Pacific Lighting estimates that transmission and distribution costs to its proposed WESCO (Western Gasification Company) venture in New Mexico with its service area in Southern California would add 32¢/Mcf to the city gate price, increasing the price to a range of $3.35 to $4.55/Mcf.

The technology involved in the production of low Btu gas is well developed and is currently applied in many commercial plants outside the United States. Actually, coal gasification was prevalent in the United States for producing 'town gas,' that is, gas produced locally for community consumption purposes only, prior to the establishment of natural gas pipelines. A limiting factor in the use of low/medium Btu gas is that it is not economically feasible to transport it more than about 50 miles. This may be an inhibiting developmental factor if a plant is intended to generate electricity to residential, commercial, and industrial users in urban areas.

Although industry is considering a number of synthetic fuels projects, none has actually proceeded to the construction stage in the United States. Six major projects involving high Btu gas from coal are currently being planned. Several low Btu gas projects related to utility and industrial fuels have been suggested, but have not yet reached the level of planning associated with high Btu gas projects. None of the projects has yet acquired the necessary financing and other approvals needed to proceed. Only a few projects have actually reached the detailed design phase.

Table III-24

COSTS OF SYNTHETIC GAS PROCESSES IN $/MCF*

Cost Category	High Btu Gas Plant		Low Btu Gas Plant	
	Low Estimates	High Estimates	Low Estimates	High Estimates
Fixed Costs	1.02	1.38	1.77	2.40
Operating and Maintenance	.82	1.01	.61	.76
Feedstock of $11** to $17/ton	1.19	1.84	.72	1.11
Total at Plant	3.03	4.23	3.10	4.27

* Derived from Draft Synthetic Fuels Commercialization Report, submitted to the President's Energy Resources Council, dated June 1975.

** Feedstock cost of coal could also be estimated at $5 to $9/ton to account for East, West regional experiences in the cost of coal production; with this lower feedstock cost, high Btu gas would range between $2.38 and $2.34/Mcf.

The major reason the projects have not proceeded is that the risks associated with initiating synthetic fuels projects are large compared with other investments providing an equal or higher rate of return. A major risk is the uncertainty concerning the future price of world oil. For instance, high Btu coal gasification projects need an equivalent of $19 per barrel to have an acceptable return on investment. Other important risks include:

- Uncertainty about air and water quality standards;
- Resource (coal, shale, biomass) availability as constrained by leasing rates and environmental concerns;
- Water availability;
- Federal regulation of price of fuels;
- Availability of labor, materials and equipment;
- Need for environmental control technology;
- Extent of socioeconomic impact;
- Unforeseen project delays.

With the proper financial incentives, the development of high and low Btu gasification plants can accelerate

rapidly after 1980 and could reach about 1,060 Bcf by 1985 and 1,440 Bcf by 1990.

The Potential for Increased Use of Substitute Natural Gas Substitute natural gas (SNG) can be made from liquid petroleum feedstock such as crude oil, naphtha, and LPG (propane and butane), through catalytic conversion of the feedstock into a methane-rich gas of high Btu content (about 850 Btu/cubic feet), and further treatment, such as methanation, CO_2 removal or propane enrichment which increases the heat value of the gas to pipeline quality. In the naphtha process, about 90 percent of the feedstock is converted into gas; the remainder is consumed as process fuel or lost; the technique is generally known as naphtha reforming.

Some existing SNG plants are primarily used for peaking purposes, operating at full design capacity for only 150 days per year. Certain other plants are running currently at less than practical operating capacity for 350 days a year, due to insufficient feedstocks as limited by government regulations. If the plants constrained by feedstock availability were provided sufficient feedstock, an additional 10 Bcf per year of SNG would be produced. If, in addition, all existing plants were run at practical operating capacity, a total of about 95 Bcf/yr of additional production could be obtained, or 0.4 percent of total natural gas use.

There are 13 SNG plants currently in operation and three under construction in the United States. Eight of these plants are naphtha reforming units, while the others are peak-shaving plants which utilize light petroleum liquids as feedstock. The combined capacity of these plants, when all are operational, is estimated at about 0.5 Tcf/yr; all 16 facilities should be on stream by 1977. In addition to these units, there are five other SNG plants in various stages of planning. The major uncertainty which appears to be delaying activation of these projects is the availability of feedstock, principally naphtha. Assuming all plants currently planned are constructed, the SNG contribution to natural gas supply could amount to approximately 1.5 Tcf by 1985; more realistically, about 1 Tcf can be anticipated.

Because of rising prices for feedstocks and the plant facilities, the cost of SNG is extremely high (between $3.50 and $5.20 per Mcf, as compared to about 52¢/Mcf for new interstate gas, and $2.30 to $3.10 for LNG), making it the most expensive source of gas supply available today. For plants operating at less than full capacity or only for part of the year, SNG cost is even higher because of the reduced levels of plant outputs over which the plant operating and maintenance costs must be prorated.

The ultimate cost to the consumer will vary depending on whether the gas is sold incrementally or on a "roll-in" basis. In the event the sale of the SNG is subject to FPC jurisdiction (i.e., the SNG is commingled with gas sold for resale in interstate commerce), the Commission has ruled in all cases to date that it will be sold on an incremental basis. For SNG subject to state regulatory jurisdiction, which is the case for most of the SNG plants operating or under construction today, "rolled-in" pricing has been the policy adopted by most states.

Problems exist with either form of pricing when SNG is being added to pipelines to supplement natural gas supplies. When priced incrementally, the gas is generally produced and purchased only on a seasonal basis to satisfy peak-shaving needs by utilities. This causes extremely high production costs for SNG and a disincentive to construct SNG plants.

Where SNG prices are allowed to be "rolled-in" with cheaper domestically produced natural gas, there exists an economic incentive to run the plants at full capacity throughout the year and thus substitute SNG for unavailable domestically produced natural gas supplies. As a result, naphtha and LPG feedstocks, in the absence of an allocation system, would be bid away from traditional users, such as farmers and industrial users, to be used in an SNG production process where about 10 percent of the feedstock is lost in conversion.

In summary, approximately 1.0 Tcf of SNG from petroleum products is forecast to be available in 1985 given current plant capacity and those expected to be constructed under incremental pricing policies. Since SNG is produced from petroleum, it is not distinguished from petroleum in FEA forecasts.

Gas From Tight Formations Natural gas is also found in tight (low permeability), thick, massive sand and shale deposits located predominantly in the Rocky Mountain states. A significant portion of this resource is believed to be in the Green River Basin of Wyoming, the Piceance Basin of Colorado and the Uinta Basin in Utah.

The FPC has estimated gas reserves in these areas at the following levels (as compared to 439 Tcf of demonstrated and inferred reserves from other areas):

	Tcf
Green River Basin, Wyoming	240
Piceance Basin, Colorado	210
Uinta Basin, Utah	150
Total	600

These formations require extensive fracturing, if the gas is to be produced on a commercial basis. There are two approaches, applying entirely different technology, potentially capable of creating the fracture systems for production. These are the nuclear explosive and the massive hydraulic fracturing methods. The nuclear explosive method has been tested and failed to provide access to the fully stimulated zone. In addition, this method has resulted in unfavorable public response regarding possible environmental and safety hazards, which could pose a major constraint in its use.

If either stimulation process can be made effective and is properly employed, cumulative recovery could reach 40-50 percent of the gas in place. Estimates of the amount of natural gas that could be produced from these formations in 1980 and 1985 are difficult to derive since the fracturing technologies have not yet been fully developed. Additionally, the actual quantities of gas in these formations are highly speculative.

Finally, the present controls on natural gas pricing at the wellhead adversely affect the willingness of industry to proceed with commercial development plans. FEA estimates that 0.2 to 0.9 Tcf/yr could be produced by 1985, depending upon the level of investment.

Gas From Devonian Shale Formations The Devonian gas shales are geologic formations underlying in an area of approximately 250,000 square miles in the Middle and Eastern sections of the United States. Trapped within the shale is an unknown, but potentially very large quantity of natural gas. In order to produce gas from these shales, it is not possible to employ the standard drilling techniques commonly used in producing natural gas; rather, advanced massive fracturing techniques are required. These techniques have been employed on a small scale, but major technological developments will be necessary before commercial quantities of gas can be extracted.

Devonian shale formations are extensive in parts of Ohio, Illinois, Indiana, Kentucky, Alabama, Tennessee, West Virginia, Pennsylvania, and New York.

If a major, rapid development program were undertaken, it might be possible for sufficient quantities of natural gas to be produced from local resources to enable these states, which, in many cases, are those most affected by the current shortage, to have an adequate gas resource base.

The principal difficulty stems from the lack of accurate data on the potentially recoverable volumes of natural gas. The U.S. Geological Survey does not include either gas from Devonian shale or tight formations in current resource estimates because, although both types of formations are known to have great potential, no feasible method for commercially extracting the gas has been found. Existing industry estimates, based on extrapolations from limited geological data, value the reserves on the order of 285 Tcf in Ohio, West Virginia, Pennsylvania, Kentucky, and New York. This estimate must be evaluated in the context of a proven gas reserve estimate of 237 Tcf for the entire United States in 1974.

Once the gas-bearing shale formations have been located, technological and economic hurdles will have to be overcome in order to develop this potential resource and to produce significant quantities of natural gas. Because of the lower delivery rates of gas from wells drilled in Devonian shale as compared with sandstone formations, large numbers of wells must be drilled in shales using current technology to produce significant quantities of gas. Columbia Gas, for example, has estimated that using today's technology to develop 250 million cubic feet daily (91 Bcf/yr) would require 3,200 wells the first year at a cost of $285 million. In the next 11 years, 3,100 wells and $280 million would be required to sustain that rate of gas production. Thus, the cost of this gas would be over $3.50/Mcf. Further research could reduce the cost of wells as well as increase their productivity. New stimulation technology could reduce the requirement for wells by as much as a factor of 10. Because of the high costs associated with the production of gas from Devonian shales, higher prices and further technological development will be necessary to obtain gas from this source.

ERDA has contracted for three experimental wells to be drilled in the West Virginia–Eastern Kentucky area. This pilot project is primarily designed to improve hydraulic fracturing techniques and evaluate the gas extraction potential from an area where much is known about the underlying geological structure.

In conclusion, Devonian gas shale formations may produce as much as .09 Tcf/yr with conventional technology by 1985 at a cost of over $3.50/Mcf. Thus, it provides little prospect for near- or mid-term relief in the context of the current shortage.

Summary The most significant impact on domestic natural gas supply is derived from the degree of price controls extended over oil and gas (see Table III-25). If existing regulations over natural gas continue and oil prices are decontrolled, about 17.9 Tcf of gas will be produced in 1985. Equally important is the fact that under these conditions the interstate natural gas market would decline to 6.6 Tcf in 1985 from 11.6 Tcf in 1974. If instead, current regulations are extended to the intrastate market and maintained at the current 52¢/Mcf level, along with regulation of oil prices, about 9.2 Tcf of natural gas can be anticipated in 1985 (almost 60 percent less than 1974 levels). However, if oil and gas prices are deregulated, 22.3 Tcf will be produced in 1985.

Selection of one of the two alternative routes to transport natural gas from Northern Alaska could provide 0.8 to 1.2 Tcf to the "Lower 48" States by the early 1980's (0.8 Tcf is included in the Reference Scenario). Also, if leasing in the offshore areas is accelerated above current expectations, an additional 0.5 Tcf can be produced by 1985.

The volumes of natural gas supplements available by 1985 are almost completely dependent on government energy policies. The announced synthetic fuels commercialization program could result in the production of 1.1 Tcf of synthetic gas by 1985. LNG imports could increase to up to about 2 Tcf by 1985, but would be 0.4 Tcf if no further project applications were approved. The availability of substitute gas from petroleum products will depend greatly upon the price of oil, the availability of feedstocks and the method of pricing when injected into pipelines and distribution gas lines. At current price levels and with an incremental pricing policy maintained, about 1.0 Tcf of SNG will be produced in 1985 (as compared to 0.5 Tcf currently).

If the natural gas resource base is made further accessible, such as through development and application of advanced fracturing technologies, natural gas from tight formations and Devonian shale would reach about 1.0 Tcf by 1985. (Only about 0.2 Tcf of gas from tight formations is included in the Reference Scenario.)

Thus, with no changes in geological expectations, about 23.6 Tcf of natural gas, 2.1 Tcf of imported LNG, 0.87 Tcf of gas from Canada, 1.0 Tcf of SNG and 1.1 Tcf of synthetic gas (from coal) could be available by 1985—a total of about 28.7 Tcf of natural gas and supplements.

Table III-25

POTENTIAL SUPPLY OF NATURAL GAS AND SUPPLEMENTS

Supply Source	Decision/Action	Price ($/Mcf)	1985 Supply (Tcf)
Lower 48 and Southern Alaskan (BAU), including the North Slope and Tight Formations	.Extend controls to intra-state gas market; maintain oil controls.	0.52	9.2
	.Extend controls to intra-state gas market; decontrol oil.	0.52	10.8
	.Maintain ceiling of $1.00 on gas and existing controls on oil.*	1.00	17.0
	.Maintain existing controls on gas; deregulate oil.*	1.24	17.9
	.Decontrol oil and new gas.*	2.03	22.3
Prudhoe Bay, Alaska	.Construct pipeline by 1982	2.50-3.00	0.8-1.2
Offshore Areas	.Accelerate leasing by 45% in acreage	2.03	0.5
Synthetic Gas From Coal	.Implement two-phase program		
	-High Btu	3.03-4.23	0.6
	-Low Btu	3.10-4.27	0.5
SNG From Petroleum Products	.Maintain incremental pricing method.	3.50-5.20	1.0
Imported LNG	.Discourage LNG imports.	2.14-3.00	0.4
	.Approve projects already submitted to FPC	2.14-3.00	1.5
	.Encourage LNG imports	2.14-3.00	2.1
Tight Formations	.Develop fracturing technologies	0.80-2.22	0.2-0.9
Devonian Shale	.Apply conventional technology.	Over 3.50	0.1

* Includes 0.8 Tcf from Prudhoe Bay since the Alaskan Pipeline is assumed constructed; also includes 0.2 Tcf from Tight Formations. These are also included in the totals shown in each respective supply source category.

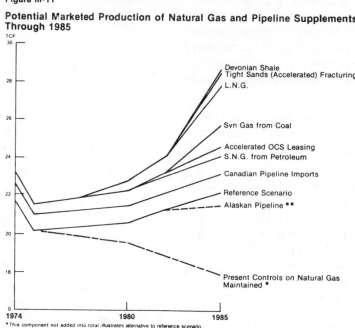

Figure III-11

Potential Marketed Production of Natural Gas and Pipeline Supplements
Through 1985

Figure III-11 shows the potential contribution of natural gas and supplements through 1985.

Natural gas production is affected significantly by the rate of leasing in the offshore areas, particularly the Gulf of Mexico, and by the actual undiscovered resources available. If the rate of leasing is accelerated by 45 percent in total acreage and the actual undiscovered resources exceed expectations by one standard deviation of the U.S. Geological Survey mean, natural gas production would reach 25.3 Tcf by 1985. If instead, the leasing rate is reduced by 32 percent in total acreage, and the actual undiscovered resources are less than expected by one standard deviation, natural gas production is forecast at about 20.5 Tcf.

The demand for natural gas in 1985 is projected at about 23 Tcf in the Reference case at current world oil prices, an increase of 10 percent over 1974 actual consumption. Although the projected unconstrained demand for natural gas in 1985 is relatively insensitive to government regulatory actions, the actual consumption of natural gas forecast in 1985 would decrease with continued price regulations over oil and gas due to the lack of available supplies, necessitating the substitution of alternate fuels and increased oil imports.

Coal

Coal Through 1975 And Short-Term Outlook

Coal is our most abundant domestic energy resource. At current consumption levels, we have enough coal

reserves to last at least 300 years. At projected 1985 consumption levels, we have enough reserves to last at least 200 years. Coal accounts for about 85 percent of our fossil-fuel resources. However, coal has accounted for a declining portion of U.S. energy consumption over the last 80 years.

The purpose of the following section of the coal chapter is to provide a perspective concerning the role coal has played and is now playing in the Nation's energy economy. The long-term outlook for the industry is discussed in the second and third major sections of this chapter.

Historical Perspective (through 1972) The Nation's coal industry began in the 18th century with bituminous coal mined in Virginia and anthracite in Pennsylvania. Coal production increased steadily throughout the 19th century. Its uses included space heating, coal gas, steam generation, and as coke in steel production. By the turn of this century, coal supplied 90 percent of the U.S. energy consumption.

However, during the first half of this century, coal consumption grew less rapidly than total energy consumption because more convenient and competitively priced domestic oil and natural gas became available, and new uses of oil (e.g., automobiles) expanded rapidly. By 1950, coal dropped to 38 percent of the Nation's energy consumption.

Since 1950, government actions have accelerated coal's declining role in the Nation's energy structure. The stimulation of nuclear electric power reduced coal's role in generating electricity. The 1966 elimination of oil import quotas for residual oil on the East Coast resulted in many large coal users converting to cheaper and more convenient foreign oil. The implementation of the Clean Air Act during the 1970's created significant uncertainties as to how much coal would be permitted to be burned and resulted in additional large coal users converting to oil. By 1972, coal accounted for only 17 percent of the energy consumed by the Nation.

Thus, while coal production has remained almost constant, the percentage of total national energy consumption supplied by coal has declined dramatically (see Figure IV-1).

Although total coal consumption in 1972 was roughly the same as in 1945, the breakdown of consumption by sector has changed. In 1945, the largest consuming sector was Class 1 railroads, burning 125 million tons. By 1972, railroad consumption of coal had dropped so far that the Bureau of Mines no longer tracks it. Retail consumption totalled 119 million tons in 1945, but only nine million tons in 1972. The other category, which includes industrial uses, also dropped from 148 million tons to 72 million tons during the 1945-1972 period. The electric utilities sector was the only sector to grow throughout the period, increasing from 72 million tons in 1945 to 349 million tons in 1972 (see Figure IV-2).

During the 1950's the growth in utility coal consumption was less than the decline in consumption by the other sectors. By 1960, total coal consumption had dropped to 4.7 million tons from the 588 million tons consumed in 1945. During the 1960's, total coal consumption increased until it hit 586 million tons in 1970. During the early 1970's, coal consumption grew at a reduced rate.

Figure IV-2

Coal Consumption By Sector, 1935–72

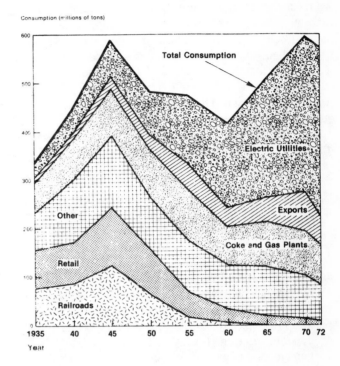

Figure IV-3

Electrical Generation By Fuel, 1955–73

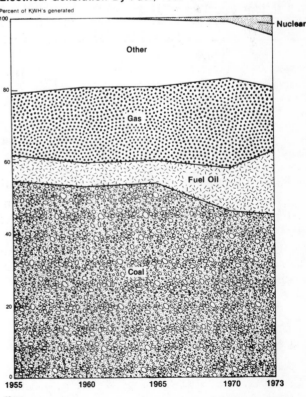

Figure IV-1

Coal's Declining Share of Total United States Energy Consumption

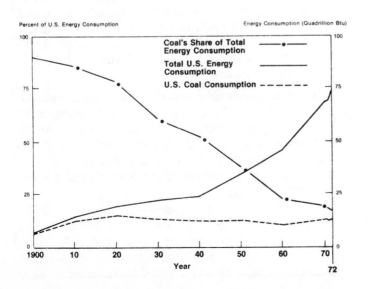

The major reason for the slowdown in the growth of coal consumption was competition from oil and nuclear power. The percentage of total kilowatt hours generated with coal has been declining since 1965 (see Figure IV-3). The elimination of oil import quotas along the East Coast and the sulfur dioxide emission limitation of the Clean Air Act pushed utilities away from coal. In addition, nuclear power has increased its share of total power generation from 0.4 percent in 1965 to 4.5 percent in 1973, largely at the expense of coal. Thus, in the early 1970's, coal's only growing market—electric utilities—was being threatened. Oil and nuclear plants could produce power more cheaply than could coal in many areas of the country.

Coal production also has undergone significant shifts since 1945. In general, coal production has shifted from East to West and from deep to surface mines. In 1945, close to 75 percent of U.S. production came from the Appalachian basin. The Interior basin produced 20 percent and the remaining 5 percent came from the Far West. By 1972, Appalachian production dropped to 65 percent, with interior and western production growing to 26 and 8 percent, respectively. In 1945, only 19 percent of U.S. production was mined using surface methods. By 1972, 49 percent of production was surface mined. This trend towards surface mines has occurred in every region of the country. Although the total amount of coal mined increased by 15 million tons between 1945 and 1972, the amount that came from deep mines declined by 164 million tons (see Table IV-1).

Recent Events (1973-75)   The Arab embargo at the end of 1973 together with a corresponding dramatic oil price increase had a substantial impact on the coal industry. Oil consumers began to explore ways to substitute coal for oil. Further, emerging natural gas shortages and the policy of the Federal Power Commission to allocate natural gas away from electric utility boilers resulted in gas consumers exploring ways to substitute coal for natural gas.

However, there were several factors that limited this substitution over the 1973-75 period. One was that very few users had the physical capability to convert to coal in the short-run, where the physical constraints included lack of boilers that could burn coal, coal and ash handling facilities, and pollution control equipment.

During the Arab embargo FEA initiated a coal conversion program to convert oil-fired utilities to coal. Only 22 units at 11 powerplants were converted. About 86 thousand barrels of oil per day were saved during February, 1974 and over five million barrels from December, 1973 through February, 1974 (corresponding to less than 2 million tons of coal). However, by the summer of 1974, most of these savings had evaporated.

These savings evaporated due to two other important constraints to rapid substitution of coal for oil and gas. One is environmental regulations. Many of the plants that converted to coal required variances from air quality regulations. At the end of the embargo, most of these variances expired.

Table IV-1

COAL PRODUCTION BY REGION AND MINING METHOD, 1945-72

		Appalachia*			Interior**			Far West***			National		
		Surface	Deep	Total	Surface	Deep	Total	Surface	Deep	Total	Surface	Deep	Total
1972	Million Tons	144.6	242.6	387.2	105.2	52.1	157.3	41.3	9.3	50.6	291.1	304.0	595.1
	Percent	37	63	100	67	33	100	82	18	100	49	51	100
1970	Million Tons	143.0	274.8	417.8	95.6	54.3	149.9	25.3	9.6	34.9	263.9	338.7	602.6
	Percent	34	66	100	64	36	100	72	28	100	44	56	100
1965	Million Tons	89.8	295.1	384.9	78.4	28.5	106.9	11.1	9.2	20.3	179.3	332.8	512.1
	Percent	23	77	100	73	27	100	55	45	100	35	65	100
1955	Million Tons	78.5	297.3	375.8	36.5	33.8	70.3	6.2	12.3	18.5	121.2	343.4	464.6
	Percent	21	79	100	52	48	100	34	66	100	26	74	100
1945	Million Tons	64.7	366.1	430.8	39.8	72.7	112.5	5.7	28.9	34.6	110.2	467.7	577.9
	Percent	15	85	100	35	65	100	16	84	100	19	81	100

  * Alabama, Georgia, Kentucky (Eastern), Maryland, Ohio, Pennsylvania, Tennessee, Virginia, West Virginia.
 ** Arkansas, Illinois, Indiana, Iowa, Kansas, Kentucky (Western), Michigan, Missouri, Oklahoma.
*** Alaska, Arizona, Colorado, Montana, New Mexico, North Dakota, Oregon, South Dakota, Utah, Washington, Wyoming.

Source: Bureau of Mines

The other important constraint is coal supply. While coal is demand-constrained in the long-run, it can be supply-constrained in the short-run since it takes 4 to 7 years to open a large new mine and the "surge capacity" of the industry (to increase production rapidly) is limited. Further, 1974 was a year in which a United Mine Workers work stoppage was anticipated, and a 28-day stoppage occurred beginning in November, 1974. Lost production was estimated to be up to 41 million tons of coal. With the threat of work stoppage during the year and the very high spot market prices associated with this threat, potential coal users were reluctant to maximize coal consumption.

Two other important constraints to the rapid substitution of coal for oil and gas are:

- The capital costs of converting existing boilers to coal and installing pollution control equipment may be so high that it is cheaper for a user (all cost considered) to burn oil.

- It takes about 5 years to plan and build a new boiler; hence, if a new boiler had not already been planned in 1973, it could not be built before about 1978.

As a result of these short-term constraints to increased coal consumption, coal use did not increase rapidly over 1972 levels (see Table IV-2). Consumption in 1973 increased about 6 percent over 1972 levels, but 1974 consumption was the same as 1973 consumption. Further,

coal production was essentially unchanged over the 1972-1974 period. Coal production built up to a rate of about 640 million tons in 1974, but about 40 million tons of this production did not occur due to UMW work stoppages.

During 1975, the coal market came back into balance. Coal consumption grew less rapidly than anticipated. Short-term constraints continued to inhibit the substitution of coal for oil and gas. The growth of electricity consumption (for which most of the coal is burned) was about 2 percent, in contrast to expected growth of 5 to 7 percent for the same period. The demand for metallurgical coal fell off, as steel production dropped. On the other hand, coal production stayed at about 640 million tons— its 1974 rate prior to the UMW work stoppage. As a result, coal users were able to rebuild inventories (drawn down during the UMW work stoppage) to about normal levels.

Coal prices reflected the state of the market over the 1973-75 period. Starting at the end of 1973, coal prices began to rise. Spot prices reached record levels in November, 1974, during the UMW work stoppage. Long-term contract prices were also negotiated (and renegotiated) at higher levels due to the tightness of the market and cost increases associated with inflation (see Table IV-3). Starting at the beginning of 1975, spot prices began to drop until they almost reached average long-term contract levels during the summer, where they remained for the rest of

Table IV-2

COAL CONSUMPTION AND PRODUCTION
(Million Tons)

	Consumption	Production	Stock Change
1970	587	603	+16
1971	551	552*	+ 1
1972	573	595	+22
1973	609	592	-17
1974	611	603*	- 6**
1975	624***	639***	+15

    * UMW work stoppage.
   ** Imports increased to two million tons.
  *** Estimate.

Source: Bureau of Mines

Table IV-3

NATIONAL AVERAGE PRICES OF DELIVERED COAL AND
RESIDUAL OIL TO ELECTRIC UTILITIES
($/Million Btu, Current Dollars)

| | Coal | | Residual Oil (No. 6) |
	Average Spot Price	Average Contract Price	Average Contract Price
April 1973	.44	.38	.68
July 1973	.44	.39	.71
October 1973	.48	.40	.87
January 1974	.76	.45	1.54
April 1974	1.04	.52	1.86
July 1974	1.25	.56	1.95
October 1974	1.39	.62	2.00
November 1974*	1.47	.67	2.00
January 1975	1.26	.68	1.98
April 1975	1.08	.74	2.12
July 1975	.98	.76	2.00
August 1975**	.98	.78	2.02

---

* Spot coal prices reached their peak.
** Last month for which data is available.

Source: Federal Power Commission Form 423.

---

the year. This drop reflects the easing of the market during 1975.

That coal prices increased at the same time as oil prices during 1974 led some analysts to conclude that coal would be priced at the Btu-equivalent of oil, with an adjustment for pollution control costs. However, this conclusion was inconsistent with the observations that coal reserves are vast and the industry is composed of enough firms that market forces will push long-term prices to a level reflecting costs plus a fair return on capital; and that even in the short-run (when coal supply is constrained by the time it takes to open new mines), not enough energy consumers have the capacity to burn coal to bid spot prices up to the Btu-equivalent price of oil.

These observations are consistent with actual price behavior. Long-term contract prices were bid up to levels reflecting mining costs with a fair return. (Average contract prices include contracts that were negotiated several years ago and are probably lower than the average of contracts signed in the last year. However, there are no indications that new contracts are being signed at a Btu-equivalence with oil.) They are essentially equivalent to the cost-based prices estimated by FEA (e.g., FEA estimates the 1985 delivered cost of utility coal to the Middle Atlantic region at about $30 a ton and the FPC reports that the average contract price for the same region was $25 a ton in August, 1975). Spot prices were bid up to levels in excess of long-term contract prices, but never to the Btu-equivalent of oil. Most significantly, these spot prices fell as the coal market loosened in 1975, an event totally inconsistent with the argument that coal will be priced equivalent to oil, for which prices did not fall (see Table IV-3).

Table IV-4

COAL* CONSUMPTION BY SECTOR
(Million Tons)

	Electric Utilities	Metallurgical Use	Industry	Residential/ Commercial	Exports
1970	319	96	88	12	71
1971	326	93	74	11	57
1972	349	87	72	9	56
1973	387	94	67	8	53
1974	388	90	64	9	60
1975**	406	83	64	7	64

* Excludes anthracite.
** Estimated.

Source: Bureau of Mines

Table IV-5

COAL PRODUCTION*
(Million Tons)

	East**			West			National
Year	Surface	Deep	Total	Surface	Deep	Total	Total
1970	221	328	549	34	10	54	603
1971	235	266	501	41	10	51	552
1972	236	294	530	55	10	65	595
1973	227	289	516	66	10	76	592
1974	245	267	512	80	11	91	603
1975***	-	-	531	97	11	108	639

* Excludes anthracite.
** East of the Mississippi River.
*** Estimated.

Source: Bureau of Mines.

At the end of 1975, the electric utility sector was still the largest consumer of coal and was the only sector that was showing substantial growth (see Table IV-4).

At the end of 1974, more than 80 percent of coal production was in the East and about half of total production was from surface mines. Surface production continues to grow faster than deep production, and western production continues to grow faster than eastern production (see Table IV-5).

Short-Term Outlook (1976-78)   The short-term outlook for coal is growth, but the rate of growth depends on a number of key uncertainties.

On the consumption side, a key uncertainty is the rate of growth of electricity consumption. If electricity continues to grow slowly, growth in coal consumption would be modest. If electricity resumes growth at historical levels (i.e., 7 percent), growth in coal consumption would be substantial. Similar uncertainties, though of smaller impact, exist in the other sectors as well. Further, FEA's coal conversion program could increase consumption by more than 15 million tons per year by 1978.

On the production side, the key uncertainties are the number of mine openings and closings. The data that exists is somewhat incomplete and difficult to interpret.

FEA has made a short-term estimate that indicates that the coal market is likely to continue to grow in balance over the 1976-78 period, with consumption growing at a rate of about 5.1 percent (see Table IV-6).

The key assumptions associated with this forecast are:

- Production will build up as indicated by various surveys of mine openings.

- Electricity will grow at an annual compound rate of about 5.5 percent from 1975.

- Utilities will add new capacity as indicated by the National Electric Reliability Council.

- FEA's coal conversion program will result in increased annual coal consumption in 1976, 1977, and 1978 of 5, 10 and 15 million tons, respectively.

- EPA will continue its Clean Fuels Policy of encouraging states to relax sulfur emission limitations that are more stringent than required to protect public health and/or of granting compliance delays to those coal burners unable to comply with sulfur emission limitations due to the lack of adequate supplies of low sulfur coal and/or stack gas scrubbers.

The majority of the increased consumption and production is expected to occur in the West (see Table IV-6). Eastern production is expected to increase by 51 million tons or by 10 percent between 1975 and 1978. However, western production is projected to increase by 64 million tons or by 60 percent during the same period. This is because eastern utilities have scheduled large increases in nuclear capacity, while western utilities are shifting out of oil and gas into coal. On the production side, this reflects large new mines in the low sulfur coal fields of the West.

It should be noted that this short-term forecast does not (and need not) reflect two important determinants of coal consumption and production in the long-run. One is the type of new capacity utilities and other large users decide to build (i.e., coal, nuclear or oil). Since it takes at least 5 years to build a powerplant, capacity through 1978 can be estimated from published sources on planned capacity additions. However, as discussed below, decisions made (and to be made) since the Arab embargo to build new coal boilers rather than oil and gas boilers will have a substantial impact on coal consumption during the 1980's.

Table IV-6

SHORT-TERM FORECAST
(Million Tons)

	Production			Consumption		
	Total	East	West	Total	East	West
1974	603	512	91	611	513	98
1975	639	531	108	624	522	102
1976	671	543	128	668	550	118
1977	715	566	149	702	564	138
1978	745	582	172	745	583	162

The other is the leasing of the western coal lands. Coal production in the West could be adversely affected in the period beyond 1980, if the problems surrounding the leasing of these lands are not solved soon.

Further, it should be noted that neither this short-term forecast, nor the long-term FEA forecast (discussed below) account for the impact on coal production and consumption of the uncertainties associated with how certain government policy issues will be resolved (e.g., strip-mining legislation, western leasing, the clean fuels deficit, and significant deterioration). These uncertainties may have a substantial adverse effect on coal production and consumption, since they render investments in coal capacity risky and hence less attractive.

Finally, in both forecasts transportation is assumed to be available to move the coal from producer to consumer. Miner productivity, both in terms of days worked and output per manday, is not projected to change by mining method. However, as the mix of mines changes with more large western mines in operation the national average productivity should improve. Similarly, problems of labor availability and attracting of capital investment were assumed not to be binding constraints. These assumptions may be over-simplifications of the situation, particularly if Federal policies relating to coal remain unresolved.

Consumption Forecasts

This section is organized into five subsections. The first discusses the 1985 Reference Scenario forecast assuming $13 per barrel imports. This scenario is employed as a benchmark, from which to measure differences. Its use as such does not mean it is considered a "best guess" at what will happen. The second subsection discusses the forecasted changes in consumption over time, i.e., 1980, 1985, and 1990. The third discusses the effects of different oil import prices on 1985 consumption. The fourth discusses the effects of different scenarios on 1985 consumption. The fifth discusses the policy implications of these findings.

Reference Scenario   The FEA Reference Scenario forecast at $13 imports indicates that consumption will be 1,040 million tons in 1985 and that the bulk of this increase will occur in the electric utility sector (see Table IV-7).

This forecast indicates a 5.0 percent growth rate over the 1974-85 period.

The FEA analysis indicates that the best way to increase the consumption of our abundant domestic resource is through electricity, where coal consumption in this sector is limited by electricity growth rates, oil prices, nuclear capacity, and environmental regulations (each of which is

Table IV-7

1985 COAL CONSUMPTION
REFERENCE SCENARIO, $13 OIL IMPORTS
(Million Tons)

Sector	1974	1985	Absolute Increase	Compound Annual Percent Growth Rate
Electric Utilities	388	715	+327	5.7
Household/Commercial	9	5	- 4	-5.5
Industrial	64	124	+ 60	6.2
Coke and Gas	90	100	+ 10	1.0
Synthetics	-	16	+ 16	-
Exports	60	80*	+ 20	2.6
Total	611	1,040	+429	5.0

* Assumed values; not estimated endogenously by model.

discussed below). The potential for increased consumption of coal in other sectors appears to be limited. Given existing environmental regulations and the large scale required to handle coal economically, no large absolute increase in coal consumption is anticipated in the industrial sector. Further, synthetic fuels from coal do not yet compete economically with natural gas and oil, even at the equivalent of $16 oil imports, and lead times for this new technology limit the market to about 16 million tons by 1985.

Within the electric utility sector, the majority of the coal consumption is forecast to be in the current major coal-burning regions, although the percentage growth in the current minor coal-burning regions is forecast to be higher (see Table IV-8).

This indicates that: the trend to oil on the East Coast would be reversed; utilities on the Southwest would be shifting out of natural gas; and utilities on the Pacific Coast would be shifting from both oil and gas to coal. The low growth rates in the central regions reflect high current coal consumption and substantial increases in nuclear capacity.

The forecast indicates that the utilities on a national basis will rely about evenly on low sulfur coal and high sulfur coal with scrubbers to comply with sulfur emission regulations on new plants. However, this mix varies widely by region (see Table IV-9).

The forecast also indicates that existing plants will burn high sulfur coal where permitted by air pollution regulations, but will switch to low sulfur (rather than install scrubbers) where required to reduce sulfur emissions. (This finding neglects the impact of long-term contracts and the cost penalties associated with burning western low sulfur coal in existing boilers designed for eastern coals. Had the FEA model been designed to account for these factors, it is likely that the forecasts would include some scrubbers on existing plants.) Where scrubbers are installed, they are installed only on baseload plants, where the high capital costs can be allocated over the maximum number of kilowatt hours.

Within the utility sector, delivered coal prices for high sulfur coal and low sulfur coal are illustrated by region in Table IV-10.

On the Atlantic Coast and East Central regions, low sulfur coal competes directly with high sulfur coal plus scrubbers for new baseload powerplants. The price of low sulfur coal is bid up to the price of high sulfur coal plus

Table IV-8

1985 UTILITY COAL* CONSUMPTION BY CENSUS REGIONS**
REFERENCE SCENARIO, $13 OIL IMPORTS
(Million Tons)

Region	1974	1985	Absolute Increase	Compounded Annual Percent Growth Rate
Northeast	2	15	+ 13	20.1
Middle Atlantic	42	105	+ 63	8.7
South Atlantic	78	136	+ 58	5.2
East North Central	133	194	+ 61	3.5
East South Central	61	77	+ 16	2.1
West North Central	37	90	+ 53	8.4
West South Central	5	42	+ 37	21.3
Mountain	27	46	+ 19	5.0
Pacific	3	10	+ 7	11.6
National	388	715	+327	5.7

* Excludes anthracite.
** Figure IV-4 gives a map of the census regions.

Figure IV-4
CENSUS REGIONS

Table IV-9

SULFUR CONTENT OF UTILITY COAL
1985 REFERENCE SCENARIO, $13 OIL IMPORTS
(Percent of Regional Coal Consumption)

Region	Existing Plants High Sulfur*	Existing Plants Low Sulfur	New Plants High Sulfur**	New Plants Low Sulfur	Total High Sulfur	Total Low Sulfur
Northeast	3.5	9.6	79.7	7.2	83.2	16.8
Middle Atlantic	24.7	17.5	34.0	23.8	58.7	41.3
South Atlantic	59.5	16.1	1.9	22.5	61.4	38.6
East North Central	21.7	40.4	33.4	4.5	55.1	44.9
East South Central	55.7	27.3	--	17.0	55.7	44.3
West North Central	48.1	22.8	--	29.2	48.1	51.9
West South Central	42.2	4.4	--	53.4	42.2	57.8
Mountain	24.1	65.9	10.0	--	34.1	65.9
Pacific	24.4	--	75.6	--	100.0	--
National	37.4	26.8	18.3	17.5	55.7	44.3

 * Without scrubbers
** With scrubbers

Note: Low sulfur coal meets the new source performance standard of 1.2 pounds of sulfur dioxide per million Btu of heat input. High sulfur coal exceeds the new source performance standard.

Table IV-10

LONG-TERM CONTRACT DELIVERED COAL PRICES TO THE ELECTRIC UTILITY SECTOR
1985 REFERENCE SCENARIO, $13 OIL IMPORTS
($/Million Btu, 1975 Dollars)

Regions	1985 Low Sulfur	1985 High Sulfur	Average Contract Price, August 1975*
Northeast	1.40	.90	1.21
Middle Atlantic	1.25	.75	1.05
South Atlantic	1.25	.80	1.01
East North Central	1.15	.65	.80
East South Central	1.15	.60	.77
West North Central	.95	.65	.57
West South Central	1.00	.70	.24
Mountain	.55	.45	.32
Pacific	--	.80	.59

* Source: FPC Form 423.

Table IV-11

COAL CONSUMPTION
REFERENCE SCENARIO, $13 OIL IMPORTS
(Million Tons)

	1974	1980	1985	1990
Electric Utilities	388	528	715	932
Household/Commercial	9	7	5	4
Industrial*	154	184	224	272
Synthetics	-	-	16	21
Exports	60	80	80	80
Total	611	799	1,040	1,309

Period	Annual Percent Growth Rate
1974-80	4.6
1980-85	5.4
1985-90	4.7

* Includes metallurgical coal consumption.

Table IV-12

ELECTRICITY CONSUMPTION GROWTH RATES
REFERENCE SCENARIO, $13 OIL IMPORTS

	Compound Annual Percent Growth Rate
1974-80	5.1
1980-85	5.7
1985-90	5.0

scrubbing. The price differential reflects the estimated cost of scrubbing—about $.50 per million Btu.

Time Path Most of the growth in coal consumption occurs in the utility sector. Coal consumption will grow slightly faster over the 1980-85 period than over the 1975-80 period, but more slowly during the 1985-90 period (see Table IV-11).

The 1974-80 growth rate is inhibited by current plant construction plans. There is not enough time to build a new coal plant by 1980, if it is not already planned. The 1985-90 growth rate is less than the 1980-85 rate because the growth of electricity consumption is forecast to be lower in the later years (see Table IV-12). However, there is a great deal of uncertainty associated with these estimates.

Nuclear capacity additions which have a substantial effect on coal consumption, are assumed to be about the same in the 1985-90 period as in the 1980-85 period. Accelerating nuclear capacity additions would reduce the rate of growth of coal consumption in the 1985-90 period further.

Most of the increased coal consumption in the low-coal consuming regions occurs during the 1980's. This again is because little or no coal capacity additions are currently planned for these regions, and there is not adequate time to plan and build coal plants by 1980. In some regions, such as the West South Central area where gas will be phased out, utility coal consumption could grow substantially by 1990 (increase from 5 to 89 million tons).

Throughout the 1975-90 period, the rate of growth of low sulfur coal consumption is substantial (see Table IV-13).

In the West, low sulfur coal consumption grows steadily over the period. This is because the supply of low sulfur coal is enormous in the West, and production costs are not expected to increase much as production is expanded. Western low sulfur coal production prices are not expected to increase enough to make western high sulfur coal plus scrubbers competitive. However, in the East, the supply of low sulfur coal is limited, and the costs of producing it are expected to increase rapidly as production is expanded. This has the effect of stimulating eastern high sulfur production (by making high sulfur coal plus scrubbers competitive with low sulfur coal); and stimulating western low sulfur production by making western coal more competitive in midwestern markets. By 1990, new technologies such as fluidized bed combustion may be in commercial operation. If so, the FEA forecast (which assumes no such technology) probably overstates low sulfur coal consumption in that year.

Table IV-13

UTILITY COAL CONSUMPTION BY SULFUR CONTENT
REFERENCE SCENARIO, $13 OIL IMPORTS
(Quadrillion Btu)

	1980		1985		1990	
Region	High Sulfur	Low Sulfur	High Sulfur	Low Sulfur	High Sulfur	Low Sulfur
East	4.9	4.1	7.0	5.0	6.8	7.6
West	1.4	1.1	1.6	1.9	1.8	3.3
National	6.3	5.2	8.6	6.9	8.6	10.9

Importantly, coal prices (in 1975 dollars) are not expected to increase substantially over the period because the national supply curve is relatively flat. As discussed above, the supply of low sulfur coal in the East is limited and has a relatively steep supply curve. However, western low sulfur coal and eastern high sulfur coal are extremely abundant and have relatively flat supply curves. Hence, increased consumption does not result in significantly higher prices. In the West, more low sulfur coal is mined without substantial price increases. In the East, low sulfur coal is mined until its price is equivalent to the price of eastern high sulfur coal plus scrubbers and/or the delivered price of western coal, then more high sulfur coal and more western low sulfur coal are mined without substantial price increases.

Effect of Oil Prices   The consumption of coal, and conversely of oil, in the electric utility sector is very sensitive to the price of oil. In the absence of regulation and if the price of oil is low enough, electric utilities will:

- Build new oil plants rather than new coal plants.

- Employ their existing oil plants more than their existing coal plants (i.e., baseload[6] coal plants and move oil plants to intermediate[7] load to the extent possible).

On the other hand, if the price of oil is high enough, electric utilities will build new coal plants and rely on existing coal plants as much as possible.

The specific oil prices where utilities will shift from one fuel to another depend importantly on the price of coal and powerplant capital and operating costs. These in turn vary by region, particularly the price of coal. Hence, it is difficult to generalize for the Nation as a whole. However, a specific region can be used to illustrate how the price of oil affects coal consumption.

The Middle Atlantic region serves as a useful illustrative region because both oil and coal are being consumed by electric utilities in large quantities. For this region, as all other regions, there are five specific oil prices that are relevant:

- *Baseloading existing plants.* Above about $8 per barrel, a utility will baseload existing coal plants rather than existing oil plants to the extent possible; this means operating them to generate as much electricity as possible given load requirements and maintenance schedules. Below about $8 per barrel, a utility will baseload existing oil plants rather than existing coal plants to the extent possible.

- *Building new plants for baseload.* Above about $9 per barrel, a utility will build a new coal plant rather than a new oil plant if additional baseload capacity is required. Below about $9 per barrel, a utility will build a new oil plant rather than a new coal plant.

- *Building new plants for intermediate load.* Above about $10.50 per barrel, a utility will build a new coal plant rather than a new oil plant if additional intermediate load capacity is required. Below about $10.50 per barrel, a utility will build a new oil plant rather than a new coal plant.

- *Substituting new coal plants for existing oil plants in baseload.* Above about $13 per barrel, a utility will build a new coal plant to be substituted for an existing oil plant in baseload. The existing oil plant would then be used as a seasonal peaking unit (with a very low capacity factor), if at all.

- *Substituting new coal plants for existing oil plants in intermediate load.* Above $19 per barrel, a utility will build a new coal plant to be substituted for an existing oil plant at intermediate-load. The existing oil plant would then be used as a seasonal peaking unit, if at all.

All of these "breakpoint" prices assume that utilities will build and operate plants in a manner that will minimize total costs and consumer rates. It is possible that financial constraints (i.e., fuel adjustment clauses, regulatory lags), and load growth uncertainties (e.g., failing to forecast rapid growth so that oil plants must be built due to inadequate time for building a coal plant) could render this assumption somewhat invalid.

All of these "breakpoint" estimates were based on the assumption that the coal plants would meet new source performance standards with low sulfur coal; assuming high sulfur coal plus scrubbers would not change the estimates substantially since the price of low sulfur coal is forecast to be bid up to the equivalent of high sulfur coal plus scrubbers, particularly in the eastern demand regions. As discussed elsewhere, the price of coal does not change substantially with different production levels. Hence, a single point estimate for coal is not misleading. Further, powerplant capital and operating costs are not expected to change substantially with different coal consumption levels.

The effects of these "breakpoints" are illustrated well by the model forecasts at different oil prices (see Table IV-14).

At $8 imported oil, the utility sector will consume about 12.5 quads of coal (579 million tons) and about 8.9 quads of oil and gas (the equivalent of about 4.0 million barrels per day). At $13 imported oil, the total quads of fossil fuel consumed change slightly, but coal consumption increases by 2.9 quads (to 715 million tons) and oil and gas consumption decreases by a similar amount (to the equivalent of 2.6 million barrels per day). This change results from the oil price passing through three breakpoints. At $8 imports, the delivered price of oil, after refining, to utilities generally exceeds $8; hence, existing

Table IV-14

ELECTRIC UTILITY SECTOR FOSSIL FUEL CONSUMPTION
1985 REFERENCE SCENARIO (Quadrillion Btu)

| | Oil Imports Price ($ per barrel) | | |
	$8	$13	$16
Coal	12.5	15.4	16.3
Oil & Gas*	8.9	5.7	5.2
Total	21.4	21.1	21.5

* Oil and gas are combined because they are generally fungible in the utility sector and their prices in a deregulated market are forecasted to equilibrate on a Btu basis.

coal plants are being operated at baseload. However the delivered price generally is less than $9; hence, new oil plants are built instead of coal plants for both base and intermediate load and no new coal plants are substituted for existing oil plants. On the other hand, at $13 imports, the delivered price of oil after refining to utilities generally exceeds $14. Hence, only new coal plants are built for base and intermediate loads and some new coal plants are built to substitute for existing oil plants in baseload. The net effect of these changes is that an additional 136 million tons of coal is consumed, and less oil and gas is consumed by the equivalent of 1.4 million barrels per day.

The difference between $13 and $16 imports is less substantial because there are essentially no additional breakpoints between $13 and $16. Coal consumption increases because total fossil fuel consumption increases (with increased electricity consumption) and because some additional new coal plants are substituted for oil and gas plants in those regions where the breakpoint around about $14 per barrel was not exceeded at $13 imports. Correspondingly, oil and gas consumption goes down slightly because some additional new coal plants are substituted for existing oil and gas plants. Hence, it is clear that the price of oil has a substantial effect on coal consumption and on oil imports.

In addition, the FEA forecasts also indicate that the price of coal does not change significantly with the price of oil (see Table IV-15).

This is because coal prices have been modeled to be cost-based since reserve ownership is generally widespread, mining technology is widely understood, and current production is not highly concentrated in a few companies. Hence, no producer can require more than a price covering costs plus a fair return on capital, because another producer could then produce coal at a lower price. In addition, coal prices do not move much with oil prices because the supply curves for coal are relatively flat. Substantial increases in coal production are possible without corresponding price increases.

Effect of Different Policy Scenarios   The effects of the various scenarios on 1985 coal consumption with $13 oil imports are illustrated in Table IV-16.

Two important observations should be noted. The first is that the total coal consumption forecasts change very little—slightly less than 10 percent below and approximately 25 percent above the Reference Scenario.

Table IV-15

DELIVERED FUEL PRICES IN 1985 TO UTILITY
SECTOR IN MID-ATLANTIC REGION
($/Million Btu, 1975 Dollars)

Oil Import Prices	Residual Oil	Low Sulfur Coal
$8/barrel	1.65	1.15
$13/barrel	2.30	1.25
$16/barrel	2.70	1.25

Table IV-16

COAL CONSUMPTION UNDER VARIOUS SCENARIOS
1985, $13 OIL IMPORTS
(Million Tons)

Sector	Reference	$9.00 Regulation	Regional Limitation	BAU Supply With Conservation	Accelerated Supply With Conservation	Electrification
Household/Commercial	5	5	5	5	5	5
Industrial	224	218	219	217	208	284
Electrical Generation	715	679	640	655	673	841
Synthetics	16	16	16	16	53	53
Exports	80	80	80	80	80	80
Total	1,040	998	960	973	1,019	1,263

The second important observation is that nearly all the changes in total coal consumption are due to changes within the electric sector. The only other sectors that change substantially are:

- The industrial sector where coal consumption is assumed to substitute for natural gas (by about 60 million tons) under the Electrification Scenario.

- The synthetics sector where coal consumption is assumed to increase by about 35 million tons under both the Accelerated Supply and Electrification Scenarios.

Both of these increases are due to policy assumptions used in specifying the scenarios.

The changes in the electric utility sector result from four factors: oil prices, nuclear capacity, electricity demand, and environmental regulations.

The effects of oil prices were discussed above. Under the $9.00 Regulation Scenario, oil prices are reduced. This increases oil consumption and reduces coal consumption in the utility sector (see Table IV-17).

The reduction in coal consumption is amplified slightly by a reduction in electricity consumption, resulting from the lower oil prices which make oil and gas more competitive with electricity.

The effect of nuclear capacity is apparent in the various scenarios. Coal consumption is inversely related to

Table IV-17

ELECTRIC UTILITY FUEL CONSUMPTION
1985, $13 OIL IMPORTS

	Reference	Regulation ($9.00)
Coal (Quadrillion Btu)	15.4	14.6
Oil and Gas (Quadrillion Btu)	5.7	6.2
Total	21.1	20.8
Average Residual Oil Price ($/Million Btu)	2.25	1.92

nuclear capacity. This is because at high oil prices, nuclear powerplants and coal powerplants generating electricity in baseload (about 65 percent of all generation) are cheaper than all other types of powerplants (see Table IV-18).

Nuclear and coal generation costs are close. The delivered price of coal varies over a wide enough range that in some regions coal plants may generate electricity for less cost than do nuclear plants. Indeed, coal and nuclear plant costs are close enough that they might be considered the same, given the uncertainty associated with the estimates. However, because of the apparent cost advantages of nuclear plants in some regions, FEA's forecasting model employs them to their maximum capacity (specified as an input constraint). Once the nuclear capacity constraint is reached in those regions, the model employs coal plants until no additional capacity is required. Hence, increased nuclear capacity results in reduced coal capacity and vice versa.

At baseload generation, each thousand MWe of coal capacity consumes about 2.8 million tons of coal per year.[8] Thus, each thousand MWe change in nuclear capacity changes coal consumption about 2.8 million tons. In the Regional Limitation Scenario, nuclear capacity is reduced about 45,000 MWe from the Reference Scenario. This reduction acts to increase coal consumption by 126.4 million tons or 2.5 quadrillion Btu (see Table IV-19). This increase, however, is more than offset by environmental and electricity demand considerations discussed below. In the Electrification Scenario, nuclear

capacity is increased about 20,000 MWe. This increase acts to reduce coal consumption by about 56.2 million tons or 1.1 quadrillion Btu (see Table IV-19). This reduction, however, is more than offset by increased electricity demand as discussed below.

Coal consumption is directly related to electricity consumption. This is because at high oil prices, coal capacity is employed to satisfy all additional generating capacity requirements, after the nuclear capacity constraints are reached (in those regions where nuclear generation costs are less than coal generation costs), except for some oil-or gas-fired turbines employed for peak load, which is estimated to account for about 2 percent of total load. For each billion kilowatt hours that electricity consumption changes, coal consumption changes by about 9.3 trillion Btu or about 0.4 million tons. The effect is well illustrated by the Electrification Scenario (see Table IV-20). The large increase in electricity consumption has the effect of increasing coal consumption by 3.1 quadrillion Btu. However, this is offset somewhat by an increase of nuclear capacity which reduces coal consumption by 1.2 quadrillion Btu. The net change in utility coal consumption, therefore, is 1.9 quadrillion Btu or about 96 million tons. The remaining 0.6 quadrillion Btu or 30 million ton increase in coal consumption results from other changes as described in the latter footnote to Table IV-20.

The effect of hypothetical environmental regulations (more stringent than currently proposed) is illustrated by the Regional Limitation Scenario with business as usual

Table IV-18

ILLUSTRATIVE BASELOAD ELECTRICITY GENERATION COSTS*
(mills/kWh, 1975 Dollars)

	Nuclear	Coal	Oil Steam
Capital	13.45	9.30	7.58
Fuel	1.80	10.11	20.70
Other	3.00	2.00	1.88
Total	18.25	21.41	30.16

* Assumes a delivered price of $1.10 per million Btu for low sulfur coal and $2.25 per million Btu for residual oil. Capital costs in 1975 dollars are $550 per kw for nuclear, $380 per kW for coal and $310 per kW for oil. A fixed charge rate of 15 percent and a capacity factor of 0.7 were assumed.

Table IV-19

EFFECTS OF CHANGES IN KEY FACTORS AFFECTING UTILITY COAL CONSUMPTION--1985, $13 OIL IMPORTS
(Quadrillion Btu)

			Scenario		
	$9.00 Regulation	Regional Limitation	BAU Supply With Conservation	Accelerated Supply With Conservation	Electrification
Impact of Change in Oil Prices	-0.5	-	-	-	-
Impact of Change in Nuclear Capacity	-0.1	+2.5	+0.2	-0.1	-1.2
Impact of Change in Electricity Consumption	0.4	-0.5	-1.2	-0.3	+3.1
Impact of Change in Environmental Regulations	-	-4.1	-	-	-
Other*	+0.2	+0.5	-0.2	-0.5	+0.6
Net Change in Utility Coal Consumption	-0.8	-1.6	-1.2	-0.9	+2.5

* Accounts for changes in generation efficiencies associated with changes in scrubber capacity, synthetics fuels, and load curves.

Table IV-20

EFFECT OF ELECTRIFICATION ON UTILITY COAL CONSUMPTION
1985, $13 OIL IMPORTS

	Scenario		Resulting Change in Coal Consumption	
	Reference	Electrification	Million Tons*	Quadrillion Btu
Nuclear Capacity (Thousand MWe)	141	162	- 61	-1.2
Electricity Consumption (Billion kWh)	3,022	3,351	+157	+3.1
Other**	-	-	+ 30	+0.6
Utility Coal Consumption	715	841	+126	+2.5

* An average heat content of 19.8 million Btu per ton was implicit in the model output.
** Accounts for changes in generation efficiencies associated with changes in scrubber capacity, synthetic fuels and load curves.

demand, where environmental regulations are specified to be (1) the requirement that all new plants burn low sulfur coal plus install scrubbers, (2) reclamation costs associated with hypothetical stripmining legislation (requiring back to original contour), and (3) a 30 percent severance tax on all western coal (see Table IV-21).

As illustrated in Table IV-21, the impact of hypothetical environmental regulations (together with a slight decrease in electricity consumption resulting from electricity price increases which, in turn, are due to the increased fuel and generation costs caused by the hypothetical environmental regulations) more than offset the increase in coal consumption resulting from reduced nuclear capacity.

The hypothetical surface mining legislation assumed in the Regional Limitation Scenario is specified to require:

- An increase of deep mining prices of $.25 associated with an abandoned mine reclamation fee.

- An increase of surface mining costs of about $.50, $.75 and $1.50 in the West, Midwest, and East, respectively (estimates in each region include a $.35 per ton reclamation tax).

In summary, the severance tax and the reclamation costs increase coal prices as illustrated in Table IV-22. These price increases affect the regional distribution of

production (discussed below under production) but have minimum impacts on coal consumption. This is because they increase the "breakpoints" discussed above under "Impact of Oil Prices" only slightly—less than 5 percent. Since the price of oil at $13 oil imports is generally well above these breakpoints, these coal price increases do not result in substantial shifts from coal to oil in the utility sector.

The major impact caused by the hypothetical environmental regulations is thus associated with the requirement that all new coal-fired plants must burn low sulfur coal and install scrubbers (rather than burn low sulfur coal or high sulfur coal plus scrubbers). These requirements increase the costs of generating electricity with coal substantially (see Table IV-23).

These large cost increases cause the "breakpoints" discussed above to increase substantially (see Table IV-24).

Thus, a great deal more oil and less coal is employed in the utility sector (see Table IV-25).

However, the specified requirement that all new plants burn low sulfur coal and install scrubbers is very stringent, and has not been seriously proposed as an air pollution control strategy. It is shown for illustrative purposes only as an attempt to place a lower bound on the effect of

Table IV-21

EFFECT OF HYPOTHETICAL ENVIRONMENTAL REGULATIONS ON UTILITY COAL CONSUMPTION 1985, $13 OIL IMPORTS

| | Scenario | | Resulting Change in Coal Consumption | |
	Reference	Regional Limitation	Million Tons*	Quadrillion Btu
Nuclear Capacity (Thousand MW)	141	96	+117	+2.5
Electricity Consumption (Billion kWh)	3,022	2,967	- 23	-0.5
Environmental Regulations	-	-	-192	-4.1
Other**	-	-	+ 23	+0.5
Utility Coal Consumption	715	640	- 75	-1.6

* An average heat content of 21.3 million Btu per ton was implicit in the model output.
** Accounts for changes in generation efficiencies associated with changes in scrubber capacity, synthetic fuels and load curves.

Table IV-22

COAL PRICES (FOB Mine)
1985, $13 OIL IMPORTS
($/Ton-1975 Dollars)

	Reference Scenario	Reclamation Costs	Severance Tax	Regional Limitation Scenario	Percent Increase
Central Appalachia (low sulfur)	24.10	1.50	-	25.6	6.2
Midwest (high sulfur)	10.80	.75	-	11.55	6.9
Western Northern Great Plains (low sulfur)	4.90	.50	1.62	7.20	43.3

government regulations on coal consumption and should be used to understand trends, rather than to support policy conclusions.

In summary, FEA forecasts that utility coal consumption is sensitive to: (a) oil prices (as they go up, coal consumption goes up); (b) nuclear capacity (as it goes up, coal consumption goes down); (c) electricity consumption (as it goes up, coal consumption goes up); and (d) en-vironmental regulations (as they are made more stringent, coal consumption goes down).

The effects of each of these four factors on coal consumption in the various scenarios is summarized in Table IV-9. As is evident, the four key factors have a substantial impact on coal consumption. However, total consumption does not vary substantially between the scenarios, because

Table IV-23

ILLUSTRATIVE COSTS OF GENERATING ELECTRICITY WITH COAL*
(Mills/kWh-1975 Dollars)

	Reference		Regional Limitation Provisions
	w/o Scrubber	w/Scrubber	
Capital	9.30	11.74	11.74
Fuel	10.11	6.85	10.97
Other	2.00	3.50	3.50
Total	21.41	22.09	26.21

* In the Reference Scenario low and high sulfur coal prices were $1.10 per million Btu delivered and $0.71 per million Btu delivered, respectively. In the Regional Limitation Scenario the price of low sulfur coal rose to $1.14 per million Btu.

Table IV-24

SHIFT IN OIL PRICE BREAKPOINTS--MID-ATLANTIC REGION*
(\$/Barrel Of Residual Oil, 1975 Dollars)

	Reference	Regional Limitation
From Existing Oil in Baseload to Existing Coal	8.00	8.00
From New Oil in Base-load to New Coal	9.00	12.00
From New Oil in Inter-mediate Load to New Coal	10.50	14.50
From Existing Oil in Baseload to New Coal	13.00	16.25

* Assumes delivered coal prices to be \$0.77 per million Btu for high sulfur coal and \$1.25 per million Btu for low sulfur coal in the Reference Scenario, and \$1.27 for low sulfur coal in the Regional Limitation Scenario.

Table IV-25

COAL AND OIL CONSUMPTION IN UTILITY SECTOR
1985, \$13 OIL IMPORTS
(Quadrillion Btu)

	Reference	Regional Limitation	Difference	
Coal	15.4	13.8	-1.6	-80 million tons* per year
Oil & Gas	5.7	9.8	+4.1	+1.9 million barrels per day
Total	21.1	23.6	+2.5	

* Assumes heat contents of 20 million Btu per ton for coal and six million Btu per barrel for oil.

the scenarios were defined such that the various factors offset each other to a large extent.

Policy Implications   The various coal consumption forecasts described above have several important policy implications.

The electric utility sector represents the greatest potential for substituting coal for oil and gas between now and 1990. This is because synthetic fuels do not yet compete economically with natural gas and oil, even at $16 per barrel. Further, it is because increased coal consumption in the industrial sector is limited by the large scale required to employ coal economically.

Coal consumption in the utility sector is extremely sensitive to oil prices. Should the price of oil (through international political events or domestic regulation) fall closer to $8 than $13 per barrel, utility oil consumption could increase substantially, to the detriment of increased coal consumption. Significantly, the potential oil savings associated with ensuring new coal rather than new oil plants are built and ensuring utilities shift loads from oil to coal to the extent practicable are greater than the potential savings from the direct conversions of oil and gas plants by an order of magnitude (e.g., about 200 million tons versus 20 million tons).

Coal consumption in the electric utility sector is very sensitive to electricity growth rates. Thus, a way of stimulating the substitution of domestic coal for oil and gas is to stimulate the substitution of electricity for oil and gas. However, the economic and environmental costs of such a strategy warrant careful consideration.

Coal consumption substitutes directly for nuclear power. Hence, the effect of increasing the use of nuclear power is generally to reduce coal consumption and vice versa. The effect of nuclear capacity on oil consumption is not significant except at low oil prices. Further, the costs of nuclear and coal electric power generation are close enough and uncertain enough that they might be considered essentially the same. Thus, it appears that there is a nuclear/coal tradeoff where the economic criteria may make little difference and where the decision between the two or the proper mix of the two may depend, therefore, on an assessment of the environmental and social costs and risks associated with them.

The effect of new and very stringent air pollution regulations could be to inhibit coal consumption and stimulate oil consumption. Although the policies examined were extreme and not currently being proposed, the analysis yields an important insight: the consideration of air pollution control strategies should include their effect on coal and oil consumption.

The FEA forecasts, together with recent market behavior, indicate that coal prices do not and will not follow oil prices.

Production Forecasts

This section discusses coal reserves and supply curves, the $13 Import Reference Scenario for 1985, the time path of the $13 Reference Scenario from 1975 through 1990, the effects of different oil prices, the effects of different strategies, and the policy implications of these production forecasts.

Reserves and Supply Curves   Most of the Nation's coal reserves on a tonnage basis are found west of the Mississippi River. However, on a Btu basis, most are

---

Table IV-26

DEMONSTRATED COAL RESERVE BASE*

	Billion Tons	Percent	Quadrillion Btu	Percent
East	202.3	46.3	5,000	52.1
West	234.4	53.7	4,600	47.9
National	436.7	100.0	9,600	100.0

* Includes anthracite.

Source: Based upon Bureau of Mines data.

found east of the Mississippi since western coal generally has a lower Btu content than eastern coal (see Table IV-26).

Approximately 46 percent of the Nation's coal reserves contain 1 percent sulfur or less by weight, and most of this is in the West. However, slightly more than one-third of the reserve base can meet new source performance standards (0.6 pounds of sulfur per million Btu). Importantly, a substantial portion of the eastern low sulfur coal is high-priced premium-grade metallurgical coal. Since coking coals are essential to the making of steel and in scarce supply worldwide, utility users are typically priced out of the market for these coals. This means that about 32 percent of the Nation's coal reserves can meet new source performance standards and are available for steam purposes (see Table IV-27).

These reserve statistics indicate that there are enormous reserves of low sulfur coal in the West and of high sulfur coal in the East. However, the supply of low sulfur coal in the East is limited.

In economic terms, this means that the supply curves for western low sulfur coal and eastern high sulfur coal are relatively flat, whereas the supply curve for eastern low sulfur coal is relatively steep (see Figure IV-5). The implications of these curves are that western low sulfur coal and eastern high sulfur coal production can be expanded a great deal without substantial cost increases, but that eastern low sulfur coal production cannot be expanded without substantial price increases.

Figure IV-5

Representative Coal Supply Curves

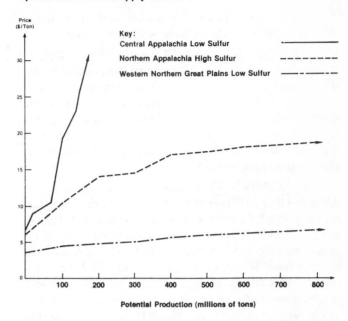

As discussed below, the results of these curves in the FEA forecasts are (a) that eastern low sulfur coal is bid up to the price of eastern high sulfur coal plus scrubbing, and (b) that prices of western low sulfur coal, eastern high sulfur coal, and eastern low sulfur coal (after it is bid up initially) do not change much over different levels of production (see Table IV-28).

Table IV-27

LOW SULFUR COAL RESERVES
(Billion Tons)

	One Percent or Less	Steam-Coal Reserves Meeting Sulfur Dioxide New Source Performance Standard*
East	32.9	7.3
West	167.3	130.3
National	200.2	137.6

* Excludes high quality metallurgical coal some of which also meets EPA's new source performance standard.

Source: Based upon Bureau of Mines data.

Table IV-28

COAL PRICES* AT DIFFERENT PRODUCTION LEVELS--1985, $13 OIL IMPORTS
($/Ton-FOB Mine, 1975 Dollars)

	Low Coal Production Regional Limitation Scenario**	Reference Scenario	High Coal Production Electrification Scenario
National Production (Million Tons)	958	1,040	1,258
Western Low Sulfur	6.50	4.90	5.50
Eastern High Sulfur	12.80	12.90	13.70
Eastern Low Sulfur	24.30	24.10	25.30

* These coal prices are for 1985, deflated to 1975 dollars. The cost of capital used to generate these prices included no inflation premium (i.e., since FEA's model makes all projections in constant dollars, a real interest rate was used). Thus, FEA's price projections will appear low when compared to current coal prices which reflect anticiapted inflation and nominal cost of capital rates of 15 to 20 percent. A rule of thumb to make current long term contract prices roughly comparable to FEA's estimate is to divide current prices by 1.2. This is the factor by which FEA's prices would increase if the higher nominal cost of capital rates had been used.

** Includes higher reclamation costs and a 30 percent severance tax in the West.

Reference Scenario The Reference Scenario forecast at $13 oil imports indicates that production will be 1,040 million tons in 1985. This represents a compound annual growth rate over 1974 levels of about 5.1 percent. The bulk of this increase occurs in the West. Further, over half is forecast to occur in one region—the Western Northern Great Plains (see Figure IV-6 for a map of coal supply regions)—with an additional 25 percent occurring in one other region—Central Appalachia (see Table IV-29).

The growth is concentrated in these regions because Central Appalachia is the only producing area in the East with substantial low sulfur reserves and the Western Northern Great Plains has vast amounts of relatively inexpensive-to-mine (on a per Btu basis) low sulfur coal reserves.

Significantly, the regional distribution of production shown in Table IV-29 is believed to be representative of what is likely to occur at the forecasted consumption level. However, the split of production between East and West is very sensitive to transportation rates, as well as factors, all of which are uncertain. Hence, these regional production estimates should be considered indicative but not precise.

Nearly all the growth in coal production is in low sulfur coal because of the sulfur emission limitations of the Clean Air Act. Many existing coal-burning facilities must reduce sulfur emissions, and all new facilities must meet new source performance standards (i.e., burn low sulfur coal or install scrubbers on high sulfur coal) (see Table IV-30).

Figure IV - 6
Coal Supply Regions

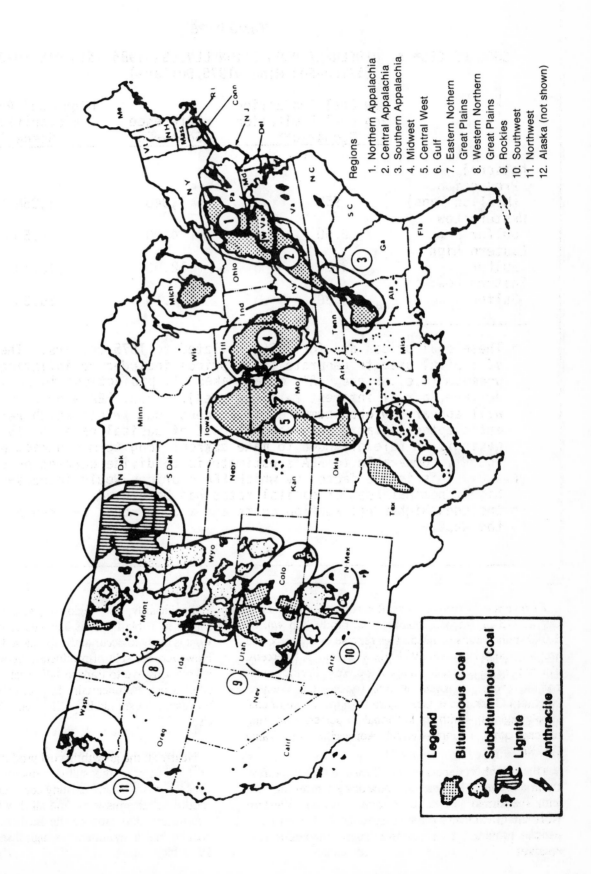

Regions

1. Northern Appalachia
2. Central Appalachia
3. Southern Appalachia
4. Midwest
5. Central West
6. Gulf
7. Eastern Nothern
   Great Plains
8. Western Northern
   Great Plains
9. Rockies
10. Southwest
11. Northwest
12. Alaska (not shown)

Legend

Bituminous Coal

Subbituminous Coal

Lignite

Anthracite

Table IV-29

COAL PRODUCTION BY REGION-- 1985 REFERENCE SCENARIO, $13 OIL IMPORTS
(Million Tons)

Regions	1974	1985	Increase	Compound Annual Percent Growth Rate
Northern Appalachia	171	183	12	0.6
Central Appalachia	184	297	113	4.4
Southern Appalachia	20	25	5	2.0
Midwest	135	156	21	1.3
Total East	510	661	151	2.4
Central West	9	9	0	0.0
Gulf	8	21	13	9.2
Eastern Northern Great Plains	8	31	23	13.1
Western Northern Great Plains	35	274	239	20.6
Rockies	14	19	5	2.8
Southwest	14	21	7	3.8
Northwest	4	4	0	0.0
Alaska	1	*	-	-
Total West	93	379	286	13.6
National	603	1,040	437	5.1

* Less than 500,000 tons.

The forecast indicates that most coal users will opt for low sulfur coal rather than high sulfur coal with flue gas desulfurization, because low sulfur coal can be mined and delivered cheaper than high sulfur coal plus scrubbing. Scrubbers are installed on facilities burning about 110 million tons of high sulfur coal.[9] Without these scrubbers, high sulfur coal production would have decreased (i.e., 1985 production of 426 million tons minus 110 million tons of scrubbed coal equals 316 million tons, which is less than 1974 production 402 million tons). Further, it is important to note that high sulfur coal in the model is anything that doesn't meet new source performance standards. Many sulfur emission limitations for existing facilities provide for coal that just slightly exceeds these standards. Hence, the average sulfur content of "high sulfur coal" will be reduced by 1985 if compliance with current sulfur emission limitations is achieved.

Just as the regional production estimates should be viewed as approximate, so should the sulfur distribution estimates. They are very sensitive to such uncertain factors as transportation rates, scrubber costs and availability, and specific regional supply curves.

The forecast also indicates that the ratio of surface production to total production will increase from about 54 to 63 percent. This is because nearly all western production, which is forecast to grow rapidly, is surface mined.

However, the ratio in the East is forecasted to drop slightly, indicating an exhaustion of inexpensive-to-mine strippable reserves in the East (see Table IV-31). Total

Table IV-30

SULFUR DISTRIBUTION OF COAL PRODUCTION
1985 REFERENCE SCENARIO, $13 OIL IMPORTS
(Million Tons)

	1974	1985	Increase	Compound Annual Percent Growth Rate
Metallurgical Coal*	111	138	26	2.0
Low-Sulfur Steam Coal	90	476	386	16.3
High-Sulfur Steam Coal	402	426	25	0.5
Total	603	1,040	436	5.1

* This is the premium quality coal used for coking and for export. It accounts for about 70 percent of domestic coking coal consumption and 85 percent of exports. The remainder of coking coal and exports comes from the low and high sulfur steam coal categories.

eastern production is projected to increase by 150 million tons from 1974 to 1985 with about 100 million tons of the increase coming from deep mines.

Again, the distribution of production by mine-type, particularly in the East, should be considered very approximate.

In the East, where low sulfur coal competes directly with high sulfur coal plus scrubbers, the FOB mine price differential reflects the cost of scrubbing to the marginal coal user (see Table IV-32).

Time Path Coal production will grow faster between 1980-85 than over the 1975-80 period, where this growth is driven up by the consumption considerations discussed above (see Table IV-33). As noted, most of the production increases over the period are concentrated in Central Appalachia and the Western Northern Great Plains. Further, most of the production increases over the 1975-80 period are forecast to be in the West. Eastern production is not forecast to increase substantially until after 1980. However, as discussed above, these regional production estimates should be considered approximate.

For example, the 1980 forecast contains some anomalies. Midwestern production is projected to decrease in 1980 and then grow by 1985. Eastern production in 1980 is less than the short-term forecast production for 1978. These anomalies are due primarily to the way the sulfur emission limitations are handled. The 1980 forecast satisfies these limitations in the least costly manner using low sulfur coal, although it involves shutting down about 100 million tons of high sulfur production, much of which would be in the Midwest.

This should not be interpreted as indicating that such mine closings will occur, but only that given the costs specified in the model, the most cost-effective way of complying with existing sulfur emission limitations by 1980 is to substitute low sulfur coal for high sulfur coal in many boilers. It appears that EPA through its program of compliance date extensions and state implementation plan revisions will not let this happen. Further, the forecast probably overstates the impact of high sulfur coal production because the model does not account for the effects of long-term contracts or the costs of burning western coal in existing boilers designed for eastern coals. However, this anomaly is instructive in indicating the kinds of impacts that might occur from certain Clean Air Act implementation strategies.

The price paths in the various regions indicate stable prices. Western low sulfur coal remains very constant, as does eastern high sulfur coal. Eastern low sulfur coal is bid up to the equivalent of high sulfur coal plus scrubbers prior to 1980, and then remains fairly constant (see Table IV-34). Importantly, these prices are all in 1975 dollars, and hence reflect only real cost increases over the period. All factor prices were assumed to inflate at the same rate.

Table IV-31

PRODUCTION BY TYPE OF MINING--1985 REFERENCE SCENARIO, $13 OIL IMPORTS
(Million Tons)

	Surface	Deep	Total	Surface as Percent Of Total
1974				
East	244.8	266.7	511.5	47.9
West	81.3	10.6	91.9	88.5
National	326.1	277.3	603.4	54.0
1985				
East	292.8	368.2	661.0	44.3
West	362.2	16.3	378.5	95.7
National	655.0	384.5	1,039.5	63.0

Table IV-32

PRICES BY REGION AND COAL TYPE--1985 REFERENCE SCENARIO, $13 OIL IMPORTS
($/Ton FOB Mine, 1975 Dollars)

Region	Low Sulfur Coal	High Sulfur Coal
Northern Appalachia	24.90	12.90
Central Appalachia	24.10	12.60
Southern Appalachia	26.00	14.50
Midwest	22.80	10.80
Central West	-	11.35
Gulf	-	4.80
Eastern Northern Great Plains	6.30	4.40
Western Northern Great Plains	4.90	3.80
Rockies	10.00	-
Southwest	8.00	4.40
Northwest	-	5.40
Alaska	6.60	-

Table IV-33

COAL PRODUCTION BY REGION--REFERENCE SCENARIO, $13 OIL IMPORTS
(Million Tons)

	1974	1980	1985	1990
Northern Appalachia	171	163	183	199
Central Appalachia	184	269	297	322
Southern Appalachia	20	24	25	24
Midwest	135	96	156	176
Total East	510	552	661	721
Central West	9	9	9	10
Gulf	8	17	21	21
Eastern Northern Great Plains	8	14	31	45
Western Northern Great Plains	35	185	274	464
Rockies	14	16	19	21
Southwest	14	5	21	21
Northwest	4	1	4	4
Alaska	1	*	*	*
Total West	93	247	379	586
National	603	799	1,040	1,307

* Less than 500,000 tons.

Table IV-34

PRICES IN SELECTED REGIONS--REFERENCE SCENARIO, $13 OIL IMPORTS
($/Ton FOB Mine, 1975 Dollars)

Region	Coal Type	1980	1985	1990
Northern Appalachia	Low Sulfur	24.40	24.90	26.20
	High Sulfur	10.70	12.90	14.20
Central Appalachia	Low Sulfur	21.20	24.10	25.80
	High Sulfur	10.40	12.60	13.80
Midwest	Low Sulfur	21.70	22.80	23.80
	High Sulfur	10.00	10.80	11.70
Western Northern	Low Sulfur	4.50	4.90	5.80
Great Plains	High Sulfur	3.80	3.80	4.50

Competition between equipment manufacturers and between coal producing regions should keep factor prices from escalating faster than the general level of inflation in the long run. However, in the short-run market imperfections may exist and enable some of the factor prices to increase faster.

Effect of Oil Prices Since the effect of different oil prices on total consumption is substantial, it is similarly substantial on total production. The fluctuations in production appear to concentrate in three regions (i.e., Northern Appalachia, Midwest, Western Northern Great Plains) (see Table IV-35).

As indicated above, coal prices do not change substantially with oil prices (see Table IV-36). These slight changes are due to changes in the level of production resulting from the impact of oil prices on coal consumption.

Effect of Different Scenarios Since the effects of the various scenarios on total consumption are not great, neither are the effects on total production (see Table IV-37). Production effects tend to be concentrated in the same three regions: low sulfur coal from the Western Northern Great Plains, high sulfur coal from Northern Appalachia and high sulfur coal from the Midwest. The sensitivity of production levels results from the flatness of the supply curves in these regions. Small changes in the equilibrium price of coal lead to large changes in production for these regions.

Table IV-35

COAL PRODUCTION BY REGION--1985 REFERENCE SCENARIO
(Million Tons)

| Regions | Oil Import Price | | |
	$8	$13	$16
Northern Appalachia	159	183	183
Central Appalachia	285	297	298
Southern Appalachia	22	25	25
Midwest	130	156	175
East	596	661	681
Western Northern Great Plains	219	274	293
Central West	9	9	9
Gulf	20	21	21
Eastern Northern Great Plains	14	31	32
Rockies	19	19	19
Southwest	16	21	24
Northwest	1	4	6
Alaska	*	*	*
Other Western Areas	79	105	111
National	894	1,040	1,085

* Less than 500,000 tons.

Table IV-36

REGIONAL VARIATION OF COAL PRICES WITH OIL PRICES
1985 REFERENCE SCENARIO
($/Ton FOB Mine, 1975 Dollars)

Region	Coal Type	Oil Import Prices $8	$13	$16
Northern Appalachia	Low Sulfur	24.70	24.90	25.30
	High Sulfur	11.20	12.90	13.30
Central Appalachia	Low Sulfur	21.60	24.10	24.50
	High Sulfur	10.90	12.60	12.90
Southern Appalachia	Low Sulfur	23.50	26.00	26.30
	High Sulfur	12.75	14.50	14.80
Midwest	Low Sulfur	22.00	22.80	23.10
	High Sulfur	10.10	10.80	11.10
Western Northern Great Plains	Low Sulfur	4.80	4.90	5.20
	High Sulfur	3.80	3.80	3.80

Table IV-37

COAL PRODUCTION UNDER VARIOUS SCENARIOS
1985, $13 OIL IMPORTS
(Million Tons)

Regions	Coal Type	1974*	Reference	$9.00 Regulation	Regional Limitation	BAU Supply With Conservation	Accelerated Supply With Conservation	Electrification
Northern Appalachia	Metallurgical	12.9	20.3	20.3	20.3	20.3	20.3	20.3
	Low Sulfur	6.1	15.2	15.2	15.5	15.2	15.2	15.5
	High Sulfur	155.6	147.1	139.1	139.1	139.1	147.1	166.1
Central Appalachia	Metallurgical	87.8	100.7	100.7	100.7	100.7	100.7	100.7
	Low Sulfur	60.0	141.1	141.1	141.1	141.1	138.5	145.6
	High Sulfur	30.7	55.5	55.5	45.2	55.5	55.5	59.6
Southern Appalachia	Metallurgical	3.9	11.2	11.2	11.2	11.2	11.2	11.2
	Low Sulfur	5.8	8.5	8.5	8.5	8.5	8.1	9.0
	High Sulfur	9.8	5.6	5.6	5.6	5.6	5.6	5.6
Midwest	Low Sulfur	5.5	14.2	14.2	14.5	14.2	13.7	14.8
	High Sulfur	133.0	141.6	132.6	160.7	132.6	147.4	175.6
Central West	Metallurgical	0.9	-	-	-	-	-	-
	High Sulfur	7.9	9.3	9.3	5.8	9.3	10.9	11.8
Gulf	High Sulfur	7.7	20.6	20.6	16.8	20.6	25.3	25.3
Eastern Northern Great Plains	Low Sulfur	1.7	25.2	20.0	14.0	20.0	20.0	25.8
	High Sulfur	6.1	6.1	6.1	-	6.1	9.3	9.3
Western Northern Great Plains	Low Sulfur	2.1	251.2	237.8	213.3	213.8	220.4	376.8
	High Sulfur	32.2	22.6	22.2	21.6	21.9	25.1	25.8
Rockies	Metallurgical	6.1	6.1	6.1	6.1	6.1	6.1	6.1
	Low Sulfur	6.9	12.7	12.7	1.9	12.7	12.7	14.7
Southwest	Low Sulfur	1.2	7.7	7.7	6.7	7.7	7.7	8.7
	High Sulfur	14.8	12.9	8.3	8.3	8.3	10.8	20.2
Northwest	High Sulfur	4.0	4.0	1.0	1.0	1.0	2.6	8.9
Alaska	Low Sulfur	0.7	0.1	0.1	0.1	0.1	0.1	0.8
National	Metallurgical	111.6	138.3	138.3	138.3	138.3	138.3	138.3
	Low Sulfur	90.0	475.9	457.3	415.6	433.3	436.4	611.7
	High Sulfur	401.8	425.3	400.3	404.1	400.0	439.6	506.2
Total		603.4	1,039.5	995.9	958.0	971.6	1,014.3	1,258.2

* Regional production by coal type estimated.

Table IV-38

COAL PRODUCTION 1985, $13 OIL IMPORTS
[Million Tons (Percent)]

	Reference	Regional Limitation
East	661 (64)	662 (69)
West	379 (36)	296 (31)
National	1,040 (100)	958 (100)

shift in the percentage of total production from West to East. (see Table IV-38).

This shift is caused principally by the 30 percent severance tax assumed to be applied to all western production in the Regional Limitation Scenario. It renders western coals less competitive with midwestern coals in the midwestern markets.

The effect of the severance tax in the Regional Limitation Scenario is somewhat offset by the reclamation costs which are higher in the East than in the West. Without the reclamation costs, the severance tax would have shifted even more production out of the West. Conversely, without the severance tax, the reclamation costs would have shifted production from East to West.

Finally, the forecast indicates that high sulfur production does not fall much under the Regional Limitation Scenario and indeed increases as a percentage of total production (see Table IV-39).

This may appear surprising considering that a specification of the Regional Limitation Scenario was that all new plants burn low sulfur coal with scrubbers, whereas the relevant specifications of the Reference Scenario were that new plants meet new source performance standards, either with low sulfur coal or with high sulfur coal plus scrubbers. However, it occurs because the requirement to scrub low sulfur coal in new plants would render new plant generation costs so expensive that utilities in some parts of the Nation would maximize the use of existing plants (even though they are generally less efficient and some would require scrubbers) because they could burn less expensive high sulfur coal.

The slight drops in production associated with the Regulation Scenario is concentrated in these regions, which together account for 75 percent of the decreases. The same is true for the Accelerated Scenario after adjustments are made for the assumed increases in synthetic fuels. Similarly, over 80 percent of the production increase associated with the Electrification Scenario is in these regions.

On the other hand, the production shifts associated with the Regional Limitation Scenario are more difficult to interpret. Low sulfur coal production from the Northern Great Plains drops substantially, but high sulfur production in the Midwest actually increases. Further, other regions are affected in unusual ways. There is a distinct

Table IV-39

SULFUR CONTENT OF STEAM COAL PRODUCTION*--1985, $13 OIL IMPORTS
[Million Tons (Percent of Total)]

	Reference	Regional Limitation With BAU Demand	Change
High Sulfur	425 (47)	404 (49)	-21
Low Sulfur	476 (53)	416 (51)	-60
Total	901 (100)	820 (100)	-81

* Excludes metallurgical coal.

This effect can be illustrated by utilities in the East North Central region, a predominantly coal burning region. Under the Reference Scenario, the forecast indicates that utilities would use those existing plants that are permitted by current air pollution regulations to burn high sulfur coal in baseload—i.e., to maximize the use of these plants. Further, existing plants required by current air pollution regulations to burn low sulfur coal or install scrubbers, would burn low sulfur coal and operate in intermediate load—i.e., to use these plants about half as much as baseload plants to minimize fuel costs. Finally, it indicates that new base load coal plants would burn high sulfur coal and install scrubbers to meet new source performance standards, while new coal intermediate load plants would burn low sulfur coal.

However, under the Regional Limitation Scenario, the new plants are not permitted to burn high sulfur coal or low sulfur coal without scrubbers. This makes generation costs from new plants very expensive. Hence, the utilities act to minimize costs by using all of the existing plants in baseload to the extent possible, installing scrubbers on those where required by air pollution regulations, because these plants are permitted to burn less expensive high sulfur coal. New plants, where expensive low sulfur coal is required, are operated only at intermediate load in order to minimize fuel costs.

The reasons for this change in coal consumption are economic. The FEA model simulates "economic dispatch"—i.e., that utilities will build and operate plants to minimize total costs. The effect of requiring new plants to burn low sulfur coal and install scrubbers is to change the relative economics of plant types, because the price of low sulfur coal is bid higher (see Table IV-40).

Note that the least expensive baseload generation (after existing plants burning higher sulfur coal without scrubbers which is always cheapest) shifts from new plants burning high sulfur coal with scrubbers in the Reference Scenario to existing plants burning high sulfur coal with scrubbers in the Regional Limitation Scenario. New plants burning low sulfur coal with scrubbers are most expensive, by a large margin.

The national average price of electricity increases from 29.73 mills per kilowatt hour in the Reference Scenario to 31.12 mills per kilowatt hour in the Regional Limitation Scenario—a 4.7 percent increase. The regional increases vary from less than 1 percent to over 10 percent (see Table IV-41). The greatest impacts occur in the Northeast, West North Central and West South Central regions where there is very little existing coal-fired generating capacity to baseload. The impact in the Mountain and Pacific regions is small since scrubbers were already required in the Reference Scenario.

Table IV-40

RELATIVE ECONOMICS OF BASELOAD COAL PLANT TYPES
EAST NORTH CENTRAL UTILITY REGION
1985, $13 OIL IMPORTS

	Reference	Regional Limitation with BAU Demand
Price of low sulfur coal ($/Million Btu)	1.11	1.21
Price of high sulfur coal ($/Million Btu)	0.63	0.68
Existing Plants Incremental Generation Costs (mills/kWh)		
- High sulfur without scrubber	8.21	8.70
- High sulfur with scrubber	13.31	13.83
- Low sulfur without scrubber	12.93	13.92
New Plant Incremental Generation Costs (mills/kWh)		
High sulfur with scrubber	12.03	-
Low sulfur without scrubber	12.21	-
Low sulfur with scrubber	16.66	17.63

Table IV-41

REGIONAL ELECTRICITY PRICES IN 1985
(Mills/kWh, 1975 Dollars)

Region	Reference	Regional Limitation with BAU Demand	Percentage Increase
Northeast	33.21	36.56	10.1
Middle Atlantic	33.43	34.90	4.4
South Atlantic	29.77	30.79	3.4
East North Central	29.79	30.91	3.8
East South Central	26.89	28.22	4.9
West North Central	28.91	31.02	7.3
West South Central	31.21	34.26	9.8
Mountain	29.26	30.15	3.0
Pacific	25.11	25.25	0.6
National	29.73	31.12	4.7

Policy Implications There are several important policy implications in these production forecasts.

First, in 1975 dollars, the price of coal is unlikely to increase rapidly, even with large increases in production, because the supply curve for coal facing any particular consuming region is relatively flat.

Second, it appears that substantial increases in low sulfur coal production from the Western Northern Great Plains will occur since it appears to be the most economical means to meet coal demand. This has implications for the rate of development in the West and for Federal western leasing policy, although coal demand could be satisfied from other regions at higher costs. However, forecast production levels in the West are very sensitive to:

- Transportation rates (which if lowered mean more production and vice versa);
- Severance taxes (which if applied mean less production);
- Reclamation requirements (where if applied uniformly across the Nation mean relatively lower cost increases in the West and more production);
- Air pollution requirements (where the specific interpretations of the Clean Air Act will determine whether western production is stimulated or inhibited).

Third, it appears that the effect of reclamation provisions associated with the hypothetical stripmining legislation specified for the FEA forecast would not have substantial effects on total coal production, but would probably shift some production from East to West.

Summary

Much has been done in the past year to refine and improve FEA's coal forecasting model. This work included substantial refinements of the coal supply curves and of the algorithms forecasting the demand for coal in each sector. Accordingly, much of the forecasting error associated with the forecasts has been reduced.

Significantly, however, the major findings this year are essentially the same as last year:

- In the long-run (although not necessarily in the short-run), coal production will be constrained by the demand for coal. The FEA Reference Scenario forecast for 1985 at $13 per barrel imported oil prices indicates that more than 1 billion tons of coal will be produced (including exports). Considerably more coal could be produced without substantial price increases, but this coal would not be consumed, because coal-using sectors are not expected to grow quickly enough to absorb it.

- The major growth in coal consumption is expected to occur in the electric utility sector. In this sector, coal consumption depends importantly on:

  —*Oil Prices:* The Reference Scenario forecast at $8 oil imports indicates that this sector will consume about 579 million tons in 1985, whereas, at $16 oil imports, 760 million tons are forecasted to be consumed—a difference of nearly 200 million tons.

  —*Electricity Growth Rates:* The Reference Scenario forecast at $13 oil imports indicates that electricity will grow at a compound annual rate of 5.4 percent between 1974-85. However, there is uncertainty associated with this estimate, and coal consumption estimates are very sensitive to electricity growth rate estimates. For each percentage point change in the compound annual electricity growth rate over the 1974 to 1985 period, forecasted coal consumption in the utility sector changes by about 150 million tons in 1985.

  —*Nuclear Capacity:* The Reference Scenario forecast at $13 oil imports indicates that nuclear capacity will be about 141 thousand megawatts in 1985. However, there is substantial uncertainty associated with this estimate as well, because the economic advantages of nuclear plants over coal plants may not be realized, nuclear plants are undergoing increasing attacks by public interest groups, and delays in nuclear construction schedules are difficult to predict. For each 10 percent change in the nuclear capacity estimate, estimated 1985 coal consumption changes by about 40 million tons.

- There is no reason to expect coal prices to equilibrate on a Btu basis with oil or gas prices, even after adjustments for pollution control costs. This is because:

  —Coal reserves are vast and reserve ownership is generally widespread enough that long-term contract coal prices are and will be cost-based.

  —The costs of producing coal do not increase rapidly as coal production is expanded.

  —The opportunities for expanding coal consumption including substituting coal for oil and gas (even through electricity) are limited.

- Environmental regulations could significantly inhibit coal consumption. Changes in current air pollution control regulations and/or deviations from current enforcement strategies could result in some substitution of oil for coal, particularly in the utility sector. Stripmining legislation could result in some mine-closings, and failure to proceed with Federal leasing of western low sulfur coal reserves could inhibit the development of coal production capacity. However, none of these environmental matters need inhibit increased reliance on coal and conversely, increased coal usage need not result in substantial adverse environmental effects. Compromises, which balance the relevant conflicting social welfare concerns, are clearly possible.

The Nuclear Fuel Cycle For Light Water Reactors

Introduction

The nuclear fuel cycle for light water reactors is a sometimes ignored, but crucial part of our energy problem. It consists of the following steps (see Figure VA-1).

- Exploration for and discovery of uranium ore reserves.
- Mining, milling and refining the ore to produce uranium concentrates (U_3O_8).
- Conversion of U_3O_8 to uranium hexafluoride (UF_6) to provide feed for uranium enrichment.
- Isotopic enrichment of UF_6 to provide reactor grade uranium fuel.
- Fabrication of nuclear fuel, including converting UF_6 to uranium dioxide, pelletizing, encapsulating in rods, and assembling the uranium dioxide into fuel elements.
- Loading of fuel into reactors and utilizing the heat for electricity generation.
- Reprocessing the spent fuel to recover remaining fissionable uranium and plutonium from radioactive wastes.
- Converting uranium to UF_6 for recycling to enrichment plants and plutonium for use in mixed (plutonium-uranium) oxide fuels.
- Radioactive waste disposal.

While the basic technology for the light water reactor fuel cycle is well developed, segments of the fuel cycle are faced with a number of complex, interrelated but solvable problems which must be resolved in a timely manner to ensure that the necessary supporting functions do not impede the utilization of nuclear power. The purpose of this section is to discuss the problems which face the nuclear fuel cycle.

Uranium Reserves And Resources

As is the case with other resource estimates, there is considerable uncertainty about the total size of the domestic uranium resource base, reflecting the extent of exploration efforts. Considerable exploration for uranium was conducted in the early 1950's by the Atomic Energy Commission and the U.S. Geological Survey with a sub-

Figure V A-1

The Light Water Reactor Nuclear Fuel Cycle

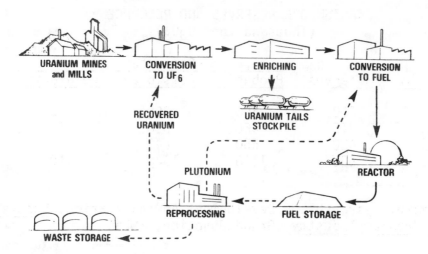

sequent major effort by private industry. In the period 1967-69, there was a sharp increase in exploration efforts well above the levels of the 1950's, followed by decreased exploration of the early 1970's due to softening in the uranium market as a consequence of slippage in uranium demands. Starting in 1973, exploration activities increased again and are expected to continue to increase in 1976.

In its latest survey of uranium resources, the Energy Research and Development Administration has divided uranium deposits into two main categories: reserves and resources. Ore reserve estimates are the most reliable figures since they are based on drill-hole and other geologic data made available to ERDA by the uranium companies. Potential resource estimates are estimates of undefined and undiscovered resources in geologic formations in the United States, and these estimates are divided into three subcategories (probable, possible, and speculative) to reflect their degree of reliability. The reliability is greatest in the probable class where there has been extensive exploration and where mines have been developed— thus defining local ore deposits. The reliability is least in the speculative class where area of favorability must be inferred solely from literature survey, geological reconnaissance of formation outcrops, and the examination of the logs and cuttings from wells drilled for petroleum and other purposes.

Since various grades of ore exist (average uranium ore from underground mines contained 0.22 and 0.20 percent U_3O_8 in 1974 and the first half of 1975 respectively) and since the ore occurs in deposits of varying thickness and scope and at varying depths, both resource and reserve estimates have been further categorized in terms of their "forward" costs of production. Forward costs are defined as those operating and capital costs yet to be incurred to

produce a particular body of ore. They do not include profit and "sunk" costs such as past expenditures for property acquisition, exploration, and mine development. The various forward costs are independent of the market price at which the reserves and estimated resources would be sold. Table VA-1 summarizes the latest estimates of uranium reserves and resources that could be recovered at various maximum forward costs. Each successive cost category includes the estimates of the lower cost category or categories.

In addition to the resources listed in Table VA-1, U_3O_8 may be recovered as a by-product of phosphate and copper production. Also, the recent price increases for alternate fuels have opened the possibility of eventual utilization of uranium available at forward costs higher than $30/1b. The Chattanooga Shale in Tennessee has a uranium content of about 60 ppm and contains in excess of 5 million tons of U_3O_8 that would be producible perhaps at a forward cost of around $100/1b. This Chattanooga Shale, plus other low grade deposits, could yield as much as 26 million tons.

Presently known uranium reserves in the contiguous U.S. are concentrated in a few states. Major mining areas are found in Wyoming, Utah, Colorado, and New Mexico; in 1974, New Mexico and Wyoming produced 75 percent of all the U_3O_8 mined (see Table VA-2).

Excluding uranium resources potentially available from abroad, the maximum nuclear capacity that can be supported based on presently available light water reactor technology will be determined by the extent of our economically and environmentally producible domestic uranium resources. Assuming 70 percent capacity utilization, from 150 to 200 short tons of U_3O_8 are needed each year to fuel a 1000 MWe light water reactor and two to three times that amount is needed to make up a complete

Table VA-1

URANIUM ORE RESERVES AND RESOURCES*
(Thousand Tons U_3O_8)

Forward Cost	Reserves	Resources			Total
		Probable	Possible	Speculative	
$ 8/lb	200	300	200	30	730
$10/lb	315	460	390	110	1275
$15/lb	420	680	640	210	1950
$30/lb	600	1140	1340	410	3490

* U.S. Energy Research and Development Administration, <u>Statistical Data of the Uranium Industry</u>, Grand Junction, 1975.

initial reactor core. A total of approximately 6000 tons of U_3O_8 is required to fuel a reactor for 30 years of operation.

The actual amount of U_3O_8 utilized will depend upon the operating characteristics and type of nuclear reactor, and two other important factors: the tails assay of the uranium enrichment plants and the recycling of uranium and plutonium from spent fuel. The 6000 ton figure assumes no recycling and a tails assay of 0.3 percent. By lowering the tails assay of the enrichment plant, more of the isotope U-235 is recovered from the feed stream,

thereby lowering the requirement for U_3O_8. Lowering the tails assay to 0.2 percent would decrease uranium requirements by about 17 percent. Utilization of unburned uranium and plutonium from spent fuel discharged from reactors could also significantly decrease reactor uranium requirements by approximately the same percentage.

Given these assumptions, some 1.4 million short tons of U_3O_8 will be needed to support the 240,000 MWe of nuclear capacity in operation under construction, or on order as of August, 1975, for their entire lives assuming

Table VA-2

DISTRIBUTION OF U_3O_8 PRODUCTION IN
ORE BY STATES, 1974

State	Tons of Ore	Tons of U_3O_8	Percent of U_3O_8 Produced
New Mexico	2,997,000	5,400	43
Wyoming	2,458,000	4,000	32
Colorado, Texas, Utah, Washington, and other states	1,661,000	3,200	25
Total	7,116,000	12,600	100

Source: Statistical Data of the Uranium Industry, ERDA GJO-100(75), January 1, 1975.

30 years of operation. As shown in Table VA-1, the total of reserves and probable resources at $30/1b or less, which have been counted on for planning purposes, exceeds 1.7 million short tons of U_3O_8, sufficient to fuel the 240,000 MWe now on order or in operation and an additional 60,000 MWe or more of capacity for 30 years of operation. Whether or not additional nuclear plants can be fueled beyond this 300,000 MWe depends on how successful the industry is in the coming years in their uranium exploration efforts.

Continued exploration and development effort will be required to convert resources into reserves. Historically, there has not been a large incentive to explore new districts, especially since the uranium market has been quite soft. In fact, for many years the Federal Government encouraged development of the uranium industry in order to meet requirements guaranteeing to buy uranium at a fixed price. However, conditions have recently changed uranium transactions into a sellers' market.

The uncertainties in the long-term availability of uranium have implications for the timing and planning of interrelated portions of the fuel cycle and for the need to develop new technology to replace it. To reduce uncertainty, the Energy Research and Development Administration has recently begun a large scale assessment of potential uranium sources in the continental U.S. and Alaska, which will not be finished for several years. These estimates will supplement existing information on undiscovered resources which are based almost entirely on data developed from previously productive geologic formations in the U.S.

Figure V A-2

Domestic Uranium Delivery Commitments

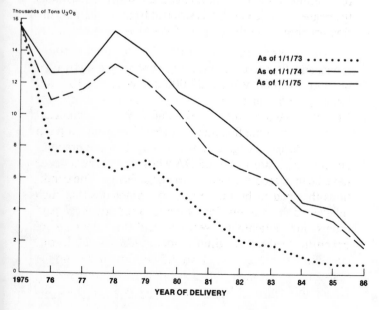

Thousands of Tons U_3O_8

As of 1/1/73 ....
As of 1/1/74 — — —
As of 1/1/75 ————

YEAR OF DELIVERY

Figure V A-3

Uranium Requirements And Delivery Commitments

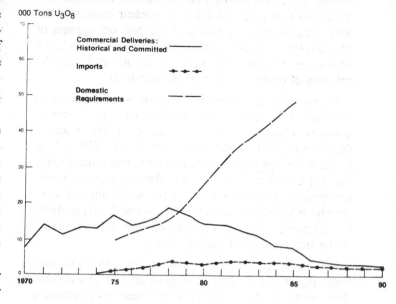

000 Tons U_3O_8

Commercial Deliveries:
Historical and Committed ————

Imports — • —

Domestic Requirements — — —

Mining

In spite of the reduction in this year's estimates of nuclear capacity expected to be in commercial operation by 1985, U_3O_8 requirements will still have significant implications for the mining industry. In the last six years about 13,000 short tons of U_3O_8 were produced annually in this country while existing milling capacity could handle as much as 17,000 short tons. By 1985 two to three times (30,000-40,000 short tons) the current annual amount of U_3O_8 will have to be produced and delivered for conversion and processing into fuels depending on the tails assay of the enrichment plants and whether plutonium and uranium are recycled. Milling capacity will have to be expanded to meet this level of annual demand. By the late 1970's, additions and modifications to existing mills will increase industry capacity to about 23,000 tons annually.

As of January, 1975, a little over 100,000 tons of U_3O_8 had been committed for delivery by 1985 (see schedule in Figure VA-2). This figure shows that uranium producers and utilities have made very few long-term delivery commitments for U_3O_8 in spite of the fact that a nuclear plant is expected to operate for 30 years. Figure VA-3 compares delivery commitments with projected annual requirements. Clearly, not all the annual requirements to fuel new and currently operating nuclear power plants have yet been contracted for. In fact, recently Westinghouse Electric Corporation contended that it was "legally excused" from honoring its contracts to deliver uranium to some customers after 1978 for the contracted price. This action could affect the delivery of up to 40,000 short tons of U_3O_8 over a period of years for which utilities had contracts with Westinghouse.

Numerous market uncertainties have dominated the industry's thinking about future investment in uranium mining. Today the industry faces a number of market uncertainties as a result of delays in nuclear capacity additions, the incremental lifting of the ban on imports of uranium for domestic use beginning in 1977, the lack of a final decision on the plutonium recycle question, and the potential of possible local nuclear moratoria.

Uranium prices will probably serve as an incentive to continue exploration and development of domestic uranium resources. The average price for material delivered in 1974 is reported to have been $7.90/1b. Projected prices under new contracts have increased sharply (see Figure VA-4). Since material for near term deliveries was largely under contract, the most significant impact of the higher prices in terms of cash flow and financial ability to continue exploration for new uranium deposits occurs in the late 1970's and early 1980's.

It is estimated that it takes about seven to eight years from exploration drilling to production and that it takes three years to open a mine and two years to construct a mill. Adequate incentives could probably reduce the time schedules for machinery and equipment. Capital costs for needed uranium mining and milling activities could be on the order of several billion dollars in the 1975 to 1990 period; however, the major portion of the capital will be required after 1982 or 1983.

The problems which threaten to create a shortfall of uranium supply at the end of this decade are not technical. Sufficient time exists, if proper incentives are provided, to

Figure V A-4

Range of Reported U₃O₈ Prices in 1974 and 1975

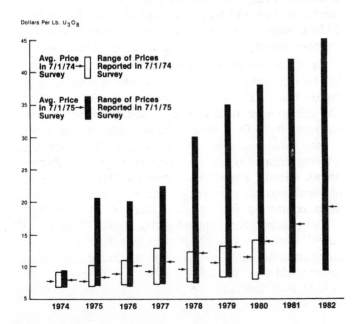

begin the expansion of existing mines and facilities and the development of new mines now. It is hoped that utilities and the uranium suppliers will meet their responsibilities in this area by establishing firm contractual arrangements which will both guarantee utilities uranium supplies at reasonable prices and guarantee uranium suppliers adequate future sales and revenues to permit them to invest in capacity expansions.

Uranium Enrichment Services

Uranium for use as fuel in light water reactors must be enriched in the fissile isotope U-235 to a concentration of approximately 3 percent by weight. Naturally occurring uranium contains only 0.7 percent U-235 by weight, the rest being U-238. In order to enrich uranium for use as reactor fuel, U_3O_8 is converted to uranium hexafluoride (UF_6) and sent to an isotopic separations plant for enrichment.

All three uranium enrichment facilities in the United States are owned and operated under contract to private industry by the Energy Research and Development Administration. They are located in Portsmouth, Ohio; Paducah, Kentucky; and Oak Ridge, Tennessee. Additional enrichment plants will be required in support of new reactor capacity probably in the mid-1980's. The timing of the need for the next increment of U.S. enrichment capacity will depend on a number of factors.

These factors include: the rate of expansion of U.S. nuclear power capacity; demand for enriching services by foreign utilities with nuclear capacity; extent of plutonium recycle; and the capacity factor at which nuclear plants operate. The supply of enrichment capability will depend upon the timing of improvements and capacity uprating of present plants, the ability to obtain adequate electric power supplies to meet the energy intensive separations requirements, the operating tails assay which determines the degree to which U-235 is stripped from natually occurring uranium; and the extent of stockpile reserves.

As of September, 1975, ERDA had signed requirements and firm fixed contracts to support the equivalent of about 315,000 MWe (208,000 domestic and 107,000 foreign) and signed conditional foreign contracts for 14,000 MWe for a total of 329,000 MWe. A significant development in the first quarter of 1975 was the adoption of a plan designed to give one-time relief to those uranium enrichment customers of ERDA whose enrichment needs have been altered because of reactor deferrals. The conditions that had to be met by the customer desiring such relief were the continuation of the required advanced payments for enrichment services and the delivery of uranium feed as originally scheduled. In addition, customers were required to pay 7.5 percent interest on the first-core enrichment value during the deferral period. Under this policy, ERDA will continue to produce the enriched uranium, holding it in a "preproduction stockpile." The objective of this policy, besides providing contract relief to enrichment customers, is the assurance of the future supply of enriched uranium through the creation of a stockpile and support of U.S. uranium mining and producing industry.

During the open season, 121 domestic customers asked for postponements averaging 23 months and 56 foreign customers asked for postponements averaging 28 months. As a result, ERDA estimates that its preproduction stockpile inventory can be increased from 20 million separative work units (SWU) to about 35 million SWU.[10] The increase in the stockpile does not postpone the need for new enriching capacity but it does make possible much firmer ERDA backup guarantees should new enrichment plants have start-up problems or should production from ERDA's facilities be curtailed due to losses of power, extended plant maintenance shutdowns or other factors.

In anticipation of meeting contract commitments to supply enrichment services, the Federal Government is making a sizeable investment over the next few years to expand the annual separative work capacity in its gaseous diffusion plants. This involves the incorporation of the most recent advances in technology, thereby increasing efficiency of the plants, and a program to permit the use of higher electric power levels. Planned capacity is expected to increase from the current level of 17 million separative work units (SWU) to nearly 28 million SWU by 1984.

With today's projections of nuclear additions and contract commitments, new enrichment capacity will be needed by the early to mid-1980's. Estimates are that it will take at least eight years to design, construct, license, test, and put a new plant into operation. Government policy since 1971 has been to encourage private industry to assume responsibility for constructing new uranium enrichment facilities. The policy is in keeping with the provisions of the Atomic Energy Act of 1954 which provided that "the development, use and control of atomic energy shall be directed so as to . . . strengthen free competition in free enterprise."

With additional legislative authorization, ERDA could enter into cooperative arrangements with private firms to enrich uranium for sale, at home and abroad. The cooperative arrangements could include:

- Supplying and warranting Government-owned inventions and discoveries in enrichment technology—for which the Government will be paid.

- Selling certain materials and supplies on a full cost recovery basis which are available only from the Federal Government.

- Buying enriching services from private producers or selling enriching services to producers from the Government stockpile to accommodate plant start-up and loading problems.

- Assuring the delivery of uranium enrichment services to customers which have placed orders with private enrichment firms.

- Assuming the assets and liabilities (including debt) of a private uranium enrichment project if the venture threatened to fail—at the call of the industry participants or the Government, and with compensation to domestic investors in the private ventures ranging from full reimbursement to total loss of equity interest, depending upon the circumstances leading to the threat of failure.

ERDA has recently taken the following administrative actions:

- ERDA is responding to a proposal from Uranium Enrichment Associates (UEA) which could lead to the construction of a $3.5 billion gaseous diffusion plant of 9 million SWU's capacity to come on line in 1983.

- ERDA has issued a request for proposals to build gas centrifuge enrichment capacity and has received proposals from Exxon Corporation, The Signal Companies, and a joint venture consisting of Atlantic-Richfield and Electro-Nucleonics Corporation (all plants to have about three million SWU's capacity). These proposals have been evaluated and meet the acceptability criteria established in ERDA's request for proposals. Detailed negotiations are now being

Figure V A-5

Separative Work Unit (SWU)

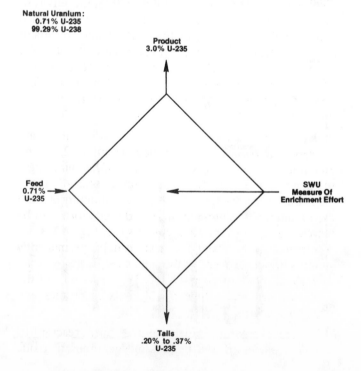

Natural Uranium:
0.71% U-235
99.29% U-238

initiated with these three groups which could lead to three cooperative agreements for the construction of gas centrifuge enrichment plants.

The proposals are based on two different separation techniques: gaseous diffusion and gas centrifuge.[11] The gaseous diffusion process is used in all three existing enrichment plants. A major advantage of gas centrifuge technology is that it uses only one-tenth of the electricity to accomplish the same amount of separation as that required by using the gaseous diffusion process. Also, plant construction lead times are shorter and capacity additions can be made in smaller increments than that required for an economic gaseous diffusion plant. However, thus far, this technology has only been applied on a demonstration scale.

The UEA-Bechtel proposal to build a gaseous diffusion plant on a 1,700 acre site near Dothan, Alabama is the farthest along, but no significant financing other than for engineering feasibility and market promotion have so far been devoted to it.

The Exxon, Signal Companies and Atlantic Richfield-Electro-Nucleonics proposals are basically for three million SWU gas centrifuge plants which have not yet been demonstrated on a commerical scale. Like the UEA venture, all would require cooperative arrangements with ERDA for technological support and temporary financial assurances.

Spent Fuel Reprocessing

The fuel cycle up to the time the fuel rods are loaded into the reactor is largely a straightforward materials handling and manufacturing operation with some environmental and radiation considerations. This is the so-called "front-end" of the nuclear fuel cycle where the major issues are: the adequacy of the resource base; the ability of industry to expand exploration and development activities and open new mines and mills; and whether sufficient new enrichment capacity will be on line to sustain future nuclear development.

Fuel discharged from light water reactors contains appreciable quantities of unburned Uranium-235 and plutonium. There are alternative ways of handling these materials. The uranium and plutonium can be chemically recovered from the spent fuel and the uranium or both the uranium and plutonium in mixed oxide form can be recycled as fuel in light water reactors (see Figure VA-1). Alternatively, the spent fuel rods can be permanently stored without recovery of the unburned fissile material. The actual mode of operation of the "back end" of the fuel cycle will be a function of both economics and regulatory policy.

To conserve domestic fuel resources, spent reactor fuel can be reprocessed and plutonium and uranium oxide fuels fabricated for reuse in light water reactors. By recycling, requirements for newly mined U_3O_8 could be decreased significantly, thus conserving a limited resource. Furthermore, plutonium generated by the light water reactor system could be used to start up and sustain a new generation of so-called breeder reactors. In one form of the breeder, fissile plutonium rather than uranium, would be used for fuel and the fission process would be used to generate both heat for electricity and more plutonium than was burned by transmutation of depleted uranium tails from the enrichment process (see Figure VA-6). In this way the existing uranium resources could be extended by a factor of 60 or more.

Industry and many electric utilities have assumed that spent fuel reprocessing and mixed oxide fuel recycle will occur. In fact, industrial firms have proceeded to build some of the necessary facilities, but have run into technical and regulatory problems.

Reprocessing has been delayed by environmental questions and regulatory uncertainties with regard to the decision to permit the use of mixed oxide (plutonium and uranium) fuels. In November, 1975, the Nuclear Regulatory Commission (NRC) announced procedures for considering the wide scale use of mixed oxide reactor fuel. It proposes to license, on an interim basis where warranted, facilities which would produce mixed oxide fuel and hopes to make a final decision on the wide scale use of mixed oxide fuel for light water nuclear reactor plants in early 1977.

It is difficult to determine the economics of spent fuel reprocessing because of a number of uncertainties. These include: the capital and operating costs associated with reprocessing, the value of the uranium recovered, the value of the plutonium recovered, the costs of safeguarding plutonium and the costs to be assessed for Federal disposal and permanent storage of the radioactive wastes. Since plutonium represents about half the energy value to be recovered from spent fuel, a decision not to permit the use of mixed oxide fuel would make fuel reprocessing more expensive for a utility than if mixed oxide fuel use were permitted.

Utilities could still opt to have their fuel reprocessed even if they were permitted to use only the recovered uranium and not the plutonium. This could be cheaper than the so-called throwaway fuel cycle where the spent fuel is stored rather than reprocessed. The choice would depend upon the relative costs of spent fuel rod disposal and terminal storage of radioactive wastes resulting from reprocessing as well as on the relative costs of recovered and newly mined uranium. Little work beyond conceptual studies has been done on terminal storage of spent fuel rods, and, therefore, the costs associated with a throwaway fuel cycle are uncertain.

Figure V A-6

Fast Breeder

The Light Water Reactor Nuclear Fuel Cycle

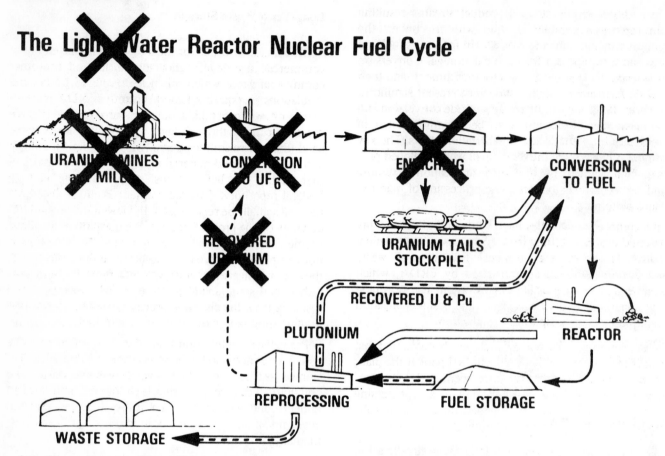

A major concern over the utilization of plutonium has been whether adequate safeguards exist to deter, prevent, or respond to the unauthorized possession or use of significant quantities of nuclear materials through theft or diversion and the sabotage of nuclear facilities. The areas of greatest difference between the present uranium fuel cycle for light water reactors (LWR) and the LWR mixed oxide fuel cycle, where additional safeguards must be considered are:

- Conversion of plutonium nitrate to plutonium oxide.

- Shipment of plutonium from reprocessing plants to mixed oxide fuel fabrication plants.

- Fabrication of mixed oxide fuel.

- Shipment of fabricated mixed oxide fuel to LWR's.

A final decision on usage of mixed oxide fuel was to be made in 1977. If it is decided that mixed oxide recycle is permissible, it is possible that the cost of safeguards could affect the economic attractiveness of using plutonium. Indications are, however, that it may be possible to adequately safeguard mixed oxide fuel without significant additional costs.

Aside from the regulatory questions related to wide-scale plutonium recycle, there are a number of technical issues which must be solved to assure that uranium and plutonium are actually chemically processed and converted to LWR fuel on a wide scale. There are currently no commercial spent fuel reprocessing facilities operating either in the U.S. or in Europe. Operation of the initial U.S. reprocessing plant by Nuclear Fuel Services (NFS) at West Valley, New York was suspended in 1971 for modification and expansion of the plant. It is scheduled to reopen sometime in 1981-82. A plant built by General Electric at Morris, Illinois scheduled to start up in 1972, never began operations because it was determined that it would not operate economically without major redesign and rebuilding. A third plant belonging to Allied General Nuclear Services (AGNS) near Barnwell, South Carolina, is nearly completed but was not expected to begin operations before 1977.

Both NFS and AGNS are using the same basic chemical process to recover uranium and plutonium from spent fuel. This process has been in use in several government facilities for many years in connection with defense programs. The key technical issues for wide scale commercial application are the processing of high exposure fuel and the associated methods of maintenance required to assure continuous economic operation over long periods.

In addition, the waste and product streams resulting from reprocessing must be dealt with to convert the uranium and plutonium to oxide form for use as fuel and the waste to solid form for terminal storage. Conversion of the uranium to gaseous form for enrichment, and then to oxide form for use as fuel does not present significant problems. Both plutonium nitrate to oxide conversion and plutonium fuel fabrication have been demonstrated in several industry pilot-scale fuel fabrication plants. The key technical problems are the scale-up of well developed processes by a factor of 10-20 and the application of remote handling techniques to enable the processing of high exposure plutonium.

No commercial facilities have yet been built to solidify the liquid wastes resulting from reprocessing for terminal storage. However, the technical feasibility of waste solidification has been demonstrated by ERDA, which has several pilot-scale facilities in operation. The key questions remaining involve selection of the best solidification techniques and scale-up to full production.

Past planning for the nuclear fuel cycle has assumed that nuclear reactors would have a spent fuel pool at the plant site with enough capacity to store spent fuel rods temporarily while awaiting transportation to a reprocessing plant where they would be chopped up and chemically treated in batches to recover plutonium and uranium.

The reactor storage pool was designed to handle a full core discharge if required for safety or operational purposes. Reactor fuel storage pools were not ordinarily designed with sufficient capacity for long-term storage of the spent fuel from the reactor. The nuclear fuel reprocessing facilities also have or were to have spent fuel storage capacity. The NFS and GE facilities are storing some spent fuel, and the GE facility has been authorized by NRC to expand its storage capacity from 100 to 750 metric tons. There has been only a small volume of spent fuel discharged to date. While the recycling and reprocessing issues are being resolved, the problem of spent fuel discharge and its disposal is beginning to grow as the volume increases as a consequence of nuclear plant operation and new capacity additions.

In a number of reactor facilities, the existing reactor pool storage capacity can be expanded. In some instances, the potential exists to expand storage capacity by 200 to 300 percent. A number of utilities have expressed interest in expanding their reactor storage facilities, and a number have already submitted applications to NRC to do so. Furthermore, the possibility exists that storage space available at the three reprocessing facilities could be expanded to handle additional spent fuel rods. However, all these measures will offer only very limited short-term relief to utilities for their spent fuel rod disposal problem.

Long-Term Waste Storage

ERDA is responsible for the long-term management of commercial high-level radioactive waste and for other commercial waste which might be identified by Federal regulations as requiring Federal custody. ERDA requirements on waste handling obligate the commercial processor to convert the high level waste solution to a stable solid (the precise composition of which is still unspecified) and to seal the solid material in high integrity canisters of manageable size before transferring the material to a Federal repository. This requirement assumes that spent fuel will actually be reprocessed. In view of the present uncertainty on the processing issue, the question of the management of commercial waste and its ultimate storage is not completely resolved. If reprocessing does not occur, the spent-fuel rods themselves will have to be stored rather than some solidified form of the aqueous wastes resulting from the chemical process necessary to separate uranium and plutonium from the spent fuel.

Permanent underground storage in a stable geologic zone is considered to be the most attractive final means of storage to take care of high level radioactive waste. The search for such acceptable sites is continuing, and once an underground location is chosen, tests will be conducted to determine if the means and location of storage is environmentally acceptable.

Clearly, long-term waste storage remains a significant issue in nuclear development. With the slippage in nuclear capacity additions and the delay in the decision to permit mixed oxide fuel use, the pressure for an immediate resolution of the storage question has been slightly alleviated but remains an urgent problem. Technical and practical problems as to the best method of terminal storage must be resolved to assure that high-level waste generated in the future can be taken care of and to reduce the criticism and apprehension created by uncertainties about this end of the fuel cycle.

Summary

The development of the nuclear fuel cycle industry is essential to the expansion of nuclear power. A number of technical and other issues related to the fuel cycle remain unresolved. These issues must be addressed soon, and satisfactorily resolved, so that they do not become obstacles to further nuclear development. This is particularly true for the so-called "back-end" of the fuel cycle.

Nuclear reactor generated electricity contributes to U.S. energy independence only to the extent that there are abundant domestic reserves and resources of uranium ore, the basic input to nuclear fuel. While there is some uncertainty as to the size of the uranium resource base for the long term, ERDA has an extensive program underway to locate the new uranium resources which will be needed if the use of light water reactors is to continue expansion to the turn of the century and beyond. In the near term, reserves are sufficient and domestic uranium producers must expand and develop new mines and milling capacity to meet future uranium requirements. Timely investment in additional mining and milling capacity has been hampered by uncertainties about future demand, ore prices, and a shortage of capital. Resolution of regulatory uncertainties, different contracting arrangements between producers and users of uranium, and greater certainty about future requirements should lead to the needed investment in exploration and facilities.

Current government owned enrichment facilities can support about 315,000 MWe assuming fuel reprocessing and plutonium recycle. Fixed contracts for 208,000 MWe domestic and 107,000 MWe foreign have been signed by ERDA. In order to permit orderly development of the LWR industry regardless of whether or not plutonium recycle is permitted, and to preserve the market position of the U.S. in world nuclear development, additional new enrichment capacity will be needed in the mid-1980's. Current plans are to meet this need through private sector construction of a new nine million SWU gaseous diffusion plant to be on line in the mid-1980's and with increments of three million SWU centrifuge plants as required by projected demands for later years.

Spent fuel reprocessing is dependent upon: 1) a favorable ruling from the Nuclear Regulatory Commission on the wide scale use of plutonium for fuel, 2) on the decision by utilities that it is economic to recover just the uranium from spent fuel in the event that plutonium use in LWR's is prohibited and, 3) on the resolution of a number of technical issues associated with reprocessing and fuel fabrication. Until the questions are resolved, the industry cannot plan with confidence. Currently, it is estimated that the earliest that spent fuel reprocessing can begin is in 1977. There may be delays beyond this date such that nuclear power plants will have to expand their spent fuel storage pools to accommodate several years of spent fuel discharges. Most spent fuel storage pools appear to be capable of significant expansion.

Because of slippages in nuclear power plant and spent fuel reprocessing schedules, the onset of high volumes of radioactive waste has been postponed a few years. This should give NRC and ERDA time to develop acceptable standards for the delivery of aqueous wastes in solidified form and to choose appropriate geologic locations for terminal storage. This does not postpone the urgent need to resolve these problems to assure the public that adequate provisions have been made for terminal radioactive waste storage.

If plutonium recycle in light water reactors is not permitted and if utilities decide to have their fuel reprocessed to recover just uranium from spent fuel, then provisions will have to be made to store both high level wastes and plutonium for possible later use in breeder reactors. If neither recycle nor reprocessing take place, then terminal storage plans will have to be made for spent fuel rods.

ENDNOTES

[1] This resource outlook is referred to as the "statistical mean" in USGS Circular 725, from which the supply possibilities described here are derived.

[2] Throughout this chapter, domestic production will be quoted at the world oil price (in constant 1975 dollars) with which it competes. When these supply possibilities mesh with the consumption input to the main PIES, the actual wellhead price of domestic production would be less than the competitive imported oil price, the difference lying mainly in the transportation cost from wellhead to refinery.

[3] Throughout, when import prices are expected to be $13, North Alaskan production is limited to reserves economically viable up to about $10 at the wellhead. This is done to represent, in this chapter, the substantially higher transport costs of North Alaskan oil.

[4] Perhaps additional recovery and inclusion of additional deposits in the recoverable resource base, at higher prices than imagined in USGS-725, would alter this assessment.

[5] Conducted by the FEA Natural Gas Task Force in the Fall of 1975.

[6] Baseload plants assumed to have capacity factors of 70 percent (i.e., operate at 70 percent of capacity over a year).

[7] Intermediate load plants are assumed to have capacity factors of about 35 percent.

[8] Assumes a capacity factor of 70 percent, a heat rate of 9,200 Btu per kWh, and a coal heat content of 20.0 million Btu per ton.

[9] This estimate is probably low because the model does not account for the existence of long-term contracts or the cost penalties of burning western coals in existing boilers designed for eastern coals.

10 It is common practice to express capacity and production rate of a uranium enrichment plant in terms of separative work units. A separative work unit (SWU) is a measure of the effort expended in an enrichment plant to separate a quantity of uranium of a given assay into two components, one having a higher percentage of U-235 and one having a lower percentage (see Figure VA-5).

11 The gaseous diffusion process essentially involves forcing uranium in the form of a gas (uranium hexafluoride) through a series of filters or barriers which separate U-235 from U-238 by virtue of the fact that lighter isotopes diffuse through these barriers at a somewhat more rapid rate than the heavy isotopes. In the gas centrifuge method, uranium hexafluoride is spun in a centrifuge and isotopic weight differences result in the separation of U-235 from U-238.

ENERGY SOURCE FACTS*

SECTION ONE

THE U.S. ENERGY SITUATION

* Energy Fact Book, the Office of Naval Research, April 1977

INTRODUCTION

Most of the energy demand in the United States is supplied by petroleum and natural gas. The domestic supply of both of these fuels is dwindling, however, and may be exhausted early in the twenty-first century.

Limited choices confront the United States. The nation will continue to rely on foreign oil in the near-term (Figure I-1). Energy independence in the mid-term could be achieved, but at a cost the nation may not be willing to pay. Long-term alternatives show great promise, but they may be too late to prevent large increases in foreign imports of liquid petroleum products.

Left to the pressures of free market economics, new alternative energy sources could ultimately be developed by private industry as traditional sources diminish and become more expensive. As long as the opportunity exists to import cheaper energy sources, which, in turn, under-cuts the price of new domestic energy sources, private industry will be reluctant to develop new sources. As a result, the nation will increasingly rely on foreign sources until those sources diminish and the profit of new domestic sources is assured.

Government policymakers recognize the problem and are trying to ensure the nation's commitment to the early development of energy alternatives. There are many alternatives that can be pursued, and each is accompanied by technical, economic, environmental, and social problems. The issues are complex and, without an integrated national plan, it is difficult to set priorities. Additionally, a national consensus, in some cases, may be needed to overcome the traditional economic barriers that confront the development of alternative fuels.

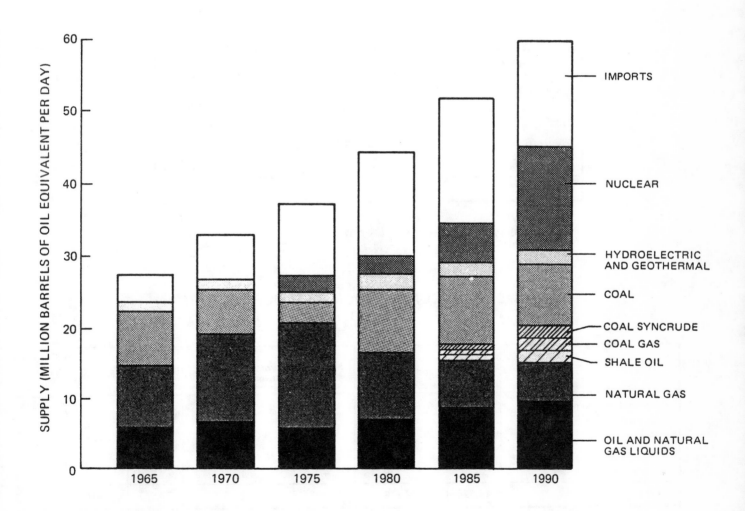

Source: American Petroleum Institute

Figure I-1. U.S. ENERGY SOURCES

ENERGY DEMAND

The United States consumes approximately 73 quadrillion (73×10^{15}) Btu's or 73 quads of energy a year. Total U.S. energy consumption in 1975 is shown in Table I-1, and 1975 energy consumption by major sectors is shown in Table I-2. Figure I-2 shows the complicated energy patterns through which primary energy sources are introduced and used by the economy. (Total energy demand in the United States peaked in 1973 and has decreased since; it is expected to rise, however, with the resurgence of the national economy.)

More than 90 percent of the demand is supplied by three fossil fuels: petroleum, natural gas, and coal. Of these, coal is the largest fossil energy resource. The United States, however, relies on its least plentiful resources—oil and gas; 76 percent of consumption is from these sources that make up only 7 percent of the nation's proved reserves. Only 18 percent of U.S. energy consumption is supplied by coal, which constitutes 90 percent of proved reserves (Figure I-3). The imbalance is caused by the valuable properties of oil and natural gas that enable these products to be produced, transported, stored, and used in ways that are cheaper, easier, safer, and cleaner than coal.

Table I-1

U.S. ENERGY CONSUMPTION, 1975[a]

Source	Demand Percent	Trillion Btu	Units
Oil and liquefied natural gas	46.4	32,719	5.64 billion barrels
Gas	28.3	19,948	18.1 trillion SCF
Coal	18.2	12,828	493.4 million tons
Hydro power	4.5	3,229	322.9 billion kwhr
Nuclear	2.6	1,833	183.3 billion kwhr
Total	100.0	70,557	−3.0% from 1974

[a]Preliminary.
Source: U.S. Bureau of Mines, 7 February 1977.

Table I-2

1975 U.S. ENERGY CONSUMPTION BY MAJOR SECTORS[a]
(Trillion Btu)

	Coal	Petroleum and Liquefied Natural Gas[b]	Natural Gas	Hydro Power	Nuclear	Total	Percent
Household and commercial	246	5,752	7,589	—	—	13,587	19.3
Industrial	3,821	5,517	8,551	35	—	17,924	25.4
Transportation	1	17,933	595	—	—	18,529	26.2
Electricity generation by utilities	8,760	3,239	3,213	3,194	1,833	20,239	28.7
Miscellaneous and losses	—	278	—	—	—	278	0.4
Total	12,828	32,719	19,948	3,229	1,833	70,557	100.0

[a]Estimated.
[b]Includes natural gas liquids, liquefied refinery gas, and still gas.
Source: Division of Interfuels Studies, Office of Assistant Director—Fuels, Bureau of Mines, U.S. Department of the Interior.

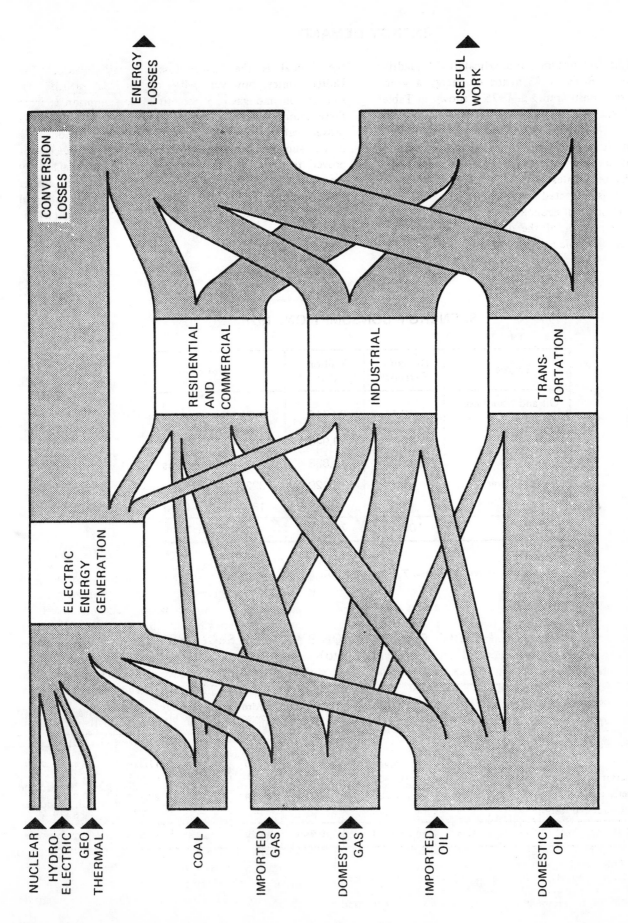

Source: *The National Energy Dilemma*, Joint Committee on Atomic Energy, 1973.

Figure I-2. ENERGY CONVERSION PATTERNS, 1980

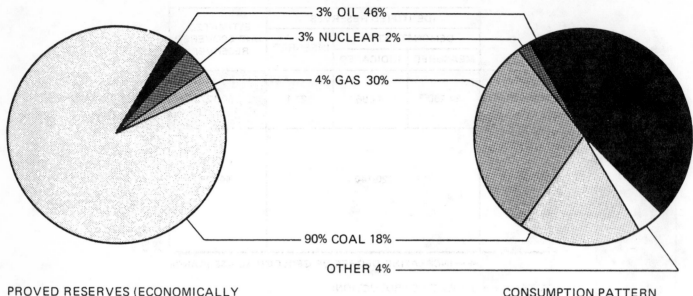

PROVED RESERVES (ECONOMICALLY
RECOVERABLE) WITH EXISTING TECHNOLOGY

CONSUMPTION PATTERN

Source: *National Energy Outlook,* Federal Energy Administration, 1976.

**Figure I-3. U.S. ENERGY SUPPLY AND DEMAND,
BY FUEL TYPE**

ENERGY SUPPLY

Oil

Figure I-4 shows estimates of U.S. oil resources and reserves. Four categories of reserves denote the degree of certainty in the estimate. Measured reserves are "proved," that is, they exist and can be recovered economically. Indicated and inferred reserves possibly exist based on examination of geological formations. Undiscovered economic reserves are postulated oil-bearing formations based on historical extrapolations.

The best estimate (90 percent confident) is that there are between 50 billion and 127 billion barrels of undiscovered economic oil reserves. Measured, indicated, and inferred reserves total 62 billion barrels of oil. Depending on the actual amount ultimately found, undiscovered economic reserves (hypothetical) constitute between 40 and 60 percent of the nation's ultimately recoverable resource estimate. These estimates are based on current technological and economic conditions. As conditions change, the portion of the resource base that is discovered reserves will also change. (Historically, estimates of ultimately

recoverable oil reserves increased as more promising geological areas were explored. Recently, this trend has been reversed. Estimates of undiscovered, recoverable oil and gas in the United States have been declining since 1965 as areas once thought to be promising have proved disappointing.)

Much of the readily recoverable onshore oil in the conterminous United States has already been tapped. If the resource estimates are correct, the United States has already consumed more than 32 percent of its original oil. New production will come from increasingly costly, but more effective, secondary and tertiary recovery methods, new areas on the outer continental shelf, and Alaska.

As the domestic supply of oil decreases, the United States will become increasingly dependent on imported oil. Today imports account for 41 percent of U.S. consumption. Nearly 84 percent of the crude oil imported in the first half of 1976 was supplied by the Organization of Petroleum Exporting Countries (OPEC). U.S. dependence on imported oil from the Arab nations (OAPEC) has increased from 31 percent in 1973 to 43 percent of

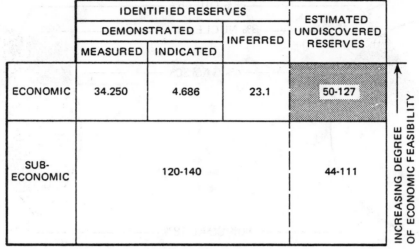

	IDENTIFIED RESERVES			ESTIMATED UNDISCOVERED RESERVES
	DEMONSTRATED		INFERRED	
	MEASURED	INDICATED		
ECONOMIC	34.250	4.686	23.1	50-127
SUB-ECONOMIC	120-140			44-111

INCREASING DEGREE OF ECONOMIC FEASIBILITY

◄— INCREASING DEGREE OF GEOLOGICAL ASSURANCE

TOTAL U.S. CUMULATIVE PRODUCTION:
106 BILLION BARRELS (12/31/74)

NOTE: RESERVES SHOWN IN BILLIONS OF BARRELS

Source: *Oil and Gas Resources, Reserves, and Productive Capacities*,
Federal Energy Administration, June 1975.

Figure I-4. U.S. CRUDE OIL RESERVES

total U.S. crude oil imports. By 2000, oil imports could constitute 83 percent of domestic oil needs.

Gas

Most of the nation's natural gas is found in and along the Gulf of Mexico. According to the U.S. Geological Survey (USGS), the United States has 439 trillion cubic feet (TCF) of known recoverable natural gas. USGS estimates that an additional 338 TCF to 722 TCF of gas may be recoverable. Thus, the United States has ultimately recoverable gas resources of 777 TCF to 1,161 TCF (133.5 to 199.5 billion barrels of oil equivalent).

Production of natural gas is started when proved and measured reserves are sufficient to support production costs. Generally, investors require that gas fields support production for at least 12 to 15 years before development becomes worthwhile. In the United States, only 237 TCF have actually been measured.

Table I-3 shows the supply and demand for natural gas in the United States for 1971 through 1975.

Coal

Coal is the nation's most abundant fossil energy resource. The United States has enough low-sulfur coal to support production growth for the next few centuries. These environmentally acceptable coal deposits are located predominantly in the Northern Rockies (Figure I-5) where, presently, there is virtually no major coal development. The most lucrative of these western deposits requires surface mining. Local and state governments are thus reluctant to permit the environmental and social disruptions that would accompany major development of these coal lands.

The percentage of demand supplied by coal has increased slightly over the last few years and should increase further from now to the end of the century, particularly as methods for converting coal to synthetic fuels are improved and new methods are discovered. (Synthetic fuels derived from coal and oil shale should begin to provide a limited alternative energy source by 1985.)

Other

Nuclear energy has supplied an increasing amount of the nation's demand for energy, rising from 1.1 percent in 1973 to 2.2 percent in 1975. Nuclear power will increase its share of the energy supply from now to the end of the century, with more exotic forms of energy contributing in a minor way.

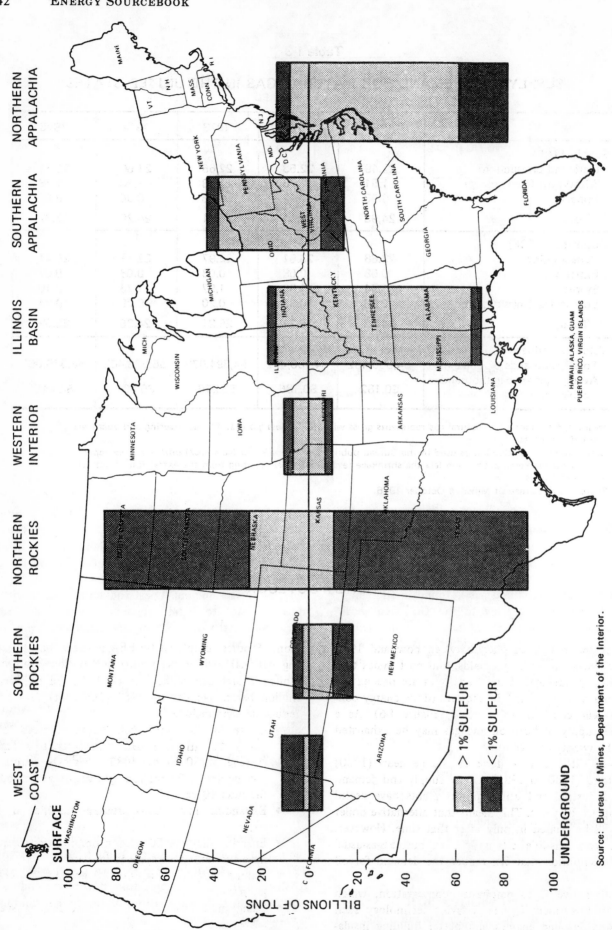

Source: Bureau of Mines, Department of the Interior.

Figure I-5. DEMONSTRATED COAL RESERVES

Table I-3

SUPPLY AND DEMAND FOR NATURAL GAS IN THE UNITED STATES

	1971	1972	1973	1974	1975
Supply (TCF)					
Marketed production[a]	22.49	22.53	22.65	21.60	20.11
Withdrawn from storage	1.51	1.76	1.53	1.70	1.76
Imports	0.93	1.02	1.03	0.96	0.95
Total	24,93	25.31	25.21	24.26	22.82
Disposition (TCF)					
Consumption	22.68	23.01	22.97	22.11	20.41
Exports	0.08	0.08	0.08	0.08	0.07
Stored	1.84	1.89	1.97	1.78	2.10
Lost in transmission, etc.	0.39	0.33	0.20	0.29	0.24
Total	24.93	25.31	25.21	24.26	22.82
Value at wellhead					
Total (thousands of dollars)	$4,085,482	$4,180,462	$4,894,072	$6,573,402	$8,945,062
Average (cents per thousand cubic feet)	$0.182	$0.186	$0.216	$0.304	$0.445

[a]Marketed production of natural gas represents gross withdrawals less gas used for repressuring and quantities vented and flared.

Note: Domestic production as used in the Bureau publication *Minerals and Materials/Monthly Survey* represents marketed production less the shrinkage (extraction loss) resulting from the extraction of natural gas liquids.

Source: U.S. Bureau of Mines, 4 October 1976.

ENERGY OUTLOOK

Most of the energy supplied between now and 1980 will come from oil wells, gas fields, and coal mines that are currently producing. (Long lead times are needed for constructing new facilities.) In the meantime, energy consumption will continue to increase (Figure I-6). As a result, the supply of both oil and gas may be exhausted early in the twenty-first century.

Relatively little can be done to change near- (1980) and mid-term (1980 to 1985) energy supply and demand patterns. Industrial and utility power plants have useful lives of up to 20 years. This means that alternative boiler systems will be phased in only after that time. However, there are two possible alternatives to business-as-usual energy comsumption that can reduce the demand for oil and gas.

One alternative is to emphasize conservation, which includes an investment in energy-saving technology such as improved gasoline engines and better building insula-

tion. Studies completed by FEA indicate that, by adopting national policies promoting energy conservation, the United States can reduce its need for oil by nearly 8 million barrels per day by 1985 (Table I-4). Measures to reduce demand include:

- Converting the automobile propulsion from its present 30:70 ratio of small to large cars to at least an average of 50:50 by 1985. This will require the production of 75 million lightweight automobiles in the next 10 years.
- Expanding mass transportation facilities in large cities.
- Ensuring that the 20 million housing units required have substantially improved insulation.
- Making industrial processes 10 percent less energy-intensive, on the average.
- Using more efficient energy space heating such as heat pumps.

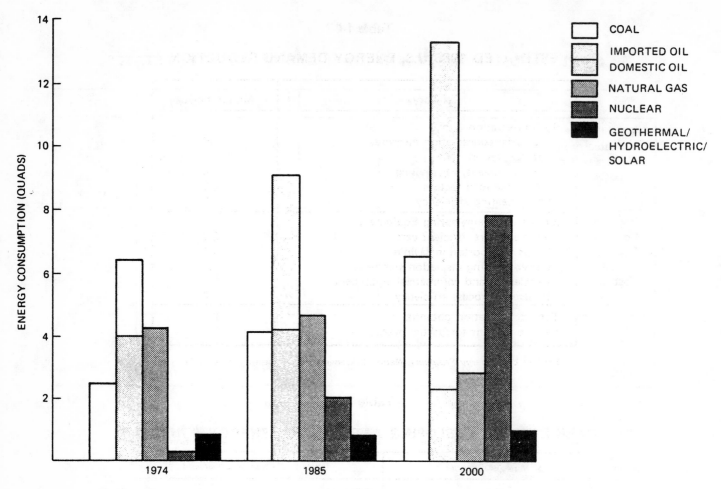

Source: *Creating Energy Choices for the Future,* Energy Research and Development Administration, 1976.

Figure I-6. PROJECTED U.S. ENERGY CONSUMPTION (NO NEW INITIATIVES)

The second alternative is to reduce dependence on oil and gas by the greater use of coal and nuclear fuel for generating electricity. Because of the long lead times required for developing new mines and constructing new power plants, the near-term reduction in oil demand would be minimal; however, a substantial mid-term reduction could be realized, as long as barriers to the direct use of coal and nuclear fuel for electricity are removed.

In the long term, a number of alternative energy sources are promising. The United States and the rest of the world are far from exhausting all the practical, available energy sources. The sources that could constitute the nation's long-term energy supplies are coal, crops, nuclear fission, nuclear fusion, geothermal, hydroelectric, ocean heat, oil shale and tar sands, solar, tides, waste heat, waste materials, water (fusion and hydrogen), and wind-power.

Although the supply of some sources is unlimited, very little can be tapped from the new, more exotic sources in this century. The development cycle of light water nu-

clear reactors is an example. It required 33 years to evolve light water reactor technology and to introduce it commercially. Although other technologies may not need a long development period, all of them will require extensive laboratory, pilot, and demonstration scale tests before they are introduced commercially.

Today, only liquid metal fast breeder reactors (LMFBR) and synthetic fuels from coal and oil shale are ready for demonstration-scale tests. It will be at least 5 to 10 years before the exact value of these two technologies is determined. The value of other less developed technologies will not be recognized for at least a decade. However, this assumes that the United States will be committed to the all out development of these technologies.

There are numerous significant barriers obstructing the development of new energy technology. An uncertain energy policy probably contributes more to the delay than the technical, economic, and social considerations. Table I-5 lists the major barriers for each of the emerging energy technologies.

Table I-4

ESTIMATED 1985 U.S. ENERGY DEMAND REDUCTION

Category	Million bbl/day
By Conservation	
Industrial conservation measures	1.5
Transportation	
Lower speeds, car pooling	1.0
Airplane load factors	0.3
Space heating efficiency	1.0
By Use of Energy-saving Equipment	
Smaller, more efficient cars	2.0
Other transportation savings	1.1
Better building insulation standards	1.1
Residential and commercial equipment	0.4
Industrial process efficiency	1.0
Total conservation potential	9.4
Less 15 percent for partial overlap	8.0

Source: *U.S. Energy Prospects,* National Academy of Engineering, May 1974.

Table I-5

BARRIERS TO DEVELOPING ALTERNATIVE ENERGY SOURCES

Technology	Issues and Areas of Uncertainty
Enhanced oil and gas recovery	Federal oil and gas pricing policies
Synthetic liquids and gases and direct utilization of coal	Federal energy policy Disposal of spent material Water consumption Strip mining and reclamation Sulfur oxide standards World oil prices Capital requirements
Geothermal	Lack of comprehensive resource information Lack of proven domestic technology Legal and regulatory complexities
Light water reactors	Limited uranium reserves
Liquid metal fast breeder reactors	Economic uncertainty Safety Radioactive waste management Insufficient engineering base (breeders) Fuel cycle performance (breeders)
Solar heating and cooling	Economic uncertainty Limited geographic applicability Need for convention backup Legal complexities
Solar electric Solar thermal electric Solar photovoltaic Wind energy Ocean thermal energy conversion	Economic uncertainty Legal complexities Lack of proven technology
Fusion	Very early in the development cycle

Source: *Creating Energy Choices for the Future,* Energy Research and Development Administration, 1976.

SECTION TWO

PETROLEUM

INTRODUCTION

Petroleum and petroleum products contribute about 44 percent to the worldwide demand for energy, nearly as much as natural gas and coal combined (Figure V-1). In the United States, petroleum and petroleum products contribute about 45 percent of energy demand (Table V-1).

Because oil is the world's primary energy source, energy problems are basically oil problems. These problems have resulted because the principal oil consumers are not the major oil producers and world oil supplies are dwindling.

Table V-1

PETROLEUM FACTS SHEET

Energy Content[1]	5.8 million Btu per barrel
Proven U.S. Reserves[2] (1976)	31.3 billion barrels (including 10 billion barrels in Alaska)
Ultimate U.S. Resources[3]	113 billion barrels of petroleum liquids as ultimately recoverable resources
U.S. Production (1976)[4]	10.1 million barrels/day (including 8.1 million barrels/day of crude oil)
Imports (1976)[4]	7.2 million barrels/day (42% of consumption)
U.S. Consumption (1976)[4]	17.3 million barrels/day
Contribution to Demand[5]	Petroleum supplied 45.3% of the 1975 U.S. energy demand

[1]"Domestic Oil and Gas Availability," *U.S. Energy Outlook,* National Petroleum Council, pages 57-133, December 1972.

[2]*Oil and Gas Journal,* page 105, December 27, 1976.

[3]National Academy of Sciences, February 12, 1975.

[4]U.S. Bureau of Mines, January 19, 1977.

[5]Federal Energy Administration.

STRATEGIC OIL DEPENDENCIES

Figure V-2 shows the major oil consumers and producers. The heavy users are the highly industrialized nations. The United States alone accounts for approximately 6 billion barrels (33 percent) of the world total consumption of 18 billion barrels annually.

The third-world nations are the predominant oil producers (Table V-2). The Middle East and Africa account for nearly 50 percent of total world oil production. Oil production in the United States represents only 16 percent of the world's total. (Domestic oil production peaked in 1970 and has been declining steadily since, although there will be a resurgence since Alaskan oil began flowing in 1977.)

The imbalance between the world's major oil consumers and its producers is likely to continue in the mid- and far-term, given the distribution of proved crude oil reserves—those that have been discovered, measured, and are ultimately recoverable. As shown in Table V-3 and Figure V-3, more than one-half of the world's crude oil reserves are in the Middle East and Africa, and only about 5 percent are in the United States.

The near-, mid-, and far-term imbalance places the United States, as an oil-dependent nation, in a precarious position. Today, U.S. imports of petroleum and petroleum products account for 42 percent of its consumption. Of this amount, 68 percent is imported from the Organization of Arab Petroleum Exporting Countries (OAPEC) (Table V-4). Another OAPEC embargo would have serious implications for the United States. Little can be done to reduce U.S. dependence on foreign oil in the near-term, other than to reduce oil consumption.

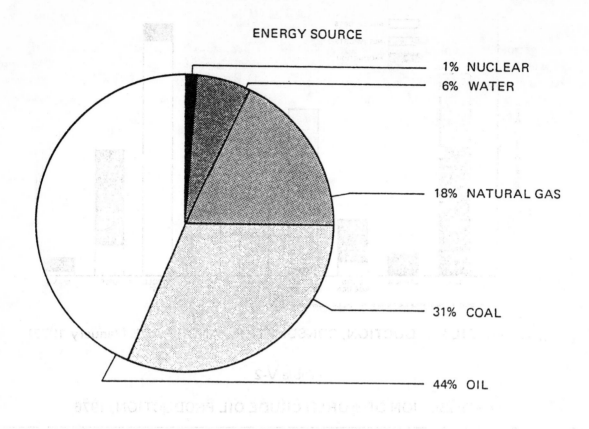

ENERGY SOURCE

1% NUCLEAR
6% WATER

18% NATURAL GAS

31% COAL

44% OIL

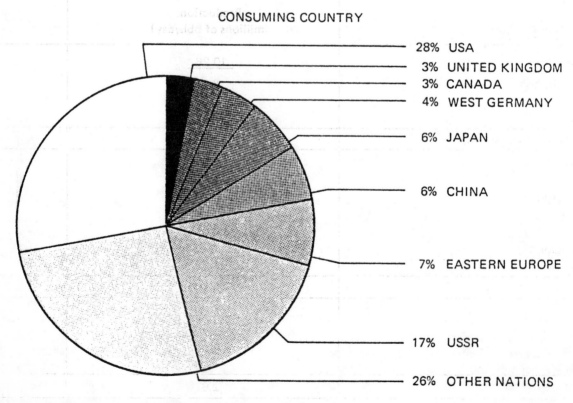

CONSUMING COUNTRY

28% USA
3% UNITED KINGDOM
3% CANADA
4% WEST GERMANY

6% JAPAN

6% CHINA

7% EASTERN EUROPE

17% USSR

26% OTHER NATIONS

Source: British Petroleum Statistical Review of the World Oil Industry, 1975.

Figure V-1. WORLD ENERGY CONSUMPTION, 1974

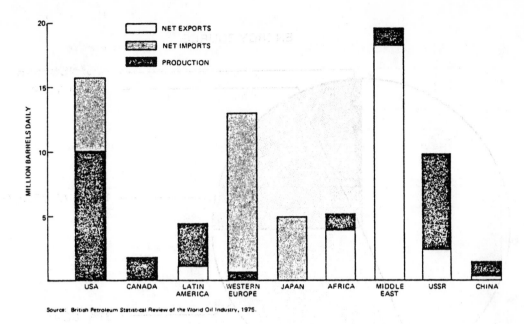

Source: British Petroleum Statistical Review of the World Oil Industry, 1975.

Figure V-2. OIL PRODUCTION, CONSUMPTION, AND TRADE (January 1975)

Table V-2

DISTRIBUTION OF WORLD CRUDE OIL PRODUCTION, 1976

Area/Country	Production (millions of bbls/day)	Percent of World Total
North America	10.26	17.9
United States	8.11	14.2
Canada	1.30	2.3
Mexico	0.85	1.5
South America and Caribbean	3.54	6.2
Middle East	21.88	38.2
Iran	5.88	10.3
Saudi Arabia	8.57	15.0
Kuwait	1.82	3.2
Iraq	2.07	3.6
Abu Dhabi	1.59	2.8
Other	1.95	3.4
Europe	0.90	1.6
Africa	5.60	9.8
Libya	1.90	3.3
Nigeria	2.02	3.5
Other	1.68	2.9
Asia-Pacific	2.67	4.7
Communist Countries	12.36	21.6
World Total Production	57.21	100.0

Source: *Oil and Gas Journal,* December 27, 1976, pp. 104, 105.

Table V-3

DISTRIBUTION OF WORLD OIL RESERVES, JANUARY 1, 1977

Area/Country	Reserves (millions of bbls)	Percent of World Reserves
North America	44,500	7.4
United States	31,300	5.2
Canada	6,200	1.0
Mexico	7,000	1.2
South America and Caribbean	22,608	3.8
Middle East	326,281	54.5
Saudi Arabia	110,000	18.4
Iran	63,000	10.5
Kuwait	67,400	11.3
Iraq	34,000	5.7
Abu Dhabi	29,000	4.8
Other	22,881	3.8
Europe	24,539	4.1
Africa	60,570	10.1
Libya	25,500	4.3
Nigeria	19,500	3.3
Other	15,570	2.6
Communist Countries	101,100	16.9
U.S.S.R.	78,100	13.0
China	20,000	3.3
Other	3,000	0.5
Asia-Pacific	19,391	3.2
World Total	598,990	100.0

Source: "Worldwide Oil at a Glance," *Oil and Gas Journal,* December 27, 1976, pp. 104, 105.

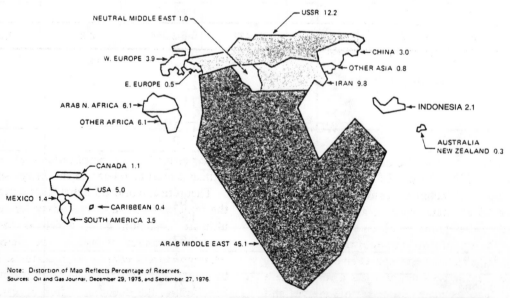

Note: Distortion of Map Reflects Percentage of Reserves.
Sources: Oil and Gas Journal, December 29, 1975, and September 27, 1976.

Figure V-3. WORLD PROVED RESERVES OF CRUDE OIL (PERCENT)

Table V-4

U.S. CRUDE IMPORTS 1970-1976
(Thousands of barrels per day)

Country of Origin	1976[a]	1975	1974	1973	1972	1971	1970
Bolivia	3	5	7	2	...	2	2
Chile	...	...	...	...	...	1	...
Colombia	...	...	...	2	5	9	20
Ecuador	48	37	42	47	...	...	...
Mexico	87	70	2	1	...	...	...
Trinidad	139	115	63	60	24	...	...
Venezuela	214	395	319	345	256	303	268
Latin America total	**491**	**642**	**433**	**457**	**285**	**315**	**290**
Algeria	438	264	180	120	87	13	6
Angola	10	71	48	48	16	4	...
Congo	9	...	2	...	...	...	...
Egypt	18	5	9	15	8	19	21
Gabon	25	27	23	...	...	...	...
Libya	423	223	4	133	110	53	47
Nigeria	964	746	698	448	244	95	48
Tunisia	18	2	12	18	7	...	...
Zaire	20	...	...	...	...	...	...
Africa total	**1,925**	**1,338**	**976**	**782**	**472**	**184**	**122**
Kuwait	6	4	5	42	36	29	33
Saudi Arabia	1,215	702	438	462	174	115	17
Neutral Zone	...	...	...	...	...	...	23
Iran	322	278	463	216	136	106	33
Iraq	9	2	...	4	4	11	...
Qatar	33	18	17	7	3	...	...
Israel	5	...	...	1	...	...	...
United Arab Emirates	222	117	69	71	74	80	63
Middle East total	**1,812**	**1,121**	**992**	**803**	**427**	**341**	**169**
Canada	395	600	791	1,001	856	721	672
Far East	535	384	285	201	167	117	70
Europe	50	17	...	...	...	...	...
Total U.S. crude imports	**5,208**	**4,102**	**3,477**	**3,244**	**2,207**	**1,678**	**1,323**

[a]Preliminary.

Source: *Oil and Gas Journal,* December 27, 1976.

WORLD OIL DEPLETION

Estimates show that the world crude oil production will probably peak about 1990. Estimates of world oil wealth depend on economic and technical feasibility of extracting oil, methods used to estimate reserves, and the degree of certainty assigned to the estimates. Much of the confusion over estimates of the world's oil resources and reserves has come from using different assumptions when incorporating these three factors into the estimates. As a result, there appears to be at least as many estimates of reserves and resources as there are estimators. Rather than favoring any single estimate, the implications of a broad range of estimates must be related to the energy situation.

Theoretical world oil exhaustion dates are calculated for the resource boundaries as a proxy for depletion dates. The ultimate depletion date, which is the time when the available resource is below the amount necessary to maintain current consumption patterns, will be determined by several interrelated and often unquantifiable factors. Specifically, the depletion dates, or transition periods, are determined by world oil production, consumption, and

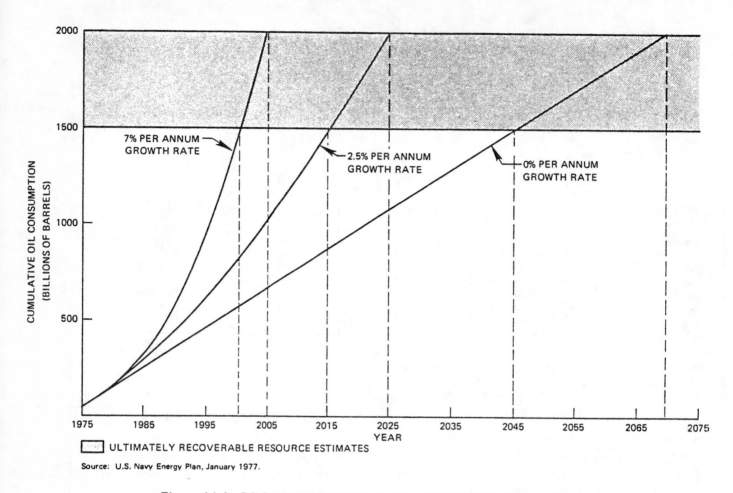

CUMULATIVE OIL CONSUMPTION (BILLIONS OF BARRELS)

7% PER ANNUM GROWTH RATE

2.5% PER ANNUM GROWTH RATE

0% PER ANNUM GROWTH RATE

ULTIMATELY RECOVERABLE RESOURCE ESTIMATES

Source: U.S. Navy Energy Plan, January 1977.

YEAR

Figure V-4. PROJECTED WORLD OIL EXHAUSTION DATES

pricing policies and, ultimately, discovered recoverable oil. The exhaustion date is when the cumulative consumption of oil exceeds the total ultimately recoverable reserves. The calculation assumes that sufficient oil is produced and available to meet the demand. In actual practice, production will decline as the reserves are used and delay the actual exhaustion date, creating a supply shortfall (that is, depletion). Calculating theoretical exhaustion dates indicates the length of time current production and consumption trends could continue until oil supplies are exhausted.

Three alternative oil consumption growth rates have been used to project world exhaustion dates (See Figure V-4). The conservative 2.5 percent annual consumption growth rate projects that, between 2015 and 2025, the entire estimated range of recoverable resources will be exhausted. If an historical growth rate of 7 percent is assumed, exhaustion will occur sometime between 2000 and 2005. In the unrealistic, but most optimistic, case of no increase in consumption, exhaustion will occur no later than 2070.

The proximity of the exhaustion date for the historical growth rate and the relative insignificance of the actual

reserve estimate, except under the no-growth case, are significant. The low-growth alternative could stretch available recoverable oil by about 25 years.

Theoretical exhaustion dates for world areas will vary significantly because of the location of oil bearing formations, local production and consumption patterns, and different trade policies. Figure V-5 gives the exhaustion dates for world regions, assuming oil consumption will have an average annual increase of 4 percent and there is no oil trade. The proximity of Western Europe's exhaustion date relates directly to its heavy dependence on foreign oil sources. Likewise, the United States is destined to face greater dependence on oil imports as its oil resources are depleted. The Soviet Union, on the other hand, has at least 20 more years of available oil than the United States.

Many countries are extending their exhaustion date by substituting foreign oil for domestic oil. Figure V-5 also depicts the exhaustion dates of these regions' domestic supplies when current import patterns are projected for the future. Figure V-6 shows, in detail, the projected oil exhaustion dates for the United States (excluding imports and alternative production policies). To extend available

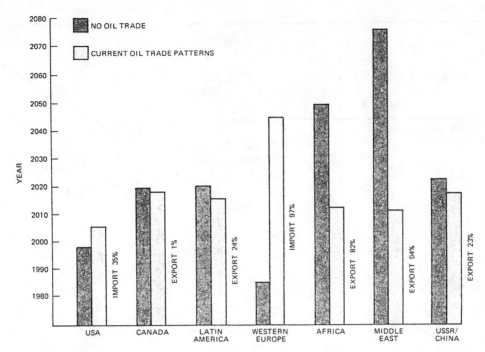

Note: Assumes 4 Percent Annual Growth in Oil Consumption.

Source: U.S. Navy Energy Plan, January 1977.

Figure V-5. REGIONAL OIL EXHAUSTION DATES

domestic oil resources, many countries, in choosing an alternative, will still depend on foreign oil. Since Western Europe relies heavily on foreign sources, their exhaustion date can be postponed to about 2040, but this region will still substantially rely on foreign sources. For the United States, heavy dependence on oil imports will only delay the exhaustion date by about six years.

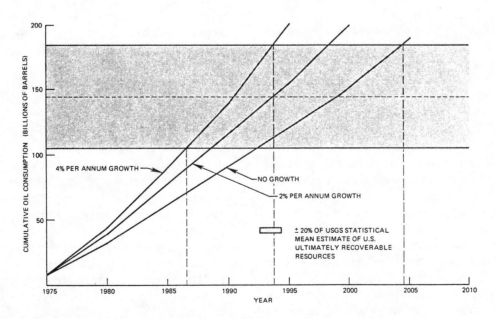

Note: Projections Exclude Imports and Alternative Production Policies

Source: U.S. Navy Energy Plan, January 1977.

Figure V-6. PROJECTED U.S. OIL EXHAUSTION DATES

SECTION THREE

OIL SHALE

INTRODUCTION

Synthetic crude from oil shale is obtained by heating oil shale—a sedimentary rock containing an organic material called kerogen—to approximately 900° F. USGS Circular 523 projects that resources of about 2.2 trillion barrels exist in the United States; of this, about 80 billion barrels are considered recoverable reserves, using existing technology. (See Table VI-1.)

Shale oil products were first obtained in France in 1838 by retorting oil shale. Other countries, including China and USSR, have successfully exploited oil shale; a plant in Manchuria was a source of fuel for the Japanese navy during World War II. Successful exploitation, how-ever, has depended almost entirely upon economic factors.

Oil shale developments have been undertaken by both industry and the U.S. Bureau of Mines. Technology has been developed and the first-generation processes are well in hand. Successful commercial development depends entirely on the ability of industry to obtain an adequate price for its products. Uncertainties in the "price" of crude oil are inhibiting commercialization. DOD efforts are directed toward providing and encouraging appropriate government incentives, and testing of the resulting fuels for operational use as they become available.

Table VI-1

SHALE OIL FACT SHEET

Gross energy content of shale oil[1]	18,330 – 18,680 Btu/lb
Recoverable reserves[2]	80 billion barrels
U.S. resources (known)[2]	2,200 billion BOE[a]
U.S. resources (total)[2]	140,000 billion BOE[a]
Concentration[1]	10.5—75 gallons/ton

[a]BOE = Barrel oil equivalent

Sources: 1. *Synthetic Fuels Data Handbook,* Cameron Engineers, 1975.
2. USGS Circular 523, 1966.

OIL SHALE RESOURCES

The quantity of oil shale in the world represents a large energy resource. As with other energy sources, how-ever, the estimates of the magnitude vary widely. Conse-quently, any estimate needs to be used with a good deal of caution, and there is significant variation between estimates. The resource estimates presented at the 1974 World Energy Conference are used in this summary, and they appear in Table VI-2. This reference shows that the bulk of the oil shale in the world is found in the U.S. The magnitude of the U.S. deposits reported generally agrees with other estimates. Detailed breakdowns of U.S. resources (USGS Circular 523) and an estimate of the recoverable reserves contained in the Green River Forma-tion in Colorado, Utah, and Wyoming appear in Table VI-3.

Table VI-2

WORLD OIL SHALE RESOURCES

Location	Resource (Megatonnes)	Resource (million bbl)	Location	Resource (Megatonnes)	Resource (million bbl)
Argentina	45	330	Jordan	7	50
Brazil	497	3,645	Luxembourg	109	795
Bulgaria	19	140	New Zealand	224	1,640
Burma & Thailand	217	1,590	Spain	6	45
Canada	24,860	182,225	Sweden	880	6,450
Chile	25	185	Turkey	2	15
China (Peoples Republic)	21,000	153,930	United Kingdom	298	2,185
Czechoslovakia	1	7	United States	145,000	1,062,850
France	237	1,740	USSR	3,388	24,835
Germany (Federal Rep.)	311	2,280	Yugoslavia	128	940
Israel	20	145	Zaire	1,550	11,360
Italy	1,087	7,965	TOTAL	199,911	1,465,347

Source: 1974 World Energy Conference.

Table VI-3

U.S. OIL SHALE RESOURCES
(Billions of barrels)

Deposits	Known Resources				Order of Magnitude of Possible Extensions of Known Resources			Order of Magnitude of Undiscovered and Unappraised Resources			Order of Magnitude of Total Resources		
	Recoverable Under Present Conditions	Marginal and Submarginal			Marginal and Submarginal			Marginal and Submarginal			Oil Equivalent in Deposits		
Range in grade; oil yield, in gallons per ton of shale	25-100	25-100	10-25	5-10	25-100	10-25	5-10	25-100	10-25	5-10	25-100	10-25	5-10
Green River Formation, Colorado, Utah, and Wyoming	80	520	1,400	2,000	600	1,400	2,000	--	--	--	1,200	2,800	4,000
Devonian and Mississippian shale, Central and Eastern United States	None	None	200	200	None	800	1,800	--	--	--	--	1,000	2,000
Marine shale, Alaska	Small	Small	Small	Small	250	200	Large	--	--	--	250	200	Large
Shale associated with coal	Small	Small	*	*	Small	Large	Large	60	250	210	60	250	210
Other shale deposits	Small	Small	Small	*	*	*	*	500	22,000	134,000	500	22,000	134,000
Total	80	520	1,600	2,200	850	2,400	3,800	550	22,000	134,000	2,000	26,000	140,000

*No estimate. Estimates and totals rounded.
Oil shale resource estimates include shale zones of the Green River Formation 10 feet or more thick yielding as little as 10 gallons of oil per ton.
Source: USGS Circular 523, 1966.

LOCATION OF U.S. OIL SHALE RESOURCES

Oil shale deposits in the U.S. are shown in Figure VI-1. The eastern and midwestern deposits are of minor importance as fuel source, however. The major U.S. oil shale resource is contained in the Green River Formation in Colorado, Utah, and Wyoming. (See Figure VI-2.) Table VI-4 shows the composition of the various shales.

Table VI-4

TYPICAL OIL SHALE COMPOSITION

ORGANIC MATTER (13.7% by weight)	% weight	MINERAL MATTER (86.3% by weight)	% weight	AVERAGE MAHOGANY ZONE OIL SHALE COMPOSITION	% weight	1 ton yields
Carbon	80.5	Carbonates	50.0	Oil	10.9	28.4 gallons
Hydrogen	10.3	Feldspars	19.0	Water	0.8	1.9 gallons
Nitrogen	2.4	Illite	15.0	Gas and Losses	2.0	400 scf
Sulfur	1.0	Quartz	10.0	Spent shale	86.3	1726 pounds
Oxygen	5.8	Analcite	5.0			
Pyrite	1.0					

Source: *Mineral Facts and Problems*, U.S. Department of Interior Bulletin 650-1970.

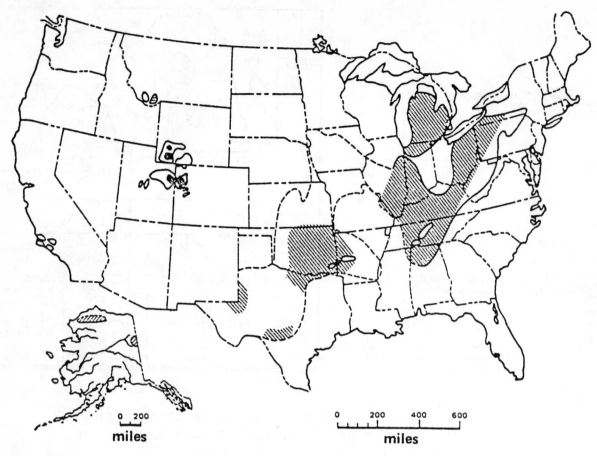

EXPLANATION

Tertiary deposits
Green River Formation
in Colorado, Utah, and
Wyoming; Monterey
Formation, California;
middle Tertiary deposits
in Montana. Black areas
are known high-grade de-
posits

Mesozoic deposits
Marine shale in Alaska

Permian deposits
Phosphoria Formation,
Montana

Devonian and Mississippian
deposits (resource esti-
mates included for
hachured areas only
in Geological Survey
Circular 523). Boundary
dashed where concealed or
where location is uncertain.

Source: *Final Environmental Statement for the Prototype Oil Shale
Leasing Program*, U.S.D.O.I. 1973, Vol. 1, p. II-5.

Figure VI-1. MAP OF PRINCIPAL REPORTED OIL SHALE
DEPOSITS OF THE UNITED STATES

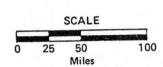

SCALE

0   25   50   100
Miles

LEGEND

Area of oil shale deposits

Area of nahcolite or trona deposits

Area of 25 gal./ton or richer oil
shale 10 ft. or more thick

Source: *Final Environmental Statement for the Prototype Oil Shale Leasing Program,* U.S.D.O.I.
1973, Vol. I, p. II-3.

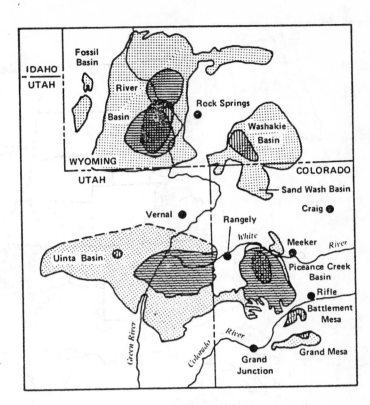

Figure VI-2. LOCATION OF OIL SHALE RESOURCES IN THE GREEN RIVER FORMATION

OIL SHALE RETORTING

Surface Retorting

The surface approach for converting the kerogen in oil shale into synthetic crude requires that the shale be mined in either a surface or underground mine; be transported to the processing plant; and be crushed and fed into a retort heated to approximately 900° F where the kerogen is converted from a solid waxy material into a liquid. The liquid hydrocarbon is collected, hydrotreated to pipeline quality, and piped to a refinery for further processing. The spent shale is deposited in landfills. Several of the more promising processing schemes are illustrated in Figures VI-3 through VI-11.

In Situ Retorting

The various in situ techniques, although not as well developed, require that a portion of the shale seam be fractured. A flame zone is then passed through the fractured material that retorts the shale in place. The liquid shale oil is collected and further processed in the same manner as in the surface technique. Problems inherent in the in situ technique include obtaining uniform fracturing, obtaining uniform heating as the flame zone moves through the fracture zone, and self-healing of the fractures. Several organizations have attempted to process shale in situ, including USBM, Sinclair Oil Co., Equity Oil Co., and Occidental Oil Co. Currently, ERDA and Occidental Oil Co. have development programs in progress. The Occidental approach is shown in Figures VI-12 and VI-13.

Multimineral Recovery

Multimineral concepts, such as the Superior Oil Process, recover not only the oil from the oil shale but also

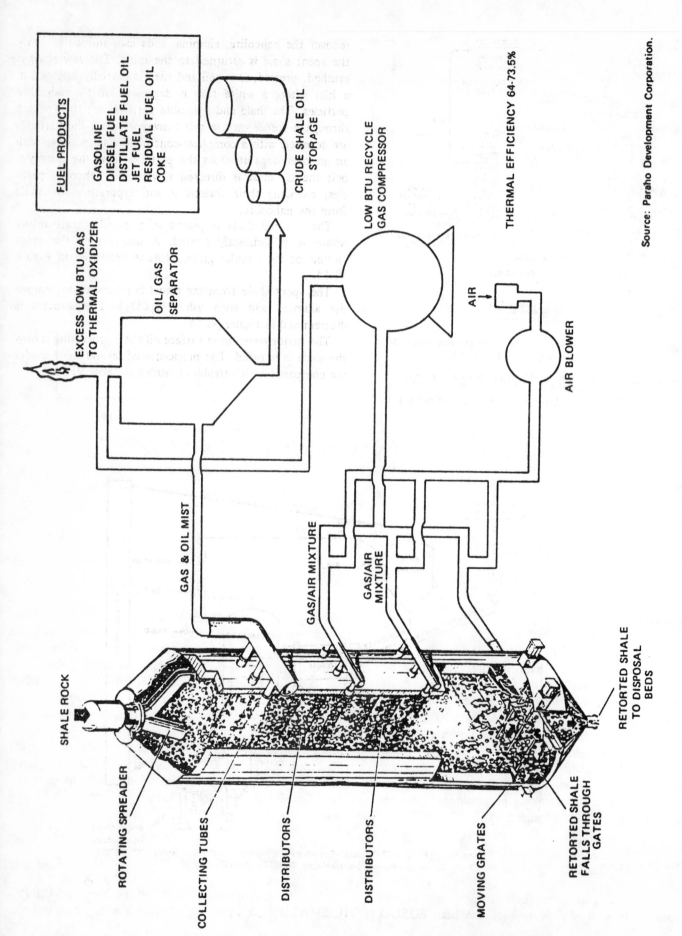

FUEL PRODUCTS

GASOLINE
DIESEL FUEL
DISTILLATE FUEL OIL
JET FUEL
RESIDUAL FUEL OIL
COKE

CRUDE SHALE OIL STORAGE

EXCESS LOW BTU GAS TO THERMAL OXIDIZER

OIL/GAS SEPARATOR

GAS & OIL MIST

LOW BTU RECYCLE GAS COMPRESSOR

GAS/AIR MIXTURE

GAS/AIR MIXTURE

AIR

AIR BLOWER

THERMAL EFFICIENCY 64-73.5%

SHALE ROCK

ROTATING SPREADER

COLLECTING TUBES

DISTRIBUTORS

DISTRIBUTORS

MOVING GRATES

RETORTED SHALE FALLS THROUGH GATES

RETORTED SHALE TO DISPOSAL BEDS

Source: Paraho Development Corporation.

Figure VI-3. SCHEMATIC OF PARAHO OIL SHALE PROCESS

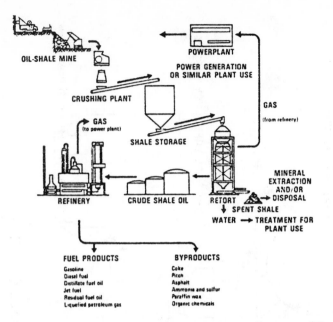

Source: *Final Environmental Statement for the Prototype Oil Shale Leasing Program,* U.S.D.O.I. 1973.

Figure VI-4. SCHEMATIC DIAGRAM OF OIL SHALE SURFACE PROCESSING

recover the nahcolite, alumina, soda ash, and water. Only the spent shale is returned to the mine. The raw shale is crushed, pressed, screened and then is partially calcined in a kiln where a white film is deposited on the nahcolite particles. The shale and nahcolite particles are then passed through a feeder onto a belt conveyor where the particles are scanned with a computer-controlled laser scanner with an air blast separator. As the particles leave the conveyor belt the air blast is directed toward the nahcolite particles, changing their trajectory and separating the shale from the nahcolite.

The crushed shale is placed in a circular grate retort where it is indirectly heated. A diagram of the cross section of the circular grate retort is presented in Figure VI-14.

The spent shale from the retort is processed to remove the alumina and soda ash (Na_2CO_3). This process is diagrammed in Figure VI-15.

The major variation in surface oil shale processing is how the shale is retorted. The properties of several shale crudes are compared with petroleum crudes in Table VI-5.

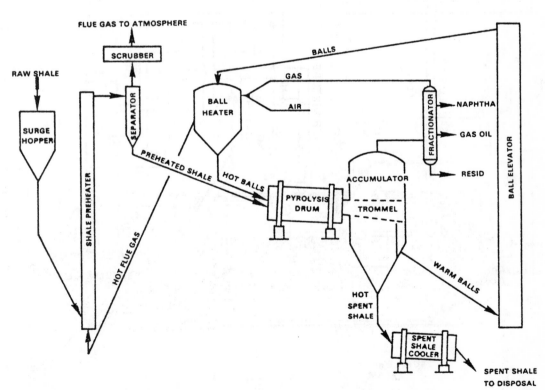

Adapted from: Albert F. Lenhart, "The TOSCO Process—Economic Sensitivity to the Variables of Production," Proceedings of the American Petroleum Institute, Refining Division, 1969.

Figure VI-5. TOSCO II OIL SHALE PLANT

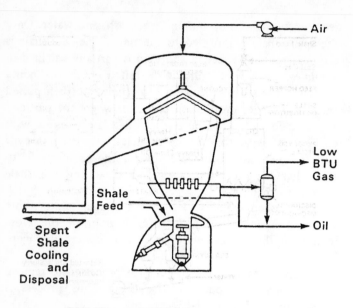

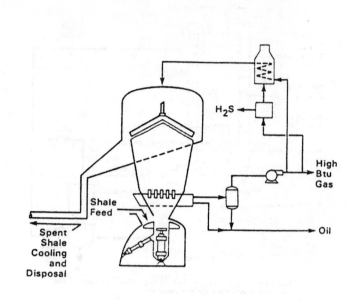

83% Thermal Efficiency
(40% Low BTU Gas, 60% Crude Oil)
Demonstrated in 1956–58 at up to
1200 Tons/Day

Figure VI-6. UNION OIL—OIL SHALE
RETORT A

69% Thermal Efficiency

Figure VI-7. UNION OIL—OIL SHALE
RETORT B

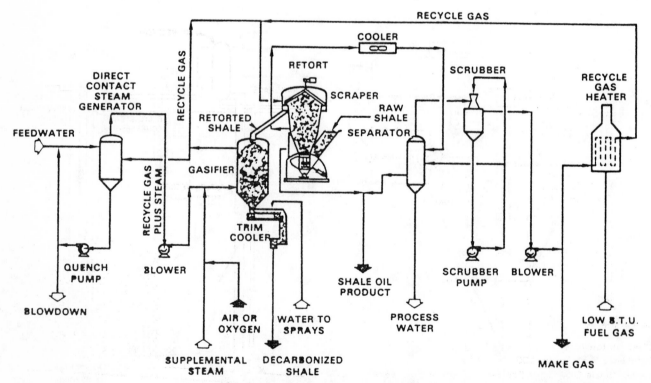

Adapted from: Fred L. Hartley, "Oil Shale: Another Source of Oil for the United States,"
Oil Daily's Third Annual Synthetic Energy Forum, New York, New York, June 10, 1974.

Figure VI-8. UNION OIL SGR OIL SHALE PLANT

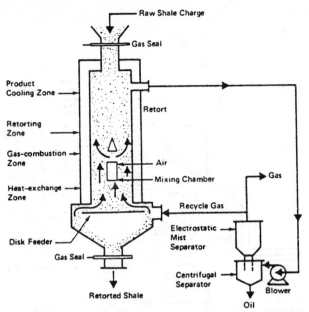

Recycle gas is mixed with air and burned within the retort. Gases flow upward and shale moves downward.

Size: 360 tons/day   Efficiency, % of Assay: 82-87

Source: *Final Environmental Statement for the Prototype Oil Shale Leasing Program*, U.S.D.O.I. 1973, Vol. 1, p. I-13.

Figure VI-9. USBM GAS COMBUSTION RETORT

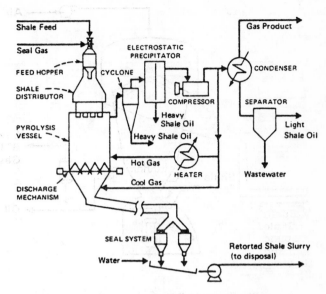

Size: 2200 tons/day
Efficiency % of Assay: Unknown

Source: "Shale Oil-Process Choices," *Chemical Engineering*, May 13, 1974.

Figure VI-10. PETROSIX OIL SHALE PROCESS

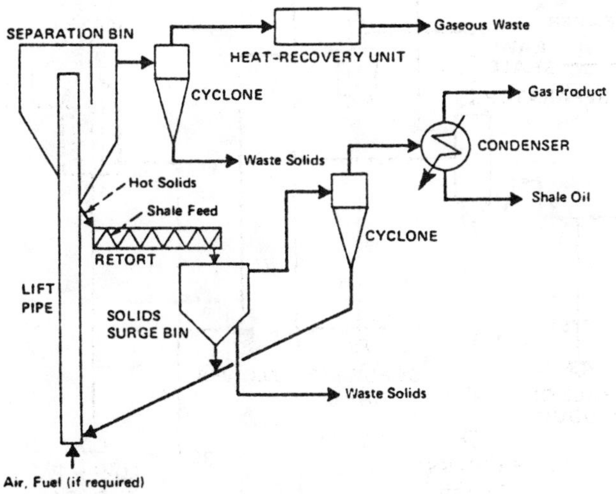

Size: 16 tons/day
Efficiency % of Assay: 100
Source: "Shale Oil-Process Choices," *Chemical Engineering*, May 13, 1974.

Figure VI-11. LURGI—RUHRGAS OIL SHALE PROCESS

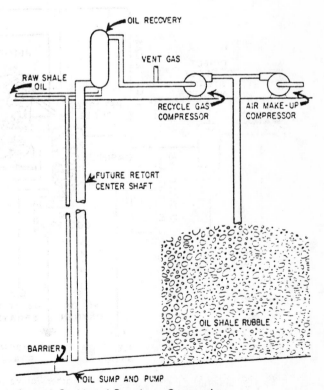

Source: Occidental Petroleum Corporation.

Figure VI-12. OCCIDENTAL IN SITU OIL SHALE PROCESS

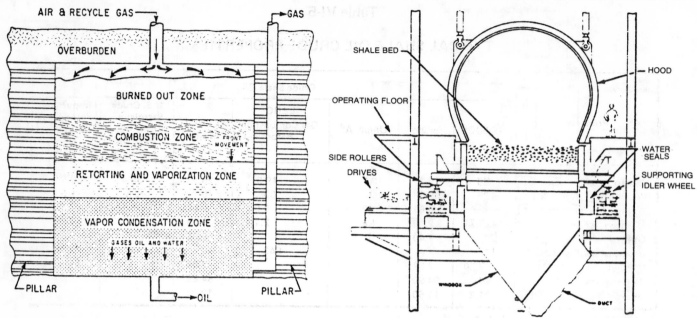

Source: Occidental Petroleum Corporation.

Source: Superior Oil Company.

Figure VI-13. OCCIDENTAL IN SITU OIL
SHALE RETORTING

Figure VI-14. CROSS-SECTION OF SUPERIOR
OIL COMPANY CIRCULAR RETORT

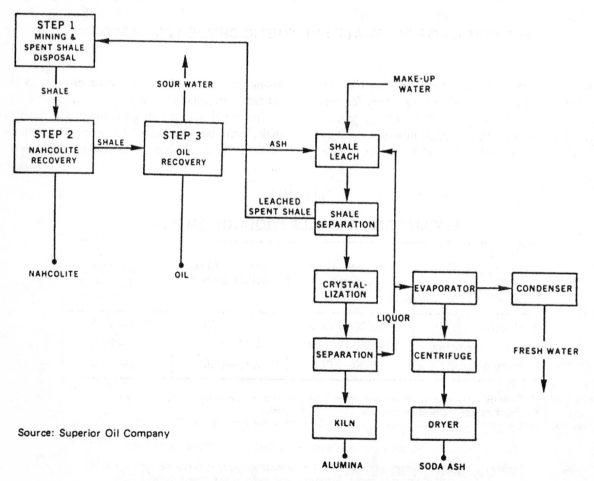

Figure VI-15. SUPERIOR OIL PROCESS

Table VI-5

TYPICAL SHALE OIL CRUDE PROPERTIES

Property	Crude Shale Oil						
	TOSCO[a]	Paraho[b]	Union A[a]	LERC[a] Gas Combustion Retort	LERC[a] In-situ	U.S. Crude Petroleum Black Bay,[c] Westfield Louisiana	Imported Petroleum Crude[d] Saudi Arabia
Gravity (° API)	28	19.3	19.7	19.5	28.4	34.4	30.8
Pour Point (° F)	75	85.0	85	80	10	< 5	+ 5
Sulphur (wt %)	0.8	0.61	1.0	0.60	0.60	0.19	2.4
Nitrogen (wt %)	1.7	2.19	1.8	2.16	1.69		
Oxygen (wt %)		1.40			0.80		
Viscosity (SUS at 100° F)	120			543	45	46	
C/H (wt/wt)	~ 7.50	7.38			7.06		
Carbon (wt %)	~84.7	84.90			84.88		
Hydrogen (wt %)	~11.3	11.50			12.02		

LERC = Laramie Energy Research Center.

[a]*Evaluation of Methods to Produce Aviation Turbine Fuels from Synthetic Crudes, Part I* (AFAPL-TR-75-10, March 1975).
[b]*The Production and Refining of Crude Shale Oil into Military Fuels,* August 1975.
[c]*Petroleum Refining,* Vol. 5, 1975.
[d]*Oil and Gas Journal,* 29 March 1976.

ECONOMICS OF OIL SHALE SYNTHETIC CRUDE TECHNOLOGY

The economics of the various synthetic fuels are clouded by uncertainties in technology, legal and regulatory factors, environmental considerations, government energy policy (or lack of policy), and very rapid inflation in key industries. These uncertainties have forced the abandonment or delay of oil shale projects in the U.S. and tar sands projects in Canada.

The rapid changes in equipment and manpower costs make even the most carefully prepared economic analyses of the synthetic fuels projects very tenuous. Nevertheless, it

Table VI-6

ESTIMATED OIL SHALE PRODUCTION COST[a]

Process	Investment Cost (dollars/barrel/day)	Operating Cost (dollars/barrel)	Selling Price (15% CDF,[c] 100% Equity) (dollars/barrel)
Modified in situ	5,000–7,000	3.50–5.00	8.00–11.00
Surface retorting	14,000–23,000	4.00–5.00	16.00–25.00
Multimineral[b]	7,000–9,000	2.75–4.00	9.00–12.00

[a]The oil produced by these methods may be pre-refined to a quality comparable with Arabian crudes for an additional $1 to $4 per barrel.
[b]Superior Oil Process is an example of multimineral shale treatment. (See Figures VI-14 and VI-15)
[c]See Figure VI-16 for selling prices at different discounted cash flow (DCF) rates.

Source: Dr. Philip White Statement on ERDA's R&D Program in Oil Shale, before the Subcommittee on Minerals, Materials, and Fuels of the Senate Committee on Interior and Insular Affairs on November 30, 1976.

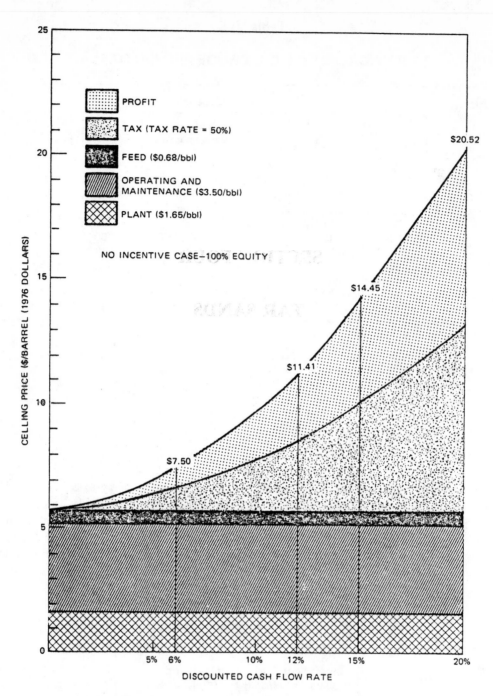

Source: *Proposed Synthetic Fuels Commercial Demonstration Program Fact Book,*
ERDA, March 1976.

**Figure VI-16. REQUIRED SHALE OIL SELLING PRICE AS FUNCTION OF
DISCOUNTED CASH FLOW**

is necessary to make such analyses in order to determine on a rough estimate basis whether synthetic fuel processes are feasible or not. Care must be exercised when using any of these estimates, however.

Synthetic fuel plants based on various oil shale processes have been designed and evaluated over the past several years. Recent estimates made by ERDA are felt to be fairly representative of the economics of the oil shale industry. These estimates appear in Table VI-9 and Figure VI-16.

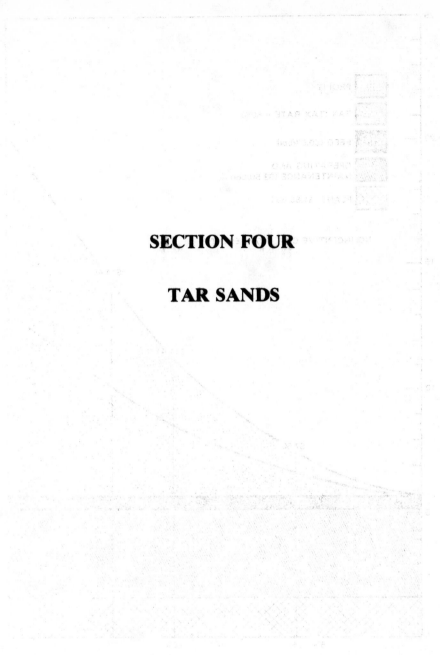

SECTION FOUR

TAR SANDS

INTRODUCTION

The terms tar sands, oil sands, bitumen-bearing rocks, oil impregnated rocks, and bituminous sands are used interchangeably to describe unique hydrocarbon-bearing deposits. The bitumen occurs in both consolidated and unconsolidated rocks, varies from viscous to solid; for practical purposes it is immobile to fluid displacement, and it cannot be recovered by primary petroleum production methods. A summary of tar sands data is presented in Table VII-1.

Early development work occurred principally in Canada. Recently efforts have been initiated to develop resources in the western United States.

Table VII-1

U.S. TAR SANDS FACT SHEET

		Percent by weight
Energy content[1]	18,000 Btu per pound[a]	
Proven reserves[2]	27 billion barrels	
Resources[3]	29 billion barrels (estimated)	
Bitumen saturation[3]	53 percent of pore volume	
Bitumen in tar sand[4]	Utah	
	Tar Sand Triangle	5
	Circle Cliffs	5
	Sunnyside	8-9
	Hill Creek	8-9
	Asphalt Ridge	8-9
	P.R. Spring	6
	Canada	
	Athabasca	12-13

[a] Bitumen in tar sands.

Sources: 1. T. F. Yen, *Shale Oil, Tar Sands, and Related Fuel Sources*, ACS Series 151, 1976.
2. *Assessment of U.S. Tar Sands as a Potential Source of Synthetic Military Fuels*, Applied Systems and Cameron Engineers, Inc., May 15, 1976, Contract N00014-76-C-0427.
3. Cecil Cupps, *et. al.*, "Field Experiment of In-Situ Oil Recovery from Utah Tar Sand by Reverse Combustion," AICHE Symposium Series No. 155, 1976.
4. Alex G. Oblad, *et. al.*, "Recovery of Bitumen from Oil-Impregnated Sandstone Deposits of Utah," AICHE Symposium Series No. 155, 1976.

WORLD RESOURCES

Tar sands are found on every continent except Australia and Antarctica and in 22 of the United States. An estimate of known resources for nine countries is shown in Table VII-2. The best defined deposits in the world are those of northern Alberta, Canada, and the "tar belt" of Venezuela. World tar sands deposits contain fuel sources equal to 65 percent of all the crude oil known and produced in the world since the discovery of petroleum. World resources of oil bearing bituminous sands are shown in Figure VII-1. (The map has been distorted to show each country's relative proportion of world tar sands deposits.)

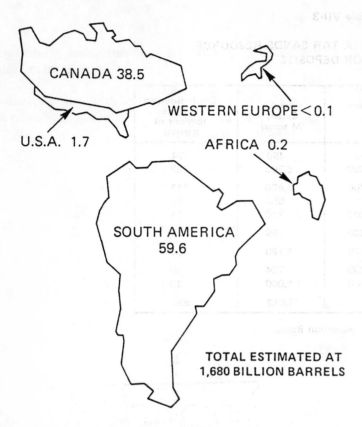

CANADA 38.5

U.S.A. 1.7

WESTERN EUROPE < 0.1

AFRICA 0.2

SOUTH AMERICA
59.6

TOTAL ESTIMATED AT
1,680 BILLION BARRELS

Source: 1974 World Energy Conference

**Figure VII-1. WORLD RESOURCE
OF TAR SANDS (PERCENT)**

Canada

Canadian oil sands extend over some 19,000 square miles of northeastern Alberta. (See Figure VII-2.) Near the Athabasca River, the oil sands are located at or close to ground level. However, most of the deposits are below an overburden of muskeg, glacial till, cretaceous bedrock, and lean oil sand varying in depth from 150 to 2,500 feet. The thickness and quality of the deposits vary considerably.

Table VII-3 summarizes the Alberta Energy Resources Conservation Board's most recent estimates by major deposit.

United States

There are approximately 27 billion barrels of oil in U.S. tar sands deposits. While 22 states contain tar sands, only six contain deposits which could be extracted commercially:

State	Millions of barrels
Alabama	1,180
California	294
Kentucky	149
New Mexico	57
Texas	130
Utah	25,100

Table VII-2

ESTIMATE OF WORLD RESOURCES FOR OIL FROM BITUMINOUS SANDS[a]
(Billions of barrels)

North America		Africa	
Canada	895.0[1]	Malagasy Republic	1.7[3]
Trinidad and Tobago	68.0[3]		
United States	27.0[2]	Europe	
		Albania	0.4[3]
South America		Rumania	0.03[3]
Colombia	1139.1[3]	USSR	0.03[3]
Venezuela	74.3[3]		

[a]Care should be taken in comparing resources among nations, since the data provided to World Energy Conference was based on different economic considerations as well as different degrees of mapping and exploration.

Sources: 1. Alberta Energy Resource Conservation Board.
2. *Assessment of U.S. Tar Sands as a Potential Source of Synthetic Military Fuels*, Applied Systems and Cameron Engineers, Inc., May 15, 1976, Contract N00014-76-C-0427.
3. *Survey of Energy Resources*, World Energy Conference, 1974.

Table VII-3

ESTIMATE OF ALBERTA TAR SANDS RESOURCE
BY MAJOR DEPOSITS

Deposit	Overburden Depth (feet)	Areal Extent (M acres)	Crude Bitumen In-Place (billions of barrels)
Athabasca	0—150	490	74
	150—2000	5,260	552
Cold Lake A	1000—2000	1,800	118
Cold Lake B	1000—2000	650	33
Cold Lake C	1000—2000	710	14
Buffalo Head Hills	500—2500	159	1
Peace River	1000—2500	1,180	50
Wabasca A	250—2000	764	30
Wabasca B	1000—2500	1,000	23
		12,013	895

Source: Alberta Energy Resources Conservation Board.

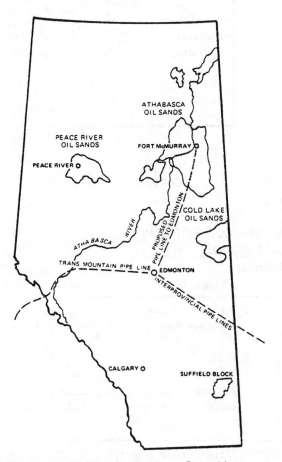

Source: *The Alberta Oil Sands Story*, Alberta Federal Intergovernmental Affairs, January 1974.

Figure VII-2. LOCATION OF ALBERTA OIL SANDS DEPOSITS

Source: *Assessment of Tar Sands as a Potential Source of Synthetic Military Fuels*, Applied Systems Corporation and Cameron Engineers, Inc., May 15, 1976.

Figure VII-3. TAR SANDS DEPOSITS IN ALABAMA

The location of the Alabama deposits are shown in Figure VII-3, California in Figure VII-4, and Utah in Figure VII-5. Table VII-4 presents the characteristics of the tar sands deposits in Alabama, California, Kentucky, New Mexico, and Texas, and Table VII-5 lists the characteristics of the tar sands deposits in Utah.

The tar sands resource of Utah has been described in detail in a survey compiled by Howard R. Ritzma in 1973.[1] There are about 97 tar sand deposits in Utah

which total 25.1 billion barrels of oil, about 93 percent of the known resources in the United States. The sulfur content of Utah tar sand bitumen varies. In the Uinta Basin, the sulfur content averages 0.56 percent by weight, while those in the central southeast region averaged 3.38 percent by weight (see Table VII-5).

[1] Howard R. Ritzma, *Utah Geological and Mineralogical Survey Map 33, Sheet 2*, April 1973.

Source: *Assessment of Tar Sands as a Potential Source of Synthetic Military Fuels*, Applied Systems Corporation and Cameron Engineers, Inc., May 15, 1976.

Figure VII-4. TAR SANDS DEPOSITS IN CALIFORNIA

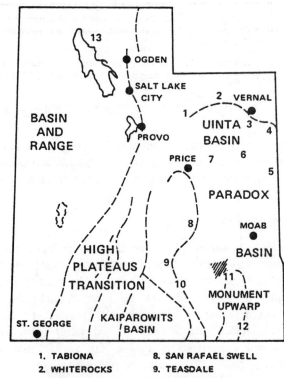

1. TABIONA
2. WHITEROCKS
3. ASPHALT RIDGE
4. RAVEN RIDGE
5. P.R. SPRING
6. HILL CREEK
7. SUNNYSIDE
8. SAN RAFAEL SWELL
9. TEASDALE
10. CIRCLE CLIFFS
11. TAR SAND TRIANGLE
12. MEXICAN HAT
13. ROZEL

Source: *The U.S. Energy Problem—Appendix S Technology of Alternative Fuels*, Intertechnology Corporation, November 1971.

Figure VII-5. TAR SANDS DEPOSITS IN UTAH

Table VII-4

U.S. TAR SAND DEPOSITS

	Oil (million of barrels)	Average Overburden (feet)		Oil (million of barrels)	Average Overburden (feet)
Alabama			Kentucky		
Hartselle Sandstone	1,180	225	Edmonson County		
			Davis-Dismal Creek	32.7	15
California			Bee Spring	7.6	30
Casmalia			Kyrock	18.4	15
North	0.5–40	None	Ollie School	7.4	15
South	46.4	0 to 40	Asphalt	47.6[a]	0 to thin
Edna	150	0 to thin	Logan County		
McKittrick	4.85–9	Up to 100	Russellville	35.3	0 to thin
Point Arena	1.2	Several hundred	Total	149.0	
Santa Cruz	10	0 to 100	New Mexico		
Sisquoc	36.9	15	Santa Rosa	57.2	0 to thin
Total	293.3		Texas		
			Uvalde	154	18

[a]200 million tons of sandstone. Assuming a bitumen content of 10 gallons per ton, this would equal a reserve of 47.6 million barrels.

Source: *Assessment of U.S. Tar Sands as a Potential Source of Synthetic Military Fuels,* Applied Systems and Cameron Engineers, Inc., May 15, 1976, Contract N00014-76-C-0427.

RECOVERY TECHNIQUES

There are two basic techniques for mining tar sands: the raw materials are mined and the bitumen processed above ground or the bitumen is recovered from the sand in-situ.

Surface Mining

The only commercial tar sands plant in operation is the Great Canadian Oil Sands (GCOS) plant, located north of Edmonton, Alberta, Canada. The facility began operations in 1967 and now produces roughly 50,000 barrels per calendar day of high quality synthetic crude oil from 130,000 tons per day of tar sands feed. Huge bucketwheel excavators strip the tar sands from the Athabasca deposit into terraces 70 feet high.

Syncrude Canada, Ltd., is building a plant in the Athabasca deposit. Surface mining with large electric draglines will be employed.

As in recovering coal, surface mining is an economical recovery technique for deposits lying close to the surface with little or no overburden. But the cost of mining one cubic yard of overburden is about the same as mining one cubic yard of high grade ore. A general rule of thumb used for Canadian operations is that the ratio of overburden thickness to ore body thickness should not exceed 1. Factors such as ore grade, overburden characteristics, and ultimate product market value can affect this ratio.

Surface mining cleanup operations are accomplished with bulldozers, scrapers, and front-end loaders. In addition to the disposal of overburden and waste sand from the separation process, large amounts of waste water from above ground extraction facilities must be handled. The GCOS facility pumps approximately 24,000 gpm of slurry into holding ponds. Some of this water may be recycled, but much of it contains clay and sand which remain in suspension indefinitely.

Underground Mining

Very little experience has been gained in underground mining of tar sands, primarily because of the abundance of surface accessible deposits in Alberta. Conventional hardrock mining is not feasible, because of the structural makeup of tar sands deposits. It may be possible to modify conventional longwall mining techniques to recover tar sands.

On the other hand, hydraulic mining might be used. The technique has been used quite successfully for underground mining of uranium ore, and is now being tested with tar sands in southern California. Figure VII-6 illustrates operation of the process. A capsule containing a high pressure nozzle, a slurry pump, and piping is lowered through a casing into a shaft drilled through the tar sands zone into the underlying formation. The nozzle directs a stream of water against the tar sands deposit, breaking the material into small pieces which are then entrained in the waste water as a slurry. The slurry drains into the sump in the underlying zone and from there it is pumped to the surface for above-ground processing.

Table VII-5

CHARACTERISTICS OF UTAH TAR SANDS DEPOSITS

Deposit	Area (square miles)	Number of Principal Pay Zone	Gross Thickness of Pay, Range (feet)	Overburden Thickness, Range (feet)	Oil (barrels)
Uinta Basin					
Argyle Canyon	7–15	3 to 6	15–85	0–500+	100–125 million
Asphalt Ridge	20–25	2 to 5	10–135	0–500+	1.048 billion
Asphalt Ridge, NW	0.15–0.20	1 to 3	20–300	0–275	10–15 million
Chapita Wells	0.35–1.0	1 to 3	5–30	0–300	7.5–8.0 million
Cow Wash	0.08–0.10	1	5–25	0–200	1.0–1.2 million
Hill Creek	115–125	1 to 3	5–35	0–500+	1.16 billion
Lake Fork	0.3–0.5	1 to 3	5–70	0–450	6.5–10.0 million
Littlewater Hills	0.5–1.75	1 or 2	5–90	0–500+	10–12 million
Minnie Maud Creek	0.5–3.5	1 to 4	5–20	0–500+	30–50 million
Pariette	1.2–1.4	1 or 2	5–32	0–300	12–15 million
P.R. Spring	240–270	2 to 6	10–80	0–500+	4.0–4.5 billion
Raven Ridge	20–25	1 to 7	5–48	0–500+	125–150 million
Rim Rock	2.5–3.5	1 to 4	5–95	0–500+	30–35 million
Spring Branch	0.1–0.2	1	5–250	0–350	1.5–2.0 million
Sunnyside	35–90	3 to 12	15–550	0–500+	3.5–4.0 billion
Tabiona	0.15	1 to 3	5–150	0–400	4.6 million
Whiterocks	0.6–0.75	1	1,000	0–500	65–125 million
Central Southeast					
Circle Cliffs, East Flank	21.1	1 to 3	5–260	0–500+	860 million
Circle Cliffs, West Flank	6.6	1 or 2	5–310	0–500+	447 million
Cottonwood Draw	10.5–12.0	1 to 3	5–65	0–500+	75–80 million
Poison Spring Canyon	0.6–0.8	1 or 3	5–24	0–500+	1.0–1.2 million
Tar Sand Triangle	200–230	1 or 2	5–300+	0–500+	16 billion
Ten Mile Wash	5.0–6.5	1 to 4	5–30	0–500+	6.0 million
White Canyon Flat	0.3–0.4	1	5–21	0–220	2.8 million

Notes: 24 deposits have been mapped and sampled in sufficient detail to provide the above information relative to possible development.

Area is generally given as a range, the minimum figure being the measured areal extent, the maximum being the indicated extent.

Number of pay zones is the number of oil-impregnated rock units five or more feet thick likely to be encountered at any one location within the measured or indicated areal extent of the deposit.

Gross thickness of pay is the total thickness of the combined pay zones likely to be encountered at any one location within the measured or indicated areal extent of the deposit. Minimum pay zone is five feet thick.

Overburden thickness is from outcrop to 1,320 feet (0.25 mile) from outcrop. Variations shown emphasize importance of topography in evaluation of these deposits.

Source: Howard R. Ritzma, *Utah Geological and Mineralogical Survey Map 33, Sheet 2,* April 1973.

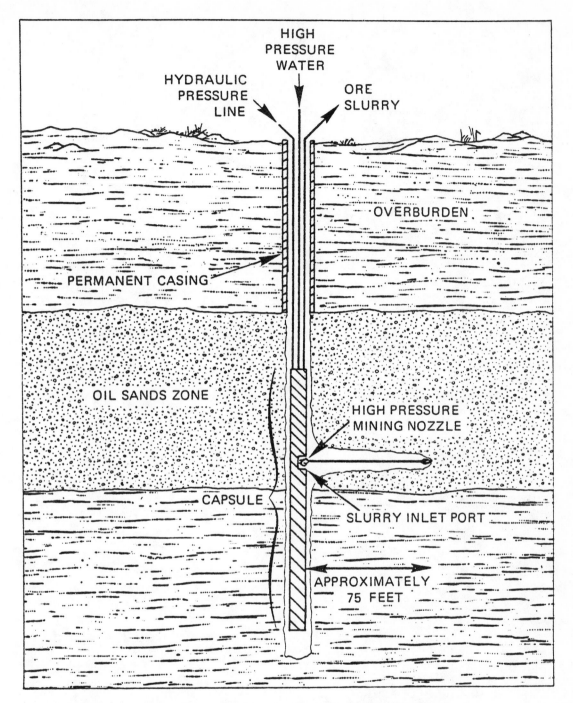

Source: *Assessment of Tar Sands as a Potential Source of Synthetic Military Fuels,*
Applied Systems Corporation and Cameron Engineers, Inc., May 15, 1976.

Figure VII-6. HYDRAULIC SLURRY MINING TECHNIQUE

SECTION FIVE

NATURAL GAS

INTRODUCTION

Natural gas is the cleanest of the fossil fuels and supplies roughly 30 percent of the nation's energy needs (Table VIII-1). Domestic natural gas production peaked in 1973 and has declined rapidly since then. U.S. natural gas production in 1976 averaged almost 10 percent less than three years ago. The finding rate (amount of gas discovered versus number of feet drilled) has declined even faster. The United States produces 11.9 billion cubic feet per day, or about 43 percent of the world's and 57 percent of the free world's total production. U.S. reserves, however, represent only about 10 percent of the world's total.

Table VIII-1

NATURAL GAS FACTS SHEET

Energy Content[a]	1032 Btu per cubic foot.
Proven U.S. Reserves (1976)[b]	220 trillion cubic feet (TCF). This stock constitutes a known inventory of natural gas stored underground against the time when the immediate needs of the industry require it to be brought to the surface.
Ultimate U.S. Resources[c]	530 TCF of ultimately discoverable resources.
U.S. Production (1976)[d]	20 TCF
Imports (1976)[e]	0.97 TCF (estimated)
U.S. Consumption (1976)[e]	19.5 TCF (estimated)
Contribution to Demand[f]	Natural gas supplied 28.4% of the 1976 U.S. energy demand.

[a]"Domestic Oil and Gas Availability", *U.S. Energy Outlook,* National Petroleum Council, pp. 57-133, December 1972.
[b]*Oil and Gas Journal,* 27 December 1976.
[c]National Academy of Sciences, 12 February 1975.
[d]*Oil and Gas Journal,* 24 January 1977.
[e]U.S. Bureau of Mines.
[f]Energy Research and Development Administration, 15 April 1976.

WORLD SUPPLY OF NATURAL GAS

The world's natural gas reserves total an estimated 2,303.8 trillion cubic feet (TCF). The distribution of these reserves, by area and country, is shown in Table VIII-2 and Figure VIII-1. The distribution of natural gas production is shown in Table VIII-3.

Estimates of ultimately recoverable natural gas resources, based on current technological and economic conditions, are given in Figure VIII-2. Using these estimates and simplifying assumptions about consumption and production policies, theoretical gas exhaustion dates can be calculated. Two possible consumption and production policies are shown on Figure VIII-3. The upper curve represents current production and consumption patterns and the lower curve represents a low-growth pattern where production and consumption are constrained. Figure VIII-3 indicates that exhaustion will take place between 2033 and 2075. If available resources prove to be only two-thirds of the estimate, then exhaustion will take place between 2022 and 2055.

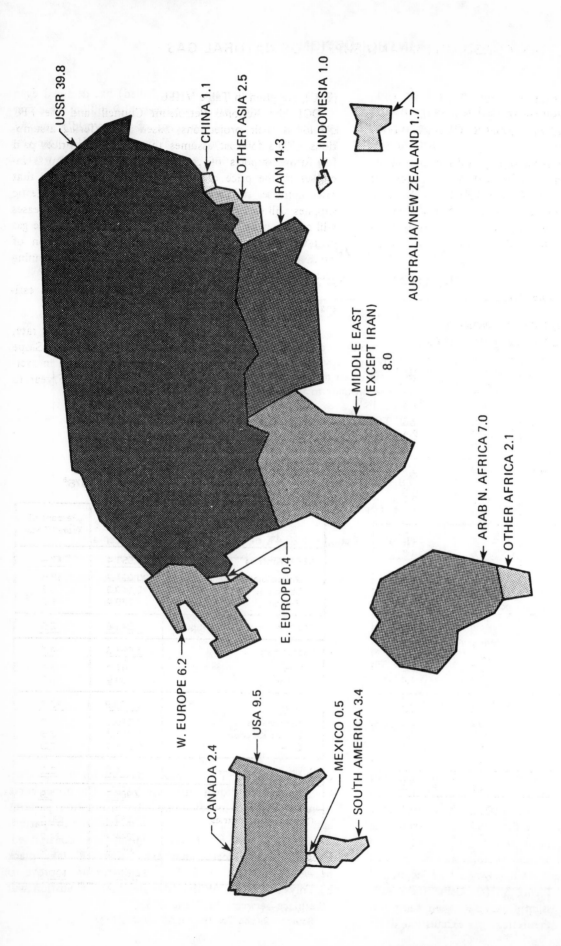

Figure VIII-1. WORLD PROVED NATURAL GAS RESERVES (PERCENT)

World Aggregate: 409.5 Billion Barrels of Oil Equivalent

Note: Distortion of Map Reflects Percentage of Reserves.

Source: *Oil And Gas Journal*, December 27, 1976.

U.S. CONSUMPTION AND SUPPLY OF NATURAL GAS

The United States consumes about 20 TCF of gas a year. Figure VIII-4 shows how this gas is used. The trend of annual consumption in the United States since 1900 is shown in Figure VIII-5.

Data on the U.S. natural gas supply and production for 1945 to 1976 are shown in Table VIII-4. Projections of the U.S. gas supply to 2000, developed by the U.S. Department of the Interior (DOI) and the National Petroleum Council, are given in Table VIII-5, and projections to 1990, developed by the Federal Power Commission (FPC), are given in Table VIII-6.

DOI, the National Petroleum Council, and the FPC developed their projections, based on differing assumptions. DOI's forecast assumes that increasing prices paid for future imports of gas will result in substantial increases in the price of domestic gas. It is assumed that price increases sufficient to elicit the additional domestic supplies will be forthcoming and that these price increases will make supplemental supplies of LNG and synthetic gas economically feasible in some locations. Production of synthetic gas from coal depends on making certain mining techniques environmentally acceptable.

The National Petroleum Council developed its estimates for four cases:

- Case I (see Table VIII-5) assumes a high finding rate, a high growth in drilling rate, Alaskan North Slope production of gas by 1978, and an increase in average annual additions to reserves of 11 TCF/year to 26 TCF/year during the 1971-85 period.

Table VIII-2

DISTRIBUTION OF WORLD NATURAL GAS RESERVES, 1976

Area/County	Reserves (TCF)	Percent of World Total
North America	288.0	12.5
United States	220.0	9.5
Canada	56.0	2.4
Mexico	12.0	0.5
South America and Caribbean	78.3	3.4
Venezuela	40.7	1.8
Ecuador	12.0	0.5
Other	25.6	1.1
Middle East	513.5	22.3
Iran	330.0	14.3
Saudi Arabia	63.0	2.7
Iraq	27.0	1.2
Kuwait	31.7	1.4
Other	61.8	2.7
Europe	141.9	6.2
Netherlands	61.9	2.7
United Kingdom	30.0	1.3
Norway	18.5	0.8
Other	31.5	1.4
Africa	209.1	9.1
Algeria	125.8	5.5
Nigeria	44.0	1.9
Libya	25.8	1.1
Other	13.5	0.6
Asia—Pacific	120.0	5.2
Communist Countries	953.0	41.4
USSR	918.0	39.8
China	25.0	1.1
Other	10.0	0.4
World Total	2,303.8	100.0

Source: *Oil and Gas Journal,* 27 December 1976, pp. 104-105.

Table VIII-3

DISTRIBUTION OF WORLD NATURAL GAS PRODUCTION, 1976[a]

Area/Country	Production (billions of cu. ft.)	Percent of World Total
North America	23,951.4	47.4
United States	20,021.7	39.6
Canada	3,140.3	6.2
Mexico	789.4	1.6
South America and Caribbean	1,243.6	2.5
Middle East	2,091.3	4.1
Iran	1,701.4	3.4
Other	389.9	0.7
Europe	6,430.9	12.7
Netherlands	3,659.0	7.2
United Kingdom	1,257.3	2.5
Other	1,514.6	3.0
Africa	1,631.5	3.2
Asia—Pacific	966.7	1.9
Communist Countries	14,260.7	28.2
USSR	11,244.7	22.2
Other	3,016.0	6.0
World Total	50,576.1	100.0

[a]Estimated.
Source: *Oil and Gas Journal,* 24 January 1977.

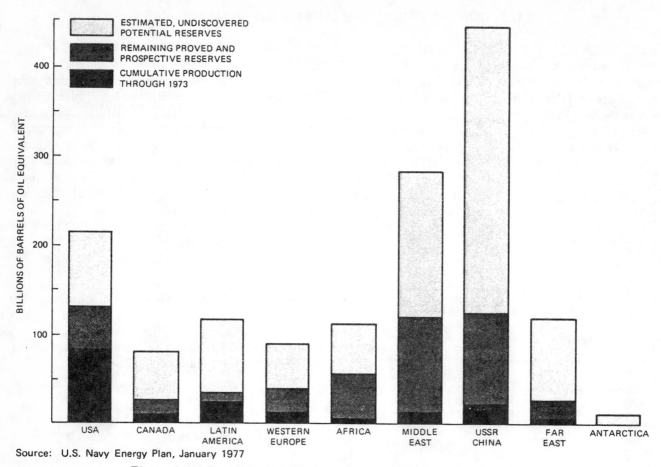

Source: U.S. Navy Energy Plan, January 1977

Figure VIII-2. ULTIMATELY RECOVERABLE NATURAL GAS

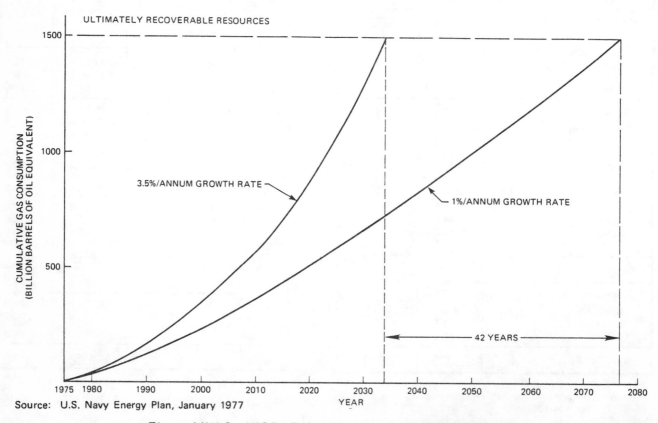

Source: U.S. Navy Energy Plan, January 1977

Figure VIII-3. WORLD NATURAL GAS EXHAUSTION

Table VIII-4

TOTAL UNITED STATES NATURAL GAS SUPPLY AND PRODUCTION FOR 1945-1976
(TCF at 60° F and 14.73 psia)

Year	Annual Gross Additions to Proved Reserves	Cumulative Discoveries	Preliminary Annual Net Production	Cumulative Net Production	Proved Reserves	Gas in Underground Storage	Proved Reserves/ Annual Production Ratio
1945	–	233.45	–	86.62	146.99	0.15	–
1946	17.63	251.09	4.92	91.54	159.70	0.15	32.46
1947	10.92	262.01	5.60	97.13	165.03	0.15	29.47
1948	13.82	275.83	5.98	103.11	172.93	0.20	28.92
1949	12.61	288.44	6.21	109.32	179.40	0.29	28.89
1950	11.99	300.42	6.86	116.18	184.58	0.34	26.91
1951	15.97	316.39	7.92	124.10	192.76	0.47	24.34
1952	14.27	330.65	8.59	132.69	198.63	0.67	23.12
1953	20.34	351.00	9.19	141.88	210.30	1.18	22.88
1954	9.55	360.54	9.38	151.26	210.56	1.27	22.45
1955	21.90	382.44	10.06	161.32	222.48	1.36	22.12
1956	24.72	407.16	10.85	172.17	236.48	1.49	21.80
1957	20.01	427.17	11.44	183.61	245.23	1.67	21.44
1958	18.90	446.06	11.42	195.03	252.76	1.73	22.13
1959	20.62	466.68	12.37	207.40	261.17	1.89	21.11
1960	13.89	480.58	13.02	220.42	262.33	2.17	20.15
1961	17.17	497.74	13.38	233.80	266.27	2.33	19.90
1962	19.48	517.23	13.64	247.44	272.28	2.49	19.96
1963	18.10	535.39	14.55	261.99	276.15	2.74	18.98
1964	20.25	555.64	15.35	277.33	281.25	2.94	18.32
1965	21.32	576.96	16.25	293.58	286.47	3.09	17.63
1966	20.22	597.18	17.49	311.08	289.33	3.22	16.54
1967	21.80	618.99	18.38	329.46	292.91	3.38	15.94
1968	13.70	632.69	19.37	348.83	287.35	3.49	14.83
1969	8.38	641.06	20.72	369.55	275.11	3.60	13.28
1970	37.20	678.26	21.96	391.51	290.75	4.00	13.24
1971	9.83	688.08	22.08	413.59	278.81	4.31	12.63
1972	9.63	697.72	22.51	436.10	266.08	4.47	11.82
1973	6.83	704.54	22.61	458.71	249.95	4.12	11.05
1974	8.68	713.22	21.32	480.03	237.13	3.94	11.12
1975	–	–	24.66	504.69	237.10	–	9.61
1976	–	–	23.95	528.64	220.00	–	9.19

Note: The small inconsistencies between annual and cumulative discoveries and between annual and cumulative production are caused by rounding of values.

Sources: American Gas Association, July 15, 1975, and *Oil and Gas Journal,* 29 December 1975, 27 December 1976, and 24 January 1977.

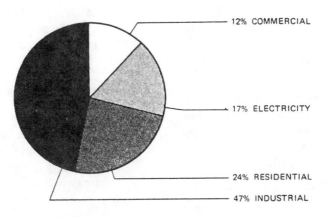

12% COMMERCIAL

17% ELECTRICITY

24% RESIDENTIAL

47% INDUSTRIAL

Source: Federal Energy Administration, September 10, 1975.

Figure VIII-4. U.S. CONSUMPTION OF NATURAL GAS BY END USE

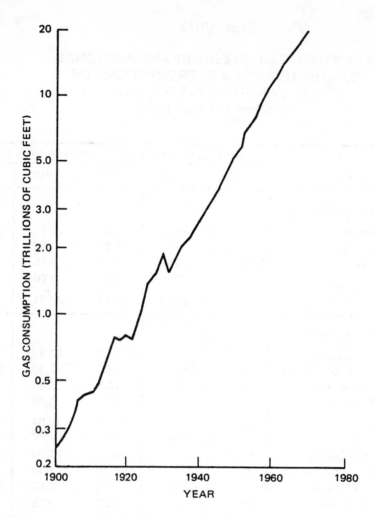

Source: Fuel and Energy Resources, 1972; Hearings Before
the Committee on Interior and Insular Affairs,
House of Representatives, April 12, 1972.

Figure VIII-5. ANNUAL CONSUMPTION OF NATURAL GAS

• Case II assumes a high finding rate, a medium growth in drilling rate, Alaskan North Slope production of gas by 1978, and an increase in average annual additions to reserves of 11 TCF/year to 21 TCF/year during the 1971-85 period.

• Case III assumes a low finding rate, a medium growth in drilling rate, Alaskan North Slope production of gas by 1978, and an increase in average annual additions to reserves of 11 TCF/year to 14 TCF/year during the 1971-1985 period.

• Case IV assumes a low finding rate, a continued current downtrend in drilling rate, Alaskan North Slope production of gas by 1983, and a decrease in average annual additions to reserves of 11 TCF/year to a 6 TCF/year during the 1971-1985 period.

Figures given for additions to reserves do not include Alaskan reserves of gas.

FPC also developed projections for four cases:

• Case I (see Table VIII-6) assumes that there will be little or no change from the current trends, with producers' prices held to $0.25 to $0.27/MCF through 1990, no development of Atlantic and Alaskan offshore areas, no gas from Alaska, only presently authorized imports, no gas from low-permeability reservoirs, and syngas only from coal and naptha.

• Case II is conservative realistic, with prices rising from $0.35/MCF in 1975 to $0.58 in 1990, development of all offshore areas, available North Slope gas, additional pipeline imports, low production from

Table VIII-5

DEPARTMENT OF INTERIOR AND NATIONAL PETROLEUM COUNCIL PROJECTIONS OF U.S. GAS SUPPLY, 1970-2000
(Trillions of Cubic Feet)

Source of Projection	Gas Supply Projections—Trillions of Cubic Feet				
	1970	1974	1980	1985	2000
Department of the Interior[a]		actual			
U.S. Production		20.84	18.88	18.21	16.53
Synthetic Gas		0	0.12	0.50	4.67
Pipeline Imports	(N/A)	0.94	0.80	0.70	1.00
LNG Imports		0	0.30	0.60	1.50
Total		21.78	20.10	20.01	23.70
National Petroleum Council[b]					
Case I: U.S. Production	21.69		26.12	31.92	
Synthetic Gas (Coal)	0	(N/A)	0.50	2.20	(N/A)
Pipeline Import	0.92		1.55	2.62	
LNG Imports	0		2.23	3.10	
Total	22.61		30.10	39.84	
Case II: U.S. Production	21.69		24.37	27.28	
Synthetic Gas (Coal)	0		0.32	1.17	
Pipeline Imports	0.92	(N/A)	1.55	2.62	(N/A)
LNG Imports	0		2.23	3.29	
Total	22.61		28.47	34.36	
Case III: U.S. Production	21.69		20.49	21.20	
Synthetic Gas (Coal)	0		0.32	1.17	
Pipeline Imports	0.92	(N/A)	1.55	2.62	(N/A)
LNG Imports	0		2.23	3.59	
Total	22.61		24.59	28.58	
Case IV: U.S. Production	21.69		17.35	14.99	
Synthetic Gas (Coal)	0		0.16	0.48	
Pipeline Imports	0.92	(N/A)	1.55	2.62	(N/A)
LNG Imports	0		2.23	3.78	
Total	22.61		21.29	21.87	

[a]*U.S. Energy Through the Year 2000,* U.S. Department of the Interior, p. 65, December 1975.
[b]*U.S. Energy Outlook,* National Petroleum Council, December 1972.

Table VIII-6

FEDERAL POWER COMMISSION PROJECTIONS OF
U.S. GAS SUPPLY, 1975-1990
(Trillions of cubic feet)

	Case I				Case II			
	1975	1980	1985	1990	1975	1980	1985	1990
Domestic Production	22.2	19.1	15.1	11.2	22.5	20.6	20.0	17.9
Syngas Production	0	0.2	0.7	1.2	0	0.3	1.1	2.2
Total U.S.	22.2	19.3	15.8	12.4	22.5	20.9	21.1	20.1
Imports	1.4	2.1	2.2	1.7	1.8	3.8	4.2	5.1
Total Supply	23.6	21.4	18.0	14.1	24.3	24.7	25.3	25.2
	Case III				Case IV			
	1975	1980	1985	1990	1975	1980	1985	1990
Domestic Productions	22.6	24.7	23.6	22.8	22.6	22.7	29.6	32.5
Syngas Production	0	0.4	1.3	3.0	0	0.6	1.9	5.1
Total U.S.	22.6	25.1	24.9	25.8	22.6	28.3	31.5	37.6
Imports	2.2	6.1	7.7	8.4	2.4	7.5	9.5	11.6
Total Supply	24.8	31.2	32.6	34.2	25.0	35.8	41.0	49.2

Source: *Future Domestic Natural Gas Supplies,* Federal Power Commission, June 1974.

low-permeability reservoirs after a five-year delay, and moderate development of a syngas industry with both foreign and domestic feedstocks.

• Case III is optimistic realistic, with prices rising from $0.42 in 1975 to $0.89 in 1990, availability of North Slope gas by 1979, substantial improvements in LNG and pipeline imports, low production from low-permeability reservoirs but with no production

delay, and development of syngas industry in line with industry forecasts.

• Case IV represents the maximum future supply that can reasonably be expected to be available from each source, including a price range assumption of $0.50 in 1975 to $1.21 in 1990. Under this case, supply will exceed FPC forecasts of future requirements.

DIRECTORY OF GAS INFORMATION SOURCES

AMERICAN GAS ASSOCIATION LIBRARY
   1515 Wilson Boulevard
   Arlington, Virginia 22209

INSTITUTE OF GAS TECHNOLOGY
   Technical Information Services
   3424 South State Street
   Chicago, Illinois 60616
   Telephone: 312-225-9600 Ext 626

NATURAL GAS PROCESSORS ASSOCIATION
   808 Home Federal Building
   Tulsa, Oklahoma 74103
   Telephone: 918-582-5112

OFFICE OF OIL AND GAS
   U.S. Department of the Interior
   18th and C Streets, N.W.
   Washington, D.C. 20240
   Telephone: 202-343-3831

NATIONAL PETROLEUM COUNCIL
   1625 K Street, N.W.
   Washington, D.C. 20006
   Telephone: 202-393-6100

OFFICE OF MINERAL INFORMATION
   U.S. Bureau of Mines
   18th and C Streets, N.W.
   Washington, D.C. 20240
   Telephone: 202-343-4964

SECTION SIX

COAL

INTRODUCTION

The most recent government estimates for U.S. coal resources remaining in the ground on January 1, 1974, are shown in Tables IX-1 and IX-2. The total, approximately 4 trillion tons, includes several categories according to degree of reliability of estimates.

In 1973, the United States contributed about 18 percent to total world coal production (3,288 million short tons); the USSR produced 22 percent, Europe, 14 percent, and the Peoples' Republic of China, 14 percent.

According to data gathered at the 1974 World Energy Conference, the United States contains about 25 to 30 percent of the world's recoverable coal beds, although estimates could be greatly increased for Asia as more land areas in the Soviet Union and the Peoples' Republic of China are explored.

Table IX-1

COAL FACTS SHEET

Classification[a]	Coals are classified as anthracite, bituminous, subbituminous, or lignite according to the amount of fixed carbon or calorific value
Energy Content[a]	Lignite 12.6—16.6 million Btu per ton Subbituminous 16.6—23 million Btu per ton Bituminous 21—28 million Btu per ton Anthracite $\sim$ 25 million Btu per ton
Proven U.S. Reserves[b] (1974)	300 billion tons recoverable by underground mining methods 137 billion tons recoverable by surface mining methods 437 billion tons total
Estimated U.S. Resources[c] (1974)	1734 billion tons mapped and explored 2238 billion tons unmapped and explored 3972 billion tons total
U.S. Production[d] (1975)	640 million tons
Exports[d] (1975)	65.7 million tons (including Canada)
Imports[d] (1975)	0.9 million ton
U.S. Consumption[d] (1975)	554.7 million tons
Contribution to Demand[e]	Coal supplied 19.0 percent of the 1975 U.S. energy demand

[a]"Standard Specification for Classification of Coals by Rank," ASTM Designation D388-66 (reapproved 1972), 1972 ASTM Standards—Part 19, pp. 54-58.
[b]"Demonstrated Coal Reserve Base of the United States, By Sulfur Category, on January 1, 1974," USDOI Bureau of Mines, May 1975.
[c]U.S. Geological Survey Bulletin No. 1412, 1975.
[d]*Mineral Industry Surveys*, USDOI Bureau of Mines, April 9, 1976.
[e]*Status of the Mineral Industries*, USDOI Bureau of Mines, 1976.

Table IX-2

TOTAL ESTIMATED REMAINING COAL RESOURCES OF THE UNITED STATES, JANUARY 1, 1974

State	Remaining Identified Resources, Jan. 1, 1974 (Overburden 0–3,000 feet)					Estimated Hypothetical Resources in Unmapped and Unexplored Areas [1]	Estimated Total Identified and Hypothetical Resources Remaining in the Ground	Overburden 3,000–6,000 feet: Estimated Additional Hypothetical Resources in Deeper Structural Basins [1]	Overburden 0–6,000 feet: Estimated Total Identified and Hypothetical Resources Remaining in the Ground
	Bituminous Coal	Subbituminous Coal	Lignite	Anthracite and Semi-anthracite	Total				
Alabama	13,262	0	2,000	0	15,262	20,000	35,262	6,000	41,262
Alaska	19,413	110,666	2	3	130,079	130,000	260,079	5,000	265,079
Arizona	21,234[4]	4	0	0	21,234	0	21,234	0	21,234
Arkansas	1,638	0	350	428	2,416	4,000[5]	6,416	0	6,416
Colorado	109,117	19,733	20	78	128,948	161,272	290,220	143,991	434,211
Georgia	24	0	0	0	24	60	84	0	84
Illinois	146,001	0	0	0	146,001	100,000	246,001	0	246,001
Indiana	32,868	0	0	0	32,868	22,000	54,868	0	54,868
Iowa	6,505	0	0	0	6,505	14,000	20,505	0	20,505
Kansas	18,668	0	6	0	18,668	4,000	22,668	0	22,668
Kentucky									
Eastern	28,226	0	0	0	28,226	24,000	52,226	0	52,226
Western	36,120	0	0	0	36,120	28,000	64,120	0	64,120
Maryland	1,152	0	0	0	1,152	400	1,552	0	1,552
Michigan	205	0	0	0	205	500	705	0	705
Missouri	31,184	0	0	0	31,184	17,489	48,673	0	48,673
Montana	2,299	176,819	112,521	0	291,639	180,000	471,639	0	471,639
New Mexico	10,748	50,639	0	4	61,391	65,556[7]	126,947	74,000	200,947
North Carolina	110	0	0	0	110	20	130	5	135
North Dakota	0	0	350,602	0	350,602	180,000	530,602	0	530,602
Ohio	41,166	0	0	0	41,166	6,152	47,318	0	47,318
Oklahoma	7,117	0	0	0	7,117	15,000	22,117	5,000[8]	27,117
Oregon	50	284	6	0	334	100	434	0	434
Pennsylvania	63,940	0	0	18,812	82,752	4,000[9]	86,752	3,600[10]	90,352
South Dakota	0	0	2,185	0	2,185	1,000	3,185	0	3,185
Tennessee	2,530	0	0	0	2,530	2,000	4,530	0	4,530
Texas	6,048	0	10,293	0	16,341	112,100[11]	128,441	11	128,441
Utah	23,186[12]	173	0	0	23,359	22,000[13]	45,359	35,000	80,359
Virginia	9,216	0	0	335	9,551	5,000	14,551	100	14,651
Washington	1,867	4,180	117	5	6,169	30,000	36,169	15,000	51,169
West Virginia	100,150	0	0	0	100,150	0	100,150	0	100,150
Wyoming	12,703	123,240	2	0	135,943	700,000	835,943	100,000	935,943
Other states [14]	610	32[15]	46[16]	0	688	1,000	1,688	0	1,688
Total	747,357	485,766	478,134	19,662	1,735,000	1,849,649	3,580,568	387,696	3,972,000[17]

Table IX-2 *(Cont'd)*

Note: Estimates include beds of bituminous coal and anthracite generally 14 inches or more thick, and beds of subbituminous coal and lignite generally 2½ feet or more thick, to overburden depths of 3,000 and 6,000 feet. Figures are for resources in the ground.

1 Source of estimates: Alabama, W. C. Culbertson; Arkansas, B. R. Haley; Colorado, Holt (1975); Illinois, M. E. Hopkins and J. A. Simon; Indiana, C.E. Wier; Iowa, E.R. Landis; Kentucky, K.J. Englund; Missouri, Robertson (1971, 1973); Montana, R. E. Matson; New Mexico, Fassett and Hinds (1971); North Dakota, R. A. Brant; Ohio, H. R. Collins and D. O. Johnson from data in Struble and others (1971); Oklahoma, S. A. Friedman; Oregon, R. S. Mason; Pennsylvania anthracite, Arndt and others (1968); Pennsylvania bituminous coal, W. E. Edmunds; Tennessee, E. T. Luther; Texas lignite, Kaiser (1974); Virginia, K. J. Englund; Utah, H. H. Doelling; Washington, H.M. Beikman; Wyoming, N.M. Denson, G. B. Glass, W. R. Keefer, and E. M. Schell; remaining States, by the author.

2 Small resources of lignite included under subbituminous coal.

3 Small resources of anthracite in the Bering River field believed to be too badly crushed and faulted to be economically recoverable (Barnes, 1951).

4 All tonnage is in the Black Mesa field. Some coal in the Dakota Formation is near the rank boundary between bituminous and subbituminous coal. Does not include small resources of thin and impure coal in the Deer Creek and Pinedale fields.

5 Lignite.

6 Small resources of lignite in western Kansas and western Oklahoma in beds generally less than 30 inches thick.

7 After Fassett and Hinds (1971), who reported 85,222 million tons "inferred by zone" to an overburden depth of 3,000 feet in the Fruitland Formation of the San Juan basin. Their figure has been reduced by 19,666 million tons as reported by Read and others (1950) for coal in all categories also to an overburden depth of 3,000 feet in the Fruitland Formation of the San Juan basin. The figure of Read and others was based on measured surface sections and is included in the identified tonnage recorded in Table IX-5.

8 Includes 100 million tons inferred below 3,000 feet.

9 Bituminous coal.

10 Anthracite.

11 Lignite, overburden 200–5,000 feet; identified and hypothetical resources undifferentiated. All beds assumed to be 2 feet thick, although many are thicker.

12 Excludes coal in beds less than 4 feet thick.

13 Includes coal in beds 14 inches or more thick, of which 15,000 million tons is in beds 4 feet or more thick.

14 California, Idaho, Nebraska, and Nevada.

15 California and Idaho.

16 California, Idaho, Louisiana, and Mississippi.

17 Four million short tons located not previously reported.

Source: *Coal Sources of the United States, January 1, 1974,* U.S. Geological Survey Bulletin No. 1412.

ASSESSING COAL RESOURCES

The estimates in the first five columns of Table IX-2, "remaining identified" resources, are based on factual information. All identified coal resources are further broken down into the "measured," "indicated" and "inferred" resource categories discussed below. The same information by coal basin appears in Table IX-3.

"Hypothetical resources" included in the last four columns of Table IX-2 are estimates of coal in the ground in unmapped and unexplored parts of known coal bases to an overburden of 6,000 feet. These estimates are determined by extrapolation from nearby areas of identified resources.

Approximately 44 percent of the total estimated remaining coal resources in the U.S. have been identified. At least 12.5 percent of these resources is considered economically recoverable, based on past recovery rates. Increased production by strip mining would increase this percentage since (1) strip-mined coal represents only 13 percent of past cumulative production and (2) average recoverability in strip mining is about 80 percent, while underground and auger mining average roughly 50 percent. Of the total identified resources, approximately 43 percent is bituminous coal, 91 percent is 1,000 feet or less below the surface, and 33 percent is in thick beds.

DEMONSTRATED COAL RESERVE BASE

Figures IX-1 and IX-2 show the coal fields of the conterminous United States and Alaska.

The "demonstrated coal reserve base" shown in Tables IX-4 and IX-5 is a selected portion of the coal in the ground in the measured and indicated category as defined below. This demonstrated reserve base is restricted primarily to coal in thick and intermediate beds less than 1,000 feet below the surface that were deemed to be economically and legally available for mining at the time of the determination.

Measured resources — Tonnage of coal in the ground based on assured coal-bed correlations and on closely spaced observations about one-half mile apart. Computed tonnage judged to be accurate within 20 percent of the tonnage.

Indicated resources — Tonnage of coal in the ground based partly on specific observations (measured resources) and partly on reasonable geologic projection. The points of observation and measurement are about one mile apart for beds of known continuity.

Demonstrated resources — Combined tonnage in the measured and indicated resource categories.

Inferred resources — Tonnage of coal in the ground based on an assumed continuity of coal beds downdip from and adjoining areas containing measured and indicated resources.

As shown in Table IX-4 and IX-5, about 46 percent of the reserve base coal contains less than 1 percent sulfur, and 84 percent of this low-sulfur coal is also of lower rank; it has been estimated that, on a calorific basis, only 10 to 15 percent (44 to 55 billion tons) of the nation's coal reserve base would be acceptable by present SO_2 pollution standards: 1.2 lb SO_2^{-}/lb^6 Btu, without sulfur removal or gas scrubbing.

Details on the U.S. bituminous and lignite industry are provided in Tables IX-6 and IX-7; data on U.S. consumption of bituminous coal and lignite are given in Table IX-8, and coal consumption by sector, 1935-1972, is shown in Figure IX-3. Table IX-9 shows the U.S. coal production potential for 1985, assuming that imported oil costs $13 per barrel. Table IX-10 shows reserves and resources of solid fossil fuels by nation.

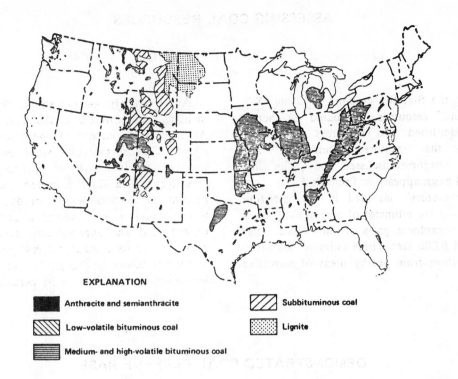

EXPLANATION

■ Anthracite and semianthracite

▨ Low-volatile bituminous coal

▤ Medium- and high-volatile bituminous coal

▨ Subbituminous coal

▦ Lignite

Figure IX-1. COAL FIELDS OF THE CONTERMINOUS UNITED STATES

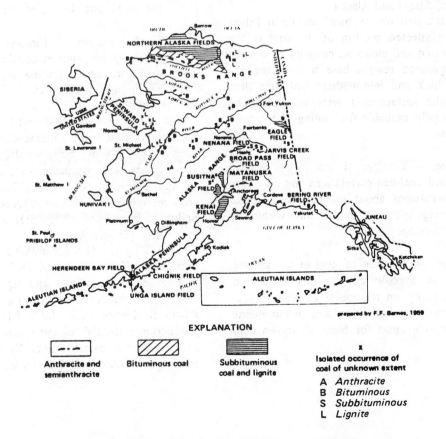

prepared by F.F. Barnes, 1969

EXPLANATION

Anthracite and semianthracite

Bituminous coal

Subbituminous coal and lignite

x
Isolated occurrence of coal of unknown extent
A *Anthracite*
B *Bituminous*
S *Subbituminous*
L *Lignite*

Figure IX-2. COAL FIELDS OF ALASKA

Table IX-3

IDENTIFIED COAL RESOURCES, JANUARY 1, 1974[a]
(Billions of Short Tons)

Basin or Region	Overburden 0—3,000 feet			
	Demonstrated Reserve Base, 0—1,000 ft Overburden[b] (from Table IX-1)		Resources in Thin Beds and Inferred Resources, 0—1,000 ft Overburden; and Identified Resources in All Beds 1,000—3,000 ft Overburden	Total Remaining Identified Resources (from Table IX-1 rounded)
	Tons	Percent		
Northern Appalachian basin (Pa., Ohio, W. Va., and Md.)	93	21	132	225
Southern Appalachian basin (eastern Ky., Va., Tenn., N.C., Ga., and Ala.)	20	5	36	56
Michigan basin	. . .	. . .	. . .	. . .
Illinois basin (Ill., Ind., and western Ky.)	89	20	126	215
Western interior basin (Iowa, Kansas, Mo., Okla., Ark., and Texas)	19	4	63	82
Northern Rocky Mountains (N. Dak., S. Dak., Mont., Wyo., and Idaho)	178	41	606	784
Southern Rocky Mountains (Colo., Utah, Ariz., and N. Mex.)	24	6	211	235
West Coast (Alaska, Wash., Oreg., and Calif.)	14	3	123	137
Total	437	100	1,297	1,734

Note: Leaders (. . .) indicate negligible amount of coal. Figures are for reserves and resources in the ground. At least half of the reserve base is recoverable.

[a] Includes coal reserve base and total remaining identified coal resources of the United States. The reserve base is a selected portion of the identified resources deemed to be suitable for mining by 1974 methods. The figures in the table are for coal in the ground. At least 50 percent of the coal in the ground is recoverable, and this portion is termed "reserves," as distinguished from the reserve base. To avoid any possible ambiguity, "reserves" may also be termed "recoverable reserves."

[b] Includes coal in the measured and indicated (demonstrated) category in beds 28 inches or more thick for bituminous coal and anthracite, and 5 feet or more thick for subbituminous coal and lignite. Maximum overburden is 1,000 feet for subbituminous coal, bituminous coal, and anthracite, and 120 feet for lignite. May include coal outside these parameters if such coal is being mined or is considered to be commercially minable (U.S. Bureau of Mines, 1974).

Source: *Coal Sources of the United States, January 1, 1974*, U.S. Geological Survey Bulletin No. 1412.

Table IX-4

DEMONSTRATED SURFACE MINING COAL RESERVE BASE OF THE UNITED STATES, JANUARY 1, 1974[a]

(Millions of Tons)

State	Sulfur Content				
	≤ 1.0%	1.1–3.0%	> 3.0%	Unknown	Total[b]
Alabama	35.4	83.2	1.6	1,063.2	1.183.7
Alaska	7,377.6	21.0	0.0	0.0	7,399.0
Arizona	173.3	176.7	0.0	0.0	350.0
Arkansas	37.9	152.8	17.1	55.2	263.3
Colorado	724.2	146.2	0.0	0.0	870.0
Illinois	60.4	1,493.0	9,321.3	1,347.8	12,222.9
Indiana	105.3	559.2	907.3	101.6	1,674.1
Kansas	0.0	309.2	695.6	383.2	1,388.1
Kentucky, East	1,515.7	929.9	86.8	915.3	3,450.2
Kentucky, West	0.2	177.8	2,017.5	1,708.8	3,904.0
Maryland	28.6	66.6	16.2	34.6	146.3
Michigan	0.0	0.5	0.1	0.0	0.6
Missouri	0.0	47.8	1,635.8	1,730.0	3,413.7
Montana	38,182.4	2,175.2	46.4	2,166.7	42,561.9
New Mexico	1,681.0	579.3	0.0	0.0	2,258.3
North Carolina	0.0	0.0	0.0	0.4	0.4
North Dakota	5,389.0	10,325.4	268.7	15.0	16,003.0
Ohio	18.9	991.0	2,524.9	117.9	3,653.9
Oklahoma	120.5	88.1	38.8	186.2	434.1
Oregon	0.5	0.3	0.0	0.0	0.8
Pennsylvania	138.6	718.4	231.5	89.5	1,181.4
South Dakota	103.1	287.9	35.9	1.0	428.0
Tennessee	65.5	163.2	55.2	34.1	319.6
Texas	659.8	1,884.6	284.1	444.0	3,271.9
Utah	52.3	149.1	42.6	18.0	262.0
Virginia	411.6	218.1	2.1	46.7	679.2
Washington	172.5	307.7	25.8	2.2	508.1
West Virginia	3,005.5	1,422.8	270.4	509.6	5,212.0
Wyoming	13,192.8	10,122.3	425.5	105.3	23,845.3
Total[b]	73,252.3	33,597.4	18,950.9	11,076.1	136,885.7

[a]The reserve base is a selected portion of the identified resources deemed to be suitable for mining by 1974 methods. The figures in the table are for coal in the ground. At least 50 percent of the coal in the ground is recoverable, and this portion is termed "reserves," as distinguished from the reserve base. To avoid any possible ambiguity, "reserves" may also be termed "recoverable reserves."
[b]Data may not add to totals shown due to rounding.

Source: *Mineral Industry Surveys*, USDOI, Bureau of Mines, May 1975.

Table IX-5

DEMONSTRATED UNDERGROUND MINING COAL RESERVE BASE OF THE UNITED STATES, JANUARY 1, 1974[a]
(Millions of Tons)

State	Sulfur Content				
	≤ 1.0%	1.1–3.0%	> 3.0%	Unknown	Total[b]
Alabama	589.3	1,016.7	14.8	176.2	1,798.1
Alaska	4,080.8	163.2	0.0	0.0	4,246.4
Arkansas	43.3	310.3	29.2	19.1	402.4
Colorado	6,751.3	640.0	47.3	6,547.3	13,999.2
Georgia	0.3	0.0	0.0	0.2	0.5
Illinois	1,034.7	5,848.4	33,647.6	12,908.4	53,441.9
Indiana	443.5	2,746.6	4,355.1	1,402.5	8,948.5
Iowa	1.5	226.7	2,105.9	549.2	2,884.9
Kentucky, East	5,042.7	2,391.9	212.7	1,814.0	9,466.5
Kentucky, West	0.0	386.6	7,226.4	1,107.1	8,719.9
Maryland	106.5	623.9	171.2	0.0	901.9
Michigan	4.6	84.9	20.8	7.0	117.6
Missouri	0.0	134.2	3,590.2	2,350.5	6,073.6
Montana	63,464.2	1,939.8	456.2	0.0	65,834.3
New Mexico	1,894.3	214.1	0.9	27.5	2,136.5
North Carolina	0.0	0.0	0.8	31.3	31.3
Ohio	115.5	5,449.9	10,109.4	1,754.1	17,423.3
Oklahoma	.154.5	238.5	202.6	264.3	860.1
Oregon	1.0	0.0	0.0	.0	1.0
Pennsylvania	7,179.7	16,195.2	3,568.1	2,864.7	29,819.2
Tennessee	139.3	370.0	101.4	53.9	667.1
Utah	1,916.2	1,397.6	6.8	460.3	3,780.5
Virginia	1,728.5	945.4	12.0	283.3	2,970.7
Washington	431.0	957.8	13.2	42.9	1,445.9
West Virginia	11,086.6	12,583.4	6,552.9	4,142.9	34,377.8
Wyoming	20,719.5	4,535.1	1,275.6	2,955.0	29,490.8
Total[b]	126,928.8	59,400.2	73,720.2	39,761.6	299,839.7

[a]The reserve base is a selected portion of the identified resources deemed to be suitable for mining by 1974 methods. The figures in the table are for coal in the ground. At least 50 percent of the coal in the ground is recoverable, and this portion is termed "reserves," as distinguished from the reserve base. To avoid any possible ambiguity, "reserves" may also be termed "recoverable reserves."
[b]Data may not add to totals shown due to rounding.

Source: *Mineral Industry Surveys,* USDOI, Bureau of Mines, May 1975.

Table IX-6

STATISTICS OF THE BITUMINOUS COAL AND LIGNITE INDUSTRY IN THE UNITED STATES

	1971	1972	1973	1974	1975 Preliminary
Production (thousand short tons)	552,192	595,386	591,738	603,406	640,000
Value (thousands)	$3,904,562	$4,561,983	$5,049,612	$9,486,209	$12,093,750
Consumption (thousand short tons)	494,862	516,776	556,022	552,709	554,749
Stocks at end of year:					
Industrial consumers and retail yards (thousand short tons)	89,985	116,500	103,022	95,528	127,159
Stocks on upper lake docks (thousand short tons)	1,205	939	822	1,051	1,185
Exports[a] (thousand short tons)	56,633	55,997	52,903	59,926	65,669
Imports (thousand short tons)	111	47	127	2,080	940
Price indicators, average per net tons:					
Cost of coking coal at merchant coke ovens	$15.26	$17.67	$19.77	$34.20	$40.00
Railroad freight charge[b]	$3.70	$3.67	$3.71	4.71	$5.25
Value F.O.B. mines (sold in open market)	$6.66	$7.35	$8.06	$15.13	$18.20
Value F.O.B. mines	$7.07	$7.66	$8.53	$15.72	$18.75
Method of Mining:					
Underground (total, in thousand short tons)	275,888	304,103	299,353	277,309	289,788
Cut by hand and shot from solid	4,700	4,198	4,288	4,947	4,800
Cut by cutting machine	111,693	113,766	107,024	91,490	96,000
Cut by continuous mining machines	152,943	178,375	178,600	171,297	178,588
Cut by longwall machines	6,552	7,763	9,442	9,574	10,400
Percentage mined by underground methods	50.0	51.1	50.6	46.0	45.3
Percentage mechanically loaded	98.2	99.0	99.3	99.7	99.7
Surface (total, in thousand short tons)	276,304	291,284	292,384	326,097	350,212
Percentage mined by surface methods	50.0	48.9	49.4	54.0	54.7
Mechanically cleaned (thousand short tons)	271,401	292,829	288,918	265,150	264,000
Percentage mechanically cleaned	49.1	49.2	48.8	43.9	41.3
Number of mines	5,149	4,879	4,744	5,247	5,100
Capacity at 235 days (thousand short tons)	618,000	622,000	613,000	653,458	692,000
Average number of men working daily:[c]					
Underground mines	109,311	112,252	111,083	119,416	140,000
Surface mines	36,353	37,013	37,038	47,285	54,550
Total	145,664	149,265	148,121	166,701	194,550
Average number of days worked:					
Underground mines	210	222	231	205	218
Surface mines	212	217	215	208	214
Total	210	221	227	206	217
Production per man per day:[c]					
Underground mines (short tones)	12.03	11.91	11.66	11.31	9.50
Surface mines (short tons)	35.88	36.33	36.67	33.16	30.00
Total	18.02	17.74	17.58	17.58	15.15

[a] Bureau of the Census, U.S. Department of Commerce.

[b] Interstate Commerce Commission.

[c] Estimates based on data supplied by Health and Safety Analysis Center, Mining Enforcement and Safety Administration.

Source: *Mineral Industry Survey*, USDOI, Bureau of Mines, Weekly Coal Report No. 3056, April 9, 1976

Table IX-7

PRODUCTION AND AVERAGE MINE VALUE OF BITUMINOUS AND LIGNITE COAL, BY TYPE OF MINING, 1974

State	Production by Type of Mining (thousand short tons)			Average F.O.B. Mine Value by Type of Mining (dollars)	
	Underground	Surface	All[a]	Underground	Surface
Alabama	7,053	12,771	19,824	30.30	17.09
Alaska	–	700	700	–	W
Arizona	–	6,448	6,448	–	W
Arkansas	–	455	455	–	21.28
Colorado	3,260	3,636	6,896	13.89	5.33
Illinois	31,256	26,960	58,216	11.12	8.70
Indiana	139	23,587	23,726	W	8.36
Iowa	379	211	590	W	9.15
Kansas	–	718	718	–	7.61
Kentucky	63,497	73,700	137,197	19.48	14.98
Maryland	90	2,247	2,337	W	20.79
Missouri	–	4,623	4,623	–	6.36
Montana	–	14,106	14,106	–	3.90
New Mexico	529	8,864	9,392	W	W
North Dakota	–	7,463	7,463	–	2.19
Ohio	14,365	31,044	45,409	13.70	11.68
Oklahoma	–	2,356	2,356	–	10.51
Pennsylvania	42,249	38,213	80,462	22.63	17.83
Tennessee	3,106	4,435	7,541	13.70	21.04
Texas	–	7,684	7,684	–	W
Utah	5,858	–	5,858	12.24	–
Virginia	22,767	11,559	34,326	25.87	23.11
Washington	15	3,898	3,913	28.70	W
West Virginia	82,220	20,242	102,462	21.76	21.21
Wyoming	526	20,177	20,703	10.19	4.88
Total	277,309	326,097	603,406	19.86	12.25

W = Withheld to avoid disclosing individual company confidential data.
[a]Data may not add to totals shown because of independent rounding.

Source: *Mineral Industry Survey,* USDOI, Bureau of Mines, Weekly Coal
Report, November 21, 1975.

Table IX-8

U.S. CONSUMPTION OF BITUMINOUS COAL AND
LIGNITE, BY CONSUMER CLASS AND RETAIL DELIVERIES, 1975
(Thousands of Short Tons)

Month	Electric power utilities[a]	Bunker foreign and lake vessel[b]	Beehive coke plants	Oven coke plants	Steel and rolling mills[c]	Other manufacturing and mining industries[d]	Retail deliveries[e]	Total[f]
January	35,710	1	112	7,191	416	5,290	1,121	49,841
February	31,983	1	108	6,923	359	5,662	690	45,726
March	32,690	—	108	7,772	302	5,678	703	47,253
April	30,147	3	100	7,327	254	5,340	396	43,567
May	30,128	4	89	7,193	210	4,776	283	42,683
June	33,120	3	81	6,840	147	4,201	335	44,727
July	36,186	2	91	6,547	114	4,070	486	47,496
August	37,759	2	94	6,470	137	4,322	318	49,102
September	32,361	2	97	6,190	135	4,666	378	43,829
October	32,717	3	94	6,565	171	4,689	324	44,563
November	33,199	2	89	6,396	227	5,308	324	45,545
December	37,249	1	62	6,654	243	5,757	,324	50,290
Total	403,249	24	1,125	82,068	2,715	59,759	5,682	554,622

[a]Federal Power Commission

[b]Bureau of the Census, U.S. Department of Commerce. Ore and Coal Exchange.

[c]Estimates based upon reports collected from a selected list of representative steel and rolling mills.

[d]Estimates based upon reports collected from a selected list of representative manufacturing plants.

[e]Estimates based upon reports collected from a selected list of representative retailers. Includes some coal shipped by truck from mine to final destination.

[f]The total of classes shown approximates total consumption. The calculation of consumption for production, imports, exports, and changes in stocks is not as accurate as the "Total of classes shown" because certain significant items of stocks are not included in monthly stocks. These items are: Stocks on lake and tidewater docks, stocks at other intermediate storage piles between mine and consumer, and coal in transit.

Source: *Mineral Industry Survey*, USDOI, Bureau of Mines, Weekly Coal Report No. 3060, May 7, 1976.

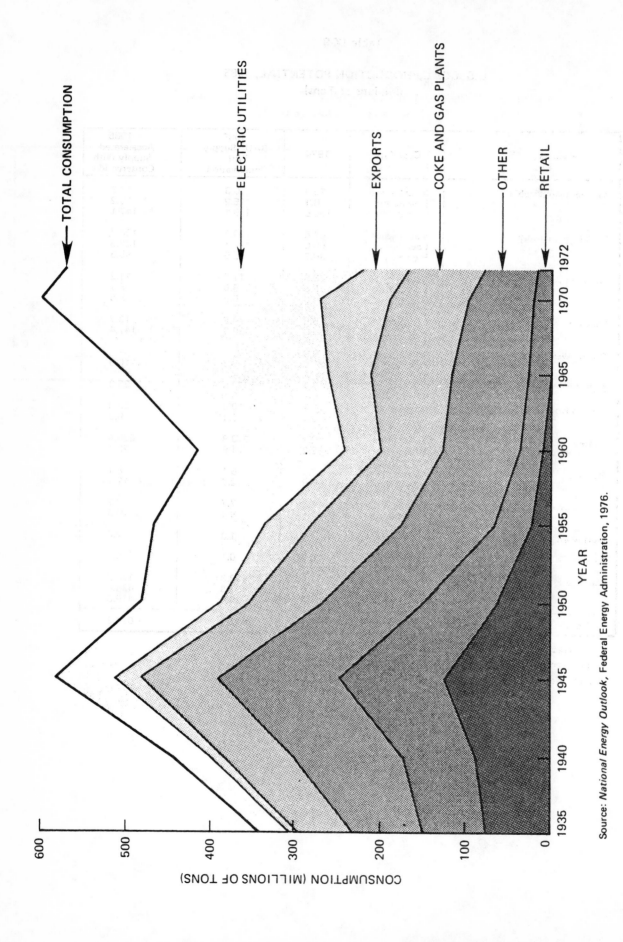

Source: *National Energy Outlook*, Federal Energy Administration, 1976.

Figure IX-3.   COAL CONSUMPTION BY SECTOR, 1935-1972

Table IX-9

U.S. COAL PRODUCTION POTENTIAL, 1985
(Millions of Tons)

Regions	Coal Type	1974	1985 BAU[a] Supply With Conservation	1985 Accelerated Supply With Conservation
Northern Appalachia	Metallurgical	12.9	20.3	20.3
	Low Sulfur	6.1	15.2	15.2
	High Sulfur	155.6	139.1	147.1
Central Appalachia	Metallurgical	87.8	100.7	100.7
	Low Sulfur	60.0	141.1	138.5
	High Sulfur	30.7	55.5	55.5
Southern Appalachia	Metallurgical	3.9	11.2	11.2
	Low Sulfur	5.8	8.5	8.1
	High Sulfur	9.8	5.6	5.6
Midwest	Low Sulfur	5.5	14.2	13.7
	High Sulfur	133.0	132.6	147.4
Central West	Metallurgical	9.9	—	—
	High Sulfur	7.9	9.3	10.9
Gulf	High Sulfur	7.7	20.6	25.3
Eastern Northern Great Plains	Low Sulfur	1.7	20.0	20.0
	High Sulfur	6.1	6.1	9.3
Western Northern Great Plains	Low Sulfur	2.1	213.8	220.4
	High Sulfur	32.2	21.9	25.1
Rockies	Metallurgical	6.1	6.1	6.1
	Low Sulfur	6.9	12.7	12.7
Southwest	Low Sulfur	1.2	7.7	7.7
	High Sulfur	14.8	8.3	10.8
Northwest	High Sulfur	4.9	1.0	2.6
Alaska	Low Sulfur	0.7	0.1	0.1
National	Metallurgical	111.6	138.3	138.3
	Low Sulfur	90.0	433.3	436.4
	High Sulfur	401.8	400.0	439.6
Total		603.4	971.6	1,014.3

[a]Business as usual.

Note: Production assumes imported oil will cost $13/barrel.

Source: *National Energy Outlook,* Federal Energy Administration, February 1976, p. 207.

Table IX-10

RESERVES AND RESOURCES OF SOLID FOSSIL FUELS, BY NATION
(Millions of Short Tons)

Nation	Reserves		Total Resources	Nation	Reserves		Total Resources
	Recoverable	Total			Recoverable	Total	
Africa				**Europe** *(Cont'd)*			
South Africa	11,642	26,646	48,773	East Germany	27,830	33,201	33,055
Rhodesia	1,529	1,936	7,274	Yugoslavia	18,577	19,774	23,926
Swaziland	2,002	2,224	5,524	Czechoslovakia	6,999	15,151	23,573
Zaire	792	792	792	Sweden	33	10,406	10,439
Botswana	557	557	557	Hungary	1,842	3,685	7,040
Mozambique	88	110	440	Bulgaria	4,826	4,826	5,753
Tanzania	198	340	407	Netherlands	2,024	4,076	4,076
Nigeria	248	494	494	Spain	1,807	2,422	3,918
Zambia	56	81	169	Iceland	—	2,200	2,200
Morocco	16	16	106	Romania	1,265	4,367	2,156
Malagasy	43	86	101	Greece	748	999	1,732
Malawi	—	—	42	France	504	1,548	1,548
Egypt	14	28	28	Denmark	22	617	639
Algeria	6	10	22	Ireland	460	464	493
Total Africa	17,191	33,320	64,728	Belgium	140	278	278
				Austria	70	163	195
Asia				Norway	2	2	167
People's Rep. of China	88,000	330,000	1,100,000	Italy	36	121	121
India	12,738	25,476	91,275	Portugal	36	46	46
Japan	1,129	9,491	9,491	Total Europe	144,612	401,663	718,176
Turkey	2,228	3,182	8,010				
Indonesia	3,394	2,335	2,786	**USSR**	150,260	300,520	6,284,960
Pakistan	189	884	2,135				
Bangladesh	571	858	1,640	**North America**			
North Korea	598	979	1,595	United States	199,959	399,918	3,216,953
Taiwan	287	527	726	Canada	6,091	9,937	119,634
Iran	212	424	424	Mexico	692	5,848	13,200
Burma	8	14	315	Greenland	1	2	2
Thailand	130	258	258	Total North America	206,743	415,705	3,349,789
Philippines	42	82	97				
Afghanistan	—	—	94	**Central and South America**			
Vietnam	7	13	13	Peru	116	232	7,660
Total Asia	107,304	374,525	1,218,858	Colombia	120	165	5,863
				Chile	64	107	4,340
Oceania	26,970	82,169	219,619	Brazil	1,969	3,582	3,582
				Venezuela	12	15	958
Europe				Argentina	110	171	611
West Germany	43,528	109,472	314,765	Honduras	—	—	6
United Kingdom	4,258	108,765	179,095	Total Central and South America	2,391	4,272	23,020
Poland	24,904	42,761	66,660				
Finland	4,719	36,300	36,300				

Source: Survey of World Energy Resources, World Energy Conference, 1974.

SECTION SEVEN

COAL GASIFICATION

INTRODUCTION

Gas manufactured from coal was first produced in the late 18th century by heating coal in the absence of air. The first coal-gas company, which distributed its product for lighting, was chartered in London in 1812; the first U.S. company was chartered in Baltimore in 1816.

"City gas" (carburetted water gas mixed with coal and coke-oven gas) had been the common source of fuel for cooking, domestic hot water, and street lighting in metropolitan centers for 150 years, until it began to be replaced by natural gas and electricity. City gas had a heating value of about 475 to 560 Btu per cubic foot (scf).[1] The substitution of natural gas, with a heating value of about 1,000 Btu per scf, permitted much more thermal energy to be supplied through the city-gas pipelines.

In the early days, synthetic gas was produced first by destructive distillation, that is, by heating the coal to a temperature at which it decomposed chemically. The gas produced had a heating value of about 550 Btu per scf. Subsequent to distillation, additional gas of lower heating value (300 Btu/scf) was produced by reacting the solid distillation residue (char) with air, steam, or mixtures of them. The heating value of the gas could be enriched further by spraying oil onto hot bricks, thus producing what is known as "carburetted blue gas" or "water gas."

Because the companies originally sold a coal gas with a heating value of about 550 Btu/scf, burners were designed to handle a gas of that quality. With burner designs fixed, manufactured gas, no matter how it was produced, was usually adjusted to that heating value.

The gas companies also manufactured a "producer gas" which was even cheaper than carburetted water gas. It had a heating value of 110 to 160 Btu/scf, which meant that it could not be widely distributed because the cost would be prohibitive. Producer gas served well, however, in industries that required a locally produced clean fuel for combustion or a source of heat for manufacturing.

Starting in about 1850 and continuing until World War II, the technology of making water gas and producer gas was improved steadily in the United States. After manufactured gas lost its markets in the United States, the technology was further improved in Europe, when coal was still the only indigenous fuel found in any significant quantity. New processes were investigated, taking advantage of technical advances in other fields such as the development of large-scale oxygen plants, new methods of handling solids in reactions with gas, and improved construction materials. At about the time the technology had reached a stage where plants could be installed, however, natural gas was discovered in the North Sea and in North Africa. In addition, most of the European nations decided to shift from an economy based on high-cost indigenous coal to one based on what was at the time low-cost imported petroleum. Few coal gasification plants embodying new technology were installed, and interest in further improving the technology lagged.[2]

[1] Standard cubic foot, that is a cubic foot of gas at standard temperature and pressure: 0° C and atmospheric pressure.
[2] Robert H. Perry and Cecil H. Chilton, *Chemical Engineers' Handbook*, pp 19-20, and *Evaluation of Coal Gasification Technology*, Office of Coal Research, p iv.

CONVERTING COAL TO GAS

Because of recent energy shortages, the United States has renewed its interest in developing the technology that will permit rapid commercialization of processes for converting coal to low-, medium-, and high-Btu gas. Low-Btu gas, with a heating value of 100 to 250 Btu per scf, is the cheapest of the gaseous fuels produced from coal and can be used economically only on site, either as a fuel feedstock or for electric power generation in combined gas-steam turbines. On an equivalent-Btu basis, conversion of coal to low-Btu gas is less complex than conversion to high-Btu gas, and the capital costs are lower.

Medium-Btu gas (250 to 550 Btu per scf) is usually a feed gas for producing high-Btu gas.

High-Btu gas from coal, with a heating value of 950 to 1,000 Btu per scf, can be substituted for natural gas and can be distributed economically to consumers in the same pipelines now used to carry natural gas. Natural gas, a widely used heating fuel and industrial feedstock, is com-

posed essentially of methane and contains virtually no sulfur, carbon monoxide, or free hydrogen.

Converting coal to low-, medium-, or high-Btu gas requires a chemical and physical transformation of solid coal, a transformation made more difficult because coal's chemical and physical properties differ widely, depending on where the coal is mined. To find the most suitable techniques for gasifying coal, several conversion processes are being developed. A list of the major coal gasification processes and a brief description of each process and its development status are given in Table X-1. Although each process has unique characteristics, each requires five major steps to convert coal to gas: coal preparation and pretreatment, gasification, shift conversion, gas purification, and methanation. Figure X-1 is a generalized flow chart depicting these steps.[1]

[1] *Energy From Coal: A State-of-the-Art Review*, U.S. Energy Research and Development Administration, ERDA 76-67.

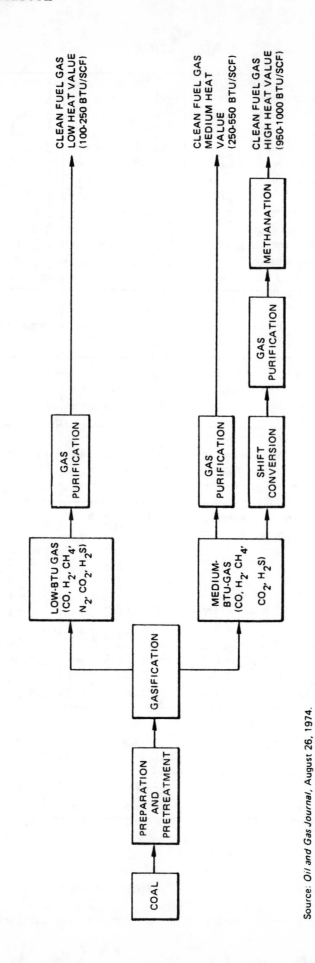

Source: *Oil and Gas Journal*, August 26, 1974.

Figure X-1. FUEL GAS FROM COAL

Table X-1

GASIFICATION PROCESSES AND STATUS

Process	Owner or Contractor and Site	Process Description	Coal Type	Input (Tons/day)	Output (10⁶ scf/day)	Status
		High-Btu Processes				
ATGAS-PATGAS	Applied Technology Corp., Pittsburgh, Pa.	Coal, crushed and dried, is injected into a molten iron bath through steam lances. Oxygen is introduced through lances located at the iron-bath surface. Coal dissolves in the molten iron where the volatiles crack and are converted into carbon monoxide and hydrogen. Sulfur in the coal migrates to a lime slag floating on the molten iron, and forms calcium sulfide. The slag, containing ash and sulfur, is continuously withdrawn from the gasifier and desulfurized with steam to yield sulfur and desulfurized slag. The raw gas from the gasifier can be used as medium-Btu fuel or upgraded to high-Btu fuel.	All U.S. coals			The process has been under investigation in laboratories since 1967, and has been demonstrated in short-duration runs in a 2-foot internal diameter gasifier. Plans for further development involve a larger gasifier to demonstrate long-duration operation.
BI-GAS	Bituminous Coal Research, Inc., Pittsburgh, Pa.	Coal is introduced into the upper section of a two-stage reactor where it is contacted with hydrogen-rich gas and partially gasified. The hydrogen-rich gas is produced in the lower section of the reactor by the slagging gasification of recycle char with oxygen and steam. The product gas must be methanated to produce high-Btu gas.	All U.S. coals	120	2-3	Construction of the pilot plant was completed in mid-1976, and shakedown and operation started.
Chevron	Chevron Research Co.	High-Btu gas is produced from a wide range of organic feeds such as lignite and organic waste materials. The organic feed is reacted with steam at 300-800 psi and 1,700°-1,400° F in the presence of an alkali metal catalyst (e.g., K_2CO_3). High-Btu gas is produced by the catalytic steam-reforming of the products of degradation of the feed.				Details of the development of the process are not available.

Table X-1

GASIFICATION PROCESSES AND STATUS (Cont'd)

Process	Owner or Contractor and Site	Process Description	Coal Type	Input (Tons/ day)	Output (10^6 scf/ day)	Status
CO$_2$ Acceptor	Consolidation Coal Co., Pittsburgh, Pa.	Coal is charged to a devolatilizer and is contacted at 300 psi with hydrogen-rich gas from a gasifier vessel. Calcined dolomite (the acceptor) is added to both vessels, where it reacts with carbon dioxide. Acceptor regeneration and ash removal is done in an air-blown regeneration vessel where spent char is combusted. The product gas must be purified and methanated to produce high-Btu gas.	Lignite Subbitu-minous	40 (pilot plant	2	The objective of CO$_2$ acceptor process development is to keep the pilot plant operating to identify and resolve process and equipment problems relevant to commercialization. Process efficiency of 77 percent has been demonstrated. The pilot plant is being operated on an integrated basis with the liquid phase methanation process.
Electrofluidic Gasification	Iowa State Univ. Ames, Iowa	A fluidized bed of conducting particles is heated by passing an electrical current through the bed. The bed itself acts as a resistor between electrodes placed in contact with the bed. Reacting steam and coal char in the reactor provide a wide range of hydrogen-carbon monoxide mixtures, as well as mixtures containing methane suitable for upgrading to high-Btu gas.				Four- and 12-inch-diameter reactors have been successfully operated. The process is being integrated with pilot plant tests of the HYGAS process electro-gasifier.
Exxon	Esso Research and Engineering Co., Baytown, Texas	Coal is reacted with steam in a fluidized-bed gasifier at 1,500° F–1,700° F. A stream of circulating char is withdrawn from the gasifier and partially burned with air in a char heater. The heated char is returned to the gasifier after separation from the flue gas. The medium-Btu gas produced can be upgraded to high-Btu gas.	All U.S. coals			A 0.5 ton/day pilot plant has been in operation for several years.
Garrett's Coal Gasification	Garret Research & Development Co., La Verne, Calif.	Coal is introduced into a simple reactor at atmospheric pressure where gas is produced by rapid devolatilization of coal. Large amounts of excess char are produced.	All U.S. coals			Garrett, in conjunction with Colorado Interstate Gas, initiated development of the coal-gasification process in 1971. The process has been successfully evaluated in a pilot plant. The results of the pilot plant testing provided data that were evaluated by Combustion Engineering subsidiary, Lummus Co., to provide a detailed design for a 40,000 ton/day commercial plant. The plant would yield

Table X-1

GASIFICATION PROCESSES AND STATUS (Cont'd)

Process	Owner or Contractor and Site	Process Description	Coal Type	Input (Tons/ day)	Output (10⁶ scf/ day)	Status
Garrett's Coal Gasification (Cont'd.)						250 million scf/day of pipeline quality gas and sufficient char to feed a 1,200 MW power plant. Garrett plans a 250 ton/day demonstration plant to be located near a power utility. Design and construction of the commercial plant could be started during operation of the demonstration plant. Operation of the commercial-scale pyrolysis reactor has been simulated with the operation of a continuous 3-16 lb/hour laboratory-scale reactor, which had the same configuration as the projected commercial unit except that its heat source was electrical. Results have indicated yields of pipeline-gas equivalents ranging from 4,500 scf/ton of MAF coal at 1,500° F to 7,500 scf/ton at 1,700° F, depending on coal type. Commercial-scale operation should yield an additional 1,000 scf/ton at 1,700° F of pipeline-gas equivalent by recycling the tar produced in the pyrolysis step to the reactor for further cracking. The commercial plant could be on-stream in 1980.
Hydrane	U.S. Bureau of Mines, Pittsburgh Energy Research Center, Pittsburgh Pa.	Crushed raw coal is fed to a two-zone hydrogenation reactor operated at 1,000 psi and 1,650° F. In the top zone, the coal falls freely through a hydrogen-rich gas containing some methane from the lower zone. About 20% of the carbon is converted to methane. The char from the top stage falls into the lower zone where hydrogen feed gas maintains the particles in a fluidized state and reacts with about 34% more of the carbon to make methane. Char from the lower zone is reacted with steam and oxygen to generate the needed hydrogen.				A second-generation hydrane process is in the engineering evaluation and design phase of development. This phase is scheduled to continue through the third quarter of FY 1978. Construction of a process development unit is scheduled to begin early in FY 1977 and continue through FY 1979, at which time the operation phase will begin. Laboratory studies are being conducted to acquire yield data, test operability using various coals, and obtain hy drogasification kinetic scale-up data.

Table X-1

GASIFICATION PROCESSES AND STATUS (Cont'd)

Process	Owner or Contractor and Site	Process Description	Coal Type	Input (Tons/ day)	Output (10⁶ scf/ day)	Status
HYGAS	Institute of Gas Technology, Chicago, Ill.	Ground, dried coal is pretreated with air, slurried with by-product oil, and fed to a two-stage fluidized-bed hydrogasifier operating at 1,000-1,500 psia. Hydrogen-rich gas for the reaction can be furnished by processes using electric energy or oxygen, or by the steam-iron process. Gas from the reactor must be purified and methanated to produce high-Btu gas.	All U.S. coals	75 (pilot plant)	1.5	The pilot plant is being operated to obtain data. Improvements in oil/gas separation and oil recovery are being developed. An ash-agglomerating gasifier that could improve overall char utilization of the process is in operation. A decision to connect the steam-iron unit for hydrogen production from char will be made in FY 1977.
Koppers-Totzek	Heinrich Koppers GmbH Essen, W. Germany	Raw coal is dried, ground, and charged to a gasifier by a screw conveyor with a mixing head in which oxygen and steam are added. The reactor operates at atmospheric pressure and at 2,700° F. The product gas, mostly hydrogen and carbon monoxide, can be methanated to produce high-Btu gas.	All U.S. coals			There are 16 Koppers-Totzek plants around the world, none of which is in the United States; five new plants are being built. An interesting new development of Heinrich Koppers and Imperial Chemical Industries (I.C.I.), Billingham, U.K., is a combined carbon monoxide-shift conversion and methanation unit. This unit's reactor uses a nickel catalyst that simultaneously promotes both shift and methanation reactions. Testing of this reactor by I.C.I. on a pilot scale has indicated that commercially acceptable lifetimes for the catalysts can be expected. A demonstration plant will be built in Germany to produce 2.6 scf/day from a coal feed of 145 tons/day. The Koppers—I.C.I. combined shift conversion and methanation reactor will be installed in the demonstration plant to upgrade the Koppers-Totzek gasifier raw gas to pipeline gas. Estimates for a Koppers-Totzek plant producing 250 million scf/day of high-Btu gas indicate a coal feed rate of 25,000 short tons/day to a battery of 24 Koppers-Totzek gasifiers.

Table X-1

GASIFICATION PROCESSES AND STATUS (Cont'd)

Process	Owner or Contractor and Site	Process Description	Coal Type	Input (Tons/ day)	Output (10⁶ scf/ day)	Status
Koppers-Totzek (Cont'd.)						In the United States, Northern Illinois Gas Co. and the State of Illinois are studying the process, among others, for application at their proposed 80-90 million scf per day synthetic natural gas demonstration plant to be completed in Illinois in the early 1980s.
Lurgi Pressure Gasification	Lurgi Gesellschaft fur Warme-und Chemotechnik mbH Frankfurt, West Germany	Crushed coal is fed to the gasifier vessel through lock hoppers, and travels downward as a moving bed. The process operates at 350 to 450 psi. Steam and oxygen are introduced through a revolving steam-cooled grate, which also removes ash at the bottom of the gasifier. The hydrogen-rich gas passes up through the coal bed, producing some methane by hydrogenation of coal. The product gas is purified and methanated to produce high-Btu gas.	Noncaking coals			The first commercial plant was constructed in 1936 and, to date, 14 plants (comprising 58 units) have been built and additional plants, either with or without a methanation step, are under construction or in the planning stages.
Molten Salt	M. W. Kellogg Co. Piscataway, N.J.	Crushed and dried coal, oxygen, and steam are injected into a high-purity alumina reaction vessel with molten sodium carbonate. Coal-steam reaction is catalyzed by the molten salt contained in the reactor. The product gas can be purified and methanated to produce high-Btu gas.	All U.S. coals			In early tests of the process, under Office of Coal Research sponsorship from 1964 to 1967, two vessels were used. In the first, steam and coal were reacted in a molten-salt bath to yield synthesis gas. In the second vessel, the residual carbon in the circulating molten carbonate was burned with air to reheat the sodium carbonate for recirculation. Because of problems arising from the corrosive nature of the salt, the small-scale tests of this process, were discontinued. W.M. Kellogg Co., continued their research and developed a noncorrosive alumina reactor lining to overcome the corrosion problem, and incorporated the use of a single reactor vessel, which not only eliminates circulation of the molten salt, but also simplifies gas handling and reduces further processing requirements.

Table X-1

GASIFICATION PROCESSES AND STATUS (Cont'd)

Process	Owner or Contractor and Site	Process Description	Coal Type	Input (Tons/day)	Output (10^6 scf/day)	Status
Molten Salt (Cont'd.)						Because of these new developments, the Office of Coal Research sponsored additional work, with special emphasis on the suitability of the process as a method for generating a fuel gas suitable for magnetohydrodynamic generating systems. The process is now being tested in a process development unit 10 times larger than earlier vessels.
Multiple Catalyst	Univ. of Wyoming Laramie, Wyo.	Methane is produced directly from coal and steam with the methanating -catalyst bed placed in the middle of the reactor and heated to the desired temperature by a Lindberg furnace. The temperature is monitored by thermocouples located in the thermo-well inside the reactor. The methane-rich product gas passes through a motor valve which allows the pressure to be controlled.				The concept was developed at the Univ. of Wyoming and supported for 5 years by OCR. Babcock and Wilcox have undertaken further development of a better catalyst system, which could assure long catalyst life. The U.S. Bureau of Mines has conducted bench-scale experiments on the catalytic reaction of coal and steam at 1,900° F using tungsten-sulfide as a catalyst.
Self-Agglomerating Ash	Battelle Memorial Institute, Columbus Laboratories, Columbus, Ohio	Coal is reacted with steam in a two-stage fluidized-bed system. Air is used for combustion of part of the coal to provide heat for the gasification process. The process operates at up to 100 psi to produce a synthesis gas suitable for conversion to high-Btu pipeline gas by methanation.	Bituminous	25	0.8	Construction of the process development unit was completed in mid-1976, and shakedown started. The unit will be operated through mid-1977. The process engineering and economics data generated will be used to design a larger unit.
Synthane	U.S. Bureau of Mines, Pittsburgh Energy Research Center, Bruceton Pa.	Coal is fed into a reactor incorporating three processing steps: a free-fall oxygen-steam pretreatment zone, a dense fluid-bed carbonizer, and a dilute fluid-bed gasifier. Hydrogen-rich gas for the reaction is produced by the use of oxygen in the reactor. The process operates at 500 to 1,000 psia. The product gas can be purified and methanated to produce high-Btu gas.	All U.S. coals	70 (pilot) plant	1.4	Pilot plant design and construction were completed in 1975 and are currently in the shakedown phase. The plant is being operated to obtain enough data for designing a commercial plant.

Table X-1

GASIFICATION PROCESSES AND STATUS (Cont'd)

Process	Owner or Contractor and Site	Process Description	Coal Type	Input (Tons/day)	Output (10⁶ scf/day)	Status
Two-stage Fluidized Gasification	Midlands Research Station, United Kingdom	Coal is subjected to hydrogenation in two stages: a rapid reaction at 1,470° F.-1,560° F and a slower reaction at 1,650° F.-1,740° F at 750 psi. The char produced then passes to a fluidized-bed gasifier operating at 1,900° F, which produces a gas which is upgraded by catalytic methanation to pipeline quality.				Work has been done using fluidized-bed models under different operating conditions. From the results, a pilot plant to produce 4 million scf/day of synthesis gas was designed.
Wellman-Galusha	McDowell-Wellman Co. and Wellman-Galusha Co.	Crushed coal, dried and fed by an oxygen-steam mixture, is introduced through a revolving grate at the bottom of the reactor. Gasifiers are available with or without an agitator, which reduces channeling and maintains a uniform bed. The ash is removed continuously through a slowly revolving grate at the bottom of the reactor. The gas produced can be upgraded to high-Btu gas.				The process has been commercial for over 30 years. Two units are operating in the U.S. serving large industrial plants. McDowell-Wellman Co. is under contract to determine the feasibility of constructing a fixed-bed gasifier for operation on caking coals.
Winkler	Davy Powergas, Inc. Lakeland, Florida	Crushed coal is dried and fed to a fluidized-bed gasifier through a variable-speed screw feeder. Coal reacts with oxygen and steam to produce offgas rich in carbon monoxide and hydrogen. Because of the high temperatures, all tars and heavy hydrocarbons are reacted. Unreacted carbon carried over by gas is converted by secondary steam and oxygen in the space above the fluidized-bed. Raw gas leaving the gasifier is passed through a further waste-heat recovery section. Fly-ash is removed by cyclones, wet scrubbers, and an electrostatic precipitator. Gas is then compressed, shifted, purified, and methanated.				The process has been in use commercially at 16 plants in a number of countries since its development in Europe 50 years ago. The plants produce low-Btu fuel gas and synthesis gas. Davy Powergas, Inc., is currently developing a high-pressure modification of the Winkler process which should increase the thermal efficiency.

Table X-1

GASIFICATION PROCESSES AND STATUS (Cont'd)

Medium- and Low-Btu Processes

Process	Owner or Contractor and Site	Process Description	Coal Type	Input (Tons/ day)	Output (10^6 scf/ day)	Status
Advanced System	Westinghouse Electric Corp. Pittsburgh, Pa.	Crushed, dried coal is fed into a central draft tube of a devolatilizer-desulfurizer. Coal and recycled solids are carried upward from a combustor by hot gases flowing at a velocity greater than 15 feet per second. Recycle solids flow downward in a fluidized bed surrounding the draft tube at rates up to 100 times the coal feed rate. Heat is provided by hot combustor gases. A lime sorbent is added to the gasifier to remove sulfur. Spent sorbent is removed, stripped of char, regenerated, and recycled to the gasifier. Char is removed from the top section of the gasifier and fed to the combustor. Raw product gas passes through a cyclone to remove fines and then through a heat-recovery unit.				This process is being tested in a 1,200 lb/hour pilot plant at Waltz Mill, Pa. Westinghouse, in late 1972, began a 9-year research and development program expected to cost $80 million, cosponsored by Bechtel Corp., AMAX Coal, Peabody Coal Co., and the Public Service Co. of Indiana. Eleven electric power utilities are also sponsoring the program as associate members. A 60-ton/hour commercial, low-Btu gasification and electric power plant is under construction at the Dresser Station of the Public Service Co. of Indiana at Terre Haute, Indiana. This project, sponsored by ERDA, will utilize a combined-cycle coal gasification-power system fueled by the Westinghouse gasifier. The plant is expected to be operational during 1978.
BCR Fluid-bed Three-stage Pressurized	Bituminous Coal Research Monroeville, Pa.	This process consists of three fluidized beds. Raw coal is fed into Stage 1. This stage acts as a pretreatment stage, devolatilizing the coal with the offgas from Stage 3. From Stage 1 the coal flows by gravity to Stage 2 where it is gasified with air and steam. Stage 3 functions as a char combustion step, operates at the highest temperature, and maximizes char utilization.	All U.S. coals	1		Construction of a one-ton per day process development unit was completed late in 1975. The unit will be operated for two years, and will be used to study and optimize the multistage system. Data generated from operation will be used for scale-up design. Laboratory research has been done to further refine the process.
Combined Cycle	Babcock & Wilcox Co. Alliance, Ohio	Coal and air are fed to a pressurized, water-cooled gasifier where they react to form a combustible gas. After cleaning, the gas is fired in a combustor that discharges to a high-temperature gas turbine, which, in turn, exhausts to the steam generating portion of the cycle to power a steam-turbine generator.				A 480 ton/day pilot plant is planned to be installed at a power generation utility site yet to be selected. Testing in a 60 ton/ day plant has been under evaluation since 1961.

Table X-1

GASIFICATION PROCESSES AND STATUS (Cont'd)

Process	Owner or Contractor and Site	Process Description	Coal Type	Input (Tons/ day)	Output (10^6 scf/ day)	Status
Combined Cycle	Foster-Wheeler Corp., Livingston N.J.	The process utilizes an entrained-bed, two-stage slagging pressure gasifier. The low-Btu fuel gas produced by the reaction of coal, steam, and air is cleaned and fired in a combustor that discharges to a gas turbine. The hot gas expanding through the turbine is sent to the steam-generating portion of the cycle to power a steam-turbine generator.				A research and development program initiated in 1972 will culminate in the operation of a 1,200 ton/day demonstration plant at Northern States Power Co.'s Lawrence Plant near Sioux Falls, S.D. Foster-Wheeler is developing a detailed conceptual design of the demonstration plant.
Entrained Fuel	Combustion Engineering, Inc. Windsor, Conn.	The gasifier consists of two sections: a combustion chamber that burns coal and recycle char to provide heat to the gasifier, and a reducing chamber where coal is reacted with steam to produce low-Btu gas. The gasifier is an entrained-bed reactor operating at atmospheric pressure. The product gas with a heating value of 125 Btu/scf leaves the gasifier a 1,600° F and enters the heat-recovery train. The gas is cooled further to 300° F.		120		A 120 ton/day plant is being built and is scheduled for completion in 1977. The plant will be operated to determine the technical and economic feasibility of the process. Continuous operation will be attempted to demonstrate equipment reliability. Cost and performance estimates for a commercial-size plant will be determined.
Fixed Bed	M. W. Kellogg Co., Piscataway	This process uses a low-pressure fixed-bed, revolving-grate gasifier to produce a low-Btu fuel gas with air, and a medium-Btu fuel gas with oxygen. By-product tar and oil are used as plant fuel or chemical feedstock.				The company is presently studying the formation of a consortium to erect a demonstration plant at an, as yet, un-selected utility site.
GEGAS	General Electric Research and Development Center, Schenectady, N.Y.	This process utilizes a moving fixed-bed air-blown gasifier operating at 120 psi and 1,000° F. An extrusion process is used for coal feeding and off-gases are cleaned of hydrogen sulfide.				The process has been tested at a 50 lb/hour facility. A pilot plant will be built at a utility site. G.E. will initiate construction and operation of a pilot-plant head ex-changer to determine the effects of high-temperature coal gasification products discharging through an MHD generator.

Table X-1

GASIFICATION PROCESSES AND STATUS (Cont'd)

Process	Owner or Contractor and Site	Process Description	Coal Type	Input (Tons/day)	Output (10^6 scf/day)	Status
HRI Fluidized Bed	Hydrocarbon Research, Inc. Princeton, N.J.	Steam and oxygen fluidize a bed with a fuel depth of 25 feet operating at pressures up to 400 psia, and at 1,450°F to 1,650°F to produce a synthesis gas of 320 Btu/scf.				Work was done in the 1960s using a 26-inch diameter fluidized-bed gasifier.
Kerpely Producer	U.S. Bureau of Mines, Louisiana, Missouri	Coal passes through a lock hopper down into a fixed-bed cylindrical unit, and is gasified by a steam-oxygen (or air) blast through a revolving grate, which removes the ash continuously. The unit operates at atmospheric pressure to produce a 260 Btu/scf gas with oxygen or a 130 Btu/scf gas with air.				A 7-foot internal diameter unit was operated by the U.S. Bureau of Mines. About 2 million scf/day of 260 Btu/scf synthesis gas with oxygen blasts were produced.
Molten Salt	Atomics International Norwalk, Conn.	Coal is gasified in a molten pool of sodium carbonate sulfide and sulfate through which air is blown. The product gas has a heating value of 150 Btu/scf. Conducting gasification reactions in the molten salt medium permits the attainment of very high oxidation rates and traps ash and sulfur in the melt.	All U.S. coals			Development tests, including hydraulic, quench tests, ash settling, solubility characteristics and regeneration of the molten salt, were conducted in FY 1975. A 24 ton/day process development unit has been designed.
Ruhrgas Vortex	Ruhrgas A.G. West Germany	High-ash coal or lignite, crushed to a 1/16-inch top size, is fed with air, preheated to 1,300°F, into a vortex chamber where it is gasified without steam and under slagging conditions. The slag passes out the bottom and the reactants pass upward into a tall shaft of larger diameter where the greater part of the gasification occurs at 3,100°F. The 100-120 Btu/scf off-gas is passed through cyclones and bag filters for dust removal and recycling of entrained gas.				The process has been in commercial use for many years to produce low-Btu fuel gas.

Table X-1

GASIFICATION PROCESSES AND STATUS (Cont'd)

Process	Owner or Contractor and Site	Process Description	Coal Type	Input (Tons/day)	Output (10^6 scf/day)	Status
Stirred Fixed Bed	U.S. Bureau of Mines, Pittsburgh, Pa.	Unsized coal is fed to the top of the gasifier, which operates at 300 psi. Steam and air are introduced below the grate at the bottom. The nominal steam: coal feed ratio is 1:2 and the air: coal ratio is 3:1. Gasifier temperatures range from 2,400°F just above the grate to 880-1200°F at the gas exit. A water cooled stirrer is used to control caking and eliminate voids. The product is low-Btu gas.	Bituminous Subbituminous Lignite	12		A low-Btu gasification process development unit is operating at Morgantown Energy Research Center. Continued operation of the gasifier at different pressures with different types and sizes of coal to determine maximum capacity will provide the necessary data for design scale-up and economic evaluation. Construction of gas scrubber, hydrogen sulfide removal, and full blown combustion/turbine subsystems will begin in FY 1977. Operation of the fully integrated process, consisting of gasifier, cleanup, combustion, and turbine, will begin in FY 1978.
Texaco Gasification	Texaco Development Co.	Pulverized coal, suspended in steam at 950°F, is fed into the top of a downflow cylindrical reactor, where it is gasified with oxygen to produce 280 Btu/scf gas. The unit operates at 260 psi and temperatures above the ash fusion point. The product gas and slag are removed at the base of the vessel.				This process has been tested in a down-flow plant and has also been utilized in the HYGAS pilot plant for producing hydrogen.
Two Stage (Submerged Coal Combustion)	Applied Technology Corp.	The process is based on the molten-iron gasification process with air/coal feed to yield a 185 Btu/scf offgas and is similar to the ATGAS/PATGAS process.				Testing has been carried out in short runs using a 2-foot internal diameter vessel. The U.S. Environmental Protection Agency is sponsoring a design study for a 50 to 100 MW power generating plant using the process low-Btu offgas.
Two-step Coal Pyrolysis	West Virginia University Morgantown, West Virginia	Coal is fed to a sand fluidized-bed for pyrolysis at 1,400°F. Char produced is separated from effluent gas and reacted with air and steam in a gasifier to produce fluidizing gases for the pyrolyzer. A small quantity of raw coal is added to the gasifier char feed where the temperature is maintained at 1,900°F.	All U.S. coals			Feasibility has been demonstrated in bench-scale experiments using a 15-inch diameter fluidized-bed reactor. A conceptual study has been made of the process for application in power generation by coupling this process with an advanced-design combined gas and steam turbine power cycle.

Table X-1

GASIFICATION PROCESSES AND STATUS (Cont'd)

Process	Owner or Contractor and Site	Process Description	Coal Type	Input (Tons/day)	Output (10^6 scf/day)	Status
U-GAS	Institute of Gas Technology	Crushed coal is pressurized in a lock hopper operating at 350 psi and 800°F, reacted with air, and fed to a fluidized-bed gasifier operating at 350 psi and 1,900°F. Air and steam are introduced through the base of the gasifier and ash removed through lock hoppers. Gases from the preheater and gasifier pass through heat-recovery and sulfur removal systems and power-recovery turbines. Gas produced has a heating value of 155 Btu/scf. Substituting oxygen for air produces a medium-Btu fuel gas.				The process has been tested in an air-blown 485 lb/hour unit, which showed the suitability of the process for both combined-cycle power generation and as a "grass-roots" source of industrial and power generation energy. A 10 to 35 ton/hour pilot plant, sufficient to fuel a 100 MW power utility, is being designed.

Sources: *Coal Conversion Technology: A review,* I. Howard-Smith and G. J. Werner, 1975, and *Fossil Energy Research Program of the Energy Research and Development Administration, FY 1977,* ERDA 76-63.

SECTION EIGHT

COAL LIQUEFACTION

INTRODUCTION

Coal has been burned directly for centuries and a fuel gas was made from coal almost 200 years ago; coal liquids derived from pyrolysis, synthesis, or hydroliquefaction were first produced about 50 years ago.

The most notable example of production of coal liquids is the German experience during World War II. Germany had built several synthetic fuel plants with a combined output of 5 million tonnes[1] per year (approximately 100,000 bbl/day). About 20 percent of the production came from the distillation (pyrolysis) of brown and bituminous coal, 12 percent came from the Fischer-Tropsch synthesis process, and 68 percent came from the direct hydrogenation of coal.

Germany's supply of petroleum was limited before World War II. Consequently, building synthetic fuel plants was a part of Germany's rearmament program. Germany, in an effort to be self-sufficient, demonstrated the ability to derive adequate synthetic fuels from coal, although these fuels were uneconomical compared with natural crude oil.

After World War II, the synthetic fuel industry dwindled. In 1956, however, a new plant started production in South Africa based on the Fischer-Tropsch synthesis technology (5,000 to 6,000 bbl/day). Also, it was reported that three of the World War II German synthetic fuel plants located in East Germany had a combined annual output in 1956 of approximately 11 million barrels of products per year (30,000 bbl/day).

The basic conversion technology required to use coal as a source of liquid fuels has existed for many years. Most of this conversion technology has not been economical when faced with competition from low-priced natural crude. However, over the last two decades, considerable research and development efforts have been expended by the United States Office of Coal Research, Bureau of Mines (now part of the Energy Research and Development Administration) and various energy companies to improve the efficiency of conversion processes, lower the cost of the facilities required, and in general make these alternate fuel sources more competitive. These research efforts have had considerable success; many new and refined process technologies now exist. The most recent development has been directed toward building pilot plants based on these improved technologies as a first step toward a full-scale commercial plant.

[1] Tonne = 1000 kg = 2204.6 lb.

CHEMISTRY OF COAL LIQUEFACTION

A simplified treatment of the chemistry of coal conversion is helpful in understanding the different coal processes. Basically, coal is a solid hydrocarbon with a hydrogen-to-carbon mole ratio of approximately 0.9 (coal can be represented as $CH_{0.9}$). In addition, coal has varying amounts of oxygen, nitrogen, sulfur, ash, and moisture. Typical equivalent chemical formulas for moisture- and ash-free (MAF) bituminous and subbituminous coals are compared in Table XI-1 to the equivalent chemical formulas for gasoline, jet fuel, light fuel oil, heavy fuel oil, coal-derived synthetic crude oil, paraffin-based natural crude (Pennsylvania pipeline), and naphthene-based natural crude (Coalinga, Calif.). Examination of the table shows that it is necessary to increase the relative amounts of hydrogen in coal to convert it to a useful liquid fuel. In reality, however, conversion is much more complicated because coal tends to be highly aromatic and requires sophisticated treatment to convert it to paraffin or olefin products. Coal, for example, makes better gasoline than it does jet or diesel fuel.

Table XI-1

EQUIVALENT CHEMICAL FORMULAS FOR VARIOUS FEEDSTOCKS AND HYDROCARBON PRODUCTS

Feed Stocks	
Bituminous Coal	$CH_{0.9}O_{0.1}S_{0.02}N_{0.01}$ + Ash + Moisture
Sub-bituminous Coal	$CH_{0.9}O_{0.2}S_{0.004}N_{0.01}$ + Ash + Moisture
Coal Derived Syncrude (H-Coal)	$CH_{1.5}O_{0.02}S_{0.001}N_{0.002}$
Paraffin Crude Oil	$CH_{2.0}$
Naphthene Crude Oil	$CH_{1.6}N_{0.01}S_{0.003}$

Products			
Gasoline	$CH_{2.1}$	Jet Fuel	CH_2
Light Fuel Oil	$CH_{1.8}$	Heavy Fuel Oil	$CH_{1.3}S_{0.002}$

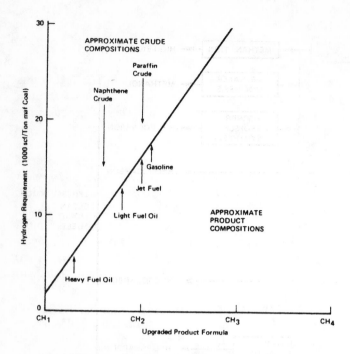

Figure XI-1. MINIMUM HYDROGEN REQUIRE-
MENTS FOR COAL LIQUEFACTION

Increasing the hydrogen-to-carbon ratio of coal can be accomplished by reducing the amount of carbon by coking or pyrolysis or by adding hydrogen from a second source to the coal molecule, as is done in solvent refining or catalytic hydrogenation. If the coal is totally gasified by partial oxidation, the resulting hydrogen and carbon monoxide can be reformed using the Fischer-Tropsch synthesis over the proper catalysts to yield almost any desired hydrocarbon product.

Estimates of hydrogen required to convert coal ($CH_{0.9}$) to the various hydrocarbon products, based on perfect conversion, are shown in Figure XI-1. The hydrogen requirements of a real plant would exceed this minimum amount because of normal process inefficiencies and the need to provide hydrogen for sulfur removal.

COAL LIQUEFACTION TECHNOLOGY

Three methods exist for converting coal into liquid hydrocarbon fuels: synthesis gas, pyrolysis (coking), and hydrogenation. Hydrogenation is frequently subdivided into noncatalytic processes such as solvent-refined coal (SRC) and catalytic processes such as H-Coal. This fact book considers the three major methods. Figure XI-2 shows a general schematic of the methods for converting coal to liquid fuels. A list of specific liquefaction processes being developed and a brief description of each process and its development status are given in Table XI-2.

Synthesis Gas

The production of synthetic fuels using the synthetic gas process is a well known, relatively simple, but generally more expensive than competing processes. The advantage of this process is that there is more control over the type of products manufactured. Consequently, this process would be preferred where part of the product mix would be used to supply a petrochemical industry.

The synthesis gas technology could also be applied to any hydrocarbon starting material. Basically, the processes partially oxidize the coal (or any other organic materials) to produce carbon monoxide and hydrogen. This synthesis gas, passed over an appropriate catalyst at a particular pressure and temperature, will form a synthetic liquid product, which is then refined into the useful fuel fractions. The ratio of carbon monoxide to hydrogen, the particular catalyst used, and the pressure and temperature all influence product distribution obtained in the processes. Modifications of the synthesis gas process have been used to manufacture methyl and higher alcohols from combustible waste.

The operating conditions and products of synthesis gas processes are shown in Table XI-3.

Pyrolysis

The thermal distillation of coal into coke, fuel gases, and liquid fuels has been done commercially for many years. Adaptation of these pyrolysis techniques to produce primarily liquid and gaseous products with a wide range of coal types has been pursued by several organizations. Some of the more noteworthy U.S. research efforts have been Project Seacoke, sponsored by ERDA and conducted by

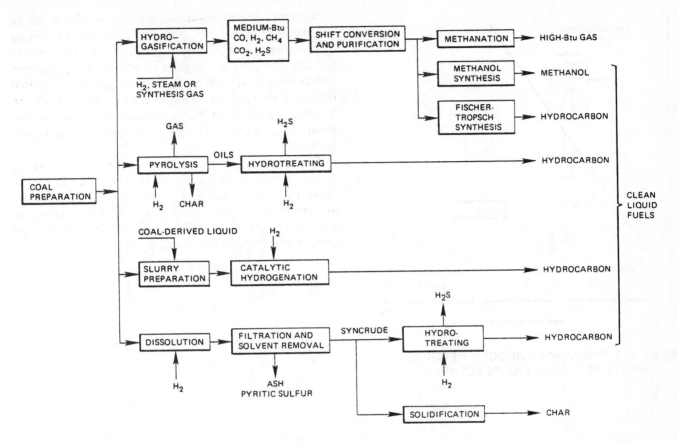

Source: *Energy From Coal, A State-of-the Art Review, U.S. Energy Research and Development Administration, ERDA 76-67.*

Figure XI-2. LIQUID FUELS FROM COAL

the Atlantic Richfield Company; Project COED, sponsored by ERDA and conducted by FMC; TOSCOAL, conducted by The Oil Shale Corporation; and the independent work conducted by Garrett, a subsidiary of Occidental Petroleum Company.

The operating conditions and products of pyrolysis processes are shown in Table XI-4.

Hydrogenation

The direct hydrogenation of coal, either with or without catalysts, appears to be one of the most promising of the evolving synthetic fuel technologies. It seems to offer higher overall thermal efficiencies and, in all probability, lower costs. The Germans used direct hydrogenation much more extensively than either pyrolysis or synthesis gas during World War II. The early German work of Bergius used a process in which pulverized coal and hydrogen were allowed to react in the presence of a catalyst at a particular pressure and temperature. By varying the choice of catalyst, the coal-to-hydrogen ratio, and the operating pressures and temperatures, a liquid product could be obtained approxi-

mating a very heavy fuel oil or a product containing mostly volatile aviation fuel and hydrocarbon gases.

The recent research efforts have all been aimed at improving the conversion yield of the hydrogenation process, in tailoring the catalyst and operating conditions for particular products, and in improving the process economics. Different approaches to the chemical reactor have also been tried. Hydrocarbon Research, Inc. (H-Coal), has used improved catalysts in a fluidized-bed reactor, whereas the U.S. Bureau of Mines (Synthoil) has been using improved catalysts in a fixed-bed reactor. In general, a direct hydrogenation process will yield 3 to 4 barrels of liquid products per ton of coal and should be operational at 70 to 80 percent thermodynamic efficiency.

Both private industry and the U.S. government are sponsoring major direct hydrogenation projects, but most projects are just moving into the pilot plant stages. Based on the present rate of progress, it will be several years before commercialization is achieved.

The operating conditions and products of hydrogenation processes are shown in Table XI-5.

Table XI-2

LIQUEFACTION PROCESSES AND STATUS

Process	Owner or Contractor, Site, and Capacity	Process Description	Status
Bergius	None	Finely ground coal is mixed with process-derived hydrocarbon liquid and a catalyst. The mixture is reacted with hydrogen at 3,000 psi to 10,000 psi. The products from the first reactor are separated into light, middle, and bottom fractions. The middle fraction is further treated over a catalyst in a vapor phase to produce petroleum-like products.	In the 1950s, a large government ammonia plant in Louisiana, Mo., was converted into two liquefaction demonstration plants, one of which used the Bergius process to produce about 200 barrels per day of gasoline. No Bergius plants are currently operating.
Catalytic Coal Liquefaction	Gulf Research and Development Co. 1 ton/day pilot plant	Dried and pulverized coal is mixed with a process-derived oil. The resultant slurry is forced through an arrangement of fixed catalysts by a stream of hydrogen at about 2,000 psi. The liquid product can be used for producing gasoline, diesel fuels, or petrochemical feedstocks.	Gulf Research and Development Co. has been testing this process for 8 years on a bench-scale level. In January 1975, the 1 ton/day pilot plant began operation. It is designed to yield 3 barrels of oil from each ton of MAF coal. A conceptual design of a larger demonstration plant is being prepared based on data from pilot plant operations.
Char-Oil Energy Development (COED)	FMC Corp. Princeton, N.J. 36 ton/day pilot plant	Coal is crushed and dried, then heated to successively higher temperatures in a series of fluidized-bed reactors. The temperature of each bed is just short of the maximum temperature to which coal can be heated without agglomerating and defluidizing the bed. The number of stages and temperatures vary with the agglomerating properties of the coal. The volatile matter released from the coal in the pyrolysis reactor is condensed in a product-recovery system.	The pilot plant has been operational since 1970. Only large-scale gasification of the pyrolysis char product remains to be demonstrated. A preliminary estimate has been made for a 24,000 ton/day COED plant to produce 26,400 barrels of oil per day, 12,000 tons of char per day, and 390 million scf of synthesis gas (400 to 500 Btu/scf) per day.
Clean Coke Process	U.S. Steel Corp. Monroeville, Pa. Five 500 lb/day process development units 100 ton/day pilot plant being designed 17,000 ton/day commercial plant planned	Coal, after beneficiation and sizing in a coal-preparation plant, is split into two fractions: part is processed through a carbonization unit where it is devolatilized, and the remainder is slurried with a process-derived carrier oil and is hydrogenated to convert a large portion of the coal to liquid. The liquid products from both units are converted into low-sulfur liquid fuels, chemical feedstocks, and three oil fractions that are recycled into other areas of the process.	Design and operation of the five 500 lb/day process development units is planned by 1977. Bench-scale studies to aid design and operation of these units are being conducted, and a 100-ton/day pilot plant is being designed. The planned commercial plant will produce, annually, 2.2 million tons of coke, 669,000 tons of oil residue, 750,000 tons of chemical products, 34,000 tons of ammonia, 49,000 tons of sulfur, 80 million gallons benzene, and 8 million gallons of tar products.
Coal-Oil-Gas (COG) (Liquefaction section)	Pittsburg & Midway Coal Mining Co. Merriam, Kansas	Crushed coal is combined with unfiltered solvent to produce a 50 weight percent slurry, which is sent to the preheat furnace. The slurry is combined with	The Ralph M. Parsons Co. was awarded a contract for designing a COG demonstration plant, based on design data supplied by the individual process

Table XI-2

LIQUEFACTION PROCESSES AND STATUS (Cont'd)

Process	Owner or Contractor, Site, and Capacity	Process Description	Status
COG (cont'd)	6 ton/day pilot plant 50 ton/day pilot plant	synthesis gas and water, then fed to the reactor. The solid phase is separated by filtration from a portion of the liquid phase, and is transferred to the gasification plant. The filtrate is fractionated to produce naphtha, distillate that is desulfurized to a ligher boiler fuel, and residual fuel oil. Solid solvent-refined coal can be produced by distillation if required.	developers. This demonstration plant is designed to process 10,000 tons of coal feed per day to produce 2,011 barrels of naphtha, 8,472 barrels of fuel oil, 11,345 barrels of heavy liquid product, 121 tons of heavy liquid plant fuel, 2,142 tons of fuel gas, and 317 tons of sulfur per day.
COGAS	COGAS Development Co. Princeton, N.J. 36 ton/day pyrolysis pilot plant 50 ton/day char heat-carrier pilot plant	Gasification-combustion of coal is integrated with multistage fluidized-bed coal pyrolysis. The products of pyrolysis are a reactive char and pyrolysis oil and gas. The char is sent to the gasifier; the oil can be upgraded by hydrogenation to a high-grade synthetic crude oil or, by using less hydrogen, to a low-sulfur fuel oil.	The pyrolysis section of the process is based on the COED process. The pilot plants at Leatherhead, England, and Princeton have successfully demonstrated most of the key features of the COGAS process, and are providing design data for an 800 to 1,000 ton/day demonstration pilot plant.
Consol Synthetic Fuel (CSF)	Consolidation Coal Co. Cresap, W.V. 20 ton/day pilot plant 900 ton/day demonstration plant planned	Crushed coal is preheated in a fluidized bed to 450° F, then slurried in process-derived solvent. The slurry is pumped to a stirred solvent-extraction vessel where extraction occurs at 765° F and 150 to 400 psi. Recycle solvent, distillate, and liquid product for hydrotreatment to naphtha are produced. Solid residue in a concentrated slurry is sent to a low-temperature carbonization reactor where the slurry is pyrolyzed at 800° F to 900° F and low pressure to recover the solvent and also to produce additional distillate by coking the residue and the extract. In the hydrotreatment section, liquid product from the fractionation step and tar from the carbonization step are hydrogenated in a catalytic reactor operating at 800° F and 3,000 psi to produce naphtha, light oil, gas, and makeup solvent.	This process was tested in the pilot plant from 1967 to 1970. The results were less favorable than predicted, based on bench-scale tests. A detailed assessment of the process indicated that it was technically sound but that major mechanical modifications were necessary to improve operating reliability. In 1974, Fluor Corp. was awarded a 3-year contract to revamp the Cresap pilot plant and supplement existing equipment with new equipment designed to produce fuel oil for power generation and industrial uses. The plant may also be modified to evaluate several coal liquefaction processes for various types of coals.
Exxon Liquefaction	Exxon Research and Engineering Co. Baytown, Texas 0.5 ton/day laboratory unit	Crushed coal is slurried with a recycle solvent, preheated to about 800° F, and pumped into the liquefaction reactor operating at about 2,000 psi. Pretreated hydrogen is also added to the reactor. The product is separated into gas, naphtha, recycle solvent, distillate, and heavy bottoms. The recycle solvent is catalytically hydrogenated and slurried with fresh coal to repeat the cycle.	Laboratory work on this process has been done since 1966. Exxon recently proposed government funding of a planned 200 ton/day plant for demonstrating critical process features.

Table XI-2

LIQUEFACTION PROCESSES AND STATUS (Cont'd)

Process	Owner or Contractor, Site, and Capacity	Process Description	Status
Fischer-Tropsch Synthesis	South African Coal, Oil, and Gas Corp., Ltd. (SASOL) 6,600 ton/day commercial plant 38,000 ton/day commercial plant	In the SASOL Fischer-Tropsch plant, coal is gasified in 13 Lurgi high-pressure, steam-oxygen gasifiers. The gas produced consists primarily of carbon monoxide and hydrogen. The gas is quenched to remove tar and oil and purified by the Rectisol (Lurgi) process. Part of the gas is passed through a fixed-bed catalytic reactor (Arge synthesis). The products are straight-chain high-boiling hydrocarbons with some medium-boiling oils, diesel oil, L.P.G., and oxygenated compounds such as alcohols. The other portion of the gas goes to the Synthol plant (Kellogg synthesis), which is a fluidized-bed catalytic iron reactor. Products are gasoline, alcohol, oil, and gas.	The SASOL plant is the only one producing liquid hydrocarbons from coal-derived synthesis gas using the Fischer-Tropsch process. The plant has been operating since 1955, and produces about 2.5 million tons of petrochemicals per year. A second SASOL plant is planned, and should come on-stream in 1979-1981. This plant should produce about 10 million tons of gasoline per year. In the United States, the Ralph M. Parsons Co. was awarded a 3-year contract in 1974 that includes preliminary design work on a Fischer-Tropsch synthesis plant to produce substitute natural gas and motor fuels. ERDA's R&D program includes the preliminary design of a process development unit to evaluate modifications to the process.
Garrett's Coal Pyrolysis	Garrett Research and Development Co. La Verne, Calif. 3.6 ton/day pilot plant	Crushed coal, in a stream of recycled gas, is pyrolyzed at 1,100° F through contact with hot char from a char heater vessel. Effluent from the pyrolysis reactor is sent to a series of cyclones for separation of gas and entrained char. A portion of the char is cooled as product char. The remaining char is sent to the char heater where a portion is burned with air to heat the contents to 1,400° F. Hot char is cycled to the pyrolysis reactor. Part of the gas from the cyclones is cooled, scrubbed, and sent to a plant for generating hydrogen, which is used in the tar hydrotreater to produce liquid fuels.	Garrett Research and Development Co. has studied pyrolysis and gasification coal for years. Results to date indicate typical yields equal to 200 percent Fischer assay and significantly higher than fluidized-bed pyrolysis processes.
H-Coal	Hydrocarbon Research, Inc. (HRI) Trenton, N.J. 3 ton/day process development unit 600 ton/day pilot plant planned	Dried, pulverized coal is slurried with process-derived oil, then compressed hydrogen is added. The mixture is heated and fed to an ebullated-bed catalytic reactor. Vapor product from the reactor is cooled and cleaned to separate the heavier components as liquid. Light hydrocarbons, ammonia, and hydrogen sulfide are absorbed from the gas stream and sent to a separator and sulfur-recovery unit. Liquid-solid product from the reactor is fed into a flash separator. Material that boils off is distilled to produce light and heavy distillates. The bottoms product from the flash separator (solids and heavy oil) is further separated in a vacuum still to produce heavy distillates and residual fuel oil.	HRI has been developing the H-Coal process since 1964, based on experience with the H-Oil process. Various plant options and systems have been developed and tested. The cost of the 600 ton/day demonstration pilot plant is expected to exceed $80 million; the government will provide two-thirds of the project cost.

Table XI-2

LIQUEFACTION PROCESSES AND STATUS (Cont'd)

Process	Owner or Contractor, Site, and Capacity	Process Description	Status
Intermediate Hydrogenation	University of Utah Salt Lake City, Utah 50 lb/hour bench-scale unit 5-10 ton/day pilot plant designed	Dry, pulverized coal is passed with catalyst stannous or zinc chloride into a reactor containing hydrogen at 2,000 to 2,500 psi. The coal is hydrogenated, and liquid fuels and gases are produced.	Successful research and development work on the process was conducted between 1969 and 1974. The University has also experimented (bench-scale) on catalytic hydrosolvation of coal and lignite to synthetic crude in a single step.
Project SEACOKE	ARCO Chemical Co. Philadelphia, Pa. Laboratory unit 10,000 barrel/day pilot plant designed	Coal, usually blended with petroleum residuum as part of the feedstock, is pyrolyzed in multistage fluidized beds to produce char, liquids, fuels, and gas. After separation of the phases, the liquid products are further catalytically hydrotreated to produce gasoline. The gas can be used in the process or sold, and the char can be used for power generation on site.	This project was operational under government sponsorship during the 1960s. A 10,000 barrel/day plant was designed for converting coal and residual fuel oil to char, syncrude, and fuel gas. In 1970, the final report on the project was issued.
Solvent-Refined Coal (SRC)	Pittsburgh & Midway Coal Mining Co. (PAMCO) Merriam, Kansas 50 lb/hour continuous flow process development unit 6 ton/day pilot plant 50 ton/day pilot plant 1,000 ton/day demonstration plant planned	Pulverized coal is slurried with coal-derived solvent, then hydrogen (produced by other steps in the process) is added. The mixture is pumped through a fired preheater and passed into a dissolver where about 90 percent of the MAF coal is dissolved. Gas is then separated from the slurry of undissolved solids and coal solution. The raw gas is sent to a hydrogen-recovery and gas-desulfurization unit. The undissolved solids are separated from the coal solution in a filtration unit. The coal solution passes to the solvent recovery unit and the final liquid product, solvent-refined coal, is produced.	Beginning in 1972, Spencer Chemical Co. (subsequently PAMCO) conducted bench-scale evaluation of the Pott-Broche process to find a clean fuel. The project has continued at an accelerated pace and much interest has been shown by both government and private companies. In 1974, Wheelabrator-Frye announced plans for a 1,000 ton/day demonstration plant costing $80 million. If successful, the plant can be expanded, over 3 years at a cost of about $350 million, to 10,000 tons/day.
Synthoil	U.S. Bureau of Mines, Pittsburgh Energy Research Center Pittsburgh, Pa. 5 lb/hour bench-scale unit 0.5 ton/day pilot plant 8-10 ton/day pilot plant under construction	Pulverized, dried coal is slurried with recycled oil. The slurry is pumped into a catalytic, fixed-bed reactor with hydrogen at high velocity to create turbulent flow conditions. The reactor is filled with immobilized catalyst pellets composed of cobalt molybdate on silica-activated alumina. The hydrogen, turbulent flow conditions, and catalytic action combine to liquefy and desulfurize the coal. The product passes through a high-pressure receiver where gas is separated and recycled after ammonia and hydrogen sulfide are removed. The raw oil is	Progressing from a bench-scale unit and a small pilot plant, the Bureau of Mines awarded a $6.9 million contract to Foster Wheeler Corp. to procure equipment and construct an 8 to 10 ton/day pilot plant (producing 1,000 gallons of fuel oil per day). Bethlehem Steel Corp. will contribute $1.1 million to the plant's cost and $0.5 million for further research, and will operate the pilot plant for 2 years. If the project is successful, a 700 ton/day plant will probably be constructed.

Table XI-2

LIQUEFACTION PROCESSES AND STATUS (Cont'd)

Process	Owner or Contractor, Site, and Capacity	Process Description	Status
Synthoil (cont'd)	700 ton/day demonstration plant being designed	centrifuged to remove ash and unreacted coal, providing a low-sulfur, low-ash fuel oil.	
Toscoal	The Oil Shale Corp. (TOSCO), Rocky Flats Research Center Golden, Colorado 25 ton/day pilot plant	Preheated coal from a dilute-phase fluidized bed is fed to a pyrolysis vessel where it is contacted with heated ceramic balls. The char produced in this reactor is screened, cooled, and stockpiled. The cooled ceramic balls pass over the screen and are reheated. The vaporized products of the pyrolysis step are condensed and fractionated. Offgas (600 Btu/scf) from the condensor can be used as a fuel gas heating the ceramic balls or processed for sale.	TOSCO has investigated the Toscoal process since 1970, drawing on experience and development work associated with the TOSCO II process for oil-shale retorting. The TOSCO II process was field tested in a 1,000 ton/day pilot plant, and construction engineering is under way on a 66,000 ton/day commercial oil-shale plant. The Toscoal process will probably parallel development of the TOSCO II process in the future.

Sources: I. Howard-Smith and G. J. Werner, *Coal Conversion Technology: A Review*, 1975.
Energy From Coal, A State-of-the-Art Review, U.S. Energy Research and Development Administration, ERDA 76-67.
Fossil Energy Research Program of the Energy Research and Development Administration, FY 1977, ERDA 76-63.

Table XI-3

SYNTHESIS GAS PROCESS

Process	Reactor Bed Type	Temperature (°F)	Pressure (psig)	Reactants	Products
Fischer-Tropsch Synthesis					
M. W. Kellogg (SASOL)	Fluidized-bed catalytic	620	330	Synthesis gas Iron catalyst	Gasoline, alcohol, oil, gas
Arge-Arbeit (SASOL)	Fixed-bed catalytic	450	360	Synthesis gas Iron/cobalt catalyst	Gasoline, L.P.G., oil, wax, gas

Source: I. Howard-Smith and G. J. Werner, *Coal Conversion Technology: A Review,* 1975.

Table XI-4

PYROLYSIS PROCESSES

Process	Reactor Bed Type	Temperature (°F)	Pressure (psig)	Reactants	Products
Char-Oil Energy Development (COED)	Fluidized bed No. 1	600	5—10	Coal Heat	Char, oil, gas, liquor
(FMC Corp.)	No. 2	850	5—10		
	No. 3	1,000	5—10		
	No. 4	1,500	5—10		
COGAS (COGAS Development Company)	Four fluidized beds	600—1,500	5—10	Coal Heat	Char, oil, gas, liquor
Garrett's Coal Pyrolysis (Garrett Research and Development Company)	Pyrolyzer	1,100	Atmospheric	Coal Hot char	Tar, product char, gas
Project SEACOKE (ARCO Chemical Company)	Flue fluidized beds	600—1,600	Atmospheric	Coal Heat	Char, gas, oil
TOSCOAL (TOSCO)	Pyrolyzer	800—1,000	Atmospheric	Coal Heat	Char, gas, oil

Source: I. Howard-Smith and G. J. Werner, *Coal Conversion Technology: A Review,* 1975.

Table XI-5

HYDROGENATION PROCESSES

Process	Process Type	Temperature (°F)	Pressure (psig)	Reactants	Products
Bergius (F. Bergius)	Solution Hydrogenation (Iron-oxide catalyst)	900	3,000–10,000	Coal Recycle oil Hydrogen	Light oils
Catalytic Coal Liquefaction (Gulf Research and Development Company)	Fixed-bed catalytic	900	2,000	Coal Oil Hydrogen	Synthetic crude oil, gas
Clean-Coke Process (U.S. Steel Corp.)	Carbonization	1,200–1,400	100		Liquid products, gas, char for coker
	Extraction Hydrogenation	900	3,000–4,000		Liquid products, gas, filter cake for gasifier
Coal-Oil-Gas (COG) (Pittsburg & Midway Coal Mining Company)	Extraction Hydrogenation	850	1,000	Coal slurry Synthesis gas Water	Naphtha, fuel, oil, SRC, fuel gas
Consol Synthetic Fuel (CSF) (Consolidation Coal Company)	Extraction Carbonization Hydrotreatment	765 925 800	150–400 10 3,000		Vapors, liquids, residue Char, pyrolysis, liquid, gas Naphtha, oil, gas, residue
Exxon Liquefaction (Exxon Research and Engineering Company)	Catalytic Hydrogenation	800	2,000	Coal H-Donor solvent Hydrogen	Naphtha, gas, distillate, heavy bottoms, recycle solvent
H-Coal (Hydrocarbon Research, Inc.)	Ebullated-bed catalytic	850	2,250–2,700	Coal Oil Hydrogen	Synthetic crude oil, gas
Intermediate Hydrogenation (University of Utah)	Entrained-flow catalytic	930–1,020	2,000–2,500	Coal Hydrogen	Liquid, gas
Solvent-Refined Coal (SRC) (Pittsburgh & Midway Coal Mining Company)	Dissolver	815	1,000	Coal Hydrogen Solvent	Solvent-refined coal
Synthoil (U.S. Bureau of Mines, Pittsburgh Energy Research Center)	Fixed-bed catalytic	850	2,000–4,000	Coal Hydrogen Oil	Fuel oil, gas

Source: I. Howard-Smith and G. J. Werner, *Coal Conversion Technology: A Review*, 1975.

SECTION NINE

NUCLEAR ENERGY

INTRODUCTION

The generation of power from nuclear reactions is accomplished by two quite distinct processes. The first (and most highly developed) is nuclear fission. In the fission process, heavy nuclei such as those of uranium and plutonium atoms are split into lighter nuclei by neutron absorption. The splitting of the heavy nuclei results in the release of additional neutrons (which sustain the fission process) and the conversion of a small fraction of mass into kinetic energy of the fission products. The kinetic energy is degraded into thermal energy and the fission process acts simply as a heat source used to make steam to generate electric power.

Although the basic process is conceptually simple, the engineering, control, and safety considerations make fission utilization a highly sophisticated industry requiring the integration of a great many technologies. As a result of the continuing development of each of the technologies involved and of each electric utility's special problems, there is little standardization of commercial nuclear power plants. On the other hand, there has been some degree of standardization in nuclear reactors for naval propulsion because of the specific requirements of marine propulsion systems and their space and structural limitations. Both commercial power generation and naval propulsion systems are discussed further in this chapter.

The second process for using nuclear reactions for power generation is fusion. Fusion is much the opposite of fission in that light nuclei such as those of the hydrogen isotopes deuterium and tritium are combined (or fused) into heavier nuclei such as those of helium. This is the process that occurs within the sun. Again, a small amount of mass is converted into kinetic energy that can be degraded into useful thermal energy. The process is conceptually simple but technically difficult because fusion can occur only under the stringent conditions of ultrahigh temperatures $(100,000,000° K)$ for the appropriate fuel confinement time and density.

Basically two approaches are being taken to achieve the conditions necessary for fusion. The first is magnetic confinement of a heated plasma. Several magnetic configurations are under investigation with fusion temperatures now attainable. The second approach to fusion is production of microexplosions that can be achieved by subjecting pellets of a deuterium-tritium mixture to intense bombardment by electron beams or by laser beams. Again, the necessary temperatures can be reached.

Power generation by means of fusion is not a near-term possibility. Many basic problems remain to be solved that will require substantial private and public investments in research.

NUCLEAR POWER GROWTH

Most of the commercial nuclear electric energy generating capacity in the United States is based on light water reactor (LWR) systems. As of June 30, 1976, there were 32 pressurized water reactors (PWR), 23 boiling water reactors (BWR) and one light water cooled, graphite moderated reactor (LGR) in commercial operation in the United States.[1] The total capacity of these plants was 39,030 MWe or about 8.5 percent of the total electric generating capacity in the United States. The growth rate for nuclear power is a function of the economic conditions of the utilities and of possible delays. Delays encountered by the electric utilities have stemmed from environmental objections, complex licensing procedures, and construction and supply limitations. Table XII-1 presents three estimates of nuclear power capacity in the United States through 2000, with the actual installed capacities for 1960 and 1970 listed.

For comparison, the 1974 year-end installed commercial nuclear capacity was 31,214 MWe and was 36,452 MWe for 1975.[2] The ability to meet nuclear capacity projections depends greatly upon the introduction of several new types of reactors. The reason for this limitation is the finite amount of uranium available from which the light water reactor fuel is obtained. The two most widely discussed alternative reactors are the liquid metal fast breeder reactor (LMFBR) and the high-temperature, gas-cooled reactor (HTGR). Both of these reactors can greatly extend the resource base. The United States has a demonstrated capacity for producing both of these reactors; one HTGR is commercially operational. The U.S. experience with LMFBRs dates back to 1946, and the first electric energy was produced by this kind of reactor in 1951.[3]

[1] *Nuclear News,* August 1976.
[2] *Nuclear News Buyers Guide,* Mid-February 1975, pp. 45-56 and Mid-February 1976, pp. 52-64.

[3] Draft Environmental Statement Liquid Metal Fast Breeder Reactor Program, U.S. Atomic Energy Commission WASH-1535, 1974.

Table XII-1

YEAR-END PROJECTED NUCLEAR CAPACITY
(Thousands of MWe)

Estimate	1960	1970	1975	1980	1985	1990	2000
High	0.02	5.8	39	71	166	290	620
Medium	0.02	5.8	39	67	145	250	510
Low	0.02	5.8	39	60	127	195	380

Source: *Information from ERDA,* Vol. 2, No. 45, November 26, 1976.

THE NUCLEAR FUEL CYCLE

The use of nuclear fuels differs from fossil fuels in two important ways:

- Before it can be used, the fuel must undergo a complex series of processing and fabrication steps to produce useful fuel elements.
- Nuclear fuels are not completely expended when used in a reactor but are removed, purified, replenished, and refabricated periodically.

These unique characteristics establish a fuel cycle that includes exploration, mining, milling, conversion, enrichment, fabrication, recovery and reprocessing, transportation, and waste disposal. Figure XII-1 shows fuel cycles for the LWR, HTGR, and LMFBR. In each case, ERDA and the nuclear industry attempt to optimize the fuel cycle from the long-range economic point of view.

Uranium 235, U-233, and plutonium 239 are the three fissile materials capable of serving as fuels in fission reactors. Of these, only U-235 occurs naturally. The other two can be produced or bred from the fertile materials thorium 232 and U-238 by neutron absorption. Uranium, as it occurs naturally, is 99.284 percent U-238, 0.711 percent U-235, and 0.005 percent U-234. Although reactors such as the Canadian CANDU can operate on natural uranium, the LWRs in use in the United States are designed to operate on uranium that is 2.0 to 3.2 percent U-235.[1]

The fuel cycle for LWRs starts with the mining and milling of uranium ore to obtain yellowcake (U_3O_8). The yellowcake is shipped from the mill to a conversion plant where it is converted into uranium hexafluoride (UF_6), a solid at room temperatures. The UF_6 is shipped to an ERDA-operated enrichment facility where the ratio of the uranium isotopes (U-235 and U-238) is changed. The portion of the UF_6 that contains a higher than natural percentage (or assay) of U-235 is the enriched uranium and the portion that contains the lower assay is the de-

pleted uranium (or tails). The enriched uranium is sent to a fuel fabrication plant where the UF_6 is converted into uranium oxide (UO_2) powder and compacted into small cylindrical pellets. The fuel assembly consists of precisely aligned cylinders that contain the fuel pellets. In this form the uranium is ready for use in a reactor. Periodically (usually once a year) LWRs are shut down and refueled. At that time, 25 to 35 percent of the fuel is replaced. The spent fuel is intensely radioactive and is stored at the power plant site for several months before shipping to a reprocessing plant. The spent fuel contains, in addition to U-235 and U-238, isotopes of plutonium and other radioactive materials. The reprocessing procedure separates the uranium and plutonium from the spent fuel and prepares the remaining wastes for storage. The uranium is still slightly enriched (0.84 to 0.94 percent) and is shipped back to the enrichment plant for recycling.

In the LWR fuel cycle shown in Figure XII-1, the dashed line indicates the path the plutonium would follow if it were to be recycled for use as LWR fuel. At the present time, plutonium is stockpiled for its anticipated future use in both LWRs and LMFBRs. The Nuclear Regulatory Commission (NRC) has proposed to announce its position on plutonium recycle early in 1977.[2]

The HTGR fuel cycle in Figure XII-1 is based on the use of both thorium and uranium. The uranium used as a fuel in the HTGR is highly enriched (93.15 percent U-235) and is in the form of uranium carbide (UC_2). Excess neutrons from the U-235 fission are absorbed by the thorium nuclei in ThC_2 and U-233 produced. The U-233 is fissile and serves as a fuel for the HTGR.

---

[1] *Nuclear Power Growth 1974-2000*, U.S. Atomic Energy Commission, WASH-1139, 1974.

[2] *Weekly Energy Report*, November 12, 1975.

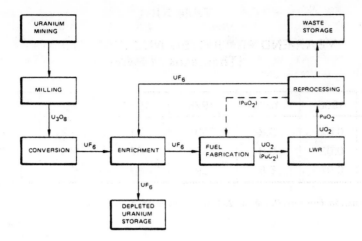

LIGHT WATER REACTOR FUEL CYCLE

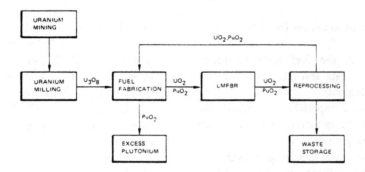

LIQUID METAL FAST BREEDER REACTOR FUEL CYCLE

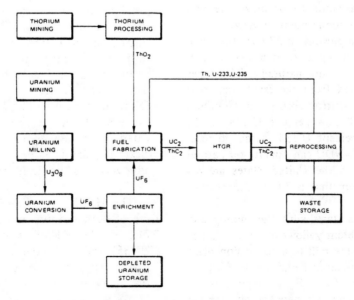

HIGH TEMPERATURE, GAS-COOLED REACTOR FUEL CYCLE

Figure XII-1. LWR, LMFBR, AND HTGR FUEL CYCLES

The LMFBR fuel cycle in Figure XII-1 uses plutonium as a fuel. The U-238 in the natural uranium that serves as the resource base provides the fertile material from which the plutonium is bred. The unique feature of the LMFBR fuel cycle is that more plutonium is bred from the U-238 than is consumed in the reactor. In the sense that plutonium is the fissioning material, more fuel is produced than consumed and the excess plutonium can be used for other reactors such as the light water reactor.

U.S. URANIUM AND THORIUM RESOURCES

The resource base of uranium and thorium for the nuclear industry is commonly expressed in terms of tons of the resource recoverable at a given cost. Recent estimates of the size of the U.S. nuclear resources are shown in Tables XII-2 and XII-3. The exact extent of thorium deposits is not well known, but thorium is probably a more abundant resource than uranium.

It has been estimated that unconventional supplies of uranium present in the United States could be recovered at costs of $100/lb U_3O_8. These include 2,700,000 tons in very low grade ore and an additional 2,500,000 tons in Chattanooga shale. Also, uranium may be recovered from seawater (0.0033 ppm U) at a recovery cost of approximately $300/lb U_3O_8.[1]

[1] *Nuclear News*, July 1975, p. 37.

Table XII-2
U.S. URANIUM RESOURCES
(Thousands of tons U_3O_8)

Recovery Cost	Reserves	Probable	Possible	Speculative
to $10/lb	270	440	420	145
to $15/lb	430	655	675	290
to $30/lb	640	1,060	1,270	590
Byproduct*	140			

*Byproduct of phosphate and copper production.

Source: *Information from ERDA*,
    Vol. 2, No. 13, April 9, 1976, pp. 5-6.

Table XII-3
U.S. THORIUM RESERVES

Recovery Cost ($/lb)	Reasonably Assured Reserves (Tons ThO_2)
to $10	65,500
to $30	200,000
to $50	3,200,000

Source: *Draft Environmental Statement LMFBR Program*, U.S. Atomic Energy Commission, WASH-1535, 1974.

U.S. ANNUAL DEMAND

The annual demand for yellowcake (U_3O_8) depends on the types of reactors in operation, the availability or unavailability of reprocessing facilities and the plutonium recycle, and the assay of the depleted uranium at the enrichment facilities. Table XII-4 presents a variety of projections of uranium requirements for different nuclear power development cases and various assumptions about the fuel cycle. Cases B and D assume that the Barnwell, S.C., reprocessing facility will begin operation in 1981 and will reach a capacity of 1,500 metric tons per year in 1982. (In cases B and D recovered uranium and plutonium are recycled to LWRs after reprocessing unless the plutonium is required by breeder reactors.) It is assumed additional reprocessing facilities will become available as needed. Cases C and E assume that the Barnwell plant begins pilot operations in 1985 and reaches a capacity of 1,000 metric tons per year in 1986. (In cases C and E recovered uranium is recycled, but the plutonium is used only in breeders.)

At the end of 1973, there were 15 U_3O_8 mills in operation or on standby in the United States with a total capacity of 28,450 tons of U_3O_8 per year.[1] In 1975, the production of yellowcake was 12,300 tons with primary uranium demand for nuclear fuels estimated at 15,600 tons.[2] Because of the projections of demand for yellowcake, the existing mining and milling capacity will be exceeded by the late 1970s.

As a result of supply and demand for uranium, the price of yellowcake has doubled in the last year. At the

[1] *Statistical Data of the Uranium Industry*, U.S. Atomic Energy Commission, GJO-100, 1974.
[2] *Commodity Data Summaries 1976*, Bureau of Mines, U.S. Department of Interior, January 1976, p. 182.

Table XII-4

U.S. URANIUM REQUIREMENTS
(Thousands of short tons of U_3O_8)

Tails Assay	Case A			Case B			Case C		
	0.20%	0.25%	0.35%	0.20%	0.25%	0.30%	0.20%	0.25%	0.30%
1976	10	11	12	11	12	13	11	12	13
1980	17	18	20	19	20	22	19	20	22
1985	29	32	35	31	34	37	36	39	43
1990	43	47	52	41	45	50	55	60	66
2000	74	81	89	65	71	80	82	90	99

Tails Assay	Case D			Case E		
	0.20%	0.25%	0.30%	0.20%	0.25%	0.30%
1976	12	13	14	12	13	14
1980	22	24	26	22	24	26
1985	36	40	44	42	45	50
1990	51	56	62	65	71	78
2000	74	82	92	86	94	105

Case A: Low projection Table XII-1; no recycle of uranium or plutonium.
Case B: Medium projection Table XII-1; uranium and plutonium recycled on constrained basis.
Case C: Medium projection Table XII-1; limited uranium recycle; plutonium not recycled in LWRs.
Case D: High projection Table XII-1; uranium and plutonium recycled on constrained basis.
Case E: High projection Table XII-1; limited uranium recycle; plutonium not recycled in LWRs.

Source: *Information from ERDA,* Vol. 2, No. 46, November 26, 1976.

end of 1975, the price of yellowcake was $30/lb for immediate delivery with a price of $40/lb for delivery in 1980.[1] However, the capital-intensive nature of the nuclear industry makes the cost of power produced almost independent of uranium costs. A $10/lb increase in the price of yellowcake increases the total fuel cycle cost about 0.8 mills/kWh.[2] Also, uranium supplies have been commited to long-term procurement contracts within the nuclear industry so that the spot price is not an accurate indicator of actual costs to the buyer. The future estimated average delivery prices under contract as of July 1, 1976 are shown in Table XII-5. The prices are for purchases contracted for from 1967 through mid-1976 and do not represent prices at which uranium can be purchased now for delivery in the future. Since the delivery commitments for future years cover only a fraction of projected requirements, the average prices for those years will change as additional uranium is contracted for.

Table XII-5

AVERAGE U_3O_8 PRICES FOR PROCUREMENT CONTRACTS

Year	Price/lb U_3O_8[a]	Delivery Commitments (tons U_3O_8)
1976	$12.05	14,900
1977	12.60	13,800
1978	14.30	17,300
1979	16.10	18,000
1980	15.95	17,400
1981	18.60	16,000
1982	19.85	15,800
1983	19.80	12,600
1984	19.55	10,200
1985	19.90	7,900
1976-1985		143,900

[a]Current dollars.

Source: *Information from ERDA,* Vol. 2, No. 44, November 12, 1976, pp. 1-2.

[1] *Nuclear News Buyers Guide,* Mid-February 1976, p. 38.
[2] "Task Force Report on Nuclear Energy," *Project Independence,* November 1974.

CONVERSION, ENRICHMENT, AND FABRICATION

Conversion

Conversion of the yellowcake (U_3O_8) to uranium hexafluoride (UF_6) takes place at two plants in the United States. These plants can process 22,400 tons per year of yellowcake and produce 28,100 tons per year of UF_6. Planned expansion of an existing facility and the construction of a new plant will double the U.S. conversion capacity.[1] The costs of conversion amount to about 1.5 percent of the cost of the total fuel cycle and have little effect on the cost of power produced.

Enrichment

Enrichment is a major component of the fuel cycle. ERDA operates three gaseous diffusion plants that take UF_6 from conversion plants and reprocessing plants and alter the isotopic mixture of U-235 and U-238. The gaseous diffusion process is both capital and power intensive. It is common practice to measure the capacity and productivity of the enrichment process in terms of separative work units. A separative work unit (SWU) is a measure of the effort expended in the plant to separate a quantity of uranium of a given assay into two components, one having a higher percentage of U-235 and one having a lower percentage. Separative work is generally expressed in kilograms to give it the same dimension as material quantities. However, it is common practice to refer to a kilogram SWU simply as an SWU. For example, if a single kilogram of uranium enriched to 3.0 percent U-235 were produced starting with natural uranium (0.711 percent U-235) and with depleted (or tails) uranium of 0.275 percent U-235, then 3.6 SWU would be required. If there was any change in the feed assay, the tails assay or the enrichment assay, the number of SWU would change. For the example cited, 6.25 kilograms of natural uranium are needed to produce a single kilogram of 3.0 percent enriched uranium.[2] Lowering the tails assay would decrease the demand for natural uranium but would increase the separation work required. ERDA operates its diffusion plants at 0.25 percent tails assay.[3]

The three enrichment plants—located at Oak Ridge, Tennessee; Paducah, Kentucky; and Portsmouth, Ohio—operate interdependently with the complex having a capacity of 17.2 million SWU per year in 1973. Operating at full capacity, the three plants consume 6,000 MWe. Because the demand for enrichment services will grow with the nuclear power industry, ERDA is pursuing two programs to increase the diffusion plant capacities. The Cascade Improvement Program (CIP) will increase capacity by 33 percent, and the Cascade Uprating Program (CUP) will raise that another 21 percent for a total capacity of 27.7 million SWU per year by 1980. At this capacity, the power demand of the complex will be about 7,400 MWe.[4]

Because of the limitations on electric power available, the enrichment facilities have been operating well below full capacity. The FY 1972 and FY 1973 power levels and production levels and the projected FY 1974 figures for the enrichment plants are shown in Table XII-6. Full production will not be achieved until about 1978.

The projected demands for separative work are shown in Table XII-7. These projections were made assuming a 0.30 percent tails assay with plutonium recycle in 1977. Without plutonium recycle, the demand for enrichment services will increase.

The current cost of enrichment is \$61.30/SWU for fixed-commitment, long-term contracts and \$66.75/SWU for requirements-type contracts. The cost of enrichment had been \$59.05/SWU for fixed-commitment contracts before October 1, 1976 and \$42.10/SWU before August 20, 1975. The price of requirements-type contracts will have increased to \$69.80/SWU on January 27, 1977.[5] By 1981, ERDA plans to increase the cost of enrichment services to about \$76/SWU.[6] An increase from \$42 to \$76/SWU increases the fuel cycle costs by about 0.9 mills/kWh.[6]

ERDA plans an expansion of its Portsmouth, Ohio, gaseous diffusion plant. After completion of CIP and CUP in 1981, the capacity will have been increased from 5.2 to 8.4 million SWU per year. The proposed increase in plant size will add 8.75 million SWU per year by the mid-1980s and will require 3,500 to 3,700 MWe of additional power.[7]

The future expansion of enrichment facilities in the United States is a matter of Congressional debate. Several proposals have been made by private industry to enter the enrichment market.

Two alternatives to gaseous diffusion are under investigation in the United States. The first, the gaseous centrifuge, is at the pilot-plant stage. This process consumes only 10 percent of the power of a gaseous diffusion plant

[1] "Task Force Report on Nuclear Energy," *Project Independence*, November 1974, and *Nuclear News*, April 1974.
[2] *AEC Gaseous Diffusion Plant Operations*, U.S. Atomic Energy Commission, ORO-684, 1972.
[3] *Energy Daily*, September 9, 1976.
[4] "Task Force Report on Nuclear Energy," *Project Independence*, November 1974 and Vincent V. Abajian and Alan M. Fishman, "Supplying Enriched Uranium," *Physics Today*, August 1973, pp. 23-29.
[5] *Information from ERDA*, Vol. 2, No. 30, August 6, 1976.
[6] "Task Force Report on Nuclear Energy," *Project Independence*, November 1974.
[7] *Information from ERDA*, Vol. 2, No. 41, October 22, 1976.

Table XII-6

ENRICHMENT OPERATIONS

	MWe	Million SWU
FY 1972	2626	8.4
FY 1973	3227	10.3
FY 1974	4069	12.7

Source: *The Nuclear Industry, 1973,* U.S. Atomic Energy Commission WASH-1174-73 UC-2.

Table XII-7

ANNUAL SEPARATIVE WORK DEMAND
(Million SWU)

	1974	1977	1980	1985	1990	2000
High	4.6	7.2	13.9	28.5	53.4	97.4
Reasonable	3.3	7.2	14.1	26.4	46.0	84.0
Low	2.5	6.2	11.3	23.0	36.3	57.4

Source: *Nuclear Power Growth 1974-2000,* U.S. Atomic Energy Commission, WASH-1139, 1974.

for the same separative work and has been demonstrated to be effective in both the United States and Europe. The second is isotope separation by lasers. This is still in the experimental stage and can only be considered to be a possible long-term enrichment method.

Fabrication

There are five operating fuel fabrication plants in the United States with a total capacity of 3,025 tons of uranium per year. Industry plans will add a capacity of 6,000 tons of uranium per year by 1980.[1] The fabrication facilities convert the UF_6 from the enrichment plant to UO_2. The UO_2 is formed into pellets and sintered before loading into zircaloy or stainless steel tubes which are welded shut. The completed fuel rods are assembled into fuel element arrays before shipping to a nuclear power plant.

[1] "Task Force Report on Nuclear Energy," *Project Independence,* November 1974.

NUCLEAR REACTORS

Both the boiling water reactor (BWR) and the pressurized water reactor (PWR) are fueled with slightly enriched UO_2 and are cooled by ordinary water. In the BWR, the pressure is maintained at about 1,000 psig and steam is generated in the primary coolant loop at 545° F. The steam is passed directly through a turbine to drive an electric generator. In the PWR, the pressure in the reactor vessel is maintained at 2,050 psig and the water does not boil. The heated water passes through steam generators where the heat is transferred to water in a secondary loop at lower pressures and steam is formed for driving the turbines. Simplified diagrams of BWR and PWR systems are shown in Figure XII-2. Some of the significant characteristics of these reactor systems appear in Table XII-8.

The high-temperature gas-cooled reactor (HTGR) diagrammed in Figure XII-3 operates on the U-233, Th-232 cycle. The primary coolant is helium, which passes through the reactor core consisting of a mixed UC_2, ThC_2 fuel. The present generation of HTGRs is designed so that the helium coolant transfers the heat of reaction to a steam generator. The primary coolant reaches 1,400° F and the steam is generated at 950° F and 2,400 psig. The high operating temperatures of the HTGR give it a thermal efficiency of nearly 40 percent. If a direct-cycle, helium-driven turbine is developed, the efficiency could be increased to as much as 50 percent.[1] Because of the slowed growth rate of the electric power industry, most of the HTGRs that were on order have been cancelled and the HTGR has yet to demonstrate economic feasibility. One of the advantages of the HTGR over the BWR and PWR is its lower demand for natural uranium. (See Table XII-8.)

The liquid metal fast breeder reactor (LMFBR)[2] is being developed because of the limited size of the uranium resource base. The LMFBR utilizes a high percentage of the energy potentially available in the uranium. Light water reactors and HTGRs use only 1 to 2 percent

[1] *Draft Environmental Statement Liquid Metal Fast Breeder Reactor Program,* U.S. Atomic Energy Commission WASH-1535, 1974.
[2] In nuclear reactor terminology the term "fast" designates that the neutrons on the average have high velocities (i.e. fast neutron spectrum); slow (or thermal) neutrons have low velocities.

Table XII-8

NUCLEAR REACTOR CHARACTERISTICS[a]

Characteristic	BWR	PWR	HTGR	LMFBR
Thermal efficiency (percent)	34	33	40	40
Raw material demand U_3O_8 (tons)	180	190	100	1.62[b]
Raw material demand ThO_2 (tons)			8.6	
Enrichment demand[c] (SWU)	84000	94000	67000	
Fresh fuel assay (percent U-235)	2.7	3.2	93	
Spent fuel assay (percent U-235)	0.8	0.9		
Reprocessing demand (tons)	30	27	11	21
Plutonium production (tons)	0.18	0.19		0.31
Primary loop pressure (psig)	1000	2050	700	200
Primary loop temperature (°F)	545	600	1400	1000
Steam loop pressure (psig)	d	800	2400	1450
Steam loop temperature (°F)	d	500	950	900

[a]For 1000 MWe plant, steady state conditions, 75 percent plant factor, no plutonium recycle except in LMFBR.
[b]Uranium feed can consist of depleted tails in stockpile, no enrichment needed.
[c]Tails assay 0.30 percent.
[d]There is no secondary loop for a BWR.

Sources: *Nuclear Power Growth 1974-2000*, U.S. Atomic Energy Commission, WASH-1139, 1974; *AEC Gaseous Diffusion Plant Operations*, U.S. Atomic Energy Commission, ORO-684, 1972; *The Nuclear Industry 1973*, U.S. Atomic Energy Commission, WASH-1174-73 UC-2; and *Draft Environmental Statement Liquid Metal Fast Breeder Reactor Program*, U.S. Atomic Energy Commission, WASH-1535, 1974.

of the available energy while the LMFBR is designed to use 60 to 70 percent of that energy. As indicated in Table XII-8, the demand for U_3O_8 for the breeder is about one hundredth of that for LWRs. This breeder reactor uses sodium as the primary coolant. A secondary sodium loop is used to transfer heat from the primary loop to the steam loop. The overall thermal efficiency of the LMFBR is expected to be about 40 percent.

The pressurized water reactor is generally accepted as the preferred nuclear power conversion system for ship propulsion. Nuclear reactors have proven successful in terms of safety and reliability on both submarines and surface ships. The U.S. Maritime Administration operated the *USS Savannah* from 1962 to 1970 to demonstrate the feasibility of commercial nuclear-powered vessels. The

reactor was a PWR that generated 20,000 shaft horsepower. Currently, there is only one operating commercial nuclear ship, the West German 10,000 shaft horsepower *Otto Hahn*. It uses an advanced PWR termed the Consolidated Nuclear Steam Generator (CNSG) in which the primary coolant flow is entirely within the reactor pressure vessel.[1] Economics in the maritime industry do not support commercial development of fleets of nuclear merchant ships.

[1] *The Nuclear Industry, 1973*, U.S. Atomic Energy Commission, WASH-1174-73 UC-2, and R. A. Grams, W. L. Sage, and G. W. Geyer, "Fuels for Marine Steam Propulsion," The Society of Marine Port Engineers 22nd Annual Fort Schuyler Forum, March 1974.

REPROCESSING AND WASTE MANAGEMENT

During reprocessing of spent fuel from nuclear power plants, the usable fissile materials are recovered and the waste materials are separated for storage. For a light water reactor, the recovered uranium is still slightly enriched and is shipped to an enrichment facility where it

serves as feedstock. For each ton of uranium reprocessed, approximately 3 grams of plutonium are recovered and stored.

No fuel reprocessing plants are in commerical operation, and power plants are storing spent fuel at their plant

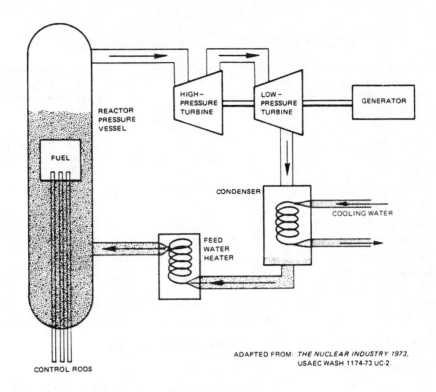

ADAPTED FROM: *THE NUCLEAR INDUSTRY 1973,*
USAEC WASH 1174-73 UC-2.

BOILING WATER REACTOR

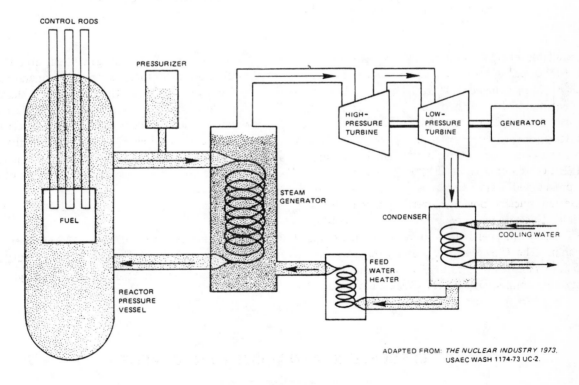

ADAPTED FROM: *THE NUCLEAR INDUSTRY 1973,*
USAEC WASH 1174-73 UC-2.

PRESSURIZED WATER REACTOR

**Figure XII-2. SCHEMATIC DIAGRAMS FOR BOILING WATER
AND PRESSURIZED WATER REACTORS**

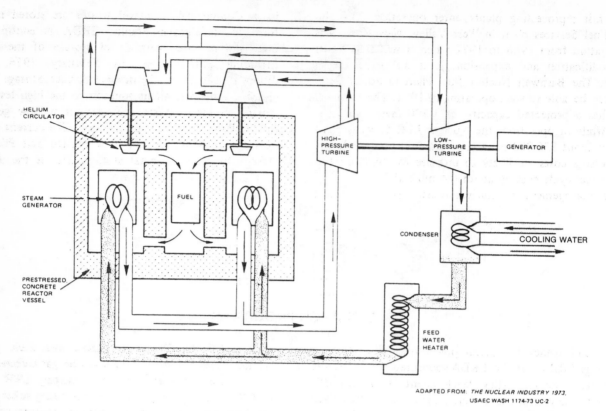

ADAPTED FROM: *THE NUCLEAR INDUSTRY 1973,*
USAEC WASH 1174-73 UC-2

HIGH-TEMPERATURE, GAS-COOLED REACTOR

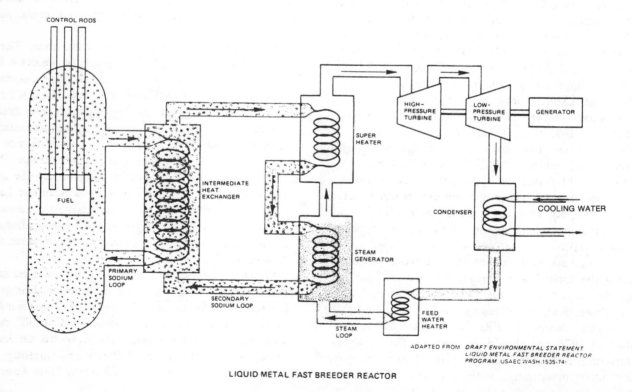

ADAPTED FROM *DRAFT ENVIRONMENTAL STATEMENT
LIQUID METAL FAST BREEDER REACTOR
PROGRAM* USAEC WASH-1535-74

LIQUID METAL FAST BREEDER REACTOR

Figure XII-3. SCHEMATIC DIAGRAMS FOR HGTR AND LMFBR REACTORS

sites until reprocessing plants enter operation. The Nuclear Fuel Services plant in West Valley, New York, was in operation from 1966 to 1971 when it was shut down for modification and expansion. It is not expected to reopen. The Barnwell Nuclear Fuel Plant in South Carolina may be able to start operating in 1981. The Barnwell plant has a projected capacity of 1,500 metric tons per year. While in operation, the Nuclear Fuel Services plant charged about $35,000 per ton of uranium processed. The reprocessing costs are likely to increase fourfold, increasing the fuel cycle cost by about 0.4 mills/kWh.

The management of nuclear wastes is an unsettled issue. Commercial high-level wastes are stored in liquid form in underground tanks. ERDA is continuing its investigations into methods of storage of these wastes, including solidification. In February 1976, ERDA dropped plans for a Retrievable Surface Storage Facility (RSSF), a nonpermanent solution to the high level waste storage problem. Waste management is now geared to solidification with geologic isolation. The current program calls for the construction of a Bedded Salt Pilot Plant (BSPP) for safe, terminal storage. This is the approach that has been taken in Europe.

RESEARCH PROGRAMS

The lead agency in nuclear power research and development is ERDA. Of the ERDA-sponsored programs, the largest are those supporting development of the LMFBR. One of the key elements in that program is the Fast Flux Test Facility (FFTF) at the Hanford Engineering Development Laboratory (HEDL). The purpose of the FFTF is to provide a neutron environment similar to that anticipated in a fast breeder reactor to test fuel elements and reactor components. Cost of the FFTF was originally estimated to be $87 million; the entire FFTF program is now expected to approach $1 billion. The second major element of the LMFBR program is the construction of a demonstration breeder, the Clinch River Breeder Reactor (CRBR), near Oak Ridge, Tennessee. The cost estimate of the CRBR program has grown to $1.7 billion, with possible start of operation in 1982. However, before starting construction, ERDA must issue a final environmental impact statement for the entire breeder program, must await the Nuclear Regulatory Commission (NRC) final environmental statement on the CRBR, and must obtain NRC authorization.

ERDA also sponsors several other breeder programs, including the Light Water Breeder Reactor (LWRB). An LWRB core is planned for the Shippingport, Pennsylvania, Atomic Power Station to demonstrate the technical feasibility of this concept in PWRs. This reactor had its core installed in 1976 and should demonstrate the feasibility of converting PWR systems to breeders. Another breeder concept under investigation is the gas-cooled, fast reactor (GCFR), which would operate on the thorium-uranium fuel cycle.

ERDA continues to support research on thermal (nonbreeder) reactors. Experimental work is being funded on the HTGR and on the very high temperature gas-cooled reactor (VTGR). Closely associated with these programs are the development of a direct-cycle gas turbine and the thorium-uranium fuel cycle. For existing LWR systems, ERDA is investigating ways of improving reliability and efficiency. Related to these programs are improvements in the enrichment facilities and the support of advanced isotope separation technologies (gaseous centrifugation and laser separation).

Fusion research is split into two basic areas. The laser fusion program is included in the ERDA weapons activities because of possible military applications. A portion of the laser fusion funds has been designated for KMS Industries, a corporation that has shown considerable expertise in laser fusion. The major element of the magnetic confinement approach to fusion is the construction of a Tokamak fusion test reactor at the Princeton Plasma Physics Laboratory. Two related programs are the intense neutron source projects at Los Alamos Scientific Laboratory (LASL) and at the Lawrence Livermore Laboratory (LLL). These programs will investigate anticipated materials problems that may occur with intense neutron fluxes at 14 MeV.

ERDA's Division of Naval Reactors is directing its efforts toward development of improved nuclear propulsion plants and reactor cores for nuclear-powered warships.

DOD has supported development of small nuclear power plants for remote bases. The Army has the lead for development of this type of reactor and currently has a 20 MW plant in operation in the Panama Canal Zone.[1]

---

[1] "A Study of the Navy's Energy Research Needs—From the Viewpoint of NRL Involvement," *NRL Memorandum Report 3027,* November 1974.

SECTION TEN

FUEL CELLS

INTRODUCTION

The fuel cell is a device in which the chemical energy of a fuel is converted directly into electrical power. As illustrated in Figure XIII-1, the reactants (fuel and oxidant) are fed continuously from the outside and the products of the reaction are continuously removed. Since it is not limited to the efficiency of the Carnot cycle as are heat engines, the fuel cell is capable of very high efficiencies.

The first hints of a fuel cell concept occurred in the early 1800s when Sir Humphrey Davy reported on the construction of simple galvanic combinations.[1] However, the first discovery of the fuel cell is usually credited to Sir William Grove in the late 1830s.[2] In his experiments, Grove demonstrated that the electrolysis of water was a reversible process and that hydrogen and oxygen could be recombined in an electrochemical cell to produce electrical power.

The first serious attempt to produce a practical device was made by Mond and Langer in the 1880s.[3] Their aim was to use a cheaper fuel than hydrogen and to replace the expensive platinum electrodes used by Grove with a much cheaper metal, such as nickel. It was during these experiments that they discovered the carbonyl process for refining nickel; this diverted their attention away from fuel cells, but led to the founding of a large nickel industry.

In the early 1900s, Bauer did work on high-temperature fuel cells with the prime objective of obtaining electricity directly from coal.[4] However, this objective was too ambitious for the time.

Among the most important work in the development of fuel cells was that started by F. T. Bacon in the 1930s. His original objective was to develop a practical energy storage device. Although the work on his hydrogen-oxygen fuel cell was interrupted by World War II, he returned to the task

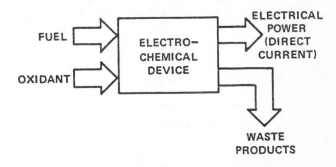

Figure XIII-1. THE BASIC FUEL CELL

afterwards and, in 1959, demonstrated a 6 KW unit.[5] It was the Bacon cell that was later further developed for use in Project Apollo by Pratt and Whitney Aircraft (now the Power Utility Division of United Aircraft Corporation—PUD/UAC).

Today much of the fuel cell research and development is being directed toward reducing costs and making fuel cells more practical. The focus of many of these programs is either to achieve high power densities for application in transportation (cars, trains, ships, buses, and trucks) or to achieve high efficiencies with available fuels for use in electrical power generation.

[1] H. Davy, *Journal of Natural Philosophy, Chemistry and the Arts*, Vol. 1 (edited by W. Nicholson), 1802, pp. 144-145.
[2] W. R. Grove, *Philosophical Magazine*, Vol. 3 Nr. 14, 1939, p. 139. W. R. Grove, "On Gaseous Voltaic Battery," *Philosophical Magazine*, Vol. 3 Nr. 21, Dec. 1842, p. 417.
[3] L. Mond and C. Langer, *Proceedings of the Royal Society*, Vol. 46, 1889, p. 296.
[4] E. Bauer and H. Ehrenberg, *Z. Elekrochen*, Vol. 10, 1912, p. 697.
[5] F. T. Bacon, *et al*, "Fuel Cells," *American Institute of Chemical Engineering* (a C.E.P. technical manual), 1963, p. 63.

BASIC HYDROGEN-OXYGEN FUEL CELL

The principle of hydrogen-oxygen fuel cell operation is shown in Figure XIII-2. Two platinum foil electrodes are immersed in a conductive acid electrolyte. One electrode is supplied with hydrogen, bubbled around it through the solution, and the other electrode is similarly supplied with oxygen. A diaphragm in the solution allows the hydrogen ions to pass through but prevents the hydrogen and oxygen from coming into direct contact with one another.

This chemical reaction occurs at the negative electrode:

$$2H \rightarrow 2H^+ + 2e^-$$

Each hydrogen molecule that contacts the negative electrode surface is dissociated into two atoms by virtue of the catalytic properties of the surface. These enter the solution as hydrogen ions, leaving behind two electrons, which pass through the external electrical circuit.

This chemical reaction takes place at the positive electrode:

$$\tfrac{1}{2}O_2 + 2H^+ + 2e^- \rightarrow H_2O$$

At the positive electrode, the oxygen combines with the free hydrogen ions from the electrolyte and gains two electrons to form water. A "cold" electrochemical reaction occurs at two separated reaction sites to replace the normal single combustion process that occurs in a hydrogen-oxygen "flame."

The simple fuel cell illustrated in Figure XIII-2 does not provide a way to remove the water that is generated as a waste product and, therefore, is not of practical value. A fuel cell that does allow the water to be removed in shown in Figure XIII-3. This fuel cell incorporates porous electrodes that allow them to be "wet" by the electrolyte.

The gas pressures must be selected carefully to avoid flooding or drying the elctrode pores, either of which would impede the reaction rate and limit the current flow.

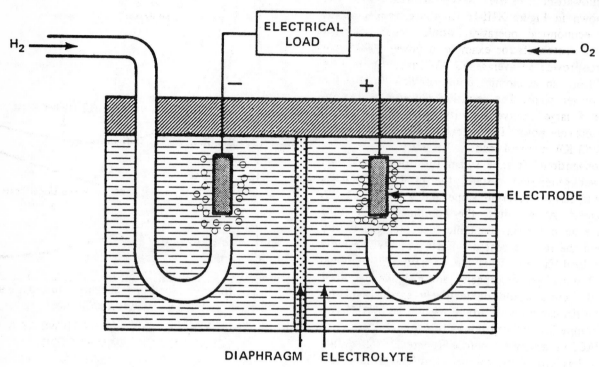

Figure XIII-2. SIMPLE HYDROGEN-OXYGEN FUEL CELL

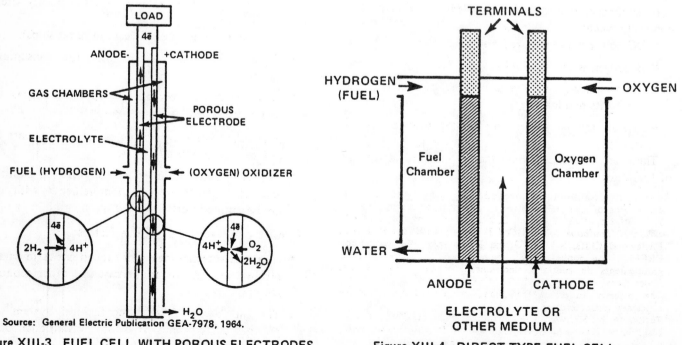

Source: General Electric Publication GEA-7978, 1964.

Figure XIII-3. FUEL CELL WITH POROUS ELECTRODES

Figure XIII-4. DIRECT TYPE FUEL CELL

ECONOMICS

The economic evaluation[1] of competing energy conversion systems in its simplest form requires the combination of fixed and proportional costs to determine a cost per kilowatt-hour (KWH). A typical situation for fuel cells is shown in Figure XIII-16. In the example shown, the most economical operation would occur at a 53 percent load factor. If, for example, a power plant were required to provide an average 53 KW load, it would be desirable, from an economics point of view, to build a 100 KW power plant. The resulting power plant would thus have a large reserve capacity. It could also economically provide power for at least a 40 percent reduction in its 53 KW nominal load.

In a conventional (e.g., a steam turbogenerator) electrical power generation system, the proportional costs curve would have a reversed slope and a somewhat different shape.[2] As a result, the combined costs curve would have an optimum economic load factor near 100 percent and the relative cost per KWH would rise rapidly for lower load factors. Thus the optimum plant would have a (1) small reserve capacity and (2) energy at the lower load factors would be relatively expensive. However, the initial capital costs would usually be much lower than the competing fuel cell power plant.

PUD/UAC, in testimony before Congress,[3] stated that technology has progressed to the point that a mass production selling price of $200 to $350 per kilowatt can be projected. These costs include both input (for fuel conditioning) and output (to convert from DC to AC power) interface devices for the fuel cell.

In summary, fuel cells compare most favorably economically when:

- DC power is the required output.

- Hydrogen is the required fuel.

- A power plant has a large peaking requirement relative to its nominal load.

- One of the favorable factors listed below could be exploited.

There are several favorable factors involved in the use of fuel cells:

[1] For more details on the methodology for making economic evaluations of fuel cells relative to other power systems consult J. Verstraete, *et al*, "Fuel Cell Economics and Commercial Applications," *Handbook of Fuel Cell Technology*, Prentice-Hall, Inc., Englewood Cliffs, N.J., 1968 and F. Courtoy, "La tarification EREFKA—son application au reglement des echanges dans les groupements de centrales electriques," *Revue Universelle des Mines*, 7eme serie, XI, No. 2, 7-15-1926.

[2] The primary cause of the change would be the differing efficiency characteristics.

[3] Testimony by Mr. William H. Podolny before the Subcommittee on Energy Research, Development, and Demonstration, Committee on Science and Technology, United States House of Representatives on February 27, 1975.

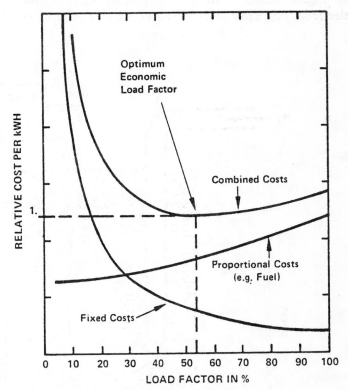

Figure XIII-16. COST VARIATIONS AS A FUNCTION OF LOAD FACTOR

- Fuel cells lend themselves to modular construction, which allows:
  - a utility to purchase the power capacity needed today with the flexibility to add capacity later as required
  - good space utilization (e.g., in naval ships).

- Higher efficiencies result in lower fuel consumption and costs.

- Fuel cells can be located near application sites, thus reducing electrical distribution costs.

- Fuel cell modules are made up of components that can be mass produced.

- Fuel cells can meet many of the noise, air pollution, and other environmental requirements with only minimum modifications.

There are also several unfavorable factors:

- It is a new technology with uncertainties in data on production and operation costs and other economic factors.

- The anticipated life of some fuel cell system components is less than that of conventional power sources.

SECTION ELEVEN

GEOTHERMAL ENERGY

INTRODUCTION

Geothermal energy is heat from the earth's interior. This energy is mostly generated from the slow decay of naturally occurring radioactive elements present in all rocks. The heat escapes very slowly from the earth's core to the crust by conductive flow through solid rocks, by convective flow in circulating fluids, and by mass transfer of magma (molten rock generated from within the earth, termed lava when expelled at the earth's surface).

Thermal gradient describes the rate at which temperature increases with depth below the earth's surface and is expressed as degrees per unit of depth. Normally, the earth's heat is diffuse, the thermal gradient averaging about 25° C/km. In many areas, though, geologic conditions have created local thermal gradients much higher than the average. These thermal reservoirs contain enough concentrated heat to make up a potential energy source.

TYPES OF GEOTHERMAL SYSTEMS

Geothermal systems are classified according to the mode of heat transfer and the temperature and pressure of the system.

In hydrothermal-convection systems, Figure XIV-1, heat is transferred from a deeper igneous source (magma) by the circulation of water or a vapor. Vapor-dominated systems,[1] meaning that pressure is controlled by vapor rather than by liquid, produce saturated or slightly superheated steam containing little or no liquid water and a small percentage of other gases such as CO_2 and H_2S.

Temperatures in these systems can reach 240° C. Unfortunately, this type of system occurs only rarely, since the steam can be easily used directly in turbines to generate electricity. As a matter of fact, steam geothermal systems have been the most successfully and widely used to date in the Geysers Field, California; Lardarello, Italy; and Matsukawa, Japan.

In liquid-dominated systems, hot water transfers heat from deep sources to a geothermal reservoir at depths shallow enough to be tapped by drill holes. Most liquid-dominated systems occur as hot springs, although other types exist. Hot water convection systems have been arbitrarily divided into three temperature ranges according to their potential end-use: above 150° C for generation of electricity;[2] 90° C to 150° C for space and process heating; and below 90° C for local use where better energy sources do not exist.[3]

Hot water systems are about 20 times more common than steam systems and are usually found in areas of volcanic origin and high seismic activity; for example, in the western United States and along the mid-Atlantic Ridge. (See Figure XIV-2.) Their brine (dissolved salts) content varies widely. Hydrothermal convection systems in the United States have been studied for years by U.S. Geological Survey (USGS). More details on the characteristics of these, as well as other systems, can be found in numerous USGS publications, including the most recent summary.[4]

When used for space heating, hot water from geothermal resources can be piped directly to the point of use. If the hot water is a highly corrosive brine, heat exchangers could be used. Other uses for such hot water include heating greenhouses, fish farming, pulp and paper processing, and as a source for extractable minerals. Desalination of geothermal hot waters might also provide fresh

[1] Sometimes inappropriately called "dry-steam deposits."
[2] Binary systems may allow use of somewhat lower temperatures for electricity generation.
[3] D. E. White, "Characteristic of Geothermal Resources," *Geothermal Energy*, P. Kruger and C. Otte (ed), Stanford University Press, 1973.
[4] *Assessment of Geothermal Resources of the United States—1975*, Circular No. 726, U.S. Geological Survey, Washington.

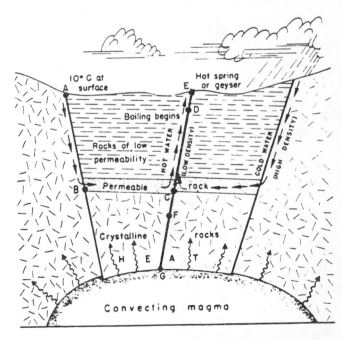

Source: D. E. White, "Characteristics of Geothermal Resources," *Geothermal Energy*, P. Kruger and C. Otte (ed), Stanford University Press, 1973.

Figure XIV-1. HYDROTHERMAL CONVECTION SYSTEM

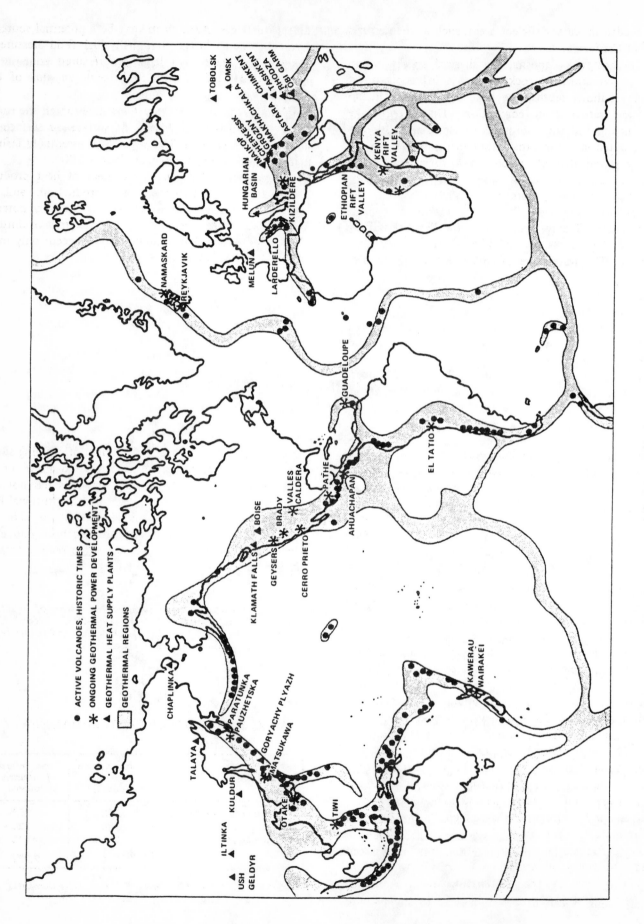

Figure XIV-2. GEOTHERMAL REGIONS OF THE WORLD

water needed in water-deficient areas, such as the Imperial Valley of California.

In dry hot rock deposits, the thermal energy is contained in impermeable rocks of very low porosity at relatively shallow depths, the heat being transferred by conduction rather than convection. The potential resources in dry hot rock are much greater than the hydrothermal potential given satisfactory methods of recovery.

Geopressured deposits result when formation waters, overlain by an insulation of 2 to 3 km of impermeable clay beds, become geopressured (high-pressured) and hotter as heat rising from the earth's interior is absorbed by the water. Geopressured zones are characterized by abnormally high pressures and low salinities. They occur worldwide. The waters are often saturated with recoverable natural gas. Also, there may be a potential source of hydraulic energy in the abnormally high fluid pressures of these areas. There is a large geopressured zone in the northeastern Gulf of Mexico beneath an area of over 278,500 km^2.

Magma or molten rock systems underlie all the earth's crust, sometimes coming near the surface, or surfacing in the form of volcanoes. This resource is essentially infinite, but no development is expected before 2000.

Normal thermal gradients are areas of heat produced by heat flows, radiogenic heat production, and the thermal conductivity of rocks. This is the only potential geothermal resource in most of the eastern two-thirds of the United States, but exploitation will occur only in the distant future, if then.

U.S. GEOTHERMAL RESOURCES

The Energy Research and Development Administration (ERDA) has estimated the recoverable geothermal heat available using present or near-term technology without regard to cost. The total of 3,004 quads shown in Table XIV-1 is approximately equal to U.S. consumption of all forms of energy for 42 years (at the present rate of 71 quads per year). One quad is a quadrillion Btu or 10^{15} Btu.

Exploration in the western United States increased rapidly from 1968 to 1976 encouraged by new public land leasing policies, increasing prices of energy, and by the successful development of geothermal energy at The Geysers. (See Figure XIV-3.) To quote from one authority:

"Extensive exploration and development are ongoing at The Geysers, and there have been significant discoveries made in the Imperial Valley, California, and at the Valles Caldera, New Mexico. Exploration is continuing at Beowawe and Brady's Hot Springs, Nevada, and Surprise Valley, California. In addition, exploration has been accelerated in portions of Utah, Idaho, Oregon, and Arizona. Discoveries have been sparse, but should increase as land becomes available and exploration is expanded."[1]

Several states have passed laws to permit leasing of state lands for geothermal exploration; however, the increased availability of land has coincided with increased legal requirements for environmental protection, resulting in conflicts and delays in the issuance of permits to drill, particularly in California. The problem of defining surface rights, mineral rights, and water rights to allow for geothermal exploration and drilling activities has not been resolved in some areas. (See Legal and Institutional Problems in this chapter.) Increased interest in U.S. geothermal energy potential has encouraged both public and private sources to make financing more readily available for exploration and related activities.

[1] James B. Koenig, *Exploration and Development of Geothermal Resources in the United States, 1968-1975.* Second United Nations Symposium for the Development and Utilization of Geothermal Resources, San Francisco, 1975.

Table XIV-1

U.S. RECOVERABLE GEOTHERMAL HEAT

Type	From Known Resources (quads)	From Inferred Resources (quads)
Hydrothermal convective	102	262
Hot dry rock	80	230
Geopressured	782	1,730
	964	2,222

Source: *ERDA Plan for Energy Research, Development, and Demonstration,* ERDA 76-1.

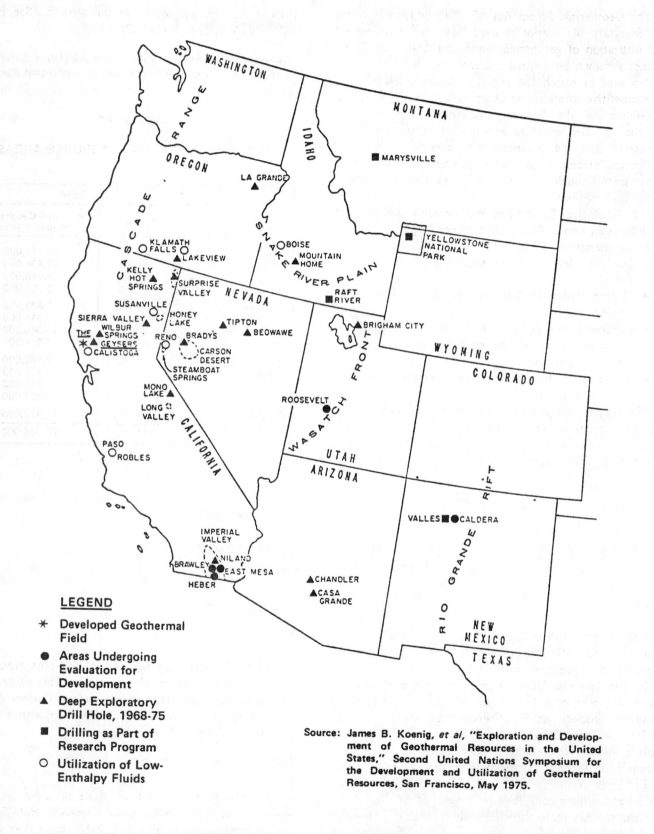

LEGEND

✳ Developed Geothermal
   Field

● Areas Undergoing
   Evaluation for
   Development

▲ Deep Exploratory
   Drill Hole, 1968-75

■ Drilling as Part of
   Research Program

○ Utilization of Low-
   Enthalpy Fluids

Source: James B. Koenig, *et al*, "Exploration and Development of Geothermal Resources in the United
States," Second United Nations Symposium for
the Development and Utilization of Geothermal
Resources, San Francisco, May 1975.

Figure XIV-3. GEOTHERMAL EXPLORATION IN THE UNITED STATES

KNOWN GEOTHERMAL RESOURCE AREAS

The Geothermal Steam Act of 1970, which authorizes the Secretary of Interior to issue leases for development and utilization of geothermal steam and related resources, defines a known geothermal resource area (KGRA) as:

"an area in which the geology, nearby discoveries, competitive interests, or other indicia would, in the opinion of the Secretary (Interior), engender a belief in men who are experienced in the subject matter that the prospects for extraction of geothermal steam or associated geothermal resources are good enough to warrant expenditures of money for that purpose."

U.S. Geological Survey has four requirements before it establishes an area as having development potential:

- Temperatures above 150° to 400° F (65° to 204° C), depending on production and use technology.
- Depths under 10,000 feet to permit economical drilling.
- Sufficient rock permeability to allow the heat transfer agent—water, steam, or both—to flow continuously at a high rate.
- Sufficient water recharge to maintain production over many years.

"In general, the average heat content of rocks is considerably higher in the Western United States than in the east. This also helps to explain why the most favorable hydrothermal convection systems and the hot young igneous systems also occur in the west."[1] (See Figures XIV-3, XIV-4, and Table XIV-2.)

[1] *Assessment of Geothermal Resources in the United States—1975,* Circular No. 726, U.S. Geological Survey, Washington.

Table XIV-2

KNOWN GEOTHERMAL RESOURCE AREAS

State	Acres	
	KGRA	Potential Geothermal Resource Areas
California	1,051,533	15,737,000
Nevada	344,027	13,468,000
Oregon	84,279	15,048,000
Washington	17,622	5,759,000
Arizona	88,160	1,473,000
Colorado	–	1,014,000
Idaho	21,844	14,845,000
Montana	12,763	3,834,000
New Mexico	152,863	7,482,000
South Dakota	–	436,000
Utah	13,521	4,511,000
Wyoming	–	824,000
Alaska	88,160	11,277,000
Total	1,874,772	95,708,000

Source: Comptroller of the Currency, 1975.

STATUS OF U.S. HYDROTHERMAL PHYSICAL DEVELOPMENT

California

The already highly developed Geysers area produces more than 500 MW of electricity from hot dry steam and is projected to produce up to 2,000 MW.

In the Imperial Valley numerous wells yielding hot water have been drilled at several locations. Some of these locations produce water of excessive mineral content. ERDA and San Diego Gas and Electric Company have built a facility to test very salty brines in a heat exchanger; this facility is undergoing pre-start-up tests.

In Long Valley several promising holes have been drilled and drilling continues.

Calistoga has more than 60 wells producing hot water used for space heating.

In Amedee two wells are used for greenhouse operations and further exploration is probable.

New Mexico

At least 15 holes have been drilled and nine producible wells have been found in Valles Caldera. This water is hot enough to flash into steam at the surface. Further drilling is likely and negotiations may begin soon with a utility company to build a 50 MW power plant.

Utah

Six wells have been drilled; three of them are good producers of hot liquids near Roosevelt Hot Springs. Further exploratory drilling is probable and power generation is under consideration.

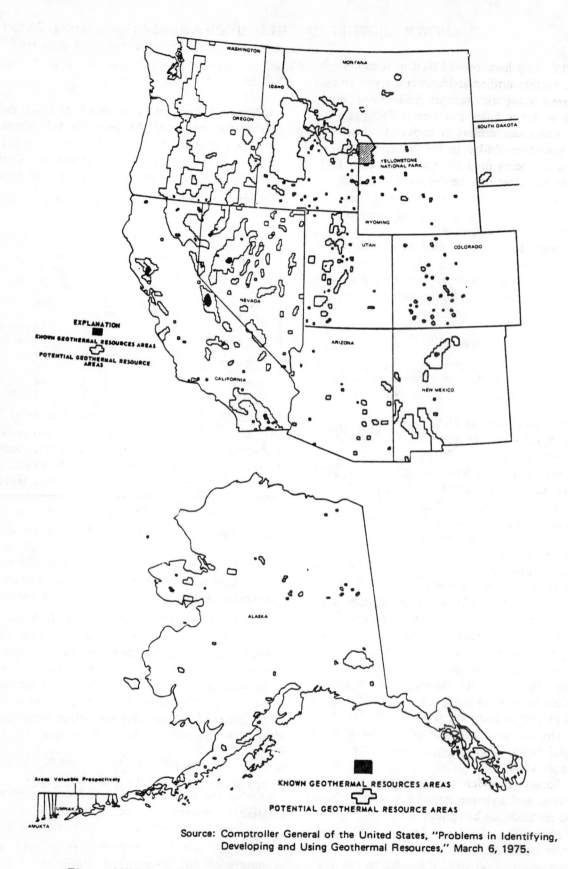

Source: Comptroller General of the United States, "Problems in Identifying, Developing and Using Geothermal Resources," March 6, 1975.

Figure XIV-4. KGRA AND POTENTIAL GEOTHERMAL RESOURCE AREAS IN THE UNITED STATES

Nevada

More than 17 holes have been drilled in four areas of Carson Desert. Further drilling and testing are expected in two of these areas along with wildcat drilling in adjoining areas. Twelve or more holes have been drilled in the Beoware area; continued drilling is expected. Dozens of shallow wells have been drilled in the Steamboat Springs area, and some are being used for space heating. Deeper holes to seek hotter water may be drilled.

Oregon

Some 400 wells have been drilled at Klamath Falls.

Most of these are used for space heating. Further development and search for hotter water are expected.

Idaho

Two wells have been drilled at Raft River, yielding low temperature water. ERDA probably will decide within a few months whether or not to build a test facility to evaluate these wells for power generation. Two wells at Boise supply water for space heating, and expansion of this use is underway.

EXPLORATION AND ASSESSMENT

Many of the exploration methods used in the petroleum and mining industries are also used for finding and assessing geothermal deposits. There has been more experience in exploration for hydrothermal systems than for other types, partially because many of these systems have surface fluid manifestations and because they are more economical energy sources. Normally, exploration and assessment include geologic examinations, fluid geochemistry, and geophysics.

Exploration for geothermal resources begins with the selection of prospective areas by geological mapping and data analysis. This is often followed by geochemical analyses of water from hot springs, fumaroles, and other surface manifestations of geothermal energy. Such geochemical analyses provide estimates of the temperature of water in the subsurface reservoir. Usually, if geological and geochemical tests indicate reasonable prospect in an area, geophysical surveys are made. A geophysical survey estimates the properties and structures of subsurface rocks by gathering physical data from instruments placed at the surface. Several types of geophysical surveys are used in geothermal exploration.

Airborne Survey—Includes aerial photography, aeromagnetic surveys, and airborne infrared surveys, although the latter two methods are being used less.

Gravity Survey—This is a measurement of the gravitational attraction of the earth at any location. The results of gravity surveys yield, among other things, the depth and profile of the basement rock underlying a sedimentary basin and the location of faults.

Magnetic Survey—This is a measurement of the intensity of the earth's magnetic field at any location. This survey provides results similar to the gravity survey.

Passive Seismic Surveys—Such surveys record naturally occurring microearthquakes or seismic ground noise. Microearthquakes are recurring low intensity earthquakes, usually not felt by humans, caused by fracturing and displacement of subsurface rock along an active fault. Such active faults are often considered to be the flow conduits of geothermal water from depth. Seismic ground noise implies continuous low intensity vibrations in the subsurface and may be associated with geothermal areas.

Geologic and Hydrologic Survey—Includes structural and stratigraphic mapping to detect recent faulting, to determine the distribution and age of young volcanic rocks, and the location and character of surface thermal manifestations. Hydrologic analysis includes temperature and discharge measurements of hot and cold springs, evaluation of surface and subsurface water movements, and collection of basic meteorologic data.

Geochemical Survey—Data obtained from chemical analysis of water and gas samples are used to determine whether the system is vapor or hot-water dominated, to estimate temperatures and chemistry of the waters at depth, and to determine the source of recharge water. Analysis of the isotopic content can be used to specify the origin of the water in hydrothermal systems.

Heat Flow Studies—Vertical temperature gradients are measured in shallow boreholes (100 to 500 feet) drilled in an area considered prospective from other surveys. Knowing the thermal conductivity (K) of the subsurface rock, which is either measured from samples of the rock or assumed from experience, the rate of vertical conductive heat flow (q) can be calculated from Fourier's Law:

$$q = -K\frac{dT}{dz}$$

where dT/dz is the vertical temperature gradient. Geothermal areas exhibit heat flow rates of several times the worldwide average of 1.5 microcalories/cm^2/sec.

A judicious selection of these geophysical surveys can locate a geothermal reservoir and define its limits. However, the resource is not proven until exploratory boreholes have been drilled. Subsurface rock samples are collected from these boreholes either as drill cuttings or core samples. Various well logs are run in the borehole. The well is allowed to produce fluids and various well tests are run. Based on the results of these tests on the exploratory borehole, a preliminary assessment can be made of the power generation potential of the reservoir.

DRILLING

Techniques used for drilling geothermal wells are similar to those used for conventional drilling for petroleum: rotary rigs efficient to 7.5 km and up to 250° C. As Koenig points out, the average well depth at The Geysers is 2.3 km and wildcat wells elsewhere have gone as deep as 3.3 km. Few significant holes are drilled to less than 1.2 km.[1] However there are some specific problems encountered in drilling geothermal reservoirs that differ from petroleum drilling:

- Higher temperatures are sometimes encountered; these can melt hard rubber fittings and valves on oil drill rigs and affect materials used for well casing.
- Many geothermal wells are drilled in harder rock than encountered in oil well drilling; this results in shorter bit life and slower penetration rates.
- Hydrothermal reservoirs having a high brine content can cause corrosion and scaling on drilling equipment.

In May 1975, the United Nations Geothermal Symposium summarized some of the more recent research in geothermal drilling technology:

"Research is being done on over 30 novel drills ranging from lasers which melt rock to explosive drills which blast holes in the rock. Subterrenes (rock-melting drills) being developed by the Los Alamos Scientific Laboratory utilize electric resistance heaters to melt holes in rocks. Subterrenes have potential for drilling into magma, lava beds, and other extremely hot rocks which exceed the temperature capabilities of conventional rotary drills. Sandia Laboratories is working on four novel drills which have potential for increasing drilling rate and bit life: spark drills, downhole changeable bits, continuous chain bits and Terra Drills which utilize projectiles to fracture the rock and roller bits to remove it. A new high-pressure erosion drill being developed jointly by Exxon and eight other oil companies utilizes fluid jets at 15,000 psi to disintegrate the rock. These high pressure bits drill two to three times faster than conventional bits and have potential for reducing the cost of drilling geothermal wells."[2]

[1] James B. Koenig, *Exploration and Development of Geothermal Resources in the United States, 1968-1975.* Second United Nations Symposium for the Development and Utilization of Geothermal Resources, San Francisco, 1975.
[2] William C. Maurer, *Geothermal Drilling.* Second United Nations Symposium for the Development and Utilization of Geothermal Resources, San Francisco, 1975.

ENVIRONMENTAL, LEGAL, INSTITUTIONAL, AND ECONOMIC CONSIDERATIONS

Environmental Considerations

Although geothermal energy has been lauded as a "clean" energy source with few environmental problems associated with its development, there is only a small amount of environmental data available on the use of geothermal energy, and almost no field experience with many of the conversion technologies. However, the effects in most cases will be less than the impact of nuclear and fossil fuel systems.

In general, the environmental effects are site-dependent—that is, the drilling takes place in the immediate vicinity of the power plant or other facility. Transportation is limited to pipes and power lines; pipes would extend no more than a few miles, and power lines would be limited by the small capacity of most geothermal plants. Most negative impacts would occur because of drilling and construction during the development period.

This section summarizes some potential negative environmental impacts. Details can be found in the *Final Environmental Impact Statement for the Geothermal Leasing Program*, Department of Interior, in *Energy Alternatives: A Comparative Analysis*, prepared for CEQ, ERDA, EPA, FEA, FPC, DOI, and NSF, May 1975, and in the *Proceedings of the NSF Workshop on Environmental Aspects of Geothermal Resources Development*, 1974.

Air Pollution—Noncondensable gases such as hydrogen sulfide, carbon dioxide, methane, ammonia, and nitrogen found in the vapor phase of a geothermal source, could cause serious air pollution if released. Hydrogen sulfide ranks as the most likely potential environmental hazard, occurring at 16 times the toxic level in undiluted geothermal steam at The Geysers, although normally the gas is dispersed in the atmosphere before it reaches a toxic level. Mercury is also a potential hazard in some geothermal fluids and would have to be monitored continuously.

Water Pollution—Introduction of highly saline or toxic geothermal fluids to surface waters, resulting from brine disposal, blowouts, or spills, could cause water and thermal pollution, although reinjection of spent fluids into the reservoir greatly mitigates the risk. Ground water contamination can result from interference with aquiferous fresh water during drilling and production.

Land Subsidence—Sinking of the earth's crust sometimes occurs when supporting fluids are removed from underground reservoirs. Subsidence has occurred in areas where very large amounts of water have been removed during geothermal development. There is a potential for this occurring in the Imperial Valley. Prevention of subsidence involves injecting replacement fluids, usually the spent geothermal fluids.

Seismic Activity—It is possible for changes in reservoir pressures to cause an increase in seismic activity. Although not well studied to date, either injection or withdrawal of large volumes of fluid may have a powerful enough effect on the stresses in a fault zone to cause a major earthquake. On the other hand, minor changes in seismic activity may relieve accumulated strain before a major earthquake occurs.

Noise Pollution—This can result during venting of geothermal steam through relief valves. Mufflers are being developed. Drilling and construction activities produce noise as well.

Land Modification—Most geothermal power plants would be in areas not now industrialized or urbanized, necessitating disruption of existing land use and possibly disturbing wildlife. However, it is also true that since such facilities would be smaller than most power plants, fossil or nuclear, and since the electricity or steam would usually not be transmitted great distances, the negative impacts on land use and wildlife would be minimal and restricted to the immediate area of the plant. Also, a developed geothermal field need not be incompatible with other land uses. For example, in Italy farms, orchards, and vineyards are interspersed among the pipelines and wells. At The Geysers, cattle graze and wildlife live in areas immediately adjacent to the power plant. Geothermal developments would not be drilled normally in recreational areas, especially in federal and state parks.

Considerable attention has been given to the environmental impacts of geothermal energy development in Japan.

Legal and Institutional Problems

In a recent workshop the National Science Foundation (NSF) has reviewed legal problems associated with the development of geothermal sources.[1] Some of the problems uncovered are:

Resource definition varies from state to state. In Hawaii, geothermal resources are defined as minerals, in Wyoming as water resources.

Ownership rights. Federal grants of public land retain mineral rights for the federal government, while some state grants include mineral rights.

Control over use of water. Some states such as Oregon, California, and Colorado have laws which prohibit transporting water out of state.

Overlapping and conflicting regulations and jurisdictions for permits, licenses, taxes, environmental control, etc., exist between federal, state, and local governments.

Leasing complications. Since almost 75 percent[2] of all KGRA's in the United States are located beneath federally owned land, most of the leasing contracts must be negotiated through the Department of Interior. Industry representatives have criticized DOI's land classification and leasing policies, maintaining that in many cases, they cause unwarranted delays in resource development.

Environmental problems. The lack of environmental impact data also tends to discourage or delay acceptance of geothermal technologies.[2]

Economic Considerations

The only geothermal operation in the United States generating data on the economics of developing a geothermal steam resource has been from The Geysers development. However, many experts agree with S. D. Worthington that "the technology and economics of The Geysers development must never be used as a measure of other locations having even modestly different characteristics."[2] And since steam developers, like those who operate The Geysers, do not normally reveal their costs, mills/kw published are usually the cost of power to the utility, not the actual cost of producing the power. Other uncertainties include:

- The extent and characteristics of the resources for most potential areas are not known with enough accuracy to predict the exploration and drilling required for development, both of which can add significantly to the total investment and discourage industry and financial institutions from committing capital for development.
- Conversion efficiencies have not been proven for most systems suggested; and these efficiencies will vary as the fluid temperatures vary from reservoir to reservoir.
- Costs for all forms of energy production are rising, making it difficult to compare geothermal costs with other energy sources.
- The geothermal industry does not have the same tax incentives as do other energy extraction industries.

Known factors that can contribute toward making geothermal energy economically competitive with other forms include:

- Continued and increased government support in R&D and federal loan guarantee programs.
- Willingness of industry to make the investments.
- Successful compliance with EPA without prohibitive expenditures on environmental control technologies.
- Continued high costs for more conventional energy sources.
- Integrated operation of geothermal power stations from exploration to production rather than purchase of steam or hot water by the utility companies from independent suppliers (the effect would be increased investment cost/kw of capacity but decreased production cost per kWh of energy).
- Improved technology for drilling and conversion methods.
- Expedition of leasing and regulatory procedures.

Many estimates of the potential contribution of geothermal electricity production to the national supply have been made under various growth scenarios. The estimates cited most recently range from 3,500 to 132,000 Mwe in 1985 (University of Oklahoma, 1975).

[1] *Proceedings Conference on Geothermal Energy and the Law*, National Science Foundation Report No. NSF-RA-S-75-003, 1975.
[2] S. D. Worthington, "Geothermal Development," *Status Report—Energy Resources and Technology*, Atomic Industrial Forum, 1975.

SECTION TWELVE

HYDROGEN

INTRODUCTION

The alternative fuels discussed in this chapter include only synthetically produced nonhydrocarbons. They all have the common properties of being synthesized from abundant materials and of having products of combustion that are not noxious and that can be assimilated into the environment at the point of use, without having to be recycled to the generating station. These alternative fuels are hydrogen, ammonia, hydrazine, methanol, and methylamines. The emphasis is on hydrogen, not because it is the simplest, cleanest and has the highest heating value per pound of any fuel, but because it is a basic ingredient for the other alternate fuels, as well as a necessary feedstock for production of synthetic hydrocarbons.

Production costs for the various alternative fuels are not treated directly; rather the energy required to produce the fuel—known as process energy—is given in kilowatt hours electric per pound (kWh$_e$/lb) or kilowatt hours thermal per pound (kWh$_t$/lb). The former is used for manufacturing processes that are basically electrochemical and the latter is used for processes that are thermochemical. Also the process energy used per Btu of fuel produced is given where appropriate in units of kWh$_e$/Btu or kWh$_t$/Btu. In all cases, the lower heating value of hydrogen is used. Production costs of the fuels can be compared from a knowledge of the cost of process energy. (Capital investment costs, financing costs, labor costs, etc., are not included.)

The source of the process energy is not discussed; it could be solar, nuclear or thermonuclear in most cases. The majority of papers on the production of alternative fuels assume the source of the process energy to be nuclear, but, with a few exceptions, no such restriction is necessary.

The production costs of alternative fuels are shown in Table XV-1. The manufacturing energy in each case is for the most likely production process. For all of the fuels, hydrogen is assumed to be produced electrolytically and the manufacturing energy is expressed in kWh$_t$/lb using the optimistic figure of 40 percent thermal to electric conversion efficiency.

Some of the more important physical properties of these alternative fuels and methane are displayed in Table XV-2.

Table XV-1

ALTERNATIVE FUELS PRODUCTION

	Combustion Energy[a] (Btu/lb)	Manufacturing Energy (kWh$_t$/lb)	Process Efficiency[b] (percent)
Hydrogen	51,536	62.5	24
Ammonia	7,986	9.2	25
Hydrazine	7,200	30.2	7
Methanol	8,600	4.35	58
Methylamines	15,085	11.2	40

[a]Lower heating value.
[b]Ratio of combustion energy to manufacturing energy.

Source: Adapted from B. Berkowitz, *et. al.,* "Alternative, Synthetically Fueled, Navy Systems," TEMPO, General Electric Company, November 1974.

Table XV-2

PROPERTIES OF ALTERNATIVE FUELS

	Hydrogen	Ammonia	Hydrazine	Methanol	Methylamines	Methane
Liquid density (lb/ft^3)	4.43	42.6	63.1	49.7	41.7	25.9
Melting point (° C)	−259.02	−77.8	1.1	−97.8	−	−182.5
Boiling point (° C)	−252.77	−33.3	113.3	64.7	−	−161.5
Heat of vaporization (Btu/lb)	191.7	590.0	548.0	473.02	280.0	219.42
Critical temperature (° C)	−239.9	132.2	380.0	240.0	−	−82.1
Critical pressure (atm)	12.80	111.0	145.0	78.5	−	45.8
Autoignition temperature in air (° C)	585	651	270	464	−	538
Explosive limit in air						
lower (%)	4.0	15.0	4.7	6.0	2.0	5.0
upper (%)	75	28	100	37	21	15
Flame speed (ft/sec)	8.8	0.034	−	1.6	−	1.2

Adapted from B. Berkowitz, *et. al.,* "Alternative, Synthetically Fueled, Navy Systems," TEMPO, General Electric Company, November 1974.
D. Mathis, *Hydrogen Technology for Energy,* Noyes Data Corporation, 1976.

HYDROGEN PRODUCTION

The most common method of producing hydrogen in large quantities today is by reforming of volatile hydrocarbons. This is not likely to be the method of production in the future because of the increased costs and reduced availability of these feedstocks. In the near term (1975 to 1985), hydrogen production will still depend on fossil fuels, but the feedstock for the chemical processes will shift to heavy petroleum fractions and coal.

Some hydrogen is produced by electrolytic decomposition of water. In the future, this may become the preferred method for obtaining bulk quantities of hydrogen. However, the electrolysis of water requires large quantities of electricity—quantities that may be available only from thermally inefficient nuclear power plants. Looking beyond electrolysis, the need for electricity for hydrogen production can be reduced by direct utilization of thermal energy through multistage thermochemical processes of high efficiency.

Other possibilities for hydrogen production include bioconversion, use of ultraviolet light from a fusion torch, and use of municipal rubbish and plants as feedstock for chemical reforming using existing technology.

Steam Reforming of Volatile Hydrocarbons

The major process for hydrogen production today is by steam reforming of volatile hydrocarbons (particularly methane because of its traditional low cost).[1] Desulfurized hydrocarbon gas is combined with steam in a reformer over a nickel (Ni) catalyst bed to produce synthesis gas (H_2 and CO). The CO is removed in a catalytic shift converter to form additional H_2 and CO_2. The overall reaction is endothermic. The two reactions and the summary reaction are:

$$C_n H_{2n+2} + nH_2O \xrightarrow[\text{Cat. 350 psig}]{815°\text{ C}} nCO + (2n + 1) H_2$$

$$nCO + nH_2O \xrightarrow[\text{Cat.}]{} nCO_2 + nH_2$$

$$\overline{C_n H_{2n+2} + 2n\ H_2O + \text{heat} \longrightarrow nCO_2 + (3n + 1) H_2}$$

The catalysts are susceptible to feedstock poisoning.

Partial Oxidation of Heavy Petroleum Fractions

This is a two-stage process in which the feedstock is partially oxidized to produce synthesis gas. The heat released in this process is used to aid in the subsequent shift reaction of CO with H_2O to increase the yield of hydrogen:

Table XV-3

ELECTROLYTIC COST OF HYDROGEN

	Cost of Electricity (mills/kWh)		
	10	15	20
Dollars per pound H_2	0.19	0.29	0.38
Dollars per million Btu[a]	3.69	5.53	7.37

[a] Lower heating value.

$$2C_nH_m + nO_2 \longrightarrow 2n\ CO + mH_2$$

$$2n\ CO + 2n\ H_2O \longrightarrow 2n\ CO_2 + 2n\ H_2$$

$$\overline{2C_nH_m + 2n\ H_2O + nO_2 \longrightarrow 2n\ CO_2 + (2n + m) H_2}$$

In addition to requiring a hydrocarbon feedstock, this process depends on a supply of pure oxygen.[1]

Coal Gasification

The inputs for the production of hydrogen from coal are pure oxygen, water, and coal. The coal is oxidized to produce heat to promote the endothermic gasification reaction. The result is synthesis gas, which is steam treated in a shift reactor to increase the hydrogen yield. For bituminous coal, the basic reactions are:

$$3C + 2O_2 \longrightarrow CO_2 + 2CO + \text{heat}$$

$$3C + 3H_2O \xrightarrow[\text{450 psig}]{870°\text{-}1000°\text{ C}} CO + CO_2 + H_2 + CH_4$$

$$3CO + 3H_2O \longrightarrow 3CO_2 + 3H_2$$

$$\overline{6C + 2O_2 + 6H_2O \longrightarrow 5CO_2 + 4H_2 + CH_4}$$

Trace materials in the coal feedstock can poison the catalysts. As a result, extensive preparation of the coal is necessary to remove contaminants. In addition, the need for pure oxygen makes this process expensive.[1]

Electrolysis

Electrolysis is the only currently available method for large-scale production of hydrogen not requiring fossil

[1] Homer W. Carhart, et. al., "Hydrogen as a Navy Fuel," *NRL Report 7754*, June 12, 1974.

Table XV-4

OPERATING CHARACTERISTICS OF ELECTROLYZERS

	Teledyne	Lurgi	GE
Size of system compared, MW equivalent of H_2	39.9	53.3	51.6
Million SCF H_2/stream-day	10	13.44	13.0
D-c electric input (max) (kW)	58,400	69,000	65,300
Specific cell efficiency (%)	68-70	77	82.2
A-c to d-c converter efficiency (%)	97	97	97
Auxiliary system efficiency loss (%)	2	NA[a]	1
Overall efficiency (%)	64-66	74.7	78.9
Operating pressure	100 psig	440 psia	Pressure vessel designed for operating pressure up to 3000 psig
Cooling water	NA	184,940 gal/hr	Closed cycle dry cooling tower
Feedwater (gal/1000 SCF)	6.36	6.36	6.36
Nitrogen per start-up, SCF	Yes	74,640	No
Caustic potash initial charge (lb)	NA[a]	344,000	None
Labor	NA[a]	2 men/shift	NA[a]
Mode of operation	Fully automatic	Fully automatic	Fully automatic

[a]NA = not available.

Source: K. Darrow, *et. al.,* "Commodity Hydrogen Off-Peak Electricity," Proceedings, First World Hydrogen Off-Peak Electricity," *Proceedings, First World Hydrogen Energy Conference,* 1976, pp 8C-32.

fuels.[1] Large-scale electrolysis plants are in operation in many parts of the world where cheap electric power is available, mainly supplying hydrogen to the ammonia and fertilizer industries. The existing plants are modular in design and could be scaled up without difficulty.

An electrolytic process is a decomposition reaction that occurs by passing a direct electric current between two electrodes immersed in an electrolyte. Each hydrogen molecule is formed by the addition of one electron to each of two hydrogen ions in solution. In the ideal case, a voltage of 1.47 volts applied at 25° C would generate hydrogen and oxygen isothermally with 100 percent of the heating value of the electrical energy converted into the fuel value of the hydrogen. However, a water electrolysis cell can be operated at a lower applied voltage if heat is supplied to maintain the cell temperature, with the result that the fuel value of the hydrogen produced can exceed the heating value of the electical energy supplied. In practice, electrolysis cells have efficiencies of 60-70 percent. Cell efficiency can be increased by operating at higher temperatures, and advanced designs can be expected to have higher efficiencies than current cells. For the near term, a realistic figure for the energy cost of electrolytic hydrogen is 19 kWh$_e$/lb hydrogen gas. The cost of hydrogen production is related to the cost of electrical power as shown in Table XV-3.

Three types of electrolyzers are suitable for large-scale hydrogen production: the bipolar alkaline cell (manufactured by Lurgi and Teledyne), the unipolar alkaline cell (manufactured by Electrolyzer Corp.), and the bipolar solid polymer cell (manufactured by General Electric). The Lurgi bipolar alkaline cells are the only large-scale electrolyzers in commercial service. However, the solid polymer electrolyzers can provide lower capital costs and improved efficiency in the near future. Table XV-4 displays the operating characteristics of the Lurgi, Teledyne, and GE electrolyzer cells. Because the cells require direct current, ac-to-dc rectification equipment will be necessary if dc power is not available. Although quite efficient, the capital cost of such equipment is high.

Thermochemical

An alternative to the electrolytic method of generating hydrogen from water is thermochemical water splitting in which multistage reactions are used to dissociate water. Single-stage (pure thermal) dissociation occurs at 2500° C and is not considered feasible for hydrogen production. Two-stage processes have been eliminated because they too require extreme temperatures. Several multistage processes that appear technically feasible have been proposed.

The most widely discussed thermochemical process is the Marchetti process, which is based on the splitting of HBr (hydrogen bromide) produced by the hydrolysis of

[1] D. P. Gregory, *A Hydrogen-Energy System,* American Gas Association, August 1972.

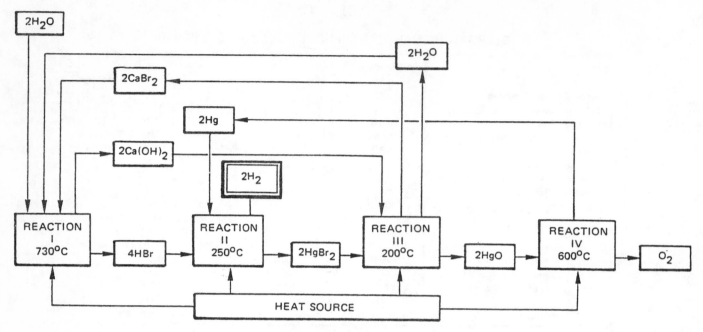

ADAPTED FROM G. DE BENI AND C. MARCHETTI. "MARK I, A CHEMICAL
PROCESS TO DECOMPOSE WATER USING NUCLEAR HEAT." AM. CHEM.
SOC. DIV. FUEL CHEMICAL PREPRINT 16, NO. 4, APRIL 1972, PP. 110-120.

Figure XV-1. THERMOCHEMICAL PRODUCTION OF HYDROGEN

$CaBr_2$ (calcium bromide).[1] The process is diagrammed in Figure XV-1. All steps in the sequence can be carried out at or below 730° C. The only inputs to the process are water and heat; the calcium bromide and mercury (Hg) are recycled. The sequence of reactions and the summation reaction are:

$$2CaBr_2 + 4H_2O \xrightarrow{730°\,C} 2Ca(OH)_2 + 4HBr$$

$$2Hg + 4HBr \xrightarrow{250°\,C} 2HgBr_2 + 2H_2$$

$$2HgBr_2 + 2Ca(OH)_2 \xrightarrow{200°\,C} 2CaBr_2 + 2HgO + 2H_2O$$

$$2HgO \xrightarrow{600°\,C} 2Hg + O_2$$

$$\overline{2H_2O \longrightarrow 2H_2 + O_2}$$

The process has a theoretical thermal efficiency of 59 percent and preliminary laboratory work indicates practical efficiencies of 40-50 percent can be expected. Here the efficiency is defined as the ratio of the higher heat value of the hydrogen produced to the thermal heat input. A serious drawback to the process is the highly corrosive nature of the compounds used (especially hydrobromic acid) and the large inventory of mercury involved.

The Marchetti process is compared with four other thermochemical hydrogen production processes in Table XV-5.

Another variation of the thermochemical process is the Von Fredersdorff process based on the conventional steam-iron-carbon monoxide process with the product CO_2 being split to regenerate the carbon monoxide and produce oxygen.[2] The latter step is carried out at low temperatures (320° C) by use of ionizing radiation from a chemonuclear reactor. The technical feasibility of the process depends heavily on the development of chemonuclear reactors.

Bioconversion

Several efforts are underway to develop a biophotolytic process for producing hydrogen. The basis for the procedure is to exploit the ability of anaerobic bacteria, which can be induced to form hydrogen during part of their metabolic cycle. In general, the bacteria do not use water directly, but reduce organic or inorganic substances to form hydrogen photosynthetically from these substrates.[3]

[1] G. De Beni and C. Marchetti, "Mark 1, A Chemical Process to Decompose Water Using Nuclear Heat," American Chemical Society Division of Fuel Chemical Preparation, Vol. 16, No. 4, April 1972, pp. 110-120.

[2] D. P. Gregory, A Hydrogen-Energy System, American Gas Association, August 1972.

[3] Privileged communication from L. O. Krampitz, Case Western Reserve University.

Table XV-5

THERMOCHEMICAL WATER DECOMPOSITION

	Marchetti Process	Cesium Oxide Process	Tin Oxide Process	Vanadium Chloride Process	Fe Chloride Oxide Process
Total Input Energy					
(Btu/lb H_2)	103000	128000	145000	347000	117000
(kWh$_t$/lb H_2)	30.2	37.5	42.5	101.7	34.3
(kWh$_t$/Btu)^a	0.00059	0.00073	0.00082	0.00197	0.00067
Thermal Efficiency^b					
Higher Heating Value	59%	48%	42%	18%	53%
Lower Heating Value	49%	41%	36%	15%	45%
Highest Endothermic Reaction Temperature (°C)	730	1050	1700	725	650
Fraction Process Heat at Highest Temperature	26%	70%	90%	30%	32%
Reactions in Closed Cycle	4	4	3	4	5

^{a}Based on lower heating value of hydrogen.
^{b}Full extent of reaction; 100% separation efficiency; no loss of intermediates; 100% internal heat recovery.

Source: Adapted from M. M. Eisenstadt and K. E. Cox. "Hydrogen Production from Solar Energy." *Solar Energy 17*, pp 59-65.

A process using algae rather than bacteria has been described for the photoproduction of hydrogen. Municipal sewage would be used as the growth medium with nitrates and phosphates as marketable by-products.[1]

[1] D. T. Blankenship, and G. D. Winget, "Hydrogen Fuel: Production by Bioconversion," *Proceedings, Eighth Inter-Society Energy Conversion Conference*, University of Pennsylvania, August 1973.

HYDROGEN DISTRIBUTION

Since most processes for hydrogen production require large heat sources, production plants will almost certainly be separated from the consumer by large distances. At the present time, hydrogen is transported from the source to the user by pipeline, truck, train and barge in both gaseous and liquid forms.

Pipeline

The transmission of gaseous hydrogen by pipeline in moderate quantities is an established industrial practice, but is normally carried out over very small distances.[1] The longest hydrogen pipeline in the U.S. is an 8-inch line 12 miles long operating at 200 psi. A comprehensive hydrogen pipeline network in the Ruhr Valley in Germany has a total length of 130 miles and has been in operation since 1940. Another hydrogen pipeline in Johannesburg, South Africa, is 50 miles long.

None of these networks is of such a length as to require in-line compressors to maintain transmission rates. Three types of compressors are applicable for service in hydrogen pipelines: piston or reciprocating compressors; radial or centrifugal turbocompressors; and screw compressors. All these can handle hydrogen without significant changes in design from those used for natural gas.

The existing network of natural gas pipelines will require extensive modification and expansion to adequately fill the needs of hydrogen transmission. Because the higher heating value of hydrogen is 325 Btu/SCF, to transmit the same energy, approximately three times the volume of hydrogen must be moved as natural gas. Higher pressures can be achieved by multi-stage compressors.

[1] D. P. Gregory, *A Hydrogen-Energy System*, American Gas Association, August 1972.

Table XV-6

COSTS OF DELIVERING ENERGY

	Electricity	Natural Gas[a]	Hydrogen Gas[b]
Transmission (Dollars per million Btu)	0.61	0.20	0.52
Distribution (Dollars per million Btu)	1.61	0.27	0.34

[a]Natural gas optimized pipeline; natural gas cost $0.25 per million Btu.

[b]Hydrogen gas optimized pipeline; hydrogen cost $3.00 per million Btu.

Source: Adapted from D. P. Gregory, *A Hydrogen-Energy System.* American Gas Association, August 1972, p. 11-5.

Ultimately, to take advantage of the potentially low transmission costs of hydrogen pipelines, a new, specially designed system will be required. A comparison of the costs of energy transmission and distribution between electricity, natural gas pipelining, and an optimized hydrogen pipeline is shown in Table XV-6.

The pipeline transmission of liquid hydrogen presents greater problems than the pipeline transmission of liquid natural gas (LNG) because the temperature at which hydrogen enters the liquid phase is $-253°$ C. Thermal insulation and in-line refrigeration plants would greatly increase the capital costs of the pipeline. The minimum work required to cool hydrogen from $21°$ C and one atmosphere to a liquid at one atmosphere is 5198 Btu/pound. However, because of thermodynamic limitations, the energy consumed in liquefying hydrogen is 15,000 to 30,000 Btu/pound, depending on the process used. Because of the temperatures involved and the refrigeration costs, pipeline transmission of liquid hydrogen may be desired only if the end use form requires liquid hydrogen.[1]

The pipeline transmission of cryogenic hydrogen has been limited to short runs at production plants and to somewhat longer lines at space program test and launch facilities.

The possibility of pipeline transmission of subcooled liquid hydrogen as a slush solid/liquid mixture has been suggested. The advantages of this scheme are an increased density of 15-20 percent over cryogenic hydrogen and the very significant additional heat sink capability, which minimizes the refrigeration required along the pipeline.

Truck, Train and Barge

The transportation of small volumes of gaseous hydrogen in high pressure containers is common.[2] However, for large volumes, this form of transmission is not practical. Transportation of cryogenic hydrogen has been carried out by truck trailers with capacities of 16,000 gallons and by railroad tank cars with capacities of 34,000 gallons. The insulation problems and the boil-off losses are disadvantages for the long distance transmission of hydrogen by these means.

The Chicago Bridge and Iron Co. has built hydrogen transportation barges for NASA with tank capacities of 240,000 gallons. The tanks consist of concentric cylinders separated by 23 inches of evacuated perlite. The boil-off losses from these tanks is about 0.25 percent per day.[2]

[1] D. P. Gregory, *A Hydrogen-Energy System*, American Gas Association, August 1972.

[2] Homer W. Carhart, *et. al.,* "Hydrogen as a Navy Fuel," *NRL Report 7754*, June 12, 1974.

HYDROGEN UTILIZATION

Heating

Two types of combustion are possible for hydrogen. The first is by conventional burners modified to account for the particular physical and chemical properties of hydrogen. The second is by catalytic or surface combustion, which can occur below the normal flame temperature and avoid the formation of nitrogen oxides. Catalytic burners eliminate the open flame (particularly serious for hydrogen since the flame is invisible) and produce only water vapor. This eliminates the necessity of venting the exhaust gases with the accompanying loss of heat. Catalytic space heating systems would be decentralized and resemble electrical appliances in flexibility.

Electrical Power Generation

Hydrogen can be converted to electricity by fuel cells and by direct thermal-mechanical systems. Hydrogen is the ideal fuel for efficient production of electricity in fuel cells.

Direct thermal-mechanical systems for electric power production include central steam plants, gas turbine generators and diesel generators. These systems can be converted to hydrogen without great difficulty. The efficiency of these systems can be increased by supplying pure oxygen for the combustion. For base-loading, hydrogen-oxygen fired plants could have efficiencies as high as 55 percent.

The expense of pipelining oxygen (a by-product of the electrolysis and thermochemical production of hydrogen) is prohibitive over distances greater than 30 miles. If liquid hydrogen is the chosen method for transporting energy, the recovery of the hydrogen liquefaction energy can make it possible to separate stoichiometric amounts of oxygen from air on site with little additional energy.[1]

Vehicles and Aircraft Propulsion

Considerable work, dating from the late 1920s, has been done on the use of hydrogen in internal combustion engines. The use of hydrogen in piston engines appears to be quite possible by the application of fuel injection and proper ignition timing.

In 1956, Pratt and Whitney converted a standard J57 aircraft engine to operate with hydrogen. At a later date, a B-57 was flown with one engine operating on hydrogen from a liquid hydrogen fuel tank. Engine conversions to hydrogen appear to present few problems.[2]

Although handling and on-board storage of hydrogen is a serious problem for any vehicle, liquid hydrogen as a fuel for transportation is technically possible. In fact, it may be the only fuel for long-range, high-performance hypersonic transports and might be adaptable for use by jumbo jets. Small, vacuum-insulated tanks have been constructed for use in automobiles which can contain boil-off for up to 18 hours.

[1] W. R. Parrish, *et. al.*, "Selected Topics on Hydrogen Fuel," NBS Special Publication 419, May 1975.
[2] R. J. Schoeppel, *Chemical Technology* Vol. 2, No. 476, 1972.

SECTION THIRTEEN

SOLAR ENERGY

INTRODUCTION

Solar energy is an ideal energy source in many ways. Solar energy conversion systems generate neither air nor water pollution and negligible thermal pollution. Solar energy is abundant and perpetually renewable. Approximately 1,390 watts of energy arrive on each square meter of surface just outside the earth's atmosphere, and solar energy is equivalent to about 1,000 watts per square meter, directly facing the sun at the earth's surface on a clear day.

The annual U.S. energy demand for the early 1970s has been estimated at between 12 to 15×10^{12} kwh (after process losses).[1] Theoretically, a desert area of 50 miles by 50 miles would receive this equivalent energy each year. A desert area of 30 miles by 30 miles (equal to 85 percent of Rhode Island) would receive enough solar energy to meet U.S. conventional energy demands in the early 1970s. While these hypothetical examples provide a perspective of the intensity of solar energy available compared to total national energy requirements, they are misleading. Available solar energy conversion devices have nominal conversion efficiencies of 10 percent for photo-

voltaic solar cells or thermionic devices and less than 70 percent for water and air heating panels.

Thermal electric systems require high operating temperatures (about 1,000° F) relative to ambient temperatures. Concentrator collectors can produce these temperatures, but collector heat losses increase as mean collector temperatures exceed ambient temperatures. Overall solar-thermal electric system efficiencies may be, at best, about like those of photovoltaic conversion efficiencies; that is the overall collector area requirements for a solar-thermal electric plant will be nominally the same as those for a photovoltaic system to produce the same power.[1]

The most important near-term applications of solar energy include:

- Direct solar heating and cooling.
- Thermal generation of electricity.
- Photovoltaic generation of electricity.

[1] B. J. Brinkworth, *Solar Energy for Man*, 1972, Sections 1.3 to 1.6 and p. 240.

TERRESTRIAL SOLAR ENERGY CHARACTERISTICS

The sun is neither a continuous nor a constant source of energy. Relative to any point on earth, the sun rises in the east, crosses the sky at 15° per hour, and sets in the west. On any day, the sun reaches a maximum altitude at mid-day, depending on the season of the year. Because of the earth's 23½° tilt, the solar altitude in the northern hemisphere is at its highest on June 21 and its lowest (at mid-day) on December 21. Correspondingly, the number of daylight hours available at the peak of summer are proportionally greater than the number of daylight hours at the peak of winter.

Solar radiation is usually measured in Langleys per minute or Langleys per day. A Langley of radiation energy is equivalent to one calorie of heat per square centimeter.

Approximately 700 stations in the world continuously record solar radiation intensity. These stations measure direct and scattered radiation on a horizontal surface. About 100 stations record radiation received on a surface maintained normal to the sun. However, most available solar radiation charts indicate the diffuse and normal intensity incident on a stationary, horizontal surface. A typical average solar radiation level for temperature regions is one Langley per minute for a surface tilted toward the sun on a clear day. This level of solar intensity can result in an accumulation of 500 Langleys for a

Table XVII-1
COMMON SOLAR ENERGY INTENSITY CONVERSION FACTORS

1 Langley/min	=	1 cal/(cm^2 . min)
	=	221 Btu/(ft^2 . hr)
	=	0.700 kw/m^2
Assuming 500 min/day of solar radiation, 1 Langley/min	=	500 Langleys/day
	=	500 cal/(cm^2 . day)
	=	1841.7 Btu/ft^2 . day)

500-minute day (approximately eight hours). Table XVII-1 shows some useful energy conversions.

Regions between 15° and 35° latitude either side of the equator receive the greatest amount of solar energy with a minimum mean radiation of 500 Langleys per day. The southern United States, Mexico, Hawaii, India, Saudi Arabia, southern China and northern Africa all fall in the maximum solar energy band in the northern hemisphere. Australia, southern Brazil and southern Africa fall in the corresponding maximum solar energy band in the southern hemisphere.

The equatorial belt between 15° N and 15° S receives between 300 to 500 Langleys per day throughout the year, which is somewhat less than the tropical regions receive. This equatorial belt includes the East Indies, southeast Asia, Central America, northern Brazil and central Africa.

Between 35° and 45° latitudes, radiation can average 400 to 500 Langleys per day during the summer; however there is a significant seasonal drop in solar intensity during the winter. The seasonal variation can be reduced by utilizing collectors that are maintained normal to the sun. Falling in this moderate solar energy band is most of the continental United States, southern Europe, the Mediterranean Sea, Japan and most of the People's Republic of China.

Regions north of 45° N receive a limited amount of annual solar energy, which is particularly low in winter months. This region of limited solar energy includes northern Europe, Scandinavia, Alaska, most of Canada and most of the Soviet Union. In those latitudes, half the total annual solar radiation may be diffuse with a higher proportion of diffuse energy in the winter than in the summer. Also, at those high latitudes, the maximum solar altitudes are low, particularly in winter; consequently, vertical surfaces facing the equator can receive greater amounts of solar energy than can horizontal surfaces. In Hamburg, West Germany, for example, solar radiation falling on a southfacing vertical surface can be over two and one-half times that falling on a horizontal surface.

Another form of solar radiation is that which is reflected from the ground, particularly from snow or water, and long wavelength infrared radiation released by warm ground temperatures to a cooler atmosphere. The reflected sunlight, known as albedo, may be an important factor in using solar heating in certain locations.

Many environmental factors affect the average solar energy that the earth receives in any given location. Cloud cover interferes with solar radiation; the solar intensity on mountaintops above the clouds normally would be greater than that in a neighboring valley, and a foggy location near the sea would receive diminished solar energy. Air pollution also severely limits the amount of solar radiation received.

Long-range weather characteristics, such as cloudy day sequences in northern regions, constitute important statistical information that can affect the design of solar energy systems. In locations such as New England, where up to 10 successive days of cloud cover may occur, large-capacity thermal storage systems may be required if solar energy is to be used as a primary heating system.[1]

Figure XVII-1 shows the annual or seasonal solar energy intensity characteristics of specific regions. Other more specific insolation data has been published in *Solar Energy*.[2] These maps indicate the amount of energy that falls on a horizontal surface, a common measurement of solar energy intensity. However, this kind of statistical information is only a very preliminary indicator of available solar energy.

Figure XVII-2 indicates the variation in solar energy that occurs through the seasons based on measurements of various directional orientations at a New England latitude. The measured solar intensities for various months of the year as shown in Figure XVII-2 indicate that orientation of the collector panels critically affects the amount of convertible solar energy available during a given season. This figure indicates that a horizontally oriented collector receives less than one-half the solar energy that a south-facing vertical collector receives in December. Either orientation is similar in performance in March and September; consequently, if the primary function of a solar collector is to provide heat for late fall, winter and early spring months, then vertically oriented collectors would be more useful for New England latitudes.

Empirical data indicating solar intensity on vertical surfaces or other selected orientations is limited. However, the solar intensity on a vertical or inclined surface can be derived from horizontal surface intensities through trigonometric relationships between the receiving surface and the sun's rays. The inclined surface intensities calculated by geometric relationships have been developed to compensate, to some extent, for clouding, albedo, and diffusion effects. Empirical performance has been correlated with the mathematical models developed resulting in a firm basis for estimating the solar intensity on any south-facing inclined surface. The hourly intensities derived from these models can be summed to result in expected daily insolation levels. The mean daily insolation can then be estimated for any month. The characteristic solar intensity levels of a given region directly affect the collector size required to generate the desired heat or electrical energy. The physical practicality and the economic justification for purchasing a collector are closely related to minimizing collector size and optimizing orientation for a maximum of energy conversion.[3]

[1] Farrington Daniels, *Direct Use of the Sun's Energy*, Chapter 3, 1974.
[2] Ivan Bennett, "Monthly Maps of Mean Daily Insolation for the United States," *Solar Energy*, IX, 3, 1965.
[3] B. Y. H. Liva and R. C. Jordon, "A Rational Procedure for Predicting the Long-Term Average Performance of Flat-Plate Solar Energy Collectors," *Solar Energy*, VII, 2, 1963.

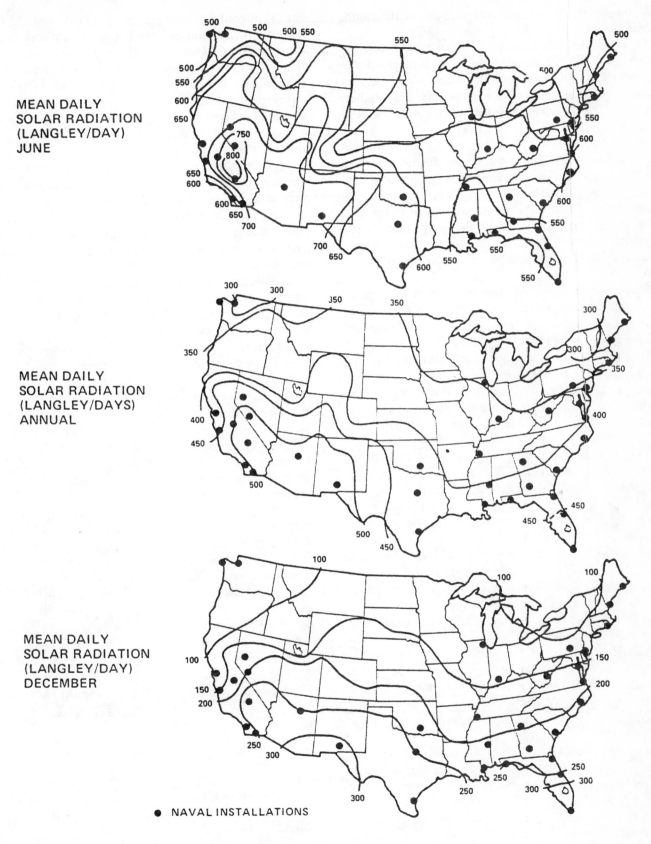

MEAN DAILY
SOLAR RADIATION
(LANGLEY/DAY)
JUNE

MEAN DAILY
SOLAR RADIATION
(LANGLEY/DAYS)
ANNUAL

MEAN DAILY
SOLAR RADIATION
(LANGLEY/DAY)
DECEMBER

● NAVAL INSTALLATIONS

Source: *Solar Power*, IX, 3, 1963.

Figure XVII-1. SOLAR ENERGY DISTRIBUTION IN THE U.S.

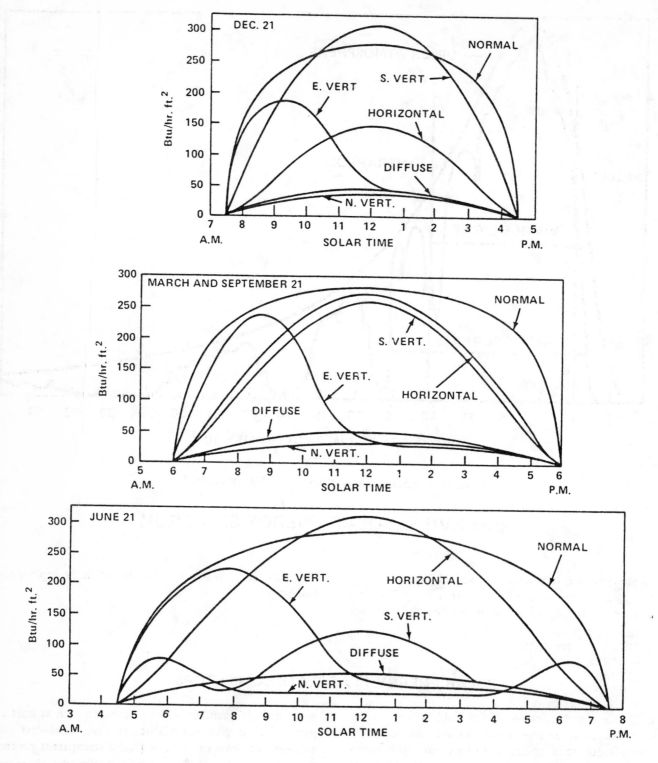

Incident solar energy on clear days, latitude 42° N. (Reported by I. F. Hand, U.S. Weather Bureau, Milton, Mass, January, 1950.)

Source: I. F. Hand, U.S. Weather Bureau, Milton, Mass.

Figure XVII-2. INCIDENT SOLAR ENERGY ON CLEAR DAYS IN NEW ENGLAND, LATITUDE 42° N

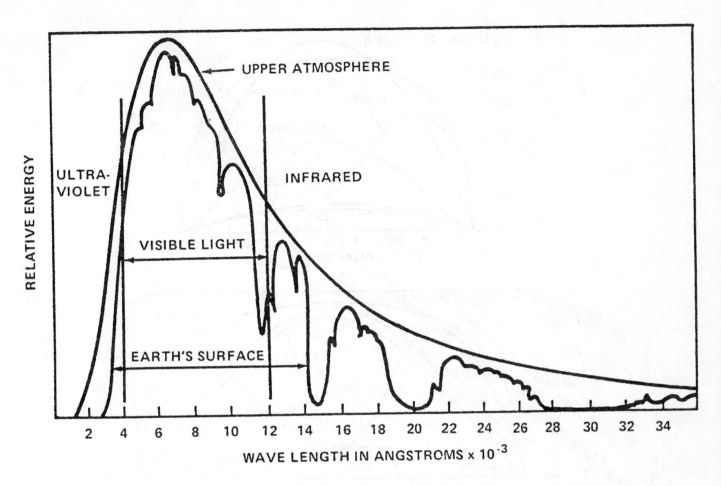

Source: Eppley Laboratory, Inc., Newport, R. I.

Figure XVII-3. SOLAR ENERGY SPECTRUM

Several types of instruments are available for measuring and recording the characteristics of solar energy. To measure solar intensity as a function of wavelength, as shown in Figure XVII-3, requires the use of fairly sophisticated equipment.

SOLAR ENERGY FLAT-PLATE COLLECTORS

The simplest and most readily available type of solar energy collector is a large black surface that converts short wavelength solar radiation to long-wave heat radiation. The heat is conducted from the collector to air or water, which can then be used for space heating or for producing hot water for a variety of applications.

A typical flat-plate collector is illustrated in Figure XVII-6. A large flat plate of sheet metal is painted black on the side that will face the sun. Tubing bonded to the sheet metal circulates water to the plate, which collects heat conducted from the plate. The flat plate is enclosed in an air-tight chamber, which is covered with at least one pane of clear glass (or plastic) so that short-wave solar radiation can pass easily through the transparent covering. The black surface will tend to convert the short-wave solar radiation to long-wave infrared radiation, which is emitted from the black surface. The glass coverings are poor conductors of heat, which trap the infrared radiation and, therefore, reduce heat loss from the flat-plate collector. Flat-plate collectors can produce water temperatures of 150° F to 200° F under normal solar intensity,

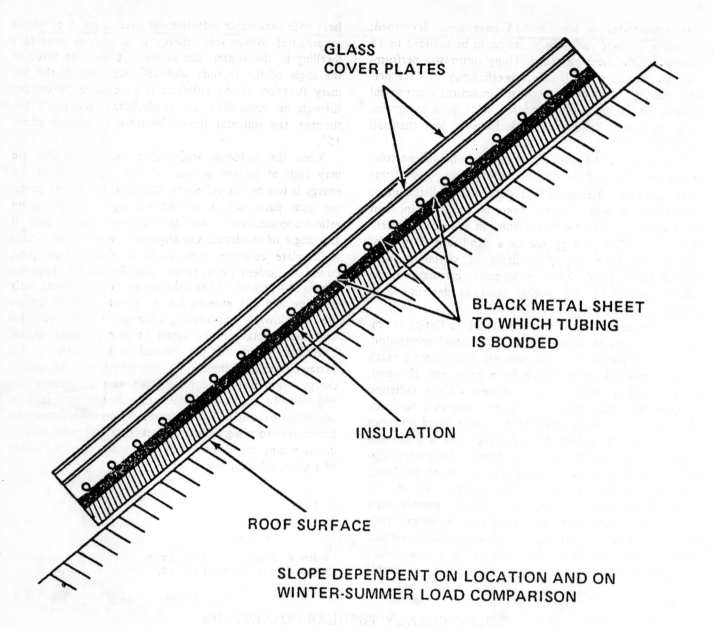

Figure XVII-6. SOLAR ENERGY FLAT-PLATE COLLECTOR

and temperatures approaching boiling are feasible on exceptionally hot days.

As solar radiation is converted by the flat-plate collector, a steady-state temperature is reached where the rates of heat recovery and loss are balanced by heat gain. Heat loss by convection to the surrounding air increases as wind velocity increases particularly at high collector

temperatures. Radiation losses also increase with high collector temperatures. Transmission losses through the glass-pane covers can be 15 to 20 percent. Between 80 and 95 percent of the solar energy passing through the glass pane covers can be absorbed. By using two or three layers of glass covering and insulating the panel, convection and conduction losses can be minimized. Selective surfaces with emissivities as low as 0.15 have been developed; therefore, infrared radiation losses could be reduced to 15 percent of the heat absorbed. Using optimistic performance factors, an overall collector efficiency of 68.5 percent may be achievable. However, practical commercial designs, which must keep material costs to a minimum, result in overall efficiencies considerably less than 50 percent.[1]

The flat-plate collector can convert both diffuse solar energy, which is generally omnidirectional, and direct solar radiation. Meteorological data which distinguishes the diffuse portion from the direct solar energy incident on a horizontal surface is available. In the northern latitudes, the diffuse energy can be a significant portion of the average solar energy available in winter months. Consequently, for flat-plate performance calculations, the diffuse energy for any region must be determined in calculating panel efficiency.

The amount of normal radiation that a flat-plate collector can convert to heat depends on panel orientation. A panel normal to the sun's rays will accumulate a maximum of available solar energy for a given size. However, since flat-plate collectors can convert diffuse radiation without the complicated mechanisms required to track the sun's path, they are usually fixed in inclined positions facing south to collect diffuse energy and a maximum practical portion of the available direct solar energy. Fixing the position of the flat-plate collector simplifies design but compromises the total daily energy that can be accumulated from solar radiation. Although mathematical models have been developed to determine normal radiation for a given orientation, a south-facing, fixed-position collector generally should be oriented for a compromise solar altitude that would convert solar energy to usable heat with reasonable effectiveness over as much of winter as practical. Where solar energy is to provide heat to a dwelling in the winter, the collector should be tilted at the angle of the latitude plus 15°. However, if the primary function of the collector is to provide air cooling through an absorption air conditioning system in the summer, the collector should be tilted at latitude minus 15°.

When the incidence angles to a collector surface are very high at certain periods of any day, much of the energy is lost by the reflective characteristics of the covering glass panes set at an oblique angle. Double panes reflect approximately twice the energy of a single pane at any angle of incidence. Consequently, where light strikes a flat-plate collector with single or double glass pane covers at incident angles greater than 70° or 80°, approximately 40 percent of the light energy is lost. During early morning and late evening hours, normal solar intensities are very low. A south-facing collector will receive these very weak solar energy levels at high incident angles. Therefore, much of the normal solar energy at the extreme hours of the day is lost. However, the normal energy component of the oblique rays can contribute cumulatively to the total daily solar energy that may be converted by a flat-plate collector. Orientation losses and transparent-covering reflection losses should be considered in estimating the daily energy accumulation performance of a given collector size.

[1] Walter E. Morror, Jr., "Solar Energy—Its Time Is Near," *Technology Review*, December 1973, pp. 31-43.

SOLAR ENERGY TUBULAR COLLECTORS

The tubular collector, another type of solar collector, is still in the developmental stage. Commercial production of tubular collectors is expected to begin in one or two years. The tubular collector is made of three concentric glass tubes, using manufacturing techniques similar to those for fluorescent light tubes. (See Figure XVII-7.) The feeder tube is the innermost cylinder; the absorber tube surrounds it; and the cover tube is outermost. The transparent cover tube allows light to pass to the absorber tube through the evacuated space between the tubes. The absorber tube has a selective surface coating which enables it to absorb energy from the sun. The collector fluid flows in through the feeder tube and collects heat from the selective surface of the absorber tube as the fluid returns between the tubes.

Because of its tubular construction, high vacuum, and selective coating, the tubular collector can produce temperatures above 240°F, with greater efficiency than flat-plate collectors. Low ambient temperatures and high winds have minimal effects on tubular collector performance because of the vacuum insulation. Also, the tubular symmetry and low loss coefficient enable these collectors to heat fluids to useful temperatures for longer periods of the day and under more diffuse conditions.

Tubular collectors are placed on trough-shaped reflective backgrounds to increase performance. Each tube in the collector panel rests in a shallow aluminum parabolic trough providing a moderate degree of concentration without having to track the movement of the sun. The reflective surface directs more of the sun's diffuse and direct rays to the tubular collector than a flat reflective background.

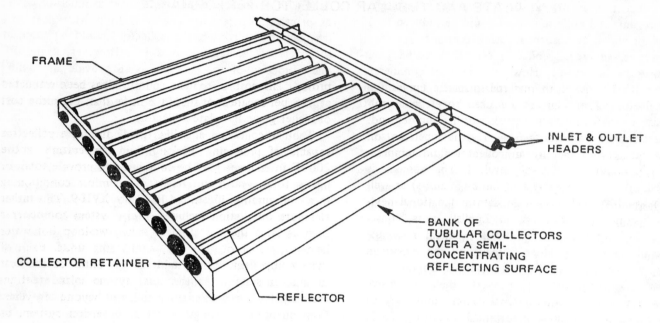

FRAME

INLET & OUTLET
HEADERS

BANK OF
TUBULAR COLLECTORS
OVER A SEMI-
CONCENTRATING
REFLECTING SURFACE

COLLECTOR RETAINER

REFLECTOR

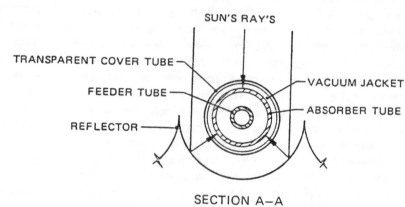

SUN'S RAY'S

TRANSPARENT COVER TUBE

FEEDER TUBE

VACUUM JACKET

ABSORBER TUBE

REFLECTOR

SECTION A—A

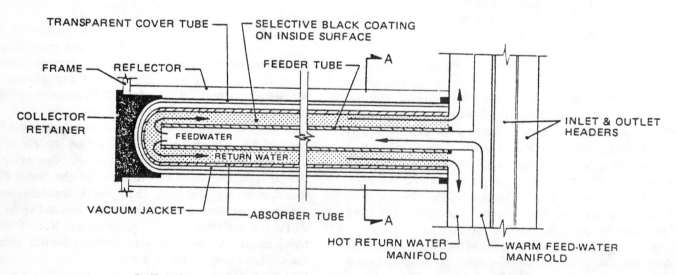

TRANSPARENT COVER TUBE

SELECTIVE BLACK COATING
ON INSIDE SURFACE

FEEDER TUBE

FRAME   REFLECTOR

A

COLLECTOR
RETAINER

FEEDWATER

RETURN WATER

INLET & OUTLET
HEADERS

VACUUM JACKET

ABSORBER TUBE

A

HOT RETURN WATER
MANIFOLD

WARM FEED-WATER
MANIFOLD

CUT-AWAY SECTION OF A TYPICAL TUBULAR COLLECTOR

Figure XVII-7. TUBULAR COLLECTOR

FLAT-PLATE AND TUBULAR COLLECTOR PERFORMANCE

Figure XVII-8 shows thermal performance curves for solar collectors. These curves are used to estimate collector size to match insolation levels and heating demand. The parameter of the abscissa, $T_f - T_a/I$, is dependent on ambient temperature, T_a; mean collector fluid temperature, T_f; and solar insolation level, I. The abscissa is measured in international system units (SI units) as well as English units. Much insolation data and national heating and cooling statistics are in English units; consequently, English units are the most practical reference units until the U.S. Weather Bureau and the American Society of Heating, Refrigerating, and Air Conditioning Engineers (ASHRAE, Inc.) convert their extensive national statistics into international system units. (Since SI is becoming widely used in technical literature, the SI scale is shown for reference in Figure XVII-8.) Collector efficiency is the ratio of the heat collected to the incident energy on a unit area of the collector. Not all manufacturer's collector performance characteristics are depicted as shown in Figure XVII-8; however, National Bureau of Standards (NBS) uses this performance notation and most published performance characteristics can be translated into these parameters.

Typical design regions are indicated in Figure XVII-8. By regulating fluid flow, a solar collector should be able to produce temperatures greater than 140° F if it is to provide water heating or to supply heat to a water tank for thermal storage for a space heating system. At a solar insolation of one Langley per minute (221 Btu/ft² hr) and a winter ambient temperature of 40° F, $(T_f - T_a)/I = 0.45°$ F hr ft²/Btu. Notice that at 140° F, the efficiency of a tubular collector system slightly exceeds that of a flat-plate collector. A solar collector which heats air under similar conditions may produce temperatures of approximately 100° F during winter months; at lower output temperatures, the flat-plate collector is more efficient than a tubular collector.

The overall efficiency of cooling systems will tend to increase as heat source temperatures increase. Consequently, the goal for solar cooling system design is to provide temperatures well in excess of 200° F from the solar collector. At higher output temperatures, the tubular collector can perform at much higher thermal efficiencies than a flat-plate collector. Based on these performance characteristics, tubular collectors appear to be more versatile; they can perform as well as flat-plate collectors for heating water in all seasons and yet produce the higher temperatures for efficient solar cooling in the summer. However, tubular collectors are relatively new and un-

proved. The cost of tubular collectors has been estimated at $25 per square foot, which is more than twice the cost of higher grade flat-plate collectors.

Tubular collectors and high grade flat-plate collectors capable of producing working fluid temperatures above 200° F in summer may be configured to provide total, or nearly total, year-round residential comfort conditioning in a configuration illustrated in Figure XVII-9. This rather elaborate installation includes special system components such as large thermal storage tanks, two-loop hot water heaters, and absorption air conditioning units. Each of these component options adds to the initial capital cost of a solar system. As the total system initial cost increases, payoff periods may extend well beyond ten years. Consequently, a high-grade solar conversion system, as depicted in Figure XVII-9, may provide a large portion of winter space heating, summer cooling, and year-long water heating—possibly over 75 percent of a residence's total annual energy requirements. But the system may not pay for itself in fuel savings in less than 15 years.

Air heating collectors produce low temperatures and, therefore, should operate at the higher collector heating value; they may be operated with limited thermal storage in a bed of crushed rock. Although air systems are limited to space heating, they are simple and inexpensive compared to the more elaborate water heating systems. Because of their low initial cost, simple air heating systems pay for themselves in a shorter time, but they provide a smaller portion of the overall heat demand.

The selection and sizing of a solar system for any application is a complex procedure which must account for many factors. A few of the many considerations in comparing various solar collector types and systems can be deduced from the performance curves in Figure XVII-8.

A step-by-step approach for estimating the size and cost of a solar collector system based on the use of the performance curves of Figure XVII-8 has been published by the Civil Engineering Laboratory of the Naval Facilities Engineering Command. Their report, *Solar Heating of Buildings and Domestic Hot Water* (Technical Report No. R835, January 1976, by E. J. Beck, Jr. and R. L. Field) is based on design procedures developed by leading authorities in solar energy conversion.[1]

---

[1] S. A. Klein, *et al*, "A Design Procedure for Solar Heating Systems," *Solar Energy*, V 18 (1976), pp. 113-127.

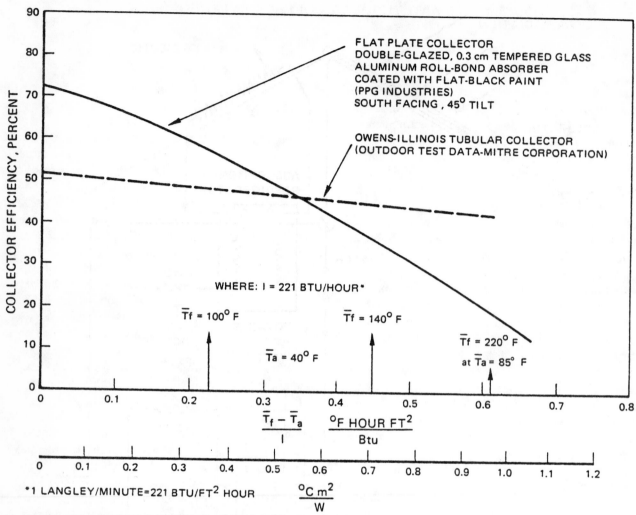

Source: Civil Engineering Laboratory, Naval Facilities Engineering Command,
Technical Report No. R835, January 1976.

Figure XVII-8. FLAT-PLATE AND TUBULAR COLLECTOR PERFORMANCE CHARACTERISTICS

SOLAR COOLING

Solar cooling systems have the advantage that demand and supply tend to be in phase. When the sun shines hottest, the need for refrigeration and air conditioning is greatest. Cooling units that are being considered for integration with solar collectors to provide space cooling include absorption cycles, organic Rankine cycles, and dessicant absorption units. Solar powered systems for space cooling require a refrigeration or cooling cycle that will give good performance at the relatively low temperature levels provided by low cost solar collectors, and equipment suitable for low-cost production and long life operation with minimum maintenance.

The efficiency or coefficient of performance (COP) of any air conditioning system is a function of maximum cycle temperature (the temperatures produced by the solar collector or other heat source) and the condensing temperature. The greater the difference of these two temperatures, the higher the COP. Tubular collectors and high-grade flat-plate collectors using selective surfaces and two or three transparent covers may be able to produce the cycle temperatures required for a relatively efficient and practical air cooling or dehumidification system.

Of the various cooling systems in consideration, the absorption cycle is being applied in several demonstration projects sponsored by ERDA. HUD solar driven organic Rankine cycles are under development and may not be available commercially for some time. However, active dessicant systems such as the Munters Environmental Control may be available for solar dehumidification and cooling in the near future.

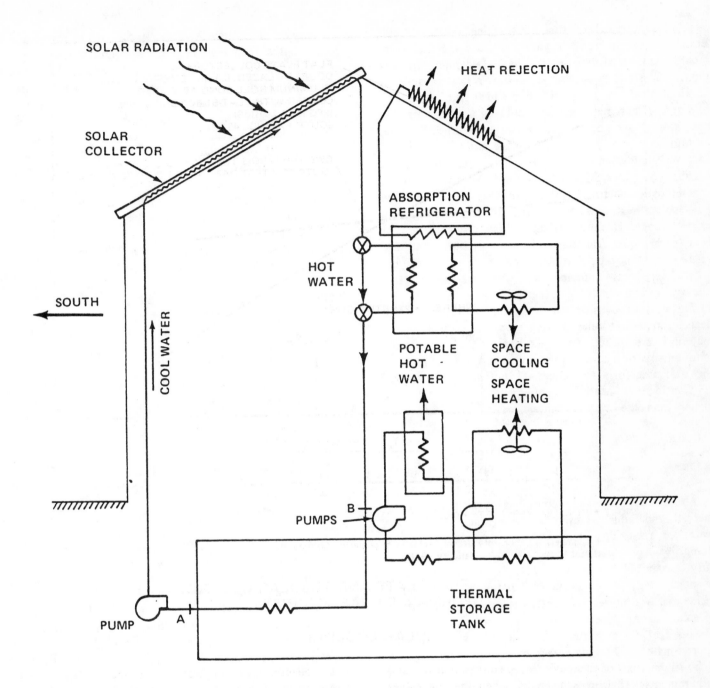

Figure XVII-9. HOUSEHOLD SOLAR HEATING AND COOLING SYSTEM

LOW-TEMPERATURE ENERGY STORAGE

The flat-plate collector used for residential space heating, Figure XVII-9, utilizes a storage system that provides a day or two of heating capacity to compensate for night-heating requirements and overcast conditions. Thermal storage systems may be either sensible-heat storage or latent-heat storage types. Sensible heat storage means heating a material and causing a temperature rise, then releasing the accumulated heat as the material cools to ambient temperature. Water has the highest specific heat (62 Btu/ft³ ° F) of any thermal storage material up to 200° F. Raising the temperature of 3 cubic feet of water (22.5 gallons) 100° F stores the heat equivalent of one pound (~pint) of fuel oil (heating value ~18,600 Btu/lb). Crushed stone is an inexpensive material commonly used for storing sensible heat. Depending on how tightly the stone is packed, it can have a heat capacity of 25 to 36 Btu/ft^3 °F, about half the heat storage capacity of water. Other materials that could be used for sensible heat storage are not as cheap as water or crushed stone.

Another form of thermal storage utilizes the latent heat or phase-change properties of various compounds. Glauber's salt ($Na_2SO_4 \cdot 10H_2O$) has high heat of fusion characteristics at transition temperatures of 90° F. These salts have a heat capacity of 9,700 Btu/ft^3 resulting from phase change. However, Glauber's salt cannot retain its heat for any practical length of time, and 24-hour storage of heat may not be feasible. Other materials displaying latent heat storage superior to Glauber's salt are available but usually at a much higher cost.

The cost of thermal storage systems is critical in the decision to adopt solar heating even when the cheapest materials are used. To meet average winter heating requirements of a dwelling usually requires use of most of the roof area for solar collectors. In January and February, residential heating requirements are considerably higher than the average winter heating load, and solar intensity is at its lowest during those two exceptionally cold months. The high heat demand and the low solar intensity of the two coldest months amplify the size requirements of solar panels required. Because roof-size limitations restrict the amount of heat that can be collected practically from solar radiation during the coldest two months, very little or no reserve can be accumulated for overnight use. Solar heating must be supplemented with an electrical or fossil-fuel fired home heating system during exceptional demand. With the requirement for an auxiliary heating system, it becomes difficult to justify the capital investment for a thermal storage system with a capacity greater than the average overnight heating demand. Practical solar heating systems are sized for compromise conditions to accumulate possibly up to 24 hours of reserve heat during "average" winter heating and solar intensity months. A tank of 157 cubic feet of water elevated 100° F· in temperature may be able to provide one day of reserve heat for a typical house. This 4.5x4.5x8 foot tank would require a large closet in a basement.[1]

[1] H. F. Hottel and J. B. Howard, *New Energy Technology, Some Facts and Assessments*, 1973.

ECONOMIC CONSIDERATIONS FOR HEATING AND COOLING SYSTEMS

About half the energy consumed by residential, commercial, and industrial users is in the form of hot air, hot water, or low-quality steam.[1] A very large portion of this domestic energy demand could be met without particularly advanced development. Flat-plate collectors could produce nearly all of the energy required for individual residential heating requirements. The primary disadvantage of solar heating panels is their size. A one-floor house 30 by 30 feet in a central U.S. location would require approximately 500 square feet of collector area to provide 70 percent of winter space-heating and hot water requirements. Thermal storage by heating water would require a tank capacity of 750 to 1,000 gallons. The total system could cost from $5,000 to $15,000. Where electric heating is the alternative, $500 to $800 a year can be saved in fuel costs. Where oil heating is the alternative, $200 to $350 can be saved.[2] Consequently, solar heating may become economically competitive with electric heating in the near future as the cost of electric energy increases and as the cost of mass produced solar heating systems decreases.

In view of estimates that existing houses will provide approximately 50 percent of the housing needs in 2000,[3] newly constructed solar homes will probably not be able to contribute significantly to residential or building heating requirements for the near future. However, many houses may be able to retrofit modular systems on existing roof surfaces. Panels of limited size could be installed on roofs or elsewhere on the property to provide possibly only 25 to 30 percent of winter heating requirements. If the scope of supplemental heating were kept within these limits, a home could be heated while the sun shines and no thermal storage system would need to be incorporated. With this approach, at least daytime heating requirements could be offset to some extent. The overall effect could be a significant reduction in annual heating requirements and costs by the individual homeowner. The initial capital cost of a limited-size panel then may be justified over a long-term fuel cost savings. As the cost of fuel for heating increases, individual houses, schools, commercial buildings, and factories may convert to limited solar heating to offset conventional fuel requirements. Several relatively portable units, some containing limited thermal storage, are currently being sold. Various commercial units are being introduced for residential application.

[1] *Exploring Energy Choices—A Preliminary Report*, Energy Policy Project of the Ford Foundation, 1974, pp. 1-4; S. David Freeman, "Energy," *The New Era*, August 1974, p. 206.
[2] "Solar Energy for Space Heating and Hot Water," ERDA Division of Solar Energy Pamphlet No. SE101, May 1976.
[3] S. David Freeman, "Energy," *The New Era*, August 1974, p. 206.

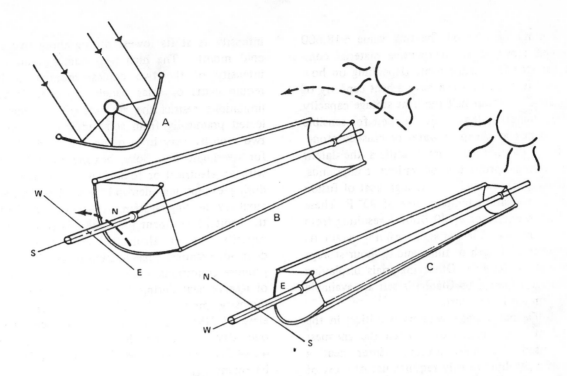

Figure XVII-10. PARABOLIC CONCENTRATOR CONFIGURATIONS

HIGH-TEMPERATURE CONCENTRATOR COLLECTORS

A concentrator collector focuses the sun's energy on a relatively small area, creating very high temperatures at the focal point. The typical concentrator collector is a parabolic prism reflector with a heat absorbing pipe at the focal line. See Figure XVII-10. Water flowing through the collector pipe is heated to steam, which can be used to drive a turbine to produce power. Temperatures above 4,000° C can be generated by a parabolic collector; however, steam temperatures of only 600° C are required for the turbines used by electric utilities. Concentrator collectors can be configured to convert solar to electric energy.[1]

The collector pipe at the focal point of the parabolic concentrator reaches a steady-state temperature at which the rates of heat recovery and losses are balanced by the heat gain. As with flat-plate collectors, the highest collector efficiencies can be achieved when the concentrator collector temperatures approach ambient.

The concentrator collector cannot convert diffuse energy and must continuously face the sun if high conversion efficiencies are to be maintained throughout the day. Ideally, the line bisecting the concave angle formed by the parabolic prism (or a surface of revolution) collector must be parallel to all planes formed by the sun's rays to maximize conversion of available normal radiation. A two-axis tracking collector can be mechanically synchronized by clockwork to follow the east-west travel of the sun and can be automatically adjusted to the sun's seasonal altitude changes. Although this is the most efficient concentrator collector configuration, it is the most complex mechanically. A practical compromise uses one-axis tracking, which will either pivot to east-west solar travel at a fixed inclination angle or pivot to altitude change about an east-west axis (B and C in Figure XVII-10). The one-axis tracking collector is simpler than the two-axis collector, yet can be designed to perform nearly as well for the high-intensity periods of the day.

A common solar power plant configuration using concentrator collectors is illustrated in Figure XVII-11. Banks of parabolic concentrators would be used to "farm" a large area of solar energy to produce the large quantity of steam required to drive a major electric utility.

Another common solar power plant configuration is the tower collector shown on Figure XVII-12. In this configuration, a large area of two-axis flat reflectors are coordinated to direct sunlight to a central collector where the solar energy is further concentrated to produce the high-cycle temperatures required of an efficient thermal

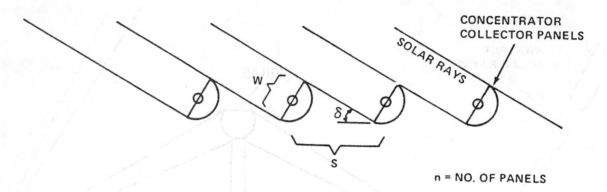

FOR $\delta = 30°$, S = 2w

THEREFORE, FOR PANEL LENGTH L, TOTAL PANEL AREA, Ap = nwL.
HOWEVER, TOTAL PLAN AREA BECOMES:

Ao = nLS, FOR n >> 1; THAT IS, FOR n > 20.

(FOR SMALL n, ON AREA = LS CAN BE DEDUCTED FROM THE
GENERAL EQUATION FOR Ao.)

Figure XVII-11. SOLAR FARM AREA RELATIVE TO COLLECTOR AREA

power plant. These solar farms would require large land areas to provide central-station power levels. A 1,000 MW(e) continuous-duty power station would require a collector area of 16 km^2, assuming a steam system efficiency of 25 percent. However, banks of collectors on a solar farm will tend to shade each other during early morning and late evening hours when solar incident angles are very oblique. Consequently, if full collector utilization is to occur at solar altitude angles of 30 degrees or more, collectors will have to be spaced at least one panel apart, as shown on Figure XVII-11. As a result, the land area required can be double the collector area required if collector effectiveness is to be maximized for full-day solar energy conversion. The 1,000 MW(e) power station would therefore require approximately 32 km^2, which is over 11 square miles. The reflectors of the tower top concentrating configuration in Figure XVII-12 are subject to the same spacing and plan area requirements of parabolic collectors.[1]

Because daytime peak loads of a typical power station are nearly twice as high as the continuous base loads,[2] a 1,000-megawatt solar plant may be more practical in off-setting some part of the daytime peak power require-

ments. Used this way, the solar plant would not have to be oversized to produce the storable energy for operating continuously during dark or overcast hours. A 1,000-megawatt intermittent load plant would require a collector area of approximately 8 km^2 (assuming a solar intensity of 1 Langley/min, a collector efficiency of 70 percent and a steam plant efficiency of 25 percent). The 16 km^2 land area required would be one-half that required for a continuous duty 1,000-megawatt plant. The overall area conversion efficiency of this example would be 17.5 percent, based on relatively optimistic assumptions. With more realistic collector efficiencies of less than 50 percent, overall area conversion efficiencies of the solar thermal powerplant will be less than 12 percent, which is only roughly competitive with photovoltaic area conversion efficiencies. The intermittent load solar powerplant would operate only when sufficient solar energy were available to supplement power requirements.

[1] Walter E. Morror, Jr., "Solar Energy—Its Time Is Near," *Technology Review*, December 1973, pp. 31-43.
[2] Federal Power Commission, *The 1970 National Power Survey, Part 1*, 1971, Chapter 3.

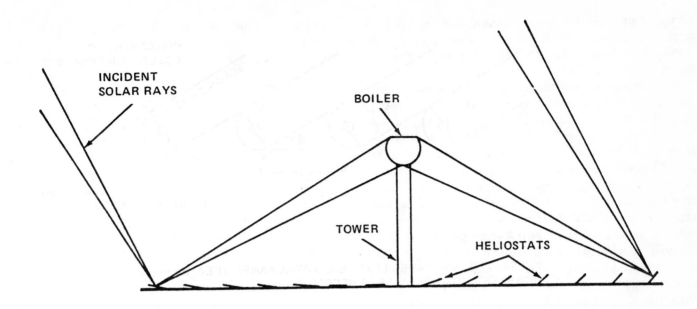

Figure XVII-12. TOWER TOP COLLECTOR

HIGH-TEMPERATURE STORAGE

Energy storage systems used with concentrator collector powerplants are similar to those described for flat-plate collectors. However, efficient steam turbine generator systems require steam at 600° C (1,100° F). Scrap iron and magnetite (iron ore) are sensible-heat storage materials capable of storing thermal energy at these high temperatures.[1] A thermal storage tank filled with a large number of small iron pieces heated to 1,500° F will have a heat capacity of approximately 20,000 Btu/ft^3 (30 percent voids are assumed). Steam at 600° C (1,100° F) can be generated by this tank. An electric energy demand of 1 MW-hr is equivalent to 3.4x10^6 Btu (ideal conversion); therefore, 100 MW-hrs of electric energy would require an iron thermal storage tank volume of 51,000 ft^3 (based on a typical electric powerplant efficiency of 33 percent). In cubic form, such a tank would be 37 feet on every side. The iron in the tank would weigh over 7,100 short tons. Using iron or iron ore as a heat storage material for a solar thermal electric powerplant does not appear practical for even the simplest application because of size and weight.

Lithium hydride, a latent heat storage material, changes phase from solid to liquid at 1,200° F to 1,300° F. The heat of fusion of this material is 92,000 Btu/ft^3.[1] With this form of heat storage, 100 MW-hr of electric energy would require a storage tank volume of 11,000 ft^3. In cubic form, this tank would be 22 feet on

each side and would weigh about 30 tons. Although this tank would be much smaller and lighter than an equivalent iron thermal storage tank, lithium hydride thermal storage requirements would still require enormous volumes for large solar thermal electric powerplants. This high-temperature latent heat storage material is also more costly than other thermal storage materials. In addition, transferring the heat of the phase change as molten lithium hydride crystallizes poses engineering problems. Latent heat storage does not appear practical for a solar thermal electric powerplant.

Electrochemical storage would appear to be a more direct method of storing electric energy for solar electric power stations. Several advanced battery concepts are being developed, having specific energy capacities of 200 watt-hours per pound.[1] A one megawatt-hour energy demand would require advanced batteries weighing 5,000 pounds. Lead-acid batteries would weigh 10 times as much as advanced batteries for the same energy demand. The cost of the materials for advanced batteries prohibits their practical consideration. Even though the cost per unit weight of conventional batteries may be relatively low, the greater quantities that would be required for

[1] H. F. Hottell and J. B. Howard, *New Energy Technology, Some Facts and Assessments*, 1973.

storing comparable energy levels would also result in high costs. Therefore, batteries do not appear practical for storing the large quantities of energy required by a central power station.

Rock or molten salt thermal storage systems for solar electric powerplants have been suggested.[1] This type of thermal storage would produce steam at only a few hundred degrees Fahrenheit. Much larger conventional turbines would be required to use the low-energy steam that would be produced at these temperatures. A plant operating with a maximum steam temperature of 300°F would have a thermal efficiency half that of a conventional plant using steam at 1,000° F. The inefficiency of a low-energy steam cycle would further amplify the size of the turbines required. The initial capital cost of a low-energy steam plant would be considerably higher than conventional power machinery. Although a rock or molten salt thermal storage system could be designed, such a system would not be practical or feasible for central power stations.

Instead of storing solar energy, it could be used to manufacture synthetic gaseous or liquid fuels. A solar electric powerplant could manufacture hydrogen by electrolysis with a portion of the day time electric power production.[1] The hydrogen could then be stored in metal hydrides to be used as a fuel during night time and overcast operations.

Yet another possibility is that the concentrator panel could be used directly to provide the high temperatures to manufacture low-Btu gas or high-Btu methane from coal or solid waste. Methane could be liquefied to reduce the storage volume; the methane could then be piped in gaseous form to be used as a natural gas substitute for residential heating. Low-Btu gas could be compressed and stored for use by central power stations for power production during off-solar hours. Using solar energy to produce synthetic fossil fuels may be the most practical approach to energy storage, because the energy storage density of fossil fuels is very high compared to that of thermal or electrochemical energy storage systems. Synthetic fossil fuels are also more readily usable by conventional power systems. However, the feasibility and practicality of using solar energy to produce synthetic fossil fuels cannot be determined at this time.

---

[1] Walter E. Morror, Jr., "Solar Energy—Its Time Is Near," *Technology Review*, December 1975, pp. 31-43; *Solar Energy Projects of the Federal Government*, Federal Energy Administration, January 1975.

ECONOMIC CONSIDERATIONS FOR ELECTRIC POWER SYSTEMS

If a major electric utility power station to provide 1,000 Mw continuously were driven by focusing solar collectors with an overall system efficiency of 25 percent, a collector area of at least 16 km² would be required.[1] However, because of collector spacing requirements, the land surface area required would be 30 km² (7,400 acres) which is a square area having 3.4-mile sides. Even if the cheapest construction materials were used for collector panels, the overall cost of a solar power station would be excessive. Focusing collectors having been optimistically estimated to cost $60 per square meter.[1] However, the collector size is only part of the capital cost of solar power plants. Since the sun is an intermittent source of energy and power demand does not cease at night or during overcast or during short winter days, some form of energy storage to provide possibly 100 days of energy reserve would be required for solar central power stations; such storage requirements pose massive engineering problems, even for moderate-capacity power stations.

Closely related to the engineering problems are the economic problems of constructing these large solar energy farms. A 1,000 Mw, continuous-duty prototype solar power plant has been estimated to cost approximately $1.4 billion (1973 dollars), which corresponds to $1,400 per kw of capacity.[1] By comparison, nuclear power plants have typical construction capital costs of $500 to $615 per kw of capacity.[2] As new, more efficient or more economical solar collectors and energy storage systems are developed, the cost penalty usually associated with the improved performance characteristics will have to compete with the size and cost of state-of-the-art systems. Unless a technological breakthrough somehow dramatically reduces the large physical sizes required by major solar electric power systems, the hardware commitment involved will dominate the capital investment requirements of solar power systems. In summary, major solar electric power systems face economic as well as technical barriers. The best possible practical application of solar energy for electric requirements may be as peak-load boost plants.

---

[1] Walter E. Morror, Jr., "Solar Energy—Its Time Is Near," *Technology Review*, December 1973, pp. 31-43.
[2] Seymour Baron, "The LMFBR: The Only Answer," *Mechanical Engineering*, December 1974, pp. 12-20; S. David Freeman, *Energy, The New Era*, August 1974, p. 206.

KEY FACTORS AFFECTING COMMERCIALIZATION
OF SOLAR ENERGY TECHNOLOGIES

FACTORS INHIBITING COMMERCIALIZATION OF SOLAR ENERGY	FACTORS OR ACTIONS PROMOTING COMMERCIALIZATION OF SOLAR ENERGY
Legal Solar system installations may be hampered by restrictions of existing local building codes. Three-dimensional zoning to protect solar collectors against shading by neighboring development and to prevent nuisance reflections must be worked out, tested, and adopted. A fourth dimension, temporal variations in illumination, must be defined and assessed. Some solar technologies are regionally specific in their application and may produce benefits usable only in particular areas, thus raising the question of equitable distribution of the benefits from federally funded programs. A paradox exists in the patent rights area in that the investments by private companies need to be protected in terms of exclusivity of RD&D results while at the same time assuring the widespread dissemination of these results to ensure extensive commercialization. Several international problems associated with solar energy systems include the questions of international boundaries and jurisdictions, the security of marine facilities and the establishment of policies on export of solar energy technologies. A dense concentration of solar systems in a small area may pose some aesthetic and legal problems that will need to be resolved through new concepts in community planning.	**Legal** To date, several states have enacted legislation that promotes the installation and use of solar energy and enhances its economic viability. This was accomplished by modifying building codes and tax deduction rights as well as by allocating funds for solar energy promotion. PL 93-577 provides a framework for a flexible patent policy to expedite commercial application of inventions and innovations developed under the federal program. The fact that exclusivity will be granted by the government for commercial application of specific technologies will be a major incentive for private industrial involvement in solar technologies.
Institutional Inexperience of building code administrators in dealing with new requirements. Local, state, and federal regulatory authorities will have to understand and accept solar technologies to assist in removing the barriers to implementation. The building design, construction and marketing industry is diverse, complicated, fragmented, and highly resistant to innovation. Even with technical and economic problems resolved, solar systems could still fail in the marketplace. Tendency of contractor to bid conservatively on any new technology. Lack of standardization of component parts for solar systems adds confusion to the industry and makes rational operation difficult. Traditional labor-management jurisdictional procedures vary widely across the nation and may hamper introduction of solar systems into the building industry.	**Institutional** ERDA is launching a major public information program using both electronic and print media. Educational resource grants and manpower training programs are being established by ERDA. PL 93-409 establishes a Solar Heating and Cooling Information Data Bank under Secretary of HUD to promote and perform the collection and dissemination of information related to solar energy. Technology transfer teams, expert in each solar technology, are being formed by ERDA. A solar energy advisory group and an interagency panel are being created by ERDA. Information centers at solar energy field sites are being formed by ERDA. ERDA Technical Information Center, Oak Ridge, Tennessee 37830, will serve as the central archive and wholesale distribution center for the results of the Federal Program for Solar Heating and Cooling.

FACTORS INHIBITING COMMERCIALIZATION OF SOLAR ENERGY	FACTORS OR ACTIONS PROMOTING COMMERCIALIZATION OF SOLAR ENERGY
Institutional (cont) To develop sufficient industrial capability to manufacture solar heating and cooling systems, architects, engineers and the building trades must have information available on design, installation, and operation of these systems. Lack of data and system simulation capabilities required to optimize solar system designs for use in specific buildings and locations. Expanding solar industry must find way of self-policing if government role is to be minimized. Reluctance of private and government financial institutions to provide mortgages for new dwellings or retrofit installations involving solar systems.	**Institutional (cont)**
Societal Lack of trained personnel to install, start-up, and operate solar systems. The tendency of the purchaser in the housing market is to place a higher priority on first costs, whereas the advantages of solar systems are realized over a long-term payout. Uncertainties in the minds of potential users and the general public because of unavailable or unknown information on the eventual costs, reliabilities, lifetimes and other operational factors associated with solar systems. Consumer resistance to the new technology. Consumer concern about warranties and maintenance of solar energy products. Before solar technologies can become market successes they must shed their "experimental" image which was created in part because solar energy development has been centered around the experimental community rather than in industry. Vulnerability of the market to rapid introduction of poor quality equipment, and the absence of laws, criteria, consumer information, etc., to protect the public and industry from such equipment.	**Societal** Manpower requirements should not be significantly different from those for conventional energy technology, although specialized training will be required. In its programs, ERDA will ensure the participation of those segments of the economy whose acceptance of solar technology will be essential to its general adoption. National solar energy demonstration program aims at providing a government-supported market for new technology, which should encourage independent industry participation and private investment in later cycles.
Environmental Although the sun's energy is non-polluting, there will be environmental impacts related to conversion and storage of this energy and to the construction of facilities. Because certain solar energy systems require large land areas, careful consideration must be given to site prepara-	**Environmental** Use of solar energy does not require solid waste disposal, fuel storage, or pipelines, transmission lines or other forms of fuel transportation, and does not create potential hazards. Solar energy, applied to heating and cooling, does not

FACTORS INHIBITING COMMERCIALIZATION OF SOLAR ENERGY	FACTORS OR ACTIONS PROMOTING COMMERCIALIZATION OF SOLAR ENERGY
Environmental (cont) tion, land use and potential environmental impacts in the development of any large central or distributed solar power systems that are not located on the roofs or walls of structures. Alternative land and water uses may restrict site availability for solar energy system use. Sizable solar installations within certain areas may cause local atmospheric perturbations. Need for local governments to develop new land-use patterns based on "sun rights."	**Environmental (cont)** introduce any new materials requirements, is pollution free, and reduces pollution to the degree that it replaces conventional energy sources. Recent legislative trends that have increased the responsibility of energy producers for detrimental environmental impacts should generally improve the competitive position of solar energy as compared to other energy sources.
Economic Solar technologies are still in the early stages of demonstration. Limitations in build-up of an industrial capability to supply and maintain solar systems at a cost and level of performance and reliability that will provide economic viability. Energy costs and availability are subject to substantial volatility. Energy pricing policies may give competitive edge to other systems. Need to develop ways to achieve maximum beneficial effect on utility systems: load leveling, new rate structures, etc. Higher initial cost of solar heating and cooling systems, which needs to be amortized by savings in operating costs over the lifetime of the systems. The need for energy backup systems during bad weather for solar energy installations increases the cost over conventional heating and cooling or conservation alternatives. Need for long-term guaranteed markets in order to achieve the cost reductions necessary for economic viability through improvements in industrial productivity. The risk facing a private company is accentuated by the fact that many companies may have access to the same information, and may develop similar technologies which will be in competition, limiting each company's potential market share. Potential inability of producers to obtain adequate capital to finance production of solar equipment and to develop markets.	**Economic** Analyses of life-cycle costing indicate that in the near future, solar heating may have an advantage over conventional systems in many areas of the country. The quantity of solar heating and cooling systems purchased by the Federal Government for new buildings and renovations could be substantial enough to foster the development of a solar industrial capability. Large-scale commercial production is expected to cut capital costs by a factor of 50 or greater for photovoltaic applications and to a significant but lesser degree for other technologies. Architectural techniques geared to making buildings into total energy conserving systems will reduce costs by ensuring proper physical placement of the structure, sufficient insulation, proper building materials, and proper room placement. This approach should also eliminate the necessity for expensive conventional backup systems. To promote the solar market, tax incentives, interest subsidies, and loan guarantees applied to solar system installations are being considered. To promote solar equipment manufacturing, an industrial tax credit and an accelerated write-off of capital costs (60 months) are being considered. Since future fossil fuel supplies are uncertain, solar energy technologies have basic advantages over conventional ones because they offer long term stable energy prices based principally on initial capital costs. In the short term, the opportunity exists for exporting solar technologies developed in the United States. In the future, the nation's solar energy production may exceed domestic needs and permit export of energy in such forms as hydrogen or synthetic fuels. The principal material resources for solar systems, aluminum, copper, steel, plastics, and glass, all have alternative replacements and thus it is not expected that materials will be supply-limited.

Sources for Key Factors Affecting Commercialization of Solar Energy Technology

National Program for Solar Heating and Cooling, ERDA-23A, October 1975.

Norman Lutkefedder, "International Solar Industry Expo 75," 27-29 May 1975.

Solar Energy Research Program Alternatives, Mitre Corporation, NSF/RA/N-73-111B, NTIS distributed (PB-231 141), December 1973.

Solar Energy Projects of the Federal Government, FEA/C-75/247, January 1975, (PB-241 620) National Energy Information Center.

A National Plan for Energy Research, Development and Demonstration, ERDA-48, Vol. 1, June 1975.

Definition Report: National Solar Energy Research. Development and Demonstration Program, ERDA-49, June 1975.

Peter E. Glaser, Solar Climate Control, Congressional Record, September 3, 1975.

SECTION FOURTEEN

WIND ENERGY

INTRODUCTION

Next to sunlight, wind is the most commonly experienced and universally distributed manifestation of solar energy on earth. Wind is the movement of the atmosphere in a pair of gigantic convection loops, one in the northern hemisphere and the other in the southern hemisphere. The basic wind flow is along the surface of the earth from the polar regions to the tropics where it is heated and rises, then returns at high altitude toward the poles where it is cooled, sinks, and returns again along the surface to the tropics, completing the cycle. This basic flow is modified by the earth's rotation so that, in the northern hemisphere, the prevailing surface winds are from the northeast in the trade-wind belts near the tropics, and from the northwest in the temperate zone. Secondary and tertiary factors further modify these essentially constant winds; heat is added over deserts and removed over large bodies of water, generating variations and modifications in the wind. Boundary layer effects, mountain ranges, local obstructions, etc., add to the confusion to the extent that large microgeographic variations as well as variations over time in fixed locations exist in the wind's direction and speed.

Despite the combined disturbing effects of the secondary and tertiary factors, the variations are normally of quite short duration, and the long-term average winds are very constant. Hourly readings may exhibit extreme variations, and daily averages commonly vary widely. But monthly and yearly averages are surprisingly constant. In fact, Thomas and other researchers have reported that even weekly averages show a great deal of constancy.[1]

Figure XVIII-1 illustrates the long-term average wind velocities in the United States.

Man has long recognized and utilized wind energy. Windmills were known in China and Japan as early as 2000 B.C. and have been in common use for at least 700 years in parts of Europe; wind energy systems were in wide use in the western United States until about 1950. Some are still to be found in remote regions, pumping water into stock tanks or generating electricity for individual farm houses. Figure XVIII-2 summarizes U.S. energy production since 1840 and compares the contribution of wind energy with that of other energy sources.

From 1935 to 1955, a number of large experimental wind-powered generators were constructed. Most of these units were located in Europe; the Smith-Putnam unit at Grandpa's Knob, Vermont, was the only U.S. effort. Putnam's narrative[2] of the Smith-Putnam wind turbine project remains a classic study of wind-power engineering. On October 19, 1941, this unit was the first ever to feed wind-generated power synchronously into a utility power grid. Rated at 1250 Kw in a 30-mile-per-hour wind, it was operated experimentally for 1100 hours over four and one-half years. Put out of commission by a blade failure in March 1945, the project was discontinued for economic reasons.

[1] Percy H. Thomas, *Electric Power From the Wind: A Survey,* Federal Power Commission, Washington, D.C., 1945.
[2] Palmer C. Putnam, *Power From the Wind,* New York: Van Nostrand Reinhold Co., 1948.

EXTRACTING ENERGY FROM THE WIND

The total kinetic energy of a moving body is expressed by:

$$E = \tfrac{1}{2}mV^2 \qquad (1)$$

But if we are speaking of a fluid body, the mass m must be expressed in terms of the density (mass per unit volume) ρ and the volume of the fluid that passes a given reference point per unit time. Thus, for a fluid such as air, $m = \rho A V$, where A is the cross-sectional area of interest. $A = \pi D^2/4$ for a circular configuration of diameter D such as a turbine. Combining terms gives

$$E = 1/8\,\rho\,\pi\,D^2\,V^3 \qquad (2)$$

which gives the total kinetic energy contained in a wind stream D units in diameter.

Equation (2) suggests that extracting power from the wind reduces wind velocity. The Betz momentum theory describes the deceleration of air traversing a windmill disk, and has been demonstrated. A column of air velocity V arriving at a windmill is slowed, and its boundary becomes an expanding envelope; see Figure XVIII-3. The interference factor a is the proportion by which the wind is slowed in traversing the windmill disk $(0 \leqslant a \leqslant 1)$. It can be shown that the wind ultimately slows by a factor of $2a$, at which time the pressures have equalized and the diameter of the air stream has expanded correspondingly.

Disregarding drag and rotational losses, the maximum power obtainable from the wind can be shown to be

$$P_m = 4a(1\text{-}a)^2 P = \tfrac{1}{2}\rho\,\pi\,D^2\,V^3\,[a(1\text{-}a)^2], \qquad (3)$$

which is maximized when $a = 1/3$ and the term $4a(1\text{-}a)^2 = 16/27$, or 0.592. Thus, the maximum power that can be removed from the wind is only 59.2 percent of the total power contained in the wind. The factor $4a(1\text{-}a)^2$ is termed the power coefficient, C_p. C_p is usually defined as the ratio of the power delivered by a wind turbine to the power contained in the wind.

Under normal conditions, the total power contained in an air stream of one meter cross-sectional area is, from

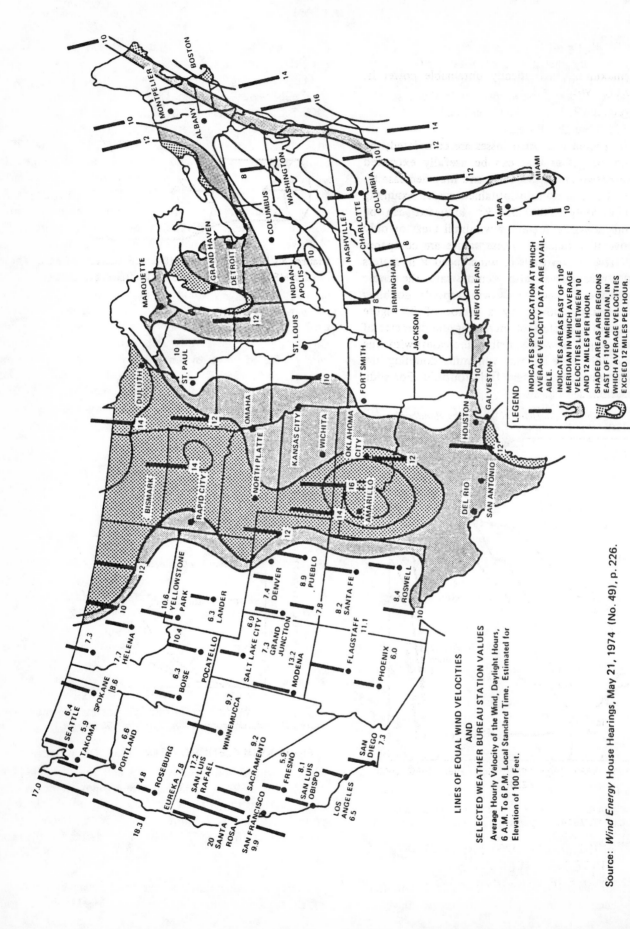

LINES OF EQUAL WIND VELOCITIES
AND
SELECTED WEATHER BUREAU STATION VALUES

Average Hourly Velocity of the Wind, Daylight Hours,
6 A.M. To 6 P.M. Local Standard Time. Estimated for
Elevation of 100 Feet.

Figure XVIII-1. AVERAGE WIND VELOCITIES IN THE UNITED STATES

Source: *Wind Energy House Hearings*, May 21, 1974 (No. 49), p. 226.

equation (2),

$$P_t = 0.000613 \ V^3,$$

so that the maximum theoretically obtainable power is, from equation (3) with $a = 1/3$,

$$P_m = 0.000364 \ V^3.$$

When drag, rotational and other losses are considered, the actual amount of power that can be usefully extracted will vary with design and application and may decrease by 20 to 50% of the theoretically obtained value. Assuming 70% efficiency, only $0.000255 \ V^3$ kilowatts can be extracted from a square meter of windmill area, or only about 41% overall efficiency. These values are compared in Figure XVIII-4 as functions of wind speed V in meters per second. These curves also demonstrate the cubic relationship between power and wind speed: doubling wind speed increases power by a factor of 8. Figure XVIII-5 illustrates the effect of increasing the diameter of the windmill. Since power available increases with the square of the diameter of the windmill, doubling the diameter increases the power available fourfold. For additional information, see Fales.[1]

[1] E. N. Fales, *"Windmills," Mechanical Engineers Handbook.*

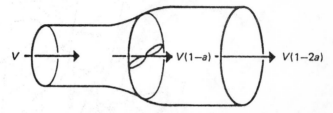

Figure XVIII-3. DIMINUTION OF WIND VELOCITY WHEN TRAVERSING A WINDMILL DISK

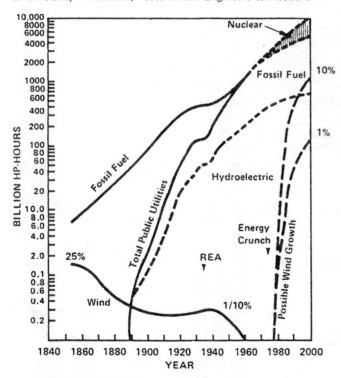

Source: *NSF/NASA/Utility Wind Energy Conference Report,*
December 17, 1974.

Figure XVIII-2. U.S. ENERGY PRODUCTION SINCE 1840 — EXCLUDING ENERGY FOR TRANSPORTATION

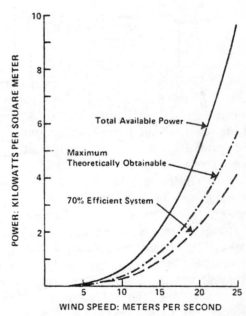

Note: 25 Meters/Second Is Approximately 56 Miles/Hour

Figure XVIII-4. ENERGY CONTENT OF WIND

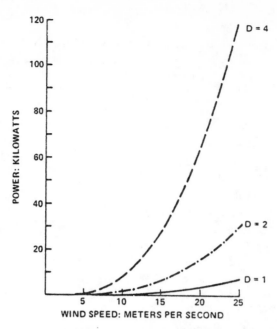

Figure XVIII-5. WIND POWER AS A FUNCTION OF TURBINE DIAMETER

ENERGY CONVERSION

Although in the earliest applications of wind energy there was direct mechanical coupling of the wind turbine to the driven machinery or water pump, such applications severely limit site selection and system configuration, and are of limited potential today. Consequently, all large-scale experimental systems are designed to generate electricity. Although this is less efficient than direct mechanical drive, the advantages more than compensate for the energy conversion losses, particularly in energy transmission and storage. Compressed air conversion offers some of the advantages of electrical generation in that the compressor is relatively light-weight and can be mounted in the power head, and short-range energy transmission and storage are easily done. This concept is within technological capability, but has not yet been fully tested.

When electrical power is to be generated at remote sites or for local consumption not connected with a power grid, the system can be relatively simple. Either AC or DC may be generated as required. Figure XVIII-10 illustrates several system design schemes.

If the electrical power generated is to be used to supplement a power grid, the output must be fixed-frequency AC (50 or 60 Hz, depending on location). Figure XVIII-11 illustrates three possible schemes. They are significantly more complicated than all but the third

design in Figure XVIII-10. While the use of variable-pitch blades to drive consistant speed turbines is costly and complicated, it does provide a blade-feathering capability for securing the turbine and protecting it during high winds. Other systems of speed control do not have this feature, and other means of protection must be provided.

Even though high wind speeds give disproportionately high outputs, it is often not economical to design electrical generating equipment to absorb all the rotor power at maximum wind speeds. Since high winds occur only infrequently, it is more cost-effective to use a small generator that maintains a flat rating and, in most cases, does not seriously degrade overall system performance. K. H. Bergey testified before the House Subcommittee on Energy,[1] that, based on University of Oklahoma wind data, a generator of only half the size required to absorb the maximum wind turbine output will still produce 90 percent of the total wind-turbine power potential at the site. He also noted that the choice of startup speed has very little effect on total power output since the energy content of low-speed winds is quite small.

[1] *Wind Energy,* Hearing before the Subcommittee on Energy of the Committee of Science and Astronautics May 21, 1974, 93rd Congress.

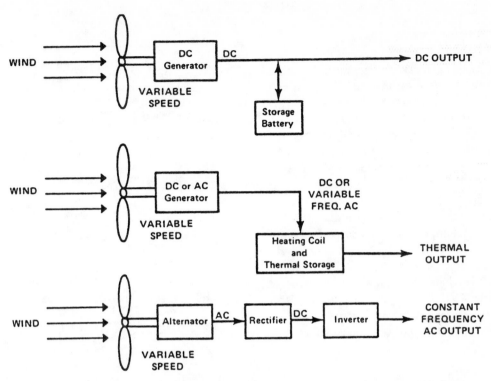

Source: R. Rama Kumar and W. Hughes, *Proceedings of the Second Workshop on Wind Energy Conversion Systems,* Washington, D.C., June 9-11, 1975, NSF-RA-N-75-050.

Figure XVIII-10. SCHEMES TO CONVERT WIND ENERGY TO ELECTRICITY

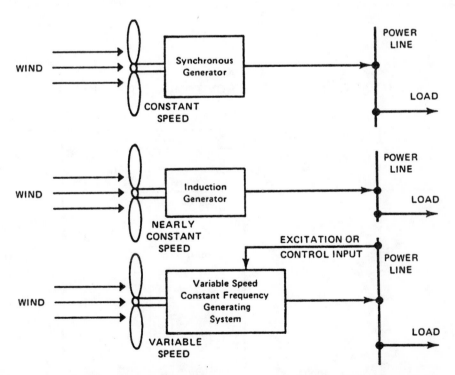

Source: R. Rama Kumar and W. Hughes, *Proceedings of the Second Workshop on Wind Energy Conversion Systems,* Washington, D.C., June 9-11, 1975, NSF-RA-N-75-050.

Figure XVIII-11. SCHEMES TO USE WIND ENERGY AS A
SUPPLEMENTARY ELECTRICAL ENERGY SOURCE

ENERGY STORAGE

Some source of supplementary energy must be available when wind speed is below turbine cut-off speed and when demand is greater than can be provided by the prevailing wind. An energy storage system may also take advantage of those periods when available wind-generated power exceeds demand. Thus, an energy storage/retrieval system is essential if the full potential of wind power is to be realized.

When wind-generated power is used to supplement a power grid, the energy storage problem is reduced to the existing fuel storage problem; but in a self-sufficient wind-power system, excess energy must be stored when available and retrieved during periods of insufficient wind. Table XVIII-1 lists the characteristics of current storage techniques, and Table XVIII-2 compares the energy density of representative storage systems. Figure XVIII-12 compares the investment required for storage of equivalent energy forms.

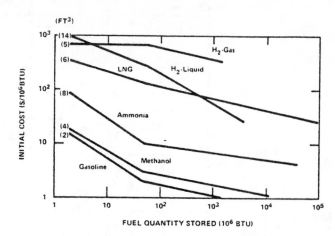

Source: W. Hauze, *Wind Energy Conversion Systems Workshop Proceedings,* June 11-13, 1973, PB-231-341.

Figure XVIII-12. FUEL STORAGE INVESTMENT (1972 BASIS)

Table XVIII-1
CHARACTERISTICS OF ENERGY STORAGE TECHNOLOGY

| Technology | Typical Economic Module (MWe) | Characteristics | | Remarks |
		Earliest Commercial Availability	Storage Efficiency (%)	
Batteries	1	1975-82	70-80	Proven Technology
Flywheels	1	1985	70-90	
Hydrogen/Fuel Cells	1	1985	40-60	Storage Options for Hydrogen
Compressed-Air (Adiabatic)	10 (30 MwH)	1982	70-80	High-Grade Thermal
Compressed-Air (Isothermal)	10	1975	NA	Required Fuel
Pumped Hydro	100 (?)	1975	70-75	Special Situations
Superconducting Magnets	500	1995	90	

Source: M. Zlotnick, *Proceedings of the Second Workshop on Wind Energy Conversion Systems,* Washington, D.C., June 9-11, 1975, NSF-RA-N-75-050.

Table XVIII-2
ENERGY DENSITY OF REPRESENTATIVE STORAGE SYSTEMS

Means of Storage	Storage Conditions		Energy Density Btu/ft^3
Mechanical			
Flywheel	Optimized Steel		< 43,000
Pumped Storage	100 ft head		14
Thermal			
Hot Rocks/Metal	60-500° F		8,000-12,000
Molten Salts	60-500° F		10,000-20,000
Steam	15 psi	212° F	40
	120 psi	347° F	340
	500 psi	467° F	1,270
Water	15 psi	212° F	9,000
	130 psi	347° F	16,000
	500 psi	467° F	21,000
Chemical			
Hydrogen			
• Gas	15 psi	60° F	280
	1,000 psi	60° F	18,500
• Liquid	15 psi	-425° F	200,000
• Hydride (Mg$_2$Ni or FeTi)			250,000
Ammonia			340,000
Methanol			430,000
Gasoline			830,000
Batteries			10,000-80,000

Source: W. Hauze, *Wind Energy Conversion Systems Workshop Proceedings*, June 11-13, 1973. PB-231-341.

FEDERAL WIND ENERGY PROGRAM

The objective of the federal wind energy program is to advance through research, development, tests, and demonstrations, the technologies necessary for implementation by the mid-1980's of commercial wind energy conversion (WEC) systems. [1]

Near-Term: 1985

A successful RD&D program whose results would be implemented at an early date by industry could be capable of supporting commercial energy production of 2.5 to 5 x 10^9 kW$_e$h per year, saving from 3 to 6 million barrels of petroleum per year.

Mid-Term: 2000

Continued commercial implementation of the WEC technology being developed could supply from 120 to 210 x 10^9 kW$_e$h of energy annually, saving between 230 million and 410 million barrels of petroleum per year. The equivalent power production capacity contributed by WEC systems, as normalized to an improved equivalent load factor of 0.7, would be 20 to 35 GW$_e$.

Long-Term: Beyond 2000

By 2020, with continued commercial implementation of WEC technology, power capacity from these systems could be further increased, depending upon availability of suitable wind sites.

The general strategy of the WEC program is to advance the development of WEC technology and performance, stimulate industrial efforts to lower the production cost of WEC units through the use of prefabrication and other techniques, and accelerate, through demonstrations, the application and integration of reliable, economical wind energy systems capable of rapid commercial implementation. This will require the early involvement of potential manufacturers and users to ensure the definition of proper requirements and facilitate the application of WEC systems.

Initial emphasis will be placed on developing and testing systems to establish the feasibility of using large unshrouded horizontal-axis wind turbines for generating

[1] *A National Plan for Energy R&D: Creating Energy Choices for the Future*, ERDA76-1, Vol. 2, June 1976.

electricity at prices competitive with conventional generating systems. Alternative WEC technologies also being developed include vertical-axis rotors, ducted systems, and vortex generators. Alternative energy applications of WEC systems are being considered, and small-scale systems are also being developed for farms and rural homes. With the exception of small-scale heating and irrigation systems, most applications will likely use electricity as an intermediate step, although in some cases unconditioned power may be used leading to lower system costs.

The first systems will be developed for high wind zones with later systems for the larger, more moderate wind zones. The geographical regions for initial applications of WEC have been selected, and major farm demonstrations are planned for the early 1980's.

The principal federal role is to assist the private sector in development of improved WEC technology, and to provide a stimulus for private industry to produce such systems and for utilities and others to use them in suitable applications.

Program Organization

To accomplish the many tasks involved, this structure of program elements was adopted:[1]

1. Program development and technology
   - Mission analyses
   - Applications/systems analyses
   - Legal/social/environmental issues
   - Wind characteristics
   - Technology development
   - Advanced system concepts

2. Farm and rural home systems

3. 100 kW scale systems

4. MW scale systems

5. Large-scale multiunit systems

[1] Energy Research and Development Administration, *Federal Wind Energy Program Summary (Interim)*, May 1, 1975.

SECTION FIFTEEN

OCEAN ENERGY

INTRODUCTION

The amount of energy potentially available in the sea — both visible and invisible — is practically limitless. Some of the estimates of this energy are truly staggering: 25 billion kw of energy are constantly being dissipated along the world's shorelines by waves; tides could be harnessed to produce 1240 billion kwh per year; the Gulf Stream off Florida has a volume flow of over 50 times the total discharge of all the rivers of the world; enough electricity could be generated from heat engines operated on the temperature differential between surface and deeper ocean waters to provide more than 10,000 times the world's yearly electric power requirements.[1]

The transformation of hydraulic water power energy into mechanical and electrical energy is a relatively simple and efficient process. The efficiency of a hydraulic turbine can be as high as 96 percent. Water power requires a simple energy conversion process, compared with thermal, chemical, or nuclear conversion.

Various approaches to extracting some part of this vast energy potential are discussed in this chapter under five headings: tidal energy, wave energy, ocean current energy, ocean thermal energy conversion (OTEC), and salinity gradient energy.

[1] A. Fisher, "Energy from the Sea—Part II, Topping the Reservoir of Solar Heat," *Popular Science*, June 1975.

TIDAL ENERGY

Tidal energy is one of the oldest forms of energy used by man. A tidal mill built centuries ago in the Deben Estuary, in Great Britain, and mentioned as early as 1170, is still in operation. Engineering ingenuity has resulted in a large number of schemes which make tidal power a very reliable source of energy. The energy is available, at will, as peak power or as steady power regardless of the time for ebb and flow. It is predictable, as far ahead as needed, as are the movements of the celestial bodies which govern the tides.

Tidal energy requires large capital investments, but compared to thermal or nuclear power plants which will have to be replaced every 30 years, tidal power installations, once built, may last forever with small maintenance costs.

The tidal power generating facilities which are now in operation are the tidal power plant of Rance in France and Kislaya Guba on the White Sea, in the USSR. The average tidal range at Rance is 9 meters, and at Kislaya Guba, 4 meters.

Tidal power is being seriously considered today by many countries for alternate sources of energy. Active investigations are being undertaken in France at the Bay of Mt. St. Michel, in Canada at the Bay of Fundy, in England in the Bristol Channel, in Korea and in the USSR. In the United States, both ERDA and the U.S. Army Corps of Engineers are reappraising the Passamaquoddy project in Maine originally submitted in 1963.

The Source of Tides

Tides are caused by the attraction of the earth by the moon and the sun. The attraction of the moon is 2.2 times more significant than that of the sun. The moon's gravity acts on the entire earth mass but pulls the nearest part away from its center. The furthest part is also pulled away because it is subjected to smaller gravitational force than its center. Thus a high tide is produced beneath the moon and at the "anti-moon." High tides occur on opposite sides of the earth, and, because the earth rotates, each side experiences two high tides and two low tides every day.

This simplified picture is complicated by several phenomena:

- The sun's attraction reacts with the moon's attraction. When the sun's attraction reinforces the moon's, spring tides occur; when it opposes it, neap tides are produced.
- The orbit of the moon and the sun with respect to the earth are not quite circular but elliptical with varied inclinations with respect to the earth. The tidal amplitude is largest when the moon or sun is closest to the earth.
- The earth is not covered uniformly by water, and each basin has its own varying dynamic response.
- The solid earth itself undergoes tidal distortion, typically 0.5 meter. What is observed to be ocean

tide is actually ocean tide minus earth tide. Earth tides also interact with ocean tides in a complex and still not fully-understood manner.

Tidal amplitude in deepwater is not very well known, but the subject is of less practical importance. The wide deep ocean basins respond directly to the external gravitational disturbances created by the moon and the sun. The shallow seas and bays surrounding the continents are subjected to and respond to the tidal motion prevailing in the deep ocean. The responses of the shallow tidal basins are a function of size and depth. Large tidal ranges are generally the result of a matching of periods between deepwater tidal excitation and the free natural oscillation of large embayments.

Much progress is now being made in predicting shallow water amplitude by analyzing deepwater tides and shallow water response to deepwater excitation. But the tidal basin boundaries are not fully reflective, like vertical walls, but contain a dissipative feature. Turbulent energy dissipation is a non-deterministic phenomenon.

Despite all these complexities, tidal amplitudes and time predictions along the coastline can be made with great accuracy. The error never exceeds 50 cm in tidal range or one-half hour in phase.

Tidal amplitudes are predicted by harmonic analysis and correlation between the measured range at a given location and the moon-sun location with respect to the earth. Tidal component coefficients are associated with each periodic motion of celestial bodies such as:

		Hours	Coefficient
M_2	Principal lunar period	12.42	0.908
S_2	Principal solar period	12.00	0.422
N_2	Larger lunar elliptic	12.66	0.174
K_2	Lunar-solar semidiurnal	11.97	0.078/0.036
O_1	Principal lunar diurnal	25.82	0.376
M_f	Lunar fortnightly	327.86	0.156

As a result, shallow water tidal motions are one of the most predictable phenomena on earth.

Tidal Power Plants

Tidal power plants consist of three basic components: the power house or housing for the generating units; the

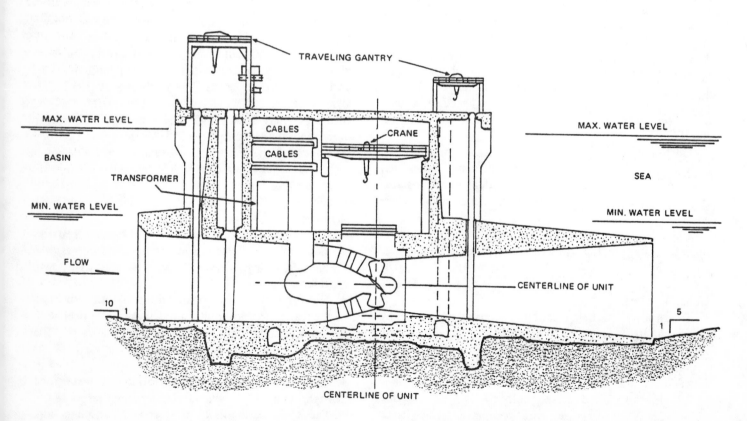

Figure XX-7. CROSS SECTION OF A POWER PLANT EQUIPPED WITH A BULB-TYPE TURBINE

sluiceways with their gates for filling or emptying the controlled basins; and the dikes, usually rockfill, constituting the closure between power houses and sluiceways and between either of these and the abutments of the development.

Figure XX-7 shows the cross section of a power plant equipped with a bulb-type turbine, constructed in situ behind temporary cofferdams. A prefabricated element or a caisson floated in place costs less to contruct. The dike must be high enough so that no appreciable overtopping will occur under the most extreme combinations of high water and waves. The sluiceways must be equipped with gates that can be operated frequently, quickly, and reliably.

In a tidal power plant, power is developed at low to very low heads. The only turbines that are adaptable to such plants are the axial flow, high specific speed types including Kaplan bulb, straight-flow and tube designs.

There are very few reliable and detailed cost estimates on tidal power plants. The total cost of the Rance tidal power station in 1960 was $100 million (1960 evaluation) for 240,000 kw of installed power and an annual production of 560 million kwh with a value of $420/kw of equipped power based on the total estimated cost of production.[1] Later, the value was increased to $500/kw of equipped power. The cost per kilowatt-hour produced is $0.0026, based on 1973 calculations.

The total cost of the Passamaquoddy tidal power project as designed and evaluated in 1963 was $759 million for 1 million kw of power installed. The estimated yearly production was to be 1000 kwh/yr, or $759 per kw of equipped power. Canada believed this project to be uneconomical because the interest rates used were higher than those applied in the United States. The current cost of construction of the Passamaquoddy tidal power project is now being reassessed under the direction of ERDA and the New England Division of the U.S. Army Corps of Engineers.

Operational Tidal Power Plants

There are only two tidal power plants in operation in the world: one is in the Rance Estuary in Brittany, France; the other is on the White Sea at Kislaya Guba in the USSR. Both installations have been marked by new technology developments.

The Rance installation, inaugurated in November 1966, demonstrated that varying power demand could be matched with tidal energy making the tidal plant a valuable component of a grid system regardless of season.

This was achieved through the systematic use of the reversible bulb-housed turbine generator unit with variable pitch runner blades.

The Kislaya Guba plant, actually only a small experimental station, is significant for the method of its construction. Based on the Russian experience in construction of floating reinforced concrete docks, and similar work in Holland and West Germany, unit plants were built on land, and floated into place, thus avoiding the expensive, difficult and lengthy operation of building a cofferdam.

Rance Tidal Power Plant[1]

The Rance Estuary is located on the coast of Brittany in France (Figure XX-8) where the average tide is 11.40 meters. The Rance tidal power plant has been a pioneering achievement: it has demonstrated the effectiveness of the group-bulb turbine system, and has provided data for studies in physical oceanography, construction at sea, and corrosion and protective measures.

The plant has now been in operation for ten years and has required very little maintenance. As previously mentioned based on 1973 calculations, the cost per kwh produced is $0.0026. It should be pointed out that if the float-in-place method of construction were to be used, a plant like Rance could be built at a much reduced cost.

Exploitation of tidal power would be much improved if we could produce energy not only during ebb tide, but also during the flow period leading to ebb. The new bulb-group concept was used at Rance allowing the turbine to work in both directions by reversing the blade. Furthermore, using the generator as a motor, the turbines were also able to work as pumps in either direction. Finally, by having the blades parallel to the axis of the turbine, group-bulb turbines could also operate as sluice gates. The flexibility of such a system considerably increases the efficiency of tidal power extraction, since the groups are able to work as turbines and pumps in both directions and as gates.

The great advantage of pumping becomes evident when one considers that if energy is expended to overfill or empty the pools behind the dam, this requires only a small amount of energy since the head is only one meter. This water however could be released later at a head of 7 meters, therefore giving a considerable gain in energy. Furthermore, this gain can be considerably increased if the pumping can be done during hours of low energy demand so that energy can be produced during the peak load. A group of 24 of these group-bulb turbine generators were installed at Rance tidal power station, each

[1] G. Maubousin, "L'Usine Maremotrice de la Rance," *Tidal Power*, T. J. Gray and O. K. Gashus (eds.), New York: Plenum Press, 1972.

[1] R. Gibrat, *L'Energie des Marees*, Presses Universitaires de France, Paris, 1966.

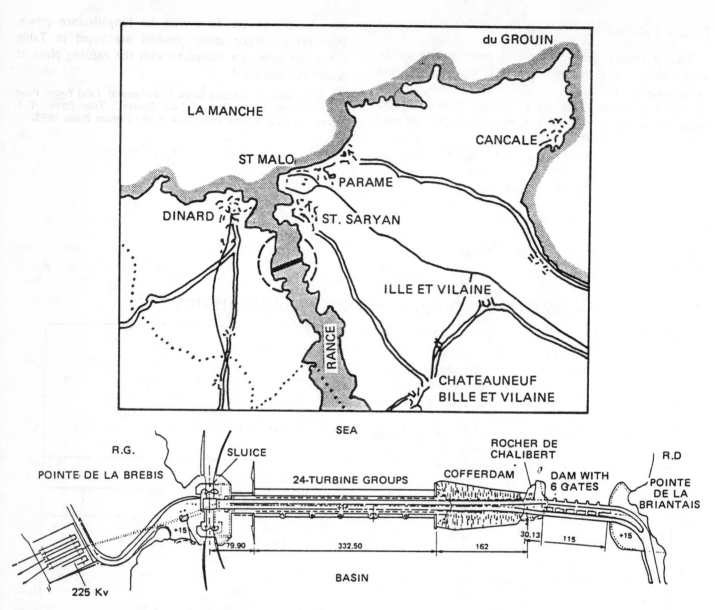

Figure XX-8. THE RANCE ESTUARY AND LOCATION OF THE TIDAL PLANT

with a power of 10,000 kilowatts. The main characteristics of these groups are shown in Table XX-2.

Kislaya Guba Experimental Plant

The USSR has a tidal power potential of 210 billion kWh/year of the world's estimated 1240 billion kWh.[1] The use of the 40 billion kWh/year power resources of the White Sea could be incorporated into the integrated power system of the European part of the country.

The Kislaya Guba tidal power plant, 600 miles north of Murmansk, is located in a narrow neck 50 meters wide that connects the sea with the Ura-Guba Bay. The site

was selected because of the relative simplicity of the installation and its proximity to a power system, although the height of the tide here only varies from 1.3 to 3.9 meters. The tidal power plant was built at an industrial center and was delivered to the site in a finished form with the equipment already assembled.

The power of this small experimental plant was determined only by the requirements of the experiment. Two units were installed, one Russian and one French. The French unit is a bulb-housed, reversible-flow turbine-generator with a capacity of 400 kW. The diameter of its runner is 3.3 meters; its speed is 72 rpm; and it is connected via a speed booster to a 600-rpm synchronous generator.

Future Tidal Power

Serious studies are underway at many points in the world where the tidal conditions indicate good potential for generating electric power. (See Figures XX-9, 10, and 11.) In some cases the distances of the tidal sites from users of electric power prevent their economic use until new techniques are discovered for long-distance power transmission. Major study projects are listed in Table XX-3 and some are compared with the existing plant at Rance in Table XX-4.

[1] L. B. Bernshtein, "Kislaya Guba Experimental Tidal Power Plant and Problems of the Use of Tidal Energy," *Tidal Power*, T. J. Gray and O. K. Gashus (eds.) New York: Plenum Press, 1972.

Table XX-2

RANCE GROUP-BULB TURBINE CHARACTERISTICS

Turbine:	Kaplan type with 4 adjustable blades Diameter: 5.35 meters Power: 10 mw Speed: 94-380 rpm
Generator:	Rotating in air at pressure 2 kg/cm^2 (absolute) Power: 10 mw at cos φ = 1

	Head (meters)						
	11	9	7	5	3	2	1
Discharge Basin - Sea m^3/sec	110	130	175	260	200	—	—
Power, 1000 Kw	10	10	10	8	3.2	—	—
Turbine Discharge Sea - Basin m^3/sec	130	155	230	195	135	—	—
Power, 1000 Kw	10	10	95	5.5	2	—	—
Pump Discharge Sea - Basin m^3/sec	—	—	—	—	170	195	225

Table XX-3

TIDAL POWER PROJECT STUDIES

Country	Location	Physical Characteristics	Tidal Range	Electric Power
United States	Cook Inlet, Alaska (near Anchorage)[a] (See Figure XX-9)	230 miles long, varying from 60-13 miles wide. Five possible sites.	15-24 feet	A. 75,000 Gwh/year B. 10-12,000 Gwh/year C. 60 Gwh/year D. 916 Gwh/year E. — (See Figure XX-9)
United States — Canada	Passamaquoddy, Bay of Fundy, Maine/New Brunswick[b] (See Figure XX-10)	Double-basin: Passamaquoddy Bay (101 square miles) and Cobscoo Bay (41 square miles)	12-27 feet	1843 million kWh/year
Canada	Bay of Fundy	Double-basin (See Table XX-4)	23-54 feet	(See Table XX-4)
Argentina	Valdes Peninsula[c] (See Figure XX-11)	Single-basin with canal	—	75,000 Gwh/year
Great Britain	Severn River, Bristol Channel,[d] and Solway Firth	Single-basin, with locks for navigation, and pumped storage	—	4 billion Kwh/year 10,432 Gwh/year 3.2 billion Kwh/year
France	Bay of Mount-Saint-Michel	Double-basin (See Table XX-4)	12-41 feet	(See Table XX-4)
Korea	Garorim Bay[e]	Unknown	Unknown	Unknown
USSR	Okhotsk Sea	Unknown	Unknown	10 million kw

Sources:

[a] E. M. Wilson and M.C. Swales, "Tidal Power from Cook Inlet, Alaska," *Tidal Power*, T. J. Gray and O. K. Gashus (eds.), New York: Plenum Press, 1972.

[b] F. L. Lawton, "Tidal Power in the Bay of Fundy," *Tidal Power*, T. J. Gray and O. K. Gashus (eds.), New York: Plenum Press, 1972. S. L. Udall, *The International Passamaquoddy Tidal Power Project and Upper Saint John River. Hydroelectric Power Development.* (Report to President John F. Kennedy), Department of Interior, July 1, 1963.

[c] H. E. Fentzleff, "The Tidal Power Plant San Jose, Argentina," *Tidal Power*, T. J. Gray and O. K. Gashus (eds.), New York: Plenum Press, 1972.

[d] E. M. Wilson, B. Severn, and M. C. Swales, *The Bristol Channel Barrage Project,* 11th Conference on Coastal Engineering, London, 1968.

[e] *Feasibility Study of Tidal Power Plan, R-74-51,* Korean Institute of Science and Technology, Ministry of Science and Technology, Seoul, Korea, 1974.

Table XX-4

COMPARISON OF TIDAL PROJECTS

Characteristics of the Basins	U.S. – Canada	Canada – Bay of Fundy			France	
	Passamaquoddy	Petit Codiac Memramcook	Cumberland Shepody	Minas Basin	Rance	Mont Saint-Michel
Scheme	2 basins	2 basins	2 basins	1 basin	1 basin	2 basins
Tidal range (ft)	12 to 27	24 to 54	23 to 51	24 to 53	11 to 38	12 to 41
Area (square miles) High	101	12	45	300	8	200
Low	41	9	28	—	—	—
Length of dam (miles)	6.8	2	6	4	—	—
Natural energy (M Gwh)	16,000	7,300	35,000	160,000	2,000	60,000
Installed power	300,000 kw	201,000 kw	450,000 to 1,800,000 kw	1 to 8 million kw	240,000 kw	3,000,000 kw
Number of sluice gates	160	61	38 to 76	—	6	—
Guaranteed power	95,000 kw	54,000 kw	150,000 to 300,000 kw	—	—	—
Annual production in M kwh	1,900	1,310	2,140 to 7-9,000	Up to 30 or 40,000	600	25,000

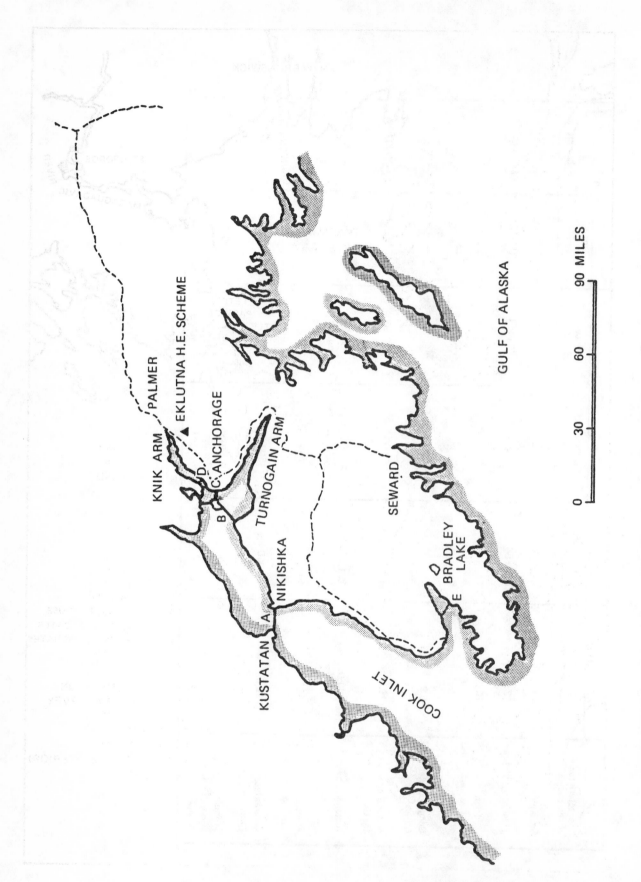

Figure XX-9. POTENTIAL SITES FOR TIDAL POWER DEVELOPMENT COOK INLET

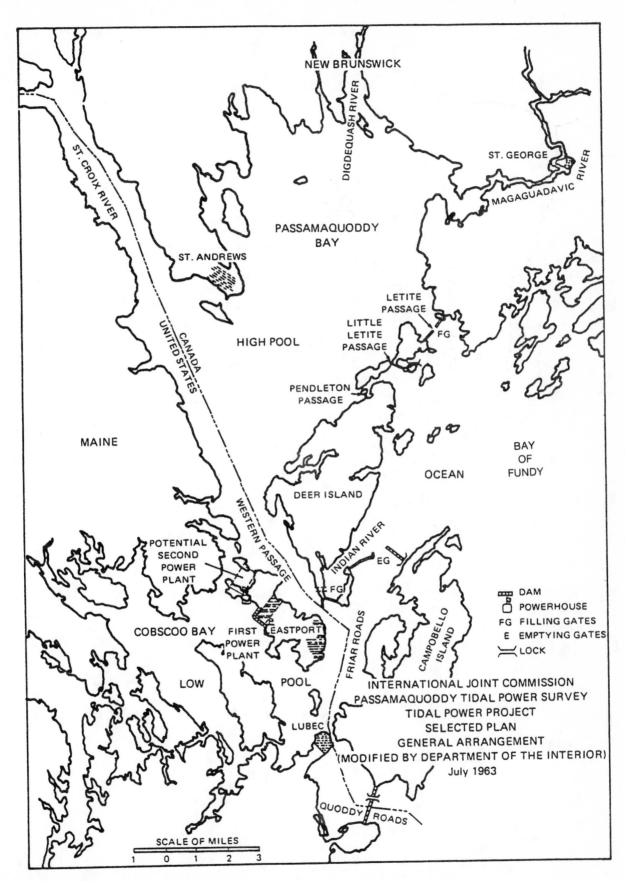

Figure XX-10. PASSAMAQUODDY TIDAL POWER PLANT

SECTION SIXTEEN

BIOMASS CONVERSION

INTRODUCTION

Biomass conversion, or bioconversion, is the process of utilizing solar energy captured by photosynthesis. On a moisture-free basis, organic materials from algae to wood wastes have a remarkably uniform heat content of 7000-9000 Btu/lb. To utilize the solar energy captured in the biomass, several systems have been developed. Research to expand the capability of bioconversion processes is underway. The most readily available source of biomass energy is the waste generated daily by industrialized society. In addition to the many schemes for utilizing this waste, there are proposals for both land and ocean farms to produce bioenergy crops.

BIOMASS SOURCES

Biomass suitable for conversion into energy comes from a variety of sources: some originates from urban and industrial wastes, some from agricultural and forestry wastes. In addition to these sources, there is the possibility of growing organic matter specifically for energy production by land, fresh water, and ocean farming. At this time the most readily available biomass resource is in the form of wastes. Estimates of the quantity of usable waste vary greatly, and definitive figures are not available. One source estimates that the solid wastes generated in the United States in 1970 totaled 4.5 billion tons, of which about 13 percent represented the dry combustible fraction. Table XXI-1 lists the material content of the moisture-free fraction. Not all of this is collectable or usable, and there is considerable seasonal variation, particularly for crop residues.

Municipal solid waste (MSW) represents the most collectable portion of the usable resources and many energy waste recovery systems have been designed to utilize MSW. Table XXI-2 gives the breakdown of typical MSW on a percentage basis. The composition and quantity vary from season to season and from location to location. The high heating value of the composite MSW shown in the table is about 4500 Btu/lb. On a moisture- and ash-free basis, the heating value is about 8000-9000 Btu/lb.

Agricultural and forestry wastes are available in far greater quantities than MSW. However, these wastes are generally dispersed and low in heat content in their moist form. Collection and transportation of these wastes to central locations is not economically attractive.

The current disposition of agricultural and forestry wastes is shown in Table XXI-3. Of the total residues of 474 million dry tons, 418 million tons are considered available for use. The seasonal nature of farming makes 35 million tons of the agricultural and forestry residues available in the first quarter of the year, 50 million in the second, 174 million in the third, and 159 million in the fourth quarter.

Table XXI-1

QUANTITY AND FUEL VALUE OF DRY COMBUSTIBLE SOLID WASTE DISCARDED IN 1970

Waste Source	Quantity (10^9 lb)	Fuel Value (10^{15} Btu)
Urban and Industrial		
Household and municipal	168.4	1.348
Commercial and institutional	62.1	0.496
Manufacturing plant	23.5	0.188
Demolition	7.7	0.062
Wood related	51.3	0.411
Textile and fabric	0.6	0.005
Non-fabric synthetic materials	0.9	0.011
Food processing	1.5	0.008
Miscellaneous manufacturing	0.2	0.001
Sewage solids	13.8	0.083
Agricultural and Forestry		
Crop residues	644.0	5.152
Animal waste	72.0	0.482
Forestry residue	232.0	1.856
Total	1278.0	10.103

Sources: George L. Huffman, "Processes for Conversion of Solid Wastes and Biomass Fuels to Clean Energy Forms," *Conference on Capturing the Sun Through Bioconversion*, Washington, D.C., March 10-12, 1976.

John Alich, Jr., "Agriculture and Forestry Wastes," *Conference on Capturing the Sun Through Bioconversion*, Washington, D.C., March 10-12, 1976.

Energy plantations have been proposed as possible sources of biomass material for conversion into energy, such as synthetic natural gas. The matrix in Table XXI-4 indicates the areas of land mass that would be required to meet various amounts of the current U.S. demand for

Table XXI-2

SAMPLE MSW COMPOSITION IN THE UNITED STATES

Component	Percent by Weight	Percent Moisture by Weight	Btu/Pound[a]
Food Waste			
Garbage	10.0	72.0	6,484
Fats	2.0	0	16,700
Rubbish			
Paper	42.0	10.2	7,572
Leaves	5.0	50.0	7,096
Grass	4.0	65.0	7,893
Street sweepings	3.0	20.0	6,000
Wood	2.4	20.0	8,613
Brush	1.5	40.0	7,900
Greens	1.5	62.0	7,077
Dirt	1.0	3.2	3,790
Oils, paints	0.8	0	13,400
Plastics	0.7	2.0	14,368
Rubber	0.6	1.2	11,330
Rags	0.6	10.0	7,652
Leather	0.3	10.0	8,850
Unclassified	0.6	4.0	3,000
Noncombustibles			
Ashes	10.0	10.0	
Metals	8.0	3.0	
Glass and ceramics	6.0	2.0	

[a] On a moisture- and ash-free basis.

Source: *The Problem of Waste Disposal*, College of Engineering, University of Michigan, 1972.

natural gas if it were to be produced from an energy crop; 169,000 square miles is about 5.6 percent of the land mass of the conterminous states. Table XXI-5 summarizes observed yields for selected plant species. The rate of plant growth is in part determined by the availability of water. As a general rule, about 500 tons of water are required to produce a single ton of dry plant matter. To obtain a yield of 10 (dry) tons/acre-year, 44 inches of rain (or its equivalent as irrigation) must be provided. For comparison, rainfall over the southeastern United States averages 48 inches per year.

Table XXI-3

AGRICULTURAL AND FORESTRY WASTES

	Crop (10^9 lb)	Animal (10^9 lb)	Forestry (10^9 lb)
Total residue	644	72	232
Collected	14	52	150
Returned to soil	10	35	
Fed without sale	3		
Sold	1	8	50
Wasted		9	75
Used as fuel			25

Adapted from: John Alich, Jr., "Agriculture and Forestry Wastes," *Conference on Capturing the Sun Through Bioconversion*, Washington, D.C., March 10-12, 1976.

Table XXI-4

POTENTIAL SNG PRODUCTION BY LAND FARM

Percent of Present Demand[a]	Area Required (square miles)		
	10 Tons/Acre-Year	25 Tons/Acre-Year	50 Tons/Acre-Year
1.66	12,000	5,000	2,800
10	72,000	30,100	17,000
50	361,000	150,500	84,500
100	723,000	301,000	169,000

[a] Approximately 22×10^{12} SCF/year.

Source: George L. Huffman, "Processes for Conversion of Solid Wastes and Biomass Fuels to Clean Energy Forms," *Conference on Capturing the Sun Through Bioconversion*, Washington, D.C., March 10-12, 1976.

Because of the demand for water in biomass production, fresh water and ocean farming concepts have been proposed Single-cell algae in nutrient-rich fresh waters exhibit growth rates as high as 70 (dry) tons/acre-year with 16-32 (dry) tons/acre-year reasonable for a 365-day growing season. Water hyacinth in the southeastern states can grow as rapidly as 60 (dry) tons/acre-year. A methane production fresh water farm with a capacity of 72 billion SCF/year would require 16,000 miles of canals on 348 square miles of land if water hyacinth were to be cultivated.[1]

Because of the limited availability of land area suitable for land or fresh water farming, studies are being conducted on ocean farming. The principal algae under consideration is the giant California kelp, which converts solar energy to biomass energy with a 2 percent efficiency under proper growing conditions. Because the surface waters in which the kelp would be grown are nutrient-deficient, the necessary nutrients would be supplied by the upwelling of enriched waters from 500- to 1000-foot depths. Plans call for a 100,000 acre farm by 1985-1990. The kelp will be anchored to a submerged raft of polypropylene lines. If anaerobic digestion is used to extract methane from the harvested kelp, the productivity of the ocean farm will be about 160,000 SCF/acre-year. A farm 470 miles on a side could supply the U.S. demand for natural gas. The American Gas Association is particularly interested in ocean farming of kelp. Considerable basic research has been done and indications are that the concept is reasonable.

[1] Richard S. Greeley and Peter C. Spewak, "Land and Fresh Water Farming," *Conference on Capturing the Sun Through Bioconversion*, Washington, D.C., March 10-12, 1976.

Table XXI-5

ABOVEGROUND, DRY BIOMASS YIELDS OF
SELECTED PLANT SPECIES

Species	Location	Yield (tons/acre-year)
Annuals		
Exotic forage sorghum	Puerto Rico	30.6
Forage sorghum (irrigated)	New Mexico	7-10
Forage sorghum (irrigated)	Kansas	12
Sweet sorghum	Mississippi	7.5-9
Exotic corn (137-day season)	North Carolina	7.5
Silage corn	Georgia	6-7
Hybrid corn	Mississippi	6
Kenaf	Florida	20
Kenaf	Georgia	8
Perennials		
Sugarcane	Mississippi	20
Sugarcane (state average)	Florida	17.5
Sugarcane (best case)	Texas (south)	50
Sugarcane (10-year average)	Hawaii	26
Sugarcane (5-year average)	Louisiana	12.5
Sugarcane (5-year average)	Puerto Rico	15.3
Sugarcane (6-year average)	Philippines	12.1
Sugarcane (experimental)	California	32
Sugarcane (experimental)	California	30.5
Alfalfa (surface irrigated)	New Mexico	6.5
Alfalfa	New Mexico	8
Bamboo	Southeast Asia	5
Bamboo (4-year stand)	Alabama	7
Black cottonwood (2-year old)	Washington	4.5
Red alder (1- to 14-year old)	Washington	10

Source: John Alich, Jr. and Robert Inman, "Energy from Agriculture," at
*Clean Fuels from Biomass, Sewage, Urban Refuse, and Agricultural
Wastes*, Orlando, Florida, January 26-30, 1976.

FACILITIES AND RESEARCH

Table XXI-13 lists some of the major energy and resource recovery facilities in operation or planned. In addition to these, there are numerous smaller facilities in operation for waste processing and energy generation. A glance at the table reveals considerable interest in energy recovery systems by industry, municipalities, and government.

Not listed in Table XXI-6 are two facilities planned for the processing of animal wastes into pipeline quality gas. Calorific Recovery Anaerobic Processes of Oklahoma City and ERA, Inc., of Lubbock, Texas, plan on using feedlot wastes to produce a primary product to be used as either a feed supplement or a fertilizer. Calorific will process 70,000 tons/year of manure and generate 641 million SCF of methane; ERA will process 80,000 tons/year of manure to obtain 438 million SCF of methane.

In addition to the research conducted by industry, ERDA and EPA have funds allocated for the development of the biomass resource. ERDA funds $3,830,000 of research in fuels from biomass as part of its solar energy program. The ERDA FY 77 request for biomass research was $3,000,000. These funds support programs in biomass sources (agriculture, silviculture and marine), conversion technologies (anaerobic digestion, enzymatic hydrolysis, fermentation, pyrolysis, hydrogenation and direct combustion), and advanced concepts such as the direct photosynthetic production of hydrogen.

Four major waste conversion processes have been under long-term EPA development: Combustion Engineering's CPU-400 Process, the St. Louis waste as a supplementary fuel, the Occidental (formerly Garrett) Pyrolysis Process, and the Monsanto Landgard System.

ENVIRONMENTAL CONSIDERATIONS

Many of the bioconversion schemes have beneficial impacts on the environment. The resource recovery and reduced demand on landfill sites favor MSW energy recovery systems for urban areas. In addition, the fuels derived from MSW are generally low in sulfur, making them attractive to the utility industry.

Negative environmental impacts are possible from land and ocean farming. The removal of agricultural wastes from the fields could, in the long run, adversely affect soil productivity. Development of monocultures for land and ocean farming could open the way for serious blights. Extensive irrigation could have regional effects. Also, there is a possibility that the use of deep waters for supplying nutrients in ocean forms could release large quantities of carbon dioxide to the atmosphere with possible global impacts.

Table XXI-6

MSW ENERGY RECOVERY SYSTEMS

Location	Key Participants	Process[b]	Capacity (ton/day)	Description
Existing Facilities—Electrical Generation				
Ames, IA	City of Ames; Henningson, Durham, and Richardson, Inc.	Cofiring with coal	200	Baling, shredding, magnetic separation, air classification, screening, other mechanical separation; 8 MW equivalent power
Menlo Park, CA	Combustion Power Corp.	Fluidized-bed combustor	75	Direct power generation from exhaust gases of combustor; 1 MW equivalent power
So. Charleston, WV	Linde Div., Union Carbide Corp.	Pyrolysis	200	Medium-Btu gas produced by Purox oxygen converter, shredding, 6 MW equivalent power
St. Louis, MO	City of St. Louis; EPA; Union Electric	Cofiring with coal	300	Prepared MSW fuel; 12 MW equivalent power
Existing Facilities—Steam Generation				
Baltimore, MD	City of Baltimore; Monsanto Envirochem Systems, Inc.; EPA	Pyrolysis	1000	Langard process: shredding, pyrolysis, water quenching, magnetic separation; steam at 200,000 lb/hr, 430° F, 330 psig
Baltimore County, MD	Baltimore County, Md., Environmental Services, Teledyne National	RDF	600-1500	Shredding, air-classification, magnetic separation
Braintree, MA	City of Braintree	Incineration	240	Steam at 60,000 lb/hr, 250 psig, saturated
Chicago, IL	City of Chicago	Incineration	1600	Steam at 440,000 lb/hr, 275 psig, saturated
East Bridgewater, MA	City of Brockton and nearby towns; Combustion Equipment Assoc.; East Bridgewater Association	RDF	400	Shredding, drying, air classification, magnetic separation, mechanical separation, sterilization; used in industrial boiler
Franklin, OH	City of Franklin, EPA, Black-Clawson	Paper fibers	150	Wet pulping, magnetic separation by a proprietary process.
Harrisburg, PA	City of Harrisburg	Incineration	600	Steam at 185,000 lb/hr, 456° F, 250 psig
Nashville, TN	Nashville Thermal Transfer Corp.; I. C. Thomasson and Assoc., Inc.	Incineration	720	Steam at 220,000 lb/hr, 620° F, 400 psig
New Orleans, LA	City of New Orleans, Waste Management, WCRR	Incineration	650	Shredding, air-classification, magnetic separation
Norfolk, VA	U.S. Navy	Incineration	360	Steam at 100,000 lb/hr, 275 psig, saturated

[a] This is a status summary of some of the energy and resource projects in the United States.
[b] RDF (refuse derived fuel) is listed when the method of combustion is not specified.

Sources: *Fuels from Municipal Refuse for Utilities*, Bechtel Corporation, March 1975.
NCRR Solid Waste Management Briefs, June 1976; *Pollution Engineering*, May 1976.

Table XXI-6 (Cont.)

Location	Key Participants	Process	Capacity (ton/day)	Description
Orchard Park, NY	Torrax, Inc.	Pyrolysis	75	Aggregate, crude metal, glass wool recovery; steam at 16,000 lb/hr, 470° F, 500 psig
Saugus, MA	Ten communities including Saugus and part of northern Boston; Refuse Energy Systems Corp.	Incineration	1200	Waterwall incineration, magnetic separation; steam at 370,000 lb/hr, 875° F, 890 psig sold to General Electric
Facilities Committed				
Akron, OH	City of Akron; Glaus, Pyle, Schomer, Bruns and DeHaven; Ruhlin Construction Co.; Babcock and Wilcox	RDF	1000	Shredding, air classification, magnetic separation
Bridgeport, CT	Connecticut Resources Recovery Authority; Occidental Petroleum; Combustion Equipment Assoc.	Cofiring with coal	2200	Shredding, magnetic separation, air classification, mechanical separation; 25 MW equivalent power
Chicago, IL	City of Chicago; Ralph M. Parsons Co.; Consoer, Townsend and Assoc.	Cofiring with coal	1000	Shredding, air classification, magnetic separation; 23 MW equivalent power
Danvers, MA	Clean Community Corp.	RDF	2000	Prepare RDF as primary fuel for new boilers; sell steam and electricity; 50 MW equivalent power
Palmer Township, PA	Palmer Township, Elo and Rhodes, Pennsylvania Dept. of Environmental Resources	RDF	160	Shredding, air classification, magnetic separation
Hempstead, NY	City of Hempstead; Hempstead Resource Recovery Corp.	Incineration	2000	Wet pulping, magnetic and mechanical separation; 40 MW equivalent power
Milwaukee, WI	City of Milwaukee; Americology Div. of American Can Co.; Bechtel, Inc.	Cofiring with coal	1300	Shredding, air classification, magnetic separation; 31 MW equivalent power
Monroe County, NY (Rochester)	Monroe County; Raytheon Service Co.	Cofiring with coal	2000	Shredding, air classification, magnetic separation, mechanical separation
Pompano Beach, FL	Waste Management, Inc.; ERDA; Jacobs Engineering Co.	Anaerobic digestion	50-100	Sewage sludge to be mixed with MSW for methane production
San Diego County, CA	San Diego County; EPA; Occidental Petroleum	Pyrolysis	200	Shredding, air classification, magnetic, mechanical separation, froth flotation; pyrolysis oil for cofiring with oil; 4 MW equivalent power

Table XXI-6 (Cont.)

Location	Key Participants	Process	Capacity (ton/day)	Description
St. Louis, MO	Union Colliery Co.	Cofiring with coal	8000	Shredding, air classification, magnetic separation, nuggetizing; 200 MW equivalent power
Facilities Planned				
Cleveland, OH	City of Cleveland	Undetermined	2000	Steam for use in utility; magnetic metals
Cuyahoga Valley, OH	Cuyahoga County Commissioners	Incineration	2000	Steam for industrial use, magnetic metals
State of Delaware	State of Delaware; EPA	Pyrolysis and anaerobic digestion	500 +230 sewage sludge	Shredding, air classification, magnetic and mechanical separation; produce RDF and agricultural products
Hartford, CT	United Illuminating; Connecticut Resources Recovery Authority; Combustion Equipment Corp.	Cofiring with coal	800	RDF used as primary fuel; 12 MW equivalent power
Knoxville, TN	Tennessee Valley Authority	Undetermined	3000	Energy for use in utility, magnetic metals, aluminum
Lyndhurst, NJ	Combustion Equipment Assoc.; N.J. Public Service Electric and Gas	Cofiring with coal	200	5 MW equivalent power
Seattle, WA	City of Seattle	Pyrolysis	1500	Gas produced with possible methanol or ammonia production; 30 MW equivalent power
Scranton, PA	Research-Cottrell, Inc.; Community Central Energy Corp.	RDF	600	Shredding, air classification, drying, magnetic separation; aluminum separation; steam production from RDF
Westminster, CO	Energy Conversion Systems; Public Service Co. of Colorado	Incineration	450	11 MW equivalent power
Projects Under Study				
Berlin, CT	Cities of Berlin, Hartford, New Haven; Connecticut Resources Recovery Authority	Undetermined	2200	Energy and materials
Beverly, MA	Cities of Beverly and Salem	Undetermined	1000	RDF or steam for use in industry and utility
Eugene, OR	Lane County	Undetermined	1000	24 MW equivalent power

Table XXI-6 (Cont.)

Location	Key Participating	Process	Capacity (ton/day)	Description
Facilities Planned—cont'd				
Honolulu, HI	City of Honolulu; Hawaiian Electric Co.	Incineration	2000	Steam-electric unit; 48 MW equivalent power
Miami, FL	Dade County	Undetermined	3000	75 MW equivalent power
Montgomery County, MD	Montgomery County; Potomac Electric Power Co.	Cofiring with coal	1000	25 MW equivalent power
Oakland, CA	East Bay Municipal Utility District; Pacific Gas and Electric Co.	Pyrolysis	1200	Pyrolysis gas converted to methane; 25 MW equivalent power
Staten Island, NY	City of New York; Consolidated Edison	Cofiring with coal	1500	35 MW equivalent power
TVA Service Area	TVA; several communities	Cofiring with coal	8000	200 MW equivalent power
Washington, D.C.	City of Washington; Potomac Electric Power Co.	Cofiring with coal	300	9 MW equivalent power
Toledo, OH	Ohio Water Development Authority, Northwest Ohio Solid Waste Management	RDF	1000	Shredding, air-classification, magnetic separation

ENERGY SOURCE ECONOMICS*

Synthetic Fuels From Coal

Fossil fuels release energy when their hydrogen content is oxidized by combustion. Whether in liquid, gaseous, or solid form, all such fuels are mixtures of carbon and hydrogen. By altering the ratios of carbon and hydrogen and by reforming these atoms into different molecules, it is possible to tailor synthetic fuels of desirable properties. There are a dozen or more processes under study for conversion of coal to more convenient forms—clean, low-BTU gas (less than 200 BTUs per cubic foot) for electric power generation; synthetic gas of pipeline quality (1000 BTUs per cubic foot), which can substitute for our present methane natural gas; methanol, also known as wood or methyl alcohol, which could serve as a future motor fuel in place of gasoline; synthetic crude oil, which could be used as refinery feedstock; and even a clean solid fuel with a low ash and sulfur content and a higher energy value than most of our present coals.

It must be emphasized that since all of these processes involve very large plants in order to realize economies of scale, their capital costs will be high. For example, the El Paso Natural Gas Company is building a $300 million plant in New Mexico to produce 250 million cubic feet of "syngas" per day. The cost of this plant comes to about $1200 for each million BTUs of daily production of synthetic gas. El Paso calculates that it can produce pipeline quality gas at a cost of about $1.21 per million BTUs (1000 cubic feet) at the plant, or about three times the present wellhead price for natural gas sold in interstate commerce.

While high-BTU gas could replace the natural gas now used in stoves and furnaces, it is more likely that a low-BTU synthetic gas will come into increasing use for generating electricity. Since the low-BTU gas has only one-fifth the heating value of methane, it cannot be transported economically over long distances by pipeline; instead it must be consumed close to the point of production. However, no oxygen is required to produce it, and other steps necessary in the high-BTU gasification process can be eliminated. Hence its cost at the plant gate would be about 20% less than high-BTU gas, or about $0.90 per

million BTUs using the cheapest western coals, according to the Cornell Workshop study. As shortages of natural gas become increasingly acute, it is expected that electric utilities and industrial users, who now account for two-thirds of all natural gas consumption, will shift increasingly to the cheaper low-BTU gas, and leave natural gas and the high-BTU synthetic production to residential users.

Processes for the manufacture of methanol and "syncrude" from coal involve more elaborate chemical treatment than gasification. Capital costs are expected to range from $1400 to $1600 for each million BTUs of daily production capacity, according to a 1972 study of new energy forms conducted by the National Petroleum Council. At that time it reckoned that a methanol plant using the most modern technology could produce methanol at a cost of $1.50 to $2.00 per million BTUs. However, since liquid fuels are cheaper to transport over long distances than gaseous fuels, the ultimate cost of methanol or syncrude to the user would not bear the same 30% differential over syngas expected in the manufacturing process itself.

Methanol is of particular interest because of its potential for replacing motor gasoline and diesel fuels. Although it has only about one-half the energy per pound as gasoline and would provide only about 55% to 60% as much mileage per gallon as gasoline, a manufacturing cost of about $0.15 per gallon, based on the price of coal before the oil embargo, could be competitive on a BTU basis with the refinery cost of gasoline derived from crude costing $7 to $10 a barrel. One difficulty with methanol is cold weather starting, but many experts believe this can be solved. Methanol will burn more cleanly than gasoline, emitting only a fraction of the carbon monoxide and nitrogen that come from engines burning gasoline.

A number of schemes have been proposed for establishing a synthetic fuel industry based on coal gasification and liquefaction. Some would require massive amounts of government assistance. For example, one proposal calls for building 66 plants to produce oil and gas from coal, with a total production capacity equivalent to about 4.1 million barrels of oil per day. The cost is estimated at $98 billion. Common to this and other proposals is an agreement by the government to buy the plant's entire output over its useful life at a floor price—say, $1.50 per million BTUs. The operator would be free to sell his product on the open market if the price is higher than the govern-

* The Economics of America's Energy Future, Henry Simmons, U.S. Energy Research and Development Administration, 1975

ment-guaranteed level. But if energy prices remain relatively high or continue their upward trend, the market price would stay above the floor price and the government would not have to subsidize the production of synthetic fuel.

It should be pointed out that ambitious plans for such crash programs could provide only a minor fraction of present and projected energy needs. For example, one plan under consideration by the Cornell Workshops proposed 36 synthetic fuel plants at a cost of about $500 million each—24 plants producing 250 million cubic feet of high-BTU gas per day and 12 others extracting shale oil at the rate of 100,000 barrels per day. Such an array would produce a volume of gas and oil equal to only about 6% of total U. S. energy consumption in 1973, and less than 4% of the projected consumption for 1985.

Improved technology can significantly reduce the costs of converting coal into more desirable fuels. Coal is hydrogen-poor, compared to the other fuels, but all conversion processes exact an energy penalty. In the case of gasification, for example, about 35% of the original heat content of the coal is lost. It may ultimately be possible to make up some of this loss through the introduction of combined cycle power generation processes, in which gas turbines and steam turbines are coupled in tandem so that the jet exhaust of the former raises steam in the boiler of the latter. It is thought that such systems might achieve overall energy efficiencies of 50% or more, compared to 42% for the best single-stage power stations today, but is doubtful that the energy penalty of converting coal to gas can be reduced much below 20%.

The high costs for coal-derived energy must necessarily persist according to the National Petroleum Council, since coal handling, gas handling, processing, scrubbing, and compression are far more capital-intensive than the handling of hydrogen-rich liquids such as petroleum. The NPC said, "It is fundamentally incorrect to believe that capital requirements for producing gaseous energy forms from coal can ever be reduced to levels which are typical for refining liquid petroleum fractions."

Another problem in estimating the costs of synthetic fuels is the extreme sensitivity of their costs to the price of coal. The 1972 NPC study of the cost of synthetic fuels assumed prices as low as $0.20 per million BTU for western coals during the 1975-82 period, and $0.25 for the 1982-2000 period. However, coal prices on long-term contracts have increased quite sharply, so many of the earlier forecasts have become outdated.

Because of the sharp increases in coal prices and the inflationary price increases occurring throughout the whole capital goods sector of the economy, earlier optimism that synthetic fuels might compete with gas and oil at present world prices has diminished. Although synthetic fuels may not be economic in the short-term future, they may become more competitive as the supply of petroleum and natural gas diminishes. Moreover, it is also desirable for the U. S. to build them on a major scale for reasons of national security and political independence in world affairs. A synthetic fuel industry is, therefore, an integral part of achieving self-sufficiency in energy.

Oil Shale

In three states of the western U. S.—Colorado, Wyoming, and Utah—there are deposits of shale containing about 1.4 trillion barrels of oil—about six times the proven, probable, and speculative U. S. reserve of both on- and off-shore oil. According to the U. S. Bureau of Mines, this shale oil occurs in deposits at least 10 feet in thickness and yields 10 to 25 gallons of crude oil per ton of shale.

The thickest and richest deposits of shale are in the Piceance Basin of western Colorado; these range more than 10 feet in thickness and 20 gallons or more per ton. Underlying an area of about 600 square miles, this shale contains a total of 720 billion barrels of oil, according to the Interior Department. It represents a major U. S. energy resource.

Two methods are under consideration for extracting shale oil. One calls for mining the shale, crushing it, and then retorting the material to a temperature of about 900°F to decompose the solid organic material (kerogen) to crude oil. This technique would require vast amounts of water to dispose of spent material, and it would pose severe environmental problems.

A second method for shale oil extraction is *in situ* retorting. This would be accomplished by drilling and excavation to prepare a body of shale for underground retorting and pumping the liquid oil yield to the surface. The underground technique would involve handling only about one-fourth as much material as the surface method, and it would avoid the serious problem of spent shale disposal, but its technology is not as far advanced as that of mining and surface retorting.

Water availability may ultimately place a ceiling of 3 to 5 million barrels a day on shale oil production, according to government estimates. If the bulk of this oil is obtained by mining and surface retorting, it will present a severe materials handling problem. For every 1 million barrels of oil of daily production capacity, it is estimated that 570 million tons of material will have to be mined each year. This would be as much as all of the material handled by the entire U. S coal-mining industry in 1973. Compounding the problem is the fact that the shale must be handled twice—first it must be mined and then it must be disposed of in an environmentally acceptable manner.

Another problem is the technology of extracting oil from shale. While this has proven in surface retorts on a scale of 1000 tons per day, commercial retorts would have to be at least 10 times larger. With respect to *in situ* extraction, demonstrations have been conducted on a very much smaller scale, with output of only about 35 gallons a day.

If shale oil can make a major contribution to national energy needs, its price is expected to be significantly less than oil synthesized from coal. The Cornell Workshops Study estimated a cost of $0.80 per million BTUs for shale oil extracted from the richest beds (yielding more than 35 gallons per ton), and it has suggested that this might be driven downward to perhaps $0.70 as the industry becomes experienced in the new operation.

It is not clear how rapidly shale oil production can come into operation. According to the National Academy of Engineering report, "The lead times and the serious problems facing the industry force the Task Force to conclude that *the maximum target production rate by 1985 cannot realistically exceed 0.5 million barrels per day.* Even this target is an extremely large undertaking, involving the capital expenditure of some $3 billion to $5 billion in a new and unfamiliar technology."

Geothermal Power

There are several hundred hot springs, fumaroles (openings in volcanic areas from which smoke and gases arise), and geyser complexes located mainly in the western states of the U.S. Geological studies of these regions have disclosed the existence of subsurface steam and pressurized hot water that can be drilled into so that the energy can be either converted to electric power by means of steam turbines and generators or used directly for other purposes.

The Geysers field near San Francisco is the only geothermal site presently in commercial use in the U.S. It has a capacity of 400 electrical megawatts and expansion to 900 megawatts is planned. A single well in this field can produce more than 100 tons of steam an hour at a temperature of 400°F and a pressure of 140 pounds per square foot. The cost of this steam, including the disposal of the spent steam, has been reckoned at about $0.35 a ton, or only one-third the cost of comparable steam generated in a conventional power plant burning fuel oil at a cost of $7 a barrel.

The success of The Geysers as a geothermal power source has raised expectations that significant amounts of power can be extracted from other geothermal sources in the U.S. and that this new industry will expand rapidly because of cost advantages of geothermal heat compared to heat produced by nuclear reactions and fossil fuels. The National Petroleum Council has estimated that 19,000 megawatts of geothermal power capacity—all of it in

California and Nevada—could be on line in the U.S. by 1985. Other estimates of the potential have ranged up to 132,000 megawatts by 1985, or about 15% of total anticipated U.S. installed electrical capacity at that time. To spur the exploitation of this new energy resource the Congress has enacted the Federal Geothermal Leasing Act to make available millions of acres of promising federal lands for prospecting and development.

Several caveats should be noted with respect to geothermal power. In the first place, The Geysers and two of the other geothermal power sites now in operation in the rest of the world produce dry steam, which is the most desirable product. Some geologists estimate that relatively few geothermal sites will yield dry steam. A larger number produce hot water or a mixture of steam and water. An even larger number of hot dry rock reservoirs contain no usable quantities of water, but might be used to produce heat if water were passed through them. While low-pressure steam can be separated from the flow and additional steam of still lower pressure can be obtained by a flashing process, the capital costs and therefore the ultimate cost of electrical kilowatts produced from these fields will be greater than for dry-steam fields. Low-pressure turbines will cost more per kilowatt of generating capacity because the use of steam in large quantities at pressures and temperatures far below steam produced in conventional fuel-burning plants requires large turbines to transform the heat to mechanical energy.

A second problem with geothermal power relates to the impurities in the wet steam produced at many sites. For example, wells drilled in parts of the Salton Sea area of California can produce 60 tons of steam an hour from a brine containing 20% to 30% by weight of dissolved salts and other solids. Not only do these mineral impurities cause corrosion and the buildup of deposits in pipes and equipment, but they also present a severe disposal problem. It appears, however, that the latter problem can be solved in many fields by re-injecting the effluent back underground through wells designed for this purpose. Fortunately, many geothermal wells yield fluids having much lower mineral content, so that flashed steam may be used directly in a turbine. Furthermore, a variety of techniques are being developed to control scale formations.

While there is considerable debate over the severity of these problems and therefore the rate at which geothermal power generation can develop, the vast potential of geothermal resources appears to warrant a serious effort to exploit them in economically and environmentally acceptable ways. Localized, relatively shallow geothermal heat sources like The Geysers and the Salton Sea fields constitute only the smallest fraction of the available heat in the upper 6 miles of the earth's crust. This amounts to about 560 quads of BTUs, or seven times the total U. S. energy consumption in 1973, according to the NPC. However, millions of quads of BTUs, supplied by tectonic processes and radioactive decay in the earth itself, are held by hot water in sedimentary basins at depths of more than 2 miles, by the heat trapped in rocks down to a depth of 6 miles, and by magma chambers within a few miles of the earth's surface.

In the case of the water in deep, permeable sedimentary basins, the NPC suggests that the total detectable heat stored in such basins in the U. S. at depths below 2 miles may equal the heat of combustion of 10 trillion barrels of oil, or about 100 times the Nation's total petroleum reserves. "It seems conceivable that (the heat) may overshadow even the overall total for oil," the NPC observed, but it remains to be seen whether this energy can be harnessed for practical use.

Solar Energy

No source of energy is as clean, abundant, and inexhaustible as sunlight and some of its secondary effects, such as the winds and the differences in temperature between the tropical ocean surface and the waters in the depths. The idea of harnessing this energy is inherently attractive because it is a "gentle" technology that emits almost zero pollutants and exacts a far smaller penalty on our environment than some other energy-production activities.

Historically, solar energy has played a major role in civilization. Up to the 20th century, for example, it was the wind that propelled most of the world's ocean commerce, and until the 1940s the wind provided electricity for tens of thousands of American homes. Ironically, low-cost fossil fuels drove wind-generated electricity out of business. More recently, silicon photovoltaic cells have been employed in camera light meters and to generate electricity for spacecraft.

In theory, an earth-based solar collector 1/500th of the area of the United States (an area slightly smaller than Massachusetts) receives an amount of solar energy that, if converted at 20% efficiency, would provide for all of the Nation's present consumption of electricity. Statistics like these have caused some people to conclude that much higher priority should be assigned to solar energy and that some present approaches to energy needs should be dropped or sharply curtailed.

In fact, however, there are technical, economic, and institutional barriers to the immediate and widespread use of solar energy. Overcoming these barriers will take decades of work. Thus it would be irresponsible and foolhardy for the United States to ignore other opportunities to satisfy its short-term energy needs.

The technical barriers to using solar energy are associated with two facts about the sun's rays: They are spread diffusely over the surface of the earth and they are inter-

mittent; the sun shines only by day and is frequently obscured by clouds. To harness large amounts of solar energy, collectors must be spread over a large area, and the larger the facility, the higher the cost. With most techniques, only a portion of the collected solar energy is used immediately. The rest must be stored. The cost of storage is usually a significant fraction of the cost of operating the installation. Thus one of the main areas of research and development that must be pursued to improve the outlook for solar energy utilization has to do with finding ways to store large amounts of energy at low cost.

The economic barriers to utilization of solar energy result from the fact that high initial costs are required for solar energy facilities, even though the operating costs are low. Someone has to borrow money to build these facilities. This is often a problem even for governments and large businesses. For individual homeowners, it is even more of a problem.

The institutional barriers of using solar energy result from outmoded thinking. People and institutions do not usually give serious consideration to lifetime energy costs when they construct a facility or a residence. Because of the historic low costs of fossil fuels, there has been no economic incentive to establish industries that manufacture, install, guarantee, and maintain solar energy equipment. Consequently, the banks and other lending institutions have nowhere to turn for advice if someone wants a loan for a solar installation.

To alleviate economic and institutional barriers, governments may offer special financial incentives such as guaranteed loans to encourage the use of the new technology. A number of other measures can also be adopted; for example, revision of building and zoning codes, rapid amortization allowances for federal income tax purposes, and local property tax exemptions for buildings with solar plants.

Six major approaches to using this energy source are being followed in the national solar energy program under the leadership of ERDA. Two approaches involve the direct utilization of the sun's light and heat. The others are techniques for converting solar energy into electricity. The six, listed in order of their potential for large-scale near-term benefits, are:

- Heating and cooling
- Wind energy conversion
- Bioconversion to fuels
- Solar thermal conversion
- Photovoltaic conversion
- Ocean thermal energy conversion.

Solar energy for heating and cooling is the most immediately promising application because it is technically simple and because roughly one quarter of all United

States energy consumption is for space heating, water heating, and air conditioning—at a cost of more than $25 billion a year. Furthermore, the use of air conditioning is continuing to increase. In 1974, the government began major efforts to demonstrate solar heating and cooling on a large scale and to carry out necessary research and development. Several initial installations have been made in public school buildings.

Also in 1974, the Solar Heating and Cooling Demonstration Act was passed. This legislation provides for major demonstrations of solar heating technology within 3 years and combined solar heating and cooling technology within 5 years.

In early 1975, ERDA completed an interim report on a national plan to achieve the purposes of this legislation. The plan, submitted to the Congress, called for the construction and operation of systems in a large number of residential and commercial buildings, both publicly and privately owned. Cooperative efforts by 13 federal departments and agencies would lead to the installation of units in 400-2400 buildings. In addition, the plan provided for research and development, collection, and widespread

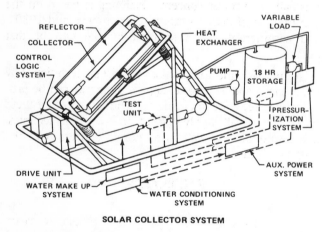

SOLAR COLLECTOR SYSTEM

Highly reflective curved metal plates cause the sun's rays to converge on the glass tube in the center. Fluid in the tube is heated by the sun and circulates through the tubes. The fluid goes through the heat exchanger where the heat is stored and the fluid is recirculated to pick up more heat.

dissemination of information on solar heating and cooling, and activities to remove obstacles based on economic factors and traditional ways of thinking. With the creation of a government-supported market through 1979, the plan pointed toward achieving conditions under which a solar heating and cooling industry can develop.

Wind is another area that promises relatively short-range use of solar energy if economic and institutional barriers can be overcome. If ways can be found to use wind-generated energy directly or to store it at low cost, this source can provide needed additional electrical generating

capacity in areas of the country where there are relatively high winds.

A series of experimental wind energy machines are now being built. In the near future more advanced versions of these machines will be installed at generating facilities at various locations. The purpose will be to learn how to solve the problem of introducing electricity generated from the varying winds into utility grids requiring steady service to customers and to verify the technical and economic characteristics of such systems.

Still another technique of using solar energy is to accentuate the natural processes of photosynthesis in plant life. There are many ways to do this; again the problems are mainly economic and institutional.

The ERDA program of bioconversion to fuels is working to establish the commercial practicability of producing significant quantities of plant materials at feasible costs. The goal is to convert these materials and other organic products now considered wastes into clean fuels. The four major sources of materials being examined are urban solid wastes, agricultural residues, and terrestrial and marine crops. End products that may result include synthetic natural gas, alcohol fuels, solid fuels, heat, electricity, ammonia nitrogen fertilizer, and petrochemical substitutes.

The economic analysis of bioconversion has one interesting aspect. If the entire cost of production has to be recovered by the sale of the end products, solar energy might find it difficult to compete with conventional energy. But if a portion of the cost is charged to environmental protection and disposal of wastes, the prospects for solar energy systems seem more promising.

Numerous bioconversion experiments and studies are under way with ERDA support. One study involves the growth of giant kelp as an ocean energy crop. Under examination is a plan to place a 7-acre kelp farm off the California coast to determine operating and performance characteristics of kelp beds on floating structures. An important feature of this work is the design of the artificial supports that would be necessary and the determination of whether this could be done at sufficiently low cost to make the plan economically attractive. Another type of project now being designed is a pilot plant to evaluate a process for producing pipeline quality fuel gas from urban solid wastes.

Somewhat longer time scales are associated with the other techniques for generating electricity from solar energy. One such approach will employ high-temperature thermal conversion. Experiments are under way to use various means to collect and concentrate the sun's rays on pipes coated with materials that would absorb the sunlight as completely as possible and reduce re-radiation of heat outward. But this application illustrates some of the economic barriers very graphically. A 1000-megawatt power plant of this design would require a collection area of about 10 square miles if located in the southwestern United States, where solar radiation is high. Estimates of the cost of such installations vary widely. For example, one estimate suggests that such capacity might be constructed for about $750 per kilowatt, which would result in costs of about $0.02 per kilowatt-hour for electric

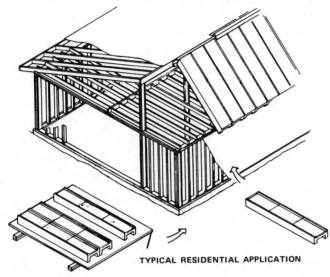

TYPICAL RESIDENTIAL APPLICATION

The flat plate solar collector unit can be architecturally integrated into a building (cutaway view above). The unit is weathertight and insulated. It is easily installed and maintained by building craftsmen.

power at the bus bar.[1] Other estimates run as high as three to four times as much. No one will really be able to estimate such costs with any degree of accuracy before demonstration plants are built and operated for a period of time.

Another long-range potential contributor of electric power is the photovoltaic technique used in photographic light meters and solar cells in space. The cost challenge is illustrated by the solar cell array on the Skylab space station orbited in 1973 and occupied by teams of astronauts for periods ranging up to 84 days. The array was designed to produce 10 kilowatts and cost about $2 million per kilowatt to build. This is about 4000 times the cost of power generation capacity using coal-fired or nuclear plants on earth.

Of course, systems designed for use in space must meet much higher quality-control standards than would be necessary on earth, where equipment can be maintained periodically and repaired when necessary. It is estimated that present mass production techniques might produce silicon solar cell arrays at a cost of $10,000 per kilowatt and that this could be reduced to $2500 by developing an inexpensive process for producing cadmium sulfide cells. The goal of the photovoltaic program is to drive costs down ultimately to about $500 per kilowatt.

The longest-range application of solar energy involves making use of differences of 40°F or more between the temperatures at the tropical ocean surface and a half-mile below. These differences can be used to drive turbines that operate through the boiling and condensation of liquids such as propane or ammonia. Research has progressed through the solution of some design problems, and engineering organizations have evaluated the feasibility of various concepts. Planning is based on the construction of demonstration plants by the mid-1980s, and commercial implementation by the end of that decade.

In summary, the sun provides at least six techniques by which clean and abundant supplies of energy can be provided to meet *some* of our needs. The utilization of these opportunities will involve efforts to overcome technical and institutional as well as economic barriers over the next few decades.

ENDNOTE

[1] A bus bar is one of the main bars or conductors carrying an electric current.

CHAPTER FOUR

OPTIONS FOR AMERICAN INDUSTRY

ENERGY CONSERVATION DATA FOR NINE INDUSTRIES*

Energy Consumption Base: Executive Summary Tables for all Industries

Comparison of Energy Consumption Data for the Nine Industries

This study details the material and energy consumptions for the manufacture of fifteen major products in nine industries. This section summarizes and compares key data on energy consumption and reviews the items of particular interest covered in subsequent detailed studies of the industries involved.

The estimates of energy consumption presented in this report include the energy required for all production steps occurring within the United States, from the extraction of raw materials out of the ground to the production of the specific product. The data do not include the energy required to transport materials between production steps which are typically located at different places in the country, nor does it include the energy requirements for imported materials consumed.

The terms used in describing the energy use should be noted. "Primary" energy is used to refer to sources of energy such as coal, refined oil products, natural gas, etc., commonly shipped in commerce. "Secondary" sources of energy, such as electricity or steam consumed in production, are included in the energy use figures in terms of the primary energy required to produce them. "Ultimate" energy refers to energy consumed in supplying the primary energy needed in each production sequence. For example, ultimate energy figures include the energy consumed in the field production and refining of oil, and for the mining and preparation of coal which is subsequently shipped to the final user (the power plant, coke ovens, etc.) The ultimate energy figures are thus an indication of the rate of depletion of mineral resources in the U.S.

These tables of key results facilitate quick comparisons of energy use and resource depletion in nine industries. Table 3.1 displays the primary energy used to produce each product, the breakdown of primary energy by resource type and the total energy used in the industry in 1970 for the specified product.

The ultimate energy consumption for each product appears in Table 3.2, and the cost of primary energy as a percent of total product price appears in Table 3.3.

Items of Particular Interest in Relation to Energy Conservation

Technological development and shifts in product demand are clearly two examples of changes which will affect energy consumption in industry. As this study progressed, many items relating to energy consumption and conservation became apparent and are summarized in this section.

Selected Plastics

The primary energy consumption for production of low density polyethylene, high density polyethylene, and polyvinyl chloride resins is strongly dependent on the energy used in the production of ethylene, while polystyrene resin has the production of aromatics as the largest single energy consuming step. The total energy used in the manufacture of all four products studied is high and energy cost represents a high percentage of the selling price of the products:

| | PERCENTAGE BREAKDOWN OF PRIMARY ENERGY CONSUMPTION | | | |
	LDPE	HDPE	Polystyrene	PVC
Natural gas processing	15.3	16.2	4.0	7.5
Production of ethylene	63.3	66.8	16.3	30.8
Production of acetylene	–	–	–	9.4
Production of oxygen	–	–	–	1.5
Production of aromatics	–	–	52.4	–
Production of styrene	–	–	20.5	–
Production of chlorine	–	–	–	18.1
Production of vinyl chloride	–	–	–	12.7
Production of resin	21.4	17.0	6.8	20.1
Totals	100.0	100.0	100.0	100.0
Total Primary Energy Use, MMBTU/Ton	93.49	88.64	117.42	82.92
Energy Cost as Percentage of Product Price	15.4	14.5	30.3	12.0

* Energy Conservation—The Data Base: The Potential for Energy Conservation in Nine Industries, Office of Industrial Programs, Federal Energy Administration, 1975.

TABLE 3.1

PRIMARY ENERGY CONSUMPTION DATA FOR THE NINE U.S. 'INDUSTRIES'

	Notes	Primary Energy Consumption (MMBTU/ Ton Product)	Breakdown of Primary Energy Use by Type of Resource (Percentages)					Total Energy Used in 1970 in Making Product (10^{12} BTU)
			Coal	Oil	Gas	Purchased Electricity	Derivative Fuels	
Low Density Polyethylene Resin	a,b	93.49	0	23.6	67.3	18.2	(9.1)	201
High Density Polyethylene Resin	a,b	88.64	0	28.1	73.1	8.4	(9.6)	75
Polystyrene Resin	a,b	117.42	1.1	100.4	27.1	6.9	(35.5)	197
Polyvinyl Chloride Resin	a,b	82.92	9.1	19.4	55.6	23.4	(7.5)	131
Petroleum Refinery Products	a,e,d	(0.44)	--	--	--	--	--	1745
Portland Cement – Wet Process	a,b	8.04	30.4	13.7	39.9	16.0	--	378
Portland Cement – Dry Process	a,b	7.25	42.6	8.0	32.4	17.0	--	224
Primary Copper	a,b	111.84	10.1	13.5	38.4	38.0	--	170
Primary Aluminum	a,c	173.26	0.5	15.1	9.0	72.2	3.2	690
Raw Steel	a,b	19.22	81.1	6.6	13.5	8.4	(9.6)	2528
Glass Containers	a,b	18.16	35.8	7.3	48.8	14.5	(6.4)	205
Newsprint	a,b	21.95	6.6	12.8	13.5	67.1	--	73
Writing Paper	a,b	24.47	19.3	27.8	23.5	29.4	--	57
Corrugated Containers	a,b	21.74	26.2	26.2	42.1	6.9	(1.4)	216
Folding Boxboard	a,b	21.90	17.1	25.8	40.6	16.5	--	21
Virgin Styrene Butadiene Rubber	a,b	133.63	0.1	47.8	53.9	9.7	(11.5)	199

Total energy use represented by these products was 7207 x 10^{12} BTU in 1970. [See Note (f)]

<u>NOTES FOR TABLE 3.1</u>

a. The figures shown are based on average industrial practice in the U.S. during 1970-1971.

b. For all process steps other than alumina smelting and petroleum refining, electric energy was derived from the following mix of primary energy sources: 48.5% coal, 16.1% oil, 26.8% natural gas, 2.6% nuclear fuels, 6.0% hydroelectric. Taking generation and transmission losses into account, this is equivalent to 10286 BTU/KWH.

c. For alumina smelting, electric energy was derived from the following mix of primary energy sources: 39.0% coal, 12.9% oil, 21.5% natural gas, 2.1% nuclear fuels, 24.5% hydroelectric.

d. For petroleum refining, the primary energy consumption in generating electricity was taken as equivalent to 12000 BTU/KWH, which is derived from the breakdown given in note (b) above with the exclusion of the hydroelectric contribution.

e. Petroleum refining industry data expressed as MMBTU per barrel of crude oil processed. Data taken from "typical refinery" calculations (Volume II, Section 4.24 of this study). Breakdown by resource type not determined for overall industry. Typically, all energy is derived from oil, gas, and purchased electricity. Electricity use in the refinery is typically 11%. Total energy use is based on 0.44 MMBTU/bbl. and the 1970 total of crude runs to stills, 3.967 x 109 bbls (<u>API Annual Statistical Review</u>).

f. The total energy figures quoted in this table correspond to the primary energy consumption shown in the first column of numbers. These consumption figures were multiplied by the total tonnage of product manufactured in 1970. The energy totals therefore correspond to the specific definition given in this report. The numbers do not necessarily correspond to any one particular standard industrial classification code number.

TABLE 3.2

ULTIMATE ENERGY CONSUMPTION DATA
(U.S. Data)

	Ultimate Energy Consumption MMBTU/Ton of Product(a)
Low Density Polyethylene Resin	93.57
High Density Polyethylene Resin	88.70
Polystyrene Resin	115.67
Polyvinyl Chloride Resin	83.01
Petroleum Refinery Products	(b)
Portland Cement - Wet Process	8.26
Portland Cement - Dry Process	7.42
Primary Copper	115.81
Primary Aluminum	175.75
Raw Steel	19.33
Glass Containers	18.21
Newsprint	21.89
Writing Paper	24.39
Corrugated Containers	21.73
Folding Boxboard	21.85
Virgin Styrene Butadiene Rubber	132.95

Notes:
(a) These figures reflect the fact that 15% of refined oil products consumed in the U.S. in 1970 were derived from foreign crude and 12.2% of domestically refined crude oil was imported.
(b) Not calculated for the U.S. average. Depends on product slate and product specification: a typical figure would be about 42.2 MMBTU per ton of product, which includes 3 to 3.5 MMBTU per ton for internal refinery energy use.

TABLE 3.3

COST OF PRIMARY ENERGY AS A PERCENTAGE OF PRODUCT PRICE (U.S., 1970)

	Cost of Primary Energy Consumed ($/Ton Product)	Product Selling Price $/Ton	Primary Energy Cost As % of Selling Price
Low Density Polyethylene Resin	40.74	265	15.4
High Density Polyethylene Resin	40.71	280	14.5
Polystyrene Resin	72.68	240	30.3
Polyvinyl Chloride Resin	34.86	290	12.0
Petroleum Refinery Products	--	--	(a)
Portland Cement - Wet Process	3.37	17.5	19.3
Portland Cement - Dry Process	2.90	17.5	16.6
Primary Copper	43.94	1148	3.8
Primary Aluminum	56.40	574	9.8
Raw Steel	9.36	87	10.8
Glass Containers	7.20	158	4.6
Newsprint	7.94	150	5.3
Writing Paper	11.02	245	4.5
Corrugated Containers	10.20	207	4.9
Folding Boxboard	9.99	200	5.0
Virgin Styrene Butadiene Rubber	68.79	460	15.0

Note:
(a) Highly dependent on product slate specifications and market prices. Refinery energy use typically represents about 5%.

An increase in the cost of energy will thus have a severe effect on the cost of producing plastics. Unlike styrene batadiene rubber, the problems associated with recycling plastics are quite complex and recycling does not seem to be a viable means for the industry to reduce energy consumption at present. It is likely that the resins using least energy will be favored, that there will be increased competition from products made from less energy-intensive materials, and that the industry may shift away from high-cost oil and gas as feedstock materials towards coal which is plentiful, in terms of U.S. resource reserves.

Petroleum Refining

The energy consumed in converting crude oil into products for the marketplace is strongly dependent on the product slate required and on the specifications of the products. For the investigation performed for this study using linear programming techniques, the key findings were as follows:

a) Depending on the case chosen, the internal refinery energy use represents a loss of 7 percent to 12 percent by volume of the crude oil intake.

b) Energy consumption is almost constant for a product slate corresponding to a motor gasoline yield between 40 percent and 50 percent volume on crude oil. Current U.S. market demand is around 50 percent.

c) The penalty in terms of internal energy consumption becomes high when about 60 percent motor gasoline is exceeded.

d) The internal energy use does not continue to decline after the motor gasoline yield falls below about 40 percent. There is actually an increase in energy requirement since increasing quantities of high boiling range crude oil components are converted into the middle distillate range.

e) The refinery internal energy is dependent on the crude type. For the crude oils studied, the 17° API heavy crude required about 25 percent more energy than the 32° API light crude for a corresponding product slate.

f) The impacts of changing motor gasoline lead levels and octane numbers can be highly significant for refinery internal energy use. The following examples are for a fixed gasoline production volume.

To put the energy consumption figures in perspective, an increase of 22 percent (Case B) represents 0.42 quadrillion BTU's per year and an increase of 9 percent (Case C) represents 0.17 quadrillion BTU's per year when applied to the total volume of crude oil run to refinery stills in 1970.

g) The impact of changing the sulfur level in residual fuel oil was relatively small for the range of parameters covered. Changing sulfur level from a maximum of 1.0 percent to 1.6 percent by weight reduced internal refinery energy consumption by 1.5 percent for a fixed fuel oil production. The reasons for the small change in refinery energy use in the particular cases studied are that the volume production of fuel oil was only 6.5 percent of crude oil intake (although this is a typical level for the U.S. market) and that the desulfurization of gas oil components for the fuel oil blending pool is not particularly energy-intensive. The energy use is also a function of the crude oil being used. For very low sulfur fuel oils, say in the 0.5 percent sulfur range or lower, the energy requirement can rise substantially as complex processing routes become necessary.

h) A brief review of refinery capital costs indicates that these costs follow the energy consumption curve: for example, as the motor gasoline yield rises from 50 percent to 60 percent, the refinery internal energy use, and the refinery capital cost to achieve the specified product slate, rise. Minimum refinery energy use corresponds to the simpler processing sequences required to produce from 40 to 50 percent motor gasoline yield.

i) Profit margins also tend to follow the energy consumption curve: in other words, with the typical U.S. market prices, increased gasoline production gives increased profit margins. A comparison was made of a given refinery configuration when run for minimum energy use to produce 50-percent motor gasoline yield and the same configuration when run for maximum profit using recent market prices for products. The differences in profit margins (after allowing for maintenance insurance, operating labor costs and all variable operating costs) and energy consumption were as follows:

Case	Regular & Premium Lead Level cc TEL/gal	Average Pool F-1 Octane Number	Relative Energy Used
A	2.0	96.5	1.00
B	0.5	96.5	1.22
C	0.0	92.0	1.09
D	0.5	92.0	0.99

	A Minimum Energy Operation	B Maximum Profit Operation	Differences B-A	B/A
Profit margins MM$/yr.	12.5	17.3	4.8	1.38
Internal energy use, MMBTU/bbl. crude	0.489	0.555	0.066	1.13

With regard to a thermodynamic analysis of available energy performed for the refining process in general and for catalytic reforming in particular, the general conclusions are that large amounts of available energy are lost in combustion processes and that the overall efficiency of the refining process is under 5 percent in terms of available energy utilization.

The two major investigations reported previously in this section are concerned with various calculations of energy consumption using linear programming techniques and thermodynamic analysis. While these calculations offer guidance as to the most efficient manner in which a refinery may be operated, they are not intended to deal in specific detail with the day-to-day inefficiencies which occur in many operating plants and which can lead to significant waste of energy. To address directly the problem of these inefficiencies, a separate study of practical, state-of-the-art techniques for energy conservation was performed. The petroleum refining industry is perhaps unique in the variety of unit operations and types of equipment which are utilized in the manufacturing process. This study, then, of practical energy conservation measures in this industry is particularly valuable since it provides many useful techniques applicable throughout the process industries. In general, the techniques have the potential for retrofitting to existing plants as well as being worthy of consideration at the design stage of proposed plants.

The following items of equipment and systems found in all refineries, are covered in this report:

Fired heaters	Insulation
Heat exchangers	Instrumentation
Air coolers	Vacuum systems
Pumps and drivers	Cooling water systems
Fractionating towers	Steam systems
Tanks	Electrical systems

In addition, recent developments in catalysts and processes were reviewed for possible relevance to energy saving.

A summary of energy conservation measures is presented in the three-page tabulation that follows.

Cement

The two basic systems for manufacturing portland cement are the wet process and the dry process. Apart from preparation of raw materials, both processes are essentially identical. In the wet process, grinding and blending of raw materials use a slurry of the materials in water. In the dry process, the grinding and blending is performed using the materials in their natural (dry) state. Energy consumed in evaporating water in the cement clinkering stage (the cement kiln) accounts for most of the difference in energy use in the two processes:

	Primary Energy Consumption for Overall Process Sequence for Cement Manufacture, MMBTU/Ton
Wet Process	8.04
Dry Process	7.25

Conversion of wet plants to dry plants is clearly a potential source of energy savings, although there may be important technical problems depending on the nature of the raw materials.

In terms of primary energy resources consumed, the process is dependent on fossil fuels for over 80 percent of its energy requirement, the bulk of which is used in the kiln. Most of the electricity used in the process is for grinding raw materials and the clinker. Improved technology of grinding processes, including, for example, the use of air classifiers using hot kiln exit gases in the grinding of raw materials, is leading to reduced electricity consumption.

With regard to the kiln, most plants in the U.S. do not have efficient heat recovery systems in comparison with European and Japanese plants. Systems for heat recovery from hot kiln gases include steel chains installed at the inlet end of the kiln: these serve to break up the coarser lumps of raw materials as they enter the kiln and prevent aggregation of the wet raw materials in the case of wet process kilns. In addition, heat transfer from the hot gases to the cold feed is enhanced. Elaborate raw material preheater systems are well developed in European plants. Manufacturers such as Polysius, Wedag, and Humboldt in Germany, and F. L. Smidth in Denmark offer multistage gas/feed contacting devices to recover useful heat from the kiln combustion gases. Most operate on the principle of passing the gases through several cyclones, and introducing the granular feed (or a slurry) into the cyclone system near the gas exit. Typically, the feed tumbles down the preheater and enters the kiln at around 1300°F, while the gases leave the kiln at 1800°F and are cooled to 600°F. Modern systems such as this are able to cut fuel consumption as compared to the older, non-preheater kilns by substantial amounts: figures of 40 percent or so are quoted in the literature. One other technique used for improving fuel efficiency by increasing heat transfer is to raise the speed of rotation of the kiln from, say 1 RPM to 2.5 RPM, while reducing kiln inclination to maintain the correct residence time in the kiln.

It is interesting to note that about 10 percent of the heat loss occurring in the kiln is through the walls: improved insulation techniques and materials can obviously produce substantial fuel savings.

Summary of Energy Conservation Measures

NO.	EQUIPMENT OR SYSTEM	ITEM	REMARKS	NORMALLY EFFECTIVE SHORT MEDIUM OR LONG TERM (A)	NORMALLY APPLICABLE ONLY TO EXISTING OR NEW PLANTS (B)	PARAGRAPH NUMBER (SECTION 4.0, VOLUME II)
1	Fired Heaters	Control of excess air	Control of combustion	S	E	1
2	Fired Heaters	Fuel atomization	Control of combustion	S	E	1
3	Fired Heaters	Flame patterns	Control of combustion	S	E	1
4	Fired Heaters	Stack gas temperature	Control of combustion	S	E	1
5	Fired Heaters	Install convection section	Heat recovery from stack gas	ML	EN	2
6	Fired Heaters	Install air preheater	Heat recovery from stack gas	ML	EN	2
7	Fired Heaters	Cleaning of equipment, items 5 & 6	Heat recovery from stack gas	S	E	3
8	Heat Exchangers	Configuration of flows	Optimize heat recovery	ML	EN	4
9	Heat Exchangers	Area of surface required	Optimize heat recovery	ML	EN	4
10	Heat Exchangers	Minimize heat loss to air/water	Optimize heat recovery	SML	EN	4
11	Heat Exchangers	Cleaning cycles	Optimize heat recovery	S	E	7
12	Heat Exchangers	Extended surface	Improve heat transfer efficiency	SML	EN	5
13	Heat Exchangers	Porous boiling surfaces	Improve heat transfer efficiency	SML	EN	6
14	Heat Exchangers	Water washing control	See also 11	S	E	7
15	Heat Exchangers	Water scaling control	See also 11	S	E	7
16	Heat Exchangers	Biocide fouling control	See also 11	S	E	7
17	Air Coolers	Fin continuity, thermal contact	Maintain heat transfer effic.	SML	EN	5
18	Air Coolers	Hot air recirculation	Avoid loss of capacity	SML	EN	8
19	Air Coolers	Inlet air distribution	Improve heat transfer effic.	ML	N	8
20	Air Coolers	Protection of bundles	Avoid Cycling	ML	N	8
21	Air Coolers	Temperature control, variable pitch fans	Minimize energy to drive fans while controlling process temps	SML	EN	8
22	Air Coolers	Hub and tip seals	Minimize air recirculation	S	E	8
23	Pumps and Drivers	Correct pump characteristics for required service		SML	EN	9
24	Pumps and Drivers	Correct motor sizing for required service		SML	EN	9
25	Pumps	Replacement of undersized lines and control valves	Investigate equipment for internal fouling, corrosion, etc.	S	E	9
26	Pumps	Spillback or recirculation systems		SML	EN	9

Summary of Energy Conservation Measures (cont'd)

NO.	EQUIPMENT OR SYSTEM	ITEM	REMARKS	NORMALLY EFFECTIVE SHORT MEDIUM OR LONG TERM (A)	NORMALLY APPLICABLE ONLY TO EXISTING OR NEW PLANTS (B)	PARAGRAPH NUMBER (SECTION 4.0, VOLUME II)
27	Compressors	See above: Pumps		SML	EN	9
28						
29						
30						
31	Fractionating Towers	Optimum reflux ratio and number of trays		ML	N	10
32	Fractionating Towers	Reduce reflux ratio	Review product purity	SML	EN	10
33	Fractionating Towers	Feed preflash, temperature	Feed-bottoms, etc.	SML	EN	10
34	Fractionating Towers	Optimum heat exchange		SML	EN	10
35	Fractionating Towers	Product side draw	Reflux reduction may be possible	S	E	10
36	Fractionating Towers	Operating pressure		ML	N	10
37	Fractionating Towers	Vapor recompression	For optimum efficiency	SML	EN	10
38	Fractionating Towers	Tray loading		SML	EN	11
39	Tanks, Vessels	Mixing echniques		SML	EN	12
40	Tanks, Vessels	Suction heater		SML	EN	12
41	Insulation	Increase insulation thickness				
42	Paint	Maintain correct color in good condition		S	E	12
43	Instrumentation	Monitor process conditions to allow optimum operation	See other sections. Additional instruments often show good payout	SML	EN	13
44	Instrumentation	Correct sizing of control valves and orifice meter plates	Minimize pressure drop	SML	EN	9.13
45	Vacuum Systems	Review required operating pressure	Cut down on steam rise to eductors	SML	EN	14
46	Vacuum Systems	Eliminate leakage		SML	E	14
47	Vacuum Systems	Efficient condenser operation	Minimize unnecessary uncondensables loading	S	E	14
48	Vacuum Systems	Review condenser type for possible improvement	Recovery of condensate may be possible	SML	EN	14
49	Cooling Water System	Control use according to plant throughput		S	E	15

Summary of Energy Conservation Measures (cont'd)

NO.	EQUIPMENT OR SYSTEM	ITEM	REMARKS	NORMALLY EFFECTIVE SHORT MEDIUM OR LONG TERM (A)	NORMALLY APPLICABLE ONLY TO EXISTING OR NEW PLANTS (B)	PARAGRAPH NUMBER (SECTION 4.9, VOLUME II)
50	Cooling Water System	Review system pressure drop	Reduce blowdown ratio	SML	EN	15
51	Steam Systems	Efficient water treating		SML	EN	16
52	Steam Systems	Condensate recovery		SML	EN	16,18
53	Steam Systems	Useful work from steam let down		SML	EN	17
54	Steam Systems	Efficient steam trap operation		S	E	18
55	Steam Systems	Steam tracing efficiency		S	E	18
56	Steam Systems	CO boilers on fluid catalytic cracking plants		L	N	19
57	Electrical Systems	Load levelling		S	E	20
58	Electrical Systems	Power factor improvement		S	E	21
59	Power Recovery Systems	From gases, in expansion turbines		L	N	22
60	Power Recovery Systems	From liquids, in hydraulic turbines		L	N	23
61	Loss Control	Tank evaporation losses		S	E	12
62	Loss Control	Many miscellaneous items, including reduced flare losses, slop oil recovery, etc.		S	E	
63	Catalyst Development	Improved catalysts	Lower energy requirements due to lower operating temperatures, better selectivity, less hydrogen recycle, etc.	S	E	25
64	Process Development	Improved processes	--	ML	EN	26
65	Alternative Process Sequences	--	--	L	N	27

A. Short term is typically less than 6 months, Medium term is 6 months to 1 year and Long term is over 1 year.

B. The categories of existing (E) and new Plants (N) are for guidance only; exceptions will be found occasionally. Where an item is identified as applicable to both new and existing plants (EN), design of the new plant should consider that item and existing plant operations should be checked for possible "retrofit" of equipment or use of the specified technique.

Finally, one technique which may provide significant energy savings in the future is the increased use of non-energy-intensive materials such as pozzolans (naturally occurring siliceous materials or man-made fly ashes, etc.) to blend into the final cement product.

Copper

The energy consumption in the overall process for primary copper manufacture is accounted for mainly on energy used in the mining and ore beneficiation stages:

	Percent of Primary Energy Use
Mining and ore beneficiation	54.3
Smelting	40.8
Refining	4.9

The increasing use of lower grade copper ores is likely to lead to greater energy use in the beneficiation stage due to greater quantities of ores to be handled. The energy increase is likely to occur in spite of technological improvements in the ore preparation techniques themselves.

Relative to the copper smelting stage, the reverberatory furnace has been the workhorse of copper smelting for about 90 years. However, partly as a result of economic pressures and partly as a result of environmental pressures, this process is being challenged by newer techniques such as the electric furnace, "flash smelting" furnaces and the Japanese Momoda blast furnace. In the reverberatory furnace itself, oxygen enrichment of the air blast shows promise for energy reduction. Canadian and Russian experiments on full size commercial plants indicate the potential for perhaps 30 percent fuel reduction. The Momoda blast furnace technique requires about 30 percent and the electric furnace, as used in Norway and Sweden for example, around 60 percent of the fuel required by a reverberatory furnace.

The "flash smelting" technique is a continuous system combining the copper production process into one step. The furnace uses mainly the heat produced by the oxidation of the concentrate and thus requires much less additional fuel than the reverberatory furnace. The off gases from the flash smelter are used to preheat incoming combustion air or oxygen.

Other new continuous smelting processes currently under active development include the Noranda (Canada), WORCRA (Australia), Mitsubishi (Japan) and KIVCET (Russia), as well as the U.S. Bureau of Mines Autogenous Smelting System.

An interesting area is the development of hydrometallurgical processes, currently applied almost exclusively to oxide-type ores. These processes involve the conversion of copper compounds in the ore into a solution by leaching with chemicals such as sulfuric acid, ferric chloride or ammonia: the most common solvent is sulfuric acid. From solution, the copper is precipitated out or recovered by electrolysis. The hydrometallurgical processes show particular promise for the economic recovery of copper from low grade ores or mine tailings.

Finally, mention should be made of the conservation of energy by increasing recovery of secondary (scrap) copper. While refining of the scrap is generally necessary, the high energy-consuming steps of mining, beneficiation and smelting are clearly avoided. In 1970, secondary copper represented about 40 percent of the total copper produced in the U.S.

Aluminum

Over 70 percent of the energy used in the production of primary aluminum is required for the generation of electricity, most of which is used in the smelting of alumina to aluminum. With increasing energy costs, there will be a greater incentive to improve the efficiency of the electrolytic reduction cells used in this stage of manufacture. The electric energy used by U.S. producers in 1970 amounted to 15688 KWH/ton of primary aluminum. Actual operating data from countries which have historically had high power costs indicate this energy use may be reduced 15 percent to 20 percent with existing technology, at the expense of capital investment.

In 1970, almost all the bauxite and about one-third of the alumina used in the U.S. for the production of primary aluminum was imported. These imports obviously reduce the amount of U.S. domestic energy required to produce aluminum. Because of inadequate U.S. bauxite reserves, the U.S. appears likely to remain a large importer of bauxite. In addition, because of economic advantages of locating alumina production facilities at the bauxite mining area, and the desire of bauxite-producing nations to encourage this, it appears the import of alumina is likely to increase. This would clearly lower the consumption of U.S. primary energy resources. However, should it be deemed desirable for security or other reasons to reduce the dependence of the U.S. on foreign sources of aluminum, U.S. energy consumption is likely to increase substantially because of the need to process lower grade domestic ores.

Processes are being researched for producing metallurgical-grade alumina from alunite, a basic sulfate of aluminum, of which large deposits are located in Utah. The Bureau of Mines is continuing research on the recovery of aluminum and sodium from oil shale containing dawsonite and nahcolite. With recent increased interest in the production of oil from oil shale, this particular research program may receive greater attention.

Steel

An important factor in the energy consumption for the production of raw steel is the energy consumed in mining and beneficiating iron ores. High grade iron ores are being depleted rapidly worldwide, although currently the U.S. is importing significant quantities of ore with consequent savings in domestic energy resources. For 1970, it is estimated that these imports saved 0.57 MMBTU of U.S. primary energy per ton of raw steel produced, or 75×10^{12} BTU annually.

With regard to the production of iron from ores, the blast furnace appears likely to remain the principal smelting process for two or three decades. Direct reduction processes which bypass the blast furnace are, however, undergoing development and may in time receive widespread application. Improvements in the blast furnace are, of course, being made. Over the period from 1961 to 1971, the weight of coke used per ton of pig iron produced dropped from 0.71 to about 0.63, a reduction of about 12 percent. The main reasons for this reduction are:

1. Conversion to pelletizing and agglomeration or iron ore charge.

2. Improved operating practices.

3. Greater attention to burden preparation.

4. Larger blast furnaces.

5. Higher blast temperatures.

6. Hydrocarbon fuel injection.

From data given in the steel volume of this study, the following savings in energy use relative to reduced coke use may be calculated:

	MMBTU Primary Energy Savings Per Ton of Raw Steel Arising from 0.10 Ton Reduction in Coke Use Per Ton of Pig Iron
Improved operation without compensating hydrocarbon fuel injection	1.38
Substitution of equal MMBTU of hydrocarbon injection	0.56

With regard to coke manufacture itself, new technology is available for the dry quenching of the coke as it leaves the ovens with a circulating gas stream. The advantage over conventional quenching with water is that substantial heat is recovered from the hot coke and essentially all the adverse environmental impacts of the wet method are eliminated.

In steel furnace technology, there has been a drastic reduction in the relative production of raw steel from the open hearth furnace in favor mainly of the basic oxygen furnace (B.O.F.) and some increase in the use of the electric furnace. The basic oxygen process can lead to substantial energy savings although this must be tempered with the fact that the basic oxygen furnace is limited in the amount of cold scrap that can be charged since no external heat source is used to convert the iron to steel. The following comparisons may therefore be made:

	Furnace Primary Energy Consumption with No Scrap in Charge (relative to B.O.F.)	Percent Scrap in 1970 Furnace Charge	Overall Steel Mill Primary Energy Consumption with Furnaces Charging 1970 Pig Iron and Scrap (relative to B.O.F.)
Open Hearth Furnace	16.9	41.0	1.06
Basic Oxygen Furnace	1.0	30.0	1.00
Electric Furnace	25.0	98.5	0.62

New technology being developed in the iron and steel industry which may have an impact on energy conservation includes:

1. Cationic flotation of silica for more efficient removal of silica from low grade ores

2. Flocculation of iron oxide prior to flotation to minimize loss of iron during flotation

3. Conversion of low grade nonmagnetic iron ore to magnetic iron ore by roasting so as to allow magnetic separation techniques

4. Prereduction of iron ores, already in commercial operation, in order to raise the iron content of low grade ores so that smelting in the blast furnace is minimal or even bypassed altogether.

Technological development of the basic oxygen process and the electric furnace may also pay off in terms of reduced energy consumption in the making of steel.

Glass Containers

About 25 percent of the energy used to manufacture glass containers is associated with the production of natural and synthetic soda ash. In fact, the domestic soda ash industry has been turning away from the synthetic towards the natural soda ash, thereby consuming less energy per ton of soda ash. In the context of glass container manufacture, energy savings would amount to about 4 MMBTU per ton of glass containers by using all natural soda ash: this amounts to about 45.2×10^{12} BTU per year, based on 1970 data.

The use of recycled cullet to produce glass containers would have some impact on energy consumption. Currently cullet represents about 20 percent of the glass product. If this were increased to 50 percent, it is estimated that 0.51 MMBTU per ton of glass containers would be saved.

The mix of fossil fuel and electric energy currently used in glass container production may change in the near future since increasing electric energy use is the trend. Many furnaces have had electric booster heaters added to increase glass output and with good results.

The efficiency of the furnace itself is of interest. Because of the danger of reaction between the refractory lining of the furnace and the molten materials in the furnace, the heating flame is normally directed at the top of the batch rather than the bottom. This leads to low furnace efficiency unless hot exit gases are recovered and used in some way to preheat incoming combustion air. Developments in this respect have had significant results, as can be seen from the following census data:

Year	Primary Energy Consumption Per Ton of Glass Containers (relative figures)
1962	1.00
1967	0.83
1970	0.67

Selected Paper Products

In terms of energy consumption, there are several conflicting trends with regard to future consumption levels. Trends which tend to increase energy use include the increasing demand for relatively more bleached products and a simultaneous trend towards higher average brightness of the bleached product. Bleaching is in fact a highly energy-intensive operation. For example, about 16 percent of the total primary energy consumption is attributable to bleaching in folding boxboard production.

Also tending to increase energy use is the increasing emphasis on air and water pollution abatement and solid waste disposal. Operation of water treatment facilities and electrostatic precipitators is energy-intensive. For production of folding boxboard, it has been estimated that almost 4 percent extra primary energy will be needed by the average integrated mill to meet proposed air and water emission requirements.

On the other hand, projects which may decrease energy use per ton of product include the continued increase in kraft pulping due to increased demand for stronger and brighter products. Kraft pulping is less energy-intensive than other chemical and groundwood pulping. Another favorable trend is the continued increase in the ratio of sawmill residue to roundwood used in pulping. Use of the residue eliminates energy (largely electrical) which might otherwise be used for debarking and shipping. For example, in the case of an integrated mill for folding boxboard, the primary energy savings in a shift from 100 percent roundwood to 100 percent sawmill residue would be about 0.9 MMBTU/ton product.

Finally, the increased use of recycled fiber can lead to significant energy savings. As an example, it is estimated that about 30 percent of the gross energy consumption could be saved by going from virgin to deinked newsprint.

Styrene Butadiene Rubber (SBR)

SBR, like plastics, is highly sensitive to changes in hydrocarbon raw material prices and availability. The major potential for energy conservation in the SBR industry is thus likely to lie in the direction of increased rubber reclamation and re-use.

	MMBTU
Primary Energy to Produce One Ton Virgin SBR	133.63
Primary Energy to Produce One Ton Reclaimed Rubber Hydrocarbon	23.48
Savings Per Ton of Rubber	110.15

Applying this saving to the potential displacement of all synthetic rubber in passenger car tires produced in 1970, the total primary energy savings would hypothetically have been 14.3×10^{12} BTU.

INDUSTRIAL ENERGY OPTIONS BASED ON COAL AND NUCLEAR SYSTEMS*

Introduction

PURPOSE AND SCOPE

This study was a joint undertaking of the Oak Ridge National Laboratory (ORNL) and eight industrial firms representing paper, chemical process, and petroleum refining industries. The purpose of the study was to analyze alternative future sources of energy for industrial uses. The assessment includes technical, environmental, economic, and resource availability aspects of industrial energy supply. Since coal and nuclear appear to be the only domestic fuels with the potential for meeting an increased share of near-term energy demands and with an adequate long-term resource base, these were the only fuels considered.

NEED FOR ALTERNATIVES

The industrial sector, the largest energy user in the United States, accounts for about 40% of the total primary energy consumption (Fig. 1.1). Natural gas and petroleum are the primary fuels currently used by industry; of the direct fuel uses, 51% is natural gas, 27% is oil, and 22% is coal. Both natural gas and petroleum are becoming scarce, and the prices are escalating rapidly. Perhaps an even greater concern to industry is that no longer can a long-term supply of gas or oil be assured regardless of price. As a consequence, industry will have to rely more and more on the plentiful domestic fuel resources (i.e., coal and nuclear) in the future. From a national energy viewpoint, the use of coal or nuclear fuel in industry would release gas and oil for other uses and would move us an important step toward the national goal of self-sufficiency in energy. Figure 1.2 shows the industrial consumption of gas and petroleum projected by the Department of Interior for 1980,[1] and, for comparison, the projected U.S. shortfall by 1980. As will be noted, the use of substitute domestic fuels by industry would materially reduce our dependence on foreign supply.

Natural gas and petroleum are consumed in both fuel and nonfuel applications. Nonfuel uses include chemical feedstocks, lubricants, etc. Less than 7% of the natural gas and nearly 38% of the petroleum consumed by industry is used for nonfuel purposes. Although coal may eventually be converted to forms suitable for chemical feedstocks, the best opportunity for industrial energy substitutions is in the area of fuels.

---

* An Assessment of Industrial Energy Options Based on Coal and Nuclear Systems, Oak Ridge National Laboratory, 1975.
1. W.G. Dupree, Jr., and James A. West, *United States Energy Through the Year 2000*, U.S. Department of the Interior *(December 1972)*.

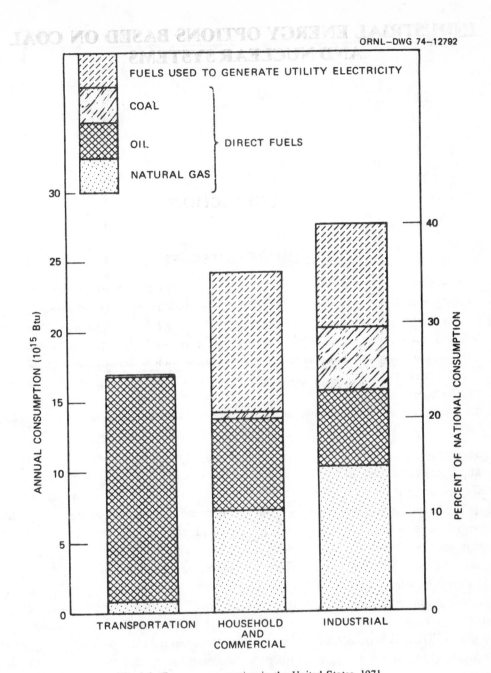

ORNL–DWG 74–12792

Fig. 1.1. Energy consumption in the United States, 1971.

The Department of Interior projections to the year 2000 reported by Dupree and West[1] assumed that the rate of increase of industrial energy consumption would average 3.3%/year. The energy increases were assumed to be borne by natural gas, petroleum, and utility-produced electricity. Although the projections were quite reasonable in 1972, recent events suggest that the use of gas as an industrial fuel will decline because reserves are inadequate to meet demands. The increased use of oil for industrial use may, in fact, come about, but this is contrary to the goal of self-sufficiency in energy.

Another possible scenario developed from the Department of Interior projections is shown in Fig. 1.3. In developing these data, the following assumptions were made.

1. Total industrial energy use and the contributions of coal and electricity to the total are the same as those reported by Dupree and West.

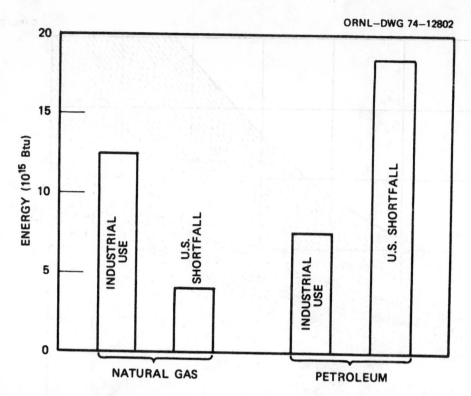

Fig. 1.2. Comparison of industrial consumption and U.S. deficit of natural gas and petroleum in 1980. (Source: West and Dupree.[1])

2. The nonfuel energy sources are the same as those reported by Dupree and West.

3. Natural gas for industrial fuel will be phased out linearly starting in 1975 and ending in 1985.

4. Oil for industrial fuel will be phased out linearly starting in 1980 and ending in 1990.

The deficit in industrial fuels resulting from the assumed phaseout of oil and gas, illustrated in Fig. 1.3, would have to be made up by coal, nuclear, and other energy sources. According to this scenario, the rate of changeover in the decade 1975 to 1985 would need to be very great. For example, the new capacity of industrial boilers and process heaters added in that period, as shown in Table 1.1, would be nearly 60% of the thermal energy capacity that will be installed by the electric utility industry in the same time period. It should be noted that nearly three-fourths of the "new" industrial energy capacity for the 1975 to 1985 period will be obtained by retrofitting existing industrial plants. There is serious doubt as to whether the assumed rate of phaseout of gas and oil is feasible because (1) some promising methods of utilizing coal or nuclear for industrial fuels are not sufficiently developed for commercial application, and (2) equipment manufacturers and the fuel resource industries will be hardpressed to meet both the industrial and electric utility demands.

The present trend in industries that burn natural gas is to convert process heaters and boilers to oil. Although most industries recognize that this could be a stop-gap measure, there are essentially no other alternatives at the present time. Thus, there is an urgent need to develop energy options based on domestic fuels for the industrial sector.

ENERGY ALTERNATIVES CONSIDERED

There are a number of energy systems options based on either coal or nuclear fuel. The nuclear options examined were large commercial nuclear power plants [light-water-cooled reactors (LWRs) or high-temperature gas-cooled reactors (HTGRs)] and a small [~300-MW(t)] special-purpose pressurized-water reactor (PWR) for industrial applications. Coal-based systems selected for study

ORNL–DWG 74–12794

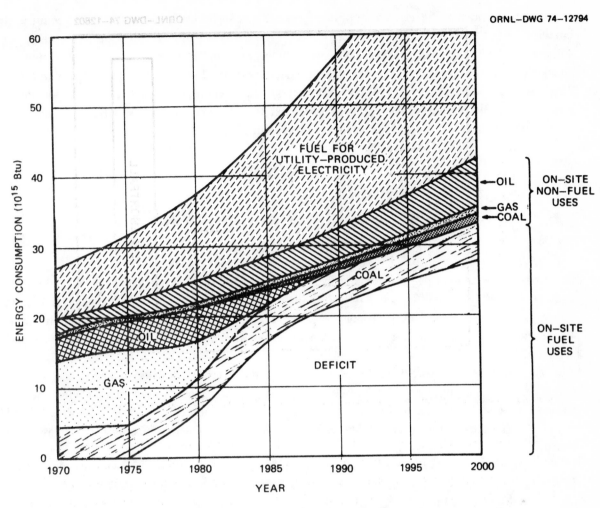

Fig. 1.3. Industrial energy supply to the year 2000 assuming phaseout of gas and oil.

Table 1.1. New industrial boiler
and process heater capacity
required to the year 2000

Period	New capacity[a] [MW(t)]	
	For period	Annual average
1975–1980	289,000	57,800
1980–1985	449,500	89,900
1985–1990	222,000	44,400
1990–1995	126,000	25,200
1995–2000	125,500	25,100
Total 1975–2000	1,212,000	48,500

[a]Boilers and process heaters assumed to operate at 90% plant factor and with a fuel-to-heat
conversion efficiency of 85%.

were those that appear capable of meeting environmental standards, especially with respect to sulfur dioxide; these are (1) conventional firing using either low-sulfur coal or high-sulfur coal with stack-gas scrubbing, (2) fluidized-bed combustion using high-sulfur coal, (3) low- and intermediate-Btu gas, (4) high-Btu pipeline-quality gas, (5) solvent-refined coal (SRC), (6) liquid boiler fuels, and (7) methanol from coal.

Although much of the assessment of energy systems is applicable to all regions of the country, the emphasis of the study was on the Gulf Coast area, since industries in this region are large energy consumers and the primary fuel is natural gas. Since both technical and economic data on energy systems are changing rather rapidly, it should be kept in mind that the assessment given in this study is based on data obtained during the first half of 1974. Furthermore, only those energy systems that have the potential for significant commercial implementation within the next 15 years were considered. Thus, energy sources such as breeder reactors, fusion, and solar were not examined.

Results

DESCRIPTION AND STATUS OF ENERGY SYSTEMS

Large Nuclear Systems

Large nuclear power plants commercially available are the boiling-water reactor (BWR), the PWR, and the HTGR. Both BWRs and PWRs use slightly enriched uranium dioxide pellets as fuel and demineralized water as coolant and moderator. The fuel of the HTGR is a mixture of uranium carbide (highly enriched in ^{235}U) and thorium oxide, the moderator and core structure is graphite, and the coolant is helium.

All present reactors were developed to serve the needs of the electric utility industry, and, with one exception, all existing or planned large reactors are single-purpose electricity-generating plants. The Consumers Power Midland, Michigan, nuclear station, which will commence operation in 1980, is designed to produce both electricity for the grid and process steam for the Dow Chemical Company complex located nearby.

Commercial nuclear steam supply systems are available in standard sizes, ranging from 1900 to 3800 MW(t) (Table 2.1). Typically, the BWRs and PWRs produce steam at 1000 psia saturated; the HTGR steam conditions are 2400 psia and 510°C (950°F).

As of Dec. 31, 1973, there were 42 large reactors operating, 56 under construction, and 101 planned or on order. The large size of the units, coupled with a relatively complex regulatory process, results in a long period of planning and construction totaling 7 to 10 years. After a reasonable shakedown period for new plants, it is expected that plant availability factors of $\sim 80\%$ can be achieved.

Small PWR

The Consolidated Nuclear Steam Generator (CNSG) is a small [$\sim$ 300-MW(t)] PWR developed by Babcock and Wilcox for nuclear ship propulsion. Part of the developmental work was sponsored by the U.S. Maritime Administration. Conceptual studies of land-based and barge-mounted versions of the CNSG were made to assess, in a preliminary way, the potential value of this reactor for industrial applications.

Table 2.1. Commercial nuclear steam supply systems

	Reactor type		
	BWR	PWR	HTGR
Number of U.S. manufacturers	1	3	1
Size range, MW(t)	1956–3833	1882–3818	2000–3000
Steam conditions, psia	1040 (sat.)	915–1125 (sat.)	2400 (950°F)

The basic technology embodied in the CNSG is similar to that for large PWRs, but the CNSG has some unique features. It is a very compact system; the compactness is accomplished by placing the once-through steam generator inside the reactor vessel and by using a pressure-suppression containment system. Primary coolant pumps are placed on the reactor vessel, thus eliminating external coolant loops. Steam is produced at 700 psia and 237°C (458°F) (50°F superheat).

Some of the unique features of the plant design, including the once-through steam generator, have already been demonstrated in the German nuclear ship "Otto Hahn"; this 38-MW(t) plant has operated successfully since 1969. The U.S. Maritime Administration is currently developing plans to apply the CNSG [313 MW(t)] to a 600,000-ton tanker. Start of construction is planned within 1 or 2 years. It would appear that only a small amount of development would be required to adapt the CNSG to industrial uses.

Since the CNSG design allows a greater degree of shop assembly than large reactors, the planning and construction period may be reduced. Planning and construction may be about 6 years for the land-based plant and 4½ years or less for the barge-mounted version. Assuming a mature technology, the plant availability factor is expected to be on the order of five percentage points higher than that for large reactors; the difference is attributable to less-frequent refueling and reduced refueling time.

Direct Coal Firing

Within environmental constraints, there are three methods of directly using coal for boilers. Low-sulfur coal can be burned in a conventional boiler with precipitators to reduce particulate emission. High-sulfur coal can be fired in a conventional boiler equipped with stack-gas scrubbers to remove SO_2 or in fluidized-bed coal combustors with limestone injection. All these methods appear to also be applicable to process heaters. Coal-fired process heaters were once common, but they are not presently being manufactured in the United States; they were displaced by gas- and oil-fired heaters. Fluidized-bed process heaters would seem feasible, but no development work is currently being done.

If coal of sulfur content low enough to meet Environmental Protection Agency (EPA) standards of 1.2 lb SO_2 per million Btu heat input is available, a wide selection of coal-fired boilers is available from U.S. manufacturers. However, particulate-removal equipment, usually an electrostatic precipitator, will be needed to meet the requirement of 0.1 lb/10^6 Btu heat input set by EPA. Conventional coal-fired boilers are available to produce steam at temperatures and pressures suitable for all industrial applications in sizes ranging from a few hundred pounds per hour to several million pounds per hour. Planning and construction periods are on the order of 2 years, and plant availability factors of near 90% are achievable.

A conventional boiler or direct coal-fired process heater burning high-sulfur coal would require stack-gas scrubbing; over 100 such processes have been proposed, and about a dozen have reached the pilot plant or demonstration phase. The scrubbing systems may be divided into three broad groups: throwaway, regenerable, and dry processes. The throwaway processes generally dispose of removed sulfur as a waste sludge of calcium salts. The regenerable and dry processes convert product solutions or solids to elemental sulfur or sulfuric acid. Many of the scrubbing processes remove SO_2 with an aqueous solution or slurry of alkaline material. The electric utility industry has placed greatest emphasis on the development and demonstration of lime and limestone slurry scrubbing, which are throwaway processes. Systems are being planned for over 20 power plants.

However, operating experience to date has not been entirely satisfactory because of scaling, plugging, erosion, and corrosion.

Fluidized-bed combustion of coal, a relatively new technology, appears to be very promising as an environmentally acceptable method of burning high-sulfur coal. Combustion is accomplished in an inert bed, consisting mainly of ash and limestone, which rests on a plate containing nozzles. Combustion air introduced through the nozzles expands the bed to a level greater than its static depth. Crushed coal is injected into the bottom of the bed. Bed turbulence aids in transferring heat to the fuel and also provides intimate mixing of fuel and air, thus promoting rapid combustion. Bed temperature is controlled at 870 to 982°C (1600 to 1800°F) by removing approximately half of the heat through heat transfer surfaces immersed in the bed. The relatively low combustion temperature sharply reduces the formation of nitrogen oxides, and the conditions of temperature and turbulence in the bed favor the reaction of sulfur oxides and limestone. Thus the injection of limestone is very effective in reducing SO_2 emissions. Fluidized-bed boilers are not now commercially available but are under development. A demonstration boiler that produces 300,000 lb of steam per hour [~100 MW(t)] is scheduled for completion in mid-1975.

Gas from Coal

There are a number of processes for producing fuel gas from coal, some of which are in the development stage and others commercially available. The fuel gases produced are classified according to the higher heating value of the gas as follows: (1) low-Btu gas, 120 to 200 Btu/scf, (2) intermediate-Btu gas, 300 to 600 Btu/scf, and (3) high-Btu gas, 900 to 1000 Btu/scf. The high-Btu gas is similar to natural gas both in composition and heating value. Table 2.2 gives a comparison of compositions and heating values of the coal-derived gases.

Low-Btu gasification is achieved by reacting coal with steam and air. Partial combustion of the coal provides the heat necessary to cause steam to react with carbon, producing hydrogen, carbon monoxide, and small amounts of methane and other hydrocarbons. In addition to combustible gases, the fuel also contains significant quantities of CO_2 and nitrogen as shown in Table 2.2. Sulfur contained in the coal appears in the gas principally as hydrogen sulfide (H_2S), which can be scrubbed from the fuel gas.

The production of intermediate-Btu gas from coal is similar to the production of low-Btu gas, except that oxygen or oxygen-enriched air is used in partially oxidizing the coal. Thus, the nitrogen content of the product gas is substantially reduced.

Table 2.2. Representative properties of low-,
intermediate-, and high-Btu gas

	Gas composition (% by volume)		
	Low Btu	Intermediate Btu	High Btu
Carbon dioxide	15	4–6	1
Carbon monoxide	15	30–41	
Hydrogen	23	37–49	5
Methane	4	1–14	92
Nitrogen	42	4–6	2
Other hydrocarbons	1	0–7	
Approx. higher heating value, Btu/scf	170	300–500	1000

There are a number of developmental processes for producing high-Btu gas from coal, but the process that is considered current technology is based on additional processing of intermediate-Btu gas. Two major steps are required. A shift conversion step reacts some of the carbon monoxide in the intermediate-Btu gas with steam to produce additional hydrogen. A methanation step reacts hydrogen with carbon monoxide to produce methane (CH_4). El Paso Natural Gas Company is planning a coal gasification plant to produce 288 million ft^3/day of pipeline-quality gas in the northwest corner of New Mexico; plans are for the plant to be completed in 1978. [Combustion of this gas would produce energy at the rate of about 3000 MW(t).]

Liquid Fuels from Coal

A number of processes are under development for the production of liquid fuels from coal. One point of emphasis in this program is the production of synthetic crude oil which could be refined into various products much like natural crude oil. The main problem in the conversion of coal to liquids is the transformation of a low-hydrogen-content solid into a liquid containing a large amount of hydrogen. The differences among the various processes are related primarily to the method of hydrogenation. Some hydrogen can be added without a catalyst, but a catalyst is generally required to make light fuel products. The Office of Coal Research is pursuing three processes for coal liquefaction, and it is expected that a commercial process will be developed by the early 1980s.

Solvent-Refined Coal (SRC)

The solvent refining process was developed to produce a low-ash, low-sulfur boiler fuel from coal with a minimum of hydrogenation. The product is a solid at room temperature. In the SRC process, crushed coal is slurried with anthracene-oil solvent and hydrogen, the mixture is heated to ~427°C (~800°F) to dissolve the coal, and the resulting solution is filtered to remove the mineral residue. The product, which is low in sulfur, can be burned as a hot liquid or can be solidified (cooled) for shipment and use as a solid fuel. Although there is some question about remelting, limited tests suggest that the product can be remelted and fired much as a heavy residual oil.

A 50-ton/day SRC pilot plant, sponsored by the Office of Coal Research, is scheduled for startup in the fall of 1974. The plant would have a coal feed rate equivalent to about 14 MW(t). A smaller 6-ton/day pilot plant, built by the Southern Company and Edison Electric Institute, was completed in September 1973. This unit, operating on Kentucky No. 14 coal with 3.9% sulfur, produces a product with about 0.6% sulfur and a heating value near 16,000 Btu/lb.

ASSESSMENT

Resources

Both coal and uranium are relatively abundant, but there are limitations to exploitation for each. Uranium, which is widely distributed in the earth's crust, is more abundant than gold or silver and about the same as molybdenum or tin. However, the average concentration in the earth's crust is rather low (2 to 4 ppm), and extraction from dilute sources would be expensive. The present source of uranium ore in the United States is contained in sedimentary strata, particularly those found in the Colorado Plateau and in the Wyoming basin. The average concentration of uranium in presently mined ore is about 2100 ppm, and the market price is $6 to $10 per pound of U_3O_8. Known and estimated reserves in conventional uranium ore deposits are expected to be depleted by the end of the century. Assuming no new mining regions are discovered, the uranium supply will then shift to more dilute sources.

The Chattanooga shales contain 25 to 80 ppm of U_3O_8, and the cost of extraction is expected to be $50 to $100 per pound of U_3O_8. Other sources of uranium include western lignite deposits (50 to 200 ppm), Conway granites (10 to 20 ppm), and the sea (0.003 to 0.004 ppm). The Chattanooga shales alone contain enough uranium to last over a century. Thus, the problem is not that we will run out of uranium but that its price and the environmental effects of mining low-grade ore will gradually increase until alternatives to present-day converter reactors may become more desirable. The expected trend in nuclear energy production cost based on converter reactors is illustrated in Fig. 2.1. However, studies by the U.S. Atomic Energy Commission (AEC) indicate that even to the year 2000, converter reactors will still be more economical than coal for base-load central-station power applications. The AEC expects that the breeder reactor, which is presently under development, will begin to relieve the stress on uranium resources by the early 1990s.

The in-place reserves of coal that is minable with present technology amounts to about 394 billion tons. Assuming present mining recovery factors, the recoverable reserves amount to 220 billion tons, with 175 billion tons deep minable and 45 billion tons strippable. Of the strippable coal, 25 billion tons are low in sulfur and are located in the Rocky Mountain states. The total recoverable coal reserves are equivalent to about a 65-year supply at a rate of consumption equal to our total national energy use in 1970. It is evident that the coal reserves are adequate to meet almost any demand in the foreseeable future. The limitations on the exploitation of this resource are (1) environmental constraints on mining, (2) coal-industry development, and (3) transportation.

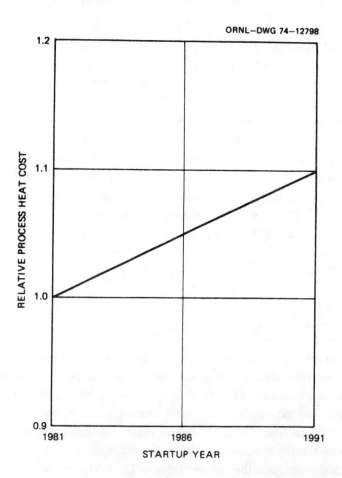

ORNL—DWG 74—12798

Fig. 2.1. Relative levelized cost of steam production with a light-water reactor as a function of startup date (utility financing).

Most of the present concern about environmental effects is related to strip mining. Because of low capital and operating costs and reduced time for mine development relative to deep mines, strip mining is on the increase and presently accounts for about half of our total coal production. Some form of national legislation to reduce the adverse effects of stripping seems inevitable. The nature of this legislation could have a strong bearing on the rate at which coal resources can be exploited, especially in the west. Aside from the environmental constraints, there are other limitations to coal industry expansion. Large deep mines require about 5 years and substantial capital for development. Much of the financing will need to come from outside the coal industry.

The transportation industry is also an important element of the coal energy supply system. Rail transportation is particularly important, and limitations on the rate of modernization and expansion of this industry will affect the rate of coal resource development. When all factors are taken into consideration, the National Petroleum Council believes that coal production can increase at 5%/year. However, it appears that a rate of over 6% will be required over the next decade to simply hold the rates of oil and gas consumption in the utility and industrial sectors at their present levels. If the goal is to displace present uses of oil and gas, the coal expansion rate must be even higher. It appears that coal supply will be hard pressed to meet demand, at least over the next decade.

General Applicability

Industrial needs for energy include steam, process heat, electricity, and chemical feedstocks. Blocks of energy vary in size from a few to several hundred thermal megawatts. Much of the current need for new energy systems is for retrofitting existing industrial plants that are presently burning gas or oil, but there is also a need for energy systems for expansion of present plants and for new "grass roots" industrial plants. The energy alternatives considered in this study exhibit different degrees of flexibility relative to meeting the various requirements for industrial energy systems.

Size

The question of how well the output of individual supply systems match the consumption of energy is of significance only for the nuclear systems. Generally, the commercial nuclear power plants produce more energy than individual industrial plants can use. Even for large petroleum refineries, which are among the most energy-intensive industrial operations, there is a mismatch between the output of commercial reactors and refinery energy needs. For example, a 500,000-bbl/day refinery would require approximately 4000 MW(t) of energy input; 2000 to 3000 MW(t) of this would be based on purchased fuels, and the remainder would be supplied by internally generated fuels. Thus, a refinery slightly larger than any presently operating in the United States could take the output of one commercial reactor. However, a single unit would not provide the reliability required; at least two or possibly three units would be needed. This leads to one important result concerning the use of large nuclear power plants for industrial energy: a multiunit station will be needed, and the output will be shared by a group of industrial plants or by one or more industrial plants and an electric utility. The latter situation is illustrated by the arrangement between Dow and Consumers Power at Midland, Mich. Another consideration in supplying energy from a nuclear power station to outlying industries is that thermal energy, whether it be steam or process heat, may need to be transported over a considerable distance.

In contrast to large commercial nuclear power plants, the output of small special-purpose reactors, such as the CNSG, could be consumed by some individual industrial plants in some cases. A two- or three-unit station would provide 600 to 1000 MW(t) of steam.

Application by energy form

Depending on the type of industrial plant, energy consumption may be in the form of electricity, steam, process heat, and chemical feedstocks. Table 2.3 shows the ranking of systems relative to the four potential energy needs. All energy sources could be used to produce electricity and steam, and all except the LWRs appear to be capable of providing process heat. Both the HTGR and the fluidized-bed combustor would require additional development before they could be applied to process heating. High- and intermediate-Btu gas and synthetic crude oil from coal could be used as sources of chemical feedstocks.

Table 2.3. Ranking of industrial systems by range of application

System	Electricity	Steam	Process heat	Chemical feedstock
High-Btu gas	X	X	X	X
Intermediate-Btu gas	X	X	X	X
Liquid fuels	X	X	X	X[a]
Low-Btu gas	X	X	X	
Solvent-refined coal	X	X	X	
Fluidized-bed combustor	X	X	X[b]	
Conventional firing	X	X	X[c]	
HTGR	X	X	X[b]	
Small LWR	X	X		
Large LWR	X	X		

[a]Synthetic crude oil can be processed in a petrochemical refinery much the same as natural. Heavy boiler fuels from coal would not be a source of chemical feedstocks.

[b]Additional development required for process heating applications.

[c]Direct coal-fired process heaters have been used but are not presently manufactured in the U.S.

Ease of retrofitting

Existing industrial plants, especially those that presently use natural gas, may need to be switched to another fuel in the future. The ranking of the energy sources by the ease of retrofitting existing gas-fired installations is as follows:

1. high-Btu gas,
2. intermediate-Btu gas,
3. liquid fuels,
4. solvent-refined coal,
5. low-Btu gas,
6. fluidized-bed combustor,
7. conventional firing with low-sulfur coal,
8. conventional firing with stack-gas cleanup,
9. HTGR,
10. small LWR,
11. large LWR.

High- and intermediate-Btu gas from coal would require the least change in existing boilers and heaters. Liquid boiler fuels or synthetic crude oil would require about the same modifications as would residual oil. Solvent-refined coal might also be fired in a modified gas boiler or heater if remelting of the solid fuel product proves practicable. Low-Btu gas appears to be questionable as a fuel for retrofitted systems because of derating and loss of efficiency; however, these factors have not been thoroughly evaluated by test. The remaining energy systems (i.e., the fluidized-bed and conventional coal systems and the nuclear systems) would require the installation of new equipment. Light-water reactors would probably be the most difficult to retrofit because in some plants industrial turbine drives would have to be changed to use the saturated steam produced by LWRs.

Energy acquisition

If an industry desires to obtain a new energy system, an important consideration is the number of options available in making the acquisition. Can the equipment be purchased independently or is the energy supply of such a nature that a joint undertaking with others is required? Table 2.4 shows the options for each of the energy systems. Generally, large reactors and the mine-mouth coal-conversion processes offer the fewest options. The output of large reactors must be shared because of their size. Mine-mouth coal-conversion plants would probably be owned by an energy company selling fuels.

When an energy system will be available is another important factor. Table 2.5 ranks the energy systems by year of availability. The only option available in 2 years or less that is based on proven technology is conventional firing using low-sulfur coal.

Table 2.4. Ranking of industrial energy systems by user's options for action

System	Purchase equipment	Cooperate with others	Purchase fuel or energy
Low- and intermediate-Btu gas	X	X	X
Small reactors	X	X	X
Fluidized-bed combustor	X	X	X
Conventional firing	X	X	X
Large reactors		X	X
Liquid fuels		X	X
Solvent-refined coal		X	X
High-Btu gas			X

Table 2.5. Ranking of industrial energy systems by date of earliest commercialization or application

System	Date
Conventional firing, low-sulfur coal	1976
Conventional firing, stack-gas cleaning[a]	1976
Low-Btu gas	1976–78
Intermediate-Btu gas	1976–78
Fluidized-bed combustor[a]	1977–79
Solvent-refined coal[a]	1979–81
Liquid fuels[a]	1981–83
Large nuclear power plants	1981–84
Small nuclear power plants[a]	1981–84
High-Btu gas[a]	1978[b]

[a]Not commercially demonstrated.
[b]Earliest commercialization date is 1978; however, the capacity will not be large enough to have any impact on total gas supply.

ENVIRONMENTAL CONSIDERATIONS

Nuclear

The environmental consideration of greatest concern with nuclear power is health and safety of the public. This issue is complex, but it basically involves protection of people against any harmful exposure to ionizing radiation. In the safety review of nuclear plants, the AEC considers both plant design features and environmental characteristics that could adversely affect the plant's safety performance or the radiological consequences of accidents. Without exception, nuclear power plants have been judged by the AEC on a case-by-case basis; thus, no general assessment can determine the acceptability of a given reactor at a given site. Nevertheless, this study addressed one general aspect of nuclear plant siting that is particularly important—the size of the proximate population. The prospect of using nuclear power for industrial energy raises the question as to whether it is reasonable to expect that such plants could be located in typical industrial areas. To provide some guidance on this question, population-risk estimates were made for several industrialized areas in Texas and Louisiana. The acceptability of the calculated population-risk factors was judged by comparison with risk factors estimated for existing approved reactor sites. It was found that all of the industrialized areas studied, with the exception of the central city regions, would be quite favorable as nuclear sites, at least on the basis of population risk.

Coal-Based Systems

All the coal-based energy systems examined in this study have the capability of meeting EPA emission standards. However, this does not mean that all systems are equal with respect to environmental impacts. Typical types and quantities of wastes resulting from the use of coal or coal-derived fuels are shown in Table 2.6. For direct-fired systems employing eastern coal, the use of lime or limestone slurry stack-gas scrubbing would result in the greatest environmental insult because the sludge produced is not even suitable as land fill unless it is subjected to further treatment for stabilization, provided some acceptable economical method can be found. Regenerable systems for stack-gas scrubbing are also commercially available or will be in the near future. Generally, these systems recover sulfur in the form of sulfuric acid or elemental sulfur, the latter being more acceptable from an environmental standpoint. Fluidized-bed combustion systems produce a solid, readily handled residue which would be suitable as land fill or possibly for road or masonry construction. The processes for coal-derived fuels produce some solid waste in the form of ash, char, or slag and elemental sulfur along with relatively small waste streams which can be renovated by biological treatment. On-site coal gasification plants will generate ash in amounts equivalent to direct-fired systems, and the ash can be handled in a conventional manner. For mine-mouth plants the solid wastes, including the inert elemental sulfur if it cannot be marketed, will be returned to the mine for fill.

The coal-conversion processes examined in this study require varying amounts of water[2] as shown in Table 2.7, which also lists water consumption rates for nuclear fuel processing and oil refining for comparison. The higher values of water consumption shown include that required for process or utility cooling, most of which is once-through. While the general trend is toward closed evaporation systems to reduce thermal pollution, these systems have a greater evaporation loss than once-through systems, and, consequently, cooling water will continue to be the largest increment of water usage. Excluding cooling requirements, the water consumption for the coal-conversion systems is modest. Typically in a liquefaction plant for producing fuel oil from coal, about 4% of the total water requirement is consumed in hydrogen production. About 25% is used for scrubbing or washing the gaseous and liquid product stream. All but a small fraction of this can be subjected to biological treatment and recovered for reuse. By comparison, the solvent-refined coal process requires only about one-fifth of the water needed for coal liquefaction processes.

---

2. *Chem. Eng. News* **52**(30), 17 (July 24, 1974).

Table 2.6. Typical wastes generated when using coal or coal-derived fuels for boiler or process heat fuel

Method of coal utilization	Characteristics of waste product	Approximate quantity of waste available in fuel (lb/10^6 Btu)
On-site utilization		
Conventional firing		
Low-sulfur (western) coal (<0.5% S, 4–8% ash)	Dry ash, gaseous SO_2	5–10 lb ash; <1 lb SO_2
High-sulfur (eastern) coal (3–12% S, 8–20% ash)		
Lime or limestone slurry SO_2 removal for stack gas	Thixotropic sludge (30–60% water) mixture of lime, $CaSO_3$, and ash	13–140 lb sludge (300 ft^3/ton sludge)
Regenerable scrubbing to remove SO_2 from stack gas	H_2SO_4 or elemental sulfur[a] and small waste stream of Na_2SO_4, $CaSO_4$, or catalyst which can be recovered	2–10 lb elemental sulfur; ≥2 lb Na_2SO_4, $CaSO_4$, or spent catalyst; 13–32 lb ash
Fluidized-bed combustion using limestone injection for SO_2 abatement	Dry residue composed of ash and $CaSO_4$	9–30 lb of dry solids
Coal-derived fuels		
Low- and intermediate-Btu gas from eastern coal	Dry ash, elemental sulfur, acid wash water (which must be treated before disposal)	13–32 lb ash, 2–10 lb sulfur, 1 lb wash water
Mine-mouth production (eastern coal)		
No. 4 and No. 6 type fuel oils	Elemental sulfur, waste gas (CO_2), char, waste water	2–10 lb sulfur, ~107 lb waste gas, ~7 lb char
Solvent-refined coal	Ash, waste water (treated), elemental sulfur	1–5 lb sulfur, 13–190 lb ash, ~60 lb waste water
High-Btu gas	Elemental sulfur, waste gas and water, slag	260 lb waste gas, 2–10 lb sulfur, ~10 lb slag, ~88 lb waste water

[a]Sulfuric acid is less desirable, since it has limited commercial value and cannot be transported economically except for short distances. Elemental sulfur has commercial value and will therefore not necessarily be discarded as other waste products.

Table 2.7. Water usage for
energy-conversion processes

Process	Usage (gal/10^6 Btu)
Uranium reactor fuel (including power plant consumption for electricity used in processing)	14
Oil refining	7
Pipeline gas from coal (Lurgi process)	
Water cooling	72–158
Partial (85% of demand) air cooling	37–79
Oil from coal	31–200
Solvent-refined coal	6–40

ECONOMICS

To provide a uniform basis for comparison, costs were estimated for producing steam with each of the energy systems considered.

Capital Investments

The capital investments that must be made at the industrial site, shown in Table 2.8, range from $48 to $192/kW(t). The mine-mouth coal-conversion processes (high-Btu gas, liquid fuels, and SRC) require the least investment at the industrial plant, but, as will be discussed later, fuel costs are relatively high. Of the coal-based systems, low- and intermediate-Btu gas processes require the largest on-site investment because the costs of the gasification equipment and boilers are both included. The nuclear plant investments do not include reboilers; these may be required to isolate the nuclear steam supply system from the industrial steam system. As will be noted, the CNSG requires the largest investment per unit of output. The barge-mounted version of the CNSG is expected to

Table 2.8. On-site capital investments required per unit
of steam production (early 1974 dollars)

System	Unit investment [$/kW(t)]
High-Btu gas	48[a]
Solvent-refined coal or liquid fuels	48[a]
Conventional firing with low-sulfur coal	58
Fluidized-bed boiler	61
Conventional firing with high-sulfur coal and stack-gas scrubbing	78
Commercial LWR, 2-unit station, 1875 MW(t) each	93
Commercial HTGR, 2-unit station, 2000 MW(t) each	105
Intermediate-Btu gas	129
Low-Btu gas	141
Barge-mounted CNSG, 2-unit station, 314 MW(t) each	154
Land-based CNSG, 2-unit station, 314 MW(t) each	192

[a]Does not include off-site investments required for mine-mouth coal-conversion processes.

cost about 20% less than the land-based system because it is assumed that barge-mounted units would be factory constructed.

Fuel Costs

The prediction of future prices of energy resources is difficult because of the current state of uncertainty concerning fossil fuels. In this study, levelized nuclear fuel cycle costs were estimated for reactor startup dates to 1991 for both utility and industrial financing conditions. The estimates of nuclear fuel costs were based on what seem to be reasonable projections of uranium ore resources and uses and expected trends in the cost of ^{235}U separation (separative work), fuel fabrication, and fuel reprocessing. Since the electric utility industry is a major consumer of both coal and nuclear fuel, it was assumed that the long-term price of coal will stabilize at a level that will make it competitive with nuclear fuel for some types of electricity generation.

The estimated nuclear fuel-cycle costs are summarized in Table 2.9. Depending on the type of reactor, the startup date, and the financing assumptions, estimated costs range from 27¢ to 68¢/10^6 Btu.

Two sources of coal were considered in this study: eastern bituminous coal of high-sulfur content from southern Illinois or western Kentucky and western subbituminous coal of low-sulfur content from Wyoming. Estimates were made for the costs of coal at the mine and delivered to the Gulf Coast area (specifically to Houston and New Orleans). The estimates are summarized in Table 2.10. Mine-mouth values of coal were selected so that coal would be competitive with nuclear energy for producing non-base-load electricity. The reference coal values are 50¢/10^6 Btu for eastern high-sulfur bituminous coal and 30¢/10^6 Btu for western low-sulfur subbituminous coal. These values are somewhat lower than present market prices, especially for eastern coal, but it was assumed that present prices represent a response to a relatively short-term supply and demand situation.

Table 2.9. Reference fuel-cycle costs (early 1974 dollars)

System	Startup date					
	1981		1986		1991	
	Utility	Industrial	Utility	Industrial	Utility	Industrial
LWR						
¢/10^6 Btu	27.3	32.7	31.0	38.0	34.6	43.4
mills/kWhr(e)	2.91	3.49	3.31	4.05	3.69	4.63
HTGR						
¢/10^6 Btu	30.2	38.7	33.0	43.0	35.9	47.3
mills/kWhr(e)	2.67	3.42	2.91	3.80	3.17	4.17
CNSG						
¢/10^6 Btu	41.4	52.4	46.7	60.3	51.8	68.1
mills/kWhr(e)	4.86	6.15	5.48	7.07	6.08	7.99

Energy Production Costs

The estimated costs of producing steam with new installations in the Houston, Tex., area are shown in Fig. 2.2. The steam production costs include capital charges, operation and maintenance, and fuel costs. The capital charges depend on the financing assumptions. The assumptions made in this study, shown in Table 2.11, are intended to be a representative set of conditions but not necessarily applicable to any particular industry.

Table 2.10. Cost of coal delivered to New Orleans
and Houston areas (early 1974 dollars)

	Cost (¢/10⁶ Btu)			
	Transportation	Coal (f.o.b. mine)	Total delivered cost	
			Base	Range
Eastern high-sulfur coal				
To New Oreleans area	18	50	68	55–81
To Houston area	24	50	74	60–88
Eastern low-sulfur coal				
To New Orleans area	18	80	98	85–110
To Houston area	24	80	104	90–118
Western subbituminous coal				
To New Orleans area	57	30	87	71–103
To Houston area				
Via New Orleans	66	30	96	78–114
Direct unit train	45	30	75	60–89

The results given in Fig. 2.2 show that large nuclear plants offer steam at the lowest cost of any energy system investigated; steam costs from large nuclear plants range from 78¢ to 144¢/10⁶ Btu, depending on reactor type, size, and method of financing. The nuclear plants are followed by the direct coal-fired systems—conventional firing and fluidized-bed combustion; steam costs range from 154¢ to 184¢/10⁶ Btu. Solvent-refined coal is the most economical of the fuels derived from coal, with an estimated steam production cost of 215¢/10⁶ Btu. The land-based version of the CNSG would produce steam for about 242¢/10⁶ Btu. A factory-built, barge-mounted CNSG would be somewhat less expensive, but no overall energy cost estimates were made for this concept. The most expensive energy systems are those based on liquid and gaseous fuels derived from coal; steam production costs range from 266¢ to 345¢/10⁶ Btu for liquid fuels and pipeline-quality gas respectively. Methanol derived from coal (not shown in Fig. 2.2), the most expensive of all boiler fuels, would result in a steam production cost of about 400¢/10⁶ Btu.

The results discussed above are for new installations, but the largest near-term market for alternative energy sources is for retrofitting existing plants. Intuitively, it would seem that the coal-derived fuels, especially low- or intermediate-Btu gas, would make a better showing for the retrofitting case than for a new installation, since existing gas-fired heaters and boilers could be retained. Nevertheless, the analysis of this case showed that it will be more economical in most circumstances to replace existing gas-fired boilers with new direct coal-fired boilers. A comparison of selected energy systems for retrofitting is shown in Fig. 2.3.

In interpreting the economic results, it should be kept in mind that the comparisons are on the basis of steam production. As discussed previously, there are marked differences among the energy systems relative to the potential for supplying other energy needs. All the coal systems might be useful for supplying process heat, whereas none of the present nuclear systems have that capability. However, the HTGR could be adapted to moderate-temperature (1000 to 1400°F) process heating. It should also be noted that the LWRs (including the CNSG) produce steam at a lower temperature than either the HTGR or coal-based systems. Although the large LWRs have low thermal energy costs, the thermodynamic availability of the thermal energy is less than that of most other steam

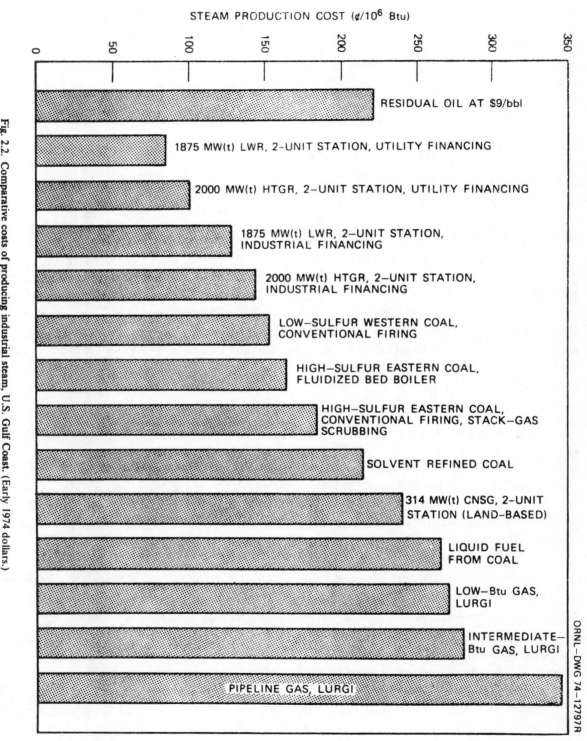

STEAM PRODUCTION COST (¢/10^6 Btu)

RESIDUAL OIL AT $9/bbl

1875 MW(t) LWR, 2-UNIT STATION, UTILITY FINANCING

2000 MW(t) HTGR, 2-UNIT STATION, UTILITY FINANCING

1875 MW(t) LWR, 2-UNIT STATION, INDUSTRIAL FINANCING

2000 MW(t) HTGR, 2-UNIT STATION, INDUSTRIAL FINANCING

LOW-SULFUR WESTERN COAL, CONVENTIONAL FIRING

HIGH-SULFUR EASTERN COAL, FLUIDIZED BED BOILER

HIGH-SULFUR EASTERN COAL, CONVENTIONAL FIRING, STACK-GAS SCRUBBING

SOLVENT REFINED COAL

314 MW(t) CNSG, 2-UNIT STATION (LAND-BASED)

LIQUID FUEL FROM COAL

LOW-Btu GAS, LURGI

INTERMEDIATE-Btu GAS, LURGI

PIPELINE GAS, LURGI

ORNL-DWG 74-12797R

Fig. 2.2. Comparative costs of producing industrial steam, U.S. Gulf Coast. (Early 1974 dollars.)

Table 2.11. Financial assumptions

	Financial parameters (%)	
	Utility	Industrial
Fraction of investment in bonds	55	30
Interest rate on bonds	8	8
Return on equity	10	15
Federal income tax rate	48	48
State income tax rate	3	3
Gross revenues tax rate	0	0
Local property tax rate	3	3
Interim replacements rate	0.35	0.35
Property insurance rate	0.25	0.25
Plant lifetime, years	30	20

sources. If the comparison were on the basis of cost per unit of shaft work capability, the large LWR cost would be near that of the HTGR.

Another factor in comparing the economics of large reactors with the other alternatives is that the cost to transport thermal energy will probably be higher than for alternative steam systems. The reason is that, since large nuclear plants are expected to serve as dual-purpose, central station electricity and industrial steam plants, the nuclear station would likely occupy a site separate from that of the industrial plant. This study indicated that steam transportation would cost 6¢ to 8¢/10^6 Btu per mile of transport.

Effects of Cost Variables on Economic Results

There are a number of cost uncertainties that could affect the absolute values of estimated energy costs as well as the relative ranking of the various energy systems investigated.

Estimated capital investments are most certain for large nuclear stations and conventional coal-fired boilers and least certain for developmental systems such as fluidized-bed boilers, small reactors, and coal-derived fuels. Whether the actual costs of these systems will be more or less than the estimates given in this study cannot be determined at the present time.

The cost of money is another important economic variable, and the effects of changes in the effective cost of money on steam production costs were investigated. The higher the cost of money, the more pronounced the gap between the least expensive (direct fired) and most expensive (coal-derived fuels) coal-based systems. The economic position of utility-owned large nuclear plants relative to coal systems is not substantially altered by changes in the cost of money up to 50% greater than the reference values given in Table 2.11. The cost of energy production for the small CNSG reactor is relatively sensitive to the cost of money, since the CNSG is capital intensive. Even so the ranking of all energy systems by cost is unchanged from that shown in Fig. 2.2 for changes in the cost of money up to 50% greater than the reference values.

Current coal prices are substantially higher than the base values used in the present study. As discussed previously, the reference coal prices were selected on the assumption that coal prices will, in the long run, readjust to a competitive position with nuclear for some central station power applications. If coal prices do not decline, (1) the cost differential between the direct-fired systems and the coal-derived fuels will become even larger, because the direct-fired systems are more efficient converters of coal to thermal energy, and (2) the relative economic position of nuclear will be substantially improved.

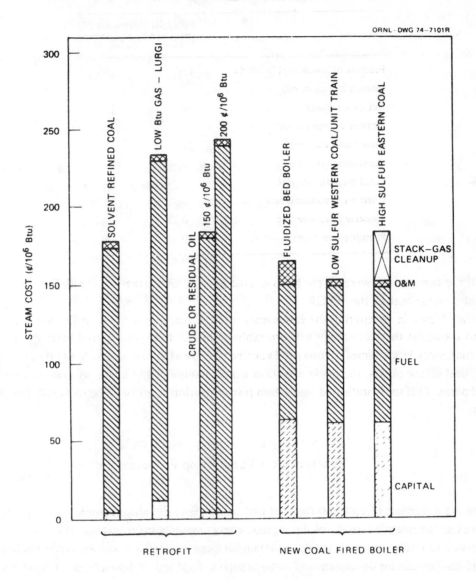

Fig. 2.3. Selected comparison of steam cost for retrofit vs new coal-fired boiler.

Conclusions

THE ENERGY NEED

Industry is faced with a period of transition in fuel sources. Presently, natural gas provides over half the on-site-produced industrial energy, but this resource is becoming scarce and is expected to be phased out as an industrial fuel within the next few years. The present trend is to substitute oil for natural gas in process heaters and boilers. Although the increased use of oil is contrary to the goal of national self-sufficiency in energy, industry has few other alternatives at the present time. Therefore, there is an urgent need to develop energy options for the industrial sector based on plentiful domestic fuels. This is especially important when it is considered that industry consumes more energy than any other economic sector.

Coal and uranium are the only major domestic fuel resources that have a reasonable long-term resource base. The technologies required to use these fuels in an economical, environmentally acceptable way are under development and in some instances being applied. However, the motivation for such development has been primarily for applications other than industrial energy: the major emphasis by both the Federal Government and the energy equipment industry has been on central station power generation. Yet, relative to central station (utility) power generation, industry consumes nearly twice the petroleum and about three times the natural gas. Thus, a stronger national emphasis on the industrial fuel need is justified.

THE ENERGY RESOURCES

The domestic uranium and coal reserves are both sufficiently large to make either fuel a reasonable long-term alternative for industrial applications. Coal reserves are particularly large, and it is likely that a major portion of the deficit in oil and gas for industry will be made up by coal. Nevertheless, there are major intermediate-term problems in exploiting our coal resources. These problems relate to environmental constraints on mining and utilization, coal-industry capitalization, and transportation. When all factors are considered, it appears that the supply of coal will be hard pressed to meet demand, at least over the next decade. The current inflated price structure appears to be a consequence of the supply-demand imbalance, but in the long term it is likely that coal will stabilize at prices lower than the present values because of competition with other fuels, particularly nuclear.

The high-grade reserves of uranium may be depleted by the end of the century. Assuming no new mining regions are discovered, the uranium supply will then shift to more dilute sources such as the Chattanooga shales. Even so, it is concluded that the total cost of nuclear energy will be relatively stable over at least the next two decades because the cost of energy production is not a strong function of uranium ore cost.

THE ENERGY SYSTEM CHOICES

Coal and nuclear fuel can each serve as a basis for a number of potentially attractive industrial energy system choices. Both fuels can and probably will help alleviate the energy deficit resulting from the decline in availability of natural gas and oil. Because of its broader range of application and relative ease of implementation, coal is expected to be the more important substitute industrial fuel over the period of interest in this study (the next 15 years). In the longer term, nuclear fuels could assume a major role for supplying industrial steam. Timing and extent of use of nuclear will depend, in part, on efforts expended to resolve institutional problems. Conclusions about specific coal and nuclear energy systems are given below.

Direct Firing of Coal

Generally, the direct firing of coal in industrial boilers and process heaters will be more economical than the use of coal-derived fuels (gases, liquids, and solids). There are three methods for directly using coal to generate steam or process heat in an environmentally acceptable manner: (1) low-sulfur coal, (2) fluidized-bed combustion, and (3) high-sulfur coal with stack-gas scrubbing.

The most realistic coal-based alternative at the present time is low-sulfur coal fired in a conventional boiler. If low-sulfur coal becomes available in sufficient quantities, this is the lowest-cost coal alternative in the Gulf Coast area.

The most promising method of using high-sulfur coal is the fluidized-bed boiler. If development goals are achieved, the process offers flexibility in fuel supply as well as low cost. Fluidized-bed combustion may also hold promise for process heating, but no development work is being done on fluidized-bed process heaters.

Wet limestone scrubbing appears to be the least expensive and best developed of the stack-gas cleanup systems. With additional development, these systems will, no doubt, become workable, but overall operating experience has been poor. Wet limestone scrubbing and other throwaway processes have one distinct disadvantage for industrial applications: the large volume of waste sludge will be difficult to dispose of in many industrial areas. For this reason, it appears that widespread industrial use of stack-gas scrubbing must await the development of economical regenerable systems.

On-Site Coal Gasification

Air-blown gasifiers producing low-Btu gas (~150 Btu/scf) and oxygen-blown gasifiers producing intermediate-Btu gas (~300 Btu/scf) are commercially available. Low-Btu gas is marginally lower in cost, but intermediate-Btu gas is a better choice for industry because (1) it can be used as a retrofit fuel for existing gas-fired boilers and process heaters and (2) it is more readily usable as a chemical feedstock. As fuels, however, low- and intermediate-Btu gases are more expensive than direct-fired coal. Extensive industrial applications of on-site coal gasifiers will require the development of a low-cost intermediate-Btu gas process.

Mine-Mouth Coal-Conversion Processes

Methods are under development for converting coal to high-quality fuels at the mine mouth; the fuels to be produced include (1) solvent-refined coal; (2) liquid fuels, including synthetic crude, boiler fuels, and methanol; and (3) pipeline-quality (high-Btu) gas.

Solvent-refined coal is potentially the least expensive of the coal-derived fuels and looks especially promising if it can be remelted and used in the same manner as residual oil.

Liquid boiler fuels may have promise for the future, but the cost is likely to exceed that of SRC.

The technology for producing methanol from coal is well developed, but the cost is too high for its use as an industrial fuel. Methanol is presently an important chemical feedstock, and this is the most likely use for coal-derived methanol.

Although high-Btu (pipeline-quality) gas from coal may find limited application in small industries, the large industrial energy user has several coal-based options that are less expensive.

Nuclear Energy

With present technology, nuclear energy can supply industrial steam and electricity. The commercially available nuclear systems are very large, ranging from about 1800 to 3800 MW(t). With further development, nuclear energy may have the capability to match most of the higher-temperature process heat applications of industry. Another developmental possibility is a smaller reactor that more nearly matches the energy demand of industrial plants. One important advantage of nuclear energy is the low fuel cost. The major drawbacks to nuclear are (1) the long lead times required in the planning and construction of power plants and (2) the difficulties in gaining site approvals and the administrative burden associated with regulatory requirements. Conclusions concerning specific nuclear alternatives are given below.

Large commercial nuclear power plants offer industrial steam and electricity at the lowest cost of the energy systems investigated. The mismatch in output of currently marketed nuclear plants and the consumption rate of individual industrial plants, coupled with the need for multiple units to provide reliability, will limit applications to joint uses of a nuclear power station. One desirable arrangement is for an electric utility to generate both electrical energy for the grid and thermal energy for local industries. This arrangement would require steam transport for a few miles in most areas.

Process heat at 1000 to 1400°F might be economically supplied from large HTGRs, but process heat HTGRs are not commercially available. Such units could be developed, if warranted by market potential, using essentially current technology. A related area of technological development that would be required is an economical means of transporting high-temperature thermal energy from the nuclear plant to the processes.

If fully developed, small [~300-MW(t)] land-based PWRs could become competitive with oil (at $10/bbl) and most coal-derived fuels for producing industrial steam and electricity. To be competitive with the lowest-cost coal systems, the capital costs of small reactors need to be reduced below present estimates. The development of factory-assembled barge-mounted units has the potential for reducing capital costs. Justification for this development by reactor manufacturers will depend on their perception of market potential. Another question that requires serious consideration is whether a large number of small reactors would be more difficult to regulate to assure the same high level of safety expected with current reactors.

Assessment of Energy Alternatives

The following general assessment of coal and nuclear energy alternatives for industrial energy is specifically directed toward large industrial energy applications in the Gulf Coast region of the U.S., where industry has been using low-cost, high-quality natural gas almost exclusively. Natural gas is now quite expensive and, more importantly, may soon be unavailable to industry for steam generation and process heating at any cost. Conversion to an alternate energy source involves an almost unmanageable number of options and decisions, many of which may be affected by national or international policies beyond the control of the industries concerned.

This assessment is intended to provide some useful guidelines for the industries involved and to contribute, along with industrial input, to a better understanding within the Federal Government of energy system development needs for industrial applications.

Each system is evaluated in terms of its application in or near Houston, Tex. Selection of this reference site has tended to make western coal more attractive as compared with some alternate site east of the Mississippi River. The reader should be cognizant of this factor in interpreting these results for alternate sites.

NUCLEAR ENERGY

Three nuclear systems were evaluated in various sizes: commercial LWRs (PWRs and BWRs), HTGRs, and the consolidated nuclear steam generator (CNSG), a small LWR development concept.

The cost of steam for a typical two-unit utility-financed reactor station is shown in Fig. 7.1. The 3750-MW(t) PWR and the 3000- and 2000-MW(t) HTGRs are standard commercial sizes. The 1875-MW(t) PWR is marketed in Europe but not in this country currently. The 1000-MW(t) HTGR is an extrapolation of our cost information and is not presently being marketed. Steam costs, including an isolation loop, vary from 78¢/10^6 Btu for the largest LWR to $1.25/$10^6$ Btu for the 1000-MW(t) HTGR. The CNSG is not illustrated with utility financing.

The cost of steam from a two-unit station with industrial financing is shown on Fig. 7.2. In this case, costs, including an isolation loop, vary from $1.08/$10^6$ Btu for the largest PWR to $2.41/$10^6$ Btu for the 314-MW(t) and CNSG.

Several comments are needed to qualify and explain these results. First, the cost difference between the equivalent PWR and HTGR sizes is compensated for by the higher quality of the steam generated in the HTGR. In terms of electricity production, these systems are equally competitive. However, the current HTGR design precludes the extraction of high-quality steam. Our estimate presumes a modification of the helium circulator design so that prime steam is available.

Transportation of the HTGR prime steam or very high-temperature, high-pressure process steam which could be generated from an isolation loop is not economically attractive. We have assumed transportation of 650 psi, 750°F steam from the HTGR without any credit for by-product power which could be produced.

Recently the General Atomic Company has proposed a "booster reheat" cycle for HTGR process steam application. This cycle provides a modest amount of power from the high-pressure turbine [130 MW(e) for a 2000-MW(t) reactor] and still provides steam from the heater at approximately 726 psia and 913°F. A major advantage of this cycle other than the improved steam conditions is that the steam pres-

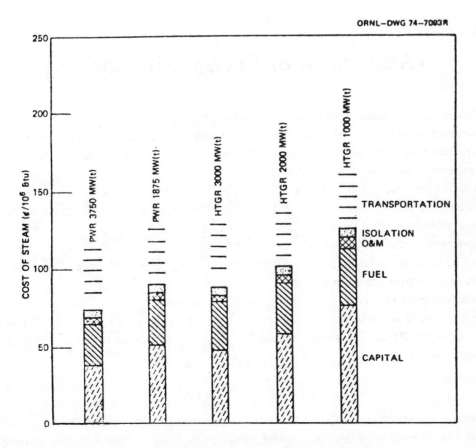

Fig. 7.1. Cost of steam from a utility-financed nuclear reactor.

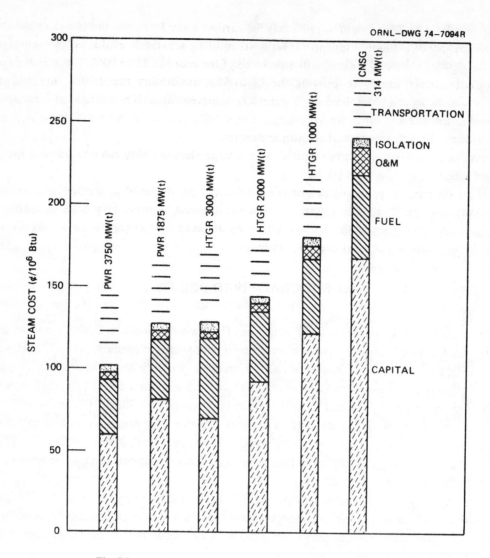

Fig. 7.2. Cost of steam from an industry-financed nuclear reactor.

sure is greater than the reactor helium pressure throughout the steam-generator/reheater. Thus the potential for radioactive contamination within the steam is greatly reduced. The question of whether a reboiler is required in this case may be debatable, but even if it is required, industrial steam conditions of 650 to 675 psia and 750°F should be available. The modified cycle is accomplished by adding a pressure control valve on the outlet line of the reheater. Other system components are identical to the conventional HTGR cycle equipment.

A quick evaluation of the effect of this improved cycle on the cost of steam from an HTGR reveals that by allowing credit of 12 mills/kWhr for the power generated (17 mills/kWhr for industrial financing) and estimating the turbine generator costs, the net effect is a reduction in cost of steam of about 14¢/10⁶ Btu for utility financing and about 19¢/10⁶ Btu for industrial financing. If the reboiler can be eliminated, there would be additional cost savings.

The incremental cost increase due to the LWR reboiler is estimated to be 5¢/10⁶ Btu. The steam conditions of the modified HTGR will probably be more favorable, although they are uncertain at this time. The same isolation loop cost (5¢/10⁶ Btu) was arbitrarily applied to the HTGR.

Steam transportation costs for the PWR and the HTGR are essentially the same. An average cost of 7¢/10⁶ Btu per mile is applied in this analysis. It is assumed, because of the nature of nuclear reactor siting, that the nuclear steam supply may be farther away from the industrial application than alternate coal-based systems. Transportation costs must be separately evaluated in each case.

The availability of a nuclear steam plant should be of the order of 85 to 90%. The question of a backup of standby steam supply to provide the 98 to 99% availability needed for the industrial applications is a difficult one. This backup is generally achieved through a multiple of small units. The more economical nuclear units are very large. The CNSG is a much more attractive unit size, but its small size results in a substantial economic penalty.

If the industrial plant is, or can be, located near a large electric utility nuclear station, there is no doubt that nuclear energy is the best buy.

It is also possible that a group of neighboring industrial plants could jointly utilize a two- or three-unit industrially financed nuclear station. Even so, it would be more attractive to induce the local utility to build and operate the facility either as an industrial energy supply only or as a dual-purpose industrial and electrical energy supply.

DIRECT COAL-FIRED BOILER

Three direct coal-fired options have been evaluated: (1) low-sulfur western coal in a conventional boiler, (2) high-sulfur eastern coal in a conventional boiler with stack-gas cleanup, and (3) high-sulfur eastern coal in a fluidized-bed boiler. The cost of steam from these systems is shown in Fig. 7.3. Two costs are presented for low-sulfur western coal as a function of coal transportation costs. The steam costs are $1.53/10^6 Btu for western coal delivered by unit train to Houston and $1.78/10^6 Btu for western coal delivered by unit train to the St. Louis area and by barge to Houston. The mine-mouth coal cost is estimated at 30¢/10^6 Btu, and the total cost of coal delivered to Houston is 75¢/10^6 Btu and 96¢/10^6 Btu for the two routes. Once again we should point out that the major effect of transportation cost on western coal must be carefully considered for alternate sites.

High-sulfur eastern coal is estimated to cost 50¢/10^6 Btu at the mine mouth and 74¢/10^6 Btu in Houston. The cost of steam for a high-sulfur eastern-coal-fired boiler with stack-gas cleanup is estimated to be $1.84/10^6 Btu. The stack-gas cleanup system cost, illustrated separately, is estimated to contribute 37¢/10^6 Btu to the total steam cost.

The fluidized-bed boiler is currently under development. The total steam cost from this boiler is estimated at $1.65/10^6 Btu. This estimate, which is admittedly a crude one, should be updated as the development and commercial design program progresses. However, it seems obvious at this time, barring some major setback in scaling up the concept, that the fluidized-bed boiler will be a most attractive approach, for direct coal-fired boilers with high-sulfur coal. It may also be applicable for process heaters using coal.

LOW-, INTERMEDIATE-, AND HIGH-Btu GAS FROM COAL

The cost of steam from a gas-fired boiler is illustrated in Fig. 7.4. Two bars are illustrated for each process; the first represents the cost of producing the gas from coal, and the second represents the cost of steam from a gas-fired boiler utilizing the gas production cost (first bar) to develop the fuel cost for the boiler.

The two processes illustrated for low-Btu gas, Wellman and Lurgi, show steam costs of $2.38 and $2.72/10^6 Btu respectively. The gas production costs are $1.57/10^6 Btu for Wellman and $1.86/10^6 Btu for Lurgi. This cost difference is almost entirely in capital cost of the equipment.

Intermediate-Btu gas costs for the Lurgi and Koppers oxygen-blown gasifiers are $2.01 and $2.38/10^6 Btu respectively. In this case the processes are quite different, and the cost difference can

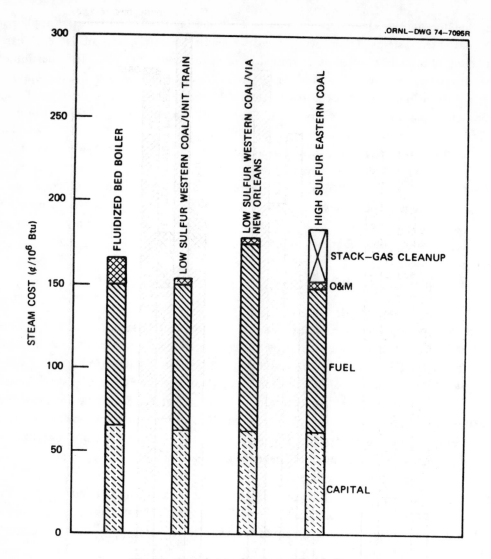

.ORNL–DWG 74–7095R

FLUIDIZED BED BOILER

LOW SULFUR WESTERN COAL/UNIT TRAIN

LOW SULFUR WESTERN COAL/VIA NEW ORLEANS

HIGH SULFUR EASTERN COAL

STACK–GAS CLEANUP

O&M

FUEL

CAPITAL

STEAM COST (¢/10^6 Btu)

Fig. 7.3. Cost of steam from a coal-fired boiler.

be explained by the much higher oxygen and electricity requirements of Koppers process. The cost of steam from the gas-fired boiler for these processes is $2.82/$10^6$ Btu for Lurgi and $3.26/$10^6$ Btu for Koppers.

High-Btu gas production by the Lurgi process is presented along with a projection of probable costs for the U.S. development processes. High-Btu gas is assumed to be a mine-mouth process at 50¢/10^6 Btu coal cost. Four major processes are under development in the U.S., and several others are receiving less emphasis. The composite projection assumes a 15% reduction in capital cost and a 5% increase in conversion efficiency as compared with the Lurgi process. The costs for high-Btu gas delivered to Houston are $2.39 and $2.19/$10^6$ Btu for the Lurgi and U.S. development processes respectively. Steam costs are $3.46 and $3.22/$10^6$ Btu respectively.

Low-quality steam is produced as a by-product for all gasification processes. The Koppers process yields more steam than the others. In our analysis, no credit or value has been assumed for this steam. However, in a paper mill, where there is a large demand for low-quality steam for drying, this by-product steam could be of significant value.

Two advantages of gasification, especially intermediate or high Btu, are ease of retrofitting and possible use as feedstock. The major disadvantage is obviously higher cost than some alternate methods of coal utilization.

ORNL—DWG 74—7096

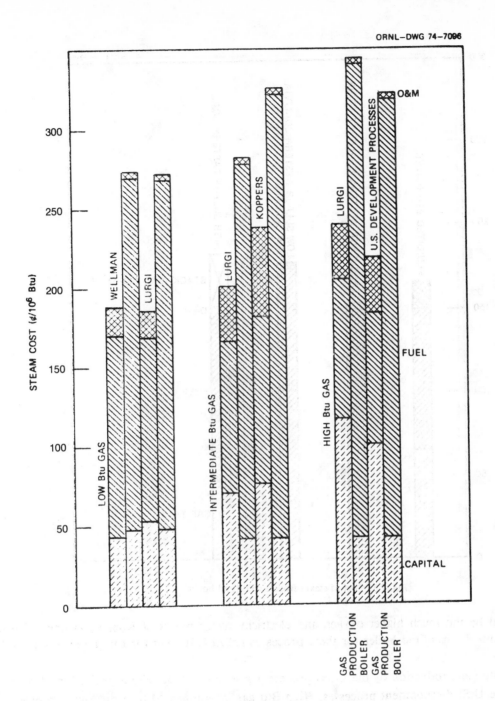

Fig. 7.4. Cost of steam from a gas-fired boiler.

SOLVENT-REFINED COAL AND LIQUID BOILER FUEL FROM COAL

The cost of steam from an oil-fired boiler using solvent-refined coal (SRC) and liquid boiler fuel from coal is shown in Fig. 7.5. For comparison, the costs of steam from an oil-fired boiler using crude or residual oil at $1.50, $2.00, and $2.50/10^6 Btu are also presented. These are approximately equivalent to $9, $12, and $15 per barrel respectively.

Solvent-refined coal is a developmental process in which the coal is dissolved in a coal-derived solvent at about 700 to 800°F with a minimum of hydrogenation. Minerals are removed by filtration, and light oils and gas are removed by distillation. Inorganic sulfur is removed in the minerals, and organic sulfur is removed as H_2S from the vent gas. The process shows great potential

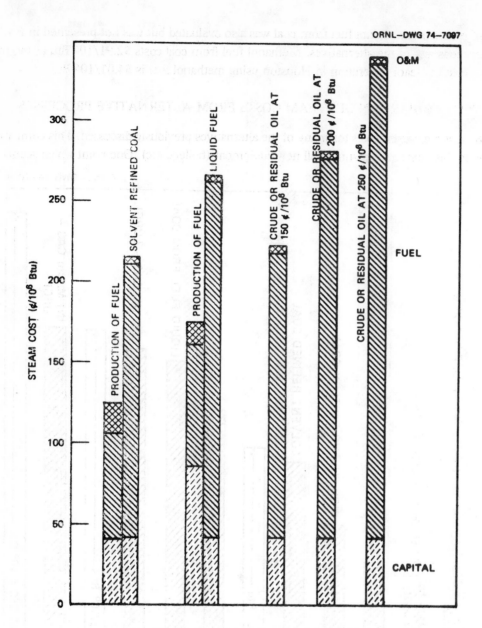

Fig. 7.5. Cost of steam from an oil-fired boiler.

for producing a low-cost clean boiler fuel from coal. Solvent-refined coal solidifies at about 300°F and apparently can be remelted at about 400°F and fed as a liquid boiler fuel or pulverized and fed like coal. The product is about 0.6 to 0.7% sulfur and 0.1 to 0.4% ash with a higher heating value of 15,650 Btu/lb. It should be suitable for oil-fired boilers or gas-fired boilers converted to oil.

Liquid boiler fuel from coal is produced by extraction-hydrogenation (the SRC process plus additional catalytic hydrogenation) or by the H-coal process.

Both the SRC and liquid fuel processes provide 10 to 20% of the product in the form of high-quality gas and light oils. Our analysis does not include any higher value credit; that is, these by-products are considered to have the same value as the SRC or liquid boiler fuel.

The cost of SRC is estimated to be $1.25/10^6 Btu at the mine mouth, and the cost of steam generation in Houston using SRC is $2.15/10^6 Btu. Liquid boiler fuel costs $1.75/10^6 Btu at the mine mouth, and the cost of steam generation in Houston using the liquid boiler fuel is $2.66/10^6 Btu.

The cost of producing methanol fuel from coal was also evaluated but was not presented in Fig. 7.5 because it far exceeds any of the alternatives. Methanol fuel from coal costs $2.91/10^6 Btu at the mine mouth, and the cost of steam generation in Houston using methanol fuel is $4.01/10^6 Btu.

SELECTED COMPARISON OF STEAM COSTS FROM ALTERNATIVE PROCESSES

Figure 7.6 illustrates steam costs for many of the alternatives previously discussed. This comparison and all analyses to this point have assumed all new equipment (boilers, etc). One point which seems ob-

ORNL–DWG 74–7098

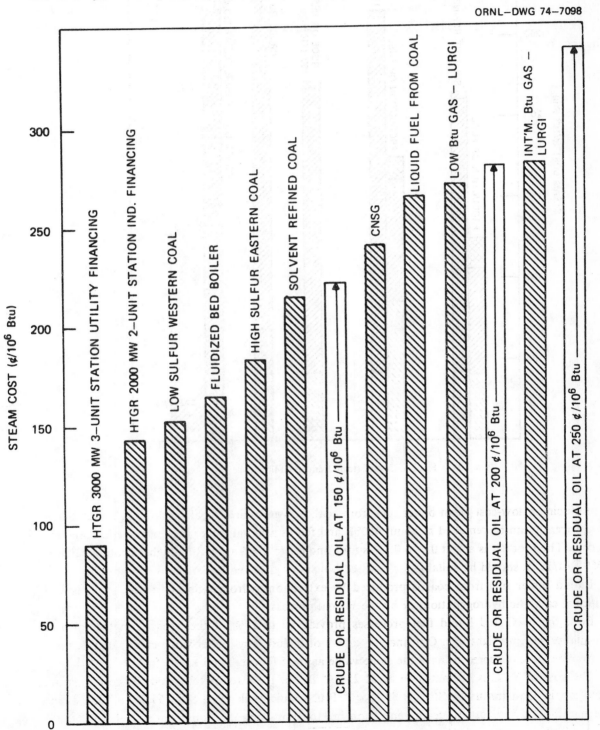

Fig. 7.6. Selected comparison of steam costs from alternative processes.

vious is that any process which is not competitive with crude or residual oil is of little near-term economic interest. Unfortunately, the long-term cost of crude oil is very uncertain.

RETROFITTING AN EXISTING GAS-FIRED BOILER (OR PROCESS HEATER)

All data to this point have been presented in terms of new capacity. The cost of steam from retrofitting an existing gas-fired boiler is presented in Fig. 7.7. High-Btu gas involves no capital expense; only fuel, operation, and maintenance costs are involved. We have assumed that conversion to intermediate-Btu gas or to oil will require 10% of the capital cost of a new boiler, and conversion to low-Btu gas will require 25% of the capital cost of a new boiler. It is presumed that adequate modifications are made, so that no loss of efficiency or capacity is incurred.

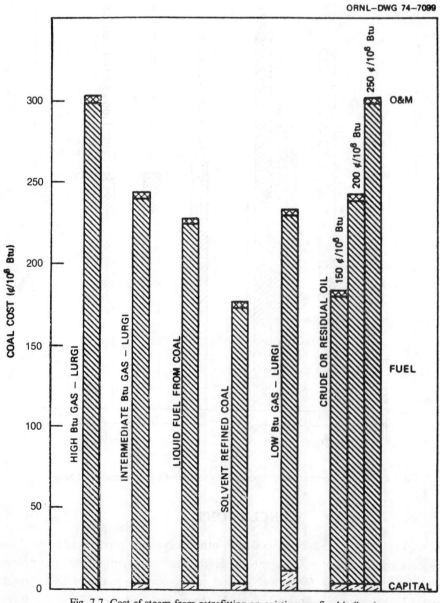

Fig. 7.7. Cost of steam from retrofitting an existing gas-fired boiler (or process heater).

It seems logical that gas-fired process heaters could also be converted to alternate fuels with similar capital expenditures.

Again, crude or residual oil is included for comparison. The cost of steam varies from $1.77/10^6$ Btu for SRC to $3.03/10^6$ Btu for high-Btu gas.

Figure 7.8 illustrates a selected comparison of steam costs for retrofitting vs new coal-fired boilers. The new coal-fired boiler for western low-sulfur coal at $1.53/10^6$ Btu and the fluidized-bed boiler at $1.65/10^6$ Btu are more favorable economically than any of the retrofit processes. Factors such as process heating or a limited plant life, which are not considered, would tend to favor the retrofit systems.

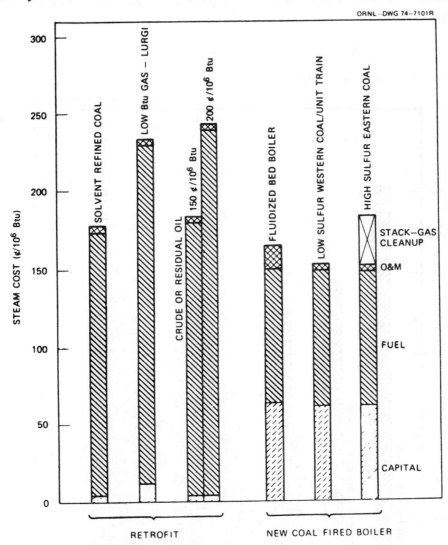

Fig. 7.8. Selected comparison of steam costs for retrofit vs new coal-fired boiler.

CONCLUSIONS

A general ranking of the various processes in other ways may provide additional insight. Table 7.1 presents a ranking by range of application. High- and intermediate-Btu gas processes are the only ones considered suitable as feedstock. Liquid fuels, low-Btu gas, and SRC could be used in process heaters. All systems are suitable for steam generation, and the HTGR and direct coal-fired systems may also be developed for process heat.

The processes, ranked according to ease of retrofit to existing gas-fired equipment, are as follows:

1. high-Btu gas,

2. intermediate-Btu gas,

3. liquid fuels,

4. solvent-refined coal,

5. low-Btu gas,

6. fluidized-bed boiler,

7. conventional boiler with low-sulfur coal,

8. conventional boiler with stack-gas cleanup,

9. HTGR.

CHAPTER FIVE

GUIDELINES FOR INDUSTRY

ENERGY MANAGEMENT GUIDE
FOR LIGHT INDUSTRY AND COMMERCE*

Introduction

The energy crisis has had considerable impact on industry and commerce in the United States, as well as in every industrialized country in the world. We are faced with the fact that the supply of easily recovered gas and oil is finite, and prices are rising to reflect this realization. We will eventually alleviate the supply problem with other developing energy sources such as solar power, or even nuclear fusion, but the relative price of energy is not likely to return to the levels of the 1960's.

Light industry and commerce [1] may be particularly caught up in this situation. For various causes in addition to energy prices, there have been increased operating and production costs, reduction in sales, reduction in profit levels, and in some cases, serious unemployment. Under such circumstances, even a moderate saving in energy costs can make the difference between a healthy business and one that is forced to close. This applies particularly to small business. The

National Federation of Independent Business reports (Sept. 1975) that in smaller businesses energy is an important item of expense. Its conservation will normally result in a direct increase in pretax profits.

While many companies have been affected adversely by the energy situation, there are many resourceful and adaptive organizations that have met these problems head on. They have learned how to make better use of the raw materials and supplies available to them, but equally important they have learned to reduce their energy usage by as much as 30 percent. This result, both in businesses that are energy-intensive and those that are not, has been accomplished through commitment to well organized and executed Energy Management Programs.

The purpose of this publication is to assist in the steps needed to carry out an effective program. The techniques are the same as those that would be applied to any aspect of a well run business. They have been derived from several successful energy management programs in both large and small industries. The program consists of four major steps:

- Organize the program
- Conduct an energy audit
- Take action to save energy
- Promote the program to your employees

---

* W.J. Kelnhofer and L.A. Wood, U.S. Department of Commerce, December 1976

[1] Light industry and commerce is defined as those businesses that are not large users of energy, and whose primary use is for heating, lighting, and refrigeration. They do not usually employ an engineering staff. Examples would include motels, food stores, laundries, garages, job shops, small assembly plants, etc.

Each step will be discussed in the material that follows. Also included is a checklist of representative energy saving opportunities, some case studies of specific Cost Saving Opportunities (CSO's), in appendix I, and a brief section on cost analysis procedures for those energy saving proposals where some capital investment is required.

Energy Management Program

Four main points, each of them discussed below, make up the energy management program. The presentation of these points should be considered as a guide; you must tailor the program to fit your own specific needs.

Organization of the Program

The success of any program will be directly related to the degree of commitment by the top management. This is true whether your firm has one employee or one hundred. In addition to commitment, top management must also provide adequate resources to meet the commitment. This means the appointment of one person to assume the responsibility as energy coordinator. This person is in charge of the energy audit, of listing and summarizing conservation opportunities, and of implementing those opportunities that are promising and are approved. The energy coordinator will be most successful if he is someone very familiar with all the operations of the firm and of its energy needs. He may be the assistant manager, the building superintendent, the manufacturing manager, or in a very small concern, the owner.

If the organization is reasonably large, it may be necessary to assist the coordinator with an energy management committee, with the coordinator sitting as chairman. The members should be able to represent authoritatively the different business functions such as manufacturing, delivery, building services, office personnel, etc. Their duties are to perform the coordination function within their separate departments.

Whatever organizational format you choose, the leadership must be strong and knowledgeable. They must be fully aware of the outlines of the energy management program, and of its importance to the business.

During the organizational phase, one should consider the use of outside engineering help to advise the coordinator and his committee. It is true that many energy saving opportunities do not require

engineering expertise; e.g., turn off unnecessary lights, weatherstrip leaky windows, and shut down equipment that is not in use. Engineering assistance is recommended, however, if a proposal is complex or if it involves a large capital investment. Outside help is also often valuable in spotting energy wastes that are not apparent to insiders because of long familiarity with things as they are. Consulting firms are available throughout the country, utility representatives are frequently available for help, and other sources of assistance are listed in a later section of this publication.

Conducting an Energy Audit

When an energy audit is completed it shows how much energy came into your business during a month, and how it was used within the plant. It may be considered as similar to the monthly closing statement of a double-entry accounting system. One series of entries consists of the amounts of energy which was purchased during the month in the form of electricity, gas, fuel oil, etc. The second series lists how this energy was used; how much in lighting, in air conditioning, in delivery trucks, in drying ovens, etc. Since the two series of entries (sides of the ledger) must balance, it may be necessary to list some estimates or some unknown losses.

The Gross Energy Audit

The first step is to determine your gross energy, the amount of energy entering your business. It is usually measured from your monthly utility and other fuel bills. It is useful to scan all of the bills for the past twelve months and summarize the monthly use and cost of energy by month for the year. The amount and the cost of each type of energy (electricity, gas, oil, etc.) should be entered separately.

Such a gross audit alone can answer several questions.

- What is your total energy cost?
- Is the cost increasing?
- Is energy an important fraction of total operating cost?
- Is energy cost apt to become more important?

In addition, an audit can become a means to judge the progress of an energy management program; a means of finding out whether energy saving measures are actually reducing the amount of energy used per unit of manufacture, per dollar of sales or any other convenient measure.

A suggested form for the monthly energy audit is shown in figure 1. It is suggested that you convert all the sources of energy used to a common unit, the British thermal unit, or Btu. (Technically the amount of energy required to raise the temperature of a pound of water by one degree Fahrenheit). This will enable you to add up the total energy used, to calculate the energy used per pound of product, or per dollar of sales, and to track month by month the results of an energy management program. Table I, below left, lists the energy content of the common energy sources.

FIGURE 1

MONTHLY GROSS ENERGY AUDIT   Date _____

Energy Source	Usage	Price	Monthly Cost	Btu's(1)	Demand (2) kW—$
Electricity	kWh	(3)			
Natural Gas	kcf(4)				
Fuel oil	gal				
Gasoline	gal				
Propane	gal				
Coal	ton				
etc.					
TOTALS			$_____	_____Btu's	

NOTES: (1) See the text for a discussion of British thermal units (Btu's).
(2) This item is discussed later in this guide.
(3) Electricity—the price needed is the dollar amount of the monthly bill divided by the kilowatt hours (kWh) used. This is important since utility bills may list a price per kWh, plus a fuel adjustment, and sometimes plus a tax, a demand charge, and a power factor penalty. If either of the latter two items are on your bill, discuss them with a consultant or an engineer from the power company.
(4) Gas is usually in thousands of cubic feet (kcf) Gas companies often use the abbreviation "Mcf" to mean the same thing, but the abbreviation "k", for kilo, is the modern preference.

TABLE I

Source	Unit	Btu's per unit
Electricity	kWh	3412
Natural gas	kcf	1,000,000
Fuel oil (#2)	gallon	140,000
Gasoline	gallon	130,000
Propane	gallon	91,000
Coal	ton	24,000,000
Steam (purchased)	1000 lb	1,000,000

The gross energy audit tells you how much energy you are using, and how this usage varies with production rate and with the time of year.

The Detailed Energy Audit

This audit is to find just what your energy is used for. The audit data leads to the evaluation of energy uses; whether each use is essential, and whether it might be reduced in amount. To conduct such an audit, consider one energy source at a time and try to find out how the month's supply was used.

In the case of electricity, the problem may be attacked rather simply. To estimate the amount used for lighting, count the number of bulbs or fluorescent tubes, read off their rating in watts (add 20 percent for the ballast used with each fluorescent) and multiply by the number of hours used per month. The answer will be in watt hours per month, so divide by 1000 to get kWh. For example 200 × 75 watt fluorescents, operating 310 hours per month, will use $\frac{200 \times 75 \times 1.20 \times 310}{1000} = 5580$ kWh per month.

Electric motors offer some difficulty for complete accuracy, but an estimate can be made from the data on the name plate and estimated use factor. If a motor is labeled at 115 volts, and a full load current of 5.5 amperes (5.5 A FL), it will use 115 V × 5.5 A = 632 watts each hour of operation at full load. Motors seldom really operate at full load, 70 percent of full load is a good average. With an actual load of 70 percent and operation for 200 hours per month, the electricity used per month is

$$\frac{632 \text{ watts} \times 0.70 \times 200 \text{ hours}}{1000} = 88 \text{ kWh.}$$

For a motor labeled "3 phase," the calculation of watts is voltage times ampere times 1.732. For example, a 220 volt, three-phase motor, rated at a full load current of 2.2 amperes, will use 220 × 2.2 × 1.732, or 838 watts at full load.

Electric heating elements are rated in watts and no correction factor is involved. The kWh usage is simply the wattage times the hours of operation per month, divided by 1000.

In some cases it may be very difficult to estimate the hours of actual operation, particularly in equipment that is controlled with a thermostat such as the compressor motor on an air-conditioner, or the heat-

FIGURE 2

MONTHLY DETAILED ENERGY AUDIT—ELECTRICAL

Date_____

Usage (except motors)	Rated Watts(1)		H	kWh	Btu
Office lighting					
Outside lighting					
Space heating					
Soldering irons					
Tank heaters					
etc.					

Motors	Rated Watts(1)	Watts(2)	H	kWh	Btu
Ventilating fans					
Exhaust fans					
Air-conditioners					
Hand tools					
Big motor #1					
Big motor #2					
etc.					

TOTALS _____ _____

DEMAND_____kW POWER FACTORS_____

NOTES: (1) Name-plate data, Watts equals volts time amperes. For fluorescent tubes, add 20 percent for the ballast; i.e., multiply the rating by 1.20. For three-phase motors, watts equals volts times amperes times 1.732.

(2) Rated watts times the fraction of full load, usually about 70 percent If the operating current has been measured, use voltage times the measured current (times 1.732 if it is a three-phase motor.)

ing elements on an electric oven. In such cases, you may need to have an electrician connect a simple electric clock across the motor terminals and read the clock every twelve hours for a day or so. The elapsed time shown on the clock at each reading will be the hours of operation for the past twelve hours of real time. It must be recognized that this type of measurement for a few days is not always representative of a yearly average energy use. Air-conditioners, for example, can be expected to vary their energy demand widely with the time of year, while a drying oven's demand pattern may depend wholly on the rate of production.

When the electric audit is finished, tabulate the results in some such fashion as figure 2, using the horizontal lines to categorize the usage in a form which you can use for later analysis. For example, one line might be office lighting, another warehouse lighting, a third air-conditioning, and a fourth ventilating fans, etc. Large uses, such as an electric furnace or a big motor, you might list separately.

The total of this tabulation, estimated for a month's usage, should be equal (within 10 percent or so) to the kWh used according to an average month's electric bill. If it isn't, you may have missed some pieces of equipment, or you may have not estimated the time of operation correctly, or if motors are a big portion of the load they may be loaded to more or less than the 70 percent which was assumed. If you have trouble reaching a reasonable balance, an electrician using a "clamp-on" ammeter can probably find the discrepancy, or a man from your local utility may be of help. If the problem is a very low power factor (less than 0.70) on a large group of motors, you may need the power company's help to locate the trouble. They will also be glad to advise as to methods of improving the power factor and thus lowering your monthly bill.

The following two paragraphs are brief explanations of electrical "Demand" and "Power Factor" charges. An understanding of these terms is helpful in reducing the electric bill.

Demand charges reflect the maximum rate at which you used electric power over some short period, usually about 15 minutes, during the month. If you are a small user, on a "domestic" contract with the utility, you probably do not pay a separate demand charge, it is averaged into the rate you pay per kilowatt hour. A larger user on a "commercial" contract will probably pay a lower rate per kilowatt hour, but will be billed a demand charge based on the maximum rate of use, and some times on the time of day at which this maximum occurred. You can minimize this charge by scheduling the major users of electricity such as very large motors or electric furnaces so that they do not all require power at the same time. In some cases, you can reduce the demand charge by operating the large power users on the night shift and not during the day. The best technique depends on your individual contract with the utility and your flexibility in scheduling operations.

Power Factor is a measure of the "phantom" currents that are needed to set up the magnetic field required for the operation of a motor. These currents are real enough; they are sometimes labeled "phantom" because they do not show up in the kilowatt hours recorded on the standard watt hour meter. They do, however, reflect lost energy in heating transmission lines and transformers. For this reason, if a high percentage of your load is electric motors, the utility may be adding an additional charge to your bill for a "low power factor." This charge can usually be eliminated by mounting the proper kind of capacitor on your larger motors. The utility will be glad to advise you as to the proper type and size.

The *oil and gas* detailed audits follow exactly the same pattern as the electrical one just described.

If the fuel being audited is used on only one piece of equipment such as a space heating furnace, the audit is quite simple. This simplicity also exists if the usage is only on a number of identical units such as small furnaces or dryers. If the usage is on a number of units of different design, however, it may be necessary to install meters on some individual pieces of equipment in order to get a suitable audit. These may be rather simple flow-meters, reading the fuel usage in terms of gallons per minute or cubic feet of gas per hour, or they may be more sophisticated (but more convenient) meters which record the total fuel used and can be read at daily or weekly intervals. Engineering consultation is suggested, so that the choice and installation of such meters is suitable for your particular case. Many firms have found that the installation of individual meters saves energy simply because the equipment operators are reminded at frequent intervals just how much expensive fuel is being used, and start thinking of energy saving ideas.

Gasoline usage should be audited by records on individual vehicles, and on individual drivers. Several companies have found that the most important factor in better mileage on trucks used for delivery is the training of the driver, and his motivation to save energy. If gasoline usage is an important item in your energy cost, good records can help you decide on the importance of better driver training, improved maintenance, using smaller vehicles, etc.

Analyzing the Energy Audit

The first question to ask when a monthly audit is complete is whether or not it balances; the quantity of energy used must be equal to the quantity that came into the plant. If 500 kcf of gas was purchased, and only 300 kcf can be accounted for, even by making some generous estimates, then the auditing technique should be refined.

The second question is to find the processes, or departments, or the pieces of equipment that are the big users of energy. This information tells one where to start first in looking for savings opportunities.

Lastly, as the audit is updated month by month, one must watch for the variations caused by the weather, by variations in product output, and of course for the reductions due to good energy management.

Taking Action on Energy Saving

This is the time when some Energy Management programs lose momentum and become ineffective. Things may look too complicated, and there seems no good place to start. But unless you start, there will be no savings in energy or in dollars.

Simple housekeeping items are always first in importance, because they are easy to see, and generally cost little money to fix.

(1) Read the check list of energy saving ideas following this section. Make sure that your energy coordinator reads it, as well as any involved department managers or section foremen.

(2) Take a walk through the facility with your people, looking for energy wastes. Ask some of the simple questions;

Why are the lights on in this room with no one in it?

Can the thermostat setting be lowered (in the winter), or raised (in the summer)?

Are there motors running idle, or empty furnaces running hot?

When was the last time the heating plant was adjusted for the best fuel/air ratio and the filters changed or cleaned?

(3) Make a list of the "no cost" energy saving ideas and assign someone to follow up on each one. You, or the energy coordinator, should follow up on him. Just this much of a program has frequently produced savings of 10 to 15 percent of the energy usage.

The *major cost saving items* are sometimes those which will require some capital investment. In such cases, the services of an independent consultant is suggested unless you have some in-house expertise. Suppose, for example, that you are operating a medium sized steam boiler which according to your detailed audit is using 30 percent of your total energy. It does not require a consultant to suggest that you should insulate any bare steam pipe, replace or repair steam traps that are leaking live steam, or operate the boiler at the minimum pressure that is actually required. It does, however, require some expertise to analyze the flue gases, estimate a heat balance on the boiler, and determine what savings might be made by adjusting the air/fuel ratio. It is not unusual to find in older boilers that 20 or 30 percent of the heat in the fuel is being wasted as hot stack gas, and that a modest investment in better combustion control equipment is capable of paying for itself in a very short time.

Promoting the Program

An energy management program that starts with a flourish and then is allowed to die because of lack of interest does not accomplish very much. Two types of follow up are needed.

(1) Measure the results:

Repeat the gross energy audit each month, and calculate the change in Btu's used per unit of product. When savings are made, determine what action caused the savings, and what programs were apparently not successful. Analyze what can be done to promote more savings, and to rescue projects which are failing.

(2) Involve your employees:

Publicize the program; explain its importance to the business and to them. Assign as many as possible to an active part in the program, even if only a small part. Reward good energy saving ideas, either with publicity or by more substantial means. Keep them up-to-date with the progress of the program. Consider telling your customers and your community about it— it could be good advertising.

Checklists for Reducing Energy Usage

Good energy management implies a reduction of energy usage by elimination of all unnecessary uses of energy and improving the remaining utilization of energy. Checklists of possibilities for accomplishing the goal are given in this section. Every item in the categorized lists will not apply to all light industry and commerce, but hopefully the suggestions will stimulate you to develop special checklists applicable to your own business.

It should not be forgotten that your employees can help significantly to accomplish your energy utilization goal. One way to encourage and guide them in this direction is to post and/or distribute the checklists that you specifically have designed.

Buildings and Grounds

- Reduce ventilation rates when possible
- Close off all unused openings and stacks
- Reduce exhaust air when possible

- Repair broken windows, skylights, doors
- Consider modern replacements for old windows
- Weatherstrip windows and doors; caulk or eliminate all cracks in building
- Insulate walls, roofs, crawl spaces, floors and foundations
- Eliminate unnecessary windows
- Use evaporative cooling on roofs to reduce air-conditioning load
- Raise building thermostat settings during cooling season [2] and lower them during heating season to maximum extent possible
- Eliminate heating/cooling from all unused buildings or rooms
- Install window shades to reduce heat gain from summer sun
- Utilize trees and shrubs as sun shades and windbreaks
- Make sure that trees and shrubs do not block air intake and exhaust openings in buildings, or proper functioning of window air-conditioners
- Use color schemes inside and out for reflection of light and solar radiation

Electricity

- Do not use electric motor larger than necessary for the job
- Reduce lighting level wherever possible. Use more efficient fixtures and bulbs
- Use timers or photo cells in lighting circuit when feasible
- Use natural light when and where possible
- Use reduced lighting during clean up operations
- Install light fixtures at as low a height as is practical
- Clean surfaces of light bulbs, tubes and reflectors periodically
- Eliminate or reduce lighting of outdoor displays and signs
- Turn off lights, typewriters, coffee pots, radios, TV sets, etc., when not in use
- Make sure that all electrical wiring is of proper size and in good condition
- Modify schedule of electrical power use to minimize electrical demand charge
- Do not let motors run idle
- Review energy efficiency ratings for all new electrical equipment
- Reduce lighting in parking lots when empty

Equipment and processes

- Schedule heating and air-conditioning system to operate only when required

---

[2] Sometimes impractical on large central systems.

- Check that all mechanical equipment is in good repair and operating properly—replace worn bearings and worn belts, have proper belt tension, lubricate as required
- Eliminate leaks in supply and return air system
- Eliminate leaks in steam and water supply or return lines, valves, steam traps, pump seals, etc.
- Install automatic controls to shut down equipment when not needed
- Properly maintain and calibrate automatic controls on all equipment
- Clean or replace dirty filters (air, water, oil, etc.,) as necessary
- Insulate bare steam, hot water and chilled water lines
- Recover energy available from exhaust air, stack gas, waste water and condensate
- Check boiler operation for proper air/fuel ratio as often as possible
- Clean and maintain boiler heat transfer surfaces often
- Inspect and repair faulty boiler insulation as required
- Do not exceed temperature required for any process, hot water, or steam supply
- Turn off power tools and support equipment when not being used
- Consider connecting exhaust fans in kitchens, wash rooms, hoods, etc., with light or equipment switch
- Clean and maintain all heating and cooling coil surfaces as often as necessary to maintain high efficiency of heat transfer
- Reduce water flow rates to a minimum in all flushing and cleaning processes
- Maintain all equipment according to manufacturer's directions
- Cover liquid treatment tanks, condensate tanks, swimming pools, etc. when not in use to minimize heat loss

Vehicles
- Maintain all vehicles in peak operating condition
- Turn off lift trucks, diesel construction equipment, delivery trucks, etc., when not in use, i.e., while loading, unloading, or waiting
- Size vehicles to the job
- Provide incentive to have customers take merchandise with them
- Organize optimum salesmen's routes and frequency of calls
- Coordinate sales calls with deliveries when possible

- Minimize same day deliveries and special deliveries
- Reduce frequency of deliveries to outlying areas
- Consolidate deliveries with other companies when possible
- Keep records on delivery vehicles, for example:

  Total route sales per period
  Total route miles per period
  Total fuel costs per period
  Route sales per vehicle mile
  Miles per gallon of fuel
  Maintenance costs per mile
  Total vehicle costs per dollar sales
  Compare data for various vehicles and drivers

Although not contributing directly to company energy savings, employees should be encouraged to form and use carpools. You might even wish to consider providing a company bus service or arranging for bus pooling with other near-by companies. These actions will help develop an energy-saving mode of thinking on the part of your employees and save them money. It will also help you to gain acceptance of other actions to save energy.

Cost Analysis Procedures

The checklist in the previous section contains some suggestions for energy saving which will require the investment of capital dollars in order to achieve savings. In some cases the savings per year may be so large, and the capital cost so small, that the desirability of the project is obvious. In other cases, a more detailed analysis is needed.

This section discusses two of a number of procedures for making a financial analysis of your cost saving opportunities. An important factor in your analysis is the amount you are paying for your energy.

The reason for determining energy costs is to allow you to make valid analysis of the actions you might need to take to save energy and money. The cost varies widely with the fuel source used. Table II shows the cost of energy at various fuel and electricity prices.

The energy costs listed assume that all of the energy content of the fuel is used, i.e., that there are no losses or inefficiencies. In actuality, there are losses, and efficiency is usually less than 100 percent. For example, in space heating with oil or gas, some of the heat is lost out the furnace stack. This results in a range of efficiency of 50 to 85 percent, with 60 percent being an average figure. Thus, if oil at $0.42 per gal-

TABLE II

	Fuel or electricity prices				Resulting energy cost, $/MBtu [a]
Electricity, $/kWh	Oil, $/gal	Gas, $/kcf	Propane, $/gal	Coal $/Ton	
0.0034	0.14	1.00	0.092	24.00	1
.0068	.28	2.00	.183	48.00	2
.0102	.42	3.00	.275	72.00	3
.0136	.56	4.00	.366	96.00	4
.0171	.70	5.00	.458	120.00	5
.0205	.84	6.00	.550	144.00	6
.0239	.98	7.00	.641		7
.0273	1.12	8.00	.733		8
.0307		9.00			9
.0341		10.00			10
.0512					15
.0682					20
.0853					25
.102					30

[a] MBtu equals one million Btu's.

lon is used for space heating at an efficiency of 70 percent, the actual cost per MBtu delivered as useful heat is $3.00 divided by 0.70, or $4.29 per MBtu. Note that electricity is by far our most expensive form of energy. But of course, it is also our most convenient and efficient form and has no replacement for some applications.

Benefit/Cost Analysis

The benefit/cost analysis can be used to decide if a capital investment is economically justified, or it can be used as a basis to choose between several alternatives after a decision to invest has been made. First, all benefits and all costs are reduced to a dollar value, and the ratio of benefits to costs is taken. If the ratio is greater than unity, the project may be economically justified and should be more fully examined.

Example—a heat recovery unit for a small heat treating plant costs $55,000 installed. It is estimated that the unit will save $12,000 annually in fuel and have a life of 10 years. Annual maintenance costs will be $500. The benefit/cost ratio is determined as follows:

Benefit = $12,000 − $500 = $11,500 per year.

Costs: Assume money is available at 10 percent interest. The annual cost will be the amortization cost, or annual payment required to repay the debt at 10 percent interest in 10 years. This is found by multiplying the total loan by a capital recovery factor, F, as found in table III. Thus, for an interest rate of 10 percent for 10 years, F = 0.1628, and cost = $55,000 × 0.1628 = $8,954 and,

Benefit/cost ratio = $11,500/$8,954 = 1.28

The investment is profitable since the benefit/cost is larger than unity.

Example—It has been decided by a small manufacturing company to make a capital investment in a wastewater, heat recovery unit. Two systems are available:

System—A:

Total Cost $14,000

Annual operation and maintenance costs $ 900

System—B:

Total Cost $12,000

Annual operation and maintenance costs $ 1,400

TABLE III

	Capital recovery factor—F				
Yr	Interest rate				
n	6.0%	7.0%	8.0%	10.0%	12.0%
5	0.2374	0.24389	0.25046	0.26380	0.27741
10	.1359	.14238	.14903	.16275	.17698
15	.1030	.10979	.11683	.13147	.14682
20	.0872	.09439	.10185	.11746	.13388
25	.0782	.08581	.09368	.11017	.12750
30	.0726	.08059	.08883	.10608	.12414
40	.0665	.07501	.08386	.10226	.12130

Both systems reduce energy utilization by the same amount, and both systems have estimated lives of 15 years. Money is available at 10 percent. Which system should provide the greater long term savings? Net Benefit per year of System A over System B = $500. Additional cost of System A over System B = $2,000. For 10 percent interest rates over 15 years, the capital recovery factor, is F = 0.1315 (from table III). Thus, the cost per year for the additional $2,000 of capital investment is:

Cost = $2,000 × 0.1315 = $263.

and

Benefit/cost = $500/$263 = 1.90

Although the original cost of System—A is 16.7 percent more than System—B, System—A will provide the greater long-term savings over the life of the system.

Time to Recoup Investment

Another approach is to determine how long it will take to recoup the investment required to accomplish a particular energy (dollar) savings. It is assumed that the annual savings is used to pay off the required loan at the current interest rate. If the investment is recouped in a period less than the life of the equipment, the investment is considered profitable. Table IV can be used to estimate the "time to recoup investment."

Example—It has been estimated that an investment of $22,000 is required to update the air-conditioning and heating system equipment and controls installed in an older five-story office building. The life of the system will be extended for ten years. The annual savings in energy purchased plus reduced maintenance cost should be approximately $5,500. Money is available at 10 percent interest. To find the time to recoup the investment the following ratio is calculated:

TABLE IV

Years to recoup investment				
Investment/ savings ratio	Interest rate			
	6%	8%	10%	12%
2	2.19	2.27	2.34	2.42
3	3.41	3.57	3.74	3.94
4	4.71	5.01	5.36	5.77
5	6.12	6.64	7.27	8.08
6	7.66	8.50	9.61	11.2
7	9.35	10.7	12.6	16.2
8	11.2	13.3	16.9	28.4

Capital investment/annual savings
$$= \$22,500/\$5,500$$
$$= 4.09$$

Referring to table IV, at an investment/savings ratio of 4, and an interest rate of 10 percent:

Time to recoup investment = 5.36 years

This is less than the extended life of the systems, and so the investment would be profitable.

These examples of cost analysis do not, of course, take into consideration some important considerations such as the value of the money spent if it were to be spent in some other way, or the impact of the state, local and Federal taxes.

It is recommended that, if an investment of any significant size is being considered, you conduct more detailed analysis of the life-cycle costs. An excellent publication which addresses this subject in considerable detail is reference 18.

"Energy Conservation in Buildings:
Techniques For Economical Design,"
($20.00), 1974
Construction Specifications Institute, Inc.
1150 17th Street, N.W.
Washington, D.C. 20036

Assistance

Probably one of the biggest mistakes the management can make is not to seek outside help and as-sistance for finding solutions to problems related to energy usage. Recognizing that energy availability and rising energy prices are national problems you can be assured that your problems are not unique. Many industrial and commercial firms are finding solutions to these problems. Most solutions to energy usage problems are not mysterious nor proprietary. No one person knows and understands them all. Some "solutions," if incorrectly applied, tend to increase energy usage rather than reduce it. Therefore, outside advice may at times be desirable and necessary.

This section lists sources of help and assistance. Indications are generally made as to the level and type of help they can provide, and suggestions are given for obtaining best results.

Private Consultants

The help of local, private engineering consultants can be valuable in many ways. First, a good energy consultant understands the problems from a technical viewpoint, but he is also sensitive to the economics involved. Probably he has already been concerned with energy management problems and his experience will be available to you. He can help you organize an energy audit procedure, suggest proper metering techniques, and help derive maximum benefit from the results. He is an "outsider" and therefore he will quickly observe practices that result in inefficient use of energy.[3] He can recommend new and efficient equipment, or suggest how to improve the operation of existing equipment. He can help to make proper cost analyses. Also, he will be familiar with local codes, and EPA and OSHA regulations. His fees may seem high, but the results of one or two days of his work may reduce your energy costs many times over.

Most private consultants who are registered professional engineers are listed in the local telephone directory. They specialize in certain areas such as mechanical work, electrical work, structural work, etc. In large cities, offices of state and national chapters of professional engineers are maintained. These offices may be listed in the classified section of the telephone directory under "Engineers". If contacted, such offices can be helpful in supplying names of qualified local consultants. Also, many local mechanical, electrical, and building contracting firms retain registered professional engineers who are available for consulting services.

---

[3] It has been proven time and time again that in-house people tend to overlook inefficient practices, but technically trained outsiders observe these practices immediately.

Utility Companies and Oil Suppliers

Most utility companies are now offering technical advice on ways to best utilize their products. Electrical power companies can advise you on proper sizing, installation, operation and maintenance of electrical equipment from appliances to air-conditioning, heating units, and motors. They can make suggestions on proper metering techniques and auditing electrical energy. They can also advise you on how to best use electricity, like reducing peak load demand, to minimize electrical bills.

Future supplies and allocations of natural gas are uncertain. The gas companies can advise you on the availability for your company and the alternatives should the supply run short. Gas companies can sometimes loan extra meters for the submetering of gas. They may also offer maintenance services for gas burning equipment.

Oil supply companies can keep you informed about future supplies. If your company has been a good customer of a supplier, chances are that you can make arrangement with him for minimum supplies during peak demand periods, unless allocation practices return. Oil supply companies may also offer maintenance services for oil burners, and they can often perform simple efficiency tests on furnaces.

Trade Associations

Trade associations whose members are concerned with manufacturing products or providing services can be of assistance in energy related problems. Many associations have already formed energy committees or councils to study the particular problems that their members are having. They have collected data on energy needs, estimated effects of the crisis, developed energy management procedures and published back-up literature for their members. Some associations have held local or regional meetings with members to discuss and exchange energy management ideas, and to discuss short and long range plans for better energy use, utilization of waste products and alternate fuels.

One of the most useful services your association can provide is to conduct a detailed survey of energy usage to make up an energy profile of your industry. Results of the survey can be used to show where you stand on energy usage relative to size, structure, location, production, etc. It forms the basis for planning a course of action for better energy management in the future. If your industry does not have an energy profile, urge your trade association to help provide one.

If your company is not a member of a trade association, and if you would like general information regarding associations related to your business, write to:

American Society of Association Executives
1101 16th Street, N.W.
Washington, D.C. 20036

Government Organizations

Government, both at the State and Federal levels, can provide information and guidance on energy related problems. Most local governments can provide names and offices to contact in their respective organizations.

On the Federal level, the Department of Commerce, the Federal Energy Administration, the Small Business Administration and the Energy Research and Development Administration can offer a great deal of assistance to light industry and commerce. There are nummerous publications available, many of which are free.

For information about Department of Commerce programs and assistance, write:

Office of Energy Programs
Department of Commerce
Washington, D.C. 20230

For information about Federal Energy Administration programs and assistance, write:

Industrial Programs, Conservation & Environment
Federal Energy Administration
Washington, D.C. 20461

Both the Department of Commerce and the Federal Energy Administration maintain a network of field offices which are sources of assistance and information. A list of the location of these offices is shown in appendix II.

The Small Business Administration maintains a large number of offices throughout the country. To obtain assistance from SBA, consult your telephone directory for the local office nearest you.

Interaction With OSHA and EPA Requirements

Almost all industry and commerce today must be aware of the safety and environmental requirements and standards issued by the Department of Labor, Occupational Safety and Health Administration (OSHA) and the Environmental Protection Agency (EPA). Attempts to meet these requirements in your business may in some cases conflict with energy management concepts. In other cases they are compatible.

Energy management actions that involve reductions in ventilation may or may not be counter to health and safety regulations. Minimum requirements for ventilation air flow rates to remove odors, contaminants, smoke, dust and abrasive particles, flammable or combustible materials, etc. must be strictly observed. However, it has been found that actual ventilation rates often far execeed minimum requirements. Sometimes, ventilation is provided continuously whether the process requiring ventilation is operating or not. Excess energy usage in these cases can be eliminated without danger to safety or health.

When large quantities of warm contaminated air must be exhausted from a building during the heating season, it can, by the use of a heat exchanger, pre-heat fresh outside air taken into the building. During the cooling season, warm outside air brought into the building can be partially cooled down with colder exhaust air.

Heating and lighting in industry have not been regulated by OSHA, but OSHA has implied that employee efficiency and comfort must be satisfied. It is well known that many buildings are kept too warm for the majority of people, and thus energy is wasted. Lighting is often inefficient, and can be replaced by improved lamps and fixtures which use less energy and still provide satisfactory illumination.

Meeting air emission standards and anti-pollution requirements established by EPA can involve large capital investments. In many cases, economic justification can be made by combining the requirement with an energy management concept that reduces energy usage. Combustible fumes that cannot be released to the environment can be burned and the released heat recovered and used for producing low pressure steam or hot water, which can be used for heating, cleaning, etc. Many industries have found that wet or dry scrubbers necessary to meet exhaust gas emission standards allow them to burn natural gas, coal, oil, and waste products such as paper and sawdust.

The energy coordinator should be familiar with and have copies of the OSHA and EPA regulations for his business. In questionable or involved situations professional assistance from a consultant may be necessary (Note references 7 and 8 in appendix II).

Appendix I

Cost Saving Opportunities (CSO's)

The main body of this guide contains checklists of suggested items to look for to reduce energy usage in your business. No specific values of reductions were given, since there are many factors varying from business to business which will affect reduction figures. However, the list of success stories of effective energy management programs in industry and commerce is growing longer, and in these stories are case histories of how energy usage was reduced and to what extent.

This appendix contains a few of the case histories showing specific ways in which reduction in energy usage and cost savings have been accomplished. They are called cost saving opportunities (CSO's)[4]. Each CSO contains a brief description of the situation, how the saving was accomplished, how much was saved, and general suggested actions that other businesses may take.

Often, similar case histories are reported by several different sources. Where appropriate, the source of the case history for the CSO is identified.

While all CSO's will not have direct application to every business, the reader should try to parallel as closely as possible the main idea behind the CSO with specific operations of his company.

CSO #1 *Savings by Use of Water Flow Control Valves*

The usage of hot and cold water is frequently more than is required. If usage can be reduced, particularly in the case of hot water, savings can be made on fuel, water, and sewage bills. Water flow control valves for showers and wash basins are available, which limit the water flow but still provide satisfactory service. They may be purchased from most plumbing supply houses.

Example:

A motor hotel in Virginia with 100 rooms installed flow control valves just before the shower head in each bathroom. The valves reduced the water flow from five gallons per minute to 2.5 gallons per minute. The cost of the valves, and installation by the maintenance crew was $700. Assuming 1.5 daily showers lasting 5 minutes each and an average occupancy rate of 70 percent, the total saving in water usage was calculated as 480,000 gallons per year.

Water Saving

Since the water rate and the sewage rate totals $1.00 per 1000 gallons, the saving due to reduced water used is $480.00 per year.

---

[4] Reference 1 contains additional case histories called energy conservation opportunities (ECO's). Many of these ECO's are applicable to light industry and commerce.

Fuel Savings

In addition to saving water, the cost of fuel needed to heat about two-thirds of this water, or 320,000 gallons, was also saved. The amount of energy needed to heat this water from 65 to 140 °F may be estimated as follows:

By definition, it takes 1 Btu to raise the temperature of one pound of water by 1 °F. Thus, to heat a pound of water from 65 to 140 °F, the energy required is 140–65, or 75 Btu's. Since water weighs 8.34 pounds per gallon, the total weight of water involved is 320,000 gal × 8.34 lb/gal, or 2,668,800 lb. The total energy required is therefore 2,668,800 lb × 75 Btu/lb, or 200.16 million Btu (MBtu).

The water would have been heated with oil at $0.35 per gallon. Reference to table II page 8, shows that oil at this price is equivalent to about $2.50 per MBtu at 100 percent efficiency. Assuming an actual efficiency of 70 percent the cost becomes $2.50 divided by 0.70, or $3.57 per MBtu.

The annual saving is 200 MBtu × $3.57/MBtu or $715 per year.

Total Savings:

Saving in water use	$ 480
Saving in fuel use	715
Total saving	$1,195 per year.

Suggested Action

Consider the possibility of installing water flow control valves on all showers and wash basins. This can be done in any motel, hotel, school, factory, business office, apartment house, or home. Several makes of flow control valves are available. Contact your local plumbing fixture supply house.

Source

Operations Bulletin (Oct. 1973)
American Hotel and Motel Association
888 Seventh Avenue
New York, N.Y. 10019

CSO #2   *Savings by Repairing or Replacing Leaky Steam Traps*

The purpose of a steam trap is to hold steam in a heat exchanger (such as a radiator, water heater, plastic molding machine, etc.) until the steam gives up its heat, and then to let the condensate (hot water) drain out and return to the boiler. It does this by means of an automatic valve which opens when a certain amount of condensate has collected behind it, and closes again when live steam starts to escape. If such a trap fails in the "valve open" position, considerable energy and money can be wasted.

The amount of energy lost depends both on steam pressures and on the size of the orifice in the valve. The following table can be used to determine the loss in terms of MBtu per 1000 hours of leakage.

Loss due to steam leaks—MBtu per thousand hours

Steam pressure	Orifice Size		
	⅛"	¼"	⅜"
20 psi	12.3	47.9	79.9
50 psi	30.8	120	200
100	61.6	240	400

This means that if a trap with a ¼" orifice on a 100 psi steam line is stuck in the open position for 12 hours a day, six days per week, the yearly loss in energy will be 3600 hours × 240 MBtu/1000 hours, or 864 MBtu per year. The cost of this energy depends, of course, on the fuel used and the efficiency with which it's used. Referring again to table II, page 8, if the boiler is fired with natural gas at $1.75 per thousand cubic feet, and the boiler efficiency is 65 percent, the cost is $1.75 divided by 0.65, or $2.69 per MBtu.

The cost of repairing or replacing such a trap will fall in the range of $50 to $200. The annual saving possible is 864 MBtu × $2.69/MBtu, or $2320 per year.

Suggested Action

It is recommended that steam traps be checked on a monthly basis. The ideal method of checking is to visually observe the discharge, perhaps by means of a special test valve. If the trap is working properly there will be a stream of hot water or of mixed water and steam lasting for a few seconds, followed by a period of no discharge for several seconds, and the cycle will repeat. If the trap is stuck in the open position, there will be a constant discharge of steam. A failure in the closed position will be indicated by no discharge, and by the fact that the equipment is not being heated.

If it is not practical to observe the discharge, one can with practice hear the pulsating discharge of a properly working trap, using a mechanics stethoscope, or in an emergency a long screw driver with the bit pressed to the trap and one's ear to the handle. An open trap will produce a continuous hiss, perhaps high enough in pitch to be almost inaudible, and will be very hot. A trap frozen shut is, of course, silent and cold.

It is possible to check traps by checking the pipe temperatures on the inlet and outlet sides. With a leaking trap both sides will be hot, and at the same temperature. A properly working trap will measure somewhat cooler on the discharge side. Good measuring equipment and great care are necessary in using this technique.

If in doubt, a representative of the trap manufacture should be contacted to recommend the best method of checking his particular traps.

Note: For additional information see ECO 3.4.5 and ECO 3.4.6. (Energy Conservation Opportunities) in reference 1., *Energy Conservation Program Guide for Industry and Commerce.*

CSO #3   *Savings by Reduction of Building Ventilation Rates*

The conditioning of outside ventilation air (heating in winter and cooling in summer) for office buildings stores, factories, etc. can account for a large percentage of the energy usage in a building. The energy required depends on the indoor-outdoor temperatures, the ventilation rates, and length of time of ventilation.

In many cases full ventilation air is provided 24 hours per day even when the building is only lightly occupied. Often, the rates of ventilation are much too high. Many case histories from all over the country show that considerable reduction in fuel usage and dollar savings can be achieved by a reduction of ventilation air rates, while still maintaining conditions of comfort.

Example

An office building in Minneapolis, Minnesota has an occupancy of 667 people and was supplied with 30 cubic feet per minute per person (30 CFM/person) of outside ventilation air 40 hours/week during the heating season. A consultant determined that the ventilation air rates could be reduced to 8 CFM/person.

Ventilation Rate Reduction =
(30 − 8) CFM/person × 667 persons
= 14,700 CFM

This reduction in the flow of cold outside air results in an energy saving; the air doesn't have to be heated from a low temperature up to 68 °F. The energy required is a function of the length and severity of the heating season in your location. Numerically, this function is "degree days," a number which can be obtained for an average winter in your locality from your heating contractor, the local weather bureau, or your supplier of gas or oil. It varies from almost 10,000 along the north border of Minnesota to less than 500 in Miami. In Minneapolis, there are about 8000 degree days per year.

The reduction in energy is also a function of the length of time that the ventilating fans are operated during the heating season. It is obvious that if cold air is blown in only 8 hours per day, less heating energy will be needed than for 24 hours operation.

Heating energy for ventilation air

Degree Days	MBtu per season per 1000 CFM of ventilation			
	40 hr/wk	72 h/wk	112 h/wk	168 h/wk
				(continuous)
2000	13.1	23.6	36.7	55.0
4000	26.2	47.1	73.3	110
6000	39.3	70.7	110	165
8000	52.4	94.3	147	220

From the above table, note that in Minneapolis at 8000 degree days per year, each 1000 CFM of ventilation provided 40 hours per week requires 52.4 MBtu of heating energy for the season. In the present example, the ventilation rate was reduced by 14,700 CFM. The yearly energy savings, therefore, was 52.4 MBtu/1000 CFM × 14,700 CFM, or 770 MBtu per year.

The cost savings can be estimated from table II, page 8. If the heating was done with oil at $0.35 per gallon, and a furnace efficiency of 70 percent, the saving was $2.50 divided by 0.70, or $3.57 per MBtu. The annual savings was $3.57/MBtu times 770 MBtu, or $2750 per year.

Suggested Action

If knowledgeable people are available in your company, have them determine present ventilation air rates, either from the ventilating fan ratings, or by measuring with an anemometer. These should be checked against minimum required rates as established by the codes for your business.

CSO #4   *Savings by Reducing Lighting in Buildings During the Cooling Season*

During the cooling season, a large portion of the cooling load comes from internal heat gains, i.e., heat given off by occupants, running motors, ovens, lights, computers, or any other equipment. If it is possible to eliminate these "heat sources" energy usage will be reduced in two ways. First, the energy usage required to operate the source is eliminated, and second the energy usage required to operate the cooling system is reduced. For office buildings, chain and department stores, and institutions, lighting reduction is very effective.

Consider a building lighted with a total of 2000 fluorescent lamps rated at 40 watts each. Assume, as often has been found to be the case, that about one third of these lamps can be turned off during the summer for eight hours per day, and that satisfactory lighting levels will be maintained. (NOTE: Because of the design of fluorescent fixtures it is usually not possible to simply remove every third lamp. The local light fixture supplier can advise as to how it should be done.)

The present power demand for lighting is 2000 lamps × 40 watts per lamp, or 80,000 watts, plus an additional 20 percent for the ballast transformers, making 96,000 watts or 96 kilowatts. Turning off one third of the lamps and their associated ballasts will therefore save 32 kW.

With a cooling season of 100 days, the energy saved per season will be 32 kW × 8 h/day × 100 days, or 25,600 kWh.

The saving in heat load on the air-conditioner is 25,600 kWh × 3412 Btu/kWh, or 87 MBtu per season.

To estimate the energy that the air-conditioner would have used to pump this heat out of the building, one must know something about the efficiency of the cooling system. This is expressed as Energy Efficiency Ratio (EER), and is numerically the number of Btu's transferred per watt hour of electricity supplied. On many newer window-type units, the back label will show an EER rating ranging from less than five for a small poorly designed unit to more than ten for a larger more efficient cooler.

If your air-conditioners are not labeled with an EER rating, they may well list a cooling capacity (in Btu per hour), and an electrical demand (in watts); in such case the EER can be readily calculated. For example, a unit rated at a cooling capacity of 8000 Btu/hour and an electrical demand of 1000 watts, has an EER of 8000 divided by 1000, or 8.0 Btu/watt hour. In some cases on large central units, the designer may have calculated a Coefficient of Performance (COP) for the cooling unit. EER = COP × 3.4. If no data are available, assume an average EER of 7.5 (COP = 2.20).

In the present example, there is a total of 87 MBtu that does not have to be pumped out of the building because of reduced lighting. Assuming an EER of 7.5, the electrical energy saving is 87 MBtu divided by 7.5 Btu/watt hour, or 11,600,000 watt hours (11,600 kWh).

The total electrical energy saved is 25,600 kWh for lighting plus 11,600 kWh for air-conditioning, or 37,200 kWh per year.

The annual cost saving, at 4.5¢ per kWh, is 37,200 kWh × $0.045/kWh, or $1,670.

Suggested Action

Reduce lighting and other heat sources as much as is practical, particularly during the air-conditioning season. Savings due to reduced lighting during the heating season will not be as great, but some savings will still be obtained.

Source

"Guidelines for Energy Saving in Existing Buildings"
Part I (GPO–041–018–000–79–8) ($5.05)
Part II (GPO–041–018–000–80–1) ($5.25)
Available from:

Superintendent of Documents
Government Printing Office
Washington, D.C. 20402

CSO #5   *Savings Due to Recovery of Waste Heat*

Whenever a hot stream of material leaves the premises, energy is being wasted and the possibility exists that energy and money can be conserved. The technique for saving, and the amount to be saved, depends on whether the stream is hot water, hot air, hot flue gas, hot bricks, or hot steel. It will usually require the services of a consultant to determine the best method of saving and to estimate the dollar amount of the savings that can be achieved. Hundreds of examples have been documented on saving waste heat from such diverse sources as hot air from paint booth exhausts, hot water from cooling welding machines, hot flue gas from a heat treating furnace, and waste heat from air compressors, refrigerators and air conditioners.

This example concerns saving waste energy from a 25-ton air-conditioner in a restaurant, $1100 per year in savings for an $800 investment.

Example—A restaurant open 12 hours per day served an average of 1000 meals per day during the summer season. Air-conditioning was required for about 84 days of the four month busy season and was furnished by a 25-ton cooling unit. The unit was equipped with a water cooled condenser, and heat was wasted in the hot water being dumped to the sewer. The restaurant also required 3500 gallons of hot water per day. This was heated electrically from 75 to 150 °F, requiring (150–75) Btu/lb × 8.34 lb/gal × 3500 gal/day × 84 days, or 184 MBtu for the air-conditioning season.

A consultant suggested recovering some of the waste heat from the air-conditioner and using it to heat water for the kitchen. He estimated that a heat exchanger installed between the compressor and the condenser could readily heat water to 150 °F, and that the heat recovery rate would be 150,000 Btu/h. He also determined that the compressor operated 50 percent of the time, or 6 hours per days, and that the total energy saved would be 150,000 Btu/h × 6 h/day × 84 days, or 75.6 MBtu. With an electrical rate of 5¢ per kWh, refer to table II, page 8, and note that this corresponds to an energy cost of almost $15 per MBtu.

The annual saving was 75.6 MBtu × $15.00/MBtu, or $1100. The cost of installing the heat exchanger with the necessary piping was less than $800.

Suggested Action

Knowing the size of the air-conditioning system in your business, consider the possibility of recovering heat from the condenser. As a rule of thumb, each ton of refrigeration represents 4,000 to 8,000 Btu of recoverable energy per hour of operation. Consultation with a technical person in this field will be worthwhile.

Application of the idea is especially attractive for large office buildings that require air-conditioning year around. Stores that need refrigeration continuously for food preservation can also apply this concept of heat recovery.

Source

"Building System Design"
January 1975 issue, page 13.

CSO #6 *Savings by Thermostat "Setback" During Unoccupied Hours*

The temperature of many plants and offices can be reduced by 10, 15, or even 20 °F during nights and weekends. The savings in energy and money can be substantial.

The amount of savings depends on (1) the average seasonal heating bill without any night setback, (2) the percent of the time that it is proposed to setback the thermostat, (3) the number of degrees that the temperature will be reduced during the unoccupied periods, and (4) the length and severity of the heating season expressed in degree days. (The number of degree days for a given locality can be obtained from the weather bureau or from a local gas or fuel oil supplier.)

The following table shows the savings to be expected at different amounts of nightly temperature setback for different climates. The table assumes that the thermostat will be at the lowered temperature 50 percent of the time. The numbers listed are percent reduction of the "normal" fuel usage at 68 °F continuously.

Percent saved by setting back thermostat 50 percent of the time

Degree days	Amount of setback			
	5 °F	10 °F	15 °F	20 °F
8000	9	18	26	32
6000	11	21	30	36
4000	13	24	34	40
2000	17	31	40	47

Example

A small office building is located in Cleveland with an average heating season of 6000 degree days. The building was normally kept warm 24 hours per day, seven days per week. The gas usage for space heating was 8100 kcf per season, at a cost of $1.50 per kcf.

It is planned in the next heating season to set the thermostat back 15 °F for 12 hours per day Monday through Friday, 16 hours on Saturday, and 24 hours on Sunday for a total of 100 hours per week. This is equal to 100 divided by 168 hours per week, or 59.5 percent of the time.

From the table above, the saving at 50 percent of the time is 30 percent of the fuel used; for 59.5 percent it is $\frac{30 \times 59.5}{50}$, or 35.7 percent of the fuel.

The estimated annual saving is 8100 kcf × $1.50/kcf × 0.357, or $4,300.

Suggested Action

Whenever possible lower building thermostats to a minimum and still maintain comfort during occupied hours. During unoccupied hours, thermostats should be lowered to whatever extent possible within the relevant building codes for plumbing, fire protection, etc. Also, radiators in vestibules, lobbies, hallways, storage areas, and unoccupied areas might be turned off permanently if possible.

Source

"Guidelines for Energy Saving in Existing Buildings"
Part I (GPO–041–018–000–79–8) ($5.05)
Part II (GPO–041–018–000–80–1) ($5.25)
Available from:

Superintendent of Documents
Government Printing Office
Washington, D.C. 20402

CSO #7 *Energy Conservation in Furnaces and Boilers*

In some businesses, a steam boiler or a high-temperature furnace may be the major user of energy and is thus definitely a prime candidate for energy saving possibilities. Many books have been written on furnace and boiler efficiency, and it is impossible to condense all the information they contain into a small space. It can be stated however, and all the authors agree, that the single greatest source of inefficiency is the energy that is lost up the stack or the chimney.

If a cubic foot of gas is burned with precisely the required amount of air, about 11 cubic feet of flue gas will go up the stack. Since this gas is hot, it represents lost energy. If the amount of air used is twice the required amount (100 percent excess air), there will be 21 cubic feet of flue gas, and the energy lost will be almost twice as great.

It is possible to calculate the stack loss, whether the fuel be gas, oil, or coal, knowing only two bits of information:

(1) The temperature of the flue gas, and
(2) The amount of excess air.

The first requires a thermometer; the second a rather simple flue gas analysis taking about an hour or less. The following table lists the stack loss as a percentage of the energy in the fuel burned for different values of stack temperature and of percent excess air.

Stack loss as percent of fuel burned

Percent Excess air	Stack temperature				
	300 °F	500 °F	700 °F	900 °F	1100 °F
0	4.0	8.0	12	.16	20
20	4.7	9.4	14	19	24
40	5.4	11	16	22	27
60	6.1	12	19	24	31
80	6.8	14	21	27	34
100	7.5	15	23	30	38

A medium sized steam boiler should operate, when burning oil, at 10 to 20 percent excess air and a stack temperature as low as practical, usually about 300 to 400 °F. Under these conditions, about 7 percent of the energy in the fuel will be lost up the stack.

Several surveys of small industrial boilers show that a large number of installations are operating at conditions which are far from the optimum. It is not unusual to find a boiler using 100 percent excess air, and indicating a stack temperature of 700 or 800 °F. Under these conditions, the stack loss will be about 25 percent of the fuel energy. Usually, such conditions can be returned to normal by appropriate testing and maintenance procedures. A high stack temperature, for example, is often caused by fouling of the interior sur-

faces, either by soot from misadjusted burners, or scale from improper feed water treatment, or both. The large quantity of excess air can be reduced by proper adjustment of the stack damper and the air inlets.

Note that too little air is also an inefficient condition since unburned or partially burned fuel will escape.

Example

Assume an oil fired boiler rated at 5,000 pounds of steam per hour, which operates 4,000 hours per year at an average load of about two thirds of its rating. If this boiler is reasonably modern, with suitable controls and well maintained, it will burn 120,000 gallons of oil per year. The stack loss, as noted in the paragraphs above, will be about 7 percent. If the boiler is not properly maintained and adjusted, the loss may increase to as much as 25 percent, and the boiler will use 145,000 gallons per year to maintain the same steam output.

The saving involved in keeping the boiler clean and well adjusted is 25,000 gallons of oil, which if priced at $0.40 per gallon amounts to $10,000 annually. The cost of such maintenance will probably be less than $1,000 per year.

Suggested Action

If a steam boiler or a process furnace is an important part of your energy budget, arrange for regular (at least quarterly) checks on stack temperature and flue gas analysis. Outside contractors will do the job, or a trained employee can perform the checks with a few hours training and $150 to $300 investment in test equipment.

NOTE: While stack loss is the largest single source of heat loss in boilers and furnaces, it is not the only source of inefficiency. See the section on Assistance for sources of help in running a complete heat balance on your boiler and determining whether other losses are wasting energy. Your boiler manufacturer can be of help in advising as to methods of saving energy.

CSO #8   *Savings by Insulating Steam and/or Water Pipes*

Large amounts of energy can be lost to the surrounding atmosphere by bare steam or hot water pipes. In all cases of bare pipes, the addition of insulation is a very attractive investment. The following table can be used to estimate the energy and cost savings which can be achieved by insulating bare pipes.

Energy saved by adding 1-½" fiber glass insulation to bare pipes

Nominal pipe size	Btu/hour/foot of pipe		
	Steam pressure		
	15 psi	50 psi	200 psi
½"	108	136	192
1"	167	237	381
2"	291	398	662
3"	413	571	962

Example

Consider 100 feet of 2" pipe carrying steam at 50 psi, with no insulation, and operating about half the time, or 4000 hours per year. The above table indicates that if this pipe is insulated with 1½" of fiberglass insulation the energy saving will be 398 Btu/h ft × 100 ft × 4000 h, or 159 MBtu per year.

If the steam boiler is fired with fuel oil at 42¢ per gallon, and operates at 65 percent efficiency, one can determine from table II, page 8, that the energy cost is $3.00 divided by 0.65, or $4.62 per MBtu.

The total saving is 159 MBtu × $4.62/MBtu, or $735 per year.

The cost of insulating 100 feet of 2" pipe will, of course, vary with location and the individual contractor; a typical cost would be $250 to $300.

Notes

(1) The above table assumes that the pipes are located inside a building at an ambient tempertaure of 75 °F. If the pipe is outside exposed to low temperatures and rain, the losses will be greater. The cost of insulation will also be slightly higher since outside insulation must carry a water-proof covering to keep it dry.

(2) The table assumes the use of 1½" insulation, which is an average thickness for many purposes; it may not, however, be the most efficient thickness if the investment is to be amortized over a number of years. For the detailed calculation of most efficient insulation thickness contact a consultant or a reputable insulation contractor, or you can perform most of the necessary calculations wtih information available in the publications of:

Thermal Insulation Manufacturers Association
7 Kirby Plaza
Mt. Kisco, New York 10549

(3) Any cold pipe which drips from atmospheric condensation or which forms frost is absorbing heat from the air. Insulation will not only relieve the nuisance, but will conserve energy used to drive the refrigeration equipment.

Federal Energy Administration
Regional Offices

REGION	ADDRESS	TELEPHONE
I	Robert W. Mitchell, Reg. Admin Analex Building—Rm 700 150 Causeway Street Boston, Massachusetts 02114	(617) 223-3701
II	Alfred Kleinfeld, Reg. Admin 26 Federal Plaza—Rm 3206 New York, N.Y. 10017	(212) 264-1021
III	J. A. LaSala, Reg. Admin 1421 Cherry St—Rm 1001 Philadelphia, Pennsylvania 19102	(215) 597-3890
IV	Donald Allen, Reg. Admin 1655 Peachtree St., N.E. 8th Floor Atlanta, Georgia 30309	(404) 526-2837
V	N. Allen Andersen, Reg. Admin 175 West Jackson Blvd Room A-333 Chicago, Illinois 60604	(312) 353-8420
VI	Delbert M. Fowler, Reg. Admin P.O. Box 35228 2626 West Mockingbird Lane Dallas, Texas 75235	(214) 749-7345
VII	Neil Adams, Reg. Admin Twelve Grand Building P.O. Box 2208 112 East 12th Street Kansas City, Missouri 64142	(816) 374-2061

Federal Energy Administration
Regional Offices (Cont.)

VIII	Dudley E. Faver, Reg. Admin P.O. Box 26247—Belmar Branch 1075 South Yukon Street Lakewood, Colorado 80226	(303) 234-2420
IX	William C. Arntz, Reg. Admin 111 Pine Street Third Floor San Francisco, California 94111	(415) 556-7216
X	Jack B. Robertson, Reg. Admin 1992 Federal Building 915 Second Avenue Seattle, Washington 98174	(206) 442-7280

Appendix II

References

A short list of reference documents is given which address the subject of energy management (the term "Conservation" is frequently used) on more or less the same technical level as does this document. Some of these documents (particularly Nos. 1 and 2) list additional references, so that if the reader wishes to study in detail any aspect of energy management he will be able to find more helpful material.

1. Energy Conservation Program Guide for Industry and Commerce

   NBS Handbook 115, issued September 1974
   ($2.90)

   NBS Handbook 115 Supplement 1, issued December 1975
   ($2.25)

   Available from:

   Superintendent of Documents
   Government Printing Office
   Washington, D. C. 20402

2. Total Energy Management—A Practical Handbook on Energy Conservation and Management

   Available from:

   National Electrical Manufacturers Association
   155 East 44th Street
   New York, N.Y. 10017

3. How to Conserve Fuel Oil, Gasoline, Solvent, Electricity and Other Essential Needs: Special Reporter, Vol 2, March 1974
   ($1.00)

   Available from:

   International Fabricare Institute
   South Chicago at Doris Avenue
   Joliet, Illinois 60434

4. A Guide to Energy Management—How to Conduct an Energy Audit, 1974
   ($5.00)

   Available from:

   American Society of Association Exectuives
   1101 16th Street, N.W.
   Washington. D. C. 20036

5. (A) Energy Management: Trade Associations and the Economics of Energy
   (30¢)

   (B) How to Start an Energy Management Program
   (25¢)

   (C) Energy Conservation Handbook for Light Industries and Commercial Buildings
   (35¢)

   These three booklets are available from:

   Superintendent of Documents
   Government Printing Office
   Washington, D. C. 20402

6. Recommended Guidelines for Supermarket Energy Conservation CRMA.EC.I.
   ($1.00)

   Available from:

   Commercial Refrigerators Manufacturers Assn.
   Executive Office
   1730 Pennsylvania Avenue, N.W.
   Washington, D. C. 20006

7. General Industry Safety and Health Regulations Part 1910 June 1974, OSHA #2206
   ($3.85)

   Available from:

   Superintendent of Documents
   Government Printing Office
   Washington, D. C. 20402

8. Construction Safety and Health Regulations Part 1926, June 1974, OSHA #2207
   ($1.55)

   Available from:

   Superintendent of Documents
   Government Printing Office
   Washington, D. C. 20402

Appendix II (Cont.)

9. Energy Management Case Histories
   (GPO–041–018–00062–3)

   Available from:

   Superintendent of Documents
   Government Printing Office
   Washington, D. C. 20402

10. Energy Management Case Histories
    (PB–246–763/AS—November 1975)

    Available from:

    National Technical Information Service
    Springfield, Virginia 22161

11. Light and Thermal Operations Guidelines
    ($2.30)

    Available from:

    Superintendent of Documents
    Government Printing Office
    Washington, D. C. 20402

12. Lighting and Thermal Operations: Building Energy Report Case Studies

    Available from:

    Superintendent of Documents
    Government Printing Office
    Washington, D. C. 20402

13. Study of the Impact of Reduced Store Operating Hours on Sales, Employment, Economic Concentration, and Energy Consumption
    PB–243 579/AS

    Available from:

    National Technical Information Service
    Springfield, Virginia 22161

14. Lighting and Thermal Operations: Energy Conservation Principles Applied to Office Lighting
    PB 244–154/AS

    Available from:

    National Technical Information Service
    Springfield, Virginia 22161

15. Guidelines for Saving Energy in Existing Buildings: Owners and Operators Manual—ECM 1
    041–018–000–79–8 ($5.05)

    Available from:

    Superintendent of Documents
    Government Printing Office
    Washington, D. C. 20402

16. Guidelines for Saving Energy in Existing Buildings: Engineers, Architects, and Operators Manual—ECM 2
    041–018–000–80–1 ($5.25)

    Available from:

    Superintendent of Documents
    Government Printing Office
    Washington, D. C. 20402

17. Guide to Energy Conservation for Food Service October, 1975
    041–018–00085–2

    Available from:

    Superintendent of Documents
    Government Printing Office
    Washington, D. C. 20402

18. Energy Conservation in Buildings: Techniques for Economical Design, 1974
    ($20.00)

    Available from:

    Construction Specifications Institute, Inc.
    1150 17th Street, N.W.
    Washington, D. C. 20036

ENERGY MANAGEMENT AND CONSERVATION FOR COMMERCIAL BUILDINGS*

* Total Energy Management: A Practical Handbook on Energy Conservation and Management, National Electrical Manufacturers Association in Cooperation with the Federal Energy Administration, March 1976.

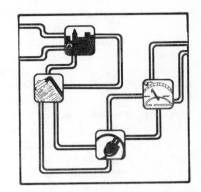

I. INTRODUCTION

Until recently, many persons in the United States considered energy to be both inexhaustible and expendable, assumptions seemingly verified by the relatively low cost of most energy forms. The problems fostered by such attitudes are exemplified in the commercial building sector of the nation's economy. Typically, buildings were designed and constructed primarily with initial costs in mind. The result has been creation of a vast inventory of commercial buildings which—by today's standards—utilize excessive amounts of energy.

It is fairly safe to say that buildings being designed now, and those to be designed in the future, will utilize many of the new techniques and systems which can lead to maximized energy efficiency. But the present building inventory is being replaced at the rate of only 2-3% per year. As a result, the majority of existing commercial buildings for many years to come will be those which were originally not designed with energy conservation in mind.

Because of this situation, conservation of energy in existing commercial buildings has become a matter of very real concern as the nation starts toward a goal of energy self-sufficiency by the mid 1980s. Due to the national security and economic aspects of this goal, the federal government has entered the arena through the Federal Energy Administration (FEA), as well as other agencies and departments. The government also has been working with organizations from the private sector to develop methodologies to help spur energy conservations in existing structures.

Two energy conservation methods have been advanced.

The first method involves implementation of specific end-use restrictions in buildings. This approach requires, as examples, adjustment of thermostats to specific levels to use less heating and cooling energy, or removal of light bulbs and lamps to reduce consumption of lighting energy. Ease of initial implementation is the primary advantage of such an approach. After all, it requires very little new education or effort to adjust a thermostat setting or remove a lightbulb. Unfortunately, the end-use restriction method has numerous drawbacks.

Key among them is this: the extent to which a system is used has no bearing on its efficiency. If for whatever reason, a system is inefficient, it will waste energy every time it is used. End-use restrictions fail to take into consideration the systems which produce the end-use product, be it heating, cooling, lighting, etc. In other words, end-use restrictions tend to ignore the significant energy savings which can be realized by making systems operate as efficiently as possible. In a similar manner, end-use restrictions fail to consider the fact that every building is a unique system whose many elements interrelate. As a result, lowering a thermostat in winter can sometimes cause consumption of more energy, not less. Likewise, removing lamps and luminaires can sometimes cause consumption of energy sources which are in the shortest supply.

Perhaps even more important, there is the serious possibility that the government eventually will mandate energy conservation standards for many types of buildings. If these standards are based primarily on end-use restrictions, the flexibility building management requires to meet the needs of energy conservation, building systems, and building users would be severely restricted. In addition, one can see that a vast bureaucratic network would be required to check compliance, consider needed exemptions, and so on. In short, end-use restrictions have the single advantage of being available quickly and with a minimum of effort. This advantage makes them ideal for immediate impact. Their drawbacks, however, make them far less effective—actually counterproductive—for anything other than very short-term applications.

The second energy conservation approach is called Total Energy Management, or TEM. In essence, TEM considers every building as a unique, complex system. To conserve energy one first must understand how the building consumes energy; how users' needs are met; how the systems' elements interrelate; how external environment affects it, and so on. By understanding how a specific building consumes energy, one can make energy conservation improvements which can be integrated into the system itself. Then, when the system is used, it runs efficiently and therefore uses the least amount of energy to get the job done.

Application of a wide variety of end-use energy modifications—which are an integral element of the TEM concept when applied with flexibility—would result in even more savings. Of equal importance, the TEM approach involves literally hundreds of different options from which a building owner/manager can pick and choose to achieve energy savings. This gives him the flexibility he needs to conserve energy while also meeting the specific needs of his building and the people who use it. This flexibility obviously would have significant impact on any government-mandated energy conservation program. The building owner could be given a conservation goal rather than operational rules and regulations. How he goes about achieving the goal would be up to him in light of his own particular set of circumstances.

Although the TEM approach is more versatile and effective than a concept which relies primarily on end-use restrictions, the latter have seemingly received far more attention. This is understandable given our current situation. End-use restrictions did not take long to develop, the problems of implementation were not considered. By contrast, analysis of the many different techniques which can be used to implement the TEM approach has required extensive research, testing and evaluation. Accordingly, it has taken much more time to develop the tools—of which this Handbook is an example—needed for TEM implementation. Now that these tools are being utilized by more and more building owners and managers, and as their experiences have been given more attention in the various media, it is expected that the TEM concept will gain rapid general acceptance and use. One of the prime reasons for this is the cost element. As even a brief review of the options in this manual will show, many of the most effective energy and energy cost conservation measures require little or no capital outlay. In fact, case study after case study has shown that significant energy savings can be obtained through minor operational changes, improved maintenance, repair of faulty equipment, etc. And while the program itself cannot be established overnight, putting in the time and effort required in the beginning can result in many elements of the program requiring little or no attention or effort later on.

As you begin reading the contents of this publication, it will become apparent that many of the specific concerns addressed by TEM are not new. What is new is the manner in which they are addressed and the methodology suggested for effective implementation. Perhaps most important, utilization of the TEM approach will enable building owners and managers to realize significant energy and energy cost savings without having to make any significant changes in the working environment each building must support.

ENERGY CONSUMPTION IN
II. BUILDINGS

If an attempt to achieve energy conservation is to be successful, it must be made in full light of the many factors which affect energy consumption. Unless these factors are known and understood, changes made may result in achievements far short of expectations or may actually do more harm than good.

Energy use in buildings is determined, basically, by climatic conditions of the area in which the building is located and the working environment and business equipment required by tenants. Neither of these factors is capable of any significant modification.

The efficiency of energy use is determined by the three basic systems which comprise any functioning building. These are: *energized systems*, such as those required for heating, cooling, lighting, ventilation, conveyance, business equipment operation, and so on; *nonenergized systems*, such as floors, ceilings, walls, roof, windows (glazing), etc., and; *human systems*, comprising maintenance, operating and management personnel as well as tenants and other users. Each of these three systems is capable of modification which can lead to a significant savings of energy. Because energized systems are those which utilize energy directly, however, the natural tendency is to concentrate energy conservation efforts in that area. To do so would be a mistake, however, because the efficiency of the equipment involved depends on numerous other factors. In other words, it can be very detrimental to a program of energy conservation to confuse the ends with the means.

Effective energy management requires that the entire pattern of energy consumption be analyzed so that changes made will be integrated into the system in full light of the interrelationships which exist and the various effects which will occur. Accordingly, the following discussion is presented to provide you with a basic understanding of certain critical factors and the way in which they interact.

It is appropriate to begin with the subject of heating and cooling since together they usually consume the largest single "block" of energy.

To start, one should not think of heating and cooling simply in terms of adding or removing heat from the inside air to achieve a given temperature. To do so would ignore what really is involved in heating and cooling, namely, compensating either for heat loss or heat gain in a building. By visualizing heating and cooling in this light, it becomes evident that modification to heating and cooling can be directed at the heating and cooling system itself, as well as those factors which contribute to heat loss and heat gain.

Heat loss and heat gain usually occur simultaneously in a building, although one usually far outweighs the other depending on the season involved. A building usually undergoes substantial heat loss during the heating season and substantial heat gain during the cooling season. Although climatic conditions—temperature, humidity, wind, solar radiation—are essentially responsible for this effect, the impact of these conditions can be modified substantially, as will be discussed.

The factors which influence heat gain and heat loss are as follows:

Infiltration: Infiltration involves passage of outside air into the building through apertures such as cracks around windows and door jambs, doors left open, etc. The amount of infiltration depends on the impact of the wind on the building and the integrity of construction. In large multistory buildings, infiltration is increased due to a vacuum effect which occurs when warmer air—which is lighter—rises to the upper portions of the building. During the heating season, infiltration contributes to heat loss because cold infiltrated air must be heated to maintain desired comfort conditions. During the cooling season, infiltration contributes to heat gain because the warmer infiltrated air must be cooled to maintain desired comfort conditions.

Transmission: Transmission refers to the amount of heat transmitted into the building or from it through the various components of the building envelope, including exterior walls, windows, and doors; roof; floor, etc. Transmission contributes to heat gain or heat loss depending upon the difference between indoor and outdoor temperature in accordance with the basic principal of heat flow which states that heat always is conducted from an area of higher temperature to an area of lower temperature. Thus, during the heating season, indoor heat is transmitted through the walls to the exterior. During the cooling season, heat is transmitted inside. The rate of the transmission depends upon the composition of the various materials utilized in construction of the building envelope.

Ventilation: As with infiltration and transmission, ventilation contributes to heat gain or heat loss (and humidification/dehumidification) depending upon the season involved. The ventilation system provides a building with fresh air by exchanging inside air for outside air. The rate of exchange is measured in cubic feet per minute or CFM. During the heating season, unconditioned cold air is brought into the building while an equivalent volume of warm air is exhausted. During the cooling season, cooled air is exhausted while warm air is brought in. Obviously, the greater the rate of ventilation, and the greater the difference between outside and indoor temperature, the more energy will be consumed by the heating or cooling system to compensate for the heat gain or heat loss involved.

Lighting: Lighting contributes to a building's heat gain in direct proportion to the wattage of the lamps involved. The heat gain involved is beneficial during the heating season in that the heat from light sources and their auxiliary supplements the heating system. During the cooling season, however, the cooling system must compensate for the heat of light.

Solar Heat: Solar heat, like the heat of light, contributes to heat gain throughout the year. The specific effect of solar heat depends on the geographical area involved, the intensity and direction of the rays, the materials which comprise the building envelope, the color and texture of exterior walls and roof, extent and type of solar controls, available shading, etc.

Equipment: Virtually all powered equipment including business machines, cooling equipment, appliances, building systems equipment, etc., contributes to heat gain because their motors or other elements generate heat.

Occupants: The number of people in a building or in a given area of a building can create a significant heat gain because human beings give heat to room air whenever the temperature around them is below 98.6°F. They also contribute to moisture content of air through perspiration and exhalation.

A building's total heat loss is equivalent to the amount of heat which the heating system must add to a given space in a given time to maintain a given temperature. The total heat gain is the amount of heat which the cooling system must remove from a given space in a given time to maintain a given temperature. In almost all cases, those factors which contribute negatively to heat loss and heat gain can be modified to a greater or lesser extent. Modification can reduce the load placed on heating and cooling equipment and so the energy required for the equipment's operation. Accordingly, while setting the thermostat to a lower or

higher temperature than otherwise would be maintained may achieve savings, reliance on this technique alone could obscure the fact that additional savings—perhaps twice as great or more—could be achieved by modifying other factors, regardless of what temperature is desired.

Modifying heat gain/heat loss factors is not the only method available for reducing the amount of heating and cooling energy required. Adjustment and modification of the heating and cooling equipment itself can achieve substantial economies. It has been shown, for example, that heating and cooling systems of even the most modern buildings often have extensive inefficiencies, usually due to faulty installation, maintenance or operation. Correction of these inefficiencies—which will not require any significant expense —can result in substantial energy savings. Other modifications also can be made. Time clocks can be added to achieve automatic night and weekend setback for certain pieces of equipment. Controls can be added to regulate ventilation equipment more efficiently. New devices can be installed to transfer heat or cooling from exhaust air to incoming air. In all cases, however, all modifications must be made in light of the various building systems involved and their effect upon each other. For example, certain energy conserving devices and techniques cannot be used because they may cause malfunctions of tenant-required equipment, such as computers. Likewise, while the amount of lighting in a given area can be reduced, the extent of reduction depends on the tasks being performed in the spaces involved, the type of persons performing the work, the ability to move desks and other furnishings to take advantage of available light in a more effective manner, the color and texture of walls, and so on. Similarly, more effective maintenance cannot be achieved unless elements of the human systems are in tune. Maintenance personnel are not likely to establish new, effective maintenance procedures unless they have direction from management. Nor are new operating procedures likely to have continuing effect unless those in charge of building operation are continually willing to do the work, and management is willing and able to continually monitor the effectiveness of the work. Human systems also can have an impact on tenant requirements, not so much in terms of changing requirements, but rather in terms of modifying the way in which systems are used to meet requirements. In other words, tenants can be encouraged to turn off lights when a room is unoccupied; to close all exterior doors securely; to close windows when heating or cooling systems are in operation, etc.

Numerous publications now available can provide you with additional information regarding interrelationships such as those described above. Many more of these interrelationships are discussed or mentioned throughout the body of this handbook. In any event, it is imperative that you—or whoever will be developing your TEM program—understand the specific system interrelationships which exist in your building and which must be taken into consideration to ensure that any measures taken lead to true conservation of energy through maximized total system efficiency.

OBTAINING INITIAL COMMITMENT AND
III. COOPERATION

Assuming that you want to proceed toward development of a Total Energy Management program for your building or buildings, it will be necessary to obtain initial cooperation. This is needed not only to obtain the commitment and assistance required for initial tasks, but also to lay the foundation for the cooperation which will be needed in actual implementation of the full TEM program. As with any management endeavor, it is suggested strongly that maximum effectiveness of the overall approach can be obtained only when one executive is selected in the beginning to head the entire project with support from subordinates as necessary. To fragment authority at the top is to confuse the lines of authority and communication stemming from above. This could affect adversely the coordination and cooperation required to implement and continue the program in an effective, expeditious manner.

Owner: Cooperation must be obtained from the owner. While he is likely to approve in principle any attempt to conserve energy and energy costs, he may balk at having to outlay initial funds for a professional survey as suggested by this manual. The owner, therefore, must be shown the benefits which will accrue to him as a result of the TEM approach. He must be convinced that the expenditure of funds will be a wise investment, especially since some of the most effective energy conservation measures are those which require no capital investment. In certain cases it may be necessary to "jump the gun" a bit and prepare an Energy Management Form (discussed in the following section) which may indicate that the energy consumption of his building is comparatively high.

Manager: The building manager must be committed to the program, and must believe firmly in its effectiveness. If he does not, then the direction which must come from him will not be what is required. The manager has the difficult responsibility of being between the owner, who wants results, and the operating and maintenance personnel, who in many cases will be producing the results. He must strive to develop an overall spirit of cooperation, therefore, and to take those actions which

are necessary to maintain this spirit throughout establishment and operation of the TEM approach. A testing program conducted to determine the effectiveness of this manual and the TEM concept itself shows that, when building management, rather than the operating engineer alone, directs the program, far more areas of concern are addressed and potential savings are expanded accordingly.

Maintenance and Operating Personnel: It is especially important to obtain the cooperation of maintenance and operating personnel early in the project. They are the ones who, in large measure, will be implementing many of the changes which will be required. In most cases, these changes will mean altering what have become habits over many years. Perhaps even more important, some operating and maintenance personnel tend to regard initial TEM procedures as a questioning of their capability. Experience has shown that, when an outside person is brought in to conduct an initial survey, he often is met with hostility and evasiveness. It may be advisable to explain the undertaking not so much in terms of "doing things better," but rather in terms of "doing things differently." An effort should be made to convince operating and maintenance personnel of the great contribution they can make to energy conservation; that energy conservation can affect profitability, and that profitability can affect all jobs. In some cases, of course, union agreements in force define specifically who is responsible for what, hours of employment, and related factors. When it is found that such agreements will be counterproductive to the goal of energy conservation, an effort should be made to work with the union involved to establish fair and equitable modifications to agreements which will help make maximum energy savings possible.

Clerical Staff: Clerical staff, or whoever is involved in developing base year data for establishment of base year EUI (discussed in the following section), must cooperate to the fullest. They must be willing to spend the extra time which may be required to find all the data required and to be sure that it is accurate. The importance of their contribution must be shown to them. This same attention to detail will be required later during implementation of the TEM concept and when data must be collected and reported on a monthly basis.

Tenants: It usually will not be necessary to obtain the cooperation of tenants during the initial phase of TEM operations unless the data required only can be obtained from them. As the project progresses, however, tenants will become more and more involved, beginning usually with conduct of the survey, more frequent inspections of facilities, requests for operational modifications, etc. In certain cases prevailing lease agreements may set certain standards which cover matters such as energy consumption and payment, lighting levels to be provided, heating, cooling conditions to be maintained, and so on. When a lease such as this will limit the degree of energy and energy dollar savings possible, every effort should be made to work with the lessee to make modifications to lease requirements—including costs, when appropriate— that will make application of TEM more effective. It should be stressed that modifications to be made will not in most cases change system performance. As examples, a lighting system can be kept highly effective—in some cases can be made even more effective—although certain lamps and/or luminaires are removed. Likewise, heating and cooling energy requirements can be reduced substantially without altering the customary temperature in the space involved.

You may find it advisable, once owner cooperation and commitment are assured, to call together all staff personnel —including clerical assistants and operating and maintenance personnel—to explain the undertaking on which you are about to embark; the contribution which can be made to the overall national goals of energy self-sufficiency, and the goals which can be achieved in terms of energy cost savings. In so doing, you also can explain how the cooperation of all individuals working together is essential for completion of the task, and so—by having a group present—instill at once a sense of team spirit which can be invaluable in helping you achieve the goal of energy conservation through Total Energy Management.

ESTABLISHING AN ENERGY CONSERVATION IV. GOAL

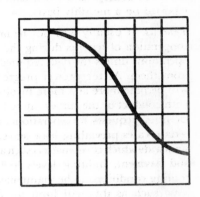

The nature of effective management is such that virtually all tasks undertaken have goals to provide direction for the undertaking, a means to measure results, and guidance for redirection of efforts. Total Energy Management is no different. A fundamental aspect of its operation, therefore, requires that managers establish energy conservation goals. The most generally accepted way of doing this is to state goals in terms of reductions of energy use over previous levels. To do this, of course, it is necessary to establish exactly what the previous levels were. Research undertaken by NEMA, NECA and Federal Energy Administration has shown that an effective way of stating previous levels is in terms of BTUs per gross conditioned square foot, which is called the Energy Utilization Index, or EUI.

The instrument used to collect the data required is the Energy Management Form shown in Figure IV-1. Although at first glance it may appear to be somewhat difficult to complete, it actually is relatively uncomplicated and straightforward. Moreover, the completed form can become a very valuable component of your TEM program because it is applicable to more than goal-setting and monitoring. Additional applications of the completed form will assist you in areas such as:

Effort Direction: If two or more buildings—similar in design and actual use—are involved, you will be able to compare the different EUIs and so determine quickly which buildings are most and least energy efficient. As a result, assuming a limited budget is involved, you will know where to concentrate initial efforts to achieve the greatest potential savings.

Basis for Comparison: By having consumption records it will be possible to compare energy consumption patterns of a given building for the same period in previous years. Even minor differences can be spotted quickly. As a result, any possible irregularities in utilities' billing or estimating procedures can be identified quickly.

Rate Savings: Establishment of EUI records will provide the information required to determine whether or not a building is receiving the lowest possible utility rates. Electric utilities in particular often have multifactor rate

schedules. Changes in the schedule or the building's energy consumption patterns may have made the rate originally established for a building inconsistent with current operations.

Estimating: By establishing the amount of energy used in a previous year, and applying any new energy rates, it will be a relatively simple task to estimate with accuracy the cost of supplying a building with the fuel required for the year ahead. This can be an essential tool in overall cash flow estimation. It can also help operating personnel establish more effective fuel delivery schedules.

Operational Overview: An EUI can quickly establish an operational overview of a given building. Variances from period to period as compared with similar periods in previous months or years can quickly serve to indicate efficiency of building systems. A mechanical problem of one sort or another also may be noticed more quickly through energy utilization data than through actual operation.

The Energy Management Form illustrated is based on a 12-month period. It is suggested for ease of data collection and analysis that a previous calendar year be utilized as the base. Although any 12-month period will do—preferably a 12-month period during which energy conservation measures were not undertaken—the calendar year approach will eliminate potential confusion in data collection and reporting. Initial data required can come either from your own records (assuming utility bill receipts are retained) or from those of the utility involved. If you utilize utility-provided data you will have to establish your base year for the 12-month period for which data is available.

1. DEVELOPING THE EUI

The process of goal-setting requires that you first establish base-year data. The procedure for recording this data and for keeping a running monthly tally for years subsequent to the base year are the same except, of course, that nonbase year data can and should be recorded as it comes in each month.

The various elements of the form shown in Figure IV-1 and computations involved are as follows:

Month (Column 1): Regardless of the billing date used by electric, steam or gas supplier, energy units consumed should be extracted from the bill for that month in which the greatest number of days occurred. If the billing period is March 2 - April 2 enter the usage under the month of March.

Heating Degree Days/Cooling Degree Days (Columns 2 and 3): Past studies indicate that daily requirements for space heat and fuel/energy consumption vary directly with the difference between 65°F and the outdoor, mean daily temperature. The outdoor mean daily temperature is the average of the maximum and minimum outdoor temperature during the 24 hours of a given day. For example, if the maximum temperature during the day is 55° degrees and the minimum is 35 degrees, the mean would be 45°F. The heating degree days involved would be 20 (65°F - 45°F). If there are 30 days in the month, and each has 20 degree days, total degree days for the month would be 600 (20 × 30). Cooling degree days are determined in the same manner, although it is readily admitted that many other factors—such as humidity, solar conditions and wind—play a significant role during the cooling season. Until such time as an accurate index is established, however, cooling degree days will have to suffice. It should be noted that EUI figures may be calculated for any given month. Monthly EUI data can be extremely useful for monitoring the effectiveness of any energy conservation technique employed. The information is inserted here because it provides a basis for comparison. For example, it would be unfair to compare the EUI of January 1974 to the EUI of January 1975 if January 1975 was twice as cold as January 1974. Information on the number of degree days in your area for each month usually can be obtained from your local electric or gas utility, oil distributor, or the U.S. Weather Bureau's local climatological reports which are issued monthly and are available for a nominal amount. Normally, heating degree day entries will be made for the months of October through May. Cooling degree days usually include the months of June through September.

Electricity—Kilowatt Hours(kWh) (Column 4): Under this column, enter the kilowatt hours shown on the electric utility bill for the appropriate month involved.

Electricity—Kilowatt Hours per Degree Day (Column 5): If electricity is used for heating, note the product of dividing kWh for heating month by the number of heating days involved. If electricity is used for cooling, divide the kWh for cooling month by the number of cooling degree days. In either case, as efficiency increases, the product decreases.

Electricity—kW Demand—Actual (Column 6) and Billed (Column 7): Electric charges for larger facilities usually are broken into two major components—the amount of electricity used (kWh) and the rate of electricity used (kW) over a preselected short period of time, usually 15 to 30 minutes. The greatest level of demand is registered during peak periods, when several major pieces of equipment are operated simultaneously. Charges for the amount of electricity used (in kWh) are based on the cost of generation of electricity. Demand charges reflect the fixed investment which a utility has in the distribution, transmission and generating equipment which must be available to meet your peak demand. In many cases, actual and billed demand are different. Actual demand is a record of what your demand really was during the month. Billed demand is the actual demand adjusted by the various rate provisions and is the demand used for the computation of charges. In Philadelphia, for example, demand rate for schedules PD and HT are billed in accordance with this provision: "During the eight months of October through May, the billing demand *will not be less* than 40% of the maximum demand specified in the contract, *nor less* than 70% of the highest billing demand in the preceding months of June through September." Given the way in which the rates are structured, use of the EUI will enable you to establish during which months an effort should be made to reduce demand and demand charges. For example, in Philadelphia, highest demand usually is recorded in July or August. If demand during both these months can be reduced, then demand charges for heating months (which cannot be less than "70% of the highest billing demand") will be lowered. Be certain to enter actual and billed demand in the correct columns. (Many smaller facilities do not pay a separate demand charge. In such cases, columns 6 and 7 should be left blank.)

Electricity—Cost—Total (Column 8): Enter the total cost of electricity for the month involved.

Electricity—Cost—Per Unit (Column 9): Obtain per unit cost by dividing total cost by kWh. This will enable you to compare costs of different months or of different buildings. This provides a possible means for determining if a billing error was made.

Purchased Steam—M (lbs.) (Column 10): Enter total steam consumption (in terms of thousands (M) of pounds) as shown on the bill.

Purchased Steam—M (lbs.)—Degree Days (Column 11): If steam is used for heating and/or cooling, divide quantity of steam by appropriate heating or cooling degree days, as for kWh.

Purchased Steam—Lbs./Hour Demand—Actual (Column 12): Enter actual demand as shown on the bill.

Purchased Steam—Lbs./Hour Demand—Billed (Column 13): Enter billed demand as shown on the utility bill. The difference between actual and billed demand is essentially similar to the difference involved for electricity.

Purchased Steam—Cost—Total (Column 14): Enter total cost as shown on the bill for the appropriate period involved.

Purchased Steam—Cost—Per Unit (Column 15): Divide total cost by quantity (M (Lbs.)) and enter.

Fuel—Oil—Quantity—Gallons (Column 16): Enter the amount of fuel oil actually *consumed* during the month, which is not necessarily the amount purchased. By knowing how much was on hand at the beginning of the month, how much was added, and how much was left at the end of the month, you will be able to determine the consumption factor.

Fuel—Oil—Cost—Total (Column 17): Multiply the per gallon cost shown on the bill by the amount of oil used during the month.

Fuel—Oil—Cost—Per Unit (Column 18): Enter the per unit cost shown on the bill.

Other Fuels: Enter as appropriate (in Columns 19, 20 and 21) the total monthly amount for each additional form of fuel—such as natural gas or coal—and calculate total cost and per unit cost as shown for electricity or oil.

Fuel—Fuel/Degree Day (Column 22): Make the necessary computation (total amount of fuel divided by number of degree days) and enter the result only if one of the "other" fuels is used for heating and/or cooling. Divide quantity of fuel used for heating during a heating month by the number of heating degree days for the month. Divide quantity of fuel used for cooling during a cooling month by the number of cooling degree days for the month.

Total Energy Cost (Column 23): Add Columns 8, 14, 17 and 20 and enter.

Building Data: The essential data required here is the gross conditioned (heated and/or cooled) square footage of the building involved. Gross conditioned square footage is determined easily by measuring inside wall-to-wall distance of each floor, including the basement (if conditioned). To determine gross conditioned, square footage of the building simply add together the gross square footage of conditioned area on all floors. Other information you may wish to insert here—or in a separate notebook—could relate to building systems, equipment and operations, deviations from normal modes of operation (which could explain differences in energy consumption patterns), etc.

BTU Conversion: Annual energy consumption is determined easily by multiplying the total annual amount of a given energy form (Columns 4, 10, 16, and 19) by the appropriate conversion factor. The result in each case is the BTU equivalent of energy consumed. Add together to determine total BTU's consumed for the year.

Energy Utilization Index: Energy utilization index (BTU's per gross square foot per year) is determined easily by dividing total annual energy consumption in BTU's consumed by the total gross square footage of the building. As mentioned above, EUIs can and should also be determined on a monthly basis.

2. SETTING THE ENERGY CONSERVATION GOAL

Once you have completed the Energy Management Form to develop base-year data, you will have an overview of the energy consumption patterns of your building. As such, you will be in a position to set your initial goals.

It is advised that your initial goal be set in terms of a quantity, for example, a 10% or 12% reduction. (Note that the reduction is in terms of energy and not energy costs. It is very possible to reduce consumption but still see energy costs rise if rate increases are significant enough.) The quantity selected should not be simply "picked from a hat." It should be a realistic, preliminary amount made in light of business objectives, economics, financial resources, personnel resources, existing methods of building operation and maintenance, and existing uses of energy and potential for conservation. This last element—potential for conservation—is of particular importance. Therefore, you should at least become passingly familiar with some of the energy conservation options discussed in this manual to determine how many can be applied to your building. Once your building survey is complete, you will be in a far better position to make your goal more specific. If an outside consultant is involved in conducting the survey (as is suggested), he probably will be able to help you set goals, too.

Goals will vary from year to year. Obviously, you cannot go along conserving the same amount or same percentage of energy year after year. Therefore, your ultimate goal eventually will be maintenance of the highest degree of energy efficiency possible and to ensure maintenance of this level by continuing review of data collected.

In evaluating the true effects of your program consider the following discussion on climatic adjustment.

3. CLIMATIC ADJUSTMENT

As already mentioned, it is difficult to compare energy consumption from one year to the next without taking into consideration those varying climatological factors—temperature, wind, humidity, precipitation, cloud cover, etc.—which have an impact primarily on a building's heating, ventilating and cooling system. What is needed, obviously, is some means whereby climatological factors can be indexed and then integrated with consumption data so energy consumption in the base year, or during a portion of the base year, can be compared to a subsequent year or period on the basis of identical climatological conditions. Although a substantial amount of research is going on to develop some type simple conversion factor or easily utilized tables and charts, none now exists. As a result, you should rely on one of two methods which can result in a reasonable basis for comparison.

The first method is to contact your local gas or electric utility. In most cases both have material on climatic factors readily available and utilize the degree day method—adjusted for local conditions—to determine their own future requirements. Chances are members of the utility's energy management staff can review data concerning your building and give you a reasonably accurate appraisal of how your EUI data can be adjusted for the impact of weather.

The second method, which can be used in conjunction with the first, requires you to gather historical energy consumption data on your building perhaps for the past five years.

Building _____

Month	Heating Deg. Days	Cooling Deg. Days	Electricity							Purchased		
			KWH	KWH/ Deg. Days	KW Demand		Cost		M (lbs.)	M (lbs.)/ Deg. Days	lbs/hr
					Actual	Billed	Total	Per Ut.			Actual
1	2	3	4	5	6	7	8	9	10	11	12
Jan.											
Feb.											
March											
1st Quarter											
April											
May											
June											
2nd Quarter											
July											
Aug.											
Sept.											
3rd Quarter											
Oct.											
Nov.											
Dec.											
4th Quarter											
Total Per Year											

Building Data

Gross Conditioned Area (ft)^2 _____

Gen Notes: _____

_____

_____

Annual Energy Consumption In BTU's
    Quantity
1. _____ kWh
    Electricity
2. _____ (M) lbs
    Purchased Steam
3. _____ MCF
    Natural Gas
4. _____ Gallons
    Oil
5. _____
    Other Fuel

_____ Year

Steam			Fuel								Total Energy Cost
			Oil			Check Gas ☐ Coal ☐ Other ☐				Fuel/ Deg. Days	
Demand	Cost		Quant. (Gal.)	Cost		Quant.	Cost				
Billed	Total	Per Unit		Total	Per Unit		Total	Per Unit			
13	14	15	16	17	18	19	20	21	22		23

	Conversion Fac.	BTU/Yr
X	3413	= _____
X	1,000,000.	= _____
X	1,030,000.	= _____
X	#2- 138,700 #6- 149,700	= _____
X	_____	= _____
	6. Total	_____

Energy Utilization Index

$$EUI = \frac{\text{Total Energy Consumption BTU's/yr}}{\text{Gross Conditioned Area (ft)}^2}$$

$$= \underline{\hspace{3cm}} \text{ BTU's/ft}^2/\text{Yr}$$

You probably will be able to rely on your own records and those which the utility may have. Obtain data on heating and cooling degree days for your area for the same period from the National Climatic Center, Asheville, North Carolina. Analyze the relationship between heating and cooling degree days (and other weather factors) and energy consumption in your building (assuming that the HVAC system, load and operating and maintenance practices have remained relatively unchanged over the period under review). The more detailed your review, the more factors which can be considered and the more accurate your adjustment can be.

CONDUCTING A BUILDING V. SURVEY

Performance of a building survey is absolutely fundamental to the successful development and implementation of a TEM program. It is essential that the survey be made by persons who know exactly what they are looking for and who can present findings in an unbiased manner. It is suggested that the program be conducted in a professional manner as by a consulting engineer. Whether the survey is conducted in-house or by a consultant, those performing it must be expert enough to recognize a possible source of wasted energy. A consulting engineer, because of his extensive experience and diversified knowledge, may recognize that the way in which the specific function is being conducted could be altered to provide significant savings. Likewise, a consulting engineer may note that maintenance is not being performed as it should be and may recommend procedures which can provide better direction. You may, of course, want to have in-house personnel undertake the survey. For this reason, the discussion presented in the following section provides, in addition to other materials, information on what to look for when making the survey.

Whoever conducts the survey first should obtain a copy of the architectural, mechanical and electrical design drawings and specifications to familiarize himself with the building's configuration and design as well as electrical and mechanical systems and equipment layout, operation and control. If such drawings are not available, it may be necessary to develop single-line diagrams of existing mechanical and electrical systems. The surveyor also should be given access to any written maintenance and operating procedures manuals supplied by equipment manufacturers or original building design professionals. He also should be familiar with utility rate schedules as well as any materials which relate to any planned building modernization programs and their applications. Much of this information can be recorded in a form such as shown in Appendix A.

Once the surveyor has familiarized himself with the various building systems and equipment data, the next step is to conduct a walk-through survey. Obviously, if the building is not owner-occupied, it first will be necessary to obtain the approval and full cooperation of tenants, as discussed in Section VII. The basic tools required for such a survey

include pen or pencil and paper, although a tape recorder may prove to be a valuable substitute. In addition, a camera could prove valuable to illustrate and document certain critical areas. Instruments required, such as light meters, psychrometers, etc., are mentioned in the following section.

The items which require investigation and analysis are discussed in full in the following section. Just a quick glance indicates that some of the most critical areas include: ventilation system operation and controls and how they can be improved; airtightness of the building and how infiltration can be reduced; heating and cooling equipment, maintenance and controls and method of improving their efficiency; lighting and lighting levels and how they can be modified; transmission characteristics and how they can be modified; tenant procedures and how they may be contributing to excessive energy consumption and so on. Assuming that in-house personnel will not be making the survey, it will be necessary for the surveyor to interview them to determine exactly how they go about performing their jobs and what ideas they have for energy conservation measures. In this regard, it is worthwhile to re-emphasize that every effort must be made to ensure that in-house operating, maintenance and other personnel do not see the survey conducted by an outside source as a challenge to their own ability or credibility. In many cases the cooperation of in-house personnel is essential for proper conduct of the survey.

The survey should result in a thorough report which details each and every fault of energized systems, nonenergized systems and human systems as they relate to excessive energy consumption. The report also should contain a list of alternative actions which can be undertaken to remedy each fault in light of building interrelationships. It also may be practical to include the expected cost of such modifications when costs are involved. In addition, the report should indicate what type of equipment and controls should be added to the various systems, or what new procedures, such as development of a lighting schedule, can be developed to reduce energy consumption. Total costs involved, payback periods and return on investment for these undertakings also can be included. In addition, you also may specify that the survey report indicate priorities (discussed in Section VII) in light of factors you establish as criteria.

Whenever a possible change is such that a significant capital outlay is involved, and/or that the retrofitting possibly may result in closing a portion of the building for a period of time, or an action of similar impact, it is suggested strongly that the action be justified by means of a feasibility study. Such studies will provide the full, in-depth information required to base a decision on all relevant facts. While the retrofitting opportunities which are subject to feasibility studies may be mentioned in a report, the feasibility study itself usually is far more detailed and prepared subsequent to review of the initial study, in full light of other alternatives which exist.

GUIDELINES FOR ENERGY VI. CONSERVATION

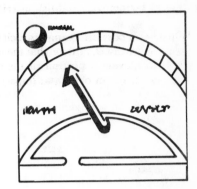

This section identifies and discusses numerous different ways in which office buildings and retail stores can be made more energy efficient. Guidance presented can be applied during the survey to establish what specifically should be looked at, as well as in determination of which energy conservation opportunities should be pursued, and how. The scope of these guidelines is necessarily broad to provide discussion of the many alternative types of sub-systems which could exist in any given building. As a result, some of the items discussed—especially in the area of heating and cooling equipment—will not be applicable to your particular building. Except as noted, however, most discussion is applicable to both retail stores and office buildings.

The specific alternatives discussed are broken into two categories: MINIMAL EXPENSE and SIGNIFICANT EXPENSE. In certain cases some of the minimal expense items are checkmarked (√) to indicate that they involve virtually no cost at all; have little or no impact on occupant comfort and business productivity, and can be implemented immediately to reduce wastage of energy. Such steps would include, for example, lowering thermostats set at abnormally high levels during the heating season; being sure that lights, equipment, machinery and appliances are turned off when an area is not in use; keeping heat exchanger surfaces and filters clean; stopping leakage of conditioned air and water, steam condensate, fuel oil and gas, etc. In all cases, such actions—in fact, all energy conservation actions—should be undertaken in a manner consistent with comfort, production, process and other requirements of building occupants.

It must be borne in mind that the cost categorization has been supplied primarily for reference purposes. While cost is a major factor in establishing which alternatives to pursue, one also must consider the benefits involved. More-over, cost factors vary from building to building, depending on the extent and capabilities of in-house personnel, accounting methods, and so on.

Before determining exactly which alternatives to pursue, it is suggested strongly that you first identify those alternatives applicable to your building. Since it is unlikely that you will be able to pursue all of them during the first or even second year of your TEM program, it probably will be most effective to determine which group of alternatives—in the aggregate—will fall within budget and yield maximum benefits.

As a last note, recognize that the following discussion addresses itself primarily to components of various systems. This approach has been utilized to reduce needless repetition in that two entirely different systems may have many components in common, such as fans, motors, etc. Nonetheless, some repetition does exist where required for better understanding of material covered. It is advised, therefore, that the index be utilized to establish all places where a given component or other subject is discussed.

1. VENTILATION

Ventilation has significant impact on a building's total energy consumption. Each cubic foot of air brought into the building must be either heated or cooled and, in some cases, humidified and/or dehumidified. It is generally agreed that many building codes demand an amount of ventilation in excess of what actually is required to provide for the safety and comfort of building occupants. Because many building code officials also recognize this, they often are willing to allow changes to ventilation systems which will drop CFM rates below those nominally required, providing that such changes are not irreversible. Of course, the approval of code authorities must be obtained before you undertake any changes which will result in violation of the applicable codes as written. Guidelines for action are as follows:

MINIMAL EXPENSE

a. Reduce outdoor air to the minimum required to balance the exhaust requirements and maintain a slight positive pressure to retard infiltration-caused heat losses and heat gains.

√b. Inspect all outdoor air dampers. They should be as airtight as possible when closed. Check operation of position indicators for accuracy.

525

install, repair, or replace position indicators as needed.

c. Reduce or eliminate the need for using outdoor air for odor control by installing chemical or activated charcoal odor-absorbing devices.

√d. Inspect filters carefully. If necessary, create a filter replacement schedule. Utilize high-efficiency, low-cost filters.

√e. Reduce exhaust air quantities as practical.

f. Close outdoor air dampers during the first and last hour of occupancy when the air must be heated or cooled, except when operating on economizer cycle.

√g. Establish a ventilation operation schedule so exhaust system operates only when it is needed most.

h. Add a warm-up cycle to air handling units with outdoor air intake. Keep outdoor air dampers closed during morning building warm-up or cool-down so only air already in the building is conditioned. Cycle can be incorporated using a two-circuit time clock to control air damper and fan operation.

i. Use exhaust hoods in food preparation and laboratory areas only while operations are underway. Add control dampers or gravity damper to keep the air path in the exhaust duct closed when fan is not operating.

j. If a food preparation area exhaust hood is oversized, adjust it so no more air than necessary is exhausted. This can be done easily by blocking off a portion of the hood, or reducing fan speed, or lowering hood, or by utilizing a combination of these techniques in compliance with applicable health regulations.

k. Consider cutting off direct outdoor air supply to toilet rooms and other potentially "odorous" areas. Permit air from other areas to migrate into such areas through door grilles and be exhausted.

l. If possible, concentrate smoking areas together so they can be served by one exhaust system.

m. Consider adding controls to shut down the ventilation system whenever the building is closed for an extended period of time, as during the evening, weekends, etc., except when the economizer cycle is in use.

n. Reduce volume of toilet exhausts in buildings which have multiple toilet exhaust fans having a total fan capacity in excess of outside air requirements. This can be done by wiring a fan interlock into toilet room lights through a timed relay, so the fan is activated only when lights are on. An administrative request plus signs to the effect that lights should be turned off when the room is not in use will help ensure that lights (and thus the fan) are off when the room is not being used. Another method involves dampering down air volume so only that amount of air required by code is removed.

o. If a large occupant load is involved, consider installing remotely adjustable outside air dampers. These permit outside air volume to be adjusted in approximate proportion to current occupancy.

p. Install baffles to prevent wind from blowing directly into an outdoor air intake.

q. Supply ventilated air to parking garages to levels indicated by CO_2 monitoring system.

SIGNIFICANT EXPENSE

r. Consider installing economizer enthalpy controls to air handling units in offices to minimize cooling energy required by using proper amounts of outdoor and return air to permit "free cooling" by outside air when possible.

s. When more than 10,000 CFM is involved, and when building configuration permits, consider installation of heat recovery devices such as a rotary heat exchanger. For some climatic conditions an "enthalpy wheel," which permits recovery of some 75% of outdoor heat load during both heating and cooling cycles, will be feasible. (See Section 11.1 of this chapter.)

t. Modify duct systems and hoods to introduce unheated outdoor or return air directly to the exhaust hood. Weigh this against changing hoods to new high velocity hoods which require less make up air.

2. INFILTRATION

Unwanted outside air infiltrates into a building through inadvertent openings in the building envelope, open doors, etc. Since outdoor air, regardless of source, must be heated or cooled (and sometimes humidified and/or dehumidified), infiltration imposes a significant load on the heating and cooling system, increasing total energy consumption. The problem of infiltration is appreciably worse in tall buildings, which usually must contend with "stack effect." This occurs because of the difference in density between warm indoor air and cold outdoor air. As indoor air is heated it becomes lighter and tends to rise, eventually leaving the building through upper floors. The hot air is replaced by a continual flow of cold air entering the building through any available opening. The upflow of air increases with the height of the structure.

The following guidelines should be observed to inspect for sources of and reduce infiltration, regardless of building height or configuration.

2.1 Windows and Skylights

MINIMAL EXPENSE

√a. Replace broken or cracked window panes.

√b. Replace worn or broken weatherstripping around operable windows. If possible, install weatherstripping where none was installed previously.

√c. Weatherstrip operable sash if crack is evident.

√d. Caulk around window frames (exterior and interior) if cracks are evident.

√e. Rehang misaligned windows.

√f. Be certain that all operable windows have sealing gaskets and cam latches that are in proper working order.

√g. Consider posting a small sign next to each operable window instructing occupants not to open window while the building is being heated or cooled.

SIGNIFICANT EXPENSE

h. Install tightfitting storm windows where practical.

2.2 Doors

MINIMAL EXPENSE

√a. Replace any worn or broken weatherstripping. Install weatherstripping where none has been installed previously.

√b. Rehang misaligned doors.

√c. Caulk around door frames.

√d. Inspect all automatic door closers to ensure they are functioning properly. Consider adjustment to enable faster closing.

√e. Inspect gasketing on garage and other overhead doors. Repair, replace or install as necessary.

√f. Consider placing a small sign next to each door leading to the exterior or unconditioned spaces advising occupants to keep door closed at all times when not in use.

√g. Consider installing signs on exterior walls near delivery doors providing instructions to delivery personnel on operation of doors.

√h. Establish rules for all building personnel regarding opening and closing of doors, directing them to keep them closed whenever possible.

i. Consider installing automatic door closers on all doors leading to the exterior or unconditioned spaces.

j. If the building has a garage but does not have a garage door, consider installing one, preferably motorized to enable easier opening and closing.

k. Consider use of a card-, key- or radio frequency-operated garage door which stays closed at all times except when in use.

SIGNIFICANT EXPENSE

l. Consider making delivery entrances smaller. The larger the opening, the more air that infiltrates when doors are open.

m. Consider using an expandable enclosure for delivery ports. It reduces infiltration when in use because it can be adjusted to meet the back of a truck reducing substantially the amount of air which otherwise would infiltrate.

n. Consider installation of an air curtain, especially in delivery areas. The device prevents penetration of unconditioned air by forcing a layer of air of predetermined thickness and velocity over the entire entrance opening. (An expert in the field should be consulted before obtaining such a device, especially when highrise structures are involved. The degree of stack effect, among other things, determines its usability.)

o. Consider installation of a vestibule for the front entrance of a building, where practical. It should be fitted with self-closing weatherstripped doors. It is critical that sufficient distance between doors is provided.

p. Consider utilizing revolving doors for the front entrance. Studies have shown that such devices allow far less air to infiltrate with each entrance or exit. Use of revolving doors in both elements of a vestibule is even more effective. If high peak traffic is involved, swinging doors can be used to supplement revolving doors.

q. In locations, where strong winds occur for long durations, consider installing wind screens to protect external doors from direct blast of prevailing winds, screens can be opaque, constructed cheaply from concrete block or can be transparent, constructed of metal framing with armored glass. Careful positioning is necessary for infiltration control.

2.3 Exterior Surfaces

MINIMAL EXPENSE

√a. Caulk, gasket or otherwise weatherstrip all exterior joints, such as those between wall and foundation or wall and roof, and between wall panels.

√b. Caulk, gasket or otherwise weatherstrip all openings, such as those provided for entrance of electrical conduits, piping, through-the-wall cooling and other units, outside air louvers, etc.

c. Where practical, cover all window and through-the-wall cooling units when not in use. Specially designed covers can be obtained at relatively low cost.

3. HEATING AND COOLING

As already mentioned, heating and cooling together usually consume the largest single "block" of energy utilized by a building during the course of a year. In most cases, however, the heating/cooling system was designed only with initial costs in mind. As a result, the energy efficiency of the system seldom was a design criterion. Moreover, most systems were designed to meet extreme conditions which possibly could occur, but which seldom do. Accordingly, many are oversized and so perform in an inefficient manner.

There are many ways in which heating and cooling systems can be made more efficient. In general, these alternatives can be divided into four categories: operating practices modifications, maintenance modifications, systems modifications, and control adjustment and modifications.

3.1 Operating Practices Modifications (General)

Significant heating and cooling energy savings can be achieved simply by modifying the manner in which heating and cooling systems are operated. Several facts should be emphasized strongly, however:

- Operational savings are limited. While changes in operational procedures can save energy and energy costs, the net amount represents but a fraction of the potential which can be saved through other, more substantive measures. In other words, do not use operational savings as an excuse not to undertake other, potentially more beneficial measures.
- Operational savings will, in some cases, cause minor deviation from accepted standards of comfort. Some deviations may be more noticed than others.
- Professional assistance and guidance should be obtained before instituting any significant operational change. As an example, in certain situations setting a thermostat to 68 degrees during the heating season can cause the cooling system to be activated, wasting more energy than is conserved. (This situation was documented in a 25-story midwestern office building at a cost of $1,000 for three hours of winter cooling.) Likewise, setting thermostats at 78°F during the cooling season can bring on heating or reheat.
- Remember that each building represents a unique situation. As such, the guidelines outlined herein should be recognized as general only. Each must be tailored for the building involved, preferably with professional guidance.

Here follow some of the guidelines for the more effective changes which can be made in operational routine to effect energy savings:

MINIMAL EXPENSE

√a.   Reduce use of heating and cooling systems in spaces which are used infrequently or only for short periods of time.

√b.   Heat office building to 68°F when occupied, to 60° when unoccupied. This does not mean that air should be cooled if the temperature exceeds 68°F. Interior office spaces tend to experience significant heat gains due to lighting, equipment and people. Systems serving most areas use a combination of recirculated inside air and some outside air. As a result, the temperature may tend to stay at or above 68°F.

√c.   Preheat building so that it achieves 65°F by the time occupants arrive. Complete warm-up during the first hour of occupancy. Lighting, people and use of equipment will aid in warm-up.

√d.   Turn heat off during last hour of occupancy.

√e.   Cool office building to 78°F when occupied. Do not utilize mechanical cooling when unoccupied. Special consideration, however, must be given to computer rooms. Generally, the primary criterion is a constant temperature/humidity relationship. Manufacturers should be contacted to determine permissible ranges. Cooling usually is required when the equipment is operated, but should not be used to lower room temperature below the range of 78°F-80°.

√f.   Begin precooling operations so the building is at 80°F, by the time occupants arrive. Complete cool-down during the first hour of occupancy.

√g.   Maintain retail store sales area temperatures at 68°F during the heating season and at 78°F during the cooling season.

√h.   Isolate storage room areas from sales area. Maintain storage areas at 60°F or lower in winter.

√i.   Shut off all heating in garages, docks and platform areas.

√j.   Consider closing outside air dampers during the first and last hours of occupancy and during peak loads.

√k.   During cooling season evening and night hours, flush the building with cooler outdoor air.

√l.   Allow natural humidity variations from 20% R.H. to 60% R.H. in occupied spaces.

√m.   When appropriate, consider closing supply registers and radiators and reducing thermostat settings or turning off the electric heaters in lobbies. corridors and vestibules.

√n.   Where sill height electric heaters are used, adjust thermostat so heat provided is just sufficient to prevent cold downdrafts from reaching the floor.

√o.   Turn off humidifiers whenever the building is closed for extended periods of time, except when process or equipment requirements take precedence.

√p.   Evaluate the necessity of humidification system and curtail humidification for areas such as hallways, equipment rooms, lobbies, laundry areas, and similar spaces.

√q.   Turn off portable electric heaters and portable fans when not needed or during unoccupied periods.

√r.   Turn on self-contained units, such as window and through-the-wall units, only when needed. Turn them off when the space is to be unoccupied for several hours.

√s.   In mild weather, lower the cooling effect by running room cooling fans at lower speeds.

√t.   Turn off all noncritical exhaust fans.

√u.   Turn off reheat in all areas during summer, except where equipment requirements necessitate humidity control.

√v.   When the sun is not shining during the heating season, close interior shading devices to reduce radiation from body to cold window surfaces.

√w. Develop an after-hours equipment operation checklist for use by custodial and other building personnel as well as occupants who may use various spaces after normal periods of occupancy.

√x. Schedule operating and maintenance work during the daytime, if possible.

√y. Wear heavier clothing during the heating season and lighter clothing during the cooling season.

√z. Reduce internal heat generation as much as possible during the cooling season. Typical sources of heat generation include lighting, people, machines, cooking equipment, etc.

SIGNIFICANT EXPENSE

aa. Adjust and balance system to minimize overcooling and overheating which result from poor zoning, poor distribution, improper location of controls, or improper control.

3.2 Operating Practices (Central Plant)

Once other changes have been made to affect the building's heating and cooling loads, certain changes can be made to central plant operating practices. The importance of several factors must be recognized.

- Certain operational changes accomplished through manual control also can be made through automatic control. Compare the efficiency and cost of both methods and consider the potential impact of likely future changes before determining which way to go.
- Obtain assistance when required. The complexity, cost and importance of central plants demand that those making changes know exactly what they are doing.
- Be certain to maintain daily operational logs to determine the effectiveness of the system, impact of a modification, and times when additional modifications may be required.

Some of the basic operational modifications which can be made to chillers and boilers are as follows:

MINIMAL EXPENSE

√a. Shutdown central heating, ventiliating and air conditioning equipment during unoccupied periods to achieve substantial savings.

Examine building for actual utilization and determine what has to be done to permit maximum shutdown of energy consuming equipment during periods when buildings have few or no occupants; during nights, weekends, and vacation periods. Experience has shown that only a small portion of a building actually requires night or 24-hour operation. Often a small unitary air conditioning system designed to serve a room or few rooms will permit substantial shutdowns of large central systems.

If central air systems are required to operate to provide the only source of heat for a building, it would occur only during a relatively few hours of the year. As such, a low limit night thermostat can be provided to start the system on a full heating mode with all outdoor air dampers closed to operate as required to keep the building at a temperature such as 60°F. A thermostat of this type is controlled by a time clock which, at a predetermined hour, starts and stops selected fan units and/or opens or closes automatic water or steam valves to maintain the desired temperature. In many cases this unit will have to operate on an infrequent basis due to the thermal storage effects of building energy. As a result, separate convector or radiation hot water systems, in buildings which have them, normally can provide adequate heat during unoccupied periods without operating large central supply air systems. Often these radiation systems can be completely shut off at all temperatures of 35°F to 45°F and above depending upon the building envelope involved: the amount of glass, wall construction, etc.

When the HVAC system is de-energized during unoccupied periods, it is essential that outside air dampers be closed tightly. Inspect them to be sure that they make a tight seal. Repair or replace them as required. Likewise, exhaust fans which interlock with outside air fans also should be closed. The only exceptions to these guidelines would be when an economizer cycle is used at night during the cooling season to use cooler outside air to lower indoor temperature instead of the mechanical cooling system.

If, after shut down, the cooling system is not capable of achieving and maintaining temperature and humidity conditions in hot spells, install controls to activate the equipment a few hours before occupancy instead of operating the system all night or throughout the entire weekend.

√b. Operate one of multiple compressors and chillers at full load, rather than two or more at part loads.

√c. Operate condenser water system at lower temperatures.

√d. Operate only the chilled water pumps and cooling tower fans necessary.

√e. Elevate chilled water temperatures when humidity conditions permit.

√f. Operate boilers at lower pressure and temperatures in accordance with space heating demand.

√g. Consider elimination of hot standby boilers since, in many cases, a boiler failure will not cause serious hardship.

√h. Operate only the heating water pumps necessary.

√i. Examine operating procedures when more than one boiler is involved. It is far better to operate one boiler at 90% capacity than two at 45% capacity each. The more boilers used, the greater the heat loss.

√j. Check flue gas analysis on periodic basis: the efficient combustion of fuel in a boiler requires burner adjustment to achieve proper stack temperature, CO_2 and excess air settings. Check settings to provide stack temperatures of no more than 150°F above steam or water temperature. There should be no carbon monoxide. For a gas fired unit, CO2 should be present at 9 or 10%. For #2 oil, 11.5–12.8%; for #6 oil, 13–13.8%.

√ k. **Adjust Air/Fuel Ratios of Firing Equipment:** The air to fuel ratio must be maintained properly. If there is insufficient air, the fire will smoke, cause tubes to become covered with soot and carbon, and thus lower heat transfer efficiency. If too much air is used, unused air is heated by combustion and exhausted up the stack wasting energy. Most fuel service companies will test your units for a token fee and provide you with specific recommendations.

3.3 Operating Practices Modification (Kitchen and Cafeteria Areas)

A variety of steps can be taken to effect more efficient use of energy in kitchen, cafeteria and other food-handling areas:

MINIMAL EXPENSE

√ a. Turn off infrared food warmers when no food is being warmed.

√ b. Inspect refrigeration condensers routinely to ensure that they have sufficient air circulation and that dust is cleaned off coils.

√ c. Inspect and repair walk-in or reach-in refrigerated area doors without automatic closers or tight gaskets.

√ d. Train employees in conservation of hot water. Supervise their performance and provide additional instruction and supervision as necessary.

√ e. Avoid using fresh hot or warm water for dish scraping.

√ f. Keep refrigeration coils free of frost build-up.

√ g. Clean and maintain refrigeration on water chillers and cold drink dispensers.

√ h. Reduce temperature or turn off frying tables and coffee urns during off-peak periods.

√ i. Preheat ovens only for baked goods. Discourage chefs from preheating any sooner than necessary.

√ j. Run the dishwasher only when it is filled.

√ k. Cook with lids in place on pots and kettles. It can cut heat requirements in half.

√ l. Thaw frozen foods in refrigerated compartments.

√ m. Fans that cool workers should be directed so they do not cool cooking equipment.

√ n. Consider using microwave ovens for thawing and fast-food preparation whenever they can serve to reduce power requirements.

3.4 Maintenance Modifications

The importance of good maintenance to a program of energy management cannot be overemphasized. Not only will effective maintenance help ensure efficient operation of equipment and systems, but it also will help prolong the usable life of equipment.

The maintenance guidelines presented herein all should be performed to at least bring systems up to efficiency. They also should be continued on a regularly scheduled basis depending on the nature of your system, frequency of operation, etc. Inspection of many of the items mentioned also will provide you with some idea about the effectiveness of the maintenance program now in effect and the condition

of your equipment, some of which may need adjustment, repair or replacement.

Realize that these guidelines are general only. Wherever possible, the manufacturer of the equipment involved should be contacted to obtain pertinent literature describing the maintenance procedures suggested. Otherwise, those who regularly install such equipment, or who design heating and cooling systems, should be asked to prepare manuals or guidelines.

3.4.1 Refrigeration Equipment

Efficiency of refrigeration equipment can be improved considerably through following proper maintenance procedures. The following guidelines are suggested:

a. Circuit and Controls

MINIMAL EXPENSE

√ i. Inspect moisture-liquid indicator on a regular basis. If the color of the refrigerant indicates "wet," it means there is moisture in the system. This is a particularly critical problem because it can cause improper operation or costly damage. A competent mechanic should be called in to perform necessary adjustments and repairs immediately. Also, if there are bubbles in the refrigerant flow as seen through the moisture-liquid indicator, it may indicate that the system is low in refrigerant. Call in a mechanic to add refrigerant if necessary and to inspect equipment for possible refrigerant leakage.

√ ii. Use a leak detector to check for refrigerant and oil leaks around shaft seal, sight glasses, valve bonnets, flanges, flare connections, relief valve on the condenser assembly and at pipe joints to equipment, valves and instrumentation.

√ iii. Inspect equipment for any visual changes such as oil spots on connections or on the floor under equipement.

√ iv. Inspect the liquid line leaving the strainer. If it feels cooler than the liquid line entering the strainer, it is clogged. If it is very badly clogged, sweat or frost may be visible at the strainer outlet. Clean as required.

√ v. Observe the noise made by the system. Any unusual sounds could indicate a problem. Determine cause and correct.

√ vi. Establish what normal operating pressures and temperatures for the system should be. Check all gauges frequently to ensure that design conditions are being met. Increased system pressure may be due to dirty condensers, which will decrease system efficiency. High discharge temperatures often are caused by defective or broken compressor valves.

√ vii. Inspect tension and alignment of all belts and adjust as necessary.

√ viii. Where applicable, lubricate motor bearings and all moving parts according to manufacturer's recommendations.

√ ix. Inspect insulation on suction and liquid lines.

b. Compressor

MINIMAL EXPENSE

√ i. Look for unusual compressor operation such as continuous running or frequent stopping and starting, either of which may indicate inefficient operation. Determine the cause and, if necessary, correct.

√ ii. Observe the noise made by the compressor. If it seems to be excessively noisy, it may be a sign of a loose drive coupling or excessive vibration. Tighten compressor and motor on the base. If noise persists, call a competent mechanic.

√ iii. Check all compressor joints for leakage. Seal as necessary.

√ v. Inspect instrumentation frequently to ensure that operating oil pressure and temperature agree with manufacturer's specifications.

c. Air-Cooled Condenser

MINIMAL EXPENSE

√ i. Keep fan belt drive and motor properly aligned and lubricated.

√ ii. Inspect refrigeration piping connections to the condenser coil for tightness. Repair all leaks.

√ iii. Keep condenser coil face clean to permit proper air flow.

√ iv. Determine if hot air is being bypassed from the fan outlet to the coil inlet. If so, correct the problem.

d. Evaporative Condenser

MINIMAL EXPENSE

√ i. Inspect piping joints and seal all leaks.

√ ii. Remove all dirt from the coil surface by washing it down with high velocity water jets or a nylon brush.

√ iii. Inspect air inlet screen, spray nozzle or water distribution holes, and pump screen. Clean as necessary.

√ iv. Use water treatment techniques if local water supply leaves surface deposits on the coil.

√ v. Follow guidelines for fan and pump maintenance.

e. Watercooled Condenser

MINIMAL EXPENSE

i. Clean condenser shell and tubes by swabbing with a suitable brush and flushing out with clean water. Chemical cleaning also is possible, although it is suggested that a water treatment company be consulted first.

f. Cooling Towers

MINIMAL EXPENSE

√ i. Perform chemical treatment to determine if solid concentrations are being maintained at an acceptable level.

√ ii. Check overflow pipe clearance for proper operating water level.

√ iii. Check fan by listening for any unusual noise or vibration. Inspect condition of V-belt. Align fan and motor as necessary.

√ iv. Follow guidelines for fan maintenance.

√ v. Keep the tower clean to minimize both air and water pressure drop.

√ vi. Clean intake strainer.

√ vii. Determine if there is air bypass from tower outlet back to inlet. If so, bypass may be reduced through addition of baffles or higher discharge stacks.

√ viii. Inspect spray filled or distributed towers for proper nozzle performance. Clean nozzles as necessary.

√ ix. Inspect gravity distributed tower for even water depth in distribution basins.

√ x. Monitor effectiveness of any water treatment program which may be underway.

g. Chillers

MINIMAL EXPENSE

√ i. Chillers must be kept clean. Inspect on a regular basis. Clean as necessary.

ii. Inspect for evidence of clogging. A qualified mechanic should be called in to service equipment in accordance with manufacturer's specifications.

h. Absorption equipment

MINIMAL EXPENSE

√ i. Clean strainer and seal tank on a regular basis.

√ ii. Lubricate flow valves on a regular basis.

√ iii. Follow manufacturers instructions for proper maintenance.

i. Self-Contained Units. (Windows and through-the-wall units; heat pump, etc.)

MINIMAL EXPENSE

√ i. Clean evaporator and condenser coils.

√ ii. Keep air intake louvers, filters and controls clean.

√ iii. Keep air flow from units unrestricted.

√ iv. Caulk openings between unit and windows or wall frames.

√ v. Check voltage. Full power voltage is essential for proper operation.

√ vi. Follow applicable guidelines suggested for compressor, air-cooled condenser and fans.

3.4.2 Heating Equipment

There are numerous different kinds of heating systems installed in existing office buildings and retail stores. Certain common maintenance guidelines to improve efficiency of operation include the following:

a. Boilers (General)

MINIMAL EXPENSE

√ i. Inspect boilers for scale deposits, accummulation of sediment or boiler compounds on water side surfaces. Rear portion of the boiler must be checked because it is the area most susceptible to formation of scale. (Scale reduces the efficiency of the boiler and possibly can lead to overheating of furnace, cracking of tube ends and other problems.

√ ii. Fireside of the furnace and tubes must be inspected for deposits of soot, flyash and slag. Fireside refractory surface also must be observed. Soot on tubes decreases heat transfer and lowers efficiency. (If your boiler does not now have one, consider installation of thermometer in the vent outlet. It can save inspection time and often can prove to be more accurate than visual inspection alone.) If gas outlet temperature rises above normal, it can mean that tubes need cleaning. Evidence of heavy sooting in short periods could be a signal of too much fuel and not enough air. Adjustment of the air/fuel ratio is required to obtain clean burning fire.

√ iii. Inspect door gaskets. Replace them if they do not provide a tight seal.

√ iv. Keep a daily log of pressure, temperature and other data obtained from instrumentation. This is the best method available to determine the need for tube and nozzle cleaning, pressure or linkage adjustments, and related measures. Variations from normal can be spotted quickly, enabling immediate action to avoid serious trouble. On an oil-fired unit, indications of problems include an oil pressure drop, which may indicate a plugged strainer, faulty regulating valve, or an air leak in the suction line. An oil temperature drop can indicate temperature control malfunction or a fouled heating element. On a gas-fired unit, a drop in gas pressure can indicate a drop in the gas supply pressure or malfunctioning regulator.

√ v. Note firing rate when log entries are made. Realize that even a sharp rise in stack temperature does not necessarily mean poor combustion or fouled waterside or fireside. During load change, stack temperatures can vary as much as 100°F in five minutes.

√ vi. Inspect stacks. They should be free of haze. If not, it probably indicates that a burner adjustment is necessary.

√ vii. Inspect linkages periodically for tightness. Adjust when slippage or jerky movements are observed.

√ viii. Observe the fire when the unit shuts down. If the fire does not cut off immediately, it could indicate a faulty solenoid valve. Repair or replace as necessary.

√ ix. Inspect nozzles or cup of oil-fired units on a regular basis. Clean as necessary.

√ x. Check burner firing period. If it's improper, it could be a sign of faulty controls.

xi. Check boiler stack temperature. If it is too high (more than 150°F above steam or water temperature) clean tubes and adjust fuel burner.

√ xii. Inspect all boiler insulation, refractory, brickwork, and boiler casing for hot spots and air leaks. Repair and seal as necessary.

√ xiii. Replace all obsolete or little-used pressure vessels.

√ xiv. Clean mineral or corrosion build-up on gas burners.

b. Boilers (Fuel Oil)

MINIMAL EXPENSE

√ i. Check and repair oil leaks at pump glands, valves or relief valves.

√ ii. Inspect oil line strainers. Replace if dirty.

√ iii. Inspect oil heaters to ensure that oil temperatures are being maintained according to manufacturer's or oil supplier's recommendations.

c. Boilers (Coal-Fired)

MINIMAL EXPENSE

√ i. Inspect coal-fired stokers, grates and controls for efficient operation. If ashes contain an excessive amount of unburned coal, its's probably a sign of inefficient operation.

d. Boilers (Electric)

MINIMAL EXPENSE

√ i. Inspect electrical contacts and working parts of relays and maintain in good working order.

√ ii. Check heater elements for cleanliness. Replace as necessary.

√ iii. Check controls for proper operation. Adjust as necessary.

e. Central Furnaces, Make-Up Air Heaters and Unit Heaters

MINIMAL EXPENSE

√ i. All heat exchanger surfaces should be kept clean. Check air-to-fuel ratio and adjust as necessary.

√ ii. Inspect burner couplings and linkages.

√ iii. Inspect casing for air leaks and seal as necessary.

√ iv. Inspect insulation and repair or replace as necessary.

√ v. Follow guidelines suggested for fan and motor maintenance.

f. Radiators, Convectors, Baseboard and Finned Tube Units

MINIMAL EXPENSE

i. Inspect for obstructions in front of the unit and remove whenever possible. Air movement in and out of convector unit must be unrestricted.

ii. Air will sometimes collect in the high points of hydronic units. It must be vented to enable hot water to circulate freely throughout the system. Otherwise, the units will short cycle (go on and off quickly), wasting fuel.

iii. Heat transfer surfaces of radiators, convectors, baseboard and finned-tube units must be kept clean for efficient operation.

g. Electric Heating

MINIMAL EXPENSE

√ i.   Keep heat transfer surfaces of all electric heating units clean and unobstructed.

√ ii.   Keep air movement in and out of the units unobstructed.

√ iii. Inspect heating elements, controls and, as applicable, fans on a periodic basis to ensure proper functioning.

√ iv.   As appropriate, check reflectors on infrared heaters for proper beam direction and cleanliness.

√ v.   Determine if electric heating equipment is operating at rated voltage as necessary.

√ vi.   Check controls for proper operation.

3.4.3 Humidification and Dehumidification Equipment

To maintain peak operating efficiency, the following maintenance guidelines should be followed.

√ a. Remove lint and dust periodically from air dampers, fan parts, spray chamber and diffuser, controls starter, and eliminator.

√ b. Check equipment for carry-over. Carry-over may by maintained by adjusting eliminator seal gap, altering damper position, or changing air velocity.

√ c. Follow guidelines suggested for "Fan and Motor Maintenance".

3.4.4 Air Handling Equipment

Proper maintenance of air handling equipment can significantly improve its efficiency. Proper maintenance guidelines include:

MINIMAL EXPENSE

√ a. Inspect ductwork for air leakage. Seal all leaks by taping or caulking.

√ b. Inspect ductwork insulation. Repair or replace as necessary.

√ c. Utilize ductwork access openings to check for any obstructions such as loose hanging insulation (in lined ducts), loose turning vanes and accessories, and closed fire dampers. Adjust, repair or replace as necessary.

√ d. Inspect damper blades and linkages. Clean, oil and adjust them on a regular basis.

√ e. Inspect air valves in dual duct mixing boxes to insure full seating and minimum air leakage.

√ f. Inspect mixing dampers for proper operation.

√ g. Clean or replace air filters on a regular basis.

√ h. Inspect air heating, cooling and dehumidification coils for cleanliness. Coils can be kept clean by using a mixture of detergent and water in a high pressure (500 psig) portable cleaning unit.

√ i. Inspect for leakage around coils or out of the casing. Seal all leaks.

√ j. Inspect all room air outlets and inlets (diffusers, registers and grilles). They should be kept clean and free of all dirt and obstructions. Clean and remove obstructions as necessary.

√ h. Inspect air washers, and evaporative air cooling equipment for proper operation. Clean damper blades and linkages if so equipped. Inspect nozzles and clean as necessary.

√ l. If electronic air cleaners are installed, check them regularly for excessive accumulations on the ionizing and grounding plate section. Replace filter media if necessary. Follow manufacturer's written instructions whenever adjustment or maintenance is required.

√ m. Inspect humidifier/dehumidifier air dampers, fan parts, spray chamber, diffuser, controls, strainer and eliminator. All must be kept free of dirt, lint and other foreign particles. Clean eleminator wheel by directing a high pressure stream of water between blades.

√ n. Adjust all VAV (variable air volume) boxes so they operate precisely. This will prevent overheating or overcooling, both of which waste energy.

√ o. Follow guidelines suggested for fan maintenance.

3.4.5 Prime Movers—Motors, Engines Turbines

Proper maintenance of motors, engines and turbines can greatly improve operational efficiency and so eliminate energy consumption. The following maintenance guidelines are suggested.

a. Motors

√ i.   Check alignment of motor to equipment driven. Align and tighten as necessary.

√ ii.   Check for loose connections and bad contacts on a regular basis. Correct as necessary.

√ iii. Keep motors clean.

√ iv.   Eliminate excessive vibrations.

√ v.   Lubricate motor and drive bearings on a regular basis. This will help reduce friction and excessive torque which can result in overheating and power losses.

√ vi.   Replace worn bearings.

√ vii. Tighten belts and pulleys to eliminate excessive losses.

√ viii. Check for overheating. It could be an indication of a functional problem or lack of adequate ventilation.

√ ix.   Balance three-phase power sources to motors. An imbalance can create inefficient motor operation and use of more energy.

√ x.   Check for overvoltage or low voltage condition on motors. Correct as necessary.

b. Engines

√ i.   Follow manufacturers recommended maintenance procedure.

√ ii. Check fuel consumption and compare with design fuel consumption.

√ iii. Record and check cooling water temperatures daily. If cooling water temperatures exceed manufacturers recommendations, check temperature controls and correct as necessary.

c. Turbines

√ i.   Follow manufacturers recommended maintenance procedures.

√ ii. Daily record steam pressure and check speed.

√ iii. Regularly check oil level, packing leakage, governor and throttle valve operation.

√ iv. Record and check bearing temperatures.

√ v.   Record and check oil cooler temperatures.

√ vi. Weekly check vibrations.

3.4.6 Fans and Pumps

Proper maintenance of fans and pumps can greatly improve operational efficiency and so eliminate unnecessary energy consumption. The following maintenance guidelines are suggested.

MINIMAL EXPENSE

a. Fans

√ i.   Check for excessive noise and vibration. Determine cause and correct as necessary.

√ ii. Keep fan blades clean.

√ iii. Inspect and lubricate bearings regularly.

√ iv. Inspect drive belts. Adjust or replace as necessary to ensure proper operation. Proper tensioning of belts is critical.

√ v.   Inspect inlet and discharge screens on fans. They should be kept free of dirt and debris at all times.

MINIMAL EXPENSE

b. Pumps

√ i.   Check for packing wear which can cause excessive leakage. Repack to avoid excessive water wastage and shaft erosion.

√ ii. Inspect bearings and drive belts for wear and binding. Adjust, repair or replace as necessary.

3.4.7 Hot and Chilled Water Piping

Proper maintenance of hot and chilled water piping will improve the efficiency of the piping system. Guidelines for effective maintenance of piping systems include:

MINIMAL EXPENSE

√ a. Inspect all controls. Test them for proper operation. Adjust, repair or replace as necessary. Also check for leakage at joints.

√ b. Check flow measurement instrumentation for accuracy. Adjust, repair or replace as necessary.

√ c. Inspect insulation of hot and chilled water pipes. Repair or replace as necessary. Be certain to replace any insulation damaged by water. Determine source of water leakage and correct.

√ d. Inspect strainers. Clean regularly.

√ e. Inspect heating and cooling heat exchangers. Large temperature differences may be an indication of air binding, clogged strainers or excessive amounts of scale. Determine cause of condition and correct.

√ f. Inspect vents and remove all clogs. Clogged vents retard efficient air elimination and reduce efficiency of the system.

3.4.8 Steam Piping

Proper maintenance of steam piping will, among other things, prevent unnecessary wastage of steam. Effective maintenance procedures include:

MINIMAL EXPENSE

√ a. Inspect insulation of all mains, risers and branches, economizers and condensate receiver tanks. Repair or replace as necessary.

√ b. Check automatic temperature-control system and related control valves and accessory equipment to ensure that they are regulating the system properly in the various zones—in terms of building heating needs, not system capacity.

√ c. Inspect zone shut-off valves. All should be operable so steam going into unoccupied spaces can be shut off.

√ d. Inspect steam traps. Their failure to operate correctly can have a significant impact on the overall efficiency and energy consumption of the system. Several different tests can be utilized to determine operations.

MINIMAL EXPENSE

√ i.   Listen to the trap to determine if it is opening and closing when it should be.

√ ii. Feel the pipe on the downstream side of the trap. If it is excessively hot, the trap probably is passing steam. This can be caused by dirt in the trap, valve off stem, excessive steam pressure, or worn trap parts (especially valve and seats). If it is moderately hot—as hot as a hot water pipe, for example—it probably is passing condensate, which it should do. If it's cold, the trap is not working at all.

√ iii. Check back pressure on downstream side.

√ v.   Measure temperature of return lines with a surface pyrometer. Measure temperature drop across the trap. Lack of drop indicates steam blow-through. Excessive drop indicates that the trap is not passing condensate. Adjust, repair or replace all faulty traps.

√ e. Inspect all pressure-reducing and regulating valves and related equipment. Adjust, repair or replace as necessary.

√ f. Inspect condensate tank vents. Plumes of steam are an indication of one or more defective traps. Determine which traps are defective and adjust, repair or replace as necessary.

√ g. Check accuracy of recording pressure gauges and thermometers.

√ h. Inspect pump for satisfactory operation, looking particularly for leakage at the packing glands.

√ i. Correct sluggish or uneven circulation of steam. It usually is caused by inadequate drainage, improper venting, inadequate piping, or faulty traps and other accessory equipment.

√ j. Correct any excessive noise which may occur in the system to provide more efficient heating and to prevent fittings from being ruptured by water hammer.

√ k. Check vacuum return system for leaks. Air drawn into the system causes unneccessary pump operation, induces corrosion and causes the entire system to be less efficient.

3.4.9. Pneumatic Air Compressor for Controls

Efficiency of pneumatic air compressors can be improved by following these guidelines:

MINIMAL EXPENSE

√ a. Inspect all connections for air leaks using a soap solution. Seal as necessary.

√ b. Note operation. If compressor seems to run excessively, it could be a sign of pressure loss at the controls or somewhere in the piping system. Determine cause and correct.

√ c. Inspect air pressure in supply tank and pressure regulator adjustment in supply line for proper limits.

√ d. Check belt tension and alignment.

√ e. Inspect air compressor intake filter pads and clean or replace as necessary.

√ f. Lubricate electric motor bearings according to manufacturer's recommendations.

3.5 Central Plant Modifications

Central plant modifications worthy of discussion in this publication relate primarily to boiler modifications. Although numerous chiller plant modifications also are possible, most require significant expense and, except in certain major installations, are economically feasible only to replace a system which has reached the end of its useful life.

Most of the following changes require significant expense. In most cases a feasibility study will be required prior to undertaking a modification.

a. Install Boiler Stack Economizer

A boiler stack economizer is a simple heat exchanger placed inside the exhaust stack which uses boiler feed water as the transfer medium. Heat captured from the exhaust gases increases the temperature of the feed water distributed to the boiler. In past years this technique was limited to systems using low or nonsulphur content fuels to avoid build-up caused when the economizer cooled exhaust gases to the sulphur dew point. Newer systems overcome this problem by incorporating a solid-state control which keeps stack temperatures above the dew point. By controlling the volume of feed water passing through the transfer coils.

b. Preheat Oil to Increase Efficiency

Preheating oil can increase efficiency by as much as 3% depending on the particular constituents of the oil involved. Heat required to attain complete atomization can be obtained through use of reclamation procedures discussed in 1.1, below. Heating oil beyond 135°F for #4 oil, 185°F for #5, or 210°F for #6 will increase efficiency even more, except care must be taken not to overheat, which could cause vapor locking and flame-out. Recommendations of the oil supplier should be followed.

c. Preheat Combustion Air To Increase Boiler Efficiency

Preheating primary and secondary air increase boiler efficiency by reducing the cooling effect when the air enters the combustion chamber and by promoting more intimate mixing of fuel and air. It is estimated that each 100°F increase in combustion air temperature increases boiler efficiency by 2%. Combustion air can be preheated up to 600°F for prevalent fuels and up to 350°F for stoker-fired coal oil and gas. The maximum temperature permissable is determined by the type of construction involved and the materials of the firing equipment. Several sources of heat are available to perform preheating. As an example, ambient air in most boiler rooms is heated incidently by boiler and pipe surfaces and collect below the ceiling. This air can be utilized directly as preheated combustion air by ducting it down to the firing level and directing it into the primary and secondary air intakes. Other methods available, discussed under Section 11.1 of this chapter involve recovering waste heat from boiler stacks, consensate, blowdown hot wells, and other sources. Manufacturer's recommendations should be followed in all cases.

d. Reduce Blowdown Losses

Blowing down a boiler has two purposes: (1) to maintain a low concentration of dissolved and suspended slides in the boiler water, and (2) to remove sludge in the boiler to avoid priming and carryover. There are two principal types of blowdown: intermittent manual blowdown and continuous blowdown. Manual blowdown (or sludge blowdown) is necessary whether or not continuous blowdown is installed, with frequency depending on the amount of solids in the boiler makeup water and the type of water treatment used. Continuous blowdown results in a steady energy drain because makeup water must be heated. In either case, blowdown energy losses can be minimized by installing automatic blowdown control and heat recovery systems. Automatic blowdown controls monitor the conductivity and PH of the boiler water periodically and blowdown the boiler only when required to maintain acceptable water quality. Further savings can be realized if the blowdown water is piped through a heat exchanger or a flash tank with a heat exchanger. In this way, for example, heat from the boiler blowdown flash tank can be used to feed reheating feed water heaters.

e. Isolate Off-Line Boilers

Light heating loads on a multiple boiler installation are often met by one boiler on line with the remaining boilers idling on stand-by. Idling boilers consume energy to meet stand-by losses. In many cases these losses are increased by a continuous induced flow of air through the idling boilers, and up the chimney. Unless a boiler is about to be used to meet an expected increase in load, it should be secured and isolated from the heating system (by closing valves) and from the stack and chimney (by closing dampers). A large boiler can be fitted with by-pass valves and regulating orifice to allow the minimum flow required to keep it warm and avoid thermal stress when it is brought on-line again. If a boiler waterside is isolated, it is important to prevent back flow of cold air through the stack which could cause the boiler to freeze.

f. Replace Boilers at or near End of Useful Life

A boiler at or near the end of its useful life should be replaced by a modern version which is matched to current and projected needs of the installation involved. In most cases new boilers on the market can obtain 80% efficiency. Even more efficiency can be gained by specifying multiple boilers and/or air-atomizing burners as appropriate. Replacement burners should be selected on the basis of long-term cost rather than first cost. Increased cost of fuel, labor and materials should be considered in developing long-term cost projections. Also consider installation of a dual-fuel system to avoid problems in the event of any shortages or curtailments.

g. Replace Existing Boilers with Modular Boilers

Most boilers achieve maximum efficiency only when running at their rated output. In most cases, however, full boiler capacity is seldom required because heat load is 60% less than full load 90% of the time. As a result, large capacity boilers in single units operate intermittently for the major part of the heating season. Although hi-low firing capabilities may reduce cycling, the boilers can only reach their design efficiency for short periods resulting in low seasonal efficiencies. A modular boiler system comprising two or more small capacity boiler units will increase seasonal efficiency. Each module is fired at 100% of its capacity only when required. Fluctuations of load are met by firing more or less boilers. Each small capacity unit has low thermal inertia (providing rapid response and low heat-up and cool-down losses) and either will be running at maximum efficiency or will be turned off. In a typical installation where single unit large capacity boilers are replaced by modular boilers, boiler seasonal efficiency may be improved from 68% to 75%. This represents a 9% savings of present fuel consumption. Use of the modular approach is particularly worthwhile in cases where the present boiler plant is at or near the end of its useful life. Replacement modular boilers should be sized to meet the reduced heating load resulting from implementation of other measures.

h. Convert from Steam Atomizing Burners to Air-Atomizing Burners

Steam atomizing burners consume at least 1.5% of total capacity to atomize the fuel oil. By contrast, air atomizing burners rely on a simple electrically driven air compressor which costs far less to operate. Accordingly, when an existing steam-atomizing burner is at or near the end of its useful life, an air atomizing replacement should be considered. In certain cases the savings to be obtained from an air-atomizing burner will warrant its installation prior to the scheduled replacement of the existing system.

i. Isolate Off-Line Chillers

Light cooling loads on a multiple chiller installation often are met by circulating chilled water through all chillers even though only one chiller is operating. This wastes pump energy by maintaining an unnecessarily high water flow rate through the system. It also forces the remaining on-line chiller to produce chilled water at low temperatures to offset the mixing effect of the bypass to meet the desired supply temperature and so causes the on-line chiller to operate at low evaporator temperatures (COP drops). Install isolating valves so off-line chillers can be isolated under light loads, thereby reducing chilled water flow rate. If multiple chilled water pumps are installed, shut off those that are unneeded. If multiple chilled water pumps are not installed, consider installing additional pumps or a multi-speed drive on the present pump.

3.6 General Systems Modifications

The only way to determine the efficiency of your heating/cooling system is to have the entire system tested and balanced in accord with the latest current procedures outlined by the American Society of Heating, Refrigerating and Air-Conditioning Engineers. The extent of testing required and its cost will depend primarily on the type of system involved (and therefore no cost categorization has been included).

In all cases the survey itself should be conducted by a qualified individual who has a thorough knowledge of heating and cooling systems, experience in testing and balancing, and the instrumentation and manpower required to collect and analyze the necessary data.

The most prevalent types of systems and steps which can be taken to make them more energy efficient are discussed as follows:

3.6.1 Terminal Reheat System

The terminal reheat system essentially is a modification of a single-zone system which provides a high degree of temperature and humidity control. The central heating/cooling unit provides air at a given temperature to all zones served by the system. Secondary terminal heaters then reheat air to a temperature compatible with the load requirements of the specific space involved. Obviously, the high degree of control provided by this system requires an excessive amount of energy. Several methods for making the system more efficient include:

a. Reduce the supply air quantity.
b. De-energize or shut off reheat coils and raise the chilled water supply air temperature in summer months in increments of 3°F. to determine the highest supply temperature which will maintain satisfactory room conditions. Temperatures which some commercial buildings have found suitable range from 60° to 70 °F.

c. Adjust ouside air, return air and mixed air damper controls in winter to raise supply air temperature to a level between 64° and 70°F.

c. Adjust outside air, return air and mixed air damper controls in winter to raise supply air temperature to a level between 64 and 70°F., depending on the conditions in the area served by the system.

d. If close temperature and humidity control must be maintained for equipment purposes, lower water temperature and reduce flow to reheat coils. This still will permit control, but will limit the system's heating capabilities somewhat.

e. If close temperature and humidity control are not required, convert the system to variable volume by adding variable volume valves and eliminating terminal heaters.

3.6.2 Dual-Duct System

The central unit of a dual-duct system provides both heated and cooled air, each at a constant temperature. Each space is served by two ducts, one carrying hot air, the other carrying cold air. The ducts feed into a mixing box in each space which, by means of dampers, mixes the hot and cold air to achieve that air temperature required to meet load conditions in the space or zone involved. Methods for improving the energy consumption characteristics of this system include:

a. Lower hot deck temperature and raise cold deck temperature.

b. Reduce air flow to all boxes to minimally acceptable level.

c. When no cooling loads are present, close off cold ducts and shut down the cooling system. Reset hot deck according to heating loads and operate as a single duct system. When no heating loads are present, follow the same procedure for heating ducts and hot deck. It should be noted that operating a dual-duct system as a single duct system reduces air flow, resulting in increased energy savings through lowered fan speed requirements.

d. Consider converting to variable volume system when energy and economic analysis to do so is favorable.

3.6.3 Multizone System

A multizone system heats and cools several zones—each with different load requirements—from a single, central unit. A thermostat in each zone controls dampers at the unit which mix the hot and cold air to meet the varying load requirements of the zone involved. Steps which can be taken to improve energy efficiency of multizone systems include:

a. Reduce hot deck temperatures and increase cold deck temperatures. While this will lower energy consumption, it also will reduce the system's heating and cooling capabilities as compared to current capabilities.

b. Consider installing demand reset controls which will regulate hot and cold deck temperatures according to demand. When properly installed, and with all hot deck or cold deck dampers partially closed, the control will reduce hot and raise cold deck temperature progressively until one or more zone dampers is fully open.

c. Consider converting systems serving interior zones to variable volume. Conversion is performed by blacking off the hot deck, removing or disconnecting mixing dampers, and adding low pressure variable volume terminals and pressure bypass.

3.6.4 Induction Systems

Induction systems comprise an air handling unit which supplies heated or cooled primary air at high pressure to induction units located on the outside walls of each space served. The high pressure primary air is discharged within the unit through nozzles inducing room air through a cooling or heating coil in the unit. The resultant mixture of primary air and induced air is discharged to the room at a temperature dependent upon the cooling and heating load of the space. Methods for conserving energy consumed by this system include:

a. Set primary air volume to original design values when adjusting and balancing work is performed.

b. Inspect nozzles. If metal nozzles, common on most older models, are installed, determine if the orifices have become enlarged from years of cleaning. If so, chances are that the volume/pressure relationship of the system has been altered. As a result, the present volume of primary air and the appropriate nozzle pressure required must be determined. Once done, rebalance the primary air system to the new nozzle pressures and adjust individual induction units to maintain airflow temperature. Also, inspect nozzles for cleanliness. Clogged nozzles provide higher resistance to air flow, thus wasting energy.

c. Set induction heating and cooling schedules to minimally acceptable levels.

d. Reschedule the temperature of the heating water and the cooling water according to the load. Avoid simultaneous heating or cooling in any one zone.

e. Reduce secondary water flow during maximum heating and cooling periods by pump throttling or, for dual-pump systems, by operating one pump only.

f. Consider manual setting of primary air temperature for heating, instead of automatic reset by outdoor or solar controllers.

g. For operation during unoccupied hours in the heating season, shut down primary air fans, raise the hot water temperature and operate the induction units as gravity convectors.

3.6.5 Variable Air Volume System

A variable volume system provides heated or cooled air at a constant temperature to all zones served. VAV boxes located in each zone or in each space adjust the quanitity of air reaching each zone or space depending on its load requirements. Methods for conserving energy consumed by this system include:

a. Reduce the volume of air handled by the system to that point which is minimally satisfactory.

b. Lower hot water temperature and raise chilled water temperature in accordance with space requirements.

c. Lower air supply temperature to that point which will result in the VAV box serving the space with the most extreme load being fully open.

d. Consider installing static pressure controls for more effective regulation of pressure bypass (inlet) dampers.

e. Consider installing fan inlet damper control systems if none now exist.

3.6.6 Constant Air Volume System

Most constant volume systems either are part of another system—typically dual duct system—or serve to provide precise air supply at a constant volume. Opportunities for conserving energy consumed by such systems include:

a. Determine the minimum amount of airflow which is satisfactory and reset the constant volume device accordingly.

b. Investigate the possibility of converting the system to variable (step controlled) constant volume operation by adding the necessary controls.

3.6.7 Single Zone System

A zone is an area or group of areas in a building which experiences similar amounts of heat gain and heat loss. A single zone system is one which provides heating and cooling to one zone controlled by the zone thermostat. The unit may be installed within or remote from the space it serves, either with or without air distribution ductwork.

a. Implementing energy conservation measures which reduce the heating and/or cooling of air handled by the HVAC system results in reduced fan power input requirements. Fan brake horsepower varies directly with the cube of air volume. Thus, for example, a 10% reduction in air volume will permit a reduction in fan power input by about 27% of original. This modification will limit the degree to which the zone serviced can be heated or cooled as compared to current capabilities.

b. Raise supply air temperatures during the cooling season and reduce them during the heating season. This procedure reduces the amount of heating and cooling which a system must provide, but, as with air volume reduction, limits heating and cooling capabilities.

c. Avoid simultaneous heating and cooling except as required for humidity control in critical areas.

d. Consider converting single zone, single duct systems to variable volume by adding variable volume boxes at each branch. Fan volume should preferably be controlled according to demand either by installing inlet guide vanes or by installing a variable speed motor or two speed.

e. Use the cooling coil for both heating and cooling by modifying the piping. This will enable removal of the heating coil, which provides energy savings in two ways. First, air flow resistance of the entire system is reduced so that air volume requirements can be met by lowered fan speeds. Second, system heat losses are reduced because surface area of cooling coils is much larger than that of heating coils, thus enabling lower water temperature requirements. Heating coil removal is not recommended if humidity control is critical in the zone serviced and alternative humidity control measures will not suffice.

3.6.8 Fan Coil System

A fan coil system usually comprises several fan coil units, each of which consists of a fan and a heating and/or cooling coil. The individual units can be located either in or remote from the space or zone being served. Guidelines for reducing energy consumption of such systems include:

a. Reduce air flow to minimally satisfactory levels.

b. Balance water flows to minimally satisfactory levels.

c. When heating and cooling loads are minimal, shut off fans so enabling the coil to act as a convector.

d. Consider installing interlocks between the heating and cooling systems of each unit to prevent simultaneous heating and cooling.

e. Consider face zoning two-pipe systems from four-pipe central system to avoid changeover losses.

3.6.9 Self-Contained Systems

Energy consumption of self-contained systems, such as rooftop, window, through-the-wall and other heating and/or cooling units, can be modified as follows:

a. If multiple units are involved, consider installation of centralized automatic shut-off and manual override controls.

b. If units are relatively old, consider replacing them with more efficient air-to-air heat pumps or similar units having a higher equivalent efficiency rating.

3.6.10 General

Regardless of the type system currently installed, consider adding to the system portable electric baseboard, unit, infrared or other types of supplemental heating units to overcome cold conditions which cannot be overcome by the current system, or to heat remote or occasionally-used areas which otherwise could be heated only through activation of all or substantially all of a central system.

3.7 Distribution Systems Modifications

A distribution system comprises the equipment and materials necessary for conveying the heating and cooling media —water, steam or air. Most versions of the nine general systems previously discussed employ one or more of the following distribution systems.

3.7.1 Hydronic Systems

Hydronic systems are those which utilize water for transferring heating and cooling. Some of the modifications which can be made to these systems are as follows:

MINIMAL EXPENSE

a. Install insulation on all hot and chilled water pipes, fittings and valves passing through unconditioned spaces to minimize heat losses and heat gains.

b. Replace fine mesh strainer baskets with ones having the largest practical openings to reduce pressure losses.

c. Remove orifice plates not regularly used for flow measurement.

d. Balance hydronic systems to attain minimally satisfactory temperature and water flow.

e. Trim impeller to actual size required on pump curve after terminal unit flows are reduced to the minimum. This will enable reductions of power requirements of actual load.

f. Install flow measurement instrumentation where none now exists. (Factory-assembled pipe-mounted instrumentation can easily be cut into the system.)

g. Check sizing of valves, filters and pipe sections. All those which are undersized should be replaced.

h. Check all pipe fittings. Replace those which are inefficient.

i. Consider adding a parallel small-GPM pump to handle heating load for dual temperature changeover systems.

j. Consider adding a variable speed drive. Although this will conserve energy, it will limit the pump's ability to handle flow to the farthest terminal units.

3.7.2 Steam Systems

Steam systems are those which utilize steam as a heat source. The steam can be provided either by an on-site boiler or by district steam. Methods for modifying the steam distribution system are as follows:

MINIMAL EXPENSE

a. Install insulation on all mains, riser, and branches, economizers, water heaters, and condensate receiver tanks where none now exists.

b. Add additional shut-off valves for more efficient zone control.

c. Install recorder pressure gauges and thermometers where none now exists to enable continual monitoring of the system.

d. Modify equipment as necessary to recover heat now going to the sewer. Such reclaimed heat from condensate can be used for boiler feedwater heating; to heat a portion of the building; to preheat water being supplied to the domestic hot water heater or be returned to the boilers.

3.7.3 Air Distribution Systems

Air distribution systems are those which use air for heating and/or cooling. Ways in which air distribution systems can be modified to effect energy conservation are:

MINIMAL EXPENSE

a. Test, adjust and balance entire air distribution system in accordance with methodology suggested in the latest ASHRAE Handbook and Product Guide.

b. Insulate all ductwork carrying conditioned air through unoccupied spaces with at least 1-½" of fibrous insulation or its thermal equivalent.

c. Reduce system resistence to air flow to a minimum by replacing those duct sections and fittings which impose unnecessary resistance on the system; replacing dirty filters with adequately sized filter media which has high efficiency and low air flow resistance; removal of unneccessary dampers and other obstructions from ductwork and replacing high resistance inlets and outlets with modern grilles and diffusers providing low resistance.

d. Reduce fan power input equipments by reducing air volume. Whenever heating and cooling loads are reduced, fan air volume reductions should be implemented to reduce fan energy consumption. Air volume can reduce fan energy consumption. Air volume can be reduced by changing the speed of rotation as follows:

- Where motor sheave is adjustable, open the "v" to reduce its effective diameter and adjust motor position or change belts to maintain proper tension.
- Change motor sheave if no further adjustment is possible.
- If motors are variable speed, set controller for reduced speed.

Following air volume reduction, determine resulting load on the fan motor. If one full load on the motor is less than 60% of the nameplate rating, consider changing the motor to a smaller one.

SIGNIFICANT EXPENSE

e. Relocate air outlets or rearrange ductwork so that air entering the space does not first come into contact with hot surfaces.

3.8 Control Adjustment and Modifications

The controls originally installed in your building probably were designed more in light of initial costs than they were for their ability to conserve energy. In addition, just five years' use without adequate maintenance—which seldom is performed—can cause controls to go out of calibration, becoming even less sensitive. A program of control adjustment and modification should consider the following guidelines:

MINIMAL EXPENSE

a. Adjust controls at the time of testing, adjusting and balancing of all heating and cooling systems.

b. Check operation of entire heating/cooling control system, including control valves and dampers. Correct all improper operations.

c. Check control system for instrument calibration and set point, actuator travel and action, and proper sequence of operation.

d. Inspect and calibrate pressure controls on dual duct system to obtain minimum static pressure during low demand and less leakage.

e. Adjust controls where applicable to prevent simultaneous operation of heating and cooling systems to achieve desired temperature.

f. Add controls to enable up to 100% shut-down of air and water to unoccupied space.

g. Inspect locations of thermostats. Relocate if they currently are positioned near outside walls, in areas that are seldom used, or if they are subject to outside drafts.

h. Consider installation of key-lock plastic covers over thermostats to prevent building occupants from adjusting settings.

i. Consider replacing pilots of gas burning equipment with electric ignition devices.

j. Limit the use of reheat to areas where humidity control is needed because of equipment needs.

k. Install thermostats for control of all heating equipment where none currently exist.

l. Consider installation of night set-back and morning start-up controls which enable you to schedule heating and cooling operations for each zone on the basis of occupancy patterns. Such controls easily can save from 10% to 30% on fuel consumption. A consultant should be utilized to determine when start-up should take place to ensure comfort for occupants when they arrive for work.

m. Consider installation of program clocks and manual overcall timers in control circuits to enable savings through scheduled operation of fans, refrigeration equipment, heating equipment and so on. Additional economies may result from decreased costs of labor and maintenance.

n. If a chilled water central plant currently is used to provide cooling, determine if the chiller plant can be shut down when outdoor temperature is below 50°. Add control valves and controllers which allow chilled water to flow from chillers to condenser water cooling tower to enable "free cooling." Similar controls must be added to condenser water system.

o. Adjust automatic timers or add time clocks to deactivate heating and cooling systems during evenings, weekends, holidays and other periods when the building is unoccupied.

p. Consider adding an automatic draft damper control to reduce heat loss through breaching when the gas or oil burner is not in operation.

q. Consider installation of automatic door closers on swinging doors leading to the exterior. Also consider such devices for garage and loading platform door operations.

r. Consider adding time clocks on self-contained heating and cooling units for automatic shut-off.

s. Consider adding a step-controller to electric heating systems with resistance elements to permit staging, resulting in more effective heat control and demand management.

SIGNIFICANT EXPENSE

t. Consider use of optimizing controls to operate equipment in most efficient modes of operation.

u. A building automation system should be investigated if your building has utility bills (electricity plus fuel) of $3,000 or more per month. Central controls involve all existing controls being wired into one central panel. In some cases, other kind of controls can be included, such as those for safety, security, etc. In some cases these controls are monitored by a person. In other cases they are monitored by computers. Typical functions performed by the system include monitoring of temperature and humidity of inside and outside air, and automatically adjusting dampers to provide that percentage of outside air which will minimize heating or cooling load. The system also can monitor electrical loads and shutoff noncritical loads (determined by the owner) whenever peak demand is approached. In many cases, central units are used to monitor not only HVAC, but also lighting, elevators, electrical system, fire protection, security, and so on, integrating all systems and providing maximum energy efficiency.

4. TRANSMISSION

Transmission losses generally can be reduced either through modification of glazing characteristics or addition of insulation.

4.1 Glazing

In all cases, preferential treatment should be given to those windows most exposed to direct sunlight or high levels of reflected sunlight.

MINIMAL EXPENSE

√a. Inspect condition of indoor shading devices such as drapes and blinds which can reduce heat gain as much as 50%. Keep indoor shading devices clean and in good repair.

√b. During the heating season, close all interior shading devices before leaving space to reduce night-time heat losses.

c. Use opaque or translucent insulating materials to block off and thermally seal all unused windows.

SIGNIFICANT EXPENSE

d. Consider adding reflective and/or heat-absorbing film to glazing to reduce solar heat gains by as much as 80%. Do be aware that such films will reduce substantially the benefits of natural lighting.

e. Consider adding reflective materials to the window side of draperies to reflect solar heat when draperies are drawn.

f. Install indoor shading devices where none now exist, even if exterior shading devices are used. They should be light-colored and opaque.

g. Consider installation of outdoor shading devices, such as sunshades, which reflect solar heat before it has a chance to enter the building, and which dissipate heat outdoors rather than indoors. Adjustable sunshades enable entrance of warming rays during the heating season.

h. Consider installation of storm windows if practical.

i. Consider reglazing with double or triple-glazing, or with heat absorbing and/or reflective glazing materials.

4.2 Insulation

It is advised strongly that expert technical assistance be obtained before undertaking any insulating to help ensure that the proper type and correct amount are installed, that cost effectiveness will result, and that any potential problems—such as moisture condensation—can be avoided.

MINIMAL EXPENSE

a. Where roof insulation is not practical, consider insulating the top floor ceiling. This can be done easily with blown insulation. In most cases, ceiling insulation also will require a vapor barrier placed on the warm side of the ceiling—if not integral with the insulation—to prevent structural damage caused by rot, corrosion or expansion of freezing water.

b. If remodeling or modernization is contemplated, consider adding insulation to all exterior walls as well as those which separate conditioned and nonconditioned spaces. Refer to ASHRAE Standard 90-75 for insulation guidelines.

c. Add or improve insulation under floors over garages or other conditioned areas. Refer to ASHRAE Standard 90-75 for insulation guidelines.

SIGNIFICANT EXPENSE

d. Consider adding roof deck insulation, especially if your building is 20 years old or older. Assuming that the roof/ceiling sandwich is not used as a return air plenum, a thermal transmission value (U—value) of 0.08-0.10 BTU/HR. Sq. Ft. °F. is considered to be an attainable goal through roof/ceiling sandwich.

5. LIGHTING

Because the lighting systems of many existing buildings were designed within the restrictions of intial cost economies, without knowledge about final space use and subdivision, and without benefit of relatively recent developments and research findings in the field, there exists significant potential for lighting system modification. These modifications can reduce substantially the energy consumed by the lighting system (and associated costs) while still providing building occupants with the quality and quantity of illumination required to perform their various task and functions.

Before undertaking any change, you must recognize that a lighting system is just that—a system. Its many elements all are interrelated with one another, just as the lighting system itself is interrelated with other systems in the building. While energy can be conserved by properly removing lamps and luminaires, realize that such action should be taken only after the entire system has been analyzed and all options evaluated. While conservation of energy is important, it must be achieved in a manner consistent with other requirements, including those of productivity and visual comfort; aesthetics; federal, state and local codes and ordinances, etc. Moreover, it is especially important to recognize that major alterations to a lighting system can have a significant impact on heating and cooling systems, most of which were designed to consider the amount of heat given off by the lighting system as originally designed. For these reasons, it is suggested strongly that competent technical assistance be obtained before any significant modifications are made and that modifications be made only in full light of the building's illumination needs, the lighting system which currently exists, and the many different options which can be utilized.

The following discussion highlights many of the actions which should or can be taken to implement an effective program of lighting energy management.

5.1 Modify Usage Patterns

An excellent initial step for a program of lighting management is to modify usage patterns based on factors developed during the initial building survey and utilizing the form shown in Appendix A. It should be noted that steps such as developing an effective lighting usage program would have to be updated and modified as changes are made to the lighting system but, for the most part, such modifications should be relatively simple once the initial steps have been undertaken.

MINIMAL EXPENSE

√ a. Establish an effective lighting usage program: a planned program to turn lights on when and where they are needed. The major advantages of such programs are that they can be tailored to the individual characteristics of the space and needs of its occupants, implemented relatively inexpensively, and implemented very quickly. The key element of a lighting usage program is a lighting schedule related to occupant usage patterns. Personnel should be assigned, trained and made responsible for the efficient utilization of lighting by means of established schedules for the control of lighting.

Define the exact nature of accupancy for each period of time. Determine the amount of lighting needed for safety and security purposes. Provide detailed instructions for system operation to responsible employees by means of charts, posting and/or color coding of switches. Train the responsible employees to assure understanding and compliance with the procedures.

For example, significant amounts of energy (and cost) can be conserved in buildings by means of lighting schedules requiring reduced lighting for daytime unoccupied (Saturdays, Sundays, and holidays), nighttime unoccupied and maintenance periods (low lighting levels).

The following two options should be considered part of the overall program.

● Campaign for better utilization by using letters, memos, signage and personal contact to encourage occupants—especially custodial personnel—to use lighting only when it is needed, to use only the amount of lighting required, and to turn off lights whenever they are not being used.

● Post a small sign or chart near each switch which identifies which lights are controlled by the switch. This enables the user to be more selective while also reducing trial-and-error which can consume significant amounts of energy as banks of lights are quickly activated and deactivated.

5.2 Work Station Modifications

Work stations can be relocated to take maximum advantage of the lighting system which exists or to supplement or enable changes to other elements of the system. Typical modifications to work station locations are as follows:

MINIMAL EXPENSE

√ a. Move desks and other work surfaces to a position and orientation that will use installed luminaries to their greatest advantage (instead of moving luminaries).

√ b. To the extent permitted by productivity requirements and related concerns, group tasks which require approximately the same levels of illumination. This may reduce the number of areas requiring higher illumination levels and provide an opportunity to reduce the total amount of lighting needed.

✓ c. Locate work stations requiring the highest illumination levels nearest the windows. (Note: Recognize that utilization of natural lighting will have an impact on heat gain, therfore requiring that the heat gain/light gain trade-off be given careful consideration. In many cases glazing can be modified to limit heat gain while still permitting entry of a significant amount of light. Such modifications are discussed earlier in this chapter under "Transmission, Glazing."

✓ d. Arrange work surfaces so that sidewall daylighting crosses the task perpendicular to the line of vision.

5.3 Maintenance Considerations

Proper maintenance of lighting system components serves to keep the system running at peak efficiency. This not only conserves energy and energy costs, but also helps maintain quality illumination and extends lamp and luminaire life. The following maintenance considerations should be reviewed.

MINIMAL EXPENSE

✓ a. Lamp efficiency deteriorates over the life of a lamp. Light output should be checked regularly with a calibrated light meter by maintenance personnel. When the light output of a group of lamps has fallen to approximately 70% of the original light output, re-lamp all fixtures in the group at the same time. This is also a good time to check whether a more efficient or lower wattage lamp is suitable.

b. Lamps should be wiped clean at regular intervals to assure maximum efficiency. Lamps which are exposed to an atmosphere with substantial amounts of dirt, dust, grease or other contaminants should be cleaned more frequently than lamps in a relatively clean atmosphere.

c. Luminaire efficiency can be maintained by properly cleaning the reflecting surfaces and shielding media. Replace lens shielding that has yellowed or become hazy with a clear acrylic lens with good non yellowing properties. For some applications, a clear glass lens can be considered if it is compatible with the luminaire and does not present a safety hazard. (Caution should be used to assure that an existing luminaire will safely support and hold the glass lens.)

d. Clean ceilings, walls and floors frequently to improve reflective qualities. When daylight is used, wash windows frequently to maintain illumination levels on tasks which require some natural illumination.

5.4 Illumination Level Modifications

There usually are at least several levels of illumination required within any building. These levels can be separated into three general categories: specific task lighting, general lighting around tasks, and general lighting for circulation or support areas.

While it is commonly understood that different visual tasks require different levels of illumination, the interiors of many offices buildings provide only uniform illumination levels which have little relationship to the amount of illumination required in specific areas.

During a building's original design, the lighting designer frequently cannot define the nature or location of specific tasks or task areas. The designer's problem is often compounded by lack of knowledge about final partition locations, floor and wall finishes and other tenant options, all of which have an impact on the final illumination results.

After a building or space is completely defined or occupied, there usually are opportunities to adjust illumination levels to improve utilization and efficiency. If the wiring and lighting system provides flexibility to allow for relocating luminaires, switching individual lamps or groups of lamps, or otherwise providing means for controlling the lighting in specifically defined areas, the adjustment can be made quickly and inexpensively. In buildings without such flexibility, it may be necessary to add switching, remove lamps, disconnect or add luminaires, or in extreme cases, remodel the entire lighting system in order to provide proper illumination for individual tasks and still accomplish the energy reduction desired.

In general office areas, nonuniform lighting systems can be applied when the average work station size is less than one worker per 50–70 square feet. If work stations are larger, a uniform lighting system is generally more practical. Larger, private offices are areas where nonuniform lighting applications could save energy. Most store lighting requires the use of uniform lighting systems within departments, but illumination levels between departments may vary depending upon the type of merchandise involved. It is also common practice in specialty shops or departments to use relatively low levels of general illumination with some merchandise highlighted by spot or flood lighting equipment. Since space usage usually changes several times over the life of a building, special consideration should be given to providing flexibility in the lighting and control systems.

The examples shown in Figure VI-1 provide some general guides for illumination levels in applications that are encountered frequently. The areas where illumination modifications can and should be made can be determined easily by use of a properly calibrated light meter. Methods to modify illumination levels, reduce energy consuption, and maintain an effective lighting system are as follows:

5.5 Lamp Modification

Lamp modification can take many forms. In some cases it may involve elimination of lamps; using those of lower wattages; changing the type involved (which would imply in most cases a change of luminaire), etc. Consider the following guidelines.

MINIMAL COST

a. Consider replacing present lamps with those of lower wattage which provide the same amount of illumination or (if acceptable in light of tasks involved) a lower level of illumination. (Lens changes or lowering the luminaire often can help facilitate this option). This

FIG. VI-1
SUGGESTED ILLUMINATION LEVELS

	Footcandles Maintained
Office Buildings:	

Private Offices

Reading handwriting in hard pencil or on poor paper, reading fair reproductions . .	100
Reading handwriting in ink or medium pencil on good quality paper	70
Reading high contrast or well-printed materials	30
Conferring and interviewing	30

General Offices

Reading handwriting in hard pencil or on poor paper, reading fair reproductions, active filing, mail sorting	100
Reading handwriting in ink or medium pencil on good quality paper, intermittent filing	70

Bank Lobby

Writing Areas	70
General Areas	50

Dental Offices

General Operatory	70
Waiting Rooms	30

Doctor's Offices

General Examination and Treatment . . .	50
Waiting Rooms	30

Conference Rooms

Conferring	30
Note-taking during projection (variable) .	30

Rest Rooms and Wash Rooms	30
Corridors, Stairways, Elevators	20

Storage Rooms

Active — Medium Materials	20
Active — Rough, Bulky Materials	10
Inactive Storage	5

Stores:

Merchandise requiring close inspection because of detail, fineness, or high value . . .	100*
General Merchandise Areas	50*
Alteration rooms, fitting rooms, dressing areas	50
Circulation areas, stockrooms	30

Illumination levels above are from Illuminating Engineering Society Handbook, 5th Edition. Guidance for special situation and more difficult and critical tasks may be found in the Handbook. It will be noted that most of the higher levels therein are intended to be provided by localized lighting involving relatively small amounts of energy. Consideration should also be given to the lighting needs of older workers with regard to illumination levels and minimum glare.

*Footcandle values on plane used to display merchandise. Horizontal plane for merchandise displayed horizontally. Vertical plane for merchandise displayed vertically.

Footcandle values above are excerpted from the IES handbook, which also provides additional information on lighting for other tasks. These illumination levels are also specified in the Model Code For Energy Conservation In New Building Construction.

method is particularly applicable where current lighting levels are higher than recommended or where uniform lighting is the most practical due to occupant density, as discussed above. This also is a simple way to provide flexibility should higher levels of illumination be required at some future time. (Note: Be certain that new lamps are compatible for use with existing ballasts in fluorescent and H.I.D. (High Intensity Discharge) luminaires.)

√ b. Remove unnecessary lamps if removal will still enable provision of illumination levels required. When lamps are removed from a fluorescent luminaire, all lamps controlled by a given ballast should be removed to prevent ballast failure or reduced lamp life. Except in the case of instant start lamps or luminaires with circuit-interrupting lamp-holders, also consider disconnecting ballasts which otherwise would continue to consume energy.

c. Select lamps which are the most efficient (efficiency is measured in lumens per watt) and which are compatible with the application. Compatibility with the luminaire, of course, also is essential. If some luminaire replacement is to be undertaken, therfore, determination of lamp type involved also should be considered.

In general, efficiencies of lamp types rank as follows, in descending order:

Lumens Per Watt (Including Ballast)

	Smaller sizes	Middle sizes	Larger sizes
High pressure sodium	84	105	126
Metal halide	67	75	93
Fluorescent	66	74	70
Mercury	44	51	57
Incandescent	17	22	24

This ranking, of course, is general only. There is overlapping of efficiencies between lamp types and even within a lamp type, for different wattages, life ratings, etc. Also there are limitations on some lamps with regard to their suitability for a specific application. Selection of the most efficient lamp must be evaluated on the basis of the specific application. Selection of the most efficient lamp must be evaluated on the basis of the specific application and the performance characteristics of the individual lamps being considered. Changing from incandescent to a more efficient light source can give paybacks in as little as one to two years depending upon local costs of energy.

5.6 Luminaire Modifications

Luminaire efficiency is measured in terms of "coefficient of utilization." While efficiency is an important consideration in luminaire selection, one also must consider visual comfort. The following guidelines are provided for the three general types of applications:

- For tasks where veiling reflections are a critical factor and visual comfort is important, the luminaire can have a coefficient of utilization of .55 or higher. It also should have high visual comfort.
- For spaces where veiling reflections are not a critical factor, but where visual comfort is still a factor, the luminaire can have a coefficient of utilization of .63 or higher, and medium to high visual comfort.
- For spaces that do not involve critical visual tasks, and where visual comfort is not a factor, the luminaire can have a coefficient of utilization of .70 or higher and low visual comfort.

More specific information regarding coefficients of utilization and visual comfort can be obtained from the Illuminating Engineering Society Lighting Handbook and from manufacturer's data for specific luminaires.

Some of the modifications to luminaires which are possible include the following.

SIGNIFICANT COST

a. Relocate luminaires to provide light on task areas at an angle outside the zone which causes veiling reflections if relocation of work station is impractical.
b. Replace outdated or damaged luminaires with modern luminaires which have good cleaning capabilities and which use lamps with higher efficiencies and good lumen maintenance characteristics.
c. Consider installing fluorescent luminaires with multiple level ballasts or adding dimming controls for incandescent luminaires in multiple-purpose spaces which require more than one level of illumination.
d. Consider lowering luminaires so they will provide recommended illumination levels on the task area at reduced wattage.
e. Where appropriate, consider installation of lenses which provide special light distribution patterns to increase lighting effectiveness. As examples, linear batwing, radial batwing, parabolic louvers or polarizing lenses may provide better visibility with the same or even reduced wattage. It is suggested that competent

technical advice be obtained to evaluate where such lenses can be used most effectively.

5.7 Control Modifications

In many cases modification of existing lighting controls, and addition of new ones, can have a considerable effect on energy consumption. Consider the following guidelines.

MINIMAL EXPENSE

a. When existing circuitry makes it impossible to utilize less than 25% of the light in a given large space whenever light is needed, and when persons work during normally unoccupied periods, consider development of a desk lamp issuance program which enables persons working during unoccupied periods to use a simple desk lamp or two instead of a large bank of luminaires.
b. When natural light is available in a building, consider the use of photocell switching to turn off banks of lighting in areas where the natural light is sufficient for the task.
c. Use photocell and/or time clock controls for outdoor lighting whenever feasible. Parking areas, building exteriors, identification signs, etc., usually require lighting for only a part of the period of darkness. Such lighting should be turned off automatically during late evening and early morning hours except for security and safety lighting.
d. Use time controls for those areas of a building which are used infrequently and only for brief periods. These controls turn off lights automatically after being activated for a set period of time.
e. Use alternate switching or dimmer controls when spaces are used for multiple purposes and require different amounts of illumination for the various activities. It is possible to provide multiple levels by providing switching for alternate fixtures, alternate sets of lamps in fluorescent fixtures, etc. Dimmer controls can be effective when it is impractical to use selective switching to obtain multiple lighting levels. This is especially true (and relatively low in cost) when incandescent lighting is involved.

SIGNIFICANT EXPENSE

f. Provide selective switching. Initial cost economies and lack of knowledge about final space subdivision often lead to the use of central panel-boards as the only means of controlling large blocks of lighting. This design approach precludes the potential for turning on only the amount of lighting that is actually needed after the space has been subdivided.

Investigate ways to provide local control of lighting. Localized switches can be provided near doorways. Remotely controlled switches can be located near panelboards to control groups of lights. Low voltage control circuits can be used to provide local control of switches located in remote locations (these controls usually are relatively inexpensive). When properly used, localized switching usually will save enough energy to provide a pay-back on the investment within a short period of time.

g. Lighting use in remote areas can be monitored by providing neon indicator lights at central stations. Personnel will be alerted to investigate and turn off lights not being used.

5.8 Heat of Light Recovery Systems

SIGNIFICANT EXPENSE

a. Heat of light recovery systems—because of the expense they entail—usually are feasible only if modernization programs are involved. While many different types are available, most provide the same basic functions. In essence, the heat produced by lighting is extracted by mechanical equipment through a ceiling cavity to the mechanical equipment room. The heat collected can be recycled to reduce heating energy needs in cold weather or discarded to reduce the cooling energy needs during warmer weather. Removal of heat in this manner usually enables luminaries and lamps to operate more efficiently and also may reduce fan horsepower requirements of the air circulation system.

6. DOMESTIC HOT AND COLD WATER

Domestic hot water often consumes from 2% to 4% of the total energy used in large office buildings. In retail stores and smaller buildings, the amount usually is smaller. Cold water, provided in drinking fountains, also is a factor in total building energy consumption. The following guidelines should be considered in an effort to conserve energy:

MINIMAL EXPENSE

√ a. Inspect water supply system and repair all leaks, including those at the faucets.

√ b. Inspect and test hot water controls to determine if they are working properly. If not, either regulate, repair or replace.

c. Inspect insulation on storage tanks and piping. Repair or replace as needed.

d. Increase the amount of insulation installed on hot water pipes and storage tanks or replace existing insulation with a type having better thermal properties ("R" value).

e. Consider replacing existing hot water faucets with spray type faucets with flow restrictors where practical.

f. Consider installing spring-activated hot water taps.

g. If water pressure exceeds 40 to 50 pounds, consider having a plumber install a pressure reducing valve on the main service to restrict the amount of hot water that flows from the tap.

h. Reduce generating and storage temperature levels to the minimum required for washing hands, usually about 100°F. Boost hot water temperature locally for kitchens and other areas where it is needed, rather than by providing higher than necessary temperatures for the entire building.

i. If cooking facilities are used only on occasion, as for certain conferences or meetings, deactivate the hot water heating system, including the gas pilot if installed, when the facilities are not being used.

j. If you have an electric domestic water heater, consider limiting the duty cycle to avoid adding water heating load to the building during periods of peak electrical demand.

√ k. If hot water is distributed through forced circulation, turn off the pump when the building is unoccupied.

√ l. Disconnect all refrigerated water fountains if acceptable to building occupants.

√ m. Discontinue sterilization of drinking water where possible and practical.

n. Consider relocating the water heater as close to the point of use as possible. The longer the run, the more hot water that sits in it—cooling down—between periods when hot water is drawn.

o. Consider replacing free running drinking fountains with spigot types which utilize a paper cup. Up to half the water drawn by free-running fountains is wasted.

7. ELEVATORS AND ESCALATORS

Despite the fact that escalators draw relatively little current under no-load operation, it generally is recognized that their continuous action does tend to waste energy. Although intermittent, as-needed operation can be obtained through use of a treadle-type switch, relatively few such installations have been made due to safety concerns. When an escalator is shut down, however, it still provides a means of transportation: stationary stairs. By contrast, an elevator cannot serve any useful purpose when it is nonoperational. When elevators are running, however, they tend to be more efficient than escalators, although they do cause indirect energy consumption due to stack effects created by the shaft and infiltration around cabs.

Following are a few of the options which should be considered in an effort to provide the elevator/escalator service required while conserving energy in the process. It should be noted that some of these options are mutually exclusive. In other words, if you pursue one given option, it would be impractical or impossible to pursue another. Determination of which options best suit your needs can be made only after careful review of traffic patterns, elevator controls, etc. If possible, contact the manufacturer, his representatives or distributors, to obtain assistance in performing such a review.

MINIMAL EXPENSE

√ a. Encourage building occupants (and perhaps visitors) to use the stairway when only a few stories are involved and when security permits.

b. Perform a traffic review to determine if a building is properly elevatored, or over- or under-elevatored in light of use during different periods of the day. If properly elevatored or overelevatored, take one or more elevators out of operation at least during periods of light traffic.

c. If your building has automatic load-shedding or demand-limiting equipment, connect elevators to the system to enable automatic shut-down of one or more to limit peak demand.

d. If elevators are taken out of service, waiting period (floor dwell time) automatically will be increased. If none are taken out of service, however, floor dwell time can be lengthened thus increasing the passenger load factor.

e. If elevators have demand type controls, adjust controls so that the fewest number of elevators travel the shortest distance that demand on the system allows.

f. Do not permit elevators to time out and shut down too rapidly. They should idle long enough so that power consumption is equal to or just less than power consumed in motor generator starting.

g. If escalators are involved, consider these alternatives:

- operate them only during peak periods, or
- shut down all "down" escalators at all times, or
- shut down all "down" escalators during periods of light traffic, or
- shut down "up" escalators on every other floor during light traffic.

SIGNIFICANT EXPENSE

g. Consider installing capacitors at points of utilization to increase power factor and so reduce kWh losses (and resulting power costs) in the internal distribution system.

h. Consider utilizing solid state motor drives instead of motor generator sets. Solid state motor drives typically provide energy savings of from 25–30% as compared to motor generator sets.

i. Consider installation of demand-type elevator controls on elevators having through trip or collective type of controls so elevators may be adjusted to ensure that the fewest number of cabs travel the shortest distance which demand on the system allows.

8. ELECTRIC POWER

Numerous elements of building systems which utilize electricity have been discussed throughout this section. Additional guidelines for reduction of electric energy consumption and losses are as follows:

8.1 General

a. Through letters, memoranda, signage, personal contact and other means, encourage all building personnel to turn off all electric equipment not in use, including portable fans, typewriters, calculators, coffee pots, etc.

√ b. Turn off window displays and revolving signs at least at the end of closing hours, possibly during low traffic periods, and perhaps at all times.

√ c. Disconnect all unnecessary apparatus and devices, for example, ventilation fans in elevators where smoking is not permitted.

√ d. Turn off equipment and devices which will be unused for a period of time, for example, vending machines (in which spoilage would not be a problem) and drinking fountains which can be turned off for the weekend. (You may wish to consider time controls to do the job for you. It would be feasible, then, to also turn off such devices during the evening hours.)

8.2 Utility Cost Management

As you probably are aware, utilities have several different rate structures and, in many cases, more than one may be applicable to your building. As you may not be aware, however, the utility does not automatically bill you at the most favorable rate. In other words, if a new rate structure has been instituted since your building was built, and if the new rate can be used in your building, it will be up to you to know whether or not the new rate is more favorable. The utility will tell you, but you are the one who must ask. As a result, it is suggested that you gather information which relates to purchased utilities, especially the electric utility. In many cases it will be discovered that a more favorable rate is available or can be made available, errors in billing have been made, meters are not working properly, or that other situations and circumstances exist which can be changed to attain positive impact.

You also should be aware of what the utility has planned for the future to aid you in your own forecasting and planning. This information can be obtained from the local utility and from your state public service commission.

8.2.1 Review Rate Structures

Many electric utilities have ten or more different services, each often subject to one or more riders. Contact an appropriate utility representative to find out what different rates, services, schedules and riders are available. Most have customer service representatives who can explain utility operations and go over yours to suggest ways of economizing. Once you are familiar with utility materials, determine for every separate service location:

- rate schedule and riders used;
- maximum demand and period of occurence;
- power factor;
- monthly and annual energy consumption;
- average cost per kWh;
- service voltage level and secondary use level, and;
- transformer and equipment ownership.

Talk with other electric customers in a position similar to your own. Determine what rate schedules they're using, what their use characteristics are, and how much they're paying. Make a complete and careful review of at least one current bill for each service and ask yourself: "Am I getting the appropriate rate?" "Is the bill computed properly?" "Why am I on this rate?" "How can I qualify for a better rate?" Seek a satisfactory answer to *each* question. Contact a utility representative for help and work with him to develop a program & rate which best meets your needs and conditions. Have him come in to review each service. Ask him if other rates apply or could be made to apply. Determine advantages and disadvantages of each. Check figures.

Your utility representative will tell you about the alternatives if you ask, but it's up to you to make a decision. If you do decide to change rates, determine what the impact will be—if any—on building systems.

8.2.2 Utility Bills

All utility bills for should be reviewed. In fact, there are companies which will do this for you, taking 50% of the refunds you obtain as their fee, (see discussion below re utility consultants).

In most cases, a bill will include charges for:

- *Energy:* Most electric utilities use a sliding block approach for energy charge, that is, so much per kWh for the first 1000 kWh, so much per kWh for the second thousand, and so on. In most cases, the more kWh you consume, the less per kWh you pay.
- *Fuel Adjustment:* Many electric utilities have imposed an additional energy cost called a fuel adjustment which reflects the increased cost of fuel. It can be a substantial charge. (Gas utilities have something similar called a purchased gas adjustment charge (PGA) which reflects adjustment to gas bills based on fluctuations in the wholesale cost of gas.)
- *Customer Related:* Some utilities add what's called customer-related costs. These comprise a special charge which reflects part of the distribution investment, part of the operating and maintenance costs, costs for accounting and collection, and so on. If it isn't billed separately, it may be included with the energy cost.
- *Demand:* The demand charge is designed to make the customer pay his fair share of the utility's fixed investment in the production, transmission and distribution equipment required to meet his maximum requirements. The charge is based on the rate at which electricity is consumed. The more used at any given time, the larger the utilities investment in generation, transmission and distribution systems has to be. For example, consider two users: A and B, both consuming an equal number of kWh each day. User A consumes electric energy 24 hours a day and user B consumes it 8 hours a day. User B requires the utility to have generating the distribution capacity equal to the ratio of 6/2 times the capacity required to supply user A. This is 3 times the capital investment that was required to serve user A, so user B is billed for this extra investment.

The consumer's actual demand is computed as the average amount of energy consumed in a predetermined demand measurement interval, usually 15 minutes (other intervals also are used by the utilities, particularly 30 minutes and 60 minutes). Regardless of the interval, the highest demand recorded during a month becomes the actual demand for the month.

Many utilities also employ a special clause which states that no matter what your actual demand may be in any given month, the demand for which you are *billed* may be no less than a certain percentage of a demand recorded typically—during the summer months, This already has been discussed in Section 1 of Chapter 4, above.

- *Low Power Factor Penalty:* Another charge sometimes applied, is a penalty for low power factor, a subject discussed below.

8.2.3 Utility Consultants

You may find it desirable to call in a utility consultant to just check your figures or, at the other extreme, to perform an all-out research effort. There are three basic kinds of consul-

tants: consulting engineers, electrical contractors, and contingency fee consultants.

A consulting engineer typically undertakes the work required for a fee so you will have a reasonably good idea of what to expect in terms of your cost. The electrical contractor usually works on the same basis or may follow the procedure used by a contingency fee consultant who is paid on the basis of how much money he saves you. A typical contract calls for a flat service fee plus additional fees for savings. In addition, the company will research your utility needs and will look for any refunds due you.

Obtain background data on at least three firms. Review the data and contact the firm's clients to see how satisfied they've been. Then meet with representatives of each of the three firms and form an opinion.

If your're going to use a consultant on a contingency fee basis, be aware that any standard contract can be modified.

While it may be true that a contingency-fee contract will result in a more thorough search being made to find you refunds and savings, realize, first, that this is not *always* true and, second, that you *may* wind up paying more on a contingency basis.

8.3 Maintenance

A proper program of electrical system maintenance can help prevent excessive energy losses, reduced equipment life, and hazardous conditions associated with poorly maintained equipment.

As an initial step, a load survey of the building's electrical distribution system should be made by a qualified professional electrical contractor. Although probably adequate when first designed and installed, the system may not now be able to carry proper current due to changes in layout and uses. Additions or shifts in motors may have affected working voltage of the system, thus affecting motor operation lighting efficiencies and conductor loading. The load survey should indicate problem areas. As examples, low voltage conditions on motors cause high amperage draw which increases line losses. Overvoltage causes some motors to become less efficient. Undersize wire increases line loss. Loose connections and bad contacts cause increased amperage draw and power loss as well as heating and arcing which is both inefficient and dangerous. Unbalanced voltages in three-phase motors can create inefficient motor operation. Power leaks to ground also can cause substantial loss of energy, arcing and, ultimately, life.

Assuming that repairs and maintenance are performed as needed, regular checks of voltage at the terminals of power and lighting circuits should be made. Constant rated voltage is necessary to obtain maximum efficiency and usable life from installed equipment.

Systematic records should be kept of all surveys, regular checks, maintenance and investigation performed, etc. In this manner you will be able to determine when correction is required, whether equipment is failing, etc.

8.4 Equipment and Control Rooms

Water, dust, heat, cold, humidity, dryness, corrosive atmospheres, vibration and toher conditions all affect the performance and usable life of electrical apparatus. For this reason, it is essential to regulate to as great a degree as possible the environment of equipment and control rooms where the majority of electric apparatus are located. It is suggested that such rooms be kept relatively dry and that appropriate ventilation be installed for enclosed rooms to prevent heat huild-up. High humidity can increase dirt build-up on electrical parts and cause inefficiencies and, in some cases, total brakdowns.

8.5 Power Transformer Management

Proper management of transformer operation and related factors can result in significant energy savings. The following guidelines should be considered:

a. Shade exterior transformer banks from solar radiation to prevent heat huild-up and resultant losses.
b. Ventilate transformer banks to keep them as cool as possible.
c. De-energize transformers whenever possible, including:

   i. Unloaded transformers
   ii. Transformers supplying unoccupied or unused spaces
   iii. Refrigeration chiller transformer during the heating season
   iv. Heating equipment transformers during the cooling season
   v. Heating and cooling transformers during periods of time which normally require no heating or cooling, as during spring and fall.

d. When replacing trasformers or adding new ones to the system, select those designed for a lower temperature rise but furnished with high temperature rise insulating materials.

8.6 Outdoor Switchgear

Because heat can increase energy losses of switchgear, consider the following guidelines for that switchgear located out-of-doors:

√ a. Provide shading
√ b. Remove or prune (in the case of shrubbery) any obstructions which tend to diminish natural ventilation.

8.7 Demand Management and Control

The effectiveness with which energy is used is rated is expressed in terms of load factor: the ratio of energy use (kWh) to highest demand (kW) x time, usually measured as 720 hours—the number of hours in 30 days. For example, if you consume 700,000 kWh in a 30-day period and during that time establish a peak demand of 1500 kW, you'd have a load factor of 64.8%

In essence, the lower the demand, the higher the load factor. The higher the load factor is, the lower the relative cost for electric service.

The techniques used most often to improve load factor are demand management and demand control. The two are not synonymous terms. Demand control refers to the electromechanical procedure of load shedding. Demand management encompasses demand control as well as other activities which can help reduce demand charges even more.

8.7.1 Analyze Operations

To determine potential for improving load factor, analyze demand records to determine when demand peaks typically occur during operating hours. Observe operations to determine what in particular is responsible for peaks. Once you find that out, determine what you can do to sequence processes or events to hold peaks down. If two pieces of equipment are started simultaneously, for example, could start-up times be sequenced so surges do not occur at the same time? Could some operations be scheduled so that one begins after the other ends?

The demand savings to be obtained this way usually require no capital expense and they can be significant.

8.7.2 Develop Load Data

The specific research data you need to develop a demand control system specification may or may not be on hand. Essentially what is needed is information on the rating of each electrical load. If comprehensive as-built drawings are available, the task should be relatively simple. If not, consider making a power survey using a recording wattmeter or other instruments to develop accurate data on how much power is being used by equipment at a particular time. Other information you should collect relates to any expansion or alternation planning which could somehow have a bearing on future demand requirements.

8.7.3 Identify Primary and Secondary Load

Each load should be identified as either primary or secondary.

A primary load is one which cannot be interrupted. A secondary load is one which can be interrupted, rescheduled or deferred and cause no problems in terms of comfort, process or productivity.

Typical secondary loads include: lighting, electric heating units, electric cooling units, chillers, air handling units, exhaust fans, water heaters, pumps, electric boilers, furnaces, ovens, incinerators, air compressors, loading dock de-icers, snow melting systems, and escalators, among others.

8.7.4 Analyze Secondary Loads

Once secondary loads are identified, determine their wattage ratings and establish an order or priority. The more essential secondary loads should be listed first so they can operate last-out-first in while lower priority loads operate first-out-last-in. Before making any decisions, analyze the impact of shedding for each load. To do this, first determine the negative impact which shedding the load will have on process, comfort, productivity or environment. Second, determine the negative impact on the equipment itself. Frequent operation of controls usually will shorten expectant life and increase maintenance costs. So the factors have to be related to savings in electrical costs.

Once controllable loads and priorities are identified, determine how much demand reduction can be allowed and the economics of various types of demand control systems.

8.7.5 Demand Control Systems

To select a specific demand control system, it should be noted that each system comprises three essential elements: input, logic, and output.

a. Input

Input to most demand control systems is in the form of pulses from the utility's kilowatt-hour meter incorporating a demand meter attachment. Each time a certain number of kilowatt hours accumulates, a pulse is generated. At the end of each interval the meter gives off an end-of-interval or EOI pulse. The pulse tells the control device that the interval is over and that new interval has begun.

b. Logic

Logic refers to the operating method by which an automated demand control device performs its function of measuring the energy being consumed in the facility and limiting demand by shedding certain secondary loads.

Demand control equipment available today ranges from relatively inexpensive units to highly sophisticated, large-scale computer systems. Some systems are not automated at all and work by shutting down equipment or sounding an alarm whenever the desired maximum demand is exceeded. Although type of unit is applicable for some installations, it does not lend itself to highly effective control. Desired maximum demand frequently is overshot because action usually can't be taken until it is too late. In most instances an automated demand control is preferable.

The five logic systems generally used are described as follows:

  i. **Ideal Rate Demand Control Logic:**
  Accumulates and compares actual rate of energy used in any demand interval to a predetermined, ideal rate of use. As actual rate of consumption approaches ideal rate, secondary loads are shed. As comsumption rate declines, secondary loads are restored.

  ii. **Converging Rate Demand Control Logic:**
  Similar to ideal rate, except ideal use curve and shed and restore lines converge at the end of each interval rather than run parallel to each other. This enables finer control over relatively small loads late in the demand interval when accumulated registered demand may be very close to the maximum desired demand setpoint.

  iii. **Instantaneous Demand Control Logic:**
  Compares actual rate of consumption at any time in the demand interval to maximum desired consumption at that time. Assume that

maximum desired consumption is 1000 kW for a demand interval. With straight-line accumulation or constant usage, the accumulated demand should be no more than 250 kW at one-fourth of the interval and 500 kW at one-half of the interval. Loads are shed and restored according to this criterion.

  iv. **Continuous Integral Demand:**
  Similar to instantaneous demand because usage is continually monitored and compared to the desired maximum rate. When actual rate approaches maximum desired rate, a secondary load is shed, but actual shedding function is carried out by a satellite cycle timer which deactivates the secondary load for a fixed period of time. This results in demand interval overlap. For example, if a secondary load which stays deactivated for six minutes is shed at 14 minutes into a 15 minute demand interval, it is going to stay shed for the first five minutes of the following interval. Continuous integral demand controllers compare the present usage to usage in previous intervals without restoring all loads at end of each interval. This reduces excessive short cycling of equipment and operations.

  v. **Predictive Demand Control Logic:**
  Measures total accumulated energy consumption from beginning of demand interval. A predicted or projected end-of-interval demand is developed based on the rate of accumulated consumption measured at each point and the rate multiplied by the time remaining in the demand interval. If the predicted demand exceeds mimum desired demand, a secondary load is shed. If a subsequent measurement indicates a large emugh margin, secondary loads are restored. Predictive method systems generally can accommodate a wide variety of load profiles and, in most cases, are more expensive than other types. They also must be compatible with utility demand metering equipment for synchronous operation.

c. Output

The output function of automated demand control systems acts on logic decisions and provides the actual control. This is accomplished by activating relays, contractors, or motor starters which shed or restore loads on the line. The sequence in which secondary loads are shed can be altered. In some cases it can be specified that a given load is the last shed and first restored, or first shed and last restored, and so on.

8.8 Power Factor Improvement

The power which must be supplied to any induction load such as induction motor, transformer, fluorescent lamp, etc., is made up of real and reactive power.

Real power, or the working power, is measured in kilowatts (kWs). The reactive, or magnetizing current, is required to produce the flux necessary for the operation of any induction equipment. Without magnetizing current, energy could not flow through the core of a transformer or across the gap of an induction motor. The unit used to measure reactive power is the kilovar or kVAR. The *vector* sum—*not* the arithemetical sum—of the real power and the reactive power is the *apparent power*, measured in kilovolt-amperes or kVA.

Power factor is a ratio of real power (kW) to apparent power (kVA) or,

$$\text{Power Factor} = \frac{\text{Real Power (kW)}}{\text{Apparent Power (kVA)}}$$

Electric utilities must provide both real and reactive power for their customers. Reactive power does not register on a kilowatthour meter, but producing it still requires the utility to put additional investment into capacitors and generating, transmission and distribution facilities.

Many utilities make up for the expense of producing reactive power by including power factor provisions in their rates. As it so happens, many utilities are defining low power as anything less than .9. Thus if a building consumes 10 million kWH per year at 3.5 cents per kWH and has a power factor of .87, its penalty would be:

$$\frac{\text{kWh/Yr}}{\text{Power Factor}} - \frac{\text{kWh/Yr}}{.9} \times \text{kWh rate}$$

$$\frac{10,000,000}{.87} - \frac{10,000,000}{.9} \times \$.035$$

$$= \$13,409.03$$

Practically speaking, a power factor improvement or at least a review of power factor economics is indicated for any building that purchases at primary level or on a large commercial power rate, or which maintains one or more of its own electric substations. More specifically, *some power factor improvement will prove worthwhile if your electric use meets one or more of the following conditions:*

- power demand is recorded on bill (in kVA);
- electric rate has a kVAR or power factor penalty clause;
- there are problems with voltage regulation or chronic low voltage, or;
- load growth limits spare capacity and you need more capacity.

Causes for low power factor typically are lightly loaded motors which draw excessive amount of reactive power and increase energy losses in the overall distribution system. Power factor correction can be made through installation of capacitors at utilization equipment locations. Costs of equipment and installation usually can be paid back quickly, if (and only if) the utility charges for reactive power supplied. It is advisable to review the need for and amount of power factor correction on specific types of loads with either the utility, equipment manufacturer, or your consultant.

9. COMPUTER FACILITIES

Recent research shows that buildings with significant computer installations frequently consume as much as 1.5 and more times the amount of energy consumed by buildings without such installations. While the computer equipment itself obviously consumes energy, researchers feel that the primary reason for the high energy consumption rate is the extent to which the computer support facilities and equipment are in use. Typically, computer operations extend into periods when a building would otherwise be unoccupied —evening, late evening, early morning, weekends, etc. in some cases computer operations continue around-the-clock. As a result, the building systems required to support computer equipment and personnel—HVAC, lighting, food service, elevator, and other systems—also must be operational and so consume energy. Given the extensive amount of work performed by computers and those who man them, as well as their high rate of productivity, suggestions that their use be reduced to conserve energy would be out-of-the-question. Nonetheless, there are steps which can be taken to at least ensure that no more energy than is necessary is used to support computer operations.

MINIMAL EXPENSE

√a. Consult manufacturers to determine permissible temperature and humidity ranges. Adjust controls of computer-support HVAC equipment to provide those conditions which are acceptable and which will result in the minimum expenditure of heating/cooling/humidification/dehumidification energy.

√b. Reduce lighting levels to those minimums suggested by the computer equipment manufacturer.

√c. Develop a checklist for use by computer personnel. Such a checklist should include directions on operation of the building's lighting, HVAC, food service elevator and other systems during periods of general building nonoccupancy. In that it is the use of other-than-computer equipment which, it is felt, contributes most to the higher energy consumption of buildings with computer installations, this particular step is of particular importance.

SIGNIFICANT EXPENSE

d. Modify the HVAC system to permit independent conditioning of air in those areas, such as computer rooms, where special conditions are required. To provide computer-required conditions to areas where such conditions are not required can result in a significant waste of energy.

e. Modify the lighting system to provide proper illumination and selective control to enable energy savings particularly during extended periods of operation when the building otherwise would be unoccupied.

f. Consider installation of systems to recover heat produced by computer equipment and computer-area lighting for use elsewhere.

10. INTERIOR SPACE UTILIZATION

The way in which interior building space is utilized by occupants can have a pronounced effect on energy utilization as well as on business productivity. Some of the potentially beneficial modifications which should be considered include:

10.1 Work Methods Improvements

MINIMAL EXPENSE

√ a. Consider combining operations and work elements, changing sequence of operations, simplifying necessary operations, eliminating unnecessary work, and establishing preferred work methods. In this way, for example, trips between floors via the elevator can be reduced if several routine tasks can be undertaken while on the floor involved, instead of making two or three trips to perform each task separately.

10.2 Equipment and Materials Relocation

MINIMAL EXPENSE

√ a. Consider locating all computer and computer-type equipment which requires close temperature and humidity control in a common space to be served by a common system.

√ b. Where practical, place all heat-producing equipment such as duplicating machines in one area to enable easier control for heating and cooling purposes.

√ c. Locate wall hangings, displays and furniture away from supply and return air grilles and registers to prevent obstruction of air flow.

SIGNIFICANT EXPENSE

√ d. Consider removing partitions to create an open space effect which will permit much freer movement of air and a reduction in lighting requirements.

10.3 Other

MINIMAL EXPENSE

√ a. Close off unused areas and rooms. Where possible, be certain that blinds or other shading devices are drawn, registers closed, etc.

√ b. If possible, have persons working after hours work in proximity to one another to lessen lighting and HVAC (heating, ventilating and air-conditioning) requirements.

√ c. When repainting, consider use of light wall surfaces to reflect both heat and light.

√ d. If possible, place in proximity to one another those persons whose tasks require similar lighting levels.

11. ADVANCED TECHNOLOGIES

For our purposes, advanced technologies are those which include waste heat reclamation systems, solar energy systems, and building automation systems. The applicability of any one of these technologies, or specific versions of them, depends on numerous different factors. Any of them, in general, require substantial capital expense. In some cases, however, paybacks can be suprisingly rapid. For example, building automation systems can cost as much as $200,000 and more. Nonetheless, numerous case histories show paybacks of three years and less; in some cases, less than two years.

11.1 Waste Heat Recovery Systems

Waste heat recovery results in utilization of heat energy that otherwise would be rejected to waste. As such, heat recovery conserves energy, reduces operating costs and reduces peak loads.

The following discussion is intended to provide some basic information on the types of heat recovery systems available and some of their general applications. See also discussion above under 3.5 (a) (Boiler Stack Economizer), 3.5 (b) (Preheat Oil To Increase Efficiency), 3.5 (c) (Preheat Combustion Air to Increase Boiler Efficiency), and 5.8 (Heat of Light Recovery Systems).

a. Rotary Heat Exchanger

The rotary heat exchanger uses a heat transfer medium in the form of a cylindrical drum or wheel. When rotated slowly between the supply air stream and exhausted air stream it absorbs heat from the warmer air stream and rejects heat to the cooler air stream. In addition to sensible heat transfer, the wheel can be hygroscopically treated with a desiccant which transfers water vapor from the humid air stream to the drier air stream. Non-hygroscopic wheels transfer water vapor when the temperature of one air stream is below the dew point temperature of the other and there is direct condensation of water vapor. During operation at temperatures below 32°F, freezing usually is prevented by preheating the supply air.

Rotary heat exchangers are normally economical for all applications of 4000 cfm or more of ventilation air. Operating at approximately 8 to 10 rpm with a face velocity of 550 fpm, the non-hygroscopic rotary exchangers recover 70 to 80% sensible heat and 40 to 60% latent. Hygroscopic or enthalpy exchangers recover 70 to 80% total heat.

The location of the supply and exhaust ductwork in close proximity of each other can be an obstacle in many applications especially when exhaust streams are contaminated. In these cases, purge sections must be added to the wheel and special filtration may be necessary in the supply air.

b. Air-to-Air Heat Exchangers

Air-to-air exchangers transfer heat directly fron one air-stream to another through direct contact on either side of a metal heat transfer surface. This surface may be either convoluted plate (more common for low temperature use in HVAC system) or tube (more common for boiler flue gas heat transfer). Air-to-air heat exchangers may be purchased as packaged units or can be custom made. They transfer sensible heat only and are not designed for cooling applications. Size is limited only by the physical dimensions of the space available.

The efficiency of each installation end cost should be calculated based on the particular circumstances that apply. Although efficiencies of air-to-air heat exchangers generally all below 50%, it must be recognized that they are relatively inexpensive, have low resistance to air flow, require no motive power input, and are trouble free and durable.

c. Run-Around System

A limitation associated with passive heat recovery devices is that the supply and exhaust duct work must be close together. In some applications this may be physically impossible. In addition, cross contamination caused by leakage from exhaust to supply streams may be unacceptable when the exhaust contains noxious or poisonous fumes, or if there is a need for cleanliness. Both of these disadvantages can be overcome by using a run-around system which consists of finned-tube water coils located in the exhaust and supply air streams, and a pump circulating water or a water/antifreeze solution between the coils. In this form the system is for sensible heat recovery only. It is seasonably reversible, preheating in the winter and precooling in the summer. As with other heat recovery devices, the coils are subject to corrosion, condensation and the possibility of freeze-up.

Coils and pump are normally selected to achieve sensible recovery efficiencies of 40% to 60%. Greater efficiencies can be achieved by adding more coils in the heat exchangers to increase their capacity. When finned tubing is added, however, the pressure drop across the coil increases and more fan power is required for the supply and exhaust system. Additional tubing also increases the pumping horsepower required, so gains in efficiency will be partially offset by increased power requirements.

If latent recovery is necessary, the system can be modified by replacing the water coils with a cooling tower surface. Therefore, an additional solution pump is needed to complete the system. This provides total heat or enthalpy transfer as the solution absorbs heat and water vapor from the air streams, and also acts as an air washer or scrubber.

d. Heat Pipe

A heat pipe, is a passive heat exchanger which involves a closed fluid cycle within a sealed tube. Cool air passing over one end of the tube is heated when it condenses the fluid enclosed in the tube. The warmer air stream passing over the other end of the tube is cooled when it evaporates the fluid contained in the tube. The action is reversible and operates whenever there is a temperature difference between either end of the tube. Any range of supply air cfm can be handled by the addition of more tubes to the heat exchanger rack. Because they contain no moving parts so there is minimal leakage between air streams. Mechanical energy is not used except in the form of increased fan horsepower to overcome static pressure losses. Note that the supply and exhaust ductwork must be brought into close proximity to each other.

e. Shell and Tube Heat Exchangers

Shell and tube heat exchangers can be used to exchange heat in liquid-to-liquid, steam-to-liquid, and gas-to-liquid configurations. All three configurations are commercially available in a wide range of sizes and outputs and with reliable heat exchange data. Particularly favorable applications are to capture energy from hot condensate, hot refrigerant gas, condenser water, and hot drain lines from kitchens and laundries. Heat exchangers should be insulated to prevent unnecessary heat loss and should be constructed of materials to suit the application.

f. Double-Bundle Condenser System

A double-bundle condenser is constructed with two entirely separate water circuits enclosed in the same shell. Hot refrigerant gas from the compressor is discharged into the condenser shell where its heat is absorbed by either one of the water circuits or by both simultaneously depending on the requirements of the system at a given time. One of the circuits is called the building water circuit and the other the cooling tower circuit. The condenser is split into two independent hydronic circuits to prevent contamination of the building water and its associated pipes, coils, pumps and valves with cooling tower water, which may contain dirt and corrosive chemicals. When a double-bundle condenser is added to a standard refrigeration machine the heat rejected by the compressor is made available to the building water circuit.

In certain applications the amount of heat reclaimed during occupied hours may exceed the daytime heating requirements of perimeter zones. This excess heat can be stored for release during times when the building is unoccupied.

The cost of installing a double-bundle condenser system is such that, in most cases, it probably will be most feasible as a replacement for a system which already is at or near the end of its useful life.

11.2 Solar Energy Systems

Solar energy obviously has tremendous potential because the energy is free. Unfortunately, the systems required to harness that energy are not free. In fact, the cost of these systems in past years has kept solar energy in the experimental and trial stages. Now that the cost of energy has risen so dramatically, however, the comparative cost of solar energy systems have become more realistic. The fact that the energy source itself is both infinite and pollution-free are two additional positive factors.

Engineering feasibility studies of solar energy systems can be performed by qualified consultants who can select equipment for analysis, estimate costs, and predict annual performance. Because the initial investment required to install one of these systems is significantly higher than that required for conventional systems, special care is necessary to ensure that life-cycle cost economics are determined accurately.

At present, solar energy is used primarily for domestic hot water heating and, to a lesser extent, space heating.

a. Domestic Hot Water Heating

Solar water heaters have been used for more than 30 years throughout the world, especially in Israel, Australia, Japan, and Florida. Current high costs of energy now have awakened a more general interest. Solar water heaters may be economically feasible in office buildings and stores with 25 or more full-time employees. Generally speaking, however, it usually is not economically feasible to use a solar system for 100% of domestic hot water requirements unless:

- the collector is used for additional services;
- hot water temperature requirements do not exceed 90°F;
- an existing storage tank is oversized for the building requirements, and
- the building is located in a temperate or hot climatic zone.

Solar water heaters are commercially available in the United States as components offered separately or together in a complete package. Components include a flat plate collector, storage tank (existing storage tanks can be used), piping, controls, circulating pump and, in climates where the collector is subjected to freezing weather, a heat exchanger with a secondary pump, piping circuit and anti-freeze.

The thermal performance of a solar water heating system depends upon:

- climatological and meterological conditions;
- solar collector size, design, and construction
- orientation of the collector and tilt angle with the horizontal;
- size of the storage tank, and
- temperature of the domestic hot water.

For normal hot water use, approximately one square foot of collector per one gallon of hot water used per day is adequate. If kitchens or other processes require hot water at elevated temperatures, collector area required is from 25% to 50% more. The solar collector can be mounted on the main roof, the roof of a building extension, or on-site. Although each installation must be considered a unique subsystem, the following solar collector installation guideline should be considered:

   i.   Provide adequate structural support to carry the dead weight (12 lbs./sq.ft.) of the collector plus wind loading.

   ii.   Orient the collector 10° west of due south if possible, but 20° either side of due south will not materially affect the performance. If the orientation must be farther to the east or west, plan on additional collector area.

   iii.   If the collector is used solely to supply hot water, a fixed tilt of latitude plus 10° will usually be optimum — variations of 10° up or down will not seriously affect yearly performance.

   iv.   Collector must not be shaded more than 10% of the time, or a larger collector area will be required.

   v.   Provide approximately one square foot of collector and one gallon of hot water storage capacity per 16 gallons of hot water used per week. If kitchens or other processes require hot water at elevated temperature, provide one square foot of collector per 20 gallons of hot water used per year.

   vi.   The existing domestic hot water heating system, even though inefficient or undersized will usually be adequate to provide heat to supplement the solar collector system.

b. Space Heating and Cooling

Prior to 1972, only about twenty solar heated buildings were erected in the United States. Of those, only one was a commercial building. Since 1972 there has been a proliferation of solar energy activity in the United States, for both new buildings and existing buildings.

The hardware for solar space heating and cooling includes solar collectors, piping, controls and storage systems which are similar to those used for domestic hot water heating, but with the following major differences:

- The required collector area and storage volumes must be larger and are more costly.
- Collectors must produce hotter water temperatures for space heating. Temperatures up to 180°F are desirable, but lower temperatures can be used.
- The orientation of the collector is more critical.
- Absorber plates with selective surfaces rather than flat black coating are be more economically feasible for heating and cooling applications than for solar water heating alone.
- Interface with existing heating and/or cooling system is critical.
- Storage systems must have a greater heat storage capacity per square foot of collector.
- Rocks or phase changing salts can be used for thermal storage instead of water in some cases.
- Collectors can be air instead of liquid heating types in selected applications.
- A full sized back-up heating system is required to supplement the solar system.

In most areas of the country for most buildings the cost of a solar energy system to provide 100% of the heating and/or cooling is prohibitive. These systems can be used to supplement more conventional systems however. Because of the extremely limited applicability of solar energy to supplement heating and cooling systems of existing buildings at this time — due primarily to cost, space and structural requirements — no further discussion is provided herein.

11.3 Building Automation Systems

A building automation system can provide constant surveillance of all building systems to enable the most efficient and effective use of energy and manpower possible. While an automated control system obviously can be used to monitor and control central system elements, it also serves to connect virtually all other energized systems of a building or complex of buildings into one central location.

Building automation, or central control systems are most applicable for larger more complex buildings or groups of buildings and vary from the relatively simple types designed to perform a few functions to the progressively more complex type performing more and more complicated functions.

Typical functions performed by a building automation system include:

- monitor all fire alarm and security devices;
- monitor operating conditions of all systems and reschedule set points to optimize energy use;

- monitor all system for off-normal conditions;
- limit peak electrical demand values by predicting trends of loads and shedding nonessential services according to programmed priorities;
- monitor continuously selected portions of any systems and store information in bulk memory for later retrieval and use in updating software;
- optimize maintenance tasks to effect maximum equipment life for minimum manpower labor and costs;
- optimize operation of all systems to obtain the maximum effect for the minimum expenditure of energy, and;
- provide inventory control of spare parts, materials, and tools used for maintenance.

Judicious use of these functions enables staff to operate all systems from the central console and have minute-by-minute control of operations. Any physical plant critical alarm will be reported automatically at the console. The operator will then be able to scan the system in alarm, analyze the fault and dispatch the correct maintenance man to effect repairs. Maintenance alarm summaries will be available on demand as well as being printed out once each day. These maintenance alarms will allow work scheduling and maximum use to be made of maintenance personnel.

Although building automation systems usually are very costly, they generally are so cost-effective that they generate rapid paybacks. Sources of cost benefit include:

i. energy cost/savings generated by energized systems optimization;
ii. energy cost savings generated by demand control;
iii. labor cost savings due to reduced manpower requirements (operating, maintenance and security personnel) and reduced manpower educational requirements (central plant operators);
iv. increased useful life of energized systems and their components due to more efficient operation and improved maintenance;
v. reduced insurance costs due to improved security and fire protection systems;
vi. improved marketability of rental space, and;
vii. added value to building.

There also are numerous other component manufacturers now involved in the field. Some of these provide the building owner or electrical contractors with all the assistance required to create a multi-manufacturer system designed specifically for the building involved.

a. System Types and Components

Building Automation systems marketed by the major temperature control manufacturers have common features and can accomplish a similar range of tasks. Each manufacturer uses coding and computer languages which are unique to the system, however, and cannot be decoded by any other system. Once a basic system has been selected and installed, however, all subsequent additions must be obtained from the original manufacturer. For this reason it is important to investigate thoroughly the expansion potential of a system in relation to future predicted requirements.

The typical system is composed of four major parts.

- Interface Panels: Located at strategic points throughout the building, usually in equipment rooms. These panels form the focal point of all signals to and from a particular area.
- Transmission System: Between the central console and all interface panels.
- Transmission System: Between the central console and all interface panels.
- Central Control Console and Associated Hardware: Located in a control room (usually close to boiler room and chief engineer's office).
- Software: Program generated by the manufacturer or another source in conjunction with the prospective user. Software input via magnetic tapes, paper tapes, or cards, contains the basic operating instructions for the computer and is stored in the form of "bits" of information either in core or bulk memory.

b. Interface Requirements

Maximum benefit of a Building Automation system is obtained when many different items of equipment are measured, monitored, and controlled. For this to be obtained, the central control system must be interfaced with the existing equipment to obtain the information in rational form and exert its control function.

Interface of two types of signal is required: binary signals which comprise only two alternatives (on/off, open/close, etc.) and analog signals which measure a value against a particular scale (temperature, pressure, etc.).

Binary signals are used as instructions to start and stop equipment, open and close valves and dampers, etc. They are also used for retrieving data such as on/off, open/closed, etc.

Analog signals are used as instructions to raise or lower temperature set points, adjust damper positions, raise or lower pressure set points, etc. They are also used for retrieving data such as temperature, pressure, humidity, etc.

When selecting a central control system, first assemble a complete list of all desired interface points under the two categories of binary and analog and arrange them in groups served by interface panels. Depending on the type of existing controls, motor starters, contactors, etc., modifications and additions may be required to allow satisfactory interface.

c. Signal Transmission

To make effective use of the computer's capabilities, information between the computer console and the interface panels must be transmitted an easily-handled format at high speed. The most convenient method of transmission is digital, where information is represented by pulses arranged serially and transmitted through a single core conductor. Digital cable is commonly coaxial, although some systems use a twisted pair of insulated wires. Multplex cable also is used. It typically comprises between 50 and 100 separate wires and has an overall diameter of one inch. It is more difficult to install in existing buildings where empty conduits and throughways are not available. Some systems use multiplex cable on the grounds that analog signals can be transmitted in unmodified form while digital transmission requires conversion of signals from analog to digital form with a small loss of accuracy at the interface panel. (Conversely, analog signals are sensitive to interference from "spikes" and other spurious signals induced by adjacent building wiring.) Obviously, the transmission methods must be analyzed based on the particular circumstances involved. Generally speaking however, digital transmission systems provide more options for later additions because multiplex systems have a finite limit to the number of points that can be connected.

d. Control Console and Hardware

Most major manufacturers' control console and hardware items, such as printers, graphic display, CRT, and input/output keyboards give comparable performance, and most offer options to suit the prospective user's particular requirements. For example, different levels of access into the computer from the keyboard are available, ranging from restriction to normal operation at the lowest level up to reprogramming for the highest level.

The central processor or computer usually is supplied with integral core memory. If core capacity will be exceeded the addition of bulk memory unit should be considered, providing the computer selected can be interfaced with external memory.

e. Software

Software or programs for common applications are available from many manufacturers, most of which have libraries of application programs developed over many years. The cost of these programs is low when compared to that of custom-written software. When selecting a central control system, investigate the extent and range of the library available.

Functions which can be provided by the system through programming include:

i.   Ventilating and Cooling Systems Optimization
Typical optimization functions performed by a computerized building control system include the following:

- Start/Stop Optimization: Includes monitoring of outdoor air temperature, solar effects (including presence of cloud cover, etc.), indoor temperature and humidity, and thermal mass of the building; calculation and analysis of data; determination of which systems should be started and stopped and when, and appropriate control functions. This particular function can result in significant energy savings when one considers the many different energy-consuming elements (fans, pumps, chillers, etc.) of the systems involved.
- Enthalpy Optimization: During the cooling season, the total heat content (enthalpy) of the outdoor and recirculated building air is monitored and compared. When enthalpy of the outdoor air is lower than that of the indoor air, a larger percentage of outdoor air is used to reduce chiller load. During the heating season, economizer cycle control is utilized to vary the percentage of outdoor and recirculated air to maintain a constant mixed air temperature to handle internal heat gains (from people, lighting,

machinery, etc.). Enthalpy optimization also can reduce energy consumption for humidification during the heating season by reducing outdoor air volumes. When heat reclamation systems are installed, selection of the best operating mode becomes somewhat more complex, but can be handled easily by a computerized control system.

- Chiller Optimization: Building Automation system can store and analyze information on operational characteristics of chillers and generate controls so most efficient chiller or combination of chillers is operated for an existing or anticipated building load. This normally is accomplished by measuring flow through the evaporator and condenser of each chiller and the reclaim coils. Differential temperature across evaporator section, condenser sections, and reclaim sections also is monitored. This enables the computer to calculate the total energy being produced by each machine. Total electrical usage is monitored continuously thus enabling instantaneous efficiency calculations. When the temperatures are monitored the minimum energy requirement for the system can be calculated. The computer then will cause the most efficient chiller or combination of chillers to be operated. Efficiency is monitored by the computer and is continuously entered into memory. In this way the system always is working with the latest information. If the need for heating or cooling energy is determined late in the day, chillers will not be started if the building soon will be unoccupied. Accordingly, chiller optimization normally is an integral part of start/stop time optimization.

- Solar Heat Optimization: A building's solar heat load is a function of solar exposure. Programming can be used to alter the HVAC system's operating characteristics as solar exposure changes with the seasons, time of day, cloud cover, etc.
- Energy and Psychrometric Calculation: The computer can be used to calculate BTU and flow data for water and steam thus eliminating a need for individual metering devices. Since characteristics of air can be determined by any two variables—dry-bulb temperature and relative humidity are used most frequently—simple programs can be developed to obtain data on other variables as needed.
- Automatic Mode Switching: Many comfort conditioning systems have individual system controls for switching from cooling season mode to heating season mode or vice versa. During intermediate fall and spring seasons conditions requiring changeover can occur at any time of day. Depending on its degree of sophistication, the system can either tell the operator when the switch-over should take place or can make the switchover automatically.

ii.   Lighting Control
An effective program of lighting control requires circuiting that enables selected or staggered portions of lighting to be extinguished while leaving enough light for activities such as after-hours cleaning, maintenance, and mul-

tishirt operations. Lobby and ornamental lighting are areas where savings can be realized, especially to hold down peak electrical demand.

iii. Electrical Demand Limiting

Most hardware which incorporates automatic power demand measurement and load-shedding accommodates a maximum of 20 loads (where a large number of motors in the one half to 20-horsepower range can be connected in series to be shed at the same time). In most cases much of the lighting in a large commercial building can be shed for a few minutes out of each interval without the occupants even being aware of the reduced lighting. The same applies to ventilation fans, sewage ejection pumps, deep freeze motors, and other miscellaneous power users. Most chillers can be throttled back for a short term during each interval without any appreciable effect on the cooling capacity.

iv. Maintenance Scheduling

Although a Building Automation system cannot perform maintenance, it can be programmed to provide printouts of regular maintenance procedures and to notify when unscheduled maintenance procedures may be required. There are at least four ways in which maintenance scheduling can be handled, as follows:

- Calendar Time Scheduling: The easiest and most direct way to schedule maintenance. For example, every 20 days maintenance men could be instructed to change all air handling unit filters or once-a-month instructions can be given to grease and lubricate certain equipment, clean luminaires, etc.
- Machine Running Time Scheduling: Since all machinery does not run on a regular schedule, calendar time scheduling is not sufficient for many items. Accordingly, the central processing unit can be set to accumulate running time of certain equipment and, after a predetermined number of running hours for each time, print out maintenance instructions.
- Efficiency Scheduling: In certain cases the amount of time equipment runs will not be an accurate indicator of its operating efficiency or need for maintenance. Since the central processor can calculate equipment operating efficiency on the basis of raw data inputs, it can be programmed to provide maintenance instruction when efficiency deteriorates to a certain predetermined level.

- Early Warning Monitor: The system can be designed to provide early warning of impending equipment failure. As one example, bearings of certain pieces of equipment can be monitored for vibration and/or temperature. Should the vibration or temperature level increase to a certain predetermined level which indicate an immediate, unscheduled maintenance problem. (It also would be feasible for the computer to stop the particular piece of equipment involved—or the entire system of which it is a component, if necessary—until the needed maintenance or repair is performed.)

v. Management Information System

Building Automation systems provide valuable management functions that can produce a significant return on investment and enable additional control of energy consumption and cost. The computer's ability to store data, compute "indirect" analog quantities directly related to energy consumption (such at BTU's, kilowatt-hours, or tons of steam), and to provide hard copy records of these values is essential to effective planning for long term energy conservation practices. For example, an energy usage profile, printed by the automation system, is a convenient graphic representation of consumption patterns by hour, day, month, or year. With a computer, virtually any desired combination of actual performance parameters can be stored and subsequently extracted in hard copy in whatever form may be most convenient for analysis. While it is difficult to place explicit dollar values on these management features, they nevertheless are useful and valuable tools for planning and implementing effective energy conservation.

vi. Security

- Door Security and Control: Achieved by a signalling device for use by those wishing to gain entrance. An intercom can be used for the operator to ascertain the identity of the person. If he is to be allowed in, the operator can activate an electromechanical device which releases the door. Closed circuit television and magnetically coded identification cards can be used to supplement or replace certain elements of this system.

- Intrusion Protection: Consists of monitoring devices attached to possible ingresses and connected to the central console. Typical devices are the familiar strips of metallic foil placed on window which activates an electric circuit if broken, as well as contact devices on doors; photo-electric beams; infrared beams; vibration detection devices; ultrasonic motion detectors; video motion detectors; microwave detectors (which sense disturbances in the electormagnetic field); electrical capacitance detectors (for small areas), and so on. Selected objects, such as file cabinets and vaults, can be fitted with devices which sense changes in electrical capacitance or vibration.

- Closed Circuit TV (CCTV) Security: CCTV cameras can be placed to monitor selected doors, isolated pedestrian tunnels, certain stairwells, large open areas (such as malls or parking lots), etc. The security or central console can have one viewer for each camera.

- Guard Communication: A transmitter-receiver can be built into the console for communication with guards carrying walkie-talkies, or the operator can signal guards to communicate by activating a pager carried, or the operator may contact the guard by means of activating a light at the guard tour station. Also, a guard can notify the operator of his position on his tour of duty by activating signals at each of his tour stations.

vii. Fire Detection

A Building Automation system is an invaluable asset for purposes of fire detection and alarm. The central processing unit can be designed to continuously monitor the entire building's fire detection and alarm network, including flame and smoke detectors, thermal fire detectors, firestats, sprinkler alarms, etc.

Any off-normal condition can be reported immediately, along with the type and location of the device triggered. Depending on the sophistication of the system, certain control functions can be implemented automatically, especially in the absence of an operator. Such functions could include notifying the nearest fire station of a problem, activation of sprinkler systems, activation of audible alarms, and even activation of selected pre-recorded tapes for building-wide transmission providing clear, distinct instructions, programmable so selected instructions are broadcast to the respective areas of the building to which they apply.

IMPLEMENTING THE
VII. PROGRAM

Implementation of a TEM program is not a "one-shot deal." While certain initial steps must be taken, true effectiveness can be obtained only when management aspects are continued on a year-round basis. The time required for successful implementation is not excessive. But even if it were, the savings to be obtained would more than offset the time and expense involved.

Here follows a relatively brief listing of guidelines to be observed for implementing both initial and continuing elements of the program once the survey has been completed.

1. SURVEY ANALYSIS

If a professional was retained to perform the initial energy survey, he also should be instructed to perform an analysis to identify actions which can be taken to effect energy conservation, providing details on those which are most feasible and general information about those which probably will not be undertaken for a while, such as addition of heat recovery equipment.

If you intend to perform the analysis yourself, consider these guidelines:

a. Determine where energy inefficiencies and wastage now exist. This does not imply modifications to the system, but rather those actions which should be taken to bring elements of the system up to the effeciency at which they should function. This in itself can save a considerable amount of energy in most buildings.

b. If a given piece of equipment is operating poorly, determine why. Is it because it: needs adjustment, repair or replacement? is not being maintained well? is being operated improperly? etc. The cause, of course, leads directly to the cure. If poor maintenance seems to be the problem, it would mean that a revised maintenance schedule may be required, or that more instruction must be given, or that the person performing the maintenance should be replaced. Many of the guidelines provided in this manual will provide direction on this subject. At all times, however, consider how any change—even bringing

the system up to full operating efficiency—will affect other elements of the same system or other systems.

c. Determine where systems can be modified in accordance with guidelines provided to achieve greater energy efficiency. In so doing, consider how the modifications should be made and what the effect will be on other systems related to it directly or indirectly.

d. Determine the problems which are likely to occur through implementation of actions, in terms of energized systems, nonenergized systems, human systems, tenant relationships, etc. The more you can think along these lines and recognize beforehand the stumbling blocks which probably will present themselves later on, the better your chances of avoiding the stumbling blocks completely. Consideration of codes and other regulations is of critical importance. There may be many more than you thought possible, depending on local circumstances, as the following list indicates:

- Building Code
- Electrical Code
- Mechanical Code (Heating, Cooling, Ventilation, etc.)
- Plumbing Code
- Fire Prevention Code
- Elevator Code
- Health Codes
- Occupational Safety and Health Administration Regulations
- Public Utility Regulations (Electricity, Steam, Gas, Water, Sewer, Telephone)
- Air and Water Pollution Regulations

While representatives of each of the agencies involved can be contacted, it may be far easier to utilize a consultant who is familiar with most of these concerns.

e. Establish the cost of each alternative and the possible amount of time it will take to implement it from start to finish.

f. Establish the amount of energy and/or money implementation of each item will save.

2. SETTING PRIORITIES

It is impossible to tell you what your priorities should be because only you know the criteria which must be used as the basis for establishing them. Compounding the problem is the fact that criteria will be modified by existing conditions. For example, it would seem logical to say that an immediate priority would be to adjust, repair, or replace all faulty equipment, controls, and so on. But this may be a waste of time and expense if the piece of equipment involved should be replaced, or if the whole system should be modified, perhaps to the extent that the faulty piece of equipment would be unnecessary. In other words, in establishing priorities, all practical actions possible must be looked at to determine which alternatives will be most effective in light of the interrelationships which exist.

In terms of energy conservation, perhaps the most logical approach is to give top consideration to those factors which relate to areas of high energy use. Using a one-to-five rating scale, where 5 represents the greatest potential for savings; the following generalized listing can be established:

- Ventilation (5)
- External Heat Gain and Heat Loss (Solar Radiation, Wind, etc.) (4)
- Lighting System (4)
- Heating and Cooling System (3)
- Transmission Heat Gain and Heat Loss (2)
- Domestic Hot Water (1)
- Power System (1)
- Internal Heat Gains (Business Equipment, People, etc) (1)

Assuming that such effort direction can be determined, the next step would be to establish criteria to direct action within each area of concern, be it ventilation or lighting. Criteria which will affect this management element include:

- potential for energy modification,
- ease of implementation,
- cost of implementation,
- suitability to perform the function,
- effects on other systems, and
- derived benefits in terms of operation and maintenance.

Cost, of course, is one of the essential priorities, but the way in which the subject can be approached depends, to a great degree, on an owner's attitude and financial position.

Costs of modification should be evaluated using life-cycle costing techniques which involve determination of total cost of ownership (including capital costs, costs of operating and maintenance, labor and material, energy and fuel costs) over the life of the equipment. Such a study can be complex, thus should be performed by an engineering economist. Before undertaking such action, therefore, you may wish to utilize one or more of the three simpler techniques which, although not as comprehensive as life-cycle costing, can be used to study alternatives. These are benefit/cost analysis, payback period analysis, and present worth analysis. Any of these cases, when forecasting costs over an extended period, consider that costs of labor and materials probably will be increasing at the rate of 8% to 10% or more per year. Energy costs also will increase, and your local utilities and/or fuel suppliers probably will be able to give you some insight on anticipated rates of increase. If you are unsure as to what rate of interest you probably will have to pay, consult a local banker or use a figure of 1% to 2% above the prime lending rate.

2.1 Benefit/Cost Analysis

Benefit/cost analysis can be utilized in two ways: to determine whether it is worthwhile to replace an existing system with a new system, and to determine which of two or more alternative new systems provides the best cost benefit.

To determine whether it would be more advisable to retain existing equipment or obtain new, more efficient equipment, the following factors must be considered:

a. Maintenance savings to be obtained by installing the new equipment.
b. Operating and energy cost savings to be obtained by installing the new equipment.
c. Salvage value of old equipment.
d. Capital cost of new equipment including legal fees, design professional fees, installation charges, cost of equipment, etc.
e. Costs of financing.
f. Changes in property taxes as a result of installing new equipment.
g. Income tax factors.
h. Changes in rental income as a result of installing new equipment.

If it can be shown on a purely monetary basis that installation of new equipment will result in savings, obviously it should be considered strongly. But more than monetary factors should be considered. One must also take into account the ease of maintenance and possibly the ability to do away with certain positions; possible lowered number of tenant complaints, greater reliability, and so on.

When utilizing benefit/cost analysis to select between two systems, a simple formula can be used to determine if the additional initial costs of the more expensive system are merited in light of long-term cost factors. The result is a benefit/cost ratio which, if it exceeds 1, indicates that extra initial expenses will result in long-term savings, as shown in the example immediately below.

Total First Cost System A	$18,000	
Total First Cost System B	20,000	
System B exceeds System A by		$2,000
Annual Operating, Maintenance and Energy Cost, System A	$1,600	
Annual Operating, Maintenance and Energy Cost, System B	1,000	
System A exceeds System B by		$ 600

Assuming a 20-year useful life for each system and a 10% interest rate, the capital recovery factor (a factor that, multiplied by the total loan amount or total principal, yields the annual payment necessary to repay debt) can be computed from Figure VII-1. In this case, it would be 0.11746. Given this, amortization cost for additional capital investment of system B would be .11746 × $2,000.

or $234.92. Therefore, the benefit/cost ratio for system B would be:

$$\frac{\text{annual savings}}{\text{amort. cost}} \frac{\$600.00}{\$234.92} = 2.55$$

Because the benefit/cost ratio exceeds 1, system B, although initially more costly, should provide more long-term savings.

2.2 Payback Period Analysis

Failure to consider cost of debt service is the most common error made when making a payback period analysis. One cannot say, for example, that an initial capital investment of $50,000 which results in an annual maintenance and operation savings of $10,000 has a payback period of five years. To do so would ignore the fact that interest must be paid on the loan, or that—if no loan is involved—the money used would otherwise be earning interest. A simple graph has been provided in Figure VII-2 to indicate payback periods. As can be seen, the vertical axis is based on the ratio of C (initial cost of a system) over S (annual maintenance and operating cost savings). The horizontal axis shows the payback period in years. Each curve represents a different rate of interest. Thus, assuming an initial investment of $3,000 and annual operating and maintenance saving of $600 (which will be applied to repaying the loan), the result is a C/S ratio of 5 which, at 10% interest, results in payback period of a little more than seven years.

If more accuracy is required, the following formula can be used:

$$n = \frac{\log \dfrac{S/rC}{S/rC - 1}}{\log (1 + r)}$$

where: C = capital cost
S = annual operating and maintenance savings
r = interest rate
n = number of years to achieve payback

Fig. VII-1 Capital Recovery Factor

Interest Rate, r

Years, n	10.0	12.0	15.0
5	0.26380	0.27741	0.29832
10	0.16275	0.17698	0.19925
15	0.13147	0.14682	0.17102
20	0.11746	0.13388	0.15976
25	0.11017	0.12750	0.15470
30	0.10608	0.12414	0.15230

2.3 Present Worth Analysis

Present worth analysis centers on the time value of money. X dollars now is not worth as much as X dollars tomorrow.

Assume, for example, that you invest $1 at 10% interest compounded annually for one year. At the end of that year the dollar would be worth $1.10. Thus, assuming a 10% interest rate, we can say that $1.10 received one year from now has a present worth of $1.

To determine the present worth of money to be received in the future, one must discount future dollars on the basis of what they could be earning doing something else. In other words, $1.10 one year from now has a present worth of $1 assuming that the next best investment would earn 10%. If all that we could do was 5%, though, then $1.10 received one year from now would be worth $1.05 today.

The computation is simple. To determine future value, multiply by unity plus the percentage rate of interest. $1 invested at 10% annual interest compounded annually will be worth $1.10 in one year (1 × 1.1); $1.21 at the end of two years (1.1 × 1.1), $1.33 after three years (1.21 × 1.1) and so on.

To determine present worth of $1 one year from now, assuming you could get a 10% investment, you divide by unity plus 10%, so, $1 one year from now discounted by the next best investment—in this case 10%—would be worth only 91 cents, or 1 ÷ 1.1. The value of one dollar received two years from now, discounting again at a 10% rate, would be 83 cents, or (÷ 1.1) 1.1, and so on, as shown here.

YEAR	PRESENT VALUE OF $1 AT 10%
1	.91
2	.83
3	.75
4	.68
5	.62

In the same manner, you can calculate the present value of $1 *per year* received each year for a number of years:

YEARS (N)	PRESENT VALUE OF $1 RECEIVED ANNUALLY FOR "N" YEARS AT 10%
1	.91
2	1.74
3	2.49

These figures are obtained simply by adding present values together. Thus, the present value of one dollar one year from now plus another dollar two years from now is equal to .91 and .73, or $1.74.

What all this means essentially is this. Building owners can make a capital investment either by investing in something that will yield interest or other income, or they can make an investment in something which will result in *cost avoidance*.

The amount of interest which the owner could obtain from an alternate investment is considered the next best investment. In other words, assuming that he can earn 10%, then 10% becomes the rate for the next best investment and is the discount rate that is used to determine present worth of any

Fig. VII-2 Payback Period

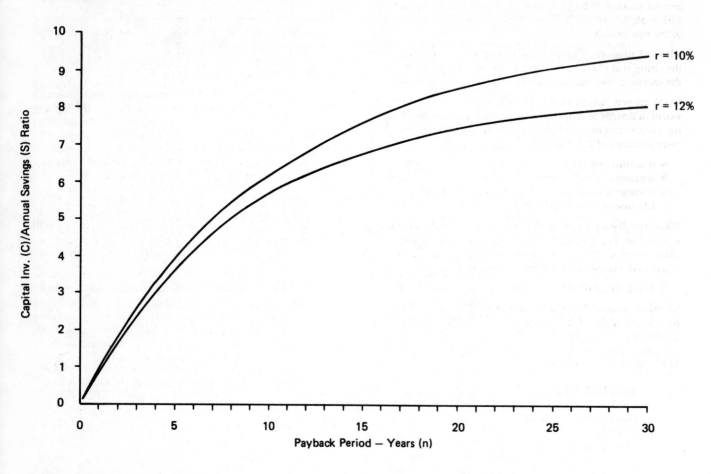

alternate use for the money. Obviously, you have to determine what the prevailing discount rate is.

Before we expand on this subject, look at the present worth table shown here:

PRESENT VALUE OF $1 RECEIVED ANNUALLY FOR N YEARS

Years (N)	6%	8%	10%	12%	14%	16%	18%	20%
1	0.94	0.93	0.91	0.89	0.87	0.86	0.85	0.83
2	1.83	1.78	1.74	1.69	1.65	1.61	1.57	1.53
3	2.67	2.58	2.49	2.40	2.32	2.24	2.17	2.11
4	3.46	3.31	3.17	3.04	2.91	2.80	2.69	2.59
5	4.21	3.99	3.79	3.61	3.43	3.27	3.13	2.99
6	4.92	4.62	4.35	4.11	3.89	3.68	3.50	3.33
7	5.58	5.21	4.87	4.56	4.29	4.04	3.81	3.60
8	6.21	5.75	5.33	4.97	4.64	4.34	4.08	3.84
9	6.80	6.25	5.76	5.33	4.95	4.61	4.30	4.03
10	7.36	6.71	6.14	5.65	5.21	4.83	4.49	4.19
15	9.71	8.56	7.60	6.81	6.14	5.56	5.09	4.67
20	11.47	9.82	8.51	7.47	6.62	5.93	5.35	4.87
25	12.78	10.67	9.08	7.84	6.87	6.10	5.47	4.95
30	13.76	11.26	9.43	8.05	7.00	6.18	5.52	4.98
40	15.05	11.92	9.78	8.24	7.10	6.23	5.55	5.00

Assuming a piece of equipment with a 20-year life, you can see that the predicted value of $1 after 20 years is $8.51 at 10% discount rate. Accordingly the present worth of $5,000 annual savings to be generated by the piece of equipment is 8.51 × $5,000, or $42,550: more than double the initial cost of the equipment.

This calculation, of course, fails to take into consideration the rising cost of energy. As energy costs escalate, the value of the energy conserved, and cost avoided, likewise increases.

PWF (present worth factor) is used to evaluate the present worth of Energy Management savings to be achieved, including consideration for of the increasing cost of energy. The three elements of PWF are:

- discount rate (D);
- economic life (L), and
- average annual rate of energy price increase over the lifetime of the equipment (P).

When the discount rate, or the rate of return for the next best investment (D), is equal to the average annual rate of energy price increase (P), the PWF—or present worth factor—is equal to the economic life of the equipment, or

When D=P, PWF=L

In other words, if average annual savings on a piece of equipment with a life expectancy of 20 years is $5,000, and the discount rate of 10% is equal to the estimated average rate of energy price increase, the present worth of savings is $100,000, derived as follows:

> When D=P, PWF=L
> L=20
> Annual Savings = $5,000
> PWF=20
> Present value of savings = PWF × Savings
>   = 20 × $5,000
>   = $100,000

When the discount rate D does not equal annual savings, you can use a formula to determine present worth or you can refer to Figure VII-3. The formula used is:

$$\text{When } D \neq P, \text{ PWF} = \left[\frac{1+P}{D-P}\right] \left\{ 1 - \left[\frac{1+P}{1+P}\right]^L \right\}$$

To see how this works, consider the following figures:

> D = 10%
> P = 6%
> L = 5 years

$$\text{PWF} = \left[\frac{1+.06}{.10-.06}\right] \left\{ 1 - \left[\frac{1+.06}{1+.10}\right]^5 \right\}$$

$$= \left[\frac{1.06}{.04}\right] \left\{ 1 - \left[\frac{1.06}{1.10}\right]^5 \right\}$$

$$= (26.5) \left[1 - (.964)^5 \right]$$

$$= (26.5)(1 - .834)$$

$$= (26.5)(.166)$$

$$= 4.48$$

Fig. VII-3 Present Worth Factors (at 10% Discount Rate)

Economic Life

	5	10	15	20	25
0%	3.79	6.14	7.61	8.51	9.08
2%	4.01	6.76	8.64	9.93	10.82
4%	4.24	7.44	9.86	11.69	13.07
6%	4.48	8.20	11.30	13.87	16.00
8%	4.73	9.05	12.99	16.59	19.87
10%	5.00	10.00	15.00	20.00	25.00
12%	5.28	11.06	17.38	24.30	31.87

It should be noted, of course, that this particular set of figures is based on a 10% discount rate. Using the example given so far—$20,000 piece of equipment that will generate an initial $5,000 per year savings and which has a 20-year lifetime, and assuming a 10% discount rate, we can see that the present worth of savings with a 6% annual energy cost increase is $69,350, derived by multiplying initial savings by a present worth factor or PWF of 13.87. For an 8% annual energy price increase, you would use the PWF of 16.59 and see that the present worth of savings is $82,950.

2.3.1 Operating and Maintenance Costs

To include the cost of operation and maintenance in your calculations, determine current cost of operation and maintenance (O&M), estimated rate of increase, and—as a result—the present worth of these costs based on the PWF.

For example, assuming that a 20-year life for the piece of equipment, and a 10% discount rate; and assuming that cost of O&M is $1,000 per year and is expected to increase at 4% per year, it can be seen that the present worth of O&M costs are $11,690, or $1,000 times the PWF of 11.69 from figure VII-3.

In the event that O&M costs will not rise on a regular average rate, for example, because the machine has to have a major overhaul every five years, the present worth of O&M can be derived accurately only by evaluating the present worth of O&M for each year it will be in effect, and adding them all up together. To determine present worth for any given year, use the formula:

$$\frac{\text{Present Worth of O\&M}}{\text{Incurred in Nth year}} = \frac{\text{O\&M Cost in the Nth year}}{(1 + \text{discount rate})^N}$$

3. INITIAL MANAGEMENT EFFORTS

Initial management efforts required for the TEM approach are not dissimilar from other initial organizational steps which must be undertaken when establishing a new venture.

First, determine what specifically is to be done to effect energy conservation. This includes allocation of resources (manpower, money, etc.), development of policies and procedures to be followed, assignment of specific accountable responsibilities, obtaining cooperation of operating personnel and tenants, determining what changes need to be made to operating and maintenance procedures and schedules, noting which equipment is to be repaired, adjusted or replaced, and so on.

Second, determine precisely what must be done to effect each change, in terms of meetings, hiring additional personnel, ordering materials, etc.

Third, determine the approximate amount of time which will be involved to effect each objective. For example, if signs must be printed, you may have to allow one week for preparation and approval of copy and graphics; two weeks for printing; one week for distribution, and three or four days for posting.

Fourth, determine when certain objectives must be completed. When you do this, of course, you automatically will determine when work on the objective should be started by using data obtained through the third step, above.

Fifth, prepare a master schedule which shows exactly what will be happening. Assign competent personnel to the various functions Examine what you have prepared for possible conflicts, such as having someone scheduled to do something during the week he is on vacation, etc. Reschedule to avoid conflicts.

Do not expect everything to run smoothly. There are bound to be problems; schedules not met; people who fail to do what they were supposed to, etc. By having a master schedule, however, you will be able to make adjustments relatively easily. As time moves on, you also will be able to develop even more specific monthly schedules, most of which will contain routine procedures refined through experience.

4. OBTAINING PERSONNEL COOPERATION

Methods for obtaining cooperation of personnel already have been discussed to an extent in chapter III of this manual. It cannot be emphasized enough, however, that all personnel involved must be reminded of the tremendous contribution they can make to the overall program. In working with specific individuals, however, you may have to gear your approach to the personality of the person involved. We will not get into the subject of interpersonal relationships to any depth because numerous other works on the subject are available. In most cases, however, you will find that some minor planning of the way in which you approach an individual will help you obtain his cooperation. If at all possible, initial contact and occasional continuing contact should be made in person. Follow-up contact can be made by telephone. If the individual involved is doing a good job, he should be told so either in person or by telephone, with any congratulatory remarks to be followed at least by a personal letter. Initial cooperation seldom will be gained by showing a person a survey report and saying something to the effect of, "Joe, this report shows me that you've been doing a lousy job." The approach almost always is more effective when the negative focus is thing—rather than person—oriented. In other words, given a survey report which indicates poor performance of maintenance operations, one could say, "Joe, this report shows that the equipment is not in very good shape. We just can't afford to replace it, so we're going to be relying on you to help us with the repairs and keep it in top-notch condition." In fact, experience has shown that maintenance and operating func-

tions generally are carried out in a less-than-effective manner. This often is due not so much to the quality of labor, but rather to lack of knowledge of specific system and equipment capabilities; performance characteristics, and operating, maintenance and control procedures. In many cases, for example, a maintenance person or operating engineer will carry out a function in a certain way because "that's the way the guy before me explained it," and "the guy before" got it from the one before him, and so on, each providing instruction perhaps in a one- or two-day period, with each instruction being subject to faults of memory. Therefore, to obtain full cooperation from personnel, and to help them turn their willingness to be of assistance into positive action, determine how they perform their functions now and where specific instruction is needed. Guidance is available from numerous sources: equipment manufacturers who can provide operating and maintenance manuals; pertinent publications and magazines; various manufacturer- and supplier-sponsored courses; continuing education programs of local colleges and universities; specific training by a consulting engineering firm or by a contractor specializing in the type equipment involved; contractor- or engineer-prepared operating and maintenance instructions if none can be obtained elsewhere; specific maintenance schedules which spell out exactly what must be done and when, etc. Simply put, you can obtain a lot more cooperation from a person if he is not being frustrated by the fact that he does not have the specific tools and knowledge required to achieve the goals you set.

5. OBTAINING TENANT COOPERATION

Obtaining cooperation from tenants was only discussed briefly in Chapter III because little is required through performance of a survey and related steps. In actual implementation, however, tenant cooperation can be of significant benefit. At the least you will want tenants to cooperate to the point of permitting entrance for routine inspection purposes. Greater understanding will be required to obtain their cooperation in matters such as turning off equipment and lighting when not in use, closing securely all doors leading to the exterior, and related matters which involve, primarily, correction of wasteful habits. Even more effort will be required to obtain cooperation when certain operating changes are made or requested, such as lowering the thermostat during the heating season and raising it during the cooling season; requesting that stairways are used for one flight trips or having the elevator stop on alternate floors only, turning off water fountains, etc.

If in the past you have communicated with tenants only to tell them to stop doing something which should not be done or to inform them of a rent increase, obviously it will be more difficult to obtain cooperation now.

It is suggested that you first establish which changes will involve tenants, either directly or indirectly. Once established, examine the different type leases in force to determine exactly who has the final say in certain matters, and perhaps who will bear the expense. So armed, meet or have a representative meet with whomever is in charge of each leased area. If feasible, present specific data relating to energy and operating costs of the building involved. Begin discussion with an explanation of the changes, expected energy cost increases and what your organization is preparing to do. Emphasize that many of the undertakings will require tenant cooperation. Identify each change which will affect tenants and explain what type effect is involved. In certain cases, of course, you will have to be prepared to negotiate changes. Try to be as flexible as possible, especially when the items concerned are of relatively low priority. Where items are important, however, try to be as firm as possible. Under no circumstances should you merely send a letter stating that a given change will be made (whether the tenant likes it or not) and that the tenant can help by doing thus and so. Personal contact is essential. An explanation of what is being done is essential.

If possible and practical, encourage the office managers to inform all employees of the impending changes and the way in which they can be of help. This, too, can be done best through personal contact, although, given the numbers probably involved, a joint meeting of one type or another will have to suffice. To prevent misinterpretation, you may request to be allowed to address the meeting yourself. In either case, materials should be prepared for distribution to employees. A typical letter-memorandum is shown.

You will find that the use of signage, as mentioned throughout this manual, also will be of assistance. Signs such as PLEASE BE SURE DOOR IS CLOSED SECURELY. PLEASE TURN OFF THIS LIGHT WHEN ROOM IS NOT IN USE. DID YOU REMEMBER TO TURN OFF THE LIGHT?, DO YOU REALLY HAVE TO USE THE ELEVATOR, OR CAN YOU USE THE EXERCISE?, PLEASE DO NOT TAMPER WITH CONTROLS. WE ALL NEED TO SAVE ENERGY., and so on, placed in strategic locations, can be most helpful.

Maintain continuing contact and involve tenants in the team effort just as you include building personnel. Let them know that their efforts and cooperation are paying off, if just by placing an easel and sign in the lobby indicating monthly energy consumption data as compared to previous periods as part of "OPERATION CONSERVATION" or whatever other title you may wish to give your overall program to help develop an esprit de corps.

MEMORANDUM (EXAMPLE)

TO: EMPLOYEES, JONES, SMITH & ASSOCIATES

FROM: JOHN DOE, XYZ MANAGEMENT

RE: "OPERATION CONSERVATION"

As you no doubt are aware, we are in the midst of a national program to conserve energy. The goal is to make our country independent in terms of energy supplies. Because of this fact, and due to the skyrocketing costs of energy, XYZ Management has embarked on, its own program called "OPERATION CONSERVATION." To make it a success, we need your cooperation and assistance.

Here are some of the specific things we'll be doing which will affect you in one way or another.

Temperature

We will be lowering the temperature to 68°F during the winter and raising it to 78°F during the summer. To compensate, wear a sweater or other warm clothing during the heating season. Wear light clothing during the cooling season.

Humidity

Because of changes being made in our air conditioning system, it may at times become a bit humid inside. We don't expect that it will happen to any great extent however.

Lighting

We will be removing lamps from certain lighting fixtures; moving others, and disconnecting some completely. Although the lighting levels will not be as high as they were before, the quality of lighting provided will be perfectly adequate for the type work being performed in the various areas affected. Of course, if you find that lighting for some reason is not adequate for your desk, please call maintenance and we'll make all necessary adjustments.

Elevators

We have eight elevators in the building. Three of them will be stopping at even-numbered floors only; three at odd-numbered floors only, and two will not be affected. This means that you may on occasion have to walk up or down a flight of stairs. It's an inconvenience, we know, but at least it will help us get the exercise we need.

We'll probably be making some other changes, too, and you'll be kept abreast of them. In the meantime, there are a few things you can do that will help us out a great deal. In many cases, we'll have signs around to remind you, too.

1. Turn off electrical equipment when not in use, such as desk lamps, typewriters, coffee pots, and so on. Certain equipment can only be turned off at the end of the day, though, but please be sure you do turn it off, especially the copying machines.

2. Turn on lights only when they're needed. Turn them off when they're not needed. While life of fluorescent lamps is reduced when they're turned off and on more frequently, the energy they use when they're on is wasted and doesn't make leaving them on worthwhile.

3. Please be sure that you close all windows and doors leading to unconditioned areas whenever the building's heating and cooling system is working. The less heat and cooling that's wasted, the more energy that's saved.

4. Whenever you can, group your errands together so you don't have to use the elevators as much. Do four things on one floor while you're there rather than making four separate trips. If possible, use the stairs instead of the elevator.

5. Please do not tamper with the thermostat. It has been carefully adjusted and calibrated.

6. Please report any leaky faucets, piping, valves etc., to the maintenance department.

7. Please close the blinds and drapes when the air conditioning is running during the day. It wastes lot of energy to have to cool down the sun. During the winter, though, open the blinds and drapes on the sunny side of the building during the day. The extra heat can be used, so can the extra light.

8. Send us your ideas and suggestions. We'll all benefit by saving energy.

We'll be keeping you posted on a month-by-month basis telling you how we're doing.we're trying to reach a goal of a 20% reduction in energy use this year and, with your help and patience, we think we can do it.

6. MONITORING YOUR PROGRAM AND KEEPING IT EFFECTIVE

Monitoring your program involves two distinct types of effort.

The first type effort consists of monitoring changes implemented in terms of the quality of implementation. If maintenance schedules are revised, for example, you should check with maintenance personnel to ensure they can handle the revised schedule. Check on equipment being maintained to ensure that maintenance is being performed well. In essence, this is doing nothing more than following procedures of good management—making sure that those responsible for carrying out specific functions carry them out in the most effective manner.

All changes implemented should be noted on a form such as shown in Figure VII-3. Duplicate copies of operating and maintenance manuals and schedules and related information also should be kept on file should replacement become necessary. The same holds for cost and inspection records.

The second type effort concerns monitoring the effectiveness of the program itself in terms of energy consumption. This can be done easiest through use of the Energy Management Form discussed in Section IV. This form will provide information on the entire system and on certain subsystems if the subsystem involved is the only subsystem which utilizes a certain form of energy. For example, if coal is used only for heating purposes, amount of energy utilized for heating can be determined exactly by referring to coal consumption records. In most cases, however, subsystem information cannot be extracted easily from the Energy Management Form, nor is there any great need that subsystem information be determined precisely. If, however, you do feel that it is imperative to determine exactly how much energy specific subsystems, such as lighting, elevators, heating, cooling etc., consume, such information can be obtained either through check metering or conduct of an empirical survey.

Check metering involves actual metering of power being supplied by the various electrical feeders to the subsystems thereby establishing how much energy each subsystem utilizes. In more contemorary buildings, where individual subsystems are supplied power independently, such metering is a relatively simple undertaking. For older buildings, however, which typically have several systems operating from one feeder, the task is far more difficult, if not practically impossible. Even when contemporary buildings are involved, however, the cost of check metering—although as mentioned a relatively simple task—can be very high.

The alternative to check metering is an empirical survey wherein a professional is retained to survey the building and its various sybsystems to establish data on all connected loads, their usage and load factors, to determine subsystem energy consumption. The larger the building involved, the more difficult and expensive the task becomes. Nonetheless, such work has and is being done. For example, one owner in the Philadelphia study revealed that he had retained a firm to undertake such work. Once data is on hand, he intends to alot to the various tenants an energy budget. Per lease agreement, each tenant would be "entitled" to a given amount of energy based on the loads used by the tenant included with the cost of rent. Any energy utilized above the stipulated amount would be paid for by the tenant. This same approach, of course, could be utilized through metering.

In either case, investment in subsystem monitoring will result in ability to know which systems utilize energy; the ability to recapture energy costs or a portion of them from tenants and, as such, an added incentive for tenants to cooperate in a program of energy conservation. While expense is involved, the exact amount required can be determined only through preliminary investigation with responsible firms. In some cases, the payback period may be short enough to warrant immediate adoption of such an approach.

In certain cases—when a building is heated and cooled by electricity—energy utilized by heating and cooling subsystems is obtained easily by installing and monitoring separate, totalized and general load meters. Data obtained from several small office buildings included in the Philadelphia study which had electric heating/cooling systems, and which utilized such meters, indicate that overall energy consumption can be categorized as:

Such figures are general only, of course, and will vary from building to building depending upon building use and operation.

The monitoring process, and the information which results from it, should be utilized to keep your TEM program as effective as possible by making improvements where data suggests improvement can be made; by undertaking alternatives which have not as yet been attempted; by revising goals where revision seems warranted, etc. In addition, it is suggested that the program be made as permanent a part of the building management function as possible. This effort would include holding periodic meetings with building and management personnel to keep them abreast of accomplishments, set-backs, future planning, and so on, as well as to request information and ideas which would benefit the program. Tenants should be treated in a similar manner to help ensure their involvement with the program and their continued willingness to make those efforts required to achieve conservation of energy.

Fig. VII-4 Energy Conservation Log

Building _____

Sheet _____ of _____

Period _____ to _____

Date of Change	Energy Conservation Measures Implemented
	Building Envelope: _____ _____ _____ Ventilation: _____ _____ _____ _____ Heating & Air Conditioning: _____ _____ _____ _____ Lighting: _____ _____ _____ _____ Elevators & Escalators: _____ _____ _____ Domestic Hot Water: _____ _____ _____ Operation & Maintenance: _____ _____ _____

CONTINUING EDUCATION

Since the field of energy conservation and Total Energy Management are relatively new, it is to be expected that the months ahead will result in development of many new products and techniques geared for conservation of energy.

Obviously, it will be to your own advantage to keep as much abreast of these developments as possible. For this reason it is suggested that you keep in close touch with appropriate national, state and local organizations as well as the various publications which relate to these fields. A listing of such organizations can be found in Appendix B.

CASE
VIII. HISTORIES

Following are two case histories each providing details on the building involved, the nature of energy conservation activities undertaken, and the results of the effort based on comparison of consumption patterns for the same period in the previous year. As can be seen, several of the guidelines mentioned in the manual have been utilized to effect substantial savings achieved on a purely voluntary basis.

BUILDING A

LOCATION:	Philadelphia, Pennsylvania
TYPE:	Office
BUILDING CONDITION:	Modernized, kept up-to-date
AREA:	556,000 gross square feet
TYPE OF HVAC SYSTEM:	1400-ton central plus 300-ton packaged
NUMBER OF FLOORS:	19
BUILT:	1926
ENERGY SOURCES:	Electricity and purchased steam for cooling and heating.
AVERAGE OCCUPANCY:	98%
HOURS OF DAILY OCCUPANCY:	7:45AM - 5:15PM

Energy Conservation Measures

Owner/manager established energy conservation measures in November 1973. These measures consisted of, among other things:

1. Setting thermostats at 68°F during the heating season.
2. Steam to noncritical building areas reduced.
3. Temperature of hot air decks in equipment rooms reduced.
4. Use of supplemental heaters banned.
5. Obstructions removed from perimeter heating units.
6. Serving cold lunch one day per week to reduce steam consumption.
7. Domestic hot water temperature reduced.
8. Reduction of lighting levels by an average of 50% in noncritical areas (e.g., restrooms, elevators, elevator lobbies, corridors, decorative lighting in lobby).
9. Lighting turned off in areas not in use (e.g., conference rooms, supply rooms, vacant offices, unoccupied space).
10. Exterior building lights turned off.
11. Employees encouraged to turn on lights only an area at a time as needed; to turn out lights when leaving a space for 20 minutes or more, and turn off lights near the end of the day.
12. Lights not used on Christmas tree ornamentation.
13. Venetian blinds and drapes closed during cold, windy days to provide additional insulation.
14. Sterilization of drinking water discontinued.
15. More efficient oven installed in kitchen.

Results of the program for the periods indicated are as follows:

	ELECTRICITY (KWH)			STEAM (MLBS)		
MONTH	*1972/1973*	*1973/1974*	*% SAVINGS*	*1972/1973*	*1973/1974*	*% SAVINGS*
DEC	573,656	477,000	16.8%	2945	1806	38.7%
JAN	644,028	506,000	26.1	4200	3794	9.7
FEB	567,000	474,000	16.4	3120	2987	4.3
MARCH	595,440	506,000	15.0	3664	2455	33.0
			Av.17.5%			Av.20.7%

BUILDING B

LOCATION:	Philadelphia, Pennsylvania
TYPE:	Office
BUILDING CONDITION:	Modernized
AREA:	574,000 gross square feet
TYPE OF HVAC SYSTEM:	1800-ton central plus 80-ton package
NUMBER OF FLOORS:	17
BUILT:	1912 (Addition 1932)
ENERGY SOURCES:	Electricity, purchased steam and natural gas for cooling and heating.
AVERAGE OCCUPANCY:	95-98%
HOURS OF DAILY OCCUPANCY:	8:30AM - 4:30PM

Energy Conservation Measures

Owner/manager established conservation measures in September 1973. These measures consisted of, among other things:

1. Building thermostats set to 75°F during cooling season.
2. Outside air intake dampers set to minimum position.
3. Lowered temperature of domestic hot water.
4. Lighting levels reduced in corridors, wardrobes, washrooms and unoccupied areas by delamping of fluorescent fixtures, and relamping with "energy saver lamps."
5. Certain fluorescent lamps in office areas replaced by "energy saver lamps."
6. Operating schedules modified.
7. Elevator service reduced during off-peak hours.
8. Cleaning hours changed from 10PM-6:30AM to 4PM-12:30AM.
9. Lighting levels reduced during cleaning hours.

Results of the program for the period indicated are as follows:

	ELECTRICITY (KWH)			STEAM (MLBS)		
MONTH	1973	1974	% SAVINGS	1973	1974	% SAVINGS
JAN	1,012,000	996,000	1.6%	3747.9	3530.0	5.8%
FEB	1,062,000	1,067,000	(.5%)	4273.8	4120.3	3.6%
MAR	1,016,000	922,000	9.3%	2728.9	2668.4	2.2%
APR	980,000	924,000	5.7%	2232.9	1631.8	26.9%
MAY	1,006,000	962,000	4.4%	1679.6	1455.1	13.4%

As can be seen, electricity consumption for the period January-May 1974 was 4% less than for the same period one year earlier. Steam consumption was reduced 8.6%.

APPENDIX A

BUILDING INFORMATION
FOR
TOTAL ENERGY MANAGEMENT

Surveyed by: _____

Survey Date: _____

I. **GENERAL INFORMATION**

   IDENTITY:

   Name of building _____

   Address _____

   _____

   Type(s) of occupancy _____

   _____

   Name of owner(s) _____

   Person(s) in charge of building _____

   _____

   PHYSICAL DATA:

   No. of floors _____ Gross Conditioned floor area _____

   Conditioned floor area, special use:

   _____ Ft^2 Computer Facility _____ Ft^2 Shops

   _____ Ft^2 Cafeteria _____ Ft^2 Other (describe _____

   _____ Ft^2 Bank _____

   Construction type:

   Walls (masonry, curtain, frame, etc.)

   N _____ S _____ E _____ W _____

   Roof:

   Type: Flat _____ Color: Light _____

   Pitched _____ Dark _____

   Windows:

   Type: _____ Fixed Sash _____ double hung: _____ Casement _____

   Doors:

   Door types and numbers
North _____	No _____	Type _____
East _____	No _____	Type _____
West _____	No _____	Type _____
South _____	No _____	Type _____

   Type designation: _____ 1-single; 2-vestibule; 3-revolving

   Glazing:

Exposure	*Type	%Glass/Exterior wall area
N	_____	_____
S	_____	_____
E	_____	_____
W	_____	_____

   *Type: Single, double, insulating, reflective, etc.

Glass shading employed outside (check one):

Fins _____ Overhead _____ None _____ Other _____

Glass shading employed inside (check one):

Shades _____Blinds _____ Drapes, open mesh _____

Drapes opaque _____ None _____ Other _____

Solid Exterior Surfaces:

Description of Surface	Thickness of Insulation (inches)	Type Insulation	Appropriate Surface Area (Ft^2)
Ceiling(s)/roof(s)			
Floor(s)			
Wall(s)			

Air Leakage (check as appropriate):

Structural damage (through the wall/ceiling cracks) _____

Broken or defective windows _____

Ventilation/Exhaust openings that remain open all the time _____

_____

Tightness around windows and doors _____

_____

Note other major observed air leaks _____

_____

_____

SKETCH OF BUILDING SHOWING PRINCIPLE DIMENSIONS & ORIENTATION:

II. BUILDING OCCUPANCY AND USE

	Weekdays		Saturdays		Sundays, Holidays	
	No. Of Occupants	Period of Occupancy	No. Of Occupants	Period of Occupancy	No. Of Occupants	Period of Occupancy
General Office						
Custodial operation						
Maintenance operation						
Computer operation						
Cafeteria						
Banks						
Retail Store						
Other (describe)						
_____						
_____						
_____						

III MAINTAINED INDOOR ENVIRONMENTAL CONDITIONS

	Occupied hours				Unoccupied hours			
	Temp (°F)		Rel. Humidity (%)		Temp (°F)		Rel. Humidity (%)	
	Summer	Winter	Summer	Winter	Summer	Winter	Summer	Winter
General office areas								
Computer Rooms								
Special process areas								

IV SYSTEMS AND EQUIPMENT DATA

HEATING, VENTILATING AND AIR CONDITIONING SYSTEMS: See page 575-578.

AIR HANDLING SYSTEMS

UNIT DESIGNATION	AREA OR ZONE SERVED	APPROX. SQ FT. SERVED	UNIT OR SYSTEM Type (roof top, Multi-zone, fan coil, Self contained, etc)	HP TOTALS Supply Fans	HP TOTALS Return Fans	METHOD OF CONTROL Temp On-Off		CFM Total Supply	CFM Outdoor Air	OUTDOOR AIR Controlled By	HOURS/DAY SYSTEM IS "ON" Weekdays	HOURS/DAY SYSTEM IS "ON" Saturdays	HOURS/DAY SYSTEM IS "ON" Sundays & Holidays

FANS:

Location,	Horsepower	Type	Function (Supply, Exhaust, etc.)	Method of Operation (Time Clock, Manual, etc.)

Source of Heating Energy:

Hot Water _____ Steam _____ Electric resistance _____

Other_____

Heating Plant:

Boiler No. _____ Rating _____ MBH

_____   _____

_____   _____

Boiler Type:

Firetube_____ Watertube _____ Elec. resist. _____

Electrode_____ Other _____

Fuel Used _____ Standby _____

Hot Water Supply_____ °F, Return _____

Steam Pressure _____ psi

Pumps No. _____ Total HP_____

Extent and condition of metering equipment: _____

_____

_____

_____

Room Heating Units:

Type: Baseboard _____ Convectors _____ Fin Tube _____

Ceiling or Walls Panels _____ Unit Heaters _____ Other _____

Heating equipment condition and maintenance _____

_____

_____

_____

Cooling Plant:

Compressors and Chillers				
No	Type (Centrifugal, reciprocating, absorption)	Capacity (tons)	Motor horsepower	Area Served
____	_____	_____	_____	_____
____	_____	_____	_____	_____
____	_____	_____	_____	_____
____	_____	_____	_____	_____
____	_____	_____	_____	_____
____	_____	_____	_____	_____

Heat dissipation device:

Evap. Condenser _____

Air cooled condenser _____

Cooling Tower _____

Condenser/Cooling Tower Fan HP_____

Chilled water pumps _____ Total HP _____

Condenser water pumps _____ Total HP_____

Extent and Condition of metering equipment: _____

_____

_____

Self Contained Units:

Type: window type air conditioners _____ Thru-the-wall units_____

No. of Units _____ Basic module served _____

Total Capacity (Tons) _____

Horsepower/unit _____

Cooling Equipment Condition and maintenance: _____

_____

_____

_____

Distribution Systems:

Condition of Steam Systems (Leakage, insulation etc.) _____

_____

_____

_____

Condition of hot and chilled water systems (leakage, insulation etc.)_____

_____

_____

_____

Condition of Refrigerant piping (leakage, insulation etc.) _____

_____

_____

_____

Condition of Air distribution systems (Leakage, insulation etc.)_____

_____

_____

_____

Automatic Controls:

Type _____

Condition _____

_____

_____

_____

_____

_____

ENERGY CONSERVATION DEVICES:

Type:

Condenser water used for heating _____

Demand limiters _____

Energy storage _____

Heat recovery wheels _____

Enthalpy control of supply-return-exhaust damper _____

Recuperators _____

Condensate used for heating domestic hot water _____

Others _____

LIGHTING:

Area Served Interior:	Type (Fluorescent, Incandescent etc.)	Watts/Ft.^{2}	Method of Control (on-off from breaker panel, wall switches, control switching)
Gen. office	_____	_____	_____
Storage	_____	_____	_____

Corridors _____ _____ _____

Lobbies _____ _____ _____

Computer Rm. _____ _____ _____

Kitchens _____ _____ _____

Toilets, etc. _____ _____ _____

_____

Exterior:	Type	Total kW	Method of Control
Parking lot	_____	_____	_____
Decoration	_____	_____	_____
_____	_____	_____	_____
_____	_____	_____	_____

Equipment condition and maintenance: _____
_____
_____

ELECTRIC POWER SYSTEM:

KVA of transformers and main secondary voltages supplies to buildings _____
_____

Power Company monthly records for 3 years-kWh, Demand, Power Factor. _____
_____
_____
_____
_____
_____

DOMESTIC HOT WATER HEATING:

Size _____ Rated input _____

Energy Source: Gas _____ , Oil _____ , Electric _____ , Other _____

Aquastat setting _____°F

General:

Types of usage — Location of usage, estimated GPD, distance from heater.
_____
_____
_____

Temperature — check several locations, including dishwashing area control (reduced temperature during nonoccupancy?)
_____
_____
_____

Type and condition of heat exchange equipment.
_____
_____
_____

OTHER EQUIPMENT (Elevators, Escalators, Data Processing, Kitchen, etc.)

Equip. Description	Quantity	Size/Capacity in BTU, kW, HP, etc.
_____	_____	_____
_____	_____	_____
_____	_____	_____
_____	_____	_____
_____	_____	_____
_____	_____	_____
_____	_____	_____

V OPERATING SCHEDULE:

Equip. Description	Unit or Area Served	Weekdays	Saturdays	Sundays or Holidays
Refrigeration cycle mach.				
_____	_____	_____	_____	_____
_____	_____	_____	_____	_____
_____	_____	_____	_____	_____
Fans — Supply, return exhaust, etc.				
_____	_____	_____	_____	_____
_____	_____	_____	_____	_____
_____	_____	_____	_____	_____
_____	_____	_____	_____	_____
_____	_____	_____	_____	_____
_____	_____	_____	_____	_____
_____	_____	_____	_____	_____
_____	_____	_____	_____	_____

	Unit or Area Served	Weekdays	Saturdays	Sundays or Holidays
HVAC auxiliary equip.				
_____	_____	_____	_____	_____
_____	_____	_____	_____	_____
_____	_____	_____	_____	_____
_____	_____	_____	_____	_____
_____	_____	_____	_____	_____
_____	_____	_____	_____	_____
_____	_____	_____	_____	_____

Lighting — Interior

_____   _____   _____   _____   _____
_____   _____   _____   _____   _____
_____   _____   _____   _____   _____
_____   _____   _____   _____   _____
_____   _____   _____   _____   _____
_____   _____   _____   _____   _____
_____   _____   _____   _____   _____
_____   _____   _____   _____   _____
_____   _____   _____   _____   _____

Exterior

_____   _____   _____   _____   _____
_____   _____   _____   _____   _____
_____   _____   _____   _____   _____

Domestic hot water ht.   _____   _____   _____

Elevators

_____   _____   _____   _____   _____
_____   _____   _____   _____   _____
_____   _____   _____   _____   _____

Escalators

_____   _____   _____   _____   _____
_____   _____   _____   _____   _____
_____   _____   _____   _____   _____

Other (describe)

_____   _____   _____   _____   _____
_____   _____   _____   _____   _____
_____   _____   _____   _____   _____

APPENDIX B

SOURCES OF INFORMATION ON ENERGY MANAGEMENT

Here follows a list of sources from whom further information on energy management may be obtained.

1. Societies, Associations, & Institutes

- Air-Conditioning and Refrigeration Institute, 1815 N. Ft. Myer Dr., Arlington, VA 22209
- Air Cooling Institute, P.O. Box 2121, Wichita Falls, TX 76301
- Air Diffusion Council, 435 N. Michigan Ave., Chicago, IL 60611
- Air Distribution Institute, 221 N. LaSalle St., Chicago, IL 60601
- Air Moving and Conditioning Association, 30 W. University Dr., Arlington Heights, IL 60004
- American Boiler Manufacturers Association, 1500 Wilson Blvd., Suite 317, Arlington, VA 22209
- American Consulting Engineers Council, 1155 15th St., N.W., Rm. 713, Washington, DC 20005
- American Gas Association, 1515 Wilson Blvd., Arlington, Va. 22209
- American Industrial Hygiene Association, 210 Haddon Ave., Westmont, NJ 08108
- American Institute of Architects, 1735 New York Ave., N.W., Washington, DC 20006
- American Institute of Consulting Engineers (See American Consulting Engineers Council)
- American Institute of Plant Engineers, 1021 Delta Ave., Cincinnati, OH 45208
- American National Standards Institute, Inc., 1430 Broadway, New York, NY 10018
- American Society of Heating, Refrigeration and Air Conditioning Engineers, Inc., 345 E. 47th St., New York, NY 10017
- American Society of Mechanical Engineers, 345 E. 47th St., New York, NY 10017
- American Society of Plumbing Engineers, 16161 Ventura Blvd., Suite 105, Encino, CA 91316
- American Society for Testing and Materials, 1916 Race St., Philadelphia PA 19103
- Associated Air Balance Council, 2146 Sunset Blvd., Los Angeles, CA 90026
- Associated General Contractors of America, 1957 E. St., N.W., Washington, DC 20006
- Better Heating-Cooling Council, 35 Russo Pl., Berkeley Heights, NJ 07922
- BRAB Building Research Institute, 2101 Constitution Ave., Washington, DC 20418
- Building Owners & Managers Association International, 1221 Massachusetts Ave., N.W., Washington, D.C.
- Building Research Advisory Board, National Research Council, National Academy of Sciences-National Academy of Engineering, 2101 Constitution Ave., N.W., Washington, DC 20418
- Construction Specifications Institute, 1150 Seventeenth St., N.W., Suite 300, Washington DC 20036
- Conveyor Equipment Manufacturers Association, 1000 Vermont Ave., N.W., Washington, DC 20005
- Cooling Tower Institute, 3003 Yale St., Houston, TX 77018

- Edison Electric Institute, 90 Park Ave., New York, NY 10016
- Electrical Apparatus Service Association, Inc., 7710 Carondelet Ave., St. Louis, MO 63105
- Electrification Council, The, 90 Park Ave., New York, NY 10016
- Heat Exchange Institute, 122 E. 42nd St., New York, NY 10017
- Hydronics Institute, 35 Russo Pl., Berkeley Heights, NJ 07922
- Illuminating Engineering Society, 345 E. 47th St., New York, NY 10017
- Institute of Electrical & Electronics Engineers, Inc., 345 E. 47th St., New York, NY 10017
- Instrument Society of America, Stanwix St., Pittsburgh, PA 15222
- International District—Heating Association, 5940 Baum Sq., Pittsburgh, PA 15206
- Mechanical Contractors Association of America, Inc., 5530 Wisconsin Ave., Suite 750, Washington, DC 20015
- National Association of Oil Heating Service Manager, Inc., 60 E. 42nd St., New York, NY 10017
- National Association of Plumbing, Heating & Cooling Contractors, 1016 20th St., N.E., Washington, DC 20036
- National Association of Power Engineers, Inc., 176 W. Adams St., Suite 1411, Chicago, IL 60603
- National Association of Refrigerated Warehouses, 1210 Tower Bldg., 1401 K St., N.W., Washington, DC 20005
- National Coal Association, Coal Bldg., 1130 17th St., N.W., Washington, DC 20036
- National Electrical Contractors Association, 7315 Wisconsin Ave., Washington, DC 20014
- National Electrical Manufacturers Association, 155 E. 44th St., New York, NY 10017
- National Environmental Systems Contractors Association, 221 N. LaSalle St., Chicago, IL 60601
- National Insulation Contractors Association, 8630 Fenton St., Suite 506, Silver Spring, MD 20910
- National LP-Gas Association, 79 W. Monroe St., Chicago, IL 60603
- National Mineral Wool Insulation Association, Inc., 211 E. 51st St., New York, NY 10022
- National Oil Fuel Institute, Inc., 60 E. 42nd St., New York, NY 10017
- National Society of Professional Engineers, 2020 K St., N.W., Washington, DC 20006
- Producers' Council, Inc., 1717 Massachusetts Ave., Washington, DC 20036
- Refrigeration Service Engineers Society, 2720 Des Plaines Ave., Des Plaines, IL 60018
- Society of American Value Engineers (SAVE), 2550 Hargrave Dr., Smyrna, Ga. 30080
- Standards Engineers Society, P.O. Box 7507, Philadelphia, PA 19101
- Steam Heating Equipment Manufacturers Assoc., c/o Samuel J. Reid, Barnes & Jones, Inc., P.O. Box 207, Newtonville, MA 02160

- Thermal Insulation Manufacturers Association, Inc., 7 Kirby Plaza, Mt. Kisco, NY 10549
- Underwriters' Laboratories, Inc., 333 Pfingsten Rd., Northbrook, IL 60062
- Water Conditioning Foundation, 1780 Maple St., P.O. Box 194, Northfield, IL 60093

2. Local Sources

- Chapters of above mentioned societies, associations and institutions
- Utilities
- Chambers of Commerce
- Construction industry organizations
- Building code authorities
- Libraries

- Architectural engineers, contractors, suppliers and others with whom you work on a regular basis.

2. U.S. Government Sources

- Federal Energy Administration, Office of Energy Conservation and Environment, 12th & Pennsylvania, N.W., Washington, D.C. 20461
- Department of Commerce, Office of Energy Programs, 14th & Constitution Ave., Washington, D.C. 20230
- General Services Administration, Public Building Service, 18th & F St., N.W., Washington, D.C. 20405
- National Bureau of Standards, Office of Energy Conservation, Building 226, Rm. B114, Washington, D.C. 20234

WASTE HEAT MANAGEMENT*

* Waste Heat Management Guidebook, U.S. Department of Commerce and Federal Energy Administration, February 1977

SOURCES AND USES OF WASTE HEAT*

Definitions

Waste heat has been defined as heat which is rejected from a process at a temperature enough above the ambient temperature to permit the manager or engineer to extract additional value from it. Sources of waste energy can be divided according to temperature into three temperature ranges. The high temperature range refers to temperatures above 1200 F. The medium temperature range is between 450 F and 1200 F, and the low temperature range is below 450 F.

High and medium temperature waste heat can be used to produce process steam. If one has high temperature waste heat, instead of producing steam directly, one should consider the possibility of using the high temperature energy to do useful work before the waste heat is extracted. Both gas and steam turbines are useful and fully developed heat engines.

In the low temperature range, waste energy which would be otherwise useless can sometimes be made useful by application of mechanical work through a device called the heat pump. An interesting application of this is in petroleum distillation, where the working fluid of the heat pump can be the liquid being distilled. (This application was developed by the British Petroleum Co.)

Sources of Waste Heat

The combustion of hydrocarbon fuels produces product gases in the high temperature range. The maximum theoretical temperature possible in atmospheric combustors is somewhat under 3500 F, while measured flame temperatures in practical combustors are just under 3000 F. Secondary air or some other dilutant is often admitted to the combustor to lower the temperature of the products to the required process temperature, for example to protect equipment, thus lowering the practical waste heat temperature.

Table 1.1 below gives temperatures of waste gases from industrial process equipment in the high temperature range. All of these result from direct fuel fired processes.

TABLE 1.1

Type of Device	Temperature F
Nickel refining furnace	2500 - 3000
Aluminum refining furnace	1200 - 1400
Zinc refining furnace	1400 - 2000
Copper refining furnace	1400 - 1500
Steel heating furnaces	1700 - 1900
Copper reverberatory furnace	1650 - 2000
Open hearth furnace	1200 - 1300
Cement kiln (Dry process)	1150 - 1350
Glass melting furnace	1800 - 2800
Hydrogen plants	1200 - 1800
Solid waste incinerators	1200 - 1800
Fume incinerators	1200 - 2600

Table 1.2 gives the temperatures of waste gases from process equipment in the medium temperature range. Most of the waste heat in this temperature range comes from the exhausts of directly fired process units. Medium temperature waste heat is still hot enough to allow consideration of the extraction of mechanical work from the waste heat, by a steam or gas turbine. Gas turbines can be economically utilized in some

* W.M. Rohrer, Jr., University of Pittsburgh and K.G. Kreider, National Bureau of Standards

cases at inlet pressures in the range of 15 to 30 lb/in²g. Steam can be generated at almost any desired pressure and steam turbines used when economical.

TABLE 1.2

Type of Device	Temperature F
Steam boiler exhausts	450 - 900
Gas turbine exhausts	700 - 1000
Reciprocating engine exhausts	600 - 1100
Reciprocating engine exhausts (turbocharged)	450 - 700
Heat treating furnaces	800 - 1200
Drying and baking ovens	450 - 1100
Catalytic crackers	800 - 1200
Annealing furnace cooling systems	800 - 1200

Table 1.3 lists some heat sources in the low temperature range. In this range it is usually not practicable to extract work from the source, though steam production may not be completely excluded if there is a need for low pressure steam. Low temperature waste heat may be useful in a supplementary way for preheating purposes. Taking a common example, it is possible to use economically the energy from an air conditioning condenser operating at around 90 F to heat the domestic water supply. Since the hot water must be heated to about 160 F, obviously the air conditioner waste heat is not hot enough. However, since the cold water enters the domestic water system at about 50 F, energy interchange can take place raising the water to something less than 90 F. Depending upon the relative air conditioning lead and hot water requirements, any excess condenser heat can be rejected and the additional energy required by the hot water provided by the usual electrical or fired heater.

TABLE 1.3

Source	Temperature F
Process steam condensate	130 - 190
Cooling water from:	
Furnace doors	90 - 130
Bearings	90 - 190
Welding machines	90 - 190
Injection molding machines	90 - 190
Annealing furnaces	150 - 450
Forming dies	80 - 190
Air compressors	80 - 120
Pumps	80 - 190
Internal combustion engines	150 - 250
Air conditioning and refrigeration condensers	90 - 110
Liquid still condensers	90 - 190
Drying, baking and curing ovens	200 - 450
Hot processed liquids	90 - 450
Hot processed solids	200 - 450

How to Use Waste Heat

To use waste heat from sources such as those above, one often wishes to transfer the heat in one fluid stream to another (e.g., from flue gas to feedwater or combustion air). The device which accomplishes the transfer is called a heat exchanger. In the discussion immediately below is a listing of common uses for waste heat energy and in some cases, the name of the heat exchanger that would normally be applied in each particular case. Commercially available types of waste heat exchangers are reviewed below.

The equipment that is used to recover waste heat can range from something as simple as a pipe or duct to something as complex as a waste heat boiler. This study categorizes and describes some waste recovery systems that are available commercially suitable for retrofitting in existing plants, with lists of potential applications for each of the described devices. These are developed technologies which have been employed for years in some industries.

(1) Medium to high temperature exhaust gases can be used to preheat the combustion air for:

> Boilers using air-preheaters
> Furnaces using recuperators
> Ovens using recuperators
> Gas turbines using regenerators

(2) Low to medium temperature exhaust gases can be used to preheat boiler feedwater or boiler makeup water using *economizers*, which are simply gas-to-liquid water heating devices.

(3) Exhaust gases and cooling water from condensers can be used to preheat liquid and/or solid feedstocks in industrial processes. Finned tubes and tube-in-shell *heat exchangers* are used.

(4) Exhaust gases can be used to generate steam in *waste heat boilers* to produce electrical power, mechanical power, process steam, and any combination of above.

(5) Waste heat may be transferred to liquid or gaseous process units directly through pipes and ducts or indirectly through a secondary fluid such as steam or oil.

(6) Waste heat may be transferred to an intermediate fluid by heat exchangers or waste heat boilers, or it may be used by circulating the hot exit gas through pipes or ducts. Waste heat can be used to operate an absorption cooling unit for air conditioning or refrigeration.

Organizing a Waste Heat Management Program

Every plant has some waste heat. A waste heat management program, that is, a systematic study of the sources of waste heat in a plant and opportunities for its use, would normally be undertaken as part of a comprehensive energy conservation program.

The organization and management of a waste heat recovery program is an integral part of the overall energy conservation program, but the engineering effort and the capital requirement for waste heat recovery are considerably greater than those for most other energy saving opportunities. Thus, decisions about individual projects become more difficult to make. Expenses for engineering studies and economic analysis are substantial and thus a greater commitment to optimum energy utilization is demanded. On the other hand the rewards in the form of reduced energy costs may also be greater and this constitutes the incentive for committing resources to waste heat recovery.

Implementing Waste Heat Management

The first steps to be taken are to survey the plant's process units in order to discover opportunities for recovering and using waste heat. On the next page is a survey form, suitable for direct fired or unfired units, which will contain all the information needed to obtain a heat balance for any industrial process unit. The flow chart for the process and its heat balances are then studied to determine where opportunities for waste heat recovery exist. The results of engineering and economic studies for each process unit are next evaluated and summarized, using appropriate additional information and proposals from manufacturers of waste heat recovery equipment. Whenever possible, the individual processes should be submetered for fuel consumption and instrumented so as to monitor equipment performance. It is essential if full benefit is to be obtained from the capital investment that the equipment be kept in optimum operating condition and this can only be assured through adequate instrumentation and an active testing program.

References

NBS Handbook 115 (1974): Energy Conservation Program Guide for Industry and Commerce (EPIC), by R. Gatts, R. Massey, and J. Robertson.

WASTE HEAT SURVEY

SURVEY FORM FOR INDUSTRIAL PROCESS UNITS

NAME OF PROCESS UNIT _____ INVENTORY NUMBER _____

LOCATION OF PROCESS UNIT, PLANT NAME _____ BUILDING _____

MANUFACTURER _____ MODEL _____ SERIAL NUMBER _____

	NAME	FIRING RATE	HHV		COMB. AIR	FUEL	STACK	CO_2	O_2	CO	CH	N_2
				TEMPERATURE OF				FLUE GAS COMPOSITION % VOLUME				
PRIMARY FUEL												
FIRST ALTERNATIVE												
SECOND ALTERNAT												

	FLOW PATH 1	FLOW PATH 2	FLOW PATH 3	FLOW PATH 4
FLUID COMPOSITION				
FLOW RATE				
INLET TEMPERATURE				
OUTLET TEMPERATURE				
DESCRIPTION				

ANNUAL HOURS OPERATION _____ ANNUAL CAPACITY FACTOR, % _____

ANNUAL FUEL CONSUMPTION: PRIMARY FUEL _____; FIRST ALTERN. _____ SEC. ALTERN. _____

PRESENT FUEL COST: PRIMARY FUEL _____; FIRST ALTERN. _____ SEC. ALTERN. _____

ANNUAL ELECTRICAL ENERGY CONSUMPTION, KWHR. _____

PRESENT ELECTRICAL ENERGY RATE _____

ECONOMICS OF WASTE HEAT RECOVERY*

Introduction

This section of the manual deals with concepts and analytical techniques which can guide the industrial plant manager in evaluating the economic efficiency of investments in waste heat utilization. It explains in textbook fashion, and demonstrates in simplified but realistic examples, the use of alternative methods of evaluating and comparing energy-saving investments. The methods which are treated range from very simple, first-level techniques such as determination of the payback period, to more comprehensive techniques such as benefit-cost analysis, life-cycle cost analysis, and the internal rate of return method. The discussion covers the treatment of taxes, inflation, and uncertainty in data estimates and assumptions. The kinds of financial data needed to perform the economic analyses are identified, and the appropriateness of the different evaluation methods for analyzing various kinds of investment decisions is explained.

Details of a financial analysis will, of course, be unique to each firm. The general procedures and types of data requirements, however, will be essentially uniform for the many different types of firms or industries which might wish to evaluate investment in waste heat recovery. Hence, this chapter is intended to serve the requirements of commercial firms of all types.

This discussion of investment evaluation techniques presupposes that a prime objective of a business firm is profit maximization.[1] Successful investment in waste heat recovery increases profits generally by reducing fuel costs, and in some cases by generating revenue. It is assumed that the expected profitability of investment in waste heat recovery systems is a critical factor in determining if firms will adopt the systems.

The material is presented in five main sections. The first discusses the kinds of benefits and costs associated with waste heat recovery. The second treats several "partial" (i.e., incomplete), but popular methods for evaluating investment alternatives. These methods, e.g., the payback method and return on investment method, are explained, illustrated, and evaluated in terms of their advantages and disadvantages.

The third section covers more comprehensive methods for evaluating investment alternatives. These methods take into account costs and benefits over the life of the waste heat recovery system and discount cash flows to a common time for comparison. They require somewhat more data and effort than the partial methods, but generally result in more correct assessments of investment opportunities than do the partial methods.

The fourth section discusses some of the complicating factors which may arise in economic evaluations, including income tax effects, inflation, and risk and uncertainty. Methods of dealing with these factors are outlined and illustrated.

The fifth section points out the different kinds of investment decisions, such as making choices among mutually exclusive projects. It discusses the nature of the decision when one investment project is prerequisite to other activities of the firm, such as might be the case where curtailment of fuel allocations causes investment in waste heat recovery to be needed to prevent production cutbacks. The appropriate evaluation method for each situation is given.

---

[1] Other possible objectives of a business firm include cost minimization for a given outcome, minimization of risk of loss, maximization of sales, and creation of a desirable public image. Most firms probably have several objectives, but profit maximization is likely to be one of the most important.

* R. Ruegg, Center for Building Technology, National Bureau of Standards

Benefits and Costs

In general, the motivation for industrial firms to invest in waste heat recovery is that they expect the resulting benefits to exceed investment costs. Factors that have recently made such investments attractive are rising fuel costs and curtailment of regular fuel sources which threaten production cutbacks and changeover to other energy sources. In addition, mandatory pollution controls and rising labor costs cut into profits and cause firms to look more closely for ways to control costs.

The kinds of potential benefits which may result from waste heat recovery are listed in table 3.1. These benefits were suggested by a preliminary look at existing applications; however, only one, fuel savings, was found in every case examined. The other benefits, savings in capital and maintenance costs on existing equipment, pollution abatement, labor savings, product improvement, and revenue from sales of recovered heat, appear limited to certain applications.

Fuel savings result when waste heat is recovered and used in substitution for newly generated heat or energy. For example, heat from stack flue gas may be recovered by an economizer and used to preheat the input water, thereby reducing the amount of fuel needed for steam generation.

Savings in capital costs for certain items of existing equipment (i.e., regular equipment apart from that required for waste heat recovery) may be possible if recovered heat reduces the required capacity of the furnace or other heating/cooling equipment.[2] For example, installation of rooftop thermal recovery equipment on buildings with high ventilation requirements can enable significant reductions in the size, and cost, of the building's heating and cooling system. This potential for savings is probably limited to new plant installations, and does not appear to have received much consideration in industrial applications of heat exchangers.

Reduced maintenance and repair on certain items of existing equipment may, in some instances, be a further benefit of investment in waste heat recovery. The principal impact on the maintenance of existing equipment is likely to result from the planning, engineering, and installation phases of investment in waste heat recovery, when the existing equipment and plant processes are often scrutinized. Existing faults may be identified and corrected; and improved maintenance practices may be extended to existing equipment. While these same effects could be achieved independently of waste heat recovery by a separate inspection of the existing equipment, planning for waste heat recovery provides a catalyst for the inspection. Furthermore, cost of the informational gain is probably significantly

---

[2] On the other hand, use of heat recovery equipment may increase capital costs of regular equipment by imposing higher temperature loads on it. This effect of increasing costs is included in the listing of costs.

TABLE 3.1 *Possible benefits from waste heat recovery* [a]

Fuel savings
Reduced size, hence lower capital cost,
    of heating/cooling equipment
Reduced maintenance costs for
    existing equipment
Reduced costs of production labor
Pollution abatement
Improved product
Revenue from sales of recovered
    heat or energy

[a] Not all of these benefits will necessarily result from investment in waste heat recovery; in fact, fuel savings may be the only benefit in many applications. However, examples of the other kinds of benefits shown were found in existing applications.

reduced when inspection is performed jointly with the planning for waste heat recovery. Additional effects from waste heat recovery which may reduce maintenance costs include a lowering of the temperature of stack gases.

Another kind of benefit which may result from investment in waste heat recovery is savings in labor costs. Labor savings can result, for example, from a lowering of furnace changeover time (i.e., the time needed to alter furnace temperatures required for a change in production use) by preheating combustion air with waste heat. Savings may also result from faster furnace start-ups, accomplished by similar means. By reducing the amount of labor "downtime," unit labor costs are reduced. (A tradeoff may exist between idling the furnace at higher temperatures during off-duty hours and incurring labor "downtime" during furnace start-ups. If the existing practice is to idle the furnace at high temperatures in order to avoid "downtime," the savings from using waste heat recovery to preheat air would be in terms of fuel reductions rather than lower labor costs.)

Pollution abatement is a beneficial side effect which may result from recovery of waste heat. For example, the pollution abatement process in textile plants will often be facilitated by waste heat recovery. Pollutants (plasticizers) are usually collected by circulating air from the ovens (where fabrics are coated or backed with other materials) through electrostatic precipitators. The air must, however, be cooled to accomplish collection of pollutants. Recovery of waste heat from the air leaving the furnace prior to its entering the precipitators will, consequently, not only provide heat or energy which can be used elsewhere to reduce fuel costs, but will also aid in the collection of pollutants. If it were not for heat recovery, it would be necessary to cool the air by other means, which would generally entail additional fuel consumption. Thus, there is a twofold impact on fuel use from this application of heat recovery.[3] Another instance of pollution abatement as a side effect of waste heat recovery occurs if pollutants are reduced by the higher furnace temperatures resulting from preheating combustion air with waste heat.

The pollution abatement side effects represented by the two preceding examples are distinguishable from the use of systems to recover heat from a pollution abatement process, where recovery of heat does not in itself contribute to pollution abatement. For example, the recovery of waste heat from the incineration of polluting fumes is a method of reducing the cost of pollution abatement by producing a useful by-product from the abatement process. However, the waste heat recovery does not itself contribute to the pollution abatement process and therefore does not yield multiple benefits; the only benefit is the value of the fuel savings from using the recovered heat in other processes.

Product improvement is a further potential side effect of waste heat recovery. For example, by achieving a more stable furnace temperature and a reduction in furnace aeration, use of a recuperator to preheat combustion air may reduce the undesirable scaling of metal products. In absence of preheating combustion air, it would be necessary to invest in improvements to furnace controls or in some other means of preventing scaling; to secure the same product quality.

A final potential benefit from waste heat recovery, as suggested by existing applications, is the generation of revenue from sales of recovered waste heat or energy. In some cases, the recoverable waste heat cannot all be used by the plant itself. Recovery may still be advantageous if there are adjoining plants which are willing to purchase the recovered heat. In this case, the potential benefits are revenue-generating, rather than cost-reducing, and would be measurable in terms of dollars of revenue received.

With the following information—records of past operating levels and expenses, the efficiency of the proposed heat recovery equipment, the level of expected furnace operation, the demand for recycled heat, and the expected price of fuel—it should be possible to predict fairly closely the savings in fuel costs that would result from substituting waste heat for newly-generated heat or energy. Certain of the other potential benefits, such as labor cost savings and product improvement, might be more difficult to estimate.

To evaluate the desirability of an investment, measures of costs are needed to compare with the benefits. Table 3.2 shows the type of costs which may arise in connection with waste heat recovery. As may be seen, costs may begin before the waste heat recovery system is installed and extend

---

[3] Here we consider only the benefits in fuel savings resulting from pollution abatement effects of waste heat recovery, and not the benefits to the surrounding area from cleaner air emanating from the plant. The emphasis is on private benefits and costs, i.e., those accruing directly to the firm, because private decision makers have traditionally not taken into account all social benefits and costs associated with their investment decisions, i.e., those benefits and costs that accrue to society at large. With the advent of environmental impact statements, however, pollution abatement benefits have become more important to private decision makers.

TABLE 3.2.   *Potential costs to consider in investing in waste heat recovery* [a]

Type of costs	Examples of costs
1. Pre-engineering and planning costs	Engineering consultant's fee; in house manpower and materials to determine type, size, and location of heat exchanger.
2. Acquisition costs of heat recovery equipment	Purchase and installation costs of a recuperator.
3. Acquisition costs of necessary additions to existing equipment	Purchase and installation costs of new controls, burners, stack dampers, and fans to protect the furnace and recuperator from higher temperatures entering the furnace due to preheating of combustion air.
4. Replacement costs	Cost of replacing the inner shell of the recuperator in N years, net of the salvage value of the existing shell.
5. Costs of modification and repair of existing equipment	Cost of repairing furnace doors to overcome greater heat loss resulting from increased pressure due to preheating of combustion air.
6. Space costs	Cost of useful floor space occupied by waste heat steam generator; cost of useful overhead space occupied by evaporator.
7. Costs of production downtime during installation	Loss of output for a week, net of the associated savings in operating costs.
8. Costs of adjustments (debugging)	Lower production; labor costs of debugging.
9. Maintenance costs of new equipment	Costs of servicing the heat exchanger.
10. Property and/or equipment taxes of heat recovery equipment	Additional property tax incurred on capitalized value of recuperator.
11. Change in insurance or hazards costs	Higher insurance rates due to greater fire risks; increased cost of accidents due to more hot spots within a tighter space.

[a] In addition, attention should be given to the length of intended use, expected lives of related equipment, and the flexibility of alternative equipment to future modification and expansion.

throughout the period of continued plant operation. In most cases, the major cost item is likely to be the acquisition and installation of the heat exchanger, and should be relatively easy to estimate.

It is important that only those costs and benefits which are attributable to an investment be included in the analysis of that investment. For example, if a plant is required by mandate to add a pollution control apparatus, the decision to add a waste heat recovery system to the pollution control system should not be influenced by the costs of the pollution control system. As a further example, costs of equipment replacement or repair not necessitated by the addition of the waste heat recovery system should not be incorporated into the waste heat evaluation, although it may be undertaken jointly for convenience.

Partial Methods of Evaluation

The simplest procedures which are used by firms to try to evaluate alternative kinds and amounts of investments are visual inspection,[4] payback period, and return on investment—approaches which are termed "partial" here because they do not fully assess the economic desirability of alternatives. These partial methods may be contrasted with the more complete techniques, discussed in the following section, which take into account factors such as timing of cash flows, risk, and taxation effects—factors which are required for full economic assessment of investments.

Despite their shortcomings, the partial techniques of analysis may serve a useful purpose. They can provide a first level measure of profitability which is, relatively speaking, quick, simple, and inexpensive to calculate. They may therefore be useful as initial screening devices for eliminating the more obviously uneconomical

[4] There are some investments whose desirability is apparent merely by inspection, and which do not require further economic analysis. An example is an investment characterized by negligible or low costs and a highly certain return. But actions which require significant initial investment and yield benefits over time—as recovery of waste heat is typically characterized —usually require more extensive analysis than visual inspection.

investments. These partial techniques (particularly the payback method) may also provide needed information concerning certain sensitive features of an investment. But where partial methods are used, the more comprehensive techniques may also be needed to verify the outcome of the evaluations, and to rank alternative projects as to their relative efficiency.

Following are descriptions, examples, and limitations of the payback method and the return on investment method, two of the more popular partial methods.

Payback Method[5]

The payback (also known as the payout or payoff) method determines the number of years required for the invested capital to be offset by resulting benefits. The required number of years is termed the payback, recovery, or break-even period.

The measure is popularly calculated on a before-tax basis and without discounting, i.e., neglecting the opportunity cost of capital.[6] Investment costs are usually defined as first costs, often neglecting salvage value. Benefits are usually defined as the resulting net change in incoming cash flow, or, in the case of a cost-reducing investment like waste heat recovery, as the reduction in net outgoing cash flow.

The payback period is usually calculated as follows:[7]

Payback Period (PP)

$$= \frac{\text{First Cost}}{\text{Yearly Benefits—Yearly Costs}} \quad (3.1)$$

For example, the payback period for a furnace recuperator which costs $10,000 to purchase and install, $300/yr on average to operate and maintain, and which is expected to save by preheating combustion air an average of 2000 Mft^3 of burner gas per year at $0.70/$Mft^3$ (i.e., $1400/yr), may be calculated as follows:

$$PP = \frac{\$10,000}{\$1400-\$300} = 9.1 \text{ yr.}$$

The *disadvantages* of the payback method which recommend against its use as a sole criterion for investment decisions may be summarized as follows:

(a) The method does not give consideration to cash flows beyond the payback period, and thus does not measure the efficiency of an investment over its entire life.

Consider, for example, the two alternative investments A and B, presented in table 3.3. Using the undiscounted payback method, a firm would prefer Investment A, which has a payback period of 1.7 yr, to Investment B, which has a payback of 2.2 yr. Yet, depending upon the true opportunity cost of capital (i.e., the discount rate), Investment B, which continues to yield benefits beyond Investment A, may be a more profitable choice. (For example, with an opportunity cost of 10 percent, Investment A would yield $20,832 in total benefits, and Investment B, $22,383 in total benefits in present value terms.)

(b) The neglect of the opportunity cost of capital, that is, failing to discount costs occurring at different times to a common base for comparison, results in the use of inaccurate measures of benefits and costs to calculate the payback period, and, hence, determination of an incorrect payback period. This problem is illustrated by the example of two alternative investments shown in table 3.4. Payback analysis using undiscounted values would result in indifference between Investments C and D. They both have a payback of 2 yr, and yield total benefits, undiscounted, of $25,000. But because Investment D yields more benefits toward the beginning than Investment C, and thereby allows the investor to realize a larger return on earnings, Investment D would be the preferred choice. In present value terms, with an opportunity cost of 10 percent, Investment C would yield total benefits of $20,697, and Investment D, $21,524.

In short, the payback method gives attention to only one attribute of an investment, i.e., the number of years to recover costs, and, as often calculated, does not even provide an accurate

---

[5] The payback method is treated in greated detail in Eugene L. Grant and W. Grant Ireson, *Principles of Engineering Economy*, 4th Ed., pp. 347, 528-529 (New York: The Ronald Press Co., 1970).

[6] The opportunity cost of capital is the return which could be earned by using resources for the next best available investment purpose (e.g., from an investor's standpoint, this might be the earning of interest on savings accounts), rather than for the purpose at hand. It represents an extra return, beyond merely covering other costs, which is necessary in order to make an investment competitive with other opportunities. This concept is discussed further in the following section of this chapter.

[7] This method has the implicit assumption that the expected proceeds from an investment are constant from year-to-year. If expected yearly proceeds are not equal, the customary approach is either (1) to average yearly benefits and costs and use the above formula, or (2) to add the proceeds in successive years until their total equals the first cost.

TABLE 3.3.   *An illustration that payback analysis does not take into account cash flows beyond the payback period*

Investment	First Cost	Yearly benefits			Payback period	Total present value benefits [a]
		Year 1	Year 2	Year 3		
Investment A	$20,000	$12,000	$12,000	$0	1.7 years	$20,832
Investment B	20,000	9,000	9,000	9,000	2.2 years	22,383

[a]Calculated for a discount rate of 10 percent, compounded annually.

TABLE 3.4.   *An illustration that the undiscounted payback method can result in inaccurate measures*

Investment	First cost	Yearly benefits			Payback period	Total present value benefits [a]
		Year 1	Year 2	Year 3		
Investment C	$20,000	$5,000	$15,000	$5,000	2 years	$20,697
Investment D	20,000	15,000	5,000	5,000	2 years	21,524

[a] Calculated for a discount rate of 10 percent, compounded annually.

measure of this. It is a measure which many firms appear to overemphasize, tending toward shorter and shorter payback requirements. Firms' preference for very short payback to enable them to reinvest in other investment opportunities may in fact lead to a succession of less efficient, short-lived projects.

Despite its limitations, the payback period has *advantages* in that it may provide useful information for evaluating an investment. There are several situations in which the payback method might be particularly appropriate:

(a) A rapid payback may be a prime criterion for judging an investment when financial resources are available to the investor for only a short period of time.

(b) The speculative investor who has a very limited time horizon will usually desire rapid recovery of the initial investment.

(c) Where the expected life of the assets is highly uncertain, determination of the break-even life, i.e., payback period, is helpful in assessing the likelihood of achieving a successful investment.

The shortcomings that result from failure to discount costs and the omission of important cost items can be overcome simply by using a more accurate calculation of payback. Essentially what is desired is to find the number of years, R, for which the value of the following expression is equal to zero:

$$C = \sum_{j=1}^{R} \frac{B_j - P_j}{(1 + i)^j} \qquad (3.2)$$

where

$$
\begin{aligned}
C &= \text{Initial investment cost,} \\
B_j &= \text{Benefits in year } j, \\
P_j &= \text{Costs in year } j, \\
R &= \text{Break-even number of years, and} \\
i &= \text{Discount rate.}
\end{aligned}
$$

Where yearly net benefits are uneven, an iterative process can be used to determine the solution. If, on the other hand, yearly net benefits are expected to be about uniform, the following formula[8] can be used to facilitate the calculation:

$$R = \frac{-\log\left(1 - \dfrac{iC}{M}\right)}{\log(1+i)}, \qquad (3.3)$$

where

R = Break-even number years,

M = Yearly net benefits,

C = Initial investment cost, and

i = Discount rate.

Return on Investment Method[9]

The return on investment (ROI) or return on assets method calculates average annual benefits, net of yearly costs such as depreciation, as a percentage of the original book value of the investment.

The calculation is as follows:

Return on Investment (ROI)

$$= \frac{\text{Average Annual Net Benefits}}{\text{Original Book Value}} \times 100. \qquad (3.4)$$

As an example, the calculation of the ROI for an investment in a waste heat economizer is as follows:

Original Book Value   = $15,000
Expected Life   = 10 yr
Annual Depreciation,
    using a straight-line method $= \dfrac{\$15,000}{10} = \$1500$

Yearly Operation, Maintenance
    and Repair Cost   = $200

Expected Annual Fuel Oil Savings   = $5000

$$\text{ROI} = \frac{\$5000 - (\$1500 + \$200)}{\$15,000} \times 100$$

$$= 0.22 \times 100 = 22 \text{ percent}$$

The return on investment method is subject to the following principal *disadvantages*, and, therefore, is not recommended as a sole criterion for investment decisions:

(a) Like the payback method, this method does not take into consideration the timing of cash flows, and thereby may incorrectly state the economic efficiency of projects.

(b) The calculation is based on an accounting concept, original book value, which is subject to the peculiarities of the firm's accounting practices, and which generally does not include all costs. The method, therefore, results in only a rough approximation of an investment's value.

The *advantages* of the return on investment method are that it is simple to compute and a familiar concept in the business community.[10]

---

[8] Educational Facilities Laboratories, *The Economy of Energy Conservation in Educational Facilities*, pp. 67-68, Library of Congress Catalog No. 73-83011, (New York: FFL, Inc., 1973).

[9] This method is described in greater detail in the Electric Energy Association's Manual, *The Financial Analysis Section of Alternative Choice Comparison for Energy System Selection*, (New York, n.d.).

[10] A variation of this method is the return on average investment method, in which the average yearly benefit, before taxes and net of depreciation, is divided by the average book value over the life of the project, (defined as the original book value plus the final book value, divided by 2. Thus, with no remaining salvage value at the end of 10 yr, the return on average investment in the example would be 44 percent.

COMMERCIAL OPTIONS IN WASTE HEAT
RECOVERY EQUIPMENT*

Introduction

Industrial heat exchangers have many pseudonyms. They are sometimes called recuperators, regenerators, waste heat steam generators, condensers, heat wheels, temperature and moisture exchangers, etc. Whatever name they may have, they all perform one basic function; the transfer of heat.

Heat exchangers are characterized as single or multipass gas to gas, liquid to gas, liquid to liquid, evaporator, condenser, parallel flow, counter flow, or cross flow. The terms single or multipass refer to the heating or cooling media passing over the heat transfer surface once or a number of times. Multipass flow involves the use of internal baffles. The next three terms refer to the two fluids between which heat is transferred in the heat exchanger, and imply that no phase changes occur in those fluids. Here the term "fluid" is used in the most general sense. Thus, we can say that these terms apply to nonevaporator and noncondensing heat exchangers. The term evaporator applies to a heat exchanger in which heat is transferred to an evaporating (boiling) liquid, while a condenser is a heat exchanger in which heat is removed from a condensing vapor. A parallel flow heat exchanger is one in which both fluids flow in approximately the same direction whereas in counterflow the two fluids move in opposite directions. When the two fluids move at right angles to each other, the heat exchanger is considered to be of the crossflow type.

The principal methods of reclaiming waste heat in industrial plants make use of heat exchangers. The heat exchanger is a system which separates the stream containing waste heat and the medium which is to absorb it, but allows the flow of heat across the separation boundaries. The reasons for separating the two streams may be any of the following:

(1) A pressure difference may exist between the two streams of fluid. The rigid boundaries of the heat exchanger can be designed to withstand the pressure difference.

(2) In many, if not most, cases the one stream would contaminate the other, if they were permitted to mix. The heat exchanger prevents mixing.

(3) Heat exchangers permit the use of an intermediate fluid better suited than either of the principal exchange media for transporting waste heat through long distances. The secondary fluid is often steam, but another substance may be selected for special properties.

(4) Certain types of heat exchangers, specifically the heat wheel, are capable of transferring liquids as well as heat. Vapors being cooled in the gases are condensed in the wheel and later re-evaporated into the gas being heated. This can result in improved humidity and/or process control, abatement of atmospheric air pollution, and conservation of valuable resources.

The various names or designations applied to heat exchangers are partly an attempt to describe their function and partly the result of tradition within certain industries. For example, a recuperator is a heat exchanger which recovers waste heat from the exhaust gases of a furnace to heat the incoming air for combustion. This is the name used in both the steel and the glass making industries. The heat exchanger performing the same function in the steam generator of an electric power plant is termed an air preheater, and in the case of a gas turbine plant, a regenerator.

However, in the glass and steel industries the word regenerator refers to two chambers of brick checkerwork which alternately absorb heat from

* W.M. Rohrer, Jr., University of Pittsburgh

the exhaust gases and then give up part of that heat to the incoming air. The flows of flue gas and of air are periodically reversed by valves so that one chamber of the regenerator is being heated by the products of combustion while the other is being cooled by the incoming air. Regenerators are often more expensive to buy and more expensive to maintain than are recuperators, and their application is primarily in glass melt tanks and in open hearth steel furnaces.

It must be pointed out, however, that although their functions are similar, the three heat exchangers mentioned above may be structurally quite different as well as different in their principal modes of heat transfer. A more complete description of the various industrial heat exchangers follows later in this chapter and details of their differences will be clarified.

The specification of an industrial heat exchanger must include the heat exchange capacity, the temperatures of the fluids, the allowable pressure drop in each fluid path, and the properties and volumetric flow of the fluids entering the exchanger. These specifications will determine construction parameters and thus the cost of the heat exchanger. The final design will be a compromise between pressure drop, heat exchanger effectiveness, and cost. Decisions leading to that final design will balance out the cost of maintenance and operation of the overall system against the fixed costs in such a way as to minimize the total. Advice on selection and design of heat exchangers is available from vendors.

The essential parameters which should be known in order to make an optimum choice of waste heat recovery devices are:

- Temperature of waste heat fluid
- Flow rate of waste heat fluid
- Chemical composition of waste heat fluid
- Minimum allowable temperature of waste heat fluid
- Temperature of heated fluid
- Chemical composition of heated fluid
- Maximum allowable temperature of heated fluid
- Control temperature, if control required

In the rest of this chapter, some common types of waste heat recovery devices are discussed in some detail.

Gas to Gas Heat Exchangers

Recuperators

The simplest configuration for a heat exchanger is the metallic radiation recuperator which consists of two concentric lengths of metal tubing as shown in figure 5.1 below.

The inner tube carries the hot exhaust gases while the external annulus carries the combustion

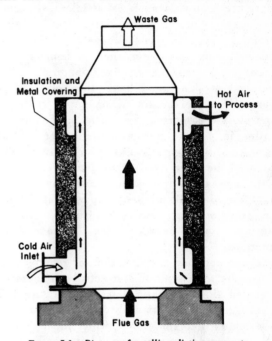

FIGURE 5.1　*Diagram of metallic radiation recuperator.*

air from the atmosphere to the air inlets of the furnace burners. The hot gases are cooled by the incoming combustion air which now carries additional energy into the combustion chamber. This is energy which does not have to be supplied by the fuel; consequently, less fuel is burned for a given furnace loading. The saving in fuel also means a decrease in combustion air and therefore, stack losses are decreased not only by lowering the stack gas temperatures, but also by discharging smaller quantities of exhaust gas. This particular recuperator gets its name from the fact that a substantial portion of the heat transfer from the hot gases to the surface of the inner tube take place by radiative heat transfer. The cold air in the annulus, however, is almost transparent to infrared radiation so that only convection heat transfer takes place to the incoming air. As shown in the diagram, the two gas flows are usually parallel, although the configuration would be simpler and the heat transfer more efficient if the flows were opposed in direction (or counterflow). The reason for the use of parallel flow is that recuperators frequently serve the additional function of cooling the duct carrying away the exhaust gases, and consequently extending its service life.

The inner tube is often fabricated from high temperature materials such as stainless steels of high nickel content. The large temperature differential at the inlet causes differential expansion, since the outer shell is usually of a different and less expensive material. The mechanical design must take this effect into account. More elaborate designs of radiation recuperators incorporate two sections; the bottom operating in parallel flow and the upper section using the more efficient counterflow arrangement. Because of the large axial expansions experienced and the stress conditions at the bottom of the recuperator, the unit is often supported at the top by a free standing support frame with an expansion joint between the furnace and recuperator.

A second common configuration for recuperators is called the tube type or convective recuperator. As seen in the schematic diagram of figure 5.2, the hot gases are carried through a number of parallel small diameter tubes, while the incoming air to be heated enters a shell surrounding the tubes and passes over the hot tubes one or more times in a direction normal to their axes.

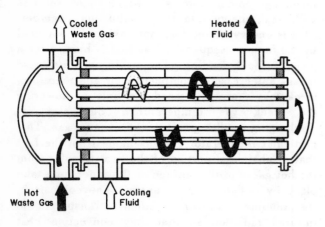

FIGURE 5.2 *Diagram of convective-type recuperator.*

If the tubes are baffled to allow the gas to pass over them twice, the heat exchanger is termed a two-pass recuperator; if two baffles are used, a three-pass recuperator, etc. Although baffling increases both the cost of the exchanger and the pressure drop in the combustion air path, it increases the effectiveness of heat exchange. Shell-and tube-type recuperators are generally more compact and have a higher effectiveness than radiation recuperators, because of the larger heat transfer area made possible through the use of multiple tubes and multiple passes of the gases.

The principal limitation on the heat recovery of metal recuperators is the reduced life of the liner at inlet temperatures exceeding 2000 F. At this temperature, it is necessary to use the less efficient arrangement of parallel flows of exhaust gas and coolant in order to maintain sufficient cooling of the inner shell. In addition, when furnace combustion air flow is dropped back because of reduced load, the heat transfer rate from hot waste gases to preheat combustion air becomes excessive, causing rapid surface deterioration. Then, it is usually necessary to provide an ambient air by-pass to cool the exhaust gases.

In order to overcome the temperature limitations of metal recuperators, ceramic tube recuperators have been developed, whose materials allow operation on the gas side to 2800 F and on the preheated air side to 2200 F on an experimental basis, and to 1500 F on a more or less practical basis. Early ceramic recuperators were built of tile and joined with furnace cement, and thermal cycling caused cracking of joints and rapid deterioration of the tubes. Later developments introduced various kinds of short silicon carbide tubes which can be joined by flexible seals located in the air headers. This kind of patented design illustrated in figure 5.3 maintains the seals at comparatively low temperatures and has reduced the seal leakage rates to a few percent.

Earlier designs had experienced leakage rates from 8 to 60 percent. The new designs are reported to last 2 yr with air preheat temperatures as high as 1300 F, with much lower leakage rates.

An alternative arrangement for the convective type recuperator, in which the cold combustion air is heated in a bank of parallel vertical tubes which extend into the flue gas stream, is shown schematically in figure 5.4. The advantage claimed for this arrangement is the ease of replacing

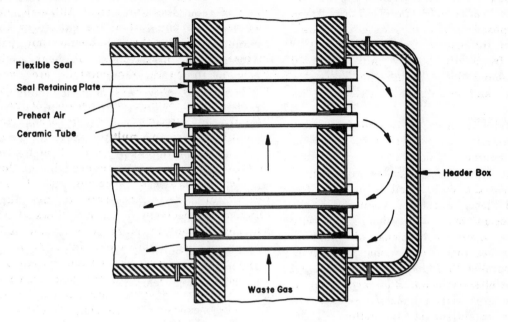

Flexible Seal
Seal Retaining Plate
Preheat Air
Ceramic Tube

Header Box

Waste Gas

FIGURE 5.3 *Ceramic recuperator.*

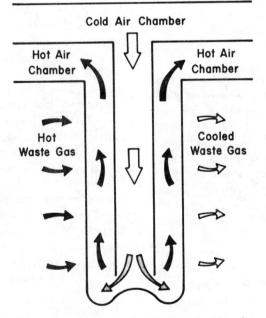

Cold Air Chamber

Hot Air
Chamber

Hot Air
Chamber

Hot
Waste Gas

Cooled
Waste Gas

FIGURE 5.4 *Diagram of vertical tube-within-tube recuperator.*

individual tubes, which can be done during full capacity furnace operation. This minimizes the cost, the inconvenience, and possible furnace damage due to a shutdown forced by recuperator failure.

For maximum effectiveness of heat transfer, combinations of radiation type and convective type recuperators are used, with the convective type always following the high temperature radiation recuperator. A schematic diagram of this arrangement is seen in figure 5.5.

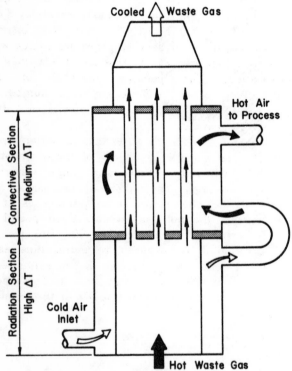

FIGURE 5.5 *Diagram of combined radiation and convective type recuperator.*

Although the use of recuperators conserves fuel in industrial furnaces, and although their original cost is relatively modest, the purchase of the unit is often just the beginning of a somewhat more extensive capital improvement program. The use of a recuperator, which raises the temperature of the incoming combustion air, may require purchase of high temperature burners, larger diameter air lines with flexible fittings to allow for expansion, cold air lines for cooling the burners, modified combustion controls to maintain the required air/fuel ratio despite variable recuperator heating, stack dampers, cold air bleeds, controls to protect the recuperator during blower failure or power failures, and larger fans to overcome the

additional pressure drop in the recuperator. It is vitally important to protect the recuperator against damage due to excessive temperatures, since the cost of rebuilding a damaged recuperator may be as high as 90 percent of the initial cost of manufacture and the drop in efficiency of a damaged recuperator may easily increase fuel costs by 10 to 15 percent.

Figure 5.6 shows a schematic diagram of one radiant tube burner fitted with a radiation recuperator. With such a short stack, it is necessary to use two annuli for the incoming air to achieve reasonable heat exchange efficiencies.

Recuperators are used for recovering heat from exhaust gases to heat other gases in the medium to high temperature range. Some typical applications are in soaking ovens, annealing ovens, melting furnaces, afterburners and gas incinerators, radiant-tube burners, reheat furnaces, and other gas to gas waste heat recovery applications in the medium to high temperature range.

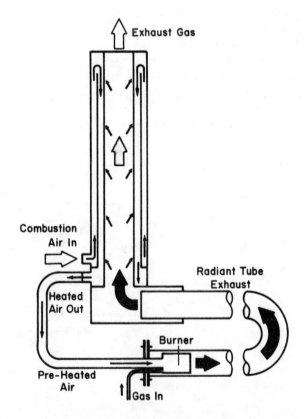

FIGURE 5.6 *Diagram of a small radiation-type recuperator fitted to a radiant tube burner.*

Heat Wheels

A rotary regenerator (also called an air preheater or a heat wheel) is finding increasing applications in low to medium temperature waste heat recovery. Figure 5.7 is a sketch illustrating the application of a heat wheel. It is a sizable porous disk, fabricated from some material having a fairly high heat capacity, which rotates between two side-by-side ducts; one a cold gas duct, the other a hot gas duct. The axis of the disk is located parallel to, and on the partition between the two ducts. As the disk slowly rotates, sensible heat (and in some cases, moisture containing latent heat) is transferred to the disk by the hot air and as the disk rotates, from the disk to the cold air. The overall efficiency of sensible heat transfer for this kind of regenerator can be as high as 85 percent. Heat wheels have been built as large as 70 ft in diameter with air capacities up to 40,000 ft³/min. Multiple units can be used in parallel. This may help to prevent a mismatch between capacity requirements and the limited number of sizes available in packaged units. In very large installations such as those required for preheating combustion air in fixed station electrical generating stations, the units are custom designed.

The limitation on temperature range for the heat wheel is primarily due to mechanical difficulties introduced by uneven expansion of the rotating wheel when the temperature differences mean large differential expansion, causing excessive deformations of the wheel and thus difficulties in maintaining adequate air seals between duct and wheel.

Heat wheels are available in four types. The first consists of a metal frame packed with a core of knitted mesh stainless steel or aluminum wire, resembling that found in the common metallic kitchen pot scraper; the second, called a laminar wheel, is fabricated from corrugated metal and is composed of many parallel flow passages; the third variety is also a laminar wheel but is constructed from a ceramic matrix of honeycomb configuration. This type is used for higher temperature applications with a present-day limit of about 1600 F. The fourth variety is of laminar construction but the flow passages are coated with a hygroscopic material so that latent heat may be recovered. The packing material of the hygroscopic wheel may be any of a number of materials. The hygroscopic material is often termed a dessicant.

Most industrial stack gases contain water vapor, since water vapor is a product of the combustion of all hydrocarbon fuels and since water is introduced into many industrial processes, and part of the process water evaporates as it is exposed to the hot gas stream. Each pound of water requires approximately 1000 Btu for its evaporation at atmospheric pressure, thus each pound of water vapor leaving in the exit stream will carry 1000 Btu of energy with it. This latent heat may be a substantial fraction of the sensible

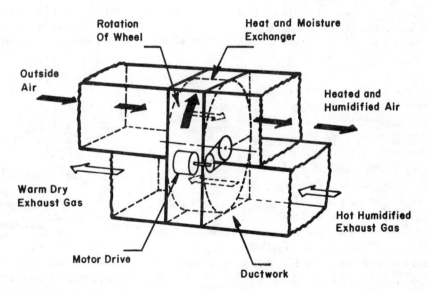

FIGURE 5.7 *Heat and moisture recovery using a heat wheel type regenerator.*

energy in the exit gas stream. A hygroscopic material is one such as lithium chloride (LiCl) which readily absorbs water vapor. Lithium chloride is a solid which absorbs water to form a hydrate, $LiCl \cdot H_2O$, in which one molecule of lithium chloride combines with one molecule of water. Thus, the ratio of water to lithium chloride in $LiCl \cdot H_2O$ is 3/7 by weight. In a hygroscopic heat wheel, the hot gas stream gives up part of its water vapor to the coating; the cool gases which enter the wheel to be heated are drier than those in the inlet duct and part of the absorbed water is given up to the incoming gas stream. The latent heat of the water adds directly to the total quantity of recovered waste heat. The efficiency of recovery of water vapor can be as high as 50 percent.

Since the pores of heat wheels carry a small amount of gas from the exhaust to the intake duct, cross contamination can result. If this contamination is undesirable, the carryover of exhaust gas can be partially eliminated by the addition of a purge section where a small amount of clean air is blown through the wheel and then exhausted to the atmosphere, thereby clearing the passages of exhaust gas. Figure 5.8 illustrates the features of an installation using a purge section. Note that additional seals are required to separate the purge ducts. Common practice is to use about six air changes of clean air for purging. This limits gas contamination to as little as 0.04 percent and particle contamination to less than 0.2 percent in laminar wheels, and cross contamination to less than 1 percent in packed wheels. If inlet gas temperature is to be held constant, regardless of heating loads and exhaust gas temperatures, then the heat wheel must be driven at variable speed. This requires a variable speed drive and a speed control system using an inlet air temperature sensor as the control element. This feature, however, adds considerably to the cost and complexity of the system. When operating with outside air in periods of high humidity and sub-zero temperatures, heat wheels may require preheat systems to prevent frost formation. When handling gases which contain water-soluble, greasy or adhesive contaminants or large concentrations of process dust, air filters may be required in the exhaust system upstream from the heat wheel.

One application of heat wheels is in space heating situations where unusually large quantities of ventilation air are required for health or safety reasons. As many as 20 or 30 air changes per h may be required to remove toxic gases or to prevent the accumulation of explosive mixtures. Comfort heating for that quantity of ventilation air is frequently expensive enough to make the use of heat wheels economical. In the summer season the heat wheel can be used to cool the incoming air from the cold exhaust air, reducing the air conditioning load by as much as 50 percent. It should be pointed out that in many circumstances where large ventilating requirements are mandatory, a better solution than the installation of heat wheels may be the use of local ventilation systems to reduce the hazards and/or the use of infrared comfort heating at principal work areas.

Heat wheels are finding increasing use for process heat recovery in low and moderate temperature environments. Typical applications would be curing or drying ovens and air preheaters in all sizes for industrial and utility boilers.

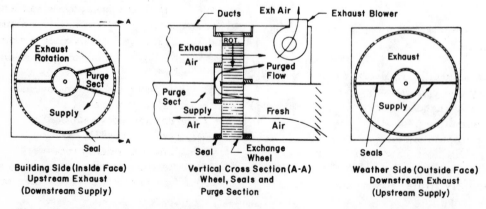

FIGURE 5.8 *Heat wheel equipped with purge section to clear contaminants from the heat transfer surface.*

Air Preheaters

Passive gas to gas regenerators, sometimes called air preheaters, are available for applications which cannot tolerate any cross contamination. They are constructed of alternate channels (see fig. 5.9) which put the flows of the heating and the heated gases in close contact with each other, separated only by a thin wall of conductive metal. They occupy more volume and are more expensive to construct than are heat wheels, since a much greater heat transfer surface area is required for the same efficiency. An advantage, besides the absence of cross-contamination, is the decreased mechanical complexity since no drive mechanism is required. However, it becomes more difficult to achieve temperature control with the passive regeneration and, if this is a requirement, some of the advantages of its basic simplicity are lost.

Gas-to-gas regenerators are used for recovering heat from exhaust gases to heat other gases in the

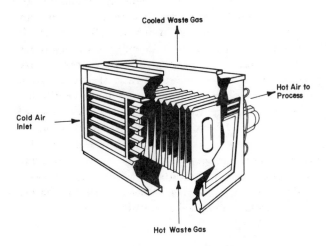

FIGURE 5.9 *A passive gas to gas regenerator.*

low to medium temperature range. A list of typical applications follows:

- Heat and moisture recovery from building heating and ventilation systems
- Heat and moisture recovery from moist rooms and swimming pools
- Reduction of building air conditioner loads
- Recovery of heat and water from wet industrial processes
- Heat recovery from steam boiler exhaust gases

- Heat recovery from gas and vapor incinerators
- Heat recovery from baking, drying, and curing ovens
- Heat recovery from gas turbine exhausts
- Heat recovery from other gas-to-gas applications in the low through high temperature range

Heat-Pipe Exchangers

The heat pipe is a heat transfer element that has only recently become commercial, but it shows promise as an industrial waste heat recovery option because of its high efficiency and compact size. In use, it operates as a passive gas-to-gas finned-tube regenerator. As can be seen in figure 5.10, the elements form a bundle of heat pipes which extend through the exhaust and inlet ducts in a pattern that resembles the structured finned coil heat exchangers. Each pipe, however, is a separate sealed element consisting of an annular wick on the inside of the full length of the tube, in which an appropriate heat transfer fluid is entrained. Figure 5.11 shows how the heat absorbed from hot exhaust gases evaporates the entrained fluid, causing the vapor to collect in the center core. The latent heat of vaporization is carried in the vapor to the cold end of the heat pipe located in the cold gas duct. Here the vapor condenses giving up its latent heat. The condensed liquid is then carried by capillary (and/or gravity) action back to the hot end where it is recycled. The heat pipe is compact and efficient because: (1) the finned-tube bundle is inherently a good configuration for convective heat transfer in both gas ducts, and (2) the evaporative-condensing cycle within the heat tubes is a highly efficient way of transferring the heat internally. It is also free from cross contamination. Possible applications include:

- Drying, curing and baking ovens
- Waste steam reclamation
- Air preheaters in steam boilers
- Air dryers
- Brick kilns (secondary recovery)
- Reverberatory furnaces (secondary recovery)
- Heating, ventilating and air conditioning systems

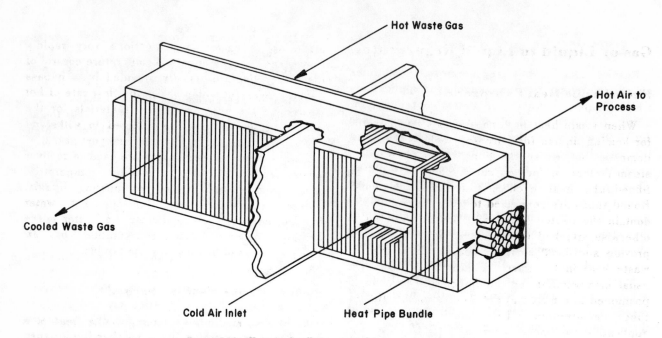

FIGURE 5.10   *Heat pipe bundle incorporated in gas to gas regenerator.*

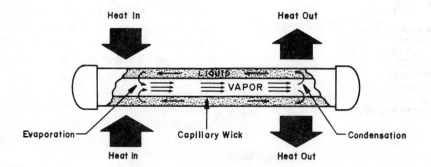

FIGURE 5.11   *Heat pipe schematic.*

Gas or Liquid to Liquid Regenerators

Finned-Tube Heat Exhangers

When waste heat in exhaust gases is recovered for heating liquids for purposes such as providing domestic hot water, heating the feedwater for steam boilers, or for hot water space heating, the finned-tube heat exchanger is generally used. Round tubes are connected together in bundles to contain the heated liquid and fins are welded or otherwise attached to the outside of the tubes to provide additional surface area for removing the waste heat in the gases. Figure 5.12 shows the usual arrangement for the finned-tube exchanger positioned in a duct and details of a typical finned-tube construction. This particular type of application is more commonly known as an economizer. The tubes are often connected all in series but can also be arranged in series-parallel bundles to control the liquid side pressure drop. The air side pressure drop is controlled by the spacing of the tubes and the number of rows of tubes within the duct. Finned-tube exchangers are available prepackaged in modular sizes or can be made up to custom specifications very rapidly from standard components. Temperature control of the heated liquid is usually provided by a bypass duct arrangement which varies the flow rate of hot gases over the heat exchanger. Materials for the tubes and the fins can be selected to withstand corrosive liquids and/or corrosive exhaust gases.

Finned-tube heat exchangers are used to recover waste heat in the low to medium temperature range from exhaust gases for heating liquids. Typical applications are domestic hot water heating, heating boiler feedwater, hot water space heating, absorption-type refrigeration or air conditioning, and heating process liquids.

Shell and Tube Heat Exchanger

When the medium containing waste heat is a liquid or a vapor which heats another liquid, then the shell and tube heat exchanger must be used since both paths must be sealed to contain the pressures of their respective fluids. The shell contains the tube bundle, and usually internal baffles, to direct the fluid in the shell over the tubes in multiple passes. The shell is inherently weaker than the tubes so that the higher pressure fluid is circulated in the tubes while the lower pressure fluid flows through the shell. When a vapor contains the waste heat, it usually condenses, giving up its latent heat to the liquid being heated. In this application, the vapor is almost invariably contained within the shell. If the reverse is attempted, the condensation of vapors within small diameter parallel tubes causes flow instabilities. Tube and shell heat exchangers are available in a wide range of standard sizes with many combinations of materials for the tubes and shells.

Typical applications of shell and tube heat exchangers include heating liquids with the heat contained by condensates from refrigeration and air conditioning systems; condensate from process steam; coolants from furnace doors, grates, and pipe supports; coolants from engines, air compressors, bearings, and lubricants; and the condensates from distillation processes.

Waste Heat Boilers

Waste heat boilers are ordinarily water tube boilers in which the hot exhaust gases from gas

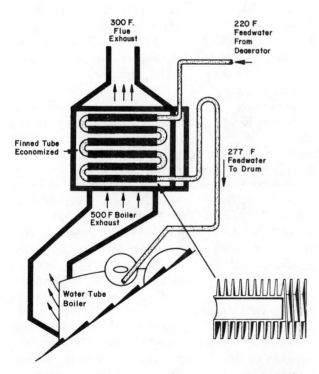

FIGURE 5.12 *Finned tube gas to liquid regenerator (economizer).*

turbines, incinerators, etc., pass over a number of parallel tubes containing water. The water is vaporized in the tubes and collected in a steam drum from which it is drawn off for use as heating or processing steam. Figure 5.13 indicates one arrangement that is used, where the exhaust gases pass over the water tubes twice before they are exhausted to the air. Because the exhaust gases are usually in the medium temperature range and in order to conserve space, a more compact boiler can be produced if the water tubes are finned in order to increase the effective heat transfer area on the gas side. The diagram shows a mud drum,

a set of tubes over which the hot gases make a double pass, and a steam drum which collects the steam generated above the water surface. The pressure at which the steam is generated and the rate of steam production depend on the temperature of the hot gases entering the boiler, the flow rate of the hot gases, and the efficiency of the boiler. The pressure of a pure vapor in the presence of its liquid is a function of the temperature of the liquid from which it is evaporated. The abridged steam tables precisely tabulate this relationship between saturation pressure and temperature. Should the waste heat in the exhaust gases be insufficient for generating the required amount of process steam, it is sometimes possible to add auxiliary burners which burn fuel in the waste heat boiler or to add an afterburner to the exhaust gas duct just ahead of the boiler. Waste heat boilers are built in capacities from less than a thousand to almost a million ft³/min of exhaust gas.

Typical applications of waste heat boilers are to recover energy from the exhausts of gas turbines, reciprocating engines, incinerators, and furnaces.

Gas and Vapor Expanders

Industrial steam and gas turbines are in an advanced state of development and readily available on a commercial basis. Recently special gas turbine designs for low pressure waste gases have become available; for example, a turbine is available for operation from the top gases of a blast furnace. In this case, as much as 20MW of power could be generated, representing a recovery of 20 to 30 percent of the available energy of the furnace exhaust gas stream. Maximum top pressures are of the order of 40 lb/in²g.

Perhaps of greater applicability than the last example are steam turbines used for producing mechanical work or for driving electrical generators. After removing the necessary energy for doing work, the steam turbine exhausts partially spent steam at a lower pressure than the inlet pressure. The energy in the turbine exhaust stream can then be used for process heat in the usual ways. Steam turbines are classified as back-pressure turbines, available with allowable exit pressure operation above 400 lb/in²g, or condensing turbines which operate below atmospheric exit pressures. The steam used for

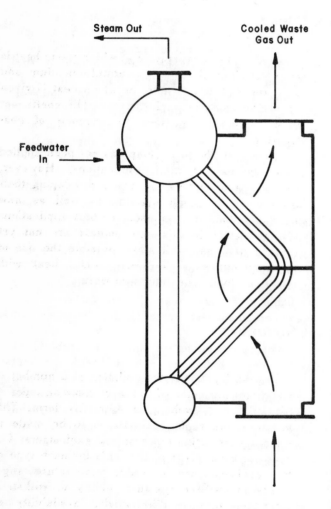

FIGURE 5.13 *Waste heat boiler for heat recovery from gas turbines or incinerators.*

driving the turbines can be generated in direct fired or waste heat boilers. A list of typical applications for gas and vapor expanders follows:

- Electrical power generation
- Compressor drives
- Pump drives
- Fan drives

Heat Pumps

In the commercial options previously discussed in this chapter, we find waste heat being transferred from a hot fluid to a fluid at a lower temperature. Heat must flow spontaneously "downhill"; that is, from a system at high temperature to one at a lower temperature. This can be expressed scientifically in a number of ways; all the variations of the statement of the second law of thermodynamics. Thermodynamics is reviewed subsequently. The practical impact of these statements is that energy as it is transformed again and again and transferred from system to system, becomes less and less available for use. Eventually that energy has such low intensity (resides in a medium at such low temperature) that it is no longer available at all to perform a useful function. It has been taken as a general rule of thumb in industrial operations that fluids with temperatures less than 250 F are of little value for waste heat extraction; flue gases should not be cooled below 250 F (or, better, 300 F to provide a safe margin), because of the risk of condensation of corrosive liquids. However, as fuel costs continue to rise, such waste heat can be used economically for space heating and other low temperature applications. It is possible to reverse the direction of spontaneous energy flow by the use of a thermodynamic system known as a heat pump. This device consists of two heat exchangers, a compressor and an expansion device.

A liquid or a mixture of liquid and vapor of a pure chemical species flows through the evaporator, where it absorbs heat at low temperature and in doing so is completely vaporized. The low temperature vapor is compressed by a compressor which requires external work. The work done on the vapor raises its pressure and temperature to a level where its energy becomes available for use. The vapor flows through a condenser where it gives up its energy as it condenses to a liquid. The liquid is then expanded through a device back to the evaporator where the cycle repeats. The heat pump was developed as a space heating system where low temperature energy from the ambient air, water, or earth is raised to heating system temperatures by doing compression work with an electric motor driven compressor. The performance of the heat pump is ordinarily described in terms of the coefficient of performance or COP, which is defined as:

$$COP = \frac{\text{Heat transferred in condenser}}{\text{Compressor work}}$$

which in an ideal heat pump is found as:

$$COP = \frac{T_H}{T_H - T_L}$$

where T_L is the temperature at which waste heat is extracted from the low temperature medium and T_H is the high temperature at which heat is given up by the pump as useful energy. The coefficient of performance expresses the economy of heat transfer.

In the past, the heat pump has not been applied generally to industrial applications. However, several manufacturers are now redeveloping their domestic heat pump systems as well as new equipment for industrial use. The best applications for the device in this new context are not yet clear, but it may well make possible the use of large quantities of low-grade waste heat with relatively small expenditures of work.

Summary

Table 5.1 presents the collation of a number of significant attributes of the most common types of industrial heat exchangers in matrix form. This matrix allows rapid comparisons to be made in selecting competing types of heat exchangers. The characteristics given in the table for each type of heat exchanger are: allowable temperature range, ability to transfer moisture, ability to withstand large temperature differentials, availability as packaged units, suitability for retrofitting, and compactness and the allowable combinations of heat transfer fluids.

TABLE 5.1

OPERATION AND APPLICATION CHARACTERISTICS

OF INDUSTRIAL HEAT EXCHANGERS

COMMERCIAL HEAT TRANSFER EQUIPMENT	Low Temperature Sub-Zero – 250°F	Intermediate Temp. 250°F – 1200°F	High Temperature 1200°F – 2000°F	Recovers Moisture	Large Temperature Differentials Permitted	Packaged Units Available	Can Be Retrofit	No Cross-Contamination	Compact Size	Gas-to-Gas Heat Exchange	Gas-to-Liquid Heat Exchanger	Liquid-to-Liquid Heat Exchanger	Corrosive Gases Permitted with Special Construction
Radiation Recuperator			●		●	1	●	●		●			●
Convection Recuperator		●	●		●	●	●	●		●			
Metallic Heat Wheel	●	●		2		●	●	3	●	●			●
Hygroscopic Heat Wheel	●			●		●	●	3	●	●			
Ceramic Heat Wheel		●	●		●	●			●	●			●
Passive Regenerator	●	●			●	●	●	●		●			●
Finned-Tube Heat Exchanger	●	●			●	●	●	●	●		●		4
Tube Shell-and-Tube Exchanger	●	●			●	●	●	●	●		●	●	
Waste Heat Boilers	●	●				●	●	●			●		4
Heat Pipes	●	●			5	●	●	●	●	●			●

1. Off-the-shelf items available in small capacities only.

2. Controversial subject. Some authorities claim moisture recovery. Do not advise depending on it.

3. With a purge section added, cross-contamination can be limited to less than 1% by mass.

4. Can be constructed of corrosion-resistant materials, but consider possible extensive damage to equipment caused by leaks or tube ruptures.

5. Allowable temperatures and temperature differential limited by the phase equilibrium properties of the internal fluid.

In regard to moisture recovery, it should be emphasized that many of the heat exchangers operating in the low temperature range may condense vapors from the cooled gas stream. Provisions must be made to remove those liquid condensates from the heat exchanger.

It is possible to list the manufacturers of industrial waste heat recovery equipment with their mail and cable addresses and telephone numbers, and then categorize their products according to type and function. However, the list would unlikely be complete and the information would not stay current. Rather than risk the almost impossible task of keeping up with changes in this presently volatile manufacturing field, it is more practical to compile a list of useful references from the technical periodical literature and from the product directories.

Technical Periodicals

Heating/Piping/Air Conditioning
Reinhold Publishing Corporation
10 S. LaSalle Street
Chicago, IL 60603

Industrial Gas Magazine *
209 Dunn Avenue
Stamford, CT 06905

Industrial Heating
National Industrial Publishing Company
Union Trust Building
Pittsburgh, PA 15219

Plant Engineering
Technical Publishing Company
1301 S. Grove Avenue
Barrington, IL 60010

*One issue published annually as a product directory.

Heating/Combustion Equipment News
Business Communications, Inc.
2800 Euclid Avenue
Cleveland, OH 44115

Power Magazine
McGraw-Hill Publications Company
New York, NY 10020

Manuals and Product Directories

ASHRAE Handbook and Product Directory—1973, Systems
Published every four years by:
American Society of Heating, Refrigerating,
  Ventilating & Air Conditioning
  Engineers, Inc.
345 East 47th Street
New York, NY 10017

ASHRAE Guide and Data Book—1975, Equipment
Published every four years by:
American Society of Heating, Refrigerating,
  Ventilating & Air Conditioning
  Engineers, Inc.
345 East 47th Street
New York, NY 10017

Thomas Register of American Manufacturers
Thomas Publishing Company
461 Eighth Avenue
New York, NY 10001

SOURCES OF ASSISTANCE FOR DESIGNING
AND INSTALLING WASTE HEAT SYSTEMS*

Just as there are many applications for waste heat recovery systems and many types of systems, there are many sources of assistance. One of the best sources in the initial stages for determining the possibilities and feasibility of a project are consulting energy-use engineers whom you may retain to assist you in making a survey of your plant. If you are not aware of specific consulting engineers in your area, the energy suppliers may be able to suggest two or three from which to choose. In some locations there are professional societies that have local energy conservation or efficient energy utilization committees that may have a list of consultants from which to select. A list of some organizations and their national office addresses are listed below:

American Society of Heating Refrigerating and
    Air Conditioning Engineers, Inc.
United Engineering Center
345 East 47th Street
New York, NY 10017

American Society for Engineering Education
One Dupont Circle
Washington, DC 20036

Institute of Electrical and Electronics Engineers,
    Inc.
United Engineering Center
345 East 47th Street
New York, NY 10017

American Consulting Engineers Council
1555 15th Street, N.W.
Washington, DC 20005

National Society of Professional Engineers
2029 K Street, N.W.
Washington, DC 20006

Edison Electric Institute
90 Park Avenue
New York, NY 10016

An energy consultant should be able to help you in identifying the best cost/effectiveness ideas and major possibilities for energy reduction. Where desired he may carry the responsibility for you in designing and supervising the changes required to implement waste heat utilization.

Another source of assistance is the equipment manufacturers and their representatives. Generally, a wealth of information regarding application details, approximate costs, installation procedures and other equipment changes is available. Quite often they will have recent case histories similar to the one applicable to your plant.

The responsibility for a project that involves two or more suppliers of equipment for an existing process is sometimes difficult to assign without a consulting engineer. On some projects such as the installation of a large recuperator on an existing furnace the major equipment supplier may take responsibility for the other changes.

* W. Rudoy, University of Pittsburgh

APPENDIX

APPENDIX A

ENERGY CONSERVATION:
POLICY CONSIDERATIONS FOR THE STATES*

* The Council of State Governments, November 1976

States and Energy Conservation

The nature and magnitude of the energy demand-supply-price problems suggest the need for a "division of labor" between the federal government and the States as they address the energy problem and seek to minimize its impacts. The basic long-term factors of supply and price must be addressed at the national level by the federal government working with the private sector. National energy flows, and the large interlinked energy companies reflect the openness and complexity of the U.S. economy. The intricacies of the energy system and its interrelationships with environmental policies and economic activities require that much of the leadership for coordinated energy policies come from the federal government.

The need for national leadership does not mean the States are not or should not be concerned with energy policy. Several States are devoting significant funds and efforts to research directed at development of new energy resources and improved supply. Because of their unique economic and constitutional position, States already have been required to oversee the allocation of energy fuels to meet the serious supply shortfalls following the oil embargo.

In spite of the past and current state efforts to address energy supply problems, energy conservation is an even more appropriate policy option for the States. The State has limited resources and legal authority to influence energy supply and price, but it does have appropriate power to affect energy conservation strategies. Among the 50 States, there are considerable differences in the mix of economic sectors, markets, geographic regions, and political and social behavior. Each State thus has a greater flexibility for designing and administering energy conservation policies and programs most suited to its needs.

VARIATION IN ENERGY IMPACTS AND STATE RESPONSES

Most States have been seriously and negatively affected by the supply-demand-price aspects of the energy problem. The inflationary prices of the energy problem hit government budgets on the expenditure side by raising the cost of goods and services procured and provided by state and local governments. To the extent that energy-related inflation contributes to a slowdown in business and economic activity within a State, tax revenues are also negatively affected. Certain state agency budgets such as highway and transportation agencies, with their significant dependence on motor fuel tax revenues, may be especially hard hit if higher fuel/energy prices reduce consumption of motor fuel.

For States in certain regions of the country, the impact of the energy problem is more widespread and serious than the general problem of inflation. Special problems may also arise according to the climate and economic conditions, the source and type of fuel supply, or the distribution network serving a State. In the New England region, the uncertainty of supply and the high prices of imported fuels have caused significant economic dislocations and have contributed to the gradual erosion of the economic base of that region. Several States in the Rocky Mountain region with vast reserves of energy resources anticipate costly environmental and socioeconomic impacts, which may not be offset in the near term by increased state revenues, should they become net energy producing States.[1]

Variations among the States and regions are frequently overlooked in energy conservation research and federal energy programs. Consequently, the resulting suggestions or mandates for energy conservation practices and policies may mislead state policymakers into adopting programs which are ill-suited or of little significance for particular States.

The practices most likely to result in actual energy savings are likely to vary among and within the States. The feasibility of certain energy conservation practices depends upon climate, institutional, and market conditions. The sectors and end uses where potential energy savings are feasible, and the particular conserving techniques most likely to realize those savings differ according to supply patterns and climatic conditions within a State. These factors affect both the achievable energy savings and the likely socioeconomic and environmental impacts of selected energy conserving measures.

Designing programs to address particular energy consumption patterns and conservation opportunities within a State is complicated by the relative lack of state level data. Most research on energy conservation options is based upon nationally aggregated data on energy flows by sector. Assertions of the potential for energy conservation in the transportation, electric generating, industrial, and residential and commercial sectors are frequently predicated on gross estimates of the magnitude of energy consumed and wasted for that sector nationwide. Therefore, recommendations for energy conservation frequently gloss over the technological, economic, market-related, or administrative difficulties of implementing energy conserving practices as they relate to individual States.

PROPOSALS FOR ENERGY CONSERVATION PRACTICES

Using the magnitude of wasted energy as a criterion, the transportation and the electrical generation sectors are the most suitable targets for public and private sector efforts at energy conservation. The transportation sector, which accounts for approximately 25 percent of United States energy use, has an extremely high ratio of rejected to useful energy (10.7 million b/d oil equivalent is rejected and 3.6 million b/d oil equivalent is useful). The electricity generation sector, which represents slightly over 25 percent of total United States energy use in 1973 and requires the equivalent of approximately 19.3 million b/d of oil, loses almost two-thirds of the energy through conversion. In contrast, the residential/commercial and industrial sectors are relatively efficient users of energy. Only 2.4 million b/d of the 9.5 million b/d oil equivalent required for the residential/commercial sectors is rejected energy. The figures for the industrial sector are 3.4 million b/d to 103 million b/d oil equivalent (see Table 1).

Reacting to the relative energy conservation implied by this aggregate data, policy analysts have espoused numerous practices to capitalize on the potential. Numerous practices and strategies in the industrial, residential and commercial sectors have been analyzed for their effectiveness in increasing the efficiency of energy use within the sectors.[3] In the industrial sector, the general practices include the following:

(1) increased recycling of energy intensive materials;
(2) use of waste heat from power plants for direct heat and process steam;
(3) improved energy efficiency of industrial processes; and
(4) use of solid waste for fuel.

In the residential and commercial sectors, recommended practices include the following:

(1) increased building insulation;
(2) heat pumps or fossil-fired furnaces in place of resistance heat;
(3) energy efficient air conditioners;
(4) total energy systems for heat and electricity;
(5) reduction of lighting levels; and
(6) energy efficient appliances.

The transportation sector is a frequent subject of energy conservation research and policy recommendations.[4] Practices to reduce energy inefficiency in the transportation sector range from the immediate changes in the load factor of vehicles (e.g., carpools and van pool programs) to longer term practices of increasing the energy efficiency of vehicles and shifting the model mix to a greater reliance on more energy efficient modes (e.g., subways and dial-a-ride). The various energy conserving practices in the transportation sector have significant implications for personal and business travel habits and for the manufacture of vehicles which must be considered by policy analysts.

Numerous energy conservation proposals involve measures (e.g., total energy systems, siting of buildings, transportation networks) with implications for spatial patterns of land use. The initial stages of energy conservation research and development preclude firm proposals for using land use as an approach and program tool to the goal of energy conservation. Yet basic reconsiderations of the land use configurations of existing transportation and community development patterns are necessary if energy conservation is to be a long-term policy concern.

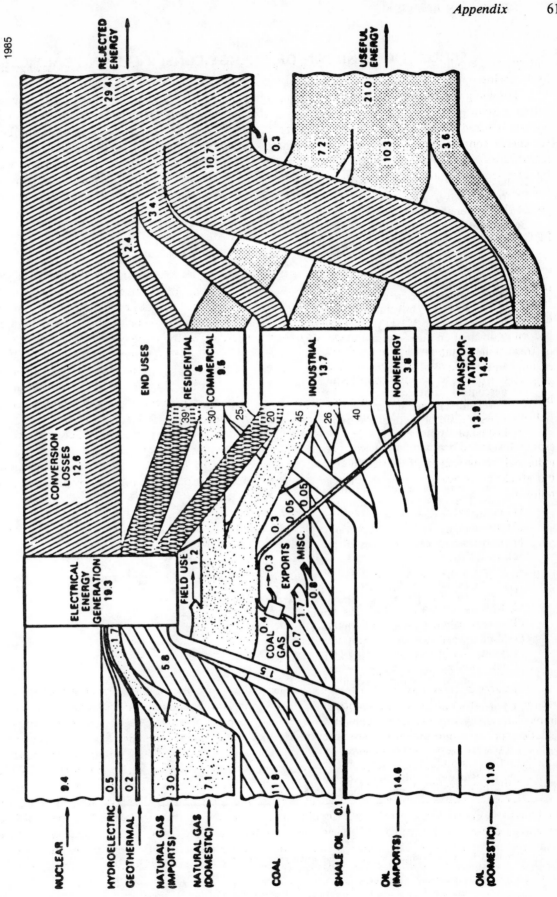

(UNITS: MILLION BBLS./DAY OIL EQUIVALENT)

1985

REJECTED ENERGY → 29.4

USEFUL ENERGY → 21.0

0.3

7.2

10.3

3.6

10.7

3.4

12.4

END USES

CONVERSION LOSSES 12.6

RESIDENTIAL & COMMERCIAL 9.6

INDUSTRIAL 13.7

NONENERGY 3.8

TRANSPORTATION 14.2

ELECTRICAL ENERGY GENERATION 19.3

1.7

5.8

1.5

FIELD USE 1.2

COAL GAS 0.4

EXPORTS 0.3

MISC. 0.8

0.3

0.05

0.05

1.7

0.7

.39 .11 .30 .25 .11 .20 .11 .45 .26 .40

13.0

11.8

NUCLEAR → 9.4

HYDROELECTRIC → 0.5

GEOTHERMAL → 0.2

NATURAL GAS (IMPORTS) → 3.0

NATURAL GAS (DOMESTIC) → 7.1

COAL → 11.8

SHALE OIL → 0.1

OIL (IMPORTS) → 14.6

OIL (DOMESTIC) → 11.0

Table 1
U.S. ENERGY FLOWS

*SOURCE: Joint Committee on Atomic Energy. Certain Background Information for Consideration When Evaluating the "National Energy Dilemma". 93rd Congress, 1st Session. Washington, D.C.: Government Printing Office, 1973.

Table 2
A SCHEMATIC RUNDOWN OF ENERGY-CONSERVATION PRACTICES*

Conservation practice	Conservation of:		
	Raw energy resources	End-use energy consumption	capacity Electric generating
1. Reduced population and income	X	X	X
2. Improved conversion efficiency (as in conventional electric generation)	X	O	O
3. Better load balancing	O[a]	O	X
4. Shift in energy end use towards form involving higher conversion efficiency (e.g., from electric to gas heating)	X	O	X
5. Shift in intermediate energy conversion towards a higher-efficiency technology (conceivably from conventional electricity generation to MHD or fuel cell)	X	O	O[b]
6. More efficient end-use energy utilization in satisfying given "need":[c]			
(a) Improved end-use technical efficiency, as in shift from incandescent to fluorescent lighting, lower horsepower automobiles, mass transit, or more efficient household motors	X	X	X[d]
(b) Reduced heat and light needs via improved building design and insulation	X	X	X[e]
(c) Eliminating waste (e.g., turning off unused lights, or raising summer thermostat when home is unoccupied)	X	X	X[e]
7. Shift towards less energy-intensive end-use activities:			
(a) Where purpose of a given activity can be achieved with greatly reduced fuel or power use (e.g., walking instead of riding, electronic communicating instead of traveling)	X	X	[f]
(b) Shift towards consumption of goods and services containing less embodied energy (e.g., more steel, less aluminum, natural instead of synthetic fibers)	X	X	X
(c) Tolerating increased discomfort (e.g., by waste heat utilization or by change in product–output specifications)[g]	X	X	X
8. Shift towards less energy-intensive, but still economic, production practices (e.g., by waste heat utilization, or by change in product–output specifications)[g]	X	X	X

*SOURCE: Joel Darmstadter, Conserving Energy: Prospects and Opportunities in the New York Region (Resources for the Future, John Hopkins University Press, Baltimore, 1975), p. 38.

(a) Slight savings may accrue from not having to use inefficient peaking equipment.

(b) There may not be a saving in kilowattage, but perhaps one of site requirements.

(c) "Need" may have to be defined in physiological or normative terms.

(d) Except if the shift were to electrified mass transit, in which case electricity consumption (even if not energy consumption as a whole) would go up and so, therefore, would electric generating capacity.

(e) The extent of the saving in electric generating capacity depends on whether electric heating and cooling are involved.

(f) Effect is unclear.

(g) Less proliferation of models and increased durability could also produce raw energy savings.

TRENDS IN STATE ACTIONS FOR ENERGY CONSERVATION

In response to the frequently severe impacts of the energy problem on state economies and on state and local government budgets, States initiated policies and programs for energy conservation prior to the federal government's belated recognition of the need to address the demand aspect of the energy problem.[5] The attention each State devotes to energy conservation as part of an overall energy policy reflects the type and severity of energy problems experienced within that State. States such as New York, Massachusetts, and California, with a high level of energy consumption, have a more immediate and direct interest in energy conservation than do the energy rich States. For some of the energy-producing States, energy conservation as a state policy concern is overshadowed by resource development programs. For others, such as the Rocky Mountain area States, energy conservation is an issue, but less serious an issue than is the pressure for resource development in the area.

The separate efforts undertaken by state agencies, commissions, and Legislatures and by local governments number in the hundreds. The types of energy conservation activities undertaken by the States include thermostat and lighting cutbacks in public buildings; public education for energy conservation; efforts to encourage efficient use of energy through peak-load pricing of utilities, life cycle costing, and energy budgets for state facilities; voluntary or mandatory appliance labeling; and incentives for the adoption of alternative energy systems.

A sampling of legislative action since 1974 indicates the momentum and trends of state energy conservation activities.[6] The legislation does not present the full picture of state activities in energy conservation, but it does provide the framework in which most programmatic actions have been carried out. A range of options is available to policymakers for designing policies and programs to promote energy conservation. These include regulation of public and private activity, economic incentives or disincentives, public education and suasion, and research. In most States, the policy approach includes a blend of these.

In 1974, fewer than one-half of the States adopted energy conservation bills. The most frequent state action that year was creation of fuel allocation offices and energy agencies to deal with the petroleum distribution problems prompted by the oil embargo. During 1975, the proportion of States enacting energy conservation legislation increased to two-thirds, and the emphasis shifted from fuel allocation efforts that would affect the energy consumption levels within a State.

The most frequent conservation legislation in 1975 occurred in the area of public utilities (especially electric) regulation and encouragement of solar energy systems by financial incentives or research funds. Legislation in these two areas accounted for one-half of the energy-related bills enacted in 1975. Other conservation efforts adopted by some States were voluntary or mandatory measures to encourage more efficient use of energy, particularly through standards for building construction. The most common policy approach in this period was regulatory, with almost 40 percent of the energy conservation legislation calling for some form of regulation. State-mandated studies of conservation measures constituted almost 25 percent of the enactments.

State legislative action in 1976 has built on the previous record of state initiative for energy conservation. State energy conservation legislation enacted in the first half of 1976 shifted emphasis as States began to implement previously legislated programs and to develop energy conservation plans under the federal programs. The amount of legislation addressed to solar energy systems declined significantly, while legislation dealing with energy conservation in buildings increased. The sectors addressed by States in 1976 are more diverse than in 1975, but the residential-commercial sector remains a common target of legislated programs. Legislation addressed to regulation, study, or incentives for energy conservation in buildings began to emerge in a few States.[7]

The most significant change in 1976 is occurring in the policy approaches adopted for state energy conservation activities. Reliance upon regulation, common in 1973-75, has declined as States begin to implement existing regulatory programs. The use of economic incentives to encourage voluntary conservation measures remains strong, but the heavy emphasis on solar energy systems in 1975 is balanced with greater attention to the use of existing technology for energy conservation in buildings. The most significant change in policy approaches is the new emphasis placed on state government's directed or supported study of energy conservation activities. As the attitude toward energy conservation shifts from a "crisis

Table 3

STATE ENERGY CONSERVATION LEGISLATION*
1973-June 1976 Enactments by Target Sector

Policy approach	Residential/Commercial	Transportation	Industrial	Energy industry	Government	Mixed	Total
Regulation	17	1	2	18	4	7	49
Economic incentives	24	2	1	5	0	5	37
Economic disincentives	1	2	0	1	0	2	6
Voluntary educational programs	2	1	0	0	0	4	7
Study	6	0	1	5	1	33	46
Direct government action	0	3	0	5	2	10	20
Total	50	9	4	34	7	61	165(a)

*SOURCES: Council of State Governments, information developed from *Energy Legislation Update*, 1973-76; and, *ECP Report*, Energy Conservation Project, Environmental Law Institute, Washington, D.C. Information is current to July 1976.

(a) Total sample size of enacted bills.

Table 4
STATE ENERGY CONSERVATION LEGISLATION*
1973-June 1976 Enactments by Program Category

Policy approach	Labeling (a)	Utilities (b)	Building construction (c)	Solar energy systems (d)	Alternate energy systems (e)	Energy agency commissions (f)	Transportation (g)	Efficient energy use (h)	Total
Regulation	1	21	12	1	4	2	0	3	44
Economic incentives	1	4	8	16	3	0	1	3	36
Economic disincentive	0	2	1	0	0	0	1	2	6
Voluntary educational programs	3	0	0	0	0	0	0	4	7
Study	0	6	2	11	3	18	0	4	44
Direct government action	0	11	1	1	2	1	3	1	20
Total	5	44	24	29	12	21	5	17	157†

*SOURCES: Council of State Governments, information developed from Energy Legislation Update, 1973-76; and, ECP Report, Energy Conservation Project, Environmental Law Institute, Washington, D.C. Information is current to July 1976.

†Total sample size

(a) Labeling: Requires appliances, automobiles, and other products to have a label concerning the energy use or efficiency of the product.

(b) Utilities: Actions and proposals concerned with rate structures, taxing measures, and regulations of public and private utilities.

(c) Building/Construction: Programs and policies concerned with energy use in public and private construction projects (e.g., insulation, building codes).

(d) Solar Energy Systems: Actions and proposals concerned with the development, installation and use of solar energy systems.

(e) Alternative Energy Sources: Actions and proposals concerned with energy systems other than solar (e.g., geothermal, bioconversion, wind, osmosis, etc.).

(f) Creation of state energy agencies and research commission.

(g) Transportation: Actions and proposals concerning the creation and funding of alternative transportation systems (e.g., bus, train, subways).

(h) Efficient energy use: Policies and programs designed to promote efficient use of energy in both the public and private sectors (e.g., fuel economy in automobiles, government purchasing, life-cycle costs calculations).

mentality" to one of recognizing the need for programs, state officials are more aware of the need for a better understanding of energy conservation practices and possible government actions to encourage them.

The functional areas and sectors which state programs are addressing are reinforced by the provisions of the federal Energy Policy and Conservation Act of 1975 (PL94-163). While the States under EPCA have latitude in developing plans for reducing the projected 1980 level of energy consumption by 5 percent, the mandated program areas for state energy conservation follow closely those in which several States and local governments have already taken action. These are:

—Lighting efficiency standards for public buildings;
—Programs for carpools, vanpools, and public transportation;
—Energy efficiency in state procurement;
—Thermal efficiency standards and insulation requirements for new and renovated buildings; and
—Traffic regulations permitting right turn on red.[8]

POLICY DEVELOPMENT FOR STATE ENERGY CONSERVATION

The current energy conservation activities of the States and the federal government reflect certain general assumptions of where in the total energy flow system energy savings can be achieved, and how these energy savings will be realized. The federal EPCA sets the parameters for immediate state energy conservation activities. Through the federal program, state energy officials get historic data or energy consumption and forecasts of consumption through 1980. The federal program is less likely, and even unable, to assist state officials in determining the most efficacious energy conservation programs for their individual States. However, techniques and methods which may be generally useful to States in devising and implementing mandated and other programs with energy conservation potential are being developed by the Federal Energy Administration in conjunction with the States.

To the States is left the difficult task of determining the details of how the energy conservation measures will be developed and implemented. The States face the challenge of ascertaining, with the limited data available to their policymakers and program analysts, policy guidelines in two broad areas:

(1) Specific technical measures most likely to result in energy savings in various sectors and end uses, and
(2) Policy strategies and program measures most likely to lead to energy-conserving behavior on the part of the general public or specific target audiences.

Policy Considerations for State Energy Activities

If the goal of state officials is adoption of the most cost-effective energy conservation policies and programs, attention should focus on the sectors and functional uses in which:

(1) Technological potential for energy savings is high;
(2) Public acceptance is likely;
(3) State authority and ability to act is strong; and
(4) An acceptable environmental-economic-equity trade-off can be obtained.

These four general criteria provide guidelines for determining an overall energy conservation strategy. Specific policy approaches—regulatory, incentive, educational/informational—should reflect a balancing of the technological, economic, and political-administrative factors and should be optimal in terms of dollar costs, energy savings, environmental and social impacts, and administrative considerations.

Development of such optimal programs requires information across a range of topics—much of which is unknown or currently unavailable in a form useful to policymakers. Actual and projected energy consumption and supply levels and the major factors contributing to changes in these levels should be available as baseline data. An understanding of the market forces relating to energy consumption and of possible obstacles to the working of these forces is also necessary to the design of effective policy. Knowledge of consumers' willingness to adopt energy conserving behavior is another guide in the choice and design of specific policies and programs. Information on the likely social, economic and environmental impacts of various conservation measures is a necessary input to balanced energy conservation programs.

Institutional considerations also influence the determination of cost-effective state energy conservation activities. The choice of the appropriate market or nonmarket conservation strategies is influenced by the economic structure of the State and its energy distribution pattern. The structure of the national economy and energy systems, as well as the dynamics of federal-state-local government relations, should enter into the determination of which sectors and uses are the most likely targets, and which government level should assume responsibility.

Most technical and general analytical studies of the energy conservation opportunities in various sectors provide laundry lists and general conclusions on the energy conservation practices available to state officials. They seldom provide state policymakers with specific information on the practices and policies most appropriate to that State. For example, many studies of energy conservation in buildings have suggested a lowering of required lighting levels in order to reduce energy consumption. Yet in buildings where excess heat produced by electric lights has been designed to complement the central heating system, turning off lights may increase the energy used by the heating system.

Obtaining data with the level of detail needed to understand and effectively control energy consumption on a state-by-state basis is a costly undertaking and often impossible in light of the proprietary nature of some data sources. Consequently, state energy programs tend to place a low priority on the collection of data, relying instead on intuition, federal mandates, and peer example to formulate policy alternatives.

Consideration and balancing of all the myriad factors related to energy policy decisions has caused energy officials in many States to construct models that would assist in determining the impacts—social, economic, environmental—as well as the projected effectiveness of various energy conservation strategies. There are several problems which inhibit the usefulness of these models and other uses of data in energy conservation programming.

First, about one-half the States reporting an actual or planned modelling capability in 1975 indicated that the offices responsible for the modelling effort had no formal connection with state policymakers, either legislative or executive.[9]   Second, the data on which the models are based is taken from a variety of sources with varying levels of quality. Some of the historic data pertaining to energy consumption prepared by FEA is based on national figures which have been disaggregated first to a regional, then to a state level. The assumptions on which these disaggregations are predicated are open to question, as are the consumption forecasts, which also use this data as a baseline. Third, much of the data that could be used to describe economic or social impacts of, or public response to, alternative policies is simply unavailable or inadequate for the task. Research is under way to determine the likely outcomes of general conservation policies, but given the national dimensions of the energy problem, the macro level at which most data is available, and the inextricable relationship of energy to the national economy, the impacts of specific measures within specific States will be difficult to ascertain.

Footnotes

1. The relative lack of existing public infrastructure, the special nature of the terrain, the serious water problem, and the high percentage of federal and Indian land holdings in the Rocky Mountain region minimizes any comparison of the impacts of resource development in these States to that in energy producing States such as Kentucky, Louisiana, Texas, and Oklahoma.

2. "Sectors" are the economic sectors as defined by the Bureau of Economic Analysis. The classification used in energy analysis includes transportation, industrial, residential/commercial, electrical energy generation, and government. End uses refers to the functional uses (e.g., lighting, heating, industrial processes, etc.) for which energy is consumed within the sectors. Thus, end use categories cut across sector classification.

3. These strategies are listed, along with supporting studies (1972-73), in Joel Darmstadter's *Conserving Energy: Prospects and Opportunities in the New Region* (Resources for the Future: Baltimore, 1975) p. 43.

4. See Margaret Fels and Michael Munson, "Energy Thrift in Urban Transportation for the Future" in *The Energy Conservation Papers,* Robert H. Williams, ed., Ford Foundation Energy Policy Project (Ballinger: Cambridge, Massachusetts, 1975).

5. ERDA singled out energy conservation as an area for increased attention and high priority for national action in its second annual report, 1976; but primary responsibility for energy conservation technologies remains with the private sector. The initial forecast model for energy demand, developed by FEA failed to include the effects of state actions on energy demand. The state role in the national energy conservation effort is recognized with the passage of the Energy Policy and Conservation Act of 1975 and its aid to States in the development of energy conservation plans.

6. The illustrative sample of state energy conservation legislation 1973-76 was developed by the Council of State Governments, based upon the CSG survey of state energy legislation, *Energy Legislation Update 1973-1976,* and *ECP Report,* Energy Conservation Project, Environmental Law Institute.

7. Regulation predominates in legislation directed to new buildings. Of the 49 enacted bills in 1975 dealing with energy conserving buildings, 21 involved some form of regulation. Regulatory legislation includes requirements for energy feasibility standards on state constructed, financed or leased buildings, the use of life cycle costing or energy impact studies on state buildings, and state or local building codes incorporating an energy conservation component.

Authorization for economic incentives for energy efficient buildings is less frequent and typically provides tax incentives in the purchase of insulation used in the retrofitting of existing buildings.

Support for solar and other alternative energy systems is a frequent policy option. Over one-half of all the new solar-related laws offer incentives for the purchase and use of solar systems. Incentive programs include income tax credits or deductions, sales tax exemptions for solar-related hardware, and exemption of the added value attributable to solar systems from assessed value for property tax.

See Robert M. Eisenhard, *Building Energy Authority and Regulation Survey: State Activity* (Office of Building Standards and Code Services, National Bureau of Standards, Washington, D.C., March 1976). Legislation current to November 1975. Also based upon the Council of State Government's representative sample of energy conservation legislation, 1973-76.

8. Energy Policy and Conservation Act, Title III, Part C, "State Energy Conservation Programs."

9. A National Governors' Conference survey indicates that nearly two-thirds of the States had or were planning in mid-1975 modelling techniques for addressing energy problems. J. D. DeForest, *State Energy Information Systems: A Survey*, Washington, 1975.

APPENDIX B

THE DEPARTMENT OF ENERGY ORGANIZATION ACT

Public Law 95–91
95th Congress

An Act

To establish a Department of Energy in the executive branch by the reorganization of energy functions within the Federal Government in order to secure effective management to assure a coordinated national energy policy, and for other purposes.

Aug. 4, 1977
[S. 826]

Be it enacted by the Senate and House of Representatives of the United States of America in Congress assembled, That this Act may be cited as the "Department of Energy Organization Act".

Department of Energy Organization Act. 42 USC 7101 note.

TABLE OF CONTENTS

TABLE OF CONTENTS—Continued

TITLE VI—ADMINISTRATIVE PROVISIONS

SEC. 2. (a) As used in this Act, unless otherwise provided or indicated by the context, the term the "Department" means the Department of Energy or any component thereof, including the Federal Energy Regulatory Commission. 42 USC 7101.

(b) As used in this Act (1) reference to "function" includes reference to any duty, obligation, power, authority, responsibility, right, privilege, and activity, or the plural thereof, as the case may be; and (2) reference to "perform", when used in relation to functions, includes the undertaking, fulfillment, or execution of any duty or obligation; and the exercise of power, authority, rights, and privileges.

(c) As used in this Act, "Federal lease" means an agreement which, for any consideration, including but not limited to, bonuses, rents, or royalties conferred and covenants to be observed, authorizes a person to explore for, or develop, or produce (or to do any or all of these) oil and gas, coal, oil shale, tar sands, and geothermal resources on lands or interests in lands under Federal jurisdiction.

TITLE I—DECLARATION OF FINDINGS AND PURPOSES

FINDINGS

SEC. 101. The Congress of the United States finds that— 42 USC 7111.

(1) the United States faces an increasing shortage of nonrenewable energy resources;

(2) this energy shortage and our increasing dependence on foreign energy supplies present a serious threat to the national security of the United States and to the health, safety and welfare of its citizens;

(3) a strong national energy program is needed to meet the present and future energy needs of the Nation consistent with overall national economic, environmental and social goals;

(4) responsibility for energy policy, regulation, and research, development and demonstration is fragmented in many departments and agencies and thus does not allow for the comprehensive, centralized focus necessary for effective coordination of energy supply and conservation programs; and

(5) formulation and implementation of a national energy program require the integration of major Federal energy functions into a single department in the executive branch.

PURPOSES

SEC. 102. The Congress therefore declares that the establishment of a Department of Energy is in the public interest and will promote the general welfare by assuring coordinated and effective administration of Federal energy policy and programs. It is the purpose of this Act— 42 USC 7112.

(1) to establish a Department of Energy in the executive branch;

(2) to achieve, through the Department, effective management of energy functions of the Federal Government, including consultation with the heads of other Federal departments and agencies in order to encourage them to establish and observe policies consistent with a coordinated energy policy, and to promote maximum possible energy conservation measures in connection with the activities within their respective jurisdictions;

(3) to provide for a mechanism through which a coordinated national energy policy can be formulated and implemented to deal with the short-, mid- and long-term energy problems of the Nation; and to develop plans and programs for dealing with domestic energy production and import shortages;

(4) to create and implement a comprehensive energy conservation strategy that will receive the highest priority in the national energy program;

(5) to carry out the planning, coordination, support, and management of a balanced and comprehensive energy research and development program, including—

(A) assessing the requirements for energy research and development;

(B) developing priorities necessary to meet those requirements;

(C) undertaking programs for the optimal development of the various forms of energy production and conservation; and

(D) disseminating information resulting from such programs, including disseminating information on the commercial feasibility and use of energy from fossil, nuclear, solar, geothermal, and other energy technologies;

(6) to place major emphasis on the development and commercial use of solar, geothermal, recycling and other technologies utilizing renewable energy resources;

(7) to continue and improve the effectiveness and objectivity of a central energy data collection and analysis program within the Department;

(8) to facilitate establishment of an effective strategy for distributing and allocating fuels in periods of short supply and to provide for the administration of a national energy supply reserve;

(9) to promote the interests of consumers through the provision of an adequate and reliable supply of energy at the lowest reasonable cost;

(10) to establish and implement through the Department, in coordination with the Secretaries of State, Treasury, and Defense, policies regarding international energy issues that have a direct impact on research, development, utilization, supply, and conservation of energy in the United States and to undertake activities involving the integration of domestic and foreign policy relating to energy, including provision of independent technical advice to the President on international negotiations involving energy resources, energy technologies, or nuclear weapons issues, except that the Secretary of State shall continue to exercise primary authority for the conduct of foreign policy relating to energy and nuclear nonproliferation, pursuant to policy guidelines established by the President;

(11) to provide for the cooperation of Federal, State, and local governments in the development and implementation of national energy policies and programs;

(12) to foster and assure competition among parties engaged in the supply of energy and fuels;

(13) to assure incorporation of national environmental protection goals in the formulation and implementation of energy programs, and to advance the goals of restoring, protecting, and enhancing environmental quality, and assuring public health and safety;

(14) to assure, to the maximum extent practicable, that the productive capacity of private enterprise shall be utilized in the development and achievement of the policies and purposes of this Act;

(15) to provide for, encourage, and assist public participation in the development and enforcement of national energy programs;

(16) to create an awareness of, and responsibility for, the fuel and energy needs of rural and urban residents as such needs pertain to home heating and cooling, transportation, agricultural production, electrical generation, conservation, and research and development;

(17) to foster insofar as possible the continued good health of the Nation's small business firms, public utility districts, municipal utilities, and private cooperatives involved in energy production, transportation, research, development, demonstration, marketing, and merchandising; and

(18) to provide for the administration of the functions of the Energy Research and Development Administration related to nuclear weapons and national security which are transferred to the Department by this Act.

RELATIONSHIP WITH STATES

SEC. 103. Whenever any proposed action by the Department conflicts with the energy plan of any State, the Department shall give due consideration to the needs of such State, and where practicable, shall attempt to resolve such conflict through consultations with appropriate State officials. Nothing in this Act shall affect the authority of any State over matters exclusively within its jurisdiction.

42 USC 7113.

TITLE II—ESTABLISHMENT OF THE DEPARTMENT

ESTABLISHMENT

SEC. 201. There is hereby established at the seat of government an executive department to be known as the Department of Energy. There shall be at the head of the Department a Secretary of Energy (hereinafter in this Act referred to as the "Secretary"), who shall be appointed by the President by and with the advice and consent of the Senate. The Department shall be administered, in accordance with the provisions of this Act, under the supervision and direction of the Secretary.

42 USC 7131.

Secretary of Energy, appointment and confirmation.

PRINCIPAL OFFICERS

SEC. 202. (a) There shall be in the Department a Deputy Secretary, who shall be appointed by the President, by and with the advice and consent of the Senate, and who shall be compensated at the rate provided for level II of the Executive Schedule under section 5313 of title 5, United States Code. The Deputy Secretary shall act for and exercise the functions of the Secretary during the absence or disability of the Secretary or in the event the office of Secretary becomes vacant. The Secretary shall designate the order in which the Under Secretary and other officials shall act for and perform the functions of the Secretary during the absence or disability of both the Secretary and Deputy Secretary or in the event of vacancies in both of those offices.

Deputy Secretary, appointment and confirmation. 42 USC 7132.

(b) There shall be in the Department an Under Secretary and a General Counsel, who shall be appointed by the President, by and with the advice and consent of the Senate, and who shall perform such

Under Secretary and General Counsel, appointment and confirmation.

functions and duties as the Secretary shall prescribe. The Under Secretary shall bear primary responsibility for energy conservation. The Under Secretary shall be compensated at the rate provided for level III of the Executive Schedule under section 5314 of title 5, United States Code, and the General Counsel shall be compensated at the rate provided for level IV of the Executive Schedule under section 5315 of title 5, United States Code.

ASSISTANT SECRETARIES

Appointment and confirmation.
42 USC 7133.

Sec. 203. (a) There shall be in the Department eight Assistant Secretaries, each of whom shall be appointed by the President, by and with the advice and consent of the Senate; who shall be compensated at the rate provided for at level IV of the Executive Schedule under section 5315 of title 5, United States Code; and who shall perform, in accordance with applicable law, such of the functions transferred or delegated to, or vested in, the Secretary as he shall prescribe in accordance with the provisions of this Act. The functions which the Secretary shall assign to the Assistant Secretaries include, but are not limited to, the following:

Functions.

(1) Energy resource applications, including functions dealing with management of all forms of energy production and utilization, including fuel supply, electric power supply, enriched uranium production, energy technology programs, and the management of energy resource leasing procedures on Federal lands.

(2) Energy research and development functions, including the responsibility for policy and management of research and development for all aspects of—

(A) solar energy resources;

(B) geothermal energy resources;

(C) recycling energy resources;

(D) the fuel cycle for fossil energy resources; and

(E) the fuel cycle for nuclear energy resources.

(3) Environmental responsibilities and functions, including advising the Secretary with respect to the conformance of the Department's activities to environmental protection laws and principles, and conducting a comprehensive program of research and development on the environmental effects of energy technologies and programs.

(4) International programs and international policy functions, including those functions which assist in carrying out the international energy purposes described in section 102 of this Act.

(5) National security functions, including those transferred to the Department from the Energy Research and Development Administration which relate to management and implementation of the nuclear weapons program and other national security functions involving nuclear weapons research and development.

(6) Intergovernmental policies and relations, including responsibilities for assuring that national energy policies are reflective of and responsible to the needs of State and local governments, and for assuring that other components of the Department coordinate their activities with State and local governments, where appropriate, and develop intergovernmental communications with State and local governments.

(7) Competition and consumer affairs, including responsibilities for the promotion of competition in the energy industry and for the protection of the consuming public in the energy policymaking

processes, and assisting the Secretary in the formulation and analysis of policies, rules, and regulations relating to competition and consumer affairs.

(8) Nuclear waste management responsibilities, including—

(A) the establishment of control over existing Government facilities for the treatment and storage of nuclear wastes, including all containers, casks, buildings, vehicles, equipment, and all other materials associated with such facilities;

(B) the establishment of control over all existing nuclear waste in the possession or control of the Government and all commercial nuclear waste presently stored on other than the site of a licensed nuclear power electric generating facility, except that nothing in this paragraph shall alter or effect title to such waste;

(C) the establishment of temporary and permanent facilities for storage, management, and ultimate disposal of nuclear wastes;

(D) the establishment of facilities for the treatment of nuclear wastes;

(E) the establishment of programs for the treatment, management, storage, and disposal of nuclear wastes;

(F) the establishment of fees or user charges for nuclear waste treatment or storage facilities, including fees to be charged Government agencies; and

(G) the promulgation of such rules and regulations to implement the authority described in this paragraph,

except that nothing in this section shall be construed as granting to the Department regulatory functions presently within the Nuclear Regulatory Commission, or any additional functions than those already conferred by law.

(9) Energy conservation functions, including the development of comprehensive energy conservation strategies for the Nation, the planning and implementation of major research and demonstration programs for the development of technologies and processes to reduce total energy consumption, the administration of voluntary and mandatory energy conservation programs, and the dissemination to the public of all available information on energy conservation programs and measures.

(10) Power marketing functions, including responsibility for marketing and transmission of Federal power.

(11) Public and congressional relations functions, including responsibilities for providing a continuing liaison between the Department and the Congress and the Department and the public.

(b) At the time the name of any individual is submitted for confirmation to the position of Assistant Secretary, the President shall identify with particularity the function or functions described in subsection (a) (or any portion thereof) for which such individual will be responsible.

Responsibilities, identification.

FEDERAL ENERGY REGULATORY COMMISSION

SEC. 204. There shall be within the Department, a Federal Energy Regulatory Commission established by title IV of this Act (hereinafter referred to in this Act as the "Commission"). The Chairman shall be compensated at the rate provided for level III of the Executive Schedule under section 5314 of title 5, United States Code. The other members of the Commission shall be compensated at the rate provided for level IV of the Executive Schedule under section 5315 of

42 USC 7134.

title 5, United States Code. The Chairman and members of the Commission shall be individuals who, by demonstrated ability, background, training, or experience, are specially qualified to assess fairly the needs and concerns of all interests affected by Federal energy policy.

ENERGY INFORMATION ADMINISTRATION

Establishment.
42 USC 7135.

SEC. 205. (a)(1) There shall be within the Department an Energy Information Administration to be headed by an Administrator who shall be appointed by the President, by and with the advice and consent of the Senate, and who shall be compensated at the rate provided for in level IV of the Executive Schedule under section 5315 of title 5, United States Code. The Administrator shall be a person who, by reason of professional background and experience, is specially qualified to manage an energy information system.

(2) The Administrator shall be responsible for carrying out a central, comprehensive, and unified energy data and information program which will collect, evaluate, assemble, analyze, and disseminate data and information which is relevant to energy resource reserves, energy production, demand, and technology, and related economic and statistical information, or which is relevant to the adequacy of energy resources to meet demands in the near and longer term future for the Nation's economic and social needs.

(b) The Secretary shall delegate to the Administrator (which delegation may be on a nonexclusive basis as the Secretary may determine may be necessary to assure the faithful execution of his authorities and responsibilities under law) the functions vested in him by law relating to gathering, analysis, and dissemination of energy information (as defined in section 11 of the Energy Supply and Environmental **15 USC 796.** Coordination Act of 1974) and the Administrator may act in the name of the Secretary for the purpose of obtaining enforcement of such delegated functions.

(c) In addition to, and not in limitation of the functions delegated to the Administrator pursuant to other subsections of this section, there shall be vested in the Administrator, and he shall perform, the functions assigned to the Director of the Office of Energy Information and Analysis under part B of the Federal Energy Administration **15 USC 790,** Act of 1974, and the provisions of sections 53(d) and 59 thereof shall **790b, 790h.** be applicable to the Administrator in the performance of any function under this Act.

(d) The Administrator shall not be required to obtain the approval of any other officer or employee of the Department in connection with the collection or analysis of any information; nor shall the Administrator be required, prior to publication, to obtain the approval of any other officer or employee of the United States with respect to the substance of any statistical or forecasting technical reports which he has prepared in accordance with law.

Annual audit.

(e) The Energy Information Administration shall be subject to an annual professional audit review of performance as described in sec-**15 USC 790d.** tion 55 of part B of the Federal Energy Administration Act of 1974.

(f) The Administrator shall, upon request, promptly provide any information or analysis in his possession pursuant to this section to any other administration, commission, or office within the Department which such administration, commission, or office determines relates to the functions of such administration, commission, or office.

(g) Information collected by the Energy Information Administration shall be cataloged and, upon request, any such information shall be promptly made available to the public in a form and manner easily adaptable for public use, except that this subsection shall not require disclosure of matters exempted from mandatory disclosure by section 552(b) of title 5, United States Code. The provisions of section 11(d) of the Energy Supply and Environmental Coordination Act of 1974, and section 17 of the Federal Nonnuclear Energy Research and Development Act of 1974, shall continue to apply to any information obtained by the Administrator under such provisions. *Information, availability to public.*

15 USC 796.

42 USC 5916.

(h)(1)(A) In addition to the acquisition, collection, analysis, and dissemination of energy information pursuant to this section, the Administrator shall identify and designate "major energy-producing companies" which alone or with their affiliates are involved in one or more lines of commerce in the energy industry so that the energy information collected from such major energy-producing companies shall provide a statistically accurate profile of each line of commerce in the energy industry in the United States. *Major energy-producing companies, identification and designation.*

(B) In fulfilling the requirements of this subsection the Administrator shall—

 (i) utilize, to the maximum extent practicable, consistent with the faithful execution of his responsibilities under this Act, reliable statistical sampling techniques; and

 (ii) otherwise give priority to the minimization of the reporting of energy information by small business.

(2) The Administrator shall develop and make effective for use during the second full calendar year following the date of enactment of this Act the format for an energy-producing company financial report. Such report shall be designed to allow comparison on a uniform and standardized basis among energy-producing companies and shall permit for the energy-related activities of such companies— *Financial report, format.*

 (A) an evaluation of company revenues, profits, cash flow, and investments in total, for the energy-related lines of commerce in which such company is engaged and for all significant energy-related functions within such company;

 (B) an analysis of the competitive structure of sectors and functional groupings within the energy industry;

 (C) the segregation of energy information, including financial information, describing company operations by energy source and geographic area;

 (D) the determination of costs associated with exploration, development, production, processing, transportation, and marketing and other significant energy-related functions within such company; and

 (E) such other analyses or evaluations as the Administrator finds is necessary to achieve the purposes of this Act.

(3) The Administrator shall consult with the Chairman of the Securities and Exchange Commission with respect to the development of accounting practices required by the Energy Policy and Conservation Act to be followed by persons engaged in whole or in part in the production of crude oil and natural gas and shall endeavor to assure that the energy-producing company financial report described in paragraph (2) of this subsection, to the extent practicable and consistent with the purposes and provisions of this Act, is consistent with such accounting practices where applicable. *Accounting practices, development. 42 USC 6201 note.*

(4) The Administrator shall require each major energy-producing company to file with the Administrator an energy-producing company *Annual financial report.*

financial report on at least an annual basis and may request energy information described in such report on a quarterly basis if he determines that such quarterly report of information will substantially assist in achieving the purposes of this Act.

(5) A summary of information gathered pursuant to this section, accompanied by such analysis as the Administrator deems appropriate, shall be included in the annual report of the Department required by subsection (a) of section 657 of this Act.

Definitions.

(6) As used in this subsection the term—

(A) "energy-producing company" means a person engaged in:

(i) ownership or control of mineral fuel resources or non-mineral energy resources;

(ii) exploration for, or development of, mineral fuel resources;

(iii) extraction of mineral fuel or nonmineral energy resources;

(iv) refining, milling, or otherwise processing mineral fuels or nonmineral energy resources;

(v) storage of mineral fuels or nonmineral energy resources;

(vi) the generation, transmission, or storage of electrical energy;

(vii) transportation of mineral fuels or nonmineral energy resources by any means whatever; or

(viii) wholesale or retail distribution of mineral fuels, nonmineral energy resources or electrical energy;

(B) "energy industry" means all energy-producing companies; and

(C) "person" has the meaning as set forth in section 11 of the Energy Supply and Environmental Coordination Act of 1974.

(7) The provisions of section 1905 of title 18, United States Code, shall apply in accordance with its terms to any information obtained by the Administration pursuant to this subsection.

ECONOMIC REGULATORY ADMINISTRATION

42 USC 7136.

SEC. 206. (a) There shall be within the Department an Economic Regulatory Administration to be headed by an Administrator, who shall be appointed by the President, by and with the advice and consent of the Senate, and who shall be compensated at a rate provided for level IV of the Executive Schedule under section 5315 of title 5, United States Code. Such Administrator shall be, by demonstrated ability, background, training, or experience, an individual who is specially qualified to assess fairly the needs and concerns of all interests affected by Federal energy policy. The Secretary shall by rule provide for a separation of regulatory and enforcement functions assigned to, or vested in, the Administration.

(b) Consistent with the provisions of title IV, the Secretary shall utilize the Economic Regulatory Administration to administer such functions as he may consider appropriate.

COMPTROLLER GENERAL FUNCTIONS

42 USC 7137.

15 USC 771.

SEC. 207. The functions of the Comptroller General of the United States under section 12 of the Federal Energy Administration Act of 1974 shall apply with respect to the monitoring and evaluation of all functions and activities of the Department under this Act or any other Act administered by the Department.

OFFICE OF INSPECTOR GENERAL

SEC. 208. (a)(1) There shall be within the Department an Office of Inspector General to be headed by an Inspector General, who shall be appointed by the President, by and with the advice and consent of the Senate, solely on the basis of integrity and demonstrated ability and without regard to political affiliation. The Inspector General shall report to, and be under the general supervision of, the Secretary or, to the extent such authority is delegated, the Deputy Secretary, but shall not be under the control of, or subject to supervision by, any other officer of the Department.

*Inspector General, **appointment and confirmation.** 42 USC 7138.*

(2) There shall also be in the Office a Deputy Inspector General who shall be appointed by the President, by and with the advice and consent of the Senate, solely on the basis of integrity and demonstrated ability and without regard to political affiliation. The Deputy shall assist the Inspector General in the administration of the Office and shall, during the absence or temporary incapacity of the Inspector General, or during a vacancy in that Office, act as Inspector General.

*Deputy Inspector General, **appointment and confirmation.***

(3) The Inspector General or the Deputy may be removed from office by the President. The President shall communicate the reasons for any such removal to both Houses of Congress.

(4) The Inspector General shall, in accordance with applicable laws and regulations governing the civil service, appoint an Assistant Inspector General for Audits and an Assistant Inspector General for Investigations.

*Assistant Inspector General for Audits and Assistant Inspector General for Investigations, **appointment.***

(5) The Inspector General shall be compensated at the rate provided for level IV of the Executive Schedule under section 5315 of title 5, United States Code, and the Deputy Inspector General shall be compensated at the rate provided for level V of the Executive Schedule under section 5316 of title 5, United States Code.

(b) It shall be the duty and responsibility of the Inspector General—

Duties and responsibilities.

(1) to supervise, coordinate, and provide policy direction for auditing and investigative activities relating to the promotion of economy and efficiency in the administration of, or the prevention or detection of fraud or abuse in, programs and operations of the Department;

(2) to recommend policies for, and to conduct, supervise, or coordinate other activities carried out or financed by the Department for the purpose of promoting economy and efficiency in the administration of, or preventing and detecting fraud and abuse in, its programs and operations;

(3) to recommend policies for, and to conduct, supervise, or coordinate relationships between the Department and other Federal agencies, State and local governmental agencies, and nongovernmental entities with respect to (A) all matters relating to the promotion of economy and efficiency in the administration of, or the prevention and detection of fraud and abuse in, programs and operations administered or financed by the Department, and (B) the identification and prosecution of participants in such fraud or abuse;

(4) to keep the Secretary and the Congress fully and currently informed, by means of the reports required by subsection (c) and otherwise, concerning fraud and other serious problems, abuses, and deficiencies relating to the administration of programs and operations administered or financed by the Department, to recommend corrective action concerning such problems, abuses, and deficiencies, and to report on the progress made in implementing such corrective action; and

(5) to seek to coordinate his actions with the actions of the Comptroller General of the United States with a view to avoiding duplication.

(c) The Inspector General shall, not later than March 31 of each year, submit a report to the Secretary, to the Federal Energy Regulatory Commission, and to the Congress summarizing the activities of the Office during the preceding calendar year. Such report shall include, but need not be limited to—

(1) an identification and description of significant problems, abuses, and deficiencies relating to the administration of programs and operations of the Department disclosed by such activities;

(2) a description of recommendations for corrective action made by the Office with respect to significant problems, abuses, or deficiencies identified and described under paragraph (1);

(3) an evaluation of progress made in implementing recommendations described in the report or, where appropriate, in previous reports; and

(4) a summary of matters referred to prosecutive authorities and the extent to which prosecutions and convictions have resulted.

(d) The Inspector General shall report immediately to the Secretary, to the Federal Energy Regulatory Commission as appropriate, and, within thirty days thereafter, to the appropriate committees or subcommittees of the Congress whenever the Office becomes aware of particularly serious or flagrant problems, abuses, or deficiencies relating to the administration of programs and operations of the Department. The Deputy and Assistant Inspectors General shall have particular responsibility for informing the Inspector General of such problems, abuses, or deficiencies.

(e) The Inspector General (1) may make such additional investigations and reports relating to the administration of the programs and operations of the Department as are, in the judgment of the Inspector General, necessary or desirable, and (2) shall provide such additional information or documents as may be requested by either House of Congress or, with respect to matters within their jurisdiction, by any committee or subcommittee thereof.

(f) Notwithstanding any other provision of law, the reports, information, or documents required by or under this section shall be transmitted to the Secretary, to the Federal Energy Regulatory Commission, if applicable, and to the Congress, or committees or subcommittees thereof, by the Inspector General without further clearance or approval. The Inspector General shall, insofar as feasible, provide copies of the reports required under subsection (c) to the Secretary and the Commission, if applicable, sufficiently in advance of the due date for the submission to Congress to provide a reasonable opportunity for comments of the Secretary and the Commission to be appended to the reports when submitted to Congress.

(g) In addition to the authority otherwise provided by this section, the Inspector General, in carrying out the provisions of this section, is authorized—

(1) to have access to all records, reports, audits, reviews, documents, papers, recommendations, and other material available to the Department which relate to programs and operations with respect to which the Inspector General has responsibilities under this section;

(2) to require by subpena the production of all information, documents, reports, answers, records, accounts, papers, and other data and documentary evidence necessary in the performance of the functions assigned by this section, which subpena, in the case of contumacy or refusal to obey, shall be enforceable by order of any appropriate United States district court; and

(3) to have direct and prompt access to the Secretary when necessary for any purpose pertaining to the performance of functions under this section.

OFFICE OF ENERGY RESEARCH

SEC. 209. (a) There shall be within the Department an Office of Energy Research to be headed by a Director, who shall be appointed by the President, by and with the advice and consent of the Senate, and who shall be compensated at the rate provided for level IV of the Executive Schedule under section 5315 of title 5, United States Code. *Director. 42 USC 7139.*

(b) It shall be the duty and responsibility of the Director— *Duties and responsibilities.*

(1) to advise the Secretary with respect to the physical research program transferred to the Department from the Energy Research and Development Administration;

(2) to monitor the Department's energy research and development programs in order to advise the Secretary with respect to any undesirable duplication or gaps in such programs;

(3) to advise the Secretary with respect to the well-being and management of the multipurpose laboratories under the jurisdiction of the Department, excluding laboratories that constitute part of the nuclear weapons complex;

(4) to advise the Secretary with respect to education and training activities required for effective short- and long-term basic and applied research activities of the Department;

(5) to advise the Secretary with respect to grants and other forms of financial assistance required for effective short- and long-term basic and applied research activities of the Department; and

(6) to carry out such additional duties assigned to the Office by the Secretary relating to basic and applied research, including but not limited to supervision or support of research activities carried out by any of the Assistant Secretaries designated by section 203 of this Act, as the Secretary considers advantageous.

LEASING LIAISON COMMITTEE

SEC. 210. There is hereby established a Leasing Liaison Committee which shall be composed of an equal number of members appointed by the Secretary and the Secretary of the Interior. *Establishment. 42 USC 7140.*

TITLE III—TRANSFERS OF FUNCTIONS

GENERAL TRANSFERS

SEC. 301. (a) Except as otherwise provided in this Act, there are hereby transferred to, and vested in, the Secretary all of the functions vested by law in the Administrator of the Federal Energy Administration or the Federal Energy Administration, the Administrator of the Energy Research and Development Administration or the Energy Research and Development Administration; and the functions vested *Federal Energy Administration and Energy Research and Development Administration. 42 USC 7151.*

Federal Power Commission.

by law in the officers and components of either such Administration.

(b) Except as provided in title IV, there are hereby transferred to, and vested in, the Secretary the function of the Federal Power Commission, or of the members, officers, or components thereof. The Secretary may exercise any power described in section 402(a)(2) to the extent the Secretary determines such power to be necessary to the exercise of any function within his jurisdiction pursuant to the preceding sentence.

TRANSFERS FROM THE DEPARTMENT OF THE INTERIOR

42 USC 7152.

16 USC 825s.

SEC. 302. (a)(1) There are hereby transferred to, and vested in, the Secretary all functions of the Secretary of the Interior under section 5 of the Flood Control Act of 1944, and all other functions of the Secretary of the Interior, and officers and components of the Department of the Interior, with respect to—

(A) the Southeastern Power Administration;

(B) the Southwestern Power Administration;

(C) the Alaska Power Administration;

(D) the Bonneville Power Administration including but not limited to the authority contained in the Bonneville Project Act of 1937 and the Federal Columbia River Transmission System Act;

16 USC 832.
16 USC 838 note.

(E) the power marketing functions of the Bureau of Reclamation, including the construction, operation, and maintenance of transmission lines and attendant facilities; and

(F) the transmission and disposition of the electric power and energy generated at Falcon Dam and Amistad Dam, international storage reservoir projects on the Rio Grande, pursuant to the Act of June 18, 1954, as amended by the Act of December 23, 1963.

68 Stat. 255.
77 Stat. 475.

(2) The Southeastern Power Administration, the Southwestern Power Administration, the Bonneville Power Administration, and the Alaska Power Administration shall be preserved as separate and distinct organizational entities within the Department. Each such entity shall be headed by an Administrator appointed by the Secretary. The functions transferred to the Secretary in paragraphs (1)(A), (1)(B), (1)(C), and (1)(D) shall be exercised by the Secretary, acting by and through such Administrators. Each such Administrator shall maintain his principal office at a place located in the region served by his respective Federal power marketing entity.

(3) The functions transferred in paragraphs (1)(E) and (1)(F) of this subsection shall be exercised by the Secretary, acting by and through a separate and distinct Administration within the Department which shall be headed by an Administrator appointed by the Secretary. The Administrator shall establish and shall maintain such regional offices as necessary to facilitate the performance of such functions. Neither the transfer of functions effected by paragraph (1)(E) of this subsection nor any changes in cost allocation or project evaluation standards shall be deemed to authorize the reallocation of joint costs of multipurpose facilities theretofore allocated unless and to the extent that such change is hereafter approved by Congress.

Federal leases.

(b) There are hereby transferred to, and vested in, the Secretary the functions of the Secretary of the Interior to promulgate regulations under the Outer Continental Shelf Lands Act, the Mineral Lands Leasing Act, the Mineral Leasing Act for Acquired Lands, the Geo-

43 USC 1331 note.
30 USC 181 note, 351 note.

thermal Steam Act of 1970, and the Energy Policy and Conservation Act, which relate to the—

    (1) fostering of competition for Federal leases (including, but not limited to, prohibition on bidding for development rights by certain types of joint ventures) ;

    (2) implementation of alternative bidding systems authorized for the award of Federal leases;

    (3) establishment of diligence requirements for operations conducted on Federal leases (including, but not limited to, procedures relating to the granting or ordering by the Secretary of the Interior of suspension of operations or production as they relate to such requirements) ;

    (4) setting rates of production for Federal leases; and

    (5) specifying the procedures, terms, and conditions for the acquisition and disposition of Federal royalty interests taken in kind.

    (c) There are hereby transferred to, and vested in, the Secretary all the functions of the Secretary of the Interior to establish production rates for all Federal leases.

    (d) There are hereby transferred to, and vested in, the Secretary those functions of the Secretary of the Interior, the Department of the Interior, and officers and components of that Department under the Act of May 15, 1910, and other authorities, exercised by the Bureau of Mines, but limited to—

    (1) fuel supply and demand analysis and data gathering;

    (2) research and development relating to increased efficiency of production technology of solid fuel minerals, other than research relating to mine health and safety and research relating to the environmental and leasing consequences of solid fuel mining (which shall remain in the Department of the Interior) ; and

    (3) coal preparation and analysis.

ADMINISTRATION OF LEASING TRANSFERS

    SEC. 303. (a) The Secretary of the Interior shall retain any authorities not transferred under section 302(b) of this Act and shall be solely responsible for the issuance and supervision of Federal leases and the enforcement of all regulations applicable to the leasing of mineral resources, including but not limited to lease terms and conditions and production rates. No regulation promulgated by the Secretary shall restrict or limit any authority retained by the Secretary of the Interior under section 302(b) of this Act with respect to the issuance or supervision of Federal leases. Nothing in section 302(b) of this Act shall be construed to affect Indian lands and resources or to transfer any functions of the Secretary of the Interior concerning such lands and resources.

    (b) In exercising the authority under section 302(b) of this Act to promulgate regulations. the Secretary shall consult with the Secretary of the Interior during the preparation of such regulations and shall afford the Secretary of the Interior not less than thirty days, prior to the date on which the Department first publishes or otherwise prescribes regulations. to comment on the content and effect of such regulations.

    (c)(1) The Secretary of the Interior shall afford the Secretary not less than thirty days, prior to the date on which the Department of the Interior first publishes or otherwise prescribes the terms and conditions on which a Federal lease will be issued, to disapprove any term

30 USC 1001 note.
42 USC 6201 note.

Production rates.

30 USC 1, 3, 5–7.

Federal leasing of mineral resources.
42 USC 7153.

Indian lands.

Regulations.

Terms and conditions, disapproval.

or condition of such lease which relates to any matter with respect to which the Secretary has authority to promulgate regulations under section 302(b) of this Act. No such term or condition may be included in such a lease if it is disapproved by the Secretary. The Secretary and the Secretary of the Interior may by agreement define circumstances under which a reasonable opportunity of less than thirty days may be afforded the Secretary to disapprove such terms and conditions.

(2) Where the Secretary disapproves any lease, term, or condition under paragraph (1) of this subsection he shall furnish the Secretary of the Interior with a detailed written statement of the reasons for his disapproval, and of the alternatives which would be acceptable to him.

Environmental impact statements.
42 USC 4332.

(d) The Department of the Interior shall be the lead agency for the purpose of preparation of an environmental impact statement required by section 102(2)(C) of the National Environmental Policy Act of 1969 for any action with respect to the Federal leases taken under the authority of this section, unless the action involves only matters within the exclusive authority of the Secretary.

TRANSFERS FROM THE DEPARTMENT OF HOUSING AND URBAN DEVELOPMENT

Energy conservation standards for new buildings.
42 USC 7154.
42 USC 6833.

SEC. 304. (a) There is hereby transferred to, and vested in, the Secretary the functions vested in the Secretary of Housing and Urban Development pursuant to section 304 of the Energy Conservation Standards for New Buildings Act of 1976, to develop and promulgate energy conservation standards for new buildings. The Secretary of Housing and Urban Development shall provide the Secretary with any necessary technical assistance in the development of such standards.

42 USC 6831 note.

All other responsibilities, pursuant to title III of the Energy Conservation and Production Act, shall remain with the Secretary of Housing and Urban Development, except that the Secretary shall be kept fully and currently informed of the implementation of the promulgated standards.

(b) There is hereby transferred to, and vested in, the Secretary the functions vested in the Secretary of Housing and Urban Development pursuant to section 509 of the Housing and Urban Development Act of

12 USC 1701z–8.

1970.

COORDINATION WITH THE DEPARTMENT OF TRANSPORTATION

15 USC 2002.

SEC. 305. Section 502 of the Motor Vehicle Information and Cost Savings Act is amended at the end thereof by adding the following new subsections:

Average fuel economy standards.

"(g) The Secretary shall consult with the Secretary of Energy in carrying out his responsibilities under this section. The Secretary shall, before issuing any notice proposing under subsection (a), (b), (d), or (f) of this section, to establish, reduce, or amend an average fuel economy standard, provide the Secretary of Energy with a period of not less than ten days from the receipt of the notice during which the Secretary of Energy may, upon concluding that the proposed standard would adversely affect the conservation goals set by the Secretary of Energy, provide written comments to the Secretary concerning the impacts of the proposed standard upon those goals. To the extent that the Secretary does not revise the proposed standard to take into account any comments by the Secretary of Energy regarding the level of the proposed standard, the Secretary shall include the unaccommodated comments in the notice.

"(h) The Secretary shall, before taking action on any final standard under this section or any modification of or exemption from such standard, notify the Secretary of Energy and provide such Secretary with a reasonable period of time to comment thereon.".

Notice.

TRANSFER FROM THE INTERSTATE COMMERCE COMMISSION

Sec. 306. Except as provided in title IV, there are hereby transferred to the Secretary such functions set forth in the Interstate Commerce Act and vested by law in the Interstate Commerce Commission or the Chairman and members thereof as relate to transportation of oil by pipeline.

Transportation of oil by pipeline. 42 USC 7155. 49 USC prec. 1 note.

TRANSFERS FROM THE DEPARTMENT OF THE NAVY

Sec. 307. There are hereby transferred to and vested in the Secretary all functions vested by chapter 641 of title 10, United States Code, in the Secretary of the Navy as they relate to the administration of and jurisdiction over—

certain naval petroleum reserves. 42 USC 7156. 10 USC 7421.

(1) Naval Petroleum Reserve Numbered 1 (Elk Hills), located in Kern County, California, established by Executive order of the President, dated September 2, 1912;

(2) Naval Petroleum Reserve Numbered 2 (Buena Vista), located in Kern County, California, established by Executive order of the President, dated December 13, 1912;

(3) Naval Petroleum Reserve Numbered 3 (Teapot Dome), located in Wyoming, established by Executive order of the President, dated April 30, 1915;

(4) Oil Shale Reserve Numbered 1, located in Colorado, established by Executive order of the President, dated December 6, 1916, as amended by Executive order dated June 12, 1919;

(5) Oil Shale Reserve Numbered 2, located in Utah, established by Executive order of the President, dated December 6, 1916; and

(6) Oil Shale Reserve Numbered 3, located in Colorado, established by Executive order of the President, dated September 27, 1924.

In the administration of any of the functions transferred to, and vested in, the Secretary by this section the Secretary shall take into consideration the requirements of national security.

TRANSFERS FROM THE DEPARTMENT OF COMMERCE

Sec. 308. There are hereby transferred to, and vested in, the Secretary all functions of the Secretary of Commerce, the Department of Commerce, and officers and components of that Department, as relate to or are utilized by the Office of Energy Programs, but limited to industrial energy conservation programs.

Industrial energy conservation programs. 42 USC 7157.

NAVAL REACTOR AND MILITARY APPLICATION PROGRAMS

Sec. 309. (a) The Division of Naval Reactors established pursuant to section 25 of the Atomic Energy Act of 1954, and responsible for research, design, development, health, and safety matters pertaining to naval nuclear propulsion plants and assigned civilian power reactor programs is transferred to the Department under the Assistant Secretary to whom the Secretary has assigned the function listed in section 203(a)(2)(E), and such organizational unit shall be deemed to be an organizational unit established by this Act.

42 USC 7158. 42 USC 2035.

42 USC 2035.

42 USC 2037.

(b) The Division of Military Application, established by section 25 of the Atomic Energy Act of 1954, and the functions of the Energy Research and Development Administration with respect to the Military Liaison Committee, established by section 27 of the Atomic Energy Act of 1954, are transferred to the Department under the Assistant Secretary to whom the Secretary has assigned those functions listed in section 203(a)(5), and such organizational units shall be deemed to be organizational units established by this Act.

TRANSFER TO THE DEPARTMENT OF TRANSPORTATION

Van pooling and carpooling.
42 USC 7159.

42 USC 6361.

SEC. 310. Notwithstanding section 301(a), there are hereby transferred to, and vested in, the Secretary of Transportation all of the functions vested in the Administrator of the Federal Energy Administration by section 381(b)(1)(B) of the Energy Policy and Conservation Act.

TITLE IV—FEDERAL ENERGY REGULATORY COMMISSION

APPOINTMENT AND ADMINISTRATION

Establishment.
42 USC 7171.

Members.

SEC. 401. (a) There is hereby established within the Department an independent regulatory commission to be known as the Federal Energy Regulatory Commission.

(b) The Commission shall be composed of five members appointed by the President, by and with the advice and consent of the Senate. One of the members shall be designated by the President as Chairman. Members shall hold office for a term of four years and may be removed by the President only for inefficiency, neglect of duty, or malfeasance in office. The terms of the members first taking office shall expire (as designated by the President at the time of appointment), two at the end of two years, two at the end of three years, and one at the end of four years. Not more than three members of the Commission shall be members of the same political party. Any Commissioner appointed to fill a vacancy occurring prior to the expiration of the term for which his predecessor was appointed shall be appointed only for the remainder of such term. A Commissioner may continue to serve after the expiration of his term until his successor has taken office, except that he may not so continue to serve for more than one year after the date on which his term would otherwise expire under this subsection. Members of the Commission shall not engage in any other business, vocation, or employment while serving on the Commission.

(c) The Chairman shall be responsible on behalf of the Commission for the executive and administrative operation of the Commission, including functions of the Commission with respect to (1) the appointment and employment of hearing examiners in accordance with the provisions of title 5, United States Code, (2) the selection, appointment, and fixing of the compensation of such personnel as he deems necessary, including an executive director, (3) the supervision of personnel employed by or assigned to the Commission, except that each member of the Commission may select and supervise personnel for his personal staff, (4) the distribution of business among personnel and among administrative units of the Commission, and (5) the procurement of services of experts and consultants in accordance with section 3109 of title 5, United States Code. The Secretary shall provide to the Commission such support and facilities as the Commission determines it needs to carry out its functions.

(d) In the performance of their functions, the members, employees, or other personnel of the Commission shall not be responsible to or subject to the supervision or direction of any officer, employee, or agent of any other part of the Department.

(e) The Chairman of the Commission may designate any other member of the Commission as Acting Chairman to act in the place and stead of the Chairman during his absence. The Chairman (or the Acting Chairman in the absence of the Chairman) shall preside at all sessions of the Commission and a quorum for the transaction of business shall consist of at least three members present. Each member of the Commission, including the Chairman, shall have one vote. Actions of the Commission shall be determined by a majority vote of the members present. The Commission shall have an official seal which shall be judicially noticed.

Acting Chairman, designation.
Quorum.
Seal.

(f) The Commission is authorized to establish such procedural and administrative rules as are necessary to the exercise of its functions. Until changed by the Commission, any procedural and administrative rules applicable to particular functions over which the Commission has jurisdiction shall continue in effect with respect to such particular functions.

Rules.

(g) In carrying out any of its functions, the Commission shall have the powers authorized by the law under which such function is exercised to hold hearings, sign and issue subpenas, administer oaths, examine witnesses, and receive evidence at any place in the United States it may designate. The Commission may, by one or more of its members or by such agents as it may designate, conduct any hearing or other inquiry necessary or appropriate to its functions, except that nothing in this subsection shall be deemed to supersede the provisions of section 556 of title 5, United States Code relating to hearing examiners.

Hearings.

(h) The principal office of the Commission shall be in or near the District of Columbia, where its general sessions shall be held, but the Commission may sit anywhere in the United States.

(i) For the purpose of section 552b of title 5, United States Code, the Commission shall be deemed to be an agency. Except as provided in section 518 of title 28, United States Code, relating to litigation before the Supreme Court, attorneys designated by the Chairman of the Commission may appear for, and represent the Commission in, any civil action brought in connection with any function carried out by the Commission pursuant to this Act or as otherwise authorized by law.

(j) In each annual authorization and appropriation request under this Act, the Secretary shall identify the portion thereof intended for the support of the Commission and include a statement by the Commission (1) showing the amount requested by the Commission in its budgetary presentation to the Secretary and the Office of Management and Budget and (2) an assessment of the budgetary needs of the Commission. Whenever the Commission submits to the Secretary, the President, or the Office of Management and Budget, any legislative recommendation or testimony, or comments on legislation, prepared for submission to Congress, the Commission shall concurrently transmit a copy thereof to the appropriate committees of Congress.

Appropriation authorization.
Legislative recommendations, copies to congressional committees.

JURISDICTION OF THE COMMISSION

SEC. 402. (a) (1) There are hereby transferred to, and vested in, the Commission the following functions of the Federal Power Commission or of any member of the Commission or any officer or component of the Commission:

Transfer of functions.
42 USC 7172.

(A) the investigation, issuance, transfer, renewal, revocation, and enforcement of licenses and permits for the construction, operation, and maintenance of dams, water conduits, reservoirs, powerhouses, transmission lines, or other works for the development and improvement of navigation and for the development and utilization of power across, along, from, or in navigable waters under part I of the Federal Power Act;

16 USC 792.

(B) the establishment, review, and enforcement of rates and charges for the transmission or sale of electric energy, including determinations on construction work in progress, under part II of the Federal Power Act, and the interconnection, under section 202(b), of such Act, of facilities for the generation, transmission, and sale of electric energy (other than emergency interconnection);

16 USC 824.
16 USC 824a.

(C) the establishment, review, and enforcement of rates and charges for the transportation and sale of natural gas by a producer or gatherer or by a natural gas pipeline or natural gas company under sections 1, 4, 5, and 6 of the Natural Gas Act;

15 USC 717,
717c, 717d,
717e.

(D) the issuance of a certificate of public convenience and necessity, including abandonment of facilities or services, and the establishment of physical connections under section 7 of the Natural Gas Act;

15 USC 717f.

(E) the establishment, review, and enforcement of curtailments, other than the establishment and review of priorities for such curtailments, under the Natural Gas Act; and

15 USC 717w.

(F) the regulation of mergers and securities acquisition under the Federal Power Act and Natural Gas Act.

16 USC 791a.

(2) The Commission may exercise any power under the following sections to the extent the Commission determines such power to be necessary to the exercise of any function within the jurisdiction of the Commission:

(A) sections 4, 301, 302, 306 through 309, and 312 through 316 of the Federal Power Act; and

16 USC 797,
825, 825a,
825e–825h,
825k–825o.

(B) sections 8, 9, 13 through 17, 20, and 21 of the Natural Gas Act.

15 USC 717g,
717h,
717l–717p,
717s, 717t.

(b) There are hereby transferred to, and vested in, the Commission all functions and authority of the Interstate Commerce Commission or any officer or component of such Commission where the regulatory function establishes rates or charges for the transportation of oil by pipeline or establishes the valuation of any such pipeline.

(c)(1) Pursuant to the procedures specified in section 404 and except as provided in paragraph (2), the Commission shall have jurisdiction to consider any proposal by the Secretary to amend the regulation required to be issued under section 4(a) of the Emergency Petroleum Allocation Act of 1973 which is required by section 8 or 12 of such Act to be transmitted by the President to, and reviewed by, each House of Congress, under section 551 of the Energy Policy and Conservation Act.

15 USC 753.
15 USC 757,
760a.
42 USC 6421.

(2) In the event that the President determines that an emergency situation of overriding national importance exists and requires the expeditious promulgation of a rule described in paragraph (1), the President may direct the Secretary to assume sole jurisdiction over the promulgation of such rule, and such rule shall be transmitted by the President to, and reviewed by, each House of Congress under section 8 or 12 of the Emergency Petroleum Allocation Act of 1973, and section 551 of the Energy Policy and Conservation Act.

(d) The Commission shall have jurisdiction to hear and determine any other matter arising under any other function of the Secretary—

Hearing.

    (1) involving any agency determination required by law to be made on the record after an opportunity for an agency hearing; or

    (2) involving any other agency determination which the Secretary determines shall be made on the record after an opportunity for an agency hearing,

except that nothing in this subsection shall require that functions under sections 105 and 106 of the Energy Policy and Conservation Act shall be within the jurisdiction of the Commission unless the Secretary assigns such a function to the Commission.

42 USC 6213, 6214.

(e) In addition to the other provisions of this section, the Commission shall have jurisdiction over any other matter which the Secretary may assign to the Commission after public notice, or which are required to be referred to the Commission pursuant to section 404 of this Act.

Notice.

(f) No function described in this section which regulates the exports or imports of natural gas or electricity shall be within the jurisdiction of the Commission unless the Secretary assigns such a function to the Commission.

Limitation.

(g) The decision of the Commission involving any function within its jurisdiction, other than action by it on a matter referred to it pursuant to section 404, shall be final agency action within the meaning of section 704 of title 5, United States Code, and shall not be subject to further review by the Secretary or any officer or employee of the Department.

Review, limitation.

(h) The Commission is authorized to prescribe rules, regulations, and statements of policy of general applicability with respect to any function under the jurisdiction of the Commission pursuant to section 402.

Rules, regulations, and statements of policy.

INITIATION OF RULEMAKING PROCEEDINGS BEFORE COMMISSION

SEC. 403. (a) The Secretary and the Commission are authorized to propose rules, regulations, and statements of policy of general applicability with respect to any function within the jurisdiction of the Commission under section 402 of this Act.

42 USC 7173.

(b) The Commission shall have exclusive jurisdiction with respect to any proposal made under subsection (a), and shall consider and take final action on any proposal made by the Secretary under such subsection in an expeditious manner in accordance with such reasonable time limits as may be set by the Secretary for the completion of action by the Commission on any such proposal.

(c) Any function described in section 402 of this Act which relates to the establishment of rates and charges under the Federal Power Act or the Natural Gas Act, may be conducted by rulemaking procedures. Except as provided in subsection (d), the procedures in such a rulemaking proceeding shall assure full consideration of the issues and an opportunity for interested persons to present their views.

16 USC 791a.
15 USC 717w.

(d) With respect to any rule or regulation promulgated by the Commission to establish rates and charges for the first sale of natural gas by a producer or gatherer to a natural gas pipeline under the Natural Gas Act, the Commission may afford any interested person a reasonable opportunity to submit written questions with respect to disputed issues of fact to other interested persons participating in the rulemaking proceedings. The Commission may establish a reasonable time for both the submission of questions and responses thereto.

Written questions and responses.

REFERRAL OF OTHER RULEMAKING PROCEEDINGS TO COMMISSION

42 USC 7174.

Public comment.

SEC. 404. (a) Except as provided in section 403, whenever the Secretary proposes to prescribe rules, regulations, and statements of policy of general applicability in the exercise of any function which is transferred to the Secretary under section 301 or 306 of this Act, he shall notify the Commission of the proposed action. If the Commission, in its discretion, determines within such period as the Secretary may prescribe, that the proposed action may significantly affect any function within the jurisdiction of the Commission pursuant to section 402(a)(1), (b), and (c)(1), the Secretary shall immediately refer the matter to the Commission, which shall provide an opportunity for public comment.

(b) Following such opportunity for public comment the Commission, after consultation with the Secretary, shall either—

(1) concur in adoption of the rule or statement as proposed by the Secretary;

(2) concur in adoption of the rule or statement only with such changes as it may recommend; or

(3) recommend that the rule or statement not be adopted.

Recommendations, publication.

The Commission shall promptly publish its recommendations, adopted under this subsection, along with an explanation of the reason for its actions and an analysis of the major comments, criticisms, and alternatives offered during the comment period.

(c) Following publication of the Commission's recommendations the Secretary shall have the option of—

(1) issuing a final rule or statement in the form initially proposed by the Secretary if the Commission has concurred in such rule pursuant to subsection (b)(1);

(2) issuing a final rule or statement in amended form so that the rule conforms in all respects with the changes proposed by the Commission if the Commission has concurred in such rule or statement pursuant to subsection (b)(2); or

(3) ordering that the rule shall not be issued.

The action taken by the Secretary pursuant to this subsection shall constitute a final agency action for purposes of section 704 of title 5, United States Code.

RIGHT OF SECRETARY TO INTERVENE IN COMMISSION PROCEEDINGS

42 USC 7175.

SEC. 405. The Secretary may as a matter of right intervene or otherwise participate in any proceeding before the Commission. The Secretary shall comply with rules of procedure of general applicability governing the timing of intervention or participation in such proceeding or activity and, upon intervening or participating therein, shall comply with rules of procedure of general applicability governing the conduct thereof. The intervention or participation of the Secretary in any proceeding or activity shall not affect the obligation of the Commission to assure procedure fairness to all participants.

REORGANIZATION

42 USC 7176.
5 USC 901.

SEC. 406. For the purposes of chapter 9 of title 5, United States Code, the Commission shall be deemed to be an independent regulatory agency.

ACCESS TO INFORMATION

SEC. 407. (a) The Secretary, each officer of the Department, and each Federal agency shall provide to the Commission, upon request, such existing information in the possession of the Department or other Federal agency as the Commission determines is necessary to carry out its responsibilities under this Act.

42 USC 7177.

(b) The Secretary, in formulating the information to be requested in the reports or investigations under section 304 and section 311 of the Federal Power Act and section 10 and section 11 of the Natural Gas Act, shall include in such reports and investigations such specific information as requested by the Federal Energy Regulatory Commission and copies of all reports, information, results of investigations and data under said sections shall be furnished by the Secretary to the Federal Energy Regulatory Commission.

16 USC 825c, 825j.
15 USC 717i, 717j.

TITLE V—ADMINISTRATIVE PROCEDURES AND JUDICIAL REVIEW

PROCEDURES

SEC. 501. (a)(1) Subject to the other requirements of this title, the provisions of subchapter II of chapter 5 of title 5, United States Code, shall apply in accordance with its terms to any rule or regulation, or any order having the applicability and effect of a rule (as defined in section 551(4) of title 5, United States Code), issued pursuant to authority vested by law in, or transferred or delegated to, the Secretary, or required by this Act or any other Act to be carried out by any other officer, employee, or component of the Department, other than the Commission, including any such rule, regulation, or order of a State, or local government agency or officer thereof, issued pursuant to authority delegated by the Secretary in accordance with this title. If any provision of any Act, the functions of which are transferred, vested, or delegated pursuant to this Act, provides administrative procedure requirements in addition to the requirements provided in this title, such additional requirements shall also apply to actions under that provision.

42 USC 7191.
5 USC 551.

(2) Notwithstanding paragraph (1), this title shall apply to the Commission to the same extent this title applies to the Secretary in the exercise of any of the Commission's functions under section 402 (c)(1) or which the Secretary has assigned under section 402(e).

(b)(1) In addition to the requirements of subsection (a) of this section, notice of any proposed rule, regulation, or order described in subsection (a) shall be given by publication of such proposed rule, regulation, or order in the Federal Register. Such publication shall be accompanied by a statement of the research, analysis, and other available information in support of, the need for, and the probable effect of, any such proposed rule, regulation, or order. Other effective means of publicity shall be utilized as may be reasonably calculated to notify concerned or affected persons of the nature and probable effect of any such proposed rule, regulation, or order. In each case, a minimum of thirty days following such publication shall be provided for an opportunity to comment prior to promulgation of any such rule, regulation, or order.

Publication in Federal Register.

Statement.

Minimum comment period.

(2) Public notice of all rules, regulations, or orders described in subsection (a) which are promulgated by officers of a State or local government agency pursuant to a delegation under this Act shall be

Notice.

provided by publication of such proposed rules, regulations, or orders in at least two newspapers of statewide circulation. If such publication is not practicable, notice of any such rule, regulation, or order shall be given by such other means as the officer promulgating such rule, regulation, or order determines will reasonably assure wide public notice.

(3) For the purposes of this title, the exception from the requirements of section 553 of title 5, United States Code, provided by subsection (a)(2) of such section with respect to public property, loans, grants, or contracts shall not be available.

(c)(1) If the Secretary determines, on his own initiative or in response to any showing made pursuant to paragraph (2) (with respect to a proposed rule, regulation, or order described in subsection (a)) that no substantial issue of fact or law exists and that such rule, regulation, or order is unlikely to have a substantial impact on the Nation's economy or large numbers of individuals or businesses, such proposed rule, regulation, or order may be promulgated in accordance with section 553 of title 5, United States Code. If the Secretary determines that a substantial issue of fact or law exists or that such rule, regulation, or order is likely to have a substantial impact on the Nation's economy or large numbers of individuals or businesses, an opportunity for oral presentation of views, data, and arguments shall be provided.

(2) Any person, who would be adversely affected by the implementation of any proposed rule, regulation, or order who desires an opportunity for oral presentation of views, data, and arguments, may submit material supporting the existence of such substantial issues or such impact.

(3) A transcript shall be kept of any oral presentation with respect to a rule, regulation, or order described in subsection (a).

(d) Following the notice and comment period, including any oral presentation required by this subsection, the Secretary may promulgate a rule if the rule is accompanied by an explanation responding to the major comments, criticisms, and alternatives offered during the comment period.

(e) The requirements of subsections (b), (c), and (d) of this section may be waived where strict compliance is found by the Secretary to be likely to cause serious harm or injury to the public health, safety, or welfare, and such finding is set out in detail in such rule, regulation, or order. In the event the requirements of this section are waived, the requirements shall be satisfied within a reasonable period of time subsequent to the promulgation of such rule, regulation, or order.

(f)(1) With respect to any rule, regulation, or order described in subsection (a), the effects of which, except for indirect effects of an inconsequential nature, are confined to—

(A) a single unit of local government or the residents thereof;

(B) a single geographic area within a State or the residents thereof; or

(C) a single State or the residents thereof;

the Secretary shall, in any case where appropriate, afford an opportunity for a hearing or the oral presentation of views, and provide procedures for the holding of such hearing or oral presentation within the boundaries of the unit of local government, geographic area, or State described in paragraphs (A) through (C) of this paragraph as the case may be.

(2) For the purposes of this subsection—

(A) the term "unit of local government" means a county, municipality, town, township, village, or other unit of general government below the State level; and

(B) the term "geographic area within a State" means a special purpose district or other region recognized for governmental purposes within such State which is not a unit of local government.

(3) Nothing in this subsection shall be construed as requiring a hearing or an oral presentation of views where none is required by this section or other provision of law.

(g) Where authorized by any law vested, transferred, or delegated pursuant to this Act, the Secretary may, by rule, prescribe procedures for State or local government agencies authorized by the Secretary to carry out such functions as may be permitted under applicable law. Such procedures shall apply to such agencies in lieu of this section, and shall require that prior to taking any action, such agencies shall take steps reasonably calculated to provide notice to persons who may be affected by the action, and shall afford an opportunity for presentation of views (including oral presentation of views where practicable) within a reasonable time before taking the action.

Definitions.

Notice.

JUDICIAL REVIEW

SEC. 502. (a) Judicial review of agency action taken under any law the functions of which are vested by law in, or transferred or delegated to the Secretary, the Commission or any officer, employee, or component of the Department shall, notwithstanding such vesting, transfer, or delegation, be made in the manner specified in or for such law.

(b) Notwithstanding the amount in controversy, the district courts of the United States shall have exclusive original jurisdiction of all other cases or controversies arising exclusively under this Act, or under rules, regulations, or orders issued exclusively thereunder, other than any actions taken to implement or enforce any rule, regulation, or order by any officer of a State or local government agency under this Act, except that nothing in this section affects the power of any court of competent jurisdiction to consider, hear, and determine in any proceeding before it any issue raised by way of defense (other than a defense based on the unconstitutionality of this Act or the validity of action taken by any agency under this Act). If in any such proceeding an issue by way of defense is raised based on the unconstitutionality of this Act or the validity of agency action under this Act, the case shall be subject to removal by either party to a district court of the United States in accordance with the applicable provisions of chapter 89 of title 28, United States Code. Cases or controversies arising under any rule, regulation, or order of any officer of a State or local government agency may be heard in either (A) any appropriate State court, or (B) without regard to the amount in controversy, the district courts of the United States.

(c) Subject to the provisions of section 401(i) of this Act, and notwithstanding any other law, the litigation of the Department shall be subject to the supervision of the Attorney General pursuant to chapter 31 of title 28, United States Code. The Attorney General may authorize any attorney of the Department to conduct any civil litigation of the Department in any Federal court except the Supreme Court.

42 USC 7192.

Jurisdiction.

Removal.

28 USC 1441.

Litigation, supervision by Attorney General. 28 USC 501.

REMEDIAL ORDERS

Violations.
42 USC 7193.

15 USC 751 note.

Sec. 503. (a) If upon investigation the Secretary or his authorized representative believes that a person has violated any regulation, rule, or order described in section 501(a) promulgated pursuant to the Emergency Petroleum Allocation Act of 1973, he may issue a remedial order to the person. Each remedial order shall be in writing and shall describe with particularity the nature of the violation, including a reference to the provision of such rule, regulation, or order alleged to have been violated. For purposes of this section "person" includes any individual, association, company, corporation, partnership, or other entity however organized.

"Person."

Final order, appeal, prohibition.

(b) If within thirty days after the receipt of the remedial order issued by the Secretary, the person fails to notify the Secretary that he intends to contest the remedial order, the remedial order shall become effective and shall be deemed a final order of the Secretary and not subject to review by any court or agency.

Contestation, notice.

(c) If within thirty days after the receipt of the remedial order issued by the Secretary, the person notifies the Secretary that he intends to contest a remedial order issued under subsection (a) of this section, the Secretary shall immediately advise the Commission of such notification. Upon such notice, the Commission shall stay the effect of the remedial order, unless the Commission finds the public interest requires immediate compliance with such remedial order. The Commission shall, upon request, afford an opportunity for a hearing, including, at a minimum, the submission of briefs, oral or documentary evidence, and oral arguments. To the extent that the Commission in its discretion determines that such is required for a full and true disclosure of the facts, the Commission shall afford the right of cross examination. The Commission shall thereafter issue an order, based on findings of fact, affirming, modifying, or vacating the Secretary's remedial order, or directing other appropriate relief, and such order shall, for the purpose of judicial review, constitute a final agency action, except that enforcement and other judicial review of such action shall be the responsibility of the Secretary.

Stay.

Hearing.

Cross examination.

Final order. Enforcement and review.

Time limits.

(d) The Secretary may set reasonable time limits for the Commission to complete action on a proceeding referred to it pursuant to this section.

(e) Nothing in this section shall be construed to affect any procedural action taken by the Secretary prior to or incident to initial issuance of a remedial order which is the subject of the hearing provided in this section, but such procedures shall be reviewable in the hearing.

Savings provision.

(f) The provisions of this section shall be applicable only with respect to proceedings initiated by a notice of probable violation issued after the effective date of this Act.

REQUESTS FOR ADJUSTMENTS

42 USC 7194.

15 USC 761 note.

15 USC 791 note.
42 USC 6201 note.

Sec. 504. (a) The Secretary or any officer designated by him shall provide for the making of such adjustments to any rule, regulation or order described in section 501(a) issued under the Federal Energy Administration Act, the Emergency Petroleum Allocation Act of 1973, the Energy Supply and Environmental Coordination Act of 1974, or the Energy Policy and Conservation Act, consistent with the other purposes of the relevant Act, as may be necessary to prevent special hardship, inequity, or unfair distribution of burdens, and shall by rule, establish procedures which are available to any person for the purpose of seeking an interpretation, modification, or recission of, exception to, or exemption from, such rule, regulation or order. The Secretary or any such officer shall additionally insure that each decision on any application or petition requesting an adjustment shall specify the standards of hardship, inequity, or unfair distribution of burden by which any disposition was made, and the specific application of such standards to the facts contained in any such application or petition.

(b)(1) If any person is aggrieved or adversely affected by a denial of a request for adjustment under subsection (a) such person may request a review of such denial by the Commission and may obtain judicial review in accordance with this title when such a denial becomes final.

Denial, judicial review.

(2) The Commission shall, by rule, establish appropriate procedures, including a hearing when requested, for review of a denial. Action by the Commission under this section shall be considered final agency action within the meaning of section 704 of title 5, United States Code, and shall not be subject to further review by the Secretary or any officer or employee of the Department. Litigation involving judicial review of such action shall be the responsibility of the Secretary.

Hearing.

REVIEW AND EFFECT

SEC. 505. Within one year after the effective date of this Act, the Secretary shall submit a report to Congress concerning the actions taken to implement section 501. The report shall include a discussion of the adequacy of such section from the standpoint of the Department and the public, including a summary of any comments obtained by the Secretary from the public about such section and implementing regulations, and such recommendations as the Secretary deems appropriate concerning the procedures required by such section.

Report to Congress.
42 USC 7195.
Contents.

TITLE VI—ADMINISTRATIVE PROVISIONS

PART A—CONFLICT OF INTEREST PROVISIONS

DEFINITIONS

SEC. 601. (a) For the purposes of this title, the following officers or employees of the Department are supervisory employees:

Supervisory employees.
42 USC 7211.
5 USC 5332 note.
5 USC 5312–5316.

(1) an individual holding a position in the Department at GS–16, GS–17, or GS–18 of the General Schedule or at level I, II, III, IV, or V of the Executive Schedule, or who is in a position at a comparable or higher level on any other Federal pay scale, or who holds a position pursuant to subsection (b) or (d) of section 621, or who is an expert or consultant employed pursuant to section 3109 of title 5, United States Code, for more than ninety days in any calendar year and receives compensation at an annual rate equal to or in excess of the minimum rate prescribed for individuals at GS–16 of the General Schedule;

(2) the Director or Deputy Director of any State, regional, district, local, or other field office maintained pursuant to section 650 of this Act;

(3) an employee or officer who has primary responsibility for the award, review, modification, or termination of any grant,

contract, award, or fund transfer within the authority of the Secretary; and

(4) any other employee or officer who, in the judgment of the Secretary, exercises sufficient decisionmaking or regulatory authority so that the provisions of this title should apply to such individual.

"Energy concern."

(b) For purposes of this title the term "energy concern" includes—

(1) any person significantly engaged in the business of developing, extracting, producing, refining, transporting by pipeline, converting into synthetic fuel, distributing, or selling minerals for use as an energy source, or in the generation or transmission of energy from such minerals or from wastes or renewable resources;

(2) any person holding an interest in property from which coal, natural gas, crude oil, nuclear material or a renewable resource is commercially produced or obtained;

(3) any person significantly engaged in the business of producing, generating, transmitting, distributing, or selling electric power;

(4) any person significantly engaged in development, production, processing, sale, or distribution of nuclear materials, facilities, or technology;

(5) any person—

(A) significantly engaged in the business of conducting research, development, or demonstration related to an activity described in paragraph (1), (2), (3), or (4); or

(B) significantly engaged in conducting such research, development, or demonstration with financial assistance under any Act the functions of which are vested in or delegated or transferred to the Secretary or the Department.

List of energy concerns, publication.

(c) (1) The Secretary shall prepare and periodically publish a list of persons which the Secretary has determined to be energy concerns as defined by subsection (b). The absence of any particular energy concern from such list shall not exempt any officer or employee from the requirements of sections 602 through 606 of this Act.

(2) At the request of any officer or employee of the Department the Secretary shall determine whether any person is an energy concern as defined by subsection (b).

Energy concerns, knowledge of interest or positions.

(d) For the purposes of sections 602(a), 603(a), 605(a), and 606 an individual shall be deemed to have known of or knowingly committed a described act or to have known of or knowingly held a described interest, status, or position if the employee knew or should have known of such act, interest, status, or position. For the purposes of section 602(a) an officer or employee shall be deemed to have known of or knowingly held an interest in an energy concern if such interest is sold or otherwise transferred to his spouse or dependent while such officer or employee is, or within six months prior to the date on which such officer or employee becomes, an officer or employee of the Department. The placing of an interest under a trust by an individual shall not satisfy the requirement of section 602 or waive the requirements of section 603 as to such interest unless none of the interests placed under such trust by such individual consists of known financial interests in any energy concern.

DIVESTITURE OF ENERGY HOLDINGS BY SUPERVISORY OFFICIALS

42 USC 7212.

SEC. 602. (a) No supervisory employee shall knowingly receive compensation from, or hold any official relation with, any energy concern, or own stocks or bonds of any energy concern, or have any pecuniary interest therein.

(b) Personnel transferred to the Department pursuant to section 701 of this Act shall have six months to comply with the provisions of subsection (a) with respect to prohibited property holdings. Any person transferred pursuant to section 701 of this Act shall notify the Secretary or his designee of all known circumstances which would be violative of the restrictions set forth in subsection (a) not later than thirty days after the date of such transfer, as determined by the United States Civil Service Commission.

Transferred personnel, compliance. Notice.

(c) Where exceptional hardship would result, or where the interest is a pension, insurance or other similarly vested interest, the Secretary is authorized to waive the requirements of this section for such period as he may prescribe with respect to any supervisory employee covered. Such waiver shall:

Waiver.

(1) be published in the Federal Register;

(2) contain a finding by the Secretary that exceptional hardship would result or that there is such a vested interest; and

Publication in Federal Register.

(3) state the period of the waiver and indicate the actions taken to minimize or eliminate the conflict of interest during such period.

(d) Any supervisory employee who continues to receive income from any energy concern, or continues to own property directly or indirectly in any such concern shall disclose such income or ownership pursuant to section 603.

DISCLOSURE OF ENERGY ASSETS

SEC. 603. (a) Each individual who at any time during the calendar year serves as an officer or employee of the Department shall disclose to the Secretary—

Report.
42 USC 7213.

(1) the amount of income and the identity of the source of income knowingly received by such individual, his spouse, or dependent from any energy concern, and

(2) the identity and value of interest knowingly held in any such concern

during such calendar year. Such report shall be filed not later than thirty days after commencing service in the Department and on May 15 following each such calendar year. Each report under this subsection shall be in such form and manner as the Secretary shall, by rule, prescribe.

(b) The Secretary shall—

(1) act, within ninety days after the effective date of this Act, by rule to establish the methods by which the requirement to file written statements specified in subsection (a) will be monitored and enforced, including appropriate provisions for the filing by such officers and employees of such statements, for the recording by the reviewing official of any action taken to eliminate any potential conflict, and for the signing of such statement by the reviewing official; and

(2) include, as part of the report made pursuant to section 657, a report with respect to such disclosures and the actions taken in regard thereto during the preceding calendar year.

(c) In the rules prescribed in subsection (b), the Secretary shall identify specific positions, or classes thereof, within the Department which are of a nonregulatory or nonpolicymaking nature at or below GS–12 of the General Schedule and shall exempt such positions and

Exempt positions.

5 USC 5332 note.

the individuals occupying those positions from the requirements of this section.

(d) Each individual required to file a report under this section who during any calendar year ceases to be an officer or employee of the Department shall file a report covering that portion of such year beginning on January 1 and ending on the date on which he ceases to be such an officer or employee, and such report shall be filed with the Secretary not later than thirty days after such date.

Extension.

(e) The Secretary may grant one or more reasonable extensions of time for filing any such report under this section but the total of such extensions shall not exceed ninety days.

REPORT ON PRIOR EMPLOYMENT

42 USC 7214.

SEC. 604. (a) Within sixty days of becoming a supervisory employee of the department, each supervisory employee shall file with the Secretary, in such form and manner as the Secretary shall prescribe, a report identifying any energy concern which paid the reporting individual compensation in excess of $2,500 in any of the previous five calendar years. The individual shall include in the report—

Contents.

(1) the name and address of each source of such compensation;

(2) the period during which the reporting individual was receiving such compensation from each such source;

(3) the title of each position or relationship the reporting individual held with each compensating source; and

(4) a brief description of the duties performed or services rendered by the reporting individual in each such position.

Exceptions.

(b) Subsection (a) shall not require any individual to include in such report any information which is considered confidential as a result of a privileged relationship, recognized by law, between such individual and any person; nor shall it require an individual to report any information with respect to any person for whom services were provided by any firm or association of which such individual was a member, partner, or employee unless such individual was directly involved in the provision of such services.

POSTEMPLOYMENT PROHIBITIONS AND REPORTING REQUIREMENTS

42 USC 7215.

SEC. 605. (a)(1) Except as provided in paragraph (2) or (3), no supervisory employee shall, within one year after his employment with the Department has ceased, knowingly—

(A) make any appearance or attendance before, or

(B) make any written or oral communication to, and with the intent to influence the action of;

the Department if such appearance or communication relates to any particular matter which is pending before the Department.

Exceptions.

(2) Paragraph (1) shall not apply to any appearance, attendance, or communication made, during any part of such year that such individual is employed by, and is on behalf of, the United States; nor shall it apply to an appearance or communication by the former supervisory employee where such appearance or communication is made in response to a subpena, or concerns any matter of an exclusively personal and individual nature such as pension benefits.

National interest exception.
Publication in Federal Register

(3) Paragraph (1) shall not prohibit a former supervisory employee with outstanding scientific or technological qualifications from making any appearance, attendance, or written or oral communica-

tion in connection with a particular matter in a scientific or technological field if the Secretary or the Commission, as the case may be, makes a certification in writing, published in the Federal Register, that the national interest would be served by such action or appearance by such former supervisory employee.

(b) (1) Each former supervisory employee of the Department shall file with the Secretary, in such form and manner as the Secretary shall prescribe, not later than May 15 of the first and second calendar years following the first full year in which such person ceased to be an officer or employee of the Department, a report describing any employment with any energy concern during the period to which such report relates, including any employment as a consultant, agent, attorney, or otherwise, except that the requirements of this subsection shall not apply to any former supervisory employee who, at the time such employment with the Department ceases, has any contract, promise, or other agreement with respect to future employment with any energy concern, if (A) the former supervisory employee describes such agreement in any report filed within thirty days after the individual ceases to be an employee of the Department, and (B) the former supervisory employee amends the report by May 15 of either of the next two years during which he has accepted employment with another energy concern. Report.

(2) Each report filed pursuant to paragraph (1) of this subsection shall contain the name and address of the person filing the report, the name and address of the energy concern with which he holds or will hold employment during any portion of the period covered by the report, a brief description of his responsibilities for the energy concern, the dates of his employment, and such other pertinent information as the Secretary may require. Contents.

PARTICIPATION PROHIBITIONS

SEC. 606. (a) For a period of one year after terminating any employment with any energy concern, no supervisory employee shall knowingly participate in any Department proceeding in which his former employer is substantially, directly, or materially involved, other than in a rulemaking proceeding which has a substantial effect on numerous energy concerns. 42 USC 7216.

(b) For a period of one year after commencing service in the Department, no supervisory employee shall knowingly participate in any Department proceeding for which, within the previous five years, he had direct responsibility, or in which he participated substantially or personally, while in the employment of any energy concern.

(c) Whenever the Secretary makes a written finding as to a particular supervisory employee that the application of a particular restriction or requirement imposed by subsection (a) or (b) in a particular circumstance would work an exceptional hardship upon such supervisory employee or would be contrary to the national interest, the Secretary may waive in writing such restriction or requirement as to such supervisory employee. Any waiver made by the Secretary of a restriction imposed under subsection (b) shall also be filed with any record of the Department proceeding as to which the waiver for purposes of participation is granted. No such waiver shall in any instance constitute a waiver of the requirements of section 207 of title 18, United States Code. Waiver.

PROCEDURES APPLICABLE TO REPORTS

Reports, availability to public.
42 USC 7217.

SEC. 607. (a) (1) Except as provided in this section, the Secretary shall make each report filed with him under section 603, 604, or 605 available to the public within thirty days after the receipt of such report, and shall provide a copy of any such report to any person upon written request.

Fee.

(2) The Secretary may require any person receiving a copy of any report to pay a reasonable fee in any amount which the Secretary finds necessary to recover the cost of reproduction or mailing of such report, excluding any salary of any employee involved in such reproduction or mailing. The Secretary may furnish a copy of any such report without charge, or at a reduced charge, if he determines that waiver or reduction of the fee is in the public interest because furnishing the information primarily benefits the public.

(3) Any report received by the Secretary shall be held in his custody and made available to the public for a period of six years after receipt by the Secretary of such report. After such six-year period, the Secretary shall destroy any such report.

Audit.

(b) The Civil Service Commission shall, under such regulations as are prescribed by the Commission, conduct, on a random basis, a sufficient number of audits of the reports filed pursuant to sections 603, 604, and 605, as deemed necessary and appropriate in order to monitor the accuracy and completeness of such reports.

Findings and waivers file, availability to public.

(c) The Secretary shall maintain a file containing all findings and waivers made by him pursuant to section 602(c), 603(c), 605(a), or 606(c) and all such findings and waivers shall be available for public inspection and copying at all times during regular working hours in accordance with the procedures of this section.

SANCTIONS

42 USC 7218.

SEC. 608. (a) Any individual who is subject to, and knowingly violates, section 603 shall be fined not more than $2,500 or imprisoned not more than one year, or both.

(b) Any individual who violates section 602, 603, 604, 605, or 606 shall be subject to a civil penalty, assessed by the Secretary in accordance with applicable law or by any district court of the United States, not to exceed $10,000 for each violation.

(c) Notwithstanding any penalty imposed under subsection (a), any violation of section 605(a) shall be taken into consideration in deciding the outcome of any Department proceeding in connection with which the prohibited appearance, attendance, communication, or submission was made.

(d) Nothing in this title shall be deemed to limit the operation of section 207 or section 208 of title 18, United States Code. Nor shall any waiver issued pursuant to section 602(c) constitute a waiver of the requirements of such provision.

PART B—PERSONNEL PROVISIONS

OFFICERS AND EMPLOYEES

42 USC 7231.

SEC. 621. (a) In the performance of his functions the Secretary is authorized to appoint and fix the compensation of such officers and employees, including attorneys, as may be necessary to carry out such functions. Except as otherwise provided in this section, such officers and employees shall be appointed in accordance with the civil service laws and their compensation fixed in accordance with title 5, United States Code.

(b)(1) Subject to the limitations provided in paragraph (2) and to the extent the Secretary deems such action necessary to the discharge of his functions, he may appoint not more than three hundred eleven of the scientific, engineering, professional, and administrative personnel of the department without regard to the civil service laws, and may fix the compensation of such personnel not in excess of the maximum rate payable for GS–18 of the General Schedule under section 5332 of title 5, United States Code.

5 USC 5332 note.

(2) The Secretary's authority under this subsection to appoint an individual to such a position without regard to the civil service laws shall cease—

    (A) when a person appointed, within four years after the effective date of this Act, to fill such position under paragraph (1) leaves such position, or

    (B) on the day which is four years after such effective date, whichever is later.

(c)(1) Subject to the provisions of chapter 51 of title 5, United States Code, but notwithstanding the last two sentences of section 5108(a) of such title, the Secretary may place at GS–16, GS–17, and GS–18, not to exceed one hundred seventy-eight positions of the positions subject to the limitation of the first sentence of section 5108(a) of such title.

5 USC 5101

(2) Appointments under this subsection may be made without regard to the provisions of sections 3324 of title 5, United States Code, relating to the approval by the Civil Service Commission of appointments under GS–16, GS–17, and GS–18 if the individual placed in such position is an individual who is transferred in connection with a transfer of functions under this Act and who, immediately before the effective date of this Act, held a position and duties comparable to those of such position.

(3) The Secretary's authority under this subsection with respect to any position shall cease when the person first appointed to fill such position leaves such position.

(d) In addition to the number of positions which may be placed at GS–16, GS–17, and GS–18 under section 5108 of title 5, United States Code, under existing law, or under this Act and to the extent the Secretary deems such action necessary to the discharge of his functions, he may appoint not more than two hundred of the scientific, engineering, professional, and administrative personnel without regard to the civil service laws and may fix the compensation of such personnel not in excess of the maximum rate payable for GS–18 of the General Schedule under section 5332 of title 5, United States Code.

(e) For the purposes of determining the maximum aggregate number of positions which may be placed at GS–16, GS–17, or GS–18 under section 5108(a) of title 5, United States Code, 63 percent of the positions established under subsections (b) and (c) shall be deemed GS–16 positions, 25 percent of such positions shall be deemed GS–17 positions, and 12 percent of such positions shall be deemed GS–18.

SENIOR POSITIONS

Sec. 622. In addition to those positions created by title II of this Act, there shall be within the Department fourteen additional officers in positions authorized by section 5316 of title 5, United States Code, who shall be appointed by the Secretary and who shall perform such functions as the Secretary shall prescribe from time to time.

42 USC 7232.
Ante, p. 569.

EXPERTS AND CONSULTANTS

42 USC 7233.

5 USC 5332 note.

SEC. 623. The Secretary may obtain services as authorized by section 3109 of title 5, United States Code, at rates not to exceed the daily rate prescribed for grade GS–18 of the General Schedule under section 5332 of title 5, United States Code, for persons in Government service employed intermittently.

ADVISORY COMMITTEES

Establishment.
42 USC 7234.
5 USC app. I.

SEC. 624. (a) The Secretary is authorized to establish in accordance with the Federal Advisory Committee Act such advisory committees as he may deem appropriate to assist in the performance of his functions. Members of such advisory committees, other than full-time employees of the Federal Government, while attending meetings of such committees or while otherwise serving at the request of the Secretary while serving away from their homes or regular places of business, may be allowed travel expenses, including per diem in lieu of subsistence, as authorized by section 5703 of title 5, United States Code, for individuals in the Government serving without pay.

Meetings.
15 USC 776.

(b) Section 17 of the Federal Energy Administration Act of 1974 shall be applicable to advisory committees chartered by the Secretary, or transferred to the Secretary or the Department under this Act, except that where an advisory committee advises the Secretary on matters pertaining to research and development, the Secretary may determine that such meeting shall be closed because it involves research and development matters and comes within the exemption of section 552b(c)(4) of title 5, United States Code.

ARMED SERVICES PERSONNEL

42 USC 7235.

10 USC 7421 *et seq.*

SEC. 625. (a) The Secretary is authorized to provide for participation of Armed Forces personnel in carrying out functions authorized to be performed, on the date of enactment of this Act, in the Energy Research and Development Administration and under chapter 641 of title 10, United States Code. Members of the Armed Forces may be detailed for service in the Department by the Secretary concerned (as such term is defined in section 101 of such title) pursuant to cooperative agreements with the Secretary.

(b) The detail of any personnel to the Department under this section shall in no way affect status, office, rank, or grade which officers or enlisted men may occupy or hold or any emolument, perquisite, right, privilege, or benefit incident to, or arising out of, such status, office, rank, or grade. Any member so detailed shall not be charged against any statutory or other limitation or strengths applicable to the Armed Forces, but shall be charged to such limitations as may be applicable to the Department. A member so detailed shall not be subject to direction or control by his armed force, or any officer thereof, directly or indirectly, with respect to the responsibilities exercised in the position to which detailed.

PART C—GENERAL ADMINISTRATIVE PROVISIONS

GENERAL AUTHORITY

42 USC 7251.

SEC. 641. To the extent necessary or appropriate to perform any function transferred by this Act, the Secretary or any officer or employee of the Department may exercise, in carrying out the function so transferred, any authority or part thereof available by law, including appropriation Acts, to the official or agency from which such function was transferred.

DELEGATION

Sec. 642. Except as otherwise expressly prohibited by law, and except as otherwise provided in this Act, the Secretary may delegate any of his functions to such officers and employees of the Department as he may designate, and may authorize such successive redelegations of such functions within the Department as he may deem to be necessary or appropriate.

42 USC 7252.

REORGANIZATION

Sec. 643. The Secretary is authorized to establish, alter, consolidate or discontinue such organizational units or components within the Department as he may deem to be necessary or appropriate. Such authority shall not extend to the abolition of organizational units or components established by this Act, or to the transfer of functions vested by this Act in any organizational unit or component.

42 USC 7253.

RULES

Sec. 644. The Secretary is authorized to prescribe such procedural and administrative rules and regulations as he may deem necessary or appropriate to administer and manage the functions now or hereafter vested in him.

42 USC 7254.

SUBPENA

Sec. 645. For the purpose of carrying out the provisions of this Act, the Secretary, or his duly authorized agent or agents, shall have the same powers and authorities as the Federal Trade Commission under section 9 of the Federal Trade Commission Act with respect to all functions vested in, or transferred or delegated to, the Secretary or such agents by this Act.

42 USC 7255.

15 USC 49.

CONTRACTS

Sec. 646. (a) The Secretary is authorized to enter into and perform such contracts, leases, cooperative agreements, or other similar transactions with public agencies and private organizations and persons, and to make such payments (in lump sum or installments, and by way of advance or reimbursement) as he may deem to be necessary or appropriate to carry out functions now or hereafter vested in the Secretary.

42 USC 7256.

(b) Notwithstanding any other provision of this title, no authority to enter into contracts or to make payments under this title shall be effective except to such extent or in such amounts as are provided in advance in appropriation Acts.

ACQUISITION AND MAINTENANCE OF PROPERTY

Sec. 647. The Secretary is authorized to acquire (by purchase, lease, condemnation, or otherwise), construct, improve, repair, operate, and maintain laboratories, research and testing sites and facilities, quarters and related accommodations for employees and dependents of employees of the Department, personal property (including patents), or any interest therein, as the Secretary deems necessary; and to provide by contract or otherwise for eating facilities and other necessary facilities for the health and welfare of employees of the Department at its installations and purchase and maintain equipment therefor.

42 USC 7257.

FACILITIES CONSTRUCTION

42 USC 7258.

Sec. 648. (a) As necessary and when not otherwise available, the Secretary is authorized to provide for, construct, or maintain the following for employees and their dependents stationed at remote locations:

(1) Emergency medical services and supplies;

(2) Food and other subsistence supplies;

(3) Messing facilities;

(4) Audio-visual equipment, accessories, and supplies for recreation and training;

Reimbursement.

(5) Reimbursement for food, clothing, medicine, and other supplies furnished by such employees in emergencies for the temporary relief of distressed persons;

(6) Living and working quarters and facilities; and

Educational transportation.
Reasonable prices.

(7) Transportation of schoolage dependents of employees to the nearest appropriate educational facilities.

(b) The furnishing of medical treatment under paragraph (1) of subsection (a) and the furnishing of services and supplies under paragraphs (2) and (3) of subsection (a) shall be at prices reflecting reasonable value as determined by the Secretary.

Reimbursement proceeds, use.

(c) Proceeds from reimbursements under this section shall be deposited in the Treasury and may be withdrawn by the Secretary to pay directly the cost of such work or services, to repay or make advances to appropriations of funds which will initially bear all or a part of such cost, or to refund excess sums when necessary. Such payments may be credited to a working capital fund otherwise established by law, including the fund established pursuant to section 653 of this Act, and used under the law governing such fund, if the fund is available for use by the Department for performing the work or services for which payment is received.

USE OF FACILITIES

U.S. and foreign government facilities.
42 USC 7259.

Sec. 649. (a) With their consent, the Secretary and the Federal Energy Regulatory Commission may, with or without reimbursement, use the research, equipment, and facilities of any agency or instrumentality of the United States or of any State, the District of Columbia, the Commonwealth of Puerto Rico, or any territory or possession of the United States, or of any political subdivision thereof, or of any foreign government, in carrying out any function now or hereafter vested in the Secretary or the Commission.

(b) In carrying out his functions, the Secretary, under such terms, at such rates, and for such periods not exceeding five years, as he may deem to be in the public interest, is authorized to permit the use by public and private agencies, corporations, associations, or other organizations or by individuals of any real property, or any facility, structure, or other improvement thereon, under the custody of the Secretary for Department purposes. The Secretary may require permittees under this section to recondition and maintain, at their own expense, the real property, facilities, structures, and improvements involved to a satisfactory standard. This section shall not apply to excess property as defined in 3(e) of the Federal Property and Administrative Services Act of 1949.

40 USC 472.
Reimbursement proceeds, use.

(c) Proceeds from reimbursements under this section shall be deposited in the Treasury and may be withdrawn by the Secretary or the head of the agency or instrumentality of the United States involved, as the case may be, to pay directly the costs of the equipment, or facilities provided, to repay or make advances to appropriations or funds which do or will initially bear all or a part of such costs, or to refund excess sums when necessary, except that such proceeds may be credited to a working capital fund otherwise established by law, including the fund established pursuant to section 653 of this Act, and used under the law governing such fund, if the fund is available for use for providing the equipment or facilities involved.

FIELD OFFICES

SEC. 650. The Secretary is authorized to establish, alter, consolidate or discontinue and to maintain such State, regional, district, local or other field offices as he may deem to be necessary to carry out functions vested in him.

42 USC 7260.

COPYRIGHTS

SEC. 651. The Secretary is authorized to acquire any of the following described rights if the property acquired thereby is for use by or for, or useful to, the Department:

42 USC 7261.

    (1) copyrights, patents, and applications for patents, designs, processes, and manufacturing data;

    (2) licenses under copyrights, patents, and applications for patents; and

    (3) releases, before suit is brought, for past infringement of patents or copyrights.

GIFTS AND BEQUESTS

SEC. 652. The Secretary is authorized to accept, hold, administer, and utilize gifts, bequests, and devises of property, both real and personal, for the purpose of aiding or facilitating the work of the Department. Gifts, bequests, and devises of money and proceeds from sales of other property received as gifts, bequests, or devises shall be deposited in the Treasury and shall be disbursed upon the order of the Secretary. Property accepted pursuant to this section, and the proceeds thereof, shall be used as nearly as possible in accordance with the terms of the gift, bequest, or devise. For the purposes of Federal income, estate, and gift taxes, property accepted under this section shall be considered as a gift, bequest, or devise to the United States.

42 USC 7262.

CAPITAL FUND

SEC. 653. The Secretary is authorized to establish a working capital fund, to be available without fiscal year limitation, for expenses necessary for the maintenance and operation of such common administrative services as he shall find to be desirable in the interests of economy and efficiency, including such services as a central supply service for stationery and other supplies and equipment for which adequate stocks may be maintained to meet in whole or in part the requirements of the Department and its agencies; central messenger, mail, telephone, and other communications services; office space, central services for document reproduction, and for graphics and visual aids; and a central library service. The capital of the fund shall consist of any appropriations made for the purpose of providing capital (which appropriations are hereby authorized) and the fair and reasonable value of such stocks

Establishment.
42 USC 7263.

Contents.

of supplies, equipment, and other assets and inventories on order as the Secretary may transfer to the fund, less the related liabilities and unpaid obligations. Such funds shall be reimbursed in advance from available funds of agencies and offices in the Department, or from other sources, for supplies and services at rates which will approximate the expense of operation, including the accrual of annual leave and the depreciation of equipment. The fund shall also be credited with receipts from sale or exchange of property and receipts in payment for loss or damage to property owned by the fund. There shall be covered into the United States Treasury as miscellaneous receipts any surplus found in the fund (all assets, liabilities, and prior losses considered) above the amounts transferred or appropriated to establish and maintain said fund. There shall be transferred to the fund the stocks of supplies, equipment, other assets, liabilities, and unpaid obligations relating to the services which he determines will be performed through the fund. Appropriations to the fund, in such amounts as may be necessary to provide additional working capital, are authorized.

Transfers.

SEAL OF DEPARTMENT

42 USC 7264.

SEC. 654. The Secretary shall cause a seal of office to be made for the Department of such design as he shall approve and judicial notice shall be taken of such seal.

REGIONAL ENERGY ADVISORY BOARDS

Establishment.
42 USC 7265.

SEC. 655. (a) The Governors of the various States may establish Regional Energy Advisory Boards for their regions with such membership as they may determine.

Observers.

(b) Representatives of the Secretary, the Secretary of Commerce, the Secretary of the Interior, the Chairman of the Council on Environmental Quality, the Commandant of the Coast Guard and the Administrator of the Environmental Protection Agency shall be entitled to participate as observers in the deliberations of any Board established pursuant to subsection (a) of this section. The Federal Cochairman of the Appalachian Regional Commission or any regional commission under title V of the Public Works and Economic Development Act shall be entitled to participate as an observer in the deliberations of any such Board which contains one or more States which are members of such Commission.

42 USC 3181.

Recommendations.

(c) Each Board established pursuant to subsection (a) may make such recommendations as it determines to be appropriate to programs of the Department having a direct effect on the region.

(d) If any Regional Advisory Board makes specific recommendations pursuant to subsection (c). the Secretary shall, if such recommendations are not adopted in the implementation of the program, notify the Board in writing of his reasons for not adopting such recommendations.

DESIGNATION OF CONSERVATION OFFICERS

42 USC 7266.

SEC. 656. The Secretary of Defense, the Secretary of Commerce, the Secretary of Housing and Urban Development, the Secretary of Transportation, the Secretary of Agriculture, the Secretary of the Interior, the United States Postal Service, and the Administrator of General Services shall each designate one Assistant Secretary or

Assistant Administrator, as the case may be, as the principal conservation officer of such Department or of the Administration. Such designated principal conservation officer shall be principally responsible for planning and implementation of energy conservation programs by such Department or Administration and principally responsible for coordination with the Department of Energy with respect to energy matters. Each agency, Department or Administration required to designate a principal conservation officer pursuant to this section shall periodically inform the Secretary of the identity of such conservation officer, and the Secretary shall periodically publish a list identifying such officers.

List, publication.

ANNUAL REPORT

SEC. 657. The Secretary shall, as soon as practicable after the end of each fiscal year, commencing with the first complete fiscal year following the effective date of this Act, make a report to the President for submission to the Congress on the activities of the Department during the preceding fiscal year. Such report shall include a statement of the Secretary's goals, priorities, and plans for the Department, together with an assessment of the progress made toward the attainment of those goals, the effective and efficient management of the Department, and progress made in coordination of its functions with other departments and agencies of the Federal Government. In addition, such report shall include the information required by section 15 of the Federal Energy Administration Act of 1974, section 307 of the Energy Reorganization Act of 1974, and section 15 of the Federal Nonnuclear Energy Research and Development Act of 1974, and shall include:

Report to President for transmittal to Congress.
42 USC 7267.,
Contents.

15 USC 774.
42 USC 5877.
42 USC 5914.

(1) projected energy needs of the United States to meet the requirements of the general welfare of the people of the United States and the commercial and industrial life of the Nation, including a comprehensive summary of data pertaining to all fuel and energy needs of residents of the United States residing in—

Energy needs.

(A) areas outside standard metropolitan statistical areas; and

(B) areas within such areas which are unincorporated or are specified by the Bureau of the Census, Department of Commerce, as rural areas;

(2) an estimate of (A) the domestic and foreign energy supply on which the United States will be expected to rely to meet such needs in an economic manner with due regard for the protection of the environment, the conservation of natural resources, and the implementation of foreign policy objectives, and (B) the quantities of energy expected to be provided by different sources (including petroleum, natural and synthetic gases, coal, uranium, hydroelectric, solar, and other means) and the expected means of obtaining such quantities;

Energy supply.

(3) current and foreseeable trends in the price, quality, management, and utilization of energy resources and the effects of those trends on the social, environmental, economic, and other requirements of the Nation;

Trends.

(4) a summary of research and development efforts funded by the Federal Government to develop new technologies, to forestall energy shortages, to reduce waste, to foster recycling, to encour-

Research and Development.

age conservation practices, and to increase efficiency; and further such summary shall include a description of the activities the Department is performing in support of environmental, social, economic and institutional, biomedical, physical and safety research, development, demonstration, and monitoring activities necessary to guarantee that technological programs, funded by the Department, are undertaken in a manner consistent with and capable of maintaining or improving the quality of the environment and of mitigating any undesirable environmental and safety impacts;

(5) a review and appraisal of the adequacy and appropriateness of technologies, procedures, and practices (including competitive and regulatory practices) employed by Federal/State, and local governments and nongovernmental entities to achieve the purposes of this Act;

Recommendations.

(6) a summary of cooperative and voluntary efforts that have been mobilized to promote conservation and recycling, together with plans for such efforts in the succeeding fiscal year, and recommendations for changes in laws and regulations needed to encourage more conservation and recycling by all segments of the Nation's populace;

(7) a summary of substantive measures taken by the Department to stimulate and encourage the development of new manpower resources through the Nation's colleges and universities and to involve these institutions in the execution of the Department's research and development programs; and

Foreign entities operating in the U.S., activity summary.

(8) to the extent practicable, a summary of activities in the United States by companies or persons which are foreign owned or controlled and which own or control United States energy sources and supplies, including the magnitude of annual foreign direct investment in the energy sector in the United States and exports of energy resources from the United States by foreign owned or controlled business entities or persons, and such other related matters as the Secretary may deem appropriate.

LEASING REPORT

Submittal to Congress.
42 USC 7268.

SEC. 658. The Secretary of the Interior shall submit to the Congress not later than one year after the date of enactment of this Act, a report on the organization of the leasing operations of the Federal Government, together with any recommendations for reorganizing such functions may deem necessary or appropriate.

TRANSFER OF FUNDS

42 USC 7269.

SEC. 659. The Secretary, when authorized in an appropriation Act, in any fiscal year, may transfer funds from one appropriation to another within the Department, except that no appropriation shall be either increased or decreased pursuant to this section by more than 5 per centum of the appropriation for such fiscal year.

AUTHORIZATION OF APPROPRIATIONS

42 USC 7270.

SEC. 660. Appropriations to carry out the provisions of this Act shall be subject to annual authorization.

TITLE VII—TRANSITIONAL, SAVINGS, AND CONFORMING PROVISIONS

TRANSFER AND ALLOCATIONS OF APPROPRIATIONS AND PERSONNEL

SEC. 701. (a) Except as otherwise provided in this Act, the personnel employed in connection with, and the assets, liabilities, contracts, property, records, and unexpended balance of appropriations authorizations, allocations, and other funds employed, held, used, arising from, available to or to be made available in connection with the functions transferred by this Act, subject to section 202 of the Budget and Accounting Procedure Act of 1950, are hereby transferred to the Secretary for appropriate allocation. Unexpended funds transferred pursuant to this subsection shall only be used for the purposes for which the funds were originally authorized and appropriated.

42 USC 7291.

31 USC 581c.

(b) Positions expressly specified by statute or reorganization plan to carry out function transferred by this Act, personnel occupying those positions on the effective date of this Act, and personnel authorized to receive compensation in such positions at the rate prescribed for offices and positions at level I, II, III, IV, or V of the executive schedule (5 U.S.C. 5312–5316) on the effective date of this Act, shall be subject to the provisions of section 703 of this Act.

EFFECT ON PERSONNEL

SEC. 702. (a) Except as otherwise provided in this Act, the transfer pursuant to this title of full-time personnel (except special Government employees) and part-time personnel holding permanent positions pursuant to this title shall not cause any such employee to be separated or reduced in grade or compensation for one year after the date of enactment of this Act, except that full-time temporary personnel employed at the Energy Research Centers of the Energy Research and Development Administration upon the establishment of the Department who are determined by the Department to be performing continuing functions may at the employee's option be converted to permanent full-time status within one hundred and twenty days following their transfer to the Department. The employment levels of full-time permanent personnel authorized for the Department by other law or administrative action shall be increased by the number of employees who exercise the option to be so converted.

42 USC 7292.

(b) Any person who, on the effective date of this Act, held a position compensated in accordance with the Executive Schedule prescribed in chapter 53 of title 5, United States Code, and who, without a break in service, is appointed in the Department to a position having duties comparable to those performed immediately preceding his appointment shall continue to be compensated in his new position at not less than the rate provided for his previous position, for the duration of his service in the new position.

5 USC 5301.

(c) Employees transferred to the Department holding reemployment rights acquired under section 28 of the Federal Energy Administration Act of 1974 or any other provision of law or regulation may exercise such rights only within one hundred twenty days from the effective date of this Act or within two years of acquiring such rights, whichever is later. Reemployment rights may only be exercised at the request of the employee.

15 USC 786.

AGENCY TERMINATIONS

42 USC 7293.   SEC. 703. Except as otherwise provided in this Act, whenever all of the functions vested by law in any agency, commission, or other body, or any component thereof, have been terminated or transferred from that agency, commission, or other body, or component by this Act, the agency, commission, or other body, or component, shall terminate. If an agency, commission, or other body, or any component thereof, terminates pursuant to the preceding sentence, each position and office therein which was expressly authorized by law, or the incumbent of which was authorized to receive compensation at the rates prescribed for an office or position at level II, III, IV, or V of the Executive Schedule (5 U.S.C. 5313–5316), shall terminate.

INCIDENTAL TRANSFERS

42 USC 7294.   SEC. 704. The Director of the Office of Management and Budget, in consultation with the Secretary and the Commission, is authorized and directed to make such determinations as may be necessary with regard to the transfer of functions which relate to or are utilized by an agency, commission or other body, or component thereof affected by this Act, to make such additional incidental dispositions of personnel, assets, liabilities, contracts, property, records, and unexpended balances of appropriations, authorizations, allocations, and other funds held, used, arising from, available to or to be made available in connection with the functions transferred by this Act, as he may deem necessary to accomplish the purposes of this Act.

SAVINGS PROVISIONS

42 USC 7295.   SEC. 705. (a) All orders, determinations, rules, regulations, permits, contracts, certificates, licenses, and privileges—

(1) which have been issued, made, granted, or allowed to become effective by the President, any Federal department or agency or official thereof, or by a court of competent jurisdiction, in the performance of functions which are transferred under this Act to the Department or the Commission after the date of enactment of this Act, and

(2) which are in effect at the time this Act takes effect,

shall continue in effect according to their terms until modified, terminated, superseded, set aside, or revoked in accordance with law by the President, the Secretary, the Federal Energy Regulatory Commission, or other authorized officials, a court of competent jurisdiction, or by operation of law.

(b)(1) The provisions of this Act shall not affect any proceedings or any application for any license, permit, certificate, or financial assistance pending at the time this Act takes effect before any department, agency, commission, or component thereof, functions of which are transferred by this Act; but such proceedings and applications, to the extent that they relate to functions so transferred, shall be continued. Orders shall be issued in such proceedings, appeals shall be taken therefrom, and payments shall be made pursuant to such orders, as if this Act had not been enacted; and orders issued in any such proceedings shall continue in effect until modified, terminated, superseded, or revoked by a duly authorized official, by a court of competent jurisdiction, or by operation of law. Nothing in this subsection shall be deemed to prohibit the discontinuance or modification of any such proceeding under the same terms and conditions and to the same extent that such proceeding could have been discontinued or modified if this Act had not been enacted.

(2) The Secretary and the Commission are authorized to promulgate regulations providing for the orderly transfer of such proceedings to the Department or the Commission.

Regulations.

(c) Except as provided in subsection (e)—

(1) the provisions of this Act shall not affect suits commenced prior to the date this Act takes effect, and,

(2) in all such suits, proceedings shall be had, appeals taken, and judgments rendered in the same manner and effect as if this Act had not been enacted.

(d) No suit, action, or other proceeding commenced by or against any officer in his official capacity as an officer of any department or agency, functions of which are transferred by this Act, shall abate by reason of the enactment of this Act. No cause of action by or against any department or agency, functions of which are transferred by this Act, or by or against any officer thereof in his official capacity shall abate by reason of the enactment of this Act.

(e) If, before the date on which this Act takes effect, any department or agency, or officer thereof in his official capacity, is a party to a suit, and under this Act any function of such department, agency, or officer is transferred to the Secretary or any other official, then such suit shall be continued with the Secretary or other official, as the case may be, substituted.

SEPARABILITY

SEC. 706. If any provision of this Act or the application thereof to any person or circumstance is held invalid, neither the remainder of this Act nor the application of such provision to other persons or circumstances shall be affected thereby.

42 USC 7296.

REFERENCE

SEC. 707. With respect to any functions transferred by this Act and exercised after the effective date of this Act, reference in any other Federal law to any department, commission, or agency or any officer or office the functions of which are so transferred shall be deemed to refer to the Secretary, the Federal Energy Regulatory Commission, or other official or component of the Department in which this Act vests such functions.

42 USC 7297.

PRESIDENTIAL AUTHORITY

SEC. 708. Except as provided in title IV, nothing contained in this Act shall be construed to limit, curtail, abolish, or terminate any function of, or authority available to, the President which he had immediately before the effective date of this Act; or to limit, curtail, abolish, or terminate his authority to delegate, redelegate, or terminate any delegation of functions.

42 USC 7298.

AMENDMENTS

SEC. 709. (a) The Federal Energy Administration Act of 1974 is amended:

(1) by repealing sections 4, 9, 28, and 30;

(2) in section 7—

(A) by striking out subsections (a) and (b) and redesignating subsection (c) as subsection (a);

15 USC 761 note.
Repeals.
15 USC 763, 768, 786, 761 note.
15 USC 766.

(B) by striking out subsections (d), (e), (f), (g), and (h);

(C) by striking out "(i)(1)" and by striking out subparagraphs (A), (B), (C), (E), and (F) of subsection (i)(1) and redesignating subparagraph (D) of such subsection as subsection (b);

(D) by striking out, in the matter redesignated as subsection (b), "the rules, regulations, or orders described in paragraph (A)" and inserting in lieu thereof "any rule or regulation, or any order having the applicability and effect of a rule as defined in section 551(4) of title 5, United States Code, pursuant to this Act";

(E) by striking out, in such subsection, "paragraph (2) of this subsection" and inserting in lieu thereof "subsection (c)";

(F) by redesignating paragraph (2)(A) of subsection (i) as subsection (c) and by striking out subparagraph (B) of subsection (i)(2); and

(G) by striking out paragraph (3) of subsection (i) and by striking out subsections (j) and (k);

15 USC 790a. (3) in section 52(a)—

(A) by striking out "and" at the end of paragraph (2);

(B) by striking out the period at the end of paragraph (3) and inserting in lieu thereof "; and"; and

(C) by adding after such paragraph (3) the following new paragraph:

15 USC 717w.
16 USC 791a. "(4) the States to the extent required by the Natural Gas Act and the Federal Power Act."; and

15 USC 790d. (4) in section 55(b)—

(A) by striking out "seven" and inserting in lieu thereof "six";

(B) by inserting "and" after "Federal Trade Commission:"; and

(C) by striking out "one shall be designated by the Chairman of the Federal Power Commission; and".

Repeal.
42 USC 5818. (b) The Energy Reorganization Act of 1974 is amended by repealing section 108.

Repeal.
42 USC 2036. (c)(1) The Atomic Energy Act of 1954 is amended by repealing section 26.

42 USC 2201 note. (2) Section 161(d) of the Atomic Energy Act of 1954 shall not apply to functions transferred by this Act.

12 USC 1701z–8. (d) In section 509 (c)(6) and (e) of title 5 of the Housing and Urban Development Act of 1970, add "the Secretary of Housing and Urban Development." to those individuals and agencies with whom the Secretary of the Department of Energy must consult.

(e) The Energy Conservation Standards for New Buildings Act of 1976 is amended as follows:

42 USC 6833. (1) in section 304(c), by inserting "the Secretary of Housing and Urban Development," after "the Administrator,"; and

42 USC 6839. (2) in section 310, by inserting "Secretary of Housing and Urban Development," after "the Administrator,".

Loans, criteria. (f) The Rural Electrification Act of 1936 is amended by adding a new section 16 to title I thereof to read as follows:

7 USC 916. "SEC. 16. In order to insure coordination of electric generation and transmission financing under this Act with the national energy policy, the Administrator in making or guaranteeing loans for the construction, operation, or enlargement of generating plants or electric transmission lines or systems, shall consider such general criteria consistent with the provisions of this Act as may be published by the Secretary of Energy.".

(g) Section 19(d)(1) of title 3, United States Code, is amended by inserting immediately before the period at the end thereof the following: ", Secretary of Energy".

ADMINISTRATIVE AMENDMENTS

Sec. 710. (a) Section 101 of title 5, United States Code is amended by adding at the end thereof the following:

"The Department of Energy.".

(b) Subsection (a) of section 5108 of title 5, United States Code, is amended by striking out "an aggregate of 2,754" and inserting in lieu thereof "an aggregate of 3,243".

(c) Section 5312 of title 5, United States Code, is amended by adding at the end thereof the following:

"(14) Secretary of Energy.".

(d) Paragraph (22) of section 5313 of title 5, United States Code, is amended to read as follows:

"(22) Deputy Secretary of Energy.".

(e) Section 5314 of title 5, United States Code, is amended by striking out, in paragraph (21), "Federal Power Commission" and by inserting in lieu thereof "Federal Energy Regulatory Commission", and by amending paragraph (60) to read as follows:

"(60) Under Secretary, Department of Energy".

(f) Section 5315 of title 5, United States Code, is amended by striking out, in paragraph (60), "Federal Power Commission" and inserting in lieu thereof "Federal Energy Regulatory Commission", by striking out paragraph 102, and by adding at the end of the section the following:

"(114) Assistant Secretaries of Energy (8).

"(115) General Counsel of the Department of Energy.

"(116) Administrator, Economic Regulatory Administration, Department of Energy.

"(117) Administrator, Energy Information Administration, Department of Energy.

"(118) Inspector General, Department of Energy.

"(119) Director, Office of Energy Research, Department of Energy.".

(g) Paragraphs (135) and (136) of section 5316 of title 5, United States Code, are amended to read as follows:

"(135) Deputy Inspector General, Department of Energy.

"(136) Additional Officers, Department of Energy (14).".

TRANSITION

Sec. 711. With the consent of the appropriate department or agency head concerned, the Secretary is authorized to utilize the services of such officers, employees, and other personnel of the departments and agencies from which functions have been transferred to the Secretary for such period of time as may reasonably be needed to facilitate the orderly transfer of functions under this Act.

42 USC 7299.

CIVIL SERVICE COMMISSION REPORT

Sec. 712. The Civil Service Commission shall, as soon as practicable but not later than one year after the effective date of this Act, prepare

Transmittal to Congress.
42 USC 7300.

and transmit to the Congress a report on the effects on employees of the reorganization under this Act, which shall include—

(1) an identification of any position within the Department or elsewhere in the executive branch, which it considers unnecessary due to consolidation of functions under this Act;

(2) a statement of the number of employees entitled to pay savings by reason of the reorganization under this Act;

(3) a statement of the number of employees who are voluntarily or involuntarily separated by reason of such reorganization;

(4) an estimate of the personnel costs associated with such reorganization;

(5) the effects of such reorganization on labor management relations; and

(6) such legislative and administrative recommendations for improvements in personnel management within the Department as the Commission considers necessary.

ENVIRONMENTAL IMPACT STATEMENTS

SEC. 713. The transfer of functions under titles III and IV of this Act shall not affect the validity of any draft environmental impact statement published before the effective date of this Act.

TITLE VIII—ENERGY PLANNING

NATIONAL ENERGY POLICY PLAN

SEC. 801. (a) The President shall—

(1) prepare and submit to the Congress a proposed National Energy Policy Plan (hereinafter in this title referred to as a "proposed Plan") as provided in subsection (b);

(2) seek the active participation by regional, State, and local agencies and instrumentalities and the private sector through public hearings in cities and rural communities and other appropriate means to insure that the views and proposals of all segments of the economy are taken into account in the formulation and review of such proposed Plan;

(3) include within the proposed Plan a comprehensive summary of data pertaining to all fuel and energy needs of persons residing in—

(A) areas outside standard metropolitan statistical areas; and

(B) areas within standard metropolitan statistical areas which are unincorporated or are specified by the Bureau of the Census, Department of Commerce, as rural areas.

(b) Not later than April 1, 1979, and biennially thereafter, the President shall transmit to the Congress the proposed Plan. Such proposed Plan shall—

(1) consider and establish energy production, utilization, and conservation objectives, for periods of five and ten years, necessary to satisfy projected energy needs of the United States to meet the requirements of the general welfare of the people of the United States and the commercial and industrial life of the Nation, paying particular attention to the needs for full employment, price stability, energy security, economic growth, environmental protection, nuclear non-proliferation, special regional needs, and the efficient utilization of public and private resources;

(2) identify the strategies that should be followed and the resources that should be committed to achieve such objectives, forecasting the level of production and investment necessary in each of the significant energy supply sectors and the level of conservation and investment necessary in each consuming sector, and outlining the appropriate policies and actions of the Federal Government that will maximize the private production and investment necessary in each of the significant energy supply sector; consistent with applicable Federal, State, and local environmental laws, standards, and requirements; and

(3) recommend legislative and administrative actions necessary and desirable to achieve the objectives of such proposed Plan, including legislative recommendations with respect to taxes or tax incentives, Federal funding, regulatory actions, antitrust policy, foreign policy, and international trade.

(c) The President shall submit to the Congress with the proposed Plan a report which shall include— **Report to Congress.**

(1) whatever data and analysis are necessary to support the objectives, resource needs, and policy recommendations contained in such proposed Plan;

(2) an estimate of the domestic and foreign energy supplies on which the United States will be expected to rely to meet projected energy needs in an economic manner consistent with the need to protect the environment, conserve natural resources, and implement foreign policy objectives;

(3) an evaluation of current and foreseeable trends in the price, quality, management, and utilization of energy resources and the effects of those trends on the social, environmental, economic, and other requirements of the Nation;

(4) a summary of research and development efforts funded by the Federal Government to forestall energy shortages, to reduce waste, to foster recycling, to encourage conservation practices, and to otherwise protect environmental quality, including recommendations for developing technologies to accomplish such purposes; and

(5) a review and appraisal of the adequacy and appropriateness of technologies, procedures, and practices (including competitive and regulatory practices) employed by Federal, State, and local governments and nongovernmental entities to achieve the purposes of the Plan.

(d) The President shall insure that consumers, small businesses, and a wide range of other interests, including those of individual citizens who have no financial interest in the energy industry, are consulted in the development of the Plan. **Consultation.**

CONGRESSIONAL REVIEW

SEC. 802. (a) Each proposed Plan shall be referred to the appropriate committees in the Senate and the House of Representatives.

(b) Each such committee shall review the proposed Plan and, if it deems appropriate and necessary, report to the Senate or the House of Representatives legislation regarding such Plan which may contain such alternatives to, modifications of, or additions to the proposed Plan submitted by the President as the committee deems appropriate.

Plan, referral to congressional committees. 42 USC 7322. Report to Congress.

TITLE IX—EFFECTIVE DATE AND INTERIM APPOINTMENTS

EFFECTIVE DATE

Publication in Federal Register. Regulations. 42 USC 7341.

SEC. 901. The provisions of this Act shall take effect one hundred and twenty days after the Secretary first takes office, or on such earlier date as the President may prescribe and publish in the Federal Register, except that at any time after the date of enactment of this Act, (1) any of the officers provided for in title II and title IV of this Act may be nominated and appointed, as provided in those titles, and (2) the Secretary and the Commission may promulgate regulations pursuant to section 705(b)(2) of this Act at any time after the date of enactment of this Act. Funds available to any department or agency (or any official or component thereof), functions of which are transferred to the Secretary or the Commission by this Act, may with the approval of the Director of the Office of Management and Budget, be used to pay the compensation and expenses of any officer appointed pursuant to this subsection until such time as funds for that purpose are otherwise available.

INTERIM APPOINTMENTS

42 USC 7342.

SEC. 902. In the event that one or more officers required by this Act to be appointed by and with the advice and consent of the Senate shall not have entered upon office on the effective date of this Act, the President may designate any officer, whose appointment was required to be made, by and with the advice and consent of the Senate, and who was such an officer immediately prior to the effective date of the Act, to act in such office until the office is filled as provided in this Act. While so acting such persons shall receive compensation at the rates provided by this Act for the respective offices in which they act.

TITLE X—SUNSET PROVISIONS

SUBMISSION OF COMPREHENSIVE REVIEW

Submittal to Congress. 42 USC 7351.

SEC. 1001. Not later than January 15, 1982, the President shall prepare and submit to the Congress a comprehensive review of each program of the Department. Each such review shall be made available to the committee or committees of the Senate and House of Representatives having jurisdiction with respect to the annual authorization of funds, pursuant to section 660, for such programs for the fiscal year beginning October 1, 1982.

CONTENTS OF REVIEW

42 USC 7352.

SEC. 1002. Each comprehensive review prepared for submission under section 1001 shall include—

(1) the name of the component of the Department responsible for administering the program;

(2) an identification of the objectives intended for the program and the problem or need which the program was intended to address;

(3) an identification of any other programs having similar or potentially conflicting or duplicative objectives;

(4) an assessment of alternative methods of achieving the purposes of the program;

(5) a justification for the authorization of new budget authority, and an explanation of the manner in which it conforms to and integrates with other efforts;

(6) an assessment of the degree to which the original objectives of the program have been achieved, expressed in terms of the performance, impact, or accomplishments of the program and of the problem or need which it was intended to address, and employing the procedures or methods of analysis appropriate to the type or character of the program;

(7) a statement of the performance and accomplishments of the program in each of the previous four completed fiscal years and of the budgetary costs incurred in the operation of the program;

(8) a statement of the number and types of beneficiaries or persons served by the program;

(9) an assessment of the effect of the program on the national economy, including, but not limited to, the effects on competition, economic stability, employment, unemployment, productivity, and price inflation, including costs to consumers and to businesses;

(10) an assessment of the impact of the program on the Nation's health and safety;

(11) an assessment of the degree to which the overall administration of the program, as expressed in the rules, regulations, orders, standards, criteria, and decisions of the officers executing the program, are believed to meet the objectives of the Congress in establishing the program;

(12) a projection of the anticipated needs for accomplishing the objectives of the program, including an estimate if applicable of the date on which, and the conditions under which, the program may fulfill such objectives;

(13) an analysis of the services which could be provided and performance which could be achieved if the program were continued at a level less than, equal to, or greater than the existing level; and

(14) recommendations for necessary transitional requirements in the event that funding for such program is discontinued, including proposals for such executives or legislative action as may be necessary to prevent such discontinuation from being unduly disruptive.

Approved August 4, 1977.

LEGISLATIVE HISTORY:

HOUSE REPORTS: No. 95-346, pt. I (Comm. on Government Operations) and No. 95-346, pt. II (Comm. on Post Office and Civil Service), both parts accompanying H.R. 6804, and 95-539 (Comm. of Conference).

SENATE REPORTS: No. 95-164 (Comm. on Governmental Affairs) and No. 95-367 (Comm. of Conference).

CONGRESSIONAL RECORD, Vol. 123 (1977):
    May 18, considered and passed Senate.
    June 2, H.R. 6804 considered in House.
    June 3, considered and passed House, amended, in lieu of H.R. 6804.
    Aug. 2, House and Senate agreed to conference report.

WEEKLY COMPILATION OF PRESIDENTIAL DOCUMENTS, Vol. 13, No. 32:
    Aug. 4, Presidential statement.

APPENDIX C

ENERGY:
ISSUES FACING THE 95TH CONGRESS*

* General Accounting Office, April 1977

Chapter 1

Introduction

During the recent Presidential campaign, President Carter raised a number of issues regarding the Nation's energy policies and promised some new initiatives and legislation during the 95th Congress. Some of the issues raised during the campaign included:

- The priority that should be given to conservation and advanced energy supply technologies, such as solar energy.

- The pace and timing for expanding the use of nuclear fission, including questions about the nonproliferation of nuclear weapons from peaceful uses of atomic energy.

- The need to reorganize the Federal energy agencies.

- The possible need to decontrol domestic crude oil and natural gas prices.

- The possibility of expanding the use of coal consistent with solving any environmental and socioeconomic problems.

- The role the Liquid Metal Fast Breeder Reactor (LMFBR) and synthetic fuels from coal play in meeting energy needs.

Because of possible new initiatives by the Carter Administration, the Chairman, Subcommittee on Energy and Power, House Committee on Interstate and Foreign Commerce, asked us to assess current major energy programs. He said that the Subcommittee needed such an assessment to respond effectively to new initiatives as well as develop alternatives of its own.

This report provides our assessment of the major energy issues and problems facing the 95th Congress and the major energy agencies based on our past efforts during the 94th Congress. Because this report discusses the major issues as they apply to each major energy agency, it will serve to augment the previous report and hopefully will aid the Congress in setting priorities for reviewing each agency's programs and in formulating energy policy.

Over $11 billion will be spent in fiscal year 1977 on Federal energy programs. Currently, five executive agencies are responsible for carrying out the majority of these programs.

- Federal Energy Administration (FEA)
- Department of the Interior
- Federal Power Commission (FPC)
- Nuclear Regulatory Commission (NRC)
- Energy Research and Development Administration (ERDA)

In addition, other Federal agencies—such as the Departments of Commerce and Housing and Urban Development, General Services Administration, and the Tennessee Valley Authority—either have their own internal energy-related programs or have an interagency agreement with one of the five major agencies to carry out their programs. For example, the National Aeronautics and Space Administration carries out part of ERDA's solar energy research and development program.

Also, there were several programs recently enacted by the 94th Congress and other proposals which would substantially expand the activities and the cost of the Federal energy effort. These include:

- The Energy Conservation and Production Act (Public Law 94-385), which established a number of new programs with authorized funding of about $360 million. Included was a program for obligation guarantees of up to $2 billion to encourage energy conservation measures and renewable resource energy measures in private, State, and local buildings and industrial plants.

- The Energy Policy and Conservation Act (Public Law 94-163), which established a number of new programs, including the Strategic Petroleum Reserve which has an estimated Federal cost of $8 to $20 billion, and a $750 million loan guarantee program to develop new underground coal mines.

- The Federal Coal Leasing Amendments Act (Public Law 94-377), which established new policies for leasing coal on Federal lands.

- The Naval Petroleum Reserves Production Act of 1976 (Public Law 94-258), which opened some of these reserves for production and sale on the open market.

- The recently proposed Surface Mining Control and Reclamation Act of 1977 (H.R. 2 and S. 7) which, if passed, will establish strong environmental controls over surface mining and will provide for reclamation of previously mined land.

- Recently proposed amendments to the Outer Continental Shelf Lands Act (S. 9 and H.R. 1614), which would significantly alter the present system of leasing oil and gas resources on the Outer Continental Shelf.

- The proposed Energy Independence Authority (S. 2532 and H.R. 10267-94th Congress) which would administer Federal loan and loan guarantee programs with a potential total of $100 billion.

- The proposed synthetic fuels program (H.R. 12112-94th Congress), which would involve Federal guarantees of obligations estimated to total about $3.5 billion.

- The proposed uranium enrichment program (S. 2035 and H.R. 8401-94th Congress), which would authorize ERDA to contract with private industry to produce enriched uranium and guarantee up to a commitment of $8 billion that uranium enrichment technology supplied by the Government will work.

Some of the programs proposed in the 94th Congress have been reintroduced in the 95th Congress. For example, several bills have been introduced to provide ERDA with broad loan guarantee authority for non-nuclear technologies, including synthetic fuels (e.g., H.R. 36, H.R. 37, H.R. 38, H.R. 1142, S. 37, and S. 429). On the other hand, bills to establish an Energy Independence Authority and to authorize contracts with private industry to produce enriched uranium have not yet been reintroduced. Whether these bills will be introduced in the same form is uncertain.

Over the past 3 to 4 years, the strength of the Organization of Petroleum Exporting Countries (OPEC) has grown starting with the oil embargo by those countries in 1973. As a result, international oil prices have increased by over 400 percent. In that time, the Federal Government has responded to the energy problem in many and varied ways. New regulations have been formulated, new programs initiated, new legislation passed, and many voluminous reports written.

Unfortunately, the short term effects of Federal actions have not been encouraging. The Nation is more dependent upon foreign energy sources today than it was 3 years ago. A longer term assessment of these effects is even more difficult. Certainly the Federal response has not been disciplined by a clearly enunciated and cohesive national energy policy. The effects of the energy shortage and the Nation's growing dependence on foreign sources have again been brought to the forefront by the unusually cold winter of 1977 and natural gas shortages in the eastern and midwestern parts of the country.

Our past efforts during the 94th Congress in the energy area were aimed at evaluating the efficiency and effectiveness of the various energy agencies' operations as well as identifying and assessing the alternative courses of action for solving several critical energy issues.

In addition, the Congress mandated us to evaluate and make recommendations on programs being carried out under the Federal Energy Administration Act of 1974 (Public Law 93-275), the Energy Reorganization Act of 1974 (Public Law 93-438), the Energy Policy and Conservation Act, and the Energy Conservation and Production Act.

Among other things, we are required to (1) evaluate and monitor the operations of the Federal Energy Administration, including its reporting activities, (2) audit, review, and evaluate the activities of NRC and report our findings by January 1980, (3) report annually to Congress on programs carried out under Title IV of the Energy Conservation and Production Act for conserving energy in existing dwelling units, nonresidential buildings, and industrial plants, and (4) participate in establishing a Professional Audit Review Team to annually review the activities of FEA's Office of Energy Information and Analysis.

In addition, Title V of the Energy Policy and Conservation Act required us to conduct energy data verification examinations and report annually to the Congress on the results of our work. The act gave the Comptroller General substantial new authority to conduct such examinations of the books and records of:

(1) companies legally required to submit energy information to FEA, FPC, or Interior; (2) companies engaged in the energy business and who furnish information to any Federal agency which uses the information in carrying out its official functions; and (3) vertically integrated petroleum companies with respect to energy related financial information. In carrying out the authorities of Title V, the Comptroller General is authorized to sign and issue subpoenas, require written answers to interrogatories, administer oaths, enter business premises and facilities to inventory and sample energy resources and examine and copy books and records, and assess and collect penalties.

We have developed the following broad program areas which include the five major agencies' energy programs.

Conservation	Pipeline rights-of-way
Petroleum and natural gas regulatory programs	Outer Continental Shelf
	Public lands
Energy information and analysis	Fossil energy development
Strategic Petroleum Reserve	Nuclear power development
Federal energy organization	Renewable resources development
Electricity	International concerns

Based partly on past work and partly on our continuing assessment of critical national issues, we identified those key energy issues that, in our view, are most in need of attention. The following chapters of this report discuss our assessment of the major issues facing the 95th Congress as they relate to each of the 5 executive energy agencies and the 13 program areas listed above. Each chapter will also discuss our past efforts within each program area and our currently planned work aimed at helping to answer some of these questions and concerns. This report is designed to serve as a reference document to aid the Subcommittee, the Congress, and the public in gaining a better understanding of our energy problems. It should also serve to highlight those areas where congressional actions may be required.

Chapter 2

Federal Energy Administration

The Federal Energy Administration was created as a temporary agency in 1974 by the Federal Energy Administration Act of 1974, primarily to manage short-term fuel shortages using existing allocation and price control authorities. At that time, several energy responsibilities previously existing in the Department of the Interior and the Cost of Living Council were transferred to FEA. Since that time, the Congress has given FEA new and additional program responsibilities in the areas of energy conservation, Strategic Petroleum Reserve, renewable resources, and energy data. FEA's authority was extended through December 1977.

The issues facing FEA in the immediate future fall within four broad areas of FEA's responsibility: conservation, petroleum regulatory programs, energy information and analysis, and Strategic Petroleum Reserve. Our views on the major questions within each of these areas are discussed below. Our past efforts at FEA are discussed on page 690.

Issues Facing The 95th Congress

Conservation

There are basically three kinds of conservation actions:

- Eliminating energy waste through belt-tightening or leakplugging actions. Simple actions include turning down the thermostat and observing the highway speed limits. Complex actions include demand-management approaches, whereby electric utilities can discourage consumers from wasting energy.

- Developing more efficient energy-use systems such as automobile engines and industrial systems.

- Changing lifestyles and living patterns to reduce energy use, yet still achieving the same social and personal objectives. These include living closer to work and using forms of communication which eliminate the need for travel.

During the 1973-74 oil embargo, the Federal Government realized that new domestic energy sources would take at least a decade to develop and started showing genuine interest in energy conservation. To create an economic, social, and political atmosphere that encourages conservation, the Federal Government (1) sets energy performance standards (e.g., for new automobiles and buildings), (2) requires specific reductions in Government energy uses as an example to the Nation, and (3) provides financial incentives for the private sector. FEA is responsible for developing and monitoring the implementation by the Government and private industry of equitable voluntary and mandatory energy conservation programs.

A number of energy conservation programs were enacted in the 94th Congress. These programs raise several questions about the role and impact of energy conservation in a national energy policy. We believe the following questions are most important in assessing that role.

How effective are the conservation programs that have been enacted? Various types of conservation programs were enacted in the Energy Policy and Conservation Act and the Energy Conservation and Production Act. The effectiveness of these programs must be assessed to assist the Congress in determining what more needs to be done to achieve an acceptable national energy consumption growth rate.

We have ongoing and future work planned which should assist the Congress in its deliberations on this issue. One ongoing effort—a study of Federal efforts to achieve energy conservation—attempts to determine (1) whether energy conservation programs are working, (2) what further incentives and/or requirements could result in more effective energy conservation, and (3) what the Federal role should be in establishing energy conservation policies and priorities. A second ongoing effort will assess the four specific energy conservation programs authorized under Title IV of the Energy Conservation and Production Act in terms of energy savings, effectiveness, and expenditures of Federal funds. These four programs provide:

- Weatherization assistance to low income and low income handicapped and elderly persons ($200 million total funding authorized).

- Additional financial assistance to States for developing and implementing energy conservation plans ($105 million total funding authorized).

- Various forms of financial assistance to owners of existing dwelling units to encourage the implementation of energy conservation and/or renewable resource measures ($200 million total funding authorized).

- Loan guarantees to those purchasing and implementing energy conservation and/or renewable resource measures in any building or industrial plant ($60 million total funding authorized).

Only two of these programs—weatherization assistance and financial assistance to the States—were funded by the previous Administration's fiscal year 1978 budget. The new Administration's 1978 budget, however, would, if enacted by Congress, fund the entire title IV program.

Another ongoing effort—a review of the Community Services Administration's low-income weatherization program—will assess the effectiveness of this specific program.

A related question concerns whether essentially voluntary programs will be enough to get industry to conserve energy. Industry uses about 40 percent of the Nation's energy. FEA has established targets for energy conservation and requires key industries to report on their successes in meeting the targets. These targets call for industry to improve its energy efficiency by an average of about 15 percent based on 1972 usage. The stringency of the targets and industries' success in meeting them will help determine the need, if any, for mandatory standards.

Questions could be raised about the wisdom of using 1972 as the base year for measuring industries' success in meeting the targets. Industry has already taken a number of steps to conserve energy as a result of the 1973-74 oil embargo and subsequent energy crises. Thus, changing the base to a more recent year may be desirable.

As part of our ongoing study of Federal efforts to achieve energy conservation, we are assessing the effectiveness of voluntary industrial conservation programs and identifying actions that could be taken to achieve greater industrial energy savings.

Will existing energy performance standards for new automobiles adequately encourage energy conservation in the transportation sector?   Transportation accounts for about 25 percent of total energy use and is a major area where opportunities exist for significant energy savings. Achieving many of these savings requires changing the automobile's basic engine and body design, using alternative transport methods (buses, special lanes, etc.), and using the most energy efficient transport methods for particular purposes. This could mean, for example, that short airline routes might be discouraged in favor of train or bus service.

In one of our ongoing efforts, we are exploring the types of actions beyond performance standards that could be taken to reduce energy use in the transportation sector.

To what extent will institutional barriers inhibit energy conservation?   A major unresolved question is whether reducing our energy growth rate will also result in reducing our economic growth rate. Many studies indicate that in the recent past, energy growth and economic growth have gone and will continue to go hand-in-hand. Other studies argue that energy growth and economic growth can be successfully decoupled. The question has not been satisfactorily resolved, and it must be if this Nation is to lower energy growth rates substantially without sacrificing the major national goals.

In addition, there is a whole range of questions regarding the degree to which changes in building codes, utility rate structures, and other areas will be accepted. Conservation actions may or may not result in substantial changes in lifestyles, greater Government regulation, and a lessening of competition in certain transportation modes (i.e., fewer airline companies with more passengers). All of these factors must be considered in establishing a desirable level of energy conservation.

Our ongoing review of Federal efforts to achieve energy conservation will identify institutional barriers which are inhibiting greater energy conservation and assess the possible implications of overcoming those barriers.

Can the Federal Government do more to encourage in-house energy conservation?   The Federal Government must demonstrate its commitment to energy conservation and provide leadership by achieving a significant level of energy conservation in its in-house activities. The Federal Government uses from only 2 to 3 percent of the energy consumed in the United States. However, its example-setting implications are clearly important because, if the Government does not set the pace, it can hardly expect the private sector to follow.

We currently have underway two studies of the Federal Government's in-house conservation activities. In these studies, we are assessing the efforts being made by Federal agencies in assisting Government contractors to establish effective energy management programs and the Department of Defense's management of its Energy Conservation Investment Program. In the future, we plan to begin a review of the efforts being made to retrofit existing Federal Office buildings with energy saving equipment and techniques.

Petroleum And Natural Gas Regulatory Programs

FEA's responsibilities in this area include (1) assuring lawful and equitable distribution and pricing of crude oil and petroleum products, (2) monitoring the supply and demand of energy resources, (3) directing allocation actions, and (4) assuring compliance with FEA regulations. FEA does not have any regulatory responsibility over the use of natural gas.

Before the implementation of the Energy Policy and Conservation Act, which provides for the gradual phase-out of price controls over petroleum products and crude oil, a great deal of public and congressional interest existed in FEA's compliance and enforcement efforts. As a result, a great deal of our work at FEA was directed toward this program area. Since passage of the Energy Policy and Conservation Act interest has declined and this area requires less of our effort.

How effective will FEA's energy conservation and gasoline rationing contingency plans be in minimizing the impact of a crude oil supply shortage? FEA is required to develop a variety of energy conservation contingency plans, including gasoline rationing, which can be placed quickly into use if there are future embargos or other disruptions to the energy supply. These plans would be put into effect only after congressional approval and if required by a supply interruption. The types of action that can be taken and their potential effectiveness in alleviating possible energy shortages has been the subject of some debate, particularly during and following the oil embargo of 1973-74. They become even more important in view of the Nation's growing dependency on imported crude oil.

During the 95th Congress, we plan to begin a study to evaluate the basis for and potential effectiveness of FEA's contingency plans. We plan to determine (1) how and why FEA selected specific plans for development, (2) the scope and applicability of the plans (i.e., how many energy-consuming sectors are affected), (3) the potential impact and energy savings of each plan, and (4) potential difficulty or ease with which the plans can be implemented. In addition, we intend to assess the relationship of the conservation and gasoline rationing contingency plans to the Strategic Petroleum Reserve plan (see p. 688) since all three programs are designed to deal with future supply interruptions.

Fossil Energy Development

There has been a great deal of debate over the best way to increase the supplies of or reduce the demand for scarce resources of fossil fuels—particularly petroleum and natural gas. There are several options available for reaching demand reducing or supply increasing objectives including the use of increased taxes, tax incentives, and regulatory controls. The use of these options also has implications on the development and commercialization of new energy technologies, such as renewable resource technologies.

In addition to questions about the use of such options, there is a question about the need for increased domestic petroleum refining capacity in the future.

What are the effects of pricing, tax, and other regulatory actions on the production and price of energy supplies? The extent to which crude oil price controls should be continued in view of the Nation's growing dependence on imported crude oil and whether decontrol would result in increased domestic production are major questions facing the 95th Congress. Related questions concern the options available for influencing the price of and demand for energy and the impact these options will have on other areas, such as imported crude oil prices and conservation efforts. Some specific options include excise taxes on gasoline, tax credits for weatherizing homes or installing solar heating equipment, and various types of pricing structures such as peak load pricing for electricity.

In addition, recent Federal actions, such as coal mine health and safety regulations, air and water quality regulations, and the repeal of depletion allowances affect national energy supplies and prices.

State and local governments are also using taxes as a means of regulating energy development. For example, New Mexico, Montana, Wyoming, and Alaska have increased taxes on coal, oil, and gas. Just how State actions interface with Federal actions and their likely influence on energy resource development will be important questions in the years to come.

We are currently studying the effects of State taxes on Alaskan oil. In this effort, we are reviewing the development of Alaskan oil resources and the financial implications of existing and proposed State and local taxes on such development and on the supply of oil. We are also examining the interrelationship of Federal, State, and local taxes and their effect on energy development.

In another effort, we plan to examine existing and proposed tax structures as they affect the supply of all energy sources. We hope to give consideration to various tax policies—such as depletion allowance, investment tax credits, and excise taxes—and the extent to which these and other tax policies encourage or discourage the development of energy sources.

In other efforts, we plan to examine the cause and effect relationships between higher domestic crude oil prices and increased production. We plan to examine and evaluate (1) current Federal pricing incentives to encourage increased domestic oil production using primary, secondary, and tertiary recovery techniques, (2) the need for additional Federal pricing incentives, and (3) the impact of total decontrol of domestic crude oil prices.

What levels of domestic refining capacity are desirable? A critical issue affecting future domestic energy production is the availability of and need for future domestic refining capacity. There are several questions which need to be addressed relative to this issue, including:

- What are the refining capacity projections for the future?

- Does the United States need this projected refining capacity?

- What is the relationship of existing capacity to future capacity?

- Should the United States build more domestic refining capacity or should it rely more on foreign capacity?

Our current plans are to look at the domestic refining situation as it relates to these questions in an attempt to identify specific areas for further examination.

Energy Information And Analysis

Since the 1973 Arab oil embargo, the Congress has been concerned over the availability of accurate and reliable information on which to base energy policy decisions. While the Federal Energy Administration Act of 1974 gave FEA significant energy data collection responsibilities, a number of Federal agencies continue to collect energy information in various forms to meet the needs of their specific programs. This has resulted in fragmented energy data collection and analysis. Over the years, various forms of legislation were proposed to solve this problem. The Energy Conservation and Production Act, passed on August 14, 1976, established a separate energy data component in FEA with the authority to oversee the Federal Government's energy data collection effort. The act also established a Professional Audit Review Team to oversee FEA's data activities, with a GAO representative—appointed by the Comptroller General—serving as chairman of the team.

Is energy data credible? The key issue in this area is still one of credibility. A related concern is whether the provisions of the Energy Conservation and Production

Act will be successful in solving the problem. Because of the enactment of these energy data provisions, it is unlikely that additional energy data legislation will be immediately forthcoming from the 95th Congress.

We will continue monitoring FEA's data collection and analysis activities to determine whether the actions taken are resulting in more accurate, timely, and credible energy information for making policy decisions. Our work in this area, however, will supplement and not duplicate the work of the Professional Audit Review Team.

We are also currently examining the energy accounting practices used by the petroleum industry required under the Energy Policy and Conservation Act. Our objective is to gain an insight into several companies' accounting systems for oil exploration and production. It will enable us to better assist the Securities and Exchange Commission in carrying out its responsibilities under the act to develop industry energy accounting practices which will permit the compilation of an energy data base.

Strategic Petroleum Reserve

The Energy Policy and Conservation Act requires FEA to create a Strategic Petroleum Reserve containing an estimated 500 million barrels of crude oil and/or petroleum products by December 1982 to help diminish U.S. vulnerability to the effects of a severe interruption in energy supplies. As part of the Reserve, the act requires that an Early Storage Reserve be established to contain at least 150 million barrels of oil or products by December 1978. The act also gives FEA authority to establish a Regional Petroleum Reserve and an Industrial Petroleum Reserve. The quantities of oil to be contained in these reserves are to be part of, and not in addition to, the Strategic Petroleum Reserve.

Major issues concerning FEA's plan for a Strategic Petroleum Reserve relate to the nature and type of storage, how oil should be acquired to fill the Reserve and how it should be financed. Our previous work in this area identified three basic questions which must be analyzed and addressed in developing and approving a Strategic Petroleum Reserve plan.

- Is there a need for the type of Strategic Petroleum Reserve as outlined by FEA? Industry stockpiles could be used at significant savings.

- If so, how will the oil be purchased to fill the reserve? Royalty and Elk Hills Naval Petroleum Reserve oil, rather than oil purchased on the open market, may be viable alternatives.

- What ways other than general tax revenues are available to finance a Strategic Petroleum Reserve?

A user fee placing the cost on those who use the product may be a better option.

We discuss each of these questions in more detail starting on page 691.

Our work in this area during the 95th Congress will focus on FEA's efforts to answer these questions. Also since FEA currently plans to store the oil in salt caverns, primarily located in the Gulf Coast area, we have recently begun a study of the cost and feasibility of such storage.

International Concerns

This Nation's growing dependence on imported energy makes it vulnerable to international, political, and economic pressures—such as those exerted by the oil embargo—and reduces its freedom in foreign and domestic policymaking.

The oil embargo demonstrated the Nation's vulnerability to reliance on foreign oil imports. FEA estimated that the embargo caused a $10 to $20 billion drop in the Gross National Product and a rise in unemployment of 500,000. The embargo and accompanying four-fold increase in imported oil prices were the principal causes of the worst U.S. recession since World War II. Worldwide impacts have been similarly severe.

FEA was created in 1974 primarily to manage short term fuel shortages. Thus, international actions have a heavy impact on its policymaking and coordination functions.

Will the Nation be able to import oil and gas in sufficient quantities to meet future demand requirements at reasonable prices? Although many large-scale and sophisticated studies have been conducted which attempt to project U.S. demand and indigenous supply capacity in the mid-term future, the results vary considerably. An ingredient common to most of the studies is the implicit assumption that international oil supplies will adequately satisfy U.S. import needs, regardless of the size of those needs. Most experts agree that the world's proven oil and gas reserves are adequate to match the world's mid-term demand needs; however, whether key supplier nations will be prepared to exploit their reserves to the level required to meet world demand is uncertain.

On the other hand, if major new discoveries materialize, major investments in alternative new energy supplies may be lost as a result of substantially reduced prices for energy on the world market. This raises a question of whether the United States should maximize domestic petroleum production now or maintain domestic reserves for future contingencies and use imported energy while foreign supplies exist and the prices are relatively stable.

Other important problems are related. As a member of the International Energy Agency, the United States is somewhat protected from oil shortages by a system which would allocate available oil among member nations. In the event the International Energy Agency breaks down, would U.S. contingency plans get the Nation through another oil embargo? What are the implications of growing economic interdependence between the major oil importing and producing nations?

In one major ongoing review, we are studying the relationship between the international oil companies and OPEC governments. Some of the issues we are examining include (1) the nature of the OPEC price maintenance mechanisms, (2) the role of oil company purchasing decisions on OPEC or individual member price setting behavior, (3) the effect of long term contracts which award access to crude oil on preferential terms, (4) the effects of OPEC ambitions to obtain access to refining and distribution operations and the extent to which these ambitions are facilitated by OPEC's leverage over major oil companies, and (5) the oversight role of the U.S. Government in the international oil market. We are using our authority under Title V of the Energy Policy and Conservation Act in this effort (see p. 684) and expect to issue a report on this review in the next few months. We are also currently studying the potential for expanding oil field potential in free world non-OPEC countries and selected International Energy Agency's programs and activities. In the future, we plan also to examine energy's role in U.S. bilateral relations with selected OPEC nations.

Is the Government doing all it can to coordinate and cooperate with other nations in the areas of energy conservation? The United States is lagging behind other nations in reducing energy consumption. These nations may therefore be implementing conservation actions which could also be implemented in this country. We are currently reviewing foreign energy related technological development and conservation practices with a view toward identifying ways to reduce U.S. energy consumption.

Is the Government doing all it can to minimize the possibility of foreign energy policies impairing vital U.S. national interests? Given the significant changes in the international order arising from the new international energy situation, it is important to determine whether vital U.S. interests have been or are in danger of being impaired. These recent changes raise questions about the impact of growing monetary reserves of producer nations and increasing direct investments in the United States by these nations. Such investments may improve relations with key producing countries, but their impact on the United States is not clearly understood. There are also questions about the security implications of exporting vast quantities of sophisticated military weapons and hardware to Middle East oil producer nations and whether such exports are necessary to alleviate balance of payments problems or to provide future bargaining leverage with foreign oil suppliers.

Past Efforts

Conservation

Because most Federal efforts to encourage energy conservation have only recently been initiated in such legislation as the Energy Policy and Conservation Act passed in December 1975, and the Energy Conservation and Production Act passed in August 1976, FEA's conservation programs are in their infancy. Thus, our past efforts in this area have been limited.

Nevertheless, we have issued several major reports on conservation during the 94th Congress. For example, one report dealt with residential energy conservation (RED-75-377, 6/20/75), while another dealt with Federal in-house conservation efforts (LCD-76-229, 8/19/76).

The first report discussed such problems and issues as the emphasis on lowest initial cost in residential construction, obstacles preventing introduction of technological changes to promote energy efficiency, limited use of the Department of Housing and Urban Development's minimum property standards to encourage energy conservation, and limited research to improve the energy efficiency of a housing unit. We recommended that the Congress consider a combination of mandatory and voluntary actions to increase the level of energy conservation in the residential sector and that the Department of Housing and Urban Development emphasize energy conservation and establish thermal standards for federally insured homes. Many of the recommended actions were incorporated in the Energy Policy and Conservation Act and the Energy Conservation and Production Act.

The second report on Federal in-house energy conservation actions concluded that although some conservation actions had been taken by Federal agencies, much more could be done. This report, which was based on a review of conservation actions at 77 Government installations, identified a lack of (1) commitment to energy conservation, (2) leadership, and (3) complete and accurate data to assess progress in meeting energy conservation goals. We made recommendations to FEA, in conjunction with other Federal agencies, in the areas of energy program management, energy consumption data, vehicle operations, facilities energy use, and mission and training operations. FEA generally agreed with our recommendations and the Congress addressed some of the problems in

the Energy Policy and Conservation Act. Specifically, the act directed the President to develop mandatory energy conservation standards for federally owned or leased facilities.

In another report to the 95th Congress (CED-77-27, 2/14/77), we discussed the Department of Transportation's 55 mile-per-hour speed limit program and concluded that, although the program has been somewhat successful in decreasing the average driving speeds, the Department's efforts to increase State enforcement of the speed limit are limited. We made recommendations aimed at improving the program's acceptance and effectiveness.

In addition, we reviewed Federal efforts to improve the fuel economy of new automobiles (EMD-77-13, 1/13/77) and found that, although substantial improvement in new automobiles' fuel economy has occurred over the last 3 model years, continued improvements depend largely on how well Federal emissions and safety standards can be balanced with often conflicting fuel economy standards. We noted that the present Federal approach to regulate automobile design is a piecemeal and conflicting decisionmaking process and recommended several actions for achieving a balanced set of automobile standards.

We also evaluated and submitted comments to the Senate Finance Committee on H.R. 6860 — a bill to establish import limitations on foreign oil — as passed by the House of Representatives. We concluded that only two of the bill's provisions — mileage standards for automobiles and housing insulation — were likely to achieve measurable reductions in energy consumption, and that imposition of import quotas without commensurate reductions in petroleum demand could result in severe shortages and have an adverse effect on the economy.

Petroleum And Natural Gas Regulatory Programs

As noted earlier, congressional and public interest in FEA's regulatory activities in the pricing, distribution, and allocation of crude oil and petroleum products has declined since passage of the Energy Policy and Conservation Act providing for a gradual phaseout of controls on crude oil and petroleum products. Thus, we have also placed less emphasis on this area but will be monitoring FEA's efforts on a continuing basis to identify possible areas for improvement.

During the 94th Congress, we issued several major reports concerning FEA's compliance and enforcement efforts and its administration of various compliance and allocation programs. These reports discussed problems in FEA's auditing procedures, regulation development and implementation, efforts to protect the independent sector of the petroleum industry, and administration of the State petroleum set-aside program. We made several recommendations which the agency generally followed.

Energy Information And Analysis

In a 1976 report (OSP-76-21, 6/15/76), we pointed out that many problems continue to exist in the energy data area and that establishing a Department of Energy and Natural Resources with an independent data component offers the best long-term organizational solution to energy problems, including energy data problems. In the interim, we concluded that FEA could be strengthened to make it a more credible and objective focal point for Federal energy data efforts.

As a result of this report and a similar report issued in 1974, the Energy Conservation and Production Act included a number of measures providing for a credible and objective focal point for collecting energy data. It established within FEA an Office of Energy Information and Analysis and a National Energy Information System. As noted earlier, it also created a Professional Audit Review Team to conduct a thorough annual performance audit review of the procedures and methodology of the office. The Chairman of the team is appointed by the Comptroller General.

In another recently issued report (EMD-77-6, 3/17/77) on domestic resource and reserve estimates of coal, crude oil, natural gas, and uranium, we concluded that these estimates could be greatly improved and that additional information should be obtained concerning oil and gas in the Outer Continental Shelf areas, the availability of economically recoverable uranium, the effect of the cost-price relationship on the recovery of energy resources, the quantities of recoverable coal resources, and the ownership and control over energy sources. We made several recommendations aimed at making improvements in all of these areas.

Strategic Petroleum Reserve

On December 15, 1976, FEA submitted the Strategic Petroleum Reserve plan to the Congress for its approval. In a February 16, 1977, report entitled 'Issues Needing Attention in Developing the Strategic Petroleum Reserve', (EMD 77-20), we discussed questions in three key areas which we believe need further analysis by FEA and warrant the attention of the Congress in its deliberations on approving the plan (also see p. 688).

- Is there a need for the type of Strategic Petroleum Reserve as outlined by FEA? Potential exists for using industry stockpiles of crude oil and product stocks for the reserve at significant dollar savings. According to a Government report to the International Energy Agency, U.S. industries maintain commercially held stocks of crude oil and products equivalent to 120 days of oil imports. For these inventories to be used effectively as part or all of a Strategic Reserve, the Government would have to impose controls so that specified quantities of oil are maintained and appropriately used in the event of an embargo. This system would be similar to the Government controlled and industry-owned oil storage programs of France and Japan. We concluded that further analysis of this possible alternative is needed before a Strategic Reserve plan is approved.

- If there is a need for a reserve, how will the oil be purchased to fill it? FEA intends to fill the reserve through purchase of oil on the open market at a price near the national average composite price. However, other options exist for acquiring the oil in addition to open market purchase. Oil produced from Outer Continental Shelf and onshore Federal leases, and oil from Elk Hills Naval Petroleum Reserve, under certain circumstances, offer substantial cost savings to the Federal Government. If price controls remain in effect, significant savings can be incurred if royalty oil were purchased for the reserve. If oil prices are decontrolled, savings could result from purchasing Elk Hills oil. FEA said it would consider using Elk Hills oil if it were economical, but disagreed that royalty oil should be used.

- What ways other than general tax revenues are available to finance a Strategic Petroleum Reserve? Although FEA's plan does not specify how the reserve is to be financed, it implies that general tax revenues, largely personal and corporate income taxes, will be the source of financing. FEA is currently studying several options for financing the reserve. The benefits of the reserve accrue directly to those who buy imported crude oil and the products derived therefrom by providing protection against the economic costs they would occur in the event of a supply interruption. Thus, we said that consideration should be given to having those who will benefit directly from the reserve bear its cost. This could be accomplished through imposing a user fee. We did not analyze all available options for imposing a fee; however, we identified two options—a tariff on imported crude oil and an excise tax on gasoline. We expressed the view that fees collected should be placed in the general fund of the U.S. Treasury and remain subject to congressional oversight.

We testified on our report before the Subcommittee on Energy and Power, House Committee on Interstate and

Foreign Commerce on February 16, 1977, and will continue to monitor the Strategic Petroleum Reserve program because of its magnitude and importance as a cornerstone of national energy policy.

Chapter 3

Federal Power Commission

The Federal Power Commission is responsible for regulating the interstate aspects of the electric power and natural gas industries. In fulfilling this function, FPC is responsible for assuring an adequate supply of natural gas and electric power at reasonable rates. FPC also licenses the construction and operation of non-Federal hydroelectric projects and investigates the environmental impact of the activities it regulates. FPC's regulatory authority is limited, however, to wholesale rates and services. Jurisdiction over retail natural gas and electric rates and services resides with the individual States. Our views on the major issues facing FPC are discussed below. Our past efforts at FPC are discussed on page 694.

Issues Facing the 95th Congress

Electricity

FPC is responsible for assuring that the interstate sale of electrical power in the wholesale market is offered at rates and conditions that are fair and equitable to both buyers and sellers. FPC's hydroelectric licensing program attempts to insure that the Nation's water resources are used for the maximum public benefit. To effectively carry out its responsibilities, FPC has its own data collection and forecasting program.

The major issues facing FPC in this session of Congress relate to the current structure of the electric utility industry and to FPC's ratemaking policies.

Is there a need to restructure the electric utility industry and to amend the Federal Power Act? The Federal Power Act, as amended (16 U.S.C. 792-825) which governs the operation of the wholesale portion of the electric utility industry, has not changed substantially since 1935; yet, there have been numerous changes in the factors which affect that industry. In recent years, fuel prices have increased dramatically, inflation has increased operating and construction costs, and the subsequent economic recession has dampened demand for electric energy and has caused significant changes in the utility industry.

Industry leaders are unsure as to the best course of action to pursue, both in the near and far term, because of such uncertainties and problems as (1) the lack of Federal and State coordination resulting in conflicting requirements, fragmented policies and procedures, and jurisdictional differences, (2) inadequate and different demand forecasting methodologies, (3) lack of standardized reserve levels or reliability criteria, (4) inadequate financing for operations and expansion, (5) possible imposition of load management and pricing alternatives with concomitant socioeconomic implications, (6) uncertain effects and costs of new technologies, and (7) the potential conflict of environmental and conservation requirements with industry objectives.

As a result, there is concern as to whether the Nation's 3,600 municipal, cooperative, State, Federal, and private utilities can cooperate sufficiently to build the kinds of systems needed for the future, or whether further Federal planning and intervention is needed.

We are currently examining the problems and issues confronting the electric utility industry to identify and assess the various factors affecting the industry's future, their interrelationship, and the pros and cons of alternative courses of action.

Petroleum And Natural Gas Regulatory Programs

In regulating natural gas sold in interstate commerce, FPC is responsible for, among other things, authorizing the construction, extension, acquisition, and/or operation of facilities and regulating natural gas rates and services, including curtailments in times of gas shortages. FPC does not have any regulatory responsibility over the use of petroleum.

FPC's problems in the natural gas area are being dramatized by the current energy crisis occurring as a result of an abnormally cold winter. The natural gas shortage and the resulting decline in deliveries and dedications to the interstate market is the most difficult problem facing FPC. As with electricity, FPC is also faced with the responsibility of insuring adequate supplies at a reasonable price while, at the same time, maintaining the financial viability of natural gas producers and pipelines.

Is there a need to increase the effectiveness of FPC's natural gas policies?   The most immediate and pressing energy problem facing the Nation is the shortage of natural gas. Recently, emergency legislation was passed to provide the President with additional powers to alleviate critical shortages in several states. These shortages have occurred because of a steady decline in the interstate natural gas supply which has caused many interstate pipelines to curtail gas deliveries to their customers. As a result of the gas shortage, there has been extensive debate about whether to deregulate the price of natural gas and/or improve the effectiveness of FPC's curtailment policy.

The continued disagreement about whether to deregulate natural gas has made the gas industry unsure of its actions. Clearly, price regulation affects the entire energy system, not just the regulated component. At present, low regulated prices may contribute to making it uneconomical to develop new energy sources; surely they discourage conservation actions. It may not be so much a question of regulation versus deregulation, however. Most of the consequences of deregulation could occur under continued regulation with higher regulated prices which approximated market prices. Price is the key to the supply and economic implications of deregulation and, in theory at least, prices could rise by comparable amounts in the context of either deregulation or continued regulation. The question of deregulation then, is not so much a question of increasing natural gas supplies as it is a question of the social and economic desirability of government-determined versus market-determined natural gas prices.

FPC's direct curtailment policy applies only to sales by the interstate pipeline companies and does not extend to intrastate pipelines, distributing companies and end users. As a result of this jurisdictional limitation, the effectiveness of FPC's curtailment policy in limiting the adverse effects of shortages is limited.

FPC has recently taken action to increase deliveries to the interstate market including:

- establishing a new national rate structure,
- permitting pipeline companies to make interest-free advance payments to producers, and
- permitting curtailed industrial customers to compete in the intrastate market for gas supplies.

The recently enacted emergency gas legislation is also aimed at increasing interstate deliveries.

Our ongoing work includes reviews of FPC's advance payment program, the adequacy and reliability of natural gas reserve information, and the natural gas curtailment program, including an assessment of activities under the recently enacted emergency natural gas legislation. In this latter study, we plan to review the use of emergency purchases by interstate pipelines and the allocation of natural gas between these pipelines with a view towards developing recommendations for dealing with the natural gas shortages.

Are FPC's methods of determining reasonable electric and natural gas rates fair?   FPC is responsible for assuring an adequate supply of electric power and natural gas at the lowest reasonable rates. FPC's reasonable rate determinations depend heavily on the assessment of the utilities' operating costs, investment in the business, and profit. The demand for electric power and the natural gas shortage has justifiably focused attention on methods used by FPC to determine reasonable rates. Maintaining the financial viability of the electric and natural gas utility industries to provide service without excessive costs to the consumers is a difficult task. We plan to begin separate reviews of FPC's electrical and natural gas ratemaking processes during the 95th Congress.

What can be done to alleviate regulatory lag? This question applies to FPC's electricity and natural gas regulatory functions and concerns the delay in disposing of the massive backlog of natural gas and electric rate cases in addition to numerous and complex gas curtailment cases.

FPC has been unable to cope with its increasing workload, which arose primarily in the last 3 or 4 years as a result of the energy crisis. At the end of February 1976, there were over 140 natural gas pipeline rate increase cases totaling about $2.2 billion annually under suspension and subject to potential refund and over 100 electric rate cases totaling over $500 million annually under suspension.

Regulatory lag may cause problems, including increased rates, inadequate service, and the possibility that refunds may or may not be returned to consumers. We plan to study the effects of regulatory lag and identify actions that can be taken to solve or alleviate the problem.

Are FPC's surveillance and enforcement activities adequate to protect the consumer and the general public? This question also applies to both electricity and natural gas regulatory programs and concerns FPC's effectiveness in insuring that laws, regulations, Commission orders, and conditions attached to permits, licenses, and certificates are being properly followed. On several occasions, FPC has been criticized for footdragging and failing to enforce compliance with its regulations. If these allegations are true, consumers and the general public are not being protected as intended by the Congress.

We plan to evaluate the effectiveness of FPC's surveillance and enforcement activities during the 95th Congress.

Fossil Energy Development

What should the role of liquefied natural gas be in meeting U.S. energy needs? FPC's role in fossil energy development is somewhat limited. Because of the natural gas shortage, however, an increasing reliance will have to be placed on supplemental supplies, such as liquefied natural gas imports. Such imports, if relied on, must be used to the best advantage because of balance of payments and security of supply concerns. Using liquefied natural gas imports must also be balanced against using imported oil to determine which fuel offers the most advantages. Problems, such as the need for specialized tankers and receiving terminals, must also be considered. In short, large scale liquefied natural gas imports may involve problems similar to those created by large oil imports.

Using liquefied natural gas also has certain major safety problems and concerns. In this respect, we are assessing the potential dangers associated with transporting and storage of this gas as well as other dangerous gases, such as naphtha.

In August 1976, the Energy Resources Council recommended a limit on liquefied natural gas imports and a continuation of Federal financial assistance to liquefied natural gas projects. If import controls are placed on liquefied natural gas, a decision must be made on the best way to control these imports. We have recently initiated a study to determine how liquefied natural gas can best be utilized in meeting the Nation's energy needs, actions available to control imports, and the strategy that should govern the use of these controls. In a related effort, we plan to examine, as a case study, problems faced by U.S. liquefied natural gas importers in obtaining approval for developing and shipping liquefied natural gas from Indonesian fields.

Energy Information And Analysis

Is FPC's information system adequate for making good management decisions? Beginning in 1973, FPC began developing an automated data processing system to provide timely and accurate information for use in carrying out its decisionmaking responsibilities. The use of this system raises several questions, such as (1) is the information necessary for good decisions being collected? (2) is the information accurate? and (3) does the system focus on the most critical problems?

If the new system is not providing FPC with accurate, adequate, and timely information, FPC's decisionmaking process will be hampered thus adversely affecting the regulated industry and the consumer. The need for reliable information on which to base decisions was highlighted by the recent gas shortage and allegations that major natural gas producers are withholding information on natural gas supplies to obtain a higher price. This allegation has been raised for several years, particularly since the recent shortages, and has yet to be resolved.

During the 95th Congress we plan to assess how well FPC's new information system is being used to meet the needs of FPC, the public, and the Congress. We are also currently reviewing the adequacy and reliability of natural gas reserve information for use by FPC, the Congress, and the Government in making decisions on the natural gas question.

Past Efforts

Electricity

Our past efforts in FPC's electric power regulation program have been aimed primarily at FPC's hydroelectric licensing program and its steadily growing applications backlog. In a September 23, 1975, report (RED-76-13), we noted that most of the licensing time required was outside FPC's control. On the other hand, we found that some of the time required was within FPC's control and was due to processing delays, such as (1) automatic extension of reporting deadlines after allowing applicants 30 to 90 days to comply with requests for needed information, (2) never attempting to prosecute those who have failed to provide needed information, and (3) a lengthy and timeconsuming process for obtaining comments from other Federal agencies. We made several recommendations aimed at reducing the processing delay and at formalizing the role of other Federal agencies in the licensing process. FPC has subsequently taken action to implement our recommendations. However, formal procedures for obtaining other agencies' comments have not yet been established.

Petroleum And Natural Gas Regulatory Programs

Our efforts during the 94th Congress regarding natural gas dealt primarily with the possible deregulation and curtailment of this valuable resource. In one report (OSP-76-11, 1/14/76) we analyzed the consequences in terms of increased supplies and increased prices from deregulation of natural gas. Although we did not make any recommendations, our basic conclusion was that natural gas production, even with deregulation, was likely to decline. We said, however, that deregulation could slow the rate of decline by providing an additional 1.5 trillion cubic feet of new natural gas supply in 1985, but this would have to be weighed against a cumulative additional cost to the consumers of about $75 billion between

1975-85. We also pointed out that continued regulation would result in almost the entire decline in supplies being borne by the interstate market whereas deregulation would tend to distribute this decline between inter- and intrastate markets.

We also reported (RED-76-11, 9/18/75) that the reliability of FPC's projections of the amounts of natural gas currently under contract between producers and pipeline companies which could be released as a result of Federal price deregulation was questionable. In our view, this occurred because FPC did limited verification to determine if the data on which the projections we¯e based was complete and accurate. FPC has taken action to correct this situation which should provide more current and accurate contract information and enhance its decision-making process.

Regarding FPC's natural gas curtailment policy, we reported on September 19, 1975 (RED-76-18) that FPC lacks the authority to obtain end-use and economic impact information necessary to evaluate the effectiveness of its curtailment program because its jurisdiction does not extend to intrastate commerce. We noted that FPC, with FEA, was attempting to obtain the needed information, and we recommended that FPC report to the Congress on the results of its efforts and on additional actions, if any, needed to obtain the data.

In another report dealing with the impact of natural gas curtailments during the winter of 1975-76, (RED-76-39, 10/31/75) we said that if the winter were normal and if alternative fuels were available, the natural gas shortage was not expected to result in widespread unemployment and extensive plant closures. The report provided the Congress with information regarding the need for emergency natural gas legislation.

In addition to our reports on deregulation and curtailments, we reported on September 13, 1974, (B-180228) that FPC (1) made improper extensions to its 60-day limits on emergency gas sales, (2) did not have complete and accurate data on the volume and price of emergency sales used in its decisionmaking process, (3) failed to take timely action on applications under its optional certificate procedure—which allows a producer to charge higher rates until final action is taken on its application—resulting in higher gas prices than may have been just and reasonable, and (4) allowed widespread noncompliance by FPC officials with its standards of conduct regulations intended to prevent conflicts of interest.

We recommended that FPC obtain additional information on the volume and price of emergency sales and improve its internal procedures to adequately evaluate its emergency sales program. We followed up on these recommendations in a May 24, 1976, report (RED-76-108) and found that FPC had, for the most part, implemented our recommendations.

Chapter 4

Department Of The Interior

The Department of the Interior is the Federal custodian of the Nation's natural resources, particularly the public lands which contain about half of this country's remaining energy resources. Thus, the Department's role in this Nation's energy future is immensely important. It has major responsibilities in domestic energy exploration, extraction, and marketing as well as land use, environmental protection, conservation, and safety. The Department has major programs in the areas of pipeline rights of way, including the trans-Alaska pipeline; tract selection and leasing regulation of the Outer Continental Shelf and public lands onshore; and generation and marketing of electricity through such organizations as the Bureau of Reclamation and Bonneville Power Administration. Following is a discussion of the major issues facing the Interior Department. Our past efforts are discussed on page 699.

Issues Facing The 95th Congress

Pipeline Rights Of Way

The Department is responsible for issuing transmission rights-of-way permits for pipelines after making environmental impact analyses. It is also responsible for construction and post construction monitoring to determine compliance with the permit. Currently, the major program in this area is the construction and eventual operation of the trans-Alaska pipeline, which will deliver Alaskan oil to the lower 48 States.

Thus, the most significant issue in this program area relates to the trans-Alaska pipeline and how decisions and actions taken on that effort will affect other oil and gas pipeline construction decisions.

What are the environmental and socioeconomic ramifications of pipeline construction? Since inception, there have been disagreements over the potential socioeconomic and environmental effects of the trans-Alaska pipeline. Problems encountered and possible environmental and socioeconomic effects of the trans-Alaska pipeline will certainly influence decisions on other major pipeline construction decisions. For example, the opening of Outer Continental Shelf areas to energy development will probably require pipelines to onshore facilities. Problems, such as divided Federal authority, lack of information on the number and location of pipelines to be required, and the environmental and economic impact, could hamper the success of Outer Continental Shelf development if not properly assessed and addressed.

In an ongoing review, we are examining the management of and reasons for cost increases in the trans-Alaska oil pipeline with a view toward identifying shortcomings in the management of that effort which could be avoided in constructing a trans-Alaska natural gas pipeline. When issued, our report should outline lessons learned in constructing the oil pipeline which could be applied to the gas pipeline.

We are also monitoring the progress of the trans-Alaska pipeline construction, including the Department's handling of environmental, system design, and quality control problems and are studying the Outer Continental Shelf pipeline issues.

Outer Continental Shelf

The Outer Continental Shelf contains an estimated 16 to 49 billion barrels of recoverable oil and 146 to 181 trillion cubic feet of natural gas. The Department estimated that 301 million barrels of oil and 3.8 trillion cubic feet of natural gas would be produced from Outer Continental Shelf resources in fiscal year 1977.

In leasing Outer Continental Shelf lands, the Department performs resource appraisals and environmental investigations for tract selection and valuation, awards leases, and monitors the operation of the producer and lessee, including safety, quantity verification, and royalty assessment and collection. Because of the shortages of oil and natural gas, this program is being accelerated.

Since the inception of the program in 1953, for example, 13.2 million acres have been leased on the Outer Continental Shelf for oil and gas development. By comparison, the Department expected to offer 4.4 million acres for lease in fiscal year 1977. Until recently, leasing on the Outer Continental Shelf was confined to the Gulf of Mexico and Southern California. However, recent and planned leasing off the Atlantic and Alaskan coasts has aroused public concern over the program's management, the fair value return to the Treasury, and the environmental consequences of possible oil spills.

In our view, the primary issues relating to Outer Continental Shelf development concern the program's direction, the need for reliable data on which to base decisions, and the environmental and socioeconomic impacts of the program.

What should our Outer Continental Shelf leasing goals be and how do they relate to national energy needs? One of the overriding issues facing Outer Continental Shelf development concerns how offshore oil and gas fit into the overall U.S. energy plans and goals. The Nation is committed to an accelerated Outer Continental Shelf leasing program as a major means of increasing energy self-sufficiency. Our past work in this area, however, has shown that the Department's plans are not clearly defined or related to other national objectives and goals, such as those set forth in FEA's Project Independence. Unfortunately, the Department has not responded favorably to our past recommendations in this area. One review now in progress addresses conflicts among various groups—Federal, State, local, and industry—on Outer Continental Shelf development. In this review, we plan to determine the need for additional steps which might spur the Department to action.

Is sufficient geologic and geophysical data available on Outer Continental Shelf resources? The Outer Continental Shelf leasing program is hindered by the lack of knowledge about the extent of Outer Continental Shelf resources. For example, estimates of recoverable oil range from 16 to 49 billion barrels.

The Department has programs to obtain additional data on Outer Continental Shelf reserves, and legislation was introduced last year that would have required federally financed exploration. The proposed legislation, however, failed to pass. We have reported on this problem in the past. For example, as discussed on page 699, our most recent report on Outer Continental Shelf sale no. 35 in California noted a need for more reliable data on Outer Continental Shelf resources and made several recommendations for improvement. We are currently looking at the broader question of overall Outer Continental Shelf needs in our ongoing review of Outer Continental Shelf conflicts discussed above.

Additional related issues to be resolved in this area include questions about Federal versus private exploration, whether to make exploration data available to others, and whether fair market value is being received for leasing public resources. Adequate data is needed to answer these questions.

What are the environmental and socioeconomic impacts of Outer Continental Shelf development? Outer Continental Shelf development has brought considerable opposition from coastal States and other private interests resulting in some delays in lease sales. There are many environmental and socioeconomic questions yet to be answered, and in our view, these issues have not received adequate consideration in the past. Spills have occurred, and less consideration seems to be given to the long-term impact of lease decisions on marine life and on the socioeconomics of a particular area. The impact on nearby cities can be significant and land use becomes a consideration because of onshore activities that accompany offshore development. One recent sale on the east coast, for example, was canceled by a court primarily for environmental reasons.

A somewhat related issue concerns the possible need for deepwater port facilities. Super tankers cannot enter U.S. ports resulting in the additional expense of transferring the oil to smaller ships. Other nations have constructed deepwater ports with pipelines to carry the oil to shore. This procedure may be less costly, but there are important questions about its socioeconomic and environmental impact.

We are currently reviewing the need for environmental data in our previously cited study of Outer Continental Shelf conflicts. We are also studying the pros and cons of constructing deepwater port facilities. We plan to begin a study of the usefulness of baseline and monitoring programs for protecting the environment and in managing the Outer Continental Shelf leasing program.

Public Lands

The Department has numerous responsibilities and programs dealing with public lands. Many of these activities—such as mapping resource appraisals and assuring compliance with mining safety standards—also extend into private lands. According to Department estimates, energy reserves on Federal land amount to 1.8 billion barrels of oil and natural gas liquids and 16.2 trillion cubic feet of natural gas. The Federal Government also owns and administers approximately 70 percent of the oil shale resources and owns 60 percent of the Nation's western coal resources. Federal lands in 1974 accounted for 6 percent of domestic production, and efforts are underway to increase this production. Decisions on leasing public lands will be a major determinant of both the amount and type of energy the country uses.

The major issues in this area relate to the manner in which public lands will be developed, the adequacy of the resource information, and the role of Alaskan fossil fuel resources.

How should development of energy resources on public lands proceed? In our view, firmer decisions need to be made on development and production requirements for the various energy resources on public lands. Other issues relate to the need for timely lease development, efforts to improve tract valuation, need to evaluate nonproductive leases, the socioeconomic impacts on growing communities, and environmental impacts.

We have several ongoing and planned efforts in this area, including evaluations of (1) the relationship between the major end uses of coal and the Federal coal leasing program and (2) the likely socioeconomic impacts of leasing in the Rocky Mountain area. We are also examining the land use planning and the classification of Federal lands and plan to study the effects of withdrawing public lands for wilderness areas on other land uses, such as energy development.

Is the data base sufficient for adequate program development? The Department's knowledge of energy resources and reserves on public lands is speculative, making it difficult to prepare reliable plans and accurately assess the potential for U.S. self-sufficiency. This lack of knowledge can also reduce the number of bids and value of bids on lease offers. Although there are several factors to consider in deciding whether more intensive exploration is needed—such as whether it offers a favorable cost benefit ratio—such exploration would provide for firmer leasing schedules, production estimates, and tract valuation.

The Federal Coal Leasing Amendments Act requires a comprehensive departmental survey of coal resources on Federal lands. We are currently using our authority granted under Title V of the Energy Policy and Conservation Act to verify the accuracy of the Department's coal reserve estimates under Federal lease with private industry.

What is and will be the role of Alaskan energy resources? Alaska's problems and potential are so unique as to warrant being discussed separately. Alaska has large known oil and natural gas resources and potentially large coal reserves but, besides petroleum, little development is taking place. Its vast areas of undeveloped land and its extremely fragile ecology are greatly threatened by large-scale resource development. Furthermore, since the high cost of constructing transportation systems has made it uneconomical for private interests to build competing systems, the Federal Government will continue to be involved in deciding how to transport Alaskan energy resources to the lower 48 States.

The trans-Alaska pipeline is now completed, but many problems experienced in that effort will more than likely be faced in attempting to move other Alaskan resources to the lower 48 states. For example, a natural gas pipeline may be built from Alaska. Questions and concerns about that pipeline have yet to be resolved and problems experienced in constructing the oil pipeline will also be faced in building a gas pipeline.

Also, the transfer of federally owned lands to native groups and the State of Alaska as well as the transfer of presently unappropriated public domain lands into the forest, parks, refuge, and wild and scenic rivers system will likely significantly impact on the development of Alaskan energy resources.

The Federal Government may also have to assist in determining the ultimate destination in the lower 48 States for Alaskan oil when production starts in 1977. Current industry plans call for the oil to be delivered to the west coast and may result in a glut of oil there. The Government may have to approve a plan to ship some of the oil east or to export it.

As discussed on page 695, we are currently examining the management of and reasons for cost increases in the trans-Alaska oil pipeline to identify any problems which could be avoided in constructing a gas pipeline. In the future, we plan to study the agency's efforts to identify Alaskan resources and to increase the production and marketability of these resources.

Fossil Energy Development

Some of the issues relating to expanding the use of coal and to developing other fossil fuel resources do not relate specifically to the Department's responsibilities over public lands, but they are being discussed here because of the large amounts of fossil fuel resources on Federal lands.

How can the socioeconomic and environmental impact of accelerated domestic energy production be minimized? With the bulk of our energy resources lying on Federal lands, the Department's public lands leasing policies will also have a major impact on society and the environment. For example, there are major questions about the environmental and socioeconomic impacts associated with expanded use of coal which could be especially severe in the western states where coal is being strip mined at an accelerating pace to help boost the Nation's output of electric power. Montana, for example, increased its strip mine production from an estimated 3 million tons in 1970 to 23 million tons in 1975. The influx of labor to support the large strip mine operations and the resultant demand for increased services pose serious problems for many previously stable small western communities. Likewise, the agricultural way-of-life of many western areas will be subject to drastic changes. These socioeconomic consequences are compounded by the damage strip mining does to the land. Major surface mining legislation has been passed in recent years but has been vetoed twice. Major debate centers on the question of the

proper tradeoff between environmental concerns and their impact on production and employment.

There is also growing concern over the long-term effects of burning fossil fuels, even if all pollutants could be removed. Fossil fuels are mainly carbon and, when burned, release carbon dioxide into the atmosphere. Since carbon dioxide acts as a one-way filter, its increased concentration in the atmosphere poses a potential problem by permitting the sun's rays to reach the earth but not allowing heat to escape. Atmospheric heat buildup may well turn out to be the major problem of and argument against increased use of fossil fuels. Analysis of the potential impacts of such a heat buildup is only in its infancy. Much must be learned about this phenomenon, and quickly, if a major program to increase the use of fossil fuels is to achieve social acceptance.

As discussed under the following question, a major study underway will provide a broad overview of the issues influencing coal's future in this country. As part of that study, we are addressing the environmental and socioeconomic problems with increased coal production. Another ongoing effort is studying the socioeconomic impact of potential coal and other energy resource development in the Rocky Mountain area.

Also, the Federal Coal Leasing Amendments Act requires the Department to consider the environmental and socioeconomic impacts on an area when leasing land for coal development. It requires the Department to prepare a comprehensive land use plan and requires mining companies, within 3 years after the lease is awarded, to submit a mining and land reclamation plan. In the future, we plan to determine how well the Department's regulations governing reclamation and mining plans have been implemented and whether an adequate review of mining plans is performed to ensure that the environment will be protected.

How can the U.S. make better use of its coal resources? The coal industry has been financially depressed until just recently, and little effort has gone into technology for improved extraction, transportation, and combustion of coal. A number of promising new techniques to extract a higher percentage of coal from the ground are being used by other countries, but the United States has not adopted them to any great extent. Locating electric generating plants near the coal mine instead of near the population being served could keep electricity costs down, but this technique is in very limited use in this country. Coal slurry pipelines could transport coal efficiently, but a number of technical, environmental, and legal problems must be resolved before it can become a major, feasible way of delivering coal to users.

In a major study now underway, we are analyzing the promises and uncertainties of future development of U.S. coal. The study is addressing four major questions:

- Where does the United States stand now and who are the key participants in U.S. coal development?

- Based on selected scenarios, where will U.S. coal development be in 1985 or 2000?

- What is required to meet the energy goals in the scenarios?

- What are the issues and constraints and what are the alternatives to solve them?

Electricity

Is the existing structure of the Federal power marketing agencies suitable to meeting the future needs of the Nation? The Federal power marketing programs are based on the principles that (1) energy shall be marketed to encourage the widest possible use, (2) it shall be made available at the lowest possible rates (consistent with sound business principles), and (3) preference in power sales shall be given to public bodies and cooperatives.

These principles were established at a time when energy was abundant. As a result, electricity sold by the power marketing agencies has generally been cheaper than other energy sources and has encouraged electricity consumption. The power marketing agencies' decisions on prices and whether to construct additional generating facilities may not be consistent with overall Federal energy policies and goals which encourage conservation and reducing energy use. The programs of those agencies will need reexamination in the light of changing national needs.

We plan during the coming year to examine the operating philosophies of the Federal power marketing agencies in relationship to national energy goals and the potential for increasing the efficiency and production of electricity from these plants.

Currently, we have a similar study underway on the Tennessee Valley Authority's activities. In this effort, we are assessing how the Tennessee Valley Authority's goals relate to National energy and environmental goals. We are considering actions that may be taken to better define or change the agency's overall goals.

Past Efforts

Outer Continental Shelf

We issued three major reports during the 94th Congress dealing with various aspects of the Department's efforts to develop Outer Continental Shelf resources (RED-75-343, 3/19/75; RED-75-359, 6/30/75; and RED-76-48, 11/21/75). These reports were directed largely at difficulties in achieving the Administration's

leasing objectives. We concluded that (1) the acreage leasing goals were unrealistic and did not consider national energy goals and plans, (2) shortages of materials, equipment, manpower and capital can limit the timing of Outer Continental Shelf production, and (3) a Government-financed and -directed exploring program is essential because information on reserves is inadequate and hinders proper tract selection and valuation.

In a recent report to the 95th Congress (EMD-77-19, 3/7/77) on Outer Continental Shelf sale no. 35 in California, we noted that the Department's policy of leasing Outer Continental Shelf resources as quickly as possible encourages industry to tie up its capital in lands with minimal potential and may lower the value received. We concluded that the Department should have more reliable data on potential Outer Continental Shelf resources and recommended that the Department (1) direct an exploration program to provide a systematic plan for appraising and selecting Outer Continental Shelf tracts and (2) limit lease offers to those tracts on which sufficient data has been collected.

We also aided the Congress in its consideration of the Coastal Zone Management Act Amendments (Public Law 94-370) which authorized $1.2 billion in Federal aid to help coastal states deal with the effects of offshore gas and oil development. We supported this act in April 9, 1975, testimony before the Senate Committees on Commerce and Interior and Insular Affairs because it would assist coastal states in the orderly development of their coastal zones and would provide grants for planning, training, and research.

We also assisted the Congress—through written comments and testimony before the Subcommittee on Energy Research, Development, and Demonstration, House Committee on Science and Technology, and joint hearings before the Senate Committees on Commerce and Interior and Insular Affairs—in its consideration of the Outer Continental Shelf Lands Act Amendments (S. 521-94th Congress). The bill, which did not pass, would have significantly altered the present system of leasing oil and gas resources on the Outer Continental Shelf. Similar bills (S. 9 and H. R. 1614) with the same essential elements have been introduced in the 95th Congress.

Public Lands

Our efforts during the past 2 years in this program area have been directed primarily at the Department's coal leasing program. We reported (RED-76-79, 4/1/76) that the Department had not determined when and how much land should be leased to meet national coal production goals. We recommended that the Department (1) develop a systematic coal drilling program for resource appraisal and provide planned and coordinated drilling through federally financed activities and (2) determine the demands that will be placed on Federal coal resources and establish a leasing schedule.

We also recommended in this report that the Congress amend the Mineral Leasing Act of 1920 to provide for (1) awarding leases only on a competitive basis and (2) issuing prospecting permits under which persons would explore for coal but would have no exclusive rights to leases. Our recommendations were subsequently incorporated into the Federal Coal Leasing Amendments Act. We recommended also that the act be amended to provide for more frequent adjusting of the lease terms, but this recommendation was not adopted.

We examined Federal geothermal resources (RED-75-330, 3/6/75) and concluded that through 1985, these resources will not be a major energy source and through 2000, projections are uncertain. We also concluded that more reliable information was needed before designating Federal lands as known geothermal resource areas, and that leasing regulations should be changed to promote early exploration and development of leased lands.

Until recently, the general policy of private development of energy resources on public lands did not apply to the Naval Petroleum Reserves. This policy, however, has been reevaluated in view of the limited capacity of the reserves and the desire to use them to reduce foreign imports. We have issued two reports on these reserves (LCD-75-321, 7/29/75; LCD-76-313, 5/14/76) in which we identified a need for reliable resource estimates and for clear statements of how the reserves will be used. In March 17, 1975, testimony before the House Ways and Means Committee, we advocated developing two of the reserves as part of a national emergency energy reserve and recommended that the third reserve be fully explored for eventual commercial leasing. Subsequently, the Naval Petroleum Reserves Production Act of 1976 was enacted providing that oil from reserves 1, 2, and 3 will be produced and sold on the open market. Responsibility for management of Reserve 4, located in Alaska, was to be turned over to the Interior Department on June 1, 1977. The act authorizes the President to study the possible uses for the reserve and, in so doing, requires that he consider the impacts of further development and production.

Chapter 5

Nuclear Regulatory Commission

The Nuclear Regulatory Commission was established in January 1975 by the Energy Reorganization Act of 1974 to provide an independent agency to regulate the commercial nuclear industry. This responsibility previously rested with the former Atomic Energy Commission.

NRC is primarily responsible for regulating the construction and operation of commercial nuclear powerplants and most activities associated with the nuclear fuel cycle to assure that they do not pose an undue risk to public health and safety. NRC carries out these responsibilities by developing standards and regulations, issuing licenses, and inspecting and enforcing licensee compliance with regulations. NRC expends almost half of its budget on reactor safety research. The questions facing NRC are discussed below. Our past efforts are discussed on page 703.

Issues Facing The 95th Congress

Nuclear Power Development

Nuclear powerplants currently provide about 8 percent

of the country's total electricity; in some local areas this figure is as high as 42 percent. As of December 1976, there were 62 commercial nuclear powerplants licensed to operate in this country, and another 72 under construction. In addition, public utilities had applied for construction permits for 67 powerplants and had placed orders with manufacturers for 16 more.

However, nuclear fission power continues to be one of the most controversial energy issues in this country. Consequently, its future contribution is not yet decided, and could range from an outright moratorium to, some optimists believe, providing up to 45 percent of the Nation's total electrical needs by the year 2000. Decisions made in the next 5 years may well be pivotal in deciding the future of nuclear fission.

Because NRC is responsible for regulating the commercial nuclear industry to protect public health and safety, it, as well as the Energy Research and Development Administration, are the agencies which are faced with the critical issues facing nuclear power development.

The arguments against nuclear energy have been taken to the courts and to the voters. Two recent Court of Appeals decisions challenged NRC's licensing process by requiring that applicants give full consideration to (1) the environmental problems of operating reprocessing plants and disposing of wastes and (2) the alternative of energy conservation. Antinuclear groups have garnered enough support to get nuclear "moratorium" and/or control initiatives on ballots in a number of States. In every instance, these initatives were defeated. The voting showed, however, that a large and vocal minority does not favor increased growth of nuclear power. Nevertheless, it also shows that most voters in these States believe nuclear power should be developed further as an alternative to foreign energy imports.

These recent court decisions underline the fact that NRC can no longer consider license applications solely on a case-by-case basis, and only in terms of reactor health and safety. NRC is being pressured more and more to consider broad programmatic questions, including

- safety and security problems,

- adequate disposal of radioactive wastes,

- the need for new nuclear plants in light of overall trends in the development of alternative energy sources, and

- socioeconomic and environmental impacts.

Is NRC an independent, aggressive, and effective regulator of the nuclear industry? Intervenors frequently criticize NRC because it allegedly accepts, without question, the information provided by utilities in their license applications and thus appears to be "too soft on" or "in bed with" the industry it is supposed to regulate. Many see little change since the 1974 reorganization of the Atomic Energy Commission into ERDA and NRC.

Although most regulatory agencies are subject to some criticism, it appears that the persistence of this image may adversely affect the future development of nuclear power. In future work, we plan to consider the relationship of NRC to the nuclear industry by (1) identifying and applying qualitative and quantitative methods to evaluate this relationship and (2) comparing the NRC relationship with the nuclear industry to other regulatory agencies and the industries they regulate.

A related question concerns whether NRC's licensing process can be streamlined to reduce the 8 to 10 years lead time it takes to license and build a reactor. This long lead time adds to the already high capital cost of nuclear powerplants and many utilities have deferred or canceled construction of planned reactors due, in part, to increased capital costs. The previous Administration directed NRC to take steps to reduce this lead time, and NRC has adopted administrative measures within its present legal authority and has proposed changes in its legislative authority. These changes, however, have not yet been adopted.

Are nuclear powerplants safe? Powerplant safety is the single most critical issue facing the nuclear industry.

Opponents point out that NRC has not demonstrated that the "worst possible" accident—a fuel core melt which would result in a release of radioactivity to the environment and pose serious threats to public health and safety—will never occur. NRC maintains that the chances of such an accident are so remote that there is no need to consider it when reviewing and approving applications for permits to build and operate nuclear powerplants.

NRC fulfills its nuclear safety responsibilities through its licensing processes and procedures, a quality assurance program, and a program for powerplant security against theft and sabotage.

We are currently identifying and evaluating the processes and procedures used by NRC in considering applications for nuclear powerplant construction and operation, including the degree of independent evaluation and research conducted versus the amount of reliance placed on the applicant's information, the amount of staff participation and input in the process, and the degree to which generic safety questions are being addressed or suppressed.

NRC's quality assurance program is designed to monitor the licensee's activities to determine if it is adhering to previously approved design, construction, fabrication, and operating standards. This is accomplished through a series of inspections, starting very early in the design phase and carried throughout the life of the powerplant. In regulating and inspecting commercial nuclear facilities, NRC's philosophy is that the licensee has the prime responsibility for assuring that its facility is adequately designed, constructed, and operated. Thus, the major quality assurance/quality control activities are carried out by the licensee or his contractors.

We are currently evaluating the type and extent of NRC's quality assurance inspection program to determine whether (1) the present NRC philosophy assures adequate public protection against potential nuclear hazards caused by poor design, construction, or operating practices, (2) the system is adequate for evaluating the effectiveness of the quality assurance program, (3) inspectors are used effectively, and (4) a firm stand is taken with utilities when deficiencies are found.

NRC is also responsible for assuring that adequate safeguards exist against theft of special nuclear material or other highly dangerous nuclear materials from a plant or the sabotage of that plant. Over the past decade terrorism has increased, both here and abroad. As a result, nuclear powerplant security is of utmost importance for the protection of public health and safety, as well as the vast investment in plant and equipment.

We are currently evaluating the adequacy of the protection provided to determine whether (1) plant security requirements are uniform, (2) NRC inspectors are consistent, and (3) NRC regulations should be more stringent.

Related questions concern whether the NRC and ERDA reactor safety research programs are addressing the right safety questions and whether problems associated with decontaminating and decommissioning nuclear facilities in the future are being addressed.

In view of the increasing controversy over nuclear power, it would seem logical that safety research projects be geared toward either confirming or improving the safety of nuclear powerplants and nuclear fuel cycle activities. We intend to begin a study of NRC's research program during the coming year.

Decommissioning and decontamination is the process by which nuclear facilities, after the end of their useful life, are decontaminated and/or disposed of safely and completely. NRC is responsible for assuring that all users of radioactive materials licensed by them carry out this process. ERDA is responsible for decommissioning and decontaminating its own facilities. We plan to evaluate NRC's and ERDA's decommissioning and decontamination programs with a view towards recommending possible actions that can be taken now to better plan for this eventuality.

Does the nuclear option involve unacceptable damage to the environment?   Under the National Environmental Policy Act of 1969 (42 U.S.C. 4321), Federal agencies must prepare a detailed environmental impact statement for all significant actions affecting the environment. NRC prepares such statements preparatory to issuing licenses for nuclear facilities—including power reactors, testing facilities, fuel reprocessors, and isotopic enrichment plants, as well as when new regulations are promulgated.

We are currently evaluating the adequacy of NRC's assessment of the environmental impacts and associated long-term problems of nuclear powerplants. We are determining among other things whether the agency decision-makers and the interested public have sufficient information to assess the environmental impacts of a proposed facility. We are also considering whether NRC (1) substantiates environmental data submitted by applicants, (2) evaluates the projected cumulative effects of nuclear power proliferation, (3) considers specific energy conservation methods and their possible impact on power consumption when considering the need for power, and (4) addresses adequately the decommissioning of these facilities after their useful life.

Are there advantages to collocating commercial nuclear fuel cycle facilities?   The Energy Reorganization Act of 1974 directed NRC to consider the feasibility and practicability of nuclear energy centers. Collocating facilities into nuclear parks could eliminate much of the required nuclear materials transportation and consequent safeguards risks. The energy center thus has some advantages in protecting against terrorists and saboteurs.

The larger controlled area would also give more time to implement emergency measures to protect offsite populations and make it more difficult for intruders to penetrate the plants. On the other hand, this concept would pose a new set of problems, including vulnerability to overt attack and siting and transmission problems.

During the 95th Congress we intend to determine the economic and practical potential for this concept.

Do nuclear plants generate electricity cheaper than their fossil fueled competitors?   Nuclear proponents maintain that electricity produced from nuclear power is significantly cheaper than from its chief competitors—coal and oil. They maintain that lower operating costs more than offset higher capital costs. NRC, in preparing environmental impact statements, usually finds the 40 year cost of electricity is cheaper via the nuclear option. Some experts disagree, however.

Many factors in addition to capital investment and operating costs must be considered in comparing nuclear power to other energy alternatives. Perhaps the most important factor is the level of Government support which may be required in future years to sustain a large commercial nuclear fission program. The comparative performance of nuclear versus other alternatives must also be considered. For example, a recently published study maintains that nuclear power is more costly than alternatives—except for oil in the northeast—because the nuclear plants experience higher outage rates.

In the future, we plan to evaluate the direct and indirect costs of commercial nuclear powerplants and compare these costs to available alternatives. We also plan to point out the difficulty in quantifying some of the costs, such as the cost of permanent waste disposal and decommissioning. Currently, the cost of waste disposal, decommissioning, and reprocessing are highly uncertain and are not included in computing the cost of generating electricity with nuclear power. Such omissions clearly enhance nuclear energy's competitive position relative to other sources of electrical energy, such as coal.

International Concerns

Regardless of the position this country takes on nuclear power, other countries are developing energy policies heavily dependent on nuclear fission power. This is particularly true for many European countries which have limited energy resources. This international commercialization of nuclear power and the development of new nuclear technologies poses critical problems for this Nation's security, particularly as it relates to questions about nonproliferation of nuclear weapons, safeguards, and export controls.

Is the Government doing all it can to see that international safeguards are established which are sufficient to prevent nuclear proliferation and the diversion of nuclear materials to terrorist groups? The Congress continues to prod the executive branch in this area, urging it to undertake greater efforts. Perhaps the greatest danger affecting U.S. security and world peace is the spread of nuclear weapons beyond the six nations which now have nuclear weapons capability. Such proliferation is made possible by, among other things, the sharing of certain peaceful nuclear technology, such as reprocessing and enrichment facilities. Several proliferation control measures were debated during the 94th Congress, although none were passed.

Some of the questions most in need of answers include: Has the Government fully explored the possibilities for cooperation with other nuclear nations to halt the spread of nuclear technologies? If cooperative efforts fail, are alternative courses of action open to the Government? For example, could the United States produce and sell enough enriched uranium to maintain a dominant supplier position? Could or should the Government promote international nuclear reprocessing facilities to meet the enriched uranium needs of present non-nuclear weapons nations? Further examination of U.S. and international safeguards, nuclear suppliers' export policies, and the arms control implications of new nuclear-related technologies and transfers of this technology is needed. A related question concerns the need for more stringent export controls until stronger nonproliferation measures can be implemented. We are currently identifying and assessing the major issues affecting U.S. efforts to control nuclear proliferation. In addition, we have initiated a review of the nuclear export policies of major supplier nations with a view towards identifying areas where the United States can strengthen its nuclear export policies and procedures.

Past Efforts

Nuclear Power Development

Our major reports on NRC activities during the 94th Congress dealt primarily with nuclear safety and problems associated with disposing of wastes from nuclear operations.

In two reports (RED-76-68, 5/26/76; EMD-76-4, 8/25/76), we said that two NRC safety research projects—the loss-of-fluid test facility and the Plenum Fill experiment—experienced management deficiencies and delays, including schedule slippages, program redirection, and escalated costs. We concluded that neither project could reach its anticipated objective.

In another report (RED-76-54, 1/12/76) on waste disposal, we noted that neither ERDA—which has research and development responsibilities for nuclear waste management—nor NRC had established site selection criteria for low level radioactive waste burial grounds and has not defined earth science characteristics even though some sites had been operating for over 30 years. Some sites were releasing radioactivity to the environment. Based on our recommendations, ERDA budgeted funds for fiscal year 1977 to develop site selection criteria for its own burial grounds.

Between 1952 and 1966, uranium mill tailings—a low level sand-like material resulting from the extraction of uranium from uranium ore—were used extensively for construction fill material in Grand Junction, Colorado. In a May 21, 1975, report (RED-75-365), we noted that Federal and State efforts to provide financial assistance for remedial actions were stymied because all property owners could not be notified. Although uranium mills must be licensed by NRC or State agencies operating under agreement with NRC, there is no Federal enforcement once the license is terminated. Since tailings stabilization methods to date have been ineffective, we felt there was a need for continued regulation and long-term control to insure their integrity.

In a report to the 95th Congress on NRC efforts to reduce the long lead time (8 to 10 years) it takes to license and build a reactor (EMD-77-15, 2/25/77), we concluded that NRC is not going to succeed in reducing lead times through administrative procedures primarily because State and local governments' licensing requirements are not compatible with NRC licensing procedures. We recommended that NRC work with the States to develop common licensing procedures. NRC generally agreed with our recommendations.

In another report to the 95th Congress on the issues related to the closing of the only commercial reprocessing facility that has operated in the United States (EMD-77-27, 3/8/77), we concluded that the technology for solidifying and disposing of waste at the West Valley, New York, facility has not been developed and years of additional research are needed before any decisions on the final disposition of this waste can be made. We also concluded that it is economically infeasible to reopen this facility and that additional research is needed before decisions can be made on what to do with the high-level liquid wastes presently stored at the facility. We recommended that NRC and ERDA develop a policy on Federal assistance to New York for the West Valley site. We testified on our report before the Subcommittee on Conservation, Energy and Natural Resources, House Committee on Government Operations, on March 8, 1977.

In all of these reports, we made recommendations aimed at either increasing or improving management effectiveness of these programs. The agencies agreed to take positive actions on our recommendations and in one case, NRC stopped work on a safety research project pending completion of a conceptual design study.

International Concerns

In the past, our efforts on the international development of nuclear energy have concentrated primarily on the nonproliferation and safeguards questions. Four reports were issued to the 94th Congress on various aspects of these subjects. The most recent report, issued on September 14, 1976 (ID-76-60), summarized several previous reports we had issued on international safeguards and nonproliferation. We said that although the United States has sought improvements in international safeguards and physical security of nuclear materials and equipment, much more could be done. We also discussed shortcomings in the controls over the diversion of nuclear material for weapons purposes. We made several recommendations designed to

- improve the effectiveness of International Atomic Energy Agency safeguards,
- provide the United States and other nations with more information concerning safeguards effectiveness,

- upgrade the capabilities of the International Atomic Energy Agency safeguards staff, and
- urge all Agency member nations to establish adequate sanctions against nations diverting nuclear material for nuclear explosive purposes.

Other reports issued discuss, among other things, various policy options for deterring nuclear proliferation, export controls over nuclear materials and technology, physical security of nuclear materials and equipment transferred abroad, the role of the International Atomic Energy Agency in safeguarding nuclear material, and the effectiveness of international safeguards. We made a number of recommendations in these reports aimed at strengthening U.S. and international controls over the peaceful use of atomic energy and the International Atomic Energy Agency's role in international nuclear safeguards. There was general agreement with many of the issues raised in our reports and the affected agencies have begun to take action to implement our recommendations. For example, the executive branch has initiated specific programs to strengthen international safeguards.

Chapter 6

Energy Research And Development Administration

The Energy Research and Development Administration was created by the Energy Reorganization Act of 1974 to bring together in a single agency the major Federal energy research and development activities. ERDA is responsible for (1) directing and conducting research and development on domestic sources of energy, (2) carrying out nuclear energy functions related to fuel production and national defense, and (3) conducting basic research in the physical, biomedical, and environmental sciences. In fiscal year 1977, ERDA is providing about 80 percent of the total Federal funding for energy research and development. Because of its broad research and development responsibilities, ERDA's programs include efforts in the nuclear power development, fossil energy development, renewable resource, and conservation program areas. Our views on the major issues within each of these areas are discussed below. Our past efforts at ERDA are discussed on page 708.

Issues Facing The 95th Congress

Nuclear Power Development

ERDA's present top priority research and development project is the Liquid Metal Fast Breeder Reactor, a nuclear

fission reactor that will "create" more fuel than it uses. Estimates of U.S. uranium resources are speculative, and foreign sources are uncertain. The LMFBR, with its fuel "breeding" capability, could be the solution to any problem with uranium supplies. However, there are significant problems involved with commercializing the LMFBR. It is many years and billions of dollars away from commercial use. The energy output of nuclear fission, at least over the next 20 years, will continue to be almost exclusively from light water reactors. In addition, if nuclear energy and the LMFBR are to be viable options, the nuclear fuel cycle must be closed by solving the waste disposal and reprocessing problems.

The nuclear fuel cycle involves (1) mining uranium, (2) processing it through several steps—including enrichment—into fuel for the powerplant, (3) reprocessing the used fuel, and (4) ultimately disposing of highly radioactive wastes. Because of the highly radioactive nature of most nuclear materials, they must be adequately safeguarded against the possibility of terrorism and sabotage at all times.

ERDA's responsibilities in this area include (1) making assessments of the extent of uranium resources and encouraging industry to develop these resources, (2) assisting industry in overcoming technical and institutional uncertainties in the areas of fuel reprocessing, recycling, and waste management, (3) developing and demonstrating efficient and effective safeguards systems for both light water and advanced reactor fuel cycle systems, and (4) developing and demonstrating advanced enrichment technology.

How close are NRC and ERDA to solving the fuel reprocessing and waste disposal problems necessary to close the nuclear fuel cycle? Commercial reprocessing facilities would separate waste products in spent fuel discharged from nuclear powerplants and convert the remaining spent fuel into useful uranium and plutonium products. No commercial reprocessing plants operate in the United States today, nor has reprocessing been successfully demonstrated on a commercial scale. Similarly, a solution to the problem of long-term storage of highly radioactive nuclear wastes has not been found. Failure to solve the waste management and reprocessing problems means that large amounts of highly radioactive spent fuel must be stored at the nuclear powerplants. This situation has forced many nuclear powerplants to expand their onsite storage capability for wastes of all types. Other reactors may be faced with possible shutdown because of a lack of adequate storage space.

To compound the problem, Nuclear Fuel Services, Inc.—the only fuel reprocessor close to being ready for operation—recently withdrew from the reprocessing business leaving this country with the problem of disposing of over a half million gallons of radioactive waste. We reported on this problem on March 8, 1977 (see p. 703).

An important question to be addressed by the 95th Congress will be whether commercial fuel reprocessing should go forward. On April 7, 1977, President Carter announced that because of associated safety and safeguards problems, commercial reprocessing in the United States will be deferred indefinitely. Technical alternatives to nuclear fuel reprocessing, which may reap many of the benefits, but involve less risk, are also being studied.

We are currently studying the reprocessing question as it relates to the Nation's nuclear nonproliferation objectives and plan to assess the status and pros and cons of various reprocessing alternatives during the 95th Congress.

All operations that produce or use nuclear materials generate radioactive waste. Solving the waste management problem is crucial to continued nuclear growth. However, possible solutions have been debated for 20 years, and the problem remains unsolved.

Radioactive wastes are generally classified as either high- or low-level wastes. Because high-level wastes are highly radioactive, the Nation must develop techniques for permanent isolation of these wastes in a way that requires little reliance on human surveillance for very long periods of time—centuries to millenia. An estimated 75

million gallons of high-level wastes are currently stored at temporary locations.

In addition, low-level wastes are generally disposed of in shallow land burial sites. Some of the six existing commercal sites are no longer accepting this material, however, and it is uncertain how long the remaining ones can handle the increased capacity.

NRC is responsible for protecting public health and safety through regulating the possession, use, and disposal of radioactive materials while ERDA is responsible for researching, developing, and demonstrating facilities and techniques for treating, storing, and disposing of radioactive wastes. ERDA is also responsible for the eventual operation of waste storage facilities.

We are currently assessing the obstacles faced by ERDA in solving the spent fuel storage and commercial high-level waste problems as well as the possible timing for a realistic solution to these problems. We are also assessing the waste management problem as it relates to this country's nuclear nonproliferation objectives.

ERDA has also produced 215 million gallons of high-level liquid waste from its weapons and research programs. We plan to begin a review during 1977 of ERDA's efforts to dispose of those wastes.

How reliable are ERDA's estimates of domestic uranium supplies and how available are foreign sources? Another crucial factor affecting the growth of nuclear power and the need and timing for commercializing the LMFBR is the availability of uranium. In the past, the nuclear industry assumed that uranium would continue to be available in abundant quantities and at reasonably low prices. However, recent market activity resulting in rapidly escalating prices has caused uranium consumers and producers to more closely examine the uranium supply situation. Many utilities are without uranium contracts to fill the lifetime requirements of their reactors, and producers may be unable to meet the demand. ERDA projections indicate that without fuel reprocessing there may be a shortage of uranium after 1990. The foreign supply may also be uncertain. Because many industrialized foreign countries—such as Japan and West Germany—must rely heavily on nuclear power and do not have adequate supplies of uranium of their own, worldwide demand may exceed the supplies of the major supplier nations. The restrictive export policies of some of these supplier nations further complicates the situation.

On the other hand, some experts believe, contrary to ERDA's assessments, that an adequate supply of uranium exists for meeting this country's nuclear power needs under any conditions. These conflicting opinions have helped to make utilities unsure of their actions.

We are currently assessing the factors affecting worldwide uranium supply and demand. We are examining, among other things, the reliability of the estimated domestic uranium resource base, how this base can be increased, and what present and future Government actions would be beneficial.

How urgent is the need for additional uranium enrichment capacity and how should that capacity be provided? Before uranium can be used in a nuclear reactor, it must be enriched in the fissionable isotope uranium -235. Currently, most of the worldwide enrichment capacity exists at three ERDA enrichment plants. An add-on to one of these plants is currently in the design phase.

There was a great deal of debate during the 94th Congress as to when additional capacity would be needed to meet growing domestic and foreign demand and how that capacity should be provided—Government or private ownership. We have reported on this subject on several occasions (see p. 708) and are currently assessing the need and timing for additional enrichment capacity and identifying ways that current capacity can be extended. We also plan to begin a review of ERDA's efforts to develop and commercialize new enrichment technologies.

How reasonable are ERDA's uranium enrichment pricing policies? ERDA receives considerable revenues for its enrichment services. These revenues are used to offset ERDA's operating expenses. In fiscal year 1977 ERDA expected to receive about $660 million for its enrichment services. ERDA's price for these services is governed by the Atomic Energy Act of 1954 (42 U.S.C. 2201) which requires cost recovery over a reasonable period of time.

Legislation was introduced during the 94th Congress to increase the price of enrichment services to a "commercial" rate. Proponents for this change contend that the existence of the artificially low ERDA price stifles industry interest in investing in private enrichment facilities. They also argue that it represents a subsidy to the nuclear industry and thus provides a competitive advantage to nuclear power over other energy alternatives. We plan to evaluate ERDA's enrichment pricing policy during the 95th Congress. In addition, our current review of the need and timing for additional enrichment capacity will address certain specific pricing policies relating to ERDA's uranium feed stockpile.

Fossil Energy Development

ERDA's fossil energy development activities are directed toward researching, developing, and demonstrating technologies to expand the use of coal and oil shale and improve recovery methods for oil, natural gas, and oil shale.

ERDA's coal research effort includes programs in coal conversion and coal utilization. In its coal conversion program, ERDA is attempting to develop processes to convert coal into synthetic fuels that substitute for those derived from oil and gas. Its coal utilization program is directed at developing environmentally acceptable processes to produce energy by burning coal directly. These include improved coal combustion systems, advanced power systems with gas turbines, and magnetohydrodynamic electric power.

ERDA's oil shale program is attempting to reduce the water requirements of the oil shale industry, increase the recoverable reserve base through improved production technology, and insure that environmental safeguards are built into the process.

In its oil and natural gas recovery programs, ERDA is attempting to demonstrate the technical and economic feasibility of advanced (tertiary) techniques to increase the yield of currently producing oil wells and to produce gas in areas where commercial gas production on a large scale is not now possible.

Is ERDA addressing all research and development options to solving the environmental and socioeconomic problems associated with expanded use of coal? This issue is closely related to the problem of minimizing the environmental and socioeconomic impacts of accelerated energy development discussed on page 698. This question, however, concerns ERDA and Environmental Protection Agency efforts to research and develop improved technology to reduce air pollution caused by burning coal directly.

Such technology may reduce air pollution either by removing pollutants before the coal is burned or by removing them before smoke is released to the atmosphere.

Current technology using stack gas scrubbers to clean coal emissions from coal-fired plants is inadequate and expensive to implement. The Environmental Protection Agency is attempting to improve scrubber technology, while ERDA is placing major emphasis on developing fluidized bed combustion.

Our ongoing study (see p. 698) of the issues influencing the future of coal addresses this question and, during the 95th Congress, we plan to determine whether research and development options to improve the environmental and socioeconomic acceptability of coal have been adequately considered.

What is the future role of synthetic fuels from coal and oil shale? This Nation has huge resources of oil shale that can be converted into synthetic crude oil, and coal that can be processed into both synthetic crude oil and natural gas. Although technologies for these processes are generally proven, development costs are enormous and the ultimate cost of synthetic fuels is uncertain.

Consequently, the contribution that synthetic fuels can be expected to make over the next 25 years or so and the role it will play in reducing oil imports is far from certain. Further, if the United States is, as some claim, already in a transition period from oil and gas to renewable resources, it may not make sense for the Government to spend billions of dollars to develop a synthetic fuels industry that might soon be outdated.

We are currently reviewing the objectives, status, and potential of ERDA's synthetic fuel demonstration program—paying particular attention to the extent that environmental, technical, socioeconomic, and regulatory information needed for eventual commercialization is being obtained. Also, our previously cited review of the issues influencing the future of coal will consider this question.

Renewable Resources Development

Federal funding for renewable resource technologies has increased dramatically over the past few years. Yet, there is considerable debate about the contribution these technologies can make toward meeting this Nation's energy needs and the research and development priority being assigned to them by ERDA.

What is the long-term potential of geothermal energy? and is a Federal loan guarantee program or other incentive needed? Recent public concern about dwindling supplies of oil and gas has resulted in legislation intended to advance the date by which renewable energy sources, such as geothermal energy, can be made available. Several pieces of energy legislation enacted in the 93rd Congress give ERDA authority to conduct a wide range of activities intended to make available economically competitive and environmentally acceptable geothermal technologies to the Nation as soon as possible. ERDA can also provide loan guarantees up to $200 million for financing geothermal projects.

For the most part, however, ERDA believes that geothermal energy will have little, if any, impact before 1985 and that accelerating the development of this technology will contribute little in the near term. From 1985 until 2000, ERDA does not expect geothermal to have an appreciable impact in meeting energy needs. Others disagree with these estimates.

During the coming year, we plan to identify the potential near-, mid-, and long-term use of geothermal energy as a renewable energy source, and determine the proper role the Federal Government should play in developing geothermal energy.

How does ERDA plan to solve the institutional barriers associated with implementing new technologies into the current energy system? Increased use of renewable energy technologies as a partial substitute for existing energy technologies will require advance planning. Possible economic and social dislocations that result from changes in energy sources must be minimized. Because many of these technologies can be decentralized and used on a smaller scale than current systems, changes in investment characteristics also must be anticipated. Other considerations, such as land and water use, public acceptance, and legal and institutional barriers must be identified as the technology is being researched and developed if rapid development of such technologies is to take place.

This year our work will include a review of such institutional barriers as environmental, socioeconomic, and legal constraints to commercializing solar and geothermal energy. We will also assess ERDA's role in overcoming these barriers.

How are priorities determined for these new technologies? ERDA's funding of and priority assigned to renewable resource research and development has been the subject of some controversy. Some believe that ERDA is emphasizing high cost nuclear technologies at the expense of renewable resource development. Thus, an important question is whether renewable resource technologies should be developed at a faster pace.

A related question concerns the way ERDA established its priorities to assure that it is emphasizing the most promising technologies and approaches. We are planning efforts during the 95th Congress in ERDA's solar, geothermal, and fusion research and development programs which will address this question as it applies to these specific technologies. For example, we are currently reviewing ERDA's fusion research program and will attempt to determine the funding priority that should be given to that program.

What are the environmental impacts associated with implementing these technologies and what is being done to identify and overcome them? The environmental effects of solar energy technologies have not yet been fully determined and assessed, and potentially serious problems associated with nuclear fusion and geothermal energy must be studied further. Will nuclear fusion, for example, introduce as many problems as nuclear fission? What is being done to assure that necessary environmental controls are developed?

Environmental studies are essential to identify and solve potential impacts as these technologies are developed to avoid delays in their implementation once the economic and technical problems are solved. As part of broader studies, we are currently assessing ERDA efforts in identifying, assessing, and overcoming the environmental impact associated with fusion and geothermal research and development.

How effective are new demonstration programs, such as the solar heating and cooling program, in meeting program goals? One goal of ERDA's solar heating and cooling program is to bring about commercial acceptability by the early 1980s. To this end, solar heating equipment is currently being demonstrated by the Department of Housing and Urban Development, with ERDA funding, in about 120 homes, apartments, and office buildings around the country. This program, as well as some geothermal programs, should be evaluated to determine how well they are being conducted, and if they will be able to meet program goals.

Conservation

While FEA has responsibility for commercializing existing energy conservation technologies, ERDA is responsible for researching and developing new technologies.

ERDA is conducting a variety of activities in energy conservation research, development, and demonstration geared primarily toward reducing energy waste by developing more efficient energy technologies. Its activities include efforts to increase the efficiency of consumer products, electrical transmission and distribution systems, manufacturing systems, agricultural and food process industries, and automobiles. As part of its conservation program, ERDA is attempting to develop improved energy storage systems.

Is the near-term priority role established by ERDA for new energy conservation technologies the appropriate one? ERDA has designated conservation research, development, and demonstration as a high-priority program for the near-term. ERDA plans provide that energy conservation opportunities now ready for commercialization will receive special attention. The President's Council on Environmental Quality, however, has criticized ERDA for placing too much emphasis on off-the-shelf technologies and questioned the adequacy of ERDA's planning for mid- and long-term conservation efforts.

The 95th Congress, in authorizing funds for ERDA's program, will be faced with the question of whether ERDA is placing too much emphasis on off-the-shelf, conservation technologies at the expense of new higher payoff technologies. We plan to begin a review during the 95th Congress of ERDA's conservation research and development program. As part of that effort, we will attempt to determine whether ERDA's priorities are appropriate.

What is the appropriate Federal role in automotive conservation research, development, and demonstration? The Federal role in automotive conservation research, development, and demonstration has been to support the development of high risk, advanced propulsion systems which could be demonstrated in the early 1980s and commercialized later in the decade. Several

bills were introduced in the 94th Congress to accelerate the development of these advanced systems. One recently enacted law authorizes $160 million for a 6-year electric car research and development program. Another bill, which passed both the House and Senate but did not become law, would have authorized $100 million for the first 2 years of a 5-year Government research, development, and demonstration program for new auto systems and advanced alternatives to existing autos.

Some questions could be raised, however, about the energy efficiency of some of these proposals. For example, an electric car may reduce the use of petroleum in the transportation sector, while at the same time, it increases total energy use. Such questions will need to be fully assessed and resolved before a commitment is made.

There has also been considerable debate over what the proper Federal role should be. Hearings were held on this issue in 1975 and 1976 and numerous studies have been made. Opponents of Government involvement contend it is not needed because the industry has the necessary resources. These opponents believe that industry will make economically efficient research and development decisions. Proponents of increased Government involvement say it is needed because the industry resists new technology and drags its feet on the introduction of advanced engines. These proponents believe that new technology needs to be pushed by Government regulation and federally funded research and development.

Past Efforts

Nuclear Power Development

ERDA's activities in nuclear power research and development are directed primarily at researching, developing, and demonstrating improvements in (1) the nuclear fuel cycle, (2) nuclear safeguards, and (3) advanced fission power reactors—such as the LMFBR. Thus, our efforts in nuclear research and development have been directed at these programs.

Nuclear fuel cycle and safeguards The need for and timing of additional enrichment capacity and how that capacity will be provided has been a subject of debate over the past several years. We addressed various aspects of this issue in several reports issued during the 94th Congress (RED-76-36, 10/31/75; RED-76-55, 11/28/75; and RED-76-110, 5/10/76). In those reports, we concluded that:

- There should be a greater risk-sharing between the Government and private enrichers in cooperative agreements between ERDA and private companies wishing to provide future enrichment capacity.

- The Government should provide the next increment of enrichment capacity with an add-on plant.

- ERDA's existing enrichment plants should be operated as a Government corporation.

- Legislation may be required to commercialize advanced enrichment technologies.

As a result of these reports, significant changes were made to proposed legislation authorizing cooperative agreements between ERDA and private industry for private uranium enrichment facilities, (S. 2035-94th Congress). The proposed legislation did not pass in the 94th Congress principally because of opposition to a prosposal by one private company to build an enrichment plant using existing technology. This proposal would have involved significant Government risk, and we opposed it in all our reports on the subject.

The development and use of adequate systems to safeguard nuclear material during all phases of the nuclear fuel cycle is essential to establishing a viable nuclear power industry. In a July 22, 1976, report on ERDA's system to control and protect highly dangerous nuclear material (EMD-76-3), we discussed many serious shortcomings in the system such as the need for additional guards, alarms, doorway detectors, night vision devices, and improved communication equipment. We made several recommendations aimed at improving the system and, according to ERDA, it has initiated corrective actions. We are currently following up on these actions.

Fission power reactors ERDA's priority and most expensive effort in researching and developing fission power reactors is the LMFBR program. Over the past two years, we have issued nine reports addressing various aspects of this program. Three of the reports provided broad analyses of the LMFBR reactor program's problems, potential, and prospects for commercialization. In one of our reports (OSP-76-1, 7/31/75), we concluded that there has been premature concern and emphasis on commercializing the LMFBR at a time when the Nation is years away from demonstrating that commercial LMFBR plants can be operated reliably, economically, and safely. We also concluded that a decision does not need to be made about whether the LMFBR should be a major source of electrical energy in the United States until some point in the future—perhaps 7 to 10 years.

In a followup report (EMD-77-5, 11/29/76), we discussed the actions necessary for commercial development of the LMFBR if the Nation decides that such development is desirable. We concluded that:

- If basic uncertainties of safety, safeguards, and environmental effects are resolved early and forthrightly, the start of LMFBR commercialization by the mid-1990s is feasible. This can be achieved, however, only through an integrated approach to the development of four required technologies: reactor, fuel fabrication, plutonium reprocessing, and radioactive waste disposal.

- 1990 may be the earliest time by which licensability and routine performance can be demonstrated for all four required technologies.

- Because of the time required for development of fuel cycle technologies, the year 2000 represents the most likely time frame for commercialization of the LMFBR, with four to six LMFBRs in commercial operation.

- Additional funding for the LMFBR program is not likely to hasten the initial commercial availability of technology. However, early development of program plans and increased commitment of resources could accelerate by 1 or 2 years the research, development, and demonstration of the three supporting fuel cycle technologies required for LMFBR commercialization.

We recommended several improvements to the program to better achieve LMFBR commercialization objectives if such commercialization is approved as a desirable national objective.

We also reported (EMD-76-12, 9/30/76) on our evaluation of a pro-nuclear ERDA pamphlet issued as part of a claimed internal LMFBR motivational program 2 to 4 months before a nuclear referendum in California on June 8, 1976. We concluded that the pamphlet was not objective, was propaganda, and thus was not a proper document for issuance to the public or any internal program. We noted that the pamphlet was printed and distributed far in excess of the program needs and that ERDA placed little or no restrictions on its distribution. As a result, it was distributed beyond the scope of the program and was used by some recipients in an attempt to influence voters in California. We made several recommendations aimed at preventing the recurrence of such distributions in the future. As a direct result of this report, ERDA recalled outstanding copies of the pamphlet and two bills were introduced just before congressional adjournment to place restrictions on Federal agencies issuing materials which affect State elections.

Fossil Energy Development

Most of our work on ERDA's fossil energy development programs has focused on the status and obstacles to commercialization of synthetic fuels from coal and oil shale (RED-76-81, 5/3/76) and with Administration proposals to provide financial incentives for commercial development of synthetic fuels (RED-76-82, 3/19/76; EMD-76-10, 8/24/76). We concluded that processes which produce synthetic fuels are commercially available but are not competitive with conventional oil and gas when discounted to present price equivalents. We took the position that loan guarantees for commercial development of synthetic fuels should not be provided at this time. Instead, we suggested that full priority be directed to developing improved synthetic fuels technologies. When commercialization does become a prime objective, consideration should be given to approaches other than loan guarantees for gaining the interest of private industry. We believe that these reports and subsequent testimony had an impact on proposed legislation to provide financial incentives for synthetic fuel commercialization (H.R. 12112-94th Congress).

We also issued a report on the status and problems to be resolved in coal research (RED-75-322, 2/18/75). Our report identified potential problems in areas such as mining technology, manpower, transportation, and environment that must be solved before coal's potential can be realized.

Our most recent report on ERDA's fossil energy research and development program dealt with its management of the enhanced oil and gas recovery program (EMD-77-3, 1/28/77). We identified problems in and made recommendations aimed at improving ERDA's management of that program.

Renewable Resources Development

ERDA efforts to research and develop new, essentially inexhaustible, energy resources fall into three broad categories; solar energy, geothermal energy, and nuclear fusion. We have made reviews in two of these areas during the past Congress.

Solar energy ERDA is supporting research and development in a wide range of solar technologies. ERDA is placing the most emphasis, however, on demonstrating solar heating and cooling systems. These include systems to heat and cool residential and commercial buildings and to dry agricultural crops. Other longer range development activities include solar thermal electric conversion, photovoltaic energy conversion, and fuels from biomass.

Our reports (RED-75-376, 6/10/75; EMD-77-8, 11/30/76), on solar energy research and development have discussed the status of the program and the need for establishing a formal priority system for developing and demonstrating the various solar technologies. ERDA has taken action to improve its management systems.

Fusion power ERDA's fusion research and development program is aimed at developing and demonstrating the production of commercial electric power using nuclear fusion. In a May 22, 1975, report (RED-75-356), we discussed the status of the program and noted that ERDA's management system was hampering the development of fusion technologies and that ERDA needed to establish priorities for different fusion approaches to have a better basis for managing the program.

Chapter 7

Multiagency Issues

Changing from an economy dependent largely on oil and gas to one dependent on new and different energy sources will require enormous capital outlays. Similarly, efforts to increase the production of oil and gas through improved extraction methods and by developing new sources of oil and gas—such as the trans-Alaska oil pipeline and the proposed trans-Alaska gas pipeline—will also required huge amounts of capital. Thus, a major question, which affects almost all of the energy agencies, concerns the proper Federal role in assisting and encouraging private industry to develop and commercialize these various energy sources.

In addition, the need to reorganize the Federal energy structure and to develop a national energy policy was a major issue during the presidential campaign, and the Administration has introduced legislation to reorganize the Federal energy agencies (S. 826). Such proposals may affect each agency discussed in the report.

Issues Facing the 95th Congress

What is the appropriate Government role in commercializing new energy technologies? The Government is already heavily involved in researching, developing, and demonstrating new energy technologies. However, questions about when a process is commercial and what the Government's involvement should be in assisting or encouraging private industry to commercialize that process are key issues. Related questions concern the types of assistance that should be given—such as direct financial assistance, loan guarantees, and indirect incentives.

Almost every major energy agency has programs aimed at providing financial incentives for commercializing new technologies or will soon be faced with this problem. FEA is responsible for commercializing conservation and renewable resource technologies, and ERDA has responsiblity for providing loan guarantees for geothermal energy. Several bills, such as the proposed Energy Independence Authority Act and the synfuels' commercialization legislation, were introduced during the 94th Congress to provide Federal assistance. Similar such bills have been reintroduced in the 95th Congress. Industry's role in providing additional uranium enrichment capacity has been an issue since the early 1970s. The need for government assistance in further commercialization of nuclear power—particularly in the areas of waste management and reprocessing—and in constructing a trans-Alaska gas pipeline will certainly be a matter of debate in the years to come.

We have a number of ongoing and planned studies, mentioned previously, which will address parts of this question. These include reviews of (1) the effectiveness of FEA attempts to commercialize conservation and renewable resource technologies, (2) the economics of nuclear power, (3) ERDA efforts to develop and commercialize geothermal energy, and (4) ERDA's efforts to develop and commercialize advanced uranium enrichment technologies.

How should the Federal energy organization and processes be improved? The inability to solve many energy problems stems at least in part from the diffusion of major energy programs among several Federal agencies. For example, ERDA is responsible for research, development, and demonstration of energy technologies, while FEA formulates short-term energy policy, and the Department of the Interior makes decisions regarding the development of energy resources on Federal lands. There are also two national energy planning systems: FEA's—which produced the original 1974 "Project Independence Report" and the 1976 "National Energy Outlook"—and ERDA's—which produced "A National Plan for Energy Research, Development, and Demonstration: Creating Energy Choices for the Future", and the 1976 revision of the plan. As a result of such fragmentation, policymaking and management of Federal energy activities have not proceeded as effectively as they might have, and at times work at cross purposes.

For example, there seems to be some confusion as to FEA's and ERDA's roles. This confusion is particularly pronounced in assigning responsibility for new technology commercialization. FEA and ERDA have not fully coordinated and defined their respective roles in this area. As a result of this confusion, FEA and ERDA, in April 1976, entered into a memorandum of understanding to formalize the working relationship between them. Although a step in the right direction, the memorandum of understanding leaves open the question of commercialization responsibility. Timely availability of newly developed technologies cannot proceed smoothly without a clear understanding of how the key agencies responsible for energy are to proceed and interact with the private sector to actually achieve viable commercial adaptation of new technologies into the economy.

As far back as 1971, the President proposed a Department of Energy and Natural Resources, but the Congress has not approved such a reorganization. The most recent proposal was introduced on March 1, 1977, to create a Department of Energy (S. 826). While it is not possible to centralize all energy-related programs, the major ones can and should be consolidated as a further step towards a nationalized energy decisionmaking system.

We have expressed long-standing support for such centralization of energy activities and have suggested possible organizations in testimony in April 1976 before the Senate Committee on Government Operations.

As discussed below, we recently reported on, among other things, the reorganization of energy functions. In that report we expressed our general support for the Administration's recent energy reorganization proposal and made several suggestions for inclusion in the bill. We will continue to monitor the Federal energy organization and decisionmaking process and expect to provide input to the Congress on these efforts to reorganize the Federal energy program.

Past Efforts

In a recently issued report (EMD-77-31, 3/24/77) on the activities of the executive agencies having primary responsibility for policy decisionmaking—FEA, ERDA, FPC, and Department of the Interior—we identified national goals and related decisions to the goals and considered the consistencies or inconsistencies of the decisions. We noted that there was a need for better coordination among agencies carrying out energy functions and for establishing a system of priorities among energy goals.

In addition, the report discussed the organization of energy functions of the Federal Government, including the Administration's recent proposal to establish a Department of Energy (S. 826). We concluded that the Administration's proposal has considerable merit, and we generally endorsed its enactment. However, we discussed several issues which we believed the Congress should address in enacting such legislation:

- Make clear the continued existence of the Professional Audit Review Team to provide an independent review of and reporting on Federal energy data functions. (see p. 684)

- Give the proposed Department of Energy responsibility for the automobile fuel economy standards program with the Department of Transportation having an advisory role.

- Specify more clearly the Department of Energy's responsibility for energy production formulation, planning, and programing to provide an appropriate basis for interface with agencies having health and safety responsibilities.

- Make clear the relationship between the Department of Energy and the Department of the Interior with respect to whether the Secretary of the Interior has veto power in the leasing of specific areas.

- Establish a high-level council to coordinate energy and energy-related issues and reconcile energy goals with other national goals.

- Reaffirm GAO's authority to continuously monitor, evaluate, and report to the Congress on the policies, plans, and programs of the Department of Energy.

We also said that the Congress needs to examine how energy regulatory functions should be treated in reorganizing energy functions. The Administration's proposal would include in the new department only economic regulatory functions and certain other functions of the Interstate Commerce Commission and the Securities and Exchange Commission. It would not include health and safety regulation.

The Congess should choose one of three options listed below:

- Include energy regulation, both economic and health and safety related, in the new Department of Energy. Both regulatory activities could be separate entities, but under a single Assistant Secretary. Statutory provisions should be included to assure maximum insulation of regulatory decisions from the policy process.

- Include only economic regulation in the new Department of Energy because of the perceived importance of establishing energy price regulatory policies which are consistent with other energy goals and consolidate energy health and safety regulation in a separate independent Energy Health and Safety Regulatory Agency. Strong statutory provisions should be included to assure maximum insulation of economic regulatory decisions from the policy process.

- Continue to separate energy regulation, both economic and health and safety related, from energy policy formulation. Should this be done, we believe that creation of a single energy regulatory agency is desirable.

In addition, in an August 24, 1976 report (EMD-76-10), we provided a framework and perspective for considering actions by the Federal Government which would contribute to solving energy problems over the next 10 to 25 years. In so doing, we discussed the factors that must be considered in choosing between technologies and financing mechanisms for commercializing those technologies.

Chapter 8

Summary

The Nation's energy problems are long term in nature. The harsh winter of 1977 and the resultant shortage of natural gas once again brought the realities of the Nation's energy problems to the forefront. Because energy is so pervasive, finding solutions acceptable to all areas of society is difficult, and will require political consensus among competing areas of national concern, such as balancing economic and environmental goals and objectives. In such sensitive areas, concensus is very hard to achieve.

In this report, we have summarized our views on the significant energy issues facing the Congress and the Nation. Those views were based partly on our past efforts in the area and partly on our continuing assessment of critical national issues.

Our basic objective in developing this report was to provide the Congress, the executive branch, and the public with a perspective and framework for analyzing the many diverse and sometimes conflicting energy problems facing the Nation. We feel that its principal use will be by the Congress and congressional committees in setting legislative priorities, reviewing and considering the programs and needs of the individual energy agencies, and developing a cohesive national energy policy.

We recognize that there will likely be some major changes in the organization and structure of the Federal energy agencies in the coming months. Nevertheless, the issues discussed in this report will continue to be relevant to the Congress as it considers the questions of Federal energy reorganization, energy priority and goal setting, and the resolution of tradeoffs and conflicts inherent in establishing priorities and goals.

Also, although this report is directed primarily to the Congress and the executive agencies, the issues discussed must also be addressed by everyone concerned with energy—including the academic community, scientists, industry, and concerned citizens. Hopefully, this report will help develop a public awareness of the critical energy issues and in providing those outside Government with a basis for providing input into the development of a cohesive national energy policy.

INDEX

INDEX